LAND USE LAW

in North Carolina

David W. Owens

FOURTH EDITION

For Phil Green, Bob Stipe, and Rich Ducker, who each
devoted decades of exemplary service at the Institute
of Government, now the School of Government, to
advance our understanding of land use law
and
for Ellen, Jonathan, Andrew, and Adam, who each
endured decades of land use law stories at home with
uncommon grace and good humor.

The School of Government at the University of North Carolina at Chapel Hill works to improve the lives of North Carolinians by engaging in practical scholarship that helps public officials and citizens understand and improve state and local government. Established in 1931 as the Institute of Government, the School provides educational, advisory, and research services for state and local governments. The School of Government is also home to a nationally ranked Master of Public Administration program, the North Carolina Judicial College, and specialized centers focused on community and economic development, information technology, and environmental finance.

As the largest university-based local government training, advisory, and research organization in the United States, the School of Government offers up to 200 courses, webinars, and specialized conferences for more than 12,000 public officials each year. In addition, faculty members annually publish approximately 50 books, manuals, reports, articles, bulletins, and other print and online content related to state and local government. The School also produces the *Daily Bulletin Online* each day the General Assembly is in session, reporting on activities for members of the legislature and others who need to follow the course of legislation.

Operating support for the School of Government's programs and activities comes from many sources, including state appropriations, local government membership dues, private contributions, publication sales, course fees, and service contracts.

Visit sog.unc.edu or call 919.966.5381 for more information on the School's courses, publications, programs, and services.

Aimee N. Wall, DEAN
Jeffrey B. Welty, SENIOR ASSOCIATE DEAN FOR FACULTY AFFAIRS
Anita R. Brown-Graham, ASSOCIATE DEAN FOR STRATEGIC INITIATIVES
Willow S. Jacobson, ASSOCIATE DEAN FOR GRADUATE STUDIES
Kara A. Millonzi, ASSOCIATE DEAN FOR RESEARCH AND INNOVATION
Lauren G. Partin, SENIOR ASSOCIATE DEAN FOR ADMINISTRATION
Sonja Matanovic, ASSOCIATE DEAN FOR STRATEGIC COMMUNICATIONS
Jen Willis, ASSOCIATE DEAN FOR ADVANCEMENT AND PARTNERSHIPS

FACULTY

Whitney Afonso
Gregory S. Allison
Lydian Altman
Rebecca Badgett
Maureen Berner
Frayda S. Bluestein
Kirk Boone
Mark F. Botts
Brittany LaDawn Bromell
Peg Carlson
Melanie Y. Crenshaw
Connor Crews
Crista M. Cuccaro
Leisha DeHart-Davis
Shea Riggsbee Denning
Sara DePasquale
Kimalee Cottrell Dickerson
Phil Dixon, Jr.
Jacquelyn Greene
Timothy Heinle
Margaret F. Henderson
Cheryl Daniels Howell
Joseph Hyde
James L. Joyce
Robert P. Joyce
Diane M. Juffras
Kimberly Kluth

Kirsten Leloudis
Adam Lovelady
James M. Markham
Christopher B. McLaughlin
Jill D. Moore
Jonathan Q. Morgan
Ricardo S. Morse
C. Tyler Mulligan
Kimberly L. Nelson
Kristi A. Nickodem
David W. Owens
Obed Pasha
William C. Rivenbark
Dale J. Roenigk
John Rubin
Jessica Smith
Meredith Smith
Michael Smith
Carl W. Stenberg III
John B. Stephens
Charles Szypszak
Shannon H. Tufts
Emily Turner
Amy Wade
Richard B. Whisnant
Teshanee T. Williams
Kristina M. Wilson

Cover photos by Wollwerth Imagery, Jason Schronce, and Rick; stock.adobe.com.

Printed in the United States of America

27 26 25 24 23   1 2 3 4 5

ISBN 978-1-64238-077-4

Book Summary

Contents

PART 2 Land Use and Development Regulations

PART 3 Legislative Decisions

PART 4 Quasi-Judicial Decisions

PART 5   Application and Enforcement of Regulations

PART 6   State and Federal Statutory and Constitutional Limits

PART 7 Judicial Review

APPENDIXES

INDEXES

Illustrations and Tables

ILLUSTRATIONS

TABLES

Preface

Beginning with the 1952 publication of Phil Green's landmark *Zoning in North Carolina*, the School (previously Institute) of Government established a strong tradition of works focusing on land use law. Through the years a wide variety of publications in this area have been prepared. Publications by faculty members Bob Stipe, Michael Brough, Richard Ducker, Adam Lovelady, and Jim Joyce comprehensively document the evolution of land use law in this state.

The fourth edition of *Land Use Law in North Carolina* continues this tradition with detailed coverage of the many legal issues related to land-development regulation. This book is intended as a legal reference work for those interested in the law related to development regulation in North Carolina. It builds on and expands the material originally covered in its previous three editions.

The previous groundbreaking contributions of my School of Government colleagues, as well as the helpful review, comment, and editorial assistance provided by faculty and staff members, is gratefully acknowledged. Fleming Bell, Frayda Bluestein, Anita Brown-Graham, Jim Drennan, Richard Ducker, Bob Farb, David Lawrence, Adam Lovelady, Tyler Mulligan, Jeff Welty, and Richard Whisnant all offered valuable assistance in the preparation of this book and the work it builds upon. The work herein has greatly benefited from their contributions.

David Owens
Chapel Hill
May 2023

Historical Background

PART 1

CHAPTER 1

Introduction

Land use and development regulation is one of the most visible activities—and controversial powers—of local government. Few issues involving city and county government are as likely to pack a hearing room, generate front-page newspaper stories, or result in long and acrimonious litigation.

Development regulations tend to be controversial from the day they are proposed. Some landowners, bitterly opposed to their adoption, turn out in large numbers to object to the government's telling them how they may use land that has been in their families for generations. Invariably the proposed regulations are thought to be too strict by some of those affected and not strict enough by others. The professionals can be counted on to complain as well—from developers who feel that the paperwork and the review process are too onerous to land use planners who feel that the regulations stifle creative solutions to modern land use problems.

Zoning has emerged as the principal land use–management tool of local governments and is therefore the focus of much of the law described in this book. Over the past eighty years, more than 550 cities and counties in North Carolina[1] have adopted zoning ordinances to regulate land use, building location, site design, and density of development. Zoning has become widely used because it is the most effective tool that citizens working collectively as a local government can employ to establish the future character of their community. Other development regulations also play an important role and are addressed in this book—subdivision regulations, housing and building codes, and various special-purpose regulations. It is increasingly common for many of these development regulations to be consolidated into a single ordinance, often termed a "unified development ordinance." This allows use of a common set of definitions, boards, and appeals processes.

A considerable body of law has developed regarding the land use regulatory decisions of local governments.[2] To protect both public and landowner interests, state legislation requires that special procedures and safeguards be followed in the adoption or amending of land use ordinances, requirements that do not apply to other ordinances. North Carolina appellate courts have issued hundreds of opinions interpreting these requirements and settling disputes between local governments, landowners, and neighbors regarding the adoption and application of these ordinances.

This book covers the range of legal issues involved with land use law in North Carolina.

---

1. A 2012 School of Government survey indicated that of the 650 cities and counties in the state at that time, 559 had adopted zoning ordinances. Eighty-seven percent of the state's cities and 79 percent of the counties had adopted zoning ordinances. An additional thirty-one smaller municipalities had elected to be subject to county zoning. Based on this survey data, it was estimated that about 92 percent of the state's total population live in zoned areas. David W. Owens and Dayne Batten, *2012 Zoning Survey Report: Zoning Adoption, Administration, and Provisions for Design Standards and Alternative Energy Facilities*, Planning and Zoning L. Bull. No. 20 (UNC School of Government, 2012), 3–4. Additional counties adopted zoning after this survey. In 2019, sixty-nine counties had county-wide zoning, twelve had partial-county zoning, and nineteen had no county zoning for the unincorporated areas.

2. This book discusses land use law as applied in North Carolina. Although land use law is similar in most states, the various state legislatures and state courts have adapted and applied the principles differently. The reader who is interested in or familiar with the law in other states is therefore cautioned against overgeneralization.

Part One provides a brief overview of land use regulations and the geographic jurisdiction for their application. Chapter 2 begins with the way local land use regulatory decisions are categorized, introduces the legal implications of those categorizations, and provides an overview of the various boards, staff members, and others involved with land use regulation. Chapter 3 provides a review of the history and evolution of development regulations. Chapter 4 reviews the legal authority for local regulation of development. Chapter 5 addresses the geographical jurisdiction for land use regulation—the areas in which cities and counties may exercise their power to regulate land use and development.

Part Two provides a review of the form and typical content of the most common development regulations. Chapters in this section review zoning ordinances, subdivision regulations, building and housing codes, and growth-management and environmental regulations.

Part Three covers legislative decisions. Chapter 11 outlines the process that local governing boards must follow in adopting, amending, and repealing ordinances. Specific limitations on the power to adopt small-scale zoning amendments—spot zoning, contract zoning, and conditional zoning—are discussed in Chapters 12 and 13.

Part Four addresses quasi-judicial decisions. Chapter 14 delineates which decisions fall into this category and sets out the basic constitutional and statutory requirements that apply to these decisions. Chapter 15 provides a step-by-step review of the procedural requirements for all quasi-judicial decisions. The remaining chapters of Part Four review the law as applied to various quasi-judicial decisions including special use permits, variances, and appeals of staff determinations and administrative decisions.

Part Five deals with the applicability of development regulations to existing and partially completed developments and other administration and enforcement issues. Chapter 19 reviews the vested rights of landowners, specifically their constitutional and statutory rights to continue development after regulations that would restrict it have been amended. Chapter 20 reviews ordinance provisions that address nonconformities—limitations on situations that were legal when initiated but are inconsistent with current regulatory requirements. Chapter 21 addresses administration and enforcement of land use regulations. It also includes a discussion of the liability of staff and board members, as well as the units of government directly, for land use regulatory decisions.

Part Six reviews state and federal limits on local land use regulations. Chapters 22 and 23 address state and federal statutory requirements. The remaining chapters in this part review constitutional limitations—takings, due process, equal protection, and First Amendment limitations on regulation of adult business, religious land uses, and signs.

Part Seven covers judicial review of land use decisions. Chapter 29 addresses procedural issues, including standing and statutes of limitations, the standards for judicial review, and degree of judicial deference accorded various decisions.

Background information on both North Carolina zoning statutes and North Carolina litigation is presented in several appendixes: digests of 890 North Carolina land use and development regulation cases (Appendix A); a chronology of amendments to zoning-enabling statutes (Appendix B); a directory of statutes related to land use (Appendix C); and conversion charts that show the placement of pre-2019 statutes in Chapter 160D of the North Carolina General Statutes and their original location (Appendix D).

CHAPTER 2

Framework for Decision-Making

Types of Land Use Decisions

Local governments make many decisions in the process of adopting, amending, administering, and enforcing land-development regulations. These range from a planning board's decision to recommend adoption of an initial zoning ordinance to an enforcement officer's decision to issue a notice of violation when the terms of an ordinance have not been followed.

These governmental decisions are grouped by the planning legislation and by the courts into four categories: legislative, quasi-judicial, advisory, and administrative.[1] This categorization is important, as different procedures apply depending on which type of decision is involved. In 2019, the General Assembly codified the definitions for the types of development-regulation decisions in Chapter 160D, Section 102 of the North Carolina General Statutes (hereinafter G.S.).[2]

Legislative

Legislative decisions are those that set general policies. Decisions to adopt, amend, or repeal an ordinance (which includes the zoning map) are included in this category, as are decisions to approve a development agreement.[3] While there are detailed statutory procedural requirements for legislative decisions, the substance of the decision is generally discretionary.

Hearings are required as part of the decision-making process, but they are legislative rather than evidentiary. The purpose of a legislative hearing is to solicit public opinion regarding the desirability of the policy to be chosen. By contrast, the purpose of the evidentiary hearings required for quasi-judicial decisions is to seek reliable evidence to determine facts rather than to set new policies.[4]

---

1. Cnty. of Lancaster v. Mecklenburg Cnty., 334 N.C. 496, 507, 434 S.E.2d 604, 612 (1993); Kerik v. Davidson Cnty., 145 N.C. App. 222, 227, 551 S.E.2d 186, 190 (2001).

2. The defined terms include *administrative*, *legislative*, and *quasi-judicial* decisions as well as *legislative* and *evidentiary* hearings.

3. Chapter 160D, Section 102(19) of the North Carolina General Statutes (hereinafter G.S.).

4. Massey v. City of Charlotte, 145 N.C. App. 345, 550 S.E.2d 838, *review denied*, 354 N.C. 219, 554 S.E.2d 342 (2001) (holding conditional rezoning a legislative decision); *Kerik*, 145 N.C. App. 222, 551 S.E.2d 186 (holding rezoning a legislative decision); Brown v. Town of Davidson, 113 N.C. App. 553, 439 S.E.2d 206 (1994) (holding rezoning a legislative decision not subject to quasi-judicial procedures); Sherrill v. Town of Wrightsville Beach, 81 N.C. App. 369, 373, 344 S.E.2d 357, 360 (1986) (holding rezoning a legislative act).

Quasi-Judicial

Quasi-judicial decisions involve the application of ordinance policies to individual situations rather than the adoption of new policies.[5] In a landmark North Carolina zoning case, *Lee v. Board of Adjustment*, the court ruled that the board of adjustment, acting in a quasi-judicial capacity, "is not left free to make any determination whatever that appeals to its sense of justice. It must abide by and comply with the rules of conduct provided by its charter—the local ordinance enacted in accord with . . . State zoning law."[6]

Examples of quasi-judicial decisions include variances, permits for special uses (even if issued by the governing board or planning board), certificates of appropriateness under historic-district regulations, appeals, and interpretations. These decisions involve two key elements: the finding of facts regarding the specific proposal and the exercise of some judgment and discretion in applying predetermined policies to the situation. Some decisions, such as site-plan or plat approvals, that are typically administrative become quasi-judicial if the ordinance includes standards for them that require judgment and discretion.[7]

Quasi-judicial decisions may be assigned by the ordinance to the board of adjustment, planning board, or governing board, but they may not be assigned to a staff administrator.[8]

Advisory

Advisory decisions are those rendered by bodies that may make recommendations on a matter but have no final decision-making authority over it. They are designed to provide advice on pending legislative decisions, such as the advice given by planning boards to governing boards on a rezoning petition. Referral of all proposed zoning amendments, whether text or map, to the planning board for review and comment is mandatory for cities and counties in North Carolina.[9] It is relatively common for pending quasi-judicial decisions to also be referred to an advisory board for review and comment.[10]

---

5. G.S. 160D-102(28). The definition provides that this is "[a] decision involving the finding of facts regarding a specific application of development regulation and that requires the exercise of discretion when applying the standards of the regulation."

6. 226 N.C. 107, 111, 37 S.E.2d 128, 132 (1946) (holding a use variance to be illegal, constituting an improper de facto amendment of the ordinance, which requires a legislative zoning decision). See Chapter 14 for detailed discussion of the definition of *quasi-judicial decision*.

7. G.S. 160D-102(28).

8. A few states allow staff determinations on these matters. For example, California statutes allow variance and special use permits to be determined by the zoning administrator or the board of adjustment. CAL. GOV'T CODE § 65901 (West 2018).

9. G.S. 160D-604. Prior to 2005, this was not required for cities. However, referral of proposed amendments to the planning board was an almost universal feature of city zoning ordinances.

10. In 2005, the School of Government conducted a survey of North Carolina local governments' practices regarding special use permits. Sixty-seven percent of the responding cities and counties reported that these quasi-judicial decisions were referred to the planning board for review and comment prior to consideration by the board making the decision. DAVID W. OWENS, SPECIAL USE PERMITS IN NORTH CAROLINA ZONING 9 (UNC School of Government, Special Series No. 22, Apr. 2007). While not illegal, these referrals are problematic in that very limited use can be made of the advice by the decision-making board. Any evidence presented solely to the advisory board would be hearsay. A recommendation as to how the facts fit the applicable standard would be the ultimate conclusory finding that must be made by the decision-making board, using evidence properly before it. G.S. 160D-301(b)(6) codifies this limited role of advisory reviews of quasi-judicial decisions. See Chapter 15 for additional discussion of this issue.

Administrative/Ministerial

Administrative decisions (sometimes termed *ministerial decisions*) are the day-to-day matters related to implementation of a land-development regulation.[11] Typically handled by staff, these include issuance of permits for permitted uses, most site-plan reviews,[12] initial interpretations of ordinances, and initiation of enforcement actions.[13]

While these often involve some fact-finding, they apply only objective, nondiscretionary standards.[14] If all of the technical standards of the ordinance are met, approval must be issued. No evidentiary hearing is required as part of the decision-making process, and the staff has no authority to impose or consider factors beyond the standards of the ordinance.[15] Even if the final decision is assigned to the governing board, if the decision is ministerial in nature, the board must approve the application as a matter of law if the applicant shows compliance with all of the objective decision-making standards.[16]

Characterization of Particular Decisions

The categorization of a decision as legislative, quasi-judicial, or administrative is a question of law, ultimately determined by the courts.[17] Thus, the way a decision is labeled in an ordinance is not necessarily dispositive of the question of which legal category a decision falls into. For example, a rezoning applying an overlay zoning district (such as a historic district) is normally a legislative decision, but if an ordinance is structured in such a way that a person is entitled to the designation upon establishing specified conditions, the decision can be characterized as quasi-judicial.[18] On borderline calls, however, the court gives some deference to the ordinance's categorization of the decision.[19]

The categorization of decisions depends on the nature of the decision, not the body making the decision. This is a frequent point of confusion. For example, a governing board may believe that if it makes a special use permit decision rather than the board of adjustment, it may dispense with oaths, witnesses, findings of fact, and the other requirements that must be observed for quasi-judicial decisions. This is not the case. A special use permit decision is a quasi-judicial decision no matter who is deciding it.

---

11. G.S. 160D-102(1).

12. Usually the site-plan review is used to verify compliance with objective standards in the ordinance, but some include discretionary standards and are thus quasi-judicial decisions.

13. *See, e.g.,* Quadrant Corp. v. City of Kinston, 22 N.C. App. 31, 205 S.E.2d 324 (1974).

14. For example, in *Ornoff v. City of Durham*, 221 N.C. 457, 20 S.E.2d 380 (1942), the court held that the original Durham zoning ordinance gave the board of adjustment no authority to exercise discretion regarding nonconforming uses—if the use was in existence in March 1926 it could be continued. Therefore, the zoning administrator made an initial determination of the facts, and an aggrieved party could secure judicial review with a jury trial on contested facts.

15. Nazziola v. Landcraft Props., Inc., 143 N.C. App. 564, 545 S.E.2d 801 (2001) (holding subdivision plat approval an administrative decision).

16. Sanco of Wilmington Serv. Corp. v. New Hanover Cnty., 166 N.C. App. 471, 601 S.E.2d 889 (2004) (where plat-approval standards are entirely objective, decision is ministerial and board has no authority to deny or condition approval when standards have been met).

17. Courts in some states have determined that small-scale rezonings—changing the zoning classification for an individual parcel of land, for example—should be considered quasi-judicial rather than legislative, as they analyze it as applying policy to a set of facts rather than setting policy. The leading example is *Fasano v. Board of County Commissioners*, 507 P.2d 23 (Or. 1974). See Chapter 12 for further discussion of this case in the context of spot zoning.

18. Northfield Dev. Co. v. City of Burlington, 136 N.C. App. 272, 523 S.E.2d 743, *aff'd per curiam*, 352 N.C. 671, 535 S.E.2d 32 (2000). Devaney v. City of Burlington, 143 N.C. App. 334, 337–38, 545 S.E.2d 763, 765, *review denied*, 353 N.C. 724, 550 S.E.2d 772 (2001). For a further discussion of the quasi-judicial nature of these decisions, see Chapter 14.

19. Cnty. of Lancaster v. Mecklenburg Cnty., 334 N.C. 496, 510, 434 S.E.2d 604, 614 (1993).

It is also important to note that it is the standards used in an individual ordinance that control the characterization of the decision. For example, in most ordinances a preliminary plat approval is an administrative or ministerial decision because the standards applied are entirely objective (e.g., standards on right-of-way widths, street and utility construction, and lot configuration).[20] However, a local government may add discretionary standards for plat approval (e.g., that the subdivision not have significant adverse impact on traffic or that its design be compatible with surrounding neighborhoods). If this is done, the normally administrative plat approval decision is converted to a quasi-judicial one.[21]

Another instance of a shifting characterization of a decision is the inclusion of a default decision upon failure to act on an application in a timely fashion. For example, decisions on a certificate of appropriateness under a historic-district ordinance are quasi-judicial, as the key standard is a determination of whether a proposed project is "congruent" with the historic character of the district, which involves application of judgment and discretion. However, the state statute requires that decisions on these applications be made in a timely fashion.[22] If, in response to this mandate, an ordinance provides that an application is automatically approved in the absence of a decision within a specified period, then once that period runs out, the issuance of the certificate of appropriateness becomes administrative or ministerial, as there is no longer any discretion or judgment to be exercised.[23]

Implications of Characterization

Different legal requirements and procedures are observed for each type of decision.[24] Because legislative decisions have such an important impact on both the general public and individual landowners, the enabling statutes require broad public notice of the proposed decision, encourage full public discussion and deliberation, and leave broad discretion in the hands of local elected officials regarding what these public policies should be.[25] On the other hand, in the case of quasi-judicial decisions, the focus shifts to the constitutional requirements imposed to ensure that predetermined public policies are fairly and reasonably applied to individual cases. The courts are concerned that an impartial decision be made based solely on legitimately acquired and considered evidence, a clear rationale for the decision, and an expeditious judicial review to guarantee that these required protections of individual rights have been observed.[26]

These considerations result in different statutory, constitutional, and due-process requirements for the various types of decisions. Different types of notice are required, different types of hearings are conducted, and different standards of judicial review apply. Table 2.1 summarizes some of these important differences between legislative and quasi-judicial decisions.

---

20. *Sanco*, 166 N.C. App. 471, 601 S.E.2d 889.

21. Guilford Fin. Servs. v. City of Brevard, 356 N.C. 655, 576 S.E.2d 325 (2003), *per curiam, adopting dissent in* 150 N.C. App. 1, 563 S.E.2d 27 (2002). For example, the development regulations of the Town of Wake Forest used standards involving judgment and discretion for major site-plan and major subdivision approvals—requiring that there be "adequate infrastructure" to support the development and that it "not be detrimental to the use or development of adjacent properties." The use of these standards made the decision on approval quasi-judicial. Schooldev East, LLC v. Town of Wake Forest, 284 N.C. App. 434, 876 S.E.2d 607 (2022).

22. G.S. 160D-947(d) requires that decisions be made "within a reasonable time, not to exceed 180 days" from receipt of an application.

23. Meares v. Town of Beaufort, 193 N.C. App. 49, 56, 667 S.E.2d 244, 249–50 (2008).

24. See David W. Owens, *Zoning Hearings: Knowing Which Rules to Apply*, POPULAR GOV'T, Spring 1993, at 26 for further discussion and illustrations of these differences.

25. See Chapter 11 for a detailed discussion of the procedural requirements for legislative decisions.

26. Humble Oil & Refin. Co. v. Bd. of Aldermen, 284 N.C. 458, 202 S.E.2d 129 (1974). See Chapter 15 for a detailed discussion of the procedural requirements for quasi-judicial decisions.

Table 2.1   Key Differences Between Legislative and Quasi-Judicial Decisions

	Legislative	Quasi-Judicial
Decision maker	Governing board (others may advise)	Board of adjustment, planning board, or governing board
Notice of hearing	Newspaper and mailed notices to owners and neighbors, posted notice for rezoning	Mailed to owners and neighbors; posted on-site
Type of hearing	Legislative	Evidentiary
Presentations at hearings	Reasonable limit on number of speakers and time allowed	Testimony limited to relevant, nonrepetitive evidence
Types of evidence / restrictions on participants	Evidence not required; member discussion of issue outside of hearing allowed	Substantial, material evidence in record; witnesses under oath, subject to cross-examination; no ex parte communication
Findings	None required, but statement on plan consistency and rationale required	Written findings of fact supported by evidence in the record required for contested facts
Voting majority	Simple majority of entire board	Four-fifths to grant a variance; simple majority for special use permit, appeals
Standard for decision	Establishes standard	Only applies standards previously set in ordinance
Conditions	Not allowed (unless conditional zoning involved)	Allowed if based on standard in ordinance
Filing judicial challenge	Time limit: 2 months from decision for rezoning; 1 year for others	Time limit: 30 days from mailing and filing written decision
Conflict-of-interest disqualification	Direct substantial financial interest or close relationship with affected landowner	Any financial interest, close relationship with a party, or personal bias
Vested right	None created	Created if substantial expenditures rely on it
Judicial review	Highly deferential arbitrary-and-capricious standard	Significant review for errors of law, adequacy of evidence

It should be noted, however, that local ordinances sometimes apply procedures mandated for one type of decision to other types of decisions.[27] For example, requirements in individual zoning ordinances sometimes apply aspects of quasi-judicial decision-making to legislative decisions. Many local zoning ordinances also apply some of the standards for legislative decisions to quasi-judicial decisions, such as the requirement that notices of hearings be published and mailed to adjacent landowners.

The type of decision used for a particular action is a policy choice to be made when framing the development regulation. Factors that should be considered in making that choice include:

- Are there unresolved policy questions to be addressed? A legislative decision is the process to use if decisions have not yet been made about what land uses and density levels would be appropriate, what design standards are needed, how to provide necessary infrastructure, or how to deal with environmental impacts. If clear policy choices have been made and standards set,

---

27. Procedural requirements imposed by ordinances, as well as those imposed by the general zoning-enabling act, are binding. George v. Town of Edenton, 294 N.C. 679, 242 S.E.2d 877 (1978); *Humble Oil*, 284 N.C. 458, 202 S.E.2d 129.

administrative decisions are appropriate. A closely related question is how much involvement by elected officials is desired. Elected officials make legislative decisions but have little if any involvement in administrative ones.

- Is speed, predictability, or certainty a key factor? An administrative decision is the quickest and most predictable for landowners and neighbors, while a quasi-judicial decision takes longer and requires more rigorous analysis. The legislative decision is by its very nature the least predictable and often slowest process. If the local government wants to encourage development or redevelopment of a particular type at a specific site and already knows the standards that should be met, an administrative review rather than a rezoning would be the choice to make.

- How much citizen engagement is desired? Legislative decisions allow for the most citizen engagement, quasi-judicial decisions allow those directly affected to present evidence, and administrative decisions are largely determined by staff without consulting the public. Politically sensitive policy issues are best discussed broadly in a legislative context, not resolved by staff members applying technical review standards. A rezoning allows broad public discussion, while most citizens will not learn of an administrative decision until after it has been made. Participation in a quasi-judicial hearing is limited to presentation of competent evidence, which often requires expertise that is not readily available to laypersons (and imposes real costs on both applicants and neighbors).

- How much does the decision turn on detailed technical analysis, and how likely is it that the facts will be contested? An administrative review is well suited to gather substantial information and conduct technical analysis. The quasi-judicial process is well suited to resolve contested facts, especially where both sides to a land use dispute are well represented. It is useful in this context to consider both the type of issues to be resolved and the type of decision maker needed. Professional staff make administrative decisions, quasi-judicial decisions are usually made by appointed boards, and legislative decisions are entrusted to elected officials. Legislative bodies sometimes struggle when limited to an adjudicative quasi-judicial process.

- How much flexibility and discretion is desired? Legislative decisions allow the greatest discretion, administrative decisions the least.

- Is there a need to tailor site-specific conditions? The legislative decision can be used for this in North Carolina (though not in some other states). The legislative process is better suited for setting broader community policies. The quasi-judicial process is useful when it is known that some conditions or exactions may well be needed, but a detailed, individualized review is needed to determine their precise design or scale.

- Is ease of administration and enforcement a concern? Administration of standardized, uniformly applied rules is far simpler than developing and keeping track of rules that change over time and vary from parcel to parcel.

The choice to be made involves trade-offs. A legislative decision allows a greater range of discretion and broad public engagement but is not quick or predictable. A quasi-judicial decision allows for a careful, searching inquiry into the facts but is formal and legalistic, limiting possibilities for informal discussion among applicants, citizens, and decision makers. An administrative decision is quick and efficient but requires more advance work on the ordinance to assure that all of the desired standards are in place before an application is made (such as specifying necessary infrastructure improvements, design standards for a form-based regulation, or technical standards to be met), and it provides little opportunity for governing-board or citizen involvement. Efficiency and engagement are not mutually exclusive considerations, but sometimes one or the other will take precedence.

Table 2.2   Notice Requirements

Type of Action	Type of Notice	Recipient	Timing
Final staff determination	Personal service, email, or mail Posting by owner (optional)	Person requesting Property owner	When determination is made
Hearing on quasi-judicial decision	Mail Post site	Applicant Property owner Abutting property owners	10–25 days before hearing
Quasi-judicial decision	File with clerk Personal service, email, or mail	Applicant Property owner Others making written request prior to effective date	Effective date of decision
Hearing on ordinance-text amendment	Newspaper Certified mail if near military base	Public Base commander	10–25 days before hearing
Hearing on rezoning	Newspaper Mail Post site Certified mail if near military base	Property owner Adjacent property owner Base commander	10–25 days before hearing

Notices of Hearings and Decisions

When hearings are scheduled on proposed decisions under local development regulations and when decisions are made, state law and local ordinances require public notices to be made. The required notice may be in the form of newspaper notices, mailed notices, posting the site, and sometimes personal delivery. The statutes specify which type of notice must be provided, whom it is provided to, and when it must be made.

Each of these notice requirements is discussed in detail in the following chapters. Table 2.2 summarizes these notice requirements.

Actors in the Process

A number of different local government bodies participate in land use regulation. The city council or county board of commissioners, the planning board, and the zoning board of adjustment all play key roles. In addition, local government staff provide essential support in ordinance administration and enforcement.

North Carolina law gives each local government considerable flexibility in determining how to allocate zoning decisions to various boards and agencies; the three boards described below commonly take charge of major aspects of zoning.[28]

---

28. The statutory provisions regarding boards established for purposes of planning and development regulation are collected in Article 3 of Chapter 160D of the General Statutes. The statutory provisions for each

Jurisdictions with small populations often combine several of these boards. This is most often done in rural counties or small towns. In these settings the board of adjustment, for example, often has a very modest workload, only hearing a couple of cases per year. Therefore, the governing board may conclude it is impractical to appoint a separate board with minimal activity. The combination can be accomplished in several ways. One option is to merge multiple boards into a single board, such as having a "zoning commission" that performs the duties of both the planning board and board of adjustment. A second option is to retain multiple boards but to appoint the same members to both groups, such as having the same membership for both the planning board and board of adjustment. Some care is needed in these combination options as there are different statutory requirements applicable to different boards (e.g., the board of adjustment must have at least five members with set terms, while the planning board is only required to have three members and there is no requirement for set terms). If the ordinance retains both boards, both sets of statutory requirements must be met.

In some instances, the governing board itself may take on the duties of other boards, most commonly the board of adjustment.[29] While this can be done for many boards, the option is not available for some functions of the planning board, as there is a statutory requirement that the governing board receive a written recommendation from the planning board prior to amending a zoning ordinance. This statutory mandate would be meaningless if the board is making a recommendation to itself. For this reason, G.S. 160D-604(e) requires the board that reviews and comments on proposed regulations to be separate from the governing board.

The statutes explicitly provide for this flexibility in several instances. G.S. 160D-302(b) provides that the zoning ordinance may designate the planning board or governing board to "perform any or all of the duties" of a board of adjustment. G.S. 160D-103 allows development regulations to "employ any organization structure, board, commission, or staffing arrangement authorized by law to any or all aspects" of its development ordinance.[30]

Members of these boards are "officers" of the city or county. Each member must take an oath of office.[31] The oath of office can be administered by the mayor or chair of the board of county commissioners, the city or county clerk, or any notary public.[32] State law also limits the number of offices any one person can hold at one time. An elected or appointed official can hold only one additional office in state or local government.[33] If an official holds a second position by virtue of holding the first position (generally referred to as being an *ex officio member* of the second board), that is considered part of the duties of office of the first board and not a second office.[34]

---

board—planning boards, boards of adjustment, historic-preservation commissions, and others—use a common format setting out requirements regarding board composition and duties.

29. See, e.g., *Murdock v. Chatham County*, 198 N.C. App. 309, 679 S.E.2d 850 (2009), *review denied*, 363 N.C. 806, 690 S.E.2d 705 (2010), where the board of county commissioners also sat as the board of adjustment.

30. Other boards have more-specialized provisions on coordination or integration of functions. G.S. 160D-303(b) allows the functions of a historic-preservation commission to be assigned to a planning board or community appearance commission, but only if that board has members with specified expertise. That statute also allows the functions of the planning board or community appearance board to be assigned to the historic-preservation commission for activity within a historic district.

31. G.S. 160D-309. G.S. 11-7 provides a form for the oath of office. Failure to take the oath before assuming the duties of the office may subject the member to a $500 penalty and removal from office. G.S. 128-5. Also see Chapter 21 for information about the importance of the officer-employee distinction regarding potential liability.

32. G.S. 11-7.1. The statute also allows the oath of office to be administered by a judge, magistrate, clerk of court, or member of the General Assembly.

33. G.S. 128-1.1.

34. G.S. 128-1.2.

Governing Board

The local governing board—the city council or county board of commissioners—controls local zoning. This governing board makes final policy decisions on zoning.[35] It decides whether or not to have zoning, amends the ordinance as needed, and appoints the members of the other citizen boards involved.[36]

For the most part, the governing board acts by simple majority vote. The statutes formerly required that if there was a qualifying protest petition regarding a proposed zoning-map amendment, a three-fourths vote was required to adopt a protested change.[37] That provision is no longer in the statutes.

Planning Board

The planning board or planning commission provides advice to the governing board on zoning issues.[38] These are typically boards of citizens who usually meet once or twice a month. The planning board can be of any size (it must have at least three members) and may be constituted however the governing board deems appropriate.[39]

Cities and counties may establish residency qualifications for planning-board membership, but state law does not require board members to reside within the appointing jurisdiction.[40] If a city has extraterritorial planning jurisdiction, the city planning board must include proportional representation on the planning board for residents of that area.[41] Unlike boards of adjustment, state law does not mandate a set term of office for planning boards, though many ordinances include a specified term. If a term is not specified, the members serve at the pleasure of the appointing body.[42] Appointed members hold over in office until their successors are chosen and qualified.[43]

The governing board must appoint a planning board before adopting a zoning ordinance and must refer all proposed zoning amendments to the planning board for review and comment.[44]

---

35. A few jurisdictions in North Carolina have legislative authorization to delegate some rezoning decisions to the planning board for final decision. This is discussed in Chapter 11.

36. G.S. 160D-310. The governing board may establish reasonable procedures to solicit, review, and make appointments.

37. See Chapter 11 for a detailed discussion of voting on legislative decisions.

38. There are several national handbooks often used as guides for planning-board members. *See, e.g.*, C. Gregory Dale et al., The Planning Commissioners Guide (2d ed. 2013); Albert Solnit, The Job of the Planning Commissioner (3d ed. 1987); Herbert H. Smith, The Citizen's Guide to Planning (1979).

39. G.S. 160D-301. From 1923 to 1967, the statutes required recommendations on zoning adoption from an appointed "zoning commission." In 1967, this was changed to require a recommendation from the planning board. From 1971 to 2004, the statutes used the term "planning agency" to refer to a planning board. Unlike the provisions for boards of adjustment, these statutes do not make explicit reference to alternate members. It is not unusual for cities and counties to deem it appropriate to make provisions for alternate planning-board members. These members typically serve in the place of absent members but may also be called upon if the board hears quasi-judicial matters and a member is disqualified due to a conflict of interest on an individual matter.

40. G.S. 160A-60 provides that residence within the appointing jurisdiction is not a qualification for appointed office unless the city charter or a city ordinance requires it. Likewise, G.S. 153A-25 allows the county board of commissioners to set residency qualifications for members of appointed boards but does not mandate county residence as a qualification. Members are to take an oath of office. G.S. 153A-26; 160A-61.

41. G.S. 160D-307. See Chapter 5 for more details on extraterritorial planning and development regulation.

42. In *Kinsland v. Mackey*, 217 N.C. 508, 512, 8 S.E.2d 598, 600 (1940), the court found that where the term of office of a public officer is not prescribed by law, the office is held during the pleasure of the authority making the appointment. This case involved the position of tax collector for Canton. The court also noted that in the absence of a statutory limitation, the power of removal is incident to the power of appointment, is discretionary, and may be exercised without notice or hearing. Removal from office has long been held to be an incident of the appointment authority. *In re* Hennen, 38 U.S. 230, 239 (1839).

43. G.S. 160A-62.

44. See Chapter 11 for a detailed discussion of the duties of the board in ordinance amendment.

In the early days of local land-development regulation, the principal responsibility assigned to the planning board was the development of a comprehensive plan,[45] along with conducting studies on population growth, economic development, traffic, parking, recreation, housing, and provision of public facilities.[46] Even then, these boards also played an active role in preparing or revising zoning ordinances and reviewing proposed rezonings and subdivision plats. In 1953, Philip Green, a professor at what was then the Institute of Government, suggested that the planning board's role should be twofold—gathering important background information to guide policy making by the city council and assisting in carrying the plans into effect.[47]

The statutes now provide that the planning-board duties include:

- working on the comprehensive plan and other plans, including preparing, reviewing, maintaining, monitoring, and updating plans and conducting research, data collection, mapping, and analysis;
- facilitating and coordinating citizen engagement in planning;
- recommending policies, regulations, and other measures for plan implementation;
- reviewing and commenting on regulatory amendments;
- providing a preliminary forum for review of quasi-judicial decisions; and
- exercising such other administrative or advisory functions as directed by the governing board.[48]

Both cities and counties must refer all proposed zoning amendments to the planning board for review.[49] While the governing board is not bound by the recommendation, the planning board is directed by G.S. 160D-604 to provide a written recommendation on whether the proposed amendment is consistent with an adopted comprehensive or other applicable plan. The board may comment on any other

---

45. Municipal planning boards were first authorized in 1919. S.L. 1919-23 authorized planning boards "to make careful study of the resources, possibilities and needs of the city or town, particularly with respect to the conditions which may be injurious to the public welfare or otherwise injurious, and to make plans for the development of the municipality."

46. A 1952 survey of planning activity in North Carolina reported that preparation of a "master plan" was the most popular activity for planning boards. Philip P. Green, Jr., *City Planning and Zoning Moves Ahead*, POPULAR GOV'T, Sept. 1952, at 10. The 1947 legislation authorizing the Winston-Salem/Forsyth County planning commission not only authorized the commission to prepare a plan but also required many public improvements (to streets, squares, parks, open space, public buildings, and major public utilities) to be submitted to the commission for approval and allowed delegation of approval of subdivision plats to the commission. S.L. 1947-677.

47. Green suggested six tasks for policy-making assistance: (1) developing information on current land uses, future land use needs, and projected annexations; (2) providing population-growth projections; (3) identifying strengths and weaknesses in the local economy; (4) assessing traffic congestion and parking needs and the impacts on new streets; (5) assessing housing demand, identifying substandard areas, and advising on means to provide decent housing; and (6) coordinating other plans, such as for school siting, parks, roads, and public utilities. He also suggested five tasks related to plan implementation: (1) preparation of a zoning ordinance and review of proposed amendments; (2) review of subdivision plats; (3) advice on preparation of a capital-improvements plan; (4) review of proposed city projects; and (5) review of redevelopment plans. Philip P. Green, Jr., *The City Planning Board: What Should the City Council Expect of It?* POPULAR GOV'T, Feb. 1953, at 7–8. *See also* Philip P. Green, Jr., *Improving Local Planning Boards*, POPULAR GOV'T, Apr. 1972, at 14–16 (suggesting that planning boards focus on community goal setting).

48. G.S. 160D-301(b).

49. G.S. 160D-604. The previous county statute, G.S. 153A-344(a), always required such a referral. Prior to 2005, most city zoning ordinances also required referral of proposed zoning amendments to their planning boards, but state law did not require it. G.S. 160A-387 was amended in 2005 to also mandate referral of proposed zoning text and map amendments to the planning board for review and comment. S.L. 2005-418, § 7(a). See Chapter 11 for a detailed discussion of ordinance adoption and amendment procedures.

matter deemed appropriate. Some governing boards also assign to their planning boards either advisory[50] or final decision-making authority for permits for special uses. Planning boards may help with a number of nonzoning matters, such as development of a comprehensive plan, community- and economic-development programs, or plat reviews under a subdivision ordinance. The governing board may also assign to the planning board any or all of the functions of a board of adjustment.[51]

Board of Adjustment

The board of adjustment (sometimes termed the *board of appeals*) was created as a judicial-like body to decide individual zoning disputes without the time and expense involved with formal litigation.[52] The board of adjustment is not involved in setting policies. Rather, this board interprets and applies the standards that have been placed in development regulations by the governing board.

The board of adjustment hears individual quasi-judicial cases, such as appeals, requests for permits for special uses, and variance petitions.[53] The statutes require a four-fifths vote of the board of adjustment to approve a variance.[54] Decisions of the board are appealed directly to the courts.

The governing board appoints at least five members to this board.[55] Each member must have a set three-year term and the terms may be staggered. Cities and counties may establish residency qualifications for membership, but state law does not require board members to reside within the appointing jurisdiction.[56] If a city has extraterritorial planning jurisdiction, the city board of adjustment must include proportional representation on the board for residents of that area.[57]

Since boards of adjustment typically hear variances where a supermajority vote is required and impartial decision makers are a necessity, the statutes make express provision for alternate members for boards of adjustment.[58] Alternate members may serve (1) in the absence of a member, (2) due to the temporary disqualification in an individual case where the member has a conflict, or (3) to fill a

---

50. The advisory nature of planning-board review of rezoning requests has long been a source of frustration for some planning boards. The entire Fayetteville Planning Board resigned in protest in 1948 when its role was limited to making recommendations rather than decisions on zoning petitions. *The Clearinghouse*, POPULAR GOV'T, July 1948, at 20.

51. G.S. 160D-302(a).

52. Authorization for a board of adjustment was included in the initial zoning-enabling statute in North Carolina in 1923. S.L. 1923-250.

53. The board must hear these matters arising from zoning regulations. G.S. 160D-302 provides it may also hear and decide matters arising under other development regulations. Each of these quasi-judicial proceedings is discussed in detail in Chapters 16 through 18. G.S. 160D-302(a) also specifically authorizes local governments to designate other specialized boards to hear technical appeals. Some local governments have such technical boards to hear appeals on stormwater plans, subdivision plats, or other engineering and technical matters.

54. G.S. 160D-302(a). These statutes were amended in 2005 to provide that vacancies and board members who are not participating in a particular matter due to a conflict of interest are not considered in computing the required majority. S.L. 2005-418, §§ 8(a) and 8(b). See Chapter 15 for further discussion of voting in quasi-judicial matters.

55. G.S. 160D-302(a).

56. G.S. 160A-60 provides that residence within the appointing jurisdiction is not a qualification for appointed office unless the city charter or a city ordinance requires it. Likewise, G.S. 153A-25 allows the county board of commissioners to set residency qualifications for members of appointed boards but does not mandate county residence as a qualification. Members are to take an oath of office. G.S. 153A-26; 160A-61. Appointed officers hold over in office until their successors are chosen and qualified. G.S. 160A-62. The state constitution also provides that elected and appointed officers hold over in office until their successors are chosen and qualified. N.C. CONST. art. VII, § 10.

57. G.S. 160D-307. See Chapter 5 for more details on extraterritorial planning and development regulation.

58. G.S. 160D-302(a). *See generally* Patricia E. Salkin, *Planning for Conflicts of Interest in Land Use Decisionmaking: The Use of Alternate Members of Planning and Zoning Boards*, 31 REAL EST. L.J. 375 (2003); Patricia E. Salkin, *Providing for Alternate Members on Planning and Zoning Boards: Drafting Effective Local Laws*, 61 PLAN. & ENVTL. L. 3 (2009).

vacancy on the board pending appointment of a replacement member. The method of appointment of alternate members and their terms are the same as for regular members. An alternate member has the same powers and rights as a regular member when actively serving at a meeting. Many jurisdictions have alternate members attend each meeting, while some only call upon alternates to attend when it is known in advance of the meeting that their services will be needed. If an alternate member is present at a quasi-judicial hearing but not serving in place of a regular member, the alternate member should simply observe rather than actively participate in the hearing or discussion of the case.

A board member may not be removed during the member's term of office except for good cause.[59] The grounds for removal must be substantial, such as criminal misconduct in office, willful or intentional failure to discharge the duties of office, persistent and substantial conflicts of interest, incapacities that preclude discharge of the member's duties on the board, and the like.[60] Technical or inconsequential violations of the law or disagreement with the substance of the member's decisions are not sufficient cause for removal.[61] This provides some degree of independence for board members, allowing them to judiciously apply the law without fear of immediate political reaction by elected officials. While the statutes are silent as to the procedures that must be followed for removal of a member, it would be prudent to provide a timely and adequate notice of the proposed removal to the member, give the member a reasonable and fair opportunity to be heard on the matter, and have a fair and impartial decision by the board making the removal decision.[62]

The governing board does, however, always have the option of amending the ordinance to repeal authorization for a board of adjustment altogether.[63] This has the effect of dismissing the entire board, which can later be reestablished and reconstituted with different members. This action requires notice and a public hearing, as ordinance amendments are necessary to do this.

---

59. A member appointed to office for a fixed term can only be removed for good cause. State *ex rel.* Bryan v. Patrick, 124 N.C. 651, 33 S.E. 151 (1899) (holding members of state Board of Internal Improvements with two-year terms could not be removed from office by the legislature without cause). For a general discussion of the authority to remove an appointed official for cause during a term of office, see *James v. Hunt*, 43 N.C. App. 109, 117–21, 258 S.E.2d 481, 486–88 (1979) (addressing removal of gubernatorial appointee to State Cemetery Commission). *See generally* Wiener v. United States, 357 U.S. 349 (1958); Humphrey's Executor v. United States, 295 U.S. 602 (1935); Myers v. United States, 272 U.S. 52 (1926).

60. For a list of potential grounds of "just cause" removal from office in the analogous context of county social-services-board members, see John L. Saxon, *The County Board of Social Services (Part III): Appointment, Terms, Term Limits, and Removal from Office*, Soc. Servs. L. Bull. No. 36 (UNC School of Government, June 2002), at 7–8. State personnel law allows removal of employees with permanent status for cause, and personnel regulations define "just cause" in this context as either "grossly inefficient job performance" or "unacceptable personal conduct." Title 25, Chapter 01I, Section 2301(c) of the North Carolina Administrative Code.

61. *See, e.g.*, Steeves v. Scotland Cnty. Bd. of Health, 152 N.C. App. 400, 567 S.E.2d 817 (2002).

62. Early case law in North Carolina held that a board member appointed to office for a fixed term had a property interest in continuation in office. Hoke v. Henderson, 15 N.C. 1, 10–11 (1833). However, in *Mial v. Ellington*, 134 N.C. 131, 46 S.E.2d 961 (1903), the court rejected that view after a detailed review of contrary views in the federal courts and in other states. Thus, a board member being dismissed for cause may not have the full range of constitutional due-process rights discussed in Chapter 14. Still, considerations of equity and fairness, as well as potential constitutional constraints, would indicate that a city council or board of county commissioners should observe basic procedural safeguards in making a removal decision.

63. Bd. of Adjustment v. Town of Swansboro, 334 N.C. 421, 432 S.E.2d 310 (1993). The governing board amended the zoning ordinance to abolish the board of adjustment and then immediately reestablished a reconstituted board. The members of the original board sued, contending this action illegally shortened their terms of office. The court held that the existence of a board of adjustment is not mandated and the governing board retains the option of abolishing the board at any time.

Table 2.3   Typical Assignment of Functions

Body	Primary Role	Other Possibilities
Governing board (city council, county board of commissioners)	Legislative decisions: Adopts ordinances, amendments, policy statements, budgets; approves acquisitions; makes appointments to other bodies	May approve plats and special use permits
Planning board (planning board; planning commission)	Advisory decisions: Sponsors planning studies; recommends policies, advises governing board; coordinates public participation; must recommend initial zoning ordinance and review and provide written recommendations on all amendments	May also serve as board of adjustment; may approve or review plats
Board of adjustment (board of appeals)	Quasi-judicial decisions: Hears zoning appeals, variances, special use permits	
Staff (zoning administrator, planning department, inspections department, manager, clerk)	Administrative decisions: Issues permits, conducts technical studies, initiates enforcement, advises manager	

Staff

City or county managers hire the staff members who support the zoning function.[64] In a few instances in North Carolina, the planning staff is hired directly by the planning board. Staff in the planning department, inspections department, and manager's office provide support to the planning-and-development-regulation process, preparing drafts of regulations, processing permits, enforcing ordinances, and keeping the records of the citizen boards.[65] Local governments can also secure staff assistance from private consultants, regional councils of government, or others.

Table 2.3 illustrates a typical allocation of zoning responsibilities among these groups.

Staff committees may also be assigned formal roles in land use decision-making. The most common example is a technical-review committee that may be assigned responsibility for review and approval of preliminary subdivision plats. These committees typically have representation from various city and county departments, such as planning, transportation, utilities, public safety, and parks and recreation.

Other Boards and Commissions

There are a number of other entities that play some role in land-development regulation. A historic-preservation commission,[66] for example, reviews permits related to specially designated historic districts or landmarks. Community appearance commissions,[67] economic-development commissions,

---

64. It has long been recognized that a land-development regulation is effective only if it is properly administered and enforced. "The manner of enforcement of the ordinance has at least as much effect upon the future characteristics of the community as the terms of the ordinance." PHILIP P. GREEN, JR., ZONING IN NORTH CAROLINA 255 (1952).

65. G.S. 160D-402(b). See Chapter 21 for a detailed discussion of the staff role in administration and enforcement of development regulations.

66. G.S. 160D-303.

67. G.S. 160D-304.

redevelopment commissions,[68] and housing authorities rarely work directly in regulatory implementation but often closely coordinate their work with regulatory programs.[69]

Nongovernmental Groups

A wide variety of nongovernmental community groups are often actively engaged in local land-development issues, including neighborhood associations, nonprofit community-development corporations, and advocacy groups for builders, real estate agents, business groups, environmental organizations, and others. While these groups do not have official decision-making authority, they are often influential in crafting local land-development policies.

Intergovernmental Coordination

North Carolina local governments have extensive authority to coordinate planning and development regulation with one another.[70] Often coordination of planning efforts is a task assigned to the planning board[71] or is done through informal coordinating committees.

More formal and ongoing coordination can be done by contracts and agreements made by two or more local governments. Joint planning boards and staffing arrangements can be created if desired. Both Winston-Salem/Forsyth County[72] and Charlotte–Mecklenburg County[73] have had joint planning commissions for over fifty years.[74] Other jurisdictions have merged their staffing for planning or land-development-regulation implementation.[75] Regional-planning commissions[76] and councils of government[77] may undertake cooperative planning efforts.[78]

---

68. G.S. 160A, §§ 504 to 512.

69. G.S. 160D-306 allows a local government to establish any additional advisory boards it deems appropriate. G.S. 160D-305 allows the duties of a housing-appeals board to be assigned to the board of adjustment.

70. G.S. 160D-503 explicitly authorizes coordinated planning efforts. G.S. 160A-460 to -464 also authorizes local governments to jointly exercise "any power, function, public enterprise, right, privilege, or immunity" of the local governments. G.S. 160A-460.

71. Such coordination has a long history. The Institute of Government reported in 1952 that following joint meetings of all the involved boards, the City–County Planning Board for Winston-Salem/Forsyth County had been assigned the task of coordinating the planning functions of the planning board, the school board, the housing authority, and the urban-redevelopment commission. *Notes from North Carolina Cities*, POPULAR GOV'T, Apr. 1952, at 2.

72. The joint board was formed pursuant to a local act. S.L. 1947-677.

73. The city and county planning boards were merged in 1954 under the general authority for joint operations. The combined board featured five members appointed by the city and five members appointed by the county. The city's annual appropriation of $20,000 and the county's of $7500 were transferred to the joint board, and there was an agreement that henceforth the city would fund 60 percent and the county 40 percent of the joint board budget. *Notes from North Carolina Cities*, POPULAR GOV'T, Oct. 1954, at 5.

74. At various times, Clinton–Sampson County, Durham City–County, Edenton–Chowan County, Fayetteville–Cumberland County, Sanford–Lee County, and Wilmington–New Hanover County have had merged city-county planning and development regulation programs.

75. For example, a combined building-inspections department provides zoning-staff services for Mecklenburg County and seven municipalities within the county.

76. G.S. 153A, §§ 391 to 398.

77. G.S. 160A, §§ 470 to 478. *See generally* Kloster v. Region D Council of Gov'ts, 36 N.C. App. 421, 245 S.E.2d 180, *review denied*, 295 N.C. 466, 246 S.E.2d 215 (1978).

78. For additional background on regional planning, see James H. Svara, *Regional Councils as Linchpins in North Carolina*, POPULAR GOV'T, Spring 1998, at 21.

CHAPTER 3

Evolution of Government Regulation of Development

Early Development Planning and Regulation

Cities in North Carolina have undertaken land use planning since colonial times. Many of the state's towns were laid out in a carefully planned fashion. The plans generally set a street network[1] and provided for creation of lots to be sold. Many plans also included other features such as public squares and delineated places for churches, markets, courthouses, cemeteries, schools, town commons, and residences. These early plans included a variety of development styles, from Raleigh's rectangular grid of streets and squares to Salem's avenues radiating from a central plaza and New Bern's triangular form at the confluence of two rivers.[2]

In colonial times and in early statehood, municipal government authority in North Carolina was provided by individual city charters and special acts for each municipality rather than by general state law.[3]

Rudimentary building regulations date from the state's colonial period. Much of the early regulation focused on fire safety in an era of wooden buildings and limited firefighting capacity. For example, Edenton was authorized in 1740 to forbid the use of wooden chimneys in town.[4] By the mid-1800s, many

---

1. The street width most commonly required in early statehood was 66 feet. A few towns (such as Raleigh and Bath) increased major street width to 100 feet; a few (such as Asheville) provided for streets as narrow as 33 feet. William Garner Roberts, Jr., Determinants of the Physical Characteristics of the Eighteenth-Century North Carolina Town 30 (1963) (unpublished M.A. thesis, University of North Carolina at Chapel Hill). Plans were often specified in town charters adopted by acts of the General Assembly.

2. JOHN H. CLEWELL, HISTORY OF WACHOVIA IN NORTH CAROLINA (1902); ADELAIDE L. FRIES, RECORDS OF THE MORAVIANS IN NORTH CAROLINA (1922); DAVID L. SWAIN, EARLY TIMES IN RALEIGH (1867); V.H. TODD & JULIUS GOEBEL, CHRISTOPH VON GRAFFENRIED'S ACCOUNT OF THE FOUNDING OF NEW BERN (1920).

3. The first town to be chartered in the state was Bath in 1705, followed by Edenton in 1722, Beaufort and New Bern in 1723, and Wilmington in 1760. See Charles D. Liner, *The Evolution of Governmental Roles and Responsibilities*, in STATE AND LOCAL GOVERNMENT RELATIONS IN NORTH CAROLINA 4 (2d ed. 1995). For much of the state's early history, each incorporated town had a unique set of legislatively delegated powers. A 1949 study noted:

> For a hundred and fifty years after the incorporation of the first town in North Carolina, towns were created, extended, or abolished by special acts of the General Assembly; and powers and duties were given and taken away in the same fashion. If every one of them was not a law unto itself, at least it had a set of laws unto itself.

REPORT OF THE COMMISSION ON PUBLIC-LOCAL AND PRIVATE LEGISLATION 27 (1949). For an overview of the evolution of municipalities in North Carolina, see Warren J. Wicker, *Introduction to City Government in North Carolina*, in MUNICIPAL GOVERNMENT IN NORTH CAROLINA 3–28 (David M. Lawrence & Warren J. Wicker eds., 2d ed. 1995). *See also* Mary P. Smith, Municipal Development in North Carolina, 1665–1930 (1930) (unpublished Ph.D. dissertation, University of North Carolina at Chapel Hill).

4. LAWS OF NORTH CAROLINA, 1740, ch. 1. For a more complete review of the development of both private-nuisance law and early government regulation of development, see PHILIP P. GREEN, JR., ZONING IN NORTH CAROLINA 5–73 (1952).

cities were authorized by charter to prohibit wooden buildings in certain parts of town.[5] In 1905, all incorporated towns in the state were required to establish fire limits,[6] and by 1917, cities were granted the authority to regulate the erection of fences and billboards, the storage of combustible and explosive materials, the removal of dangerous buildings, and the installation of plumbing and electrical facilities.[7]

In addition to these construction standards, regulations on the location, type, and intensity of land uses, primarily designed to limit the impacts of what were deemed to be noxious land uses, became increasingly common in the United States in the late 1800s.[8] An early notable local ordinance, passed in 1885, was a Modesto, California, regulation restricting laundries to certain portions of town—an attempt, some observers now contend, to segregate Chinese immigrants.[9] In 1908, Los Angeles pioneered creation of use districts in the city to regulate the location and operation of various land uses.[10] By 1913, Wisconsin, Minnesota, and New York had authorized cities to exclude manufacturing and commercial uses from certain residential districts.[11] In larger urban areas, such as Washington, D.C., in 1899 and Boston in 1904, the advent of building technology for skyscrapers led to the adoption of height limits in different districts of the city.[12] In North Carolina, ordinances regarding objectionable uses were adopted by many cities in the decades before zoning, limiting the location of hogpens,[13] sawmills,[14] livery stables,[15] hospitals,[16] gas stations,[17] pool halls,[18] dance halls,[19] and lumberyards.[20]

---

5. *See, e.g.*, State v. Johnson, 114 N.C. 846, 19 S.E. 599 (1894); State v. Tenant, 110 N.C. 609, 14 S.E. 387 (1892); Privett v. Whitaker, 73 N.C. 554 (1875).

6. S.L. 1905-506, §§ 7, 8.

7. S.L. 1917-136.

8. Among the very early precursors to land use regulation was an 1838 Michigan statute authorizing cities to "assign certain places for the exercising of any trade or employment offensive to the inhabitants." Mich. Rev. Stat. § 45 (1838).

9. *In re* Hang Kie, 10 P. 327 (Cal. 1886). Similar restrictions by San Francisco restricting hours of operation, location, and operation of laundries were upheld in the face of allegations of ethnic discrimination. Barbier v. Connolly, 113 U.S. 27 (1884); Soon Hing v. Crowley, 113 U.S. 703 (1885). Seymour Toll noted the violent anti-Chinese agitation of the time and the "strong overtones of nativism" motivating these regulations. Seymour I. Toll, Zoned American 27 (1969).

10. *See* Hadcheck v. Sebastian, 239 U.S. 394 (1915) (upholding ordinance establishing residential district and excluding brickyard from it); *Ex parte* Quong Wo, 161 Cal. 220, 119 P. 714 (1911) (upholding Los Angeles regulatory scheme prohibiting laundries and warehouses in residential districts). For a review of the evolution of land use regulation in Los Angeles, see Andrew H. Whittemore, *Zoning Los Angeles: A Brief History of Four Regimes*, 27 Plan. Perspectives 393 (2012).

11. *See, e.g.*, Cronin v. New York, 82 N.Y. 318 (1880) (regulating slaughterhouse location); Shea v. City of Muncie, 148 Ind. 14, 46 N.E. 138 (1897) (regulating location of alcohol sales).

12. The Boston height limit was upheld in *Welch v. Swasey*, 214 U.S. 91 (1909). The height limits were modest by modern standards—125 feet on wide central streets and 80 feet on all other streets. Baltimore and Indianapolis also had building height limits for certain portions of the cities in the early 1900s. *See generally* Mel Scott, American City Planning Since 1890 75–76, 152 (1969); Gordon Whitnall, *History of Zoning*, 155 Annals Am. Acad. Pol. & Soc. Sci. pt. II at 1, 9–10 (1931); W.L. Pollard, *Outline of the Law of Zoning in the United States*, 155 Annals Am. Acad. Pol. & Soc. Sci. pt. II at 15, 16–20 (1931).

13. State v. Hord, 122 N.C. 1092, 29 S.E. 952 (1898).

14. Barger v. Smith, 156 N.C. 323, 72 S.E. 376 (1911).

15. State v. Bass, 171 N.C. 780, 87 S.E. 972 (1916). *See also* Reinman v. City of Little Rock, 237 U.S. 171 (1915) (upholding ordinance excluding stables from specified areas).

16. Lawrence v. Nissen, 173 N.C. 359, 91 S.E. 1036 (1917).

17. Gulf Refin. Co. v. McKernan, 179 N.C. 314, 102 S.E. 505 (1920). *See also* Pierce Oil Corp. v. City of Hope, 248 U.S. 498 (1919) (upholding regulation prohibiting oil and gasoline storage in specified areas).

18. Brunswick-Balke-Collender Co. v. Mecklenburg Cnty., 181 N.C. 386, 107 S.E. 317 (1921).

19. State v. Vanhook, 182 N.C. 831, 109 S.E. 65 (1921).

20. Turner v. City of New Bern, 187 N.C. 541, 122 S.E. 469 (1924).

By the early 1900s, a substantial body of private law regarding land use had emerged as well, the result of numerous lawsuits over land uses that neighbors considered nuisances—suits involving the location of millponds, distilleries, stables, cotton gins, gristmills, sawmills, cemeteries, guano factories, freight yards, hospitals, and gasoline filling stations.[21] However, this body of law was reactive, usually dealt with a single issue or type of land use, and only resolved disputes between neighbors.[22] For the most part, nuisance law did not address broader public concerns regarding land development.[23]

---

21. *See, e.g.*, Aydlett v. Carolina By-Products Co., 215 N.C. 700, 2 S.E.2d 881 (1939) (odor from factory using slaughterhouse by-products constituted public nuisance). Many of the early nuisance cases are cited in Appendix A.

In its landmark case upholding the legality of zoning, the U.S. Supreme Court noted that in assessing validity of a particular zoning restriction,

> the maxim "sic utere tuo ut alienum non laedas," which lies at the foundation of so much of the common law of nuisances, ordinarily will furnish a fairly helpful clew. And the law of nuisances, likewise, may be consulted, not for the purpose of controlling, but for the helpful aid of its analogies in the process of ascertaining the scope of, the power.

Vill. of Euclid v. Ambler Realty Co., 272 U.S. 365, 387 (1926). Although the background principles of property and nuisance law were once thought to be primarily of historical interest, the Supreme Court has indicated that they can be important in resolving constitutional challenges alleging a regulatory taking. The Court has held that a regulation that renders property totally valueless is a taking unless the restriction prohibits activity already barred by state nuisance law. Lucas v. S.C. Coastal Council, 505 U.S. 1003 (1992). See Chapter 24 for further discussion of this issue.

22. Restrictive covenants are another private–land use regulatory device that can anticipate and prevent problems rather than only react to them. The use of this tool in North Carolina largely dates to the 1920s. *See* GREEN, *supra* note 4, at 23–34. The use of covenants, particularly with residential subdivisions, is very common in North Carolina. Covenants, however, are a private matter between the property owners and may not be enforced by local governments as a development regulation. Covenants that violate constitutional or statutory provisions, such as a restriction on property sales based on race, are void and unenforceable. *See, e.g.*, Shelley v. Kraemer, 334 U.S. 1 (1948). For a review of the evolution of the law of covenants regarding apartment houses in the period leading to the *Euclid* decision, see Maureen E. Brady, *Turning Neighbors into Nuisances*, 134 HARV. L. REV. 1609 (2021).

The Real Property Marketable Title Act provides that when an owner has a thirty-year unbroken chain of title, any restrictive covenants not within the chain of title, other than those that restrict the property to residential use, are extinguished. Chapter 47B, Section 3(13) of the North Carolina General Statutes (hereinafter G.S.). Other covenants that have not been recorded in the chain of title, such as those related to the size and number of structures, placement of the structures on the lot, future subdivision of lots, or other architectural limits on structures are all extinguished after thirty years. C Investments 2, LLC v. Auger, 383 N.C. 1, 881 S.E.2d 270 (2022).

For a discussion of the relationship between private covenants and public development regulations, see Hannah J. Wiseman, *Public Communities, Private Rules*, 98 GEO. L.J. 697 (2010).

23. The contemporary use of nuisance law in this manner arises in several contexts. One involves civil actions by neighbors alleging a private nuisance. For example, in *Broadbent v. Allison*, 176 N.C. App. 359, 626 S.E.2d 758, *review denied*, 361 N.C. 350, 644 S.E.2d 4 (2006), the court upheld a finding that a private airstrip caused substantial and unreasonable interference with the use and enjoyment of neighboring property. Also see the agricultural nuisance cases noted in Chapter 22. Second are public-nuisance actions, which can arise based on local ordinances to prohibit nuisances or nuisance-like conditions (such as overgrown-lot restrictions or junk-car regulations) or as individual nuisance-abatement suits. G.S. 19, §§ 1 through 8.3 provide a statutory framework for nuisance-abatement actions, which are generally applied against land uses where illegal activity has been alleged. *See, e.g.*, State v. Campbell, 169 N.C. App. 829, 610 S.E.2d 799 (2005) (overturning conviction based on drug sales and police calls as a breach of the peace).

Early Zoning Activity

Zoning emerged in an era of considerable political and civic reform[24] as a more comprehensive, forward-looking, and rational approach to addressing the public interest in the development of urban and urbanizing areas.[25] It was designed to replace reliance on single-purpose ordinances and private litigation for land use management.

The country's first comprehensive zoning ordinance was adopted by New York City in 1916.[26] The early twentieth century was a time of remarkable growth in the city. The introduction of steel-beam construction and elevators made possible high-density development that rapidly transformed lower Manhattan.[27] The drafter of New York's zoning ordinance noted these reasons for its adoption: (1) the advent of the subway had significantly increased congestion in Manhattan, leading to loss of air and light and creating dark urban canyons; (2) the unchecked spread of incompatible uses was leading to the premature depreciation of settled areas; and (3) development patterns needed to be more stable.[28] Some observers have contended that passage of the ordinance was motivated largely by an interest in

---

24. There is considerable debate in the planning profession about how reform-oriented zoning came to be practiced. A number of observers have decried the lack of comprehensive planning as a basis for zoning; the use of zoning to protect the status quo, particularly the value of established and speculative property; and the sometimes capricious and parochial manner in which zoning has been applied in the thousands of U.S. communities that have adopted this land use–management tool. RICHARD F. BABCOCK, THE ZONING GAME: MUNICIPAL PRACTICES AND POLICIES (1966); RICHARD F. BABCOCK & CHARLES L. SIEMON, THE ZONING GAME REVISITED (1985); DONALD L. ELLIOTT, A BETTER WAY TO ZONE: TEN PRINCIPLES TO CREATE MORE LIVABLE CITIES (2008); R. ROBERT LINOWES & DAN T. ALLENSWORTH, THE POLITICS OF LAND USE PLANNING: PLANNING, ZONING, AND THE PRIVATE DEVELOPER (1973); DANIEL R. MANDELKER, THE ZONING DILEMMA: A LEGAL STRATEGY FOR URBAN CHANGE (1971); TOLL, *supra* note 9. *See also* Charles M. Haar & Michael A. Wolf, *Euclid Lives: The Survival of Progressive Jurisprudence*, 115 HARV. L. REV. 2158 (2002); Harvey M. Jacobs & Kurt Paulsen, *Property Rights: The Neglected Theme of 20th-Century American Planning*, 75 J. OF AM. PLAN. ASS'N 134 (2009).

25. One of the early models for zoning ordinances was the districting scheme developed for Frankfurt, Germany, in 1891. Other German cities, including Berlin, Hamburg, Stuttgart, Mannheim, Hanover, Nuremberg, and Munich, adopted zoning-like regulations in the 1892–1903 period. Thomas H. Logan, *The Americanization of German Zoning*, 42 J. OF AM. PLAN. ASS'N 377, 379–81 (1976). The German experiences were influential in the design of early U.S. zoning ordinances. FRANK B. WILLIAMS, THE LAW OF CITY PLANNING AND ZONING 210–17 (1922). The use of a form of zoning in the 1909 English town planning act was also influential. Part II, Housing and Town Planning Act of 1909.

26. New York City, N.Y., Building Zone Resolution. The ordinance is reprinted in GEORGE B. FORD, NEW YORK CITY BUILDING ZONE RESOLUTION RESTRICTING THE HEIGHT AND USE OF BUILDINGS AND PRESCRIBING THE MINIMUM SIZES OF THEIR YARDS AND COURTS (1917). *See generally* S.J. MAKIELSKI, JR., THE POLITICS OF ZONING: THE NEW YORK EXPERIENCE (1966); TOLL, *supra* note 9; MICHAEL A. WOLF, THE ZONING OF AMERICA: *EUCLID V. AMBLER* (2008); ZONING AND THE AMERICAN DREAM: PROMISES STILL TO KEEP (Charles M. Haar & Jerold S. Kayden eds., 1989); Raphael Fischler, *The Metropolitan Dimension of Early Zoning: Revisiting the 1916 New York City Ordinance*, 64 J. OF AM. PLAN. ASS'N 171 (1998); Herman L. Weisman, *Zoning Administration in New York City*, 2 ST. JOHN'S L. REV. 105 (1928).

27. One of the city's best-known early tall buildings, Daniel Burnham's Flatiron Building, was constructed in 1902 and, at 22 stories, stood some 285 feet tall. This height was roughly the same as the steeple on the city's Trinity Church, constructed in 1846. However, dramatic change soon came to the city. The subway system opened in 1904, allowing increased concentration of employment and residences. Builders took advantage of new technologies to greatly increase the height of new buildings. The Singer Building, completed in 1908, was 612 feet high. The Woolworth Building in lower Manhattan was completed in 1913, with 60 stories and a height of 793 feet, at the time the world's tallest building. The competition for "world's tallest building" continued unabated in New York after the introduction of zoning, with the title passing to 40 Wall Street in 1930 (71 stories, 927 feet high), the Chrysler Building in 1930 (77 stories, 1,046 feet high), and the Empire State Building in 1931 (102 stories, 1,252 feet high). However, buildings constructed after the adoption of zoning regulations in 1916 were required to have less density on higher floors in order to preserve light and air for their neighbors. This requirement resulted in the buildings' distinctive stepped-back appearance.

28. EDWARD M. BASSETT, ZONING: THE LAWS, ADMINISTRATION, AND COURT DECISIONS DURING THE FIRST TWENTY YEARS 23–26 (2d ed. 1940).

excluding garment factories and warehouses (and their low-income workers) from the valuable Fifth Avenue commercial district.[29] Others note that the New York ordinance discussed and addressed broader issues, including preservation of residential neighborhoods, segregation of social groups, management of urban infrastructure, and control of municipal finances.[30]

The ordinance established three use districts (residential, business, and unrestricted), five height districts, and five area districts (setting yard and setback requirements). In the earliest application of New York's ordinance, this was called *districting*. However, the term *zoning* soon became the popular and generally accepted means of labeling these land use and development regulations.[31] The New York City ordinance became the model for zoning ordinances enacted by local governments around the country.

The use of local zoning ordinances to regulate land uses rapidly spread across the United States in the 1920s.[32] The U.S. Department of Commerce actively promoted the concept, publishing and distributing a standard zoning-enabling law that was adopted by most states.[33] In 1926 the U.S. Supreme Court upheld the basic constitutionality of the zoning concept in *Village of Euclid v. Ambler Realty Co.*[34] By 1937, every state had authorized zoning. With this statutory basis and judicial acceptance, the stage was set for widespread adoption of zoning.[35] The number of U.S. cities with zoning ordinances increased from 48 in 1921 to 218 by 1923 and to 525 by 1927.[36] In 1936, more than 1200 municipalities had adopted zoning. By 1937, 75 percent of the U.S. population lived in zoned areas.[37]

The movement toward land use planning and development regulation in North Carolina took a similar path in this period, as the state began shifting from an overwhelmingly rural state in the nineteenth century to a state of many small towns and cities in the twentieth century (see Table 3.1).

---

29. *See, e.g.*, Makielski, *supra* note 26, at 7–40; Toll, *supra* note 9, at 115–87.

30. Fischler, *supra* note 26. For a discussion of the role of zoning and land use regulation as a tool of enforcing residential racial segregation, see Richard Rothstein, The Color of Law: A Forgotten History of How Our Government Segregated America 39–57 (2017); Andrew H. Whittemore, *The Experience of Racial and Ethnic Minorities with Zoning in the United States*, 32 J. of Plan. Lit. 16 (2016). Also see the discussion of affordable housing and inclusionary zoning in Chapter 9, fair housing in Chapter 23, and legitimate objectives for regulation in Chapter 25.

31. Bassett, *supra* note 28, at 21.

32. The proportion of U.S. residents residing in cities passed 50 percent for the first time in 1920. By 2000, that figure had reached nearly 80 percent.

33. U.S. Dep't of Commerce, A Standard State Zoning Enabling Act (1924). This act was first issued in mimeographed form in August 1922. In a number of states, action to authorize zoning had anticipated the model act: ten states had authorized zoning by 1919, and another nine did so in 1921. By 1930, some thirty-five states had adopted legislation modeled on this act.

34. 272 U.S. 365 (1926). The Court confirmed the legality of land use regulations shortly thereafter in two additional decisions. In *Gorieb v. Fox*, 274 U.S. 603 (1927), the Court upheld a street setback requirement. In *Nectow v. City of Cambridge*, 277 U.S. 183 (1928), the Court again upheld the zoning concept as a valid exercise of the police power but ruled the ordinance invalid as applied. Thereafter, for almost fifty years, the U.S. Supreme Court left the zoning field to state courts. Prior to *Euclid*, state courts had both upheld and invalidated local zoning. *See, e.g.*, Goldman v. Crowther, 128 A. 50 (Md. 1925) (invalidating zoning); Carter v. Harper, 196 N.W. 451 (Wis. 1923) (upholding zoning).

35. For a detailed review of state court rulings on the validity of early zoning ordinances, see Newman F. Baker, *The Constitutionality of Zoning Laws*, 20 Ill. L. Rev. 213 (1925). *See also* Bassett, *supra* note 28; Alfred Bettman, *The Constitutionality of Zoning*, 37 Harv. L. Rev. 837 (1924); James Metzenbaum, *The History of Zoning: A Thumbnail Sketch*, 9 W. Res. L. Rev. 36 (1957).

36. It was estimated that 40 percent of the country's population resided in zoned areas in the early 1920s. Bettman, *supra* note 35, at 834–35.

37. Bassett, *supra* note 28, at 8; Scott, *supra* note 12, at 193–94, 249; Toll, *supra* note 9, at 281.

Table 3.1   N.C. Population Residing in Cities and Towns

Year	% Residing in Cities and Towns
1800	3.2
1850	4.7
1900	17.0
1950	40.9
2021	58.0

In 1800, North Carolina had only four cities with populations over 1000.[38] By 1860, there were still only twenty-five cities in the state, and only twelve of these had populations over 1000.[39] Indeed, in 1920, on the eve of the introduction of zoning, North Carolina did not have a single city with a population over 50,000. Yet dramatic change was underway, as the percentage of the state's population living in cities doubled in the first half of the twentieth century, climbing from 17 percent in 1900 to 41 percent in 1950. By 1950, there were fifty-three cities and towns in the state with populations over 5000.[40] The state's population growth continued and accelerated after 1950, especially in urban areas. The state's official 2021 population estimates indicated 142 municipalities with populations over 5000 (with 21 having populations over 50,000). As of July 2021, 58 percent of the state's 10,155,942 residents resided in a municipality (and 20 percent of the total state population resided in the five municipalities with populations over 250,000).[41]

The initial legislative authorization for planning in North Carolina came in 1919 with the authorization of city planning commissions.[42] Durham, Greensboro, High Point, Raleigh, and Winston-Salem appointed groups of citizen leaders in the 1920s to consider how growing cities could be more attractive and more efficient. However, general and active land use planning did not spread across North Carolina until the late 1940s.[43] With the support of federal grant money, land use planning became commonplace for many North Carolina local governments in the 1960s.[44]

Zoning authority was granted to cities in 1923 with the adoption of the state's zoning-enabling statute.[45] Among the early zoning ordinances adopted in the state were those of Raleigh in 1923; Durham,

---

38. These were New Bern (2467), Wilmington (1689), Fayetteville (1656), and Edenton (1302). Only an additional four towns had populations over 500: Raleigh (669), Salisbury (645), Washington (601), and Tarboro (523). Smith, *supra* note 3.

39. Guion G. Johnson, *The Ante-Bellum Town in North Carolina*, 5 N.C. Hist. Rev. 372 (1928). There were only sixteen cities in the entire United States with populations over 50,000 in 1860.

40. Albert Coates, *The Place of the City in the Government of North Carolina*, Popular Gov't, Dec. 1959, at 1.

41. The state's official annual population figures are published online at *State Demographer*, North Carolina Office of State Budget and Management, https://www.osbm.nc.gov/facts-figures/demographics.

42. S.L. 1919-23.

43. As part of the postwar push for planning, the authority to create planning boards was extended to counties in 1945. S.L. 1945-1040. For a detailed review of the evolution of planning in North Carolina, see Koleen Alice Haire Huggins, The Evolution of City and Regional Planning in North Carolina, 1900–1950 (1967) (unpublished Ph.D. dissertation, Duke University). *See also* Philip P. Green, Jr., Organizing for Local Governmental Planning in North Carolina (2d ed. 1989).

44. For an illustrative guidebook prepared by the Institute of Government for North Carolina planners of this period, see Robert E. Stipe, An Introduction to Municipal Planning (1968).

45. S.L. 1923-250. The North Carolina statute closely followed the model act promulgated by the U.S. Department of Commerce. The state also adopted the Model Airport Zoning Act in 1941. S.L. 1941-250. The law is codified at G.S. 63, §§ 30 to 37. Using procedures substantially similar to the general zoning-enabling act, cities and counties were authorized to create zones around airports to limit the height of structures and trees. As local governments subsequently adopted general zoning ordinances, these provisions were usually incorporated into the zoning ordinance, but several jurisdictions retain separate airport zoning ordinances pursuant to this separate authority.

Philip P. Green, Jr., land use law professor at the Institute of Government (1949–1988), speaking at the 1966 North Carolina Annual Planning Conference.

Greensboro, High Point, and Southern Pines in 1926; Chapel Hill and Rocky Mount in 1928; Elizabeth City and Fayetteville in 1929; and Winston-Salem in 1930.[46] By 1938, Goldsboro, Thomasville, and Warrenton had also adopted zoning.[47] However, the Depression and World War II substantially reduced development levels in the state, and land use regulation was relatively dormant in this period, as were a number of the programs initiated in the 1920s.

Zoning in the Post–World War II Era

The immediate postwar period brought new development and renewed interest in local land use regulation.[48] Philip Green, newly hired at the Institute of Government to provide land use–law assistance, reported in 1948 that most of the state's cities had rewritten their zoning codes in the 1944–1948 period and were beginning to staff their zoning and planning programs (though he reported that there were

---

46. Kay H. Huggins, *City and Regional Planning in North Carolina, 1900–1929*, 46 N.C. Hist. Rev. 377, 395 (1969).

47. Patrick Healy, Jr., A Zoning Manual for North Carolina Towns and Cities 3 (N.C. League of Municipalities Report No. 27, 1938).

48. The Institute of Government reported in 1946 that thirty of the state's cities already had zoning ordinances in place, another ten were actively developing ordinances, and "hit-or-miss city growth is fast going out of style in North Carolina." *Monthly Survey*, Popular Gov't, Mar. 1946, at 7. Later that year, the Institute reported, "During post-war 1946, with city-planning being talked up as never before, the caption used on a Dunn Dispatch editorial seems indicative of a prevailing attitude: 'Let's zone the town.'" *The Clearinghouse*, Popular Gov't, Oct. 1946, at 7. A 1952 Institute survey indicated that of thirty-six active planning boards in the state, twenty-four had been

Table 3.2 Municipalities Adopting Zoning Ordinances (2012)

Population	Number Responding	% of Respondents
<1000	216	71
1000–4999	203	96
5000–9999	49	100
10,000–24,999	48	100
25,000–49,999	17	100
50,000+	17	100
Total	**550**	**87**

only three planning directors in the state and only nine full-time local staff members statewide working on planning and zoning).[49]

By 1950, virtually every city in the state with a population over 10,000 had adopted zoning.[50] As the state began rapid population growth thereafter, zoning spread to counties and smaller municipalities. By 1985, 349 of the state's 495 cities, some 71 percent, had adopted zoning ordinances.[51] Over time, even less-populous municipalities began to adopt zoning ordinances. A 2012 survey by the School of Government indicated that most of the state's cities with populations over 1000 had adopted zoning ordinances.[52] Table 3.2 sets out the adoption rate for zoning by municipal population as of 2012.

Because zoning originally addressed urban issues, county zoning in North Carolina came later.[53] Several of the state's more urbanized counties undertook zoning shortly after World War II. Forsyth

---

established since 1946 (as had thirteen of the twenty-five boards of adjustment). Philip P. Green, Jr., *City Planning and Zoning Moves Ahead*, POPULAR GOV'T, Sept. 1952, at 10.

49. Philip P. Green, Jr., *City Planning in North Carolina*, POPULAR GOV'T, Dec. 1949, at 8–9. Only Durham, Greensboro, and Charlotte had full-time planning staff, with recruitment underway in Winston-Salem.

50. Kinston adopted zoning in 1950, leaving only one other city in the state with a population over 10,000 without zoning. *Zoning Ordinance*, POPULAR GOV'T, June 1950, at 3. By 1968, Green was able to conclude, "Zoning is probably the single most important legal device available for carrying out the land use plan of a community." PHILIP P. GREEN, JR., AN INTRODUCTION TO MUNICIPAL ZONING (1968).

51. Unpublished survey by the Division of Community Assistance, N.C. Dep't of Commerce (1992) (on file with the Division of Community Assistance).

52. David W. Owens & Dayne Batten, *2012 Zoning Survey Report: Zoning Adoption, Administration, and Provisions for Design Standards and Alternative Energy Facilities*, PLAN. & ZONING L. BULL. No. 20 (UNC School of Government, 2012). For earlier surveys of these issues, see DAVID W. OWENS & NATHAN BRANSCOME, AN INVENTORY OF LOCAL GOVERNMENT LAND USE ORDINANCES IN NORTH CAROLINA 3 (UNC School of Government, Special Series No. 21, May 2006); DAVID W. OWENS & ANDREW STEVENSON, AN OVERVIEW OF ZONING DISTRICTS, DESIGN STANDARDS, AND TRADITIONAL NEIGHBORHOOD DESIGN IN NORTH CAROLINA ZONING ORDINANCES 1 (UNC School of Government, Special Series No. 23, Oct. 2007). A 2018 School of Government survey confirmed that this high rate of municipal adoption of zoning was largely unchanged. It also found that county zoning was applied in many of the small-population cities that had not adopted municipal zoning. Of the responding cities with populations under 1000, 78 percent reported the city had adopted zoning, 14 percent had county zoning applied within the city, and only 8 percent had no zoning within the city. See Chapter 6 for a more detailed description of contemporary zoning ordinances. David W. Owens, *2018 Survey Report: Adoption and Administration of Local Development Regulations, Conditional Zoning, and Subdivision Administration*, PLAN. AND ZONING L. BULL. No. 30 (UNC School of Government, Dec. 2020), at 4–5.

53. A bill to authorize county zoning (H.B. 710) was introduced in 1945, but it was defeated in committee. The General Assembly did authorize county planning boards in 1945 (H.B. 711, codified as G.S. 153-9). Six counties were exempted from this authorization.

Figure 3.1 Zoning by North Carolina Counties

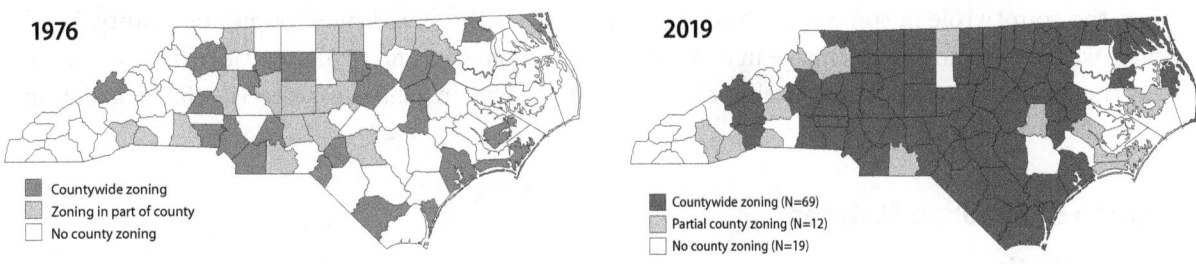

1976

Countywide zoning
Zoning in part of county
No county zoning

2019

Countywide zoning (N=69)
Partial county zoning (N=12)
No county zoning (N=19)

County received authority to undertake zoning in 1947, and Durham County was granted that authority in 1949.[54] However, general enabling authority for county zoning was not adopted until 1959.[55]

As counties have increasingly been called on to address the issues and conflicts generated by land use and development, the number of North Carolina counties exercising zoning authority has grown. By 1979, 44 of the state's 100 counties had adopted some zoning.[56] As of 2022, eighty-one counties had adopted zoning.[57] The trend toward increased county zoning is indicated by the fact that the number of counties with countywide zoning increased from forty-one in 1998 to sixty-nine in 2019.[58] The change in geographic distribution of county zoning in the state is illustrated in Figure 3.1.

When both city and county zoning are considered, over 90 percent of the state's population resides in jurisdictions subject to zoning.[59]

---

54. S.L. 1947-677 (Forsyth County); S.L. 1949-1043 (Durham County). Other local acts had authorized activity in individual counties. *See, e.g.*, S.L. 1949-400 (Clay County); S.L. 1951-1193 (Dare County). By late 1948, Forsyth County had prepared a draft zoning ordinance that would place all of the county's unincorporated area into one of six zoning districts: rural, residential A, residential B, business, commercial, or industrial. *The Clearinghouse*, Popular Gov't, Nov. 1948, at 13. Guilford County applied zoning to all of its rural areas in 1964 and adopted the state's first countywide subdivision ordinance in 1965.

55. S.L. 1959-1006. Earlier local legislation had authorized joint city-county planning and zoning in several more-urbanized counties. For a contemporary analysis of the form of county planning at this time, see Philip P. Green, Jr. & Robert E. Stipe, *County Planning and Development*, Popular Gov't, Mar.–Apr. 1960, at 2.

56. In 1979, twenty-five counties had countywide zoning and nineteen had zoning in part of the county's jurisdiction. Richard D. Ducker, *Land-Use Planning in Rural Areas*, Popular Gov't, Summer 1980, at 29. For a detailed review of the status of city and county land use–ordinance adoption in 2006, see Owens & Branscome, *supra* note 52.

57. Another indicator of the spread of zoning in North Carolina has been the development of a voluntary professional organization of zoning officials to provide continuing education and professional development. The North Carolina Association of Zoning Officials was chartered in 1981 and by 2004 had nearly 400 members. It began a certification program for zoning-enforcement officers in 1991.

58. For the most part, the unzoned counties are those with low population densities. Twenty-eight of the thirty counties with no zoning in 2003 had population densities below the state average of 163 persons per square mile (the two exceptions were Vance and Alamance); twenty-two of the unzoned counties had population densities under 75 persons per square mile.

Also, the boundary between having a zoning ordinance and having other general ordinances that regulate land uses is not always clear. See, for example, the characterization of Alamance County's watershed-protection ordinances in *Town of Green Level v. Alamance County*, 184 N.C. App. 665, 646 S.E.2d 851, *review denied*, 361 N.C. 704, 655 S.E.2d 402 (2007). Subsequent to that litigation, the county adopted a "High Impact Land Uses/Polluting Industries Ordinance," citing both the statutory authorization for general ordinances and zoning ordinances. While this ordinance does not create separate zoning districts, it is applicable in all unincorporated areas and sets development standards and permit requirements for thirteen specified land uses. Several unzoned or partially zoned counties in the western part of the state have similar ordinances.

59. Owens & Batten, *supra* note 52, at 5.

Ironically, several of North Carolina's most urban counties have a reduced role in zoning. As cities have annexed territory, new cities have incorporated, and even small towns have taken on their own zoning, the county role in some areas has begun to decline. The state's most populous county, Mecklenburg, was one of the first to engage in county zoning and now has no regulatory jurisdiction for land use, as the land within the county is either within a city or within a city's extraterritorial jurisdiction.

Evolution of Enabling Statutes

Early Organization

North Carolina's planning-and-development-regulation statutes have evolved over the past century. After adoption of building regulations and zoning authority in the early twentieth century, authorization for other regulations was gradually enacted, such as authorization for housing codes in 1939[60] and municipal subdivision regulation in 1955.[61] In 1959, many of the city-enabling statutes were extended to counties.[62] Municipal extraterritorial jurisdiction was also authorized in 1959. Specialized provisions were added in subsequent decades, including open-space protection in 1963, historic-preservation and landmark protection in 1971,[63] community appearance in 1971, floodplain zoning in 1979, and authority to negotiate and approve development agreements in 2005. For the most part, these enabling statutes were incorporated into the general provisions for cities and counties.

The basic statutory framework for county government was first enacted in 1905 and for city government in 1917. In the late 1960s, the General Assembly directed a local government study commission to examine and modernize the statutes affecting cities and counties.[64] As part of this effort, the various statutes affecting municipal planning and development regulation were collected as Article 19 of G.S. Chapter 160A when that chapter was created in 1971.[65] The same was done for county planning and development regulation in Article 18 of Chapter 153A when that chapter was created in 1973.[66] Although subject to many amendments and refinements, this basic organization structure of the enabling statutes adopted in the early 1970s was followed until the enactment of Chapter 160D.

---

60. S.L. 1939-287.

61. S.L. 1955-1334.

62. County planning boards were first authorized in 1945. S.L. 1945-1040. County zoning and subdivision regulation were authorized in 1959. S.L. 1959-1006 (zoning); S.L. 1959-1007 (subdivision). Several more urban counties had previously been authorized to exercise this authority by local bills.

63. S.L. 1971-884. Winston-Salem, Edenton, Bath, and Halifax secured authorization to require certificates of appropriateness for exterior alterations to historic structures in 1965. Several additional jurisdictions secured approval for similar regulation between 1965 and 1971. S.L. 1965-504. Regulations to authorize protection of individual landmark buildings were also enacted in 1971. S.L. 1971-885.

64. The Local Government Study Commission was created by the 1967 General Assembly to conduct a thorough study of the entire local government system in the state. Res. 1967-76, H.R.J. Res. 944, 1967 Gen. Assemb. (N.C. 1967). Institute of Government faculty members were the principal staff members for the commission. The commission made recommendations for state constitutional amendments regarding local governments in 1969. In the two following legislative sessions, the commission made recommendations for statutory amendments regarding city and county government.

65. S.L. 1971-698. This 1971 recodification was the first such comprehensive revision since 1917. This act recodified significant portions of G.S. Chapter 160 into a new Chapter 160A. It also made numerous amendments and reorganized statutes within the new chapter.

66. S.L. 1973-822. This law, which created G.S. Chapter 153A, largely aligned county planning-and-development-regulation statutes with the city statutes adopted in 1971 as Chapter 160A.

Chapter 160D

The North Carolina Bar Association in 2013 embarked on the development of a proposal to completely reorganize the state's planning-and-development-regulation statutes.[67] The objective was to develop a new organizational structure for these statutes that was coherent and easy to follow. In addition, this initiative proposed to edit the entire body of law to secure greater clarity, removing archaic, obsolete, and confusing language and recommending greater uniformity and consistency among the various statutes. Where consensus among the various affected parties was possible, the group sought to incorporate common-sense reforms and solutions to nagging problems and ambiguities in the statutes.

After multiple years of review and comment of the draft legislation, the proposal was introduced in 2015 but not enacted.[68] An updated version of the bill was introduced in 2017, but again not enacted.[69] A third updated version of the bill was introduced in 2019.[70] The Senate merged the relatively noncontroversial reorganization bill proposed by the Bar Association with a more controversial set of amendments to the zoning statutes.[71] Although merged into a single bill (Parts I and II of S.B. 355), the individual parts were debated independently throughout the legislative process. The reorganization bill in Part II was eventually adopted in 2019 essentially as introduced.[72]

The new legislation created Chapter 160D. This consolidates the previous county-enabling statutes in Article 18 of Chapter 153A and the city-enabling statutes in Article 19 of Chapter 160A into a single, unified new Chapter 160D. Related statutes on city and county development regulation previously scattered throughout the statutes were also relocated to Chapter 160D. These include, for example, provisions for land use regulation of adult businesses and family care homes. In addition, statutes remaining in other chapters, such as the seldom-used 1941 Model Airport Zoning Act, were amended to use the procedures for ordinance adoption, administration, and enforcement that are set out in Chapter 160D. This created a uniform set of statutes applicable to cities and counties and common to all local government development regulations.

Chapter 160D placed the development-regulation statutes into a more coherent organization. Provisions that affect all development regulations (such as definitions and provisions related to moratoria, vested rights, and conflicts of interest) are grouped in one article, followed by articles that address geographic jurisdiction, creation and duties of boards, administration of regulations, the process for adoption and amendment of regulations, and judicial review of regulations. There are also detailed articles for each major type of development regulation, including planning, zoning, subdivision, building and housing codes, environment, historic preservation, and community development.

---

67. For a more detailed review of the legislative history and substance of this initiative, see David W. Owens & Adam S. Lovelady, Chapter 160D: A New Land Use Law For North Carolina (2019).

68. H.B. 548. In the 2015 session, the House generally reached agreement on the substance of the bill but adopted it as a study committee in order to resolve final details in the 2016 session. However, the bill was not taken up at all in 2016.

69. S.B. 419. The bill was passed in the Senate but not considered by the House.

70. S.B. 422 and H.B. 448.

71. S.B. 355.

72. S.L. 2019-111, pt. II, § 2.10 of this law directed the General Statutes Commission (GSC) to study and recommend legislation to the 2020 session of the General Assembly to integrate Parts I and II of this 2019 legislation, along with any additional legislation enacted in 2019 that affected the statutes incorporated into Chapter 160D, into an updated version of Chapter 160D prior to its effective date. In May 2020, the GSC approved its report and draft legislation. General Statutes Commission, Report to the 2020 Regular Session of the 2019 General Assembly of North Carolina on Incorporating Land-Use Laws Adopted in 2019 into Chapter 160D of the General Statutes as Required by S.L. 2019-111 (May 7, 2020). The GSC-proposed legislation was enacted and became effective June 19, 2020, which then became the effective date for Chapter 160D. S.L. 2020-25. Given the impacts of the COVID-19 pandemic on scheduling and adopting local government–ordinance updates to secure conformance with Chapter 160D, cities and counties were given the option of having the new law become effective in their jurisdiction upon adoption of their updated ordinance, provided that was not later than July 1, 2021.

Chapter 160D is organized under fourteen articles:

- Article 1, General Provisions;
- Article 2, Planning and Development Regulation Jurisdiction;
- Article 3, Boards and Organizational Arrangements;
- Article 4, Administration, Enforcement, and Appeals;
- Article 5, Planning;
- Article 6, Process for Adoption of Development Regulations;
- Article 7, Zoning Regulation;
- Article 8, Subdivision Regulation;
- Article 9, Regulation of Particular Uses and Areas;
- Article 10, Development Agreements;
- Article 11, Building Code Enforcement;
- Article 12, Minimum Housing Codes;
- Article 13, Additional Authorities; and
- Article 14, Judicial Review.

While not making major policy changes or shifts in the scope of authority granted to local governments, Chapter 160D includes many clarifying amendments and consensus reforms in the statutes.[73]

Range of Development Regulations Used

Land use and development regulations have been adopted by most North Carolina local governments. Zoning and subdivision regulations are the most widely used ordinances for both cities and counties. Special-purpose regulations that address junk and abandoned cars, signs, manufactured-home parks, noise, telecommunication towers, junkyards, flood-hazard areas, and adult-entertainment facilities are also in wide use; a 2005 survey by the School of Government indicated that each sort of special-purpose regulation was generally being imposed by at least two-thirds of the jurisdictions responding to the survey.[74] These special-purpose regulations were sometimes included in a zoning ordinance or unified development ordinance and were sometimes adopted as a separate ordinance. Table 3.3 summarizes the overall frequency of adoption of these regulations.

While the general frequency of adoption of most types of ordinances was similar for cities and counties, there were several notable exceptions. Since many smaller cities contracted with counties for building-code enforcement and several large cities had merged building inspections with the county, only 37 percent of cities handled building-code enforcement, as compared to 100 percent of the counties (note that local governments are required by law to enforce the North Carolina State Building Code but have the option of allowing another unit of government to conduct the required inspections and permitting within their jurisdiction).

Some regulations were more frequently adopted by cities than counties. Those with substantially higher municipal adoption rates included those that are more traditionally considered municipal concerns, such as nuisance-lot regulations and housing codes.

---

73. The enacting legislation for Chapter 160D states that it "clarifies and restates the intent of existing law and applies to ordinances adopted before, on, and after the effective date" of the law. S.L. 2019-111, § 3.2. However, the law made numerous substantive modifications to existing law although it did not alter the scope of authority granted to local governments, nor did it make major policy changes. As discussed in legislative discussions at the time of adoption, the changes to existing law were "substantive" but not "substantial."

74. OWENS & BRANSCOME, *supra* note 52, at 2.

Table 3.3   Frequency of Use of Ordinances

Type of Ordinance	% of Cities	% of Counties
Zoning	89	77
Junk car	84	80
Subdivision	83	88
Sign	82	81
Nuisance lot	81	27
Manufactured-home park	79	93
Noise	77	69
Telecommunication tower	70	78
Junkyard	69	80
Flood hazard	68	98
Adult entertainment	67	74
Housing code	52	27
Stormwater	46	35
Watershed	46	82
Building code	37	100
Sediment and erosion control	32	44
Historic district/landmark	30	21
Adequate public facility	29	21
Airport perimeter	15	59

The frequency of adoption for virtually every type of ordinance increases as the population of the jurisdiction increases. The more-populous cities and counties with higher population in unincorporated areas were far more likely to have adopted any form of land use regulation than their less-populous counterparts.

CHAPTER 4

Authority for Local Regulation of Development

Explicit Grants of Authority

Local governments in North Carolina have no inherent power.[1] The courts in North Carolina have uniformly concluded that municipalities and counties are created by the state and can exercise only those state powers that have been delegated to them by the General Assembly. The state constitution provides that the General Assembly shall provide for the "organization and government" of cities and counties and "may give them such powers and duties . . . as it may deem advisable."[2] With this authority, the General Assembly can create[3] and abolish cities and counties.[4] The General Assembly can delegate or revoke such authority as deemed appropriate and may set procedural requirements for the use of delegated authority.

The General Assembly has made a general grant of regulatory authority to both cities and counties. Section 160A-174 of the North Carolina General Statutes (hereinafter G.S.) allows a city to "by ordinance define, prohibit, regulate, or abate acts, omissions, or conditions detrimental to the health, safety, or welfare of its citizens and the peace and dignity of the city, and may define and abate nuisances." G.S. 153A-121 provides substantially similar authority for counties.

The General Assembly has also authorized a variety of specific regulatory authority under this "general police power."[5] Among the regulations for which specific authority is provided are ordinances on nuisance abatement, noise control, emission of pollutants, outdoor advertising, sewage tie-ons, flea markets, places of amusement, adult businesses, domestic and dangerous animals, explosive materials,

---

1. For a national survey of state-local allocation of responsibility and oversight for land use regulations, see David D. Foster & Anita A. Summers, *State Executive/Legislative and Judicial Activities and the Strength of Local Regulation of Residential Housing*, 40 URB. LAW. 1, 2–9 (2008).

2. N.C. CONST. art. VII, § 1. A similar provision was included in the 1868 constitution as article VIII, § 4. *See also* Hunter v. City of Pittsburgh, 207 U.S. 161, 178–79 (1907) (discussing the continued existence of a municipal corporation and holding that the scope of its authority is a matter of state law, unconstrained by the Federal Constitution).

3. "The Legislature has full and complete power to create a municipal corporation and to determine when and how the corporation may come into existence, the powers which it may exercise, the area in which the corporation may act, . . . and other incidental matters." Starbuck v. Town of Havelock, 252 N.C. 176, 113 S.E.2d 278, 280 (1960).

4. For example, in 1881 the General Assembly provided that if the town of Fayetteville's debts were not reduced by half by a set date, the future existence of the town as a municipal corporation would be put to the voters. The debt was not reduced, the voters elected to disband the town, and the town as a corporate entity ceased to exist. Lilly v. Taylor, 88 N.C. 489, 490–91 (1883). As for counties, the North Carolina Supreme Court held in 1886 that they

> possess such corporate powers and delegated authority as the Legislature may deem fit to confer upon them, and such power and authority must be exercised in the way, and only for the purpose prescribed by legislative enactment; and moreover, they are always subject to legislative control, and their powers may be abolished, enlarged, abridged, or modified.

Comm'rs of Dare Cnty. v. Comm'rs of Currituck Cnty., 95 N.C. 189, 191–92 (1886). The legislature also has the authority for city-county mergers. N.C. CONST. art. VII, § 3.

5. Chapter 153A, Section 121 of the North Carolina General Statutes (hereinafter G.S.); G.S. 160A-174.

firearms, and junked or abandoned vehicles.[6] G.S. 153A-124 and 160A-177 explicitly provide that the enumeration of these powers to regulate particular activities shall not be deemed to be exclusive or a limiting factor on the general authority to adopt ordinances.

In addition to the general ordinance-making authority, the legislature has granted explicit authority to cities and counties for a wide variety of land-development regulations, including zoning, subdivision control, building codes, housing codes, and a variety of specialized-growth-management and environmental regulations.[7]

The grant of zoning authority allows local governments to regulate the location of particular land uses, regulate the size of structures and lots, require provision of open space and buffers, provide landscaping, and protect historic, cultural, environmental, and community resources. The grant of subdivision-review authority allows local governments to require that developers provide adequate water, sewer, transportation, and recreation facilities for their developments. Other grants of authority address additional, specific management issues.

In addition to these grants of authority, the legislature can grant, restrict, or modify the powers available to individual jurisdictions. These laws that are applicable to individual jurisdictions are commonly referred to as "local bills." For example, while counties have not been given the authority to impose school impact fees, the legislature has explicitly authorized Chatham County to do so.[8] While the state constitution limits the subject matter of local bills,[9] these local modifications in state law are relatively common on issues related to development regulation.

---

6. The enumeration of these ordinance-making subjects is at G.S. 153A-125 to -144 and G.S. 160A-178 to -201.

7. For a review of the scope of each of these explicitly delegated authorities, see Chapters 6 through 10. Chapter 160D includes a broad definition of "development" and of "development regulation." G.S. 160D-102(12) provides that development" includes:

Any of the following:
a. The construction, erection, alteration, enlargement, renovation, substantial repair, movement to another site, or demolition of any structure.
b. The excavation, grading, filling, clearing, or alteration of land.
c. The subdivision of land as defined in G.S. 160D-802.
d. The initiation or substantial change in the use of land or the intensity of use of land.

This definition explicitly provides, however, that it does not alter the scope of regulatory authority. G.S. 160D-102(14) provides that a "development regulation" includes a

unified development ordinance, zoning regulation, subdivision regulation, erosion and sedimentation control regulation, floodplain or flood damage prevention regulation, mountain ridge protection regulation, stormwater control regulation, wireless telecommunication facility regulation, historic preservation or landmark regulation, housing code, State Building Code enforcement, or any other regulation adopted pursuant to this Chapter, or a local act or charter that regulates land use or development

8. S.L. 1987-460. Orange County was granted similar authority, but it was subsequently revoked. The authority to adopt impact fees is discussed in more detail in Chapter 9.

9. N.C. Const. art. II, § 24. Among the fourteen subjects on which local legislation is prohibited are those authorizing the laying out, opening, altering, maintaining, or discontinuing streets and those regulating labor, trade, mining, or manufacturing. The court in *Town of Boone v. State*, 369 N.C. 126, 794 S.E.2d 710 (2016), held that this provision did not limit local bills' expanding or deleting municipal extraterritorial jurisdictions. A reasonable classification of geographic areas is permissible, as in, for example, laws applicable only to the coastal area of the state. Adams v. N.C. Dep't of Nat. & Econ. Res., 295 N.C. 683, 249 S.E.2d 402 (1978). A variety of local acts have been invalidated as unconstitutional under this provision. *See, e.g.*, City of Asheville v. State, 369 N.C. 80, 794 S.E.2d 759 (2016) (impermissible to transfer city water system to regional district); City of New Bern v. New Bern–Craven Cnty. Bd. of Educ., 338 N.C. 430, 450 S.E.2d 735 (1994) (impermissible to transfer building-inspection responsibility from city to county); High Point Surplus Co. v. Pleasants, 264 N.C. 650, 142 S.E.2d 697 (1965) (local act allowing regulation of Sunday sales impermissible); Orange Speedway, Inc. v. Clayton, 247 N.C. 528, 101 S.E.2d 406 (1958) (local act authorizing regulation of automobile race track impermissible). For a historical overview of the law related to

Overlapping Grants of Authority

Some grants of authority specify particular procedures that must be followed and place particular restrictions on the exercise of that authority. Where the legislature has made specific provision for local regulation, cities and counties are required to follow the limits and procedural requirements set by the legislature. The question arises, however, to what extent a city or county can elect to use the less demanding or less restrictive general ordinance-making power if there is an overlapping specific grant of authority.

Early cases addressing this issue held that where cities and counties have multiple sources of authority, they are free to elect either and must follow only the mandatory procedures for adoption required for the source of authority chosen. The courts applied this rule to hold that sign regulations,[10] adult-entertainment-siting regulations,[11] and moratoria[12] that could have been incorporated into a zoning ordinance may be adopted as a separate general ordinance and, if that is done, the notice and hearing requirements for zoning adoption do not apply.[13] More recent cases, however, have held that where there is a specific statutory grant of authority, that grant is controlling, and the general ordinance-making power is inapplicable for that specific type of regulation. The North Carolina Supreme Court has emphasized that it is the nature of the ordinance and the subjects it regulates, rather than the precise statutory authorization cited by the local government, that controls the statute to be followed.

The authority to adopt development moratoria illustrates this principle's application in the area of development regulation. Prior to the 2005 adoption of explicit statutory authority, Iredell County adopted a moratorium on permitting quarries using its general-ordinance authority. The moratorium adoption did not follow the public notice and hearing requirements of the zoning statute. In *Vulcan Materials Co. v. Iredell County*,[14] the court held that because the building-permit system, the county's land use plan, and the zoning authorities were essential to this regulatory scheme, it must be adopted in accordance with the notice and hearing requirements for zoning. The court applied this rationale again in *Sandy Mush Properties, Inc. v. Rutherford County*.[15] Rutherford County had no zoning but was considering adopting a "Polluting Industries Development Ordinance" under its general ordinance-making power. The county adopted a 120-day moratorium on initiation of heavy industries near schools and near the end of the moratorium adopted a "School Zone Protective Ordinance" to make this restriction permanent. Both were adopted pursuant to G.S. 153A-121, the general ordinance-making authority. The court invalidated the moratorium, however, for failure to follow the notice and hearing requirements for land use–related ordinances.

Chapter 160D codifies this principle. G.S. 160D-101(a) states that the provisions in the chapter apply not only to regulations that are explicitly authorized by the chapter but also to "any other local ordinance that substantially affects land use and development."[16]

---

local legislation, see Joseph S. Ferrell, *Local Legislation in the North Carolina General Assembly*, 45 N.C. L. Rev. 340 (1966).

10. Transylvania Cnty. v. Moody, 151 N.C. App. 389, 393–95, 565 S.E.2d 720, 724–25 (2002); Summey Outdoor Advert., Inc. v. Cnty. of Henderson, 96 N.C. App. 533, 538, 386 S.E.2d 439, 443 (1989), *review denied*, 326 N.C. 486, 392 S.E.2d 101 (1990).

11. Maynor v. Onslow Cnty., 127 N.C. App. 102, 488 S.E.2d 289, *review denied*, 347 N.C. 400, 496 S.E.2d 385 (1997).

12. PNE AOA Media, LLC v. Jackson Cnty., 146 N.C. App. 470, 554 S.E.2d 657 (2001). *But see* Sandy Mush Props., Inc. v. Rutherford Cnty., 164 N.C. App. 162, 595 S.E.2d 233 (2004).

13. See Chapter 11 for further discussion of ordinance-adoption procedural requirements.

14. 103 N.C. App. 779, 407 S.E.2d 283 (1991).

15. 164 N.C. App. 162, 595 S.E.2d 233 (2004). *See also* Union Land Owners Ass'n v. Cnty. of Union, 201 N.C. App. 374, 689 S.E.2d 504 (2009) (finding no authority for county to adopt voluntary mitigation payments as school impact fees). The authority for moratoria and impact fees are discussed in Chapter 9.

16. This section also allows cities and counties to apply any of the definitions and procedures authorized by Chapter 160D to any general-police-power ordinance and to "employ any organizational structure, board,

Scope of Implied Delegation of Authority

When a development-regulation ordinance contains a novel management technique that is not expressly mentioned in the enabling legislation, the question is raised whether legal authorization has been granted to use that technique.[17] In cases where a local government has taken an action that is not explicitly authorized by the statutes, the courts must determine whether that particular power is an aspect of the authority that has been granted by the General Assembly.

In his classic 1872 treatise on municipal law, Judge John F. Dillon set forth a standard for the construction of state grants of authority to local governments that has since come to be known as Dillon's Rule. This rule has frequently been cited by North Carolina courts in determining whether local governments have been delegated the authority to undertake a particular action:

> It is a general and undisputed proposition of law that a municipal corporation possesses, and can exercise, the following powers, and no others: First, those granted in *express words*; second, those *necessarily or fairly implied* in, or incident to, the powers expressly granted; third, those *essential* to the declared objects and purposes of the corporation—not simply convenient, but indispensable. Any fair, reasonable doubt concerning the existence of power is resolved by the courts against the corporation, and the power is denied.[18]

In the 1971 comprehensive revision and modernization of the state's municipal-government statutes, the legislature determined that grants of state power to local government should be broadly rather than strictly construed.[19] G.S. 160A-4 was adopted to read as follows:

> It is the policy of the General Assembly that the cities of this State should have adequate authority to execute the powers, duties, privileges, and immunities conferred upon them by law. To this end, the provisions of this Chapter and of city charters shall be broadly construed and grants of power shall be construed to include any additional and supplementary powers that are reasonably necessary or expedient to carry them into execution and effect: Provided, that the

---

commission, or staffing arrangement" authorized by Chapter 160D in the administration of those other ordinances. G.S. 160D-101(c).

17. For a more extensive review of the judicial interpretation of the scope of delegated authority to local governments in North Carolina, see Frayda S. Bluestein, *Do North Carolina Local Governments Need Home Rule?* 84 N.C. L. Rev. 1983 (2006); David W. Owens, *Local Government Authority to Implement Smart Growth Programs: Dillon's Rule, Legislative Reform, and the Current State of Affairs in North Carolina*, 35 Wake Forest L. Rev. 671 (2000).

18. John F. Dillon, Treatise on the Law of Municipal Corporations § 55 (1872). Dillon quotes at length from an 1839 Massachusetts case setting forth these general limitations, *Spaulding v. Lowell*, 23 Pick. 71, 74 (1839). He also recognized that it is the intent of the legislative body that is at issue in statutory construction cases, albeit with a continuing admonition toward strict construction:

> The extent of the powers of municipalities, whether express, implied, or indispensable, is one of construction. And here the fundamental and universal rule . . . is, that while the construction is to be just, seeking first of all for the legislative intent in order to give it fair effect, yet any ambiguity or fair, reasonable, substantial doubt as to the extent of the power is to be determined in favor of the State or general public, and against the State's grantee.

John F. Dillon, Commentaries on the Law of Municipal Corporations § 239 (5th ed., 1911) (paraphrased approvingly in City of Asheville v. Herbert, 190 N.C. 732, 735, 130 S.E. 861, 863 (1925)).

19. In some respects, this statute returned North Carolina to the broad reading of statutory grants of regulatory authority applied by the courts prior to 1890. *See, e.g.*, Whitfield v. Longest, 28 N.C. (6 Ired.) 268, 273–74 (1846); Hellen v. Noe, 25 N.C. (3 Ired.) 493, 499–500 (1843); Shaw v. Kennedy, 4 N.C. (Taylor) 591, 591–92 (1817). Even during the period when Dillon's Rule was most rigorously imposed in North Carolina, it was applied more stringently to interpretation of grants of authority for taxes and fees and local government service provision than to grants of regulatory authority. Owens, *supra* note 17, at 682–87.

exercise of such additional or supplementary powers shall not be contrary to State or federal law or to the public policy of this State.

The 1973 revision of the county statutes adopted a substantially similar provision for counties as G.S. 153A-4. G.S. 160D-110(a) makes both the city and county provisions applicable to Chapter 160D.

These statutes do not convert North Carolina to a "home rule" state (those states where the state constitution or state statutes delegate full authority to local governments to regulate their internal affairs). The General Assembly rejected that approach in 1949 and 1955. Local governments must still have a basic authorization to act in a given area. However, this legislation is important because the legislature has clearly stated that when it does grant powers to local governments, that power is to be broadly interpreted.[20]

These statutes differ from Dillon's Rule in two important respects. First, they replace the general admonition that any doubt about a grant of authority be resolved against the grant with an express direction for broad construction. Second, they change the standard for implied powers from those that are "necessarily or fairly implied" by express grants to those additional and supplementary powers that are "reasonably necessary or expedient" to carry express grants into effect. Where local governments have been authorized to act, the legislature has unambiguously expressed its intent that these delegations are to be liberally construed.

In addition to these specific directions for a broad construction, the 1971 statutory revision for cities and the 1973 revision for counties also specifically provided that the enumeration of specific regulatory authority should not be deemed to be exclusive or otherwise limit the general authority of cities and counties to adopt ordinances.[21]

Several cases have applied the statutory rule of broad construction in assessing the scope of local governments' regulatory authority.

In *River Birch Associates v. City of Raleigh*,[22] the court upheld the required conveyances of open space in subdivisions to private homeowners' associations. The city used G.S. 160D-804 as authority for this requirement. This statute provides that a subdivision ordinance may require the dedication or reservation of recreation areas serving residents of the immediate neighborhood within the subdivision. The developer correctly contended that a "dedication" requires conveyance to the public and a "reservation" involves a retained interest by the grantor. The developer further contended that since a required conveyance to a third party (the homeowners' association) is neither a dedication nor a reservation, the city was without statutory authority to require it. The court ruled that legislative grants of power must be broadly construed to carry into effect the legislative intent to secure to the residents of the subdivision the benefits of the recreation areas, and thus that the city's regulatory authority to require a dedication or reservation of open space implied the authority to compel conveyance of title to the open space to a homeowners' association that would assume control and maintenance responsibility for the land.

In *Homebuilders Ass'n of Charlotte v. City of Charlotte*,[23] the court upheld the imposition of user fees for a variety of city services, including rezonings, special use permits, plat reviews, and building

---

20. Several cases decided after the adoption of this statutory amendment do not explicitly address its impact on the scope of delegated powers. *See, e.g.,* Porsh Builders, Inc. v. City of Winston-Salem, 302 N.C. 550, 276 S.E.2d 443 (1981) (holding that statutory requirement for sale of redevelopment land to the "highest responsible bidder" conveyed little if any discretion to the city in defining what constituted a responsible bid).

21. G.S. 153A-124; 160A-177.

22. 326 N.C. 100, 388 S.E.2d 538 (1990).

23. 336 N.C. 37, 442 S.E.2d 45 (1994). *See also* Maready v. City of Winston-Salem, 342 N.C. 708, 467 S.E.2d 615 (1996) (upholding city use of economic-development incentives to private businesses); Moores v. Greensboro Minimum Hous. Standards Comm'n, 198 N.C. App. 384, 679 S.E.2d 480 (2009) (upholding authority to delegate hearing appeals and making final orders in housing-code appeals to housing-appeals commission). *But cf.* Bowers v. City

inspections, even though the city had no express statutory authority to impose them. The court held that G.S. 160A-4 required that grants of authority to cities be interpreted to include additional and supplementary powers that are expedient to execution of the city's regulatory powers. The court noted that such fees must be reasonable, generally not to exceed the cost of the regulatory program.

The court in *Massey v. City of Charlotte*[24] held that the zoning-enabling statutes authorized the use of conditional-use districts but did not mandate their use nor by implication limit the use of other types of zoning decisions (such as the purely legislative conditional zoning used by Charlotte in that case), especially when the zoning statutes were read with the mandate for broad construction in mind.[25]

In *King v. Town of Chapel Hill*,[26] the court upheld parts of an ordinance regulating the towing of cars parked without permission in private parking areas but also invalidated other portions of the ordinance. The ordinance specified the size and content of warning notices to be posted in parking lots, set vehicle-release requirements, and set maximum fees to be charged. The second ordinance prohibited the use of mobile phones while operating a motor vehicle. The court noted that where enabling legislation is clear and unambiguous, there is no room for judicial construction and the plain and definite meaning of the statute must be applied. The broad rule of construction is only applicable when the grant of authority is ambiguous. In this case the source of authority for the towing ordinance was the general police power that authorized regulations to protect or promote the health, safety, and general welfare. The court held that this grant of authority was inherently ambiguous and could not be placed within fixed, definite limits. Therefore, it was given a broad construction. However, even with a broad construction the implied authority must be exercised within constitutional limits. This requires a rational, real, substantial relation to protection of public health, safety, and general welfare. The court found that the warning-sign requirements met that standard.[27]

In *Patmore v. Town of Chapel Hill*,[28] the court upheld a neighborhood-conservation-overlay-district regulation that, among other things, limited parking to four cars per residential lot. The court held that it was appropriate to apply broad construction to G.S. 160D-701, the zoning statute, as the regulation was reasonably related to the statutorily approved purposes of regulating population density and traffic congestion. Since this was a zoning regulation addressing the land use problem of residential overoccupancy, it was not preempted by statutes that regulated parking in public vehicular areas.

Other decisions have illustrated the difficulty of determining the precise scope of implied powers and reflect the court's reluctance to relinquish close judicial oversight of the extent of implied powers

---

of High Point, 339 N.C. 413, 451 S.E.2d 284 (1994) (holding that the city had no authority to pay higher retirement benefits to law-enforcement officers than amount set by statute).

24. 145 N.C. App. 345, 550 S.E.2d 838, *review denied*, 354 N.C. 219, 554 S.E.2d 342 (2001).

25. *Id*. at 351, 353–55, 550 S.E.2d at 844–46. For a further discussion of *Massey* and conditional zoning, see Chapter 13.

26. 367 N.C. 400, 758 S.E.2d 364 (2014).

27. Consistent with the cases noted below regarding strict construction of ordinances pertaining to taxes and fees, the court held that the Town did not have the authority to create a fee schedule for the towing without express statutory authority. The court did uphold the ordinance provision prohibiting a "cash only" policy (which required tow operators to accept credit or debit cards for payment of towing fees) as reasonably related to citizen safety and welfare because it allowed vehicle owners who illegally parked to have quick and easy access to their towed vehicles. But the Town was held not to have the authority to cap the fee by prohibiting towers from passing debit- and credit-card charges on to the vehicle owners.

28. 233 N.C. App. 133, 757 S.E.2d 302, *review denied*, 367 N.C. 519, 758 S.E.2d 874 (2014). The court distinguished this regulation from the rule of strict construction applied to a county's authority to impose school impact fees (discussed below) on the grounds that this regulation was a bona fide zoning regulation, unlike the regulation voided in *Lanvale Properties*. For a critique of that analytic approach, see Heyward Earnhardt, Note, *More's the Pity: Patmore v. Town of Chapel Hill and the Continuing Uncertainty over North Carolina Judicial Construal of Local Authority*, 37 N.C. Cent. L. Rev. 216 (2015).

in the area of fees and local government finance. The statutes and cases have emphasized that when fees or taxes are involved, the scope of any implied authority is very narrow.[29]

Two of these cases involved challenges to the financing of Durham's comprehensive stormwater-management program. The city's program included a physical drainage system and various other non-capital components, including educational programs, guidance manuals, used-oil recycling, collection of household hazardous waste, and litter-enforcement programs. The city assessed fees on all developed property to finance its comprehensive program, with the fees based on the impervious area of the assessed land. Landowners[30] challenged the city's use of these fees rather than general-tax revenues to fund the program.

In *Smith Chapel Baptist Church v. City of Durham*,[31] the court initially upheld the city's authority to impose these fees to operate its entire stormwater program. The court held that while the public-enterprise statutes did not give the city authority to impose these fees, the authority could be based on the state constitutional provision establishing protection of the environment as a proper function of local governments,[32] with cities having implied supplementary power to impose reasonable fees for program implementation.[33] After rehearing, the court issued a new opinion that superseded this initial opinion. In its second decision,[34] the court held that the language of G.S. 160A-314(a1) "clearly and unambiguously"[35] provided that city stormwater utility fees were limited to the costs of constructing and operating the physical aspects of stormwater and drainage systems rather than the full cost of maintaining a comprehensive stormwater-quality-management program.[36] The court refused to apply the rule of broad construction, reasoning that where there was no ambiguity in the statute, the plain-meaning rule applied and there was no need for the court to resort to an interpretation, strict or broad.[37]

The case law on impact fees likewise illustrates the need for explicit authority to impose development-related taxes and fees.

---

29. See Chapter 9 for additional discussion of impact fees and Chapter 24 for discussion of the constitutional limits on exactions.

30. The plaintiff churches were subject to the utility-fee assessment but exempt from property taxes. G.S. 105-278.3.

31. 348 N.C. 632, 502 S.E.2d 364 (1998).

32. N.C. CONST. art. XIV, § 5.

33. "[W]hen a city has the power to regulate activities, it has a supplementary power reasonably necessary to carry the program into effect." *Smith Chapel*, 348 N.C. at 636, 502 S.E.2d at 367.

34. 350 N.C. 805, 517 S.E.2d 874 (1999). After the 1998 election, the court in 1999 had a different makeup and the decision on rehearing reflected its different judicial philosophy and partisan composition. The court applied a similar rationale to limit the scope of authority granted to the N.C. Department of Transportation in review of driveway permits under G.S. 136-18(29). The court held the statute unambiguously grants authority to regulate the size, location, design, and construction of driveway permits, but includes no authority to require off-site improvements or to obtain another property owner's approval of the access design. High Rock Lake Partners, LLC v. N.C. Dep't of Trans., 366 N.C. 315, 735 S.E.2d 300 (2012). In 2018, the General Assembly explicitly limited the authority of cities to require schools to pay for any road improvements other than those related to ingress and egress from the school. G.S. 160A, §§ 307.1, 383(d).

35. *Smith Chapel* at 811, 517 S.E.2d at 878. In dissent, Justice Henry E. Frye, who had concurred with the result in the initial decision, contended that the court was taking an "unduly narrow view of the City's authority." *Id.* at 819, 517 S.E.2d at 883.

36. Upon reconvening after the second *Smith Chapel* decision, the legislature, at the recommendation of the Environmental Review Commission, clarified the statute at issue. S.L. 2000-70 revised the statutes involved to explicitly provide that stormwater-management systems that can be funded through utility fees include "any cost necessary to assure that all aspects of stormwater quality and quantity are managed in accordance with federal and State law, regulations, and rules." The changes in the city and county statutes were made effective retroactively to July 15, 1989, the date of the original adoption of this authority.

37. For further discussion of how the rules of construction apply to development regulations, see Chapter 18.

The court in *Lanvale Properties, LLC v. County of Cabarrus* invalidated a school impact fee imposed as a mitigation measure for developments proposed in areas with inadequate school capacity.[38] The county initially adopted these adequate-public-facility requirements as part of its subdivision ordinance and later moved the requirements to its zoning ordinance. The provisions prohibited approval of residential subdivisions if there was inadequate school capacity for the projected development, but the proposed subdivision could be (and routinely was) approved upon entering a consent agreement to pay a fee to be used for the capital costs of providing additional school capacity. The court held that the county lacked statutory authority under the county's zoning authority to impose a mitigation fee to remedy inadequate school capacity. The court noted that while assuring adequate provision of public facilities was a legitimate objective of zoning, the means authorized to address that objective included regulating the use of land, density, setbacks, and the like. Only those exactions expressly authorized could be imposed and there was no statutory authority for a school impact fee. The court viewed these fees as a revenue mechanism, not a land use regulation.

Earlier cases from the court of appeals regarding school impact fees had similar results. In *Durham Land Owners Ass'n v. County of Durham*,[39] the county asserted that the statutory grant of authority to fix fees for "performing services or duties required by law" gave the county authority to impose a school impact fee on new residential construction. The court held that provision of schools, while mandated by the state, is a general governmental obligation rather than a service provided to an individual for which the county can charge a fee. In *Union Land Owners Ass'n v. County of Union*,[40] the court held that even where a legitimate regulatory objective was being met, the means used to advance that objective could not be implied to extend beyond the powers granted. That case involved an adequate-public-facilities provision that gave developers the option of paying a voluntary mitigation fee if there was inadequate school capacity. The court held that the tools enumerated in the zoning and subdivision statutes did not include the authority to assess what was essentially a school impact fee even though school capacity itself was a legitimate legislative concern.[41]

The court has applied the same rule of interpretation of the scope of authority regarding fees for public utilities imposed under the public-enterprise statutes. In *Quality Built Homes Inc. v. Town of Carthage*, the court invalidated a utility-impact fee that was assessed regardless of the property owner's actual use of the utility system. The court found that the municipal public-enterprise statute only authorized fees for "services furnished," not for prospective services that might be provided in the future.[42]

The rules of preemption and standard canons of statutory interpretation also sometimes limit local government flexibility regarding land-development regulations.[43] For example, while Dillon's Rule is no longer applicable, the plain-meaning rule requires the court to give full effect to clear legislative direc-

38. Lanvale Props., LLC v. Cnty. of Cabarrus, 366 N.C. 142, 731 S.E.2d 800 (2012). The regulation provided that if available student capacity was inadequate, the development application would be denied or conditions imposed to mitigate impacts, including deferring or phasing final approval until school capacity became available, reducing density, or entering a consent agreement to make school-impact-fee payments to provide needed school capacity. Adequate-public-facility ordinances are discussed in more detail in Chapter 9.

39. 177 N.C. App. 629, 630 S.E.2d 200, *review denied*, 360 N.C. 532, 633 S.E.2d 678 (2006). The Mississippi Supreme Court reached a similar conclusion in *Mayor of Ocean Springs v. Homebuilders Ass'n*, 932 So. 2d 44 (Miss. 2006). Authority for exactions in subdivision ordinances is discussed further in Chapter 7.

40. 201 N.C. App. 374, 689 S.E.2d 504 (2009).

41. For a critique of this rationale, see Michael F. Roessler, *Public Education, Local Authority, and Democracy: The Implied Power of North Carolina Counties to Impose School Impact Fees*, 33 Campbell L. Rev. 239 (2011).

42. 369 N.C. 15, 789 S.E.2d 454 (2016). *See also* Point S. Props., LLC v. Cape Fear Pub. Util. Auth., 243 N.C. App. 508, 778 S.E.2d 284 (2015) (no authority to impose utility-impact fees when the property involved was not served by the utility and no specific plan for service had been adopted).

43. See Chapter 18 for a review of cases interpreting statutes and ordinances and Chapter 22 for a discussion of preemption and state legislative limitations on local discretion.

tions. Where the legislature has provided specific direction to local governments, that direction must be followed.[44] A local government may not use its general authority or a rule of broad construction to circumvent limitations specifically imposed by statute.[45]

Incorporation by Reference

A local development regulation "incorporates by reference" a secondary document when it declares that the secondary document is a part of the regulation and applies just as if it were fully set out in the regulation itself. This gives the secondary document the same force and effect as the regulation.

Definitions in state and federal law are among the more common items incorporated by reference into development regulations. A city zoning regulation, for example, may include locational restrictions on adult businesses or family care homes. The land uses that are subject to the restrictions must be defined in the regulation. Rather than including detailed definitions, however, the regulation may simply state that the rules apply to all "sexually oriented businesses as defined by G.S. 160A-181.1(f)" or to all "family-care homes as defined in G.S. 168-21." These cross-references are useful in keeping local regulations consistent with state law.

Maps and designations promulgated by the state for federal agencies are also frequently incorporated. Floodplain-zoning regulations often incorporate officially promulgated flood-insurance-rate maps (FIRMs) prepared for the National Flood Insurance Program. FIRMs are used to define the zones within which flood-hazard regulations apply. Another example would be a county ordinance that applies certain development restrictions within an "ocean-hazard area of environmental concern as designated by the N.C. Coastal Resources Commission." A city could apply its stormwater-management standards to a 100-foot buffer on either side of a perennial or intermittent stream "as shown on the most recent version of the 1:24,000 scale (7.5 minute) quadrangle topographic maps prepared by the United States Geological Survey."[46] In each of these instances, the maps prepared by others become an integral part of the local development regulation.

A third example is the use of documents and standards promulgated by nongovernment agencies. These are often technical standards or model codes prepared by national groups. For example, a local zoning ordinance may provide that a density bonus shall be available for any building that "meets or exceeds the minimum U.S. Green Building Council's LEED Silver criteria."

---

44. *See, e.g.,* Cnty. of Lancaster v. Mecklenburg Cnty., 334 N.C. 496, 509, 434 S.E.2d 604, 613 (1993) (counties may not delegate decisions required by statute to be made by planning board to an individual staff member); Five C's, Inc. v. Cnty. of Pasquotank, 195 N.C. App. 410, 672 S.E.2d 737 (2009) (where statute explicitly lists the grounds for local regulation of manufactured housing, County has no authority to regulate on the basis of other factors).

45. In *BellSouth Communications, Inc. v. City of Laurinburg*, 168 N.C. App. 75, 606 S.E.2d 721 (2005), a case addressing the scope of the public-enterprise statutes and municipal authority to operate a fiber-optic network, the court reviewed and reconciled the statute and cases thusly:

> The narrow Dillon's Rule of statutory construction used when interpreting municipal powers has been replaced by N.C. GEN. STAT. § 160A-4's mandate that the language of Chapter 160A be construed in favor of extending powers to a municipality where there is an ambiguity in the authorizing language, or the powers clearly authorized reasonably necessitate additional and supplementary powers to carry them into execution and effect. However, where the plain meaning of the statute is without ambiguity, it must be enforced as written.

Id. at 82–83, 606 S.E.2d at 726 (citations omitted).

46. See *Cary Creek Ltd. Partnership v. Town of Cary*, 203 N.C. App. 99, 690 S.E.2d 549 (2010), for an example of this type of cross-reference.

Statutory Authority

Courts in most states have upheld incorporation of existing statutes and ordinances into local ordinances. As state and federal laws are official documents readily and widely available and are applicable whether or not they are incorporated into an ordinance, it seems reasonable that they can be incorporated by reference into local development regulations. Some cases have held that statutory authorization is necessary to incorporate material other than state and federal laws, while others have a general rule allowing incorporation by reference if the document to be incorporated is sufficiently identified and made a part of the public record.

North Carolina has several statutory authorizations for incorporation by reference that apply to development regulations.

G.S. 160A-76(b) authorizes incorporation by reference into city ordinances "any published technical code or any standards or regulations promulgated by any public agency." G.S. 153A-47 provides substantially similar authority for counties.

There is some ambiguity in these statutes. Authority to incorporate nongovernmental material into local ordinances assumes that the "technical codes" and perhaps "standards" that may be incorporated by reference are not limited to ones adopted by public agencies. Given the use and placement of the conjunction or in the statute, it is reasonable to interpret the sentence to mean that the phrase "promulgated by any public agency" applies only to "regulations." If so, this allows incorporation of technical codes and standards promulgated by nongovernmental entities.[47] The material to be incorporated under the authority of G.S. 160A-76(b) or 153A-47 must have been "published." This suggests there needs to be a specific document that is readily available to the general public (in either paper or electronic form) that includes the specific provisions that are being made a part of the city or county ordinance.

In addition to these general authorizations for incorporation by reference, several statutes address the issue for particular items. For example, G.S. 160D-704(b) specifically authorizes ordinances that provide regulatory incentives for energy conservation to reference "generally recognized standards established for such purposes," such as use of the Green Building Council standards when allowing a zoning-density bonus. Another critical example is use of flood-insurance maps. State law mandates use of "the current floodplain maps prepared pursuant to the National Flood Insurance Program or approved by the Department [of Public Safety]" to define the base floodplain that must be included in flood-hazard areas in local regulations.[48] G.S. 160D-105(b) provides that development regulations may incorporate by reference maps officially adopted by state or federal agencies, including approved updates to those maps.

Copy of Incorporated Material

When material is incorporated by reference into an ordinance, that material does not appear in the ordinance. How does a citizen know just what is required for compliance with the ordinance? Failure to comply with the detailed requirements of the incorporated material is a violation of the ordinance, so it is important that enforcement officers, the regulated community, and citizens know exactly what is required.

---

47. An alternative interpretation of the statutory authorization focuses on the placement of the word *any* and would have the "promulgated by any public agency" limitation applicable to standards and regulations but not to technical codes. In either interpretation, nongovernmental technical codes could be incorporated by reference. These statutes do not explicitly address maps and other technical documents, but these are sufficiently similar to technical codes and standards that they can also likely be incorporated by reference even if not officially adopted as formal state or federal rules.

48. G.S. 143, §§ 215.52(a)(1b), 215.56(c).

G.S. 160A-76(b) and 153A-47 address this need when technical codes, standards, or regulations are incorporated by reference into a city or county ordinance. An official copy of the incorporated material must be available for inspection in the office of the city or county clerk. Similarly, G.S. 160D-105(b) requires that the city or county clerk maintain the map for public inspection. It would be prudent for the city or county to file an official copy of any other material incorporated by reference with the city clerk, to be maintained with comparable materials such as the code itself.

Readily available reference copies on the city or county website and in planning offices would also be useful, even if not legally required.

Incorporation of Future Amendments

While existing external material can be incorporated by reference, what about future amendments to that material? Do cities and counties have the option of automatically including future amendments to that material in the incorporated material? It is often useful to do so in order to keep the local ordinances and the incorporated material in sync without the necessity of amending the local ordinance to explicitly reference every subsequent update of the incorporated material.

Prior to the enactment of Chapter 160D, this aspect of the issue was more difficult to resolve. It raised the question of whether incorporation of material that does not yet exist unlawfully delegates the local government's legislative authority.[49] In addition to this constitutional concern, in North Carolina the statutory authority to incorporate future amendments into city and county ordinances was not certain. G.S. 160D-105(b) resolved this uncertainty by explicitly allowing a development regulation to incorporate by reference a specific map (the 2017 version, for example) or the most recent officially adopted version of the map. When zoning-district boundaries are based upon incorporated maps, the local ordinance may provide that the zoning-district boundaries are automatically amended to remain consistent with the incorporated map, provided the clerk maintains the incorporated map for public inspection.[50]

Any incorporation by reference should be specific about which option is intended (current version only or version as may be subsequently amended). For example, the ordinance could incorporate by reference a technical code adopted on a specified date or it could incorporate that technical code "including subsequent amendments." If subsequent amendments are to be incorporated, that places an obligation on the local government staff to regularly update the official copy maintained by the city clerk.

---

49. Case law nationally is divided on the degree to which this can be done. Some cases hold that any incorporation of future amendments is not permissible as it allows the entity responsible for the incorporated material to effectively amend the local ordinance in ways unknowable to the local government's elected officials. An alternative is to tie the legality of incorporating future amendments to the nature of the material incorporated. For example, some courts allow incorporation of future amendments of material that has a purpose independent of the ordinance that incorporates it (such as definitions in state and federal statutes or independently produced technical codes) but do not allow incorporation of future amendments of material created for the sole purpose of implementing the ordinance (such as having a conditional rezoning be subject to future conditions to be developed and approved by the landowner and neighbors).

50. The statutes on local-ordinance incorporation by reference did not address future amendments. The state Administrative Procedure Act does. G.S. 150B-21.6 allows incorporation by reference in state agency rules of any code, standard, or regulation adopted by another state or federal agency or a "generally recognized organization or association." This law expressly gives rule-making agencies the option to include subsequent amendments and editions of the incorporated material. The rule must clearly state which option is to be applied. Coastal Ready-Mix Concrete Co. v. Bd. of Comm'rs, 299 N.C. 620, 625, 265 S.E.2d 379, 382 (1980). If the principles in G.S. 150B-21.6 are applied to local ordinances, these ordinances have the option of either incorporating only the current edition of the material or incorporating future amendments as well.

CHAPTER 5

Geographic Jurisdiction for Land-Development Regulation

Cities and counties in North Carolina may undertake land use planning and apply land-development regulations only in the geographic areas over which the legislature has delegated authority to them. There is no overlapping of land-development-regulatory jurisdiction in North Carolina. Exclusive jurisdiction for an area is assigned to a particular city or county.

As a general rule, municipalities may exercise authority within their city limits and counties may exercise authority in the unincorporated area outside city jurisdiction.[1] The exception to this general rule is that municipalities may extend regulations under certain circumstances to a limited area immediately outside their city limits.

Municipalities

Chapter 160D, Section 201 of the North Carolina General Statutes (hereinafter G.S.) is the basic statute that sets territorial jurisdiction for all municipal land-development regulations. G.S. 160D-201(a) provides that all planning-and-development-regulation powers may be exercised by any city within its corporate limits. Most of the specific enabling statutes for land-development regulations simply repeat the authority to enact regulations within a city's "territorial jurisdiction."[2]

The 1923 zoning-enabling act[3] granted cities the authority to zone within their corporate or city limits.[4] The provision of that act mandating that zoning be in accordance with a comprehensive plan

---

1. The General Assembly can modify these general rules for individual cities and counties. The most-common local modifications are those for extraterritorial areas, as discussed below. Another example is Chapter 63A, Section 18 of the North Carolina General Statutes (hereinafter G.S.), which gives the North Carolina Global TransPark Authority zoning jurisdiction over its cargo-airport complex near Kinston and the area within six miles of the site.

While it is not explicitly addressed by statutes or case law, cities and counties can likely apply development regulations to water bodies as well as land areas within their respective jurisdictions. *See* N.C. Dep't of Justice, Office of the Att'y Gen., Advisory Opinion: Zoning; Municipal Corporations; Coastal Area Management Act, Op. N.C. Att'y Gen., Aug. 12, 1982 (town zoning can be applied to water bodies within the town's extraterritorial-planning jurisdiction); N.C. Dep't of Justice, Office of the Att'y Gen., Advisory Opinion: Zoning; Coastal Area Management Act, Op. N.C. Att'y Gen., July 27, 1982 (county zoning can be applied to regulate "floating homes" located on public waters).

2. *See, e.g.*, G.S. 160D-801 (subdivision); G.S. 160D-701 (zoning). G.S. 160D-960 provides that community appearance commissions may operate within a local government's "planning and development regulation jurisdiction." An exception to this general rule is the authority to adopt maintenance codes for nonresidential buildings. These regulations may be applied jurisdiction-wide, in specified municipal service districts or in areas designated for improvement and investment in an adopted comprehensive plan. G.S. 160D-1129(a).

3. S.L. 1923-250.

4. G.S. 160A-22 provides that an official copy of the city's corporate limits must be retained permanently in the office of the city clerk. Copies of the map certified by the clerk are admissible in evidence in court.

The General Assembly has occasionally limited municipal zoning authority for particular cities by local legislation. For example, when the Town of Saint James was incorporated, the legislature provided that Brunswick County

was interpreted by the North Carolina Supreme Court to require that zoning be applied throughout a municipality. Zoning may not be applied to only part of a city.[5] That rule is now codified as G.S. 160D-201(c), which requires that city zoning and subdivision regulations, if adopted at all, must be applied jurisdiction-wide.

A municipality may also apply its ordinances to city-owned property outside the city limits.[6] If a city owns an airport and has a separate airport zoning ordinance, the city may elect to extend the coverage of that ordinance to protect the approaches to the airport, even if the approaches are not within the city's corporate limits or its extraterritorial–land use jurisdiction.[7]

Counties

The initial authority to regulate county development in North Carolina was extended to individual counties by special act of the General Assembly. Forsyth County received authority to undertake zoning in 1947, and Durham County was granted that authority in 1949.[8]

Authority to enact county zoning was extended to most counties in the state in 1959.[9] Every county now has general authority to enact land-development regulations throughout the part of the county that lies outside of municipal jurisdiction.[10] The court of appeals confirmed in *Cumberland County v. Eastern Federal Corp.*[11] that a county's exercise of zoning power only in the unincorporated portion of the county had a reasonable basis and did not violate the equal-protection provisions of the state or federal constitutions.

G.S. 160D-201(b) allows county development regulations to be adopted throughout the county except in areas subject to municipal planning-and-development-regulation jurisdiction.[12] Once a city has estab-

would have zoning jurisdiction within the town for ten years. S.L. 2005-305 amended that to grant the town zoning authority earlier but still prohibited the town from exercising extraterritorial jurisdiction (ETJ) until 2010.

G.S. 160A, §§ 37(f2) and 49(f2) provide that when agricultural or forestry land subject to use-value taxation is annexed into a city, it is considered a part of the city for land use regulation but not for other purposes while it still qualifies for use-value taxation.

5. Shuford v. Town of Waynesville, 214 N.C. 135, 138, 198 S.E. 585, 587 (1938). In addition to the statutory requirement, the constitutional guarantees of equal protection and due process likely mandate citywide zoning. See Chapter 25 for a discussion of these constitutional issues.

6. G.S. 160A-176.

7. G.S. 63-31(d).

8. S.L. 1947-677 (Forsyth County); S.L. 1949-1043 (Durham County). Other local acts authorized activity in individual counties. *See, e.g.*, S.L. 1949-400 (Clay County); S.L. 1951-1193 (Dare County). The Dare County authorization allowed zoning of selected areas of the county upon petition of 15 percent of the property owners of the area. A similar authorization for Guilford County was introduced in 1951 (H.B. 1128) but not adopted. In other instances, county regulation was authorized to deal with particular development issues. Cumberland County was given zoning authority in 1957 to protect the area around the newly established Methodist College outside of Fayetteville. S.L. 1957-1455. By 1958, six counties had been granted authority to enact zoning (Cumberland, Dare, Durham, Forsyth, Guilford, and Perquimans). In addition, all counties had been granted authority for airport zoning (in 1941) and floodplain zoning (in 1956).

9. S.L. 1959-1006. This law exempted thirty-one counties from its coverage.

10. G.S. 153A-320.

11. 48 N.C. App. 518, 269 S.E.2d 672, *review denied*, 301 N.C. 527, 273 S.E.2d 453 (1980).

12. G.S. 130A-55(17) allows certain sanitary districts to adopt zoning ordinances that have the same jurisdiction and effect as municipal ordinances. To qualify, the sanitary district must adjoin an incorporated area and also be within three miles of two other cities. Application of this authority is quite rare. Also, G.S. 63-31 allows both cities and counties to adopt airport zoning regulations for "the area surrounding any airport" within the jurisdiction. The city or county may also apply the airport zoning regulations extraterritorially, if necessary, to protect the approaches to airports owned by the city or county. G.S. 63-31(d). Although many airport zoning provisions have been incorporated into general zoning ordinances, separate airport zoning regulations continue to exist.

lished an extraterritorial ordinance, the county loses jurisdiction in that area for its land use–related powers, including regulations or programs related to zoning, subdivisions, building codes, community development, historic districts or landmarks, open space, housing codes, or community appearance.[13] Unlike land-development regulations, a county's general-police-power ordinances may be applied in the extraterritorial area[14] (and a city may not extend its general-police-power ordinances beyond its corporate limits). However, if a city elects not to apply a particular type of development regulation in its extraterritorial area, the county may elect to exercise that type of regulation in the area.[15]

Whether property is or is not within a county is a factual question that determines the threshold issue of applicability of a county zoning ordinance.[16] An illustration of this is provided by *Guilford County Planning & Development Department v. Simmons*.[17] The board of adjustment denied a variance for chicken houses located along the Guilford-Alamance county border. The trial court held that the site of the buildings was in Alamance County. The court of appeals held that failure of the defendant to file a judicial appeal of the board of adjustment's decision that the property was in Guilford County did not waive the fundamental question, whether the board had subject-matter jurisdiction. The court held that where there was conflicting information about the location of the county boundary line, the finding of fact by the trial court that the property was outside the county was not to be disturbed if it was supported by competent evidence.

G.S. 160D-202(f) enables counties to exercise land-development-regulatory power within a city's boundaries upon request from the city's governing board. The request from the city and the acceptance by the county must be in the form of a resolution formally adopted by each governing board.[18] Any such request or approval may be revoked at any time by mutual agreement of both jurisdictions or with two years' written notice by either of the entities acting alone.

Counties also have the option of regulating only part of the unincorporated portion of the county.[19] Prior to the adoption of Chapter 160D, G.S. 153A-342 required that such an area originally contain at least 640 acres and have at least ten tracts in separate ownership. Subsequent additions to these areas could be of any size. Some counties used this authority to adopt zoning in areas immediately around cities, around lakes and recreation areas, or in densely populated townships while leaving the more rural portions of the counties unregulated. The limitation of a minimum 640-acre area was not continued in G.S. 160D-201 or G.S. 160D-702, providing greater flexibility for partial-county regulation.

A county must be careful to clearly delineate its intentions regarding the scope of its jurisdiction.[20] In *State v. Baggett*,[21] the court dismissed criminal charges regarding violation of an adult-entertainment-

---

13. G.S. 143-215.57 establishes an exception to this general rule for floodplain regulations. If a city exercises ETJ, it may apply city floodplain regulations to that area, even if they are included in a separate ordinance rather than incorporated into the city zoning ordinance. However, if the city elects not to exercise floodplain regulations in the extraterritorial area, the county may apply its own floodplain regulations to that area.

14. G.S. 153A-122.

15. G.S. 160D-202(b). This provision was added to the statutes with the adoption of Chapter 160D. S.L. 2019-111.

16. Guilford Cnty. Plan. & Dev. Dep't v. Simmons, 102 N.C. App. 325, 401 S.E.2d 659, *review denied*, 329 N.C. 496, 407 S.E.2d 533 (1991).

17. 115 N.C. App. 87, 443 S.E.2d 765 (1994).

18. G.S. 160A-360(g).

19. See Figure 3.1 in Chapter 3 for a map of the counties in the state that have elected to adopt either countywide or partial-county zoning.

20. A county general-police-power ordinance can be applied to any part of the county not within a city's corporate limits. G.S. 153A-122. This includes a city's ETJ. By contrast, a county development regulation cannot be applied within a city's extraterritorial area unless the city requests that the county apply it or if the city is not applying that particular development regulation in the ETJ. G.S. 160D-202(b), (f).

21. 133 N.C. App. 47, 514 S.E.2d 536 (1999).

siting ordinance because it was not clear whether or not this ordinance, adopted under the county's general-ordinance-making authority, was intended to apply within the city's extraterritorial area.

Municipal Extraterritorial Authority

General Law

A city may not extend its regulatory or police powers beyond the city limits without specific legislative authority. The state supreme court ruled in 1894 that the town of Washington did not have the authority to regulate the throwing of dead fish from a pier into the Pamlico River.[22] The city limits extended only to the low-water mark of the river, so the portion of the pier over the river itself was not within the city's regulatory jurisdiction. Because no expanded police-power jurisdiction had been granted by the legislature, the city could not enforce its ordinance outside its city limits. The court noted, however, that the city's police-power jurisdiction could, with legislative approval, be set at other than the city limits:

> [T]he Legislature unquestionably had the power to extend the jurisdiction of the town for police purposes to the middle of the river or to the opposite bank, and . . . the effect would have been to extend the boundary for the exercise of the power to prohibit nuisance delegated to the town across the adjacent bed of the river, while the territorial limit of its authority for all purposes other than the exercise of police powers would have been the low water mark on the north bank.[23]

The concept of state-authorized municipal regulation of extraterritorial areas to protect public health and safety is widespread and has a considerable lineage.[24] Many states extended this idea to allow extraterritorial-planning and land-development regulations.[25]

---

22. State v. Eason, 114 N.C. 787, 19 S.E. 88 (1894).

23. *Id.* at 792–93, 19 S.E. at 89.

24. An early example is an 1825 Georgia statute allowing the city of Savannah to prohibit rice farms within a mile of the city limits. The city adopted such a regulation to promote "dry culture" of the swamplands near the city as a public-health-protection measure. The city's extraterritorial regulation was upheld in *Green v. Mayor of Savannah*, 6 Ga. 1 (1849). Also see *Harrison v. Mayor of Baltimore*, 1 Gill 264 (Md. 1843), upholding the authority of the city to apply health regulations within three miles of the city. The authority had been applied to quarantine and disinfect an arriving ship with Irish immigrants infected with smallpox and typhoid fever.

Municipal extraterritorial regulation to prevent nuisances, protect water supplies, and regulate various particular land uses and practices (such as uses generating pollution or posing risks to public health, safety, welfare, or morals) have also long been common. This includes regulations on the location of high-impact land uses—slaughterhouses, packing houses, tanneries, storage of explosives, distilleries, intensive livestock concentrations, and the like—and places where "unseemly" and illegal activities might take place, particularly gambling, prostitution, or the sale of alcohol. The scope of activities that could be regulated and the geographic extent of extraterritorial authority varied widely from state to state. *See* Russell W. Maddox, Extraterritorial Powers of Municipalities in the United States 58–69 (1955); William Anderson, *The Extraterritorial Powers of Cities* (pt. 2), 10 Minn. L. Rev. 564, 577–78 (1926).

25. A 1952 report indicated that eight states—Alabama, Indiana, Kentucky, Nebraska, North Carolina, South Carolina, Tennessee, and West Virginia—had granted some or all of their cities extraterritorial-zoning authority. Am. Soc'y of Plan. Officials, Extraterritorial Zoning 6 (PAS Report No. 42, Sept. 1952). During this period, however, relatively few cities exercised extraterritorial zoning. One national study reported that over 95 percent of cities with populations over 25,000 zoned the land within their corporate limits, but less than 10 percent had authority for extraterritorial zoning. John C. Bollens, *Controls and Services in Unincorporated Urban Fringes*, 21 Mun. Y.B. 53, 54–55 (1954). At least two-thirds of the states had granted municipalities extraterritorial-planning authority at this time. Frank S. Sengstock, Extraterritorial Powers in the Metropolitan Area 61–63 (1962). For additional background, see Maddox, *supra* note 24; Louis F. Bartelt, *Extraterritorial Zoning: Reflections on Its Validity*, 32 Notre Dame L. Rev. 367 (1957). The question of whether and how to extend extraterritorial

The court upheld a legislative grant of extraterritorial power in 1912 in *State v. Rice*.[26] Special legislation had granted the city of Greensboro authority to impose sanitary regulations up to one mile beyond the city limits. The city, acting under this authority, had adopted an ordinance that prohibited keeping hogs in the city or within a quarter mile of the corporate limits. In its deliberations of a challenge to the ordinance, the court concluded that the legislature had "unquestioned authority" to grant the city extraterritorial jurisdiction. This one-mile extraterritorial authority for sanitary ordinances was extended statewide in 1917,[27] and G.S. 160A-193 now allows cities the authority to summarily abate public-health and safety nuisances within one mile of their corporate limits.[28]

A principal concern with granting municipalities extraterritorial power has been the lack of political representation for extraterritorial residents.[29] The legal aspects of this concern, if not the political and policy considerations involved, were largely resolved when the U.S. Supreme Court concluded that federal constitutional guarantees of due process and equal protection are not violated when states grant municipalities extraterritorial jurisdiction without extending the right to vote in municipal elections to extraterritorial residents.[30]

In the *Rice* case, the state supreme court addressed this contention. Because the police power was a state authority that was being exercised, the court dismissed the complaint.[31] The court reached the same conclusion in 1957 for an extraterritorial-zoning ordinance adopted by Raleigh pursuant to a specific grant of authority in local legislation.[32]

In the absence of a specific grant of extraterritorial authority, cities have no inherent extraterritorial power. A 1955 case, *State v. Owen*,[33] addressed an attempt by Winston-Salem to apply its zoning ordinance extraterritorially. The court ruled that a general grant of a one-mile extraterritorial jurisdiction in the city's 1927 charter applied only to the police force and criminal-law enforcement. The court further held that a subsequent grant of extraterritorial-zoning authority did not apply retroactively, ruling that

---

planning and regulatory authority continues to be debated in many states. *See, e.g.*, Lori Schwartzmiller, Comment, *This Land Is Whose Land? The Feasibility of Extraterritorial Jurisdiction in West Virginia's Land Use Planning Laws*, 109 W. Va. L. Rev. 929 (2007).

26. 158 N.C. 635, 74 S.E. 582 (1912).

27. S.L. 1917-136.

28. While not directly related to development regulations, G.S. 160A-286 provides that city police officers have law-enforcement powers within one mile of the corporate limits of the city.

29. "The crux of the arguments opposing the conferring of unlimited police powers over noncorporate territories is that such a grant involves government without the consent of the governed." Sengstock, *supra* note 25. This concern was a key aspect of several early judicial invalidations of broad grants of extraterritorial regulatory authority. *See, e.g.*, Smeltzer v. Messer, 311 Ky. 692, 225 S.W.2d 96 (1949); Malone v. Williams, 118 Tenn. 390, 103 S.W. 798 (1907).

Those opposing extraterritorial exercise of municipal police powers often express this contention as "no taxation without representation." Since residents of a city's ETJ do not pay city taxes and have mandated representation on city planning boards and boards of adjustment, they actually have "representation without taxation," a fact that rarely mollifies those opposed to being included in the city's regulatory jurisdiction. For an example of interest in this complaint, see H.B. 66, 2d Ex. Sess. (N.C. 1993), which proposed allowing residents in the extraterritorial-zoning area to vote in municipal elections.

30. Holt Civic Club v. City of Tuscaloosa, 439 U.S. 60, 70–75 (1978).

31. "There is nothing in our Constitution which restricts the Legislature in the exercise of its police power from conferring upon the municipal authorities of Greensboro such [extraterritorial] power." *Rice*, 158 N.C. at 638, 74 S.E. at 583.

32. City of Raleigh v. Morand, 247 N.C. 363, 100 S.E.2d 870 (1957), *appeal dismissed*, 357 U.S. 343 (1958). The case is discussed in Philip P. Green, Jr., *Supreme Court Upholds Extra-Territorial Zoning*, Popular Gov't, Mar. 1958, at 6. *See generally* David E. Hunt, *The Constitutionality of the Exercise of Extraterritorial Powers by Municipalities*, 45 U. Chi. L. Rev. 151 (1977).

33. 242 N.C. 525, 88 S.E.2d 832 (1955).

a 1953 local act that granted three miles of extraterritorial-zoning jurisdiction did not validate a zoning ordinance adopted by the city in 1948.

Authority to Regulate Extraterritorial Land Use

As zoning and other land use regulations first came into widespread use in North Carolina, this activity was almost exclusively a municipal concern. While most cities of any size were adopting zoning, only a few counties were doing so. As the post–World War II development boom took off, a good deal of the development occurred along the urban fringe, often in unregulated areas just outside of city corporate limits, and often in what was characterized at the time as "relatively chaotic fashion."[34] The result in North Carolina, as in many states, was to authorize city "perimeter zoning," which is now known as municipal extraterritorial jurisdiction (often referred to as *ETJ*).

Authority to adopt zoning ordinances in the one-mile area surrounding the city was granted to Raleigh, Chapel Hill, Gastonia, and Tarboro in 1949.[35] In succeeding years, a number of additional cities secured local legislation authorizing extraterritorial zoning.[36]

The Municipal Government Study Commission examined the issue in 1958 and came to this conclusion:

> The Commission recognizes that municipalities have a special interest in the areas immediately adjacent to their limits. These areas, in the normal course of events, will at some time be annexed to the city, bringing with them any problems growing out of chaotic and disorganized development. Even prior to that time they affect the city. Health and safety problems arising outside the city do not always respect city limits as they spread . . . . Subdividers of land outside the city commonly wish to tie into city water and sewerage systems. New industrial and commercial development may, for a variety of reasons, take place just outside the corporate limits. Visitors to the city receive their first impression from these outlying areas.[37]

The study commission recommended that all cities with populations of 2500 and larger be granted a one-mile area of ETJ. The commission noted the concern that residents of these areas were not entitled to vote in city elections and recommended mandatory representation of extraterritorial residents on city planning boards and boards of adjustment "[t]o meet this objection in a practical and yet legal manner."[38]

---

34. Philip P. Green, Jr., *The Zoning of Areas Outside City Limits*, POPULAR GOV'T, Oct. 1953, at 7. Green offered three options for addressing development regulation in these areas: city extraterritorial zoning, county zoning, or special-district zoning.

Cities had previously also been granted some authority over land subdivisions within one mile of city limits. A 1929 statute provided that land within one mile of a city could not be subdivided until the city governing board approved a map of the subdivision and its proposed layout of streets and sidewalks. S.L. 1929-186. When the subdivision-enabling statute was adopted in 1955, cities were authorized to regulate land subdivision within one mile of their corporate limits. S.L. 1955-1334.

35. S.L. 1949-540 (Raleigh), S.L. 1949-629 (Chapel Hill), S.L. 1949-700 (Gastonia), S.L. 1949-1192 (Tarboro).

36. For example, in 1951, this authority was extended to Statesville, Farmville, Mooresville, Chapel Hill, and Kinston. S.L. 1951-238 (Statesville), S.L. 1951-441 (Farmville), S.L. 1951-336 (Mooresville), S.L. 1951-273 (Chapel Hill), S.L. 1951-876 (Kinston). In 1953, Winston-Salem was given a three-mile ETJ. S.L. 1953-777. By 1958, nineteen municipalities had secured local legislation authorizing extraterritorial zoning (Carrboro, Chapel Hill, Charlotte, Elizabeth City, Farmville, Gastonia, Goldsboro, Greensboro, High Point, Jacksonville, Kinston, Mooresville, Raleigh, Salisbury, Snow Hill, Spencer, Statesville, Tarboro, and Winston-Salem).

37. REPORT OF THE MUNICIPAL GOVERNMENT STUDY COMMISSION OF THE NORTH CAROLINA GENERAL ASSEMBLY 39 (Nov. 1958).

38. *Id.* at 40. The commission report noted that such an arrangement would provide "outside residents an appropriate and essential role in both the legislative process [given the planning board's role in recommending

The commission went on to recommend that cities with larger populations be granted up to five miles of ETJ, provided the county agreed. The legislature adopted the bulk of the study commission's recommendations and granted statewide authority for municipal extraterritorial–land use regulation in 1959.[39]

The statute on ETJ has undergone a number of amendments since its enactment. In 1961, the population required to exercise this power was reduced to 1250.[40] A number of technical revisions were made to the statute in 1965, including allowing interlocal agreements on extraterritorial boundaries.[41] The current statutory scheme, a tiered ETJ of one to three miles based on city population, was adopted in 1971.[42] The original extraterritorial authorization exempted bona fide farms from zoning coverage because this exemption existed for county zoning. The farm exemption in the extraterritorial area of cities was deleted in the 1971 recodification but reinserted into the statutes in 2011.[43] Subsequent amendments have included:

- provision for vested rights when jurisdiction shifts,[44]
- allowance for annual updates to be used in determining city populations,[45]
- clarification of the process for assumption of authority in extraterritorial areas by a county when a city relinquishes jurisdiction,[46] and
- deletion of provisions allowing a separate advisory board of extraterritorial residents in lieu of expanding the planning board and board of adjustment to include extraterritorial representation.[47]

---

regulations] and the administration of the ordinance [given the board of adjustment's role with variances]." *Id.* at 40a.

39. S.L. 1959-1204. General enabling authority for county zoning had been adopted earlier in the 1959 legislative session. S.L. 1959-1006. Nineteen counties were exempted from the coverage of the law authorizing extraterritorial zoning. City charters or local legislation can restrict use of ETJ for particular cities. *See, e.g.,* S.L. 2007-334 (restoring the power to exercise ETJ to River Bend). Prior to the 1971 recodification of municipal statutes into G.S. 160A, the extraterritorial authority was in the zoning part of G.S. 160, which led to common use of the term *extraterritorial zoning* as opposed to *extraterritorial jurisdiction.* Authority for cities to enforce the State Building Code in the ETJ was granted in 1969. S.L. 1969-1065. This law allowed city authority to do so only in the ETJ and only if the city had requested the county to enforce the Code there and the county had failed to do so.

40. S.L. 1961-548. This law also added a provision granting cities the authority to appoint the extraterritorial members of the planning board and the board of adjustment if the county failed to make such appointments.

41. S.L. 1965-864. Other changes included provisions that initial zoning of extraterritorial areas was not subject to protest petitions, that extraterritorial members of boards could vote on matters within the city, and that extraterritorial members could reside outside the area being zoned if necessary to secure the requisite number of members.

42. S.L. 1971-698. This comprehensive reorganization of municipal statutes, which created Chapter 160A of the General Statutes, applied the same ETJ rules for all development regulations, not just zoning. Also see S.L. 2006-246, which uses a one-to-three-mile "municipal sphere of influence" in allocating responsibility for city and county stormwater-management regulatory programs.

43. S.L. 2011-363. This law created G.S. 160A-360(k) to provide that property being actively used for bona-fide-farm purposes is exempt from a municipality's ETJ. Land used for farm purposes can be included within the geographic area of a city's extraterritorial boundary. That land is then exempt from city jurisdiction while in active farm use but becomes subject to city jurisdiction upon the cessation of that use. This law also provides that property in active farm use may not be annexed into a city without the written consent of the property owner. This section of the statutes was further amended in 2014 to provide that farmland in the extraterritorial area is subject to county floodplain regulation. S.L. 2014-120. See Chapter 22 for a discussion of the definition of "bona-fide-farm use."

44. S.L. 1973-525.

45. S.L. 1977-882.

46. S.L. 1977-912.

47. S.L. 1983-584. The deleted provisions allowed for a separate advisory board to review text and map amendments for development ordinances and to make recommendations on subdivision plats, special and conditional use permits, and variances proposed for properties in the extraterritorial area. G.S. 160A-362 continues to provide,

In 1996, the statutes were amended to require mailed notice to affected property owners whenever zoning jurisdiction was extended to an extraterritorial area. These amendments also added a requirement for proportional representation of extraterritorial residents on city planning boards and boards of adjustment.[48]

When a city adopts an extraterritorial-boundary ordinance, the city acquires jurisdiction for all of its ordinances adopted under Chapter 160D, and the county loses its jurisdiction for the same range of ordinances.[49] This includes not only zoning and subdivision ordinances but also housing and building codes and regulations on historic districts and historic landmarks, open spaces, community development, erosion and sedimentation control, floodways, mountain ridges, and roadway corridors. The city does not acquire, nor does the county lose, jurisdiction for regulations adopted under the general-ordinance-making power of G.S. 160A-174, such as a nuisance-lot, junked-car, or noise ordinance. This can lead to confusion, as some regulations could be adopted as part of a zoning ordinance or as a general ordinance. For example, if sign regulations are a section of a city zoning ordinance, they apply in the extraterritorial area; however, if they are part of a separate sign ordinance, they do not.

An additional degree of flexibility for application of county development regulations in the extraterritorial area was incorporated into the statute with the adoption of Chapter 160D. A city with an extraterritorial area may elect to extend some but not all of its development regulations in the extraterritorial area.[50] For example, a city might apply its zoning and subdivision regulations in the ETJ area but elect to apply its housing code only within the corporate limits. This is legally permissible as there is no mandate that a city apply all of its development regulations in the extraterritorial area. In this situation both the city and county could have a housing code, but if the city elects not to apply it in the ETJ and the county has no jurisdiction to do so, property in the ETJ would be subject to neither the city nor the county housing code. G.S. 160D-202(b) addresses this by providing that if a city does not extend a particular type of development regulation to the ETJ, the county may elect to exercise that development regulation in the ETJ. The county is not mandated to do so, but the prohibition of doing so is removed, leaving the county with the flexibility to apply its regulation there if desired.

Most North Carolina cities, particularly those with populations greater than 2500, have taken advantage of the statutory authority to regulate extraterritorial land use. A 1995 North Carolina League of Municipalities survey indicated that 64.5 percent of all municipalities responding to the survey had adopted extraterritorial zoning.[51] A survey completed by the School of Government in 2005 indicated little change in the following decade, as 62 percent of responding municipalities had adopted extraterritorial zoning.[52] By 2012, the number of municipalities reporting use of extraterritorial zoning had slightly increased to 65 percent.[53] A 2012 School of Government report estimated that about 500,000

---

however, that any such advisory board created before July 1, 1983, constitutes compliance with the requirement of providing extraterritorial input into city decision-making until that advisory board is abolished.

48. S.L. 1996-746.

49. G.S. 160D-201(b). In a few instances, other statutes explicitly provide that municipal regulations may be applied in its extraterritorial-development-regulation jurisdiction. *See, e.g.*, G.S. 143-215.57(b) (authorizing application of municipal floodplain regulation in the ETJ); G.S. 160A, §§ 176.1, 176.2 (application of municipal ordinances on swimming and surfing in Atlantic Ocean adjacent to corporate limits or extraterritorial area).

50. See *infra* text accompanying note 89 for details on municipal application of development regulations in the ETJ area.

51. Ngoc Nguyen & Lee M. Mandell, Results of the 1995 Municipal Ordinance Survey (June 1995) (based on a survey of 327 of the state's 524 cities).

52. David W. Owens, The North Carolina Experience with Municipal Extraterritorial Jurisdiction 9 (UNC School of Government, Special Series No. 20, Jan. 2006). While some jurisdictions have exercised ETJ for some time, two-thirds of the cities reported initial adoption of ETJ after 1980. *Id.* at 10.

53. David W. Owens & Dayne Batten, *2012 Zoning Survey Report: Zoning Adoption, Administration, and Provisions for Design Standards and Alternative Energy Facilities*, Plan. & Zoning L. Bull. No. 20 (UNC School of

Table 5.1 Percentage of Reporting Cities Exercising ETJ, by Population

Population	1995	2005	2012	2018
>10,000	89	85	83	84
2500–10,000	79	69	70	--
1000–2499	68	71	69	--
<1000	38	34	39	34

people resided in municipal extraterritorial areas.[54] All of the surveys indicate that larger cities are far more likely to exercise ETJ. A 2018 survey by the School of Government indicated these rates have held steady as 66 percent of responding cities reported they exercised ETJ.[55] The rates, broken down by population and year, are summarized in Table 5.1.

In addition to this general authorization of ETJ, there are special provisions applicable to individual jurisdictions that have been adopted by local legislation. Notable among these are the agreement of the municipalities in Mecklenburg County to allocate extraterritorial areas based on negotiated spheres of influence for future annexation;[56] a joint-planning area and allocation of future jurisdiction by Chapel

---

Government, 2012), 7. With changes in annexation law, some municipalities in 2012 reported relinquishing ETJ areas. When asked about changes in their ETJ areas in the previous five years, 61 percent reported no change and 16 percent reported adding jurisdiction, but 22 percent reported deleting jurisdiction due to annexation, returning the area to county jurisdiction, or transferring the area to another city. *Id.* at 7–9.

54. *Id.* at 8.

55. David W. Owens, *2018 Survey Report: Adoption and Administration of Local Development Regulations, Conditional Zoning, and Subdivision Administration*, PLAN. & ZONING L. BULL. No. 30 (UNC School of Government, Dec. 2020), at 8. As with prior surveys, the adoption rate for ETJ substantially increases once the population of the municipality passes 1000. Only 34 percent of cities with populations under 1000 reported ETJ adoption, compared with 79 percent of those with populations between 1000 and 10,000, 77 percent of those with populations from 10,000 to 25,000, and 84 percent of those with populations over 25,000.

56. Local provisions on municipal ETJ in Mecklenburg County have evolved over the years. In 1955, Charlotte was granted ETJ for a specified area for both its zoning and subdivision regulations. S.L. 1955-123; S.L. 1955-124. In 1959, these specified areas were revised to include additional territory. S.L. 1959-113; S.L. 1959-114. The statewide authorization of ETJ in 1959 extended authority for ETJ to the other municipalities in the county. In 1971, however, the General Assembly removed ETJ from all municipalities in Mecklenburg County. S.L. 1971-860, §§ 12–14. The provisions of this bill stripping Charlotte and the other municipalities of ETJ was a last-minute addition to a bill on the Charlotte Firemen's Retirement System. The bill had passed the House of Representatives, and these provisions were added as a floor amendment as the Senate considered the bill in the waning days of the General Assembly's 1971 session. Under this act, municipalities did retain a municipal advisory role in the extraterritorial area, as the county was required to refer all proposed zoning amendments and special or conditional use permit applications to them for a recommendation for actions arising within their respective former extraterritorial areas. There was a gradual reinstatement of ETJ in the county in the following years. In 1977, a one-mile extraterritorial area was restored for Cornelius, Davidson, and Huntersville. S.L. 1977-393. (Also see S.L. 1983-966 for Huntersville.)

In 1983, the General Assembly authorized the use of binding annexation agreements among the municipalities in Mecklenburg County. S.L. 1983-953. Use of annexation agreements was later extended to three additional counties and then extended statewide in 1989. G.S. 160A-58.21 to -58.28. These annexation agreements then became the foundation for the allocation of ETJ in Mecklenburg County. The concept used is similar to the "spheres of influence" used in California local government law (where each county has a Local Agency Formation Commission that sets areas of future municipal jurisdiction to be used in mandatory land use plans, service areas, annexations, and municipal "prezoning" of unincorporated areas). In 1991, Charlotte and the municipalities in the southern portion of the county (Matthews, Mint Hill, and Pineville) were given authority to exercise ETJ for areas that were both within one mile of the municipalities' respective corporate limits and in areas referred to as "Sphere[s] of Influence" in annexation agreements between the municipalities. S.L. 1991-161. The same authority was then in 1992 provided

Hill, Carrboro, and Orange County;[57] and a substantial number of local bills affecting the geographic scope of extraterritorial areas for particular jurisdictions.[58]

The legislature's authority to make individual, local modifications to ETJ was challenged by the Town of Boone when it was stripped of its ETJ authorization in 2014.[59] In *Town of Boone v. State*,[60] the court held that since the state constitution granted the state authority to provide for "the organization . . . and the fixing of boundaries" of local governments,[61] this allowed the General Assembly to set corporate limits and ETJ boundaries (if any). The court further held that the General Assembly was allowed to vary this authorization by local act on a case-by-case basis to meet the needs of different communities. While article II, section 24 of the North Carolina constitution prohibited the General Assembly from enacting local legislation that related to health and sanitation, it did not prohibit the General Assembly from setting the boundaries within which those powers could be exercised.[62]

---

to Cornelius and Davidson (S.L. 1992-884), revised in 1994 for Mint Hill (S.L. 1994-590), revised for Cornelius and Davidson, and extended to Huntersville in 1997 (S.L. 1997-106), and in 2001 updated for Charlotte's annexation agreements with municipalities in the northern portion of the county (Cornelius, Davidson, and Huntersville) (S.L. 2001-228).

57. S.L. 1987-233. The agreement is described in Richard D. Ducker, *The Orange County Joint Planning Agreement*, POPULAR GOV'T, Winter 1988, at 47. The three units of government were granted authority to exercise the land use planning and regulatory powers of any of the three units, jointly or by delegation, with a mutually-agreed-upon area. Chapel Hill, Carrboro, and Orange County subsequently entered such a joint-planning agreement for the two cities, their extraterritorial areas, and a 45,000-acre rural buffer or transition area. The agreement addressed land use–plan classifications, development density, annexation, and provision of urban services within the rural buffer.

58. A number of local governments have secured local legislation to modify the area of potential ETJ. The most common amendment has been to allow towns with populations under 10,000 to add a second mile of ETJ. Local variations enacted since 1973 include: Apex (1993), Archdale (2005), Asheville (2013), Belmont (1991), Blowing Rock (1985), Boone (2014), Burgaw (2009), Canton (1983), Caswell Beach (1983), Chadbourn (2004), Charlotte (2001, 1991), Chocowinity (2006, 1999), Cornelius (1997, 1992, 1977), Davidson (1997, 1992, 1977), Dunn (1998), Faison (2009, 1991), Farmville (1999), Grifton (1993), Huntersville (1997, 1984, 1977), Kings Mountain (1999), Knightdale (1985), Lake Waccamaw (1973), Landis (2006), Maggie Valley (1996), Magnolia (2007), Marshville (2006), Matthews (1999, 1991), Minnesott Beach (2001), Mint Hill (1994, 1991), Mocksville (1990), Mooresville (1997, 1991), Montreat (1991), Morehead City (1997), Mount Airy (2001), Mount Holly (1991), Nashville (1985), Newport (1997), Oak Ridge (2009), Pilot Mountain (1990), Pinebluff (1999), Pinehurst (1992), Pineville (1991), Pittsboro (1989), River Bend (1997), Roanoke Rapids (2005), Rockingham (2001), Siler City (1989), Smithfield (1977), Stanley (1991), Troutman (2017), Wake Forest (1985), Wallace (1996), Warsaw (1990), Washington (1981), Weaverville (2014), Wendell (2009), Whiteville (2000), Williamston (1997), Wingate (2006), and all municipalities in Johnston County (1986), Moore County (1985), and Pamlico County (1977). G.S. 160D-202(i) provides that the statute does not repeal or modify any extraterritorial boundaries that have been set by more-precise local legislation.

In *Town of Pinebluff v. Moore County*, 374 N.C. 254, 839 S.E.2d 833 (2020), the court interpreted the local legislation authorizing a two-mile ETJ for the town to retain the provision that gives the county discretion to disapprove that jurisdiction in areas where the county was already exercising zoning, subdivision, and building-code enforcement.

59. S.L. 2014-120. When the general authorization for extraterritorial-planning-and-development jurisdiction was adopted in 1959, local legislation provided that Boone did not have such power. In 1961, this authority was extended to Boone, but the town did not exercise it until 1981. At that time the town requested approval from the county for a two-mile area, but the county refused to grant it, so the town's ETJ was set at one mile.

60. 369 N.C. 126, 794 S.E.2d 710 (2016).

61. N.C. CONST. art. VII, § 1.

62. *Boone*, 369 N.C. 126, 794 S.E.2d 710. Also see *City of Asheville v. State*, 369 N.C. 80, 794 S.E.2d 759 (2016), decided contemporaneously with *Boone*, where the court invalidated a legislatively mandated transfer of Asheville's water system to a utility district as violating the prohibition of local acts relating to health, sanitation, and the abatement of nuisances under article II, section 24(1)(a) of the North Carolina constitution.

Table 5.2   Maximum Areas of ETJ

City Population	Maximum ETJ
<10,000	1 mile
10,000–25,000	2 miles
>25,000	3 miles

Geographic Area Covered

G.S. 160D-202 grants municipalities the authority to exercise ETJ and includes specific standards for delineating an ETJ's geographic area. A single boundary must be used for all of a city's extraterritorial–land use powers.[63]

The maximum size of an ETJ is determined by its population. G.S. 160D-202(a) provides that the extraterritorial area may extend up to one mile from the city's primary corporate limits for cities with populations of less than 10,000. If county approval is secured, a city with a population of 10,000–25,000 may extend its jurisdiction for up to two miles; a city with a population of more than 25,000, up to three miles. The maximum areas of extraterritorial zoning are summarized in Table 5.2. In addition, a city may choose to exercise only part of its potential jurisdiction.

A 2005 survey by the School of Government indicated that most municipalities only exercised this jurisdiction within one mile of the city limits. Of the 195 cities reporting use of ETJ, 85 percent had one mile or less of ETJ, 10 percent had one to two miles, and only 5 percent had two to three miles.[64] G.S. 160D-202(e) provides that the area chosen must be based on "existing or projected urban development and areas of critical concern to the city, as evidenced by officially adopted plans for its development."[65] To the extent feasible, the boundaries of an area are to be identified by "geographic features identifiable on the ground" but without extending beyond the statutory mileage maximums. Boundaries typically follow property lines but are not required to do so. Cities have the option of excluding areas in another county, areas separated from the city by barriers to growth, or areas where growth will have minimal impact on the city. Neither the boundary ordinance nor the public notice for the hearing on the boundary ordinance needs to be based on a detailed legal survey. However, the boundary must be described with sufficient precision that landowners can tell whether or not their properties are covered without hiring a surveyor.

---

63. The same extraterritorial boundary is used for all of the city's land use–related police powers that are applied outside the city limits. Also, G.S. 160A-176 provides that city ordinances may be applied to city-owned property outside city limits.

64. OWENS, *supra* note 52. The state's annexation statutes were substantially amended in 2011. S.L. 2011-396. These amendments significantly limited municipal authority to annex territory without the consent of the residents of the area to be annexed. *See* Judith Welch Wegner, *North Carolina's Annexation Wars: Whys, Wherefores, and What Next*, 91 N.C. L. REV. 165 (2012). As a result, some municipalities relinquished substantial portions of their ETJs.

65. The statute does not define *officially adopted plan*. See the discussion of the comprehensive-plan requirement in Chapter 22. This provision likely requires some formal study, and adoption by resolution of the governing board, of a document setting forth the city's development concerns. Also, while there is no mandatory relationship between annexation and ETJ, it is common for a city to base its ETJ on anticipated future annexation of these areas. In a 2005 survey by the School of Government (published in 2006), two-thirds of the municipalities with ETJ reported that these areas were likely to be annexed. Nine percent reported plans to annex the areas within ten years, while 57 percent reported that they were likely to be annexed but that no definite timetable had been set for annexation. OWENS, *supra* note 52.

Three North Carolina cases illustrate the degree of precision needed in defining extraterritorial boundaries. In *Sellers v. City of Asheville*,[66] the application of Asheville's zoning ordinance to an extraterritorial area was held to be invalid in part because of an inadequate description of the extraterritorial area. The wording in the ordinance earmarked "the territory beyond the corporate limits for a distance of one mile in all directions," but the map showed only sweeping curves. The purpose of the statutory mandate in G.S. 160D-202(e), the court held, was to define boundaries "to the extent feasible, so that owners of property outside the city can easily and accurately ascertain whether their property is within the area over which the city exercises its extraterritorial-zoning authority."[67] That an owner could secure a surveyor to measure one mile from the corporate boundaries was held to be insufficient to meet the statutory requirements. The use of a very general map was also held to be inadequate in *Town of Lake Waccamaw v. Savage*.[68] The court there found that "the sweeping curves drawn around the lake and town are in no way definable. No distances are shown on the map and the lines themselves do not coincide with any geographical feature on the ground."[69] *In re Raynor*[70] provides an example of a public-notice description of an extraterritorial area that was held to be adequate. That notice characterized the area as encompassing "approximately 1 mile in width ringing the present Garner [ETJ] between Jones Sausage Road east and south across U.S. 70 and White Oak Road to N.C. 50." The notice proceeded to "roughly describe" the boundaries, using roads as references.[71]

Regarding the annexation of areas that are not contiguous with the city (often referred to as *satellite annexations*), G.S. 160A-58.4 allows zoning to be applied therein as in all other parts of the city. The city may not extend ETJ to the land adjacent to those areas, however, unless that land is within the extraterritorial area authorized for the city's primary corporate limits.[72]

When the ETJs of two cities overlap, the boundary of each is set at the midway point unless the cities agree otherwise.[73]

Process to Establish Extraterritorial-Planning Jurisdiction

G.S. 160D-202 also includes a detailed process that must be followed by a city in establishing ETJ. These requirements are summarized in Table 5.3.

G.S. 160D-202(e) requires that the extraterritorial area be set by an ordinance adopted by the city governing board. This boundary ordinance is subject to newspaper-notice, mailed-notice, and public-hearing requirements.

Several cases have addressed the detail required in the notice of the hearing. In *Sellers*, the application of the city's zoning ordinance to an extraterritorial area was held to be invalid in part because the public notice had been inadequate. The newspaper notice had not mentioned that the proposed ordinance was the city's initial effort to exercise its extraterritorial prerogative in the area. The court found the notice to be too vague to give any diligent landowners reasonable cause to suspect that the ordinance affected their properties. Similarly, in *Town of Swansboro v. Odum*,[74] the town's attempt to extend its

66. 33 N.C. App. 544, 236 S.E.2d 283 (1977).
67. *Id.* at 550, 236 S.E.2d at 287.
68. 86 N.C. App. 211, 356 S.E.2d 810, *review denied*, 320 N.C. 797, 361 S.E.2d 89 (1987).
69. *Id.* at 215, 356 S.E.2d at 812. In the town's action seeking a mandatory injunction to compel removal of a sign that violated its sign ordinance, the court upheld summary judgment for the landowner.
70. 94 N.C. App. 91, 379 S.E.2d 880, *review denied*, 325 N.C. 707, 388 S.E.2d 458 (1989).
71. *Id.* at 96, 379 S.E.2d at 883.
72. G.S. 160D-202(a).
73. G.S. 160D-202(e).
74. 96 N.C. App. 115, 384 S.E.2d 302 (1989).

Table 5.3   Summary of Requirements for ETJ

1. Prepare adequate boundary description. Boundary may extend for up to three miles, depending on the city's population.

2. Publish newspaper notice of public hearing; the notice must appear once a week for two successive weeks, the first time at least ten but not more than twenty-five days before hearing.

3. Mail notice to individual property owners in affected area. The notice must include information on the effect of the ETJ, the right to participate in the hearing on the matter, and the right to apply to serve on the city's planning board and board of adjustment. The notice must be mailed at least thirty days prior to the hearing. Mailed notice is also required for application of zoning to the area. A single notice may be provided for a single hearing on both the boundary change and the zoning amendment.

4. Secure county agreement if county is exercising its zoning power and regulating subdivisions in affected area. Secure county approval if the area extends beyond one mile from the city limits. County approval must be in the form of a written resolution adopted by the board of county commissioners.

5. Adopt ordinance by city governing board setting extraterritorial-planning jurisdiction and delineating its boundary.

6. File copy of boundary map with city clerk and register of deeds.

7. Amend city zoning ordinance to add area to zoning maps. This action must comply with the notice and hearing requirements for all zoning-map amendments (but one notice can be mailed for the zoning and boundary amendment).

8. Appoint extraterritorial members to planning board, board of adjustment, and historic commission (if historic districts or landmarks are in extraterritorial area). The number of extraterritorial members must be proportional to the population of the extraterritorial area relative to the city's internal population.

zoning to an extraterritorial area was held to be invalid on several grounds.[75] For one, the public notice for the hearing on the extraterritorial ordinance had simply stated, "The purpose of the hearing shall be to answer questions and receive input as to extra-territorial jurisdiction as authorized by G.S. 160A-360." For another, the required public hearing had been held in January, but the ordinance had not been adopted until the following September. The court held:

> Its notice of the . . . public hearing failed to apprise defendants—or any other property own-
> ers within the affected area—of the nature and character of the proposed actions, failed to
> describe in any way the area in question, and failed to comport with the clear requirements of
> G.S. § 160A-364 in that it was not published in two successive calendar weeks. Furthermore,
> plaintiff's ordinance was adopted in a proceeding held over eight months subsequent to its
> initial hearing, and without either further public hearing or notice. Finally, plaintiff never
> recorded a boundary description as required by G.S. § 160A-360(b).[76]

The ordinance was ruled to be void and thus ineffective against the defendant.

Mailed notice to affected property owners is required when zoning jurisdiction is being extended to an extraterritorial area.[77] G.S. 160D-202(d) dictates that a mailing be made thirty days prior to the date of the hearing on the boundary ordinance. That notice must specify the effect of the jurisdiction's extension, advise the owners of the hearing on the proposal and their right to participate in the hearing, and advise owners of their right to seek appointment as extraterritorial members of the city's planning board and board of adjustment. A separate public hearing can be held but is not required when jurisdic-

---

75. The town had brought a suit to enforce a zoning restriction that prevented placement of a mobile home on the defendant's property, which was within the ETJ claimed by the town.

76. *Swansboro*, N.C. App. 155 at 117, 384 S.E.2d at 304. See Chapter 29 regarding the statute of limitations for challenging the validity of zoning amendments.

77. S.L. 1996-746.

tion is actually extended and the city zoning map is amended to apply city zoning to the new territory. Published and mailed notice is also required for the zoning amendment. G.S. 160D-602(a) allows, but does not require, a single hearing to be held on the ETJ-boundary amendment and the zoning amendment. If a combined hearing and notice is used, the notice is to be mailed at least thirty days prior to the date of the hearing.

In certain instances, county approval must be given for a city to exercise its extraterritorial powers. G.S. 160D-202(a) requires county approval whenever a city with a population of more than 10,000 seeks to extend its ETJ beyond one mile. G.S. 160D-202(c) requires that county approval be secured for the extension of a city's ETJ into any area where the county is enforcing zoning and subdivision regulations. This includes the one-mile area adjacent to the city.[78] County ordinances for both of these regulatory functions must be in place in the affected area to trigger the approval requirement.

In most instances, the application of these statutes is clear. However, for those counties with no county zoning or only partial-county zoning, the question arises whether some ordinance other than a traditional zoning ordinance can trigger the requirement of county approval. In *Town of Green Level v. Alamance County*,[79] the county, which had not adopted a general zoning ordinance, attempted to block the town's extension of ETJ. The town in 2003 proposed to adopt an extraterritorial-boundary ordinance to extend its zoning. The county contended that its 1997 water-supply-watershed ordinance was a "zoning ordinance" and thus required the town to secure county approval of the proposed ETJ. The town disagreed and began the process to adopt an extraterritorial-boundary ordinance. The county then quickly amended the watershed ordinance on April 19, 2004, to apply a "Rural Community District" to the disputed area. The town adopted its extraterritorial-boundary ordinance and brought a declaratory-judgment action to determine whether the town ordinance was effective. The court held that the watershed-critical areas and balance of watershed areas depicted in the 1997 watershed area did not extend into the disputed area. Although that ordinance also spoke of "stream buffers," no streams had been mapped by the county in this area and the county had not enforced any buffer requirements in the area. Thus, the ordinance could not be considered county zoning of the area. The court went on to hold that the county's 2004 amendment was arbitrary and capricious in that it was adopted to block the town jurisdiction rather than to promote a legitimate health, safety, or welfare purpose. The record indicated that the county made no reference to a comprehensive plan in its adoption, contained no references to water-quality protection, and allowed various industrial uses inconsistent with a rural community.

G.S. 160D-202(h) requires that county approval, as well as any other request, approval, or agreement on ETJ by a city or a county, be established by a formally adopted resolution of the governing board. The statute does not establish any standards for county approval or disapproval, so whether to allow a municipality to extend its extraterritorial area in these situations is left to the discretion of the county board of commissioners.[80] The statute is silent as well on the timing of the required county approval; it can be secured at any time before the proposed effective date of adoption or amendment of the extraterritorial ordinance.

---

78. Before the 1971 revisions to extraterritorial-zoning authority, no county approval for city ETJ was required. G.S. 160A-360(e), requiring county approval for areas covered by county zoning, subdivision, and building-code enforcement, applies to extensions of extraterritorial areas occurring after 1971.

79. 184 N.C. App. 665, 646 S.E.2d 851, *review denied*, 361 N.C. 704, 655 S.E.2d 402 (2007). The county in 2006 adopted a "High Impact Land Uses/Polluting Industries Ordinance" under its general-ordinance and zoning-ordinance authority. That ordinance, which was not a factor in this litigation since it was adopted subsequent to the extraterritorial dispute, is applicable in all unincorporated areas and does not create zones, but it does set permit requirements and development standards for thirteen specified land uses.

80. A county may establish policies it will follow in reviewing municipal requests for approval of ETJ. Wake County, for example, requires cities to present a plan to extend services to the proposed area and to annex the area within ten years of securing jurisdiction.

G.S. 160D-202(e) requires that the adopted boundary map be recorded with the register of deeds for any affected county and that the map be retained permanently in the office of the city clerk.

Where there has been substantial compliance with the notice provisions regarding establishment of an extraterritorial area, and those affected have received actual notice of the hearing, technical failures in the adoption process do not invalidate the ordinance. In *Potter v. City of Hamlet*,[81] the plaintiff challenged the adoption of ETJ some four years earlier on the grounds that the boundary map had not been filed with the county register of deeds. The court noted that there had been proper newspaper notice of the hearing, that the plaintiff's predecessor in title had received a mailed notice of the hearing, that several hearings were actually held, that the ordinance had a metes-and-bounds boundary description attached, and that a map of the area was displayed in the city clerk's office. Thus, the court found the city had substantially complied with the notice requirements and the failure to file a copy with the register of deeds did not invalidate adoption of the extraterritorial area.[82]

Another important requirement for a city exercising extraterritorial authority is that the membership of its planning board, its board of adjustment, and any board exercising its functions in the extraterritorial area be expanded to include extraterritorial representation. G.S. 160D-307 requires the appointment of a proportional number of residents of the extraterritorial area to both bodies.[83] For example, if a city with a population of 5000 has a five-member planning board, one extraterritorial member is required for each 1000 extraterritorial residents. If the number of residents of the extraterritorial area itself is insufficient, other county residents may be appointed.[84] The statute does not specify how the population of the extraterritorial area is to be computed to make this calculation.[85] In the absence of a specific directive, it has been held that the mechanics of how this is accomplished is left to the judgment and discretion of the city, and the courts will not interfere unless the means chosen are manifestly unreasonable and oppressive.[86]

The board of county commissioners of each affected county appoints extraterritorial members to the municipal planning board and board of adjustment. If the board of county commissioners fails to make the appointments within ninety days of receiving a resolution from the city governing board requesting that the appointments be made, the city governing board may make the appointments.

Extraterritorial members act only on matters affecting the extraterritorial area unless the city ordinance specifically grants them equal authority on matters within the city.[87] The overwhelming majority

---

81. 141 N.C. App. 714, 541 S.E.2d 233, *review denied*, 353 N.C. 379, 547 S.E.2d 814 (2001).

82. *Id.*, 541 S.E.2d 233. The court also found the action barred by the statute of limitations, so its comments regarding substantial compliance are dicta. For a brief period, state law also required that all planning and development ordinances be recorded. That requirement was added to G.S. 160A-364 in 1971 but was repealed by S.L. 1973-425, § 58.

83. Originally, the number of extraterritorial members had to equal the number of nonextraterritorial members. S.L. 1959-1204. The requirement of a specific number of extraterritorial members was deleted in the 1971 comprehensive revision of the municipal statutes. S.L. 1971-698. However, the statute was again amended in 1996 to require proportional representation. S.L. 1996-746.

84. A 2005 School of Government survey indicated that in the decade since adoption of the proportional-representation requirement, the state's cities had generally, but not uniformly, complied. Where the representation is not proportional, however, it is far more common to have overrepresentation of extraterritorial residents than to have underrepresentation. For planning boards, 59 percent of the cities reported overrepresentation and 24 percent reported underrepresentation. For boards of adjustment, 53 percent reported overrepresentation and 28 percent underrepresentation. Owens, *supra* note 52.

85. G.S. 160D-307 does specify that the population estimates must be updated no less frequently than after each decennial census.

86. Macon Cnty. v. Town of Highlands, 187 N.C. App. 752, 758, 654 S.E.2d 17, 21 (2007).

87. G.S. 160D-307(c).

of cities in North Carolina with ETJ—over 90 percent—allow extraterritorial members to vote on all matters coming before the boards.[88]

It is important to note that there are two steps in the process of establishing extraterritorial zoning and that they can be accomplished concurrently or separately. The first step is the establishment of the ETJ as discussed above. The second step is the actual zoning of the extraterritorial area. This must be accomplished by amendment of the city's zoning map to include the ETJ. G.S. 160D-202(g) provides for a sixty-day transition period, during which prior county zoning remains in place and enforceable.

Similarly, amendments to other land-development ordinances being applied in an extraterritorial area need to be made to ensure that their provisions regarding the geographic area covered include the extraterritorial area. In a 2005 survey by the School of Government, 99 percent of the North Carolina municipalities exercising extraterritorial authority reported applying zoning to this area. Other frequently applied land-development ordinances included subdivision regulation (92 percent), manufactured-home-park regulation (88 percent), sign regulation (87 percent), telecommunication-tower regulation (74 percent), floodplain zoning (69 percent), adult-entertainment-location regulation (69 percent), junkyard regulation (54 percent), watershed-protection regulation (50 percent), stormwater-management regulation (45 percent), sediment-and-erosion-control regulation (37 percent), and historic-district regulation (17 percent). Fifty-nine percent also reported that the city administers the State Building Code in the extraterritorial area (and 32 percent applied their housing codes in this area).[89]

Effects of Changes in Jurisdiction

The authority to exercise land-development-regulatory power in a particular geographic area changes upon the incorporation of a city, annexation of territory, extension of ETJ, or agreement between a city and a county to modify their respective jurisdictions. This issue was addressed in *Taylor v. Bowen*.[90] After an area outside of Fayetteville had been zoned for residential use by Cumberland County, the city annexed the area and zoned it for residential use. Subsequently, the county attempted to rezone it for commercial use. The court held the county's action to be ineffective because the zoning power of the county did not survive the annexation. Prior zoning does not carry over or bind the legislative discretion of the jurisdiction assuming jurisdiction.

G.S. 160D-202, §§ (g) and (h) provide for an orderly transition of authority between cities and counties. Specifically, when a city acquires territory that has been subject to county regulations, the county's regulations and power of enforcement remain in place until sixty days have elapsed or the city adopts regulations, whichever comes sooner. This gives the city time to provide public notice, hold hearings, and deliberate carefully before adopting regulations for the area. County regulation of the area expires when the municipal regulation becomes effective or sixty days after the transfer of jurisdiction, whichever comes first. If, for example, the city has not adopted zoning for its newly acquired territory within this sixty-day period, the land becomes unzoned. The same process and time periods apply if territory is being transferred from city to county jurisdiction.

The effect of a change in jurisdiction on an individual project is controlled by G.S. 160d-202(j), which provides that the property becomes fully subject to the new regulation with one important exception: any vested right that has been established under the original regulation continues to be valid under the new regulation.

88. David Owens & Adam Brueggemann, A Survey of Experience with Zoning Variances 10 (UNC School of Government, Special Series No. 18, Feb. 2004).

89. Owens, *supra* note 52, at 10–11.

90. 272 N.C. 726, 158 S.E.2d 837 (1968).

A shift in jurisdiction also affects subsequent enforcement of an ordinance provision or permit. Although the terms of approval survive the jurisdiction change, the new jurisdiction assumes administrative and enforcement responsibilities.[91]

Davidson County v. City of High Point[92] illustrates some of the complexities of changing jurisdiction. In this case, the city expanded a sewage-treatment plant that was located in the county's zoning jurisdiction. The city was required to obtain a special use permit from the county. The permit contained a condition requiring county approval for extension of sewer services to county residents. The city subsequently annexed several areas and extended sewer service to them without the county's approval. The court held that in this instance, the condition in the special use permit was unenforceable because the county had no zoning authority within the city and the area in question had become part of the city upon annexation.[93] Therefore, although the basic permit and its conditions might still be in effect, the scope of its application had changed as the city's boundary had changed.

Split Jurisdiction

Occasionally an individual parcel of land is split by jurisdictional boundaries. Part of the parcel is in one city or county and part is in a separate city or county. The general rule in this situation is that each local government has jurisdiction over planning and development regulation for the portion of the property that lies within its territorial jurisdiction.

One qualification to the general rule is provided by G.S. 160D-404(c)(2).[94] It applies if a city development regulation is to be applied or enforced outside of its territorial jurisdiction. Since a city has no authority to apply a regulation outside its jurisdiction, it appears that this situation would only arise if a project were located partially inside the city jurisdiction and city provisions were also being applied to the portion of the development outside the city jurisdiction. The statute states that if this is done, the city and the property owner must certify that the city rules are not being applied under coercion and that the city has not made its approval of the portion of the project within its jurisdiction contingent upon the application of its rules to the portion outside its jurisdiction.

G.S. 160D-203[95] provides an option that allows a single jurisdiction to apply and enforce development regulations for a parcel that is split between multiple jurisdictions. If the landowner and both units of government agree, exclusive planning-and-development-regulation jurisdiction for the entire parcel may be assigned to one jurisdiction. That agreement applies only to development regulations. It does not change jurisdiction boundary lines, taxation, or any other nonregulatory matter. The agreement on application of a single jurisdiction's development regulation must be approved by a resolution formally

---

91. G.S. 160D-202(j). In *Town of Black Mountain v. Lexon Insurance Co.*, 238 N.C. App. 180, 768 S.E.2d 302 (2014), *review denied*, 771 S.E.2d 307 (2015), the court held that performance guarantees for completion of required infrastructure that were made to the county when a subdivision was approved could be assigned to and enforced by the city after annexation of the affected property. The bonds in question did not contain language restricting their assignability.

92. 321 N.C. 252, 362 S.E.2d 553 (1987). The case is reviewed in James G. Farris, Jr., Note, *Davidson County v. City of High Point: The North Carolina Supreme Court Solves a City-County Conflict*, 66 N.C. L. Rev. 1266 (1988).

93. The court also dismissed the county's claim that the city's acceptance of the permit estopped it from later challenging the condition, holding that the city was not attacking the condition's validity, only the interpretation that it applied to subsequently annexed areas. The supreme court did not address the court of appeals's conclusion (*Davidson County*, 85 N.C. App. 26, 354 S.E.2d 280 (1987)) that only governmental "buildings," not "public enterprises," such as sewer services, are appropriate subjects for zoning regulations.

94. This provision was added to the statutes by S.L. 2015-246, § 3.

95. This provision was added to the statutes with the adoption of Chapter 160D. S.L. 2019-111.

adopted by both governing boards and be recorded with the register of deeds within fourteen days of adoption of the last required resolution.

Pending Jurisdiction

When land is being considered for a shift in jurisdiction from one city or county to another, there are often development proposals for that property involved as well. For example, a landowner in the unincorporated area of a county may petition for annexation by a city and seek to have the property rezoned from a county to a city district at the same time.

G.S. 160D-204[96] addresses the coordination of pending shifts in jurisdiction with concurrent requests for development approvals. It provides that a jurisdiction can begin the process of applying its development regulations and may accept and process applications and application fees for development in anticipation of a jurisdiction shift. The jurisdiction considering the application may provide notice for required hearings and hold them prior to the shift. However, this can only be done after the process to change jurisdiction has been formally proposed. Final decisions on ordinance adoption or on permit applications can only be made after the jurisdiction changes. Acceptance of jurisdiction, adoption of regulations, and decisions on permit applications may be made at the same time and have a common effective date.

---

96. *Id.*

Land Use and Development Regulations

PART 2

CHAPTER 6

Zoning Regulations

Most North Carolina cities and counties have zoning regulations. Virtually all cities with populations over 1000 and 81 of the state's 100 counties have zoning regulations.[1]

Given the strong respect for private-property rights and concern about government regulation, why has zoning grown to the extent that over 90 percent of the state's population resides in zoned areas? An early architect of zoning in the United States, Edward Bassett, observed, "No one thought of it as a cure for all municipal shortcomings and disorders, and the most that was hoped for was that it might bring a fair degree of stabilization in the place of increasing chaos."[2] The desire for stability, predictability, and protection of property values explains a good deal of zoning's attraction.

Providing stability and predictability in the dynamic and financially as well as emotionally charged area of real-estate development has turned out to be a prodigious task. Individual landowners are intensely interested in development regulations because limits on what can be built on their property and on how construction must proceed have a substantial financial effect on them. Rezoning property from a residential to a commercial district, for example, will often double or triple the land's value. Landowners also rely on zoning regulations to protect their most valuable investment: their homes. Neighbors, citizen groups, and the general public are strongly interested in zoning decisions because these decisions greatly influence a range of public issues, including future traffic congestion, neighborhood property values, and the overall character of a community. Businesses, industries, and local governments also have a strong interest in these decisions because zoning affects the availability, efficiency, and cost of government services, such as water and sewer systems, roads, and parks. Zoning has therefore become one of the most closely watched components of local government.

The zoning regulation of the 1920s was a fairly simple proposition.[3] It separated residential, business, and industrial uses. It limited the height of buildings and set minimum lot sizes and building setbacks. And that was about all that was included in early zoning regulations. The nation's first comprehensive zoning regulation, the 1916 New York City ordinance, accomplished this with seven pages of text.[4] Chapel Hill's 1928 "Building Zone Ordinance," a standard ordinance of the time, was fourteen pages

---

1. David W. Owens, *2018 Survey Report: Adoption and Administration of Local Development Regulations, Conditional Zoning, and Subdivision Administration*, Plan. and Zoning Law Bull. No. 30 (UNC School of Government, Dec. 2020), at 4. In addition, an earlier 2011 survey noted that thirty smaller municipalities had elected to be subject to county zoning. David W. Owens and Dayne Batten, *2012 Zoning Survey Report: Zoning Adoption, Administration, and Provisions for Design Standards and Alternative Energy Facilities*, Plan. & Zoning L. Bull. No. 20 (UNC School of Government, 2012), at 3–4.

2. Edward Bassett, *Zoning for Humanitarian Institutions*, 155 Annals Am. Acad. Pol. & Soc. Sci. pt. II, at 34, 35 (1931).

3. The history and evolution of zoning nationally and in North Carolina is reviewed in Chapter 3.

4. The ordinance was published in a pamphlet of fourteen pages; half of those were unofficial editorial notes and diagrams. The ordinance had three use districts (residential, business, and unrestricted); five height districts; and five area districts (setting yard and setback requirements). George B. Ford, New York City Building Zone Resolution Restricting the Height and Use of Buildings and Prescribing the Minimum Sizes of Their Yards and Courts (1917).

long.[5] Zoning regulations did not change a great deal in their first several decades of use. The Charlotte zoning regulation of 1951 was only fourteen pages long.

Zoning regulations have changed dramatically since 1950. A contemporary zoning regulation is a far more complicated proposition. The regulation itself typically ranges from 100 pages for a small jurisdiction to over 600 pages of text, charts, and diagrams for a large city.[6] Despite this dramatic increase in bulk, the modern zoning regulation[7] remains conceptually similar in many respects to the regulation of eighty years ago, albeit with considerably greater flexibility and sophistication.

While the original authorization for local zoning required that the regulations be in accordance with a comprehensive plan, until recently there was no state mandate for a formal, separate plan prior to the adoption of zoning regulations. However, state statutes now require that cities and counties adopt and reasonably maintain a comprehensive plan or land use plan as a precondition to exercising zoning authority.[8]

Every regulation is unique, as each local government decides how many zoning districts it wants, what to call them, what uses to allow, and what development regulations to impose. The applicable state enabling statute leaves the exact form and substantive content of the regulation largely to the discretion of local elected officials. Even so, there is a basic framework for zoning that is almost uniformly followed. That basic framework is discussed in this chapter.

Use Districts

Early Zoning Regulations

The principal characteristic of a zoning regulation is division of the city or county's land area into districts with a separate set of development regulations for each zone or district. Ordinances adopted under the general police power must be uniformly applied throughout the jurisdiction. Zoning regulations must be uniformly applied within each district, but variation between districts is permissible.

The zoning regulation defines the districts and sets the land uses and regulations for each district. The zoning map (see Figure 6.1), which is a part of the regulation, applies those districts to land within the jurisdiction.[9] Changing land from one district classification to another, termed a *rezoning*, is the most frequent zoning-regulation amendment in many jurisdictions.

---

5. Even with amendments, by 1938 the Chapel Hill ordinance had added only an additional two pages of text. A model zoning ordinance promulgated for North Carolina jurisdictions in 1938 was nine pages long. PATRICK HEALY, JR., A ZONING MANUAL FOR NORTH CAROLINA TOWNS AND CITIES 16–24 (N.C. League of Municipalities, Report No. 27, July 1938).

6. Most larger jurisdictions now post searchable copies of their development regulations online. In 2022, the online edition of the Winston-Salem/Forsyth County Unified Development Ordinance (UDO) was 748 pages and the Raleigh UDO was 572 pages.

7. There is no typical zoning ordinance, but many follow a standard format. *See, e.g.*, FRED H. BAIR, JR. & ERNEST R. BARTLEY, TEXT OF A MODEL ZONING ORDINANCE WITH COMMENTARY (1966).

8. Chapter 160D, Section 501(a) of the North Carolina General Statues (hereinafter G.S.). S.L. 2019-11, § 2.9(c) provided that this prerequisite for zoning must be met by July 1, 2022. That date was extended to July 1, 2023, for municipalities with populations of 1500 or less by S.L. 2022-75. S.L. 2020-25 modified this mandate to clarify that either a land use plan or a comprehensive plan could be adopted to satisfy the requirement to have a plan prior to exercising zoning authority. See Chapter 22 for a detailed discussion of plans and their relationship to zoning regulations.

9. G.S. 160D-105(a) requires that the official zoning map be maintained for public inspection in the office of the city or county clerk (or in another office specified in the zoning regulation). The official zoning map can be in digital or paper format.

Figure 6.1 Zoning Map

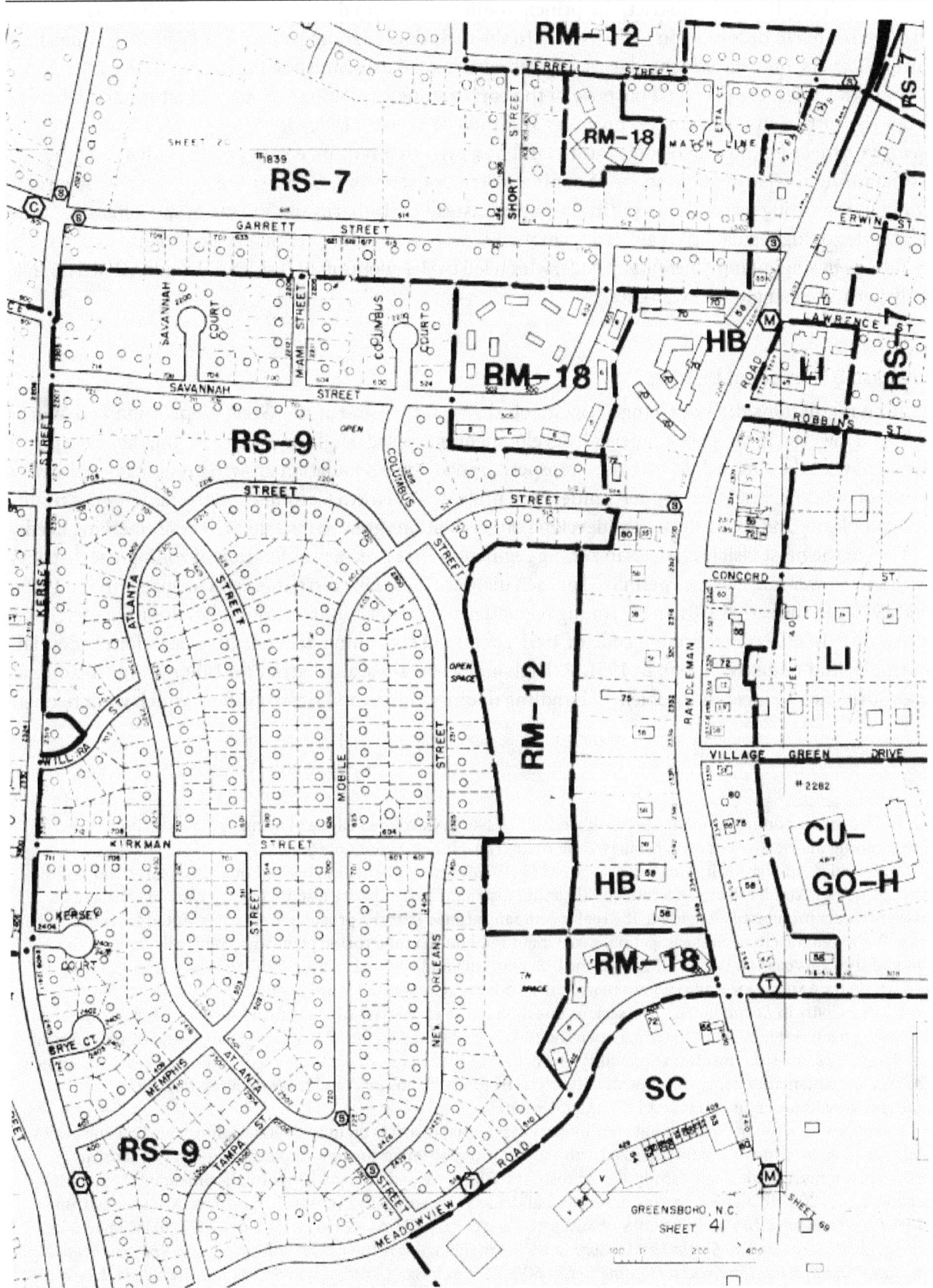

A zoning map applies the zoning districts created in the ordinance text to all property within the jurisdiction of the city or county.

While setbacks, height limits, off-street parking requirements, sign limits, and other regulations typically vary from district to district, the principal difference from district to district is the range of land uses permitted to be located in each district. In the early days of zoning, a city was typically divided into three districts: one for residential uses, one for commercial uses, and one for industrial uses.[10]

In many cities, the principal purpose of the early zoning regulation was to protect residential areas from the intrusion of "offensive" business and industrial uses. Indeed, in the 1926 *Euclid v. Ambler Realty Co.* decision, Justice George Sutherland observed that nuisance law provided a helpful guide to ascertaining the permissible scope of zoning restrictions, noting, "A nuisance may merely be a right thing in the wrong place—like a pig in the parlor instead of the barnyard."[11] One of the "offensive" uses that early zoning regulations regulated, as in the *Euclid* case, was the presence of high-density apartment buildings in single-family neighborhoods, which led to the adoption of residential zoning districts that only permitted single-family homes.[12]

Increasing Number of Districts

Zoning regulations did not change very much through the time of the Great Depression and World War II. However, in the postwar period, development increased. Highway construction, the widespread availability of the automobile, increased prosperity, and simple population growth brought an entire new range of development issues, opportunities, and problems to North Carolina and the nation. As a result, the complexity and sophistication of development regulations grew in response to these emerging needs.

One of the most visible changes in zoning regulations has been a proliferation of zoning-use districts with a narrower range of uses permitted in each district. These new districts began to appear in the 1950s and 1960s. In the early 1950s, many zoning regulations were amended to create subdivisions in each basic category.[13] The Charlotte zoning code of 1951 contained six zoning districts (two each for residential, business, and industrial uses). In 1951, Raleigh adopted a separate district for office and institutional uses "designed to meet the problem of handling doctors' offices and similar offices which want to open

---

10. The model zoning ordinance promulgated by the North Carolina League of Municipalities in 1938 called for three zoning districts—residence, business, and industrial. HEALY, *supra* note 5.

11. Euclid v. Ambler Realty Co., 272 U.S. 365, 388 (1926). The ordinance challenged in *Euclid* placed most of the tract owned by Ambler Realty in a residential zoning district. The ordinance also included a class of enumerated uses that were prohibited altogether. The realty company argued that the property was better suited for industrial uses. Although the city won the litigation, a major automobile-manufacturing plant was eventually built on the 68-acre site. This case and its ramifications for U.S. planning and zoning law are discussed at some length in ZONING AND THE AMERICAN DREAM: PROMISES STILL TO KEEP (C. Haar & J. Kayden eds., 1989).

12. The Court in *Euclid* noted, "The serious question in the case arises over the provisions of the ordinance excluding from residential districts apartment houses, business houses, retail stores and shops, and other like establishments. This question involves the validity of what is really the crux of the more recent zoning legislation, namely, the creation and maintenance of residential districts, from which business and trade of every sort, including hotels and apartment houses, are excluded." 272 U.S. 365, 390.

A century later, the impact of single-family-only residential districts on urban sprawl, affordable housing availability, and environmental quality sparked a zoning reform movement to allow duplexes, triplexes, or similar residences in most or all single-family zoning districts. Charlotte and Raleigh, for example, amended their zoning regulations in 2022 to allow such greater residential density. *See generally* DANIEL G. PAROLEK, MISSING MIDDLE HOUSING: THINKING BIG AND BUILDING SMALL TO RESPOND TO TODAY'S HOUSING CRISIS (2020); Michael Manville et al., *It's Time to End Single-Family Zoning*, 86 J. AM. PLAN. ASS'N 106 (2020); John Infranca, *The New State Zoning: Land Use Preemption Amid a Housing Crisis*, 60 B.C. L. REV. 823 (2019); David Schleicher, *Stuck! The Law and Economics of Residential Stagnation*, 127 Yale L.J. 78 (2017).

13. PHILIP P. GREEN, JR., ZONING IN NORTH CAROLINA 95–97 (1952).

in residential districts."[14] In 1954, the Shelby zoning regulation was amended to add a "neighborhood business" district and to divide its single residential district into three residential districts.[15] Raleigh in 1954 added a shopping-center district and a buffer commercial district to its zoning regulation.[16] Between 1952 and 1992, Charlotte's zoning regulation went from five to sixty zoning districts; Greensboro's, from seven to thirty-eight; and Raleigh's, from five to fifty-seven.

Many of the initial zoning regulations adopted in the 1920s had *cumulative districts*. These regulations established a hierarchy of uses, with residential being the most-protected or "highest" use and industrial being the least-protected or "lowest use." The lower districts permitted any uses allowed in a higher district. For example, a commercial district would allow both commercial and residential uses but not industrial uses. By the 1960s, many communities had substantially restricted the cumulative nature of the districts.[17] For example, low-density commercial uses would be allowed in a high-density commercial district, but residential uses were prohibited.

The opposite of a cumulative district is an exclusive or *special-purpose district*, allowing only a very narrow range of uses. In the 1960s, many jurisdictions began to add these districts, most often for industrial or high-density districts. For example, if a community has a limited area highly suitable for industrial development (given topography, utility availability, rail or highway access, or the like), it may place that land in a district that prohibits all uses other than industrial. It is increasingly common in rural areas with limited public services to have zoning districts that prohibit any intensive land uses or those that would interfere with productive agricultural uses.[18]

Another important trend in the evolution of zoning regulations in the post–World War II era was the introduction of greater flexibility into the regulations, particularly in the way individual proposed land uses were treated.[19] Rather than treating all land uses as either prohibited or permitted in a particular district, zoning regulations were amended to allow for a case-by-case review of individual developments as "special uses."

Other common innovations of the time incorporated into zoning regulations in the 1960s were provision of transitional zones between divergent types of uses, special provisions for large-scale developments, and performance standards for industrial uses.

---

14. *Notes from North Carolina Cities*, POPULAR GOV'T, Nov. 1951, at 4. The new "O and I district" was first applied to the Cameron Village area, near where Rex Hospital was then sited. *Id.*

15. *Notes from North Carolina Cities*, POPULAR GOV'T, Apr. 1954, at 3.

16. *Notes from North Carolina Cities*, POPULAR GOV'T, Oct. 1954, at 5.

17. One of the first North Carolina zoning ordinances to shift away from cumulative districts was Greensboro's 1951 update of its 1926 zoning ordinances. *Notes from North Carolina Cities*, POPULAR GOV'T, Dec. 1951, at 4.

18. In *Tonter Investments, Inc. v. Pasquotank County*, 199 N.C. App. 579, 681 S.E.2d 536, *review denied*, 363 N.C. 663, 687 S.E.2d 296 (2009), the court upheld use of an agricultural zoning district that prohibited all residential land uses. The court noted that the county based the restriction on the remote nature and lack of roads in most of this zoning district, the potential strain on provision of essential public services to potential residents, the very limited prior residential uses within the district, and the aerial application of pesticides within the district. The court therefore found a clear relationship between the restriction and protection of public health and safety.

19. *See, e.g.*, CONSTR. & CIVIC DEV. DEP'T, CHAMBER OF COMMERCE OF THE U.S., ZONING AND CIVIC DEVELOPMENT 16–19 (1950). This report, recommending use of updated zoning ordinances, was prepared by the U.S. Chamber of Commerce with the assistance and cooperation of the American Institute of Planners and the American Institute of Architects.

Contemporary Zoning Regulations

Contemporary zoning regulations often contain several types of use districts. These include conventional districts, overlay districts, floating districts, conditional districts, and form-based districts.[20]

Conventional Districts

The most common type of zoning district in a contemporary zoning regulation is the conventional district. These districts are sometimes referred to as "general-use districts," "base districts," or "underlying districts." They are basic zoning districts with a variety of permitted land uses in each district. Conventional districts may also include some uses allowed only by special use permits.

Over time, the number of conventional districts in zoning regulations has steadily increased. For example, instead of a single residential district, a contemporary zoning regulation may have a half-dozen residential districts: one designated for single-family residences on large lots; a second one for single-family residences on small lots; a third for duplexes; a fourth for small apartment buildings; a fifth for high-rise apartment buildings; and a sixth for manufactured housing.[21]

The typical North Carolina zoning regulation contains ten or so conventional districts. Most regulations have three to ten residential districts, two to six commercial districts, several industrial and office districts, and perhaps a few additional specialized districts. For municipalities, more-populous cities not surprisingly have a greater number of districts. Respondents to a 2006 School of Government survey indicated that the median number of conventional districts for cities with populations under 1000 was six, while the median for cities with populations over 25,000 was 21.5.[22]

Overlay Districts

Zoning regulations may also include overlay districts. These are special zoning districts that apply development standards in addition to the requirements of the conventional or underlying district. Overlay districts are used to apply a particular set of development standards to multiple districts. For example, all of a city's flood-hazard areas may be placed in a floodplain overlay district that imposes requirements for flood proofing structures and for locating them outside of floodways. These standards are supplemental to the requirements of the basic residential, commercial, or industrial districts in which the land is zoned.[23] It is important to note that a development regulation may also have regulations that are applicable to specified areas without making those areas separate zoning districts, especially where the standards apply jurisdiction-wide regardless of zoning district.[24] Examples include requirements to

20. G.S. 160D-703(a) is a specific authorization for zoning districts. It provides that the districts may include (but are not limited to) conventional districts, conditional districts, overlay districts, and form-based districts.

21. This stricter segregation of uses, though politically popular, has increasingly lost favor with planning professionals, and the ordinances of the 1990s tended to allow greater flexibility and more mixed uses. This was often accomplished, however, by adding new, flexible districts while retaining the older, narrower districts.

22. DAVID W. OWENS & ANDREW STEVENSON, AN OVERVIEW OF ZONING DISTRICTS, DESIGN STANDARDS, AND TRADITIONAL NEIGHBORHOOD DESIGN IN NORTH CAROLINA ZONING ORDINANCES 2–3 (UNC School of Government, Special Series No. 23, Oct. 2007).

23. Local governments have the option of adopting many of these special provisions either as overlay districts within the zoning ordinance or as separate, independent ordinances. For example, G.S. 63, §§ 30 to 37 authorizes airport-approach-protection regulations, such as use and height limits, that may be adopted as a separate airport zoning ordinance. The procedure that must be followed to adopt this airport zoning was made consistent with the process for regular zoning with the adoption of Chapter 160D in 2019. S.L. 2019-111.

24. G.S. 160D-703(d) expressly authorizes use of zoning standards that apply uniformly across a jurisdiction rather than only to particular zoning districts.

maintain sight triangles at all road intersections and requirements to maintain buffers adjacent to all surface waters for water-quality protection.[25]

Respondents to a 2006 School of Government survey indicated that a substantial majority of North Carolina jurisdictions with zoning had overlay districts.[26] Overall, two-thirds of responding jurisdictions reported use of overlay districts. They were particularly widely used by counties and more-populous cities. Among jurisdictions with overlay districts, the most commonly used were flood-hazard and water-supply-watershed-protection overlay districts,[27] both of which were used by over half of those jurisdictions. Historic districts,[28] corridor-protection districts, and central-business-district-overlay zones were also relatively common, with each being used by at least a third of the jurisdictions with overlay zones. Among the miscellaneous other types of overlay district used in the state were manufactured-housing, airport,[29] and neighborhood-conservation districts.

Floating Districts

A zoning regulation may also include floating districts. They are not specifically mentioned in the enabling statute but are clearly permissible as they are a specialized form of conventional or overlay district. Floating districts are defined in the text of the regulation, which includes details about acreage, infrastructure, and design standards, but are applied or mapped only upon petition of landowners.[30] Examples include mobile-home-park districts, shopping-center districts, and mixed-use districts.[31]

One of the more common types of floating districts is the *planned-unit-development* (PUD) district. These districts were added to many zoning regulations in the 1950s and 1960s. They usually require a minimum acreage and an overall concept plan for development of the entire tract prior to rezoning. Initially, PUDs were primarily residential planned communities,[32] but they later came to be used for commercial and industrial projects. PUDs have increasingly been used for mixed-use developments that

---

25. *See, e.g.,* Cary Creek Ltd. P'ship v. Town of Cary, 203 N.C. App. 99, 690 S.E.2d 549, *review denied*, 364 N.C. 600, 703 S.E.2d 549 (2010). The town's protection rules for water-supply watersheds required a protected buffer along all streams but did not make the buffer area a separate overlay district. *See also* Town of Green Level v. Alamance Cnty., 184 N.C. App. 665, 646 S.E.2d 851, *review denied*, 361 N.C. 704, 655 S.E.2d 402 (2007) (holding stream buffers in county water-supply-watershed-protection ordinance were not zoning districts).

26. Owens & Stevenson, *supra* note 22.

27. Flood-hazard and watershed districts are discussed in more detail in Chapter 10.

28. Historic districts and landmark regulations are discussed in more detail in Chapter 22.

29. The Federal Aviation Administration recommends restrictions on residential uses in areas adjacent to airports that would experience airport noise of 65 decibels or more. Airports receiving federal funding undertake airport-noise-compatibility planning that includes preparation and regular updating of noise-exposure maps. 14 C.F.R. § 150.21 (2022). Both Raleigh and Morrisville, for example, have airport overlay districts to limit residential development adjacent to Raleigh-Durham International Airport.

30. An early leading case upholding the use of floating zones is *Rodgers v. Village of Tarrytown*, 302 N.Y. 115, 96 N.E.2d 731 (1951). *See also* Sheridan v. Plan. Bd., 159 Conn. 1, 266 A.2d 396 (1969) (upholding use of floating zones); Bellemeade Co. v. Priddle, 503 S.W.2d 734 (Ky. 1974) (upholding use of floating zones); Mayor of Rockville v. Rylyns Enters., Inc. 372 Md. 514, 814 A.2d 469 (2002) (floating zones at "far end of the flexibility continuum" relative to conventional districts). The Pennsylvania court, however, invalidated a floating zone as illegal spot zoning. Eves v. Zoning Bd., 401 Pa. 211, 164 A.2d 7 (1960).

31. A common critique of traditional zoning often made by academic planners is that it rigidly segregates permitted uses. *See, e.g.,* Sonia Hirt, *The Devil Is in the Definitions: Contrasting American and German Approaches to Zoning*, 73 J. Am. Plan. Ass'n 436 (2007). As David R. Godschalk notes in rejoinder, however, many of these critiques ignore the mixed uses, flexibility, design-based standards, and other innovations in contemporary zoning regulations. David R. Godschalk, *Comment on Hirt: U.S. Zoning: Mixed Use by Design*, 73 J. Am. Plan. Ass'n 451 (2007).

32. An early form of the planned-unit development was the large residential subdivision with common open space and recreation centers. Fed. Hous. Admin., Land Planning Bulletin No. 6, Planned-Unit Development with a Homes Association (1963). *See also* Frank S. So et al., Planned Unit Development Ordinances (Am. Plan. Ass'n, Plan. Advisory Serv. Report No. 291, 1973).

incorporate single-family, multifamily, commercial, and institutional uses in a comprehensively planned development.[33] Clustered development and common open space are also common elements of a PUD. The provision of an overall plan and design for the development within a PUD allows greater flexibility for the developer, balanced with detailed local review and approval of the proposed development.

Respondents to a 2006 School of Government survey indicated that floating districts were used in North Carolina, though less frequently than overlay districts. While two-thirds of the jurisdictions used overlay districts, only about a third used floating districts.[34] As with overlay districts, the use of floating districts was related to population size, as these districts were more commonly used by more-populous municipalities. The most commonly used floating district in North Carolina was the PUD district.[35] The other floating districts used, in order of frequency, were manufactured-home-park districts, mixed-use districts, traditional-neighborhood-design districts, and miscellaneous others.

Conditional Districts

Conditional districts are a special form of floating district that includes detailed site-specific development rules.[36] Unlike the districts noted above, which are common in zoning regulations around the country, the law on whether and how conditional districts can be used varies considerably among the states. In North Carolina, the statutes allow use of these districts, but only upon petition of the landowner.

Developed in the 1990s, legislative conditional zoning incorporates all of the site-specific standards directly into the zoning-district regulations and applies that zoning district only to the single parcel that is the subject of the rezoning petition. While some jurisdictions include all of the conditions in the text of the zoning regulation, the more common practice is to incorporate them by reference to a mandated site plan.[37]

Conditional districts are widely used in North Carolina. A 2006 School of Government survey indicated that the majority of rezoning petitions—57 percent—considered by responding jurisdictions in the previous year were for rezonings to conventional zoning districts. However, over a third of all rezoning petitions were reported to include site-specific conditions; 37 percent of all rezoning petitions were for conditional districts.[38] These results are shown in Figure 6.2.[39]

---

33. *See* Daniel R. Mandelker, *New Perspectives on Planned Unit Developments*, 52 REAL PROP., TR. & EST. L.J. 229 (2017); DANIEL R MANDELKER, PLANNED UNIT DEVELOPMENTS (Am. Plan. Ass'n, Plan. Advisory Serv. Report No. 545, 2007).

34. OWENS & STEVENSON, *supra* note 22, at 4.

35. Kildare Farms in Cary, a 967-acre mixed-use development approved in the early 1970s, is often cited as the first large PUD approved in North Carolina that incorporated various housing types and commercial development.

36. See Chapter 13 for a discussion of conditional districts.

37. While use of a mandated site plan for all conditional districts is common, some jurisdictions simply incorporate by reference a list of site-specific conditions for each individual conditional rezoning. For example, if the zoning regulation creates a "Highway Commercial-Conditional" zoning district, the text would provide that the specific conditions for each property placed in that district are adopted with each individual rezoning.

38. DAVID W. OWENS, ZONING AMENDMENTS IN NORTH CAROLINA 5 (UNC School of Government, Special Series No. 24, Feb. 2008).

39. Prior to 2020, there were two forms of conditional zoning used in North Carolina. The statutes and case law authorized use of "conditional use districts." These were districts with no permitted uses, allowing only uses with a conditional use permit (which was typically considered concurrently with the rezoning to the conditional use district). This hybrid legislative/quasi-judicial process was eliminated with the adoption of Chapter 160D. See Chapter 13 for a detailed discussion of conditional zoning.

Figure 6.2 Type of Rezoning Sought in 2006

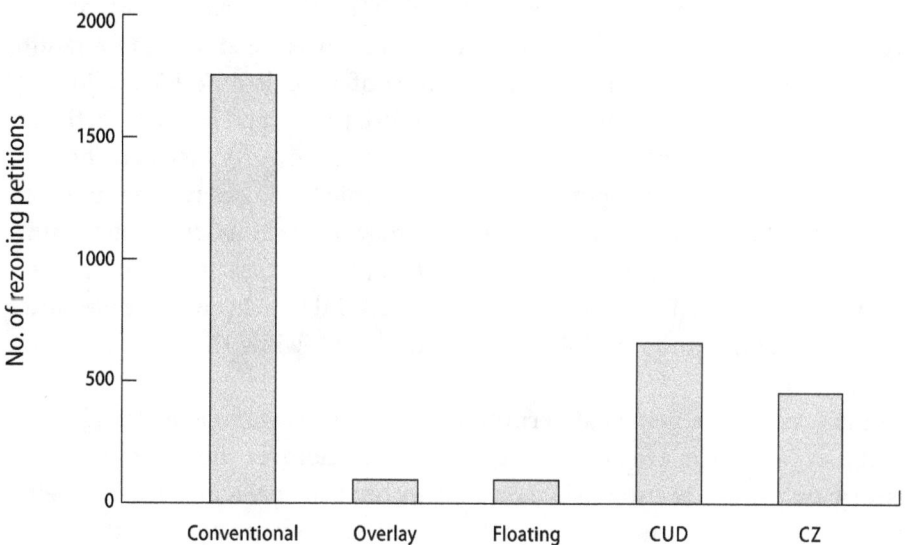

Form-Based Districts

Form-based districts began to be adopted in North Carolina in recent years. These districts were explicitly authorized with the adoption of Chapter 160D in 2019.[40] Chapter 160D, Section 703(a)(3) of the North Carolina General Statutes (hereinafter G.S.) defines these as districts "that address the physical form, mass, and density of structures, public spaces, and streetscapes." These districts are based on the form of the development rather than on the land use involved. They are discussed in more detail in Chapter 9.

Regulation of Uses Within Districts

Within each zoning district, the regulation specifies which land uses are permitted. The regulation usually lists the particular uses allowed, often in considerable detail.[41] Occasionally, a regulation will specifically list uses that are prohibited in a particular district.

---

40. S.L. 2019-111, Part II.

41. Many ordinances use the national standardized categorization and definitions of land uses of the Standard Industrial Classification system published by the Occupational Health and Safety Administration, Department of Labor.

Questions also arise as to whether a particular activity is a "use" subject to differential treatment by a zoning ordinance. For example, does renting an individual room in a single-family home on a nightly basis make the use a commercial one rather than a residential one? Is the result different if the whole house is rented on a nightly or weekly basis to transient occupants? See Chapter 22 for a discussion of short-term rentals of residential property. State enabling statutes generally give broad discretion to local governments to define "uses" and how they are regulated, but state mandatory directives are sometimes made.

Some early zoning cases in other jurisdictions held that a lawful use cannot be totally excluded from an entire jurisdiction or that such exclusion warrants strict judicial scrutiny.[42] The North Carolina courts have not so held. The issue was raised in *Kass v. Hedgpeth*[43] but not resolved, as the ordinance in question (which would have prevented expansion of a tobacco warehouse) was ruled invalid for failure to observe proper zoning-regulation-adoption procedures. The court of appeals in *Robins v. Town of Hillsborough* noted that the burden is on the local government to establish that a total ban of a particular use is not arbitrary and capricious.[44] The North Carolina Supreme Court, however, decided the case on other grounds and vacated that portion of the opinion.[45] So, while some land uses receive statutory or constitutional protection, absent that protection a particular use may be excluded in some circumstances. Since the ordinance is presumed valid, an exclusion is to be upheld unless it is arbitrary and capricious. For example, a small jurisdiction may prohibit a particular lawful use throughout the entire jurisdiction,[46] such as a small resort community prohibiting industrial uses, while the same exclusion would be unreasonable for a major city.

Uses that are incidental or accessory to a principal permitted use, such as a garage or storage shed being placed on the same lot as a residence, are also typically allowed wherever the principal use is allowed. However, an accessory use cannot be established on a lot without the principal use first being present.[47] Whether a use is customarily incidental to a principal use is an interpretation of the intent of the regulation and a question of law.[48] In making this determination, the zoning administrator must consider the actual use being undertaken, not the potential use.[49]

Proposals for uses that are not explicitly permitted or prohibited pose a special problem. Some regulations, particularly for smaller jurisdictions, do not have a long or detailed list of permitted uses. Other jurisdictions may have attempted to reduce the complexity of the regulation and make it more user-friendly by simplifying the list of permitted uses. A regulation may have been adopted before a particular use existed or before anyone anticipated that such a use would ever be proposed in the jurisdiction. At one time, many regulations addressed this issue by including a provision that any land use not specifically permitted in a district was prohibited in that district. Another common approach to this problem was the inclusion of a provision that any use not explicitly mentioned should be treated the same as the most

---

42. *See, e.g.*, People *ex rel.* Trust Co. of Chi. v. Vill. of Skokie, 408 Ill. 397, 97 N.E.2d 310 (1951) (invalidating ordinance that totally excluded outdoor motion-picture theaters); Kropf v. City of Sterling Heights, 391 Mich. 139, 215 N.W.2d 179 (1974); Exton Quarries, Inc. v. Zoning Bd. of Adjustment, 425 Pa. 43, 228 A.2d 169 (1967) (invalidating ordinance totally excluding quarries where there was no showing of harmful effects). *But see* Cadoux v. Plan. & Zoning Comm'n, 162 Conn. 425, 294 A.2d 582 (1972) (upholding ordinance limiting entire jurisdiction in residential uses). The underlying question is often whether the exclusion is reasonably related to a legitimate governmental objective.

43. 266 N.C. 405, 38 S.E.2d 164 (1946).

44. Robins v. Town of Hillsborough, 176 N.C. App. 1, 9–10, 625 S.E.2d 813, 819 (2006).

45. 361 N.C. 193, 200, 639 S.E.2d 421, 425 (2007).

46. An early example of a case upholding the decision of a small residential community to totally exclude heavy industry is *Duffcon Concrete Products, Inc. v. Borough of Cresskill*, 1 N.J. 509, 64 A.2d 347 (1949). More-recent cases focus on exclusion of particular intrusive uses. *See, e.g.*, Consol. Rock Prods. Co. v. City of L.A., 57 Cal. 2d 515, 20 Cal. Rptr. 638, 370 P.2d 342 (1962); Gernatt Asphalt Prods., Inc. v. Town of Sardinia, 87 N.Y.2d 668, 642 N.Y.S.2d 164, 664 N.E.2d 1226 (1996).

47. Harry v. Mecklenburg Cnty., 136 N.C. App. 200, 523 S.E.2d 135 (1999) (where ordinance specifies that a pier is an accessory use, a pier may not be constructed as a principal use in the absence of other structures on the lot).

48. Hayes v. Fowler, 123 N.C. App. 400, 473 S.E.2d 442 (1996) (bed-and-breakfast facility is not an accessory use to the permitted residential use). *See also* Four Seasons Mgmt. Servs., Inc. v. Town of Wrightsville Beach, 205 N.C. App. 65, 695 S.E.2d 456 (2010) (applying ordinance distinction between accessory uses and accessory structures).

49. Dobo v. Zoning Bd. of Adjustment, 149 N.C. App. 701, 710–13, 562 S.E.2d 108, 114–16 (2002), *rev'd on other grounds*, 356 N.C. 656, 576 S.E.2d 324 (2003). A large sawmill was being operated in the rear yard of a residence. Although the saw was large enough for commercial use, the fact that the evidence indicated that it had been used only for noncommercial purposes precluded a finding that it was a commercial or industrial use.

nearly similar use.[50] Still others provided that "any other similar use" is permitted in a district in addition to those listed, or a regulation may include some catchall uses, such as "all other commercial uses" or "all other industrial uses." In these instances, the zoning administrator must make a determination on similarity, and that determination can be appealed to the board of adjustment and on to the courts.

The option of simply prohibiting any unlisted use is no longer permissible in North Carolina. The court of appeals originally expressed skepticism about presumptions prohibiting uses in *Land v. Village of Wesley Chapel*.[51] The issue was whether a shooting range had been lawfully established in the county (prior to annexation) so as to be a lawful nonconformity. The regulation did not specifically list shooting ranges as a regulated use. It included a presumption that "all legitimate uses" of land were permitted in the jurisdiction. It directed that the list of permissible uses be liberally interpreted to include other uses with similar impacts[52] and stated that unlisted uses that did not have similar impacts were prohibited. The zoning administrator contended that the most nearly similar listed use was "privately-owned outdoor recreational facility," which required a special use permit that the plaintiff had not secured. The court held that the provision allowing the zoning administrator to determine similarity of impacts left the administrator with too much discretion where no similar use was listed. As the regulation included only "nebulous" categories of use, the regulation failed to clearly place the public on notice as to how a particular use would be treated, thus rendering this provision arbitrary and capricious. Given the strength of the common law presumption that ambiguity should be resolved in favor of free use of property, the court refused to accept the administrator's interpretation that a shooting range should be treated the same as an outdoor recreational facility.

The supreme court subsequently endorsed this approach to consideration of unlisted uses. *Byrd v. Franklin County*[53] also presented the question of zoning regulation of a shooting range where the zoning regulation did not expressly list shooting ranges in its table of uses. Unlike the regulation in *Land*, this regulation did not have a presumption that unlisted uses were allowed and that an unlisted use should be treated as the most nearly similar use. Rather, the Franklin County regulation provided that any use not specifically listed as permitted was prohibited. The dissent in the court of appeals decision, subsequently endorsed by the supreme court, concluded that such a prohibition of all uses not explicitly permitted "is in derogation of the common law and is without legal effect."[54]

These cases emphasize the importance of careful and precise drafting of use restrictions in order to provide notice to landowners and neighbors about what is and is not allowed in a particular zoning district. A zoning regulation should include a detailed list of specific uses that is regularly updated and specify whether they are permitted. Particular attention should be given to providing explicit direction for the treatment of controversial or newly emerging land uses. Consideration should also be given to including general "catchall" categories for unlisted uses (such as "other retail uses" or "other industrial and manufacturing uses not specifically listed"). If staff members are directed to treat unlisted uses as

---

50. For a variation of this approach, see *Fairway Outdoor Advertising, LLC v. Town of Cary*, 225 N.C. App. 676, 683–84, 739 S.E.2d 579, 583 (2013), where the Cary ordinance provided that the planning director "may" permit an unlisted use upon making specified findings.

51. 206 N.C. App. 123, 697 S.E.2d 458 (2010).

52. A similar direction to treat unlisted uses as those listed uses with the most-similar impacts was an important factor in the interpretation of the scope of permitted uses in *Fort v. County of Cumberland*, 235 N.C. App. 541, 761 S.E.2d 744, *review denied*, 367 N.C. 798, 766 S.E.2d 688 (2014).

53. 368 N.C. 409, 778 S.E.2d 268 (2015), *reversing* 237 N.C. App. 192, 765 S.E.2d 805 (2014), *per curiam for reasons stated in dissent*.

54. 237 N.C. App. 192, 202, 765 S.E.2d 805, 811 (2014).

those with similar impacts, the regulation should provide guidance on how that determination is to be made, listing the factors to be considered.[55]

A major change to zoning in the past fifty years has been the addition of greater flexibility regarding authorized uses. Originally, particular land uses were either permitted or prohibited in each district. Contemporary regulations typically prohibit some uses, permit others, and allow still others if certain conditions or requirements can be met (termed *special uses, conditional uses,* or *special exceptions*). In order to reduce confusion regarding terminology, Chapter 160D requires that local regulations use the term *special use permit* for all these permits.[56] The ordinance must contain set standards to be followed in determining whether special uses are to be permitted as well as procedures for evidentiary hearing on each of these quasi-judicial zoning decisions.[57]

Most zoning regulations include a *table of permitted uses* (see Figure 6.3). These tables specify how a particular land use is regulated in each zoning district. For example, a multifamily apartment building may be automatically permitted in some residential districts, allowed only with a special use permit in other residential districts, and not allowed at all in industrial districts.

Height, Bulk, and Area Regulations

In addition to regulating where particular land uses can be located, zoning regulations typically have standards on the height and size of structures, lot design and layout, and density of development. These are often referred to as "dimensional standards."

Building-height restrictions are usually set for each zoning district,[58] but smaller jurisdictions may impose a uniform height limit throughout the jurisdiction.[59] Each regulation typically specifies how the height limit is measured (for example, specifying measurement from the lowest grade or the average grade). The regulations also typically specify exceptions to the limits, such as chimneys, antennae, church steeples, and the like.

Minimum setbacks from property lines are typically required for structures.[60] Varying setbacks are often applied for different zoning districts. Property-line setbacks also usually vary for the front, sides, and rear of the property. Setbacks may be imposed to prevent locating structures in hazardous or environmentally sensitive areas, such as setbacks from flood-hazard areas, streams, or drinking-water wells. Other setbacks may have a public-safety component, such as the common requirement that telecommunication towers be set back from the property line at a distance equal to the height of the structure

---

55. Typical factors, for example, include the type, density, and intensity of development; environmental impacts; and the anticipated amount of traffic, noise, light, vibration, odor, and similar impacts on neighboring properties.

56. G.S. 160D-102(30), § 2.9(b), S.L. 2019-111 provides that any conditional use permit or special exception shall be deemed a "special use permit" consistent with the provisions of Chapter 160D.

57. See Chapter 16 for a discussion of special use permits.

58. Welch v. Swasey, 214 U.S. 91 (1909).

59. For example, several beach communities in North Carolina have imposed a 65-foot height limit for all buildings. Occasionally, a controversy will arise over what building parts should be included within the height limit. *See, e.g.,* Coastal Ready-Mix Concrete Co. v. Bd. of Comm'rs, 299 N.C. 620, 265 S.E.2d 379 (1980). Ordinances may exclude structures such as flagpoles, mechanical appurtenances, church steeples, or telecommunication towers from some height limits. The General Assembly has also imposed height limits by local legislation. *See, e.g.,* S.L. 2006-126 (65-foot height limit for Kure Beach and 64-foot limit in Hendersonville, subject to approval in referendum) and S.L. 2006-60 (clarifying previous height limits applicable in Oak Island).

60. *Gorieb v. Fox*, 274 U.S. 603 (1927), is an early case upholding the use of setback requirements. Some ordinances have different setbacks for principal and accessory structures (such as allowing a toolshed or garage to be placed closer to a rear property line than is allowed for a house). Some contemporary ordinances also establish maximum setbacks, or "build to" lines, particularly in urban commercial areas.

Figure 6.3 Table of Permitted Uses

USE TYPES	Ref SIC	AG	RS40	RS30	RS20	RS15	RS12	RS9	RS7	RS5	RM8	RM12	RM18	RM22	RM26	LO	GOM	GOH	NB•	LB•	GB•	HB•	CB	SC	CP•	LI•	HI	PI•	LUC
RECREATIONAL USES																													
Public Parks	7990	D	D	D	D	D	D	D	D	D	D	D	D	D	D	D	D	D	D	D	D	D	D	D	D	D	D	D	1
Public Recreation Facilities	7990	D	D	D	D	D	D	D	D	D	D	D	D	D	D	D	D	D	D	D	D	D	D	D	D	D	D	D	2
Riding Stables	7999	S	S																								S		2
Shooting Ranges, Indoor	7999	S																			D	D				D	D		3
Shooting Ranges, Outdoor	7999	S																									S		5
Skating Rinks	7999																				P	P	P	P		P			3
Sports Instructional Schools	7999	S																			P	P	P	P	D	P	P		3
Sports & Recreation Clubs, Indoor	7997																				P	P	P	P	P	P			3
Swim and Tennis Clubs	7997	S	S	S	S	S	S	S	S	S	S	S	S	S	S	D	D								D				3
EDUCATIONAL AND INSTITUTIONAL USES																													
Ambulance Services	4119	P														P	P		P	P	P	P	P	P	P	P	P		3
Auditoriums, Coliseums, or Stadiums	0000																				P	P	P		P				3
Cemeteries/Mausoleums	0000	D	D	D	D	D	D	D	D	D	D	D	D	D	D	D	D	D	D	D	D	D	D	D	D	D	D		2
Churches	8661	P	D	D	D	D	D	D	D	D	D	D	D	D	D	P	P	P	P	P	P	P	P	P	P	P	P		3
Colleges or Universities	8220																				P	P							3
Correctional Institutions	9223	S																								S	S		4
Day Care Centers, Adult (5 or less, Hom. Occ)	8322	D	D	D	D	D	D	D	D	D	D	D	D	D	D	D	D	D	D	D	D	D	D	D	D	D	D		1
Day Care Centers, Adult (6 or More)	8322	S									D	D	D	D	D	D	D	D	D	D	D	D	D	D	D	D			3
Day Care Centers, Child (5 or less, Hom. Occ)	8351	D	D	D	D	D	D	D	D	D	D	D	D	D	D	D	D	D	D	D	D	D	D	D	D	D	D		1
Day Care Centers, Child (6 or more)	8351	S									D	D	D	D	D	D	D	D	D	D	D	D	D	D	D	D			3
Elementary or Secondary Schools	8211	D	D	D	D	D	D	D	D	D	D	D	D	D	D														3
Fire Stations	9224	P	P	P	P	P	P	P	P	P	P	P	P	P	P	P	P	P	P	P	P	P	P	P	P	P	P	P	3
Fraternities or Sororities (Univ. or College)	0000																D	D		D	D	D				D			3
Government Offices	9000																P	P	P	P	P	P	P	P	P	P	P	P	3
Hospitals	8062																												3
Libraries	8231															P	P	P	P	P	P	P	P	P	P				3
Museums or Art Galleries	8412															P	P	P	P	P	P	P	P	P					3
Nursing and Convalescent Homes	8050													S	S	P	P		P	P	P								3
Orphanages	8361	S												S	S	P	P												3
Police Stations, Neighborhood	9221	P	P	P	P	P	P	P	P	P	P	P	P	P	P	P	P	P	P	P	P	P	P	P	P	P	P		3
Post Offices	0000																P	P	P	P	P	P	P	P	P	P	P	P	3
Psychiatric Hospitals	8063																P	P		P	P	P							3
Retreat Centers	0000	S																		P	P	P	P	P					3

P=USE BY RIGHT D= DEVELOPMENT STANDARDS S= SPECIAL USE PERMIT REQUIRED Z=OVERLAY ZONING REQUIRED
*= INDICATES ADDITIONAL DISTRICT REQUIREMENTS SEE SECTION 30–4–5.3

or that buildings, signs, and other structures be located at a safe distance from streets and do not block sight lines at intersections.[61] Some regulations impose maximum setbacks or "build to" lines, particularly in urban areas, to require building locations closer to streets. In addition to setbacks for principal structures, many regulations include smaller setbacks for fences, signs, and accessory buildings.

Minimum lot sizes and minimum street frontages for each lot are also typical regulatory requirements.[62]

Zoning regulations may also address the size of permissible structures. The most common provision is setting a maximum square footage for buildings in order to regulate the intensity and density of permitted uses. For example, a neighborhood-commercial zoning district will usually set a maximum floor area for commercial uses in that district, with larger structures allowed only in more intensive commercial districts. Several beach towns set a maximum square footage for single-family residential structures in low-density residential zoning districts in order to limit construction of extremely large

---

61. In addition to zoning authority, road setbacks and intersection sight line protections can be adopted as general police-power regulations. G.S. 160A-306. That provision requires that measurements for sight lines at intersections must begin within the roadway or at the edge of the pavement of a proposed or existing street.

62. Prohibition of odd-shaped lots is also common. For example, a "flag lot" that has a very small road frontage and an extended narrow accessway to a wide rear portion of the lot is often prohibited.

vacation rental homes. Regulations may also relate maximum building size to lot size through use of a floor-area ratio, a maximum impervious-surface coverage for a lot, or a requirement that a minimum amount of open space be retained. State law does, however, prohibit zoning regulations from setting a minimum (as opposed to a maximum) square footage for residential structures.[63]

Development regulations other than zoning may also include dimensional standards. For example, stormwater regulations often regulate the amount of impervious surface coverage on a lot, a cell-tower regulation may have height limits, and subdivision regulations may have dimensional standards for new lots. When there are multiple dimensional standards in different regulations, G.S. 160D-706(a) provides that the more-stringent regulation applies. Zoning dimensional standards can be more restrictive than other development regulations or state statutory standards, and if so, the zoning restriction applies.[64] But if another local or state regulation is more restrictive, the zoning rule does not override it, and the more-stringent standard applies.

Other Regulatory Provisions

In addition to use and dimensional requirements, it is common for zoning regulations to include a wide variety of additional development regulations. Off-street parking, landscaping, and sign regulations are among the more common additional regulations. Growth-management and environmental restrictions are also common and are addressed in subsequent chapters.[65]

Landscaping requirements typically apply to nonresidential land uses. For example, new businesses and industries may be required to have a planted buffer to provide a separation between uses or to assist in protecting water quality. Zoning regulations may require provision of landscaping along the street front or in parking areas to enhance the community's appearance. The size of the area to be landscaped and the type of plants to be used may be specified.

In order to prevent street congestion or impositions on neighbors, regulations often require new development to provide a minimum amount of off-street parking on-site.[66] For example, a restaurant may be required to provide one parking place for every four seats, an office building may be required to provide one parking place for each 250 square feet of floor space, an industry may be required to provide two parking places for every three employees, and a residential use may be required to provide two parking places for each residential unit. The zoning regulation will usually specify the size of the

---

63. G.S. 160D-702(c), created by S.L. 2019-174. The restriction applies to any structure built to the one- and two-family residential building code. The same restriction was also added to the subdivision statute. This limit on zoning restrictions on small houses does not apply to private restrictive covenants. Small homes are also still subject to the State Building Code, which regulates matters such as the minimum floor area for each habitable room and minimum ceiling heights. N.C. State Building Code, Residential Code, §§ R304.1, R304.3, R305.

Section 1.17 of S.L. 2019-111 also amended G.S. 160D-706(b) to provide that city and county development regulations may not use definitions of specified terms—building, dwelling, dwelling unit, bedroom, and sleeping unit—that are inconsistent with the definitions of those terms in a rule adopted by a state agency, including those contained in the State Building Code.

64. S.L. 2021-168, § 2, clarified that the authority for more stringent zoning regulations is subject to G.S. 160A-174(b) regarding preemption (see Chapter 22 for discussion of that issue).

65. See, for example, the discussion of adequate-public-facility ordinances, design standards, and "form-based codes" in Chapter 9.

66. In response to critiques that these required off-street parking requirements have led to far more parking than is necessary for commercial developments and to increased stormwater runoff and unnecessary increases in housing prices in urban areas, a number of jurisdictions have reduced or even eliminated their minimum parking requirements. *See generally* DONALD SHOUP, THE HIGH COST OF FREE PARKING (2011).

Table 6.1   Municipalities Adopting Sign Regulations

Population	Number Responding	% of Respondents
<1000	85	59
1000–4999	121	91
5000–9999	40	95
10,000–24,999	43	84
25,000–49,999	9	100
50,000+	16	94
Total	314	82

Table 6.2   Counties Adopting Sign Regulations

Unincorporated Population	Number Responding	% of Respondents
<20,000	25	52
20,000–49,999	39	87
50,000+	26	100
Total	90	81

parking places,[67] whether they must be paved, and where on the site they can be located. Some regulations may also include a maximum number of parking places that can be provided.

Zoning regulations often include limits on signs though sometimes a separate sign ordinance covers these regulations. Typical sign regulations include limits on location (for example, no billboards allowed in residential zoning districts and a minimum distance required between billboards); size (maximum height and square footage); and type (for example, prohibitions on flashing lights, portable signs, or windblown signs).[68] While state law also regulates outdoor advertising near federal highways (see Chapter 136, Sections 129 to 140.1 of the North Carolina General Statutes), the state regulatory scheme does not preempt local sign regulations.

A 2005 survey by the School of Government indicated that sign regulations were very common in North Carolina.[69] As Tables 6.1 and 6.2 indicate, nearly all cities with populations over 1000 and counties with unincorporated populations over 20,000 reported adoption of sign regulations.

Performance standards for various land use impacts may also be established. First employed for industrial uses, the performance standards can address maximum noise, vibration, dust, smoke, glare, and the like. Contemporary regulations may extend these standards to all land uses and may incorporate performance standards for traffic, stormwater retention, vegetation protection, and the like.

---

67. G.S. 160D-702 provides that a zoning regulation may not require that a maximum parking space be any larger than nine feet wide by twenty feet long unless it is "for handicap, parallel, or diagonal parking." The law expressly provides that it preempts any contrary local development regulation.

68. Regulation of signs raises constitutional issues that are discussed further in Chapter 28.

69. DAVID W. OWENS & NATHAN BRANSCOME, AN INVENTORY OF LOCAL GOVERNMENT LAND USE ORDINANCES IN NORTH CAROLINA 7 (UNC School of Government, Special Series No. 21, May 2006).

Development regulations are also sometimes crafted to create incentives for particular types of development activity. One of the more common incentives is the density bonus. For example, a particular zoning district may allow ten dwelling units per acre but also provide that the density can be increased to twelve units per acre under prescribed circumstances. This technique may be used to encourage development attributes that go beyond regulatory minimum-development standards or that use innovative development techniques. Examples include provision of more open space, incorporation of energy-efficient development,[70] provision of affordable housing, or use of clustered development.

Zoning regulations can also require the dedication of land, funds, and construction of public facilities in order to address the impacts created by permitted development. Although more typically imposed as part of subdivision-plat approvals, G.S. 160D-702 allows zoning regulations to apply exactions and performance guarantees "to the same extent and with the same limitations" as is the case with plat approvals.[71]

---

70. G.S. 160D-704(a) allows all cities and counties to provide density bonuses and other incentives in land use regulations for those who achieve significant energy conservation in new development or reconstruction projects. In 2007, five local governments received express authority to provide zoning incentives for new development that is energy efficient. S.L. 2007-241. In 2008, this was extended to ten additional jurisdictions. S.L. 2008-22. In 2009, the explicit authority was extended to all cities and counties. S.L. 2009-95. G.S. 160D-704(b) also explicitly allows cities and counties to charge reduced building-permit fees for buildings that meet or exceed specified green-building certifications. G.S. 143-135.35 to -135.40 set standards for water and energy conservation in public buildings.

71. Explicit authorization of use of zoning exactions is also made for special use permit decisions by G.S. 160D-705(c). Exactions are discussed in detail in Chapter 7.

Subdivision Regulations

Subdivision ordinances regulate the creation of new lots or separate parcels of land. Subdivision regulations typically address new residential developments but can also be applied to commercial, industrial, or mixed-use developments. The subdivision regulation does not, however, address the ultimate land uses proposed for the subdivided land.[1]

As with zoning, there were early national model acts that served as the foundation for most state subdivision-enabling statutes.[2] There has long been, however, more substantial variation from state to state with subdivision and platting statutes than is the case with zoning.[3] North Carolina cities were first authorized to adopt subdivision regulations in 1929.[4] This authority was extended to counties in 1959.[5]

Most cities in North Carolina with populations over 1000 have adopted subdivision regulations, and counties are even more likely to have adopted a subdivision regulation than a zoning regulation. A 2018 survey by the School of Government indicated that of the responding jurisdictions, 97 percent of the municipalities and 94 percent of the counties had adopted subdivision regulations.[6]

---

1. Jones v. Davis, 163 N.C. App. 628, 594 S.E.2d 235 (2004). The court held that where individual lots were being created, the fact that the lots would be used for rental-mobile-home placement was irrelevant to subdivision approval.

2. U.S. Dep't of Commerce, A Standard City Planning Enabling Act 24–32 (1928). The model code provided that subdivision regulations "may provide for the proper arrangement of streets in relation to other existing or planned streets and to the master plan, for adequate and convenient open spaces for traffic, utilities, access of fire-fighting apparatus, recreation, light and air, and for the avoidance of congestion of population, including minimum width and area of lots." It allowed for inclusion of standards for the construction of roads; construction of water, sewer, and other utilities, and for provision that this infrastructure "be installed as a condition precedent to the approval of the plat."

3. For a summary of the history of subdivision regulation, see Robert H. Freilich & Michael M. Schultz, Model Subdivision Regulations 1–13 (2d ed. 1995); Marygold Shire Melli, *Subdivision Control in Wisconsin*, 1953 Wis. L. Rev. 389 (1953); John W. Reps, *Control of Land Subdivision by Municipal Planning Boards*, 40 Cornell L.Q. 258 (1955); John W. Reps & Jerry L. Smith, *Control of Urban Land Subdivision*, 14 Syracuse L. Rev. 405 (1963); Note, *Land Subdivision Control*, 65 Harv. L. Rev. 1226 (1952); Note, *Platting, Planning and Protection—A Summary of Subdivision Statutes*, 36 N.Y.U. L. Rev. 1205 (1961).

4. S.L. 1929-186. For a more detailed review of subdivision law and practice in North Carolina, see Adam S. Lovelady, Land Subdivision Regulation in North Carolina, 2015 (UNC School of Government, 2016). For an early review of subdivision law in North Carolina, see Philip P. Green, Jr., *Legal Status of Subdivision Regulation*, Popular Gov't, Apr. 1955, at 9–11. *See also* Richard D. Ducker, Subdivision Regulations in North Carolina: An Introduction (UNC Institute of Government, 1980).

5. S.L. 1959-1007.

6. For municipalities, 92 percent reported adopting a municipal subdivision regulation while an additional 5 percent reported that county subdivision regulations were applied within the city. The use of subdivision regulations by North Carolina local governments has long been common, especially for municipalities with larger populations. David W. Owens, *2018 Survey Report: Adoption and Administration of Local Development Regulations, Conditional Zoning, and Subdivision Administration*, Plan. and Zoning L. Bull. No. 30 (UNC School of Government, Dec. 2020), at 5–6. An earlier 2005 survey by the School of Government indicated that of the jurisdictions responding to the survey, 83 percent of the municipalities and 88 percent of the counties had adopted a subdivision regulation. David W. Owens & Nathan Branscome, An Inventory of Local Government Land Use Ordinances in North Carolina 4 (UNC School of Government, Special Series No. 21, 2006). A 1966 survey indicated 96 percent

A subdivision regulation may be adopted as a separate ordinance or combined with zoning and other development regulations into a single ordinance regulating multiple aspects of land development (often termed a "unified development ordinance").

Purpose and Content

Subdivision regulations serve a variety of purposes. For example, they facilitate record keeping of land ownership by setting clear standards for surveying lots,[7] marking them on the ground, and recording plat maps with the register of deeds. Subdivision regulations also usually include standards on the size and shape of new lots and the layout of public facilities (such as street location, intersection design, and the like). Further, most subdivision regulations require the provision of essential infrastructure (such as roads, utilities, recreational lands, and open space[8]) and the details of how it is to be laid out and constructed.[9] Subdivision regulations will often require dedication of land and improvements for this infrastructure to the public agency that will be responsible for its operation (or the provision of fees in lieu of provision of these improvements). Any proposed dedication, however, must be clearly demarcated as such on the plat.[10]

In addition to creating public ownership of dedicated lands and facilities, recording a plat and selling lots with reference to it also creates private rights to use of streets and other public spaces by lot purchasers. These rights exist even if a transfer to public ownership fails. Purchasers of lots in platted subdivisions acquire a right to have streets, playgrounds, and parks kept open for reasonable use, and this right cannot be revoked except by agreement.[11] Also, where representations are made to purchasers that undivided sections will remain as open space or for joint use of purchasers, the purchasers may have

---

of responding North Carolina cities with populations over 10,000 had adopted a subdivision regulation (and virtually all of these applied the ordinance both within the corporate limits and within an extraterritorial area). Div. of Cmty. Plan., Dep't of Conservation Dev., Local Development Policies: A Survey of Current Practices in North Carolina 6 (1967). For all responding municipalities, the report noted the number with subdivision regulations had increased from 40 percent in 1958 to 47 percent in 1966. *Id.* at 24.

7. Chapter 39, Sections 32.1 to 32.4 of the North Carolina General Statutes (hereinafter G.S.); G.S. 47, §§ 30 to 32.2.

8. *See generally* Randall G. Arendt & Holly Harper, Conservation Design for Subdivisions: A Practical Guide to Creating Open Space Networks (1996); Randall Arendt et al., Growing Greener: Putting Conservation into Local Plans and Ordinances (1999); Randall Arendt et al., Rural by Design: Maintaining Small Town Character (1994).

9. *See, e.g.,* Beechridge Dev. Co., LLC v. Dahners, 350 N.C. 583, 516 S.E.2d 592 (1999) (holding a "public easement" granted as part of subdivision-plat approval includes use of the easement for a public sewer line); Batch v. Town of Chapel Hill, 326 N.C. 1, 387 S.E.2d 655 (1989), *cert. denied*, 496 U.S. 931 (1990) (holding town may require developer to coordinate with present and future road plans as set forth in the adopted thoroughfare plan).

10. Harry v. Crescent Res., Inc., 136 N.C. App. 71, 523 S.E.2d 118 (1999) (court will not imply that remnant lots are limited to open-space use). *But see* Gaither v. Albemarle Hosp., 235 N.C. 431, 70 S.E.2d 680 (1952) (upholding finding that undivided, unbuildable strip of land between road and river was intended to be dedicated to public use).

11. Hawthorne v. Realty Syndicate, Inc., 300 N.C. 660, 268 S.E.2d 494 (1980); Realty Co. v. Hobbs, 261 N.C. 414, 421, 135 S.E.2d 30, 35–36 (1964); Conrad v. Land Co., 126 N.C. 776, 36 S.E. 282 (1900); *Harry*, 136 N.C. App. 71, 523 S.E.2d 118; Gregory v. Floyd, 112 N.C. App. 470, 435 S.E.2d 808 (1993); Hinson v. Smith, 89 N.C. App. 127, 365 S.E.2d 166, *review denied*, 323 N.C. 365, 373 S.E.2d 545 (1988); Stines v. Willyng, Inc., 81 N.C. App. 98, 344 S.E.2d 546 (1986); Whichard v. Oliver, 56 N.C. App. 219, 387 S.E.2d 461 (1982). *See generally* Charles Szypszak, The Law of Municipal Streets and Utility Easements in North Carolina (2019); David M. Lawrence, Property Interests in North Carolina City Streets 7–9 (1985).This principle predates subdivision regulation. *See, e.g.,* Home Real Estate Loan & Ins. v. Town of Carolina Beach, 216 N.C. 778, 7 S.E.2d 13 (1940) (street dedication resulting from platting land and selling lots with reference to the plat).

legal rights even though such rights are not clearly indicated on the plat.[12] The subdivision regulation may also include provisions for performance guarantees to assure provision of required infrastructure.[13]

There is a law—Chapter 136, Section 102.6 of the North Carolina General Statutes (hereinafter G.S.)—that establishes additional requirements regarding any subdivision either outside of a city or within a city that involves state roads, whether or not a local subdivision regulation is in place. When the subdivision creates a new street or changes an existing street, this statute requires a plat to be recorded that delineates the street or road and designates whether it is private or public. If any street is designated as public, the plat is deemed to be a conclusive offer of dedication. Any street proposed for the state highway system is required to be reviewed by the North Carolina Department of Transportation and must meet minimum standards set by the Board of Transportation.[14] State and local regulations that require permits for access to state and local roads (often termed "driveway permits") can also have an important impact on subdivision design.[15]

Definitions and Exemptions

State statutes define the land divisions subject to coverage by local subdivision regulations. The North Carolina statutes[16] provide that the division of a "tract or parcel of land into two or more lots, building sites, or other divisions when any one or more of those divisions are created for the purpose of sale or

---

12. River Birch Assocs. v. City of Raleigh, 326 N.C. 100, 388 S.E.2d 538 (1990); Shear v. Stevens Bldg. Co., 107 N.C. App. 154, 418 S.E.2d 841 (1992). See Chapter 24 for a discussion of the scope of exactions that can be required.

13. G.S. 160D-804(g)(3) was amended in 2005 to provide that performance guarantees can include, but are not limited to, surety bonds and letters of credit. These statutes also require that the developer of an individual project be allowed to choose the particular means of guarantee to be used from among options provided by the city or county. S.L. 2005-814, §§ 2(a) and 2(b).

14. This statute applies only to subdivisions made on and after October 1, 1975. The rules for state roads are set out in Title 19A, Chapter 2C, Sections .0101 to .0213 of the North Carolina Administrative Code (hereinafter N.C.A.C.). For an illustration of the conflicts that can arise when a subdivision street is not accepted as a public street, see *Ocean Hill Joint Venture v. Currituck County*, 178 N.C. App. 182, 630 S.E.2d 714, *review granted*, 360 N.C. 648, 636 S.E.2d 808 (2006), *review improvidently granted*, 361 N.C. 228, 641 S.E.2d 302 (2007) (road owned and maintained by property owners' association proposed to be closed to public when traffic from adjacent subdivision increased).

15. Authority for access permits for state roads is provided by G.S. 136-18(29). *See* High Rock Lake Partners, LLC v. N.C. Dep't of Trans., 366 N.C. 315, 735 S.E.2d 300 (2012). Municipal authority for driveway access to city streets is provided by G.S. 160A-307. Related municipal authority is provided in G.S. 160A-306 for classification of city streets and establishment of building-setback distances from rights-of-way.

16. G.S. 160D-802(a). A variety of local modifications have been adopted. Recent examples include: S.L. 2004-46 (Pitt County, exempting divisions among heirs and transfers within an immediate family and repealing previous modifications for Harnett County); S.L. 2003-79 (Chowan County, exempting division of land as part of estate settlement but allowing denial of other permits if other regulations not met); S.L. 2002-141 (Chowan County, ordinance applicable only to divisions into three or more lots and exempting gift of single lot by parent to child); S.L. 2001-189 (Richmond County, allowing categories of subdivision approval); S.L. 2000-11 (Richmond County, exempting divisions into parcels greater than five acres with no right-of-way dedication); S.L. 1999-125 (Jones County, exempting divisions into parcels greater than five acres with no right-of-way dedication); S.L. 1998-37 (Stanly County, revising large-lot exemption from five acres to ten acres); S.L. 1996-565 (affecting divisions within the Rose Hill extraterritorial area); S.L. 1995-78 (Davie County, changing large-lot exemption to parcels greater than five acres and exempting certain intrafamily and court-ordered transfers); S.L. 1995-337 (Montgomery County, various exemptions, including intrafamily transfers and divisions over five acres with no right-of-way dedication); S.L. 1994-574 (Stanly County, exempting certain divisions over five acres); S.L. 1994-638 (Robeson County, exempting some divisions greater than two-and-a-half acres); S.L. 1994-131 (Robeson County, exempting certain intrafamily transfers); S.L. 1994-195 (repealing Lincoln County modification); S.L. 1992-972 (Transylvania County modifications). There has been some trend toward eliminating some of these local variations. *See, e.g.*, S.L. 2007-207 (repealing a 1993 exemption applicable to Pasquotank County); S.L. 2007-237 (deleting prior exemption in Stanly County for lots of at least 20,000 square feet with at least 100 feet of road frontage); S.L. 2006-189 (repealing exemptions created for Rutherford County).

building development (whether immediate or future)"[17] and all divisions involving the "dedication of a new street or a change in existing streets" are subdivisions subject to regulation.[18]

Since the division must be for the purpose of sale or development, courts have held that divisions for other purposes are not subject to subdivision regulation. For example, a division of land for the purpose of dividing an estate among the heirs has been held not to be a subdivision under the statutory definition.[19] Creation of multiple lots for future development, even if the lots remain in single ownership, is a "subdivision" subject to regulation. Examples include lots in a mobile-home park or outparcels in a commercial development.[20]

The statutory definition of a subdivision also includes the following exemptions:[21]

1. the combination or recombination of portions of previously subdivided and recorded lots where the total number of lots is not increased and the resultant lots meet or exceed the standards of the municipality as shown in its subdivision regulations;

2. the division of land into parcels greater than ten acres where no street right-of-way dedication is involved;[22]

3. the public acquisition by purchase of strips of land for the widening or opening of streets or for public-transportation-system corridors;[23]

4. the division of a tract in single ownership whose entire area is no greater than two acres into no more than three lots, where no street right-of-way dedication is involved and where the resultant lots meet or exceed the standards of the municipality, as shown in its subdivision regulations; and

5. the division of a tract to settle an estate.[24]

Before the register of deeds can record a plat that is exempt from local subdivision regulation, a review officer must review the plat and certify that it is in fact exempt.[25]

Three Guys Real Estate v. Harnett County[26] illustrates the effect of the statutory exemption from subdivision regulation. The owner of a 231.37-acre parcel proposed to divide the land into twenty-three

---

17. The N.C. Attorney General's office in 1975 expressed the view that one lot created for sale or development is not a subdivision if no streets are created and there is no intent to sell or develop the remainder of the larger tract from which the single new lot was created. N.C. Dep't of Justice, Office of the Att'y Gen., Advisory Opinion: Counties; Subdivision Ordinance, Op. N.C. Att'y Gen. (March 4, 1975). The opinion says that any additional lots created out of that larger parcel would constitute a subdivision, even if done one at a time. However, many local governments considered that even the first lot would constitute a subdivision since there would now be two lots (the original parcel and the new lot) existing as of the creation of even one lot for conveyance out of the larger tract. The statute was amended in 2005 to clarify that even the first lot out is subject to subdivision regulation. The statute now explicitly provides that if any one lot is created for the purpose of sale or development, it is a subdivision. S.L. 2005-426, §§ 4(a) and 4(b).

18. G.S. 160D-802.

19. Williamson v. Avant, 21 N.C. App. 211, 203 S.E.2d 634, *cert. denied*, 285 N.C. 596, 205 S.E.2d 727 (1974).

20. Jones v. Davis, 163 N.C. App. 628, 594 S.E.2d 235 (2004) (lots in mobile-home park).

21. The exemptions are listed in G.S. 160D-802(a).

22. This exemption originally was for the creation of lots of five acres or more with no street dedication. See G.S. 160-226.6, created by S.L. 1955-1334. The 1971 comprehensive revision of the municipal statutes changed this to ten acres. S.L. 1971-698. The same change was made for counties. G.S. 153-266.7, created by S.L. 1959-1007, provided for a five-acre exemption, and this was adjusted to ten acres by S.L. 1973-822. For a collection of cases from other states interpreting similar statutory definitions, see JAMES A. KUSHNER, SUBDIVISION LAW AND GROWTH MANAGEMENT §§ 5:7 to 5:15 (2d ed. 2004).

23. The provision for public-transportation-system corridors was added effective July 1, 2003, by S.L. 2003-284, § 29.23(a).

24. Provision added by S.L. 2017-10, essentially codifying *Williamson*, 21 N.C. App. 211, 203 S.E.2d 634.

25. G.S. 47, §§ 30(f)(11), 30.2.

26. 345 N.C. 468, 480 S.E.2d 681 (1997).

lots and proposed no street rights-of-way or other access to the lots. After suit was filed, a revised plat showed access by a series of private-driveway easements. The county refused to approve the plat, noting the hazards to public safety caused by the lack of adequate access. The North Carolina Supreme Court, however, concluded that the statutory exemption of G.S. 160D-802(a)(2) was clear and unambiguous: if all lots created by a subdivision exceeded ten acres and there was no public-right-of-way dedication involved, the subdivision was exempt from any and all county subdivision regulation.

The fact that a division of land is exempt from the definition of a subdivision for the purposes of a city or county land-subdivision regulation does not, however, exempt the development from other types of local development regulation. In *Tonter Investments, Inc. v. Pasquotank County*,[27] for example, the plaintiff owned three tracts and proposed to subdivide them into lots of greater than ten acres each with no street right-of-way dedications. The parties agreed that such a division would be exempt from the county's land-subdivision regulation. Prior to any development of the lots, the county amended its zoning regulation to prohibit residential uses in the county's A-2 zoning district (where two of the plaintiff's tracts were located) and to allow residences in the A-1 zoning district (where the plaintiff's third tract was located) only if the lot had a specified minimum frontage on a state road and was within 1000 feet of a public water supply.[28] The plaintiff contended that the *Three Guys* rationale precluded these zoning restrictions. The court disagreed, holding there was no evidence that the legislative intent to exempt these large-lot divisions from land-subdivision regulation constituted an "unfettered exemption from all county regulations, including zoning regulations."[29]

Plat Review

North Carolina enabling statutes for the most part do not mandate particular procedural requirements for subdivision review and approval processes.

Types of Plats

G.S. 160D-801 notes that a subdivision regulation may provide for review and approval of sketch plans and preliminary plats, as well as final plats, and allow the regulation to be adopted as part of a unified development ordinance. The statutes also allow for differing review procedures for differing classes of subdivisions, provide that expedited reviews may be set for specified classes of subdivisions,[30] and for a specific class of subdivision noted below, mandate an expedited review. Decisions on preliminary and final plats may be made by the governing board, the planning board, a technical-review committee or

---

27. 199 N.C. App. 579, 681 S.E.2d 536, *review denied*, 363 N.C. 663, 687 S.E.2d 296 (2009).

28. In 2011, the General Assembly amended the county-zoning statute to restrict use of this approach. S.L. 2011-384 enacted G.S. 160D-903(b) to provide that counties may not prohibit single-family detached homes on lots greater than ten acres in size in zoning districts where more than 50 percent of the land is used for agriculture or silviculture (unless it is a commercial or industrial zoning district allowing a broad variety of commercial or industrial uses). The law provides that any ordinance provision inconsistent with this limitation is void and unenforceable as of the effective date of the law. This law also mandates a study of the extent to which counties should be able to require that lots exempt from subdivision regulation be accessible to emergency-service providers.

29. *Tonter*, 199 N.C. App. at 583, 681 S.E.2d at 539. *See also* Town of Nags Head v. Tillett, 314 N.C. 627, 336 S.E.2d 394 (1985) (holding that statutory provisions for enforcement of land-subdivision ordinance do not limit enforcement options under zoning ordinance).

30. The statutory references to sketch plans, preliminary plats, differing classes of subdivisions, and unified development ordinances were added by S.L. 2005-418, §§ 2(a) and 2(b). The references to expedited review of specified classes of subdivisions were added to G.S. 160D-801 by S.L. 2005-426, §§ 4(a) and 4(b). The typical subdivision-review process is described in *River Birch Associates v. City of Raleigh*, 326 N.C. 100, 111–12, 388 S.E.2d 538, 544–45 (1990).

other designated body, or even a designated staff person.[31] Within these broad parameters, each city and county fashions its own review process.

A preliminary *sketch plan* may be required as a first step. This is often reviewed only by the planning staff to ensure there are no glaring problems before the owner spends time and money preparing plats for the subsequent stages of approval.

The key decision in the subdivision-approval process is the *preliminary plat*. Despite the name of this step toward securing approval, there is little that is "preliminary" about it. The preliminary plat application usually requires detailed survey plats of all the lots and engineering details on all the proposed and required improvements. The preliminary plat is widely circulated among various government agencies to assure compliance with standards within their areas of expertise. For example, in cities, the utilities department will check the water and sewer specifications, the transportation department will review proposed streets, the fire department may check streets for acceptability for use by fire trucks and the adequacy of fire-hydrant location, and the sanitation department may review the preliminary plat for acceptable refuse-collection access. In counties, the preliminary plat is reviewed by the health department regarding acceptability for wells and septic tanks and by the N.C. Department of Transportation for roads that will be dedicated to the state. Preliminary plat approval is often delegated to the planning board or a staff technical-review committee.

Preliminary plat approval authorizes the owner to install the required public improvements and make other site improvements. G.S. 160D-807(b) allows contracts to sell or lease lots in approved preliminary plats for which final approval has not yet been secured.[32] In these instances, the buyer must receive a copy of the preliminary plat at the time of contracting and must receive a copy of the final plat prior to closing. The prospective buyer must be clearly notified that final plat approval has not yet been secured, that approval is not guaranteed, and that the contract may be terminated if the final plat is materially different from the preliminary plat.

After the required improvements are installed, the city or county inspects them for compliance with the regulation. If they meet the standards and are built as proposed, *final plat approval* is given. Approval is required if the work is consistent with the terms of the regulation and the preliminary plat approval. Although there is little discretion involved with final plat approval, this decision is usually made by the city council or county board of commissioners. Submission of the final plat is an offer of dedication of indicated improvements, and with final plat approval the city or county formally accepts the dedication of streets and utilities. After the review officer designated under G.S. 47-30.2 certifies that the plat either meets plat and subdivision standards or is exempt, the final plat may be recorded with the register of deeds.[33]

---

31. G.S. 160D-803. The provisions allowing decisions by a staff person were added to these statutes in 2005. S.L. 2005-418, §§ 3(a) and 3(b).

32. S.L. 2005-426, §§ 3(a) and 3(b). These statutes also allow contracts to sell or lease based on a preliminary plat when the contract is with a person engaged in the business of constructing residential, commercial, or industrial buildings on the affected property. In this instance, the actual conveyance may not occur until final plat approval is secured. G.S. 160D-807(c).

33. Building permits may be denied for lots that have been illegally subdivided. G.S. 160D-807(a).

Approval Process

If all of the standards for subdivision approval are objective, the plat-approval decision is properly characterized as administrative. If the standards for decision include discretionary standards, the plat-approval process is quasi-judicial.[34] The vast majority of North Carolina jurisdictions use only objective standards for plat reviews, but several have opted to use discretionary standards and a quasi-judicial review process. Several rural counties have also zoned much of their land area for low-density residential use, thereby as a practical matter requiring a rezoning prior to (or concurrent with) many subdivision plat reviews.

G.S. 160D-801 provides that decisions on both preliminary and final plats must be based only on standards explicitly set forth in the regulation. These statutes were further amended to provide that if the standards employed require the exercise of judgment, the criteria used must provide adequate guiding standards for decision makers.[35] In these quasi-judicial determinations, the applicant for subdivision approval has the burden of production of evidence for compliance with the standards. Once the applicant makes the requisite prima facie showing of compliance, approval is required in the absence of contradictory evidence in the record. If the standards are entirely objective, and if the owner submits adequate evidence that the regulation requirements have been met, the owner is entitled to plat approval.[36]

The necessity of adequate evidence in the record to support a quasi-judicial subdivision decision is illustrated by *Blue Ridge Co. v. Town of Pineville*.[37] The town denied approval of a subdivision plat based on a conclusion that the proposal failed to meet two subdivision-regulation standards: (1) that the subdivisions be consistent with adopted public plans (including policy plans and plans for public facilities, such as roads, parks, and schools) and (2) that new subdivisions be designed to "protect and enhance the stability, environment, health and character of the neighboring area."[38] The town council based its denial regarding the first standard on school overcrowding and its denial regarding the second on traffic concerns. The court held there was insufficient evidence in the record to support a denial based on school overcrowding. The court noted that it was uncertain that there was in fact an adopted plan or policy specifically addressing this point. Furthermore, the regulation did not require a school-impact analysis, and in any event, the overcrowding existed even without this subdivision. As for traffic impacts, an expert testified that the increase in traffic would not create an undue safety problem, while opponents, the court noted, offered no mathematical studies but only speculative and generalized concerns.

For the most part, the substantive standards in subdivision regulations are left to the local government's discretion, as is the case with zoning standards. However, G.S. 160D-804 does impose several

---

34. G.S. 160D-803(c). *See also* Guilford Fin. Servs., L.L.C. v. City of Brevard, 356 N.C. 655, 576 S.E.2d 325 (2003), *per curiam, adopting dissent in* 150 N.C. App. 1, 563 S.E.2d 27 (2002). Both the majority and dissent in the court of appeals held that the preliminary plat decision involved was quasi-judicial and subject to the same fair-trial and due-process requirements as quasi-judicial zoning decisions.

35. S.L. 2005-418, §§ 2(a), (b). As for the adequacy of guiding standards, see the discussion on this point relative to standards for special use permits in Chapter 16. G.S. 160D-705 provides for judicial review of quasi-judicial plat reviews in the same manner as for quasi-judicial zoning decisions.

36. Sanco of Wilmington Serv. Corp. v. New Hanover Cnty., 166 N.C. App. 471, 601 S.E.2d 889 (2004) (with ministerial plat approvals, petitioner is entitled to approval as a matter of law upon establishing compliance with standards); Nazziola v. Landcraft Props., Inc., 143 N.C. App. 564, 545 S.E.2d 801 (2001) (plat-approval decision must be based only on the clearly identified standards for decision set out in the ordinance). The same limitation applies to other land use regulatory decisions, such as site-plan approval. *See, e.g.,* Knight v. Town of Knightdale, 164 N.C. App. 766, 596 S.E.2d 881 (2004) (town council can base site-plan-approval decision only on the standards specifically enumerated in the ordinance).

37. 188 N.C. App. 466, 655 S.E.2d 843, *discretionary review denied, dismissed as moot,* 362 N.C. 679, 669 S.E.2d 742 (2008).

38. *Id.* at 471, 655 S.E.2d 843 at 846.

restrictions. First, the regulation may not set a minimum structure size for one- and two-family residences. Second, the regulation may not require the burial of power lines if the line existed above ground at the time of plat approval.[39]

Expedited Plat Review

G.S. 160D-802(c)[40] provides that for qualifying subdivisions, a local government may require only a plat for recordation (a final plat).

To qualify for this expedited approval, the property involved must be five acres or more. At least ten years must have passed since the property was previously subdivided through expedited review. The subdivision must not be exempt as a ten-acre exemption. The subdivision must result in no more than three lots. The resulting lots must meet applicable lot-dimension requirements and must have a permanent means of ingress and egress designated on the plat. Finally, the resulting lots must comply with applicable zoning requirements.

No sketch-plan review or preliminary plat review may be required for qualifying subdivisions. As with any other subdivision, before a review officer may sign off for a qualifying plat to be recorded, the plat must be approved by the local government's subdivision officer. The subdivision officer must determine whether the plat meets the standards to be a qualifying subdivision. This expedited review is similar to the "minor plat" review and approval processes provided by some subdivision regulations.

Appeals of Plat Decisions

Appeals of final decisions on plat approvals are governed by G.S. 160D-1403.

If the approval decision is quasi-judicial, the appeal is made to superior court in the nature of certiorari in the same manner as other quasi-judicial development-regulation decisions.[41]

If the approval decision is administrative, the appeal process depends on the entity making the decision.[42] The same rules apply to appeals of any other administrative decision made in the course of implementation of subdivision regulations. If the administrative decision is made by the governing board or planning board, the appeal is made to superior court for declaratory or equitable relief. These appeals must be made in writing thirty days from receipt of written notice of the decision. If the administrative decision is made by staff or a staff committee (such as a technical review committee), then the appeal is made to the board of adjustment under G.S. 160D-405.[43]

---

39. G.S. 160D-804(h), (i). Both of these limits were added by S.L. 2019-174.

40. Provisions added by S.L. 2017-10, § 2.5.

41. G.S. 160D-1403(a). This statute provides that G.S. 160D-406, regarding quasi-judicial procedures, applies to these appeals. That section further incorporates the standard provisions of G.S. 160D-1402, regarding judicial review of quasi-judicial decisions, and G.S. 160d-1405(d), regarding the time for appeals.

42. G.S. 160D-1403(b).

43. See Chapter 19 for a discussion of appeals of staff administrative decisions.

Performance Guarantees

Most subdivision regulations require the installation of necessary infrastructure to support the planned development. A subdivision regulation may require completion of all infrastructure prior to final plat approval (which was common in the past) or require the development to proceed in phases, with final approval given for each phase only when the infrastructure for that phase is complete.[44]

Under many regulations, if the required streets, water mains, sewer lines, sidewalks, stormwater-management systems, and other infrastructural elements are not fully complete and accepted at the time of final plat approval, the development can still proceed if a financial guarantee is provided. The guarantee provides financial assurance that the mandated infrastructure will be completed in an acceptable fashion.[45] Use of performance guarantees is permitted but not required. If performance guarantees are used, which is now the standard practice, G.S. 160D-804.1[46] provides guidance on their use.

The statute allows performance guarantees only for completion of the required improvements, not for repairs or maintenance.[47] It requires that the following three options be available as performance guarantees:

1. a surety bond issued by any company authorized to do business in North Carolina,
2. a letter of credit issued by any financial institution licensed to do business in North Carolina, and
3. any other form of guarantee that provides security equivalent to a surety bond or letter of credit.[48]

The developer has the option to choose any of these means of providing a guarantee. A guarantee may be up to 125 percent of the estimated cost of completing the improvements (100 percent of the estimated cost of labor and materials and 25 percent for inflation and administrative costs). The local government

---

44. The standard enforcement provisions for ordinance violations are also available to deal with noncompliance. See Chapter 21 for more details on ordinance-enforcement options.

45. In *Town of Black Mountain v. Lexon Insurance Co.*, 238 N.C. App. 180, 768 S.E.2d 302 (2014), *review denied*, 771 S.E.2d 307 (2015), the court held that performance guarantees running to the county could be assigned to the city when the affected property was annexed and the authority to enforce the subdivision ordinance thereby shifted from the county to the city. A subsequent purchaser of the property subject to a performance bond would generally have no rights under that bond unless the agreement explicitly provided for that. In *Brookline Residential, LLC v. City of Charlotte*, 251 N.C. App. 537, 796 S.E.2d 369 (2017), the plaintiff acquired land that contained a partially built subdivision with an outstanding performance bond for completion of the streets. The plaintiff redesigned the project and then tried to compel the city to use the performance bond to build at least part of the remaining street. The court refused to order the city to call the bond, noting the plaintiff was not a party to the bond, was not assigned rights under the bond, and was not a third-party beneficiary of the bond.

The scope of the guarantor's obligation is determined by terms of the contractual guarantee itself. Developers Sur. & Indem. Co. v. City of Durham, No. 1:11CV515, 2014 WL 4677181 (M.D.N.C. Sept. 18, 2014). In this case the plaintiff provided a surety bond for completing streets and stormwater-management facilities within a subdivision. When the developer defaulted, the city called the bond. The court held that the terms of the surety bond were controlling as to the scope of the plaintiff's obligations. In this instance, the bond only required the completion of improvements already constructed, not the completion of those improvements not yet initiated.

46. This subsection was added to the statutes by S.L. 2015-721. It was further amended by S.L. 2019-79 and recodified and further amended by S.L. 2020-25, § 20(b). G.S. 160D-1006(f) makes this provision applicable to development agreements as well as subdivision regulations. Performance guarantees associated with erosion and stormwater control are not subject to this statute.

47. There is separate statutory authority for some maintenance guarantees. Local governments will need to find distinct authority for such maintenance guarantees. G.S. 153A-454 and 160A-459 provide authority for financial arrangements to ensure adequate maintenance and replacement of stormwater-management facilities.

48. G.S. 160D-804.1(1). Examples include cash in escrow, a trust agreement, or some other financial instrument. The statute does not specify who decides what types of guarantee provide equivalent security.

may require the performance guarantee to be posted at the time of plat recordation or at a later date. A developer may post a single guarantee or multiple guarantees for different types of infrastructure. The initial term of the guarantee is to be for one year unless the developer elects a longer term.

The developer is required to make good-faith progress towards completions and extensions may be made when needed and new guarantees issued. If the guarantee is extended or a new guarantee provided, the amount is to be based only on the cost and duration to complete the remaining infrastructure.[49] When the work is completed, the local government is required to release the guarantee and provide written acknowledgment that the required improvements have been completed.

In the event that a developer fails to meet milestones set through the guarantee agreement, and the developer is not making good-faith efforts, a local government can call the guarantee and use the funds to complete the unfinished improvements.[50]

After acknowledgment by the local government that the improvement is complete, the local government must return or release the guarantee in a timely manner. Many local governments will release the guarantee in stages as various stages of the infrastructure is completed.

Exactions

The statutes authorize a variety of development exactions as a condition of plat approval. G.S. 160D-804 authorizes counties and municipalities to require provisions for:

- streets (dedication of rights-of-way, construction, or fees in lieu of construction),[51]
- utilities (dedication of rights-of-way),[52]
- recreation, park, and open-space areas (dedication or reservation of sites and fees in lieu of site dedication or development),[53]
- community-service facilities (construction and bonds for compliance), and
- schools (reservation of sites for subsequent public purchase).

---

49. G.S. 160D-804.1(1b).

50. G.S. 160D-804.1(5) specifies who has a claim or rights under any performance guarantee. These are the local government to whom the guarantee is provided, the developer at whose request or benefit the guarantee was given, and the entity issuing the guarantee. This clarification was added by S.L. 2017-40, § 3.

51. There is not a general authority for these fees in lieu of street construction for counties since counties, unlike cities, do not provide streets. Ownership and maintenance of roads outside of municipalities is generally assumed by the state if the roads are built to state standards and accepted by the N.C. Department of Transportation (NCDOT). G.S. 136-102.6(d) requires NCDOT to accept the roads within ninety days of a petition to do so if the department determines that the roads meet state standards. G.S. 160D-804(c)(3) does give counties the authority to collect funds for road development in subdivisions located in municipal extraterritorial areas and then pass those funds to the city.

Although they infrequently did so, local governments in the past could also adopt a transportation-corridor official map to protect future rights-of-way. G.S. 136-44, §§ .50 to .54. Building permits for projects within an officially designated right-of-way could be delayed for up to three years. However, the authority to adopt official maps has been repealed, as discussed below in this chapter.

52. Fees established for public-enterprise functions can address the costs of providing infrastructure to development. G.S. 153A-277; 160A-314. *See* Town of Spring Hope v. Bissette, 53 N.C. App. 210, 280 S.E.2d 490 (1980).

53. S.L. 2007-339 allows Chatham County to impose recreational fees in development agreements. S.L. 2007-321 allows Cary to impose recreational fees on multifamily residential developments that do not involve land subdivision. S.L. 2008-76 allows Chapel Hill to require payment of fees instead of accepting dedications of land for recreation areas of less than four acres and to do the same for projects requiring a special or conditional use permit.

In addition to requiring provision of public infrastructure, the subdivision regulation can require the design and layout of the development to be coordinated with planned public streets and other facilities.[54]

G.S. 160D-804(c) has been interpreted to preclude requirements that a street be constructed outside of the land area of the proposed subdivision, even if it is adjacent to and serving the subdivision.[55] In *TAC Stafford, LLC v. Town of Mooresville*, the court held that the town lacked statutory authority under the subdivision-enabling statute to require any off-site transportation improvements.[56]

The authority to require provision of land and facilities and payment of fees for infrastructure needs created by new subdivisions includes authority to impose reasonable fees for transportation, water, sewer, recreation, and open-space needs generated by growth.[57] Local governments can also impose special assessments on benefited properties to pay for improvements for streets, sidewalks, and water, sewer, and drainage systems.[58]

However, while North Carolina statutes authorize these fees for public-enterprise functions, the statutes do not include enabling legislation for impact fees that are common in other states.[59] In *Durham Land Owners Ass'n v. County of Durham*,[60] the court held that counties did not have statutory authority to impose a school-impact fee without explicit and specific authorization. Several dozen North Carolina cities and counties have secured local acts authorizing the use of impact fees to provide for various types of public facilities.[61] Only a portion of the affected local governments have actually adopted fee ordinances, however. Some of these include Raleigh in 1987 (covering roads, parks, and greenways),

---

54. Batch v. Town of Chapel Hill, 326 N.C. 1, 12, 387 S.E.2d 655, 662 (1989).

55. Buckland v. Town of Haw River, 141 N.C. App. 460, 541 S.E.2d 497 (2000). The court noted that the statute explicitly allows collection of fees in lieu of street construction for such outside street improvements. *See also* Pansy Rd., LLC v. Town Plan. & Zoning Comm'n, 283 Conn. 369, 926 A.2d 1029 (2007). S.L. 2006-103 authorizes Chapel Hill to require payment of fees for public transit as well as for streets.

56. 282 N.C. App. 686, 872 S.E.2d 95, *rev. denied*, 880 S.E.2d 696 (2022). The plaintiff had spent $993,584 to comply with off-site transportation-mitigation measures. The town was required to return the funds paid directly to the town, but moneys paid to other landowners to acquire off-site rights-of-way were held not to be an exaction paid to the government, so the town could not "return" those fees.

57. G.S. 160D-804(c), (d); S. Shell Inv. v. Town of Wrightsville Beach, 703 F. Supp. 1192, 1206 (E.D.N.C. 1988), *aff'd*, 900 F.2d 255 (4th Cir. 1990) (upholding authority to charge impact fee for water and sewer services). Also, a city can set utility fees in its sound judgment. Atl. Constr. Co. v. City of Raleigh, 230 N.C. 365, 53 S.E.2d 165 (1949). The authority to impose impact fees for public services other than public enterprises is far less clear. The cases nationally are split on this authority in the absence of explicit statutory authorization (and about half of the states have provided such authorization). *See* DANIEL R. MANDELKER, LAND USE LAW § 9.21 (5th ed. 2003). See Chapter 9 for a discussion of impact fees generally.

G.S. 162A-200 to -215 defines permissible system-development fees that may be charged for water and sewer services. These statutes set how the fees are calculated, how a fee schedule is adopted, when a fee is assessed, and how fees may be spent. System-development fees may be assessed only on new development, not existing development. This article was added to the statutes by S.L. 2017-138. Also, G.S. 153A-210.1 to .7 and G.S. 160A-239.1 to .7 authorize special assessments upon petition by landowners to finance critical infrastructure needs, including transportation, parking, water, sewer, parks, recreation, and other public needs. These funds may be used to reimburse private parties who initially provide this infrastructure.

58. G.S. 160A, §§ 216 to 238.

59. For general background on impact fees, see Brian W. Blaesser & Christine M. Kentopp, *Impact Fees: The "Second Generation,"* Wash. U. J. URB. & CONTEMP. LAW 38 (1990); David A. Dana, *Land Use Regulation in an Age of Heightened Scrutiny*, 75 N.C. L. REV. 1243 (1997); Martin L. Leitner & Susan P. Schoettle, *A Survey of State Impact Fee Enabling Legislation*, 25 URB. LAW. 491 (1993); James C. Nicholas, *Impact Exactions: Economic Theory, Practice, and Incidence*, 50 LAW & CONTEMP. PROBS. 85 (1987). See Chapter 9 for a discussion of the authority to impose impact fees and the limitations on their use.

60. 177 N.C. App. 629, 630 S.E.2d 200, *review denied*, 360 N.C. 532, 633 S.E.2d 678 (2006).

61. See Chapter 9 for a list of these authorizations.

Durham in 1987 (streets, parks, recreation facilities, and open space), Cary in 1989 (roads), and Orange County in 1993 (school-impact fees).[62]

The exactions required are constitutionally limited to those rationally related to impacts or needs generated by the proposed development.[63]

When a subdivision developer is constructing required improvements, the government and developer may agree that it is cost-effective for the developer to construct improvements that exceed those needed to address the impact of the proposed development (such as constructing a utility line with excess capacity to serve future development). In these instances, G.S. 153A-451 and 160A-499 authorize the parties to enter a reimbursement agreement so that the government subsequently pays the costs of the excess capacity provided.[64] To use this option, a city or county must first adopt an ordinance setting the procedures and terms for approval of reimbursement agreements. The improvements to be constructed must be included in the local government's capital-improvement plan.

A local government and a developer may also enter into a contract for the developer to construct public-enterprise improvements that are adjacent or ancillary to a private project, with the local government reimbursing the developer for those improvements not mandated by development regulations.[65]

Transportation Corridor Official Map Act

In 1987, the General Assembly adopted the Roadway Corridor Official Map Act, later renamed the Transportation Corridor Official Map Act. The law, codified at G.S. 136-44.50 to -44.54, allowed transportation corridors to be identified by those entities responsible for public road and transportation improvements.[66] The law required duly noticed public hearings and formal adoption of the maps, with the adopted maps filed with the applicable county register of deeds.

Filing an official map with the register of deeds had several key consequences. Work was required to begin on environmental-impact statements or preliminary engineering within one year of adopting the maps.[67] Once an official map was filed, the law prohibited approval of building permits or new subdivisions within the corridor.[68] However, no application for a building permit or plat approval could be delayed more than three years after submittal of a corridor-map determination.[69]

---

62. The authority for Orange and Chatham counties to adopt school impact fees was granted by S.L. 1987-460. Orange County's authority to do so was repealed by S.L. 2017-36.

63. Dolan v. City of Tigard, 512 U.S. 374 (1994); Nollan v. Cal. Coastal Comm'n, 483 U.S. 825 (1987); Anderson Creek Partners, L.P. v. Cnty. of Harnett, 382 N.C. 1, 876 S.E.2d 476 (2022). These constitutional limitations are discussed in Chapter 24.

64. While the reimbursement agreement is not subject to bidding laws applicable to local government contracts, the developer must solicit bids if the work would have required competitive bidding under state law. G.S. 153A-451(a); 160A-499(d).

65. G.S. 153A-280; 160A-320. This, for example, would allow a city to agree to pay for an oversized sewer line in order to accommodate other future developments, saving money by having the line built now instead of paying later for a separate project. G.S. 160A-309 permits cities to similarly contract for intersection and roadway improvements that are adjacent or ancillary to private development projects. In both instances, if the amount of the contract is under $250,000, the project is not subject to the public-bidding statutes if the local government finds that coordination of separately constructed improvements would be impractical or that the cost of the contract would not exceed the cost of the local government's conducting the improvements with its own workforce.

66. This included cities, the N.C. Department of Transportation, regional transportation authorities, the N.C. Turnpike Authority, and two projects for the Wilmington Urban Area Metropolitan Planning Organization.

67. G.S. 136-44.50(d).

68. G.S. 136-44.51(a).

69. G.S. 136-44.51(b). The law also allowed for variances to be granted if no reasonable return could be made from the land (G.S. 136-44.52), and it allowed landowners to petition for initiation of acquisition if the limits on

Landowners affected by a 1997 official-map designation for a proposed thirty-four-mile-long loop road around northern Winston-Salem sued the state, alleging the act made their property unmarketable and was an unconstitutional taking of their property. The state supreme court held that filing a corridor-protection map under the Official Map Act was an exercise of the power of eminent domain rather than an exercise of the police power, thus necessitating compensation.[70] Therefore the landowners were entitled to compensation running from the time the official map was recorded.[71]

The General Assembly responded by suspending the Official Map Act program in 2016[72] and repealing it in 2019.[73]

development imposed an undue hardship (G.S. 136-44.53). Official maps had previously been authorized and upheld in other states. *See, e.g.,* Palm Beach Cnty. v. Wright, 641 So. 2d 50 (Fla. 1994); Headley v. City of Rochester, 5 N.E.2d 198 (N.Y. 1936).

70. Kirby v. N.C. Dep't of Transp., 368 N.C. 847, 786 S.E.2d 919 (2016). The court emphasized that *property* included the rights to improve, develop, and subdivide, which were severely and indefinitely restricted by the Official Map Act. The court noted that police-power regulations must have an appropriate connection to protection of life, health, and property, while the eminent-domain power took property because the action was advantageous or beneficial to the public. The court found that the Official Map Act was directly tied to condemnation of land for transportation projects. The principal public benefit was a reduction in acquisition costs rather than any prevention of injury under the police power. Thus, the court held the filing of an official map to be an act of eminent domain rather than a legitimate police-power regulation. The court remanded the matter for a determination of damages, to be measured by the diminution in fair-market value of the land as a whole immediately before and after the taking. For an earlier dispute regarding reservation of a right-of-way for a Winston-Salem beltway, see Wilson Realty Co. v. City and Cnty. Plan. Bd., 243 N.C. 648, 92 S.E.2d 82 (1956).

Other cases have also found similar map-act requirements to be a taking. *See* Urbanizadora Versalles, Inc. v. Rivera Rios, 701 F.2d 993 (1st Cir. 1983) (four years on map without acquisition a taking although a "reasonable" term would be valid); Jensen v. City of New York, 42 N.Y.2d 1079, 399 N.Y.S.2d 645, 369 N.E.2d 1179 (1977); Ward v. Bennett, 214 A.D.2d 741, 625 N.Y.S.2d 609 (App. Div. 1995). *See also* Daniel Mandelker, *Interim Development Controls on Highway Programs: The Taking Issue,* 4 J. LAND USE & ENVTL. L. 167 (1989); David A. Thomas & Robert S. Payne, *Long-Range Highway Corridor Preservation: Issues, Methods and Model Legislation,* 13 BYU J. PUB. L. 1 (1998).

71. After *Kirby,* substantial litigation followed regarding just what rights are taken upon filing an official map and the amount of compensation due. See Dep't of Transp. v. Stimpson, 258 N.C. App. 382, 813 S.E.2d 634 (2018); Beroth Oil Co. v. N.C. Dep't of Transp., 256 N.C. App. 401, 808 S.E.2d 488 (2017).

72. S.L. 2016-90. This law amended G.S. 136-44.50 to place a moratorium until July 1, 2017, on the adoption of any new corridor official maps and rescinded all previously adopted maps.

73. S.L. 2019-35.

CHAPTER 8

Building and Housing Codes

One of the oldest and most widely employed forms of land-development regulation is the building code. Since colonial times, government has regulated construction practices to ensure public health and safety.[1] Because they have been used so widely for so long, the building inspections and permits that are used to ensure compliance with these codes often serve as the organizing tools for inspections and permits for other development regulations. Minimum-housing codes, which set minimum standards of habitability for residences, are optional in North Carolina and are less widely used than the State Building Code.

Building Codes

Building codes regulate how new construction must be conducted.[2] These codes include detailed standards for structural safety, insulation, and electrical, plumbing, and heating systems.[3] State law also regulates certain practices within buildings that may pose a threat to public safety.[4] There are exemptions to building code coverage for some farm buildings and small projects.[5]

---

1. The 1740 charter for the Town of Edenton prohibited wooden chimneys. Laws of 1740, ch. 1, § 13. Construction and fire-safety standards were common in the eighteenth and nineteenth centuries.

2. It is within the police power "to establish minimum standards, materials, designs, and construction of buildings for the safety of the occupants, their neighbors, and the public at large." State v. Walker, 265 N.C. 482, 484–85, 144 S.E.2d 419, 421 (1965) (upholding conviction for initiation of building repairs without the requisite building permit).

3. Chapter 143, Section 138(b) of the North Carolina General Statutes (hereinafter G.S.) authorizes the State Building Code to address a wide variety of building standards, including location, height, and floor areas; lighting and ventilation; means of ingress and egress; construction practices; permissible materials, loads, and stresses; rules for chimneys, heating appliances, elevators, and other mechanical systems; plumbing, heating, and air-conditioning systems; electrical systems; activities within buildings that pose a danger of fire or explosion; and "such other reasonable rules pertaining to the construction of buildings and structures and the installation of particular facilities therein as may be found reasonably necessary for the protection of the occupants of the building or structure, its neighbors, and members of the public at large." Additional safety standards are imposed on high-rise buildings. The replacement of windows, doors, porches, decks, like-kind electrical devices, and plumbing (if there is no change in the plumbing's size or capacity) in single-family homes are generally exempt. G.S. 143-138, 160D-1110.

4. For example, G.S. 14-413 prohibits use of indoor pyrotechnics unless the local fire marshal has certified their safety.

5. G.S. 143-138(b4) provides that farm buildings outside of municipalities are not covered. G.S. 143-138(b5) and 160D-1110(c) provide that no building permit is required for minor construction projects in single-family residences and farm buildings (costing less than $20,000) if no load-bearing structural work or addition or change in the design of plumbing, heating, air-conditioning, or electrical systems is involved. G.S. 143-138(b21) excludes work costing $20,000 or less within twelve consecutive months in commercial buildings, provided the work is in accordance with the current building code.

In North Carolina all cities and counties are required by state law to enforce the North Carolina State Building Code.[6] Rather than simply enable local regulation, as is the case with most land-development regulations, there have long been state mandates for building codes.[7]

The building code is uniform throughout the state; each local government enforces the code approved by the N.C. Building Code Council. The code used is based on the International Building Code, with North Carolina modifications. No local variations in the code are allowed other than fire-prevention codes and floodplain-management regulations approved by the state.[8] The North Carolina Supreme Court has held, for example, that a city may not impose fire-sprinkler requirements beyond those found in the State Building Code.[9] Several local governments have obtained local legislation authorizing sprinkler requirements.[10]

The state also sets standards for building inspectors. Each inspector must pass the appropriate state examination to be licensed to conduct particular types of inspections.[11]

The approval process under the State Building Code includes submission of plans for the structure to be built, issuance of a building permit, periodic inspections during the course of construction to ensure adherence to the code, and issuance of a certificate of occupancy[12] at the conclusion of building to verify that all requirements have been met and to authorize activation of utilities and occupancy of the building. All initial reviews of building permits conducted by local governments for one- and two-family residential structures must be performed within fifteen business days of submission of an application.[13]

---

6. G.S. 160D-1102. The first North Carolina State Building Code was published in 1936. It was ratified and adopted by the General Assembly in 1941.

7. In 1905, all cities with populations over 1000 were directed to have a building inspector to enforce state construction standards. N.C. Pub. Laws 1905, ch. 506. For a brief overview of the history of building codes in the state, see PHILIP P. GREEN, JR., LEGAL ASPECTS OF BUILDING CODE ENFORCEMENT IN NORTH CAROLINA 1–4 (2d ed. 1987).

8. G.S. 143-138(e). This precludes the adoption, for example, of local "green building" standards requiring that buildings be constructed to specified environmental standards. For examples of such regulatory requirements, see Erin Burg Hupp, *Recent Trend in Green Buildings Laws: Potential Preemption of Green Building and Whether Retrofitting Existing Buildings Will Reduce Greenhouse Gases and Save the Economy*, 41 URB. LAW. 489 (2009).

9. Greene v. City of Winston-Salem, 287 N.C. 66, 213 S.E.2d 231 (1975).

10. S.L. 1998-85 (Wrightsville Beach); S.L. 1998-13 (Nags Head); S.L. 1997-761 (Carrboro); S.L. 1997-316 (fraternity- and sorority-house sprinklers in Charlotte, Greensboro, and Raleigh); S.L. 1995-571 (fraternity and sorority houses in Carrboro and Chapel Hill); S.L. 1981-911 (Carrboro and Chapel Hill for buildings over fifty feet in height). Prior to the adoption of statewide requirements for smoke detectors, several local governments secured local legislation to authorize their required provisions. S.L. 1989-829 (Edenton); S.L. 1987-911 (Kill Devil Hills and Nags Head); S.L. 1987-226 (Boone and Blowing Rock).

11. G.S. 160D-1103. Oversight and disciplinary provisions for State Building Code–enforcement officials are provided by the N.C. Code Qualification Board. G.S. 143-151.8 to -151.21. G.S. 160D-1104(e) requires that every inspection department provide a process for informal internal reviews of inspection decisions. At a minimum, these reviews must include: (1) an initial review by the inspector's supervisor; (2) a listing of the name, phone number, and email address of the supervisor with each permit issued, along with a notice of the availability of the review process; and (3) the procedures the department will follow when a permit holder requests an informal internal review.

12. G.S. 160D-1104. The statute uses the terminology "certificates of compliance." Some local ordinances also use the terms "certificate of occupancy" or "certificate of completion." Other statutes use these terms as well, such as "certificate of occupancy" in G.S. 160D-1110(h). In G.S. 160D-1116, a "certificate of compliance" is issued after a final inspection of all work done under a building permit, and a "temporary certificate of occupancy" allows use of all or part of a building prior to its final completion.

Unless specifically authorized, a local government may not withhold a building permit or certificate of compliance in order to compel compliance with a permit or ordinance affecting another property. G.S. 160D-1110(h). Building permits may be denied for lots that have been illegally subdivided. G.S. 160D-807(a).

13. G.S. 160D-1110(b).

Each local government that conducts building-permit inspections must designate a person to be responsible for daily oversight of the program.[14]

State law specifies that building permits expire in six months if work is not commenced and expire if work is ceased for twelve months after it is commenced.[15] Permits may also be revoked. The statutes direct mandatory revocation for substantial departure from approved plans, for refusal to comply with applicable laws, or for false statements or misrepresentations made in securing the permit; permit revocation is permissible (but not mandated) for mistakenly issued permits.[16]

In addition to regulating new construction, state statutes allow cities and counties to inspect existing buildings for defects and to order corrections of code violations. When inspectors find an unsafe structure, they may order the structure vacated, repaired, or demolished.[17]

Chapter 160D, Sections 1119 to 1125 of the North Carolina General Statutes (hereinafter G.S.) provide for periodic inspections of buildings, condemnation of unsafe buildings, orders to take corrective action, appeals of these orders, and enforcement options should the unsafe conditions not be remedied.[18] The owner of a building subject to condemnation as unsafe must be given written notice of the hearing on that determination.[19]

G.S. 160D-1117 and -1207 limit periodic inspections of buildings for unsafe, unsanitary, or otherwise hazardous conditions. Inspections for existing residential buildings are allowed when there is reasonable cause to believe those conditions exist based on past violations, complaints, or actual knowledge of those conditions. Periodic inspections may also be made in target areas designated by the governing board. The targeted areas may not exceed one square mile or 5 percent of the jurisdiction's area, whichever is greater. The areas must reflect a neighborhood-revitalization strategy and consist of properties meeting the definition of a "blighted" area or parcel under the urban-redevelopment law.

A more recent development in North Carolina has been the local adoption of maintenance codes for nonresidential buildings. Somewhat analogous to housing codes for residential structures, these codes set minimum standards for maintenance, sanitation, and safety designed to prevent buildings from deteriorating to the point of becoming dangerous and unsafe. While some cities and counties had adopted "commercial maintenance codes" earlier, the statutory authority to do so was unclear before 2007. In that year the General Assembly enacted G.S. 160D-1129 to explicitly authorize such ordinances.[20] These statutes set up a process by which cities and counties can order the repair, closing, or demolition of dilapidated nonresidential buildings. The laws specify that an officer may investigate a building that appears to have been improperly maintained and, if a violation is discovered, may serve a complaint on the owner. Following an administrative hearing, the officer may order remedial action.

---

14. G.S. 160D-1102(a). This requirement was created by S.L. 2022-11, § 9(a). The same legislation also created G.S. 160D-1102(c), which requires an annual report in 2023, 2024, and 2025 from each local government on how it uses building-permit fees.

15. G.S. 160D-1111.

16. G.S. 160D-1115. For a discussion of the impacts of mistakenly issued or revoked permits on vested rights, see Chapter 19.

17. G.S. 160D-1122.

18. *Walker v. City of Charlotte*, 276 N.C. 166, 171 S.E.2d 431 (1970), upheld the basic constitutionality of such regulations. Also see Six at 109, LLC v. Town of Holden Beach, 238 N.C. App. 469, 767 S.E.2d 400 (2014) (upholding order to demolish an unsafe structure). The limit on periodic inspections also applies to dwellings used for short-term rentals. S.L. 2019-73.

19. Actual notice is not a substitute for the mandated statutory notice. Newton v. City of Winston-Salem, 92 N.C. App. 446, 374 S.E.2d 488 (1988). If the owner cannot be located, the local government may post the property and provide published notice. Farmers Bank v. City of Elizabeth City, 54 N.C. App. 110, 282 S.E.2d 580 (1981). *See also* Coffey v. Town of Waynesville, 143 N.C. App. 624, 547 S.E.2d 132 (2001) (upholding demolition order).

20. These regulations may be applied jurisdiction-wide, in specified municipal-service districts, or in areas designated for improvement and investment in an adopted comprehensive plan. G.S. 160D-1129(a).

If appropriate repairs are not made, the governing board may order the structure to be repaired or vacated and closed. If remedial action is not taken, the governing board can order the demolition of the offending structure provided the owner is given a reasonable opportunity to bring the structure into compliance. If the owner has not made repairs within two years[21] of an order to repair or close the building, the governing board can determine the owner has abandoned the intent to repair. The board may then order the repair or demolition of the building upon finding "the continuation of the building or structure in its vacated and closed status would be inimical to the health, safety, and welfare of the municipality in that it would continue to deteriorate, would create a fire or safety hazard, would be a threat to children and vagrants, would attract persons intent on criminal activities, or would cause or contribute to blight and the deterioration of property values in the area."[22] The law specifically allows ejectment actions and liens on the property as enforcement mechanisms.[23]

The General Assembly has also created a program to deal with abandoned manufactured-housing units. G.S. 130A-309.113 authorizes (but does not mandate) counties to implement a program for the management of abandoned manufactured homes—those that are (1) vacant or in need of extensive repair and (2) that pose an unreasonable danger to the environment or to public health, safety, or welfare. If a county elects to have a program, it must prepare a plan that sets out the method it will use to identify abandoned manufactured homes, how the homes will be deconstructed, how materials will be removed for reuse or recycling, and how those not deconstructed will be disposed of. Once a plan is adopted, the county notifies the owner of the abandoned manufactured home and the owner of the land where it is located that the home must be properly disposed of by the homeowner within ninety days. The notice must be in writing and must provide for a hearing before a designated public officer in the county no less than ten and no more than thirty days after the notice is served. If, after the hearing, the officer determines that the manufactured home is in fact "abandoned," the officer can order it to be disposed of within ninety days. If the homeowner fails to comply, the county can take enforcement action, including entering the property and arranging to have the unit deconstructed and disposed of according to the plan. If the land is owned by a separate party, the landowner can be ordered to allow entry onto the property to permit removal and disposal of the unit. The unit owner can be held liable for the costs incurred by the county, including administrative and legal costs as well as the direct and indirect costs of disposal. These provisions do not apply to the retail sales lots for manufactured homes nor to a solid-waste-disposal facility that has no more than ten manufactured homes being stored (provided the units are deconstructed or removed within a year of receipt).

Cities and counties can also use their regular nuisance-abatement programs to deal with abandoned manufactured homes[24] and other public-safety situations.[25]

Housing Codes

Housing codes set minimum standards that must be met for structures to be used for residential purposes. For example, a housing code may require a minimum square footage of space for each occupant, availability of adequate sanitary facilities, an adequate heating source, and avoidance of unsafe conditions (such as exposed wiring or holes in the floor).

---

21. The time period is five years for vacant manufacturing facilities or industrial warehouses.

22. G.S. 160D-1129(g).

23. G.S. 160D-1129(i) and (j), respectively.

24. The program was enacted by S.L. 2008-136. Originally codified as G.S. 130A-309.99A to -99H, it was renumbered as G.S. 130A-309.111 to -309.118 at the direction of the Revisor of Statutes.

25. G.S. 160A-193.

Table 8.1   Municipalities Adopting Housing Codes

Population	Number Responding	% of Respondents
<1000	82	21
1000–4999	115	50
5000–9999	37	62
10,000–24,999	44	86
25,000–49,999	9	89
50,000+	16	94
Total	**303**	**52**

Table 8.2   Counties Adopting Housing Codes

Unincorporated Population	Number Responding	% of Respondents
<20,000	29	31
20,000–49,999	42	17
50,000+	26	39
Total	**97**	**27**

G.S. 160D-1201 authorizes cities and counties to adopt housing codes. The statute allows the minimum-housing code to address structural dilapidation and defects, general disrepair, lighting, sanitary facilities, fire hazards, ventilation, and general cleanliness.

Unlike State Building Code enforcement, adoption of a housing code is not mandatory in North Carolina.[26] Housing codes are adopted at the option of each city and county. While frequently adopted by cities with populations over 10,000, housing codes in North Carolina are less often adopted by counties and cities with populations under 1000. The rates of adoption of housing codes reported in a 2005 School of Government survey[27] are set out for municipalities and counties in Tables 8.1 and 8.2.

Cities and counties with housing codes can order repairs to be made to substandard residential structures; structures not repaired can be ordered to be closed or demolished. The statutes provide a detailed administrative process that must be followed in housing-code enforcement.[28] An official appointed to enforce the code makes a preliminary inspection of the property upon receipt of a complaint or on the official's own motion. If that inspection indicates the property is unfit for human habitation, the officer issues a complaint stating the charges regarding habitability and provides notice to the owner of a hearing before the officer. This is an administrative hearing rather than a formal evidentiary hearing

---

26. For an example of an early standard housing code, see N.C. League of Municipalities, The North Carolina Model Housing Code (1978 ed.). There are, however, mandatory minimum state and federal standards for housing provided for migrant farm workers. See G.S. 95-225. Federal regulations established under the Occupational Safety and Health Act are set out at 29 C.F.R. § 1910.142 (2010).

27. David W. Owens & Nathan Branscome, An Inventory of Local Government Land Use Ordinances in North Carolina 5 (UNC School of Government, Special Series No. 21, May 2006).

28. G.S. 160D-1203. See Chapter 21 for additional discussion of enforcement of housing codes.

as would be required for a quasi-judicial decision.[29] Following the hearing, if the officer concludes the property is indeed unfit for habitation, the officer makes a written finding regarding the deficiencies and serves an order to repair, vacate, or demolish the property on the owner. The owner must be afforded a reasonable opportunity to repair the structure.[30] If the owner does not comply with the order, the officer may post the property to prohibit its occupation and the unit of government may undertake the repairs or demolition if those actions are authorized by the governing board.[31] The ordinance may provide for appeals of the officer's orders to a housing-appeals board or the board of adjustment.[32] Occupation of a building that has been posted is a criminal offense, and the local government may initiate a civil action to remove any inhabitants who do not comply with an order to vacate. Any of these orders may be appealed to superior court.[33]

Many local governments coordinate housing-code enforcement with various revitalization programs, such as financial assistance to low-income residents for home repairs.

---

29. In this context, the court has held that provision of an administrative hearing, with the right of appeal to a housing-appeals board or the board of adjustment, satisfies due-process requirements. Patterson v. City of Gastonia, 220 N.C. App. 233, 725 S.E.2d 82 (2012). An appeal of the officer's order is heard as a quasi-judicial matter by the designated appeals board. Failure to appeal an officer's order to the appeals board precludes judicial review as a failure to exhaust administrative remedies.

30. Horton v. Gulledge, 277 N.C. 353, 177 S.E.2d 885 (1970). This election of remedy does not apply to buildings condemned under the unsafe-building statute.

31. This is often referred to as "condemning the property," but it should not be confused with an action to acquire title by eminent domain. The order only prohibits occupation of the structure deemed unfit for habitation. The governing board's authorization to proceed with repairs, demolition, or posting the property must be enacted by an ordinance recorded with the register of deeds. G.S. 160D-1203, §§ (4), (5).

32. G.S. 160D-1208. Failure to make such an appeal is a failure to exhaust administrative remedies, and that will preclude subsequent judicial review. Cheatham v. Town of Taylortown, 254 N.C. App. 613, 803 S.E.2d 658 (2017) (applying G.S. 160A-446 provision for appeals of orders adopted under a minimum-housing code).

33. G.S. 160D-1208(c).

CHAPTER 9

Growth-Management Regulations

Substantial population growth has been the rule in North Carolina since World War II. The state's population grew from 4.1 million in 1950 to nearly 10.5 million in 2019. As in the rest of the country, much of this growth has been on the urban fringes, prompting concern about the economic, environmental, social, and cultural impacts of "urban sprawl."[1] Coping with the impacts of growth is a critical land use issue in many communities.

A variety of land-development regulations are employed by cities and counties to address growth-management concerns. Legislation in some states specifically authorizes a variety of these management tools.[2] For the most part, this has not been done in North Carolina, so local governments generally rely on their implied authority to undertake the regulations.[3]

This chapter addresses some of the principal growth-management tools used in North Carolina: development moratoria, adequate-public-facility ordinances, urban-growth boundaries, inclusionary zoning, and urban-design standards.[4]

Moratoria

Given the time needed to complete the procedures required for adoption or amendment of development regulations or to even rezone property, local governments sometimes adopt moratoria on development to preserve the status quo while plans are made, management strategies are devised and debated, ordinances are revised, or other development-management concerns are addressed.[5] Moratoria are also

---

1. There is a considerable body of literature documenting and discussing the implications of these national growth trends. *See, e.g.,* DAVID RUSK, CITIES WITHOUT SUBURBS (2d ed. 1995); Lee R. Epstein, *Where Yards Are Wide: Have Land Use Planning and Law Gone Astray?* 21 WM. & MARY ENVTL. L. & POL'Y REV. 345 (1997); Oliver A. Pollard III, *Smart Growth: The Promise, Politics, and Potential Pitfalls of Emerging Growth Management Strategies,* 19 VA. ENVTL. L.J. 247 (2000); Edward H. Ziegler, *Sustainable Urban Development and the Next American Landscape: Some Thoughts on Transportation, Regionalism, and Urban Planning Law Reform in the 21st Century,* 43 URB. LAW. 91 (2011). For a review of the underlying population growth that fuels local government concerns, see V. Jeffrey Evans & Barbara Vestal, *Local Growth Management: A Demographic Perspective,* 55 N.C. L. REV. 427 (1977).

2. For example, in New Hampshire, the enabling legislation specifically authorizes local use of innovative land-use controls that may include (but are not limited to) timing incentives, phased development, intensity and use incentives, transfer of density and development rights, planned-unit development, cluster development, impact zoning, performance standards, flexible and discretionary zoning, environmental-characteristics zoning, inclusionary zoning, impact fees, village-plan-alternative subdivision, and integrated-land-development-permit options. N.H. REV. STAT. ANN. § 674:21.

3. See Chapter 4 for a discussion of the scope of implied authority in North Carolina.

4. These tools are discussed in Richard D. Ducker & David W. Owens, *A Smart Growth Toolbox for Local Governments,* POPULAR GOV'T, Fall 2000, at 29.

5. Use of temporary development moratoria is not rare in North Carolina, but they have not been adopted routinely. Nearly 20 percent of the state's cities and counties responding to a 2008 School of Government survey reported adoption of a moratorium in the previous three years. DAVID W. OWENS, DEVELOPMENT MORATORIA: THE LAW AND PRACTICE IN NORTH CAROLINA 8–9 (UNC School of Government, Special Series No. 26, 2009). The

sometimes used when there are insufficient public services necessary to support development, such as inadequate water supply or wastewater-treatment capacity.

Local governments and the courts have long recognized the planning value of temporary moratoria in certain circumstances. The U.S. Supreme Court noted, "[M]oratoria . . . are used widely among land-use planners to preserve the status quo while formulating a more permanent development strategy. In fact, the consensus of the planning community appears to be that moratoria . . . are an essential tool of successful development."[6] Even so, the impact of a moratorium on individual landowners can be significant for at least the duration of the moratorium. Thus, it is not surprising that controversy and sometimes litigation follow a decision to apply a development moratorium.

Some states allow use of expedited procedures to adopt an interim zoning ordinance, sometimes referred to as "stopgap zoning."[7] These interim ordinances typically allow existing land uses to be continued and similar uses established while more detailed and future-oriented ordinances are being prepared. This is not allowed in North Carolina. In this state, all zoning ordinances must be adopted in accordance with the procedures described in Chapter 11.

Authority and Process Before 2005

Before 2005, there was no explicit statutory authority in North Carolina to adopt development moratoria. The single exception was adult-business siting. When the General Assembly amended the statutes in 1998 to clarify city and county authority to adopt regulations on siting and operation of adult establishments, the statute included explicit authority to adopt moratoria on the opening or expansion of adult businesses while the issue was studied and appropriate regulations deliberated.[8]

Courts in most other states that addressed the scope of implied statutory authority for development moratoria have held that local governments have implied authority to adopt reasonable moratoria.[9]

---

moratoria were most often of short duration (typically six months) and were normally focused on particular types of development. The most common reason cited for moratoria was the need to develop regulations for a particular land use, followed by needs to update plans and the lack of infrastructure to support development. *Id.* at 10–12. Given the statutory limitations discussed below on the use of residential-development moratoria if the purpose is to update plans or regulations, the use of moratoria has declined since the 2008 survey. However, they are still employed in North Carolina. For example, the Village of Bald Head Island adopted a moratorium on commercial development in 2022 while its master plan and regulations were being updated.

6. Tahoe-Sierra Pres. Council, Inc. v. Tahoe Reg'l Plan. Agency, 535 U.S. 302, 337–38 (2002). Moratoria "have been found to play an important role in municipal planning. They aid in 'bridging the gap between planning and its implementation into legal measures.' They may, as here, be used to preserve the status quo while study of the area and its needs is completed. This moratorium on land use serves a significant public purpose." Schaefer v. City of New Orleans, 743 F.2d 1086, 1090 (5th Cir. 1984) (upholding ten-and-one-half-month moratorium on permits for fast-food restaurants in a specified neighborhood while study conducted). *See generally* Robert Freilich, *Interim Development Controls: Essential Tools for Implementing Flexible Planning and Zoning*, 49 J. Urb. L. 65 (1971).

7. *See, e.g.*, Pawn Am. Minn., LLC v. City of St. Louis Park, 787 N.W.2d 565 (Minn. 2010) (upholding moratorium on pawnshops adopted pursuant to interim-zoning statute, with moratorium applicable while zoning revisions were considered).

8. Chapter 160D, Section 902 of the North Carolina General Statutes (hereinafter G.S.).

9. While a few states have explicit legislative authorization for moratoria, in most states the authority is implied. For an illustrative case upholding implied authority for moratoria, see *Wisconsin Realtors Ass'n v. Town of West Point*, 309 Wis. 2d 199, 747 N.W.2d 681 (Ct. App. 2008). The court there held that the town had implied authority for a moratorium on subdivision-plat approvals while updates to a comprehensive plan and a subdivision ordinance were underway. *See also* Droste v. Bd. of Cnty. Comm'rs, 159 P.3d 601 (Colo. 2007) (finding implied authority for ten-month moratorium in portion of county while plan prepared); Arnold Bernhard & Co. v. Plan. & Zoning Comm'n, 194 Conn. 152, 479 A.2d 801 (1984) (upholding nine-month zoning moratorium); Collura v. Town of Arlington, 367 Mass. 881, 329 N.E.2d 733 (1975) (upholding two-year moratorium on apartment buildings in portion of town). For statutes explicitly authorizing moratoria, see Cal. Gov't Code § 65858 (moratoria adopted without notice allowed for 45 days; with notice, up to 22.5 months, four-fifths majority required to adopt); Minn. Stat. Ann.

It was generally assumed by the courts prior to 2005 that North Carolina local governments had the implied power to adopt reasonably limited moratoria under both their general police power and their zoning authority.[10] In *PNE AOA Media, LLC v. Jackson County*,[11] the court held that the county had the authority to adopt a moratorium on new billboards under the general police power. In *Tri-County Paving, Inc. v. Ashe County*,[12] the court upheld the county's adoption of a one-year moratorium on asphalt plants and other "polluting industries." In *Robins v. Town of Hillsborough*,[13] the town in 2003 adopted a moratorium on the location of asphalt plants within the city and its extraterritorial area after the plaintiff had submitted an application for such a plant. While the decision largely addressed the issues related to processing a pending-complete application, the North Carolina Supreme Court assumed the town had authority to impose the moratorium.

Apart from the authority to adopt moratoria, the key legal question in North Carolina before 2005 was determining which process a local government was required to follow in adopting a moratorium—the process used for general ordinances or the more involved process mandated for land-development regulations.

The general ordinance-making authority could be used to adopt moratoria when unexpected threats to public health and safety arose, necessitating quick action to prevent harm to public interests while a permanent ordinance was being prepared, debated, and adopted.[14] This authority could also be used when the ultimate regulation to be adopted after the moratorium was to be a general ordinance rather than a zoning ordinance. For example, in *PNE AOA Media*,[15] the court held that a moratorium on

---

§ 394.34 (allowing interim zoning for one year, with one-year extension while plans and studies conducted); MONT. CODE ANN. § 76-2-206 (allowing interim zoning for one year, with single one-year extension permissible); UTAH CODE ANN. § 17-27a-504 (allowing temporary land use regulation of up to six months); WASH. REV. CODE ANN. § 36.70.790 (interim regulation allowed while studies, plans, ordinance amendments are considered). *See generally* DANIEL R. MANDELKER, LAND USE LAW § 6.06 to 6.10 (6th ed. 2018); PATRICIA E. SALKIN, *Chapter 35: Moratoria, in* AMERICAN LAW OF ZONING (5th ed. 2022). Not all courts have held that there is an implied power for moratoria. *See, e.g.*, Naylor v. Twp. of Hellam, 565 Pa. 397, 773 A.2d 770 (2001) (no implied power for subdivision-plat-approval moratorium while comprehensive plan updated). Also, a local moratorium must not exceed the bounds of delegated state authority. *See, e.g.*, Biggers v. City of Bainbridge Island, 162 Wash. 2d 683, 169 P.3d 14 (2007) (city imposition of moratorium inconsistent with state shoreline-management law).

10. In *Tate Terrace Realty Investors, Inc. v. Currituck County*, 127 N.C. App. 212, 488 S.E.2d 845, *review denied*, 347 N.C. 409, 496 S.E.2d 394 (1997), the county denied a special use permit and sketch plan for a 429-lot subdivision on the grounds that the available public-school facilities were inadequate to serve the development, essentially imposing a moratorium pending the provision of adequate services. The court upheld the county's action but did not address the validity of the moratorium in its decision. Likewise, in *Kirkpatrick v. Village Council of Pinehurst*, 138 N.C. App. 79, 530 S.E.2d 338 (2000), a case on expansion of a nonconforming campground, the village had adopted a moratorium on commercial building pending update of a comprehensive plan and a development ordinance. The court upheld the village's action, but again did not expressly address the moratorium.

11. 146 N.C. App. 470, 554 S.E.2d 657 (2001). The county was considering adoption of a sign regulation under its general ordinance-making authority.

12. 281 F.3d 430 (4th Cir. 2002).

13. 361 N.C. 193, 639 S.E.2d 421 (2007). Processing of the application was suspended during the moratorium. Prior to expiration of the moratorium, the town amended its ordinances to prohibit the location of asphalt plants throughout the town's jurisdiction. As a result, the town terminated consideration of the application. The key issue on appeal was whether the application should be considered under the rules in effect at the time of application or those in effect after the expiration of the moratorium. The court held that the town ordinance itself mandated a decision on the application within a reasonable time. Since the town had not made a decision, the court remanded the application for a decision under the rules in effect at the time of application.

14. G.S. 153A-121; 160A-174(a). See Chapter 4 for a discussion of overlapping statutory authorities.

15. 146 N.C. App. 470, 554 S.E.2d 657. At the time, the county did not have a zoning ordinance. *See also* Maynor v. Onslow Cnty., 127 N.C. App. 102, 488 S.E.2d 289, *appeal dismissed*, 347 N.C. 268, 493 S.E.2d 458, *review denied*, 347 N.C. 400, 496 S.E.2d 385 (1997) (upholding general ordinance-adoption procedures for adult-business-location regulations); Summey Outdoor Advert., Inc. v. Cnty. of Henderson, 96 N.C. App. 533, 386 S.E.2d 439 (1989), *review denied*, 326 N.C. 486, 392 S.E.2d 101 (1990) (upholding general ordinance-adoption procedures for sign regulations). The Georgia court reached a similar conclusion in *City of Roswell v. Outdoor Systems, Inc.*, 274 Ga. 130, 549 S.E.2d 90 (2001).

new billboards while a sign ordinance was being considered was not subject to the notice and hearing requirements applicable to zoning amendments.

However, if the moratorium was more closely related to traditional land use regulations, the courts required that those procedures be used in adopting the moratorium. In *Vulcan Materials Co. v. Iredell County*,[16] the plaintiff applied for building permits associated with a planned quarry in an unzoned portion of the county. The county then adopted a sixty-day moratorium on building permits while it took steps to extend zoning to this area. The moratorium limited permits to those that would be consistent with the county's land use plan, which had been adopted more than two years earlier. The moratorium adoption did not follow the public-notice and hearing requirements of the zoning statute. The court held that because the building-permit system, the county's land use plan, and zoning authorities were essential to this regulatory scheme, it must be adopted in accordance with the notice and hearing requirements for zoning.[17]

The court subsequently applied the *Vulcan* analysis in other "land use related" contexts. In *Sandy Mush Properties, Inc. v. Rutherford County*,[18] Rutherford County had no zoning but was considering adoption of a "Polluting Industries Development Ordinance" under its general ordinance-making power. The county published a single advertisement for a hearing on the proposed ordinance, which would limit new or expanded heavy industries within 2000 feet of a church, school, or residence. At the hearing, the county board of commissioners decided not to adopt the proposed ordinance; instead, it adopted a 120-day moratorium on initiation of heavy industries within 2000 feet of a school (and near the end of the moratorium, it adopted a "School Zone Protective Ordinance" to make this restriction permanent). Both the moratorium and school-protection ordinance were explicitly adopted pursuant to Chapter 153A, Section 121 of the North Carolina General Statutes (hereinafter G.S.), the general ordinance-making authority, for which no public hearing is required. However, the court invalidated the moratorium for failure to follow the notice and hearing requirements for land use–related ordinances. The court reasoned that the moratorium was in effect a temporary land use plan that divided the county into two areas—one area in which heavy industry was allowed and a second, smaller area near schools where heavy industries were at least temporarily prohibited. This fact, along with the use of the building-permit system for its enforcement, led the court to conclude that the moratorium must be adopted following the procedures for land use regulations. Thus, the nature of the ordinance and the subjects it regulated, rather than the precise statutory authorization cited by the local government, controlled which process was to be followed for adoption. Likewise, in *Thrash Ltd. Partnership v. County of Buncombe*,[19] the court held that a county ordinance regulating multifamily dwellings that applied

16. 103 N.C. App. 779, 407 S.E.2d 283 (1991).

17. *Id.*, 407 S.E.2d 283. Although prevailing in the litigation, the plaintiff allowed its option on the land to expire and a quarry was not built on the site. The county subsequently adopted countywide zoning.

18. 164 N.C. App. 162, 595 S.E.2d 233 (2004). The plaintiffs had applied for a building permit for a crushed-stone quarry on a 180-acre tract within 2000 feet of a school. An initial, incomplete application was filed after the public notice on the Polluting Industries Development Ordinance but before the moratorium was adopted. A revised, complete application was filed after the moratorium was adopted but before the School Zone Protective Ordinance was adopted. The application was denied because of the moratorium. In later proceedings this dispute returned to the court of appeals two more times. The court held that the building permit for the quarry office was still valid, as construction was tolled during the moratorium and the judicial review of it. However, the vested rights extended only to the office building, as that permit did not purport to authorize the more extensive mining use of the site. On remand the court of appeals affirmed this result. Sandy Mush Props., Inc. v. Rutherford Cnty., 181 N.C. App. 224, 638 S.E.2d 557, *remanded by* 361 N.C. 569, 651 S.E.2d 566, *affirmed by* 187 N.C. App. 809, 654 S.E.2d 253 (2007), *review dismissed*, 363 N.C. 577, 681 S.E.2d 339 (2009). For further discussion of the effects of multiple permit requirements on vested rights, see Chapter 19.

19. 195 N.C. App. 727, 673 S.E.2d 689 (2009).

differential rules based on altitude of proposed location of the dwellings must comply with adoption and amendment procedures for land use regulation.

This pre-2005 case law remains relevant for those moratoria not addressed by the statute discussed below. However, given the breadth of that statute's coverage, few development-related moratoria will fall into this category.

Authority and Process After 2005

In 2005, the General Assembly amended the zoning-enabling statutes to explicitly authorize use of development moratoria and set a number of rules regarding their use.[20]

G.S. 160D-107 allows temporary development moratoria to be placed on any city's or county's development approval. This statute authorizes moratoria on "any development approval required by law." This includes all zoning permits, land-subdivision plats, building permits, sign permits, and any other approvals required prior to development.

Any confusion in the case law regarding which process is to be followed in adoption is clarified by this statute, which provides that if there is an imminent threat to public health and safety, the moratorium may be adopted without notice or hearing. Otherwise, a moratorium with a duration of sixty days or less requires a single public hearing with a notice published not less than seven days in advance of the hearing; a moratorium with a duration of more than sixty days (and any extension of a moratorium so that the total duration is more than sixty days) requires a public hearing with the same two published notices required for other land use regulations. The initial notice of the hearing must be published at least ten but not more than twenty-five days prior to the day of the hearing, and the second notice must be published in a separate calendar week.

The moratorium must be adopted as an ordinance by the city or county. The ordinance establishing it must expressly include the following four items:

1. a clear statement of the problems or conditions necessitating the moratorium, what courses of action other than a moratorium were considered by the city or county, and why those alternatives were not deemed adequate;[21]
2. a clear statement of the development approvals subject to the moratorium and how a moratorium on those approvals will address the problems that led to its imposition;
3. an express date for termination of the moratorium and a statement setting forth why that duration is reasonably necessary to address the problems that led to its imposition;[22] and
4. a clear statement of the actions, and the schedule for those actions, proposed to be taken by the city or county during the moratorium to address the problems that led to its imposition.

---

20. S.L. 2005-426, §§ 5(a), 5(b).

21. Courts in other states have held that the fact that adoption of a moratorium was motivated by a particular development application does not make the moratorium arbitrary or unreasonable. *See, e.g.,* Pawn Am. Minn., LLC v. City of St. Louis Park, 787 N.W.2d 565 (Minn. 2010).

22. This general requirement is consistent with national case law that the permissible length of a moratorium must be reasonable and is generally considered on a case-by-case basis. *See, e.g.,* Almquist v. Town of Marshan, 308 Minn. 52, 245 N.W.2d 819 (1976) (moratorium valid if it is adopted in good faith, is not discriminatory, is of limited duration, furthers a legitimate need, and is followed by prompt action to address that need). *See also* Condor Corp. v. City of St. Paul, 912 F.2d 215 (8th Cir. 1990); Schiavone Constr. Co. v. Hackensack Meadowlands Dev. Comm'n, 98 N.J. 258, 486 A.2d 330 (1985); Simpkins v. Gaffney, 315 S.C. 26, 431 S.E.2d 592 (1993); State *ex rel.* SCA Chem. Waste Serv. v. Konigsberg, 636 S.W.2d 430 (Tenn. 1982). See SALKIN, *supra* note 9, § 35:2, for a collection of state cases assessing reasonableness of moratoria duration. *See generally* Matthew G. St. Amand & Dwight H. Merriam, *Defensible Moratoria: The Law Before and After the* Tahoe-Sierra *Decision*, 43 NAT. RESOURCES J. 703 (2004).

The statute contains several exemptions from the coverage of moratoria and limits on their use. The most significant of these is that the "permit choice" rule applies if a completed application for the development was submitted prior to the effective date of the moratorium.[23] In these instances, action of the application is suspended while the moratorium is in effect, but when permit processing resumes, the applicant has the option of having the proposed project considered under the rules in effect at the time of the application or at the time of the permit decision. A moratorium may not be applied to residential land uses if the purpose of the moratorium is to preserve the status quo while plans or ordinances are developed or updated.[24] Absent an imminent threat to public health and safety, moratoria may not be applied to projects with legally established vested rights—those with a valid outstanding building permit, an outstanding approved site-specific vesting plan, or substantial expenditures that have been made in good-faith reliance on a prior valid administrative or quasi-judicial permit or approval.[25] Moratoria do not apply to certain projects for which complete applications have been accepted by the city or county prior to the call for a public hearing[26] to adopt the moratorium. These include special use permits and preliminary or final plats. If a preliminary plat application is subsequently approved while a moratorium is in effect, that project can also proceed to final plat approval. Moratoria may not be applied to colocation of small wireless facilities.[27]

Renewal or extensions of moratoria are also limited by this statute. Extensions are prohibited unless the city or county has taken all reasonable and feasible steps to address the problems or conditions that led to imposition of the moratorium. An ordinance extending a moratorium must explicitly address this point, in addition to the four points noted above, and set forth any new facts or conditions warranting the extension.

Finally, the statute provides for expedited judicial review of moratoria. Any person aggrieved by the imposition of a moratorium may petition the court for an order enjoining its enforcement.[28] These actions are to be set for immediate hearing and are to be given priority scheduling by both trial and appellate courts. The burden is on the city or county in these challenges to show compliance with the procedural requirements of the statute regarding moratoria adoption.

Constitutional Limitations on Moratoria

Opponents of development moratoria have argued that a regulation that even temporarily precludes the possibility of development approvals constitutes an unconstitutional taking of private property without compensation.[29]

---

23. G.S. 160D-107(c). Importantly, the permit-choice rule only applies if the application was complete at the time of imposition of the moratorium. Ashe County v. Ashe County Planning Bd., 284 N.C. App. 563, 876 S.E.2d 687 (2022). See Chapter 19 for a discussion of the permit-choice rule.
24. This limit was added to the statutes in 2011 by S.L. 2011-286.
25. These vested rights are discussed in Chapter 19.
26. The statutes do not define what constitutes a "call for public hearing." It is likely the time at which the governing board authorizes staff to proceed with advertisement for the hearing or when the formal notice of hearing is otherwise initiated. Also note that the subsequently adopted permit-choice rule, discussed in Chapter 19, allows an applicant for any development approval to select the old or revised rules if the rules change after an application is submitted.
27. G.S. 160D-107(c). See Chapter 22 for more detailed discussion of state statutory limits on development regulations for wireless telecommunication facilities.
28. Courts in other states have held that adoptions of moratoria are legislative actions of local governments and must be challenged in an appropriate manner. See, e.g., Geisler v. City Council, 769 N.W.2d 162, 166 (Iowa 2009) (adoption of six-moratorium on multifamily residences in overlay district cannot be challenged through writ of certiorari).
29. See Chapter 24 for a discussion of the taking issues.

The U.S. Supreme Court has held that a temporary moratorium on development approvals is not in and of itself an unconstitutional taking. *Tahoe-Sierra Preservation Council, Inc. v. Tahoe Regional Planning Agency*[30] involved development moratoria imposed on sensitive lands adjacent to Lake Tahoe while studies, planning, and development regulations were being prepared. There were two moratoria challenged in this suit, which together prevented development in the most-sensitive portions of the Lake Tahoe watershed for thirty-two months. (Other moratoria not involved in this litigation effectively extended these moratoria to six years). The plaintiff urged the Court to hold that all moratoria, no matter how short or long, violated the constitutional prohibition on taking private property without just compensation on the rationale that no economically productive use of their property could be made during the moratorium. The Court refused to accept this reasoning. The Court held that the balancing test enumerated in *Penn Central Transportation Co. v. City of New York*[31] should be applied in virtually all cases contending that a regulation is a taking. The Court ruled that the examination of the economic impact of the moratorium could not be applied to the period of the moratorium alone, further limiting the attempt of property owners to segment property interests when making a taking analysis.[32] Consideration of "fairness and justice" is critical, and in *Tahoe-Sierra* a careful analysis of all the factors involved led to a conclusion that there was no taking. The Court noted that temporary moratoria allowed time for necessary studies, public participation, and deliberation, and that the complexity of the management issues involved with developing a complex bi-state management plan justified the moratorium at issue.[33] While noting that moratoria lasting longer than a year might well warrant special skepticism, the Court concluded that the longer period was justified in this situation.

It is legally possible, though unusual, that a moratorium can constitute an unconstitutional taking. An indefinite moratorium can constitute a taking if it deprives the landowners of all economically beneficial use of the property,[34] though it is only the extraordinary moratorium that will fall into this category. For example, in *Monks v. City of Rancho Palos Verdes*,[35] the city imposed a moratorium on construction of new homes in the vicinity of previous landslides in 1978. Plaintiffs owned lots that had been subject to the moratorium for thirty years. A California appellate court found that the moratorium removed all economically beneficial use of the property and that the facts did not support that these uses would be precluded by the state's common law of public nuisance, thus the moratorium constituted an

---

30. 535 U.S. 302 (2002). *See also* Wild River Estates, Inc. v. City of Fargo, 2005 ND 193, 705 N.W.2d 850 (twenty-one-month moratorium on building permits in floodway pending adoption of flood-hazard map not a taking).

31. 438 U.S. 104, 123–24 (1978). With this test, the courts examine a challenged regulation on a case-by-case basis to consider the character of the governmental action and the economic impact on the landowner (with a particular focus on the distinct investment-backed expectations of the owner).

32. When undertaking a taking analysis, the property as a whole, not just the regulated portion or the time period of the regulation, must be considered. Concrete Pipe & Prods. v. Constr. Laborers Pension Trust, 508 U.S. 602 (1993); Machipongo Land & Coal Co. v. Commonwealth, 569 Pa. 3, 799 A.2d 751 (2002).

33. Most prior state-court decisions reached similar results. *See, e.g.,* Tocco v. N.J. Council on Affordable Hous., 242 N.J. Super. 218, 576 A.2d 328 (App. Div. 1990) (eighteen-month moratorium while local government considered the few vacant sites in the community for potential development of affordable housing not a taking). *See also* Mont Belvieu Square, Ltd. v. City of Mont Belvieu, 27 F. Supp. 2d 935 (S.D. Tex. 1998) (six-month moratorium on all building permits except for single-family development pending decision on whether to adopt a comprehensive plan not a taking); Oblin Homes, Inc. v. Vill. of Dobbs Ferry, 935 F. Supp. 497 (E.D.N.Y. 1998) (thirteen-month moratorium not a due-process violation).

34. This categorical "total taking" test for a regulatory taking is set forth in *Lucas v. South Carolina Coastal Council*, 505 U.S. 1003, 1027 (1992).

35. 167 Cal. App. 4th 263, 84 Cal. Rptr. 3d 75 (2008).

unconstitutional taking. A moratorium imposed in order to depress or freeze property values pending potential public acquisition has been held to be an unconstitutional taking by a Florida court.[36]

While rare, other constitutional issues may arise with regard to moratoria. For example, First Amendment and parallel state constitutional rights might be implicated. In *City of Woodinville v. Northshore United Church of Christ*,[37] the city had adopted a moratorium on all temporary-use permits within its R-1 residential district. The defendant church had two years earlier sponsored a tent encampment in a city park for homeless persons (the program involved encampments that moved around the county, staying in individual locations for ninety-day periods). During this twelve-month moratorium, the church applied for a temporary-use permit to host the encampment on its property. The town denied the permit due to the moratorium. The Washington Supreme Court held that the moratorium placed a substantial burden on the church's religious freedom and thus violated the state's constitutional provision on free exercise of religion. The Sixth Circuit Court of Appeals in *Bronco's Entertainment, Ltd. v. Charter Township of Van Buren*[38] rejected a due-process and First Amendment–free-speech challenge to a six-month moratorium as applied to an adult business.

Adequate-Public-Facility Ordinances

Adequate-public-facility ordinances (AFPOs) tie development approval to the availability of essential public services. Development is not permitted at a particular site unless and until a defined level of public services is available.[39]

This requirement can be imposed in a variety of ways. One is to adopt a long-term capital-improvement program and then to sequence development approvals as the required services become available.[40] Another approach is to set a specific limit on the quantity of development approvals that will be issued in a particular time, such as a set number of housing units to be approved per year, with the permitted

36. Joint Ventures, Inc. v. Dep't of Transp., 563 So. 2d 622 (Fla. 1990). This case involved a reservation of land for future purchase. The state imposed a five-year moratorium (which could be extended an additional five years) on any development permits on a 6.5-acre tract that the Department of Transportation needed for stormwater drainage for a future highway-widening project. The court concluded this was essentially the same as deliberately attempting to depress land values in anticipation of condemnation of the property.

37. 166 Wash. 2d 633, 211 P.3d 406 (2009) (noting that the Washington constitution's protections are broader than the Free Exercise Clause of the U.S. Constitution). The Washington court has long vigorously protected religious free-exercise rights under the state constitution. *See* Munns v. Martin, 131 Wash. 2d 192, 930 P.2d 318 (1997) (invalidating fourteen-month delay imposed on conversion of historic church building to a pastoral center). See Chapter 27 for a discussion of regulation of religious land uses.

38. 421 F.3d 440 (6th Cir. 2005). See Chapter 26 for a discussion of regulation of adult businesses. *See also* Samson v. City of Bainbridge Island, 683 F.3d 1051 (9th Cir. 2012) (thirty-one-month moratorium on dock and pier construction not a due-process violation).

39. The converse of an adequate-public-facilities review is an affirmative direction of infrastructure spending in areas most suited for planned growth, such as Maryland's priority-funding areas designated under the state's 1997 Smart Growth Areas Act. MD. CODE ANN., STATE FIN. & PROC. §§ 5-7B-01 to -10. See Gerrit-Jan Knaap & John W. Frece, *Smart Growth in Maryland: Looking Forward and Looking Back*, 43 IDAHO L. REV. 445, 456–64 (2007); Rebecca Lewis et al., *Managing Growth with Priority Funding Areas: A Good Idea Whose Time Has Yet to Come*, 75 J. AM. PLAN. ASS'N 457 (2009). An advocacy group unsuccessfully challenged a highway-funding decision under this law in *1000 Friends of Md. v. Ehrlich*, 170 Md. App. 538, 907 A.2d 865 (2006). *See generally* JOHN M. DEGROVE, PLANNING POLICY AND POLITICS: SMART GROWTH AND THE STATES (2005).

40. The leading case upholding the validity of such a development timing ordinance is *Golden v. Planning Board*, 285 N.E.2d 291 (N.Y. 1972) (upholding phased-development ordinance in the Town of Ramapo). For additional background and analysis of the case and its implications for growth management, see John R. Nolon, Golden *and Its Emanations: The Surprising Origins of Smart Growth*, 35 URB. LAW. 15 (2003).

volume tied to projected increases in service availability.[41] A third approach is to require an analysis of service availability and development impacts, with development approvals allowed only where adequate public services are available and denied where the project would lead to a degradation of services.[42] These programs are widely used by local governments in many parts of the country. To date, however, they have been sparingly applied in North Carolina.[43]

The statutes grant cities and counties the authority to regulate development "to facilitate the adequate provision of transportation, water, sewerage, schools, parks, and other public requirements."[44] This provides authority to use zoning tools to implement regulatory adequate-public-facility requirements.[45]

Several North Carolina jurisdictions make adequacy of public services a criterion in rezoning and various other decisions related to project approval.[46] In *Tonter Investments, Inc. v. Pasquotank County*,[47] the plaintiffs contested a zoning-ordinance requirement that prohibited residences in an agricultural zoning district unless the lot had a minimum specified frontage on a state road and was within 1000 feet of a public water supply. The court held that such a restriction, "passed with the goal of ensuring that all new structures in Pasquotank County will have adequate access to drinking water, as well as roads that can handle traffic and emergency vehicles," clearly fit within the permissible goals of a zoning

---

41. An annual-quota program for issuance of building approvals was upheld in *Construction Industry Ass'n of Sonoma County v. City of Petaluma*, 522 F.2d 897 (9th Cir. 1975).

42. This "concurrency" requirement is mandated in Florida. FLA. STAT. ANN. § 163.3180. The requirement was amended in 2011 to make concurrency requirements for transportation, schools, parks, and recreation facilities optional, with requirements related to water, sewer, solid waste, and drainage still mandatory. For a critique of the 2011 amendments, see Kacie A. Hohnadell, Community Planning Act: The End of Meaningful Growth Management in Florida, 42 STETSON L. REV. 715 (2013). *See generally* Thomas G. Pelham, *Transportation Concurrency, Mobility Fees, and Urban Sprawl in Florida*, 43 URB. LAW. 105 (2011); Thomas G. Pelham, *From the Ramapo Plan to Florida's Statewide Concurrency System: Ramapo's Influence on Infrastructure Planning*, 35 URB. LAW. 113 (2003); S. Mark White & Elisa L. Paster, *Creating Effective Land Use Regulations through Concurrency*, 43 NAT. RESOURCES J. 753 (2003).

43. While formal APFOs are not common in North Carolina, it is common for the availability of adequate services to be a critical issue both in rezonings that would allow more intensive development and in the consideration of individual special use permits; 29 percent of municipalities and 22 percent of counties responding to a 2005 School of Government survey reported some use of adequate-public-facility requirements. DAVID W. OWENS & NATHAN BRANSCOME, AN INVENTORY OF LOCAL GOVERNMENT LAND USE ORDINANCES IN NORTH CAROLINA (UNC School of Government, Special Series No. 21, May 2006).

44. G.S. 160D-701.

45. For a discussion of the use of this regulatory approach relative to schools, see Richard Ducker, *Adequate Public Facility Criteria: Linking Growth to School Capacity*, SCH. L. BULL. (UNC School of Government, Winter 2003), at 1. See Chapter 4 for a general discussion of the scope of local authority.

46. In 1994, Currituck County adopted availability standards in its unified development ordinance for school, fire-and-rescue, law-enforcement, and other county facilities. The standards apply to large residential subdivisions, multifamily residential developments, and other uses requiring conditional or special use permits. Cabarrus County's unified development ordinance, adopted in 1998, includes standards for the same types of facilities covered by the Currituck County ordinance and applies to residential subdivisions and uses requiring conditional use permits. Cary's ordinance, also adopted in 1998, includes adequacy-of-service standards for schools and roads, and applies to all subdivisions and site-plan approvals.

47. 199 N.C. App. 579, 681 S.E.2d 536, *review denied*, 363 N.C. 663, 687 S.E.2d 296 (2009). In 2011, the General Assembly amended the county-zoning statute to restrict use of this approach. S.L. 2011-384 enacted G.S. 160D-903(b) to provide that counties may not prohibit single-family detached homes on lots greater than ten acres in size in zoning districts where more than fifty percent of the land is used for agriculture or silviculture (unless it is a commercial or industrial zoning district allowing a broad variety of commercial or industrial uses). This law also mandates a study of the extent to which counties should be able to require that lots exempt from subdivision regulation be accessible to emergency-service providers.

regulation. In *Tate Terrace Realty Investors, Inc. v. Currituck County*,[48] the court did not directly address the question of enabling authority but did uphold Currituck County's denial of a residential development because county school capacity was inadequate to serve the proposed development.

Impact Fees

Impact fees are assessments made by local governments on the owners or developers of land to recoup the capital costs for services needed to serve new development.[49] In many parts of the country, impact fees, rather than general-tax revenues, are used to finance the new roads, water, sewers, fire stations, public-safety services, parks, schools, and other public facilities that must be provided to service new development.[50]

The authority to condition regulatory authority on the adequacy of public facilities does not, however, include any implied authority to impose impact fees to address inadequate facilities.[51]

Local governments in North Carolina have authority to impose fees for a variety of "public enterprise" functions, such as the provision of water and sewer services.[52] The subdivision statute also authorizes requirements to provide land, construct facilities, and pay fees in lieu for streets; utilities; recreation, park, and open-space areas; and community-service facilities within an approved subdivision.[53] The authority to impose public-enterprise fees, however, is contingent on the actual or planned provision of services. The state supreme court, in *Quality Built Homes Inc. v. Town of Carthage*,[54] invalidated a

---

48. 127 N.C. App. 212, 488 S.E.2d 845 (1997). See also Blue Ridge Co. v. Town of Pineville, 188 N.C. App. 466, 655 S.E.2d 843, review denied, 362 N.C. 679, 669 S.E.2d 742 (2008) (inadequate evidence in record to support denial of subdivision approval due to school overcrowding).

49. Various terms are used for these fees. They are sometimes referred to as facility fees, in-lieu fees, mitigation fees, or tap fees. On impact fees generally, see ARTHUR C. NELSON, ed., DEVELOPMENT IMPACT FEES: POLICY RATIONALE, PRACTICE, THEORY AND ISSUES (1988); Brian Blaesser & Christine M. Kentopp, *Impact Fees: The "Second Generation,"* 38 WASH. U. J. URB. & CONTEMP. L. 55 (1990); Mark Fenster, *Regulating Land Use in a Constitutional Shadow: The Institutional Contexts of Exactions*, 58 HASTINGS L.J. 729 (2007); Fred Jacobsen & Jeff Redding, *Making Development Pay Its Way*, 55 N.C. L. REV. 407 (1977); Julian C. Juergensmeyer & Robert M. Blake, *Impact Fees: An Answer to Local Governments' Capital Funding Dilemma*, 9 FLA. ST. U. L. REV. 415 (1981); Arthur C. Nelson, *Development Impact Fees*, 54 J. AM. PLAN. ASS'N 3 (1988); Arthur C. Nelson, *Development Impact Fees: The Next Generation*, 26 URB. LAW. 541 (1994).

50. *See, e.g.*, CAL. GOV'T CODE §§ 66000 to 66025. For a typical application of such a statute, see *Homebuilders Ass'n of Tulare/Kings Counties, Inc. v. City of Lemoore*, 185 Cal. App. 4th 554, 112 Cal. Rptr. 3d 7 (2010). Approximately half of the states have authorized use of impact fees. They include: Arizona, California, Colorado, Georgia, Idaho, Illinois, Indiana, Maine, Maryland, Nevada, New Hampshire, New Jersey, New Mexico, Oregon, Pennsylvania, Rhode Island, Texas, Vermont, Virginia, Washington, West Virginia, and Wisconsin. Ronald H. Rosenberg, *The Changing Culture of American Land Use Regulation: Paying for Growth with Impact Fees*, 59 SMU L. REV. 177, 247 (2006). Many state courts have also held that local governments have implied authority to impose impact fees for utility services and that such fees are not a tax. *See, e.g.*, St. Clair Cnty. Home Builders Ass'n v. City of Pell City, 61 So. 3d 992 (Ala. 2010). A 2000 study found that 59 percent of cities with populations over 25,000 used impact fees. U.S. GEN. ACCOUNTING OFFICE, COMMUNITY DEVELOPMENT: LOCAL GROWTH ISSUES–FEDERAL OPPORTUNITIES AND CHALLENGES 43 (2000).

51. Also see the discussion of authority for exactions with subdivision-plat approvals in Chapter 7 and the discussion of the limitations of the Takings Clause in Chapter 24.

52. The statutory framework for how water- and sewer-impact fees, termed *system development fees*, are calculated, adopted, and assessed is set by G.S. 162A-200 to -215.

53. See the discussion of subdivision exactions in Chapter 7. Similar authority for zoning approvals is discussed in Chapter 6.

54. 369 N.C. 15, 789 S.E.2d 454 (2016). Subsequent cases applied this rationale to invalidate capacity fees charged for future system development. Daedalus, LLC v. City of Charlotte, 282 N.C. App. 452, 872 S.E.2d 105, *review denied*, 876 S.E.2d 285 (2022); Kidd Constr. Grp., LLC v. Greenville Util. Comm'n, 271 N.C. App. 392, 845 S.E.2d 797 (2020).

utility-impact fee that was assessed for water and sewer expansion at the time of subdivision approval. These fees were in addition to "tap fees" to access the systems and regular monthly charges for water and sewer customers. The impact fees were assessed regardless of the property owner's actual use of the systems or whether the town actually expanded the system. The court noted that the municipal-public-enterprise statute[55] only authorizes fees for "services furnished," omitting the "to be furnished" authorization present in the county-public-enterprise statute.[56] This same rationale was applied in *Point South Properties, LLC v. Cape Fear Public Utility Authority*,[57] when developers successfully challenged an imposition of utility-impact fees when the property involved was not served by the utility and no specific plan for service had been adopted.

In the mid-1980s, a number of North Carolina local governments secured local legislation authorizing other impact fees.[58] In the absence of specific authority to impose an impact fee, the courts have been unwilling to imply such authority.

The leading case on the scope of local government statutory authority to impose impact fees other than authorized public-enterprise fees is *Lanvale Properties, LLC v. County of Cabarrus*. The county adopted adequate-public-facility requirements as part of its subdivision ordinance and later moved the requirements to its zoning ordinance.[59] The provisions prohibited approval of residential subdivisions

55. G.S. 160A-314. Following the *Quality Built Homes* decision, the General Assembly amended the public-enterprise statute to allow "system development fees." G.S. 162A-201, effective October 1, 2017, created by S.L. 2017-138.

56. G.S. 162A-88. The court noted that the city had not secured local legislation to authorize impact fees, as several other local governments had done. For an example of local legislation authorizing a municipal fee for services to be furnished, see JVC Enterprises, LLC v. City of Concord, 376 N.C. 782, 855 S.E.2d 158 (2021). In McNeill v. Harnett County, 327 N.C. 552, 398 S.E.2d 475 (1990), the court held that counties can also enter an interlocal agreement, with a water and sewer district to operate a system on behalf of the district and then exercise the district's rights, powers, and functions in operating the system. The court subsequently held that a county "capacity use fee" to partially recover from new customers the costs of expanding capacity of the utility services were not "user fees" but were properly characterized as "impact fees" and monetary land-use exactions. Anderson Creek Partners, LP v. County of Harnett, 382 N.C. 1, 876 S.E.2d 476 (2022). See the discussion of exactions in Chapter 24.

57. 243 N.C. App. 508, 778 S.E.2d 284 (2015). The court noted a general intent to provide service at some "unspecified time in the indefinite future" is an insufficient basis to comply with the G.S. 162A-88 authorization of fees from services "furnished or to be furnished." *Id.* at 522, 778 S.E.2d at 292–93. *See also* Bill Clark Homes of Raleigh, LLC v. Town of Fuquay-Varina, 281 N.C. App. 1, 869 S.E.2d 1 (2021) (improper to dismiss claim that capacity fee was ultra vires as the allegation was that it was based on ordinance as well as a development agreement). The federal court applied this holding in a federal case involving this same claim regarding the same utility. Tommy Davis Constr., Inc. v. Cape Fear Pub. Util. Auth., 807 F.3d 62 (4th Cir. 2015).

58. These jurisdictions were most often authorized to adopt impact fees to address streets, parks, open spaces, recreational facilities, and stormwater facilities. Local variations included authority to assess fees for emergency medical facilities, fire stations, schools, cultural facilities, libraries, administration buildings, emergency shelters, and facilities for water, sewer, and solid waste. S.L. 1991-324 (Orange County amendments); S.L. 1991-660 (Dunn); S.L. 1989-430 (Knightdale); S.L. 1989-476 (Durham); S.L. 1989-502 (Wake Forest); S.L. 1989-606 (Zebulon); S.L. 1989-607 (Southern Pines); S.L. 1988-986 to -988 (Dare County municipalities amendments); S.L. 1988-996 (Rolesville); S.L. 1988-1021 (Catawba County); S.L. 1987-68 (Wendell); S.L. 1987-460 (Chatham and Orange counties, Pittsboro); S.L. 1987-514 (Raleigh); S.L. 1987-668 (Knightdale, Zebulon); S.L. 1987-705 (Hickory); S.L. 1987-801 (Cary); S.L. 1987-802 (Durham); S.L. 1986-936 (Chapel Hill, Hillsborough); S.L. 1985-357 (Carrboro); S.L. 1985-498 (Raleigh); S.L. 1985-536 (Kill Devil Hills, Kitty Hawk, Manteo, Nags Head, and Southern Shores). Only a handful (notably Raleigh, Durham, and Cary) of those authorized to do so actually used that authority. For a description of the Raleigh program for transportation-impact fees, see William R. Breazeale, *Raleigh's Facility-Fee Program*, POPULAR GOV'T, Fall 1989, at 2.

59. Lanvale Props., LLC v. Cnty. of Cabarrus, 366 N.C. 142, 731 S.E.2d 800 (2012). The plaintiff proposed a residential development on a fifty-four-acre site in the city of Locust. The county refused to issue building permits unless the plaintiff complied with adequate-public-facility requirements in the county zoning ordinance. In 2004, the county secured local legislation to allow application of the "school adequacy review" in the county subdivision ordinance in municipalities as well as the county. In 2007, the county substantially modified the

if there was inadequate school capacity for the projected development, but the proposed subdivision could be approved upon entering a consent agreement to pay a fee[60] to be used for the capital costs of providing additional school capacity.

The state supreme court held that the county lacked statutory authority under the county's zoning authority to impose a voluntary mitigation fee to remedy inadequate school capacity. The court noted that the purposes of zoning ordinances include facilitating the adequate provision of specified public facilities, including schools.[61] However, the grant of powers in the zoning statute specifies the regulations that can be used to address that legitimate purpose. These include regulating lots, setbacks, density, building size, and the use of land and buildings.[62] The school-capacity regulation adopted by the county did not fall within these authorized regulations. Rather, the court found the ordinance to be a "carefully crafted revenue generation mechanism."[63] The court further held that there was no implied authority for the provisions.[64] Similarly, the court in *China Grove 152, LLC v. Town of China Grove* held that the town had no authority under the subdivision statute to impose an impact fee to subsidize its law enforcement, fire protection, and parks.[65]

A series of earlier decisions by the court of appeals likewise found no implied authority for school impact fees. In *Durham Land Owners Ass'n v. County of Durham*, the court ruled that counties do not

---

adequate-public-facility-review process and moved the requirements to the county zoning ordinance (with a cross-reference in the subdivision ordinance). The provisions provided for a detailed process for review of school capacity to support proposed development. If available student capacity was inadequate, the provisions provided for denial of the application or imposition of conditions to mitigate impacts, including reducing density, deferring or phasing final approval until school capacity became available, or entering a consent agreement to provide needed school capacity.

60. The initial fee in 1998 was $500 per residential unit. In 2003, the fee was increased to $1008 per unit. In 2004, the county increased the fee to $4034 per single-family unit and $1331 per multifamily unit. In 2008, the fee was increased to $8617 per single-family unit with lesser amounts for townhouse and multifamily housing.

61. G.S. 160D-701.

62. G.S. 160D-702(a).

63. *Lanvale Props.*, 366 N.C. at 161, 731 S.E.2d at 814. The court held it would be inappropriate to sever the mitigation-fee provisions from the remainder of the adequate-public-facility provisions, as the entirety of the adequacy-review provisions had "little or nothing" to do with zoning. The court noted that subdivision regulations can address some aspects of provision of public facilities in the land-subdivision-approval process but held that the scope of the zoning authority is distinct from the scope of authority under subdivision ordinances.

64. The court held that the broad-construction rule of G.S. 153A-4 was not applicable, as that rule of statutory construction is only to be applied in interpretation of ambiguous statutes. The court held that here the scope of the zoning authority was not ambiguous and plainly did not include an authorization of provisions requiring developers to pay an adequate-public-facilities fee. The court further held that the local legislation secured by the county did not confer authority to adopt these provisions. It noted that the legislature had explicitly granted authority for a school impact fee to Orange and Chatham counties and had rejected a grant of explicit authority three times for Union County. Orange and Chatham counties secured local legislation authorizing school impact fees. S.L. 1987-460. Orange County's authority to impose a school impact fee was repealed in 2017. S.L. 2017-36. For a review of the Orange County experience, see Richard Ducker, *Using Impact Fees for Public Schools: The Orange County Experiment*, SCH. L. BULL. (UNC School of Government, Spring 1994), at 1. These local bills argue against interpreting this law to implicitly authorize such a fee. The court noted that the circumstances surrounding the adoption of this local bill indicated it was an effort to resolve city-county jurisdictional confusion rather than to grant the county new authority. Even if the local bill were read to confer authority for an adequacy review, the court held, this did not include "unfettered authority to enact this revenue-driven ordinance," noting the county substantially expanded the scope of the provisions subsequent to the adoption of the local bill, converting it from "a simple adequacy review process into a complex revenue generating system." *Lanvale Props.*, 366 N.C. at 167, 731 S.E.2d at 817.

65. China Grove 152, LLC v. Town of China Grove, 242 N.C. App. 1, 773 S.E.2d 566 (2015). In addition to returning the improperly collected fee, the town was required to pay interest on it under G.S. 160A-363(e).

have any implied authority to impose school impact fees.[66] The court held that the provision of schools was a general governmental obligation rather than a service provided to an individual for which a fee could be charged and that, while the authorization in G.S. 153A-102 to fix fees did allow a county to set a fee for a service provided by an employee, it did not provide authority for fees to fund a general governmental obligation such as schools. The court further found that, while permit-application and review fees were appropriate under the statutory authorization of general ordinances and zoning ordinances, that authority did not reach to fees to fund basic governmental services.[67]

The use of mandatory school impact fees is not authorized even if the fee is only an option to avoid project denial or if it is agreed to as a condition on an individual approval. In *Union Land Owners Ass'n v. County of Union*, the county adopted an adequate-public-facilities section within a land use ordinance that included a calculation of a proposed development's impact on school capacity. If the development's impact would overburden school capacity, the ordinance provided several options, including reducing the scale of the proposed development, phasing its construction to match school-construction schedules, or having the developer provide funding or construction to address the school-capacity issues. The county also adopted a resolution establishing a procedure to calculate the "voluntary mitigation payment" that the developer could pay to offset school-capacity deficiencies. The court held that the county lacked authority to adopt this ordinance under its general police power, zoning, or subdivision-regulation authority. Since the zoning and subdivision statutes directly addressed real-estate development, concluded the court, the general ordinance-making authority did not provide an independent source of authority for an adequate-public-facilities ordinance. As in *Lanvale*, the court noted that consideration of development impacts on the efficient and adequate provision of public services (including schools) was expressly within the permissible objectives of a zoning ordinance. However, local governments can only employ the tools provided in the statute to address this objective. The tools enumerated in the statute (building sizes, lot sizes, setbacks, density, land uses, etc.) were not sufficiently broad to include the tools used in this ordinance, held the court. Similarly, while the adequacy-of-facilities objectives were within those that could be addressed by a subdivision ordinance, the tools authorized there did not include a requirement for developers to address school-facility needs by payments, land donation, or school construction. Therefore, the court held that inclusion of a "voluntary mitigation payment" and other, similar measures rendered the ordinance beyond the scope of the county's delegated authority. The court found that this was an improper, indirect attempt to impose a school impact fee, which could clearly not be done directly.[68]

---

66. Durham Land Owners Ass'n v. Cnty. of Durham, 177 N.C. App. 629, 630 S.E.2d 200, *review denied*, 360 N.C. 532, 633 S.E.2d 678 (2006). Courts in other states have likewise been reluctant to imply authority for school impact fees or any implied expansion of explicitly delegated authority. *See, e.g.,* Home Builders Ass'n of Cent. Ariz. v. City of Apache Junction, 198 Ariz. 493, 11 P.3d 1032 (Ct. App. 2000); Bd. of Cnty. Comm'rs v. Bainbridge, Inc., 929 P.2d 691 (Colo. 1996).

67. *Durham Land Owners Ass'n,* 177 N.C. App. at 637, 630 S.E.2d at 205. After the plaintiffs in this case obtained a refund of school impact fees paid but received no interest on the funds that had been held in escrow by the county, G.S. 153A-324(b) and 160A-363(e) were enacted to require local governments to pay interest on illegally imposed taxes, fees, or monetary contributions not specifically authorized.

68. Union Land Owners Ass'n v. Cnty. of Union, 201 N.C. App. 374, 689 S.E.2d 504 (2009), *discretionary review denied, dismissed as moot,* 364 N.C. 442, 703 S.E.2d 148 (2010). Other states have reached a similar conclusion regarding implied authority for impact fees under state subdivision statutes. *See, e.g.,* Hylton Enters. v. Bd. of Supervisors, 220 Va. 435, 441, 258 S.E.2d 577, 581 (Va. 1979). Another decision by the N.C. court of appeals reached a similar conclusion. In *Amward Homes, Inc. v. Town of Cary,* 206 N.C. App. 38, 698 S.E.2d 404 (2010), *aff'd per curiam by evenly divided court,* 365 N.C. 305, 716 S.E.2d 849 (2011), the town adopted an adequate-public-school-facilities ordinance that required a certificate of adequate school facilities or an exemption prior to approval of large residential developments. Although the ordinance did not include an explicit school-impact-fee schedule, the mayor allegedly informed the developers that the town council would not approve the development without payment of school impact fees (this requirement was later added to the ordinance). The court of appeals held that the town had

It is important to distinguish regulatory and funding requirements when considering adequate-public-facility requirements. A city or county clearly has the authority to make the adequacy of necessary public facilities a significant factor in land use regulatory restrictions. Whether there are or will be adequate school capacity, roads, utilities, and essential public-service facilities is a lawful and legitimate consideration in rezoning decisions.[69] It can be made a decision-making standard for special use permits, subdivision-plat approvals, and other development-regulatory reviews. Assuming the local government has done appropriate planning and analysis to support the decision at issue, it has the legal authority to deny or delay development approvals that would overburden public facilities.[70] The local government cannot, however, use development regulations to require payment of impact fees to provide those services unless the particular fee involved has been expressly authorized by the General Assembly. While there may be some latitude for good-faith negotiations on public-private cost-sharing for provision of public facilities with development agreements and conditional zoning, any mandatory impact fee needs legislative authorization.

Urban-Growth Boundaries and Service Areas

An urban-growth boundary separates land that may be developed for urban purposes from land that may not.[71] A local government designs such a boundary to accommodate the urban growth projected to occur in the area during the immediate planning period. Although an urban-growth boundary may be adjusted from time to time, areas beyond the boundary are meant to remain rural or undeveloped. Such boundaries are generally intended to prevent urban sprawl, protect open space and agricultural land in rural areas, and enhance the vitality of downtowns, urban neighborhoods, and existing urban areas.

A closely related concept is the "urban service area," a geographic area within which urban governmental services are or will be provided and outside of which such services will not be extended. Urban-service areas are most often used with extensions of water and sewer services.[72] An example of the use of this

---

no authority to impose or accept school impact fees pursuant to its adequate-public-school-facilities ordinance. Since the town had established a custom of requiring these fees, the fact that this particular fee was imposed by a condition on an individual approval rather than directly by ordinance provision did not make it legal. As this decision was affirmed by an equally divided state supreme court, the decision has no precedential value. It is, however, consistent with the subsequently decided *Lanvale Properties* decision.

69. Courts nationwide generally find it appropriate for a local government to consider the availability of sewer service for all phases of a development when considering a rezoning petition. *See, e.g.*, Christmas v. Town of Smyrna, No. M2009-02580-COA-R3-CV, 2010 WL 4962900 (Tenn. Ct. App. Dec. 6, 2010).

70. In *FC Summers Walk, LLC v. Town of Davidson*, No. 3:09-CV-266-GCM, 2010 WL 4366287 (W.D.N.C. Oct. 28, 2010), the town's adequate-public-facilities ordinance set requirements for the availability of law enforcement, fire protection, and parks to support proposed development. The plaintiff developer received staff determinations that (1) services were inadequate and (2) it could wait until services were available or pay its pro rata share of the costs to advance the deficient services. The federal district court concluded that while state law was relatively settled regarding school impact fees, the state law on adequate-public-facility requirements for the public safety, and parks requirements at issue here, were important and unsettled. The court therefore abstained and remanded the case to state courts.

71. *See generally* G. Easley, Staying Inside the Lines (Am. Plan. Ass'n, Plan. Advisory Serv. Report No. 440, 1992). Definition of urban-growth boundaries has long been a key component of the mandatory-planning program in Oregon and Washington. *See* Or. Rev. Stat. § 199.410; Wash. Rev. Code Ann. § 36.70A.110(1). *See also* Steve P. Calandrillo et al., *Making "Smart Growth" Smarter*, 83 Geo. Wash. L. Rev. 829 (2015) (advocating use of urban-growth boundaries).

72. Cities and counties in North Carolina have broad authority to establish and operate utility systems to provide water and wastewater services. G.S. 153A-277; 160A-311. This includes authority to set rates and service areas. *See* Gen. Textile Printing & Processing Corp. v. City of Rocky Mount, 908 F. Supp. 1295 (1995); Town of Spring Hope v. Bissette, 305 N.C. 248, 287 S.E.2d 851 (1982). Every place of residence is required to be served by a wastewater system, be it a public utility or a private system, approved by the local health department. G.S. 130A-335.

management tool in North Carolina is the "rural buffer" established by Orange County, Carrboro, and Chapel Hill in the 1980s. These jurisdictions entered into an interlocal agreement concerning planning jurisdiction, enforcement of land-development ordinances, extension of water and sewer lines into the area by the Orange Water and Sewer Authority, and future annexation of territory.[73]

North Carolina counties and cities operating water and sewer systems within city limits take on the special obligation of a public-service corporation to provide equal service to properties within their corporate limits.[74] Once such a utility holds itself out as providing service in an area, it generally must serve all of those in the area who request it. Refusal to extend service within its boundaries must be based on a utility-related reason, such as inadequate system capacity, geographic barriers to service, or inadequate financial resources to provide additional service. It is unclear whether a local government that does take on the special utility obligation of a public-service corporation may refuse to extend service on the ground that doing so would be inconsistent with a growth-management plan. Courts elsewhere have reached mixed conclusions on this question.[75]

However, a North Carolina municipality has no obligation to furnish service outside its city limits and has broad discretionary power to determine whether and on what terms it does so.[76] A North Carolina municipality may refuse to extend water or sewer service beyond an urban service area or urban-growth boundary to the extent that such an area or boundary is located outside city limits. In *United States Cold Storage v. Town of Warsaw*,[77] the town contracted to provide water and sewer services to a facility outside of its corporate limits. The parties agreed that the town would not annex the property for at least eight years. After that period expired, the town requested that the plaintiff voluntarily annex to the town and stated that if that were not done, the town would cease to provide water and sewer services.[78] The court affirmed that the town could terminate services as the town had no legal obligation to provide water and sewer services outside its corporate limits provided it did not unfairly discriminate among similarly situated nonresidents. There was no showing of discrimination against the plaintiff, as the town made voluntary annexation a condition of provision of service to all its commercial customers who were outside the town limits.

---

73. The jurisdictions secured local legislation, as the agreement limits the powers of the three units. S.L. 1987-233. For a detailed review of the agreement, see Richard D. Ducker, *The Orange County Joint Planning Agreement*, POPULAR GOV'T, Winter 1988, at 47. Durham employs a system of "development tiers" in its development regulations, ranging from a rural tier without urban services to a downtown tier. DURHAM, N.C., UNIFIED DEVELOPMENT ORDINANCE, § 4.1.2 (2018).

74. Dale v. City of Morganton, 270 N.C. 567, 571, 155 S.E.2d 136, 141 (1967) (obligation to provide utility services to city residents without discrimination); Fulghum v. Town of Selma, 238 N.C. 100, 76 S.E.2d 368 (1953). Also, the court in *Browning-Ferris Industries of South Atlantic, Inc. v. Wake County*, 905 F. Supp. 312 (E.D.N.C. 1995), held the county's actions in refusing use of a county sewer interceptor for a project with vested rights to be arbitrary and capricious, as the concerns that formed the bases for the county's objections were outside the county's regulatory jurisdiction.

75. *Compare* Dateline Builders, Inc. v. City of Santa Rosa, 146 Cal. App. 3d 520, 194 Cal. Rptr. 258 (1983) (holding that refusal of city to provide service because project was outside growth area as designated by city-county growth-management plan was necessary and proper exercise of city's police power) *with* Robinson v. City of Boulder, 190 Colo. 357, 547 P.2d 228 (1976) (holding that city was obligated to extend service despite city's determination that development in area would conflict with city-county growth-management plan). *See also* Associated Home Builders v. Livermore, 18 Cal. 3d 582, 135 Cal. Rptr. 41, 557 P.2d 473 (1976); Smoke Rise, Inc. v. Wash. Suburban Sanitary Comm'n, 400 F. Supp. 1369 (D. Md. 1975).

76. *Fulghum*, 238 N.C. 100, 76 S.E.2d 368. *See* G.S. 160A-312.

77. 246 N.C. App. 781, 784 S.E.2d 575 (2016).

78. The contract for extension of services had no express limit on termination by either party.

Affordable Housing, Inclusionary Zoning, and Social Equity

Affordable-Housing Initiatives

One consequence of rapid development is a concomitant rise in housing prices. Although homeowners usually view this as good news, rapidly escalating housing prices make it difficult for less-affluent persons to enter the housing market. Often it is not just the poor who have difficulty finding housing: schoolteachers, firefighters, police officers, and many middle-class workers also struggle to find adequate housing in the fast-growing areas where they work.[79] So a number of cities and counties have sought means to provide more "workforce" and affordable housing in their communities.

In addition, there has been a history of discrimination against racial and ethnic minorities in past land use regulations.[80] Some local governments used zoning and development regulations to prevent low- and moderate-income housing from being located in more-affluent neighborhoods. Separating housing by race, ethnicity, and income (often referred to as "exclusionary zoning") was a goal of some early zoning schemes and the by-product of others.[81]

This has since the 1970s prompted interest in remedial action to address these inequities. The state Fair Housing Act declares that it is unlawful housing discrimination to discriminate in land use decisions or permitting based on race, color, religion, sex, national origin, handicapping condition, familial status, or the fact that a development contains affordable housing.[82] The statute does allow a dispersal requirement, if needed, to limit high concentrations of affordable housing.

---

79. The 2000 U.S. Census indicated that 21 percent of North Carolina's population lives in households that pay more than 30 percent of household income for housing (a standard definition of unaffordable housing). Also see the discussion of affordable housing in Chapter 22.

80. In *Clinard v. City of Winston-Salem*, 217 N.C. 119, 6 S.E.2d 867 (1940), the court invalidated a zoning regulation that had segregated residential zoning districts by race. The court had earlier invalidated an ordinance that prohibited a person from residing in a block where a majority of the houses were occupied by persons of a different race. State v. Darnell, 166 N.C. 300, 81 S.E. 338 (1914). For additional information on racially restrictive zoning, see Christopher Silver, *The Racial Origins of Zoning: Southern Cities from 1910–40*, 6 Plan. Perspectives 189 (1991).

81. For an overview of the issue, see Andrew H. Whittemore, *Exclusionary Zoning: Origins, Open Suburbs, and Contemporary Debates*, 87 J. Am. Plan. Ass'n 167 (2021). A substantial body of legal literature developed on exclusionary zoning and efforts to combat it. *See, e.g.*, Richard F. Babcock and Fred P. Bosselman, Exclusionary Zoning: Land Use Regulation and Housing in the 1970s (1973); Vicki Been, *City NIMBYs*, 33 J. Land Use & Envtl. L. 217 (2018); Paul Davidoff & Linda Davidoff, *Opening the Suburbs: Toward Inclusionary Land Use Controls*, 22 Syracuse L. Rev. 509 (1971); Robert C. Ellickson, *Suburban Growth Controls: An Economic and Legal Analysis*, 86 Yale L. J. 385 (1977); J.R. Kemper, *Exclusionary Zoning*, 48 A.L.R. 3d 1210 (1973); John Mangin, *The New Exclusionary Zoning*, 25 Stan. L. & Pol'y Rev. 91 (2014); Lawrence Gene Sager, *Tight Little Islands: Exclusionary Zoning, Equal Protection, and the Indigent*, 21 Stan. L. Rev. 767 (1969).

For a judicial response mandating local acceptance of a regional fair share of affordable housing, see *Southern Burlington County NAACP v. Township of Mount Laurel*, 67 N.J. 151, 336 A.2d 713 (1975), *cert. denied*, 423 U.S. 808 (1975). Also see the discussion of fair housing in Chapter 23 and racial/ethnic discrimination as regulatory objectives in Chapter 25.

82. G.S. 41A-4(g). G.S. 41A-4(f) also requires local governments to allow reasonable modifications of residences and to make reasonable accommodation where necessary to allow disabled persons' equal use and enjoyment of housing. See Chapter 23 for a discussion of "reasonable accommodation" in the context of the federal Fair Housing Act.

A variety of techniques are available to local governments to address affordable-housing concerns.[83] Zoning can allow more multifamily housing in appropriate areas.[84] Regulations that increase the cost of development can be carefully scrutinized to see whether standards might be relaxed and the development-approval process for affordable housing streamlined. A density bonus may be provided for developments that commit to providing a specified minimum amount of affordable housing.[85] Some local governments have used public funds to locate and construct not only traditional public housing but also housing for middle-income public-service workers.[86]

Some communities also use regulatory incentives for affordable housing. For example, if a specified proportion of a development will provide affordable housing, it becomes eligible for expedited permit processing or a density bonus. Other communities move beyond incentives to inclusionary-zoning mandates. Carrboro, Chapel Hill, and Davidson, for example, require that new residential developments above a certain size include a specified percentage of smaller or affordable houses.[87] Communities in other states[88] directly mandate that large residential developments include a minimum number of houses with sales prices that meet affordable-housing targets.[89]

---

83. ANITA R. BROWN-GRAHAM, AFFORDABLE HOUSING AND NORTH CAROLINA LOCAL GOVERNMENTS (2006); LOCALLY INITIATED INCLUSIONARY ZONING PROGRAMS: A GUIDE FOR LOCAL GOVERNMENTS IN NORTH CAROLINA AND BEYOND (Anita R. Brown-Graham ed., 2004); C. TYLER MULLIGAN & JAMES L. JOYCE, INCLUSIONARY ZONING: A GUIDE TO ORDINANCES AND THE LAW (UNC School of Government, 2010). For national overviews, see THE LEGAL GUIDE TO AFFORDABLE HOUSING DEVELOPMENT (Tim Iglesias & Rochelle E. Lento eds., 2d ed. 2011); James A. Kushner, *Affordable Housing as Infrastructure in the Time of Global Warming*, 43 URB. LAW. 179 (2011); Jenny Schuetz et al., *31 Flavors of Inclusionary Zoning*, 75 J. AM. PLAN. ASS'N 441 (2009).

84. Various zoning reforms have been initiated across the nation to promote additional affordable housing. Several states have mandated increased residential density, such as requiring zoning to allow duplexes or accessory dwelling units in single-family zoning districts or mandating increased residential density and decreased parking requirements along transit corridors. *See, e.g.,* CAL. GOV'T CODE § 65852.21 (mandating increased residential density); 2021 Conn. Pub. Acts No. 21-29, § 6 (mandating allowance of one accessory dwelling unit by right for any single-family home); MASS. GEN. LAWS ch. 40A, §§ 3A, 5 (2021) (local governments in specified area must allow multifamily housing in at least one zoning district; simple majority rather than two-thirds majority required to allow accessory dwelling units); S.B. 8 § 1, 81st Leg. Assemb., Reg. Sess. (Or. 2021) (allowing affordable housing on land zoned for commercial or religious assembly uses); WASH. REV. CODE ANN. § 36.70A.540 (multiple affordable-housing mandates). *See generally* DANIEL G. PAROLEK, MISSING MIDDLE HOUSING: THINKING BIG AND BUILDING SMALL TO RESPOND TO TODAY'S HOUSING CRISIS (2020); John Infranca, *The New State Zoning: Land Use Preemption Amid a Housing Crisis*, 60 B.C. L. Rev. 823 (2019); Dwight Merriam, *Affordable Housing: Three Roadblocks to Regulatory Reform*, 51 URB. LAW. 343 (2022).

85. For a review of regulatory incentives to promote affordable housing and the provision of other amenities, such as additional open space or park land, see George C. Homsy & Ki E. Kang, *Zoning Incentives: Exploring a Market-Based Land Use Planning Tool*, 89 J. AM. PLAN. ASS'N 61 (2023).

86. Several local bills authorize provision of affordable rental housing for teachers and government employees. *See, e.g.,* S.L. 2009-154 (Brevard, Rosman, and Transylvania County); S.L. 2009-161 (Edgecombe County); S.L. 2006-61 (Bertie County); S.L. 2006-86 (Hertford County); S.L. 2004-16 (Dare County).

87. For information on the Chapel Hill program, see TOWN OF CHAPEL HILL, QUESTIONS AND ANSWERS ABOUT CHAPEL HILL'S INCLUSIONARY ZONING ORDINANCE (July 2010). The town in 2000 adopted a policy in its comprehensive plan that required residential developments with rezonings to include 15 percent affordable housing. The development ordinance was amended in 2010 to require development applications with five or more housing units to provide 15 percent of the units at prices that were affordable to low- and moderate-income households (10 percent in the Town Center area). The Davidson ordinance requires new developments with eight or more housing units to include at least 12.5 percent affordable housing.

88. Two of the largest and best-known inclusionary-zoning programs are in the Washington, D.C., metropolitan area—Montgomery County, Maryland, and Fairfax County, Virginia. For a review of the issues and programs involved, see John J. Delaney, *Addressing the Workforce Housing Crisis in Maryland and Throughout the Nation: Future Housing Supply and Demand Analysis for the Greater Washington Area*, 33 U. BALT. L. REV. 153 (2004).

89. Nationally, the case law on legal challenges to affordable-housing mandates is mixed. A facial challenge to a Napa, California, requirement that 10 percent of newly constructed residential units be affordable was rejected in *Home Builders Ass'n of Northern California v. City of Napa*, 90 Cal. App. 4th 188, 108 Cal. Rptr. 2d 60 (2001). *See*

North Carolina cities and counties have the legal authority to undertake most of these initiatives. The public-investment and regulatory-incentive programs are likely permissible with existing general grants of authority, though several local governments have secured local legislation to specifically authorize use of affordable-housing bonuses.[90] How far local governments can go with regulatory mandates for affordable housing is unclear. To date, North Carolina courts have been wary of allowing land-development regulations to address socioeconomic concerns directly.[91] Still, securing adequate housing for all segments of the community and promoting geographic diversity for all segments of the housing market are legitimate governmental objectives. It may well be permissible to require development to show that it will be consistent with these broad community objectives. Also, to the extent that large new commercial, office, or industrial developments create a need for additional affordable housing, it would be constitutionally permissible to require the developers to assist in providing that housing through, for example, mandatory contributions to a housing trust fund. However, North Carolina statutes do not explicitly authorize such requirements.[92]

Employment and Other Linkage Requirements

Local governments in North Carolina have infrequently used "linkage" requirements, which tie approval of development to the provision of jobs and services for disadvantaged members of the community.[93] For example, a large commercial development might be required to employ a specified number of low-income residents during construction or as workers in the eventual business.

---

generally ALAN MALLACH, INCLUSIONARY HOUSING PROGRAMS: POLICIES AND PRACTICES (1984); David L. Callies, *Mandatory Set-Asides as Land Development Conditions*, 43 URB. LAW. 307 (2011); Barbara E. Kautz, Comment, *In Defense of Inclusionary Zoning: Successfully Creating Affordable Housing*, 36 U.S.F. L. REV. 971 (2002). Restrictions on transient occupancy to protect the stock of affordable rental units were upheld in *Cope v. City of Cannon Beach*, 317 Or. 339, 855 P.2d 1083 (1993). An inclusionary mandate was invalidated on state-constitutional grounds in *Board of Supervisors v. DeGroff Enterprises*, 214 Va. 235, 198 S.E.2d 600 (1973). Rent-control provisions have routinely been upheld in a number of states. *See, e.g.*, Kavanau v. Santa Monica Rent Control Bd., 16 Cal. 4th 761, 66 Cal. Rptr. 2d 672, 941 P.2d 851 (1997). *But see* Town of Telluride v. Lot Thirty-Four Venture, LLC, 3 P.3d 30 (Colo. 2000); Apartment Ass'n of S. Cent. Wis. v. City of Madison, 2006 WI App 192, 296 Wis. 2d 173, 722 N.W.2d 614 (requirement that 15 percent of units in new rental housing be affordable preempted state rent-control statute). North Carolina statutes prohibit local rent-control ordinances. G.S. 42-14.1.

90. S.L. 1994-588 (Winston-Salem, Forsyth County); S.L. 1991-119 (Wilmington); S.L. 1991-246 (Orange County); S.L. 1991-503 (Durham city and county).

91. For example, the court of appeals ruled that Chapel Hill could not use zoning to regulate the conversion of apartments to condominiums, holding that form of ownership was not a legitimate concern of land use regulation. Graham Court Assocs. v. Town Council of Chapel Hill, 53 N.C. App. 543, 281 S.E.2d 418 (1981). The court also invalidated a Harnett County rezoning that was based on concerns about crime (and, allegedly, on the ethnicity of potential residents of manufactured-housing parks), noting that, in zoning, it is arbitrary and capricious to consider impacts other than those on land use. Gregory v. Cnty. of Harnett, 128 N.C. App. 161, 493 S.E.2d 786 (1997).

92. Although such exactions would meet the constitutional requirement of being reasonably related to the impacts generated by the development approval, the more difficult question in North Carolina is one of statutory authority. Exactions can be required for streets, utilities, and recreational lands and for construction of "community service facilities," but provision of affordable housing may not fit any of these categories. In *Epcon Homestead, LLC v. Town of Chapel Hill*, No. 1:20CV245, 2021 WL 2138630 (M.D.N.C. May 26, 2021), the plaintiff challenged a requirement that they contribute $803,250 to an affordable-housing trust fund as a condition of approval of a special use permit for a sixty-three-unit housing development. The case was dismissed, however, for failure to file the action within the applicable three-year statute of limitations. At the time of writing, an appeal is pending at the 4th Circuit Court of Appeals.

93. These requirements are more common in other states. *See, e.g.*, Commercial Builders v. City of Sacramento, 941 F.2d 872 (9th Cir. 1991), *cert. denied*, 504 U.S. 931 (1992) (upholding housing fee to support low-income workers for permitted project); Russ Bldg. P'ship v. City & Cnty. of S.F., 199 Cal. App. 3d 1496, 246 Cal. Rptr. 21 (1987) (upholding transit fee imposed on central-city developments); Holmdel Builders Ass'n v. Twp. of Holmdel, 121 N.J.

In North Carolina it is not unusual for a developer to offer such a plan voluntarily during the development-approval process and for local governments to consider it informally as a factor in the potential community benefits of a project. However, the legality of requiring it is less clear. Although a local government may require that a developer address the impacts it is creating (for example, by helping the people who will work there secure public transportation or adequate day care), requiring that the developer provide jobs to a specified community likely goes beyond what a local government can legally mandate.

Design Standards and Form-Based Codes

Traditional Neighborhood Design

Local governments increasingly adopt regulations that facilitate (or even require) a greater mix of land uses, a more pedestrian orientation to residential and commercial areas, and a greater attention to the design of new developments.[94]

The segregation of uses in conventional zoning ordinances is a policy choice by elected officials, not a statutory mandate. A city or county can amend its development regulations to allow mixed uses, be they residential uses above commercial storefronts in existing downtowns or new developments with single-family and multifamily development interspersed with commercial and office uses arrayed in a walkable fashion.[95] Some suggest paying far less regulatory attention to where specific land uses are located and greater attention to the bulk and design of the built environment.[96]

Development regulations can be amended to permit traditional neighborhood development and to revise infrastructure requirements, such as allowing narrower streets, mandating an interconnected street layout, and providing sidewalks or alleyways.[97] Several local governments in North Carolina (including Belmont, Chapel Hill, Cornelius, and Davidson) have amended their regulations to facilitate or allow these kinds of traditional neighborhood-design features. In rural and suburban contexts, ordinances increasingly allow clustered development: the overall density of development may not be

---

550, 583 A.2d 277 (N.J. 1990) (upholding fee for low-income housing). *See generally* David A. Marcello, *Community Benefit Agreements: New Vehicle for Investment in America's Neighborhoods*, 39 Urb. Law. 657, 660–61 (2007).

94. The U.S. Green Building Council has adapted its certification program for high-performance green buildings to include a certification program for neighborhood development, the Leadership in Energy and Environmental Design for Neighborhood Developments. U.S. Green Bldg. Council, LEED Reference Guide for Green Neighborhood Development (2009). The rating system addresses project location, design, and construction.

See generally Peter Calthorpe, The Next American Metropolis: Ecology, Community, and the American Dream (1993); Peter Katz, The New Urbanism: Toward an Architecture of Community (1994); Smart Growth: Form and Consequences (Terry S. Szold & Armando Carbonell eds., 2002); Douglas R. Porter et al., The Practice of Sustainable Development (2000); Douglas R. Porter et al., Making Smart Growth Work (2002); Eric M. Braun, *Growth Management and New Urbanism: Legal Implications*, 31 Urb. Law. 817 (1999); Brian Ohm & Robert J. Sitkowski, *The Influence of New Urbanism on Local Ordinances: The Twilight of Zoning?*, 35 Urb. Law. 783 (2003); Andrés Duany & Emily Talen, *Transect Planning*, 68 J. Am. Plan. Ass'n 245 (2002); James A. Kushner, *Smart Growth, New Urbanism and Diversity: Progressive Planning Movements in America and Their Impact on Poor and Minority Ethnic Populations*, 21 UCLA J. Envtl. L. & Pol'y 45 (2003).

95. *See generally* Local Gov't Comm'n, Smart Growth Zoning Codes: A Resource Guide (2003).

96. *See, e.g.,* Andrés Duany & Emily Talen, *Making the Good Easy: The Smart Code Alternative*, 29 Fordham Urb. L.J. 1445 (2002). See the discussion of "form-based codes" below.

97. Robert J. Sitkowski, *Enabling Legislation for Traditional Neighborhood Regulations*, Land Use L. & Zoning Dig. 3 (Oct. 2001). N.C. Department of Transportation rules allow construction of narrower streets with on-street parking within subdivisions outside cities. These rules set the minimum standards for roads that are turned over to the state for maintenance. Title 19A, Chapter 2C, Sections .0201 to .0213 of the North Carolina Administrative Code.

increased, but that development is concentrated into a portion of the overall project, and other areas are retained as open space and natural areas.[98]

A national criticism of zoning is that it prohibits or inhibits the use of innovative design schemes such as traditional neighborhood development. This does not appear to be the case in North Carolina where, with the exception of municipalities with populations under 10,000, a majority of responding jurisdictions in a 2006 School of Government survey allowed traditional neighborhood-design projects.[99] These projects were particularly prevalent in more populous cities, with 88 percent of cities with populations over 25,000 allowing for such developments. Most jurisdictions that permit these tools to be used, however, retain a degree of case-by-case approval of individual projects. Most jurisdictions that allow traditional neighborhood design require a rezoning to do so.

Design Standards

Cities and counties also address the design of individual structures.[100] Initially, this was addressed as voluntary, advisory reviews. In 1971, the General Assembly authorized the creation of community appearance commissions.[101] These boards provide advisory reviews of building designs. They develop plans for landscaping, community beautification, and streetscape projects.

---

98. *See, e.g.,* RANDALL G. ARENDT, CONSERVATION DESIGN FOR SUBDIVISIONS: A PRACTICAL GUIDE TO CREATING OPEN SPACE SUBDIVISIONS (1996).

99. DAVID W. OWENS & ANDREW STEVENSON, AN OVERVIEW OF ZONING DISTRICTS, DESIGN STANDARDS, AND TRADITIONAL NEIGHBORHOOD DESIGN IN NORTH CAROLINA ZONING ORDINANCES 6 (UNC School of Government, Special Series No. 23, Oct. 2007).

100. Aesthetics is a legitimate basis for local regulation. State v. Jones, 305 N.C. 520, 290 S.E.2d 675 (1982) (upholding junkyard-screening requirement); A-S-P Assocs. v. City of Raleigh, 298 N.C. 207, 258 S.E.2d 444 (1979) (upholding historic-district regulations). For a review of the law on aesthetics as an objective of regulation prior to these cases, see H. Rutherford Turnbull, III, *Aesthetic Zoning*, 7 WAKE FOREST L. REV. 230 (1971). See Chapter 25 for a discussion of the constitutional aspects of protecting aesthetic values as a legitimate governmental objective and Chapter 22 for further discussion of historic preservation and landmarking ordinances. Local governments also use regulatory appearance codes to prevent dilapidated commercial buildings in redevelopment areas or community entranceways. For general background on the issue, see CHRISTOPHER J. DUERKSEN, AESTHETICS AND LAND-USE CONTROLS: BEYOND ECOLOGY AND ECONOMICS (Am. Plan. Ass'n, Plan. Advisory Serv. Report No. 399, 1986); MARK L. HINSHAW, DESIGN REVIEW: GUIDING BETTER DEVELOPMENT (Am. Plan. Ass'n, Plan. Advisory Serv. Report No. 454, 1995); LANE KENDIG, TOO BIG, BORING, OR UGLY: PLANNING AND DESIGN TOOLS TO COMBAT MONOTONY, THE TOO-BIG HOUSE, AND TEARDOWNS (Am. Plan. Ass'n, Plan. Advisory Serv. Report No. 528, 2004); RICHARD HEDMAN, FUNDAMENTALS OF URBAN DESIGN (1984); Douglas G. French, *Cities Without Soul: Standards for Architectural Controls with Growth Management Objectives*, 71 U. DET. MERCY L. REV. 267 (1994); James P. Karp, *The Evolving Meaning of Aesthetics in Land-Use Regulation*, 15 COLUM. J. ENVTL. L. 307 (1990); Kenneth Regan, Note, *You Can't Build That Here: The Constitutionality of Aesthetic Zoning and Architectural Review*, 58 FORDHAM L. REV. 1013 (1990); Shawn G. Rice, Comment, *Zoning Law: Architectural Appearance Ordinances and the First Amendment*, 76 MARQ. L. REV. 439 (1993); Julie A. Tappendorf, *Architectural Design Regulations: What Can a Municipality Do to Protect Against Unattractive, Inappropriate, and Just Plain Ugly Structures?*, 34 URB. LAW. 961 (2002). Courts in other states have upheld application of design standards. *See, e.g.,* State *ex rel.* Stoyanoff v. Berkeley, 458 S.W.2d 305 (Mo. 1970); State *ex rel.* Saveland Park Holding Corp. v. Wieland, 269 Wis. 262, 69 N.W.2d 217, *cert. denied*, 350 U.S. 841 (1955). A variety of nonregulatory tools are also often used to address urban-design issues. Examples include the state and federal tax credits for renovation and restoration of historic structures; the state's Main Street Program (which provides technical assistance for revitalization of small-town commercial centers); creation of municipal service districts to finance downtown revitalization; and the location and design of public facilities (such as courthouses, public-safety centers, and post offices).

101. G.S. 160D, §§ 960 to 963. For a review and assessment of the work of an early North Carolina appearance commission in its first decade of existence (having been authorized prior to the statewide general authorization), see Sidney Cohn, *Community Appearance Commissions: Chapel Hill's Experience*, POPULAR GOV'T, Winter 1975, at 15.

Local governments in North Carolina apply regulatory design standards on commercial developments and in particular areas, such as historic districts,[102] important entry corridors, particular residential neighborhoods,[103] and downtown areas.[104] A 2006 survey by the School of Government indicated that there was local government interest in regulatory design standards, usually for commercial developments and in particular areas (often through the use of overlay districts).[105] The School of Government survey indicated that the use of mandatory regulatory design standards at that time was largely confined to more-populous municipalities in North Carolina, generally those with populations over 10,000. It was less common for North Carolina ordinances to address the design of residential structures outside of historic districts, though private restrictive covenants doing so were quite common.[106] A 2012 School of Government survey indicated that 42 percent of the responding cities and counties had imposed some design standards, most often in their central business district (24 percent), commercial districts (20 percent), or highway-corridor districts (20 percent). Only 3 percent reported use in residential districts other than historic districts.[107]

The General Assembly in 2015 amended G.S. 160D-702(b) to limit use of regulatory design standards for buildings subject to the N.C. Residential Code for One- and Two-Family Dwellings.[108] The restrictions

102. G.S. 160D-940 to -950 establish a detailed framework for regulating historic districts and landmarks. *See generally* David E. Hollowell, Case Note, 16 WAKE FOREST L. REV. 495 (1980); Keith N. Morgan, *Reaffirmation of Local Initiative: North Carolina's 1979 Historic Preservation Legislation*, 11 N.C. CENT. L.J. 243 (1980); C. Thomas Ross, *Practical Aspects of Historic Preservation in North Carolina*, 12 WAKE FOREST L. REV. 9 (1976); Robert E. Stipe, *A Decade of Preservation and Preservation Law*, 11 N.C. CENT. L.J. 214 (1980); Robert E. Stipe, *Tools for Historic Preservation: Advantages and Disadvantages of Easements and Zoning*, POPULAR GOV'T, Dec. 1967, at 16. See Chapter 22 for further discussion of historic-preservation and landmarking regulations.

103. See, for example, the discussion of Raleigh's neighborhood-conservation districts in Adam Lovelady, *Broadened Notions of Historic Preservation and the Role of Neighborhood Conservation Districts*, 40 URB. LAW. 147, 161–67 (2008). Local regulations in other states prohibit homes that are either too uniform or too dissimilar from neighboring homes.

104. Design standards for central business districts have long been a concern in North Carolina for both large cities and small towns. Development plans and design proposals developed in the late 1950s and early 1960s for fourteen different cities (Ahoskie, Asheville, Chapel Hill, Charlotte, Durham, Greensboro, High Point, Laurinburg, Mooresville, Raleigh, Rockingham, Salisbury, Selma, and Winston-Salem) are summarized in Ruth L. Mace, *Downtown N.C. Scoreboard*, POPULAR GOV'T, May 1962, at 6. These early efforts often focused on public improvements (such as parking, sidewalks, landscaping, and lighting), though many also suggested standards for façade improvements, canopies, and the like. *See also* Anthony Lord, *Comfort in the City*, POPULAR GOV'T, Oct. 1962, at 6 (discussing urban-design criteria).

105. OWENS & STEVENSON, *supra* note 99, at 6–7.

106. Local regulations in other states most commonly prohibit homes that are either too uniform or too dissimilar from neighboring homes. Cases in a number of other jurisdictions have upheld design-review requirements. City of Scottsdale v. Ariz. Sign Ass'n, Inc., 115 Ariz. 233, 564 P.2d 922 (Ct. App. 1977); Novi v. City of Pacifica, 169 Cal. App. 3d 678, 215 Cal. Rptr. 439 (1985) (upholding an anti-monotony provision); Reid v. Architectural Bd. of Review, 119 Ohio App. 67, 192 N.E.2d 74 (1963); State *ex rel.* Stoyanoff v. Berkeley, 458 S.W.2d 305 (Mo. 1970) (involving denial of permit for pyramid-shaped residence in a neighborhood of traditional-style homes in an affluent St. Louis suburb); City of Santa Fe v. Gamble-Skogmo, Inc., 73 N.M. 410, 389 P.2d 13 (1964) (as applied in historic area); State *ex rel.* Saveland Park Holding Corp. v. Wieland, 269 Wis. 262, 69 N.W.2d 217 (1955) (upholding regulation prohibiting structures so at variance from neighboring structures as to cause substantial depreciation of property values). Other states are less accepting of these requirements and have invalidated similar design-review requirements. R.S.T. Builders, Inc. v. Vill. of Bolingbrook, 141 Ill. App. 41, 489 N.E.2d 1151 (1986); City of W. Palm Beach v. State *ex rel.* Duffey, 158 Fla. 863, 30 So. 2d 491 (1947); Bd. of Supervisors of James City Cnty. v. Rowe, 216 Va. 128, 145, 216 S.E.2d 199, 212–13 (1975).

107. David W. Owens & Dayne Batten, *2012 Zoning Survey Report: Zoning Adoption, Administration, and Provisions for Design Standards and Alternative Energy Facilities*, PLAN. & ZONING L. BULL. No. 20 (UNC School of Government, 2012), at 14–20.

108. S.L. 2015-86.

do not apply to multifamily housing or nonresidential buildings such as commercial, institutional, or industrial buildings. The restrictions on design standards do not apply to private restrictive covenants, only to government regulation.

The restrictions on design standards apply to any regulation of "building design elements." These cannot be regulated directly or indirectly through a plan-consistency review. The prohibition covers:

1. exterior building color;
2. type or style of exterior cladding material;
3. style or materials of roofs or porches;
4. exterior, nonstructural architectural ornamentation;
5. location or architectural styling of windows and doors, including garage doors;
6. location of rooms; and
7. interior layout of rooms.

There are several items that are explicitly listed as not being "building design elements" and which can still be regulated. These are:

1. a structure's height, bulk, orientation on a lot, or location on a lot;
2. the use of buffering or screening to minimize visual impacts, mitigate impacts of light or noise, or protect the privacy of neighbors; and
3. permitted uses of land or structures subject to the Residential Code for One- and Two-Family Dwellings.

The statute provides several exceptions to the prohibition of residential-design regulations. Design standards that are voluntarily consented to by the owners of all the property may be applied if they are imposed as "part of and in the course of" seeking a zoning amendment or the approval of a zoning, subdivision, or other development regulation.[109] Design standards developed and agreed to by the owners of all affected property can be incorporated into conditional zoning, special use permits, or development agreements. There are other specific exceptions to the prohibition listed in the law. Residential-building-design elements can also be regulated in these circumstances:

1. in designated, local historic districts;
2. in historic districts on the National Register;
3. for designated local, state, or national landmarks;
4. for elements directly and substantially related to safety codes;
5. for manufactured housing; and
6. for elements adopted as a condition of participation in the flood-insurance program.

Care must be exercised against the use of design restrictions as backdoor economic protectionism. The Commerce Clause prohibits regulatory measures designed to benefit in-state commerce by burdening out-of-state competitors.[110] If a regulation directly regulates or discriminates against interstate commerce or has the effect of favoring in-state commerce, the regulation is invalid unless it advances a legitimate local purpose that cannot reasonably be served by nondiscriminatory alternatives. The burden is on the regulating local government to justify imposition of a regulation with discriminating effects.[111] Such regulations are very difficult to justify and are almost always held to be invalid. On the other hand, if the effects on interstate commerce are only indirect, the test is whether the regulation

---

109. G.S. 160D-702(b).
110. New Energy Co. of Ind. v. Limbach, 486 U.S. 269, 273 (1988).
111. Hunt v. Washington State Apple Advert. Comm'n, 432 U.S. 333, 350 (1977).

advances a legitimate local interest and whether the burden on interstate commerce clearly exceeds the local benefit.[112] Some local regulations designed to prevent "formula" design by national retailers have been invalidated as violative of the Commerce Clause.[113]

New development in existing neighborhoods sometimes leads to the call for detailed design review to assure compatibility of old and new land uses. This concern about design standards arises in a variety of contexts. Some communities want to allow carefully designed manufactured-housing units or small multifamily buildings on vacant urban lots in existing residential neighborhoods. Others want to allow basement or garage apartments as accessory uses within single-family zoning districts. Still other communities have discussed neighborhood-conservation zoning districts that allow infill while protecting an older neighborhood's character.[114] These steps sometimes require amending the list of permitted uses in zoning ordinances, adjusting setbacks or density limits to make new construction feasible on small lots, and consideration of aesthetic standards that maintain the character of the neighborhood.

Form-Based Codes

A number of communities have considered reform of their development regulations to focus on physical design features—particularly the dimensions and locations of buildings and streets—rather than on the land uses, as is done with traditional zoning.[115] These "form-based" codes typically address the form and mass of buildings and the scale and types of streets and blocks. Building heights, building placement, the design of building fronts, and the relation of buildings to streets, sidewalks, and public

---

112. Brown-Forman Distillers Corp. v. N.Y. State Liquor Auth., 476 U.S. 573, 578–79 (1986). *See also* United Haulers Ass'n, Inc. v. Oneida-Herkimer Solid Waste Mgmt. Auth., 550 U.S. 330 (2007) (applying rule to uphold landfill flow control requiring delivery to publicly owned facility).

113. *See, e.g.*, Island Silver & Spice, Inc. v. Islamorada, 542 F.3d 844 (11th Cir. 2008). The ordinance at issue prohibited "formula restaurants" and limited the square footage of "formula retail" establishments. "Formula" establishments were defined as those with standardized architecture, layout, merchandise, logos, and the like. The ordinance precluded the plaintiff from selling the site of a mixed-retail store to the Walgreens chain. The offered rationale was protection of the town's unique small-town scale and reducing traffic. The court noted that while these may be legitimate goals, there was no evidence that those unique small-town characteristics actually existed or that the ordinance would further them if they did.

114. For example, the Raleigh zoning ordinance allows use of a neighborhood-conservation overlay district in neighborhoods that are at least 75 percent developed, comprise at least 15 acres, and have a distinctive character. A neighborhood plan is prepared and new development must be consistent with that plan. Raleigh Unified Development Ordinance, § 5.4.3 (2018). Most districts set specific minimum lot sizes; minimum street frontages; front-, side-, and rear-yard setbacks; and building-height limits. Additional standards included in some districts address off-street parking, building-entrance location, driveway location, and building separations. As of 2018, nineteen such overlay districts have been designated.

115. *See* CONGRESS FOR THE NEW URBANISM, CODIFYING NEW URBANISM: HOW TO REFORM MUNICIPAL LAND DEVELOPMENT REGULATIONS (Am. Plan. Ass'n, Advisory Serv. Report No. 526, 2004); CHAD D. EMERSON, THE SMARTCODE SOLUTION TO SPRAWL (2007); DANIEL G. PAROLEK ET AL., FORM-BASED CODES: A GUIDE FOR PLANNERS, URBAN DESIGNERS, MUNICIPALITIES, AND DEVELOPERS (2008); Andrew Bauman, *Legally Enabling a Modern-Day Mayberry: A Legal Analysis of Form-Based Zoning Codes*, 50 URB. LAW. 41 (2019); Andrés Duany & Emily Talen, *supra* note 96; Duany & Talen, *supra* note 94; Robert J. Sitkowski & Brian W. Ohm, *Form-Based Land Development Regulations*, 38 URB. LAW. 163 (2006); Emily Talen, *Design by the Rules: The Historical Underpinnings of Form-Based Codes*, 75 J. AM. PLAN. ASS'N 144 (2009).

In North Carolina, Davidson has adopted a variation of a form-based code. Asheville, Chapel Hill, Raleigh, and other jurisdictions have incorporated form-based districts into their ordinances. In a 2018 survey by the School of Government, nearly 30 percent of North Carolina cities and counties reported some use of a form-based code. David W. Owens, *2018 Survey Report: Adoption and Administration of Local Development Regulations, Conditional Zoning, and Subdivision Administration*, PLAN. AND ZONING L. BULL. No. 30 (UNC School of Government, Dec. 2020), at 6–7.

Richard D. Ducker, land use law professor
at the Institute of Government, now the
School of Government (1977–2015).

open space become the focus of the regulation, as opposed to the focus on the use of land and buildings that is typical of traditional zoning regulation. It is common for some elements of a form-based code to be incorporated within a more traditional use-based zoning code.

G.S. 160D-703(a)(3) explicitly allows use of form-based zoning districts.[116] Most aspects of a form-based code are within the expressly authorized portions of delegated local government regulatory authority. The zoning-enabling statute specifically authorizes regulation of the height and size of buildings, the location of buildings and structures, and the size of open spaces. Several states have provided specific statutory authorization for form-based codes or "traditional neighborhood design" regulation.[117]

The foundation of these codes is generally a regulating plan that is based on community preferences for the physical form in which development will take place. They are often developed for a discrete geographic area, such as a downtown or a particular neighborhood. They frequently include standards for the form of buildings on a particular parcel or block as well as street-design standards. Some include more-detailed architectural standards to regulate building styles, features, details, and building materials. The use of graphics and architectural-design guidelines are another common feature of form-based codes.

It is also possible to incorporate elements of a form-based code into a more traditional zoning ordinance. An example would be establishing form-based regulations for a particular area, such as a central business district, where there is an interest in both the form and design of structures and the uses to which they are put (for example, including a requirement for ground-floor commercial use as well as design standards).

---

116. This provision was added by S.L. 2019-111.

117. Cal. Gov't Code § 65302.4; Wis. Stat. Ann. § 66.1027 (provisions regarding traditional neighborhood developments and conservation subdivisions). The California authorization provides:

> The text and diagrams in the land use element that address the location and extent of land uses, and the zoning ordinances that implement these provisions, may also express community intentions regarding urban form and design. These expressions may differentiate neighborhoods, districts, and corridors, provide for a mixture of land uses and housing types within each, and provide specific measures for regulating relationships between buildings, and between buildings and outdoor public areas, including streets.

See also Ajay Garde, Sustainable by Design? Insights from U.S. LEED-ND Pilot Projects, 75 J. Am. Plan. Ass'n 424 (2009) (reviewing the U.S. Green Building Council's early experience with neighborhood-development standards to certify sustainable neighborhoods).

CHAPTER 10

Environmental Regulations

A number of regulations address the environmental impacts of land development. Many of these regulatory programs are adopted and implemented by the federal and state government, but local governments play an increasingly significant role in this area. The local role may be in enforcing programs initiated by the state or federal government,[1] while other programs are the product of increased local interest in these matters.[2] These provisions may be integrated into a zoning or unified development ordinance,[3] or each may be adopted as a separate ordinance.

The regulations below are discussed in three groups of topics: (1) those related to protection of water quality, (2) those related to protection of coastal resources and wetlands, and (3) brief summaries of miscellaneous other programs.

Water-Quality Protection

Stormwater Controls

The federal Clean Water Act establishes requirements for regulation of harmful discharges to water bodies. North Carolina was delegated permitting authority for the Act's National Pollutant Discharge Elimination System (NPDES) in 1975. The NPDES program is administered by the Division of Water

---

1. There are increasing land use implications from traditional environmental laws. For example, the Clean Air Act requires enhanced planning as to air quality, land use, and transportation in areas that fail to meet air-quality standards. 42 U.S.C. § 7506(c). Likewise, the Clean Water Act requires attention to nonpoint sources of water pollution, such as urban stormwater runoff, that have a strong land use–regulation component. 33 U.S.C. § 1342(p). The Endangered Species Act, 16 U.S.C. §§ 1531–1544, has a significant impact if development is proposed that affects the critical habitats of threatened or endangered wildlife or plant species. *See* Babbitt v. Sweet Home Chapter of Communities for a Great Or., 515 U.S. 687 (1995).

2. *See generally* Philip Berke & Maria Manta-Conroy, *Are We Planning for Sustainable Development? An Evaluation of 30 Comprehensive Plans*, 66 J. Am. Plan. Ass'n 21 (2000); John C. Dernbach & Scott Bernstein, *Pursuing Sustainable Communities: Looking Back, Looking Forward*, 35 Urb. Law. 495 (2003); Amanda Siek, Comment, *Smart Cities: A Detailed Look at Land Use Planning Techniques That Are Aimed at Promoting Both Energy and Environmental Conservation*, 7 Alb. L. Envtl. Outlook J. 45 (2002). For general background on state environmental laws in North Carolina, see Milton S. Heath, Jr. & Alex L. Hess, III, *The Evolution of Modern North Carolina Environmental and Conservation Policy Legislation*, 29 Campbell L. Rev. 535 (2007); Milton S. Heath, Jr. & Alex L. Hess, III, *The Governors' Leadership Role in Developing Modern North Carolina Environmental Law: 1967–1983*, 84 N.C. L. Rev. 2031 (2006).

3. See Chapter 22 for a discussion of additional state statutory limitations on local land use regulations, some of which have an environmental component (e.g., density bonuses for developments with energy conservation and limits on regulation of solar collectors). While not common, some early zoning ordinances included provisions to protect natural resources. *See, e.g.*, De Mars v. Zoning Comm'n, 115 A.2d 653 (Conn. 1955) (use of large lot sizes to protect drinking water).

Resources in the Department of Environmental Quality (DEQ). This permitting program applies to both point sources (such as industrial discharges) and nonpoint sources (such as urban stormwater runoff).[4]

In response to state[5] and federal requirements,[6] in the 1990s North Carolina local governments were required to adopt comprehensive stormwater-management programs. These mandated stormwater-control programs include both structural stormwater controls and management measures such as education and used-oil-recycling programs. These programs are designed to manage both the quality and quantity of stormwater runoff.

Phase I of the stormwater-permitting program in 1990 required adoption of comprehensive stormwater-management programs in municipalities with populations over 100,000. Six large municipalities in the state were required to adopt stormwater-management programs as Phase I communities.[7] Phase II of this program[8] extended the requirement for local stormwater-management programs in 2007 to smaller municipalities and counties in urbanized areas.[9] The minimum standards for development

---

4. The federal provisions were initially established by the Water Pollution Control Act in 1948. Pub. L. 80-845. The Water Quality Improvement Act of 1970, Pub. L. 91-224, added a requirement that applicants for federal permits or licenses must provide a state certification that proposed discharges into navigable waters would not violate applicable water-quality standards (33 U.S.C. § 1341). The federal Water Pollution Control Act Amendments of 1972, Pub. L. 92-500, established the basic regulatory framework that is still in place. Section 402 of the 1972 amendments established the NPDES for discharge permits (33 U.S.C. § 1342), and Section 404 authorized the Corps of Engineers to issue permits for the discharge of dredged or fill material into navigable waters (33 U.S.C. § 1344). The Clean Water Act of 1977, Pub. L. 95-217, added requirements for a "Best Management Practices" program as part of state programs (33 U.S.C. § 1288), general permit authority and exemptions for federal wetland-fill permits, and incentives for permit streamlining. The Water Quality Act of 1987, Pub. L. 100-4, made numerous program refinements, adding the stormwater provisions noted below, cleanup of toxic wastes, and programs for estuaries of national significance, the Chesapeake Bay, and the Great Lakes. The Clean Water Act requires nonpoint source discharges to be regulated by the states. 33 U.S.C. § 1329.

5. Chapter 143, Section 214.7 of the North Carolina General Statutes (hereinafter G.S.) directs the Environmental Management Commission (EMC) to phase in stormwater-runoff rules and to develop model stormwater-management programs to be implemented by state agencies and local governments. The stormwater rules are at Title 15A, Chapter 2H, Sections 1001–1013 of the North Carolina Administrative Code (hereinafter N.C.A.C.). The EMC's initial rules applied to activities in the twenty coastal counties that require a major-development permit under the Coastal Area Management Act or a sedimentation-and-erosion-control plan if the site drains to a water classified as an *outstanding-resource water*, as well as to those areas within a half-mile of waters classified as *high-quality waters*. 15A N.C.A.C. 2H, § .1003(b). Rules for the water-supply-watershed-protection program also address stormwater management.

6. 33 U.S.C. § 1342(p). The requirements to address stormwater were added to the federal statutes in 1987 (expanding the NPDES-permit program to include industrial stormwater and municipal-separate-storm-sewer systems, often referred to as "MS4s"). Water Quality Act of 1987, Pub. L. No. 100-4 (1987). Regulations are at 40 C.F.R. §§ 122.21, 122.26, 122.28, 122.30–.37, 122.41, 122.65, 123.25, 123.35, 124.52. In some forty-six states, including North Carolina, implementation of the federal regulatory requirement is delegated to the state government.

7. 40 C.F.R. § 122.26(d). North Carolina's rules for Phase I stormwater permitting are at 15A N.C.A.C. 2H, § .0126. The jurisdictions covered by the Phase I program include Charlotte, Raleigh, Durham, Greensboro, Winston-Salem, and Fayetteville–Cumberland County. Phase I generally provides for individual permits for affected jurisdictions, while Phase II provides for general permits that include all jurisdictions meeting specified standards.

8. 40 C.F.R. §§ 122.32–.36. The state rule-making process for Phase II stormwater-management standards was lengthy and highly contested. Temporary rules were proposed in November 2002 and the initial permanent rules first adopted by the Environmental Management Commission in July 2003. However, the Rules Review Commission—and ultimately the legislature—intervened. S.L. 2004-163 was enacted to provide guidelines to be used by the Environmental Management Commission in program design. This act was later replaced by S.L. 2006-246.

9. Phase II requirements affect some 123 municipalities (including their extraterritorial areas), all of 26 counties, and portions of 19 others.

regulations under this program set maximum impervious-surface coverage on lots,[10] minimum vegetated buffers adjacent to waterways,[11] and standards for engineered stormwater-control systems.[12] The requirement for local adoption of management programs was phased in over the 2007–2011 period.[13]

North Carolina has specialized stormwater requirements for the state's coastal area. The management standards differ based on the categorization of the adjacent water body, with separate rules for (1) lands within 575 feet of outstanding-resource waters (ORWs), (2) lands within one-half mile of and draining into waters with an "SA" classification, and (3) other development in coastal counties. The rules limit the amount of impervious-surface coverage, require vegetated buffers adjacent to some waters, allow engineered solutions with some high-density options, set standards for structural stormwater controls, and provide for vesting of some previously approved projects. Coastal jurisdictions generally are to comply with these rules rather than Phase II stormwater requirements.[14]

The state has also developed an optional universal stormwater program that is an alternative to the multiple programs applicable to different portions of the state.[15] This program allows local governments to adopt ordinances that meet or exceed state minimum standards. Once approved by the Environmental Management Commission (EMC), these ordinances replace the state rules for sixteen specified stormwater-control programs.[16]

Of the six municipalities required to implement stormwater-management programs in Phase I of these requirements, five (Charlotte, Greensboro, Winston-Salem, Durham, and Fayetteville) treated

---

10. The general standard for "low density" construction in noncoastal counties is a maximum of 24 percent impervious-surface coverage for projects disturbing an acre or more. In coastal counties this standard is 12 percent impervious-surface coverage for projects within a half-mile of and draining into shellfish-resource waters, and 24 percent for projects within a half-mile of and draining into other waters. For engineered stormwater-controls for high-density projects, the standards generally require control and treatment of the rain expected over a twenty-four-hour period for the one-year storm event (or in some instances, 1.5 inches of rainfall). S.L. 2006-246, § 9(c).

11. The general standard is that built-upon areas must be set back thirty feet from all perennial and intermittent surface waters.

12. G.S. 143-214.7(b4) requires an annual certification that permitted projects conform to permit conditions. This provision was added to the statutes by S.L. 2021-158.

13. The law includes an exclusion for projects that had established vested rights prior to July 1, 2007. There is also an exclusion for redevelopment that does not increase the net amount of built-upon area and that provides equal or better stormwater control than the existing development.

14. In 2008, the General Assembly disapproved the coastal stormwater rules adopted by the Environmental Management Commission and replaced those rules with the standards set out in S.L. 2008-211. The state has also imposed specific stormwater rules on surface-parking lots in areas not subject to other stormwater-management regulations (including rules applicable to water-supply watersheds, high-quality waters, ORWs, nutrient-sensitive waters in the Neuse and Tar-Pamlico basins, the Randleman Lake watershed, and areas subject to Phase II or coastal-county stormwater rules). The requirement applies to parking areas that have land-disturbing activities (as defined by the Sedimentation Pollution Control Act) of an acre or more. G.S. 113A-71(a) provides two options for these parking areas: (1) that the parking area contain no more than 80 percent impervious surface; or (2) that the stormwater runoff generated by the first two inches of rain that falls on at least 20 percent of the parking area flow to an appropriately sized bioretention area. The bioretention area must meet standards to be set by the DEQ. Compliance with these requirements is also made a precondition for building permits for these projects.

15. The rules for the Universal Stormwater Management Program are at 15A N.C.A.C. 02H, § .1020. The Division of Water Resources has promulgated a model ordinance for this program. The general standard for noncoastal counties is to control and treat runoff from residential areas with an acre of land disturbance (one-half acre for nonresidential development) for the first inch of rain, with a 36 percent impervious-surface limit in water-supply-watershed critical areas and a thirty-foot undisturbed buffer from waters (and a location outside the 100-year floodplain). In coastal counties, the threshold for coverage is 10,000 square feet of land disturbance, and the standards include a setback of thirty feet from surface waters, control and treatment of the first 1.5 inches of rainfall, and a 36 percent impervious-surface limit for new development in areas within 575 feet of shellfishing waters.

16. The sixteen programs include the water-supply-watershed rules, the rules for high-quality and outstanding-resource waters, the Phase II stormwater rules, and the Catawba and Randleman Lake rules.

the program as a utility and imposed utility fees to cover program costs.[17] Several churches sued Durham, contending the city had no authority to charge utility fees for these programs. (As nonprofit organizations, the churches were exempt from property taxes but had to pay utility fees.) In *Smith Chapel Baptist Church v. City of Durham* (*Smith Chapel I*),[18] the North Carolina Supreme Court initially upheld the city's authority to impose these fees to operate its entire stormwater program. The court held that while the public-enterprise statutes did not give the city authority to impose the fees, the authority could be based on the state constitutional provision establishing protection of the environment as a proper function of local governments,[19] with cities having implied supplementary power to impose reasonable fees for program implementation.[20] After rehearing, the court issued a new opinion that superseded this initial opinion.[21] In its second decision, the court held that the language of Chapter 160A, Section 314(a1) of the North Carolina General Statutes (hereinafter G.S.) "clearly and unambiguously"[22] provided that city stormwater-utility fees are limited to the costs of constructing and operating the physical aspects of stormwater and drainage systems rather than the full cost of maintaining a comprehensive stormwater-quality-management program. The court refused to apply the rule of broad construction, reasoning that where there was no ambiguity in the statute, the plain-meaning rule applied and there was no need for the court to resort to an interpretation, strict or broad. Upon reconvening after the second *Smith Chapel* decision, the legislature emphatically said that it had intended to allow cities to use either utility fees or tax revenues to finance these programs.[23]

Local governments incorporate stormwater-management programs that meet or exceed state standards into their local ordinances. The regulatory provisions related to stormwater are often made a part of local zoning ordinances, subdivision ordinances, or unified development ordinances, though they are sometimes independent ordinances. In *Cary Creek Ltd. Partnership v. Town of Cary*,[24] the town's development ordinance contained stormwater-management standards that included 100-foot riparian buffers adjacent to perennial and intermittent streams identified on United States Geological Survey maps and 50-foot buffers adjacent to other surface waters. The court held that the town's buffer requirements were not preempted by state watershed-protection statutes, as G.S. 143-214.5 provided for a cooperative state-local management program and explicitly allowed local governments to adopt more stringent standards than the state-mandated minimum standards.

---

17. The sixth city, Raleigh, initially elected to use local tax revenues to pay for its program. Raleigh also subsequently used stormwater fees to finance its program.

18. 348 N.C. 632, 502 S.E.2d 364 (1998).

19. N.C. Const. art. XIV, § 5.

20. "When a city has the power to regulate activities, it has a supplementary power reasonably necessary to carry that program into effect." *Smith Chapel I*, 348 N.C. at 636, 502 S.E.2d at 367.

21. Smith Chapel Baptist Church v. City of Durham (*Smith Chapel II*), 350 N.C. 805, 517 S.E.2d 874 (1999). Given an election between the first and second opinions, the court was reconstituted with a different ideological and partisan balance prior to the rehearing.

22. *Id.* at 812, 517 S.E.2d at 879. In dissent, Justice Frye contended that the court was taking an "unduly narrow view of the City's authority." He noted that Dillon's Rule was defunct and argued that under a rule of broad construction, a stormwater "system" could include these ancillary functions as reasonably necessary or expedient aspects of the explicitly authorized system. *Id.* at 819–20, 517 S.E.2d at 883–84.

23. S.L. 2000-70 revised G.S. 153A-277 (counties), 160A-314(a1) (cities), and 162A-9 (utility districts) to explicitly provide that stormwater-management systems that can be funded through use of utility fees include "any cost necessary to assure that all aspects of stormwater quality and quantity are managed in accordance with federal and State law, regulations, and rules." The changes in the city and county statute were made effective retroactively to July 15, 1989, the date of original adoption of this authority.

24. 203 N.C. App. 99, 690 S.E.2d 549, *review denied*, 364 N.C. 600, 703 S.E.2d 441 (2010).

Basin-Wide Strategies, Nutrient Reduction, and Riparian Buffers

The state has been working toward the development of a comprehensive nutrient strategy for Jordan Lake, similar to the strategies and rules that have been put into place for the Neuse and Tar-Pamlico basins.[25] After several years of studies and informal discussions, the formal rule-making process to establish the "Jordan Lake Rules" was initiated in 2007. This led to the EMC's adoption of thirteen Jordan Lake–watershed rules in 2008 that set nitrogen- and phosphorus-reduction goals for each of the three arms of the lake.[26] These rules affect eight counties and twenty-six municipalities in this watershed. They address agriculture, stormwater management for new development, protection of riparian buffers, wastewater discharges, stormwater from state and federal entities (including the N.C. Department of Transportation), fertilizer management, and options for offsetting nutrient reductions. These rules included standards for nutrient reductions from existing development, a necessary step given the significant contributions of pollutants from this source in the Jordan Lake watershed.[27]

Rules for the Falls Lake and Upper Neuse River Basin watershed have also been under development and discussion for some time.[28]

G.S. 143-214.23A prohibits cities and counties from enacting or enforcing a riparian setback that exceeds setbacks necessary to comply with state or federal requirements.[29] In other instances, a local government may petition the EMC for permission to enact a riparian buffer more stringent than state requirements. The local request must include scientific studies that support the necessity for more-stringent buffers. Cities and counties are also directed not to treat riparian buffers as if they were public property unless they have required an easement or other property right. Privately owned land within buffer areas may be used by the owner to satisfy development regulations.

---

25. 15A N.C.A.C. 2B, §§ .0232–.0242 set rules for stormwater-management standards for certain local governments in the Neuse River basin; 15A N.C.A.C. 2B, §§ .0229 and .0255–.0261 do so for the Tar-Pamlico River basin; and 15A N.C.A.C. 2B, §§ .0243–.0244 do so for portions of the Catawba River basin. Section 17 of S.L. 2011-394 required the riparian-buffer rules in the Neuse and Tar-Pamlico basin to allow placement of single-family residences on lots of two acres or less that were existing on August 1, 2000, provided the residence was at least thirty feet from the water and no part of a septic tank system was located within the buffer.

26. 15A N.C.A.C. 2B, §§ .0262–.0273. S.L. 2013-395 delayed implementation of the Jordan Lake rules until July 1, 2016. The rules were further delayed until October 15, 2019, by S.L. 2016-94 (and this section delayed the Falls Lake rules until October 15, 2022). It also provided that impervious surfaces added within the Jordan Lake watershed between July 26, 2013, and December 31, 2020, should not be counted as built-upon areas for the purposes of calculating a city's or county's nutrient-loading targets under stormwater rules and that cities and counties are not to enforce any ordinance, condition, or contractual obligation imposed under stormwater rules for nutrient-loading targets for the Jordan Lake watershed.

27. In 2009, the legislature adopted two bills that adjusted some of these rules. S.L. 2009-216; S.L. 2009-484. These laws replaced the EMC's rule on existing development with legislatively adopted standards. All local governments were to submit Stage 1 adaptive-management programs by the end of 2009. More stringent Stage 2 programs would be required in 2014 and 2017, if needed, based on water-quality monitoring, with further measures potentially required in 2023. The laws also created a Nutrient Sensitive Waters Scientific Advisory Board. Section 14 of S.L. 2011-394 extended the deadline for some nitrogen dischargers' compliance from 2016 to 2018.

28. S.L. 2009-486 directed the EMC to develop a nutrient-management strategy for this area by January 15, 2011, with implementation to be mandated no later than thirty months after the rules became effective. The EMC was also directed to provide credits to local governments and landowners for early implementation of nutrient- and sedimentation-reduction policies and practices. The law included adjustments to compensatory mitigation and sedimentation standards for water-supply watersheds.

29. An exception is made for local ordinances adopted prior to August 1, 1997, if the ordinance includes findings that it was enacted for specified purposes beyond protection of water quality and preventing excess nutrient runoff. These specified purposes include protecting aesthetics, fish and wildlife habitat and recreational uses, or natural shorelines to minimize erosion or chemical pollution. This statutory provision was created by S.L. 2015-246.

Figure 10.1 Water-Supply Watersheds

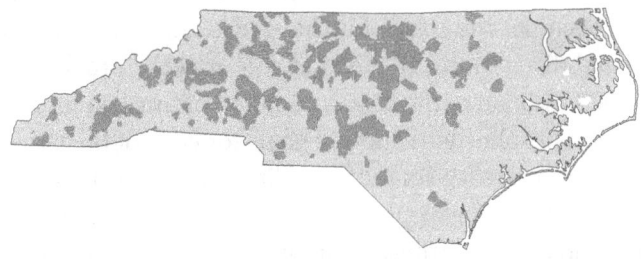

Water-Supply Watersheds

In 1989, the legislature mandated that local governments whose jurisdictions contained surface water used for public water supplies adopt minimum land use regulations to prevent harmful runoff and thereby protect the quality of those waters.[30] This law affects a substantial portion of North Carolina, as some 20 percent of the state's land area is in a water-supply watershed (see Figure 10.1). Over 250 local jurisdictions were required to adopt watershed-protection regulations, either as part of a zoning ordinance or as a separate ordinance.

The EMC classifies the state's watersheds (which establishes the level of protection that is required), sets the minimum standards for local ordinances,[31] and reviews and must approve each ordinance and any significant amendments.

The local regulations must limit certain land uses near these bodies of water (such as landfills or the storage of hazardous materials) and require density limits on development that drains into them. Density limits take the form of minimum lot sizes for residential construction and restrictions on the portion of a lot that can be used for commercial and industrial development. The statute allows the density limits to be exceeded for the redevelopment of lots with previous nonresidential development if the landowner voluntarily agrees to treat the stormwater.[32] The state rules allow local governments to adopt a "high density" option that permits more intensive development if the developer takes measures to control runoff, such as installing a pond to collect rainwater.

The validity of the watershed-protection statute was upheld in *Town of Spruce Pine v. Avery County.*[33] The court there held that legislative standards for implementing the watershed-protection program need be only as specific as circumstances permit and that procedural safeguards can be used to assure adherence to legislative standards in cases where precise standards are not feasible. The court viewed

---

30. S.L. 1989-426, codified at G.S. 143-214.5. *See* DAVID H. MOREAU et al., NORTH CAROLINA'S WATER SUPPLY WATERSHED PROTECTION ACT: HISTORY AND ECONOMIC AND LAND USE IMPLICATIONS (Water Res. Rsch. Inst. Univ. N.C., Report No. 271, 1992); Brandon Bordeaux, Comment, *Legal Analysis of the Constitutionality of the Water Supply Watershed Protection Act of 1989 and the Hyde Bill*, 29 WAKE FOREST L. REV. 1279 (1994).

31. The rules are set forth in 15A N.C.A.C. 2B, § .0104. Rules have also been adopted for the Randleman Lake water-supply watershed. 15A N.C.A.C. 2B, §§ .0248–.0252.

32. G.S. 143-214.5(d3). The provision on redevelopment was added by S.L. 2021-164.

33. 346 N.C. 787, 488 S.E.2d 144 (1997). This suit, brought by the Town of Spruce Pine (in Mitchell County) against neighboring Avery County, involved a dispute over the city's proposed location of a new water-supply intake in the North Toe River (which would trigger a requirement that Avery County adopt a watershed-protection ordinance). In 1995, during the course of this litigation, the legislature passed a bill requiring the EMC to place this particular watershed in a less restrictive WS-IV class, which the EMC did. The parties in this case agreed that the legislation, exempting a single watershed from coverage under the state watershed-protection program, was adopted without a rational basis. The court noted that although this lack of a rational basis may well have made the legislation establishing the solitary exemption unconstitutional, it did not invalidate the basic watershed-protection statute.

the complex system of watershed classification and management, the general goals for water-quality standards in G.S. 143-211, the direction in G.S. 143-214.5 to use density limits or performance standards to regulate watershed development to protect water quality, and the detailed rulemaking-hearing requirements of G.S. 150B as sufficient legislative guidance.

Coastal Resources and Wetland Protection

Coastal Management

In 1974, the legislature adopted the Coastal Area Management Act (CAMA).[34] This law established a comprehensive regional resource management program for the state's twenty-county coastal area. The act survived an early facial challenge, with the court ruling that CAMA was neither an unlawful local act nor an unconstitutional delegation of legislative authority.[35] In 1978, the North Carolina program was deemed to meet the minimum requirements of the federal Coastal Zone Management Act,[36] thereby making the state eligible for federal grants and triggering a requirement that federal actions in or affecting the state's coastal zone be consistent with the approved state program.[37]

The Coastal Resources Commission (CRC) makes program-policy decisions.[38] The Division of Coastal Management (DCM) within the DEQ provides staff.

The regulatory provisions of CAMA[39] only apply to development in a geographic area that the CRC has designated an *area of environmental concern* (AEC). These areas include all coastal waters and the

---

34. *See generally* Peter G. Glenn, *The Coastal Area Management Act in the Courts: A Preliminary Analysis*, 53 N.C. L. Rev. 303 (1974); Milton S. Heath, Jr., *A Legislative History of the Coastal Area Management Act*, 53 N.C. L. Rev. 345 (1974); Milton S. Heath, Jr. & Allen C. Moseley, *The Coastal Area Management Act: A Progress Report*, Popular Gov't, Spring 1980, at 32; Milton S. Heath, Jr. & David W. Owens, *Coastal Management Law in North Carolina: 1974–1994*, 72 N.C. L. Rev. 1413 (1994); David W. Owens, *Coastal Management in North Carolina: Building a Regional Consensus*, 51 J. Am. Plan. Ass'n 322 (1985); Thomas J. Schoenbaum, *The Management of Land and Water Use in the Coastal Zone: A New Law Is Enacted in North Carolina*, 53 N.C. L. Rev. 275 (1974); Thomas J. Schoenbaum & Ronald H. Rosenberg, *The Legal Implementation of Coastal Zone Management: The North Carolina Model*, 1976 Duke L.J. 1 (1976).

35. Adams v. N.C. Dep't of Natural & Econ. Res., 295 N.C. 683, 249 S.E.2d 402 (1978). The state statute on wetland regulation, the dredge-and-fill law, G.S. 113-229, was similarly held to be a lawful delegation of legislative authority in *In re Broad & Gales Creek Community Ass'n*, 300 N.C. 267, 266 S.E.2d 645 (1980).

36. 33 U.S.C. §§ 1451–1466. *See* Am. Petroleum Inst. v. Knecht, 609 F.2d 1306 (9th Cir. 1979) (upholding approval of California program). *See generally*, David R. Godschalk, *Implementing Coastal Zone Management: 1972–1990*, 20 Coastal Mgmt. 93 (1992).

37. 16 U.S.C. § 1456(c)(1)(A). Implementing regulations are at 15 C.F.R. § 930. *See generally* Edward M. Cheston, *Comment, An Overview and Analysis of the Consistency Requirement Under the Coastal Zone Management Act*, 10 U. Balt. J. Envtl. L. 135 (2003); Tim Eichenberg & Jack Archer, *The Federal Consistency Doctrine: Coastal Zone Management and "New Federalism,"* 14 Ecology L.Q. 9 (1987); Edward A. Fitzgerald, California Coastal Commission v. Norton: *A Coastal State Victory in the Seaweed Rebellion*, 22 UCLA J. Envtl. L. & Pol'y 155 (2004).

In *Secretary of the Interior v. California*, 464 U.S. 312 (1984), the U.S. Supreme Court held that the Department of Interior's sale of oil and gas leases on the outer continental shelf was not an activity "directly affecting" the California coastal zone, so no consistency determination was required. Subsequently, the Outer Continental Shelf Lands Act, 43 U.S.C. §§ 1331–1356a, was amended to require consistency reviews for these activities. This amendment allowed North Carolina's 1990 objection to a consistency determination that played a key role in blocking approval of Mobil Oil's exploration plan for an area the company had leased off the Outer Banks. The company subsequently obtained restitution for the $156 million it had paid for its leases. Mobil Oil Exploration & Producing Se., Inc. v. United States, 530 U.S. 604 (2000).

38. G.S. 113A-104. There is also a forty-seven-member Coastal Resources Advisory Council that advises the CRC. G.S. 113A-105.

39. G.S. 113A-113 to -128. The substantive permit standards are set forth at 15A N.C.A.C. 7H and the procedural rules are at 15A N.C.A.C. 7J. Exemptions are set forth in 15A N.C.A.C. 7K. General policy statements, which are also used in permit reviews, are set forth in 15A N.C.A.C. 7M.

land immediately adjacent to the ocean, sounds, and coastal rivers; coastal wetlands; and several other, smaller areas.[40]

CAMA permits are required for all "development" in AECs.[41] CAMA-permit applications are all considered on the basis of the standards and policies adopted by the CRC and the specific standards in the locally adopted and CRC-approved land use plans.[42] Though the substantive standards do not vary, there are three different methods by which applications are processed: (1) general permits for routine projects, (2) minor-development applications that are administered by local permit officers, and (3) major-development projects that are administered by the DCM.

General permits are authorized by G.S. 113A-118.1 and G.S. 113-229(c1).[43] General permits are not subject to the public-notice requirements that apply to all other CAMA permits. The CRC has by rule adopted general permits for seventeen types of projects.[44] These general permits are not exemptions and are not administered in the same fashion that the Army Corps of Engineers administers nationwide or general permits under the Section 404 program (described in more detail below). Each applicant for a CAMA general permit must complete an individual application. A CAMA field officer then makes a site inspection to verify the application information. If approved, the permit is immediately issued on-site.

Minor development is defined by G.S. 113A-118(c). It includes any development that occupies less than twenty acres or construction of a structure that covers less than 60,000 square feet of ground, does not involve drilling for or excavating natural resources, and most significantly, does not require any other state or federal permit.[45] Since a state dredge-and-fill permit or a federal Section 10 or Section 404 permit

---

40. The currently designated AECs are provided in 15A N.C.A.C. 7H, §§ .0205 (coastal wetlands), .0206 (estuarine waters), .0207 (public-trust waters), .0209 (estuarine shorelines) (75 feet wide for all estuarine waters, except 575 feet wide adjacent to ORWs), .0304 (ocean-hazard areas) (includes ocean-erodible area, high-hazard flood area, inlet-hazard area, and unvegetated-beach area), .0405 (small-surface water-supply watersheds) (includes Nags Head Fresh Pond and Toomers Creek in New Hanover County), .0406 (public-water-supply-well fields) (includes fields at Cape Hatteras and Elizabeth City), .0507(d) (Jockey's Ridge sand dune), .0509(e) (Permuda Island). There is also a nomination process by which individual sites can be considered for AEC designation. 15A N.C.A.C. 7H, § .0500. Each specialized AEC has specific standards for development. See Coastal Ready-Mix Concrete Co. v. N.C. Coastal Res. Comm'n, 116 N.C. App. 119, 446 S.E.2d 823, review denied, 337 N.C. 800, 449 S.E.2d 566 (1994) (applying standards related to sand removal from the Jockey's Ridge AEC).

41. G.S. 113A-103(5). In Pamlico Marine Co. v. North Carolina Department of Natural Resources & Community Development, 80 N.C. App. 201, 341 S.E.2d 108 (1986), the court held that where the decking of piers at a marina had been removed some ten years earlier with the piles left in place, rebuilding the piers was new development, not repair, and thus subject to permit requirements.

42. Legislation has also been enacted to mandate certain development standards. The prohibition against hardened erosion-control devices (bulkheads and seawalls) was codified as G.S. 113A-115.1 by S.L. 2003-427. The same act directed the CRC to issue a general permit for offshore parallel sills of stone or riprap used as estuarine-shoreline erosion-control devices when such sills are used in conjunction with existing, created, or restored wetlands. The prohibition of shoreline-hardening structures was modified by S.L. 2011-387. This law created G.S. 113A-115.1(d) to (h) to allow up to four terminal groins associated with beach-nourishment projects if specified conditions were met. These provisions on terminal groins were further modified by S.L. 2013-384. The legislature directed that rules continue to allow placement of swimming pools in oceanfront setback areas (while clarifying that cities and counties may require removal of pools found to be a public nuisance) in S.L. 2002-116. S.L. 2009-479 placed a moratorium until September 1, 2010, on requirements to remove permitted temporary erosion-control structures in any community that was actively pursuing a beach-nourishment project or inlet-relocation project on or before August 11, 2009. This act also directed the CRC to study the feasibility and advisability of the use of terminal groins. A requirement to allow redevelopment of urban waterfronts was codified as G.S. 113A-120.2 by S.L. 1997-337.

43. G.S. 113A-118.2 limits general permits in AECs classified as ORWs and primary nursery areas to minor maintenance and repair projects and to development of single-family residences.

44. 15A N.C.A.C. 7H, §§ .1100–.2700.

45. Most oceanfront development falls into the category of minor development, with permits administered by city and county local permit officers. See, for example, Long v. Currituck County, 248 N.C. App. 55, 787 S.E.2d 835, review denied, 369 N.C. 74, 793 S.E.2d 222 (2016), dealing with county zoning approval and a CAMA permit issued for a 15,000-square-foot collection of buildings used as a single-family residence with 24 bedrooms.

moves development out of the minor-development category, virtually all work in waters and wetlands requires a major-development permit. If the local government has qualified to be a permit-letting agency under G.S. 113A-117, minor-development permits are issued by a local permit officer, who is most often also the local building inspector or zoning officer.

Major-development permits are required for all other nonexempt development in AECs. Major-permit applications are submitted to the regional office of the DCM.[46]

Review of permit applications considers not only the immediate direct impacts of development on public resources but also the cumulative impacts, secondary impacts, and impact on neighbors.[47] North Carolina agencies may not, contrary to the practice of the Corps of Engineers with Section 404 permits, consider "after the fact" permit applications.[48]

Appeals of all initial CAMA and dredge-and-fill permits are made to the CRC.[49] These are contested-case appeals under the Administrative Procedure Act.[50] Appeals must be filed within twenty days of the permit decision.[51] Persons other than the applicant or the secretary of the DEQ must first petition the CRC for a hearing.[52] Failure to seek review of a CAMA-permit decision is a failure to exhaust

---

46. 15A N.C.A.C. 7J, § .0203 defines the requirements for plats and other application information that is required to be submitted.

47. *In re* Broad & Gales Creek Cmty. Ass'n, 300 N.C. 267, 266 S.E.2d 645 (1980). Related state regulatory programs are also considered in permitting decisions. *See, e.g.,* King v. State, 125 N.C. App. 379, 481 S.E.2d 330, *review denied,* 346 N.C. 280, 487 S.E.2d 548 (1997) (CAMA permit conditioned on receipt of water-quality certification, which was subsequently denied). The cumulative-impacts consideration was explicitly added to the list of grounds for permit denial in 1989 as G.S. 113A-120(10).

48. *In re* Milliken, 43 N.C. App. 382, 258 S.E.2d 856 (1979). Also see *Appeal of CAMA Permit No. 82-0010 v. Town of Bath,* 82 N.C. App. 32, 345 S.E.2d 699 (1986), a marina-regulation case that illuminates the sometimes-confusing interplay of local zoning and CAMA regulations.

49. G.S. 113A-121.1. In *Gaskill v. State* ex rel. *Cobey,* 109 N.C. App. 656, 428 S.E.2d 474, *review denied,* 334 N.C. 163, 432 S.E.2d 359 (1993), a petition was filed with the Office of Administrative Hearings to contest a civil penalty and restoration order assessed for illegal fill of a salt marsh. However, the original filing did not include an affidavit verifying the contents of the petition. A verification was subsequently filed, but after the twenty-day period for filing had passed. Because a verified petition for review was not filed within the statutory period allowed, the court held that the petition was properly dismissed for lack of subject-matter jurisdiction.

50. A contested case is heard before an administrative-law judge of the Office of Administrative Hearings, who reports a recommended decision to the CRC for final determination. In *Webb v. Department of Environment, Health, & Natural Resources,* 102 N.C. App. 767, 404 S.E.2d 29 (1991), the court held that when the CRC makes a decision contrary to the recommended decision, there does not need to be a point-by-point refutation of the hearing officer's findings as long as a specific rationale, supported by the whole record, is set forth. G.S. 150B-34(c) was subsequently amended to provide that if a recommended finding of fact is not adopted, the agency must state the "specific reason, based on the evidence" for not doing so.

51. G.S. 150B-23(f) provides that when a statute sets a specific period for filing appeals, that controls over the standard period of sixty days under the Administrative Procedure Act.

52. G.S. 113A-121.1(b). The petition must be in writing and made within the twenty-day appeal period. If the request for a hearing is not made within twenty days of the permit decision, the Commission has no subject-matter jurisdiction to hear the matter. Fonvielle v. N.C. Coastal Res. Comm'n, ___ N.C. App. ___, ___ S.E.2d ___ (2023). To be granted an appeal, the appellant must allege that the decision is contrary to a statute or rule, the person is directly affected by the decision, and the alleged facts or legal arguments are sufficient to show that the request for a hearing is not frivolous. A decision on the petition must be made by the CRC (which has delegated the decision to its chair) within thirty days of receipt. A denial of a petition is a final decision that may be appealed to superior court. If the petition is granted, the appeal must be made within twenty days of that decision.

Originally, the standard for review of the third-party-appeal petitions included a standard that the petitioner have "a substantial likelihood of prevailing." S.L. 1987-827. This standard led to much litigation. In *Rusher v. Tomlinson,* 119 N.C. App. 458, 459 S.E.2d 285 (1995), a neighboring owner appealed issuance of a CAMA permit for berthing two large vessels in the Cape Fear River in Wilmington. The court ruled that the petition for a hearing had been properly denied, as there was no requirement that an easement be secured for a berthing facility because it involved no structures over water. In *Ballance v. North Carolina Coastal Resources Commission,* 108 N.C. App. 288, 423 S.E.2d 815 (1992), the court held that it was improper to deny a request for a hearing when the permit record

administrative remedies that can lead to dismissal of subsequent collateral challenges to the permit-ted development[53] (though a constitutional claim is not barred by a failure to exhaust administrative remedies, as the administrative body has no jurisdiction to rule on these claims).[54] Attorney fees may be awarded to a prevailing party challenging a permit decision if there is no "substantial justification" for the agency's original decision.[55]

In addition to permit appeals, the CRC may consider petitions for variances from the rules.[56] This provision is modeled after the variance standard in zoning ordinances.[57] The CRC may issue a variance upon finding that (1) unnecessary hardship would result from a strict application of the rules, (2) the hardship results from conditions peculiar to the property involved, (3) such conditions were not self-created, and (4) the spirit, purpose, and intent of the rule is preserved. Variances are considered by the full CRC on expedited review if there are no contested facts and with a full contested-case hearing if there are not stipulated facts.

---

indicated that the permit was issued despite the uncontradicted recommendations for denial from five state and federal agencies and the coastal-management field staff. In *Pamlico Tar River Foundation v. Coastal Resources Commission*, 103 N.C. App. 24, 404 S.E.2d 167 (1991), the court upheld the denial of a third-party appeal but remanded the case to the trial court to determine if additional relevant evidence on the marina location was improperly excluded. In *Conservation Council of North Carolina v. Haste*, 102 N.C. App. 411, 402 S.E.2d 447 (1991), the court ruled that the petitioner's challenge of a permit to construct an erosion-control jetty at Oregon Inlet pursuant to a temporary rule was improperly denied. In 1995, G.S. 113A-121.1 was amended to replace the showing of a substantial likelihood of success with a requirement that the appeal not be frivolous. S.L. 1995-409. In *Batson v. Coastal Resources Commission*, 282 N.C. App. 1, 871 S.E.2d 120 (2022), a request to appeal a permit issued to the N.C. Department of Transportation for a replacement bridge to Harkers Island, the court applied the updated statutory standard that the appeal not be frivolous. The court noted that an appeal is not frivolous because it does not have merit or is unlikely to succeed. Rather, it is frivolous only if the proponent can present no rational argument based on the evidence or the law to support the claim.

53. Flowers v. Blackbeard Sailing Club, Ltd., 115 N.C. App. 349, 444 S.E.2d 636, *review granted*, 337 N.C. 691, 448 S.E.2d 522 (1994), *dismissed, review improvidently granted*, 340 N.C. 357, 457 S.E.2d 599 (1995). A trespass action filed by an adjacent riparian owner on the grounds that the defendant's pier obstructed the plaintiff's riparian access rights was dismissed for failure to pursue an appeal of an adverse CAMA-permit decision. The plaintiff had objected to a CAMA-permit application for the pier but did not appeal its issuance. The court held that CAMA provided a clear administrative-appeal route to a specialized agency with the expertise and ability to address the precise issues raised by the plaintiff. The court therefore held that the superior court lacked subject-matter jurisdiction because of the plaintiff's failure to exhaust this administrative remedy. A similar result obtained in *Leeuwenburg v. Waterway Investment Ltd. Partnership*, 115 N.C. App. 541, 445 S.E.2d 614 (1994). In a third case involving adjacent-riparian owners and pier alignment, the court held that where there was an irregular shoreline (here the canal frontage made a right angle at or near the property boundary), a reasonable-use test should be employed to allow both owners access to the water. Pine Knoll Assocs. v. Carden, 126 N.C. App. 155, 484 S.E.2d 446, *review denied*, 347 N.C. 138, 492 S.E.2d 26 (1997). *See also* Barris v. Town of Long Beach, 208 N.C. App. 718, 704 S.E.2d 285 (2010) (trial court has no jurisdiction to hear dispute regarding town improvements within nonexclusive street right-of-way since CAMA-permit application was made and not yet decided or appealed).

54. Shell Island Homeowners Ass'n v. Tomlinson, 134 N.C. App. 217, 517 S.E.2d 406 (1999). Also see a companion case, *Shell Island Homeowners Ass'n v. Tomlinson*, 134 N.C. App. 286, 517 S.E.2d 401 (1999).

55. Walker v. Coastal Res. Comm'n, 124 N.C. App. 1, 476 S.E.2d 138 (1996), *review denied*, 346 N.C. App. 185, 486 S.E.2d 220 (1997). The attorney fees could be awarded pursuant to G.S. 6-19.1. The court did not allow recovery of attorney fees and costs for the administrative hearing, only for the subsequent judicial appeal. In *Batson v. Coastal Resources Commission*, 282 N.C. App. 1, 871 S.E.2d 120 (2022), the court remanded the case to determine if the defendant knowingly applied an incorrect standard for review of a third-party appeal request. If so, the action would be without substantial justification and attorney fees could be awarded.

56. G.S. 113A-120.1. *See* Williams v. N.C. Dep't of Env't & Natural Res., 144 N.C. App. 479, 548 S.E.2d 793 (2001) (remanding case where CRC improperly considered other property owned by petitioner in determining there was no unnecessary hardship).

57. *See* Chapter 17. G.S. 113A-120.1 was amended in 2002 to remove the requirements that the petitioner show that strict application of the rules would result in "practical difficulties" and that the situation could not have reasonably been anticipated when the rule was adopted; the self-created-hardship limitation was added. S.L. 2002-68.

G.S. 113A-126 provides for the full range of enforcement actions for alleged violations of CAMA. Injunctive relief is available, as are criminal sanctions. Violation of CAMA is a misdemeanor. The main-stay of the enforcement program is, however, the use of civil penalties.[58] The CRC rules also require full restoration of sites that have been improperly altered.[59]

CAMA regulations limiting erosion-control measures and wetland alteration have been challenged on takings grounds. In *King v. State*,[60] which involved the denial of permits for placement of fill in wet-lands in order to build a road and subdivide an eight-acre peninsula in Topsail Sound, the court held there was not an unconstitutional taking because practical development alternatives existed. In *Shell Island Homeowners Ass'n v. Tomlinson*,[61] the court rejected a takings challenge to CAMA regulations prohibiting permanent oceanfront erosion-control structures, holding there was no property right to construct such structures. The court noted that, in any event, the plaintiff was aware of this regulatory limitation prior to acquiring title or constructing the threatened hotel and condominium structure, and this prior knowledge foreclosed a taking or inverse-condemnation claim.

G.S. 113A-123 provides for judicial review of CRC decisions.[62] The review is in the nature of certio-rari, so there is no de novo hearing. There is also no right to a jury trial in these appeals.[63] An applicant may not collaterally attack findings made by the CRC in a permit denial in a subsequent separate judicial proceeding.[64]

In addition to this regulation of development in AECs, the CAMA program has since its inception included mandated local land use planning in the twenty coastal counties.[65] In addition to serving as a traditional comprehensive plan,[66] policies in the CAMA plans that have been approved by the CRC also become mandatory standards for permits for development in AECs.[67] Approved local plans are

---

58. *In re* N. Topsail Water & Sewer, Inc., 96 N.C. App. 468, 386 S.E.2d 92 (1989), *review denied*, 326 N.C. 364, 389 S.E.2d 810 (1990) (upholding $19,000 civil penalty for willful noncompliance that resulted in substantial sedimenta-tion damage to environment). Rules set out details on the procedure for assessments and contain a detailed schedule for computing the amount of assessments. 15A N.C.A.C. 7J, § .0409.

59. 15A N.C.A.C. 7J, § .0410. State *ex rel.* Cobey v. Simpson, 333 N.C. 81, 423 S.E.2d 759 (1992).

60. 125 N.C. App. 379, 481 S.E.2d 330, *review denied*, 346 N.C. 280, 487 S.E.2d 548 (1997). See Chapter 24 for further analysis of the taking issue.

61. 134 N.C. App. 217, 517 S.E.2d 406 (1999). The interplay of coastal development regulations, especially the chal-lenges presented by sea-level rise, dynamic shorelines, and climate change, and the Takings Clause has confronted most coastal states. *See, e.g.,* J. Peter Byrne, *The Cathedral Engulfed: Sea-Level Rise, Property Rights, and Time*, 73 La. L. Rev. 69 (2012); Laura M. Padilla, *Does a Rising Tide Lift All Boats? Sea Level Rise, Land Use, and Property Rights*, 51 Tex. Envtl. L. J. 27 (2021) (focus on California coastal law and property); Margaret E. Peloso & Marga-ret R. Caldwell, *Dynamic Property Rights: The Public Trust Doctrine and Takings in a Changing Climate*, 30 Stan. Envtl. L.J. 51 (2011); James G. Titus, *Rising Seas, Coastal Erosion, and the Takings Clause: How to Save Wetlands and Beaches Without Hurting Property Owners*, 57 Md. L. Rev. 1279 (1998); Maye C. Emlein, Comment, *Rising to the Challenge: Managed Retreat and the Takings Clause in Maine's Climate Change Era*, 73 Me. L. Rev. 169 (2021).

62. *See, e.g.,* Busik v. N.C. Coastal Res. Comm'n, 230 N.C. App. 148, 753 S.E.2d 326 (2013), *review denied*, 367 N.C. 502 (2014) (interpreting oceanfront-setback regulation).

63. State v. Simpson, 325 N.C. 514, 385 S.E.2d 329 (1989); State v. Givens, 101 N.C. App. 695, 400 S.E.2d 745 (1991).

64. Weeks v. N.C. Dep't of Natural Res. & Cmty. Dev., 97 N.C. App. 215, 388 S.E.2d 288, *review denied*, 326 N.C. 601, 393 S.E.2d 890 (1990).

65. G.S. 113A, §§ 106 to 112. G.S. 113A-110 sets the process for plan preparation, local adoption, and CRC approval. The public-notice and hearing provisions for local plan adoption were amended in 2022 to align with the requirements for the adoption of comprehensive and land use plans under Chapter 160D. S.L. 2022-43.

66. See Chapter 22 for a discussion of other planning mandates and the impact of adopted comprehensive plans on land-development regulation.

67. *See, e.g.,* Everhardt & Assocs., Inc. v. Dep't of Env't, Health, & Natural Res., 127 N.C. App. 693, 493 S.E.2d 66 (1997), *review denied*, 347 N.C. 575, 502 S.E.2d 590 (1998). The plaintiffs were denied a CAMA permit on the basis of inconsistency with the Hyde County land use plan and proposed wetland fill. The court upheld the CRC's determi-nation that the proposal was inconsistent with the plan. It is proper to consider offers of proof regarding the plan and its interpretation at the administrative hearing as they are part of the whole record, held the court.

also periodically incorporated within the state's federally approved coastal-management program and thus become relevant standards for review of federal-agency permitting and grant decisions under the federal-consistency reviews noted above.

The initial-planning guidelines adopted by the CRC in 1976 were primarily aimed at establishing a local planning infrastructure and getting at least rudimentary plans into place within the tight deadlines required by the law.[68] This was necessary, as most of the rural counties and small towns involved had no comprehensive plan, and many had no land use regulations in place.[69] The rules required plan updates every five years. The CRC's planning guidelines were substantially updated prior to the 1980 initial round of plan updates. The revised guidelines defined a set of substantive issues that had to be addressed by the plans and the procedures to be followed in production and adoption of the plans, but they left most substantive policy decisions to local governments (provided that the local policies had to be consistent with state and federal laws and rules). As part of a larger initiative on addressing coastal hazards, the planning guidelines were also amended to mandate inclusion of planning for post-storm rebuilding.[70] Efforts were also undertaken to assist local governments' use of the plans to address water-quality issues.[71]

In the mid-1990s, the state undertook a substantial reassessment of the role and purposes of the local CAMA plans.[72] In 2002, the planning guidelines were revised to place increased emphasis on basing land use policies on natural-systems capabilities and limitations and a land-suitability analysis.[73] This included production of a GIS-based environmental composite map to show the capability and limitations of natural systems for development and a land-suitability map for urban development.[74] Criteria for funding of local planning efforts were updated in 2016 to give funding priority to management topics set on an annual basis by the CRC.[75]

---

68. The land use–plan guidelines are at 15A N.C.A.C. 7B. Guidelines for grants to local governments for planning are at 15A N.C.A.C. 7L.

69. Nineteen of the twenty coastal counties adopted plans by the end of 1975 as mandated. The CRC adopted a plan for Carteret County, which prepared a plan but refused to adopt it; 63 percent of the $1.66 million available for coastal program implementation in its first eighteen months of existence was devoted to local-planning grants. Heath & Owens, *supra* note 34.

70. *See* William D. McElyea et al., Before the Storm: Managing Development to Reduce Hurricane Damage (Sept. 1982).

71. Div. of Coastal Mgmt., Protecting Coastal Waters Through Local Planning (May 1986). As of January 1985, all twenty coastal counties and fifty-five coastal municipalities had adopted CAMA plans that had been approved by the CRC.

72. The Governor's Coastal Futures Committee reviewed the CAMA planning program in 1994. At that point there were twenty county plans and sixty-seven approved municipal plans. That committee recommended numerous changes in plan preparation and implementation, including the provision of adequate fiscal resources and technical assistance to local governments (including a standard package of background data for use in plan updates and GIS assistance); attention to planning and infrastructure needs in high-growth areas; enhanced emphasis on addressing cumulative and secondary impacts; increased public-education and participation mandates; mandatory local-plan implementation through land use regulations and capital-improvement budgets; increased consistency with the plans by state agencies; eligibility for various public investments tied to successful plan implementation; and stronger intergovernmental coordination of plans. N.C. Coastal Futures Comm., Charting a Course for Our Coast 19–26 (1994).

In 1998, the state placed a moratorium on plan updates and created a land use–planning review team to review the entire process and suggest program improvements. The team issued its report to the CRC in September 2000, recommending substantial changes to the CAMA planning program.

73. The prior guidelines were repealed and the new guidelines codified at 15A N.C.A.C. 7B §§ .0701–.0901.

74. Div. of Coastal Mgmt., Technical Manual for Coastal Land Use Planning (July 2002); Land Suitability Analysis User Guide Div. of Coastal Mgmt., Land Suitability Analysis User Guide (Dec. 2005).

75. 15A N.C.A.C. 7L, § .0503.

The CAMA program was expanded in the 1980s to include a land-acquisition component.[76] There are two land-acquisition programs within the program, one for protection of natural areas in an undeveloped state and the second for provision of beach access. The N.C. Coastal Reserve preserves critical natural areas in an essentially undisturbed condition.[77] The principal uses of reserve lands are for research, education, and protection of natural resources.[78] The beach-access program[79] provides accessways, parking, and restrooms along both the ocean and estuarine shorelines. The state's access program is designed to secure effective access to these public-trust areas and is implemented primarily through a system of grants to local governments. Most of the responsibility for ownership, operation, and maintenance of access facilities is held by local governments.

In addition, the state has title to lands under navigable waters and regularly flooded marshland. The state constitution and public-trust doctrine mandate the conservation and management of these lands and waters for the benefit of the public.[80] Similarly, title to lands below mean high water is vested in the state.[81] The courts and legislature have recognized that these lands are held in trust for public use, assuring public rights of swimming, fishing, and recreation.[82]

---

76. *See generally* David Owens, *Land Acquisition and Coastal Resource Management: A Pragmatic Perspective*, 24 WM. & MARY L. REV. 625, 645–66 (1983).

77. G.S. 113A-129, §§ .1 to .3. These provisions were added to CAMA by S.L. 1989-344. The policy standards for reserve lands can also be a factor in permitting. The Cape Hatteras Water Association secured a CAMA permit for construction of nine water-supply wells in the Buxton Woods State Coastal Reserve. In *Friends of Hatteras Island National Historic Maritime Forest Land Trust for Preservation, Inc. v. Coastal Resources Commission*, 117 N.C. App. 556, 452 S.E.2d 337 (1995), the court upheld the trial court's permit revocation, holding that the wells were not a "public use" as contemplated by G.S. 113A-129.1. The court concluded that the level of development required for installation and monitoring of the wells was inconsistent with the legislative intent that the land remain essentially undeveloped.

78. The N.C. Coastal Reserve consists of ten sites along the coast, including barrier islands, maritime forests, wetlands, and archeological sites. The Coastal Reserve–system sites are: (1) Currituck Banks (immediately north of Corolla); (2) Kitty Hawk Woods; (3) Buxton Woods; (4) Emily and Richardson Preyer Buckridge (along the Alligator River); (5) Rachel Carson Reserve (Carrot Island, opposite Beaufort); (6) Permuda Island (in Stump Sound); (7) Masonboro Island; (8) Zeke's Island (south of Fort Fisher); (9) Bald Head Woods; and (10) Bird Island (along the North Carolina–South Carolina border). Four of these sites (Currituck, Rachel Carson, Masonboro, and Zeke's Island) are also designated as components of the National Estuarine Research Reserve under 16 U.S.C. § 1461. The navigable waters and upland areas of the Rachel Carson Reserve were added to the Town of Beaufort corporate limits by S.L. 2019-95. S.L. 2019-108 authorized local regulation of specified navigable waters by the Town of Manteo (Shallowbag Bay) and Hyde County Silver Lake on Ocracoke Island).

79. G.S. 113A-134, §§ .1 to .3. This program was added to CAMA by S.L. 1981-925.

80. N.C. CONST. art. XIV, § 5 (amend. 1972). *See* State v. Credle, 322 N.C. 522, 532–34, 369 S.E.2d 825, 831–32 (1988). Waters that are navigable in fact are subject to the public trust. Gwathmey v. State, 342 N.C. 287, 300, 464 S.E.2d 674, 682 (1995); State v. Twiford, 136 N.C. 603, 606, 48 S.E.2d 586, 587 (1904); State v. Baum, 128 N.C. 600, 604, 38 S.E. 900, 901 (1901); Newcomb v. Cnty. of Carteret, 207 N.C. App. 527, 701 S.E.2d 325 (2010) (riparian rights and public-trust doctrine applicable to artificially created harbor); Fish House, Inc. v. Clarke, 204 N.C. App. 130, 134, 693 S.E.2d 208, 210–11 (2010) (public-trust doctrine applicable to manmade canal that is navigable in fact); Bauman v. Woodlake Partners, LLC, 191 N.C. App. 441, 681 S.E.2d 819 (2009) (where creek dammed to form lake in gated community was not navigable in fact, lake not subject to public-trust doctrine).

81. *See, e.g.*, Capune v. Robbins, 273 N.C. 581, 160 S.E.2d 881 (1968) (confirming the right of a person to paddle under a fishing pier in Atlantic Beach); Carolina Fishing Pier, Inc. v. Town of Carolina Beach, 277 N.C. 297, 177 S.E.2d 513 (1970) (involving a beach-title dispute arising from construction of the berm along Carolina Beach). G.S. 77-20(a) codifies this rule.

82. G.S. 1-45.1 lists the types of public uses generally associated with the public-trust doctrine.

The public also has a right to limited traditional public use of the dry-sand beach along the ocean-front.[83] The dry-sand beach is the area seaward of the first line of vegetation but landward of the mean high-water line.[84] While fee title to the area belongs to the upland owner, the public has rights in the nature of an easement for traditional uses (such as walking along the foreshore, sitting on the beach, and hauling fishing nets, in some areas). G.S. 77-20(d) and (e) acknowledge these traditional public-use rights to the area between the vegetation line and mean high water, as does G.S. 113A-134.1(b).

These public-use rights to the dry-sand beach were affirmed in *Nies v. Town of Emerald Isle*.[85] In this case the owner of an oceanfront lot claimed the right to exclude the public from the area above the mean high-water line, contending the town regulation allowed limited driving on the dry-sand beach and prohibited placement of obstructions in a twenty-foot-wide strip immediately seaward of the frontal

---

83. There are several legal foundations for this public right that have been used in other states—the public-trust doctrine, prescriptive easements, custom, and implied dedication. *See, e.g.,* Gion v. City of Santa Cruz, 2 Cal. 3d 29, 84 Cal. Rptr. 162, 465 P.2d 50 (1970); City of Daytona Beach v. Tona-Rama, 294 So. 2d 73 (1974); Borough of Neptune City v. Borough of Avon-by-the-Sea, 61 N.J. 296, 294 A.2d 47 (1972); State *ex rel.* Thornton v. Hay, 254 Or. 584, 462 P.2d 671 (1969).

The North Carolina standard for establishing a prescriptive easement is set forth in *Dickinson v. Pake*, 284 N.C. 576, 201 S.E.2d 897 (1974). The court in *Koenig v. Town of Kure Beach*, 178 N.C. App. 500, 631 S.E.2d 884 (2006), applied a prescriptive easement analysis to find that adjacent owners had not established rights to use of a ten-foot-wide access easement running from the street to the public beach. The court noted that the requisite elements for a prescriptive easement are (1) use is adverse or under claim of right; (2) use is open and notorious; (3) use is continuous and uninterrupted for twenty years; and (4) there is substantial identity of the easement claimed for the requisite period. The court held that there was no evidence that the use was without the owner's permission, nor was there evidence that the claimants had used the accessway for more than a few years.

In *Hovey v. Sand Dollar Shores Homeowners Association, Inc.*, 276 N.C. App. 281, 857 S.E.2d 358 (2021), review denied, ___ N.C. ___, 868 S.E.2d 869 (2022), the court addressed whether a pedestrian easement running from a subdivision road to the oceanfront had been dedicated to the public when the subdivision was platted. The court held that a transfer of property by dedication requires a clear intent to dedicate that must be unmistakable and decisive. The burden to show that clear intent is on the person propounding the existence of the dedication, a burden that was not met in this case, as the plat noted that the easement was for "public or private use as noted" and showed only the road, not the pedestrian path, as being "public."

For an example of application of dedication principles to a determination of public rights in a street as it affects development regulations, see *Wright v. Town of Matthews*, 177 N.C. 1, 627 S.E.2d 650 (2006).

Other states have also enacted legislation to confirm and clarify common-law public-use rights. Examples include Oregon (Or. Rev. Stat. § 390.610) and Texas (Tex. Nat. Res. Code Ann. § 61.011(a)).

84. The respective physical boundaries of public and private rights—the mean high-tide line and vegetation line—are dynamic. As erosion, accretion, and seasonal changes in the shoreline cause changes in the locations of these lines, the legal rights move along with the associated physical resources. *See generally,* Alyson C. Flournoy, *Beach Law Cleanup: How Sea-Level Rise Has Eroded the Ambulatory Boundaries Legal Framework*, 42 Vt. L. Rev. 89 (2017).

85. 244 N.C. App. 81, 780 S.E.2d 187 (2015), *appeal dismissed*, 369 N.C. 484, 793 S.E.2d 699 (2016), *cert. denied*, 138 S. Ct. 75 (2017). In an earlier case, adjacent-upland owners disputed any public-use rights to the dry-sand ocean beach in Currituck County. *Fabrikant v. Currituck County*, 174 N.C. App. 30, 621 S.E.2d 19 (2005). The court dismissed the claim, holding that the state had not waived governmental immunity in the context of this quiet-title action. Also see *Town of Nags Head v. Richardson*, 260 N.C. App. 325, 817 S.E.2d 874 (2018), where an issue was raised over whether the public-trust doctrine allowed the town to place sand on the defendant's property as part of a beach-nourishment project. The court held, however, that the town had not raised that issue in a timely fashion in the condemnation proceedings.

See generally Alice Gibbon Carmichael, Comment, *Sunbathers Versus Property Owners: Public Access to North Carolina Beaches*, 64 N.C. L. Rev. 159 (1985); William A. Dossett, Note, *Concerned Citizens of Brunswick County Taxpayers Ass'n v. Holden Beach Enterprises: Preserving Beach Action Through Public Prescription*, 70 N.C. L. Rev. 1289 (1992); Joseph J. Kalo, *The Changing Face of the Shoreline: Public and Private Rights to the Natural and Nourished Dry Sand Beaches of North Carolina*, 78 N.C. L. Rev. 1869 (2000); Valerie B. Spalding, *The Pearl in the Oyster: The Public Trust Doctrine in North Carolina*, 12 Campbell L. Rev. 21 (1989).

dune in order to provide safe passage for emergency vehicles. The court took notice "that public right of access to dry sand beaches in North Carolina is so firmly rooted in the custom and history of North Carolina that it has become a part of the public consciousness."[86]

Local governments can regulate beach areas (and public-trust waters). In *Slavin v. Town of Oak Island*,[87] the court held that local government regulations may be applied to both privately owned and state-owned beach areas. The court noted that while a littoral owner has a right of access to adjacent waters, this is a qualified right and is subject to reasonable regulation. Likewise, state regulations to protect public-access rights were upheld in *Weeks v. North Carolina Department of Natural Resources & Community Development*.[88] Here the court upheld denial of a CAMA permit for a 900-foot-long pier in Bogue Sound. The denial was based primarily on interference with the public's use rights in the sound.

In *Town of Nags Head v. Cherry, Inc.*[89] the court held that only the state has authority to protect the public's rights to use the state's public-trust ocean beaches. However, the General Assembly responded with enactment of G.S. 160A-203 and 153A-145.3.[90] These statutes authorize cities and counties to enforce local ordinances to protect the public's rights to use state ocean beaches and to regulate placement of personal property on state ocean beaches. Cities may enforce such ordinances on state ocean beaches within or adjacent to their municipal boundaries. Also, G.S. 160A-205 was amended in 2015[91] to provide that if a structure is on the ocean beach, is uninhabitable, and is without water and sewer services for more than 120 days, a city can prohibit, regulate, or abate the situation.

Several cases address local use of traditional accessways, street ends, and street rights-of-way as part of access provision. In *West v. Slick*,[92] the court upheld continued use of an informal, unpaved road on the Currituck Outer Banks that ran behind the frontal dunes. Even though the exact location of the accessway varied due to the effects of wind, rain, and tides, the deviation was not substantial,[93] and a prescriptive easement was held to have been created. In *Concerned Citizens of Brunswick County Taxpayers Ass'n v. Holden Beach Enterprises, Inc.*,[94] the plaintiffs claimed a prescriptive easement to secure access to Shallotte Inlet in Holden Beach. Some 3700 feet of the 5400-foot sandy trail involved had been paved and closed to the public as a private-subdivision road. The court held that a prescriptive easement over a dynamic area of windswept sands subject to ocean flooding could be established even if the exact path used changed over time. The requirement was that there be substantial identity of the

---

86. *Nies*, 244 N.C. App. 81, 92, 780 S.E.2d 187, 196. The court noted that prior law was not clear whether these rights were based on customary use or the public-trust doctrine, but they were universally accepted by the public and recognized by state statute.

87. 160 N.C. App. 57, 584 S.E.2d 100, *review denied*, 357 N.C. 659, 590 S.E.2d 271 (2003). For a critical review of this case, see Brian C. Fork, Recent Developments, *A First Step in the Wrong Direction:* Slavin v. Town of Oak Island *and the Taking of Littoral Rights of Direct Beach Access*, 82 N.C. L. Rev. 1510 (2004).

88. 97 N.C. App. 215, 388 S.E.2d 228, *review denied*, 326 N.C. 601, 393 S.E.2d 890 (1990).

89. 219 N.C. App. 66, 723 S.E.2d 156, 157, *appeal dismissed*, 366 N.C. 386, 732 S.E.2d 580, *review denied*, 366 N.C. 386, 733 S.E.2d 85 (2012). After a storm, the defendant's cottage was disconnected from utilities and left on the ocean beach. The town sought to compel removal of the damaged structure. A key aspect of the town's public-nuisance claim was that the damaged structure was blocking public access along the beach. The court held that the state government was the only body that could bring an action to enforce public-trust rights to the state's beaches and that the town had no standing to raise the issue. In *Six at 109, LLC v. Town of Holden Beach*, 238 N.C. App. 469, 767 S.E.2d 400 (2014), the court upheld an order condemning a dilapidated structure as unsafe under G.S. 160A-429, noting that *Cherry* was inapplicable as the issue was the state of the structure, not interference with public-trust rights.

90. S.L. 2013-384, § 4(a). The same authority was extended to counties by S.L. 2015-70.

91. S.L. 2015-246, § 1.5.

92. 313 N.C. 33, 326 S.E.2d 601 (1985).

93. Testimony indicated that the actual route varied as much as 300 feet, but the court found this was in keeping with the natural conditions inherent to travel along an unimproved, sandy barrier island.

94. 329 N.C. 37, 404 S.E.2d 677 (1991).

location of the trail. The court also held that seasonal use of the accessway and ineffective attempts by the owners to halt public use did not disrupt the continuous use required for a prescriptive easement. In *Williamson v. Town of Surf City*,[95] the court upheld closing a street to allow a portion to be used for a beach-access project. In *March v. Town of Kill Devil Hills*,[96] the court upheld the location of beach-access parking in a street right-of-way. However, in *Wooten v. Town of Topsail Beach*,[97] the court noted that a town may not block vehicular traffic and convert a dedicated but unimproved street right-of-way used for beach access, parking boats and trailers, and access to a private residence without complying with the applicable statutes for closing a dedicated street.

Wetlands Regulation

Wetlands, both in the coastal area and in the rest of the state, are subject to both state and federal regulatory jurisdiction.

The basic state statute on coastal-wetland regulation is G.S. 113-230, which authorizes regulation of dredging and filling in coastal wetlands.[98] This program is now administered as part of the CAMA program described above.[99] The North Carolina wetlands regulatory program applies to coastal wetlands as defined by state law (a definition less inclusive than the one covering wetlands subject to federal regulation).[100]

State courts have also upheld the authority of the EMC to regulate wetlands statewide. The court held that wetlands were "waters" as defined by G.S. 143-212(6), as that includes any "other body or accumulation of water, whether surface or underground."[101] Also, the state generally has title to lands below the mean high-water line, so tidal wetlands (as well as submerged lands) are generally owned by the state and subject to the public-trust doctrine.[102]

---

95. 143 N.C. App. 539, 545 S.E.2d 798 (2001). *See also* Town of Emerald Isle v. State, 320 N.C. 640, 360 S.E.2d 756 (1987) (upholding state legislation that required use of town street end running to Bogue Inlet to be limited to pedestrian beach access and emergency-vehicle access).

96. 125 N.C. App. 151, 479 S.E.2d 252 (1997). Note also that G.S. 136-18(40) vests the Department of Transportation with the authority to

> expand public access to coastal waters in its road project planning and construction programs. The Department shall work with the Wildlife Resources Commission, other State agencies, and other government entities to address public access to coastal waters along the roadways, bridges, and other transportation infrastructure owned or maintained by the Department.

97. 127 N.C. App. 739, 493 S.E.2d 285 (1997), *review denied*, 348 N.C. 78, 505 S.E.2d 888 (1998).

98. The wetlands covered are defined in G.S. 113-229(n)(3) to include salt marshes and tidal marshes (both lunar tides and wind tides). *See generally* Richard Whisnant, *Wetlands in North Carolina*, ENVTL. & CONSERVATION L. BULL. No. 6 (UNC Institute of Government, Dec. 1999).

99. The dredge-and-fill regulatory program, first enacted in 1969, was originally administered by the Division of Marine Fisheries and the Marine Fisheries Commission. In 1979, the program was merged with the CAMA program, with rule-making responsibility transferred to the CRC and administrative responsibility to the DCM.

100. Also, S.L. 2015-286, § 4.18 limits application of state rules on isolated wetlands to "Basin Wetlands and Bogs" and prohibits their application to isolated man-made ditches or ponds. This provision also directed the EMC to amend its rules to establish a coastal, piedmont, and mountain region for purposes of regulating impacts to isolated wetlands.

101. *In re* Request for Declaratory Ruling by Envtl. Mgmt. Comm'n, 155 N.C. App. 408, 573 S.E.2d 732 (2002), *review denied*, 357 N.C. 62, 579 S.E.2d 392 (2003). Wetlands are thus subject to regulation under G.S. 143-214.1(a).

102. N.C. CONST. art. XIV, § 5 (amend. 1972). *See* State v. Credle, 322 N.C. 522, 532–34, 369 S.E.2d 825, 831–32 (1988). Some state-owned wetland areas were sold a century ago, and the scope of just what was sold is subject to contention. *See, e.g.*, Gwathmey v. State, 342 N.C. 287, 464 S.E.2d 674 (1995). This case involved title to regularly flooded marshlands in New Hanover County that had been conveyed to private parties by the State Board of Education. The court held that the General Assembly could by special act convey fee title to submerged lands subject to the public-trust doctrine, though there is a rebuttable presumption that it has not done so. A grant free of

The basic federal statute on wetland regulation is Section 404 of the Clean Water Act.[103] This statute requires a permit prior to the discharge of dredged or fill material into the waters of the United States. The areas affected include navigable waters[104] and adjacent wetlands.[105] Wetlands include areas with a predominance of wetland vegetation, hydric soils, or saturated soils near the ground surface.[106] Isolated wetlands not connected to navigable waters are not subject to federal jurisdiction,[107] though these areas can still be subject to state regulation.

Fill in federally regulated wetlands requires a permit issued by the U.S. Army Corps of Engineers. The Corps has by rule issued a number of "general" or "nationwide" permits that authorize a class of activity deemed to have minimal environmental effect without the necessity of an individual permit.[108] These include utility crossings, minor-road crossings, and modifications of less than an acre above

---

public-trust restrictions must be made in clear and express terms, which was not the case here. Also see G.S. 146.12, which provides for state easements for docks, piers, marinas, and similar structures located on or over state-owned waters and wetlands.

103. 33 U.S.C. § 1344. The Federal Water Pollution Control Act Amendments of 1972, Pub. L. 92-500, established the basic regulatory framework. Section 404 of that act authorized the Corps of Engineers to issue permits for the discharge of dredged or fill material into navigable waters. The Clean Water Act of 1977, Pub. L. 95-217, authorized the Corps to issue general permits on a state, regional, or national basis for any category of activities that are similar in nature, will cause only minimal environmental effects when performed separately, and will have only minimal cumulative adverse impact on the environment. 33 U.S.C. § 1344(e). The act also added exemptions for normal farming, silviculture, and ranching activities. 33 U.S.C. § 1344(f). The definition of federally regulated wetlands is at 33 C.F.R. § 328.3 and 40 C.F.R. § 120. This rule has been subject to multiple amendments, reflecting both responses to litigation and the differing views of changing federal administrations. After its initial adoption in the 1970s, substantial amendments to the rule were made in 2015 (80 Fed. Reg. 37,054), 2019 (84 Fed. Reg. 56,626), 2020 (85 Fed. Reg. 22,250), and 2023 (88 Fed. Reg. 3044). Also see the "swamp buster" provisions of the Food Security Act of 1985, 16 U.S.C. §§ 3821–3824, which limit federal agricultural subsidies to any farmer who converts wetlands to agricultural land. Regulations for this provision are set forth at 7 C.F.R. §§ 12.1–.34.

104. In *Sackett v. Environmental Protection Agency*, 2023 WL 3632751 (May 25, 2023), the Supreme Court held that regulated waters of the U.S. include only those wetlands that have a continuous surface connection with navigable waters. *See also Rapanos v. United States*, 574 U.S. 715 (2006). For federal-regulatory purposes, "navigable waters" are limited to those subject to lunar tides or used for interstate or foreign commerce. 33 C.F.R. § 329.4. This is a more limited area than the waters that are navigable in fact and therefore subject to the state public-trust doctrine. Also, Section 10 of the Rivers and Harbors Act of 1899 prohibits obstruction or alteration of navigable waters. 33 U.S.C. § 403. *See* Zabel v. Tabb, 430 F. 199 (5th Cir. 1970) (upholding application of Section 10 to prohibit fill based on adverse environmental impacts).

105. United States v. Riverside Bayview Homes, Inc., 474 U.S. 121 (1985). The Fourth Circuit has held that a wetland that drains into a roadside ditch that in turn drains into a navigable river has sufficient hydrological connectivity to be considered an adjacent wetland. United States v. Deaton, 332 F.3d 698 (4th Cir. 2003). *See also* Precon Dev. Corp. v. U.S. Army Corps of Eng'rs, 633 F.3d 278 (4th Cir. 2011) (finding inadequate nexus where wetlands connected by ditches to a river seven miles away).

106. Presence of any one of the three attributes is sufficient to establish that an area is a wetland. United States v. Larkin, 852 F.2d 189 (6th Cir. 1988). The difficulty in a precise delineation of jurisdictional wetlands can lead to substantial disputes between sellers and purchasers of land regarding potential developability and land values. In *Sunset Beach Development, LLC v. AMEC, Inc.*, 196 N.C. App. 202, 211, 675 S.E.2d 46, 53 (2009), the court noted that "sophisticated businessmen with experience in real property development in coastal communities" should be aware of these considerations. Here there was alleged misconduct between the seller and a consultant making a wetlands delineation. The court found there was sufficient notice to an alert buyer of a potential problem with the accuracy of the delineation to defeat a misrepresentation claim. The court also found sufficient evidence of a breach of covenants against past environmental violations (alleged improper ditching and road building as a prelude to development rather than for forestry purposes) to defeat a motion for summary judgment.

107. Solid Waste Agency of N. Cook Cnty. v. U.S. Army Corps of Eng'rs, 531 U.S. 159 (2001). The Court held that use of these wetlands by migratory birds is not sufficient to make them "waters of the United States" in this context. *See also* United States v. Wilson, 133 F.3d 251 (4th Cir. 1997) (isolated wetlands do not substantially affect interstate commerce and are not subject to federal regulation).

108. 33 U.S.C. § 1344(e); 33 C.F.R. § 330.5(a).

headwaters. In North Carolina, the Corps has also issued a regional general permit for work permitted under CAMA.[109] Individual permit applications undergo a "public interest" review[110] by a variety of state and federal agencies and require a certification from the state that the activity will not violate water-quality[111] or coastal-management[112] standards.

Permits may not be issued where there is a practicable alternative that would have a less-adverse environmental impact or when the proposed activity does not require location in or over the water.[113] Where fill is permitted, mitigation of any wetland losses may be required. The state has established a Wetlands Restoration Program[114] to facilitate wetland-mitigation efforts through a state ecosystem-enhancement program. G.S. 143-214.7C[115] prohibits requirements for mitigation for impacts to intermittent streams except as required by federal law.

Other Environmental Regulations

Brownfield Redevelopment

There is a substantial body of federal[116] and state law on solid and hazardous wastes.[117] Among those with the most significant land use impacts are brownfield-redevelopment programs. Brownfield programs are available that encourage reuse of previously contaminated sites by limiting the new user's liability for past environmental problems.[118] The North Carolina Brownfields Property Reuse Act sets the framework for this program.[119] A prospective developer of a brownfield site can enter into an agreement with the DEQ

---

109. SAWCO 80-N-000-0291. Regional general permits are authorized at 33 C.F.R. § 325.7(e).

110. 33 C.F.R. § 320.4.

111. 33 U.S.C. § 1341(a); 33 C.F.R. § 325.2(b)(1). This is generally referred to as the *Section 401 water-quality certification* and is obtained from the EMC. G.S. 143B-282(a)(1)(u). The rules regarding these certifications are at 15A N.C.A.C. 2H, §§ .0501–.0507. Also see 15A N.C.A.C. 2B, §§ .1301–.1305 on discharges to isolated wetlands. The court upheld the authority of the EMC to regulate wetlands in *In re Request for Declaratory Ruling by the Environmental Management Commission*, 155 N.C. App. 408, 573 S.E.2d 732 (2002), *review denied*, 357 N.C. 62, 579 S.E.2d 392 (2003), holding that wetlands were "waters" as defined by G.S. 143-212(6) (as that term includes any "other body or accumulation of water, whether surface or underground"). The court also considered the language and spirit of the statutes and their purposes (and similar long-standing federal interpretations of "waters of the United States" to include wetlands).

112. Section 307(c)(1) of the Federal Coastal Zone Management Act requires federal permitting decisions in the coastal area to be consistent with approved state coastal-management programs. 16 U.S.C. § 1456(c); 33 C.F.R. § 325.2(b)(2). The approved state program in North Carolina includes state regulatory requirements, local land use plans approved under CAMA, and state guidelines adopted by the CRC.

113. 40 C.F.R. §§ 230.3(q), 230.10(a).

114. G.S. 143-214, §§ .8 to .13.

115. Created by S.L. 2015-286, § 4.27. S.L. 2015-286, § 4.18 also limits mitigation requirements for impacts to isolated wetlands unless the impact exceeds one acre east of I-95 and one-third acre west of I-95.

116. The principal federal statutes are the Comprehensive Environmental Response, Compensation, and Liability Act of 1980 (CERCLA), 42 U.S.C. §§ 9601–9675; the Resource Conservation and Recovery Act of 1976 (RCRA), 42 U.S.C. §§ 6901–6987; and the Federal Insecticide, Fungicide, and Rodenticide Act of 1988 (FIFRA), 7 U.S.C. §§ 136–136y. The Emergency Planning and Community Right-to-Know Act of 1986, 42 U.S.C. §§ 11001–11050, provides for planning of toxic emergencies.

117. For a detailed review of state law regarding solid waste, animal waste, spills of petroleum and hazardous wastes, radioactive waste, and cleanup of contaminated sites, see RICHARD WHISNANT, CLEANUP LAW OF NORTH CAROLINA: A GUIDE TO A STATE'S ENVIRONMENTAL CLEANUP LAWS (UNC School of Government, 2003).

118. *See generally* ROBERT A. SIMONS, TURNING BROWNFIELDS INTO GREENBACKS: DEVELOPING AND FINANCING ENVIRONMENTALLY CONTAMINATED URBAN REAL ESTATE (1998); WHISNANT, *supra* note 117.

119. The program is codified at G.S. 130A-310.30 to -310.40. Property-tax benefits for brownfield-redevelopment sites are provided by G.S. 105-277.13. There are also important provisions on brownfield redevelopment in federal law. In 2002, Congress amended CERCLA to provide that bona fide purchasers of contaminated properties may also

to define the remediation to be undertaken and the land use restrictions that will then be imposed. The developer is then protected from additional liability for environmental cleanup. The programs require neighborhood involvement and approval of cleanup plans by an environmental-regulatory agency. With larger-scale commercial and mixed-use redevelopment projects, public investment in parking and other improvements may be needed to make the project financially viable.

Coal-Ash Management

For most of the twentieth century, electric utilities in North Carolina and around the country used coal-ash ponds adjacent to coal-fired power plants to dispose of waste coal ash. A Tennessee Valley Authority coal-ash pond failed in 2008, leading to a massive discharge that prompted enhanced environmental scrutiny of these aging facilities. The 2014 failure of a Duke Energy pond along the Dan River brought the issue of how best to deal with the fourteen coal-ash ponds in North Carolina to the forefront.

The General Assembly in 2014 adopted the Coal Ash Management Act to create a regulatory scheme to manage coal-ash impoundments and closure plans.[120]

The state management system created for management of coal ash allows local development regulation but has a preemption provision similar to that for hydraulic fracturing (often called "fracking"). G.S. 130A-309.205 expresses a state intent to have a uniform system for managing coal-combustion materials. Local regulation of the management of coal ash is prohibited if it imposes a restriction or condition beyond those imposed by the state or that conflict in any manner with state regulations. The operator of a coal-ash-management facility may petition the EMC to review the matter and preempt that action.[121] In this review, a zoning or other development regulation[122] that imposes a generally applicable development standard to all development is presumed valid unless the EMC finds otherwise. Preemption is required if the EMC finds that all other required state and federal regulatory approvals have been secured, that local citizens and elected officials have had adequate opportunity to participate in the permitting process, and that the project would not pose an unreasonable health or environmental risk.[123]

Environmental-Impact Statements

The environmental-impact statement is a well-known feature of federal environmental law. The National Environmental Policy Act of 1969 created a mandate that federal agencies conduct a detailed analysis of the potential environmental impacts of major federal actions that significantly affect the quality of

---

be exempt from liability under federal cleanup laws if, after conducting all appropriate inquiries, it is determined that all disposal of hazardous substances occurred prior to their acquisition of the property. 42 U.S.C. § 9607(q). Rules on "all appropriate inquiries" are set forth in 40 C.F.R. § 312. Federal grants, technical assistance, and tax incentives are available for brownfield redevelopment.

120. Among other provisions, this law created the Coal Ash Management Commission. The state supreme court ruled that the provisions for legislative-branch appointments to the commission (as well as appointments to the Oil and Gas Commission and Mining Commission) constituted an unconstitutional violation of the separation of powers. State v. Berger, 368 N.C. 633, 781 S.E.2d 248 (2016). The General Assembly responded by eliminating the Coal Ash Management Commission and assigning the program for closure of coal-ash impoundments to DEQ. S.L. 2016-95.

121. G.S. 130A-309.205(b). The EMC is required to hold a hearing on the request for preemption. Published and mailed notice of the hearing is mandated.

122. Regulations specifically addressed are setback, buffer, and stormwater requirements.

123. G.S. 130A-309.205(e).

the environment.[124] The environmental-impact statement has become a significant factor when major federal grants or permit decisions are involved.

In 1971, North Carolina adopted the State Environmental Policy Act that included a narrower requirement for environmental-impact statements in state-agency decision-making. The state requirement for a statement is triggered by actions involving the expenditure of state money[125] or the use of public land[126] for projects significantly affecting the quality of the environment.[127] While the state environmental-report requirement does not apply to permitting decisions, the issuance of a certificate authorizing acquisition of land for a new reservoir is covered.[128]

G.S. 113A-8 explicitly allows cities and counties to adopt requirements that those proposing major developments[129] prepare environmental analyses similar to those required by federal law. The require-

---

124. 42 U.S.C. § 4332(2)(C). This federal requirement sparked substantial litigation and commentary in the years following its passage. Among the cases arising in North Carolina are the following: North Carolina v. FAA, 957 F.2d 1125 (4th Cir. 1992) (challenge to closing of military air space); North Carolina v. Va. Beach, 951 F.2d 596 (4th Cir. 1991) (challenging approval of water withdrawals from Lake Gaston); Providence Rd. Cmty. Ass'n v. Environmental Protection Agency, 683 F.2d 80 (4th Cir. 1982) (challenging construction of Waxhaw wastewater-treatment plant); Fayetteville Area Chamber of Commerce v. Volpe, 515 F.2d 1021 (4th Cir. 1975) (challenging bypass location); Rucker v. Willis, 484 F.2d 158 (4th Cir. 1973) (challenging marina and piers in Bogue Sound); All. Legal Action v. U.S. Army Corps of Eng'rs, 314 F. Supp. 2d 534 (M.D.N.C. 2004) (reviewing adequacy of alternatives analyzed for Piedmont Triad Airport expansion); Hunt v. N.C. Dep't of Transp., 299 F. Supp. 2d 529 (E.D.N.C. 2004) (challenging bridge-replacement project at Sunset Beach); N.C. All. of Transp. Reform, Inc. v. U.S. Dep't of Transp., 151 F. Supp. 2d 661 (M.D.N.C. 2001) (challenging funding for Winston-Salem beltway); Warren Cnty. v. North Carolina, 528 F. Supp. 276 (E.D.N.C. 1981) (challenging PCB-landfill site); Twitty v. North Carolina, 527 F. Supp. 778 (E.D.N.C. 1981) (challenging PCB-storage site); New Hope Cmty. Ass'n v. U.S. Dep't of Housing & Urban Dev., 509 F. Supp. 525 (E.D.N.C. 1981) (challenging siting of low-income-housing project); Conservation Council of N.C. v. Froehlke, 340 F. Supp. 222 (M.D.N.C. 1972) (challenging New Hope dam to create Jordan Lake). *See also* Lujan v. Nat'l Wildlife Fed'n, 497 U.S. 871 (1990); Marsh v. Or. Natural Res. Council, 490 U.S. 360 (1989); Andrus v. Sierra Club, 442 U.S. 347 (1979); Kleppe v. Sierra Club, 427 U.S. 390 (1976); Aberdeen & Rockfish R.R. v. Students Challenging Regulatory Agency Procedures (SCRAP), 422 U.S. 289 (1975).

125. G.S. 113A-9 was amended in 2015 to define a "significant expenditure" of state funds as one greater than $10 million for a single project or related group of projects. S.L. 2015-90. G.S. 113A-12 was amended in 2010 to provide that the payment of economic-development incentives did not trigger these environmental reviews. S.L. 2010-186. The amendment was triggered by lawsuits involving the application of the State Environmental Policy Act to incentives promised for a large cement factory in the Wilmington area. S.L. 2010-188 provided that this amendment to the law was not applicable to pending litigation. The company involved in the litigation later declined offered incentives in order to expedite permit processing. The list of exempted projects was further expanded in 2015 to include university, community-college, or public-school projects; mitigation projects; and numerous other state approvals. S.L. 2015-90.

126. G.S. 113A-9 was amended in 2015 to define the "use of public land" to be land-disturbing activity of more than ten acres that results in substantial, permanent changes in land cover or topography. S.L. 2015-90. G.S. 113A-12 exempts several uses of public lands from the State Environmental Policy Act. These include construction of utilities on street rights-of-way, construction of driveway connections to public streets, leases or easements granted by the state for use of existing buildings or facilities, wastewater lines on or under state-owned submerged lands, and shellfish cultivation.

127. G.S. 113A-4(2). For background on the policies included in this act, see Milton S. Heath Jr. & Alex L. Hess III, *The Evolution of Modern North Carolina Environmental and Conservation Law Policy Legislation*, 29 Campbell L. Rev. 535, 543–46 (2007).

128. *In re* Envtl. Mgmt. Comm'n, 53 N.C. App. 135, 280 S.E.2d 520 (1981) (statement required prior to approval of certificate authorizing the Orange Water and Sewer Authority to construct the Cane Creek reservoir). *See also* Lewis v. White, 287 N.C. 625, 216 S.E.2d 134 (1975) (challenging site selection for state art museum); State v. Williams & Hessee, Ltd. P'ship, 53 N.C. App. 674, 281 S.E.2d 721 (1981) (challenging condemnation of land for expansion of Eno River State Park); Orange Cnty. v. N.C. Dep't of Transp., 46 N.C. App. 350, 265 S.E.2d 890, *review denied*, 301 N.C. 94 (1980) (challenging I-40 route selection).

129. G.S. 113-9 defines a "major development project" as including, but not limited to, shopping centers, subdivisions, and industrial and commercial projects, provided each project is not less than ten contiguous acres.

ment must be established by local ordinance. The ordinance must include minimum criteria to be used in determining when a statement is required. In *Marriott v. Chatham County*,[130] the court noted that while a county has discretion in determining whether statements are required and defining minimum criteria for when statements are required, it does not have the discretion of requiring a statement without establishing minimum criteria.

Environmental Justice

Environmental justice is the effort to assure that no group of people, regardless of race, color, national origin, or income, bears a disproportionate share of the negative environmental consequences resulting from industrial, governmental, and commercial operations.[131] In North Carolina, the opposition to the disposal of PCB wastes in a Warren County landfill was an early example of increased awareness of the need to address the practice of locating undesirable and environmentally harmful land uses and activities in communities with little political power.[132]

Governor Roy Cooper in 2022 directed all state agencies to incorporate environmental justice and equity considerations in the implementation of the state's efforts to address climate change.[133]

The location and concentration of landfills in low-income neighborhoods have been of significant concern nationally.[134] In response to these concerns, G.S. 160A-325 requires cities to consider alternative sites, socioeconomic data, and demographic data before selecting a landfill for residential solid waste

---

130. 187 N.C. App. 491, 654 S.E.2d 13 (2007), *review denied*, 362 N.C. 472, 666 S.E.2d 122 (2008). The county subdivision ordinance contained a provision that allowed the planning board to require an environmental-impact statement if the development exceeded two acres in size and if the board deemed the statement "necessary for responsible review" due to the nature of the land or peculiarities in the proposed layout of the development. The county approved several large developments on tracts adjacent to parcels owned by the plaintiffs without requiring an environmental-impact statement. The plaintiffs sought to enjoin development of the property until the county amended its ordinance to provide minimum criteria for when an impact statement would be required, and they sought a writ of mandamus to compel the county to make these amendments. The court noted that G.S. 113A-8 clearly requires a local ordinance requiring environmental-impact statements to include minimum criteria to determine when statements are required. It was undisputed that the Chatham County ordinance had no such criteria. The court held that in order to have standing, the plaintiffs must show that the injury they suffered by virtue of the defendant's actions was likely to be redressed by a favorable decision. The court held that it had no authority to compel the county to adopt or amend an ordinance. Thus, if the ordinance allowing an impact statement was invalid as written and the court had no authority to order the ordinance amended, there was no likelihood the plaintiffs' injury could be redressed by a favorable decision. Therefore, the court held, the trial court properly dismissed the action for lack of standing.

131. President Clinton issued an executive order on the subject in 1994. Exec. Order No. 12,898, 3 C.F.R. § 859, reprinted as amended in 42 U.S.C. § 4321. The implementing strategy is set forth in OFFICE OF ENVTL. JUSTICE, U.S. EPA, ENVIRONMENTAL JUSTICE STRATEGY: EXECUTIVE ORDER 12, 898 (1995). *See generally* UNEQUAL PROTECTION: ENVIRONMENTAL JUSTICE AND COMMUNITIES OF COLOR (Robert D. Bullard, ed. 1994); Clifford J. Villa, *Remaking Environmental Justice*, 66 LOY. L. REV. 469 (2020); Luke W. Cole, *Empowerment as the Key to Environmental Protection: The Need for Environmental Poverty Law*, 19 ECOLOGY L.Q. 619 (1992); Alice Kaswan, *Environmental Justice: Bridging the Gap Between Environmental Laws and "Justice,"* 47 AM. U. L. REV. 221 (1998).

132. Also see the discussion of swine-farm siting and limits on nuisance suits in Chapter 22. For aspects of this issue related to zoning, see Andrew H. Whittemore, *The Experience of Racial and Ethnic Minorities with Zoning in the United States*, 32 J. OF PLAN. LIT. 16 (2016).

133. Gov. Roy Cooper, Executive Order 246, North Carolina's Transformation to a Clean, Equitable Economy, Jan. 7, 2020. To that end, each cabinet agency was directed to identify an environmental-justice lead person to coordinate the department's efforts and to seek public input on "additional executive action to advance environmental justice, equity, and affordability priorities of North Carolinians that live in, work in, or represent low- and moderate-income communities, indigenous communities, and communities of color." Id., § 9.

134. An early report documenting the scope of the issue is U.S. Gen. Accounting Office, Siting of Hazardous Waste Landfills and Their Correlation with Racial and Economic Status of Surrounding Communities (1983).

that is located within one mile of an existing sanitary landfill.[135] The city must also hold a public hearing prior to a siting decision. G.S. 130A-294(a)(4)(c)(9) requires denial of the solid-waste-facility permit upon a finding that the cumulative impact of the proposed facility would have a disproportionate adverse impact on a minority or low-income community.

Floodplains

The National Flood Insurance Act of 1968 created the National Flood Insurance Program (NFIP).[136] Under the federal law, property owners in a community are not eligible for federal flood insurance unless the local government has adopted floodplain regulations that meet minimum federal standards.[137] Regulation of flood-hazard areas is often incorporated as a section of local zoning ordinances, but it may also be adopted as a separate ordinance.[138] This program has proven to be a powerful incentive for local adoption of flood-hazard regulations. These standards generally prohibit development in the floodway, require elevation of the lowest habitable floor above the 100-year flood level in the broader floodplain, and limit location of manufactured housing in the floodplain. In *Responsible Citizens in Opposition to the Flood Plain Ordinance v. City of Asheville*, the court upheld Asheville's floodplain zoning ordinance, finding that preventing floodway obstructions and requiring flood proofing were reasonable means of accomplishing the legitimate governmental objective of protecting public safety.[139]

---

135. In *Greene Citizens for Responsible Growth, Inc. v. Greene County Bd. of Comm'rs*, 143 N.C. App. 702, 547 S.E.2d 480 (2001), the court held summary judgment to be inappropriate in a challenge to a decision to site a new landfill near an old landfill, as there was a genuine issue of material fact as to whether the board considered alternative sites.

136. Pub. L. 90-448. A series of subsequent federal laws have modified and strengthened this law. The Flood Disaster Protection Act of 1973 (Pub. L. 93-234) established a requirement for flood-insurance coverage as a condition of receiving mortgages from federally regulated lenders on property in flood-hazard areas. These mandatory insurance requirements were strengthened by the National Insurance Reform Act of 1994 (Pub. L. 103-325). The Disaster Mitigation Act of 2000 (Pub. L. 106-390) requires preparation of local hazard-mitigation plans as a condition of receipt of some disaster assistance. The National Flood Insurance Reform Act of 2004 (Pub. L. 108-264) reduced coverage for repetitive losses on an individual property. In 2004, the Federal Emergency Management Agency initiated a major effort to update and digitize the flood-insurance-rate maps that identify and categorize flood-hazard areas. *See generally* Timothy Kozlowski, Note, *Dams and Levees Are Not Enough: The Case for Recognizing a Cause of Action Against Non-Complying NFIP Communities*, 32 Wm. & Mary Envtl. L. & Pol'y Rev. 245 (2007); Edward A. Thomas & Sam Riley Medlock, *Mitigating Misery: Land Use and Protection of Property Rights Before the Next Big Flood*, 9 Vt. J. Envtl. L. 155 (2008).

137. 42 U.S.C. § 4002(b). For flood-insurance cases arising in North Carolina, see *Burch v. Federal Insurance Administration*, 23 F.3d 849 (4th Cir. 1994), and *Leland v. Federal Insurance Administrator*, 934 F.2d 524 (4th Cir. 1991). The federal government also funds substantial disaster-relief programs, including grants and incentives for land use and construction regulations to mitigate natural-hazard damage. *See, e.g.*, 42 U.S.C. §§ 5121(b), 5131, 5133, 5165. For regulations on state and local mitigation plans, see 44 C.F.R. § 201.1. For additional analysis, see Hazard Mitigation Section, N.C. Div. of Emergency Mgmt., Keeping Natural Hazards from Becoming Disasters: A Mitigation Planning Guidebook for Local Governments (May 2003); Anna K. Schwab, *Preventing Disasters Through "Hazard Mitigation,"* Popular Gov't, Spring 2000, at 2.

138. G.S. 143-215.51 to -215.61, originally adopted in 1971. A 2005 survey by the School of Government indicated that 68 percent of the responding municipalities and 98 percent of the responding counties had adopted regulations on floodplain development. David W. Owens & Nathan Branscome, An Inventory of Local Government Land Use Ordinances in North Carolina 10 (UNC School of Government, Special Series No. 21, May 2006). It is not uncommon for low-population municipalities to be covered by county floodplain regulations. G.S. 160A-360(k) provides that county floodplain regulations apply to bona fide farmland in municipal extraterritorial areas.

139. Responsible Citizens in Opposition to the Flood Plain Ordinance v. City of Asheville, 308 N.C. 255, 302 S.E.2d 204 (1983). The court held that the regulation was not a taking and did not violate equal protection. For the most part, similar regulations are routinely upheld around the country. *See, e.g.*, Adolph v. Fed. Emergency Mgmt.

The devastating floods resulting from Hurricane Floyd in the fall of 1999 prompted substantial strengthening of the state's laws regarding regulation of development in flood-hazard areas. G.S. 143-215.51 to -215.61 were modernized in 2000[140] to convert them, collectively, from a floodway-regulatory program to a floodplain-regulatory program. This law defines flood-hazard areas as the 100-year floodplain as defined on maps prepared pursuant to the NFIP or maps approved by the Department of Crime Control and Public Safety (the state maps must be prepared to NFIP standards). Local governments are authorized to designate larger areas at their discretion. New solid-waste-disposal facilities, hazardous-waste-management facilities, salvage yards, and chemical-storage facilities are prohibited in the 100-year floodplain. Local flood-hazard-prevention ordinances are to meet NFIP requirements, prohibit the restricted uses noted above, and provide that any chemical- or fuel-storage tanks in the floodplain be elevated, watertight, and securely anchored. Local governments are authorized to purchase (using condemnation, if necessary) existing structures in flood-hazard areas if necessary to prevent damage from flooding. If a city does not adopt a flood-hazard ordinance in its extraterritorial jurisdiction, the county is authorized to do so.[141]

It is common for flood-hazard areas as defined in a federally approved Flood Insurance Rate Map (FIRM) to be incorporated into local development regulations.[142] G.S. 160D-105(b) allows maps officially adopted by state or federal agencies to be incorporated by reference into local development regulations. This specifically includes flood-insurance-rate maps and watershed-boundary maps. The local regulation may incorporate either a specific adopted map or the most recently adopted map.[143] If updated state or federal maps are to be incorporated, the ordinance may provide that zoning boundaries (such as for a flood-hazard overlay zoning district) are automatically updated as well, provided a copy of the currently effective map is maintained for public inspection by the local government clerk.

The state's emergency-management laws were also amended after Hurricane Floyd to provide an updated system of emergency management during disasters.[144] The law provides for damage assessment following a disaster and establishes three levels of disasters that may be declared by the governor, depending on the extent of damage (Type I being disasters that do not meet the federal threshold for a presidentially declared major disaster, Type II being disasters that warrant such a presidential

---

Agency, 854 F.2d 732, 738 (5th Cir. 1988); First Evangelical Lutheran Church v. Cnty. of L.A., 210 Cal. App. 3d 1353, 258 Cal. Rptr. 893 (1989); Gove v. Zoning Bd. of Appeals, 444 Mass. 754, 831 N.E.2d 865 (2005); Zanghi v. Bd. of Appeals, 61 Mass. App. Ct. 82, 807 N.E.2d 221 (2004); Maple Leaf Inv'rs, Inc. v. State, 88 Wash. 2d 726, 565 P.2d 1162 (1977). For an early case invalidating a floodplain restriction that removed all value of the regulated property, see *Dooley v. Town Plan & Zoning Commission*, 151 Conn. 304, 197 A.2d 770 (1964). *See also* Turnpike Realty Co. v. Town of Dedham, 362 Mass. 221, 284 N.E.2d 891 (1972).

140. S.L. 2000-150.

141. This legislation also made the existence of a flood-hazard ordinance a factor in setting priority for allocation of moneys from the state's Clean Water Revolving Loan and Grant Fund.

142. G.S. 143-215.52 and -215.56 mandate the use of base floodplain maps that are either prepared by the National Flood Insurance Program (*see* 44 C.F.R. § 60.3) or approved by the state. Local government flood regulations must use state- and federally approved flood-hazard delineations without amendment. When flood-hazard studies that are the foundation of FIRMs are updated, the federal government publishes notice—twice in local newspapers as well as in the Federal Register—that the preliminary FIRMs are available for a ninety-day review-and-appeal period. After any appeals are addressed, the federal government issues a Letter of Final Determination; the date on which the letter is issued serves as the effective date of the updated FIRM. Local governments must make any necessary amendments to their local flood-hazard ordinances within six months of the date of the Letter of Final Determination.

143. An automatic update provision allows updated flood-hazard delineations to be automatically incorporated into local ordinances, preventing inadvertent use of outdated and inaccurate maps or zoning-district delineations. It also avoids the time and expense of local hearings and mailed notices of zoning-map amendments to incorporate new flood-hazard maps that must be used without further amendment.

144. S.L. 2001-214.

declaration, and Type III being those disasters that both warrant a presidential declaration and have a damage level so great as to prompt a special state-legislative session). A Type I disaster declaration expires in thirty days; Types II and III, in twelve months. The law provides for a program of state disaster assistance to finance recovery efforts for which federal aid is either unavailable or inadequate. This state assistance program includes both individual assistance (for items such as temporary housing, medical expenses, and housing repair) and public assistance (for items such as debris clearance, repair of roads and bridges, crisis counseling, and public transportation). G.S. 166A-6A(b)(2) provides that local governments are eligible for state public-assistance funds only if they have an approved hazard-mitigation plan and, for flood-damage assistance, are participating in the NFIP (which requires local adoption of floodplain regulations).

Hazardous Waste

G.S. 130A-293 limits zoning coverage of state-selected sites for treatment of hazardous waste.[145] The operator of a proposed hazardous-waste treatment and storage facility may petition the secretary of the DEQ to review any local ordinance, including zoning, that restricts the operation. The secretary then holds a public hearing in the affected locality to determine to what extent the local ordinance will be preempted. The findings that must be made to support a full or partial preemption are set out in the statute, as are the standards for judicial review of the decision. G.S. 104E-6.2 establishes a similar scheme for full or limited preemption of zoning regulations affecting the siting or the operation of low-level radioactive-waste facilities.

Landfills

In addition to local regulation, there are substantial state and federal regulations regarding landfills. These regulations can vary significantly depending on the range of wastes allowed in the landfill. The most-stringent rules apply to disposal of hazardous and radioactive waste, as noted above. Siting of new sanitary landfills must comply with stringent state regulations in addition to local land use regulations.[146] Special and less-stringent rules apply if the landfill is to contain only inert debris.[147] There are also special rules for animal-waste-management facilities.[148]

A local government franchise, as well as any required land use permits, is required for a sanitary landfill.[149]

---

145. For the most part, federal laws on this topic do not preempt local regulations on the release of hazardous substances. *See, e.g.*, Fireman's Fund v. City of Lodi, 287 F.3d 810 (9th Cir. 2009).

146. The basic state-permit requirement for solid-waste-management facilities is set forth in G.S. 130A-294 and G.S. 130A-295.2 to -295.6. See *Waste Industries USA, Inc. v. State*, 220 N.C. App. 163, 187–88, 725 S.E.2d 875, 892, *review denied*, 366 N.C. 241, 731 S.E.2d 686 (2012), for an illustration of evolving state-legislative criteria for landfill siting. An illustration of the interplay of state environmental and local zoning restrictions is provided by *PBK Holdings, LLC v. County of Rockingham*, 233 N.C. App. 353, 756 S.E.2d 821, *appeal dismissed*, 367 N.C. 788 (2014).

147. G.S. 130A-301.1, applicable to disposal of land-clearing- and inert-debris landfills with a disposal area of one-half acre or less. The disposal area must be located at least fifty feet from the property line.

148. G.S. 143-215.10C.

149. G.S. 130A-294(b1). Cnty. of Wake v. N.C. Dep't of Env't & Natural Res., 155 N.C. App. 225, 573 S.E.2d 572 (2002), *review denied*, 357 N.C. 62, 579 S.E.2d 386 (2003). *See also* Griffin v. Town of Unionville, No. 3:05-cv-514-RJC, 2008 WL 697634 (W.D.N.C. Mar. 11, 2008).

Mountain Resources

The Mountain Ridge Protection Act,[150] enacted in 1983, authorizes local governments to regulate development along mountain ridges.[151] The ridge law applies to construction of tall buildings on land within 100 feet of protected mountain ridges, which are those ridges whose elevation is over 3000 feet and more than 500 feet above the adjacent valley floor.[152] Permits are required for structures more than forty feet tall.[153] Permits for these buildings must be denied if they do not provide adequate water, sewer, and sedimentation control or if they fail to meet aesthetic standards set by the local government. If a local government failed to adopt a ridge-protection ordinance by January 1, 1984, buildings taller than forty feet are prohibited along the protected ridges.[154]

The question of a broader state role in mountain-area-resources planning has been debated in North Carolina for some time. G.S. 153B-3, enacted in 2009,[155] created a seventeen-member Mountain Resources Commission. The commission was to identify issues and recommend programs to address mountain-resource issues, coordinate resource planning and protection efforts, provide a forum for discussion, promote communication and education, collect research and information on provision of

---

150. G.S. 113A, §§ 205 to 214. For a legislative history of the act, a description of early implementation action, and an analysis of legal issues involved, see Milton S. Heath, Jr., *The North Carolina Mountain Ridge Protection Act*, 63 N.C. L. Rev. 183 (1984), and Robert M. Kessler, Note, *North Carolina's Ridge Law: No View from the Top*, 63 N.C. L. Rev. 197 (1984).

151. G.S. 113A-214 provided that counties could opt out of coverage by the law upon approval of the voters by referendum held by May 8, 1984. Only one county, Cherokee County, held such a referendum, and it failed.

152. Local governments have the option of covering additional ridges. Cities with populations over 50,000 (Asheville is the only mountain municipality that qualifies) may eliminate the 3000-foot-elevation requirement and may apply their ridge-protection ordinance in their extraterritorial area. G.S. 113A-208.

153. Questions have arisen regarding the application of the ridge law to wind-energy projects. The General Assembly in 2009 considered S.B. 1068, which would establish a regulatory program for location of wind turbines. This bill would not allow these windmills in areas where they would be prohibited under the Mountain Ridge Law but would exempt any windmill to serve individual residences if the windmill were no more than 100 feet from the base to the turbine hub. In 2008, the North Carolina Wind Working Group, a coalition of state agencies, nonprofit organizations, and wind-power companies, produced a model local ordinance on wind-energy-facility regulation. N.C. Wind Working Group, Model Wind Ordinance for Wind Energy Facilities in North Carolina (July 2008).

154. Eight counties elected to adopt ridge-protection ordinances. The remaining seventeen affected counties elected to allow the state prohibition of tall buildings along protected ridges to become effective.

155. S.L. 2009-485. The law also created G.S. 153B-4 to establish a thirteen-member Mountain Area Technical Advisory Council made up of professionals with environmental, engineering, planning, and governmental expertise. The Studies Act of 2009, S.L. 2009-574, also authorized the Legislative Research Commission to study issues affecting important mountain resources and to recommend policies and programs for those issues. For earlier studies, see Mountain Area Study Comm'n, Report to the 1993 General Assembly of North Carolina 15–16 (Jan. 27, 1993) (recommending continued study of voluntary planning guidelines for the mountain area); Legislative Research Comm'n: Mountain Area Study Comm., Report to the 1995 General Assembly of North Carolina 13–14 (Jan. 11, 1995) (recommending consideration of land use–guidance systems and voluntary, incentive-based models of local planning).

Other regional resource areas have also been the subject of legislation. S.L. 2010-176 established the Uwharrie Regional Resources Act, a program to "encourage quality growth and development while preserving the natural resources" of the Uwharrie region. G.S. 153C-1(c). The law created a ten-member Uwharrie Resources Commission to identify and evaluate issues, coordinate local and regional efforts to address those issues, provide a forum for discussion, communication, and education, study new strategies and tools, and make recommendations on the use, stewardship, and enhancement of important regional resources. The commission does not have independent planning or regulatory authority. This initiative grew out of legislative discussions related to the relicensing of Alcoa's Badin hydroelectric project on the Yadkin River.

infrastructure and encouragement of quality growth, and examine new strategies and tools for addressing pressures on mountain resources. The commission was abolished in 2013.[156]

Oil and Gas Development

North Carolina historically has had no commercial oil or gas extraction, but technology for shale-gas extraction or offshore oil and gas development continues to be proposed, and the state and local management structure to consider such proposals continues to evolve.[157]

The development of technology to extract natural gas from deep shale deposits led to widespread use of fracking in other parts of the country and in Canada. The fracking process involves individual wells with rigs trucked from site to site.[158] Concerns raised about the process include the potential for groundwater contamination (either from migration of injected chemicals or leakage from well casings), the adequacy of the water supply, the drilling-and-production facility's compatibility with surrounding uses, noise- and air-quality impacts from drilling, runoff and spills from drilling operations, damage to roads from the transportation of drilling equipment, and the infrastructure for processing and distribution. The intergovernmental issue of state preemption of local regulations has also been an ongoing point of discussion.

North Carolina law prohibited fracking until 2012, when the legislature removed the ban.[159] This law was further refined in 2014 to allow the Oil and Gas Commission to preempt local regulation of fracking.[160] G.S. 113-415.1 expresses a state intent to have a uniform system for managing oil and gas exploration, development, and production. It provides that local governments may not prohibit oil and gas wells within their entire jurisdiction, ban fracking, or add conditions on fracking beyond those required by state law. If a local regulation imposes generally applicable setback, buffering, or similar rules to oil and gas exploration, development, or production facility, the operator may petition the commission to review the matter and preempt that action.[161] In this review, a zoning or other development regulation[162] that imposes a generally applicable development standard to all development is presumed valid unless the commission finds otherwise. Preemption is required if the commission finds that the

---

156. S.L. 2013-413, § 43.

157. A 2012 report by the state Department of Environment and Natural Resources concluded that about thirteen counties in North Carolina were home to a potential resource, but precise estimates of the nature and extent of the resource were unknown pending exploration. Most of the report projections were based on only two test wells in Lee County. The study estimated a potential for some 360–70 wells in the state, producing some 300 drilling jobs over seven years. N.C. Dept. of Env't & Nat. Res. & N.C. Dept. of Commerce, North Carolina Oil and Gas Study Under Session Law 2011-276 (Apr. 30, 2012).

158. Three to five million gallons of water (about 10 to 30 percent of which is recovered) is injected into the deep wells with a mixture of sand and chemicals under high pressure to fracture the shale and release natural gas.

159. S.L. 2012-143. The law also revised the state Mining Commission to create a new Mining and Energy Commission and directed it to develop a modern regulatory program for shale-gas extraction. S.L. 2013-365 directed the Mining and Energy Commission to study creation of a comprehensive environmental permit for fracking. The commission was directed to work with the League of Municipalities and Association of County Commissioners to examine local regulation of oil and gas exploration and development, allowing reasonable regulations that do not have the effect of prohibiting exploration or development. The three groups are also directed to examine the costs to local governments from infrastructure impacts (roads and the like) and how those costs should be addressed. In 2014, the statute was again revised to make this the Oil and Gas Commission. S.L. 2014-4.

160. S.L. 2014-4. This provision was amended by S.L. 2015-264 to apply the preemption to "all provisions" of local ordinances regulating fracking to the extent that those regulations place any restrictions or conditions on fracking beyond state requirements.

161. G.S. 113-415.1(d) requires the Oil and Gas Commission to hold a hearing on the request for preemption. Published and mailed notice of the hearing is mandated.

162. G.S. 113-415(f). Regulations specifically addressed are setback, buffer, and stormwater requirements.

regulation would prohibit or have the effect of prohibiting oil or gas development, that all other required state and federal regulatory approvals have been secured, that local citizens and elected officials have had adequate opportunity to participate in the permitting process, and that the development would not pose an unreasonable health or environmental risk.

Development of offshore oil and gas reserves has in recent decades proven to be an important source for global energy resources. In the United States, the Gulf of Mexico has been heavily developed, and there are important offshore oil and gas developments off the California and Alaska coasts. There was active interest in exploration and potential development of oil or gas resources off the North Carolina coast in the 1980s, interest that periodically reemerges.[163]

Open-Space Acquisition

State law authorizes cities and counties to acquire land for open space and areas for public use and enjoyment.[164] The statute allows purchase of fee interests, easements, or development rights. This is routinely done with city and county subdivision-plat approvals.

Sedimentation and Erosion Control

Sedimentation-control ordinances manage soil erosion on sites undergoing development. The state Sedimentation Pollution Control Act establishes a statewide regulatory program that requires sedimentation-control plans for land-disturbing activity affecting an acre or more of land.[165] The plans must be submitted for approval at least thirty days prior to initiating the land-disturbing activity. Disturbed lands must be protected within fifteen working days or thirty calendar days (whichever is less) of completing any phase of grading. There are substantial civil penalties for failure to file a plan or to adhere to the provisions of an approved plan.[166]

The purpose of this law is the prevention of harmful sedimentation during construction, not the control of land use within buffers adjacent to water bodies. *Hensley v. North Carolina Department of Environment and Natural Resources*[167] addressed this in a challenge to an erosion- and sedimentation-control variance granted to allow the expansion of a golf course adjacent to a trout stream. The state

---

163. In 2011, the General Assembly approved S.B. 709. This bill directed the governor to pursue an interstate compact with Virginia and South Carolina relative to exploration, development, and production of offshore energy development. Governor Perdue vetoed the bill, and her veto was not overridden.

164. G.S. 160D, §§ 1301 to 1307. The authorization is for nonregulatory land-acquisition programs. It was added to the statutes in 1963 and was modeled after a California statute. A number of states adopted similar legislation in the early 1960s to take advantage of federal grants for open-space acquisition.

165. G.S. 113A, §§ 50 to 66. Regulations for the program are at 15A N.C.A.C. 4. Also, a property owner suffering damages from improperly controlled sedimentation may sue the upstream offender to recover those damages. *See, e.g.*, Whiteside Estates v. Highlands Cove, 146 N.C. App. 449, 553 S.E.2d 431 (2001), *review denied*, 356 N.C. 315, 571 S.E.2d 220 (2002) (awarding some $600,000 in damages and attorney fees). G.S. 113A-52.01 exempts a variety of activities from coverage, including crop production, livestock cultivation, poultry farming, horticulture, mulch manufacturing, and other agricultural activities.

166. Substantial civil penalties for enforcement were upheld in *In re Appeal from Civil Penalty Assessed in Violation of Sedimentation Pollution Control Act*, 324 N.C. 373, 379 S.E.2d 30 (1989). The one-year statute of limitations in G.S. 1-54(2) does not apply to the assessment of a civil penalty for these violations. Ocean Hill Joint Venture v. N.C. Dep't of Env't, Health, & Natural Res., 333 N.C. 318, 426 S.E.2d 274 (1993). While G.S. 113A-66 provides for a private civil action when there has been a violation of the act, this is available only if there has been a notice of violation issued by the government. Applewood Props., LLC v. New S. Props., LLC, 366 N.C. 518, 742 S.E.2d 776 (2013). When a builder or developer transfers a lot developed with a single-family residence, financial responsibility for compliance transfers to the new owner. G.S. 113A-54.1(f).

167. 364 N.C. 285, 698 S.E.2d 41 (2010).

approved construction of fairways and cart paths that involved removal of the tree canopy above about a half-mile of the stream buffer and enclosing about a third of a mile of the stream in pipes and culvers. The approval included strict conditions to minimize sedimentation during the construction process. The issue was whether this activity constituted "temporary" and "minimal" land disturbance. As the construction process itself was temporary and the sedimentation controls imposed would ensure minimal sedimentation, the court upheld the approval.

G.S. 113A-60 provides that local governments may, subject to state approval, adopt local ordinances that supplant the requirement for state approval of sedimentation-control plans. Local ordinances must meet (and may exceed) the state's minimum standards for sediment control.[168] As of March 31, 2022, fifty-five local governments had adopted such programs (including two joint city-county programs).[169]

Tree Protection

Tree-protection ordinances limit the removal of large trees and set standards for landscaping cutover areas. Several local governments have sought and received specific legislative authorization to adopt various tree-protection regulations.[170] In recent years, the legislative authorizations for local tree-protection regulations have become increasingly specific.[171]

State legislation adopted in 2005 also limits some local regulation of forestry activity. G.S. 160D-921 prohibits counties and cities from regulating activities associated with growing, managing, and harvesting trees on lands subject to forestry use-value property taxation or activity being conducted in accordance with a forest-management plan.[172] These statutes provide that they do not limit local regulation of activity associated with development, such as clearing land for a subdivision or commercial development. A difficult situation arises when both forestry and development are involved, which is not an uncommon combination. For example, trees may be grown on a site under a forestry-management plan until the owner determines that the site is ready for development, at which point the trees are harvested and sold, and the site is converted to nonforest use. The statutes address this situation by

---

168. G.S. 113A-60(b1) limits permit requirements for individual residential lots if there is an approved plan for the overall development, and G.S. 113A-60(b3) limits local requirements of silt fences where the land contours are such that the fence would not substantially retain sediment.

169. A significant number of additional cities and counties also have adopted some form of sediment- and erosion-control regulation. In a 2005 survey by the School of Government, one-third of the responding cities and nearly half of the responding counties reported adoption of sediment- and erosion-control regulations. OWENS & BRANSCOME, *supra* note 138.

170. *See, e.g.,* S.L. 1997-420 (Cornelius, Davidson, Huntersville, and Nags Head); S.L. 1989-478 (Chapel Hill), S.L. 1989-611 (Wrightsville Beach); S.L. 1987-921 (1988 session) (Pine Knoll Shores); S.L. 1987-242 (Southport), S.L. 1987-786 (New Hanover County and its municipalities); S.L. 1985-828 (1986 session) (Highlands); S.L. 1985-556 (Asheville and Raleigh). Bills were introduced in the 1985 General Assembly (H.B. 959 and H.B. 960) that would have allowed cities and counties to regulate "landscapes and natural features" under zoning. The bills initially were approved in the House of Representatives but were reconsidered and re-referred to committee. Neither was enacted. Similarly, a bill to authorize ordinances to regulate tree removal, H.B. 1322, was defeated in the 1979 General Assembly.

171. *See* S.L. 2003-246 (applicable to Statesville, Rockingham, and Smithfield); S.L. 2003-129 (applicable to Rutherfordton and Wake County); S.L. 2003-73 (applicable to Holly Springs); S.L. 2001-191 (applicable to Cary, Durham, Fuquay-Varina, Garner, Knightdale, Morrisville, and Spencer, authorizing regulations on clear-cutting (Raleigh was added to this group by S.L. 2003-128)); S.L. 2000-108 (applicable to Apex, Cary, Garner, Kinston, and Morrisville, authorizing regulation of planting, removal, and preservation of trees, with mandated exemption for single-family and duplex lots and for forestry activity undertaken with a forestry-management plan).

172. These provisions were created by S.L. 2005-447. These laws also explicitly provide that they do not limit local tree regulations imposed pursuant to local legislation or enacted in response to state or federal law. Cities may also regulate trees affecting their street rights-of-way.

providing that counties and cities may deny building permits, site plans, and subdivision plats in certain instances of clear-cutting the property. If the harvest results in the removal of substantially all of the trees that were protected under city or county regulation, development approval can be withheld for up to three years after the harvest (and for up to five years if the harvest was a willful violation of local ordinances). Also, G.S. 153A-123(h) and 160A-175(h) prohibit any local ordinance from regulating trees on property owned or operated by a public-airport authority.

Wind Energy

Wind energy has increasingly been viewed as an alternative energy source in North Carolina, both at the commercial and individual-user scale.[173]

Legislation was enacted in 2013 to establish a state-permitting program for wind-energy facilities.[174] State permits are required for installation and expansion of facilities with a rated capacity of at least one megawatt. The permitting process includes submission of pre-application materials, notice to relevant agencies and parties, pre-application evaluation of the site, a scoping meeting, permit application and fees, public notice, and a hearing. In addition to site-specific permit conditions that may apply, applicants must provide financial assurance for decommissioning and annual-monitoring reports.[175] The criteria for permit approval includes impacts on military and civilian air operations, impacts on cultural and natural resources, obstruction of navigation channels, applicable Mountain Ridge Protection Act protections, and compliance with other federal, state, and local requirements, including zoning.

Counties in North Carolina have approved several commercial-scale wind-power projects in the northeastern region of the state.[176]

Local governments have also adopted regulatory provisions for small-scale wind turbines.[177] The regulations typically specify where the turbines can be located and include height limits (maximum heights for the structure and minimum elevations for rotors), setbacks, fencing, and sometimes appearance standards. Stricter regulation of commercial-scale wind farms is common.

There has been increased international development of offshore wind resources. Commercial wind projects have been proposed for areas off the Mid- and North Atlantic coast. Studies indicate that the

---

173. A demonstration project was authorized by the General Assembly for location in the Pamlico Sound, but its industry sponsor withdrew from the project due to high costs of construction. *See generally* UNIV. N.C. CHAPEL HILL, COASTAL WIND: ENERGY FOR NORTH CAROLINA'S FUTURE (June 2009); Joseph J. Kalo & Lisa C. Schiavinato, *Wind Over North Carolina Waters: The State's Preparedness to Address Offshore and Coastal Water-Based Wind Energy Projects*, 87 N.C. L. REV. 1819 (2009).

174. G.S. 143-215, §§ .115 to .126. In 2017, the legislature imposed an eighteen-month moratorium on state permits for wind-energy facilities running to December 31, 2018, in order to study the impact of the facilities on military operations in the state. S.L. 2017-192.

175. The review process considers risks to civil and military air travel and operations as well as impacts to species and habitat. Review of applications must be solicited from the U.S. Army Corps of Engineers, the U.S. Fish and Wildlife Service, the N.C. Wildlife Resources Commission, and the commanding officer of potentially affected military installations.

176. The Amazon Wind Farm US East, originally known as the Desert Wind project, a commercial-scale 208-megawatt wind farm with 104 commercial-scale turbines on 22,000 acres in Pasquotank and Perquimans counties, received zoning approval and began full commercial operation in 2017. A second project proposed for Perquimans and Chowan counties received zoning approval from Chowan County, but its special use permit for the portion of the development in Perquimans County was denied. This project, Timbermill Wind, would have up to forty-eight commercial-scale turbines. Interest has also been expressed in potential offshore wind projects.

177. N.C. WIND WORKING GROUP, *supra* note 153. For an analysis of local regulatory options and a model ordinance from the wind-industry perspective, see AM. WIND ENERGY ASS'N, IN THE PUBLIC INTEREST: HOW AND WHY TO PERMIT FOR SMALL WIND SYSTEMS—A GUIDE FOR STATE AND LOCAL GOVERNMENTS (Sept. 2008). Also see the discussion in Chapter 22 on restrictions on local regulation of solar collectors.

wind potential off the North Carolina coast could support wind projects. In 2021, Governor Roy Cooper issued an executive order setting targets for future offshore wind development and established various work groups to facilitate its development.[178] The federal government has leased two areas off North Carolina's coast for offshore wind development, one at Kitty Hawk and the other at Wilmington.[179]

---

178. Gov. Roy Cooper, Executive Order 218, Advancing North Carolina's Economic and Clean Energy Future with Offshore Wind, June 9, 2021.

179. The leases are for 122,405 acres offshore of Kitty Hawk (Lease OCS-A 0508, issued in 2017 to Avangrid Renewables, located about 24 nautical miles from shore) and two areas totaling 110,091 acres some seventeen miles off Bald Head Island (Leases OCS-A 0545 and OCS-A 0546, issued in 2022 to TotalEnergies Renewables USA, LLC and Duke Energy Renewables Wind, LLC, respectively).

Legislative Decisions

PART 3

CHAPTER 11

Adoption, Amendment, and Repeal of Land Use Regulatory Ordinances

North Carolina statutes set out special mandates that must be observed by cities and counties in adopting, amending, or repealing ordinances establishing land-development regulations.[1] Failure to observe these procedural requirements voids the adoption, amendment, or repeal of the regulation. The requirements are in addition to those that must be followed for adoption of any other ordinance. They include a public hearing on the proposed action with two published notices. Also, when adopting a zoning regulation, statutory mandates require the appointment of a planning board and special hearing notices for zoning-map amendments. Any special procedural requirements set forth in the local ordinance itself must be strictly followed.

The legislative decisions are among the most frequent major land use regulatory decisions made by local governments. With zoning, map and text amendments are frequently considered by cities and counties. In a series of surveys, the UNC School of Government asked North Carolina cities and counties about the number of variances, special use permits, zoning-text amendments, and zoning-map amendments that had been considered by their jurisdictions in the previous calendar year. Although exact comparisons are not possible because the surveys were conducted in different years,[2] the surveys indicate that zoning-map amendments are by far the most commonly sought zoning approvals addressed by city and county boards.[3] The relative volume of these requests is summarized in Table 11.1.[4]

---

1. Procedural requirements regarding legislative decisions are based on statutory rather than constitutional mandates. Constitutional, procedural due-process rights are generally not applicable to the notice, hearing, and planning-board-review requirements as applicants have no property rights to a particular legislative decision. Bi-Metallic Inv. Co. v. State Bd. of Equalization, 239 U.S. 441, 445 (1915). A failure to comply with state procedural requirements for a legislative decision does not in and of itself constitute a federal due-process violation. Onyx Properties, LLC v. Bd. of Cnty. Comm'rs, 838 F.3d 1039 (10th Cir. 2016).

2. The data is from the same universe of jurisdictions—all of the cities and counties in North Carolina with zoning ordinances—and the three surveys involved all had similar response rates. The numbers are not directly comparable, as there is an interval of two years between each of the three surveys, and slightly different jurisdictions responded to each survey. But the three survey populations are sufficiently similar and sufficiently close in time to provide a good indicator of the relative frequency with which each type of decision arises.

3. DAVID W. OWENS, ZONING AMENDMENTS IN NORTH CAROLINA 4 (UNC School of Government, Special Series No. 24, 2008). These are legislative and quasi-judicial decisions made by governing boards, boards of adjustment, and planning boards. Routine administrative and ministerial decisions made by staff without hearings are even more common.

4. While the relative distribution of these approvals has been relatively consistent over time, the absolute number of applications varies significantly depending on economic conditions and overall development levels. For example, the level of applications received in 2012 and 2018 were about half of those reported in prior years. David W. Owens, *2018 Survey Report: Adoption and Administration of Local Development Regulations, Conditional Zoning, and Subdivision Administration*, PLAN. AND ZONING L. BULL. No. 30 (UNC School of Government, Dec. 2020), at 9.

Table 11.1   Frequency of Zoning Approvals Sought, by Type

Type of Approval (Year Surveyed)	Total Number Sought in Previous Year
Zoning-map amendments (rezonings) (2006)	3029
Special and conditional use permit applications (2004)	2207
Variance petitions (2002)	1806
Zoning-text amendments (2006)	1520

Applicability

The statutory public notice and hearing requirements discussed in this chapter apply to all legislative decisions regarding land use regulatory ordinances.[5] This includes not only the original adoption of the regulation but also all subsequent actions. For example, amendments to the text of the regulation to effect such changes as setback requirements, revisions of off-street parking requirements, or additions or deletions of a permitted use for a particular zoning district must follow these mandated procedures. Amendments to a zoning map to reflect the rezoning of property from one district designation to another also are covered. A map amendment does not affect the text of the zoning regulation, but that does not release the action from having to meet these requirements because the zoning map is a part of the zoning regulation. In North Carolina, a zoning-map amendment is subject to procedural requirements in addition to those mandated for all text amendments.[6]

Repeal of a land use regulation must comply with these procedures as well. *Orange County v. Heath* illustrates the application of these requirements to legislative actions beyond the original adoption of the regulation. After proper notice and a hearing, the board of county commissioners voted to rezone the petitioner's fifteen acres from a residential to a mobile-home zoning district. A week later, the board voted to rescind the rezoning and return the land to its original classification. The court ruled that the attempted rescission was invalid because the notice and hearing requirements had been applied only to the first vote to rezone, not to the second vote to rescind the rezoning.[7]

---

5. Chapter 160D, Section 601 of the North Carolina General Statutes (hereinafter G.S.) confirms that a public hearing is required prior to "adopting, amending, or repealing" any development regulation authorized by Chapter 160D.

6. These procedural requirements include the mailed-notice, posted-notice, and protest-petition provisions discussed below. While text and map amendments are usually easy to distinguish, situations can arise in which a text amendment is functionally equivalent to a map amendment. This is most likely to occur when the text amendment modifies the permitted uses in a district to such a substantial extent that it effectively has created a new zoning district. In *Modak-Truran v. Johnson*, 18 So. 3d 206 (Miss. 2009), the court reviewed a zoning-text amendment that allowed bed and breakfasts in a residential district to include a restaurant open to the general public. The court held this to be a rezoning, noting that "the labeling of an action as a 'text amendment' does not make it so if the City's actions effectively rezone a residential plot for commercial use." *Id.* at 210. The court went on to hold this to be illegal spot zoning. On the other hand, in *Takacs v. Indian Lake Borough Zoning Hearing Board*, 11 A.3d 587 (Pa. Commw. Ct. 2010), the court held that the addition of permissible uses to a zoning district (here multifamily dwellings and commercial-boat docking) was not a zoning-map amendment.

7. Orange Cnty. v. Heath, 278 N.C. 688, 180 S.E.2d 810 (1971). Before the court invalidated the rescission of the rezoning here, a stop-work order was in force to prevent the establishment of a mobile-home use. The petitioner in *Heath* subsequently brought an action to recover damages resulting from the stop-work order. The court dismissed the claim, ruling that Chapter 1A, Section 1 of the North Carolina General Statutes (Procedural Rule 65(c)), which provided that the county was not required to post a surety upon issuance of a restraining order, did not waive government immunity in this matter. *See* Orange Cnty. v. Heath, 282 N.C. 292, 192 S.E.2d 308 (1972).

The court elaborated on the applicability of these requirements to amendment and repeal of land use regulations in *Sofran Corp. v. City of Greensboro*.[8] The court emphasized the nature of the action taken by the governing board when it reconsidered a zoning matter.[9] If the reconsideration was followed by reaffirmation or insubstantial modification of the ordinance, no additional notice or hearing was required. However, if the reconsideration resulted in repeal or substantial modification, additional notice and hearing were required.

These notice and hearing requirements apply to all ordinances related to land use that are authorized by Chapter 160D of the North Carolina General Statutes (hereinafter G.S.).[10] This includes regulations establishing regulations on subdivisions, building, housing, historic districts, community appearance, sedimentation and erosion control, floodways, mountain-ridge protection, and roadway corridors as well as those setting a municipality's extraterritorial jurisdiction.[11]

These special procedural requirements do not apply to related ordinances adopted under the general ordinance making authority or to those separate ordinances adopted under other specific legislative authority.[12] However, courts have held that in certain circumstances these notice and hearing requirements apply to even general ordinances that substantially affect land use. Iredell County had adopted a land-development plan in 1987 but before 1990 did not have countywide zoning. When a rock quarry was proposed for an unzoned area, the county adopted a sixty-day moratorium on the issuance of any building permits in the unzoned portion of the county for any use that would be inconsistent with those set forth in the land use plan.[13] In *Vulcan Materials Co. v. Iredell County*,[14] the court ruled the moratorium invalid because the county had not followed the requirements for two published notices and a public hearing set forth in G.S. 153A, § 323. Although the moratorium ordinance did not explicitly state whether it was being adopted as a general-police-power ordinance or as a land use ordinance, the court ruled that because it was so closely related to zoning and building-permit ordinances, it had to be adopted following the same procedural safeguards that were imposed on zoning. Similarly, in *Sandy Mush Properties, Inc. v. Rutherford County*,[15] the court held that a 120-day moratorium on location of heavy industries near schools was invalid due to a lack of two published hearing notices. The county, which did not have zoning, contended the moratorium was adopted under its general ordinance-making authority to protect school areas while an ordinance to provide protection was developed, debated, and

---

8. 327 N.C. 125, 393 S.E.2d 767 (1990).

9. A motion to reconsider must itself be procedurally valid. In this case, such a motion was allowed under the Greensboro code if it was made by a council member no later than the day of the second regular meeting after the original action or if a qualifying referendum petition was filed within thirty days of the original action.

10. There are, however, separate notice and hearing provisions for ordinances establishing development moratoria. G.S. 160D-107(b). See Chapter 9 for a discussion of moratoria.

11. Town of Swansboro v. Odum, 96 N.C. App. 115, 384 S.E.2d 302 (1989). The court invalidated the ordinance because of several procedural irregularities: The notice was not published in successive calendar weeks. (The notices were published ten days apart.) The notice inadequately described the action proposed and the area affected. The adoption took place eight months after the hearing, and the boundary description was not recorded as required by G.S. 160D-202(e).

12. For example, G.S. 63-33 sets the procedure to be followed if an airport-approach-protection ordinance is adopted as a separate ordinance rather than being incorporated into the zoning ordinance. Many of these other statutes were amended by S.L. 2019-111 to incorporate or cross-reference the procedures required by Chapter 160D.

13. See the discussion of moratoria in Chapter 9.

14. 103 N.C. App. 779, 407 S.E.2d 283 (1991). G.S. 160D-107, which sets specific procedures for moratoria adoption, was enacted subsequent to the *Vulcan Materials* and *Sandy Mush Properties, Inc. v. Rutherford County* (discussed in text below) decisions.

15. 164 N.C. App. 162, 595 S.E.2d 233 (2004).

put into place.[16] The court held that the moratorium was a temporary land use plan that divided the county into two areas—zones in which heavy industry was allowed and the smaller areas where they were at least temporarily prohibited. This fact, along with the use of the building-permit system for its enforcement, led the court to conclude that the moratorium must be adopted following the procedures for land use regulations. Since adoption or amendment of a land use regulation requires a public hearing with two published notices and that was not done, the moratorium was held invalid under the *Vulcan Materials* analysis. The court reached the same result in *Thrash Ltd. Partnership v. County of Buncombe*, a challenge to the validity of an ordinance regulating multifamily dwellings that established differential standards depending on the elevation of the property involved. The ordinance limited density, the height of buildings, parking standards, road construction, and the area of land disturbance. The court noted that the effect of this ordinance was to make unzoned portions of the county subject to zoning prior to the adoption of a zoning ordinance applicable to those areas. It then held that the county could not evade the notice and hearing requirements of the zoning-enabling statute by simply labeling the ordinance a "general police power ordinance" rather than a "zoning ordinance."[17]

In earlier cases, the courts allowed some single-purpose, land use–related ordinances to be adopted following general police power rather than zoning procedures. For example, in both *Summey Outdoor Advertising, Inc. v. County of Henderson*[18] and *PNE AOA Media, LLC v. Jackson County*,[19] the court upheld sign ordinances adopted under the general police power. In *Maynor v. Onslow County*, the court upheld the use of general-police-power procedures in the adoption of an ordinance regulating the location of sexually oriented businesses.[20] In each of these instances, the court held that the special procedural requirements for land-development regulations were not mandated.[21] As noted above, however, courts have refused to extend this line of cases to other situations that more closely resemble traditional land use regulation.[22]

---

16. The plaintiff was proposing to locate a crushed-rock quarry near a school. At the time the plaintiff first applied for a building permit, and at the time the moratorium was adopted, the county was considering adoption of a "Polluting Industries Development Ordinance" that would have regulated heavy industries within two thousand feet of a church, school, or residence. That ordinance was eventually rejected. The county later (but within the moratorium period) adopted a "School Zone Protective Ordinance" that precluded the plaintiff's project. The county contended that this ordinance was also adopted under its general ordinance-making power, but it followed all of the hearing and notice procedural steps required for zoning ordinances in its adoption.

17. Thrash Ltd. P'ship v. Cnty. of Buncombe, 195 N.C. App. 727, 673 S.E.2d 689 (2009). The county subsequently adopted countywide zoning, following proper procedures.

18. 96 N.C. App. 533, 386 S.E.2d 439 (1989), *review denied*, 326 N.C. 486, 392 S.E.2d 101 (1990).

19. 146 N.C. App. 470, 554 S.E.2d 657 (2001).

20. Maynor v. Onslow Cnty., 127 N.C. App. 102, 488 S.E.2d 289, *appeal dismissed*, 347 N.C. 268, 493 S.E.2d 458, *review denied*, 347 N.C. 400, 496 S.E.2d 385 (1997). The ordinance in question required adult businesses to be located at least 1000 feet from dwellings, places of worship, schools, day-care facilities, parks, and other adult businesses. Similar location requirements are usually included in zoning ordinances, but Onslow County was unzoned. The court held, "When a county adopts an ordinance designed to promote the health, safety and welfare of the county's residents, N.C. Gen.Stat. § 153A-121 [the general police power] empowers the county to adopt such ordinance without complying with the procedural safeguards provided in N.C. Gen.Stat. § 153A-341 [the zoning-enabling statute]." *Maynor*, 127 N.C. App. at 106, 488 S.E.2d at 292. Other counties without zoning have used the general police power to adopt regulations on manufactured-housing parks, junkyards, and other individual land uses.

21. This issue has also arisen in other states. The Georgia Supreme Court, for example, held that the adoption of a comprehensive tree-protection ordinance did not have to follow the procedures required for zoning ordinances because a majority of the ordinance's requirements applied uniformly across the entire jurisdiction; the tree ordinance did not "regulate according to zones or districts." Greater Atlanta Homebuilders Ass'n v. DeKalb Cnty., 277 Ga. 295, 296, 588 S.E.2d 694, 696 (2003).

22. *See, e.g.*, Union Land Owners Ass'n v. Cnty. of Union, 201 N.C. App. 374, 689 S.E.2d 504 (2009) (provisions for adequate-public-facilities and mitigation-fee ordinances are governed by the zoning- and subdivision-enabling authority rather than the authority enabling the general police power).

Some of the uncertainty regarding the applicability of these development regulation procedures to the adoption and amendment of general ordinances that affect land use and development has been statutorily resolved. G.S. 160D-101(a) provides that the provisions of Article 1 of Chapter 160D (Article 1 includes definitions and provisions on vested rights, conflicts of interest, and moratoria) apply to "any other ordinance that substantially affects land use and development." Other articles of Chapter 160D are not as broadly applicable. For example, G.S. 160D-601(a) provides that mandatory procedures for adoption, amendment, and repeal of development regulations are applicable to ordinances and regulations authorized by Chapter 160D without mention of regulations affecting land use and development that are adopted under other statutory authority. Similarly, G.S. 160D-1401 and -1402 state that the provisions on judicial review apply only to challenges to regulations and decisions made under Chapter 160D.

Observance of Statutory and Ordinance Procedural Requirements

State statutes set most of the minimum procedural standards for adoption, amendment, and repeal of development regulations. However, it is not at all uncommon for local ordinances to establish additional standards.

Any supplementary procedures incorporated in the local development ordinance must be strictly followed. For example, if the ordinance specifies the timing for posting a notice of the public hearing on the site of a proposed rezoning or sets a minimum waiting period between consideration of rezoning petitions for the same land area, those requirements may not be waived.[23]

There is also occasionally an interplay between a local procedural requirement and state law. In *Murdock v. Chatham County*,[24] the county had adopted an annual calendar for public hearings on rezonings. The calendar included specified deadlines for submission of rezoning petitions for a matter to be heard at each of the scheduled hearings. This schedule required completed applications to be received a minimum of thirty days before the public hearing. As adopted by the county planning board, the 2006 calendar stated that matters could be considered at the September 18 meeting if they were filed by August 21. Counting back thirty days from the hearing would have produced a Saturday deadline for applications (August 19), so the planning board moved the deadline to the next business day (Monday, August 21). The contested application was received on August 21, which technically was just twenty-eight days before the hearing. The county staff interpreted this as meeting the locally imposed schedule. The court, however, disagreed. The county must rely on state law for the mechanics of computing the deadline, not a local interpretation of it, the court held. Under state rules,[25] since the deadline is computed counting back from the hearing, the application would have to be filed by the close of business on the Friday preceding the Saturday deadline to meet the thirty-day mandate. The fact that the filing requirement was locally adopted for the convenience of the local government did not give the county the right to waive the requirement once it was placed in the ordinance.

Consequences of Failure to Observe Requirements

If mandated procedures are not strictly followed, the purported ordinance action is invalid.

This result first obtained in 1926 in *Bizzell v. Board of Aldermen*.[26] The court there noted that during the period when the planning commission was at work on a zoning plan for Goldsboro and no public

---

23. George v. Town of Edenton, 294 N.C. 679, 242 S.E.2d 877 (1978). See the more detailed discussion on mandatory waiting periods below.

24. 198 N.C. App. 309, 679 S.E.2d 850 (2009), *review denied*, 363 N.C. 806, 690 S.E.2d 705 (2010).

25. G.S. 1A-1, Rule 6(a).

26. 192 N.C. 364, 135 S.E. 58 (1926).

notice or hearing had been held, a valid zoning ordinance was not yet in effect. The same fate befell an ordinance that the city of Waynesville hurriedly adopted in 1936 in an attempt to prohibit the construction of a gasoline filling station in its downtown. Neither a zoning commission nor a board of adjustment had been appointed—though the ordinance had been reenacted to enable that to be done—and no public hearing had been held. The court in *Shuford v. Town of Waynesville*[27] held that since the procedures mandated by the zoning-enabling legislation were not followed, the ordinance was invalid as a zoning ordinance. Failure to apply the filling-station prohibition citywide violated the uniformity requirement, so the ordinance was also invalid as a general ordinance. Thus, the court ruled that the construction of the filling station must be allowed.

When the required procedures are not followed, a purported amendment of a zoning ordinance becomes void *ab initio*, that is, treated as if it had never been enacted, and the preexisting zoning remains in effect.[28]

Appointment of a Planning Board and Recommendations on Ordinances

Because of the substantial potential impact of zoning on property owners and citizens, zoning-enabling statutes have from the outset imposed procedural requirements to force a careful and deliberate zoning-adoption process. The attorney for New York City's pioneering zoning ordinance noted in an early zoning-law text that mandatory appointment of a planning agency was a critical part of that mandate. He observed, "This is a precautionary measure to make sure that the zoning shall not be adopted hurriedly or impulsively, but only after careful study and consultation with property owners."[29]

North Carolina's original 1923 zoning-enabling act required a city to establish a zoning or city planning commission in order to avail itself of the power to zone.[30] This requirement continues in current law. G.S. 160D-604(a) mandates the creation or designation of a planning board before a local government may exercise its zoning authority.[31] Also, after July 1, 2022, a local government must have an adopted comprehensive plan as a prerequisite for exercising zoning authority.[32] G.S. 160D-501(a) states that "[a]s a condition of adopting and applying zoning regulations under this Chapter, a local government shall adopt and reasonably maintain a comprehensive plan that sets forth goals, policies, and programs intended to guide the present and future physical, social, and economic development of the jurisdiction."

---

27. 214 N.C. 135, 198 S.E. 585 (1938). *See also* Keiger v. Winston-Salem Bd. of Adjustment, 281 N.C. 715, 190 S.E.2d 175 (1972); Kass v. Hedgpeth, 226 N.C. 405, 38 S.E.2d 164 (1946).

28. *Keiger*, 281 N.C. 715, 190 S.E.2d 175.

29. EDWARD M. BASSETT, ZONING 34 (1940).

30. S.L. 1923-250, § 6. This zoning commission was charged with preparing the initial zoning regulations and districts and holding public meetings on the draft ordinance before its referral to the governing body for adoption. S.L. 1919-23 had previously authorized the creation of city planning boards. For further information on background and organizational alternatives for local government land use planning in North Carolina, see PHILIP P. GREEN, JR., ORGANIZING FOR LOCAL GOVERNMENTAL PLANNING IN NORTH CAROLINA (2d ed. 1989). Under the original Standard State Zoning Enabling Act, the zoning commission's role was limited to developing the original ordinance, and the commission expired after zoning was adopted.

31. The comparable provision for boards of adjustment, G.S. 160D-302, states only that the ordinance *may* provide for boards of adjustment. Although such boards are almost uniformly created with the adoption of zoning, there is not an explicit statutory prerequisite for them. Moreover, once a board of adjustment is created, there is no mandate to continue to have it. Existing boards may be abolished. Bd. of Adjustment v. Town of Swansboro, 334 N.C. 421, 432 S.E.2d 310 (1993).

32. The requirement for plan adoption in order to exercise zoning was added by S.L. 2019-111. That law provided a nearly three-year grace period before its effective date in order to allow a reasonable time for any jurisdictions without a plan to prepare and adopt one. See Chapter 22 for more details on comprehensive plans.

Governing boards have considerable latitude in determining the shape and makeup of a planning board. G.S. 160D-301 provides that the board may be "[a] planning board of any size (with not fewer than three members) or composition deemed appropriate, organized in any manner deemed appropriate."[33] If a city has established extraterritorial jurisdiction, it must provide for extraterritorial members on both its planning board and its board of adjustment.[34] G.S. 160A-60 gives cities the flexibility of appointing nonresidents to the planning board unless a city is specifically prohibited from doing so by its zoning ordinance or charter. G.S. 153A-25 gives county boards of commissioners the same flexibility. Most communities have created a separate board to undertake the planning function, but some have used this statutory flexibility to appoint some other body to serve in this capacity.[35] The most common variation is a single appointed body that serves as both the planning board and as the board of adjustment.

The planning board must review and approve the full text of a draft zoning ordinance and maps showing the boundaries of the proposed zoning districts. The board may, but is not required to, hold public hearings as it prepares the draft regulation. Generally, this planning-board review is required for comprehensive revisions of a zoning regulation as well as its initial adoption.[36] While referral to the planning board of adoption, amendment, and repeal of zoning regulations is mandatory, G.S. 160D-604(c) provides that a local government may also elect to send proposed amendments to any other development regulation to the planning board for review and comment.

Also, as provided by G.S. 160D-604, upon completion of its work the planning board is to make a written recommendation regarding adoption of the regulation to the governing board.

The zoning-enabling statute requires that all subsequent amendments to the zoning regulation also be submitted to the planning board for review before the governing board of commissioners takes action. G.S. 160D-604(b) gives the planning board at least thirty days to prepare recommendations on proposed amendments. As a matter of practice, virtually all city zoning regulations have long included this planning-board provision, but it was not required for municipalities until 2006.[37]

It is important that the planning board be provided an opportunity to comment on the amendments that are actually to be presented to the governing board. In *Thrash Ltd. Partnership v. County of Buncombe*,[38] the court considered the process by which the county extended its partial-county zoning coverage countywide. After the planning board reviewed a proposed zoning map, the staff continued

---

33. The statutes do not provide for a set term of membership on planning or agency boards. For boards of adjustment, the statutes mandate a term of three years. A member of a governing board may also serve on the board of a planning agency. If that member is not serving in an ex officio capacity, consideration of the dual-office-holding provisions is appropriate. N.C. CONST. art. VI, § 9; G.S. 128, §§ 1, 2.

34. G.S. 160D-307.

35. G.S. 160D-604(e) clarifies that while a local government can assign some duties of the planning board to the governing board, review and comment on ordinance amendments cannot be assigned to the governing board. (Otherwise, the board would be making a recommendation to itself.) As a practical matter, this means each jurisdiction with zoning must have a planning board or other appointed board that conducts these reviews and makes recommendations on ordinance amendments to the governing board.

36. George v. Town of Edenton, 294 N.C. 679, 687–89, 242 S.E.2d 877, 882–83 (1978).

37. S.L. 2005-418, § 7(a). Prior to this amendment, the court of appeals in *George v. Town of Edenton* had held that the requirement of planning-board recommendations on amendments applied only to initial adoption of zoning ordinances, not to subsequent amendments. George v. Town of Edenton, 31 N.C. App. 648, 653, 230 S.E.2d 695, 698 (1977). On review, however, the supreme court in dicta expressed doubt about the proper construction of G.S. 160D-604 and, while declining to resolve the issue, expressed doubt about the court of appeals' interpretation, noting that it should not be considered authoritative. *George*, 294 N.C. 679, 688–89, 242 S.E.2d 877, 882–83 (1978). Any confusion on the matter was resolved by the 2005 amendment.

38. 195 N.C. App. 678, 673 S.E.2d 706 (2009).

to entertain requests from landowners for changes to the classification of their property.[39] The court invalidated the adoption of the ordinance, as the planning board was not given the opportunity to make recommendations on the final, revised zoning map prepared by the staff.

Although it was once mandatory for planning boards to hold hearings on amendments, G.S. 160D-604 now enables planning boards to do so but does not make it a requirement. In other words, planning-board hearings about amendments are optional.[40] A number of local ordinances, however, still require planning-board hearings on rezoning proposals; others allow for joint planning-board and governing-board hearings when addressing such proposals. Even if no formal hearing is conducted by the planning board, the meeting at which the planning board reviews and makes a recommendation on proposed amendments is always required to be open to the public, and many boards allow for public comment at those meetings.

The planning board is to submit a written recommendation that specifically addresses the consistency of a proposed amendment with an officially adopted comprehensive plan, any other adopted plans, and other matters deemed appropriate by the planning board.[41]

A governing board is not bound by the recommendations of the planning board.[42] This conclusion was originally drawn via case law when, in 1963, the state supreme court upheld a governing board's discretion on whether to rezone a parcel:

> The Planning and Zoning Commission had no legislative, judicial or quasi-judicial power. Its report (recommendation) did not restrict or otherwise affect the legislative power of the City Council. The hearings before the Planning and Zoning Commission as well as the hearings before the City Council are required in order to afford "parties in interest and citizens" an opportunity to be heard with reference to proposed legislation. Whether the zoning ordinance should be amended as requested by petitioner was for determination by the City Council in the exercise of its purely legislative function.[43]

G.S. 160D-604(b) now expressly provides that the governing board is not bound by the recommendations of the planning board.

G.S. 160D-109(b) provides that planning-board members are not to vote on any recommendation regarding a zoning amendment that "is reasonably likely to have a direct, substantial, and readily identifiable financial impact on the member."[44] A member is also prohibited from voting on any zoning amendment if the owner of the property proposed to be rezoned or the applicant for a text amendment

---

39. Prior to the planning-board review, the county had sponsored a series of community meetings to secure input from citizens and had posted the information on the county website and solicited comments there. The planning board reviewed and commented on some of these proposed changes, but some 404 additional individual changes were made by staff after the planning-board review and before adoption by the county commissioners.

40. Johnson v. Town of Longview, 37 N.C. App. 61, 245 S.E.2d 516, *review denied*, 295 N.C. 550, 248 S.E.2d 727 (1978).

41. G.S. 160D-604(d). In *Sapp v. Yadkin County*, 209 N.C. App. 430, 704 S.E.2d 909 (2011), the court held that (1) this requirement is met if the mandated written statement on plan consistency is filed with the governing board before the governing board's consideration of the matter and (2) there is no requirement that a copy of the statement be attached to planning-board minutes. See the discussion of mandatory plan-consistency statements in Chapter 22.

42. The planning-board recommendations are influential, if not binding. In a 2008 School of Government survey, 61 percent of the responding jurisdictions indicated that the ultimate governing-board decision is either always or almost always consistent with the planning board-recommendation, and another 35 percent responded that this is frequently the case. OWENS, *supra* note 3, at 15.

43. *In re* Markham, 259 N.C. 566, 571–72, 131 S.E.2d 329, 334, *cert. denied*, 375 U.S. 931 (1963) (citations and emphasis omitted).

44. These provisions were added to the statutes by S.L. 2005-426, §§ 5(a) and 5(b). Conflicts of interest are discussed in more detail in Chapter 25.

has a close family, business, or associational relationship with the member.[45] This is the same conflict-of-interest standard that applies to governing-board members.

Public Hearing

Since its original adoption in 1923, the zoning-enabling act has provided for public hearings on adoption or amendment of a zoning regulation.[46] The requirement for a hearing by the governing board, with two published notices of the hearing, has been carried forward into current statutes and is applicable to all land-development regulations. Once the governing board receives a draft ordinance from the planning board, and if the governing board decides to proceed with potential adoption, it must hold a formal public hearing on the ordinance (no hearing is required if the governing board elects not to consider adoption).[47]

Public hearings must also be held on any subsequent amendment or repeal of land-development regulations. The governing board must hold the mandated hearing; a hearing by the planning board is not sufficient.[48] The hearing may be conducted as part of the governing board's regular meeting, or it may be held at a separate time and place. The costs of providing notice of the hearing are often charged to the petitioner, and this typically is a substantial component of the fee charged for proposed zoning amendments.

A question that is not explicitly addressed by North Carolina law is whether a governing-board hearing is mandatory upon the filing of a petition for amendment. A few jurisdictions in the state conduct a preliminary review by the governing board of proposed amendments prior to submitting them to public hearing. If the board determines the petition is frivolous or has no chance of approval by a majority of the board, it has the option of denying the petition without subjecting the applicant to the cost of the notice and hearing, and without subjecting opponents to the need to come to a hearing to express that opposition. The legal rationale for the ability to "wash out" a petition prior to a hearing is a reading of the statute to require that a hearing be conducted before amending the ordinance, and if the ordinance is not to be amended, there is no requirement for a hearing. Most jurisdictions, however, send any complete petition for amendment to the planning board for review and to a public hearing for comment before the governing board takes any action.

---

45. G.S. 160D-109(b). This provision was added by S.L. 2019-111. See Chapter 25 for a discussion of conflicts of interest.

46. S.L. 1923-250, § 4. Originally, a minimum fifteen-day published notice was required, as was recommended in the Standard State Zoning Enabling Act. In 1927, this provision was amended to specify that the notice of the governing board's required public hearing had to be published once a week for two successive weeks before the hearing. S.L. 1927-90. The 1923 act also required that the planning agency (then denominated as the "Zoning Commission") hold a hearing before making its recommendation for initial zoning. S.L. 1923-250, § 6.

While these hearings are subject to the Open Meetings Law, remote hearings may be conducted during a state of emergency. S.L. 2020-3, § 4.31(a). This authorization is codified at G.S. 166A-19.24.

47. G.S. 160D-601(a).

48. Keiger v. Winston-Salem Bd. of Adjustment, 281 N.C. 715, 190 S.E.2d 175 (1972).

Published Notice

A local government must publish in a newspaper of general circulation two notices of the governing board's required public hearing on a proposed adoption, amendment, or repeal of a land use regulation. The notice must be sufficiently detailed to allow citizens to discern what is being proposed and whether they would be affected.[49]

G.S. 160D-601(a) requires published notice of the required public hearing. The notice must be published in a newspaper of general circulation[50] in the community once a week for two successive calendar weeks, with the first notice being published not less than ten or more than twenty-five days before the hearing.[51] The day of publication is not counted in computing these times, but the day of the hearing is included.

The court first addressed this required public notice of the mandated hearing in 1960 in *Walker v. Town of Elkin*.[52] The town rezoned a 3.56-acre tract from a residential to a neighborhood-business district and amended the text of the zoning regulation to allow utility storage yards in that district. The newspaper notice stated that both changes would be "thoroughly discussed" and that "[a]ll persons for or against these proposed changes are invited to be present and make whatever statements they desire."[53] The court held that this was an adequate public notice.

The following year, in *Helms v. City of Charlotte*,[54] the court gave more detailed consideration to the extent of notice that was required. The only notice provided in *Helms* was a newspaper advertisement that gave a boundary description of the area being rezoned but did not include lot numbers, block numbers, or the owners' names. The plaintiff in the case, who had no actual knowledge of the hearing or the ordinance amendment (the case predated the subsequently enacted requirement of mailed notice to the affected property owners), contended that although the statutory public-notice requirements had been met, his constitutional rights of due process had been violated. The court disagreed and held that actual notice to landowners was not constitutionally required.[55]

The published notice must provide sufficient detail to apprise interested parties of the nature of the proposed action. The notice should clearly indicate (1) what property is potentially affected, (2) the nature of the proposed regulation, and (3) the time and place of the public hearing on the proposal. A

---

49. This is a common requirement in many states. *See, e.g.,* Glazebrook v. Bd. of Supervisors, 587 S.E.2d 589, 592–93 (Va. 2003) (holding notice inadequate where it stated development standards may be amended without any indication of the nature of the proposed amendments).

50. G.S. 1-597 defines a "newspaper of general circulation" for purposes of published notices. To qualify, the newspaper must have content that appeals to the public generally, it must have more than a de minimus number of actual paid subscribers, its subscribers must not be limited entirely to a single community, and it must be available to anyone desiring to subscribe. Great S. Media, Inc. v. McDowell Cnty., 304 N.C. 427, 441–42, 284 S.E.2d 457, 467–68 (1981).

51. Several local governments have received legislative authorization to substitute electronic posting of hearing notices for newspaper publication. S.L. 2003-81 allows Cabarrus County to post notices of public hearings on ordinance amendments on the Internet rather than publishing the notice in the newspaper. The county has to use the same schedule as required for published notices and will still have to do any required mailed notices. S.L. 2003-161 does the same for Raleigh and Lake Waccamaw, with the added provision that this does not relieve the cities of any required posting of notice on affected sites. S.L. 2007-86 added Apex, Garner, and Knightdale to this list, and S.L. 2008-5 added Cary.

52. 254 N.C. 85, 118 S.E.2d 1 (1960).

53. *Id.* at 86, 118 S.E.2d at 3.

54. 255 N.C. 647, 122 S.E.2d 817 (1961).

55. Subsequently, the court of appeals held, in *Capps v. City of Raleigh*, 35 N.C. App. 290, 241 S.E.2d 527 (1978), that actual personal notice of a proposed rezoning was not required and that the city could raise a laches defense based on constructive notice that met all of the statutory notice requirements. In this case, the city published notice of the public hearing, mailed notice to nearby residents, and posted signs on the property advertising the hearing.

legal description of the affected property is not required, and the full text of the proposed ordinance does not have to be published.

A mere recitation of the statutes involved coupled with a posting of the date and time of the hearing is inadequate. For example, when Asheville first extended its zoning ordinance extraterritorially, the public notice said only that the hearing concerned "the adoption of an ordinance amending and revising Ordinance No. 322, as amended, the Zoning Ordinance of the City of Asheville." The court of appeals held this to be inadequate:

> By reading the notice, even the most diligent owner of property outside the city would have no reasonable cause to suspect that his property might be affected by the city's contemplated amendment to its ordinance. To be adequate, the notice of public hearing required by G.S. 160A-364 must fairly and sufficiently apprise those whose rights may be affected of the nature and character of the action proposed.[56]

On the other hand, the court upheld the adequacy of a notice of a zoning-text amendment that added "government owned buildings, facilities, and institutions" to a list of permitted uses in the face of a challenge by neighbors objecting to the subsequent location of a state prison on the site.[57]

It is important that the proposed zoning text and map be available for inspection at the time notice is provided. If substantial changes are made in the proposed ordinance or amendments after the notice is provided and before the governing board considers the matter, an updated (and timely) additional notice is required. In *Thrash Ltd. Partnership v. County of Buncombe*,[58] the court invalidated a zoning-map amendment that extended partial-county zoning countywide because the maps were being adjusted to reflect individual landowner requests up until the day before the public hearing. The court concluded that the unavailability of final maps at the time of notice of the hearing precluded meaningful citizen comment and thus violated the statutory notice requirement.

---

56. Sellers v. City of Asheville, 33 N.C. App. 544, 549, 236 S.E.2d 283, 286 (1977). By contrast, the court upheld the adequacy of a notice of a hearing to solicit comment on the proposed zoning of areas added to the town of Garner's extraterritorial planning and development-regulation area. The notice stated that its purpose was "to consider proposed zonings and proposed long-range land use plans within the area recently added to the Town's extraterritorial jurisdiction." *In re* Raynor, 94 N.C. App. 91, 96, 379 S.E.2d 880, 883, *review denied*, 325 N.C. 546, 385 S.E.2d 495 (1989). The notice went on to sketch a "rough description" of the area by using major streets as boundaries. *Gas Mart Corp. v. Board of Supervisors*, 269 Va. 334, 611 S.E.2d 340 (2005), involved the Virginia statute on published notices for zoning hearings that requires "a descriptive summary of the proposed action." The court there noted, "the intent of the statute is to generate informed public participation by providing citizens with information about the content of the proposed amendments and the forum for debate concerning those amendments. There is no indication that the General Assembly expected affected citizens to engage in legal research in order to decide whether to participate in the hearing or to decide what their interests may be in the proposed amendment." *Id.* at 346.

57. Carter v. Stanly Cnty., 125 N.C. App. 628, 629, 482 S.E.2d 9, 13, *review denied*, 346 N.C. 276, 487 S.E.2d 540 (1997). The court observed:

> The mere fact that the notice provided was so generic that it did not pique plaintiffs' interest does not, in and of itself, make the notice violative of § 160A-364. We are mindful that, in the eyes of a property owner, abutting a state prison is quite a different thing from abutting a veteran's service office.
>
> However, we are a judicial, not a political, body. Since the Commission has adhered to the letter of the law, plaintiffs' true remedy in this case is a political one, and that we cannot give.

Id. at 635, 482 S.E.2d at 13.

58. 195 N.C. App. 678, 673 S.E.2d 706 (2009).

Individual Mailed Notice

In the mid-1980s, in response to perceived inadequacies in the constitutional and statutory requirements for publishing a newspaper notice of a mandated hearing, the General Assembly added statutory requirements pertaining to mailed notices. More specifically, in 1985, the General Assembly amended the zoning-enabling act to require individual mailed notice to the parties most directly affected by certain legislative zoning decisions.[59] In 2004, the statutes were amended to also require a mailed hearing notice to the commanding officer of any military base located within five miles of a proposed rezoning.[60]

The exact formulation of the mailed-notice requirement has been subject to frequent legislative modification. In 1987, the provision was amended to exempt the total rezoning of an entire community from the requirement for a mailed notice.[61] The exemption was itself modified in 1990 to require mailed notice in a total rezoning if the rezoning involved *downzoning*, or zoning to a less intense use.[62] The requirements for mailed notice also were subject to perhaps more modification by local legislation than any other mandated zoning procedure—some thirty-one local bills on the subject were enacted between 1985 and 1993.[63] The exemptions were rewritten in 1993 to create five exceptions to the mailed-notice

---

59. S.L. 1985-595. The statute originally used the term "zoning classification action," which was not defined in the statute, to trigger the mailed-notice requirement. Also, some local ordinances had provisions for mailed notice prior to enactment of the statewide requirement. *See, e.g.*, Lee v. Simpson, 44 N.C. App. 611, 261 S.E.2d 295, *review denied*, 299 N.C. 737, 267 S.E.2d 662 (1980).

60. S.L. 2004-75, creating G.S. 160D-601(b). This requirement was modified by S.L. 2013-59. This law amended G.S. 160D-601(b) to expand the types of development regulations that are to be submitted to the military base for review and comment. If the ordinance changes affect areas within five miles of a base perimeter, written notice is now to be provided for:
   1. zoning maps,
   2. permitted land uses,
   3. telecommunication towers and windmills,
   4. new major-subdivision preliminary plats, and
   5. an increase in the size of an approved subdivision by more than 50 percent of its land area.
The last two items concern individual project review rather than legislative amendments. If no comments are received in thirty days, the opportunity to comment is deemed to be waived.

61. S.L. 1987-807.

62. S.L. 1989-980. The legislature has extended this mailed-notice requirement to land use regulations other than zoning. G.S. 160D-202(d), created in 1996, requires mailed notice for the hearing on proposed notice of amendments to extraterritorial boundaries (which must be mailed four weeks prior to the hearing instead of the ten to twenty-five days required for zoning-map-amendment mailings). G.S. 143-214.5(d) requires cities and counties that under their general police powers adopt ordinances to protect water-supply watersheds to post a mailed notice if the ordinances impose requirements that are more stringent than the statewide minimum standards adopted by the Environmental Management Commission.

63. Burdened by the high cost of individual mailings in cases where a substantial rezoning is proposed, individual local governments sought and received legislative relief prior to the 1993 and 1995 revisions to this requirement. The most common local modification was to allow publication of a large display advertisement in a local newspaper once a week for four weeks in lieu of mailed notices. Local modifications included the following: S.L. 1995-339 (Orange County); S.L. 1995-282 (Durham); S.L. 1994-737 (Asheboro); S.L. 1993-411 (Huntersville, Cornelius, Davidson); S.L. 1993-358 (Orange County); S.L. 1993-296 (Nash County, Franklin County and its municipalities); S.L. 1993-271 (Cabarrus, Forsyth, and Iredell counties and their municipalities; Rockingham and Yadkin counties; the municipalities in Rowan County); S.L. 1993-267 (Davie and Davidson counties, Forest City, Mocksville, King, Lexington, and Thomasville); S.L. 1993-156 (Watauga County); S.L. 1993-154 (Denton); S.L. 1993-139 (Stokes County); S.L. 1993-101 (Wilkes County, Wilkesboro, Ronda, North Wilkesboro); S.L. 1993-79 (Troy, Spencer); S.L. 1991-846 (Martin County); S.L. 1991-6 (Laurinburg); S.L. 1991-596 (Faison); S.L. 1989-904 (Bailey); S.L. 1989-198 (Warsaw); S.L. 1989-205 (Rose Hill); S.L. 1989-237 (Fairmont); S.L. 1989-252 (Wake County); S.L. 1989-312 (Wilson); S.L. 1989-314 (Rocky Mount); S.L. 1989-415 (Pittsboro, Chatham County); S.L. 1989-509 (Wake Forest); S.L. 1989-512 (Durham); S.L. 1989-516 (Durham County); S.L. 1989-565 (Cherryville, Lincolnton); S.L. 1989-568 (Elm City); S.L. 1988-903 (Bethel, Robersonville); S.L. 1988-915 (Clinton); S.L. 1987-155 (Granite Falls); S.L. 1987-165 (Stokes County); S.L. 1987-247 (Grifton); S.L. 1987-339 (Clinton); S.L. 1987-455 (Cabarrus, Iredell, and Yadkin counties; the

Table 11.2 Summary of Requirements for Mailed Notice of Zoning-Map Amendments

Triggering Action	Proposed Zoning-Map Amendment
Recipients	Owner of parcel and owners of abutting parcels, as shown on county tax listing
Method of mailing	First class
Timing	Deposit in mail 10–25 days before hearing
Content	Notice of public hearing
Verification	Certification of mailing to be provided to governing board by person making mailing

requirement and to repeal most of the local modifications to the statute.[64] Finally, in 1995, the legislature completely rewrote the mailed-notice requirement and repealed all local modifications.[65]

G.S. 160D-602(a) requires individual mailed notices for hearings on proposed zoning-map amendments. These requirements are summarized in Table 11.2. The 1985 session law establishing the mailed-notice requirement states that it applies only when tax maps are available for the area to be zoned.[66] Prior to 2006, the statute exempted initial county zoning of territory from the mailed-notice requirement; that provision was repealed in 2005.[67]

The mailed notice is to be sent by first-class mail. It cannot be sent bulk rate and it does not have to be sent by registered or return-receipt mail. Some individual zoning ordinances require return receipts, and some zoning offices use it as a matter of office policy, but it is not required by statute. The certificate of the mailer serves as proof of compliance, provided there is no element of fraud.[68] The notice is to be mailed to the owners of the property proposed to be rezoned and all abutting property, as identified by the county tax records.[69] For the purpose of the required mailed notice, G.S. 160D-602 clarifies

---

municipalities in Alexander, Cabarrus, Iredell, and Rowan counties); S.L. 1987-594 (Southern Pines); S.L. 1985-879 (Henderson, Murfreesboro); S.L. 1985-936 (Chatham County and its municipalities); S.L. 1985-950 (Richmond, Scotland, Stanly, and Union counties, the municipalities therein, and Asheboro).

64. S.L. 1993-469.

65. S.L. 1993-546 specified that all previous local bills on this subject are repealed to the extent that they conflict with the revised provisions of G.S. 160A-384.

66. S.L. 1985-595, § 3. See *Frizzelle v. Harnett County*, 106 N.C. App. 234, 416 S.E.2d 421, *review denied*, 332 N.C. 147, 419 S.E.2d 571 (1992), in which the court of appeals held that the mailed-notice provision of G.S. 153A-343 did not apply because tax maps were not available for the area. However, in this case the ordinance itself required mailed notice and posting, which was not done. The court held that these ordinance requirements applied to initial adoption as well as to rezoning. The court also held that because the county had failed to raise the nine-month statute of limitations in its answer or to give notice of the statute to the plaintiff when the statute was raised in response to a summary-judgment motion, it was waived.

67. S.L. 2005-418, § 4(b).

68. In *Rakestraw v. Town of Knightdale*, 188 N.C. App. 129, 654 S.E.2d 825, *review denied*, 362 N.C. 237, 659 S.E.2d 739 (2008), the plaintiffs presented affidavits that not all of the mailed notices of a rezoning hearing were received. The court noted that the statute provides that if the mailer certifies the mailing of the notice, then that is deemed conclusive in the absence of fraud. Here the town made such a certification. As there was no evidence of fraud presented, there could be no issue of material fact regarding the mailing, and it was upheld as legally sufficient. The court reached the same conclusion in *Good Neighbors of Oregon Hill Protecting Property Rights v. County of Rockingham*, 242 N.C. App. 280, 774 S.E.2d 902, *review denied*, 368 N.C. 429, 778 S.E.2d 78 (2015), holding that when the staff member making the mailed notices certifies that they have been mailed, that certificate is deemed conclusive in the absence of an allegation of fraud.

69. The statute does not limit the mailing to owners within the jurisdiction making the rezoning. The owners of all abutting property, even if that property is in a different jurisdiction, should be mailed notice of the hearing.

that "abutting" properties include those separated only by a street, railroad, or other transportation corridor.[70] Many local zoning regulations expand these mailings, such as requiring a mailing to the owners of all properties within a specified distance of the affected property.[71] An updated title search is not required to identify the owners, as the statute specifies that the notices go to the owners as shown on the county tax listing. The notice is to be mailed within the same time period in which the initial newspaper notice is to be published—at least ten but not more than twenty-five days prior to the public hearing on the proposed rezoning. The content of the mailed notice should be the same as the content of the published notice.

The mailed notice is required for all "zoning map amendments."[72] This clearly includes rezonings that amend zoning-district boundaries. It also includes application of new overlay zones. It does not apply to text amendments or to the initial adoption of zoning for a jurisdiction, as this is an "adoption" rather than an "amendment" of the zoning map. The application of the mailed-notice requirement is less clear when an existing ordinance is amended to add new territory to the coverage of a zoning regulation, as when a city annexes territory or a county with partial-county zoning moves to full-county zoning. It is likely that application of initial city or county zoning to a parcel added to an existing regulation does require a mailed notice, as this is an "amendment" to the zoning map to add additional territory.

The mailing must be sent to the owners of property included in the zoning-map amendment and all "abutting" owners. If only part of a parcel owned by one individual is being rezoned, is that individual both the owner and the owner of the abutting property? Such an interpretation would be consistent with the case law on eligibility to file a protest petition under the former statute. However, the language of this statute specifically refers to the abutting *parcel* of land, so presumably the owner of whatever is shown as a separate parcel on the county tax maps is the appropriate recipient of the notice. Another common practice is to mail a notice to all property owners within a set distance from the parcel affected that is specified in the ordinance, such as those within 500 feet, a practice facilitated by the increasing availability of local geographic information systems.[73]

While the statute does not specifically require the local government itself to make the mailing, by far the most common practice is for the jurisdiction to make it. Some ordinances require anyone petitioning for a rezoning to make the mailing; this is accomplished by requiring the person doing the mailing to provide a certificate that it was done. An alternative sometimes used is to require the petitioner to provide stamped, addressed envelopes to the local government to deposit in the mail.[74] Other local governments just require that a list of those to receive a mailed notice be provided as part of any petition for a rezoning.

There is an alternative procedure for individual mailed notices available when large-scale rezonings are involved. The statutes provide that if the rezoning is of at least fifty properties with at least fifty different

---

70. This clarification was added by S.L. 2019-111. This 2019 amendment to the mailed-notice requirement also provides that if a rezoning is proposed in conjunction with an expansion of municipal extraterritorial jurisdiction, a single mailing may be made of the hearing on both the rezoning and the amendment of the extraterritorial-boundary map. If a single mailing is made, it is to be done at least thirty days prior to the date of the hearing, as opposed to mailing within the ten- to twenty-five-day window for mailing otherwise required for a rezoning hearing.

71. The most-used distances range from 100 to 500 feet from the boundary of affected parcels. If included in a local ordinance, these additional mailings are mandatory and must be observed.

72. See the discussion *supra* note 6 regarding the distinction between a zoning-map and text amendment.

73. In other states, a mailed notice must be sent to all owners within a fixed distance from the property being rezoned. *See, e.g.*, Mason v. Cnty. Comm'n of Franklin Cnty., 551 S.W.3d 54 (Mo. Ct. App. 2018) (applying statute requiring mailed notice of hearing to owners of property within 600 feet of rezoned property).

74. For example, under the Wilmington zoning regulation, a rezoning petition is not complete unless it includes two sets of stamped and addressed envelopes for each owner entitled to receive notice of the hearing. WILMINGTON, N.C., LAND DEVELOPMENT CODE § 18-568(A) (2022).

owners, an expanded published notice may be partially substituted for mailed notice.[75] Cities and counties have the option in these situations of substituting two half-page newspaper advertisements for the mailing. Each advertisement must appear in a separate week. However, even with this expanded publication, mailed notice must still be sent to any property owners outside of the newspaper's area of circulation, and signs must be posted on the site to advertise the hearing. Given the cost of half-page ads and the necessity of checking addresses for absentee owners, most local governments elect to use this option only for very large rezonings, such as the adoption of an entirely new zoning map for the entire jurisdiction.

Posted Notice

For many years the state statutes did not require the posting of a sign at the site of a proposed rezoning (with the exception of the expanded-published-notice option available for large-scale rezonings, discussed immediately above). In 2005, the statutes were amended to require a posted notice for all zoning-map amendments.[76] G.S. 160D-602(c) requires the county or city to prominently post a notice of the hearing on the site to be rezoned or on the adjacent street right-of-way. When multiple parcels are being rezoned, it is not necessary that each individual parcel be posted, but sufficient notices must be posted to provide reasonable notice to interested persons.

The state statute does not specify the content or size of the posted notice. In *Rakestraw v. Town of Knightdale*, the town posted a two-by-three-foot sign on the site of a proposed rezoning reading, "Town of Knightdale PUBLIC HEARING PROPERTY NOTICE—For More Information: [phone number]."[77] The court held this was adequate to identify and locate the property and that the sign need not contain the level of detail contained in published and mailed notices.

G.S. 160D-602(c) specifies the timing for posted notices. The notice is to be posted in the same time period as required for mailing notices: at least ten but not more than twenty-five days prior to the date of the hearing.[78] A substantial number of individual zoning ordinances also include a requirement of posting a notice of hearings at the site of the proposed rezoning. Most of these local requirements predate the state mandate for posted notices. Charlotte adopted such a requirement in 1954,[79] and a number of cities and counties subsequently did likewise.[80] To the extent these local provisions add to

---

75. G.S. 160D-602(b). Prior to 2006, four half-page advertisements were required.

76. S.L. 2005-418, §§ 4(a) and 4(b). There was one earlier instance of a statutory requirement for a posted notice of zoning hearings. The 1923 zoning-enabling act required a published notice in the local newspaper. However, several small towns that did not have a local newspaper elected to adopt zoning and the question arose how the published notice could effectively be done in those places. The resolution was that the statute was amended in 1927 to provide that if there was no newspaper in the town, it was to post a notice of the hearing in four prominent places at least fifteen days before the hearing. Subsequent recodifications of the statute eventually deleted this posted-notice alternative.

77. Rakestraw v. Town of Knightdale, 188 N.C. App. 129, 134, 654 S.E.2d 825, 829, *review denied*, 362 N.C. 237, 659 S.E.2d 739 (2008).

78. The specification for the timing of posted notices was added to the statute by S.L. 2019-111.

79. *The Clearinghouse*, POPULAR GOV'T, Mar. 1954, at 1.

80. For example, as provided by the Winston-Salem/Forsyth County zoning regulation:
POSTED NOTICE
i. In all cases of petitions to amend a zoning classification, the property shall be posted with a notice of public hearing by the Elected Body at least fifteen (15) days prior to the date of said public hearing. ii. Said notice shall consist of a sign(s) posted on the property at a conspicuous location(s) or on an adjacent public street or highway right-of-way, which sign shall be legible from the nearest public road. iii. Location(s) which are not conspicuous or require additional notification to the public will be required to have a directional sign(s) posted. iv. The signs are and shall remain the property of the governmental agency which provided them, and shall be prepared, posted, and reclaimed by it. v. When multiple parcels are included within a proposed amendment, a posting on each individual parcel is not required, but there shall be sufficient signs posted to provide reasonable notice to interested persons.
WINSTON-SALEM/FORSYTH COUNTY, N.C., UNIFIED DEVELOPMENT ORDINANCE § 3.2.19(A)(6)(c) (2022).

the minimum state posting requirement—such as specifying the timing for placement of the sign—they are mandatory and must be observed. If the local requirement is less demanding or contrary to the state requirements, the state statute prevails.

Actual Notice

At one time, the state statutes required actual notice to landowners for hearings on certain proposed rezonings. That provision has since been repealed.

In 2009, G.S. 160D-602(d) was amended[81] to require that actual notice of the hearing be given to the property owner[82] of land subject to a petition to amend a zoning map if that person did not initiate the rezoning petition. The requirement for actual notice did not apply if the rezoning petition was initiated by the city or county. The burden for providing this actual notice was on the third party requesting the rezoning.[83]

The statutory mandate for actual notice for third-party rezonings was repealed in 2019.[84]

Optional Additional Notice

Some local development regulations require additional mandatory means of communicating with and securing the engagement of those affected by proposed amendments to the regulations.

The most common such requirement is for someone proposing a conditional rezoning to meet with the neighbors and to summarize that meeting as part of the rezoning application. G.S. 160D-602(e) authorizes, but does not mandate, such a broader communication requirement.[85]

Conduct of the Hearing

Public hearings on legislative land use regulatory decisions must be conducted in a fair and impartial manner designed to receive citizens' comments on the substance of the proposed action.[86]

---

81. S.L. 2009-178. This former statute required that when a petition for rezoning was made by a person other than the landowner or the local government, the petition must include a certification that the landowner has received actual notice of the application and notice of the public hearing.

82. The property owner to be notified was the owner as shown on the county tax listings.

83. This requirement imposed a logistical challenge for local governments, as a third party filing a petition cannot certify at the time of application that a hearing notice has been served on the landowner because the hearing date is not set until after the application is accepted. Cities and counties therefore generally established a process to verify that the petitioner delivers the hearing notice between the time the hearing date is set and the hearing is held. The statute defined "actual notice" using the state's Rules of Civil Procedure, G.S. 1A-1, Rule 4(j). Cities and counties typically required the rezoning petitioner to submit to the unit of government a certification that actual notice has been provided, with the certification to be submitted no later than a specified time prior to the hearing (such as seven days prior to the date of the hearing).

84. S.L. 2019-111, § 1.5. This section eliminated third-party initiation of downzonings, which was the primary rationale for requiring actual notice. Actual notice can still be mandated by local ordinance provision, but it is no longer mandated by state statute.

85. This provision was added by S.L. 2019-111. When Charlotte secured a local bill authorizing conditional zoning prior to the amendment of the state zoning-enabling statute, neighborhood meetings were mandated.

86. *See, e.g.,* Collinson v. Gott, 895 F.2d 944 (4th Cir. 1990) (reasonable, viewpoint-neutral time, place, and manner restrictions on speech at public hearing permissible under First Amendment). *See generally* A. Fleming Bell et al., *Public Comment at Meetings of Local Government Boards Part Two: Common Practices and Legal Standards*, POPULAR GOV'T, Fall 1997, at 27; John Stephens & A. Fleming Bell, II, *Public Comment at Meetings of Local Government Boards Part One: Guidelines for Good Practices*, POPULAR GOV'T, Summer 1997, at 2.

The hearing mandated before governing-board action on the proposed regulation is a legislative hearing, however, not a quasi-judicial hearing. The purpose of a legislative hearing is to secure broad public comment on the proposed action.[87] The purpose of a quasi-judicial hearing on an individual project (such as a variance or a special use permit) is to gather evidence in order to make factual findings. So the special due-process safeguards required to protect the rights of the parties and to secure reliable evidence in a quasi-judicial hearing—that witnesses be under oath, rules of evidence be observed, and written findings be made at the conclusion of the hearing—are not applied to legislative hearings. With legislative hearings, the governing board is receiving comments, not hearing evidence.

The court has held that comments made at a legislative hearing on a zoning amendment are protected First Amendment speech as part of citizens' right to petition the government. In *Cheryl Lloyd Humphrey Land Investment Co. v. Resco Products, Inc.*,[88] a petition had been made to rezone the land adjacent to a quarry in order to build a residential townhouse development there. Representatives of the quarry owners appeared at the zoning hearing to object to the rezoning. They made statements regarding potential safety impacts due to the "explosive blasting" at the quarry. Although the rezoning was approved, the buyer refused to purchase the portion of the site adjacent to the quarry, citing the safety hazards identified in the zoning hearing. The seller brought suit, contending that the malicious and false statements made at the hearing constituted tortious interference with the property transaction. The court held that the right to attempt to influence the legislative choice of the town council exists regardless of the speaker's motives and protects selfish or misleading speech. Neither the maliciousness nor the falsity of the speech has any bearing on its protected status.

The general statutory guidance for legislative public hearings is G.S. 160A-81 for cities and G.S. 153A-52 for counties. These statutes allow the governing board to

> adopt reasonable rules governing the conduct of public hearings, including but not limited to rules (i) fixing the maximum time allotted to each speaker, (ii) providing for the designation of spokesmen for groups of persons supporting or opposing the same positions, (iii) providing for the selection of delegates from groups of persons supporting or opposing the same positions when the number of persons wishing to attend the hearing exceeds the capacity of the hall, and (iv) providing for the maintenance of order and decorum in the conduct of the hearing.

---

87. A 2006 survey by the School of Government indicated that hearings on zoning amendments serve this purpose in practice. Survey respondents reported that it is fairly common for persons other than the petitioner and staff to appear at a rezoning hearing. Over half (53 percent) of the responding jurisdictions reported that this happened frequently, always, or almost always. Only 16 percent reported that it rarely or never happened in their jurisdictions. OWENS, *supra* note 3, at 8. The survey also indicated that rezoning hearings for the most part remain the province of citizens, not lawyers. A majority of responding jurisdictions (54 percent) reported that attorneys rarely or never appear at a rezoning hearing on behalf of petitioners. Only 14 percent of the jurisdictions reported that this occurs frequently, always, or almost always. *Id.* at 9.

88. 377 N.C. 384, 858 S.E.2d 795 (2021).

Therefore, reasonable rules may be established to limit the number of speakers and the amount of time each speaker is given,[89] provided that the hearing is conducted in a fair and reasonable fashion.[90] Speakers can be required to limit their remarks to those addressing the subject of the hearing.[91]

This principle was confirmed in *Freeland v. Orange County*.[92] Some 500 citizens attended the required public hearing on the adoption of zoning for the Chapel Hill Township. The chair allotted one hour each to the proponents and the opponents of the zoning ordinance, with each side also having fifteen minutes for rebuttal. Sixteen proponents and fifteen opponents were heard. In a show of hands, it appeared that the attendees at the hearing were by a four-to-one ratio opposed to the adoption of zoning. Some 200 attendees indicated that they wished to speak but were not allowed to do so because of the time limitation. The governing board members entertained no questions and made no comments themselves at the hearing. The court upheld this procedure, ruling that the legislative intent was to mandate a hearing and provide a "fair opportunity" for those in attendance to present their views. However, the governing board was allowed to establish an "orderly procedure" for the hearing, for "[t]he General Assembly did not contemplate that all persons entertaining the same views would have an unqualified right to iterate and reiterate these views in endless repetition."[93]

Additional Hearings

A question occasionally arises whether re-advertisement and rehearing are required if changes are made in the proposed regulation at or after the original hearing.[94] While the governing board always retains the discretion to call for an additional hearing when it is deemed that doing so would be prudent or useful, an additional hearing is legally mandated only if there are substantial changes in the proposal after the initial notice.[95]

Heaton v. City of Charlotte[96] sets the standard for determining when the changes are sufficiently substantial that an additional hearing is required. In this instance, the landowner requested rezoning of a 42.6-acre tract. The original zoning of most of the tract was for single-family residences. The request was to rezone 28.3 acres to a multifamily-residential district and 14.3 acres to a shopping-center district. The public notice of the hearing indicated this fact and included the following statement: "The City

---

89. For example, the Raleigh zoning regulation provides that for public hearings on zoning amendments, the staff will first present information on the matter, and then those in favor of the rezoning are given eight minutes to explain their support and those opposed are given eight minutes to explain their opposition. Additional time may be allowed by the city council if requested in advance of the hearing. CITY OF RALEIGH, N.C., UNIFIED DEVELOPMENT ORDINANCE § 10.2.4(f)(4) (2018).

90. *See generally* City of Madison Joint Sch. Dist. No. 8 v. Wis. Emp't Relations Comm'n, 429 U.S. 167, 174–75 (1976) (comment periods at public hearings are a designated public forum for purposes of First Amendment free speech); Moore v. City of Creedmoor, 345 N.C. 356, 369, 481 S.E.2d 14, 22 (1997) (government may not discriminate between speakers at public hearing based on content of speech).

91. *See, e.g.,* Steinburg v. Chesterfield Cnty. Plan. Comm'n, 527 F.3d 377 (4th Cir. 2008) (speaker at hearing on proposed zoning change has no First Amendment right to speak on other issues as hearing is a limited public forum); Eichenlaub v. Twp. of Indiana, 385 F.3d 274 (3d Cir. 2004) (citizen-comment period at governing-board meeting a limited public forum). See Chapter 28 for further discussion of First Amendment principles.

92. 273 N.C. 452, 160 S.E.2d 282 (1968).

93. *Id.* at 457, 160 S.E.2d at 286.

94. A 2006 survey by the School of Government indicated that while not typical, the issue does in practice arise with some frequency. Three-quarters of the responding jurisdictions reported that additional hearings are never or only rarely held. Only 3 percent of the jurisdictions reported that this happens frequently, always, or almost always often. The remainder—22 percent—reported additional hearings are occasionally required.

95. A rule of thumb is that if the same people would have come to the hearing and offered essentially the same comments, it is unlikely that another hearing is required.

96. 277 N.C. 506, 178 S.E.2d 352 (1971). *See also* Walker v. Town of Elkin, 254 N.C. 85, 118 S.E.2d 1 (1961).

Figure 11.1 *Heaton* Case Development Outcome

In the *Heaton* case, the court held that an additional hearing was not required when the city reduced the amount of land rezoned for shopping-center use while increasing the amount for multifamily use.

Council may change the existing zoning classification of the entire area covered by the petition, or any part or parts of such area, to the classification requested, or to a higher classification or classifications without the necessity of withdrawal or modification of the petition." After the hearing, the planning commission suggested that the area for the shopping center zoning be reduced to 10 acres, with the other 4.3 acres of this tract to be included in the multifamily residential district. The city council went beyond this recommendation and limited the shopping center to 7.4 acres, with the balance of the site in the multifamily residential district. The effect of this action was to rezone the entire tract but with less land in the shopping-center district and more in the multifamily-residential district (the resultant development is shown in Figure 11.1). Neighbors who opposed the rezoning sued, contending that the council should have held another hearing on the revised zoning scheme.

After an extensive review of the law in other states, the court ruled that the notice provided had been adequate and that no additional notice or hearing had been required:

Ordinarily, if the ordinance or amendment as finally adopted contains alterations substantially different (amounting to a new proposal) from those originally advertised and heard, there must be additional notice and opportunity for additional hearing. However, no further notice or hearing is required after a properly advertised and properly conducted public hearing when the alteration of the initial proposal is insubstantial. Alteration of the initial proposal will not be deemed substantial when it results in changes favorable to the complaining parties. Moreover, additional notice and public hearing ordinarily will not be required when the initial notice is broad enough to indicate the possibility of substantial change and substantial changes are made of the same fundamental character as contained in the notice, such changes resulting from objections, debate and discussion at the properly noticed initial hearing.[97]

In this instance, the court noted that the notice had been broad enough to indicate that changes might be made, that the changes were consistent with the fundamental character of the noticed proposal, and that the changes were made as a result of comments received at the hearing. This led the court to conclude that an additional hearing

could have resulted only in repetitive statements by the same parties or parties similarly situated. . . . The very purpose of the public hearing was to guide the City Council in making changes in the original proposal consistent with the views reflected at the public hearing. This is exactly what was done.[98]

---

97. *Heaton*, 277 N.C. 506, 518, 178 S.E.2d 352, 359–60 (1971). This area was in fact subsequently developed for the shopping center and multifamily residences allowed by the rezoning.

98. *Id.* at 518–19, 178 S.E.2d at 360. *See also* Appeal of CAMA Permit No. 82-0010 v. Town of Bath, 82 N.C. App. 32, 345 S.E.2d 699 (1986).

As a general rule, property may be deleted from a proposed rezoning without an additional hearing, but property not included in the notice should not be rezoned without an additional notice and hearing. Similarly, the proposed zoning district can likely be changed to a similar but less intensive use district without a new hearing, but if the changed district allows more intensive use or substantially different uses, an additional hearing is needed.[99]

Occasionally, lengthy hearings are recessed and continued at a subsequent meeting. G.S. 160A-81 and 153A-52, the general provisions on public hearings, specifically allow public hearings to be continued without further advertisement.[100] These statutes also provide that if a quorum of the governing board is not present for the advertised hearing, the hearing shall be continued to the next regularly scheduled board meeting. Also, G.S. 160A-71(b1) provides that regular and called meetings of the governing board may be recessed or adjourned "to reconvene at a time and a place certain" (the comparable county provision, G.S. 153A-40, does not contain this same language). G.S. 143-318.12(b)(1) in the state's open-meetings law provides that if the time and the place for reconvening are announced during the properly noticed original meeting, no additional public notice is required.

The legal sufficiency of this process is illustrated by *Rakestraw v. Town of Knightdale*.[101] In *Rakestraw*, the town published, mailed, and posted notice of a hearing on a proposed rezoning to allow a large commercial project. The advertised hearing was continued to two additional dates. The additional hearing dates were announced at the advertised hearing but were not subject to additional published, mailed, or posted notices. The court held that the notice for the initial hearing was legally sufficient to include the continued-hearing dates provided there was no substantial change to the proposed ordinance as it moved toward passage.

In sum, there is no requirement that a board vote on a matter that has been subject to hearing immediately upon conclusion of the hearing. The board may defer a vote until the next meeting in order to allow additional time for governing-board deliberation after the hearing. The board may refer the matter back to the planning board for further discussion and recommendation.

Even if a new notice is not required for a continued hearing, local governments must be cautious not to allow an inordinate length of time to pass between a hearing and an action on a matter. An eight-month delay between the conclusion of the hearing and the governing-board vote on the issue was one factor used by the court to invalidate a town's extraterritorial ordinance.[102]

---

99. The court in *Thrash Ltd. Partnership v. County of Buncombe*, 195 N.C. App. 678, 673 S.E.2d 706 (2009), noted that an additional hearing is needed if the zoning district applied to property is changed after the original hearing notice. In that case, the initial zoning for multiple properties was changed in response to landowner requests between the hearing notice and the hearing.

100. Thrash v. City of Asheville, 115 N.C. App. 310, 314, 444 S.E.2d 482, 484 (1994) (affirming that city council can continue hearing to specified time and place without further advertisement). Note that G.S. 60D-406(b) applies the same rule to continuation of evidentiary hearings on quasi-judicial matters without the necessity of additional notice.

101. 188 N.C. App. 129, 654 S.E.2d 825, *review denied*, 362 N.C. 237, 659 S.E.2d 739 (2008).

102. Town of Swansboro v. Odum, 96 N.C. App. 115, 384 S.E.2d 302 (1989). If a proposed amendment is not going to be adopted, the better practice is to defeat it rather than table it indefinitely.

Protest Petitions

From 1923 through 2015, North Carolina zoning law provided that if a sufficient number of directly affected landowners formally objected to a zoning amendment, they could trigger a requirement that the amendment receive a three-fourths supermajority of the city council in order to be enacted. That provision was repealed in 2015.[103]

While landowners and neighbors are significantly affected by zoning, the choice to change zoning restrictions is a discretionary policy choice of elected officials. Neither landowners nor neighbors can be given a veto over proposed zoning changes.[104] At the outset of local land use regulation, its proponents concluded that those most directly affected by zoning needed a degree of protection from unwanted changes in the land use policies they have relied on.[105] The provision for a protest petition was thus included in the state's 1923 zoning-enabling act to provide a degree of certainty and stability in zoning while allowing the governing body sufficient flexibility to amend the ordinance to reflect changing needs and circumstances. Although infrequently used outside of large municipalities,[106] the protest petition proved controversial in application and its use was abolished in 2015.[107]

---

103. S.L. 2015-160.

104. Early land use regulatory cases dealt with neighborhood vetoes with somewhat contradictory results, although the general rule quickly emerged that making the decision subject to neighbor approval was an unlawful delegation of legislative authority. *See* State of Washington *ex rel.* Seattle Title Trust Co. v. Roberge, 278 U.S. 116 (1928) (invalidating requirement of neighborhood approval for home for elderly poor); Eubank v. City of Richmond, 226 U.S. 137 (1912) (invalidating neighbor approval for setback line). *But see* Thomas Cusack Co. v. City of Chi., 242 U.S. 526 (1917) (allowing neighbors to waive sign restriction). For a contemporary example of incorporation of neighbor objections into a land use regulatory decision using the rationale of the *Cusack Co.* case, see *Coffey v. County of Otoe*, 274 Neb. 796, 743 N.W.2d 632 (2008). The court there upheld a county ordinance that prohibited the location of a residence within one-half mile of an animal feedlot unless the residential owner agreed to and recorded a "mutual impact easement" holding the feedlot owner harmless from odor, smoke, dust, or other impacts from the feedlot. The owner of a proposed residential lot challenged the provision as an unlawful delegation of governmental authority when an adjacent feedlot owner refused to enter into such an easement, thereby blocking construction of a residence on nearby property. The court distinguished between an ordinance allowing a neighbor to create the restriction (which would be invalid) from a provision allowing a neighbor to waive a lawfully created restriction. Also see the discussion of delegation of legislative authority *infra* note 141.

The North Carolina court has specifically held that neighbors have no right to the continuation of a particular zoning restriction. McKinney v. City of High Point, 239 N.C. 232, 237, 79 S.E.2d 730, 734 (1954).

105. The protest petition was included in the nation's first comprehensive zoning ordinance, New York's 1916 ordinance. The legal architect of the New York ordinance noted that the provision for a protest petition was "a device for the protection of the property owner" and that its purpose was "to prevent easy or careless changes in the zoning regulations. . . . The 20 percent protest will often prevent impulsive or improper map changes." BASSETT, *supra* note 29, at 38. For a summary of cases from other jurisdictions, see Larry D. Scheafer, Annotation, *Zoning: Validity and Construction of Provisions of Zoning Statute or Ordinance Regarding Protest by Neighboring Property Owners*, 7 A.L.R.4th 732 (1981).

106. In a 2006 School of Government survey, two-thirds of the responding cities reported that no protest petitions had been filed in the previous year. OWENS, *supra* note 3, at 11. However, protests were much more common in those cities with large populations—50 percent of the cities with populations between 10,000 and 25,000 reported having received a protest petition, and 71 percent of the cities with populations over 25,000 had received one or more protest petitions in the previous year. Responding municipalities reported a total of 181 protest petitions filed in the previous year. Of these, 134 (75 percent) were determined to be adequate and thereby requiring a supermajority vote for adoption of the rezoning. These same municipalities reported consideration of 2167 rezoning petitions in the previous year. Thus, only 8 percent of the municipal rezoning petitions had a protest filed, and only 6 percent had a protest sufficient to require a supermajority vote for the proposed rezoning to be enacted.

107. The protest-petition provision was repealed by S.L. 2015-160. This law also made a change to the municipal voting statute to ensure a full majority of the governing board supports changes to zoning maps. G.S. 160A-75(a) generally provides that if a governing board member, who is present and not excused from voting, does not actually vote on a matter, it is counted as an affirmative vote. This law amended the statute to provide that this rule does not

In lieu of the protest petition, the statute now provides that citizens can present written statements on proposed zoning amendments to the city clerk, who must then provide copies to the city council.[108]

Initiation and Reconsideration of Amendments

Proposed amendments to zoning texts and zoning maps can arise in a number of ways.

A 2006 survey by the School of Government indicates that most text amendments are proposed by the local government staff. In that survey, the responding jurisdictions reported that 59 percent of the text-amendment petitions in the past year originated with the city or county staff;[109] 20 percent were proposed by members of the public, 10 percent by the city or county governing board, 9 percent by the planning board, and 2 percent by miscellaneous others (such as the board of adjustment, the school board, another unit of government, or a neighborhood or business association). By contrast, petitions to amend the zoning map are usually initiated by individual property owners seeking to change the zoning districts applicable to their property.

Although the state statutes are generally silent on this question,[110] some local zoning ordinances contain provisions specifying who may initiate consideration of rezonings or other zoning-ordinance amendments. Typically, such limitations provide that rezoning petitions may be initiated by any governing-board member, the planning board, or the owner of the property to be rezoned.[111] When such a petition is filed, the ordinance requires automatic consideration by the planning board, an automatic public hearing, or some similar locally imposed requirement to initiate formal consideration of the request. Even when such limitations are placed in a zoning regulation, it is likely that any other resident may request the governing board to take action,[112] but such a request will be considered similarly to any other citizen petition for legislative action—that is, whether or not to take it up will be at the governing board's discretion.[113] Of course, if the zoning regulation requires notice and hearing for all rezoning petitions, those procedures must be followed.

---

apply to votes on amendments of development regulations (those ordinances subject to the mandatory procedures of G.S. 160D-601). The seat of a member who is present but who does not vote on a zoning-map amendment is not counted as an affirmative vote (but the seat is considered in calculating the requisite majority). The rationale offered at the time was that even if there is no longer a protest petition to protect the settled expectations of the owner and neighbors in the existing zoning, at least an actual majority of all the governing-board members present should be required to enact an amendment.

108. G.S. 160D-603.

109. OWENS, *supra* note 3, at 4.

110. An exception was made for petitions for rezonings to conditional districts. G.S. 160D-703(b) provides that these districts may only be applied upon petition of the landowner. See Chapter 13 for further discussion of these districts.

111. This has long been a feature of many zoning regulations. For example, Philip Green's 1952 treatise assumes zoning amendments can only be proposed by the government or the property owner. PHILIP P. GREEN, JR., ZONING IN NORTH CAROLINA 383–84 (1952). *See also* Keith v. Town of White Lake, 175 N.C. App. 789, 625 S.E.2d 587 (2006) (planning board may initiate rezoning).

112. A local ordinance cannot include provisions that are contrary to state law. Prior to 2019, the state statutes did not expressly address "third party rezonings" (those petitions filed by someone other than the landowner or the local government). However, G.S. 153A-343(b1) and 160A-384(b1) required actual notice to owner for third-party rezoning, which presumed their availability. The court has long recognized that neither the landowner nor the neighbors have a legal right to the continuation of a particular zoning classification, as this is a legislative enactment subject to the governing board's appropriately exercised discretion. McKinney v. City of High Point, 239 N.C. 232, 237, 79 S.E.2d 730, 734 (1954).

113. In *Carroll v. City of Kings Mountain*, 193 N.C. App. 165, 666 S.E.2d 814 (2008), the court addressed implementation of an ordinance that required that rezoning petitioners be residents of the municipality. Assuming the residency requirement to be valid, the court held that provision of the petitioner's street address in the rezoning

The zoning statute was amended in 2019 to prohibit initiation of a petition to "down-zone" a property by someone other than the landowner or the local government.[114] This provision created G.S. 160D-601(d) to require the written consent of affected landowners for a rezoning or a text amendment that decreases the permitted density of development or that reduces the range of permitted uses of the property. The statute states that a downzoning shall not be "initiated nor shall it be enforceable" without the written consent of all property owners subject to the amendment. This limit does not apply if the zoning amendment is initiated by the local government.

Most local ordinances limit the frequency with which rezonings may be considered. This type of provision establishes a minimum waiting period between considerations of rezoning proposals, typically providing that once a rezoning petition has been denied for a particular parcel, no additional rezoning petitions regarding the same property will be considered for a set time. Some ordinances are broader, preventing reconsideration after any rezoning decision, including approval of a rezoning.

An ordinance provision setting a mandatory waiting period between considerations of rezonings was upheld in *George v. Town of Edenton*.[115] The town's zoning regulation contained a provision prohibiting the governing board from accepting "any other application for the same change of zoning amendment affecting the same property"[116] within six months of the denial of a rezoning petition for a given parcel. In this case, the owner petitioned for a rezoning and the governing board denied it. Several months later (but within the waiting period set by the ordinance), during the consideration of an update of the entire zoning regulation, the governing board adopted the originally proposed rezoning on the motion of a board member. The court ruled the rezoning invalid because it violated the limit on reconsideration contained in the ordinance. Neither the fact that the second action was initiated by the governing board rather than the owner nor the fact that the rezoning was done as part of the enactment of a new ordinance removed the rezoning from coverage of the required waiting period. The court emphasized the underlying purpose of the mandatory waiting period, which was to prevent an applicant from subjecting neighbors to the burden of having to protest and defend against a series of repetitious applications.[117] Some ordinances also include limits on withdrawal of petitions in order to prevent avoidance of these waiting periods. For example, the ordinance may provide that a petition may not be withdrawn after it is noticed for public hearing, after the hearing commences, after the hearing concludes, or that in these circumstances it may only be withdrawn with the approval of the board.[118]

---

petition (without explicit reference to that property being within the city zoning jurisdiction) was sufficient for a determination that the residency requirement was met, given that this was a customary practice in the city, no objections to residency were made, and the court could take judicial notice of the fact that the property was within the city.

114. S.L. 2019-111, § 1.4, effective July 11, 2019.

115. 294 N.C. 679, 242 S.E.2d 877 (1978). Other state courts have upheld similar mandatory waiting periods between rezoning petitions. *See, e.g.*, Newman v. Smith, 217 Ga. 465, 123 S.E.2d 305 (1961); DeLatour v. Morrison, 213 La. 292, 34 So. 2d 783 (1948); Tyrie v. Balt. Cnty., 215 Md. 135, 137 A.2d 156 (1957). Some states have statutory waiting periods. For example, Massachusetts requires a two-year waiting period after a proposed zoning amendment is rejected. MASS. GEN. LAWS ch. 40A, § 5. For an application of that rule, see *Penn v. Town of Barnstable*, 133 N.E.3d 846 (Mass. App. Ct. 2019).

116. *George*, 294 N.C. at 683, 242 S.E.2d at 880.

117. *Id.* at 686–87, 242 S.E.2d at 882.

118. For example, the Winston-Salem/Forsyth County ordinance requires the permission of the board to withdraw a petition for a zoning amendment after the notice of hearing has been published. WINSTON-SALEM/FORSYTH COUNTY, N.C., UNIFIED DEVELOPMENT ORDINANCE § 3.2.19(A)(9) (2022). The Greensboro ordinance allows withdrawal if it is made at least twenty-four days before the zoning commission meets to consider a zoning-map amendment. After that time, withdrawal requires approval by the commission or city council. CITY OF GREENSBORO, N.C., LAND DEVELOPMENT ORDINANCE, § 30-4-5.15 (2022).

The most frequent time periods used for a mandatory waiting period are six and twelve months. A two-year waiting period was upheld in *Clark v. City of Charlotte*.[119]

It is permissible for a local zoning regulation to establish such a waiting period for rezoning petitions made by the landowner or other citizens but not for rezoning petitions initiated by the governing board or the planning board.[120] Judicial invalidation of a rezoning due to failure to provide the required notice does not constitute a "denial" of a rezoning petition that triggers such a required waiting period.[121]

One parliamentary procedure may be available to avoid a mandatory waiting period—a motion to reconsider the initial vote on the rezoning, rather than a second motion to adopt the rezoning. Since a motion to reconsider brings the initial vote back before the governing board, if it can be employed it will not trigger the waiting period. However, most rules of procedure followed by local governing boards significantly limit when a motion to reconsider is in order. A typical requirement is that the motion to reconsider must be made at the meeting at which the original vote was taken, though some rules allow it to be made at the next succeeding meeting.[122]

A second consideration of zoning-ordinance amendments (legislative decisions) must be distinguished from reconsideration of quasi-judicial land use decisions. With regard to the latter, which involve such actions as requests for variances or applications for special use permits, the doctrine of res judicata applies, and a board may not reopen and rehear a case previously decided unless there has been some material change in conditions.[123] There is no requirement of changed conditions for legislative rezoning decisions in North Carolina.[124]

---

119. 66 N.C. App. 437, 311 S.E.2d 71 (1984). In this case, the ordinance allowed reconsideration in less than two years only upon a finding that there had been substantial changes in conditions or circumstances bearing on the application. A four-month waiting period was upheld in *Carroll v. City of Kings Mountain*, 193 N.C. App. 165, 666 S.E.2d 814 (2008). The Winston-Salem/Forsyth County ordinance provides for a two-year wait period after a denial and a one-year wait period after a rezoning has been approved. WINSTON-SALEM/FORSYTH COUNTY, N.C., UNIFIED DEVELOPMENT ORDINANCE § 3.2.19(A)(15) (2022).

120. Nelson v. City of Burlington, 80 N.C. App. 285, 341 S.E.2d 739 (1986).

121. Lee v. Union Cnty. Bd. of Comm'rs, 65 N.C. App. 810, 310 S.E.2d 122 (1984).

122. In *Mickelsen v. Warren County*, No. 5:06-CV-00360-F, 2007 WL 4245848 (E.D.N.C. Nov. 29, 2007), the plaintiffs sought a rezoning from a residential to a neighborhood-business district. The county commissioners voted in favor of the rezoning. After the plaintiffs left the county board meeting but before the meeting adjourned, one of the commissioners who had supported the rezoning had a change of heart. He made a motion to reconsider the rezoning vote and that motion was adopted. Upon reconsideration, the rezoning motion failed. The court held that the county's rules of procedure expressly allowed a motion to reconsider if made in the same meeting as the original vote and by a member of the prevailing side. The court held that this rule of parliamentary procedure is not inconsistent with state law. It held further that additional notice, hearing, and planning-board referral was not required for the second vote because under the county ordinance, the property was not actually rezoned until the change was entered on the official zoning map, a step that had not been taken in the brief period prior to the second vote. An alternative route to this same result would have been to find that with a motion to reconsider, the board was simply returning to the initial vote, with the first vote being void upon adoption of the motion to reconsider.

The model rules of procedure provided by the School of Government suggest limiting a motion to reconsider to be made at the same meeting as the original vote, including any continuation of that meeting through recess to a time and place certain. TREY ALLEN, SUGGESTED RULES OF PROCEDURE FOR A CITY COUNCIL 50–51 (4th ed. 2017). Local governments that follow ROBERT'S RULES may rule that a motion to reconsider is in order at the meeting immediately subsequent to the meeting where the original vote was taken. The state supreme court has expressed concern, however, over failure to follow proper notice and hearing requirements when an attempt is made to undo a rezoning decision at a subsequent meeting. Orange Cnty v. Heath, 278 N.C. 688, 180 S.E.2d 810 (1971). In *Sofran Corp.*, the court noted that if reconsideration, "even upon the Council's own motion," is followed by substantial modification or repeal, an additional hearing is required (though this observation did not distinguish a motion to reconsider from a new consideration of the same matter).

123. See Chapter 15 for a discussion of res judicata in quasi-judicial regulatory decisions.

124. *See, e.g.*, Carroll v. City of Kings Mountain, 193 N.C. App. 165, 666 S.E.2d 814 (2008) (noting second rezoning of same property within four months with no change of conditions on site was not arbitrary and capricious, while

Governing-Board Action

Delegation

Adoption, amendment, or repeal of a land use regulation is a legislative decision made by the elected governing board—the city council or the county board of commissioners. In practice, governing boards rarely have an interest in delegating legislative decisions. The unlawful-delegation issue is more commonly raised in the context of ordinance implementation, particularly the adequacy of guiding standards for delegated decisions on individual special use permit applications.[125] The issue does, however, occasionally arise in the context of adoption or amendment of development regulations. The legality of such delegation is uncertain.

Two cases in North Carolina held attempted delegations of local legislative regulatory decisions to be unlawful. Shortly after World War II, a time when there was virtually no zoning in rural areas of the state, the military and the state agreed that land use regulations were needed to manage development adjacent to military bases and their air fields in the coastal region.[126] In 1949, the General Assembly created the Cherry Point Marine Corps Air Station Zoning Commission to zone the rural area near the Cherry Point military base.[127] The county board of commissioners and the base commander appointed commission members, and the commission was granted the same zoning powers as a governing board.[128] In *Vance S. Harrington & Co. v. Renner*,[129] the court invalidated the zoning ordinance adopted under this statute because, among other flaws,[130] it was adopted by an unelected body, the special-zoning commission. In 1996, the court in *City of Roanoke Rapids v. Peedin*[131] invalidated smoking regulations adopted by the Halifax County Board of Health. The court held that while an unelected board of health may adopt public health and safety regulations, the board here had improperly engaged in legislative

---

invalidating rezoning on other grounds). Some cases do discuss changed conditions as a justification for rezoning. *See, e.g.*, Allgood v. Town of Tarboro, 281 N.C. 430, 189 S.E.2d 255 (1972); Gregory v. Cnty. of Harnett, 128 N.C. App. 161, 493 S.E.2d 786 (1997). The presence of changed conditions, however, is more a factor to be considered in a spot-zoning analysis than a necessary finding for all rezonings. See Chapter 12 for a more detailed discussion of this matter. Some individual zoning ordinances require that findings of fact be made before rezonings, and changed conditions can be a factor in these. For example, the Forsyth County zoning ordinance notes that the governing board may consider compatibility with surrounding uses, changed conditions, and land use–plan consistency when reviewing petitions for zoning amendments. WINSTON-SALEM/FORSYTH COUNTY, UNIFIED DEVELOPMENT ORDINANCE § 3.2.19(A)(16) (2022).

125. See Chapter 16.

126. The contemporary counterpart of this issue has been state and local interest in managing adjacent land uses to prevent incompatible uses and assuring continued safe operation of military facilities in an era of base closings and realignment. A legislative manifestation of this interest is S.L. 2004-75, amending G.S. 160D-601(b) to require notices of public hearings on proposed land use regulatory ordinances to be mailed to the military bases located within five miles of a proposed rezoning as well as to adjacent property owners. These provisions were expanded by S.L. 2013-59. In addition, S.L. 2013-206 created the Military Lands Protection Act, G.S. 143-151.70 to -151.77, to manage construction of structures over 200 feet tall near military bases.

127. S.L. 1949-455. The act was subsequently modified by S.L. 1951-757.

128. The elected county board of commissioners served as the commission's board of adjustment.

129. 236 N.C. 321, 72 S.E.2d 838 (1952). *See also* Jackson v. Guilford Cnty. Bd. of Adjustment, 275 N.C. 155, 166 S.E.2d 78 (1969) (unlawful to delegate legislative standard setting for special use permits to unelected board).

130. The county zoning-enabling statute was seven years away in 1952, so county commissioners had little residual authority to backstop the actions of the Cherry Point zoning commission. Another flaw cited by the court was the fact that the military member of the zoning commission was an out-of-state resident and therefore not qualified to serve as a public officer in North Carolina.

131. 124 N.C. App. 578, 478 S.E.2d 528 (1996).

policy choices when it balanced economic and health factors in determining whether to exempt small establishments from the regulation.[132]

The zoning statute does make one general exception to the nondelegation rule. G.S. 160D-703(b) gives local governments the option of making minor amendments to conditional zoning districts administratively. For a local government to use this option, the zoning regulation itself must define what constitutes a "minor modification." A minor modification cannot include a change in permitted uses or in the density of the overall development. Once a definition is established, staff can be authorized to approve minor modifications without sending the matter through the legislative-amendment process. Any other modification to a conditional zoning district must follow the same process for approval as is required for a zoning-map amendment. If the conditional zoning applies to multiple parcels of property, the conditions may be modified for individual parcels without the necessity of obtaining the consent of all property owners within the conditional zoning. In these instances, the modification only applies to the parcels whose owners consent.

The North Carolina legislature has also approved several local bills that allow unelected boards to make zoning amendments. These laws amend city charters or authorize ordinance provisions that allow the planning board to rezone an area. A common provision of these local authorizations is that there be a supermajority approval of a rezoning petition by the planning board. They also usually allow an affected person to request that the matter be considered by the elected board.[133] For example, the Greensboro charter provides that the city council may by ordinance delegate authority to rezone to the city zoning commission. Pursuant to that provision, the Greensboro zoning ordinance provides that if five of the seven members of the appointed zoning commission vote in favor of a rezoning, their action amends the ordinance if it is not appealed within fifteen days to the city council.[134] The legal

---

132. It is common, however, for the legislature to delegate to state commissions rulemaking authority that includes some balancing of competing policy considerations. A classic example is the rulemaking by the Coastal Resources Commission pursuant to the Coastal Area Management Act, where the commission is to make rules "to safeguard and perpetuate [the coastal areas'] natural productivity and their biological, economic and esthetic values." G.S. 113A-102(b). This was held not to be an unlawful delegation of legislative authority. Adams v. N.C. Dep't of Nat. & Econ. Res., 295 N.C. 683, 249 S.E.2d 402 (1978).

133. The practice of allowing rezoning decisions to be made by the planning board with the possibility of an appeal to the governing board is allowed in several states, notably in California.

134. CITY OF GREENSBORO, N.C., CHARTER § 5.64. Guilford County was granted similar authority in 1985. S.L. 1985-485. The 1993 General Assembly authorized similar provisions for delegation of certain rezonings in additional jurisdictions. S.L. 1993-247 (Gastonia, Cabarrus County, and its municipalities), S.L. 1993-264 (Durham). The Gastonia ordinance allows rezonings to be made by the planning commission if approved by a three-fourths vote of the commission, provided that no appeal is made to the city council within fifteen days. CITY OF GASTONIA, N.C., UNIFIED DEVELOPMENT ORDINANCE § 5.16.3 (2021). This provision is similar to zoning law in Kentucky, where the planning board's recommended decision on a zoning amendment becomes law unless the governing board overrules it. KY. REV. STAT. ANN. § 100.211.

S.L. 2017-19 allows additional jurisdictions to delegate rezoning decisions to the planning board if an appeal to the governing board is also allowed. This law applies to Randolph County and the municipalities located wholly or in part within the county. The governing board may delegate authority to conduct the required hearing and give final approval to zoning-map amendments. The delegation is done by ordinance (which may subsequently be rescinded or modified). Decisions of the planning board are made by majority vote of the members of the entire board. Once the planning board makes a decision on a rezoning, a "person aggrieved" then has fifteen days to file a written appeal with the city or county manager appealing the decision to the governing board. If appealed, the governing board considers the rezoning petition de novo (doing its own notice, hearing, and decision). S.L. 2018-124 extends authority to Davidson County to make a similar delegation to the planning board with potential appeal to the county board of commissioners. The same is authorized for Brunswick County by S.L. 2019-99. Similar local legislation allows High Point to delegate rezoning decisions to its Planning and Zoning Commission with appeals to the city council. S.L. 2022-37.

rationale supporting the argument that these are not unlawful delegations is that the zoning power is a state authority being delegated to local governments and the legislature can delegate that authority to whichever local board it chooses.[135]

An interesting variation to this approach was authorized by a charter provision enacted by local legislation for Fayetteville.[136] Under this authority, the planning board holds a hearing on a rezoning petition and makes a recommendation to the city council. Aggrieved persons have ten days in which to file an appeal of the recommendation with the council. If the recommendation is positive and no appeal is filed, the council may adopt the rezoning without further hearing. If the recommendation is negative and no appeal is filed, the planning-board action is final and the rezoning is deemed to have been denied by the council. This procedure is consistent with the mandate that any amendment of the ordinance be passed by affirmative action by the elected board. It promotes efficiency because it dispenses with the necessity of a second hearing in noncontroversial adoptions and the council agenda does not become clogged with noncontroversial petitions likely to be denied.

The requirement that legislative decisions setting land use regulatory policies be made by the governing board, following all required procedures for ordinance making, explains in part why decision-making on quasi-judicial land use decisions has a limited scope. Quasi-judicial decisions involve applying previously adopted legislative policy decisions to individual situations. Because they are *applications* of policy rather than *creations* of policy, these decisions are not subject to the procedural requirements designed to secure broad public notice of proposed changes to ordinances. Therefore, zoning variances that have the practical effect of amending a zoning ordinance are illegal because only the governing board, following the requisite procedures, may amend the zoning ordinance.[137]

Nondelegation is also a consideration when a provision allocates some aspect of decision-making to neighbors.[138] This most often arises in the context of an individual development decision, such as a provision that a property-line setback can be relaxed upon the consent of the adjoining property owner. While that delegation is questionable as a matter of sound public policy[139] and law,[140] some jurisdictions allow it. By contrast, a decision to allow neighbors to create new regulations is generally prohibited as an unlawful delegation of legislative authority.[141]

---

135. Such a rationale requires, however, that the state legislature make that choice. Thus, without local enabling legislation, a city or county would not be able to make such a delegation of its own accord, as such would be contrary to the general zoning-enabling statute which delegates this role to the governing board.

136. CITY OF FAYETTEVILLE, N.C., CHARTER § 8.17, enacted by S.L. 1981-756. The provision is implemented in the zoning ordinance at CITY OF FAYETTEVILLE, N.C., UNIFIED DEVELOPMENT ORDINANCE § 30-2.C.1 (2022).

137. "The power to zone is conferred upon the governing body of the municipality. That power cannot be delegated to the board of adjustment." James v. Sutton, 229 N.C. 515, 517, 50 S.E.2d 300, 301 (1948). *See also* Lee v. Bd. of Adjustment, 226 N.C. 107, 37 S.E.2d 128 (1946). Variances are discussed in detail in Chapter 17.

138. See F. Rebecca Sapp, Comment, *Delegation of Land Use Decisions to Neighborhood Groups*, 57 U.M.K.C. L. REV. 101 (1988). Also see the discussion of neighbor objections above at note 107.

139. While the views of neighbors can be an important consideration by the decision-making body, allowing a current neighbor to make a decision that runs with the land would bind a future purchaser of that property to acceptance of less regulatory protection than is afforded by the ordinance to other neighboring property owners. Still, the distinction between protection of public and private interests is challenging when one of the public interests involved is protection of neighboring property values and the compatibility of adjacent land uses.

140. The Court upheld a requirement that a billboard could not be erected on a residential block unless the consent of a majority of the owners was secured in *Thomas Cusack Co. v. City of Chicago*, 242 U.S. 526 (1917). State courts have frequently invalidated provisions allowing neighbors to veto individual development approvals. *See, e.g.*, Concordia Collegiate Inst. v. Miller, 301 N.Y.2d 632, 93 N.E.2d 189 (1950) (invalidating provision that allowed a school building on a residential block upon approval of eighty percent of the property owners); Spies v. Board of Appeals, 337 Ill. 507, 1669 N.E. 220 (1929) (invalidating neighbor consent to allow a store in a residential district).

141. The Court invalidated a provision that required the city to adopt a building-setback line upon the petition of two-thirds of the owners of property in a block in *Eubank v. City of Richmond*, 226 U.S. 137 (1912). Similarly,

Exercise of Discretion

The decision on the substance of land-development regulations is vested in the governing boards of cities and counties. While landowners and neighbors are to be consulted about the decision, neither constituency has a legal right to the continuation[142] (or to the change)[143] of a particular regulation.

Because actions to adopt, amend, or repeal ordinances are legislative decisions, the choice of what action to take—indeed, whether to take any action at all—is at the discretion of the governing board. As stated by the court, "Whether the zoning ordinance should be amended as requested by petitioner [is] for determination by the City Council in the exercise of its purely legislative function."[144] If persons are dissatisfied with legislative decisions, the remedy is generally at the ballot box rather than the courthouse.

There are also limits to the governing board's discretion on rezoning decisions, especially with regard to spot zoning, contract zoning, and the imposition of conditions on rezoning, as well as specific statutory and constitutional protections that must be observed by governing boards.[145] But for the most part, the basic decisions on the substance of land-development regulations are discretionary legislative acts of the local governing board.

Legislative Motives

Since these decisions are left to the judgment and discretion of elected officials, most aspects of alleged bias are not relevant in a judicial review of legislative decision-making. A member of the governing board is free to announce a position on a rezoning prior to the hearing, an action that would constitute an impermissible bias for a quasi-judicial decision.[146] Indeed, persons can and often do run for local office with campaign promises to effectuate a particular policy direction on land use and development regulations if elected.

The motives of governing-board members in making legislative decisions are generally not subject to question. The limited exceptions to this rule are a personal financial interest in the outcome of a

---

the Court in *Washington* ex rel. *Seattle Title Trust Co. v. Roberge*, 278 U.S. 116 (1928), invalidated a provision that allowed construction of a home for the aged in a residential district upon the consent of two-thirds of the property owners within 400 feet of the proposed building as an unlawful delegation of legislative power. *See also* Larkin v. Grendel's Den, Inc. 459 U.S. 116 (1982) (invalidating on Establishment Clause grounds a provision that allowed churches to veto neighboring liquor licenses). The North Carolina court in *Wilcher v. Sharpe*, 236 N.C. 308, 72 S.E.2d 662 (1952), held an ordinance prohibiting a mill without the consent of all owners within 300 feet to be an invalid delegation of legislative power to private parties.

142. In a case dismissing neighbors' challenge to a rezoning, the court held that neighbors have no vested right to the continuance of existing zoning. "A zoning ordinance is not a contract between the municipality and its citizens . . . . It is subject to amendment or repeal at the will of the governing agency which created it." McKinney v. City of High Point, 239 N.C. 232, 237, 79 S.E.2d 730, 734 (1954).

143. *In re Markham*, 259 N.C. 566, 131 S.E.2d 329 (1963), *cert. denied*, 375 U.S. 931 (1963), provides an early example. The Durham City Council denied a petition to rezone a 3.5-acre parcel adjacent to a shopping center from residential to commercial. The petitioner appealed to the courts, alleging that the refusal to amend the ordinance was arbitrary and unreasonable. The court refused to intervene.

144. *Id.* at 572, 131 S.E.2d at 334. The court ruled that the rezoning decision could not be reviewed by writ of certiorari. *See also* Marren v. Gamble, 237 N.C. 680, 75 S.E.2d 880 (1953); Ashby v. Town of Cary, 161 N.C. App. 499, 588 S.E.2d 572 (2003).

145. See Chapters 12 and 13 for a discussion of limitations on small-scale rezonings. Also see Chapters 24 through 28 for a discussion of constitutional limitations and Chapters 22 and 23 for statutory limitations on discretion.

146. Brown v. Town of Davidson, 113 N.C. App. 553, 439 S.E.2d 206 (1994). The court held that predisposition is not a due-process concern for legislative decisions. The court also dismissed a claim of racial discrimination in the town's failure to rezone the property, as there was no forecast of proof of racially discriminatory intent or purpose.

decision[147] or a deliberate intent to violate someone's constitutional rights (such as intentional racial or religious discrimination). The United States Supreme Court has noted that it is best to eschew the guesswork inherent in determining legislative motives, ruling, "It is a familiar principle of constitutional law that this Court will not strike down an otherwise constitutional statute on the basis of an alleged illicit legislative motive."[148] Courts examine the regulation itself rather than the motive of the adopting body to determine whether the regulation serves a legitimate purpose.[149]

Even so, a prudent local government will show that legitimate governmental objectives are being addressed in its legislative decisions.[150]

An example of a failure to do so leading to the invalidation of an ordinance is *Gregory v. County of Harnett*.[151] The county denied a rezoning that would have effectively prohibited a manufactured-home park on the site at issue but then a few months later approved an identical rezoning request for the site. The court held that where the record reflected no consideration of the character of the land, the suitability of the land for proposed uses, consistency with the county plan, or changed circumstances on the land, the rezoning was arbitrary and capricious.[152] By contrast, the court in *MLC Automotive, LLC v. Town of Southern Pines*[153] had no difficulty finding that a rezoning that precluded commercial development of a site had a legitimate justification. After the plaintiff had filed applications to develop the site for a collection of automobile dealerships, neighbors petitioned for and secured a rezoning to an office district that did not allow this use. In response to the plaintiff's allegation that the rezoning was done to stop its particular project, the court noted that the public objections and the town's rezoning

---

147. G.S. 160D-109(a) prohibits a governing-board member from voting on a rezoning or text amendment if the outcome would have a direct, substantial, and readily identifiable financial impact on the member and if the member has a close-family business or associational relationship with the property owner or applicant. See Chapter 25 for a discussion of conflicts of interest.

148. United States v. O'Brien, 391 U.S. 367, 382 (1968). *See also* Hart Book Stores, Inc. v. Edmisten, 612 F.2d 821, 834–35 (4th Cir. 1979), *cert. denied*, 447 U.S. 929 (1980). In *Mermaids, Inc. v. Currituck County Board of Commissioners*, the court noted, "It is not for the federal courts to look behind the proffered evidence of legislative decision-makers to discover alleged improper methods or motives." 19 F. Supp. 2d 493, 497 (E.D.N.C. 1998). In *MLC Automotive, LLC v. Town of Southern Pines*, No. 1:05CV1078, 2007 WL 128945 (M.D.N.C. Jan. 11, 2007), the court refused to allow deposition of town-council members about adoption of zoning amendments in the midst of a vested-rights dispute.

> The general rule is that courts will not take cognizance of a contention that a legislative body as a whole or individual members of it may have been prompted by unworthy motives in enacting a zoning ordinance or an amendment thereto, or in refusing to amend the ordinance. The court can consider only the legislation itself. If the legislation meets the test of reasonableness and constitutional hurdles of due process and equal protection, courts will not inquire into what may have prompted it.

4 Sara C. Bronin & Dwight H. Merriam, Rathkopf's The Law of Zoning and Planning § 67:20 (4th ed., Nov. 2018 Update) (with a collection of state cases so holding).

149. Local governmental bodies are generally entitled to absolute legislative immunity when acting in these legislative capacities. "The immunity of legislators from civil suit for what they do or say as legislators has its roots in the parliamentary struggles of 16th- and 17th-century England; such immunity was consistently recognized in the common law and was taken as a matter of course by our Nation's founders." Lake Country Estates, Inc. v. Tahoe Reg'l Planning Agency, 440 U.S. 391, 403 (1979). *See also* Bruce v. Riddle, 631 F.2d 272, 280 (4th Cir. 1980) (holding that if legislators of any political subdivision of a state function in a legislative capacity, they are absolutely immune from being sued under federal civil-rights statutes). See Chapter 21 for further discussion of liability and immunity.

150. See Chapter 25 for a discussion of legitimate objectives in land use regulation.

151. 128 N.C. App. 161, 493 S.E.2d 786 (1997).

152. *Id.* at 165, 493 S.E.2d at 789. The record also included considerable discussion about impermissible factors for the rezoning, such as alleged crime problems resulting from the "type of people" that reside in manufactured-home parks.

153. 207 N.C. App. 555, 702 S.E.2d 68 (2010), *review denied*, 710 S.E.2d 23 (2011). The twenty-one-acre site was bounded on three sides by residential neighborhoods and fronted a conservation area across the street.

action were based on a legitimate consideration of the appropriate range of uses given the character of the surrounding area.

While the court in *Gregory* expressed some concern about two differing results on essentially identical zoning decisions, a governing board has the discretion to "change its mind" about a rezoning. This is illustrated by *Carroll v. City of Kings Mountain*. In this case, the city council in September 2005 rezoned a property from a residential to a business district.[154] In January 2006, a newly elected council rezoned the property back to residential use. While the second rezoning was ultimately declared invalid for procedural reasons, the court held that given the deference accorded to legislative actions, such a reversal was not in and of itself arbitrary and capricious.

Statement on Plan Consistency and Rationale

Until 2006 a governing body was not required to make any findings to explain or justify a legislative decision.[155] However, the zoning statutes were amended in 2005 to require some documentation of the board's rationale for ordinance amendments.[156]

G.S. 160D-605 requires that, prior to adopting or rejecting any zoning amendment, the governing board must approve a statement describing whether its action is consistent with an adopted comprehensive or land use plan[157] and explaining why the board considers its action to be reasonable and in the public interest. The statement is to be adopted concurrently with action to adopt the zoning amendment.[158]

---

154. Carroll v. City of King's Mountain, 193 N.C. App. 165, 666 S.E.2d 814 (2008). The first rezoning had been initiated by the property owner. The second rezoning was initiated by neighbors and supported by the planning staff and planning board (while the owner filed a protest petition).

155. Some ordinances do add a requirement that certain findings be made or certain factors be considered in making legislative zoning decisions. For example, the Winston-Salem/Forsyth County zoning ordinance notes that the governing board may consider compatibility with surrounding uses, changed conditions, and consistency with the land use plan when reviewing zoning-amendment petitions. WINSTON-SALEM/FORSYTH COUNTY, N.C., UNIFIED DEVELOPMENT ORDINANCE § 3.2.19(A)(16) (2022).

156. S.L. 2005-426, § 7. See Chapter 22 for a more detailed discussion on plan-consistency issues. In some states, the courts have required similar documentation. For example, in *Honn v. City of Coon Rapids*, 313 N.W.2d 409 (Minn. 1981), the court noted that there must be "a rational basis for the municipal body's legislative decision" and that while formal findings are not required, the reasons for the decision must be "recorded or reduced to writing and in more than just a conclusory fashion." *Id.* at 416.

157. See Chapter 22 for a discussion of comprehensive planning as it relates to development regulations in North Carolina. The consistency-statement requirement was broadened in 2021 to reference land use plans as well as comprehensive plans. S.L. 2021-88, § 1(d).

158. The statutory language mandating governing-board statements originally provided that the statement must be "adopted prior to" governing-board action on the proposed zoning amendment. While most jurisdictions allowed for a single motion to approve the statement and the zoning amendment, a few cities interpreted this to require two separate motions, with the statement being adopted prior to consideration of the amendment. The General Assembly addressed this concern in the 2006 Technical Corrections Act. Section 28 of S.L. 2006-259 amended G.S. 160A-383 to provide that the statement be "approved when" acting on the proposed zoning amendment. A similar clarification was not made in the county statutes. In 2017, the municipal statute was again amended to revert to the original "adopted prior to" language. S.L. 2017-10, § 2.4(c). S.L. 2019-111 clarified this yet again, this time reverting to the original municipal clarification. This law amended G.S. 160D-605, to provide that the consistency statement does not have to be adopted as a separate motion prior to acting on the proposed zoning amendment. It does so by removing the language saying the statement must be approved "prior to" action on the amendment and replacing it with a direction that the statement be approved "when" making the decision.

The court in *Morgan v. Nash County*, 224 N.C. App. 60, 735 S.E.2d 615 (2012), *review denied*, 366 N.C. 561, 738 S.E.2d 379 (2013), noted that the statement of rationale had to address the action that had been taken, so it could not be approved prior to knowing what action was taken on the amendment. Thus, to require the statements to be adopted separately and prior to action on the proposed zoning amendment would be "an illogical interpretation of the statute." *Id.* at 69, 735 S.E.2d at 621.

In 2017, the General Assembly amended this requirement to direct that the governing board adopt a plan-consistency statement that takes one of three forms:

1. a statement approving the amendment and describing how it is consistent with the plan,
2. a statement rejecting the amendment and describing how it is inconsistent with the plan, or
3. a statement approving the amendment and a declaration that the plan also is amended. In this situation, the statement must also include an explanation of "the change in conditions the governing board took into account in amending the zoning ordinance to meet the development needs of the community."

In all three options, the statement was to include an explanation of why the action being taken is reasonable and in the public interest. The 2017 amendment[159] also provided that if a city or county governing board adopts a zoning amendment that is determined to be inconsistent with an adopted plan, the zoning amendment is deemed to also amend the plan. No additional request or application for a plan amendment can be required.

With the adoption of Chapter 160D in 2019, the form of the required plan-consistency statement that must be approved was simplified. First, G.S. 160D-605(a) requires only a "brief statement describing whether its action is consistent or inconsistent" with approved plans rather than one of three specified statements. A simple conclusion or checklist is still inadequate. The statement must *describe* how the action taken is or is not consistent. Formal findings and elaborate analysis are not required, but a brief description is. Second, the provision providing for automatic plan amendment if an inconsistent zoning action is taken was simplified. G.S. 160D-605(a) provides that the zoning decision only amends any future land use map in the plan, and that land use map is deemed amended to conform it to the zoning action taken. G.S. 160D-501 requires that if the future land use map is deemed amended by adoption of an inconsistent zoning action, then that amendment must be noted in the plan itself.[160]

For the most part, the process of preparing, reviewing, and approving a plan-consistency statement has become routine and unremarkable in most cities and counties. The staff typically drafts a plan-consistency analysis as part of the staff report on proposed zoning amendments.[161] That statement is reviewed and edited as needed by the planning board and submitted to the governing board. The governing board then reviews and edits the statement, approving the statement when it acts on the zoning amendment.

While the *substance* of a plan-consistency statement is not subject to judicial review,[162] whether it was actually approved by the governing board is subject to review. In *Wally v. City of Kannapolis*, the court held that having a staff analysis available for the board's review is not the same as governing-board approval of a statement.[163] The governing board must take affirmative action to adopt or approve

159. S.L. 2017-10.

160. G.S. 160D-501 also clarifies that if the plan being amended is a plan mandated by the Coastal Area Management Act, then the plan amendment is not effective until it goes through the plan-review and approval process required by the Act.

161. A 2018 School of Government survey reported that in 77 percent of the responding jurisdictions, the staff prepared the initial draft plan-consistency statement (the principal exception was in municipalities with populations under 1000, where there is often no staff available to do so). About 90 percent of the jurisdictions further reported that the planning board and governing board never or only rarely amended the draft statements. David W. Owens, *Plan-Consistency Statements*, PLAN. & ZONING L. BULL. No. 27 (UNC School of Government, Nov. 2018), at 11–12.

162. G.S. 160D-605(a). From the outset of the plan-consistency-statement requirement, the purpose has been to encourage consideration of the plan as zoning regulations are made while not creating additional litigation opportunities for those who disagree with the decision ultimately made by the governing board. Providing that the statement itself is not subject to judicial review was an attempt to avoid protracted future litigation like that on the adequacy of environmental-impact statements.

163. Wally v. City of Kannapolis, 365 N.C. 449, 722 S.E.2d 481 (2012). After voluntary annexation of a seventy-six-acre parcel, the owners had sought a conditional rezoning to allow office, light-industrial, and retail uses of the

the plan-consistency statement. In *Atkinson v. City of Charlotte*,[164] the court found that a conclusory statement noting that "this petition is found to be consistent with adopted policies" failed to meet the statutory requirement that the governing-board statement describe how the action is consistent with adopted plans and explain why it is reasonable and in the public interest.[165]

These cases requiring formal adoption of a plan-consistency statement led to legislative modification of the requirement in 2019. If a statement is not explicitly approved, G.S. 160D-605(a) provides that if the minutes of the board meeting in which the zoning amendment was acted upon show that the governing board was aware of and actually considered the plan, then the failure to formally adopt a written statement does not invalidate the action taken.[166] In effect, the statutory mandate is that the governing board consider the plan before acting—not vote on a particular form of a motion.

The required statement of rationale was also amended in 2019.[167] G.S. 160D-605(b) provides that the statement is required only for zoning-map amendments. A local government can adopt a reasonableness analysis for text amendments, but it is not required. The statute lists the factors that should be considered in this analysis. The factors are suggested and not mandated, as not all factors will be relevant to all rezoning decisions. The factors to be addressed, adapted from *Chrismon v. Guilford County*,[168] the leading North Carolina case on spot zoning, are the size and physical attributes of the site; the benefits and detriments to the landowner, neighbors, and community; how the actual and previously permitted uses of the site relate to newly permitted uses; changed conditions; and other factors affecting the public interest.

G.S. 160D-605(c) provides that the statement of reasonableness and the plan-consistency statement can be approved as a single, combined statement.

In sum, zoning amendments should be made on the basis of consistent standards and thoughtful analysis. Solicitation and consideration of public comments, review of technical studies and staff analysis, examination of consistency with city or county plans and policies, and consideration of effects on traffic, utilities, neighbors, the owner, and natural resources—all of these factors are appropriately part of the governing board's deliberation on a legislative land use regulatory decision.[169] Consideration of

---

property. The city's zoning commission recommended approval. At the city council's public hearing on the rezoning, a staff report was presented that included an analysis of plan consistency and other factors, including impacts on safety, traffic, parking, the environment, and public facilities. The governing board itself, however, did not explicitly adopt or approve the statement.

164. 235 N.C. App. 1, 760 S.E.2d 395 (2014). In this case, the city was considering a text amendment proposed by Queens College that exempted parking decks constructed as accessories to an institutional land use from the floor-area ratio requirements in single-family and multifamily zoning districts. The planning staff made a written statement that the amendment was consistent with the city's adopted policies. The planning commission's zoning committee unanimously recommended adoption, and their recommendation included a statement on plan consistency. The city council unanimously approved the statement of consistency and the proposed amendment.

165. For an example of a plan-consistency statement deemed adequate to meet statutory requirements, see *McDowell v. Randolph County*, 256 N.C. App. 708, 808 S.E.2d 513 (2017), which involved an amendment to the site plan in the conditional zoning for a lumber yard. The statement cited three specific plan policies to support the action taken.

166. This provision was added by S.L. 2019-111.

167. S.L. 2019-111. The original requirement for a statement of rationale was codified as G.S. 153A-342(b) and 160A-382(b). In addition, G.S. 153A-341(b) and 160A-383(a) required the governing board to approve a statement for every zoning text and map amendment of why the action taken was reasonable and in the public interest. This requirement was designed to assist cities and counties in assessing the case-law requirement that spot zoning must be "reasonable."

168. 322 N.C. 611, 628, 370 S.E.2d 579, 589 (1988).

169. For an example of a recommended process for consideration of rezonings, see Stuart Meck, *Making Zoning Decisions: A Guide for Local Governments in the Miami Valley Region, in* A PLANNER'S GUIDE TO LAND USE LAW 57 (Stuart Meck & Edith M. Netter eds., 1983).

these factors should be addressed in the mandatory statement to be adopted at the time of the zoning amendment. That said, it is important to distinguish the mandatory statement from the detailed findings of fact and conclusions of law required for quasi-judicial decisions.[170]

Closed Sessions

The governing board's discussion of proposed amendments to land-development regulations must be conducted in open session.[171] It is improper for a majority of the board to discuss proposed ordinance adoption, amendment, or repeal in private, even at social or informal gatherings.

The state's open-meetings law, however, contains a limited exception for closed sessions to receive legal advice that is sometimes applicable to pending legislative decisions. In *Multimedia Publishing of N.C., Inc. v. Henderson County*,[172] the court held that a board considering a proposed moratorium on racetracks could meet in closed session with the board's attorney to discuss legal issues relative to the precise drafting and wording of the ordinance. The closed-session discussion is limited to legal technicalities, such as the scope of statutory authority or the wording of the terms in an ordinance or permit condition. Once discussion moves on to the merits of the ordinance, it must be done in open session.

Voting

For the most part, the normal rules for voting on an ordinance apply to legislative decisions.[173]

For counties, G.S. 153A-45 requires a simple-majority vote to adopt a land-development regulation. This statute requires a unanimous vote to adopt county ordinances at the meeting of introduction, but ordinances requiring a public hearing, including all legislative zoning decisions, are exempt from this unanimity provision.

For cities, G.S. 160A-75 requires that ordinances be adopted by a simple majority of all members of the council not excused from voting. Prior to 2021, a two-thirds vote was required to adopt an ordinance on the date of introduction. This raised the question of what constitutes the "date of introduction." The statute is not entirely clear on that point.[174] G.S. 160A-75 provided that this is the "date the subject

---

170. *See, e.g.*, Childress v. Yadkin Cnty., 186 N.C. App. 30, 650 S.E.2d 55, 64 (2007) (distinguishing legislative rezoning from quasi-judicial findings).

171. G.S. 143-318, §§ .9 to .18. *See generally* FRAYDA S. BLUESTEIN & DAVID M. LAWRENCE, OPEN MEETINGS AND LOCAL GOVERNMENTS IN NORTH CAROLINA: SOME QUESTIONS AND ANSWERS (8th ed. 2017).

172. 136 N.C. App. 567, 575–76, 525 S.E.2d 786, 791–92, *review denied*, 351 N.C. 474, 543 S.E.2d 492 (2000). The court reached a similar conclusion in *Carolina Holdings, Inc. v. Housing Appeals Bd.*, 149 N.C. App. 579, 561 S.E.2d 541, *review denied*, 355 N.C. 298, 570 S.E.2d 499 (2002) (board considering order to demolish dilapidated buildings can hold closed session with its attorney to discuss constitutional and legal challenges that might result from its decision).

173. A board member's direct, substantial, and readily identifiable financial interest in the outcome of a legislative zoning decision mandates nonparticipation of that member. See Chapter 25 for a detailed discussion of conflicts of interest and Chapter 15 for a discussion of voting requirements for quasi-judicial decisions. As for the vote of a member who is participating in the meeting remotely, see Frayda S. Bluestein, *Remote Participation in Local Government Board Meetings*, LOCAL GOVT. L. BULL. No. 133 (UNC School of Government, Aug. 2013) (concluding that while North Carolina statutes do not expressly authorize remote participation or a vote by members participating remotely, it is likely permissible). In response to the COVID-19 pandemic, the General Assembly authorized remote meetings during a state of emergency. S.L. 2020-3, § 4.31(a). The authorization is codified at G.S. 166A-19.24.

174. As with other zoning provisions, this requirement may be modified by the General Assembly through special charter provision or local legislation. For example, S.L. 1989-918 authorizes the High Point city council to amend the zoning ordinance to provide that a two-thirds vote of the council is required to adopt a zoning amendment that has received an unfavorable recommendation from the planning agency. *See generally* TREY ALLEN, SUGGESTED RULES OF PROCEDURE FOR A CITY COUNCIL (4th ed. 2017).

matter is first voted on by the council." Some cities interpreted this to include votes to send the proposed amendment to a public hearing or to open a public hearing set by staff or operation of the ordinance, as well as a vote on whether to adopt the ordinance or amendment. Other jurisdictions followed a more conservative interpretation that does not consider the matter "voted on" until there is a vote to actually adopt the ordinance or amendment. This uncertainty was eliminated regarding action on development regulations in 2019 with an amendment to G.S. 160A-75.[175] The requirement for a supermajority on first reading was eliminated for adoption, amendment, or repeal of development regulations.

For cities, there is also a modification to the city voting rules when a zoning amendment is involved. The general rule in G.S. 160A-75 is that a failure to vote by a city-council member who is present but not excused from voting is automatically counted as an affirmative vote. That rule does not apply to votes on amendments to zoning regulations. If a city-council member who is present fails to vote on an amendment to a zoning text or zoning map, that vote is not counted as an affirmative vote. This exception to the rule effectively allows abstentions on these votes.[176]

G.S. 160D-109(a) codifies the prohibition against governing-board members voting on zoning amendments when there is a financial conflict of interest. The statute provides that a member is not to vote on any amendment that "is reasonably likely to have a direct, substantial, and readily identifiable financial impact on the member."[177] In 2019, this prohibition was expanded to include a requirement not to vote on a zoning amendment if the member has a close familial, business, or other associational relationship with the landowner of a property subject to the proposed rezoning or with the applicant for the zoning-text amendment.[178] These restrictions also apply to planning boards making recommendations on zoning amendments.

---

175. S.L. 2019-111, § 2.5(n). This amendment was made in conjunction with the adoption of Chapter 160D and its principle of having uniform city and county procedures relative to development regulations. It conforms the municipal voting rule to the prior county rule.

176. This amendment was made when the zoning protest petition was repealed. S.L. 2015-160.

177. These provisions were added to the statutes by S.L. 2005-426, § 5(a), 5(b). They codify the statement of this rule in *County of Lancaster v. Mecklenburg County*, 334 N.C. 496, 511, 434 S.E.2d 604, 614 (1993). Also see G.S. 160A-83, which requires the governing boards of cities and counties to adopt a code of ethics, and G.S. 160A-84, which requires the boards to receive two hours of ethics training within a year of being elected or reelected. See Chapter 25 for a discussion of conflict-of-interest rules. For comparable statutory limits in other states, see CAL. Gov. CODE § 87100 (public official shall not in any way attempt to use position to influence a governmental decision in which the official knows or has reason to know of a financial interest); CONN. GEN. STAT. ANN. § 8-11; *id.* § 8-21 (zoning-board member shall not participate in "any matter in which he is directly or indirectly interested in a personal or financial sense"); IND. CODE ANN. § 36-7-4-223 (plan commission and legislative body). *See also* Wyman v. Popham, 312 S.E.2d 795 (Ga. 1984) (allegation that board members had substantial business dealings with applicant for rezoning raises potential for fraud and corruption).

178. G.S. 160D-109(a). A close familial relationship is defined to mean a parent, child, brother, sister, grandparent, or grandchild, including step, half, and in-law relationships. G.S. 160D-109(f). See Chapter 25 for a discussion of conflicts of interest.

Referenda

In some states, active use is made of initiative and referendum to require that certain land use–ordinance decisions be made directly by the voters rather than elected officials.[179] There is no provision in North Carolina statutes for submission of the adoption, amendment, or repeal of ordinances directly to the voters.[180] Thus, a North Carolina city or county has no authority to submit a question of adoption, amendment, or repeal of a land use regulation to the voters.

The General Assembly has, however, granted several local governments special charter provisions that allow use of this technique.[181] The Greensboro charter provides that if 25 percent of the city's registered voters sign a referendum petition within thirty days of the adoption of any ordinance by the city council, the council must either repeal the ordinance or submit it to the voters.[182] The state supreme court has indicated that such a requirement is within the authority of local governments to fashion procedures for initiation, amendment, and repeal of zoning ordinances.[183] Another example is provided by several

---

179. The provision of an initiative or referendum option for local-ordinance adoption, amendment, or repeal is explicitly provided for by state constitution or by statute in these states. *See, e.g.,* Foster v. City Council, 201 Cal. 769, 255 P. 1118 (1927); Fla. Land Co. v. Winter Springs, 427 So. 2d 170 (Fla. 1983); City of Old Town v. Dimoulas, 2002 Me. 133, 803 A.2d 1018; La Branche v. A.J. Lane & Co., 404 Mass. 725, 537 N.E.2d 119 (1989); Greens at Fort Missoula, LLC v. City of Missoula, 271 Mont. 398, 897 P.2d 1078 (1995); Reva v. Portage, 356 Mich. 381, 96 N.W.2d 778 (1959); Kelly v. John, 162 Neb. 319, 75 N.W.2d 713 (1956); L.A. Ray Realty v. Town Council, 603 A.2d 311 (R.I. 1992); Colton v. Corbly, 318 N.W.2d 136 (S.D. 1982); R.G. Moore Bldg. Corp. v. Comm. for Repeal of Ordinance R(c)-88-13, 239 Va. 484, 391 S.E.2d 587 (1990); Smith v. Town of St. Johnsbury, 150 Vt. 351, 554 A.2d 233 (1988). If a state constitution authorizes local referenda, statutes cannot prevent the use of referenda for land use ordinances. Sevier Power Co. v. Bd. of Sevier Cnty. Comm'rs, 2008 UT 72, 196 P.3d 583. The power may also be based on home-rule authority granted to charter cities. San Diego Bldg. Contractors Ass'n v. City Council of San Diego, 13 Cal. 3d 205, 118 Cal. Rptr. 146, 529 P.2d 570 (1974), *appeal dismissed*, 427 U.S. 901 (1976). *See generally* Marcilynn A. Burke, *The Emperor's New Clothes: Exposing the Failures of Regulating Land Use Through the Ballot Box*, 84 Notre Dame L. Rev. 1453 (2009); David C. Callies et al., *Ballot Box Zoning: Initiative, Referendum and the Law*, 39 Wash. U. J. Urb. & Contemp. L. 53 (1991); Daniel P. Selmi, *Reconsidering the Use of Direct Democracy in Making Land Use Decisions*, 19 UCLA J. Envtl. L. & Pol'y 293 (2002).

The U.S. Supreme Court has held that making zoning decisions by referenda is constitutionally permissible. Eastlake v. Forest City Enters., 426 U.S. 668 (1976) (holding requirement for approval of rezoning by 55 percent of voters in referendum does not violate equal protection). *See also* City of Cuyahoga Falls v. Buckeye Cmty. Hope Found., 538 U.S. 188 (2003) (upholding submission of site-plan approval to voters). A decision made by the voters is, however, still subject to the same constitutional limitations as any other land use regulatory decision. *See, e.g.,* Fry v. Haywood, 701 F. Supp. 179 (N.D. Cal. 1988); Marco Lounge, Inc. v. Fed. Heights, 625 P.2d 982 (Colo. 1981).

180. See G.S. 160A-103 to -105 for provisions on amendment of municipal charters by referendum and petition.

181. For a summary of the authorization and use of referenda by North Carolina local governments, see David Lawrence, *Initiative, Referendum, and Recall in North Carolina*, Popular Gov't, Fall 1997, at 8. Lawrence reports that initiative or referendum authority has been authorized for Asheville, Greensboro, Lewisville, Lumberton, Morganton, Raleigh, River Bend, Wilmington, Winston-Salem, and Wrightsville Beach; in two of these jurisdictions (Greensboro and Wilmington) votes have been held on zoning issues. *Id.* at 12–14. The General Assembly has on several occasions adopted local bills authorizing referenda on land use issues. Examples include a precinct-level referendum in Alamance County on whether to have county zoning in that precinct (S.L. 1997-495), a Buncombe County advisory referendum on adoption of zoning for unincorporated areas of the county (S.L. 1999-303), an advisory referendum in Rutherford County on "high impact land-use zoning, such as heavy industrial use" (S.L. 2007-137), and an advisory referendum on countywide zoning in Caswell County (S.L. 2020-22).

182. S.L. 1959-1137, § 2.71.

183. Sofran Corp. v. City of Greensboro, 327 N.C. 125, 127, 393 S.E.2d 767, 768 (1990). The court did not clearly specify whether the referendum provision was within the general zoning grant of authority or had specifically to be authorized by local legislation. The court cited the general-statutory provisions and stated, "In accord with this statutory authorization to fashion procedures for the initiation, amendment, and repeal of zoning ordinances, the Greensboro City Charter grants referendum powers to the voters . . . ." *Id.*

beach cities that have secured local legislation to require that any increase in the height limits established by their zoning ordinances must be approved by the voters.[184]

Filing the Zoning Regulation and Map

After adoption, an accurate copy of the zoning regulation and map is to be kept by the city or county clerk.[185] Unlike the city-boundary map and the extraterritorial-boundary map, the zoning map does not have to be recorded with the county register of deeds.

G.S. 160A-77, which requires cities to maintain a code of ordinances, allows the zoning regulation to be published as a separate technical ordinance and allows the official zoning map to be retained permanently in the office of the city clerk (or other appropriate official). It is important that a local government maintain official copies of all official zoning maps, past and present, in order to show the public and the courts exactly what the applicable zoning was at any time. G.S. 160D-105(a) requires that zoning-district maps be maintained for public inspection in the office of the local government clerk or such other office as specified by the ordinance. The maps may be in paper or digital format. As a practical matter, most zoning maps are posted online, either at the local government's planning website or as part of the county's geographic information system. The official and binding map, however, is the one filed with and maintained by the clerk or other designated official.

In *Shearl v. Town of Highlands*,[186] the inability of the town to produce an official copy of a past zoning map made it impossible to ascertain what the zoning-district boundaries were when an owner was cited for a zoning violation. G.S. 153A-49 makes similar provisions for county zoning ordinances. G.S. 160A-79 establishes the procedure for pleading and proving ordinance provisions for both cities and counties.

---

184. S.L. 1989-456 provides for such a referendum for Holden Beach and Long Beach; S.L. 1991-772, for Yaupon Beach; and S.L. 1996-621, for Calabash.
185. G.S. 153A-48; 160A-78.
186. 236 N.C. App. 113, 762 S.E.2d 877 (2014).

CHAPTER 12

Spot Zoning

Zoning maps apply the use limitations and zoning requirements of individual zoning districts to particular properties. While jurisdictions occasionally undertake comprehensive updates and revisions of the zoning map, the far more typical rezoning situation arises when an individual seeks to change the zoning-district designation of a single parcel of land.[1]

Few areas of land use law have generated more confusion and litigation than individual zoning-map amendments. As former UNC School of Law dean and longtime land use law professor Judith Wegner observed, "Rezoning decisions are a chronic source of litigation, because deeply held expectations of neighborhood stability are often at war with deep-seated desires for handsome profits, against a backdrop of uncertain jurisprudence and unpredictable judicial dispositions."[2]

Limitations on small-scale rezonings can be grouped into two general headings: spot zoning and contract zoning. Many of the cases that challenge rezonings raise one or both of these issues. Spot-zoning analysis focuses primarily on the property that is being rezoned, and contract-zoning analysis focuses on the relationship between the government and the party seeking a rezoning. This chapter addresses spot-zoning issues and the following chapter covers contract-zoning issues.

Spot zoning occurs when a relatively small tract of land is zoned differently from the surrounding area. In North Carolina, spot zoning is not illegal in and of itself, as it is in some states.[3] However, to be upheld, spot zoning must be supported by a reasonable basis.

Table 12.1 summarizes reported North Carolina appellate decisions on spot zoning.

Legal Basis for Stricter Scrutiny

As a general rule, legislative decisions regarding zoning—decisions to adopt, amend, or repeal a zoning ordinance—are presumed to be valid, and the judiciary largely defers to the judgment of local elected officials on such matters.[4]

A key question in land use law is whether this presumption of validity should continue to apply when a rezoning affects only a single parcel or a very small area. Local elected officials and courts around the country have struggled with the question of how the law should treat such small-scale rezonings. While a rezoning is typically characterized as legislative in nature, the practical reality is that when the policy choice is adopted for an individual parcel, the decision often does not have the broad policy implications or public interest and oversight that is more commonly associated with legislative decisions.

---

1. The procedural requirements for rezoning regarding public notice, mailed notice, public hearings, protest petitions, and the like are discussed in Chapter 11.

2. Judith Welch Wegner, *Moving Toward the Bargaining Table: Contract Zoning, Development Agreements, and the Theoretical Foundations of Government Land Use Deals*, 65 N.C. L. Rev. 957, 977 (1987).

3. *See also* Daniel R. Mandelker, *Spot Zoning: New Ideas for an Old Problem*, 48 Urb. Law. 737 (2016).

4. Appeal of Parker, 214 N.C. 51, 55, 197 S.E. 706, 709, *appeal dismissed*, 305 U.S. 568 (1938). See Chapter 29 for a detailed discussion of the presumption of validity and standards for judicial review.

Table 12.1   Overview of Spot-Zoning Cases

Case	Court	Date	Parcel Size (acres)	Zoning Change
Spot Zoning Invalidated:				
Allred	Sup. Ct.	1971	9.26	To higher density residential
Blades	Sup. Ct.	1972	5	To higher density residential
Stutts	Ct. App.	1976	4	Residential to mobile-home park
Lathan	Ct. App.	1980	11.4	Residential to light industrial
Godfrey	Ct. App.	1983	17.45	Residential to heavy industrial
Alderman	Ct. App.	1988	14.2	Residential-agricultural to mobile-home park
Mahaffey	Ct. App.	1990	0.57	Residential to commercial
Covington	Ct. App.	1992	1 lot	Office to conditional use business
Budd	Ct. App.	1994	17.6	Residential-agricultural to special use industrial
Good Neighbors of South Davidson	Sup. Ct.	2002	50	Rural-agricultural to light and heavy industrial
McDowell	Ct. App	2007	29.95	Rural-agricultural and light industrial to heavy industrial
Etheridge	Ct. App.	2014	1.1	Agricultural to heavy-manufacturing conditional
Spot Zoning Upheld:				
Walker	Sup. Ct.	1961	3.5	Residential to neighborhood business
Zopfi	Sup. Ct.	1968	27.5, 12, 20	Commercial/residential to commercial/multifamily
Heath	Sup. Ct.	1971	15	Residential to mobile-home park
Allgood	Sup. Ct.	1972	25	Residential to commercial
Graham	Ct. App.	1981	30.3	Residential to office/conservation
Nelson	Ct. App.	1986	1 lot	Residential to business
Chrismon	Sup. Ct.	1988	5, 3	Agricultural to conditional use industrial
Dale	Ct. App.	1991	4.99	Residential to highway commercial
Purser	Ct. App.	1997	14.9	Residential to conditional use commercial
Childress	Ct. App.	2007	51	Rural-agricultural to restricted residential
Friends of Mt. Vernon Springs	Ct. App.	2008	1076	Agricultural to conditional heavy industrial
Musi	Ct. App.	2009	15 parcels	County residential to higher density town residential
Good Neighbors of Oregon Hill	Ct. App.	2015	102	Two owners, so not spot zoning
McDowell	Ct. App.	2017	29.95	Amendment of conditional-zone conditions not spot zoning

As a result, several states have ruled that spot zoning is more appropriately characterized as a quasi-judicial instead of a legislative decision.[5] In a leading example, the Oregon court held that these rezonings are so similar to quasi-judicial proceedings that many of the same safeguards should be applied, including removal of the presumption of validity of legislative zoning enactments, a required showing of consistency with the state-mandated comprehensive plan, a hearing on the matter before an impartial board, with the opportunity to present and rebut evidence, and a record with written findings.[6] A larger number of states have considered and rejected this approach, holding even small-scale rezonings are legislative in nature.[7]

The North Carolina courts have refused to characterize small-scale rezonings as quasi-judicial.[8] However, stricter judicial scrutiny is given to rezonings that affect a small geographic area or a small number of landowners than is given to rezonings implicating broad public-policy issues.[9] Heightened judicial review of spot zoning is founded on state constitutional prohibitions against the granting of exclusive privileges,[10] the creation of monopolies,[11] and the violation of due process or equal protection of the law.[12]

---

5. Decisions characterizing small-scale rezonings as quasi-judicial include *Margolis v. District Court*, 638 P.2d 297 (Colo. 1981); *Tate v. Miles*, 503 A.2d 187 (Del. 1986); *Board of County Commissioners v. Snyder*, 627 So. 2d 469 (Fla. 1993); *Cooper v. Board of County Commissioners*, 101 Idaho 407, 614 P.2d 947 (1980); and *Fleming v. City of Tacoma*, 81 Wash. 292, 502 P.2d 327 (1972). *See generally* Daniel R. Mandelker & A. Dan Tarlock, *Shifting the Presumption of Constitutionality in Land-Use Law*, 24 URB. LAW. 1 (1992); Michael S. Holman, Comment, *Zoning Amendments—The Product of Judicial or Quasi-Judicial Action*, 33 OHIO ST. L.J. 130 (1972). There was considerable support for this approach in the mid-1970s from leading land use–law commentators. *See, e.g.,* AMERICAN LAW INSTITUTE, A MODEL LAND DEVELOPMENT CODE § 2-312 (1976).

6. Fasano v. Bd. of Cnty. Comm'rs, 507 P.2d 23 (Or. 1974). In a subsequent case, the court elaborated on which governing-board decisions should be treated as quasi-judicial rather than legislative: "[W]hen a particular action by a local government is directed at a relatively small number of identifiable persons, and when that action also involves the application of existing policy to a specific factual setting, the requirement of quasi-judicial procedures has been implied . . . ." Neuberger v. City of Portland, 603 P.2d 771, 775 (Or. 1979).

7. States/decisions rejecting a quasi-judicial characterization of small-scale rezoning include *Cabana v. Kenai Peninsula Borough*, 21 P.3d 833 (Alaska 2001); *Wait v. City of Scottsdale*, 127 Ariz. 107, 618 P.2d 601 (1980); *Arnel Development Co. v. City of Costa Mesa*, 28 Cal. 3d 511, 169 Cal. Rptr. 904, 620 P.2d 565 (1980); *Hall Paving Co. v. Hall County*, 237 Ga. 14, 226 S.E.2d 728 (1976); *Neuzil v. City of Iowa City*, 451 N.W.2d 159 (Iowa 1990); *State v. City of Rochester*, 268 N.W.2d 885 (Minn. 1978); *Asian Americans for Equality v. Koch*, 72 N.Y.2d 121, 531 N.Y.S.2d 782, 527 N.E.2d 265 (1988); *Bradley v. Payson City Corp.*, 2003 UT 16, 70 P.3d 47; and *McGann v. City Council of Laramie*, 581 P.2d 1104 (Wyo. 1978). *See generally* 3 EDWARD H. ZIEGLER JR., RATHKOPF'S THE LAW OF ZONING AND PLANNING §§ 40:18 to 40:25 (4th ed., Nov. 2022 Update). An alternative approach is set forth in *Hyson v. Montgomery County Council*, 242 Md. 55, 217 A.2d 578 (1966). There the court held that while rezoning is a legislative decision, the state statute imposing procedural requirements on the rezoning hearing (that any interested party be allowed to present evidence; that a complete record be made of the hearing; that immaterial, irrelevant, and repetitious testimony be excluded; and that the matter be decided based on the record) required that a quasi-judicial-type process be followed prior to making a quasi-legislative decision. Subsequent Maryland decisions emphasize the importance of this process when making small-scale rezonings (sometimes termed "piecemeal zoning") as opposed to more comprehensive rezonings.

8. Summers v. City of Charlotte, 149 N.C. App. 509, 562 S.E.2d 18, *review denied*, 355 N.C. 758, 566 S.E.2d 482 (2002).

9. For an analogous approach, see *City of Pharr v. Tippit*, 616 S.W.2d 173, 176-77 (Tex. 1981) (rezonings are legislative, but judicial-review standards required to restrain arbitrary and capricious decisions include compliance with a comprehensive zoning ordinance, the nature and degree of adverse impacts on neighbors, the suitability of the land for the previously zoned use, and a substantial relationship to the public health, safety, welfare).

10. N.C. CONST. art. I, § 32.

11. N.C. CONST. art. I, § 34.

12. N.C. CONST. art. I, § 19. The "law of the land" provision of Section 19 is the equivalent of the Due Process Clause of the Fourteenth Amendment to the U.S. Constitution. See Chapter 25 for discussion of due-process issues.

The North Carolina cases speak primarily to substantive due process concerns with spot zoning.[13] This is consistent with long-standing doctrine that the police power must be exercised in the interest of the public overall.[14] The concern with lack of a public interest in rezonings was one of the earliest criticisms of zoning. An observer in 1931 noted:

> Many good zoning ordinances and plans have been seriously upset or entirely destroyed by the habit of making ill-considered changes to meet the needs of only one or a few property owners. Indignant protests, law suits, and suggestions for a new policy on making changes have followed. There is now general acceptance of the principle that no change, however small, should be made except after a careful and comprehensive investigation of all the factors involved and of the effects which might result.[15]

The North Carolina courts have held that spot zoning must not be arbitrary or capricious.[16] In *Blades v. City of Raleigh*, the court emphasized the need for a reasonable basis to justify spot zoning largely in terms of effects on neighboring properties:

> The whole concept of zoning implies a restriction upon the owner's right to use a specific tract for a use profitable to him but detrimental to the value of other properties in the area, thus promoting the most appropriate use of land throughout the municipality, considered as a whole. The police power, upon which zoning ordinances must rest, permits such restriction upon the right of the owner of a specific tract, when the legislative body has reasonable basis to believe that it will promote the general welfare by conserving the values of other properties and encouraging the most appropriate use thereof.[17]

In its most comprehensive review of spot-zoning limitations, the court in *Chrismon v. Guilford County*[18] concluded that a clear showing of a reasonable basis must support the validity of spot zon-

---

13. This approach is distinct from a focus on procedural due process, where more demanding quasi-judicial procedures could be employed to reduce potential abuse of zoning power. Here the inquiry is on the substance of the decision. Contract-zoning issues, which are frequently also raised in spot-zoning cases, are discussed in Chapter 13.

14. A police-power regulation adopted to advance private rather than the public interest is a violation of due process. State v. Ray, 131 N.C. 814, 42 S.E. 960 (1902) (invalidating ordinance requiring 7:30 p.m. closing of stores). Zoning ordinances must bear a substantial relation to protection of the public health, safety, morals, or general welfare. Helms v. City of Charlotte, 255 N.C. 647, 122 S.E.2d 817 (1961); *In re* O'Neal, 243 N.C. 714, 92 S.E.2d 189 (1956). *See also* Horton v. Gulledge, 277 N.C. 353, 177 S.E.2d 885 (1970).

15. Jacob L. Crane, Jr., *Progress in the Science of Zoning*, 155 ANNALS AM. ACAD. POL. & SOC. SCI., May 1931, at 194, 199 (1931). For an early North Carolina critique noting that spot zoning amounts to "special and arbitrary treatment for one or a few individuals," see Philip P. Green, Jr., *Questionable Zoning Practices*, POPULAR GOV'T, Apr. 1952, at 4. This concern of unjustified preferential treatment has been a factor in the invalidation of spot zoning in other states. *See, e.g.*, Modak-Truran v. Johnson, 18 So. 3d 206, 211 (Miss. 2009).

16. "The legislative body must act in good faith. It cannot act arbitrarily or capriciously." Walker v. Town of Elkin, 254 N.C. 85, 89, 118 S.E.2d 1, 4 (1961). The court also noted that if the conditions existing at the time of the rezoning were such as would have originally justified the proposed action, the rezoning would be upheld. The court has not, however, subsequently required any showing of changed circumstances as a prerequisite to rezonings. In *Zopfi v. City of Wilmington*, 273 N.C. 430, 438, 160 S.E.2d 325, 333 (1968), this due-process consideration was stated as a requirement that a rezoning not be arbitrary or discriminatory, that it be reasonably related to the public welfare, and that it be consistent with the purpose for which the city was authorized to enact zoning regulations. Also note that an invalid spot zoning is not a per se abuse of discretion mandating an award of attorney's fees. Etheridge v. Cnty. of Currituck, 235 N.C. App. 469, 481, 762 S.E.2d 289, 298 (2014).

17. Blades v. City of Raleigh, 280 N.C. 531, 546, 187 S.E.2d 35, 43 (1972). This analysis harks back to the "average reciprocity of advantage" concept raised in *Pennsylvania Coal Co. v. Mahon*, 260 U.S. 393, 415 (1922). Also note Justice Louis Brandeis's rejoinder in the dissent in *Mahon*. *Id.* at 422.

18. 322 N.C. 611, 370 S.E.2d 579 (1988). The case is described in detail in Philip P. Green, Jr., *Two Major Zoning Decisions:* Chrismon v. Guilford County *and* Hall v. City of Durham, LOC. GOV'T L. BULL. No. 34 (UNC Institute

ing. This shifts the presumption of validity accorded to legislative zoning decisions when a small-scale rezoning is involved.[19]

This mandated analysis was incorporated into the zoning statutes in 2005 with the addition of a requirement that a statement analyzing the reasonableness of the proposed rezoning be prepared as part of the consideration of all petitions for a conditional district or any other small-scale rezoning.[20] With other rezonings, if the reasonableness of the amendment is debatable, it is upheld. With spot-zoning amendments, the local government must affirmatively show the reasonableness of its action.[21]

In addition to being held to a standard of reasonableness in a due-process context, spot zoning is also restricted by the zoning-enabling statute. Chapter 160D, Section 701 of the North Carolina General Statutes (hereinafter G.S.) requires that zoning regulations be made in accordance with a comprehensive plan. A rezoning decision on a relatively small parcel that does not consider the effects of the rezoning within the larger community context violates this mandate.[22]

The language of individual zoning ordinances can impose additional limitations on spot zoning. For example, in the *Blades* case, the Raleigh zoning ordinance required that rezoning decisions be "based on the need to change the zoning map in accordance with the comprehensive plan or to amend the plan for the benefit of the neighborhood or city, because of changed conditions."[23]

Defining Spot Zoning

Rezonings that undergo more intensive review as spot zoning were simply and concisely defined as zoning "changes limited to small areas" in North Carolina's first case on the subject, *Walker v. Town of Elkin.*[24]

In *Zopfi v. City of Wilmington,*[25] a case that upheld the rezoning of a sixty-acre parcel into three zoning districts, the court ruled that illegal spot zoning arose "where a small area, usually a single lot or a few lots, surrounded by other property of similar nature, [was] placed arbitrarily in a different use zone from that to which the surrounding property [was] made subject."[26] Four years later, in *Blades*, a case that invalidated a five-acre rezoning, spot zoning was more completely defined thus:

> A zoning ordinance, or amendment, which singles out and reclassifies a relatively small tract owned by a single person and surrounded by a much larger area uniformly zoned, so as to impose upon the smaller tract greater restrictions than those imposed upon the larger area,

---

of Government, Nov. 1988). *See also* Smith v. Town of St. Johnsbury, 150 Vt. 351, 554 A.2d 233, 241 (1988) (multiple factors determine reasonableness of spot zoning).

19. "Defendant argues, and the Court agrees, that as a general proposition, a municipality's zoning actions are presumed to be reasonable and valid. However, when assessing a municipality's actions that are construed to be spot zoning, we note that this Court has set aside the aforementioned presumption in favor of requiring the municipality to offer a 'clear showing' that there was a 'reasonable basis' for its decision." Good Neighbors of S. Davidson v. Town of Denton, 355 N.C. 254, 258 n.2, 559 S.E.2d 768, 771 n.2 (2002) (citations omitted). *See also* Kerik v. Davidson Cnty., 145 N.C. App. 222, 551 S.E.2d 186 (2001) (applying heightened review to alleged contract zoning).

20. Chapter 160D, Section 605(b) of the North Carolina General Statutes (hereinafter G.S.).

21. In *Chrismon*, this was posed thusly: "[D]id the zoning authority make a clear showing of a reasonable basis for the zoning?" *Chrismon*, 322 N.C. 611, 627, 370 S.E.2d 579, 589 (1988).

22. Allred v. City of Raleigh, 277 N.C. 530, 178 S.E.2d 432 (1971); Alderman v. Chatham Cnty., 89 N.C. App. 610, 366 S.E.2d 885, *review denied*, 323 N.C. 171, 373 S.E.2d 103 (1988). Plan consistency is not mandatory in North Carolina, but the plan's significance is heightened in spot-zoning cases. See Chapter 22 for a further discussion of the relationship between zoning decisions and the comprehensive plan.

23. *Quoted in* Blades v. City of Raleigh, 280 N.C. 531, 547, 187 S.E.2d 35, 44 (1972).

24. 254 N.C. 85, 89, 118 S.E.2d 1, 4 (1961).

25. 273 N.C. 430, 160 S.E.2d 325 (1968).

26. *Id.* at 437, 160 S.E.2d at 332.

or so as to relieve the small tract from restrictions to which the rest of the area is subjected, is called "spot zoning."[27]

There are several aspects to this definition.

First, spot zoning can be an issue raised in initial zoning as well as in subsequent rezonings.[28]

Second, no specific minimum or maximum size of an area constitutes spot zoning. The size of the tract must be considered relative to the surrounding area.[29] A fifty-acre rezoning in a rural setting where that tract and thousands of adjacent acres have previously been zoned the same way may be spot zoning, but a five-acre rezoning in a dense urban setting with numerous zoning districts may not be spot zoning. In the North Carolina cases that have resulted in invalidation of rezonings as illegal spot zoning, the size of the tracts involved has ranged from 0.57 to 50 acres. That said, if the size of the zoning district is sufficiently large, the rezoning is simply not spot zoning. In *Friends of Mt. Vernon Springs, Inc. v. Town of Siler City*, the court held that a 1076-acre tract is not a "relatively small area" and cannot be considered spot zoning.[30]

Third, there is an emphasis on a very limited number of property owners being involved, "usually triggered by efforts to secure special benefits for particular property owners, without regard for the rights of adjacent landowners."[31] A large number of affected parties is more likely to bring the rezoning to broader public scrutiny, greater political accountability, and less need for judicial oversight. The definition used in *Blades* in fact speaks to a single owner of the affected property. This "single owner" requirement was applied in *Musi v. Town of Shallotte*,[32] a rezoning of newly annexed property consisting of fifteen parcels owned by six persons, and in *Good Neighbors of Oregon Hill Protecting Property Rights v. County of Rockingham*,[33] rezoning a two-acre parcel jointly owned by a father and son. In each case the court found that since the rezoned property was not owned by a single person or entity, it by definition could not be spot zoning.

---

27. *Blades*, 280 N.C. at 549, 187 S.E.2d at 45. For an analysis of this definition, see Philip P. Green, Jr., *Questions I'm Most Often Asked: What Is "Spot Zoning"?*, POPULAR GOV'T, Summer 1985, at 50. Green reported looking in vain for the origin of the term in early zoning cases. He concluded,

> Assiduous research in the early literature of zoning has produced no clues. It might be noted that the word "spot" itself is used in many ways with widely varying meanings: "He is on the spot." "This is a lovely spot for a picnic." "That was the high spot of his career." "That really hits the spot." "He spots the enemy." "Out, damned spot." "You have spotted my escutcheon." "My dog Spot."

Id.

28. Good Neighbors of S. Davidson v. Town of Denton, 355 N.C. 254, 257 n.1, 559 S.E.2d 768, 771 n.1 (2002). The initial zoning of the property had been made by the county and the spot zoning was the initial zoning by the city upon assuming jurisdiction after annexation. The court rejected the contention that this was not a "reclassification."

29. There is no set definition of the "surrounding area" to be considered. In many cases the comparison is to the immediately adjacent areas, but it is clear that the challenged rezoning must be viewed in context of the zoning of the immediate area. In *Musi v. Town of Shallotte*, 200 N.C. App. 379, 684 S.E.2d 892 (2009), the plaintiffs proposed examination of a one-mile radius around the rezoned area. The court looked at both a larger area and the dry-land area within a mile of the site.

30. Friends of Mt. Vernon Springs, Inc. v. Town of Siler City, 190 N.C. App. 633, 660 S.E.2d 657 (2008). The property was rezoned from agricultural-residential to heavy-industrial conditional on petition of a company seeking to operate a quarry and processing facility on the site.

31. 2 E.C. YOKLEY, ZONING LAW AND PRACTICE § 13-3 at 207 (4th ed. 1978), *quoted with approval in* Chrismon v. Guilford Cnty., 322 N.C. 611, 626, 370 S.E.2d 579, 588 (1988).

32. 200 N.C. App. 379, 684 S.E.2d 892 (2009). *See also* Covington v. Town of Apex, 108 N.C. App. 231, 423 S.E.2d 537 (1992).

33. 242 N.C. App. 280, 774 S.E.2d 902, *review denied*, 368 N.C. 429, 778 S.E.2d 78 (2015). Also see Wally v. City of Kannapolis, No. COA13-1425, 2014 WL 7472941 (N.C. Ct. App. Dec. 31, 2013, unpublished) (rezoning two parcels owned by separate entities cannot by definition be spot zoning).

Fourth, spot zoning can be involved when the proposed new zoning requirements for the small area are either more or less strict than those for the surrounding area. The key element is that the proposed zoning is different from the other zoning, "thus projecting an inharmonious land use pattern."[34] It is not spot zoning where the difference in the zoning districts is very modest. For example, in *Childress v. Yadkin County*, the court held that the "restricted residential" and "rural agricultural" (RA) districts at issue were sufficiently similar to avoid a spot-zoning characterization.[35]

Fifth, there must be a zoning-map amendment to trigger spot-zoning review. A text amendment, even when it is an amendment to the terms of a conditional zoning for a single parcel owned by a single entity, is not spot zoning. For example, in *McDowell v. Randolph County*,[36] the county approved an amendment to the site plan that allowed relocation of chemical vats in a lumberyard that was in a conditional-zoning district. The site plan was a part of the conditions for the district. The court noted that the amendment did not change the zoning of the parcel, so it by definition could not be considered spot zoning.

In sum, the heightened scrutiny of spot zoning applies when there is the appearance of possible discriminatory treatment (either favorable or negative) for a few, rather than a decision based on the larger public interest.

Factors in Validity

When adopting a "spot" zone, a local government has an affirmative obligation to establish that there is a reasonable public-policy basis for doing so.[37] Thus, the public-hearing record and minutes of the board's deliberations should reflect consideration of legitimate factors for differential zoning treatment of the property involved. Does the property have different physical characteristics that make it especially suitable for the proposed zoning, such as peculiar topography or unique access to roads or utilities? Are there land uses on or in proximity to the site that are different from the uses made of most of the surrounding property? Would the proposed range of newly permissible development be in harmony with the legitimate expectations of the neighbors? Have appropriate safeguards been incorporated to protect the interests of those affected?

In *Chrismon*, the court set out in detail four factors that are considered particularly important by the courts in determining whether there is a reasonable basis for spot zoning:

> At the outset, we note that a judicial determination as to the existence or nonexistence of a sufficient reasonable basis in the context of spot zoning is, and must be, the "product of a complex of factors." The possible "factors" are numerous and flexible, and they exist to provide guidelines for a judicial balancing of interests. Among the factors relevant to this judicial balancing are the size of the tract in question; the compatibility of the disputed zoning action with an existing comprehensive zoning plan; the benefits and detriments resulting from the zoning action for the owner of the newly zoned property, his neighbors, and the surrounding community; and the

---

34. *Chrismon*, 322 N.C. at 626, 370 S.E.2d at 588. *See also* Dale v. Town of Columbus, 101 N.C. App. 335, 399 S.E.2d 350 (1991). In some states, when the rezoning produces regulations less restrictive than those applicable to neighboring properties, the practice is termed "spot zoning," and when the restrictions are more restrictive, it is termed "inverse spot zoning."

35. 186 N.C. App. 30, 650 S.E.2d 55 (2007).

36. 256 N.C. App. 708, 808 S.E.2d 513 (2017).

37. Philip Green summarized this point as follows:

> I would like to suggest that at root "spot zoning" is nothing but giving special treatment to one or a few property owners, without adequate justification. . . . If there is a reasonable basis for treating particular property differently from nearby or similar property, that should be enough to support the validity of the zoning.

GREEN, *supra* note 27.

A rezoning to accommodate this agricultural operation was upheld in *Chrismon v. Guilford County.*

relationship between the uses envisioned under the new zoning and the uses currently present in adjacent tracts. Once again, the criteria are flexible, and the specific analysis used depends on the facts and circumstances of a particular case.[38]

The court has subsequently emphasized that a mere cataloging of benefits is inadequate. The "clear showing"[39] of reasonableness must address the totality of circumstances involved and "must demonstrate that the change was reasonable in light of its effect on all involved."[40] Thus, the statement of reasonableness approved by the board adopting a spot zoning should specify in some detail the basis for the action taken and the information before the board that supports that conclusion.

In 2019, the gist of the *Chrismon* rule was codified and made applicable to all zoning-map amendments. G.S. 160D-605(b) requires adoption of a statement of reasonableness for all zoning-map amendments. The statute lists the factors that should be considered in this analysis. The factors are suggested and not mandated, as not all factors will be relevant to all rezoning decisions. The factors to be addressed are:

1. the size and physical attributes of the site;
2. the benefits and detriments to the landowner, the neighbors, and the community;
3. how the actual and previously permitted uses of the site relate to newly permitted uses;
4. any changed conditions warranting the amendment; and
5. other factors affecting the public interest.

A review of North Carolina litigation illustrates the application of these factors to spot-zoning challenges of rezonings.

---

38. *Chrismon*, 322 N.C. at 628, 370 S.E.2d at 589 (citations omitted). Courts in other states have emphasized the need to examine similar multiple factors in spot- and contract-zoning cases. *See, e.g.,* LaSalle Nat'l Bank v. Cnty. of Cook, 12 Ill. 2d 40, 47, 145 N.E.2d 65, 69 (1957); Plains Grains Ltd. P'ship v. Bd. of Cnty. Comm'rs, 2010 MT 155, 357 Mont. 61, 238 P.3d 332 (must consider whether newly permitted use is significantly different from prevailing land uses in area, the size of the area, and whether the change benefits a few at the expense of surrounding owners or the public); Smith v. Town of St. Johnsbury, 150 Vt. 351, 554 A.2d 233 (1988).

39. *Chrismon*, 322 N.C. at 627, 370 S.E.2d at 589 (1988).

40. Good Neighbors of S. Davidson v. Town of Denton, 355 N.C. 254, 258, 559 S.E.2d 768, 771 (2002); Etheridge v. Cnty of Currituck, 235 N.C. App. 469, 762 S.E.2d 289 (2014). For a comparable analysis of whether a spot zoning is reasonable under all the circumstances, see *Riya Finnegan, LLC v. Township Council*, 197 N.J. 184, 962 A.2d 484 (2008) (invalidating rezoning of parcel from neighborhood-commercial to office district in response to neighborhood concerns about traffic from retail uses).

Size of Tract

The first factor to be considered in determining whether spot zoning is reasonable is the size of the tract. The general rule is that the smaller the tract, the more likely the rezoning will be held invalid. However, it is very important to consider the size of the tract in context: a one-acre parcel may be considered large in an urban area developed in the 1920s but very small in the midst of an undeveloped rural area.

The rezoning of an individual lot from a single-family- and multifamily-residential district to a business district was upheld in *Nelson v. City of Burlington*.[41] In this instance, the majority of property directly across the street was already zoned for business use, and the court concluded that, given the prevalence of business zoning in the immediate vicinity of this lot, there was "some plausible basis" for the rezoning.[42]

However, several cases have held the rezoning of relatively large tracts to be illegal spot zoning. A rezoning of a fifty-acre tract from RA to industrial was invalidated in *Good Neighbors of South Davidson v. Town of Denton*.[43] The site was a satellite area of the town, located in the midst of a rural and farming area some two miles from the town's primary corporate limits. A rezoning of a 29.95-acre portion of a 120.3-acre parcel from RA and light industrial to a conditional heavy industrial was invalidated in *McDowell v. Randolph County*,[44] where the surrounding land, estimated at "thousands of acres," was uniformly zoned as RA. Similarly, a rezoning of 17.6 acres from RA to industrial was held to be impermissible spot zoning in *Budd v. Davie County*.[45] The site there was some four to five miles from the nearest industrial zone, with all of the intervening property being in residential districts. A 17.45-acre rezoning was also ruled to be impermissible spot zoning in *Godfrey v. Union County Board of Commissioners*.[46] This case involved a rural tract that was zoned for single-family-residential use, as was all of the surrounding property, and the rezoning was to an industrial district. The court in *Alderman v. Chatham County*,[47] which involved the rezoning of a 14.2-acre tract from an RA district to a mobile-home park, when the surrounding 500 acres were residentially zoned, also found that unreasonable spot zoning had occurred. However, at some point the size of the tract is such that it precludes a determination that its size is a factor in determining

---

41. 80 N.C. App. 285, 341 S.E.2d 739 (1986).

42. *Id.* at 288, 341 S.E.2d at 741. The facts of this case also illustrate the importance of considering the full range of uses available in a zoning district, a factor discussed in detail in Chapter 13. The owner of the property in *Nelson* had sought the rezoning to allow construction of a small shopping center. The initial rezoning petition was denied. After the owner announced plans to construct low-income housing on the portion of the lot zoned for multifamily use, a second commercial-use rezoning petition was approved.

43. 355 N.C. 254, 559 S.E.2d 768 (2002). The court in *Childress*, 186 N.C. App. 30, 35–36, 650 S.E.2d 55, 60 (2007) also concluded that a fifty-acre rezoning where most of the surrounding property was uniformly zoned in a different district would be spot zoning if the two districts are sufficiently different. Cases in other states have likewise invalidated rezonings of relatively large parcels as improper spot zoning when the tracts were located within much larger homogeneously zoned areas. *See, e.g.,* Little v. Winborn, 518 N.W.2d 384 (Iowa 1994) (invalidating rezoning of 223-acre parcel to allow a shooting club in an agricultural area); Greater Yellowstone Coalition, Inc. v. Bd. of Cnty. Comm'rs, 2001 MT 99, 305 Mont. 232, 25 P.3d 168 (invalidating rezoning of 323-acre parcel to a mixed-use zone for a planned-unit development); Chrobuck v. Snohomish Cnty., 78 Wash. 2d 858, 480 P.2d 489 (1971) (invalidating rezoning of 635-acre parcel to allow an oil refinery in a recreational and residential area).

44. 186 N.C. App. 17, 649 S.E.2d 920 (2007). The rezoning was requested in order to allow expansion of an existing nonconforming sawmill, kiln, and pallet-making operation.

45. 116 N.C. App. 168, 447 S.E.2d 449 (1994), *review denied*, 338 N.C. 524, 453 S.E.2d 174 (1994).

46. 61 N.C. App. 100, 300 S.E.2d 273 (1983). Compare *Rose v. Guilford County*, 60 N.C. App. 170, 298 S.E.2d 200 (1982), in which the court held that summary judgment was inappropriate when the rezoning of a 100-acre tract from an agricultural to a residential district that allowed mobile homes was challenged as arbitrary and capricious on spot- and contract-zoning grounds.

47. 89 N.C. App. 610, 366 S.E.2d 885, *review denied*, 323 N.C. 171, 373 S.E.2d 103 (1988). That an adjacent sixteen-acre tract owned by the same person had been rezoned to a mobile-home park some eleven years earlier did not change the court's conclusion that the immediate rezoning was unreasonable.

reasonableness. In *Friends of Mt. Vernon Springs*, the court noted that a rezoning of a 1076-acre tract was not unreasonable and was not spot zoning.[48]

The fact that other small areas nearby have similar zoning to that proposed in a rezoning will not avoid a spot-zoning label. The tract to be rezoned is considered in relation "to the vast majority of the land immediately around it."[49]

Compatibility with Plan

The second factor in a spot-zoning analysis is compatibility with the existing comprehensive zoning plan.[50] This involves an inquiry into whether the rezoning fits into a larger context involving rational planning for the community. Whether set forth in a formal comprehensive land use plan or reflected in an overall zoning scheme, zoning regulations must be based on an analysis of the suitability of the land for development (e.g., topography, soil types, wetland locations, and flood areas), the availability of needed services (e.g., water, sewers, roads, and rail lines), and existing and needed land uses.[51] To the extent that a small-area rezoning fits into a logical preexisting plan that is clearly based on this type of analysis, it is much more likely to be upheld.

An example of a zoning scheme involving relatively small parcels that was judged acceptable because it fit the context of the land and the surrounding uses is found in *Zopfi*. The court there upheld the rezoning of a roughly sixty-acre triangle, formed by two major highways, into three zoning districts with decreasing density moving away from the point of the highway intersection. A 27.5-acre parcel at the point of the intersection was zoned commercial, the next 12 acres were zoned for multifamily-residential use, and the remainder was zoned for single-family-residential use. Similarly in *Nelson*, the rezoning of a lot from residential use to business use was upheld on the basis that the majority of the property directly across the street was already zoned for business use.

A contrast is provided by situations in which there are no discernible reasons to single out a small tract for differential zoning treatment. This is a common rationale cited by the courts when finding spot zoning to be unreasonable and thus illegal. A number of North Carolina cases illustrate this point.

An early example is *Stutts v. Swaim*. In 1967, the town of Randleman had zoned virtually all of its half-mile extraterritorial-zoning jurisdiction (some 500 acres) for one- and two-family residences. An attempt in 1968 to rezone a four-acre tract to a mobile-home zoning district, when there were no special

---

48. Friends of Mt. Vernon Springs, Inc. v. Town of Siler City, 190 N.C. App. 633, 660 S.E.2d 657 (2008). In other states rezonings of relatively large areas of land have been held to be spot zoning when they were singled out from vastly larger areas of uniformly zoned land. *See, e.g., Greater Yellowstone Coalition*, 2001 MT 99, 305 Mont. 232, 25 P.3d 168 (invalidating rezoning to a mixed-use district of 323-acre parcel located within a 13,280-acre area zoned for low-density residential use); *Chrobuck*, 78 Wash. 2d 858, 480 P.2d 489 (invalidating rezoning for an oil refinery of 635 acres located within a 7680-acre tract zoned for residential and recreational uses).

49. Mahaffey v. Forsyth Cnty., 99 N.C. App. 676, 682, 394 S.E.2d 203, 207 (1990), *review denied*, 327 N.C. 636, 399 S.E.2d 327 (1991). In *Etheridge v. County of Currituck*, 235 N.C. App. 469, 762 S.E.2d 289 (2014), the court found illegal spot zoning even though property on one side was adjoined by property zoning for general business, with the other three sides and majority of surrounding area zoned agricultural. But see *Orange County v. Heath*, 278 N.C. 688, 180 S.E.2d 810 (1971), in which the court held that rezoning a fifteen-acre tract from a residential district to a mobile-home park was not spot zoning because it adjoined a five-acre tract already in legal use as a mobile-home park.

50. See Chapters 11 and 22 for a further discussion of zoning and consistency with comprehensive plans. Plan consistency is a factor in spot-zoning reviews in several states. *See, e.g.,* Hartshorne v. City of Whitefish, 486 P.3d 693, 699–701 (Mt. 2021).

51. The court in *Childress* went so far as to rely on an affidavit submitted by the county manager to ascertain plan consistency. Childress v. Yadkin Cnty., 186 N.C. App. 30, 38, 650 S.E.2d 55, 61 (2007).

characteristics present on that site, was ruled invalid spot zoning.[52] A relatively common spot-zoning controversy arises when a rezoning is proposed to allow intensive industrial-type uses in the midst of largely residential rural areas.

In *McDowell v. Randolph County,*[53] the plaintiff secured the rezoning of nearly thirty acres to allow expansion of milling operations at an existing nonconforming lumberyard and sawmill. The proposed rezoning would have allowed a pallet-making operation, kiln, and industrial-building expansion immediately adjacent to the plaintiff's residence.[54] The court noted the drastically different statement of purposes for the residential-agricultural and industrial districts in the county's unified development ordinance. The county's growth-management plan expressly provided that industrial development should not be located where it would diminish the desirability of residential uses. The plan identified the site as within the rural growth area, to be composed predominantly of agricultural and residential uses. Both the ordinance and the plan called for substantial buffers between industrial and residential uses and the rezoning. The court concluded the rezoning was in direct contravention of these plans and policies.

In *Lathan v. Union County Board of Commissioners,*[55] an 11.4-acre rezoning from residential to light-industrial use was ruled to be invalid spot zoning. A sawmill on the site was being operated as a nonconforming use, and the rezoning was necessary to accommodate the facility's expansion. The site had no access to major highways, rail lines, or public utilities, and the planning director concluded that industrial development would be incompatible with the surrounding residential community. Nevertheless, the planning board recommended that the tract be rezoned as requested.[56] The Union County commissioners agreed with the planning board's recommendation and adopted the rezoning. The adjacent landowner then sued. The court of appeals ruled that no special features on the tract made it any more suitable than the surrounding property for industrial use. The rezoning was ruled invalid spot zoning because there was no clear showing of a reasonable basis for the rezoning.

In *Godfrey v. Union County Board of Commissioners,*[57] the comprehensive plan designated the area rezoned as a low-density residential district, and the nearest industrial uses were approximately a half-mile away. The owner sought rezoning to heavy-industrial use because he wanted to relocate a grain-bin operation to the site. The planning director recommended approval of the rezoning from residential to industrial use based on the site's accessibility to a major highway, a railroad, and public water. The planning board approved the recommendation, and the county commissioners narrowly adopted it. The court invalidated the rezoning, however, finding that the "whole intent and purpose . . . was to accommodate his plans to relocate his grain bins, not to promote the most appropriate use of the land throughout the community."[58] The court acknowledged the availability of some services that would make this tract

52. Stutts v. Swaim, 30 N.C. App. 611, 228 S.E.2d 750, *review denied*, 291 N.C. 178, 229 S.E.2d 692 (1976). There were two mobile-home parks in the extraterritorial-zoning area, and both were zoned for mobile-home use. One was three-fourths of a mile from the tract at issue; the other, two-and-one-half miles. The litigation was initiated some five-and-a-half years after the contested rezoning. The court applied a traditional laches analysis and allowed the litigation. G.S. 160A-364.1, which establishes a nine-month statute of limitations for challenging rezonings, was subsequently adopted.

53. 186 N.C. App. 17, 649 S.E.2d 920 (2007).

54. The county had issued permits allowing expansion of industrial buildings located within twenty feet of the plaintiff's residential property. The rezoning was sought when neighbors complained that this was the unlawful expansion of a nonconforming use.

55. 47 N.C. App. 357, 267 S.E.2d 30, *review denied*, 301 N.C. 92, 273 S.E.2d 298 (1980).

56. The planning board's reasons for a favorable recommendation were "(1) Because of how long it has been there. (2) You can't tell a man that he can't grow and will have to go up U.S. 74 to expand. (3) How long they have had the land." *Id.* at 359, 267 S.E.2d at 32.

57. 61 N.C. App. 100, 300 S.E.2d 273 (1983).

58. *Id.* at 104, 300 S.E.2d at 275. The court concluded that the rezoning constituted improper contract zoning as well as improper spot zoning.

suitable for industrial development but concluded that the same was true of the surrounding property, and because this tract was "essentially similar," there was no reasonable basis for zoning it differently.

A formal comprehensive plan and the recommendations of the planning board are increasingly important in spot-zoning analysis.

In *Mahaffey v. Forsyth County*,[59] a 0.57-acre tract was rezoned from a residential and highway-business district to a general-business district. The comprehensive plan designated the area as "predominantly rural with some subdivisions adjacent to farms." The planning staff and the planning board recommended against the rezoning, but the board of commissioners adopted it. In ruling the action to be illegal spot zoning, the court pointedly noted, "[T]he County Planning Board and Planning Board Staff, made up of professionals who are entrusted with the development of and adherence to the comprehensive plan, recommended denial of the petition."[60]

A similar result was reached in *Covington v. Town of Apex*,[61] in which the rezoning of a single lot from office and institutional use to conditional use business was held to be impermissible spot zoning. The court concluded that the rezoning contradicted the town's policies on location of industrial uses, as set forth in the comprehensive plan. The court also found minimal benefit to the public and substantial detriment to neighbors. In *Budd*, the rezoning of a fourteen-acre site along the Yadkin River, as well as a half-mile-long, sixty-foot-wide accessway, from RA to industrial in order to accommodate a sand-mining operation was invalidated in part because it directly contradicted the previously adopted policies for the area. The zoning ordinance's stated intent for the RA district was to maintain a "rural development pattern" with an aim "clearly to exclude commercial and industrial uses."[62] Based on such considerations, the planning board twice recommended denial of the rezoning petition. The court held that the rezoning was in direct contravention of the stated purpose of the comprehensive zoning scheme, and this factored into invalidation of the rezoning.[63]

Consistency with a comprehensive plan sometimes justifies differential zoning. In *Graham v. City of Raleigh*,[64] the rezoning of a 30.3-acre tract from a residential to an office district was upheld in part based on the need to bring the property in line with the nodal concept of development promoted in Raleigh's comprehensive plan.[65]

Formal amendment of an inconsistent comprehensive plan is not necessarily required to avoid a finding of illegal spot zoning, though a reasonable basis for the deviation must be established.[66] In *Purser*

---

59. 99 N.C. App. 676, 394 S.E.2d 203 (1990), *review denied*, 327 N.C. 636, 399 S.E.2d 327 (1991). *See also* Etheridge v. Cnty. of Currituck, 235 N.C. App. 469, 762 S.E.2d 289 (2014) (plan inconsistency was conceded by county).

60. *Id.* at 683, 394 S.E.2d at 207. In *Good Neighbors of South Davidson*, 355 N.C. 254, 559 S.E.2d 768 (2002), the court noted that the record was silent on plan consistency and thus this factor could not be urged to show the reasonableness of the action taken.

61. 108 N.C. App. 231, 423 S.E.2d 537 (1992).

62. Budd v. Davie Cnty., 116 N.C. App. 168, 175, 447 S.E.2d 449, 453, *review denied*, 338 N.C. 667, 453 S.E.2d 174 (1994).

63. However, the governing board's attempted rezoning would have made this policy, which applied to all land zoned RA, inapplicable to this site. An argument can be made, then, that the rezoning is not inconsistent with the policies in the zoning ordinance. This reemphasizes the importance of being able to point to a comprehensive plan or to other planning studies, reports, and policies extrinsic to the zoning ordinance itself.

64. 55 N.C. App. 107, 284 S.E.2d 742 (1981), *review denied*, 305 N.C. 299, 290 S.E.2d 702 (1982).

65. The character of the surrounding neighborhood was a factor also in *Finch v. City of Durham*, 325 N.C. 352, 384 S.E.2d 8 (1989), though the spot-zoning issue was not explicitly addressed in this taking challenge. The rezoning from commercial to residential use, which was upheld in a taking challenge, was supported by policies of protecting an adjacent residential neighborhood and limiting commercial development to the opposite side of the adjacent interstate highway.

66. Note, however, that the statutes now provide that if a rezoning is adopted that is inconsistent with an adopted comprehensive plan, the plan is deemed amended by the rezoning. G.S. 160D-605(a).

v. Mecklenburg County,[67] the court upheld the rezoning of a 14.9-acre tract from residential to conditional use–commercial to allow construction of a neighborhood convenience center. The county's small-area plan for the site indicated that a nearby but different site was suitable for such a center. However, testimony presented at the public hearing indicated that whereas the suitability of the other site depended on road construction, locating a convenience center on the site in question would be consistent with policies in the county's general-development plan.

Balancing Benefits and Detriments

The third factor to be considered in spot-zoning analysis is who benefits from the rezoning, who (if anyone) is harmed, and what the relative magnitudes of the benefits and harms are. If the rezoning is granted, will it greatly benefit the owner? Will the owner be seriously harmed if it is denied? After the same questions are asked of the neighbors and the community at large, the effects on all three must be balanced. In a spot-zoning challenge, the courts, not the governing board alone, review and weigh the balance of benefit and harm created by the rezoning.

The courts may be sympathetic to a rezoning that confers considerable benefit to the owner and only modest harm to others, but even a substantial benefit for the owner will not offset substantial harm to others. This principle is evident in the ruling that invalidated the rezoning challenged in *Blades*. The case involved rezoning a five-acre tract in the midst of a large single-family zoning district to a multifamily district in order to allow for the construction of twenty townhouses. The court found that no reason was offered for treating this property differently and that the character of the existing neighborhood might be greatly harmed as a result.[68] In *Etheridge v. County of Currituck*,[69] the court noted that the purported benefits of a proposed recycling center were not supported by any evidence presented at the rezoning hearing, and the benefits offered were "a generalized benefit that has no specific connection to the surrounding rural community," while the "vast majority" of speakers were in opposition and offered supporting evidence from real-estate professionals and law-enforcement officials.[70]

Chrismon illustrates the other side of this analysis. The court there noted as follows:

> [W]hile spot zoning which creates a great benefit for the owner of the rezoned property with only an accompanying detriment and no accompanying benefit to the community or to the public interest may well be illegal, spot zoning which provides a service needed in the community in addition to benefiting the landowner may be proper.[71]

In *Chrismon*, the rezoning of one 3-acre and one 5-acre tract from an agricultural district to a conditional use–industrial district in order to allow for an agricultural chemical use was upheld. The court weighed the benefit to the owner, the harm to the immediately adjacent neighbor, the broad community support for the rezoning, and the need for these services in the surrounding agricultural community; it concluded that there were "quite substantial benefits created for the surrounding community by the rezoning."[72]

---

67. 127 N.C. App. 63, 488 S.E.2d 277 (1997).

68. Blades v. City of Raleigh, 280 N.C. 531, 546, 187 S.E.2d 35, 43 (1972). *See also* Covington v. Town of Apex, 108 N.C. App. 231, 423 S.E.2d 537 (1992), *review denied*, 333 N.C. 462, 427 S.E.2d 620 (1993) (invalidating the rezoning of a former post-office site adjacent to a residential neighborhood from institutional use to an industrial district in order to accommodate an electronic-assembly operation).

69. 235 N.C. App. 469, 762 S.E.2d 289 (2014).

70. *Id.* at 473–74, 762 S.E.2d at 293–94.

71. Chrismon v. Guilford Cnty., 322 N.C. 611, 629, 370 S.E.2d 579, 590 (1988).

72. *Id.* at 633, 370 S.E.2d at 592.

The benefits to the community must be real and substantial, not merely convenient. For example, in *Mahaffey*, it was argued that rezoning a 0.57-acre tract to allow for the establishment of an auto-parts store would be beneficial to a rural community in which virtually everyone depended on automobiles. The court rejected this argument, noting, "[A]uto parts are a common and easily obtainable product and, if such a retail establishment were said to be 'beneficial to a rural community,' then virtually any type of business could be similarly classified."[73] Likewise, in *Budd*, the court ruled that generalized benefits resulting from increased business activity related to the operation of a sand mine did not offset the potential harm to neighbors caused by the influx of heavy-truck traffic into the rural residential area.[74]

A spot-zoning analysis must consider the impacts on neighbors and the surrounding community even if they are not located in the jurisdiction of the local government making the rezoning. In fact, in *Good Neighbors of South Davidson*,[75] the court indicated it would give particular attention to the weighing of benefits and detriments in this situation because the neighbors had no political recourse for addressing what they deemed to be unreasonable zoning decisions:

> [I]n the aftermath of the satellite annexation, when the authority to rezone the parcel shifted from the county to the Town of Denton, Piedmont's neighbors suddenly found themselves outside looking in. Without a say in the annexation process, they had no one to defend their zoning interests and no one to vote out of office for failing to do so. In sum, the Town of Denton could act on the property at issue without fear of political reprisal from the neighboring landowners of Davidson County. From our vantage point, there are precious few circumstances that could prove more detrimental to a surrounding community.[76]

In concluding that this rezoning constituted illegal spot zoning, the court noted that the town's failure to consider the adverse impacts on the neighbors was "rather suggestive of a cavalier unreasonableness on the part of the town."[77]

Relationship of Uses

The fourth factor in spot-zoning analysis is the relationship between the proposed uses and the current uses of adjacent properties. The greater the disparity, the more likely the rezoning is to be held illegal.

This was a consideration in the court's invalidation of the rezonings in the *Lathan*, *Godfrey*, and *Budd* cases, even though all three situations involved relatively large acreage: 11.4 acres, 17.45 acres, and 17.6 acres, respectively. In each case the rezoning was from low-density residential to industrial use. The magnitude of the change prompted the courts to look closely for a supporting rationale; they found none.[78] Likewise, in both the *Allred* and the *Blades* cases, proposals to locate high-density multifamily projects in single-family-residential neighborhoods were invalidated.

---

73. Mahaffey v. Forsyth Cnty., 99 N.C. App. 676, 683, 394 S.E.2d 203, at 208 (1990), *review denied*, 327 N.C. 636, 399 S.E.2d 327 (1991).

74. Budd v. Davie Cnty., 116 N.C. App. 168, 175–77, 447 S.E.2d 438, 453–54 (1994), *review denied*, 338 N.C. 524, 453 S.E.2d 179 (1994). The court reached the same conclusion regarding significant neighborhood harms (increased truck traffic, noise, and dust) outweighing speculative economic benefits in *McDowell v. Randolph County*, 186 N.C. App. 17, 24–27, 649 S.E.2d 920, 926–27 (2007).

75. 355 N.C. 254, 559 S.E.2d 768 (2002).

76. *Id.* at 261, 559 S.E.2d at 773.

77. *Id.* at 262, 559 S.E.2d at 774.

78. *See also Id.*, 559 S.E.2d at 773; *Budd*, 116 N.C. App. at 178, 447 S.E.2d at 455 (rezoning would "destroy the tenor of the quiet residential and agricultural neighborhood"); *Mahaffey*, 99 N.C. App. 676, 394 S.E.2d 203 (holding that the auto-parts store allowed by rezoning was a significantly different use from the surrounding rural residential neighborhood).

On the other hand, the abovementioned *Chrismon* case resulted in only a modest change in the allowed uses: the landowner could carry on the storage and sale of grain under the original zoning; the rezoning allowed the storage and sale of agricultural chemicals. Further, the site was in the midst of an agricultural area that needed such services. Thus, the court could conclude the following:

> [T]his is simply not a situation . . . in which a radically different land use, by virtue of a zoning action, appears in the midst of a uniform and drastically distinct area. No parcel has been "wrenched" out of the Guilford County landscape and rezoned in a manner that "disturbs the tenor of the neighborhood." . . . In our view, the use of the newly rezoned tracts . . . is simply not the sort of drastic change from possible surrounding uses which constitutes illegal spot zoning.[79]

In addition, limitations on the uses proposed in the zoning approval and site-specific development conditions can minimize the adverse impact on neighboring properties. For example, a conditional use district rezoning to allow a neighborhood convenience center was upheld in *Purser*, in part because "the development of the Center was governed by a conditional use site plan that was designed to integrate the Center into the neighborhood and insure that it would be in harmony with the existing and proposed residential uses on the surrounding property."[80] By contrast, the failure to condition the rezoning on provisions that would mitigate harm to neighbors was a factor in the invalidation of the rezoning in *Etheridge*.[81]

A change in the conditions is not required to justify a rezoning in North Carolina, but it can be an important factor in establishing that a proposed new zoning classification is compatible with surrounding land uses.[82] For example, in *Allgood v. Town of Tarboro*,[83] the rezoning of a twenty-five-acre tract from residential to commercial use was upheld in part on the basis that in the eight years between the initial adoption of zoning and the challenged rezoning, the surrounding area had substantially changed because of the expansion of an adjoining road, the extension of water and sewer lines, the construction of a school and an apartment complex nearby, and the annexation of the site by the city.

---

79. Chrismon v. Guilford Cnty., 322 N.C. 611, 632, 370 S.E.2d 579 591–92 (1988). *See also* Childress v. Yadkin Cnty., 186 N.C. App. 30, 650 S.E.2d 55 (2007) (upholding rezoning where principal difference in the two districts was between allowing modular rather than manufactured housing at comparable densities).

80. Purser v. Mecklenburg Cnty., 127 N.C. App. 63, 70–71, 488 S.E.2d 277, 282 (1997).

81. Etheridge v. Cnty. of Currituck, 235 N.C. App. 469, 762 S.E.2d 289 (2014). Even though this was a conditional zoning, the only condition imposed to mitigate neighborhood impacts of a recycling center was an eight-foot fence around the property.

82. When the statutory requirement for a plan-consistency statement was amended in 2017, a requirement was added to ensure that when a rezoning was adopted that was inconsistent with the adopted plan, the local government had to provide "an explanation of the change in conditions the governing board took into account in amending the zoning ordinance to meet the development needs of the community." S.L. 2017-10. This provision was deleted with the simplification of the plan-consistency-statement requirement in the 2019 adoption of Chapter 160D. S.L. 2019-111.

83. 281 N.C. 430, 189 S.E.2d 255 (1972).

CHAPTER 13

Contract and Conditional Zoning

Zoning regulations set development policies for the entire community. They specify which land uses are appropriate for a particular area and what development standards should be applied to those uses. While in many instances these general policies are adequate, there is often interest in tailoring the regulatory requirements to a particular site or development proposal. How far can a local government go in fine-tuning its development standards to individual lots and projects? Are negotiations between the local government, the landowner, and the neighbors to craft such individualized regulations appropriate? When should this be allowed? In land use issues, what safeguards are necessary to prevent the landowner from overreaching, protect the neighbors from harmful sweetheart deals, and ensure that the public's interests are considered in the process?

The most common way to address these issues is through the use of the special use permit.[1] But there are situations where there is an interest in fashioning individualized development standards early in the approval process, at the rezoning stage rather than at a permitting stage of the development-review process. Contract-zoning analysis focuses on whether and how this can be done.

The courts have increasingly allowed rezoning decisions to incorporate good-faith negotiations that accommodate the landowners' and neighbors' interests while also furthering broader public interests.[2] While the general rule that rezoning decisions must be made to further the public interest rather than to advance only private interests stands, the flexibility of local governments to tailor zoning regulations to individual sites and development projects has significantly expanded in recent decades.[3]

Despite this greater judicial acceptance of individualized regulations, care must be observed in how they are fashioned. The courts continue to hold several practices illegal in North Carolina. For example, conditions on rezoning to a conventional zoning district, failure to consider all uses being allowed in a rezoning to a general-use district, and contract zoning are all illegal. On the other hand, *conditional zoning* (CZ) can be used to accomplish many of the same objectives and is legal.[4]

As with spot zoning, conditional zoning occupies the difficult analytic position of being at the intersection of legislative and quasi-judicial zoning decisions. While it is technically a legislative amendment to the regulation, it is in fact a detailed, site-specific regulatory decision. North Carolina courts, cognizant of the hybrid nature of these decisions, have crafted an intermediate level of judicial review. The courts

---

1. See Chapter 16.

2. *See generally* Michael B. Brough, *Flexibility Without Arbitrariness in the Zoning System: Observations on North Carolina Special Exception and Zoning Amendment Cases*, 53 N.C. L. Rev. 925 (1975); Judith Welch Wegner, *Moving Toward the Bargaining Table: Contract Zoning, Development Agreements, and the Theoretical Foundations of Government Land Use Deals*, 65 N.C. L. Rev. 957 (1987). *See also* Daniel P. Selmi, *The Contract Transformation in Land Use Regulation*, 63 Stan. L. Rev. 591 (2011).

3. Statutes in several states have been adopted to specifically authorize some degree of negotiated zoning. *See, e.g.,* Ariz. Rev. Stat. § 9-462.01(E); Idaho Code § 67-6511A; Va. Code Ann. §§ 15.2-2296 to .2-2303.4. See the discussion of development agreements in Chapter 19.

4. Caution on the terminology used in these analyses is warranted. Planners, commentators, and the courts sometimes use very similar terms to describe different concepts. Therefore labels—contract zoning, contingent zoning, and conditional zoning—should be used advisedly.

have recognized the policy-choice dimension of these decisions by refusing to characterize them as quasi-judicial applications of previously determined policies. However, the courts have also recognized the site-specific, individualized character of the decisions and required that they be supported by a reasonable basis.[5]

Conditions on Conventional Rezonings

Individual, particularized conditions on rezonings to a general-use district are unenforceable in North Carolina.[6]

Section 160D-703(c) of the North Carolina General Statutes (hereinafter G.S.) provide that, except as specifically authorized, "all regulations shall be uniform for each class or kind of building throughout each [zoning] district."[7] In *Decker v. Coleman*,[8] the court held that this uniformity requirement precluded imposition of conditions on conventional rezonings. In this case, the city of Asheville rezoned a sixty-two-acre parcel from residential to commercial in order to allow construction of a shopping center. The rezoning was conditioned upon the owner's maintaining a fifty-foot buffer without any access connections between the proposed commercial use and the adjacent residential neighborhood. While such a condition may be entirely appropriate and legal for a special use permit, here the condition was attached to the rezoning decision. Since such a buffer requirement was not uniformly applied throughout the zoning district, the court held that the city had no statutory authority to apply it as a condition of rezoning a particular parcel. The court thus held the condition invalid and unenforceable.

The inclusion of an invalid condition does not always invalidate the rezoning. Barring other legal defects, the rezoning stands; its conditions do not. In *Decker*, the city council included a specific severability clause, and the court applied it to sever the condition, invalidate it, and leave the remainder of the ordinance amendment in place. The same result was reached in *Kerik v. Davidson County*,[9] where the court invalidated a buffer requirement imposed on a rezoning but held the rezoning itself valid.

Failure to Consider All Permissible Uses

A rezoning to a conventional zoning district that is based on a single project rather than on all permissible uses in the new zoning district is invalid.

Two cases from the early 1970s established this principle of North Carolina zoning law. Both cases arose in Raleigh, and both invalidated rezonings that allowed multifamily development in single-family residential neighborhoods. These early cases termed this practice *contract zoning*. The court has since dropped this characterization but has retained the result—the practice remains illegal in North Carolina.

---

5. See the discussion of the mandatory reasonableness analysis for spot zoning in Chapter 12.

6. Several states, including Georgia, Nebraska, New York, Washington, and Wisconsin, allow this practice. *See, e.g.*, Mallins v. Foley, 74 A.D.3d 1070, 903 N.Y.S.2d 492 (App. Div. 2010) (upholding continued enforcement of restrictive covenants requiring buffers that were agreed to in rezoning from residential to industrial zone). *See generally* Ronald M. Shapiro, *The Case for Conditional Zoning*, 41 Temple L.Q. 267 (1968).

7. This statute acknowledges that regulations may differ from one district to another. As well, it provides exceptions to the uniformity requirement when additional restrictions are imposed through an overlay district or a conditional district.

8. 6 N.C. App. 102, 169 S.E.2d 487 (1969).

9. 145 N.C. App. 222, 551 S.E.2d 186 (2001). The court questioned the relevance of *Decker* in *Massey v. City of Charlotte*, 145 N.C. App. 345, 351, 550 S.E.2d 838, 843, *review denied*, 354 N.C. 219, 554 S.E.2d 342 (2001), noting that it applied only to conventional zoning and was decided prior to *Chrismon*. *Kerik*, a decision contemporaneous to *Massey*, illustrates *Decker*'s continuing vitality outside of the conditional zoning context.

In *Allred v. City of Raleigh*,[10] a 9.26-acre tract was rezoned from R-4 to R-10 to allow for the construction of twin high-rise apartment towers in what had been a single-family residential area. Two previous applications for similar rezonings of this site had been denied. Consideration of the rezoning petition that was approved included extensive discussion of the particular project proposed. The planning-commission report on the project noted that the particular proposal was for "very attractive" buildings of "outstanding architectural" quality.[11] However, it recommended denial because of the proposal's inconsistency with the comprehensive plan and because of opposition from the neighborhood. After a detailed discussion of the project, in which a prominent member of the General Assembly represented the developer, the city council voted to rezone the parcel in order to "afford the community the opportunity of this splendid development."[12] The trial court and the court of appeals upheld the rezoning. However, the North Carolina Supreme Court concluded that the rezoning was based on the specific plans of the applicant, had not considered all possible uses to which the property could be devoted under the new zoning, and was thus invalid. Writing for a unanimous court, Chief Justice Bobbitt held:

> [N]otwithstanding the motivation of the City Council may be laudable, any action of the City Council that disregards the fundamental concepts of zoning as set forth in the enabling legislation may be arbitrary and capricious.
>
> In our view, and we so hold, the zoning of the property may be changed from R-4 to R-10 only if and when its location and the surrounding circumstances are such that the property should be made available for all uses permitted in an R-10 district. Rezoning on consideration of assurances that a particular tract or parcel will be developed in accordance with restricted approved plans is not a permissible ground for placing the property in a zone where restrictions of the nature prescribed are not otherwise required or contemplated. Rezoning must be effected by the exercise of legislative power rather than by special arrangements with the owner of a particular tract or parcel of land.[13]

Blades v. City of Raleigh[14] presented a similar situation leading to the same result. In this instance, a five-acre tract was rezoned from R-4 to R-6 to allow the construction of twenty "ultra luxurious townhouses" (the existing R-4 zoning allowed only single-family residences). A site plan of the proposed development was presented at the rezoning hearing, and a representative of the owner explicitly noted that other permitted uses in the proposed R-6 district (e.g., a sanatorium, a hospital, or a rest home) would not be "proper development." Even though the Raleigh city council had previously adopted a resolution that rezonings were not to be based on a specific use or plan, the court concluded, "[I]t is quite apparent that the amending ordinance was adopted solely because the applicant convinced the Council that it would use the property for the construction of town houses as specifically described. Nevertheless, the adoption of the ordinance, if it be valid, would permit use of this property for any other

---

10. 277 N.C. 530, 178 S.E.2d 432 (1971).

11. *Id.* at 536–37, 178 S.E.2d at 435 (quoting planning-commission report).

12. *Id.* at 539, 178 S.E.2d at 437 (quoting council-meeting minutes).

13. *Id.* at 545, 178 S.E.2d at 440–41. The owner of the site subject to the litigation in *Allred* was subsequently successful in having the site rezoned from R-4 to R-10. In this later, successful rezoning, the applicant presented a professional traffic analysis, a study of the compatibility of the rezoning with the thoroughfare, and a land use study. The applicant and the staff studiously avoided reference to a particular project and instead focused on all permitted uses. A protest petition was filed, but the rezoning was unanimously adopted. Single-story attached housing that was more compatible with the neighborhood than high-rise towers was eventually built on the site.

14. 280 N.C. 531, 187 S.E.2d 35 (1972).

In the *Allred* (left) and *Blades* (right) cases, rezonings from single-family to multifamily residential uses were successfully challenged by neighbors as unlawful spot zoning. In both instances, the eventual development of the site was more compatible with the surrounding neighborhoods.

purpose permitted in an R-6 district."[15] Thus, the court again unanimously invalidated the rezoning. This rule has subsequently been followed in North Carolina.[16]

In response to these cases, a number of zoning ordinances were amended in the 1970s and 1980s to explicitly forbid presentations on specific projects when petitions for rezoning to a conventional district are being considered. The Greensboro zoning ordinance formerly prohibited petitioners from offering any testimony concerning the specific intended use of the property. This resulted in frustrations for both the governing board and the applicant because they were participating in a hearing in which neither could directly discuss what they both felt to be the most relevant topic: precisely what was going to happen if the rezoning was adopted. Stephen Davenport and Philip Green recount the story of a rezoning hearing in which "the gentleman speaking in favor of a rezoning, when advised by the Chairman that the Commission could not 'hear' the testimony he was giving (about a specific use), moved closer to the microphone and continued in a louder voice (not recognizing the distinction between legal constraints and deafness)."[17]

A number of cities and counties, however, sought to retain the ability to evaluate rezoning proposals on the basis of the particular project motivating the rezoning petition, even when the rezoning proposed was to a conventional zoning district. Durham, for example, secured local legislation authorizing site

---

15. *Id.* at 550, 187 S.E.2d at 46. Luxury single-family homes were eventually constructed on this site. *See also* Godfrey v. Union Cnty. Bd. of Comm'rs, 61 N.C. App. 100, 300 S.E.2d 273 (1983) (invalidating rezoning of 17.45 acres from single-family-residential to heavy-industrial use to allow owner to relocate his grain-bin operation).

16. In *Alderman v. Chatham County*, 89 N.C. App. 610, 366 S.E.2d 885, *review denied*, 323 N.C. 171, 373 S.E.2d 103 (1988), a 14.2-acre rezoning from a residential-agricultural district to a mobile-home district was invalidated because only the density of the development, according to a restricted plan submitted by the owner, rather than all the uses permitted in the new district, was considered by the governing board. The court of appeals noted that a rezoning was invalid if it was "accomplished as a direct consequence of the conditions agreed to by the applicant rather than as a valid exercise of the county's legislative discretion." *Id.* at 619, 366 S.E.2d at 891. In several cases the courts have also held that it is improper to grant summary judgment when an allegation has been made that a rezoning decision was based on a single proposed project. Nelson v. City of Burlington, 80 N.C. App. 285, 341 S.E.2d 739 (1986); Willis v. Union Cnty., 77 N.C. App. 407, 335 S.E.2d 76 (1985); Rose v. Guilford Cnty., 60 N.C. App. 170, 298 S.E.2d 200 (1982).

17. STEPHEN E. DAVENPORT & PHILIP P. GREEN, JR., SPECIAL USE AND CONDITIONAL USE DISTRICTS: A WAY TO IMPOSE MORE SPECIFIC ZONING CONTROLS 13 (1980).

plans to be submitted with rezoning petitions.[18] The court, however, continued to apply the *Blades* and *Allred* rule that a conventional rezoning must consider all of the potential uses allowed by the new zone. The court in *Hall v. City of Durham*[19] ruled that although a site plan may be submitted, its submission does not remove the requirement that all potential uses in a new general-zoning district be fully considered. *Hall* involved the rezoning of a 12.9-acre tract from a single-family-residential district to a commercial district to accommodate construction of a four-building commercial complex with an outdoor lumberyard and a parking area. A detailed site plan submitted with the rezoning petition included the physical layout of the development, a proposed donation of adjacent property to a conservation group, and detailed restrictions on development, including a landscaped buffer, a limit on the height to which lumber would be stacked, and a constraint on the color of the buildings. Most of these detailed conditions had resulted from extensive negotiations with neighboring property owners. The city council based the rezoning on this carefully negotiated project but without considering all of the other possible uses in the new zoning district. The planning commission had recommended against the rezoning, noting that some of the twelve other uses permitted in the new district would not be compatible with the surrounding neighborhood. The court agreed and invalidated the rezoning.[20]

The fact that specific plans are presented to the governing board, however, does not in and of itself invalidate a rezoning so long as the record is clear that all permissible uses are considered.

In *Kerik v. Davidson County*,[21] the petitioner for a 140-acre rezoning sent the governing board several memos while the petition was under review, outlining the proposed uses of the property if rezoned, describing various conditions to be placed on the property, describing proposed utility service, setting out an intent to donate park land to the county, and noting the alternative plans for the site if not rezoned. The court held that this provision of information did not invalidate the rezoning, as the record revealed that the board received a list of permitted uses in the proposed districts and discussed their potential impact (and the record reflected that the planning board had similar information and discussion).

Similarly, in *Musi v. Town of Shallotte*,[22] the court held that the fact that the town council was aware of a specific plan to build multifamily condominiums on the site of a proposed rezoning did not in and of itself indicate that the council was unaware of other uses that could be undertaken under the new zoning. The court noted that the range of uses allowed in the new town zoning district were similar to those allowed in the prior county zoning (albeit at a higher density), and each council member testified in depositions that the council had considered the full range of permitted uses at the time of the rezoning.

Morgan v. Nash County provides an additional illustration. The county was pursuing a specific company for economic development and rezoned a parcel that would accommodate construction of its plant. Before voting on the rezoning, each board member was provided a list of all permitted uses in the new

---

18. *See, e.g.*, S.L. 1975-671, § 92 (Durham city). S.L. 1989-950 extended this authority to Durham County. The submission of a development plan when a petition for a rezoning is made is at the option of the landowner. The Durham ordinance also requires submission of a traffic-impact analysis when a development plan is submitted in certain zoning districts. Durham, N.C., Unified Development Ordinance § 3.3.3 (2022). Other similar local legislation includes S.L. 1989-430 (Knightdale); S.L. 1989-611 (Zebulon); S.L. 1985-498 (Raleigh). Other local governments have also adopted ordinance provisions that allow site plans to be submitted with rezoning proposals. In these instances, the applicant may submit a "simple sketch plan," analogous to the sketch plan used in many subdivision ordinances, for staff review and comment before making a formal petition for rezoning.

19. 323 N.C. 293, 372 S.E.2d 564 (1988).

20. It has been suggested that this practice be termed *insufficiently analyzed rezoning* to distinguish it from true contract zoning. Louis W. Doherty, Comment, Chrismon v. Guilford County *and* Hall v. City of Durham: *Redefining Contract Zoning and Approving Conditional Use Zoning in North Carolina*, 68 N.C. L. Rev. 177 (1989).

21. 145 N.C. App. 222, 551 S.E.2d 186 (2001). *See also* Childress v. Yadkin Cnty., 186 N.C. App. 30, 650 S.E.2d 55, 64 (2007) (discussion at hearing by petitioner as to uses of the property if rezoned not per se violation).

22. 200 N.C. App. 379, 684 S.E.2d 892 (2009).

zoning district, the list was read aloud at the hearing, and each board member signed an affidavit averring that the member considered all potential uses in the district before voting on the rezoning. The court found this adequately established that the board met its obligation to consider all permissible uses, not just the specific use being proposed.[23]

Also, a mere allegation that a particular use and not all permissible uses were considered is inadequate to invalidate a rezoning. This is illustrated by *Graham v. City of Raleigh*,[24] where a rezoning from residential to office and institutional use was upheld over a contract-zoning challenge. The governing board and the planning board had met nine times to discuss the zoning of the site, and the record demonstrated "clearly that the circumstances and conditions concerning the questioned zone changes were peculiarly within the knowledge of the city council and that they considered all permissible uses available in the Office and Institution I and III Districts in enacting the questioned ordinance."[25]

When a specific development proposal has motivated a rezoning request, many local governments explicitly note in the hearing record the full range of uses that would be allowed in a new zoning district. This is often done in a staff report that is presented to the governing board prior to a vote on the rezoning. It is not uncommon for the list to be read aloud at the hearing, along with a statement that any of the permitted uses (in addition to any specific project that has been mentioned) would be allowed if the property was rezoned. Such a recitation is sufficient to avoid invalidation of a rezoning on the basis that all potential permitted uses were not considered prior to action.

Contract Zoning

In the classic contract-zoning situation, the local government and the landowner enter into a written agreement (sometimes recorded as a deed restriction) that if the government rezones the property to a specified new zoning district, the owner will carry out a particular use and accept specified limits or conditions on that use. While a North Carolina case has yet to involve this situation directly, in *Chrismon v. Guilford County*, the court held true contract zoning impermissible:

> Illegal contract zoning properly connotes a transaction wherein both the landowner who is seeking a certain zoning action and the zoning authority itself undertake reciprocal obligations in the context of a bilateral contract. . . . [C]ontract zoning of this type is objectionable primarily because it represents an abandonment on the part of the zoning authority of its duty to exercise independent judgment in making zoning decisions.[26]

In *Hall*, the court provided further elaboration on the contract-zoning definition:

> A typical example of such reciprocal assurances occurs when the applicant assures the city council that the property will be used only for a specified purpose and no other, and the city

23. Morgan v. Nash Cnty., 224 N.C. App. 60, 735 S.E.2d 615 (2012), *review denied*, 366 N.C. 561, 738 S.E.2d 379 (2013). In fact, even though the rezoning was upheld on appeal, the developer withdrew and the poultry-processing plant was not constructed on the site.

24. 55 N.C. App. 107, 284 S.E.2d 742 (1981), *review denied*, 305 N.C. 299, 290 S.E.2d 702 (1982).

25. *Id.* at 111, 284 S.E.2d at 745. *See also* Dale v. Town of Columbus, 101 N.C. App. 335, 399 S.E.2d 350 (1991).

26. 322 N.C. 611, 635, 370 S.E.2d 579, 593 (1988). Most states traditionally held such bilateral agreements illegal. *See, e.g.*, Hartnett v. Austin, 93 So. 2d 86 (Fla. 1956); Baylis v. Mayor of Balt., 219 Md. 164, 148 A.2d 429 (1959); Houston Petroleum Co. v. Auto. Prods. Credit, 9 N.J. 122, 87 A.2d 319 (1952). Cases typically distinguish bilateral contract zoning that is illegal from permissible CZ. *See, e.g.*, Dacy v. Vill. of Ruidoso, 114 N.M. 699, 845 P.2d 793 (1992). *See generally* Nolan M. Kennedy, Jr., Comment, *Contract and Conditional Zoning: A Tool for Zoning Flexibility*, 23 HASTINGS L.J. 825 (1972); Bruce R. Bailey, Comment, *The Use and Abuse of Contract Zoning*, 12 UCLA L. REV. 897 (1965).

council, in consideration of such assurance, agrees to rezone the property in question and not to alter the zoning for a specified period of time thereafter.[27]

This definition raises the question of whether a rezoning to a conventional district that is based on a specific proposal rather than all permitted uses is indeed contract zoning. The *Blades* court termed such a decision contract zoning, but the *Chrismon* court emphasized the necessity of a reciprocal agreement in order to have a contract. An element of reciprocity was not clearly present in the *Allred* and *Blades* cases.[28] The *Hall* decision resolved this question. The court there ruled that the practice was not contract zoning but was nonetheless illegal. When rezonings to conventional districts are involved, all potential uses in the new district must be fully considered for the rezoning to be valid.

Conditional Use District Zoning

Conditional use district (CUD) zoning is involved when a landowner requests that property be placed in a new zoning district that has no permitted uses, only special uses. Once widely used in North Carolina, this practice is no longer authorized by the statutes and has been replaced with legislative conditional zoning.[29]

CUDs (sometimes termed *special use districts*) were created in the North Carolina zoning statutes in the 1980s to avoid illegal contract zoning. At that time, legislative conditional zoning was not allowed by the state's statutes or case law. CUDs were an ingenious way around this prohibition. The concept was that a parcel would be rezoned to a new zoning district that had no permitted uses at all—only special uses. The standard practice was to use a conventional district but make all its permitted uses special uses in a parallel CUD. For example, a highway-business district might have twenty permitted uses. The highway-business conditional district would have those same twenty uses allowed, but none of them would be permitted by right and all of them would be subject to getting a special use permit. These CUDs are "floating zones"; that is, they are not applied to any property until a petition to apply them is made by the landowner.[30]

Concurrently with consideration of a petition to rezone property into a CUD—a legislative rezoning decision—the governing board considered an individual application for a special use permit for a particular project within the new district. The special use permit—a quasi-judicial decision—could be addressed at a later time and could be issued by the board of adjustment or the planning board rather than the governing board. However, the typical practice was to consider the rezoning and the permit at the same time, with both decisions made by the governing board.[31]

---

27. 323 N.C. 293, 299, 372 S.E.2d 564, 568 (1988). In the example provided by the court, the attempt to limit the discretion of future boards with a binding agreement not to change the zoning is particularly troublesome. However, the owner and local government can accomplish much the same through use of either a development agreement or a vested right based on a site-specific development plan. Both are based on the ordinance in effect at the time of the agreement but vest the right to rely on that ordinance for an extended time into the future. These tools are discussed in Chapter 19.

28. This fact produced a split on the court in *Chrismon* and *Hall*. The dissenters would have held that a rezoning based on a specific proposal was illegal contract zoning whether or not there was a reciprocal agreement.

29. Chapter 160D, Section 703 of the North Carolina General Statutes (hereinafter G.S.) eliminates conditional use districts as an authorized type of zoning district. S.L. 2019-111.

30. North Carolina cases have approved the use of unmapped floating zones for planned-unit developments, planned industrial parks, and shopping centers. Allgood v. Town of Tarboro, 281 N.C. 430, 189 S.E.2d 255 (1972); Armstrong v. McInnis, 264 N.C. 616, 142 S.E.2d 670 (1965). They are now explicitly allowed by G.S. 160D-703.

31. While the statutes did not mandate concurrent hearings and decisions, that was the near-uniform practice of jurisdictions employing this tool. A few jurisdictions opted to consider the rezoning first and, if it was adopted, then proceeded to a second hearing on the special use permit. A major drawback to this approach was the uncertainty

The legal advantage of such a system was that the legislative rezoning decision was not technically based on a single project, as any number of special use permits could be considered within the district, and the problems raised in *Allred* and *Blades* were thereby avoided. The special use permit allowed specific, enforceable conditions to be imposed on the project that was approved.[32] But since the individual conditions were imposed on the permit, not the rezoning, the problems raised in *Decker* are avoided.

This technique of CUD zoning was pioneered by Greensboro in 1972,[33] explicitly authorized by local legislation for several local governments in 1973,[34] and incorporated into the general zoning-enabling act in 1985.[35] G.S. 153A-342 and 160A-382 specifically allowed use of conditional use districts but only upon the petition of the owners of all of the land to be included in the district. The rezoning and permit decisions were legally separate, but the governing board clearly had the opportunity to deny the initial rezoning request if it objected to the project presented in the special use permit application that was officially considered subsequently. Although this had the practical effect of allowing a rezoning to be based on a particular proposal, a practice ruled illegal in North Carolina in the *Allred* and *Blades* decisions, use of CUD zoning was upheld in *Chrismon*.[36]

The court in *Chrismon* concluded that CUD zoning was not illegal contract zoning per se because the promise was unilateral: the owner offered to develop the property according to a subsequently issued special use permit without receiving a reciprocal promise from the local government; at the same time, the governing board retained its independent judgment because it did not make such a promise.[37]

CUD zoning required two separate decisions,[38] with the rezoning decision meeting all of the statutory requirements for legislative decisions and the permit decision meeting all of the constitutional requirements for quasi-judicial decisions. The initial legislative decision about rezoning was based on a consideration of the policy question whether some limited alternative use was appropriate for the site. The subsequent quasi-judicial decision about a special use permit was based on whether the particular application met the standards set in the first decision.[39] If the petition for the rezoning was denied, the

---

that would result from adopting the rezoning and later denying the permit application, leaving the landowner with no permitted uses of the property. Thus, the usual practice was to consider them together, with either the rezoning and the permit approved at the same time or the rezoning denied (leaving no need to rule on the permit application).

32. For example, a condition could be placed on the permit that development of the site be initiated within a certain time or the permit expires and a new application must be submitted in order for the site to be developed. Such a condition may not generally be placed on the rezoning decision.

33. The technique and its use in Greensboro are described in DAVENPORT & GREEN, *supra* note 17. This tool was immediately popular with landowners and the city. From its inception in June 1972 through the calendar year 1978, 22 percent of all rezonings proposed in Greensboro were for CUDs. *Id.* at 17. In addition to Greensboro, other local governments making early use of the concept include Guilford County and Statesville. This technique is not available in all states. For example, the Wisconsin Supreme Court held that a zoning district with no permitted uses and only conditional uses was arbitrary and unreasonable. Town of Rhine v. Bizzell, 2008 WI 76, 311 Wis. 2d 1, 751 N.W.2d 780 (2008).

34. S.L. 1973-381 (Winston-Salem and Forsyth County); S.L. 1973-485 (Surry County and its municipalities); S.L. 1973-1283 (Charlotte–Mecklenburg County). The Greensboro ordinance was adopted under the city's general-zoning authority. Between 1973 and 1985, more than twenty local governments sought and received local legislation authorizing this practice. A number of other local governments adopted CUD zoning under the general zoning-enabling authorities.

35. S.L. 1985-607. In *Chrismon*, 322 N.C. 611, 370 S.E.2d 579 (1988), the court ruled that the zoning-enabling statutes provided adequate statutory authority for CUD zoning even before this specific authorization was adopted.

36. 322 N.C. 611, 370 S.E.2d 579. *See* Doherty, *supra* note 20.

37. Also, the decision does not bind future governing-board action, as the property can be subsequently rezoned to some other district. The owner is protected, if at all, through securing a vested right (see Chapter 19) or by the property having nonconforming status (see Chapter 20).

38. Vill. Creek Prop. Owners' Ass'n v. Town of Edenton, 135 N.C. App. 482, 520 S.E.2d 793 (1999).

39. Some ordinances more closely bound the two decisions by providing for an automatic repeal of the CUD if the authorized use itself ceased.

board did not decide the permit application, as the rezoning was necessary to create the eligibility for the special use permit.[40]

The difficulty confronting cities and counties was that this process required making two legally different decisions—the rezoning and the permit decision—at the same time and based on a single hearing, although the legal requirements and procedures for the two hearings vary significantly. A rezoning decision is entirely legislative in nature.[41] Elected officials can discuss the matter with interested citizens at any time. At the hearing anyone can speak, and the decision is left to the judgment and discretion of the elected officials, provided it is supported by a reasonable basis. The expansive range of discretion and judicial deference for the legislative aspect of the overall decision is one of the principal reasons the tool has been so popular with local elected boards. On the other hand, a special use permit decision is quasi-judicial. Board members are not to gather evidence or discuss the case outside of the hearing. The decision is to be made on the basis of evidence presented at the hearing, substantial evidence must be presented to establish that the application meets the standards in the ordinance, and written findings are required to support the decision. As a practical matter (and likely a legal mandate), since quasi-judicial standards are more rigorous, most boards followed the quasi-judicial process when making the concurrent legislative and quasi-judicial decisions in a CUD rezoning.[42]

The court in the *Chrismon* case explicitly noted that CUD rezoning was still subject to the limitations on small-scale rezonings:

> [I]n order to be legal and proper, conditional use zoning, like any type of zoning, must be reasonable, neither arbitrary nor unduly discriminatory, and in the public interest. It goes without saying that it also cannot constitute illegal spot zoning or illegal contract zoning. . . . The benefits of the flexibility of conditional use zoning can be fairly achieved only when these limiting standards are consistently and carefully applied.[43]

As the architects of the CUD system put it, this "system is not for amateurs."[44] Applying all of these rules simultaneously to a CUD rezoning petition and a special use permit application required considerable skill and diligence. Despite the complexity of the process, CUDs were widely used in North Carolina prior to the advent of purely legislative conditional zoning. Thirty-nine percent of the municipalities and 39 percent of the counties (and 77 percent of the cities with populations between 10,000 and 25,000) reported use of CUDs in a 2006 UNC School of Government survey.[45]

---

40. *See, e.g.*, Coucoulas/Knight Props. v. Town of Hillsborough, 199 N.C. App. 455, 683 S.E.2d 228 (2009), *aff'd per curiam*, 364 N.C. 127, 691 S.E.2d 411 (2010) (rezoning to conditional use district prerequisite to special use permit consideration).

41. In *Ashby v. Town of Cary*, 161 N.C. App. 499, 588 S.E.2d 572 (2003), the court affirmed that a CUD-rezoning decision is a purely legislative decision and is to be overturned only if the record before the town council at the time of decision demonstrates that the decision had no foundation in reason and bore no substantial relationship to the public health, safety, morals, or welfare. If the decision has any plausible basis in reason and relation to public safety, the decision must be affirmed.

42. *See* McMillan v. Town of Tryon, 200 N.C. App. 228, 234–38, 683 S.E.2d 747, 752–54 (2009). The ordinance involved required that a petition for a CUD rezoning be accompanied by a special use permit application and specified that the entire process be considered in a quasi-judicial manner. The court held that the town was therefore bound to that quasi-judicial process. Note that S.L. 1999-98 classified the hybrid special use permit and conditional use district rezoning as entirely legislative for Forsyth County and its municipalities. Somewhat similarly, S.L. 1973-400 authorized the City of Durham to include a development plan in legislative rezonings.

43. 322 N.C. 611, 622–23, 370 S.E.2d 579, 586 (1988) (citations omitted).

44. DAVENPORT & GREEN, *supra* note 17, at 10.

45. DAVID W. OWENS & ANDREW STEVENSON, AN OVERVIEW OF ZONING DISTRICTS, DESIGN STANDARDS, AND TRADITIONAL NEIGHBORHOOD DESIGN IN NORTH CAROLINA ZONING ORDINANCES 5 (UNC School of Government, Special Series No. 23, Oct. 2007).

G.S. 160D-703 simplifies matters and promotes greater uniformity by eliminating the authority for conditional use districts. A zoning ordinance may have legislative conditional zoning. It may also have quasi-judicial special use permits. But it may no longer combine the two into one process and decision.[46]

Conditional Zoning

Authority for Use

Many local governments struggled with the complexity of concurrently deciding a legislative rezoning and a quasi-judicial conditional use permit under the CUD zoning scheme.[47]

One alternative was to treat the entire CUD rezoning as a quasi-judicial decision, as is mandated for all small-scale rezonings in several states.[48] In *Gossett v. City of Wilmington*,[49] the court held that a provision in the city's charter providing that the entirety of a special use district rezoning and accompanying special use permit should be considered and reviewed as a quasi-judicial matter controlled. A second alternative was to consider CUD zoning as a single decision and treat it as legislative rather than quasi-judicial,[50] as is done in some other states.[51]

Several North Carolina jurisdictions adopted this later view in the 1990s, though most still used the CUD terminology. For example, the practice that evolved in Charlotte and Mecklenburg County was to treat the CZ process just as any other rezoning. No attempt was made to conduct a quasi-judicial hearing, make findings, or limit consideration to evidence presented at the hearing. Some 75 percent of the Charlotte rezonings in 1997–99 were made in this manner.

Judicial validation of the Charlotte approach in two court-of-appeals cases added the option of using true CZ, without a concomitant special use permit, for North Carolina local governments.

---

46. S.L. 2019-111 § 2.9(b) addresses the transition for CUDs created prior to the effective date of Chapter 160D. Any CUD or special use district becomes a conditional district. Any special or conditional use permit issued as part of those approvals remains valid and is deemed a special use permit after that date.

47. Courts in a number of other jurisdictions struggle with the same issues. *See, e.g.*, Giger v. City of Omaha, 232 Neb. 676, 442 N.W.2d 182 (1989); State *ex rel.* Myhre v. City of Spokane, 70 Wash. 2d 207, 422 P.2d 790 (1967) (addressing what the court termed "concomitant agreement zoning").

48. See the discussion of the characterization of decisions as legislative or quasi-judicial in Chapter 2.

49. 124 N.C. App. 777, 478 S.E.2d 648 (1996).

50. Linda A.T. Miles & Charles E. Melvin, Jr., *Law and Practice of Rezoning, in* Land Use Regulation and Planning (N.C. Bar Ass'n Found. ed., 1991). The authors conclude:

> Quasi-judicial hearings by Boards, Commissions or Governing Bodies accustomed to hearing rezonings in a legislative manner are a great potential source of confusion, unnecessary technicalities and protracted litigation over whether or not the technical requirements for a quasi-judicial hearing have been met. Typically, Boards, Commissions or Governing Bodies hearing these matters are composed of laymen who have neither the training nor the inclination for the quasi-judicial process and it is submitted that this requirement should be removed from all such proceedings except certain matters before Boards of Adjustment where custom, tradition and more detailed fact-finding and legal conclusions are more appropriately required.

Id. at I-8.

51. *See, e.g.*, Va. Code Ann. §§ 15.2-2296 to 15.2-2303.4. Proffers of conditions to be attached to the rezoning must be voluntarily made by the rezoning applicant. Bd. of Supervisors of Powhatan Cnty. v. Reed's Landing Corp., 463 S.E.2d 668 (Va. 1995). *See also* Remmel v. City of Portland, 102 A.3d 1168 (Me. 2014) (upholding conditional zoning); Old Canton Hills Homeowners Ass'n v. Mayor of Jackson, 749 So. 2d 54 (Miss. 1999) (upholding imposition of detailed conditions on a rezoning).

The first case, *Massey v. City of Charlotte*,[52] involved the rezoning of a forty-two-acre parcel from R-3 to commercial-center district to allow construction of two "big box" retailers along with five outparcels. The trial court held that while the city could undertake the two-step CUD zoning described above, the city had no authority to undertake "conditional zoning" without using a conditional use permit (and following the requisite procedure for those permits).

In response to this ruling, while the case was on appeal, Charlotte, Mecklenburg County, and the other cities within the county obtained local legislation authorizing CZ without having a quasi-judicial conditional use permit as part of the process.[53] These bills allowed creation of "conditional zoning districts" with individualized development standards adopted as part of the ordinance. Property could only be rezoned to these districts "in response to and consistent with" a petition filed by the property's owner. The petition was required to include a site plan, a specification of the actual use planned, and any rules, regulations, or conditions that would govern development of the site. The petitioner was required to conduct at least one community meeting on the proposal prior to the official hearing on the rezoning. The rezoning decision would be made "in consideration of" relevant land use plans for the area, including the comprehensive plan, strategic plans, district plans, area plans, neighborhood plans, corridor plans, and other land use–policy documents. These rezonings would not be made between the date of election of a new governing board and the time that the new board took office.

When the *Massey* case reached the court of appeals, the court held that the zoning-enabling statutes authorized use of CUDs but did not mandate their use or by implication limit the use of other types of zoning decisions (such as the purely legislative CZ used here), especially when these statutes were read with the mandate for broad construction in mind.[54] The court noted that *Chrismon* did not explicitly require an accompanying quasi-judicial decision.[55] The court also held that the petitioner's submission of detailed plans for site development did not constitute illegal contract zoning because this was a unilateral promise from the petitioner, not a bilateral agreement with obligations being made by the city. The court held that the appropriate standard of judicial review for CZ was that applicable to legislative decisions.[56]

The second case addressed the constitutional dimensions of CZ. In *Summers v. City of Charlotte*,[57] the court again held that CZ decisions are legislative rather than quasi-judicial and are within the

---

52. 145 N.C. App. 345, 550 S.E.2d 838, *review denied*, 354 N.C. 219, 554 S.E.2d 342 (2001).

53. S.L. 2000-84 did so for Charlotte, Cornelius, Davidson, Huntersville, Matthews, Mint Hill, and Pineville. S.L. 2000-77 did so for Mecklenburg County.

54. *Massey*, 145 N.C. App. at 353–55, 550 S.E.2d at 844–46. Although *Massey* held CZ to be permissible under the general zoning-enabling act, Charlotte sought and obtained local legislation to make permanent its explicit authorization to use CZ. S.L. 2001-276 did this for the seven municipalities in Mecklenburg County, and S.L. 2001-275 did this for Mecklenburg County.

55. On the contrary, the *Massey* court noted,

> [n]othing in *Chrismon* suggests that the Board [of County Commissioners] engaged in a two-step, part legislative, part quasi-judicial process which would warrant the "competent and material evidence" standard of review. Rather, the re-zoning decision and the decision regarding the conditional uses that would be allowed on the land were determined in a single proceeding.

145 N.C. App. at 351, 550 S.E.2d at 843.

56. The court cited the *Chrismon* standard that the rezoning be upheld if it is "reasonable, neither arbitrary nor unduly discriminatory, and in the public interest." *Id.* at 349, 550 S.E.2d at 842. *See also* Ashby v. Town of Cary, 161 N.C. App. 499, 588 S.E.2d 572 (2003) (CUD rezoning is to be overturned only if it has no foundation in reason and bears no substantial relationship to the public health, safety, morals, or welfare).

57. 149 N.C. App. 509, 562 S.E.2d 18, *review denied*, 355 N.C. 758, 566 S.E.2d 482 (2002). This case involved neighbors' challenges to two Charlotte rezonings. The first rezoned 11.6 acres from an office district to a mixed-use-development district allowing offices, retail establishments, multifamily residences, and a hotel. The second rezoned the 95.6-acre site of SouthPark Mall from shopping-center and office districts to a commercial-center district. Both rezoning petitions included site plans, specifications of proposed uses, and proposed site-specific

statutory authority delegated to the city. The court also found that the mandatory community meetings and formal legislative hearing provided in the course of the rezoning process afford neighbors adequate procedural due process.[58] The court held that the rezonings were not arbitrary and capricious, as they were based on fair and careful consideration of the planning board's review, technical staff reports, and public comments. The court noted that the rezonings were consistent with adopted small-area plans for the affected area and that there was no showing of bad faith or undue discrimination.

In 2005, the General Assembly amended the zoning statutes to explicitly authorize city and county use of CZ.[59] G.S. 160D-703 provides that zoning ordinances may include "conditional districts, in which site plans and individualized development conditions are imposed." Land may be placed in a conditional district only upon petition of all of the owners of the land to be included.

The use of CZ rapidly became commonplace in North Carolina following the *Massey* decision, particularly for municipalities. A 2006 School of Government survey of North Carolina cities and counties indicated that a third of the responding cities and a quarter of the responding counties used CZ.[60] In a 2018 survey, well over half the responding jurisdictions reported using conditional zoning. The responding jurisdictions reported that 57 percent of all rezonings considered in the past year were CZs.[61] Given the use of this type of district by the state's more populous jurisdictions, over a third of all rezonings considered in the previous year included site-specific conditions.[62]

The standard practice in North Carolina cities and counties using CZ is to amend the ordinance text to create a set of CZ districts to correspond with each conventional zoning district. However, rather than requiring that all uses secure a special use permit, as was done with CUD zoning, individualized conditions and site plan provisions are incorporated (usually by reference) into the zoning-district requirements for any property rezoned to a conditional district. In most instances, the provisions in the conditional district are more stringent than those in the corresponding conventional districts. The

---

development guidelines. After a series of public meetings and a legislative hearing, the city adopted both rezonings. In each rezoning the council specified that the general zoning-ordinance provisions for the respective districts, the site plans, and the additional individualized proposed regulations and conditions all constituted the binding zoning regulations for each property. As a spot-zoning allegation was not argued on appeal, the court deemed that issue abandoned by the plaintiffs.

58. In most situations procedural due process is not an issue in legislative rezoning decisions, as neither the owner nor the neighbors have a property right in the existing zoning. Here, the court noted that procedural due process only applied if a party's vested property rights were affected, and "even assuming Plaintiffs have a vested right," the notice and hearing procedures used for legislative zoning decisions were adequate. *Summers*, 149 N.C. App. at 518, 562 S.E.2d at 25.

59. S.L. 2005-426, §§ 6(a), (b).

60. OWENS & STEVENSON, *supra* note 45, at 5. Interestingly, a number of jurisdictions reported having both CZ and CUDs in their ordinances (17 percent of the cities and 8 percent of the counties).

61. The use of CZ is even more pronounced in municipalities with larger populations. Cities with populations over 25,000 reported that 79 percent of their rezonings were to conditional districts. David W. Owens, *2018 Survey Report: Adoption and Administration of Local Development Regulations, Conditional Zoning, and Subdivision Administration*, PLAN. AND ZONING L. BULL. No. 30 (UNC School of Government, Dec. 2020), at 17.

62. DAVID W. OWENS, ZONING AMENDMENTS IN NORTH CAROLINA 5 (UNC School of Government, Special Series No. 24, Feb. 2008). The responding cities and counties reported consideration of 3029 rezoning petitions. Fifty-seven percent were for rezonings to conventional districts, 21 percent to CUDs, and 15 percent to conditional districts. There was a significant difference between municipal and county experience on this point. Counties were far more likely to have petitions for conventional rezonings. Seventy percent of all rezoning petitions in counties were for conventional rezoning, compared to 52 percent for municipalities. By contrast, cities much more frequently consider CZ. Nineteen percent of all municipal rezoning petitions were for conditional rezoning, compared to only 6 percent for counties. The trend toward use of legislative CZ was even more pronounced for cities with larger populations. Cities with populations over 25,000 reported over half of their rezoning petitions were for conditional or CUD rezonings. For these cities, 32 percent of their rezoning petitions were for conditional rezoning and 22 percent were for CUD rezoning. *Id.* at 6.

conditional district may, for example, have a much narrower list of permitted uses and may increase the buffering requirements to provide additional protection to neighboring uses. In the absence of a local ordinance provision to the contrary, it is, however, legally permissible to tailor standards that are less restrictive than those in the corresponding conventional district.[63]

While the North Carolina courts have consistently held site-specific CZ cases to be legislative, it is important to note that many of these rezonings constitute spot zoning.[64] As such, the presumption of validity usually accorded legislative zoning decisions is removed, and the burden is on the local government to establish a reasonable basis for the rezoning.

Permissible Conditions

G.S. 160D-703(b) addresses the origin and nature of conditions that may be imposed.

This statute provides that specific conditions may be suggested by the owner or the government, but only those conditions mutually acceptable to both the owner and the government may be incorporated into the ordinance.[65] The owner's consent must be in writing.[66] If an owner objects to being in a conditional district, the local government cannot put the property in one. If an owner objects to a proposed condition, it cannot be included. If the owner objects to a particular condition, the local government has the choice of approving the conditional zoning without the objectionable condition or denying the conditional rezoning if the governing board concludes that rezoning without that condition would be inappropriate.

The statute also provides that any conditions or site-specific standards imposed are limited to those that address the conformance of the development and use of the site to city or county ordinances and officially adopted plans and those that address the impacts reasonably expected to be generated from the development or use of the site. In addition, the general statutory and constitutional limits on factors that can legitimately be considered in any rezoning also apply to the conditional rezonings. So, for example, a condition could not be imposed that discriminates on the basis of race, ethnicity, or religion.

---

63. Rakestraw v. Town of Knightdale, 188 N.C. App. 129, 136, 654 S.E.2d 825, 830, *review denied*, 362 N.C. 237, 659 S.E.2d 739 (2008). In *Rakestraw*, the rezoning to a highway commercial conditional district relaxed or decreased some twenty standards relative to the corresponding conventional-highway commercial district. The court noted that the town's development ordinance specifically provided that standards could be decreased relative to the corresponding conventional district and that there is no requirement in the state statutes for more rather than less restrictive standards. *See also* Sapp v. Yadkin Cnty., 209 N.C. App. 430, 704 S.E.2d 909 (2011). The county rezoned a parcel to a manufacturing-industrial CZ district and applied specific standards relative to a jail. The parallel manufacturing-industrial conventional district allowed jails as a conditional use permit with more-restrictive standards, including a prohibition against siting jails within one mile of residential property. The court held that there was no requirement that the CZ-district standards incorporated the conditional use permit standards from a parallel CZ district.

64. See Chapter 12 for a full discussion of spot zoning. While nationally there is increasing judicial acceptance of negotiated zoning decisions, many land use–law professionals remain wary. *See, e.g.,* DANIEL R. MANDELKER, LAND USE LAW § 6.59 (6th ed. 2018) (noting that despite growing judicial approval, contract and CZ is "often unwise" due to undercutting uniformity and increasing complexity of enforcement).

65. Of course, if a proposed condition is unacceptable to the owner, the petition can be withdrawn and the proposed rezoning cannot go forward. Likewise, if a condition is unacceptable to the governing board (or the owner refuses to agree to a desired condition), the petition can be denied and there is no rezoning.

66. S.L. 2019-111, §§ 1.14 and 1.15 amended this statute to specify that the landowner's consent must be in writing. If written consent is not provided to the local government at the time of adoption of the conditional zoning, a common practice is to add a provision that the zoning is not effective until written consent from the owner is delivered to the local government (which often must be done within a specified time, such as within ten days of adoption). Several local governments require an affidavit from the owner; many allow a signed letter of acceptance of the conditions.

G.S. 160D-703(b) further provides that no condition may be imposed that is not otherwise authorized by law, including taxes, impact fees, building-design standards for one- and two-family residences, and driveway-related improvements not authorized by law *unless* consented to in writing by the owner.[67]

Another means of securing and documenting written landowner consent is the use of a concurrent development agreement with the CZ. Where there is substantial cost-sharing on infrastructure to support the proposed development or there is a voluntary provision of extra public benefits, many local governments and landowners use a development agreement in conjunction with CZ. A condition included in a CZ can require compliance with all the terms and conditions of an accompanying development agreement. G.S. 160D-1003(b) allows a development agreement to be incorporated into a zoning regulation and for the development agreement and a rezoning to be considered concurrently. G.S. 160D-1006(d) allows a development agreement to include mutually acceptable provisions for financing public facilities, provided that any measures offered by the developer beyond those that could be required by the local government are expressly set out in the agreement. While these additional measures in a development agreement cannot include a tax or impact fee not otherwise authorized, they can include a wide range of possible conditions, including donations of land and construction of public and community facilities. These items cannot be mandated unilaterally by the local government but can be included with the voluntary written consent of the landowner.

The limit of G.S. 160D-703(b1) may also be applicable to CZ. This statute provides that where multi-family structures are an allowable use, a harmony requirement may not be imposed if the development includes affordable housing.[68] On its face, this limitation only applies to a harmony requirement for "permit approval." A rezoning to a conditional district is a legislative decision, not a permit approval. However, the placement of this limit in G.S. 160D-703, which is the section of the statutes on zoning districts, implies that it may be applicable to conditional-zoning decisions as well as to special use permits.

Conditions Typically Imposed

Not surprisingly, the two most used conditions are ones that limit the range of permitted uses and that require a detailed plan for future development of the site. Both types of conditions are permissible in North Carolina. Over 70 percent of the jurisdictions responding to the School of Government's 2018 survey reported that their conditional zoning either always or frequently included these two conditions.[69]

Use Restrictions. A conventional zoning district typically allows dozens of different land uses. Some of those uses may have modest land use impacts for the neighbors, while others might be problematic in a particular setting. A condition imposed on a conditional zoning can allow a specific use on a specific parcel that the owner desires while ruling out other uses that are objectionable to the neighbors or local government if placed on that property. A condition can expand the range of permitted uses, such as allowing a range of mixed uses within a building or allowing a wider range of uses within a larger site, but it more often restricts the uses that would have been allowed in a comparable conventional zoning district. Some zoning regulations allow only conditions that are more stringent than those in the corresponding conventional zoning district while others allow any modifications deemed appropriate. State law allows either approach.

---

67. The regulation also should be clear that the owner has the option to reject the conditions, as consent must be voluntary. Similarly, the regulation should be clear about the implications of rejection of the conditions, for example, noting that, if rejected, the conditional rezoning is not effective and the prior zoning remains in place.

68. This provision was added to the statute by S.L. 2021-180, § 5.16(a). It is more commonly applicable to special use permit approval standards. See Chapter 16 for a discussion of it in that context.

69. Owens, *supra* note 61, at 19.

Site plans. A site plan incorporated into a conditional rezoning can identify where roads, buildings, parking, particular uses, and buffers will be located. It can provide information on landscaping or stormwater management, although details on these aspects of the development may be addressed later in the permitting process. Securing agreement on the site plan for the forthcoming development at the rezoning stage provides clarity for the owner, developer, and neighbors as to how the development will proceed. It shows how potential adverse impacts will be addressed and minimized.

Site development details. A related set of permissible conditions are often used to address more specific aspects of the potential development. While not quite as frequently employed as the two conditions noted above, over 50 percent of jurisdictions responding to the School of Government's 2018 survey reported frequently using these types of conditions.[70]

While a commercial district might require that buildings have a twenty-five-foot setback from the rear property line, a conditional district could increase that to a fifty-foot rear-yard setback to address potential negative impacts on neighboring residential properties. Alternatively, the setback could be reduced to ten feet if that was an adequate distance for the particular development and setting. It could require a solid fence, specified landscaping, or restrictions on exterior lighting to buffer the back of the commercial development from its neighbors. How streets within the development connect to neighboring streets can be specified. A condition could set a maximum density of future residential development to assure that there are adequate streets, utilities, schools, and recreational facilities. The design of buildings can be specified to assure harmony with their surroundings, as can the precise location of the buildings, parking, and support facilities. G.S. 160D-702(b) allows the imposition of building-design standards even on single-family homes if that is voluntarily consented to by all the owners during the process of seeking rezoning approval.

Infrastructure. For some developments, particularly those that are very large, securing adequate supporting infrastructure is a key consideration in development approval. The location, construction standards, and financing of roads, utilities, schools, parks, and greenways are important for both the developer and the local government. Details on how this is to be accomplished can be incorporated into the conditions included in a conditional rezoning. These types of conditions are permissible but are less commonly imposed.

Social equity. A final set of conditions that are sometimes considered are those that address social equity concerns. While common in some states, this type of condition has to date not been frequently applied in North Carolina. However, they may be proposed to secure plan compliance or to address impacts of the development. For example, some North Carolina comprehensive plans call for a full range of housing affordability in new developments. Other plans may address the need for more affordable and work-force housing. In response, some conditional zonings and development agreements have included provisions for a specified amount of affordable housing or a commitment to make payments to a local affordable-housing trust fund.[71]

Amendment of Conditions

An amendment to the conditions included within a CZ is a text amendment to the ordinance that generally must go through the entire ordinance-amendment process. For example, in *McDowell v. Randolph County*,[72] the landowner proposed to relocate chemical vats in a lumberyard that was in a CZ district. The site plan for the lumberyard had been incorporated as a condition in the CZ. So the site-plan amend-

---

70. *Id.* at 19–20.
71. See Chapter 9 for a discussion of affordable-housing initiatives in land use regulations.
72. 256 N.C. App. 708, 808 S.E.2d 513 (2017).

ment was considered a zoning-text amendment subject to the public-hearing, planning-board-review, and plan-consistency-statement requirements applicable to any zoning amendment.

The statutes provide an exception to this rule. G.S. 160D-703(b) gives local governments the option of processing minor amendments administratively. To use this option, the ordinance itself must define what constitutes a "minor modification." A minor modification cannot include a change in permitted uses or in the density of the overall development. Once defined, staff can be authorized to approve minor modifications administratively. Any other modification must follow the same process for approval as is required for a zoning-map amendment. If the CZ district applies to multiple parcels of property, the conditions may be modified for individual parcels without the necessity of obtaining the consent of all property owners within the CZ district, but in those instances the modification only applies to the parcels whose owners consent.

Quasi-Judicial Decisions

CHAPTER 14

Quasi-Judicial Land Use Regulatory Decisions

Applicability

While there is some law on how all land use regulatory decisions are made, the legal issues are particularly rich when boards make adjudications. To what extent can a nonjudicial branch of government make a judicial type of decision? Which adjudicatory decisions require court-like proceedings? How precise must the standards be to guide these decisions? Just how judicial must the decision-making process be? What is the role of the courts in reviewing these decisions?

Land use regulatory adjudications are classified as quasi-judicial[1] when they involve the application of legislatively determined policies to individual situations. There are two key factors that trigger the quasi-judicial classification: the finding of facts regarding the specific proposal and the exercise of discretion in applying predetermined policies to the situation.[2]

In the zoning context, quasi-judicial decisions include variances, special use permits, appeals of administrative determinations, and certificates of appropriateness under historic-district regulations. Other decisions involving land use–related decisions have also been characterized as quasi-judicial when

---

1. Literally, "as if" they were judicial determinations. These are administrative decisions that are similar to but not the same as judicial decisions. "A term applied to the action, discretion, etc., of public administrative officers or bodies, who are required to investigate facts, or ascertain the existence of facts, hold hearings, and draw conclusions from them, as a basis for their official action, and to exercise discretion of a judicial nature." *Quasi-Judicial*, BLACK'S LAW DICTIONARY (5th ed. 1979). See Chapter 2 for further discussion of the categorization of land use regulatory decisions as legislative, quasi-judicial, advisory, or administrative/ministerial.

2. Chapter 160D, Section 102(28) of the North Carolina General Statutes (hereinafter G.S.); Cnty. of Lancaster v. Mecklenburg Cnty., 334 N.C. 496, 502, 434 S.E.2d 604, 612 (1993). In one of the state's first zoning cases, the court noted:

> It is evident, we think, that the board of adjustment is clothed, if not with judicial, at least with quasi-judicial power—it being its duty to investigate facts and from its investigation to draw conclusions as a basis of official action and to exercise discretion of a judicial nature. These are not mere ministerial duties. . . . [T]he exercise of judgment or discretion may be regarded as the usual test by which to determine whether an act is ministerial or judicial.

Harden v. City of Raleigh, 192 N.C. 395, 397, 135 S.E. 151, 152 (1926). *See also* Stephenson v. Town of Garner, 136 N.C. App. 444, 524 S.E.2d 608, *review denied*, 352 N.C. 156 (2000) (decisions on conditional use permits are not ministerial as they involve substantial discretion, so the board making the decision has legislative immunity).

The finding of facts and the application of general rules to specific individuals are typical considerations in classification of a decision as quasi-judicial. Justice Holmes noted, "A judicial inquiry investigates, declares, and enforces liabilities as they stand on present or past facts and under laws supposed already to exist. That is its purpose and end. Legislation, on the other hand, looks to the future and changes existing conditions by making a new rule, to be applied thereafter to all or some part of those subject to its power." Prentis v. Atl. Coast Line Co., 211 U.S. 210, 226 (1908). Most states apply similar principles in making legislative/quasi-judicial distinctions. *See, e.g.*, Idaho Historic Pres. Council, Inc. v. City Council, 134 Idaho 651, 654, 8 P.3d 646, 649 (2000) (certificate of appropriateness under historic-preservation ordinance is quasi-judicial); Thompson v. Amis, 208 Kan. 658, 662–63, 493 P.2d 1259, 1262–63 (1972) (appeal of suspended employee with civil-service protection is quasi-judicial).

the standards for decision are discretionary. These include site-plan approval,[3] an order to demolish a dilapidated structure,[4] and plat approvals.[5]

The General Assembly codified these rules in 2009.[6] Chapter 160D, Section 1402 of the North Carolina General Statutes (hereinafter G.S.) was added to the statutes to provide detailed procedures for judicial review of quasi-judicial zoning decisions. G.S. 160D-102(28) defines quasi-judicial decisions as those "involving the finding of facts regarding a specific application of an ordinance and the exercise of discretion when applying the standards of the ordinance." This provision notes that variances, special use permits, certificates of appropriateness, and appeals of administrative determinations fall into this category. It also notes that decisions that are usually administrative or ministerial (site plans and subdivision plats, specifically) become quasi-judicial if the standards for decision require a discretionary decision. G.S. 160D-808 applies the same rule to subdivision-plat reviews.

The categorization of a decision as quasi-judicial is a question of law, ultimately determined by the courts. Thus, the way a decision is labeled in an ordinance is not necessarily dispositive of the question of which legal category a decision falls into. For example, the city of Burlington labeled a decision on permission for siting manufactured-home parks as an overlay zoning district, the application of which is normally a legislative rezoning decision. However, the ordinance provided that the overlay district was permitted by right in certain zoning districts provided specified standards were met. The court determined this was more the application of policy applying predetermined standards than the creation of new policy; so even though a rezoning is generally a legislative decision, the court determined in this situation that it was really a quasi-judicial determination.[7] Similarly, Asheville included a provision in

---

3. The Town of Wake Forest development regulations used standards involving judgment and discretion for major site-plan and major subdivision approvals—that there be "adequate infrastructure" to support the development and that it "not be detrimental to the use or development of adjacent properties." The use of these standards made the decision on approval quasi-judicial. Schooldev East, LLC v. Town of Wake Forest, 284 N.C. App. 434, 876 S.E.2d 607 (2022). *See also* Knight v. Town of Knightdale, 164 N.C. App. 766, 596 S.E.2d 881 (2004) (standards for approval included consideration of adverse effects expected from the development).

4. Hillsboro Partners, LLC v. City of Fayetteville, 226 N.C. App. 30, 738 S.E.2d 819, *review denied*, 367 N.C. 236, 748 S.E.2d 544 (2013) (decision to condemn building as unsafe is quasi-judicial); Coffey v. Town of Waynesville, 143 N.C. App. 624, 547 S.E.2d 132 (2001) (city council is acting in quasi-judicial capacity when hearing appeal of a demolition order for a dilapidated structure). *See also* Carolina Holdings, Inc. v. Hous. Appeals Bd., 149 N.C. App. 579, 561 S.E.2d 541, *review denied*, 356 N.C. 298, 570 S.E.2d 499 (2002).

5. William Brewster Co. v. Town of Huntersville, 161 N.C. App. 132, 588 S.E.2d 16 (2003). The subdivision ordinance required proposed subdivisions to be consistent with the most recently adopted public plans and policies for the area and to "protect and enhance the stability, environment, health and character of neighboring areas." *Id.* at 136, 588 S.E.2d at 20. The court invalidated denial because there was no competent, substantial, material evidence in the record to support a finding that either standard was not met. *See also* Blue Ridge Co. v. Town of Pineville, 188 N.C. App. 466, 655 S.E.2d 843, *review denied*, 362 N.C. 679, 669 S.E.2d 742 (2008); Guilford Fin. Servs., LLC v. City of Brevard, 356 N.C. 655, 576 S.E.2d 325 (2003), *per curiam, adopting dissent in* 150 N.C. App. 1, 563 S.E.2d 27 (2002) (decision on a subdivision-plat approval is quasi-judicial if the ordinance includes discretionary standards for the decision).

6. S.L. 2009-421. G.S. 160D-1402(a) states that the law is applicable to appeals of quasi-judicial decisions when the appeal is in "the nature of certiorari as required by this Chapter."

The General Assembly has on occasion adopted local acts that purport to move decisions from one category to another in particular jurisdictions. *See* S.L. 1999-98 (classifying special use permit and special use district rezoning as entirely legislative for Forsyth County and its municipalities); S.L. 1973-400 (City of Durham may require development plan in legislative rezonings).

7. Northfield Dev. Co. v. City of Burlington, 136 N.C. App. 272, 282, 523 S.E.2d 743, 749, *aff'd per curiam*, 352 N.C. 671, 535 S.E.2d 32 (2000). The ordinance provided that the manufactured-housing overlay district (MHOD) must have either (1) a minimum of eight existing contiguous lots with a minimum of 65,000 square feet or (2) a single contiguous area of 95,000 square feet. The MHOD could be applied in three of the city's eight residential districts. Manufactured, modular, and site-built houses were permitted uses once the overlay designation was made.

its subdivision regulations that allowed a modification of street standards to allow narrower streets if the applicant could show an "unusual and unnecessary" physical hardship. The provision also allowed imposition of conditions on the modification to "ensure the purposes" of the standards waived. The regulation characterized the decision as ministerial, but the court held that it required judgment and discretion and was thus quasi-judicial.[8] On borderline calls, however, the court gives some deference to the ordinance's categorization of the decision.[9]

Constitutional Requirements

Quasi-judicial decision-making by local governments and administrative agencies raises three constitutional questions. First, how does this practice comport with the notion that adjudications are a function of the judicial branch of government? Second, does the lack of a jury raise a problem in determining critical contested facts? Third, and most important, does due process demand certain minimal procedures in quasi-judicial procedures and, if so, what are those procedures and when are they triggered?

Separation of Powers

The constitutions of the United States and North Carolina each establish a tripartite governmental structure with a separation of legislative, executive, and judicial powers. This raises the question of the extent to which adjudicatory functions, such as quasi-judicial decisions, can be delegated to nonjudicial agencies.

At the federal level, Article III of the Constitution provides, "The judicial Power of the United States, shall be vested in one supreme Court, and in such inferior Courts as the Congress may from time to time ordain and establish."[10] In an early New Deal case, the U.S. Supreme Court held that this did not prevent Congress from assigning quasi-judicial authority to administrative agencies. In upholding a

---

The ordinance further provided that the district was to be designated by the city council and was "permitted by right" in the three specified districts (the list of permitted uses for each of these zoning districts listed MHODs among permitted uses). Further, the ordinance had a separate basic mobile-home district.

This ordinance provision was before the court of appeals three times. In *Northfield*, the court of appeals held that while amendment of the text of the ordinance to create the overlay district was a legislative zoning decision, any subsequent decision on whether to apply the district to a particular area was "a quasi-judicial decision because it required application of the MHOD standards set out in City's zoning ordinance to individual situations. The decision to approve or reject MHOD petitions is most analogous to the decision to grant or deny variances or special use permits . . . ." *Id.* at 282, 523 S.E.2d at 750. While affirming the decision, the supreme court did not address this aspect of the court of appeals decision. When this same ordinance provision was before the court of appeals a second time, the court noted that while the council retained some discretion in making the overlay designation, bounded discretion is a part of quasi-judicial decision-making and does not convert the decision to a legislative characterization. Devaney v. City of Burlington, 143 N.C. App. 334, 338, 545 S.E.2d 763, 766, *review denied*, 353 N.C. 724, 550 S.E.2d 772 (2001). The city continued to argue that a legislative rather than quasi-judicial procedure was appropriate for MHOD decisions, a position the court rejected a third time when the *Northfield* matter returned to the court. Northfield Dev. Co. v. City of Burlington, No. COA01-1043, 2002 WL 1419623 (N.C. Ct. App. July 2, 2002, unpublished).

8. Butterworth v. City of Asheville, 247 N.C. App. 508, 786 S.E.2d 101 (2016). The modification challenged by neighbors reduced a forty-five-foot required right-of-way to twenty-five feet. The court held that if the modifications could be approved following objective standards, the decision was administrative, but if the standards required the exercise of judgment and discretion, the decision was quasi-judicial. While this ordinance required a public hearing and written reasons to be provided if the request was denied, that was short of the fair-trial standards required for quasi-judicial land use decisions by *Humble Oil & Refining Co. v. Board of Aldermen*, 284 N.C. 458, 202 S.E.2d 129 (1974). *See also* Sanco of Wilmington Serv. Corp. v. New Hanover Cnty, 166 N.C. App. 471, 475, 601 S.E.2d 889, 892–93 (2004) (comparing administrative and quasi-judicial decisions).

9. Cnty. of Lancaster v. Mecklenburg Cnty., 334 N.C. 496, 510, 434 S.E.2d 604, 614 (1993).

10. U.S. Const. art. III, § 1.

statute assigning a commission authority to adjudicate maritime workers' claims under a workers'-compensation insurance program, the Court did impose two important limitations on these delegations: (1) courts must retain authority to undertake de novo review on questions of law and (2) fact-finding by the agency must be reasonable.[11] Subsequent cases have emphasized that while Congress can take advantage of agency expertise and streamlined administrative adjudication, fair, independent, and impartial procedures are required at all stages of adjudication.[12]

The North Carolina Constitution also establishes a three-branch system of (state) government. Article I includes a basic policy on separation of powers, with its section 6 expressly stating that "[t]he legislative, executive, and supreme judicial powers of the State government shall be forever separate and distinct from each other." North Carolina's highest court has held that this provision prohibits undue comingling of the respective branches of government.[13]

The state constitution, however, provides explicit flexibility for quasi-judicial decisions. While article IV, section 1 has a provision assigning judicial powers to the courts that is comparable to the federal provision noted above, the state constitution adds an exception: "The General Assembly may vest in administrative agencies established pursuant to law such judicial powers as may be reasonably necessary as an incident to the accomplishment of the purposes for which the agencies were created. Appeals from administrative agencies shall be to the General Court of Justice."[14]

The courts have long recognized the legitimacy of assigning quasi-judicial functions to state and local agencies.[15] The state supreme court has recognized the importance and legitimacy of administrative determination of such matters:

> Legislation of this type has become necessary in many fields, and so a system of administrative procedure has been instituted in which matters of regulation and control may, and must be, tried by properly established commissions and agencies that are peculiarly qualified for the purpose. . . . This procedure is particularly efficient when the subject of inquiry is of a very technical nature, or involves the analysis of many records. After the hearings before the agencies have been conducted, the statute gives any aggrieved party his "day in court" by appeal or other recognized procedure.
>
> To permit the interruption and cessation of proceedings before a commission by untimely and premature intervention by the courts would completely destroy the efficiency, effectiveness, and purpose of the administrative agencies.[16]

11. Crowell v. Benson, 285 U.S. 22 (1932).

12. Commodities Futures Trading Comm'n v. Schor, 478 U.S. 833 (1986); N. Pipeline Constr. Co. v. Marathon Pipe Line Co., 458 U.S. 50 (1982).

13. Advisory Op. *in re* Separation of Powers, 305 N.C. 767, 295 S.E.2d 589 (1982) (statute providing legislative-committee control over governor's line-item budget transfers unduly encroaches on executive authority); State *ex rel.* Wallace v. Bone, 304 N.C. 591, 286 S.E.2d 79 (1982) (invalidating statute providing for appointment of legislators to the Environmental Management Commission as improper legislative interference with executive branch).

14. N.C. CONST. art. IV, § 3.

15. "The Legislature has always, without serious question, given quasi-judicial powers to administrative bodies in aid of the duties assigned to them, without necessarily making them courts. . . . Certainly the limited discretion given to these bodies is no part of the 'supreme judicial power' of the State." Cox v. City of Kinston, 217 N.C. 391, 394–95, 8 S.E.2d 252, 256 (1940) (upholding assignment of fact-finding and application of discretionary standards to a municipal housing authority).

16. Elmore v. Lanier, 270 N.C. 674, 677–78, 155 S.E.2d 114, 116 (1967).

More recently, the court held that the assessment of civil penalties and the exercise of discretion in setting the amount of penalties were "reasonably necessary" to the implementation of a sedimentation-control program and could be assigned to a nonjudicial body.[17]

Jury Trial

Some quasi-judicial decisions result in a monetary assessment against a person, the most common of these being a contested-civil-penalty assessment. The Seventh Amendment to the U.S. Constitution provides for preservation of the right to trial by jury in money actions.[18] However, the U.S. Supreme Court has held that the Seventh Amendment is simply inapplicable to administrative proceedings.[19]

The comparable provision in the state constitution (article I, section 25) provides for jury trials in controversies at law respecting property. The courts have held that this, however, only guarantees the right to a jury trial where this prerogative existed at common law or by statute at the time of adoption of the 1868 constitution. This precludes a demand for jury trials in the vast majority of quasi-judicial matters decided by administrative agencies.[20]

Due Process

The most important constitutional limitation on quasi-judicial decision-making is the requirement that the procedures employed provide adequate due process.[21]

By its nature, a quasi-judicial decision involves an adjudication. The two elements that constitute the definition of a quasi-judicial decision are the same two elements necessary to trigger potential due-process applicability. First, there must be some determination of contested facts.[22] Second, there must be some individualized application of the governmental policies or standards involved.[23]

Due-process protections, however, only extend to a deprivation of life, liberty, or property.[24] The courts have held that if a person is *entitled* to certain benefits upon establishing specified facts, this is "property" that must receive some degree of procedural-due-process protection.[25]

---

17. *In re* Appeal from Civil Penalty Assessed for Violations of Sedimentation Pollution Control Act, 324 N.C. 373, 379 S.E.2d 30 (1989).

18. U.S. CONST. amend. VII.

19. Atlas Roofing Co. v. Occupational Safety & Health Review Comm'n, 430 U.S. 442, 455 (1977); Curtis v. Loether, 415 U.S. 189, 194 (1974).

20. State *ex rel.* Rhodes v. Simpson, 325 N.C. 514, 385 S.E.2d 329 (1989) (no jury trial in enforcement actions under the Coastal Area Management Act and Dredge and Fill Act); Belk's Dep't Store, Inc. v. Guilford Cnty., 222 N.C. 441, 23 S.E.2d 897 (1943) (no jury trial in appeal of property-tax valuation).

21. U.S. CONST. amends. V, XIV; N.C. CONST. art. I, § 19.

22. New Motor Vehicle Bd. v. Orrin W. Fox Co., 439 U.S. 96 (1978) (due process not implicated where there are no adjudicative facts); Weinberger v. Hynson, Westcott & Dunning, Inc., 412 U.S. 609 (1973) (genuine and substantial issue of fact necessary to trigger due-process requirements).

23. Londoner v. Denver, 210 U.S. 373 (1908) (assessments for street improvements, with individual amounts assessed to be proportionate to benefits, triggers due-process requirements).

24. Henry v. Edmisten, 315 N.C. 474, 480, 340 S.E.2d 720, 725 (1986).

25. Bd. of Regents v. Roth, 408 U.S. 564 (1972) (continued employment subject to a series of one-year contracts is not protected property where no statute provided for reemployment); Perry v. Sindermann, 408 U.S. 593 (1972) (continued employment under series of one-year contracts is protected property where state law and policies provide some form of tenure); Goldberg v. Kelly, 397 U.S. 254 (1970) (continuation of welfare benefits pursuant to statutory entitlement is protected property); State *ex rel.* Utils. Comm'n v. Carolina Util. Customers Ass'n, 336 N.C. 657, 678, 446 S.E.2d 332, 344 (1994) (no local-distribution-company property interest in gas-utility-supplier refunds because there is no entitlement to their receipt, thus no due-process rights regarding their allocation).

Whether a property right exists to a particular development regulation or permit is defined by the relevant state law. For example, in *Miller v. Town of Wenham*, 833 F.3d 46 (1st Cir. 2016), the court dismissed a due-process claim

Whether there is a legitimate claim to an entitlement is defined by statute or ordinance, not the constitution. For example, if state law provides that electrical service may only be terminated for cause, a customer with service has a legitimate claim of entitlement to continued service.[26] On the other hand, a decision that is wholly discretionary creates no entitlement and is thus not subject to procedural-due-process requirements.[27] The definition of what constitutes constitutionally protected "property" is a question of state law.[28]

This question of entitlement has a significant impact in land use law. Since a person is not entitled to a change in legislative policy, due-process rights do not affect a rezoning decision.[29] By contrast, an applicant who establishes that all the standards for a special use permit or a subdivision plat approval have been met is entitled to that approval, thus triggering due-process protections in how that decision is made.

If an adjudication affects a legitimate property interest, the next question becomes, What minimum procedures must be afforded to protect constitutional due-process rights under both the federal and state constitutions?

Certain key elements of a fair proceeding are essential under the federal Constitution—notice, opportunity to present information, disclosure of the grounds of the decision, and an impartial decision maker.[30] The opportunity to be heard must be provided at a meaningful time and in a meaningful manner.[31] When an administrative agency adjudicates contested facts in a quasi-judicial setting, it must make findings of fact, not merely recite the evidence and state its conclusions.[32]

Federal due process does not require a full evidentiary hearing for all quasi-judicial decisions. Rather, the court balances the impact of the decision on the individual against the governmental interests in securing accurate information, efficiency, and the costs of hearings to determine what minimum pro-

---

by a neighbor objecting to the town's approval of a substance-abuse facility next door to his residence upon finding the plaintiff had no property interests protected by state zoning law.

26. Memphis Light, Gas, & Water Div. v. Craft, 436 U.S. 1 (1978).

27. Conn. Bd. of Pardons v. Dumschat, 452 U.S. 458 (1981).

28. Bishop v. Wood, 426 U.S. 341 (1976). For example, in the area of personnel law the North Carolina courts have held that employment in the state is presumed to be "at will"—meaning the worker can be fired for any reason or for no reason at all—and an employee has a protected property interest in continued employment only if such is provided for by contract, statute, or local ordinance. Harris v. Duke Power Co., 319 N.C. 627, 356 S.E.2d 357 (1987). Thus, a public employee who is an at-will employee has no property right to continued employment beyond specific statutory procedural requirements. Soles v. City of Raleigh Civil Serv. Comm'n, 345 N.C. 443, 480 S.E.2d 685 (1997) (city employee has no property right to continued employment); Evans v. Cowan, 132 N.C. App. 1, 510 S.E.2d 170 (1999) (upholding dismissal of at-will nurse employee by state university); Wuchte v. McNeil, 130 N.C. App. 738, 505 S.E.2d 142 (1998) (upholding dismissal of police officer); Woods v. City of Wilmington, 125 N.C. App. 226, 480 S.E.2d 429 (1997) (upholding dismissal of city employee); Williams v. Hyde Cnty. Bd. of Educ., 490 F.2d 1231 (4th Cir. 1974) (probationary teacher does not have tenure or property right to reappointment).

29. Zopfi v. City of Wilmington, 273 N.C. 430, 434, 160 S.E.2d 325, 330 (1968). See also In re Markham, 259 N.C. 566, 131 S.E.2d 329, cert. denied, 375 U.S. 931 (1963); Ashby v. Town of Cary, 161 N.C. App. 499, 588 S.E.2d 572 (2003); Summers v. City of Charlotte, 149 N.C. App. 509, 562 S.E.2d 18, review denied, 355 N.C. 758, 566 S.E.2d 482 (2002); Brown v. Town of Davidson, 113 N.C. App. 553, 439 S.E.2d 206 (1994). This is generally the case even when the legislative enactment is targeted to address an issue raised by a single permit applicant. L C & S, Inc. v. Warren Cnty. Area Plan Comm'n, 244 F.3d 601 (7th Cir. 2001) (text amendment to require special use permit for taverns is legislative act even if enacted in response to a single proposed tavern).

30. Cleveland Bd. of Educ. v. Loudermill, 470 U.S. 532 (1985); Mullane v. Cent. Hanover Bank & Trust, 339 U.S. 306, 314–20 (1950) (notice must be reasonably calculated to apprise interested parties of action).

31. Armstrong v. Manzo, 380 U.S. 545 (1965). For an example in a land use context, see Brody v. City of Mason, 250 F.3d 432 (6th Cir. 2001) (ability to speak at some, but not all, hearings on special use permit application satisfied due-process requirements). See also Peace v. Emp't Sec. Comm'n, 349 N.C. 315, 507 S.E.2d 272 (1998).

32. In re Rogers, 297 N.C. 48, 56, 253 S.E.2d 912, 917–18 (1979) (Board of Law Examiners must make findings regarding contested determination on moral character of bar applicant).

cedures are necessary.[33] For example, the right to submit written information and make an administrative appeal was held to suffice where a personal appearance, cross-examination, and right to counsel would be unlikely to add to the quality of the evidence.[34] Likewise, the Supreme Court held that while due process must be afforded, a full evidentiary hearing is not required (and might well be counterproductive) in a high-school student-suspension setting.[35] In balancing these individual and governmental interests, the Court makes a series of inquiries. Would additional procedural-due-process safeguards produce significantly better information or increase agency accuracy? How do those benefits relate to the increased fiscal and administrative costs that would be involved? The Court also acknowledged it is appropriate for the courts to defer to the good-faith judgment of the legislative and executive branches in designing appropriate and accurate administrative adjudicatory procedures.[36]

The state constitution's law-of-the-land clause provides comparable protections of procedural due process. North Carolina courts have largely adopted and applied the federal courts' due-process analysis described above to quasi-judicial decisions.[37] However, while the federal and state due-process requirements are similar, the state imposes additional requirements.[38]

In the land use law context, the North Carolina courts have held that constitutional requirements of due process mandate that fair-trial standards be observed when quasi-judicial decisions are made.[39] In *Humble Oil & Refining Co. v. Board of Aldermen*, Justice Sharp set forth specific due-process requirements mandated by the state constitution for a quasi-judicial land use regulatory decision:

> Notwithstanding the latitude allowed municipal boards, . . . a zoning board of adjustment, or a board of aldermen conducting a quasi-judicial hearing, can dispense with no essential element of a fair trial: (1) The party whose rights are being determined must be given the opportunity to offer evidence, cross-examine adverse witnesses, inspect documents, and offer evidence in explanation and rebuttal; (2) absent stipulations or waiver such a board may not base findings as to the existence or nonexistence of crucial facts upon unsworn statements; and (3) crucial findings of fact which are "unsupported by competent, material and substantial evidence in view of the entire record as submitted" cannot stand.[40]

---

33. Goldberg v. Kelly, 397 U.S. 254 (1970).

34. Matthews v. Eldridge, 424 U.S. 319 (1976) (involving termination of Social Security disability benefits). In *Weinberg v. Whatcom County*, 241 F.3d 746 (9th Cir. 2001), the court applied a *Matthews* analysis and concluded that a hearing was required in a proceeding to vacate a previously approved subdivision plat. Similarly, in *Bowlby v. City of Aberdeen*, 681 F.3d 215 (5th Cir. 2012), the court held that notice and hearing were required before revoking a zoning approval to operate a business at a specific location. (Here the town approved the use, the business opened, and the town revoked approval without notice or hearing.)

35. Goss v. Lopez, 419 U.S. 565 (1975).

36. *Matthews*, 424 U.S. at 349.

37. *See, e.g.*, Pisgah Oil Co. v. W. N.C. Reg'l Air Pollution Control Agency, 139 N.C. App. 402, 533 S.E.2d 290, *review denied*, 353 N.C. 268, 546 S.E.2d 111 (2000) (formal evidentiary hearing not required for civil-penalty assessment for alleged air-quality violation); Nat'l Advert. Co. v. Bradshaw, 48 N.C. App. 10, 268 S.E.2d 816 (1980) (formal hearing not required for revocation of state sign permit). *See generally* Peace v. Emp't Sec. Comm'n, 349 N.C. 315, 323–27, 507 S.E.2d 272, 278–81 (1998); Soles v. City of Raleigh Civil Serv. Comm'n, 345 N.C. 443, 448–50, 480 S.E.2d 685, 688–89 (1997).

38. Henry v. Edmisten, 315 N.C. 474, 480, 340 S.E.2d 720, 725 (1986) (upholding ten-day suspension of driver's license without an evidentiary hearing for those failing breath test).

39. Cnty. of Lancaster v. Mecklenburg Cnty., 334 N.C. 496, 434 S.E.2d 604 (1993); Humble Oil & Refin. Co. v. Bd. of Aldermen, 284 N.C. 458, 202 S.E.2d 129 (1974); Jarrell v. Bd. of Adjustment, 258 N.C. 476, 128 S.E.2d 879 (1963) (while some degree of informality is acceptable, the board of adjustment can dispense with no essential element of a fair trial).

40. 284 N.C. at 470, 202 S.E.2d at 137. These standards are now codified at G.S. 160D-406.

Justice Sharp went on to note that procedural safeguards, in addition to well-defined substantive standards to be followed, were essential for fair administration of quasi-judicial decisions:

> Safeguards against arbitrary action by zoning boards in granting or denying special use permits are not only to be found in specific guidelines for their action. Equally important is the requirement that in each instance the board (1) follow the procedures specified in the ordinance; (2) conduct its hearings in accordance with fair-trial standards; (3) base its findings of fact only upon competent, material, and substantial evidence; and (4) in allowing or denying the application, it state the basic facts on which it relied with sufficient specificity to inform the parties, as well as the court, what induced its decision.[41]

These procedural requirements are discussed in detail in Chapter 15.

Statutory Provisions

From their initiation in the United States in the 1920s, enabling statutes have provided for quasi-judicial determinations in zoning implementation. Section 7 of the Standard State Zoning Enabling Act promulgated by the U.S. Department of Commerce in 1924 called for a five-member board of adjustment to do the following:

1. decide appeals by aggrieved persons where there was alleged error by a zoning-enforcement officer;[42]
2. decide special exceptions to the terms of an ordinance, subject to appropriate conditions and safeguards, in harmony with its general purpose and intent and in accordance with general or specific rules included in the ordinance; and
3. authorize variances upon appeal where literal enforcement of an ordinance would result in unnecessary hardship, as long as the spirit of the ordinance was observed and substantial justice done.

Essentially similar provisions were incorporated in the zoning-enabling statute adopted for North Carolina municipalities in 1923 and for counties in 1959.[43] Variances and appeals have been heard from the outset, and in the 1960s many local governments used the "special exception" authority to incorporate special use permits into their zoning ordinances. The enabling statutes for several other land use regulatory programs provide for appeals and hearings that are of a quasi-judicial nature.[44]

---

41. *Id.* at 471, 202 S.E.2d at 138.

42. Boards may not issue advisory opinions since the board of adjustment sits as an appellate body in these cases. The staff must make an initial ruling, which an affected party can then appeal to the board. Tate v. Bd. of Adjustment, 83 N.C. App. 512, 350 S.E.2d 873 (1986).

43. G.S. 160D-406.

44. Examples include decisions on certificates of appropriateness in historic districts under G.S. 160D-947 and appeals of orders to take corrective action under the building-code statutes under G.S. 160D-1123.

CHAPTER 15

Quasi-Judicial Procedures

When a quasi-judicial decision is made, statutory and due-process requirements mandate that the decision-making process adequately protect the rights of affected persons.[1] The procedures that must be followed dictate a decision-making process that is considerably different from a legislative rezoning or the administrative approval of a permitted use or a subdivision plat.[2] The statutes and courts recognize that lay boards make these decisions and that the formal rules of evidence required for judicial proceedings are inapplicable.[3] However, the hearings must be conducted in a manner that accords all those involved with basic procedural safeguards to assure fundamental fairness.

A fair evidentiary hearing must be conducted to gather the evidence that serves as the foundation for the decision.[4] There must be competent, substantial evidence properly in the record to support the decision, with sufficiently detailed written findings to explain the basis of the decision. After the decision is made, there is a different route for judicial review, with different standards than are applicable to legislative decisions.[5]

---

1. The General Assembly in 2013 codified much of the case law regarding quasi-judicial procedures into Chapter 160A, Section 388 of the North Carolina General Statutes (hereinafter G.S.). S.L. 2013-126. The former provision on boards of adjustment and quasi-judicial proceedings in the county zoning statute was repealed and replaced with G.S. 153A-345.1, which made G.S. 160A-388 applicable to counties. With the adoption of Chapter 160D in 2019, this provision is now codified as G.S. 160D-405 and -406. See Chapter 14 for a discussion of which land use regulatory decisions are characterized as quasi-judicial. For an overview of these procedural requirements written for lay board members, see DAVID W. OWENS AND ADAM S. LOVELADY, QUASI-JUDICIAL HANDBOOK: A GUIDE FOR BOARDS MAKING DEVELOPMENT REGULATION DECISIONS (UNC School of Government, 2017).

2. In *Coventry Woods Neighborhood Ass'n v. City of Charlotte*, 202 N.C. App. 247, 688 S.E.2d 538, *appeal dismissed*, 364 N.C. 128, 695 S.E.2d 757 (2010), the court held that neighbors had no due-process rights to notice and hearing for a preliminary plat decision. This court upheld a subdivision ordinance and a plat approval made pursuant to it that, as is almost uniformly the situation in North Carolina, made no provision for notice and hearing of this administrative approval.

3. Humble Oil & Refin. Co. v. Bd. of Aldermen, 284 N.C. 458, 471, 202 S.E.2d 129, 137 (1974). Many of the statutory requirements for quasi-judicial procedures are collected in G.S. 160D-406.

The North Carolina State Bar's Authorized Practice Committee has advised that representation of clients before a board hearing a quasi-judicial land use regulatory case constitutes the practice of law under G.S. 84-2.1. Advocacy on legislative decisions, by contrast, is not deemed by the committee to be the practice of law. N.C. State Bar Authorized Practice Comm., Advisory Op. 2006-1. The State Bar has also addressed the obligations of attorneys participating in these hearings regarding potential unauthorized-practice issues. Lawyers who represent the boards making the decisions are obligated to inform the board of this issue, and lawyers serving on these boards have no obligation to prevent unauthorized practice before the board. N.C. State Bar, 2007 Formal Ethics Op. 3.

4. Devaney v. City of Burlington, 143 N.C. App. 334, 338, 545 S.E.2d 763, 765 (2001). *See also* Lipinski v. Town of Summerfield, 230 N.C. App. 305, 750 S.E.2d 46 (2013) (holding quasi-judicial appeal of interpretation of ordinance provided a meaningful notice and opportunity to be heard, meeting procedural-due-process requirements).

5. See Chapter 29 for a discussion of judicial review of quasi-judicial decisions.

Initiating a Quasi-Judicial Hearing

Time Period to Initiate Action

Where the board involved is making the initial decision (such as deciding a variance petition or a special use permit application), the process is initiated by filing a complete application with the governmental unit involved. Most jurisdictions require the application or petition to be on forms supplied by the jurisdiction, and most require the application fee and all supporting materials to be in hand before an application is considered complete and scheduled for hearing.

Appeals seeking review of administrative decisions (such as a notice of zoning violation or a staff interpretation of the ordinance) must be filed within thirty days of receipt of notice of the determination being appealed.[6] This thirty-day period to file an appeal applies to any appeal of a final, written determination made under any development regulation.[7] The time period begins to run when the affected person receives actual or constructive notice of the decision being appealed.[8] Chapter 160D, Section 403(b) of the North Carolina General Statutes (hereinafter G.S.) requires written notice of the determination to be provided to the owner of the property affected and to the person requesting the determination. The time to appeal runs from receipt of that notice. For others the time runs from the time of actual or constructive notice of the determination. The statute allows a person receiving a determination to post a notice of the decision on the site in order to provide constructive notice and start the period for making an appeal.[9] Failure to appeal within the allotted period waives any right to raise defenses to a notice of zoning violation and civil-penalty assessment in court.[10]

The issue of when the time to make an appeal to the board begins to run was a common subject for litigation prior to the 2013 codification of the rules for appeals. For example, in *Meier v. City of Charlotte*, the plaintiff questioned compliance with building-height limits as applied to a residence under construction on an adjacent lot. After on-site meetings and plan reviews, the zoning administrator mailed a letter with an interpretation of the height limit and how it applied to this project. The letter concluded that the project would comply with the zoning ordinance. The letter also required a sealed

---

6. G.S. 160D-405(d). Prior to the 2013 amendment, the appeal had to be brought in the time prescribed by the board. The time period was generally set in the ordinance or in the rules of procedure adopted by the board hearing the matter. If no specific time was specified, the appeal to the board had to be taken within a "reasonable" time of the decision being appealed. Allen v. City of Burlington Bd. of Adjustment, 100 N.C. App. 615, 397 S.E.2d 657 (1990) (appeal of interpretation of ordinance made three years after constructive notice held not to be timely); Teen Challenge Training Ctr. v. Bd. of Adjustment, 90 N.C. App. 452, 368 S.E.2d 661 (1988) (appeal filed at least three months after neighbors learned of permit issuance (and eleven months after issuance) held not within a reasonable time); Town & Country Civic Org. v. Winston-Salem Bd. of Adjustment, 83 N.C. App. 516, 350 S.E.2d 893 (1986) (appeal to board of adjustment of permit for radio towers not timely as neighbors had constructive notice of permit decision upon delivery of materials for towers to site even if no posted or personal notice of decision); *In re* Greene, 29 N.C. App. 749, 225 S.E.2d 647, *review denied*, 290 N.C. 661 (1976) (appeal of issuance of building permit not timely when made after permitted work completed). *See also* White Oak Props., Inc. v. Town of Carrboro, 313 N.C. 306, 327 S.E.2d 882 (1985). When the ordinance set different procedures for appeal of different types of decisions, the court interpreted the ordinance as a whole to determine the appropriate appeal time and process. Fairway Outdoor Advert., LLC v. Town of Cary, 225 N.C. App. 676, 739 S.E.2d 579 (2013). For a discussion of the time limits for appeals of a board's quasi-judicial decision to the courts, see Chapter 29.

7. G.S. 160D-405(c). If notice is sent by mail, the notice is deemed to have been reviewed on the third business day after deposit of the notice in the mail.

8. *Allen*, 100 N.C. App. 615, 397 S.E.2d 657 (dismissing appeal to board brought three years after neighbors had constructive notice of zoning interpretation being applied but allowing appeal on newly made determinations regarding the use).

9. G.S. 160D-403(b).

10. Grandfather Vill. v. Worsley, 111 N.C. App. 686, 433 S.E.2d 13, *review denied*, 335 N.C. 237, 439 S.E.2d 146 (1993) (appeal not filed within the thirty days allotted waives defenses).

survey be submitted prior to issuance of a certificate of occupancy to confirm that final construction complied with the plans. The court held that the letter was a final determination on interpretation that could be appealed to the board of adjustment and that the time for appeal thus began to run upon its receipt. The as-built survey that was subsequently submitted was merely for the purpose of demonstrating compliance with the interpretation; it was not itself an interpretation and accordingly did not trigger the running of the appeals clock.[11]

A board of adjustment has no authority to waive a mandatory time period within which appeals must be filed. In *Water Tower Office Associates v. Town of Cary Board of Adjustment*,[12] the town's ordinance set a thirty-day period for filing an appeal of the zoning officer's decision to the board of adjustment. The plaintiff filed an appeal after this period, but the board heard the case and affirmed the officer's decision. When the plaintiff sought judicial review, the court dismissed the action, holding that the board had no subject-matter jurisdiction as there had not been a timely administrative appeal.

G.S. 160D-405 provides that the notice of appeal should be filed with the local government clerk or another local government official as designated by the local ordinance.

Stays upon Filing

The statutes specifically provide for stays of enforcement actions pending administrative appeals. G.S. 160D-405(f) provides that an appeal *to* the board of adjustment stays all proceedings in furtherance of the action appealed *from* and the accrual of any fines assessed (with exceptions provided if the zoning officer certifies that a stay would cause imminent peril to life or property or that the violation charged is transitory in nature and a stay would seriously interfere with enforcement). In those instances, there is no stay unless the board or a court issues a restraining order. In the event that an enforcement action is not stayed due to one of these two circumstances, the person appealing can request an expedited hearing before the board of adjustment, which then triggers a requirement that the board meet to hear the appeal within fifteen days of the request being made.

The rules on stays are different for quasi-judicial appeals of actions other than enforcement. G.S. 160D-405(f) provides that the appeal of a decision granting a permit or affirming that a use is permitted does not stay further review of an application or permission to use the property. In these situations, the appellant may request a stay of a final permit decision or issuance of building permits and the board may grant it, but it is not automatically provided. Without a stay, permittees are free to proceed at their own risk while an appeal is pending.[13]

Standing to Initiate and to Participate

G.S. 160D-405(b) provides that appeals to the board may be taken by any person who has standing for judicial review or by the local government. This includes the property owner, the applicant, the local government, and any person who would suffer some special damage, distinct from the rest of the

---

11. 206 N.C. App. 471, 698 S.E.2d 704 (2010). The ordinance required appeals to be made within thirty days of receipt of an interpretation. In *Bailey & Associates, Inc. v. Wilmington Board of Adjustment*, 202 N.C. App. 177, 689 S.E.2d 576 (2010), there was a dispute over whether the period began to run when the staff commented at the concept-review stage of a project or later, when it commented on a specific site plan. The ordinance required appeals to the board of adjustment regarding interpretation of the ordinance to be made within ten days after issuance of an order from the city manager. This presented a mixed question of law and fact, with the interpretation of the terms "issuance" and "order" being questions of law and the identification of actual dates of actions taken being a question of fact.

12. 131 N.C. App. 696, 507 S.E.2d 589 (1998).

13. *Godfrey v. Zoning Bd. of Adjustment*, 317 N.C. 51, 64 n.2, 344 S.E.2d 272, 280 n.2 (1986).

community.[14] The test for standing to seek judicial review and the test for standing to participate as a party in the quasi-judicial proceeding are the same.[15]

In most cases the party initiating a quasi-judicial action will be the person or entity applying for a variance or special use permit, appealing a notice of violation, or appealing an interpretation of the zoning officer affecting the party's property. The owner of the affected property or one who has a right to develop it can make such an appeal. An option-holder who has exercised the option subject to the necessary permits being obtained to develop the property has standing to participate in a review of those zoning permits.[16] A person bound by contract to purchase the land in question also has standing.[17] While case law held that a mere optionee does not have standing,[18] G.S. 160D-1402(c)(1)(b) gives standing to a person who has an option or contract to purchase the property. Also, it has been held that the estranged wife of a month-to-month lessee whose lease had been terminated does not have an interest in property sufficient to confer standing.[19] It is not uncommon for a lessee to file an application for a special use permit or to file a variance petition. As long as the lessee has the authority under the lease to undertake the development for which approval is sought, the lessee would have standing to initiate the quasi-judicial proceeding.[20]

People who are not applicants but who are directly affected by the proceeding have standing as parties to a quasi-judicial matter if they establish that they would suffer special damage distinct from that of the rest of the community. An allegation that a person would be adversely affected by an erroneous decision in the same way as other members of the community is not sufficient to establish standing.[21] The person seeking standing as a party has the burden[22] of showing damage to the value or use and enjoyment of the property that is distinct from damage to the neighborhood or community. G.S. 160D-1402(i) requires a court to allow evidence to supplement the record regarding standing.

---

14. Standing to make a judicial appeal is discussed in Chapter 29. That discussion is relevant to the issue of standing to initiate a quasi-judicial appeal. G.S. 160D-1402(c) addresses standing for judicial review of quasi-judicial decisions.

15. In a case reviewing whether a neighbor had standing as an "aggrieved party" to appeal a historic-preservation commission's decision on a certificate of appropriateness to the board of adjustment under G.S. 160D-947(e), the court applied the same standards for appeal to the board of adjustment and the appeal from the board of adjustment to the superior court. Cherry v. Wiesner, 245 N.C. App. 339, 781 S.E.2d 871, *review denied*, 369 N.C. 33, 792 S.E.2d 779 (2016). *See also* Pigford v. Bd. of Adjustment, 49 N.C. App. 181, 270 S.E.2d 535 (1980), *review denied*, 301 N.C. 722, 274 S.E.2d 230 (1981).

16. Humble Oil & Refin. Co. v. Bd. of Aldermen, 284 N.C. 458, 202 S.E.2d 129 (1974).

17. Deffet Rentals, Inc. v. City of Burlington, 27 N.C. App. 361, 219 S.E.2d 223 (1975).

18. Lee v. Bd. of Adjustment, 226 N.C. 107, 37 S.E.2d 128 (1946). The fact that a person holds an option rather than an obligation to purchase also goes to the issue of the degree of hardship that is a prerequisite for a variance.

19. Wil-Hol Corp. v. Marshall, 71 N.C. App. 611, 322 S.E.2d 655 (1984).

20. G.S. 160D-1402(c)(1)(a). Some jurisdictions require the landowner to provide a written agreement to the proposed action or to designate the lessee an agent for purposes of the application.

21. In *Cherry v. Wiesner*, 245 N.C. App. 339, 781 S.E.2d 871, *review denied*, 369 N.C. 33, 792 S.E.2d 779 (2016), the court found the neighbor directly across the street did not have standing to appeal the granting of a certificate of appropriateness to the board of adjustment. The court noted her allegations regarding standing were that approval of the home design alleged to be incongruous with the historic-district standards would harm the value of homes in the historic district, as opposed to showing a particular harm to the value or use of the petitioner's individual home. "Vague, general allegations that a property use will impair property values in the general area also will not confer standing." *Id.* at 349, 781 S.E.2d at 878.

22. The party invoking jurisdiction has the burden of proving the elements of standing. Neuse River Found., Inc. v. Smithfield Foods, Inc., 155 N.C. App. 110, 113, 574 S.E.2d 48, 51 (2002), *review denied*, 356 N.C. 675, 577 S.E.2d 638 (2003).

If standing is contested, the issue must be presented to the board for a ruling on standing. The zoning administrator may not refuse to place the matter on the board's agenda for lack of standing. Rather, the board itself must make that legal determination.[23]

The issue of participation in a quasi-judicial hearing by someone who does not qualify as a party was not explicitly addressed by the statutes or case law prior to the adoption of Chapter 160D.[24] While only a party can make objections and cross-examine witnesses, it has long been common that a neighbor or interested citizen wants to testify or offer evidence in the evidentiary hearing. Quasi-judicial procedures are more informal than court proceedings. Those who are official "parties" are not identified, and the distinction between witnesses and parties is not as precise as it is in a judicial setting. G.S. 160D-406(d) provides that the board may allow nonparties to present competent, material, and substantial evidence that is not repetitive. The board is not required to allow nonparties to present evidence, but virtually all do so provided that each witness is under oath, is subject to cross-examination, and is presenting relevant testimony.[25]

Notice of Hearing

The constitutional due-process rights for quasi-judicial matters require that timely notice of the opportunity to be heard be afforded to interested parties.[26] Since 2013 the statutes have also included specific, detailed rules regarding published and mailed notice of evidentiary hearings required for quasi-judicial decisions.

Richardson v. Union County Board of Adjustment[27] addressed the issue of proper notice for quasi-judicial zoning decisions. The court noted that the zoning statutes at that time required "due notice" of a hearing, while the zoning ordinance involved provided for a ten-day mailed-notice requirement and specified how that period is to be computed. The court held that the more specific ordinance requirements control rather than G.S. 1A-1, Rule 6 (the more general state law regarding computation of notice). The court has also held that it is necessary for the party claiming inadequate notice of a hearing to specify how it would have benefited from a later hearing in order to establish that it was prejudiced by lack of notice.[28]

G.S. 160D-406(b) now sets a uniform notice requirement for evidentiary hearings on quasi-judicial matters. These notice provisions are similar to those required for a zoning-map amendment, with the exception that newspaper published notice is not mandated.[29] Notice of the hearing must be mailed to the person who submitted the application that is the subject of the hearing, the owner of the affected

---

23. Morningstar Marinas/Eaton Ferry, LLC v. Warren Cnty., 368 N.C. 360, 777 S.E.2d 733 (2015).

24. In *Little River, LLC v. Lee County*, 257 N.C. App. 55, 809 S.E.2d 42 (2017), the court noted that the ordinance allowed any person to appear and submit evidence in a hearing on a special use permit.

25. It would be prudent for boards allowing non-witness testimony to have clear and uniformly applied rules of procedure specifying that this is permissible and specifying that the evidence must be competent, material, relevant, and nonrepetitive. It is also prudent for the presiding officer to remind those testifying that an evidentiary hearing is not a legislative hearing, where opinion and policy advice is appropriate. Rather, witnesses are presenting evidence as to whether the proposal meets the standards in the regulation, not freely speaking their minds on a pending application.

26. Mullane v. Cent. Hanover Bank & Trust Co., 339 U.S. 306, 314 (1950).

27. 136 N.C. App. 134, 523 S.E.2d 432 (1999). *See also* Jones v. Flowers, 547 U.S. 220 (2006) (notice required in a condemnation proceeding). Note that a person claiming a procedural-due-process right to notice generally must qualify as a party. Absent a statutory mandate, neighbors generally have no constitutional right to notice of permit applications or appeal hearings. *See, e.g.*, Kelsey v. Town of Hanover, 157 N.H. 632, 638–39, 956 A.2d 297, 302–03 (2008).

28. Symons Corp. v. Quality Concrete Constr., Inc., 108 N.C. App. 17, 422 S.E.2d 365 (1992); J.D. Dawson Co. v. Robertson Mktg., Inc., 93 N.C. App. 62, 376 S.E.2d 254 (1989); Brandon v. Brandon, 10 N.C. App. 457, 179 S.E.2d 177 (1971).

29. See Chapter 11 for the notice requirements for hearings on proposed zoning-map amendments.

property (if that is not the person requesting the hearing), adjacent owners, and anyone else entitled to mailed notice under the local ordinance. A notice of the hearing must be posted on or adjacent to the site that is the subject of the hearing. Both the mailing and posting must be done ten to twenty-five days before the hearing.

G.S. 160D-406(b) provides that an evidentiary hearing may be continued without additional notice if the time, date, and place of the continued hearing is announced at a duly noticed hearing that has been convened. Also, if a quorum of the board is not present at the announced date and time of a properly noticed evidentiary hearing, then the hearing is automatically continued to the next regular meeting of the board, and no additional notice of the hearing is required.

Some ordinances impose additional notice, such as published notice, posting of the site, or mailed notice to everyone who owns property within a specified proximity to the property involved. While none of these are mandated by the constitution or state statute, once they are incorporated into the ordinance, they are binding and must be followed.

Advisory Reviews

A number of North Carolina cities and counties send special use permit applications to the planning board for an advisory review.[30] This practice, while widespread, is not without some potentially significant legal risks.

Quasi-judicial decisions must be made on the basis of competent, substantial, and material evidence that is properly in the record of the decision-making board. This raises serious questions about what the decision-making board can make of an advisory comment from the planning board. Unless the evidence presented to the planning board is also presented at the evidentiary hearing, it cannot be used in making a decision. The planning-board comment in itself is not evidence that can be considered to resolve contested facts.

G.S. 160D-301 authorizes (but does not mandate) planning-board review and comments on pending quasi-judicial matters. However, this statute significantly limits use of an advisory review by the decision-making board. The statute characterizes these advisory reviews as a "preliminary forum." A planning board making an advisory review is not conducting a formal evidentiary hearing, but is allowing an informal, preliminary discussion of the application. Given this informality, the statute goes on to provide that "no part of the forum or recommendation" may be used as the basis for a decision by the board making the quasi-judicial decision. The decision must still be based on competent evidence presented at the evidentiary hearing held by the decision-making board.

These informal advisory reviews can identify issues and concerns and provide the parties with guidance about particular evidence that should be presented at a forthcoming evidentiary hearing. But they do not constitute evidence that can be used by the decision-making board.

---

30. In a 2005 UNC School of Government survey, 67 percent of the jurisdictions reported they sent special use permit applications to the planning board for an advisory review prior to a hearing and decision by the board of adjustment or governing board. David W. Owens, Special Use Permits in North Carolina Zoning 9 (UNC School of Government, Special Series No. 22, April 2007). The rationale generally offered for this practice was that it gave the applicants and neighbors an informal chance to present their cases and get feedback, and it provided a chance for all involved to get a better sense of the issues that would be contentious when the case got to the decision-making board. This allowed for consideration of actions to address concerns that were raised, such as conditions that might be appropriate or potential modifications to the application. While this added an extra step to the review process, many jurisdictions concluded that the benefits secured outweighed the burdens it imposed on the applicant, neighbors, and staff. In more-recent years, some jurisdictions have reconsidered the legal risks associated with incorporating informal reviews into a quasi-judicial process and have amended their ordinances to delete this step.

Remote Participation

There are occasions when there is a need to conduct an evidentiary hearing remotely. Examples include lengthy events, such as the COVID-19 pandemic, and more limited or localized ones, such as a bout of severe inclement weather or the recovery period after a natural disaster. There are also occasions when there is a need for individual board members or witnesses to participate in an evidentiary hearing remotely. The active participation of remote board members and witnesses is distinct from making the hearing available for viewing by persons not in attendance. It is certainly permissible to broadcast the hearing so that persons not physically present can observe the proceedings.[31] The issue of allowing a board member or witness to participate remotely is less clear.[32]

Remote meetings of government bodies, including an evidentiary hearing on a quasi-judicial matter, are expressly authorized during a state of emergency declared by the Governor or General Assembly.[33] G.S. 166A-19.24 provides general rules for these remote meetings, where one or all of the members of the board are participating remotely. These include notice of how the public can access the meeting, establishing and maintaining a quorum, availability of documents and records being discussed, and how votes are taken and recorded.

The law expressly allows, but does not mandate, remote evidentiary hearings. However, a remote evidentiary hearing is allowed only if: (1) the right to the hearing occurs during the declared emergency; (2) all parties with standing consent to a remote hearing; and (3) all due-process rights are preserved.

In deciding whether to conduct an evidentiary hearing remotely, or to allow participation by a member or witness remotely, it is important to keep the special nature of these hearings and the constitutional due-process rights of parties in mind. A key element of a quasi-judicial decision is determination of contested facts. Parties have the right to cross-examine witnesses. Board members must assess the credibility of witnesses to determine how much weight to accord their testimony. Observing the demeanor of a witness and asking questions about their testimony is often an important dimension of making that assessment. For that reason, many boards strive to conduct these hearings in person to fully protect the due-process rights of the parties unless there is no feasible alternative available.

Gathering Evidence

Quality and Quantity of Evidence Required

There must be substantial, competent, and material evidence in the record to support the board's findings and decision.[34] As the court noted in *Godfrey v. Zoning Board of Adjustment,*

> A determination made by a board of adjustment at a hearing, if not supported by substantial evidence, constitutes an "abuse" of the discretion vested in the board by ordinance or statute; a

---

31. Some North Carolina cities and counties routinely broadcast all meetings of the governing board over local cable television, but it is uncommon for that to be done for meetings and hearings of the board of adjustment or planning board. It became more common during the COVID-19 pandemic for these meetings and hearings to be live-streamed over the Internet.

32. The legal issues raised by a member participating remotely are addressed in Frayda S. Bluestein, *Remote Participation in Local Government Board Meetings*, LOCAL GOVT. L. BULL., No. 133 (UNC School of Government, Aug. 2013) (noting that while North Carolina statutes do not expressly authorize remote participation in order to establish a quorum or to allow remote voting, it is likely permissible).

33. This provision was added to the statutes in response to the COVID-19 pandemic. S.L. 2020-3, § 4.3(a).

34. G.S. 160D-406(j). The case law regarding this requirement includes *Jarrell v. Bd. of Adjustment*, 258 N.C. 476, 128 S.E.2d 879 (1963); *Tate Terrace Realty Inv'rs, Inc. v. Currituck Cnty.*, 127 N.C. App. 212, 488 S.E.2d 845, *review denied*, 347 N.C. 409, 496 S.E.2d 394 (1997); *Baker v. Town of Rose Hill*, 126 N.C. App. 338, 485 S.E.2d 78 (1997); *Brummer v. Bd. of Adjustment*, 81 N.C. App. 307, 343 S.E.2d 603, *review denied*, 318 N.C. 413, 349 S.E.2d 590 (1986)

determination which is not supported by substantial evidence is an arbitrary decision. A decision which lacks a rational basis—where there is no substantial relationship between the facts disclosed by the record and conclusions reached by the board—is also termed "arbitrary."[35]

Jarrell v. Board of Adjustment[36] illustrates this requirement. The High Point building inspector concluded that the use of a dwelling in a single-family zoning district as a duplex had been discontinued, thereby losing any nonconforming-use protection. The owner appealed that determination to the board of adjustment. The critical question before the board was a factual one: whether the building in question was being used as a single-family or a two-family dwelling on the effective date of the ordinance. The board discussed the petition at four meetings, at which counsel represented both the owner and the protesting neighbors. The minutes of the board of adjustment reflect the considerable attention it gave to the issue:

> The Board of Adjustment, having heard evidence in the form of verbal testimony, affidavits, letters and records, over a period of four sessions, felt that it was time to make a determination on this matter. The Board has permitted contending sides to introduce voluminous records and testimony without attempting to place any restriction of the basic law of evidence upon what they wanted to present to the Board. Much of the evidence which has been placed into the record is conflicting.[37]

The court ruled that while a degree of informality is allowed and the technical rules of evidence need not be followed, basic due-process rights required the board's critical factual findings to be based on competent and substantial evidence. In this instance the witnesses were not sworn, hearsay evidence was admitted, and the testimony on critical points was characterized as "brief and vague." The court therefore remanded the matter for a new hearing.

Substantial evidence is "that which a reasonable mind would regard as sufficiently supporting a specific result."[38]

G.S. 160D-1402(j)(3) also imposes some limits on what can be deemed "competent evidence" in quasi-judicial proceedings. In determining whether there is sufficient competent evidence, the decision-making board is allowed to consider evidence that would not be admissible under the rules of evidence in a court proceeding, but only if there was no objection to its presentation or if the evidence is "sufficiently trustworthy" and is admitted under circumstances wherein reliance on it is reasonable. Several specific instances of opinion testimony by nonexpert witnesses are explicitly deemed by this statute not to be

---

(findings of fact in appeal of interpretation of ordinance must be supported by evidence); *Jennewein v. City Council of Wilmington*, 62 N.C. App. 89, 302 S.E.2d 7, *review denied*, 309 N.C. 461, 307 S.E.2d 365 (1983); *Long v. Winston-Salem Bd. of Adjustment*, 22 N.C. App. 191, 205 S.E.2d 807 (1974) (remanding case for de novo board proceeding to secure competent evidence).

35. 317 N.C. 51, 60, 334 S.E.2d 272, 278 (1986) (citations omitted). The court has held that the denial of a special exception or conditional use permit may not be based on "conclusions which are speculative, sentimental, personal, vague or merely an excuse to prohibit the use requested." Woodhouse v. Bd. of Comm'rs, 299 N.C. 211, 220, 261 S.E.2d 882, 888 (1980) (quoting Baxter v. Gillispie, 60 Misc. 2d 349, 354, 303 N.Y.S.2d 290, 296 (Sup. Ct. 1969)); Howard v. City of Kinston, 148 N.C. App. 238, 246, 558 S.E.2d 221, 227 (2002).

36. 258 N.C. 476, 128 S.E.2d 879 (1963).

37. *Id.* at 478, 128 S.E.2d at 881.

38. CG&T Corp. v. Bd. of Adjustment, 105 N.C. App. 32, 40, 411 S.E.2d 655, 660 (1992). *Robertson v. Zoning Board of Adjustment*, 167 N.C. App. 531, 605 S.E.2d 723 (2004), *review denied*, 359 N.C. 322, 611 S.E.2d 417 (2005), provides an illustration of the quantity of evidence that is sufficient to support the required findings. The court applied a whole-record review to conclude that a variance decision was not arbitrary and was based on substantial evidence. The court held that testimony, reports, photographs, and surveys in the record regarding the site topography and the location and character of improvements sufficiently supported the board's findings on these matters and its conclusion that a fence constituted a traffic-safety problem.

competent evidence, even if no objection is made at the evidentiary hearing. These include testimony about how the proposed use would affect the value of neighboring properties, whether vehicular traffic would pose a danger to public safety, and any other matter on which only expert testimony would generally be admissible under the rules of evidence.[39]

If irrelevant or incompetent evidence is received but not used as the basis for the quasi-judicial decision, receipt in itself is not a due-process violation.[40] The question is whether there is substantial, competent, and material evidence properly in the record to support the decision that is made.

Burden of Production

As a general rule, the burden of production of evidence rests with the person initiating the action. With special use permit applications, the applicant has the burden of producing sufficient evidence to show that the permit conditions will be met.[41] With variance petitions, the petitioner must likewise present evidence sufficient to establish undue hardship. When there is a dispute as to the zoning official's determination, the person challenging that determination has the burden of producing evidence to show an error was made.[42]

Subpoenas

G.S. 160D-406(g) provides specific authority for a board of adjustment to issue subpoenas. Requests for a subpoena may be made to the board chair by the applicant, the local government, and any person with standing to participate in the hearing. The chair is to issue subpoenas that are "relevant, reasonable in nature and scope, and not oppressive." The chair is also to rule on motions to quash or modify a subpoena. Appeals of rulings on subpoenas may be made to the full board. False testimony under oath is a misdemeanor.[43] If there is noncompliance with the subpoena, the board may apply to the courts for an order to comply.

Oaths

Generally, all persons presenting evidence to a board making a quasi-judicial decision should be under oath.[44] This includes the applicant, neighbors, governmental staff members, and any other persons who may be presenting information to the board, such as a surveyor, engineer, or real-estate agent. An attorney for a party sometimes directly presents facts and information to the board (as opposed to simply questioning witnesses and making arguments to the board). Although attorneys should generally not

---

39. The provision that no timely objection is required was added by S.L. 2019-111, § 1.9. Nonexpert-opinion testimony on these issues is deemed "conclusively incompetent."

40. Dobo v. Zoning Bd. of Adjustment, 149 N.C. App. 701, 709–10, 562 S.E.2d 108, 113–14 (2002), *rev'd on other grounds*, 356 N.C. 656, 576 S.E.2d 324 (2003); *Howard*, 148 N.C. App. at 244–45, 558 S.E.2d at 226.

41. See Chapter 16 for a discussion of the cases regarding burdens of production in special and conditional use decisions.

42. Lamar Outdoor Advert., Inc. v. City of Hendersonville Zoning Bd. of Adjustment, 155 N.C. App. 516, 522, 573 S.E.2d 637, 642 (2002). In this case the ordinance specifically stated that the burden of proof rested with the applicant in all proceedings under the zoning ordinance.

43. Prior to 2013, testimony presented as a result of these subpoenas could not be used against the witness in a subsequent civil or criminal trial, other than a criminal action for perjury while testifying. That provision was deleted in the 2013 revision of the statute. S.L. 2013-126.

44. Jarrell v. Bd. of Adjustment, 258 N.C. 476, 128 S.E.2d 879 (1963); Brummer v. Bd. of Adjustment, 81 N.C. App. 307, 343 S.E.2d 603, *review denied*, 318 N.C. 413, 349 S.E.2d 590 (1986).

appear as witnesses in cases they are trying, such an appearance is not absolutely prohibited.[45] If an attorney testifies as to the facts in a case, the attorney should be sworn as a witness.[46]

The chair of the board (and any member serving as the chair) and the board's clerk are authorized to administer the oath in quasi-judicial proceedings.[47] Any notary public can also administer this oath.[48] The form that is usually used is the same as for witnesses in civil cases.[49] Persons with religious objections may affirm rather than swear an oath.

If all the parties agree, the right to have witnesses under oath may be waived. In *Craver v. Board of Adjustment*, both the petitioner and objecting neighboring property owners appeared at the hearing and explained their respective positions at length. There were inquiries from the board to both parties. The petition for a permit was not verified. The petitioner was not sworn and made no request that the opponents be sworn or cross-examined. The court noted, "Obviously, when material findings of fact must be made on conflicting testimony, witnesses should be sworn." The court held, though, that if the applicant was present at the quasi-judicial hearing, the applicant's testimony was not sworn, and a full and open discussion ensued, the unsuccessful applicant could not then object that the witnesses were not sworn.[50] Where no objection is made to unsworn testimony, the right to insist on sworn testimony is deemed waived.[51] Also, failure to participate in a duly advertised hearing waives any right to object to incompetent testimony.[52]

---

45. Robinhood Trails Neighbors v. Winston-Salem Bd. of Adjustment, 44 N.C. App. 539, 261 S.E.2d 520, *review denied*, 299 N.C. 737, 267 S.E.2d 663 (1980). The attorney for an applicant for a special use permit gave sworn testimony. The objecting neighbors contended that findings could not be based on this evidence because an attorney could not serve as a witness and an advocate in the same proceeding. The court allowed the testimony, albeit with an admonition strongly discouraging the practice. By contrast, in *Mebane v. Iowa Mutual Insurance*, 28 N.C. App. 27, 220 S.E.2d 623 (1975), the court noted that once an attorney testifies in a matter, the general course will be to withdraw from further representation in the matter. Also see Rule 3.7 of the Revised Rules of Professional Conduct of the North Carolina State Bar, limiting the role of the lawyer as a witness.

46. The fact that the attorney has taken an oath of office is insufficient, as that should be distinguished from taking an oath for presentation of evidence. The same distinction would apply to a board member who is offering evidence to be considered in a particular case.

47. G.S. 160D-406(f).

48. G.S. 10B-20(a)(2). An oath of office, which is different from an oath to tell the truth in a specific proceeding, can be administered by those listed in G.S. 11-7-1.

49. G.S. 11-11. A standard practice is to have the person administering the oath do so as follows: "Do you swear [or affirm] that the evidence you shall give to the board in this action shall be the truth, the whole truth, and nothing but the truth, so help you God?" Each witness may be sworn at the time of testifying or all witnesses may be sworn at one time at the beginning of the hearing.

50. 267 N.C. 40, 42, 147 S.E.2d 599, 601 (1966). Courts have held that when a petitioner appears at a quasi-judicial hearing accompanied by counsel, offers unsworn testimony, and does not object to unsworn testimony (or seek to cross-examine the witness or to offer rebuttal evidence), the petitioner cannot object to such on judicial review. Howard v. City of Kinston, 148 N.C. App. 238, 244, 558 S.E.2d 221, 226 (2002). *See also* Guilford Fin. Servs., LLC v. City of Brevard, 356 N.C. 655, 576 S.E.2d 325 (2003), *per curiam, adopting dissent in* 150 N.C. App. 1, 563 S.E.2d 27 (2002) (where both parties are represented by counsel in quasi-judicial plat-review decision, failure to request that witnesses be under oath is a waiver of that right); Joyner v. Zoning Bd. of Adjustment, 267 N.C. 44, 147 S.E.2d 602 (1966). In *Robinhood Trails Neighbors v. Winston-Salem Board of Adjustment*, 44 N.C. App. 539, 261 S.E.2d 520, *review denied*, 299 N.C. 737, 267 S.E.2d 663 (1980), the court allowed consideration of slides shown along with unsworn testimony at the hearing, noting that the board also made a site visit, so there was no prejudice to the appellants (and since the slides were presented by the appellants' attorneys, they were hardly in a position to object to their credibility).

51. Burton v. New Hanover Cnty. Bd. of Adjustment, 49 N.C. App. 439, 271 S.E.2d 550, *cert. denied*, 302 N.C. 217, 276 S.E.2d 914 (1981); Carter v. Town of Chapel Hill, 14 N.C. App. 93, 187 S.E.2d 588, *review denied*, 281 N.C. 314, 188 S.E.2d 897 (1972).

52. Tate Terrace Realty Inv'rs, Inc. v. Currituck Cnty., 127 N.C. App. 212, 488 S.E.2d 845, *review denied*, 347 N.C. 409, 496 S.E.2d 394 (1997).

Even if the right to have sworn testimony is waived, the board must still have competent, material, and substantial evidence in the record as a foundation for its findings of facts and conclusions. Thus, the standard practice of most boards conducting quasi-judicial hearings is to place all persons offering testimony under oath.

Presentation of Testimony and Exhibits

Most ordinances require applications and petitions for quasi-judicial decisions to be made on forms provided by the jurisdiction. The applications are designed to solicit submission of written information necessary for board action. These applications, along with staff reports and analysis, become part of the record before the board.

An application that is purposefully misleading can serve as a basis for permit denial. *Freewood Associates, Ltd. v. Davie County Zoning Board of Adjustment* [53] involved a proposed nudist camp in a residential-agricultural zoning district in rural Davie County. The court upheld a denial of a special use permit where all applications and discussions with the county had referred to a "family campground" rather than a "nudist camp" in a deliberate attempt to conceal the true use of the property.

It is common for a packet of information about pending quasi-judicial cases to be distributed to the board prior to the evidentiary hearing. This allows board members to review the application and supporting materials in advance so that they are prepared at the outset of the hearing. This is particularly useful if there are lengthy technical documents or reports that need to be read prior to the hearing. It is also a good practice to include copies of the relevant regulation so that it becomes a part of the hearing record.[54] This practice, however, raised questions as to whether this is appropriate, given limits on ex parte evidence and unsworn testimony.

G.S. 160D-406(c) addresses this by explicitly allowing, but not requiring, the distribution of meeting packets to board members prior to the hearing. This statute requires the staff to transmit to the board all administrative materials relative to the pending case—the application, reports, and other written materials received by the staff. The materials can be distributed in advance of the hearing, but only if copies of all of the materials are also provided to the applicant and landowner at the same time they are distributed to the board members.[55] If these materials are not distributed prior to the hearing, then they must be presented at the hearing.

These administrative materials then become a part of the official hearing record. Parties may make objections to the inclusion or exclusion of administrative materials before or at the hearing. Rulings on any objections are to be made by the board at the hearing. G.S. 160D-406(d) provides that the board chair rules on any objections and that the ruling may be appealed to the full board. Evidentiary rulings are also subject to judicial review.

In *Town of Gastonia v. Parrish*,[56] it was held that the *best-evidence rule* applies to quasi-judicial hearings. In this instance the original zoning-classification map for the extraterritorial area had been lost, but a copy (along with oral testimony that it was an accurate copy) was ruled admissible.

---

53. 28 N.C. App. 717, 222 S.E.2d 910, *review denied*, 290 N.C. 94, 225 S.E.2d 323 (1976).

54. This is useful not only as a convenience for the board and parties, but it is needed in the event of a judicial appeal since a court cannot take judicial notice of city and county ordinances. High Point Surplus Co. v. Pleasants, 263 N.C. 587, 591, 139 S.E.2d 892, 895–96 (1965); McEwen Funeral Serv. v. Charlotte City Coach Lines, Inc., 248 N.C. 146, 150–51, 102 S.E.2d 816, 820 (1958); Thompson v. Union County, 283 N.C. App. 547, 874 S.E.2d 623 (2022).

55. Although not addressed by the statute, if other persons have sought to qualify as a party to the proceeding prior to the hearing, copies should be distributed to them in advance as well.

56. 271 N.C. 527, 157 S.E.2d 154 (1967).

The parties to the case—the unit of government, the applicant, and other parties—have the right to present evidence, cross-examine witnesses, object to evidence proposed to be presented, and make legal arguments. G.S. 160D-406(d) allows nonparties to present competent, material, and substantial evidence that is not repetitive if that is allowed by the board.[57] When allowed, it is prudent to remind witnesses that they are presenting evidence and are not parties to the action with a right to otherwise participate in the hearing.

It is permissible for a board to establish reasonable time periods for presentation of testimony and for the presiding officer to limit repetitive or irrelevant testimony.[58] While strict time limits may well be appropriate for legislative decisions (such as three minutes per speaker for a rezoning hearing), care must be taken not to unduly limit the presentation of the substantial, competent, and material evidence that is necessary to support a quasi-judicial decision.[59]

An invocation of the Fifth Amendment as the basis for not rebutting evidence does not prevent a board from making reasonable inferences based on the evidence presented. *Davis v. Town of Stallings Board of Adjustment*[60] involved review of a staff interpretation that a particular bookstore was an "adult bookstore" located where such a business was not permitted. The town staff presented evidence that a substantial number of adult videos, magazines, CDs, and novelty items were present in the store. The plaintiff invoked the Fifth Amendment and did not testify at the hearing. The board then held that the facility violated the provisions of the permit limiting the store to trade-in videos only and that it constituted an adult establishment.[61] The court held that while the plaintiff could invoke the Fifth Amendment, the board could infer in this civil matter that failure to refute damaging evidence meant the plaintiff was running an unlawful adult establishment.[62]

Cross-Examination and Rebuttal Evidence

Parties to a quasi-judicial hearing have a right to cross-examine witnesses.[63] If opponents to a variance or a special use permit present a witness, the applicant can also ask questions of that witness to probe the strengths and weaknesses of that witness's testimony. As with the right to have sworn testimony, the rights of cross-examination and presentation of rebuttal evidence are deemed waived if not raised at the hearing.[64]

---

57. While not mandated by the statute, it is prudent for boards to have clear and uniformly applied rules of procedure specifying whether nonparties may present evidence.

58. While persuasive rather than binding, the Administrative Procedure Act specifically provides that in contested case hearings "irrelevant, immaterial and unduly repetitious evidence shall be excluded." G.S. 150B-29.

59. It is not altogether uncommon for even courts to fail to explicitly distinguish between legislative and evidentiary hearings and the differing procedures for each. For example, the courts in both *Howard v. City of Kinston*, 148 N.C. App. 238, 244, 558 S.E.2d 221, 226 (2002), and *Richardson* held that the board in a quasi-judicial decision had not abused its discretion in limiting testimony but cited a rezoning case, *Freeland v. Orange County*, 273 N.C. 452, 457, 160 S.E.2d 282, 286 (1968), as authority for these limitations.

60. 141 N.C. App. 489, 541 S.E.2d 183 (2000).

61. The town's zoning ordinance used the *adult establishment* definition provided in G.S. 14-202.10(2). For a discussion of the First Amendment aspects of adult-entertainment regulation, see Chapter 26.

62. The court reached the same conclusion regarding enforcement proceedings for a general-police-power ordinance in *McKillop v. Onslow County*, 139 N.C. App. 53, 532 S.E.2d 594 (2000).

63. Humble Oil & Refin. Co. v. Bd. of Aldermen, 284 N.C. 458, 470, 202 S.E.2d 129, 137 (1974).

64. Guilford Fin. Servs., LLC v. City of Brevard, 356 N.C. 655, 576 S.E.2d 325 (2003), *per curiam, adopting dissent in* 150 N.C. App. 1, 563 S.E.2d 27 (2002) (where both parties are represented by counsel in quasi-judicial plat-review decision, failure to request cross-examination or the opportunity to present rebuttal evidence is a waiver of those rights).

Since quasi-judicial proceedings lack the formal structure and rules of judicial proceedings, exercise of the right of cross-examination can pose practical difficulties in distinguishing parties who can fully participate in the hearing and witnesses who can only offer relevant evidence. Unlike a judicial proceeding, parties in quasi-judicial hearings are often not clearly identified. While the person initiating the action (the applicant for a special use permit, the petitioner for a variance, or the appellant of a staff determination) is clearly a party, the status of others is often blurred. The staff of the local government is a party for appeals of staff determinations, but a staff member may well be only a witness in variance or special use permit cases. A neighbor may appear as a witness to oppose a project but may not have formally intervened as a party. There may be a large number of persons who want to offer testimony, some of whom have standing to be parties and some who do not. Frequently, many if not all of these persons are not represented by counsel. Further, the physical layout of the hearing usually differs from a courtroom. Rather than counsel tables and a witness stand, it is common for all of those offering testimony and asking questions to share a single podium in front of the board.

Some boards that make quasi-judicial decisions have adopted rules of procedure to provide a degree of order to this process. For example, the rules may state the order of presentations and questions.[65] But since the vast majority of these cases are conducted informally by laypersons, often with few individuals attending and with little attendant controversy, it is not uncommon for them to be conducted without set rules for determining who can offer testimony or conduct cross-examination. In these instances it is incumbent upon the presiding officer to maintain decorum and an orderly process of securing quality evidence in a manner that assures fairness to all who are affected. Time limits on presentations, requirements that persons with common interests designate a spokesperson, and admonitions to avoid repetitive, irrelevant, or incompetent testimony (as long as they are reasonably and fairly applied) are all acceptable means of providing the necessary structure to these proceedings.[66] However, since parties to a quasi-judicial proceeding have due-process rights to present evidence and cross-examine witnesses, a rigidly applied time limit on individual witnesses or a set time limit for the entire hearing (both of which are acceptable for a legislative zoning decision) would be inappropriate if applied in a way that precluded a party from fairly presenting or challenging legally sufficient evidence.

The court in *Humble Oil & Refining Co. v. Board of Aldermen* included the right to offer rebuttal evidence as an essential element of a fair hearing, so provision to allow parties who request such an opportunity must be accommodated.[67]

Rights of cross-examination apply only to the presentation of evidence. Deliberation by the board, including discussion of potential conditions to be imposed, is not covered. In *In re Raynor,*[68] the applicant appeared before the town board subsequent to its hearing on his application for a conditional use permit and offered additional permit conditions in response to concerns raised at the hearing. The neighbors challenging the issuance of the permit had no individual notice of the board meeting at which the additional conditions were offered. The court upheld the issuance of the permit, noting that the town ordinance explicitly allowed applicants an opportunity to amend their application in response to comments made at the required public hearing. The additional conditions were not deemed "evidence," so the neighbors had no due-process rights to be present and cross-examine the applicant regarding them.

---

65. A typical process would be presentation of a factual summary by the staff, followed by a factual presentation by the petitioner and presentations by opponents. At the conclusion of each person's testimony, board members, then the staff, the petitioner, and the opponents are allowed to ask the witness questions. In some instances, each group is allowed to make a final summary statement at the conclusion of the presentation of evidence.

66. *Howard,* 148 N.C. App. 238.

67. *Humble Oil,* 284 N.C. 458, 202 S.E.2d 129.

68. 94 N.C. App. 173, 379 S.E.2d 884, *review denied,* 325 N.C. 546, 385 S.E.2d 495 (1989).

Similarly, in *Ward v. Inscoe*,[69] the court held that when a board meets at a regularly scheduled time solely for the purpose of adopting findings on a conditional use permit, the parties have no constitutional right to receive personal notice, to present new evidence, or to rebut previously submitted evidence.

Board deliberation about conditions and a decision on a matter that has been heard, however, must be carefully distinguished from consideration of a substantially revised application or receipt of additional evidence. If a site plan or other significant aspects of a project are substantially revised after the close of an evidentiary hearing, the board must reopen the hearing to receive testimony and cross-examination regarding the revised application.

This principle is illustrated by *Cook v. Union County Zoning Board of Adjustment*.[70] The board there held an evidentiary hearing on a special use permit application for a large-scale-commercial use. The hearing extended over five dates. The board closed the hearing and voted to approve the permit subject to numerous changes and submission of a revised site plan. At subsequent board meetings, the applicant presented substantially revised site plans. Neighbors and the county staff (both of whom had actively participated in the initial hearings) were not allowed to ask questions or present any evidence regarding the substantially revised plans. The court held that the board's refusal to allow presentation of rebuttal evidence or cross-examination regarding the revised site plan violated both the due-process rights of the neighbors and the requirements of the ordinance that persons be given the opportunity to present evidence and ask questions.

A cautionary note about limiting the scope of discussion about a project after the hearing has been closed is provided by *Templeton Properties, LP v. Town of Boone*.[71] The town had denied a special use permit, and on appeal the case was remanded with a direction to specify its findings of fact to support that denial. When the board took up the matter, it allowed citizens who were present to speak in opposition. The court held that hearing from one side in a contested matter was in effect receipt of new evidence and violated the due-process rights of the applicant.

Hearsay Evidence

As a general rule, the person asserting a particular fact should be physically present before the board to testify on that matter. Purported statements by those who are not present, letters from those who are concerned but not present, and petitions[72] and affidavits[73] from those not present are all hearsay evidence. While hearsay evidence can be presented, a board may well accord it considerably less weight. Critical factual findings must not be based solely on hearsay evidence.[74]

The court in several cases has upheld the admission and consideration of letters from persons not testifying at the hearing. In particular, letters from government officials that provide unbiased information that is within the specialized professional knowledge of an official or that is based on records or information kept by the official's agency in the normal course of business are generally admitted. For

---

69. 166 N.C. App. 586, 603 S.E.2d 393 (2004).

70. 185 N.C. App. 582, 649 S.E.2d 458 (2007).

71. 219 N.C. App. 266, 724 S.E.2d 604 (2012).

72. Innovative 55, LLC v. Robeson Cnty., 253 N.C. App. 714, 725, 801 S.E.2d 671, 679 (2017) (petition signed by neighbors opposing special use permit not competent evidence); Humane Soc'y of Moore Cnty., Inc. v. Town of Southern Pines, 161 N.C. App. 625, 631–32, 589 S.E.2d 162, 167 (survey of neighbors' opinions not competent evidence on property-value impacts of proposed kennel).

73. *See, e.g., In re* Custody of Griffin, 6 N.C. App. 375, 170 S.E.2d 84 (1974) (affidavit is inherently weak method of proof).

74. Jarrell v. Bd. of Adjustment, 258 N.C. 476, 481, 128 S.E.2d 879, 883 (1963) (noting affidavits and letters submitted regarding prior use of a nonconformity, as well as unsworn testimony, were incompetent and thus could not form the basis of the board's critical findings).

example, a letter from a state agency may be considered, even though its author is not present, if the letter's recipient is present, testifies under oath, and is subject to cross-examination.[75] The court has also allowed consideration of technical reports on noise impacts where a civil engineer presented test results from another consultant.[76]

Another example is provided in *Tate Terrace Realty Investors, Inc. v. Currituck County*.[77] The plaintiff applied for a special use permit for a 601-lot subdivision. A standard for the permit required that a project not exceed the county's ability to provide adequate facilities, including but not limited to schools, fire and rescue, law enforcement, and other county facilities. At the initial hearing on the matter, the planning director testified under oath about comments received on the project, including a written comment from the school superintendent, and the petitioner estimated the project would increase the county's school enrollment by 10 percent. At a continued hearing in which the petitioner did not participate (the petitioner had requested a "continuance" the day prior to the hearing), a letter from the superintendent on long-range needs of the school system was presented. At its final meeting to decide the application, the board received a staff analysis recommending denial based on inadequate school facilities to support the development, and the board of commissioners made its denial on that basis. The court held that the evidence received on the impact of the development on school capacity could properly be considered.

If reports are to be considered, particularly where the author of the report is not presenting testimony in person, it is important that the report itself (rather than just a reference to it) be formally entered into the hearing record.[78] The reports so included in the record become part of the hearing record available to a court on judicial review.

Opinion Evidence

A common issue in quasi-judicial hearings is the weight to be given generalized objections and opinions from neighbors, nonexperts, and even expert witnesses. This is particularly problematic where general standards are involved (such as compatibility with the surrounding neighborhood or adverse impacts on neighboring-property value) and the testimony is not supported by site-specific facts.

G.S. 160D-1402(j)(3) specifically limits use of opinion testimony by nonexpert witnesses on how the proposed use would affect the value of neighboring properties, whether vehicular traffic would pose a danger to public safety, and any other matter on which only expert testimony would generally be admissible under the rules of evidence.

For the most part, the appearance of expert witnesses is relatively uncommon in quasi-judicial hearings in North Carolina, but the practice is on the rise, particularly for high-profile, controversial cases. A 2005 UNC School of Government survey indicated that with special and conditional use permit hearings, 55 percent of the jurisdictions reported that expert witnesses either never or only rarely appear. However, 16 percent of the jurisdictions reported that experts appear frequently, almost always,

---

75. Whiteco Outdoor Advert. v. Johnston Cnty. Bd. of Adjustment, 132 N.C. App. 465, 513 S.E.2d 70 (1999).

76. Harding v. Bd. of Adjustment, 170 N.C. App. 392, 612 S.E.2d 431 (2005). Those subsequently complaining had an opportunity to cross-examine the witness and to offer rebuttal testimony. They also made no objection to the testimony at the hearing.

77. 127 N.C. App. 212, 488 S.E.2d 845 (1997), *review denied*, 347 N.C. 409, 496 S.E.2d 394 (1997).

78. In *Williams v. North Carolina Department of Environment & Natural Resources*, 144 N.C. App. 479, 548 S.E.2d 793 (2001), a case involving a variance decision under the Coastal Area Management Act, the parties relied on stipulated facts rather than a full evidentiary hearing. The stipulations referenced several reports prepared by government agencies, but the reports themselves were not submitted into the record. On judicial review the court noted that since the reports were not in the record, they could not be considered in determining whether there was substantial, competent, material evidence in the record to support the decision.

or always.[79] This was a marked increase in the frequency of expert testimony compared to the 2003 survey of zoning variance experience, where only 8 percent of the jurisdictions reported that experts appeared frequently, almost always, or always.

When expert testimony is offered in a quasi-judicial hearing, a proper foundation must be established. In *Mann Media, Inc. v. Randolph County Planning Board*, the court noted that a rigorous standard is necessary to establish a foundation for opinion testimony. On the issue of impacts on property values, the applicant's witness was a professional appraiser; the objecting neighbors presented testimony from a contractor and a real-estate agent. The court noted that all three witnesses offered only speculative opinions about values without supporting facts or examples and ruled that this cannot be the foundation of a finding of adverse impacts.[80]

In *PHG Asheville, LLC v. City of Asheville*, the court held that if properly qualified expert testimony is offered, the decision-making board cannot reject that evidence based on its own lay assessment of the testimony's adequacy.[81] A board's concern about the reliability of the expert testimony is not grounds for rejecting the opinion testimony in the absence of contrary evidence properly in the hearing record.

Key factual findings cannot be based on the unsupported allegations and opinions of nonexpert witnesses, even if the witnesses are the property owners[82] or neighboring-property owners. It is not necessary for an objection to be made at the hearing regarding such impermissible evidence, as it is deemed to be conclusively incompetent.[83]

Two cases illustrate this point. In *Sun Suites Holdings, LLC v. Board of Aldermen*, the court held that "speculative assertions or mere expressions of opinion about the possible effects of granting a permit are insufficient to support the findings of a quasi-judicial body."[84] The court held that a general expression of a fear of potential traffic problems was inadequate evidence, and simply establishing an increase in traffic did not necessarily establish that undue or unsafe congestion would result. Similarly, a recitation of crime statistics with reference to a similar land use elsewhere in the town, without any foundation as to how they related to the subject project, was also held inadequate to support a denial. Speculative comments by a neighbor and a realtor about impacts on property values (made without supporting factual data, appraisals, or market studies) were likewise held to be insubstantial evidence on the property-value issue. In *Clark v. City of Asheboro*,[85] neighbors in opposition to a special use permit

---

79. OWENS, *supra* note 30, at 13.

80. Mann Media, Inc. v. Randolph Cnty. Planning Bd., 356 N.C. 1, 565 S.E.2d 9 (2002). *See also* Am. Towers, Inc. v. Town of Morrisville, 222 N.C. App. 638, 731 S.E.2d 698 (2012), *review denied*, 743 S.E.2d 189 (2013) (noting expert opinion must be supported by adequate methodology); SBA, Inc. v. City of Asheville, 141 N.C. App. 19, 539 S.E.2d 18 (2000). By contrast, in *Leftwich v. Gaines*, 134 N.C. App. 502, 521 S.E.2d 717 (1999), *review denied*, 351 N.C. 357, 541 S.E.2d 714 (2000), a case seeking damages due to the improper actions of a zoning official, the court allowed testimony from a plaintiff with experience in real-estate matters to be used as a foundation for setting property values. *See also* Responsible Citizens v. City of Asheville, 308 N.C. 255, 302 S.E.2d 204 (1983) (property owners should be allowed to testify as to value in action alleging floodplain regulations constituted a taking); Huff v. Thornton, 287 N.C. 1, 213 S.E.2d 198 (1975); Zagaroli v. Pollock, 94 N.C. App. 46, 379 S.E.2d 653, *review denied*, 325 N.C. 437, 384 S.E.2d 548 (1989) (allowing real-estate-developer testimony relative to property value); *Harding*, 170 N.C. App. 392, 612 S.E.2d 431 (allowing civil engineer to testify regarding noise impacts without being formally qualified as an expert).

81. 374 N.C. 133, 839 S.E.2d 755 (2020).

82. Property owners were at one time deemed competent to testify as to the value of their own property, particularly in land-condemnation cases. However, the court in *United Community Bank (Ga.) v. Wolfe*, 369 N.C. 555, 559–60, 799 S.E.2d 269, 272–73 (2017), held that although the landowner may be competent to testify as to value, the owner still must present competent, substantial evidence. The court applied this rule to the question of establishing property-value harm in order to establish standing in *Cherry Community Organization v. City of Charlotte*, 257 N.C. App. 579, 589, 809 S.E.2d 397, 404 (2018).

83. G.S. 160D-1402(j)(3). The provision that such objection is not necessary was added by S.L. 2019-111, § 1.9.

84. 139 N.C. App. 269, 276–79, 533 S.E.2d 525, 530–31, *review denied*, 353 N.C. 280, 546 S.E.2d 397 (2000).

85. 136 N.C. App. 114, 524 S.E.2d 46 (1999).

for a proposed mobile-home park testified that the park would be an eyesore and would bring crime and increased traffic to the area. The court characterized this testimony as generalized fears that park residents would be low-income residents who would constitute a danger to the neighborhood, concerns unsupported by competent evidence and thus invalid as grounds for permit denial.

By contrast, in *SBA, Inc. v. City of Asheville*,[86] the court upheld a board's conclusion that a cell tower would be inharmonious with a neighborhood when the decision was based not only on testimony of twelve neighbors that it would be an eyesore but also on a computer-generated photograph superimposing the proposed tower on a photograph of the existing neighborhood.

Ex Parte Evidence

Board members hearing quasi-judicial matters are members of the community in which these land use cases arise. They may well have personal knowledge about the site or a personal acquaintance with the parties. It is not uncommon for a board member to have had casual conversations about the case with staff, the applicant, or the neighbors prior to the hearing.[87] While the strict rules about ex parte communications that apply to the judiciary would prevent such contacts,[88] the courts have applied a rule of reason to ex parte communication in quasi-judicial proceedings.

While prior knowledge or modest communications prior to a hearing do not automatically disqualify a board member from participating in a case, a board member must not enter the hearing with a fixed opinion about the case, and the parties have a right to know all of the evidence being considered by the board. Undisclosed ex parte communications can evidence impermissible bias or rise to a level of unfairness that will lead to judicial invalidation of the decision.[89]

In addition to constitutional due-process considerations, the zoning statutes also mandate non-participation in such instances. G.S. 160D-109(d) provides that members of boards exercising quasi-judicial functions must not participate in or vote on any quasi-judicial matter if they have a fixed opinion prior to hearing the matter that is not susceptible to change or have undisclosed ex parte communications.

---

86. 141 N.C. App. 19, 539 S.E.2d 18 (2000). *See also Harding*, 170 N.C. App. 392, 612 S.E.2d 431 (allowing testimony of civil engineer regarding noise impacts where supporting reports were submitted, opportunities for cross-examination and rebuttal testimony were allowed, and no objections were made to the testimony).

87. Rule 3.5 of the Revised Rules of Professional Conduct of the North Carolina State Bar limits attorney contact with members of an adjudicative tribunal. Written communication with the board is limited to proposed orders, emergency or scheduling matters, communication made with the consent of the opposing party or attorney, and communication permitted by rule of the particular board involved. 98 Formal Ethics Op. 13 (July 23, 1999). In these limited instances, copies of the written communication are to be simultaneously shared with opposing counsel. Also see Rule 4.2(b) of the Revised Rules of Professional Conduct of the North Carolina State Bar, which in limited circumstances allows counsel to make oral presentations to elected officials (who may be serving as the decision-making board in a quasi-judicial zoning matter) in open session.

88. Canon 3(A)(4) of the Code of Judicial Conduct provides that a judge may "neither initiate nor consider" ex parte communications concerning a pending case except as authorized by law.

89. Crump v. Bd. of Educ., 326 N.C. 603, 392 S.E.2d 579 (1990). In S.L. 2013-264, the General Assembly repealed G.S. 160A-393 (regarding judicial review of quasi-judicial decisions) and 160A-377 (appeals of subdivision-plat decisions if they involve a quasi-judicial determination) for Apex. The stated purpose of the bill was to allow town board members to continue to communicate with residents on pending quasi-judicial matters. Of course, the constitutionally based prohibition on undisclosed ex parte communications in quasi-judicial decision-making continues to apply in Apex.

If a board member has prior or specialized knowledge about a case, that knowledge should be disclosed to the rest of the board and the parties during the hearing. In *Humble Oil*, the court noted that the special knowledge of board members could be considered if properly presented:

> If there be facts within the special knowledge of the members of a Board of Aldermen or acquired by their personal inspection of the premises, they are properly considered. However, they must be revealed at the public hearing and made a part of the record so that the applicant will have an opportunity to meet them by evidence or argument and the reviewing court may judge their competency and materiality.[90]

As with personal knowledge of the facts, the courts have long held that site visits by board members are permissible.[91] During the course of the hearing, board members should note any pertinent facts they discerned from the visit so as to allow all parties to know the basis of the decision and have the opportunity to present rebuttal information.[92]

Evidence submitted after the hearing may not be considered.[93] The offer to amend an application after a hearing in order to address concerns raised at the hearing does not constitute the introduction of new evidence, nor does the discussion of permit conditions with the applicant.[94] Allowing opponents of a project to reiterate their objections after the hearing has been closed can constitute the introduction of new evidence.[95] If evidence received after the hearing is not actually considered in making a decision, receipt in and of itself is not a due-process violation.[96]

It is important to note that the limitations on ex parte communication apply to contacts with the decision makers. It is common and legally permissible for applicants, neighbors, interested citizens, and the representatives of such persons to have contact with staff to the board outside of the hearing context.[97]

---

90. Humble Oil & Refin. Co. v. Bd. of Aldermen, 284 N.C. 458, 468, 202 S.E.2d 129, 136 (1974). The court noted in *PHG Asheville, LLC v. City of Asheville* that while the board "is, of course, entitled to rely upon the special knowledge of its members concerning conditions in the locality which they serve," only the knowledge that is relevant to the standards and requirements for the decision at hand may be used as the basis for its decision. 374 N.C. 133, 156, 839 S.E.2d 755, 770 (2020).

91. *See, e.g.*, Heffernan v. Zoning Bd. of Review, 50 R.I. 26, 144 A. 674 (1929).

92. *See, e.g.*, Buckminster v. Zoning Bd. of Review, 68 R.I. 515, 30 A.2d 104 (1943). With many boards, it is a standard practice for the chair to poll the board membership at the outset of the hearing as to any personal site visits (as well as inquiring of any conflicts of interest or personal bias).

93. Humble Oil & Refin. Co. v. Bd. of Aldermen, 286 N.C. 170, 209 S.E.2d 447 (1974); Ballas v. Town of Weaverville, 121 N.C. App. 346, 465 S.E.2d 324 (1996) (evidence submitted by town after the hearing regarding infrastructure improvements may not be considered).

94. *In re* Raynor, 94 N.C. App. 173, 379 S.E.2d 884, *review denied*, 325 N.C. 546, 385 S.E.2d 495 (1989).

95. Templeton Properties, LP v. Town of Boone, 219 N.C. App. 266, 724 S.E.2d 604 (2012). The court noted that hearing legal arguments is permissible but allowing witnesses from one side to reiterate their evidence and arguments is impermissible.

96. Howard v. City of Kinston, 148 N.C. App. 238, 244–45, 558 S.E.2d 221, 226 (2002).

97. A 2003 survey of variance practice in North Carolina indicated that staff in 81 percent of the state's jurisdictions provided information to applicants on variance standards, forms, and procedures; 66 percent provided information on alternatives to a variance; and 48 percent provided advice on the likelihood of obtaining a variance. David Owens & Adam Brueggemann, A Survey of Experience with Zoning Variances 13 (UNC School of Government, Special Series No. 18, Feb. 2004). A 2005 survey indicated even more staff contact with applicants for special and conditional use permits. Ninety-six percent of the jurisdictions provided information about permit standards and forms, 73 percent provided information about alternatives, and 61 percent provided advice on the likelihood of success in securing the permit. Owens, *supra* note 30, at 11. Such prehearing staff consultation and advice is common nationally. *See, e.g.*, Mun. Art Soc'y of N.Y., Zoning Variances and the New York City Board of Standards and Appeals 2 (2004) (noting prevalent pre-application-process advice and informal staff advice prior to formal decision-making).

Reopening Hearing to Receive New Evidence

The statutes on development regulations do not address the issue of whether and under what circumstances a hearing may be reopened to receive new evidence.

The comparable Rule of Civil Procedure provides that a new hearing can be granted if a motion for that is made within ten days of the entry of judgment and limits the grounds for doing so. G.S. 1A-1, Rule 59(a)(4), allows motions for a new hearing if newly discovered material evidence is found that the party making the motion could not have discovered with due diligence. Rule 60(b)(2) allows a judgment to be set aside on the same grounds. Similarly, the Administrative Procedures Act allows a court reviewing a contested case to remand a case for additional hearing, but only if the judge is satisfied that the additional evidence is not merely cumulative and could not reasonably have been presented at the original hearing.[98]

If new evidence is discovered after a quasi-judicial hearing, a party should generally petition the board that made the decision to reopen the case to take the new evidence. In *Bailey & Associates, Inc. v. Wilmington Board of Adjustment*,[99] the court indicated that this motion needs to be initially made and decided by the board making the decision, as otherwise the trial court would have no record on the issue on appeal.

G.S. 160D-1402(i) allows the trial court to take new evidence in very limited circumstances, such as when the record is not adequate to allow an appropriate determination of standing, or when there are alleged conflicts of interest, constitutional violations, or lack of statutory authority.

Local Procedural Standards

Where an individual ordinance sets additional standards for quasi-judicial procedures, they must be followed.[100]

Several zoning cases illustrate the application of this requirement. When an ordinance has a process for mandatory referral to the planning board before council action, that procedure cannot be ignored by the council.[101] If a board has a procedural rule that requires summary of the evidence by the chair with opportunities for parties to make objections or corrections, it is error not to provide that opportunity.[102] When the ordinance defines what constitutes a complete application, a board may not waive those requirements.[103] Likewise, when the ordinance sets a time period for appeals to a board of adjustment, the board has no authority to waive that deadline.[104] When the ordinance requires a rehearing to be denied if there has been no substantial change in the facts, the evidence, or the conditions in the case,

98. G.S. 150B-49.

99. 202 N.C. App. 177, 193, 689 S.E.2d 576, 588 (2010).

100. These local procedural standards are generally set forth in the locally adopted ordinance or development regulation. G.S. 160D-308 also authorizes each board to adopt rules of procedure.

101. Humble Oil & Refin. Co. v. Bd. of Aldermen, 284 N.C. 458, 202 S.E.2d 129 (1974).

102. Cardwell v. Forsyth Cnty. Zoning Bd. of Adjustment, 88 N.C. App. 244, 362 S.E.2d 843, *review denied*, 321 N.C. 742, 366 S.E.2d 858 (1987).

103. Wade v. Town of Ayden, 125 N.C. App. 650, 482 S.E.2d 44 (1997). Here the Ayden zoning ordinance required submission of "complete final plans." The applicant submitted a "sketch plan" that did not include utility, street, and other engineering data. The court held that the ordinance requirements were binding on the board and that the board had no authority to consider an incomplete application. *See also* Richardson v. Union Cnty. Bd. of Adjustment, 136 N.C. App. 134, 523 S.E.2d 432 (1999) (ordinance may grant some flexibility to administrator to accept more or less technical information than is specified for the application).

104. Water Tower Office Assocs. v. Town of Cary Bd. of Adjustment, 131 N.C. App. 696, 507 S.E.2d 589 (1998). Note that this case was decided prior to enactment of a statutory time limit for appeals to the board.

a board of adjustment may not take a case in the absence of those situations.[105] When the ordinance provides for final approval of a preliminary plat by the planning board and only the applicant is given a right of appeal to the board of commissioners, the board has no jurisdiction to hear an appeal of a plat approval made by the neighbors.[106]

If, however, the violation of the local rules is minor and does not prejudice a party, the courts will not set aside the decision. In *Durham Video & News, Inc. v. Durham Board of Adjustment*,[107] the local rules required distribution of the staff report to the petitioner ten days prior to the board hearing, but the report was in fact received two days prior to the hearing. However, the report contained only copies and summaries of information previously available to the petitioner. The court held that unless the petitioner could show some prejudice from the late receipt, no remand was needed.[108]

Record

A detailed record of the evidentiary hearing is required. Documents and physical evidence submitted at the hearing (including photographs, models, charts, and the like) should be retained and made a part of the record.

The routine summary minutes that are acceptable for legislative hearings and routine governmental meetings will not suffice. However, there is not a requirement that a verbatim transcript be prepared for each evidentiary hearing or that every hearing be recorded on tape.[109] While it is not mandated, courts strongly encourage the production of a verbatim transcript of the evidentiary hearing.[110] Thus, most boards make audiotapes of these hearings in case a transcript is desired later. The courts have observed that, while not strictly prohibited, use of a videotape of the hearing as a substitute for a written transcript is strongly discouraged.[111] However, handwritten records and detailed summaries of the testimony received are acceptable.[112]

G.S. 160D-1402(i) specifies the content of the record on appeal of quasi-judicial decisions. It provides that the record includes all documents and exhibits submitted to the board and the minutes of the meetings at which the matter was heard. Any party may request that the record include an audiotape or videotape of the meeting if that is available. Any party may also include a verbatim transcript of the

---

105. *In re* J.H. Carter Builder, Co., 95 N.C. App. 182, 381 S.E.2d 889, *review denied*, 325 N.C. 707, 388 S.E.2d 458 (1989). Also see the discussion of res judicata below in this chapter.

106. Sanco of Wilmington Serv. Corp. v. New Hanover Cnty., 166 N.C. App. 471, 601 S.E.2d 889 (2004). This was a ministerial rather than a quasi-judicial decision, but the jurisdictional issue is the same.

107. 144 N.C. 236, 350 S.E.2d 212, *review denied*, 354 N.C. 361, 556 S.E.2d 299 (2001).

108. The court reached a similar conclusion in *Charlotte Yacht Club, Inc. v. County of Mecklenburg*, 64 N.C. App. 477, 307 S.E.2d 595 (1983). The court held that affidavits regarding impacts on property value were improperly received after the hearing had been closed. The court was not mollified by affidavits from board members that the improperly received evidence was not considered. However, since the permit was denied on the grounds that the applicant had failed to meet the burden of production of evidence regarding a different standard, the error was held nonprejudicial.

109. Burton v. New Hanover Cnty. Bd. of Adjustment, 49 N.C. App. 439, 271 S.E.2d 550, *cert. denied*, 302 N.C. 217, 276 S.E.2d 914 (1981); Washington Park Neighborhood Ass'n v. Winston-Salem Bd. of Adjustment, 35 N.C. App. 449, 241 S.E.2d 872, *review denied*, 295 N.C. 91, 244 S.E.2d 263 (1978).

110. *In re* City of Raleigh (Parks & Recreation Dep't) v. City of Raleigh, 107 N.C. App. 505, 421 S.E.2d 174 (1992).

111. Howard v. City of Kinston, 148 N.C. App. 238, 242, 558 S.E.2d 221, 225 (2002); Shillington v. K-Mart Corp., 102 N.C. App. 187, 190, 402 S.E.2d 155, 157 (1991).

112. In *Piney Mountain Neighborhood Ass'n v. Town of Chapel Hill*, 63 N.C. App. 244, 304 S.E.2d 251 (1983), the court considered an ordinance requirement that the governing board review the record of the public hearing. The court held that this did not require a transcript, as members of the board were present for the hearing, had access to all documentary evidence, and were thus sufficiently familiar with the evidence to give it proper consideration.

meeting, with the cost of preparation of the transcript being the responsibility of the party choosing to include it.[113]

In *Fehrenbacher v. City of Durham*, the board of adjustment hearing on an appeal of the zoning administrator's interpretation was recorded, but a recording malfunction resulted in the first hour of the three-hour hearing being unrecorded. The plaintiffs contended the resultant inability to produce a transcript of this portion of the hearing, where they had presented evidence, resulted in an inadequate record for judicial review. However, the record included an affidavit prepared by the plaintiffs and copies of the photographs they submitted as evidence at the hearing. Since the plaintiffs failed to specifically identify any substantial evidence that was missing as a result of the recording malfunction, the court properly refused to remand the case for a new hearing.[114]

Making a Decision

Deliberation

Fifty years ago, it was not uncommon in many jurisdictions for a board of adjustment to take evidence in a hearing and to then retire to a jury room for private deliberations. That is no longer permissible. The entirety of a board's quasi-judicial hearing and deliberation must be conducted in open session. State law requires that every official meeting of a public body be open to the public.[115] The law does allow limited exceptions for closed sessions, but those will rarely arise in the context of making quasi-judicial decisions.

The exception to open sessions that is most often applied in a quasi-judicial context is a closed session to receive advice from the board's attorney that would be protected by the attorney-client privilege.[116]

---

113. See Chapter 29 for a more detailed discussion of judicial review of quasi-judicial decisions.

114. Fehrenbacher v. City of Durham, 239 N.C. App. 141, 768 S.E.2d 186 (2015). The court also noted that by its express terms, G.S. 160A-393(i) only requires that the record include an audiotape of the hearing "if such a recording was made." *Id.* at 149, 768 S.E.2d at 192.

115. G.S. 143-318.10(a). This law is discussed in detail in Frayda S. Bluestein and David M. Lawrence, Open Meetings and Local Governments in North Carolina: Some Questions and Answers (8th ed. 2017).

116. G.S. 143-318.11. In *Carolina Holdings, Inc. v. Housing Appeals Board*, 149 N.C. App. 579, 561 S.E.2d 541, *review denied*, 356 N.C. 298, 570 S.E.2d 499 (2002), the court held that the open-meetings law was not violated when the housing board went into executive session to discuss enforcement matters pertaining to an ongoing series of hearings regarding orders to repair or demolish dilapidated apartments. For a detailed discussion of this issue, see David M. Lawrence, *Closed Sessions Under the Attorney-Client Privilege*, Loc. Gov't L. Bull. No. 103 (UNC School of Government, Apr. 2002).

Impartiality

An impartial decision maker is required for quasi-judicial decisions.[117] A board member who has a financial interest in the decision; a close-family, business,[118] or associational[119] tie to a party; or a predetermined, fixed opinion that is not susceptible to change must not participate in that matter.[120]

The court has addressed this issue in a variety of contexts:

- It is not impermissible bias for board members to announce they intend to vote against a permit after the evidence has been presented in the hearing but before a vote is called and there is no evidence that these members had a fixed decision prior to the hearing.[121]
- Due process is not violated by the fact that city council members making a quasi-judicial decision on a special use permit for an amphitheater had previously participated in planning for this municipal venture and were generally enthusiastic about the project, as there was no evidence of impermissible bias (i.e., a fixed opinion that was not susceptible to change before the hearing).[122]
- The fact that a former planning-department staff member sits on the board of adjustment is not in and of itself a conflict if no evidence shows that the applicant was prejudiced by that member's participation.[123]
- The fact that a board member has a distant family relationship with a party is not per se a conflict.[124] Where the applicant for a special use permit application was married to the aunt of

117. G.S. 160D-109(d). This statute codifies the constitutional requirement for impartiality.

118. Courts in other states have generally held that a casual business relationship is not disqualifying. *See, e.g.,* Best v. La Plata Plan. Comm'n, 701 P.2d 91 (Colo. App. 1984) (fact that board member's former law firm represented developer does not create conflict); Taylor v. Town of Wakefield, 959 A.2d 217 (N.H. 2008) (fact that member of zoning board of adjustment was a former employee of former owner of lot involved in waiver request is not disqualifying). *But see* Mountain Hill, LLC. v. Twp. Comm. of Middletown, 958 A.2d 1 (N.J. Super. Ct. App. Div. 2008) (mayor disqualified because she owned a company that performed title-insurance work for developer while developer was acquiring land before submitting first of several applications for development permits; mayor had terminated business relationship four years earlier).

119. *See, e.g.,* Grabowsky v. Twp. of Montclair, 115 A.3d 815 (N.J. 2015) (when a church or other organization owns property near the site of a zoning application, public officials who currently serve in substantive leadership positions in the organization are disqualified).

120. Cnty. of Lancaster v. Mecklenburg Cnty., 334 N.C. 496, 434 S.E.2d 604 (1993). Also see the discussion of conflicts of interest in Chapter 25. This standard is also codified at G.S. 160D-109(d). *See also* A. FLEMING BELL, II, A MODEL CODE OF ETHICS FOR NORTH CAROLINA LOCAL ELECTED OFFICIALS (2010).

121. Vulcan Materials Co. v. Guilford Cnty. Bd. of Cnty. Comm'rs, 115 N.C. App. 319, 444 S.E.2d 639, *review denied*, 337 N.C. 807, 449 S.E.2d 758 (1994).

122. *In re* City of Raleigh (Parks & Recreation Dep't) v. City of Raleigh, 107 N.C. App. 505, 421 S.E.2d 179 (1992). The court reached a similar conclusion in *Lane Construction Corp. v. Town of Washington*, 2008 ME 45, 942 A.2d 1202, concluding that while the presiding officer of the board clearly did not personally support the application, there was no indication of impermissible bias. *See also* Sapp v. Yadkin Cnty., 209 N.C. App. 430, 704 S.E.2d 909 (2011). In this case, a challenge to the validity of a rezoning that allowed a new jail, the trial judge had previously issued an order to the county to show cause why a writ of mandamus should not issue regarding county provision of adequate jail facilities. The present court held that while the judge had expressed an interest in prompt resolution of the jail issue, there was no impermissible bias as there was no evidence he had any preference or opinion on the location of a new jail.

123. JWL Invs., Inc. v. Guilford Cnty. Bd. of Adjustment, 133 N.C. App. 426, 515 S.E.2d 715 (1999), *review denied*, 251 N.C. 357 (2000).

124. G.S. 160D-109(f) defines a close family relationship to be a spouse, parent, child, brother, sister, grandparent, or grandchild, including step, half, and in-law relationships.

a board member, the court held that the burden is on the party claiming bias to show some bias by the member or that the member stands to receive some benefit from the vote.[125]

- If a permit could not lawfully be issued due to noncompliance with an objective standard in the ordinance, the potential bias of a board member is irrelevant, as it could not have affected the outcome of the decision.[126]
- If a citizen who actively opposed a special use permit application is subsequently elected to the board, it is impermissible bias for that member to participate in deciding the case on remand.[127]

As a general rule, members with a bias or conflict of interest make that determination and recuse themselves. If the board making the decision is the governing board, a member with the bias or conflict generally requests that the entire board vote to approve the recusal.[128] For planning boards and boards of adjustment, the member may simply announce the recusal at the initiation of the matter. If a member does not initiate recusal and an objection to participation is raised, the remaining members rule on participation by majority vote.[129] If a party to the hearing believes there is a potential for inappropriate participation, it is permissible for the party to query the board for potential bias.[130] While an objection to participation is generally raised at the time of the hearing rather than initially on appeal, G.S. 160D-1402(i)(2) provides that a failure to object does not constitute a waiver of the right to claim an impermissible conflict on appeal.[131] G.S. 160D-1402(i) allows the hearing record on appeal to be supplemented with affidavits, testimony, or documentary evidence regarding potential impermissible conflicts of interest.[132]

---

125. Cox v. Hancock, 160 N.C. App. 473, 586 S.E.2d 500 (2003). *See also* Randolph v. City of Brigantine Plan. Bd., 963 A.2d 1224 (N.J. Super. Ct. App. Div. 2009) (test is whether relationship could reasonably be expected to impair member's objectivity or independence). In a legislative-decision context, the court in Thorne v. Zoning Comm'n, 423 A.2d 861 (Conn. 1979) held it was improper for board member to participate in consideration of rezoning where property affected was adjacent to homes of his parents and sister, and the member had previously expressed opposition to the proposed uses.

126. Rice Assocs. of S. Highlands, Inc. v. Town of Weaverville Zoning Bd. of Adjustment, 108 N.C. App. 346, 423 S.E.2d 519 (1992).

127. Dellinger v. Lincoln Cnty., 266 N.C. App. 275, 832 SE.2d 172 (2019). The case was subsequently remanded for further consideration in light of *PHG Asheville, LLC v. City of Asheville*, 374 N.C. 133, 839 S.E.2d 755 (2020). The court distinguished a citizen's general concerns about renewable energy (the application in question was for a solar farm) from opposition to a specific project.

128. G.S. 153A-44 and 160A-75, which address voting on legislative matters by county commissioners and city-council members, respectively, provide that "[n]o member shall be excused from voting except upon matters involving the consideration of his own financial interest or official conduct or on matters on which the member is prohibited from voting under G.S. 14-234 or G.S. 160D-109." G.S. 160A-75. The county version has a comparable cross-reference to the land use conflict-of-interest standards for legislative and quasi-judicial decisions.

129. G.S. 160D-109(e).

130. While a process similar to voir dire for prospective jurors is usually not available for review of board members making a quasi-judicial decision, a general inquiry of board members regarding ex parte communications and bias is appropriate. A party can make this inquiry. In many jurisdictions, the chair routinely makes such an inquiry as a standard procedure at the opening of each case.

131. This provision was added to the statutes by S.L. 2021-168, § 4. Prior to this statutory amendment, the court in *JWL Investments, Inc. v. Guilford County Board of Adjustment*, 133 N.C. App. 426, 515 S.E.2d 715 (1999), *review denied*, 251 N.C. 357 (2000), rejected a claim of improper participation where no objection was made at the hearing.

132. Prior to 2019, admission of supplemental evidence on conflicts of interest was at the court's discretion. Amendments were made by S.L. 2019-111, § 1.9, which requires the court to allow this supplemental evidence.

Given the requirement that members with a conflict not participate, the statutes make express provision for alternate members for boards of adjustment.[133] Alternate members may also serve in the absence of a member or to fill a vacancy on the board pending appointment of a replacement member. An alternate member has the same powers and rights as a regular member when actively serving at a meeting. If an alternate member is present at a quasi-judicial hearing but not serving in place of a regular member, the alternate member should simply observe rather than actively participate in the hearing or discussion of the case.[134]

Change in Board Membership

A board's vote on a quasi-judicial decision is not invalidated by the change in membership of one member between the time of the hearing and the vote if the new member has complete access to the minutes and records from the hearing.[135] A new board member who has been furnished a copy of the full record prior to the vote is eligible to vote,[136] as are members who did not attend an initial hearing on the matter but did attend a second hearing and had full access to the minutes and exhibits from the initial hearing.[137]

Several local governments have secured local legislation (and others have internal rules of procedure) that limits participation in voting on quasi-judicial matters to those members who actually attend the full hearing on the matter.[138] Where such a local rule exists, it is binding.

Voting

Formal action by the board is required for a quasi-judicial decision. This action is generally taken by a vote of the board to grant or deny the application. In *Meares v. Town of Beaufort*,[139] the court held that a letter from the board's attorney notifying the applicant that his application was not being processed due to a prior application on the site still being under appeal does not constitute a decision of the board.

---

133. G.S. 160A-388(a). The mandated supermajority discussed below also affects the need to have a full complement of voting members present for each meeting, further supporting the need for alternate members. *See generally* Patricia E. Salkin, *Planning for Conflicts of Interest in Land Use Decisionmaking: The Use of Alternate Members of Planning and Zoning Boards*, 31 REAL EST. L.J. 375 (2003); Patricia E. Salkin, *Providing for Alternate Members on Planning and Zoning Boards: Drafting Effective Local Laws*, PLAN. & ENVTL. L., Aug. 2009, at 3.

134. *See, e.g.*, Komondy v. Zoning Bd. of Appeals, 127 Conn. App. 669, 16 A.3d 741 (2011). The court allowed an alternate member to participate in the hearing of a variance and appeal of a zoning administrator's determination but held that it was inappropriate for an unseated alternate to participate in the board's deliberations. The court analogized the unseated alternate to an alternate juror who is segregated from the regular panel once a jury begins its deliberations in a civil or criminal case.

135. Brannock v. Zoning Bd. of Adjustment, 260 N.C. 426, 132 S.E.2d 758 (1963).

136. Dellinger v. Lincoln Cnty., 248 N.C. App. 317, 789 S.E.2d 21, *review denied*, 369 N.C. 190, 794 S.E.2d 324 (2016); Baker v. Town of Rose Hill, 126 N.C. App. 338, 485 S.E.2d 78 (1997).

137. Cox v. Hancock, 160 N.C. App. 473, 586 S.E.2d 500 (2003).

138. This may be particularly important where controverted facts are involved. As the court noted in reviewing a quasi-judicial administrative decision in a nonzoning context, "The duty to weigh evidence and find the facts is lodged in the agency that hears the witnesses and observes their demeanor as they testify . . . ." Freeman v. Bd. of Alcoholic Control, 264 N.C. 320, 323, 141 S.E.2d 499, 501 (1965). *See* Howard Cnty. v. Bay Harvestore Sys., 60 Md. App. 19, 478 A.2d 1172 (1984) (zoning board members not present at hearing may not participate in decision).

139. 193 N.C. App. 49, 58, 667 S.E.2d 244, 251 (2008).

All matters other than a variance decision are determined by a simple majority of the board.[140] A four-fifths majority of the board is required to issue a variance.[141] The required majority is calculated based on the entire number of members of the board, rather than just the number of members of the board present and voting on a particular matter. G.S. 160D-406(i) says the majority for a variance is "four-fifths *of the board*," and the majority for other matters is a "majority *of the members*."[142]

However, there are at least four different contexts in which less than the full complement of a board's membership is voting on a particular matter, and there are different legal consequences in calculating the requisite majority depending on which of these contexts is involved. First, a member may be absent. Second, a member may be present but voluntarily not voting. Third, a member may be present but legally required to abstain (as when the member has a conflict of interest). Fourth, a seat may be vacant. In the first two situations, members who are absent or voluntarily not voting are still "members" of the board, so those seats are included in the computation. In 2005, the General Assembly amended G.S. 160D-406(i) to provide that vacant seats and members who are disqualified from voting on a quasi-judicial matter are not considered "members of the board" for purposes of the vote computation if there are no qualified alternate members available to take the place of such members.[143] By implication, this confirms that the seats of absent members and members who are present but do not vote are included in the computation.

When a vote is taken on a quasi-judicial matter, the minutes should clearly indicate not only the vote total but also how each individual member voted.

140. Osborne v. Town of Nags Head, 235 N.C. App. 121, 760 S.E.2d 766 (2014). The court held that a motion to reconsider a prior variance decision is decided by a simple majority even though the variance itself requires a four-fifths majority to be granted. In this case, since the motion to reconsider did not receive a majority vote, the board had no jurisdiction to hear the variance petition. In *Pope v. Davidson County*, ___ N.C. App. ___, 885 S.E.2d 119 (2023), the board held that all four standards for a special use permit had been met. However, the vote on one of the standards was 3-2 in the affirmative. The board incorrectly believed that a four-fifths vote was required for each standard, so the matter was tabled until the board's next meeting. At the following meeting, the board voted to rescind their prior votes and reconsider the matter. The court held that the initial affirmative simple-majority vote that each standard had been met had the effect of issuing the permit, rendering the subsequent reconsideration an error of law.

141. G.S. 160D-406(i) (emphasis added). Before 2013, the statute also required a four-fifths vote to overturn a determination by the staff. The four-fifths requirement to reverse or modify an officer's order is still required for appeals of housing-code-enforcement issues to a housing appeals board. G.S. 160D-1208(b).

The requirement for a supermajority was imposed on the board of adjustment in the original New York City zoning ordinance that served as the national model for zoning in the United States. There, the requirement was for a five-sevenths vote to grant a variance or reverse an administrator's determination. EDWARD M. BASSETT, ZONING 119 (2d ed. 1940). Several local governments have secured local legislation to modify the four-fifths-vote requirement. These include Durham, Mecklenburg, and Union counties and the cities of Charlotte, Hendersonville, New Bern, and Wilmington.

142. G.S. 160D-406(i) (emphasis added). The statute goes on to provide that where no vote from a seat is possible because the seat is vacant or the member is not eligible to participate due to a conflict of interest, that seat is not counted in the computation. The court in *Gaudenzia, Inc. v. Zoning Board of Adjustment*, 4 Pa. Commw. 355, 287 A.2d 698 (1972), held that requiring a majority of the entire board, including absent members, was not a due-process violation.

143. S.L. 2005-418, §§ 8(a), (b). On rare occasions, all or most of the members of a board may have a conflict of interest, leaving an insufficient number of members who are eligible to vote to resolve the matter. The statutes do not address this potentiality. It may be that in that circumstance a rule of necessity would allow the conflicted members to vote. *See, e.g.,* Lake v. State Health Plan for Teachers and State Employees, 379 N.C. 162, 861 S.E.2d 335 (2021) (applying Rule of Necessity when majority of members of the supreme court might have relatives in the plaintiff class).

Decisions

G.S. 160D-406(j) provides that decisions must be in writing and must reflect the board's determination of contested facts and their application to the applicable standards. It also provides that the decision must be made in a reasonable time and must be signed by the chair or another authorized member.

Some city and county boards ask the parties or the staff to prepare draft decisions prior to the hearing. These are often referred to as "proposed findings of fact and conclusions of law." Having such a draft is legally permissible, but it is not required. Draft decisions are often a helpful forecast of evidence expected to be in the hearing record. They allow board members to assess during the hearing whether or not the evidence presented supports the proposed factual findings and decision. These draft decisions can then be discussed, amended, and adopted after the evidentiary hearing.

If a draft-decision document has not been submitted in advance, a written-decision document should be prepared immediately after the meeting. It is not practical for the oral motion made at the meeting to be adequate for these purposes. Rather, the staff or the board's attorney usually prepares a draft decision that accurately reflects the action taken by the board. A few local governments offer the prevailing party the opportunity to draft the decision document, as is often done in court proceedings, while in other instances the board chair drafts the document.

When the decision document is complete, the chair of the board reviews it to verify that it accurately reflects the board's decision. After any needed edits are made, the chair (or other authorized member of the board) approves and signs the document. The statute is ambiguous as to whether a second vote is needed on the decision document itself if there was not a written document to approve at the time of the initial vote on the substantive decision. G.S. 160D-406(j) provides, "Each quasi-judicial decision shall be reduced to writing, reflect the board's determination of contested facts and their application to the applicable standards, and be approved by the board and signed by the chair or other duly authorized member of the board." Some local governments take the phrase "be approved by the board" to mean that the substantive decision on the findings of fact and resolution of the case must be approved by the board, which is done in the vote on the substance of the decision. Thereafter, the decision document is prepared, reviewed by the chair to assure it accurately reflects the decision made, and filed after signature by the chair without an additional vote of the board. Other local governments take that phrase to mean that not only must the substantive decision be approved by vote of the board, but the formal written document that memorializes that decision must also be approved by the board. In those jurisdictions, a second board vote is made on approval of the written-decision document.

The decision is effective when it is filed with the clerk to the board or other official specified by the ordinance. The decision is to be delivered prior to its effective date to the applicant, the property owner, and any other person who has submitted a written request for a copy of the decision. The decision can be delivered by personal delivery, electronic mail, or first-class mail. The person required to make delivery is to certify that proper notice of the decision has been made.[144] It is important to note that although the decision is effective when it is filed, the time period for making an appeal to court does not start until the date the decision is filed or the date it is delivered, whichever is later.

---

144. A letter or other decision document needs to be prepared for each quasi-judicial decision. Before 2013, many boards did not officially approve the written findings until the minutes of the meeting at which the decision was made were approved. Cary Creek Ltd. P'ship v. Town of Cary, 207 N.C. App. 339, 700 S.E.2d 80, *review denied*, 365 N.C. 193, 707 S.E.2d 241 (2010) (holding eight-paragraph set of findings included in board minutes sufficient). A 2003 survey of board practices regarding adoption of findings for zoning-variance decisions indicated that about half of North Carolina boards adopted their findings as a part of the minutes of the meeting. OWENS & BRUEGGEMANN, *supra* note 97, at 15. A 2005 survey indicated the same pattern for preparation of findings on special and conditional use permits. OWENS, *supra* note 30, at 16. For an example of minutes that inadequately set forth the grounds for denial of a special use permit, see *Motorsports Holdings, LLC v. Town of Tamworth*, 160 N.H. 95, 993 A.2d 189 (2010).

Findings of Fact

A board making a quasi-judicial decision must explicitly set forth what it determines to be the essential facts on which its decision is based.[145] It is this set of key facts that must be supported by substantial, competent, and material evidence in the hearing record.

This requirement is sometimes subject to semantic confusion. It is not uncommon for a zoning ordinance to state that a special use permit or variance may be issued upon the board's "finding" that specified standards have been met. This has led some to label their conclusions regarding the standards as the board's "findings." These conclusions, however, are not the findings of fact required.[146]

The findings regarding contested facts that are adopted by the board must be sufficiently detailed to inform the parties and a reviewing court as to what induced the decision.[147] Use of a preprinted form with only a notation that the standards are or are not met is insufficient.[148] A conclusory statement that a standard has or has not been met is similarly insufficient,[149] as is a mere recitation of testimony received about a particular standard.[150] A finding may not be based solely on an unsupported assertion in the hearing that the standard has or has not been met.[151]

Findings of fact are required for permit or variance denials as well as for affirmative decisions.[152] However, a board's failure to make any factual findings does not necessitate a remand where there is no dispute as to material facts and a full understanding of the issues was presented by the record.[153] Also, an exception to the requirement for written findings of fact exists where the board dismisses an action

---

145. Ballas v. Town of Weaverville, 121 N.C. App. 346, 465 S.E.2d 324 (1996). This contrasts with legislative zoning decisions, where no findings are required. Before the revision of G.S. 160D-406 in 2013, case law had held that a formal order with findings of fact and conclusions of law was not required if the transcript and record made the board's determinations and conclusions clear. Sanchez v. Town of Beaufort, 211 N.C. App. 547, 710 S.E.2d 350, *review denied*, 365 N.C. 349, 718 S.E.2d 152 (2011).

146. The court has emphasized that labeling a determination as "findings" or "conclusions of law" does not establish whether what is actually being done is a determination of contested facts or an application of legal principles or standards to those facts. *See, e.g.*, China Grove 152, LLC v. Town of China Grove, 242 N.C. App. 1, 5–6, 773 S.E.2d 566, 569 (2015) (discussing differing standard for judicial review depending on nature of decision being reviewed).

147. This requirement was stated by Justice Sharp in *Humble Oil*: "Equally important is the requirement that in each instance the board . . . in allowing or denying the application, . . . state the basic facts on which it relied with sufficient specificity to inform the parties, as well as the court, what induced its decision." 284 N.C. 458, 471, 202 S.E.2d 129, 138.

148. Shoney's of Enka, Inc. v. Bd. of Adjustment, 119 N.C. App. 420, 458 S.E.2d 510 (1995); Cardwell v. Forsyth Cnty. Zoning Bd. of Adjustment, 88 N.C. App. 244, 362 S.E.2d 843, *review denied*, 321 N.C. 742, 366 S.E.2d 858 (1987). *See also* Ward v. Inscoe, 166 N.C. App. 586, 603 S.E.2d 393 (2004) (court had previously remanded decision on conditional use permit where board had merely recited the standards for approval rather than making required findings). The court in *Ward* held that when a board meets at a regularly scheduled time solely for the purpose of adopting findings on a conditional use permit, the parties have no constitutional right to receive personal notice, to present new evidence, or to rebut previously submitted evidence. *But see* Piney Mountain Neighborhood Ass'n v. Town of Chapel Hill, 63 N.C. App. 244, 304 S.E.2d 251 (1983) (upholding decision where findings simply repeated the requisite findings in the ordinance).

149. Premier Plastic Surgery Ctr., PLLC v. Bd. of Adjustment, 213 N.C. App. 364, 713 S.E.2d 511 (2011); Clark v. City of Asheboro, 136 N.C. App. 114, 123, 524 S.E.2d 46, 52 (1999).

150. Welter v. Rowan Cnty. Bd. of Comm'rs, 160 N.C. App. 358, 365–66, 585 S.E.2d 472, 478 (2003).

151. Showcase Realty & Constr. Co. v. City of Fayetteville Bd. of Adjustment, 155 N.C. App. 548, 573 S.E.2d 737 (2002) (holding a variance petitioner cannot simply state that reasonable use of the property cannot be made without a variance; rather, substantial evidence to support that conclusion must be presented).

152. Crist v. City of Jacksonville, 131 N.C. App. 404, 507 S.E.2d 899 (1998) (remanding case where board made no findings for denial of variance).

153. Dockside Discotheque, Inc. v. Bd. of Adjustment, 115 N.C. App. 303, 444 S.E.2d 451, *review denied*, 338 N.C. 309, 451 S.E.2d 635 (1994). See the discussion of disposition of cases on appeal in Chapter 29.

due to lack of legal authority to hear it, as where a use variance has been requested.[154] In such instances factual findings are not needed because the board has no authority to act, regardless of the facts.

Conclusions on Standards

In addition to setting out the factual basis for its decision, a board making a quasi-judicial decision must explicitly state its conclusions as to whether the applicable standards have been met, with a clear indication why that is the case. Only factors explicitly set out as the standards for decision may be considered in making a quasi-judicial decision.[155]

When multiple cases are being heard at a single hearing, it is permissible to read each of the required conclusions into the record at the beginning of the hearing. Thereafter, motions on individual permits can incorporate by reference the findings that were previously noted.[156]

Where multiple standards are involved, as is the usual case, the board should clearly indicate its conclusions regarding all of the applicable standards. To ensure clarity on this point, some boards vote sequentially on each standard, but a single vote is permissible so long as it is clear which standards it encompasses.

Baker v. Town of Rose Hill[157] illustrates the need to address each required standard. The board there originally set out its conclusions on five of the seven standards in the zoning ordinance for conditional use permits but did not explicitly address two of the applicable standards—(1) that the use should not impair the integrity or character of surrounding properties or adversely affect the safety, health, and morals of the community, and (2) that the use was essential or desirable to the public convenience or welfare—on the advice of counsel that these standards were too subjective in nature. The trial court remanded for a statement of the board's conclusions (based on the original hearing record) regarding these two additional standards.

While a written statement of the findings of fact and conclusions regarding the standards is required, there is not a requirement that the statement be adopted at the close of the hearing unless that is specifically required by the local ordinance.[158] A written statement that supports a permit decision may be included with the formal permit decision rather than being adopted at the conclusion of the hearing.[159] Due process was found not to have been violated by the fact that neither the minutes nor a transcript of the hearing had been completed when the council voted on the matter at issue a week after the hearing.[160]

---

154. Donnelly v. Bd. of Adjustment, 99 N.C. App. 702, 708, 394 S.E.2d 246, 250 (1990); Sherrill v. Town of Wrightsville Beach, 76 N.C. App. 646, 648, 334 S.E.2d 103, 104 (1985).

155. *See, e.g.*, Knight v. Town of Knightdale, 164 N.C. App. 766, 596 S.E.2d 881 (2004) (holding that town council improperly considered property-value impacts when site-plan-approval criteria listed only physical impact of proposed development as factors for decision); Nazziola v. Landcraft Props., Inc., 143 N.C. App. 564, 545 S.E.2d 801 (2001) (applying rule to subdivision-plat approvals); C.C. & J. Enters., Inc. v. City of Asheville, 132 N.C. App. 550, 512 S.E.2d 766 (1999) (applying rule to special use permit decision). *See also* Nw. Fin. Group, Inc. v. Cnty. of Gaston, 329 N.C. 180, 190, 405 S.E.2d 138, 144 (1991) (holding that approvals under mobile-home-park ordinance must be based on standards in ordinance, not on general concern about public welfare).

156. Washington Park Neighborhood Ass'n v. Winston-Salem Bd. of Adjustment, 35 N.C. App. 449, 241 S.E.2d 872, *review denied*, 295 N.C. 91, 244 S.E.2d 263 (1978).

157. 126 N.C. App. 338, 485 S.E.2d 78 (1997). The case involved an appeal of the issuance of a conditional use permit by the town board for a soybean-meal transfer facility.

158. Rauseo v. New Hanover Cnty., 118 N.C. App. 286, 454 S.E.2d 698 (1995).

159. Richardson v. Union Cnty. Bd. of Adjustment, 136 N.C. App. 134, 523 S.E.2d 432 (1999); AT&T Wireless PCS, Inc. v. Winston-Salem Zoning Bd. of Adjustment, 172 F.3d 407 (4th Cir. 1999).

160. Piney Mountain Neighborhood Ass'n v. Town of Chapel Hill, 63 N.C. App. 244, 304 S.E.2d 251 (1983).

Conditions

Appropriate individualized conditions or limitations are often imposed on quasi-judicial decisions. The statutes expressly authorize imposition of conditions on special use permits and variances. "Reasonable and appropriate conditions and safeguards" may be imposed on special use permits.[161] "Appropriate conditions" may be imposed on any variance.[162]

A 2005 survey of North Carolina local governments indicated that 89 percent of those cities and counties using special and conditional use permits at least occasionally impose conditions on individual permit approvals (and 61 percent do so frequently).[163] For example, a special use permit or variance may include site-specific limitations that were not part of the application, such as a specification of a driveway's location to prevent traffic problems or the installation of a buffer to minimize adverse impacts on neighboring property. The court in *Overton v. Camden County* (*Overton I*) noted that "[a] court will normally defer to a board of adjustment so long as a condition is reasonably related to the proposed use, does not conflict with the zoning ordinance, and furthers a legitimate objective of the zoning ordinance."[164]

It is permissible for these conditions to require adherence to other relevant regulations, including those related to securing subsequent permits or approvals. For example, it would not be uncommon to include a condition that specified state or federal permits be secured prior to the initiation of work. In *Mangum v. Raleigh Board of Adjustment*, the court upheld a board's special use permit decision that required the applicant to submit a plat showing compliance with parking requirements and to "meet all stormwater runoff, landscape, and parking requirements" before issuance of the special use permit.[165] The permit that was subsequently issued was expressly contingent upon approval of plans. The court held that this type of provisional approval was not an unlawful delegation of the board's authority, noting that there is often a "necessary interplay" between a special use permit and other governmental approvals, both in permit issuance and assurance of compliance.

It is critical, however, that the conditions be limited to those authorized by the ordinance or statute.[166] The enabling statutes provide that special use permits may be issued "in accordance with the

---

161. G.S. 160D-705(c).

162. G.S. 160D-705(d).

163. Owens, *supra* note 30, at 17. An early zoning case from New York noted, "The power to impose reasonable conditions in making exceptions under the zoning ordinance is inherent in the board." Hopkins v. Bd. of Appeals, 179 N.Y. Misc. 325, 333, 39 N.Y.S.2d 167, 175 (Sup. Ct. 1942). The early zoning cases generally held that such conditions must be reasonable. *See, e.g.,* Selligman v. W. & S. Life Ins., 277 Ky. 551, 126 S.W.2d 419 (1948). *See generally* Bassett, *supra* note 141, at 128–31 (discussing imposition of conditions on variances).

164. Overton v. Camden Cnty. (*Overton I*), 155 N.C. App. 100, 104, 574 S.E.2d 150, 153 (2002). The court reached the same conclusion in a companion case with the same parties. Overton v. Camden Cnty. (*Overton II*), 155 N.C. App. 391, 398–99, 574 S.E.2d 157, 162–63 (2002). *See also* Bernstein v. Bd. of Appeals, 60 Misc. 2d 470, 473–74, 302 N.Y.2d 141, 146 (Sup. Ct. 1969) (cited by the *Overton* court to the same effect). See Chapter 29 for additional discussion of the issue of deference in judicial review.

165. 196 N.C. App. 249, 257, 674 S.E.2d 742, 748–49 (2009). The court also noted that the board "retains the authority to review, amend, or withdraw the special use permit to assure that the mandates of the Code and the Board of Adjustment's own limiting conditions are being met" during and after construction of the project. *Id.* at 258, 674 S.E.2d at 749.

166. Nw. Prop. Group, LLC v. Town of Carrboro, 201 N.C. App. 449, 687 S.E.2d 1 (2009). The case involved a somewhat unusual decision-making process that was mandated by the ordinance. The ordinance was structured to require the town council to make three votes on the application, determining successively that the application was complete, that it complied with all applicable portions of the ordinance, and that specified conditions were to be applied. The plaintiff contended that conditions could be imposed only if the second of these motions (that the application complied with the ordinance) failed, so conditions could be imposed only to bring the project into compliance with the ordinance. While the dissent accepted this interpretation of the ordinance, the majority held that the ordinance contemplated successive votes and that conditions consistent with the standards for conditions set out in the ordinance could be imposed even with approval of the second motion.

principles, conditions, safeguards, and procedures" specified in the ordinance.[167] In *Hewett v. County of Brunswick*, the court invalidated conditions that were imposed without reference to standards clearly set out in the ordinance. The board had invalidated a permit because the application had modified the originally approved project. However, the ordinance did not have a standard to that effect.[168] Likewise, in *Overton I*,[169] the court held that it was unlawful to impose conditions on a special use permit that required termination of a nonconforming use on a separate property or required alteration of a different special use permit previously issued to a third party. In *Stegall v. Zoning Board of Adjustment*,[170] the court held that conditions imposed on a special use permit could not be enforced because a special use permit was not actually required for the proposed use. Even though the permittee had not appealed the conditions, since the permit only authorized what the applicant already had a right to do, the applicant had not secured any benefit from the permit and was therefore not bound by its terms.

A common example of a condition imposed in a quasi-judicial proceeding would be a condition that requires changes in the project proposal that are necessary to bring the project into compliance with the standards for decision that are in the statute or ordinance. If modifications are needed to bring the project into compliance with ordinance standards, and if there is substantial, competent, and material evidence to support that conclusion, appropriate limiting conditions may be imposed. The court held that this situation applied in *Overton II*,[171] where it upheld imposition of conditions on a permit for replacement of a manufactured-housing unit as reasonable and appropriate.[172]

Each condition that is imposed must be supported by adequate evidence in the record.[173] In *Northwest Property Group, LLC v. Town of Carrboro*, the court invalidated a permit condition that limited use of a side-street access to a commercial project to emergency vehicles only. Although neighbors had expressed concerns about traffic impacts at the hearing, the board made no findings justifying the imposition of such a condition.[174]

Process for Modification or Revocation

The process to modify a decision is addressed by G.S. 160D-705(c).[175] This statute allows local governments the option of approving minor modifications of quasi-judicial decisions administratively. To do so, the zoning regulation must define a "minor modification," which may not include a change in permitted

---

167. G.S. 160D-705(c).

168. 155 N.C. App. 138, 573 S.E.2d 688 (2002). The court noted that civil and criminal penalties were available to address alleged violations of the terms of the permit (such as unauthorized amendment of the project), but there was no standard in the ordinance relative to permit revocation.

169. 155 N.C. App. 100, 574 S.E.2d 150.

170. 87 N.C. App. 359, 361 S.E.2d 309 (1987), *review denied*, 321 N.C. 480, 364 S.E.2d 679 (1988).

171. 155 N.C. App. 391, 574 S.E.2d 157.

172. The conditions were: (1) the unit must be inspected for code compliance, (2) the unit must be inhabited by one individual, (3) the unit must not be vacated for more than sixty days, (4) the unit must be kept in a condition that conforms to the standards for that area, and (5) the unit must have been constructed after 1976. The court held that all of the conditions would further the purposes of the ordinance and that all of them related to the use of the property.

173. See, e.g., the discussion of the necessity for supporting evidence for a condition in *Ward*, 166 N.C. App. 586, 603 S.E.2d 393 (2004).

174. 201 N.C. App. 449, 687 S.E.2d 1 (2009). Given the absence of any findings on this point, the court remanded the case to the town council for reconsideration and adoption of findings to support any conditions that they might impose in that reconsideration. The dissent contended that there was no substantial, competent, material evidence in the record to support the contested condition, so the remand should have been to issue the permit without the contested condition.

175. This provision was added by S.L. 2019-111.

uses or in the overall density of the development. Once defined, qualified applications may be approved by the staff without the necessity of going through the quasi-judicial process. If multiple parcels of land are included within a special use permit, then the permit may be modified for individual parcels at the request of the owners of those parcels. Any other modification or any revocation of a quasi-judicial decision must follow the same procedure used for initial approval.

If a permittee requests to modify a permit condition that has been imposed, the board must review the proposed modification under the applicable standards. If the applicant presents evidence to show the proposed modification is an acceptable, satisfactory alternative to meeting those standards and requirements, it would be arbitrary and capricious to summarily deny the modification request.[176]

Impact of Decisions

Precedent

Each quasi-judicial case is a unique case that must be decided on its own merits. The general rule is that prior decisions are not legally binding on a board.[177] However, similar cases should generally produce similar results, and it is incumbent on a board to know how and why prior cases have been decided.

Where cases with very similar facts have differing results, the board must adopt findings that explain those results and why they are not arbitrary or capricious. In *Through the Looking Glass, Inc. v. Zoning Board of Adjustment*,[178] the petitioner acquired a house located on a cul-de-sac that had previously been used as a residence and floral shop. The petitioner intended to use the structure for an office for an antique business; however, office uses in this zone required a buffer and side-yard setback for the driveway that could not be met. So a variance was requested to allow continued use of a driveway. One year earlier, the board had granted a variance to the same buffer and side-yard requirements for an essentially identical lot directly across the street from the lot involved in this litigation. The court held that while a board is not required to grant a variance just because a similar variance had previously been granted in the same district, where the fact situations are the same, the result should be the same. The court remanded the case to the board for further proceedings since there were insufficient findings in the board's decision to determine why the essentially identical situations produced different outcomes.

---

176. Orange Cnty. v. Town of Hillsborough, 219 N.C. App. 127, 724 S.E.2d 560 (2012). The county secured a special use permit for an expansion of the courthouse complex. There was inadequate space on the site for the required parking, so a permit condition specified provision of parking at a remote site. The county later submitted a proposed modification to the parking-permit condition, which the town rejected. The court held that the failure to approve an acceptable alternative, with no evidentiary support of the rejections, was arbitrary and capricious.

177. *See, e.g.*, Mastroianni v. Bd. of Zoning Appeals, 36 Misc. 2d 343, 235 N.Y.S.2d 213 (N.Y. 1961) (not an abuse of discretion to deny a variance where previous applications for similar variances were granted); Hendrix v. Bd. of Zoning Appeals, 222 Va. 57, 278 S.E.2d 814 (1981) (granting variance for off-street parking to one restaurant does not require that variance be granted upon similar request).

178. 136 N.C. App. 212, 523 S.E.2d 444 (1999). A board of adjustment "passes on individual cases, of course, but each case is determined in the contemplation of the statute and the ordinance by a uniform rule." Harden v. City of Raleigh, 192 N.C. 395, 397, 135 S.E. 151, 152 (1926).

Res Judicata

Res judicata[179] applies to quasi-judicial land use decisions. Courts have long held that a board may not rehear a quasi-judicial matter previously decided.[180] This is occasionally a source of confusion with zoning ordinances, as it is not altogether uncommon to confuse rehearing a quasi-judicial matter with rehearing a legislative matter. For example, the ordinance may include a provision that a special use permit application may be resubmitted for reconsideration after a one-year waiting period, much as a rezoning petition can be resubmitted. This, however, is not permissible, as res judicata applies to the original decision and the board has no jurisdiction to rehear the same matter.

An applicant may always submit an amended application or may resubmit if there has been a material change in the ordinance standards.[181] Also, if there has been a material change in conditions, such as a new road being constructed at the site or additional development near the site over time, res judicata does not apply.[182]

While the question of whether res judicata applies is a question of law, whether the change is sufficient to preclude application of res judicata is a question of fact reviewed under a whole-record test on judicial review. A critical factor in this review is whether the change materially affects the reasons that supported the original decision such that the application can no longer be characterized as the same claim. In *Mount Ulla Historical Preservation Society, Inc. v. Rowan County*,[183] the court applied this test to hold that the board had no jurisdiction to consider an application for a special use permit for a 1200-foot radio tower on the site where a special use permit application for a 1350-foot radio tower had been denied five years earlier. While the board making the decision deemed the 150-foot lowering of the proposed tower to be a substantial change, the court found the record had no evidence to show how this would change the reasoning regarding safety impacts for air travel that was applied in the earlier decision.[184]

Appeals of quasi-judicial decisions go directly to superior court.[185] It is not appropriate to seek a second evidentiary hearing before a different local board, such as appealing a board of adjustment's decision

---

179. Literally, "a thing adjudicated." *Res judicata*, BLACK'S LAW DICTIONARY (10th ed. 2014). Res judicata is an affirmative defense to suit made up of three elements: "(1) an earlier decision on the issue, (2) a final judgment on the merits, and (3) the involvement of the same parties, or parties in privity with the original parties." *Id.*

180. Little v. City of Raleigh, 195 N.C. 793, 795, 143 S.E. 827, 828 (1928); *In re* J.H. Carter Builder, Co., 95 N.C. App. 182, 381 S.E.2d 889, *review denied*, 325 N.C. 707, 388 S.E.2d 458 (1989).

181. The fact that an initial application is still on appeal does not in and of itself preclude submission and consideration of a second application for a modified project on the same site. Meares v. Town of Beaufort, 193 N.C. App. 49, 60, 667 S.E.2d 244, 252 (2008). It may be possible for an ordinance to impose such a limitation, but it will not be applied by the courts unless the limitation is expressly and clearly included in the ordinance. In *Meares*, the court refused to find that submission of a second but different application on the same site while the initial application was pending violated public policy.

182. *In re* Broughton Estate, 210 N.C. 62, 185 S.E. 434 (1936).

183. 252 N.C. App. 436, 754 S.E.2d 237 (2014).

184. The court concluded that the whole record revealed the board "essentially considered the same information in both the 2005 and 2010 CUP applications and reached different decisions. *Res judicata* forbids such a result." *Id.* at 443, 754 S.E.2d at 243.

185. G.S. 160D-1402. See Chapter 29 for details on judicial review. G.S. 160D-405(d), -406(k), and -1405(d) provide that appeals to superior court must be made within thirty days of the later of (1) the effective date of the decision, which is when the written decision is filed with the clerk to the board or other official designated by the ordinance, or (2) after a written copy of the decision is provided to the property owner, the applicant, and any person who has submitted a written request for a copy prior to the effective date of the decision. When first-class mail is used to deliver the decision, three days is added to the time to file a petition for review. The time periods for filing an appeal are strictly enforced. McCrann v. Vill. of Pinehurst, 216 N.C. App. 291, 716 S.E.2d 667 (2011) (dismissing an appeal filed one day late).

to the governing board or vice versa.[186] In *Garrity v. Morrisville Board of Adjustment*,[187] the governing board approved a site plan for a regional solid-waste facility. Neighbors petitioned the board of adjustment for an "interpretation and administrative review" of the governing-board approval,[188] and the board of adjustment reversed the approval. The court held that the board of adjustment had no jurisdiction to review the governing-board decision. G.S. 160D-405 allows appeals to the board of adjustment of decisions by administrative officials; however, the governing board is not an "administrative official." G.S. 160D-302 allows those appeals to the board of adjustment that are specifically enumerated in the statutes or ordinance.

---

186. Appeal of decisions on a certificate of appropriateness under a historic-district or landmark-protection ordinance is an exception to this general rule. G.S. 160D-947(e) provides an option that appeals of a preservation-commission decision may be taken to the board of adjustment. This is not a de novo hearing, however, as the appeal is in the nature of certiorari and is based on the record established at the preservation-commission hearing. Appeals from the board of adjustment in these matters go to superior court. If the ordinance does not provide for review by the board of adjustment, the appeal goes to superior court, just as with other quasi-judicial decisions.

187. 115 N.C. App. 273, 444 S.E.2d 653, *review denied*, 337 N.C. 692, 448 S.E.2d 523 (1994).

188. *Id.* at 275, 444 S.E.2d at 654.

CHAPTER 16

Special Use Permits

Zoning regulations list uses that are automatically permitted in a particular zoning district. These permitted uses are often referred to as uses by right. Many zoning regulations also allow additional uses in each district that are permitted only if specified standards are met; these are known as special uses. Eighty percent of North Carolina cities and counties with zoning reported use of special use permits in a 2005 survey by the UNC School of Government. The standards for approval of these permits include those that require application of some degree of judgment and discretion, as opposed to permitted uses where only objective standards are applied.

It is important to distinguish special use permits from variances.[1] Variances are used when the strict terms of the regulation cannot be met. Special use permits are used to conduct a detailed review of individual applications to determine whether the regulation's standards have been met.[2]

A zoning regulation may require a special use permit for changes in land uses as well as for the establishment of new uses. For example, the court in *Forsyth County v. York*[3] upheld a zoning provision that required a special use permit for the conversion of a nonconforming use to another use, provided the board of adjustment found the new use to be less intensive or of essentially the same character as the prior use.

A special use permit is not a personal right but is tied to the specific parcel of property for which it is issued. These permits run with the land. Chapter 160D, Section 104 of the North Carolina General Statutes (hereinafter G.S.) provides that all development approvals made under Chapter 160D "attach to and run with the land."

---

1. "A variance is an authority to a property owner to use property in a manner forbidden by the ordinance while a special exception allows the property owner to put his property to a use expressly permitted by the ordinance." N. Shore Steak House, Inc. v. Bd. of Appeals, 30 N.Y.2d 238, 243, 282 N.E.2d 606, 609 (1972). Variances are discussed in Chapter 17.

2. An early zoning case described the special use concept thusly:

> The theory is that certain uses, considered by the local legislative body to be essential or desirable for the welfare of the community . . . are entirely appropriate and not essentially incompatible with the basic uses in any zone (or in certain particular zones), but not at every or any location therein or without restrictions or conditions being imposed by reason of special problems the use or its particular location in relation to neighboring properties presents from a zoning standpoint, such as traffic congestion, safety, health, noise, and the like. The enabling act therefore permits the local ordinance to require approval of the local administrative agency as to the location of such use within the zone. If the board finds compliance with the standards or requisites set forth in the ordinance, the right to the exception exists, subject to such specific safeguarding conditions as the agency may impose by reason of the nature, location and incidents of the particular use.

Tullo v. Twp. of Millburn, 54 N.J. Super. 483, 490–91, 149 A.2d 620, 624–25 (App. Div. 1959).

3. 19 N.C. App. 361, 198 S.E.2d 770, *cert. denied*, 284 N.C. 253, 200 S.E.2d 653 (1974). In this case, the defendant had converted an automobile-repair and used-parts business into an agricultural-implement-sales business and placed a mobile home on the site without securing a special use permit for either action.

The duration of a special use permit is set by local ordinance. If the regulation does not set a time, the default is set by G.S. 160D-403(c), which provides that local "development approvals" expire after one year if work has not substantially commenced. In G.S. 160D-102(13), the definition of a "development approval" includes special use permits.

A local government may propose to revoke a special use permit and, if so, the same hearing and decision-making process that is required for its issuance must be followed. This is also the case for any proposed major modifications of an existing special use permit. Local ordinances may define and allow for minor administrative modifications of special use permits. While not expressly addressed by the statutes, the holder of a special use permit can presumptively voluntarily relinquish a special use permit that has not expired. If this is done, the relinquishment should be in writing, and it should be acknowledged in writing by the local government.

Nomenclature

The original Standard State Zoning Enabling Act and the original North Carolina zoning-enabling act used the term "special exception" for these permits and assigned decision-making on them to the board of adjustment.[4] Contemporary zoning regulations termed these additional uses *conditional uses* or *special uses*. Some regulations retained the term *special exceptions* as well, most often using this term to address situations where limited flexibility is desired to accommodate hardships that do not rise to the level required for a variance.

These terms were interchangeable, having the same legal consequence.[5] There is no legal significance to the term used in the regulation to label these permits; the term used in an individual ordinance was a matter of local choice. Some zoning regulations used multiple terms for these permits, for example assigning decision-making for one class of these permits to one body and another class to a different body, using different names to distinguish the two (for example, sending "conditional use permits" to the elected governing board and "special use permits" to the planning board for decision).

The varying terminology for these permits—and the similarity to the term *conditional zoning*—was a source of considerable confusion.[6] To clarify matters, the General Assembly in 2019 amended the statutes with the adoption of Chapter 160D to require use of uniform terminology. G.S. 160D-102(30) assigns a single standard name, "special use permit," for this type of permit and requires that the terminology be used by all cities and counties.

G.S. 160D-102(30) provides:

---

4. The court in *In re Application of Ellis*, 277 N.C. 419, 425, 178 S.E.2d 77, 80–81 (1970), described the special exception this way:

> A special exception within the meaning of a zoning ordinance is one which is expressly permitted in a given zone upon proof that certain facts and conditions detailed in the ordinance exist. It is granted by the board, after a public hearing, upon a finding that the specified conditions have been satisfied.

5. The statutes were amended in 1967 to explicitly allow use of "special use permits." S.L. 1967-1208. Further amendment occurred in 2005. S.L. 2005-426, §§ 5(a), (b). This provision, codified as Chapter 160D, Section 705(c) of the North Carolina General Statutes (hereinafter G.S.), provides:

> The [zoning] regulations may provide that the board of adjustment, planning board, or governing board hear and decide special use permits in accordance with principles, conditions, safeguards, and procedures specified in the regulations. Reasonable and appropriate conditions and safeguards may be imposed upon these permits.

G.S. 160D-705(c).

6. David W. Owens, *A Conditional What? Clarifying Some Confusing Zoning Terminology*, COATES' CANONS: NC LOC. GOV'T L. blog (Nov. 13, 2012), https://canons.sog.unc.edu/a-conditional-what-clarifying-some-confusing-zoning-terminology/.

Special use permit. — A permit issued to authorize development or land uses in a particular zoning district upon presentation of competent, material, and substantial evidence establishing compliance with one or more general standards requiring that judgment and discretion be exercised as well as compliance with specific standards. The term includes permits previously referred to as conditional use permits or special exceptions.[7]

Decision-Making Allocation and Process

The use of special use permits was approved by the court in *Jackson v. Guilford County Board of Adjustment*.[8] The ordinance involved there allowed mobile-home parks as a special exception in an agricultural zoning district. The key question addressed by the court was whether assignment of special use permit decision-making to the board of adjustment constituted an unlawful delegation of legislative authority. Justice Lake wrote that it does not, because the governing board makes the legislative policy decision when it determines whether the use will be allowed in a certain zoning district and under what conditions:

> When a statute, or ordinance, provides that a type of structure may not be erected in a specified area, except that such structure may be erected therein when certain conditions exist, one has a right, under the statute or ordinance, to erect such structure upon a showing that the specified conditions do exist. The legislative body may confer upon an administrative officer, or board, the authority to determine whether the specified conditions do, in fact, exist and may require a permit from such officer, or board, to be issued when he or it so determines, as a further condition precedent to the right to erect such structure in such area. Such permit is not one for a variance or departure from the statute or ordinance, but is the recognition of a right established by the statute or ordinance itself. Consequently, the delegation to such officer, or board, of authority to make such determination as to the existence or nonexistence of the specified conditions is not a delegation of the legislative power to make law.[9]

North Carolina law allows the final decision on a special use permit to be assigned to the governing board, the board of adjustment, or the planning board.[10] It is common for a zoning ordinance to assign some of these to the governing board and others to either the board of adjustment or the planning board.[11] A 2005 survey by the School of Government revealed that these decisions are most commonly assigned to the governing board, frequently to the board of adjustment, and only occasionally to the planning board.[12] The decision as to which board to assign decision-making responsibility is at the discretion of each jurisdiction, but the allocation must be made in the ordinance, not on a case-by-case basis.

---

7. S.L. 2019-111, § 2.9(b), provides that any valid "conditional use permit" becomes known as a "special use permit."

8. 275 N.C. 155, 166 S.E.2d 78 (1969).

9. *Id.* at 165–66, 166 S.E.2d at 85.

10. G.S. 160D-705(c).

11. When this is done, the ordinance may characterize those going to one board for a decision as "major" special use permits and those going to a different board as "minor" special use permits.

12. David W. Owens, Special Use Permits in North Carolina Zoning 9 (UNC School of Government, Special Series No. 22, Apr. 2007). Sixty-nine percent of the responding jurisdictions assigned at least some of the decisions to the governing board, 53 percent to the board of adjustment, and only 4 percent to the planning board. The figures add up to more than 100 percent as many jurisdictions use more than one board.

The decision on a special use permit is quasi-judicial[13] and thus subject to procedural-due-process requirements, regardless of which board is making the decision. For all boards making these decisions, a simple majority of the entire board decides permit applications.[14]

It is common in North Carolina to have an advisory board review and make recommendations on special use permits.[15] The fact that a majority of jurisdictions use this process is somewhat surprising given the strict quasi-judicial process that must be used for these permits. In practice, none of these boards serve as a hearing officer, as is the practice in state administrative law. The information presented to the advisory boards is not evidence to be considered by the ultimate decision-making board. Rather, this is an informal preliminary step in the decision-making process that helps identify issues and concerns that are then addressed in the formal hearing before the decision-making board.[16]

This limited role for advisory reviews is codified in Chapter 160D. G.S. 160D-301 allows, but does not mandate, planning-board review and comments on pending quasi-judicial matters. However, the statute confirms that such reviews are a "preliminary forum." A planning board making an advisory review is not conducting a formal evidentiary hearing but is allowing an informal, preliminary discussion of the application.[17] Given this informality, the statute goes on to provide that "no part of the forum or recommendation" may be used as the basis for a decision by the board making the quasi-judicial decision. The decision must still be based on competent evidence presented at the evidentiary hearing held by the decision-making board.

The statutes on development regulations address the process to be followed in modifying or revoking a special use permit. G.S. 160D-705(c) provides that minor modifications of quasi-judicial decisions can be made administratively, but only if the local development regulation defines a "minor modification" and authorizes it to be made administratively. A minor modification may not include a change in permitted uses or in the overall density of the development. Once defined, qualified applications may be approved by the staff without the necessity of going through the quasi-judicial process. If multiple parcels of land are included within a special use permit, then the permit may be modified for individual parcels at the request of the owners of those parcels. Any other modification of a quasi-judicial decision, and any revocation of a quasi-judicial approval, must follow the same process as used for its initial issuance.

---

13. While the standards for the permit involve application of a degree of discretion, the applicant is entitled to the permit upon establishing that the standards will be met. This creates a property right in the permit that is different from the entirely discretionary decision on a rezoning, thus making decisions on special use permits quasi-judicial. See Chapter 2 for a discussion of these distinctions.

14. G.S. 160D-406(j). A four-fifths majority was once required to issue a special use permit, an artifact of this function's original assignment to the board of adjustment. The majority required was changed over several decades to a simple majority. This change was made in 1981 for city councils and boards of county commissioners. LAWS OF NORTH CAROLINA, 1981, ch. 1. The statute was amended in 2005 to make the simple-majority vote applicable to planning boards when they have been assigned decision-making authority for these permits. S.L. 2005-426, §§ 5(a), (b). This amendment also explicitly stated that all special use permit decisions are quasi-judicial and that vacant positions and members who are not participating in a decision due to a conflict of interest are not considered in computing the requisite majority. In 2013, this simple-majority requirement to approve a special use permit was extended to boards of adjustment. S.L. 2013-126.

15. A 2005 School of Government survey indicated that 52 percent of the responding municipalities and 67 percent of the responding counties send special use permits to the planning board for an advisory recommendation. OWENS, *supra* note 12.

16. In practice, some advisory boards follow quasi-judicial procedures even at their hearing, while others use a more informal process. In most instances, the written recommendation of the board is presented to the decision-making board as part of the record of the case.

17. These advisory reviews can identify issues and concerns and provide the parties with informal guidance about particular evidence that should be presented at a forthcoming evidentiary hearing. But since the reviews do not constitute evidence that can be used by the decision-making board, an increasing number of local governments are discontinuing their use.

Adequate Guiding Standards

Since decisions on special use permits involve applying legislatively established standards to individual applications, it is essential that the zoning regulation itself include adequate guiding standards for quasi-judicial decisions.[18] It would be illegal to provide for a special use permit without including standards to guide decision-making for those permits. Adequate guiding standards are required even where the governing board is making the quasi-judicial decision.[19]

If there are no standards, or if the standard provided is so general as to leave the board unbridled discretion in its decision, the courts will invalidate the ordinance provision as an unlawful delegation of legislative authority. A board may not legislate through ad hoc quasi-judicial decision-making.

Zoning-regulation provisions that have decision standards for special use permits that are so general as to offer little practical guidance for individual decisions are invalid. *Jackson* sets the basic rule:

> Delegation to an administrative officer, or board, of authority to issue or refuse a permit for the erection of a specified type of structure in a given area, dependent upon whether such officer, or board, considers such structure in such area, under prevailing conditions, conducive to or adverse to the public interest or welfare is a different matter. Such delegation makes the determinative factor the opinion of such officer, or board, as to whether such structure in such area, under prevailing conditions, would be desirable or undesirable, beneficial to the community or harmful to it. This is a delegation of the power to make a different rule of law, case by case. This power may not be conferred by the legislative body upon an administrative officer or board. . . .
>
> So much of . . . this ordinance as requires the Board of Adjustment to deny a permit . . . unless it finds "that the granting of the special exception will not adversely affect the public interest" is, therefore, beyond the authority of the Board of County Commissioners to enact and so is invalid.[20]

In re Ellis confirms that this same restriction applies to the governing board.[21] In response to the adverse ruling in the *Jackson* case, the Guilford County Board of Commissioners adopted a resolution moving special use permit decision-making from the board of adjustment to the governing board. The commissioners subsequently denied the applicant's request for a special use permit for a mobile-home park under the "public interest" standard, making no findings of fact and stating no reasons for their decision. On appeal the court ruled that governing boards have no more discretionary power for individual special use permits than does a board of adjustment:

> Like the board of adjustment, the commissioners cannot deny applicants a permit in their unguided discretion or, stated differently, refuse it solely because, in their view, a mobile-home park would "adversely affect the public interest." The commissioners must also proceed under standards, rules, and regulations, uniformly applicable to all who apply for permits.[22]

---

18. Evidence must be presented that the standards used to make the decision are actually included in the regulation. Jubilee Carolina, LLC v. Town of Carolina Beach, 268 N.C. App. 90, 834 S.E.2d 665 (2019).

19. *In re* Ellis, 277 N.C. 419, 178 S.E.2d 77 (1970). *See also* Town of Spruce Pine v. Avery Cnty., 346 N.C. 787, 488 S.E.2d 144 (1997) (upholding water-supply-watershed-protection statute, noting guiding standards need be only as specific as circumstances permit); Adams v. N.C. Dep't of Nat. & Econ. Res., 295 N.C. 683, 249 S.E.2d 402 (1979) (upholding delegation of rulemaking and quasi-judicial authority to state Coastal Resources Commission); City of Roanoke Rapids v. Peedin, 124 N.C. App. 578, 478 S.E.2d 528 (1996) (impermissible for county board of health to make legislative judgments in its rulemaking).

20. 275 N.C. at 165–167, 166 S.E.2d at 85–87. *See also* Howard v. City of Kinston, 148 N.C. App. 238, 246, 558 S.E.2d 221, 227 (2002).

21. 277 N.C. 419, 178 S.E.2d 77.

22. *Id*. at 425, 178 S.E.2d at 81.

Thus, it is clearly the nature of the zoning decision, not the identity of the decision maker, that determines what procedures and standards must be applied. When a governing board acts in a quasi-judicial capacity, it must observe quasi-judicial, not legislative, standards.

Continuing with the line of cases that have held various standards to be so general as to offer inadequate guidance to decision makers, the North Carolina Supreme Court held a requirement that a special use be consistent with the "purpose and intent" of the zoning ordinance to be an insufficient standard and thus an unlawful delegation of authority.[23] In another case the court ruled that it was improper for the Nags Head governing board to deny a special use permit for a planned-unit development on the grounds that it was inconsistent with the goals and objectives of the land use plan, even though the ordinance specifically listed the plan as one of the factors in determining the suitability of a special use permit.[24] The state appeals court also held that it was improper to deny a special use permit for an adult bookstore on the grounds that it would be incompatible with the character and use of surrounding buildings.[25] Its inclusion as a special use by the ordinance is conclusive on the policy question of general use compatibility, the court concluded.

Even so, it is permissible to use relatively general standards for decisions. In a key decision, *Kenan v. Board of Adjustment*,[26] the court of appeals approved the use of four fairly general standards for special use permits. Many North Carolina zoning ordinances now incorporate these same standards, which require that the use

1. does not materially endanger the public health or safety,
2. does meet all required conditions and specifications,
3. will not substantially injure the value of adjoining property or be a public necessity, and
4. will be in harmony with the area in which it is located and in general conformity with the comprehensive plan.[27]

Some zoning ordinances also add more detailed, specific standards for particular uses and often apply those in combination with these general standards.[28]

The standards to be applied in particular quasi-judicial decisions must be clearly identified as such by the regulation. Only those standards specifically listed as applicable may be applied when making special use permit decisions. Additional standards may not be developed on an ad hoc basis.

C.C. & J. Enterprises, Inc. v. City of Asheville[29] illustrates this rule. The city council there denied a special use permit after finding the application met all of the technical requirements and development

---

23. Keiger v. Bd. of Adjustment, 278 N.C. 17, 23, 178 S.E.2d 616, 620 (1971). *See also* Nw. Fin. Grp., Inc. v. Cnty. of Gaston, 329 N.C. 180, 190, 405 S.E.2d 138, 144 (1991) (holding approvals under mobile-home-park ordinance may not be based on general concern about hazards to public welfare).

24. Woodhouse v. Bd. of Comm'rs, 299 N.C. 211, 261 S.E.2d 882 (1980).

25. Harts Book Stores, Inc. v. City of Raleigh, 53 N.C. App. 753, 281 S.E.2d 761 (1981).

26. 13 N.C. App. 688, 187 S.E.2d 496, *cert. denied*, 281 N.C. 314, 188 S.E.2d 897 (1972).

27. *Kenan*, 13 N.C. App. at 692–93, 187 S.E.2d at 499.

28. A 2005 survey of North Carolina local governments by the School of Government indicated widespread use of these four general standards. Eighty-nine percent of the responding jurisdictions use the standard of public health and safety; 92 percent use the standard of meeting all required conditions; 84 percent use the standard of not injuring adjoining property values; and 90 percent use the standard of maintaining harmony with the surrounding area. (Sixty-nine percent also require conformity with a comprehensive plan.) Thirty-six percent of the responding jurisdictions also included more-specific standards for particular special uses. OWENS, *supra* note 12, at 11.

29. 132 N.C. App. 550, 512 S.E.2d 766 (1999). *See also* MCC Outdoor, LLC v. Town of Franklinton, 169 N.C. App. 809, 813, 610 S.E.2d 794, 797, *review denied*, 359 N.C. 634, 616 S.E.2d 539 (2005) (denial of special use permit for sign cannot be based on findings not related to ordinance standards for decision); Knight v. Town of Knightdale, 164 N.C. App. 766, 596 S.E.2d 881 (2004) (applying rule to quasi-judicial site-plan approval). This same rule applies to subdivision-plat approvals. Nazziola v. Landcraft Props., Inc., 143 N.C. App. 564, 545 S.E.2d 801 (2001).

standards in the regulation, basing the denial on a general concern about impacts on health and safety (citing street conditions, topography, access, flooding potential, and proposed density). The court held that since the ordinance did not in fact list promotion of the public health, safety, and welfare as a standard for special use permit decisions (though it would have been permissible to do so), it was inappropriate for the city council to use it as a standard in reviewing the application. A general statement of intent that "adequate standards will be maintained pertaining to the public health, safety, welfare, and convenience"[30] was not a permit standard and could not be used in decision-making. Similarly, in *PHG Asheville, LLC v. City of Asheville*, the court held that an applicant for a special use permit is not required to rebut concerns raised by board members that are not within the range of issues and data required by the relevant standards in the regulation.[31]

The same rule applies to imposition of conditions on special use permits. Only the standards actually in the regulation can be used as the basis for imposition of conditions on a special use permit that is issued. The authority to impose appropriate conditions and safeguards "cannot be used to justify unbridled discretion" in framing permit conditions.[32]

In making its decision, the board must clearly state whether each of the applicable standards has been met. A board may vote on each standard separately or on a single motion that specifies which standards have been met (so long as the board's conclusions about each standard are clearly discernable).[33]

Burden of Production and Persuasion

With special use permits, the general rule is that the applicant has the burden of presenting sufficient evidence that an application meets the standards of the ordinance.[34] Most zoning ordinances require applications for special use permits to be on forms that are designed to solicit the basic information necessary to assess compliance with the standards. A board has no jurisdiction to consider an incomplete application.[35]

If the applicant presents uncontroverted competent, substantial, and material evidence that the standards have been met, there is a prima facie entitlement to the permit, and it must be issued.[36] On the

---

30. *C.C. & J. Enterprises*, 132 N.C. App. at 553, 512 S.E.2d at 769 (quoting ASHEVILLE, N.C., CITY CODE § 30-6-1 (1993)).

31. 374 N.C. 133, 839 S.E.2d 755 (2020).

32. Hewett v. Cnty. of Brunswick, 155 N.C. App. 138, 146, 573 S.E.2d 688, 694 (2002).

33. Richardson v. Union Cnty. Bd. of Adjustment, 136 N.C. App. 134, 523 S.E.2d 432 (1999) (permissible for board to combine two of four standards in their vote on a special use permit).

34. Humble Oil & Refin. Co. v. Bd. of Aldermen, 284 N.C. 458, 468, 202 S.E.2d 129, 136 (1974). The court noted that this is analogous to making the showing necessary to overcome a directed-verdict motion during a jury trial. 284 N.C. at 470, 471, 202 S.E.2d at 137. Whether the burden of production has been met is a question of law subject to de novo review. See Chapter 29 for a discussion of judicial-review issues.

35. Wade v. Town of Ayden, 125 N.C. App. 650, 482 S.E.2d 44 (1997). The court held that the ordinance requirements on information required for an application were binding on the board and that it had no authority to consider an incomplete application. *See also Richardson*, 136 N.C. App. 134, 523 S.E.2d 432 (ordinance may grant some flexibility to administrator to accept more or less technical information than is specified for the application).

36. PHG Asheville, LLC v. City of Asheville, 374 N.C. 133, 839 S.E.2d 755 (2020) (if applicant presents uncontroverted expert testimony that standards are met, board may not reject the application based on board's own lay opinion of the experts' methodologies); Dellinger v. Lincoln Cnty. I, 248 N.C. App. 317, 789 S.E.2d 21, *review denied*, 369 N.C. 190, 794 S.E.2d 324 (2016) (to establish a prima facie entitlement to approval, the test is presentation of competent, substantial, material evidence by the applicant, and it is error to apply a "beyond a reasonable doubt" standard of proof); Blair Invs., LLC v. Roanoke Rapids City Council, 231 N.C. App. 318, 752 S.E.2d 524 (2013); Howard v. City of Kinston, 148 N.C. App. 238, 246, 558 S.E.2d 221, 227 (2002); SBA, Inc. v. City of Asheville, 141 N.C. App. 19, 27, 539 S.E.2d 18, 22 (2000); Clark v. City of Asheboro, 136 N.C. App. 114, 119–20, 524 S.E.2d 46, 50 (1999); Triple E

other hand, when an applicant fails to produce sufficient evidence for the board to make the requisite findings, the permit must be denied.[37]

Once an applicant makes the requisite showing that the standards have been met, the burden shifts to those who oppose permit issuance to present countervailing substantial, competent, and material evidence that the standards have not been met.[38] Where there is substantial evidence on both sides, the board determines which is correct, and absent other problems, that determination is accepted by the courts.[39]

In *Woodhouse v. Board of Commissioners*, one of the grounds cited for denial of a special use permit for a multifamily project was a finding that the project "outstrips community fire-fighting facilities or services." The court held that this conclusion was not supported by competent, material, and substantial evidence in the record. It held that the applicant had met the initial burden of presenting evidence of compliance with all of the ordinance requirements and standards. The applicant was not then required to additionally "first anticipate and then prove or disprove each and every general consideration," as that "would impose an intolerable, if not impossible, burden on an applicant" to negate every possible objection.[40] Rather, once the applicant meets the initial burden, the burden of showing the project would violate the health, safety, and welfare of the community shifts to opponents of the project. The courts have applied this *Woodhouse* rule to conclude the applicant has the burden of production to present evidence showing compliance with the general standards noted below, not a burden of proof to show that all these general standards are met.[41]

While opponents have a burden of producing some contrary evidence, the regulation may, to some extent, place the burden of proof on the applicant when there is conflicting evidence. For example, an ordinance may state that a permit shall only be issued upon the applicant's establishing that the proposed project *will not harm* the public safety or neighboring property values.

Assocs. v. Town of Matthews, 105 N.C. App. 354, 413 S.E.2d 305, *review denied*, 332 N.C. 150, 419 S.E.2d 578 (1992); Harts Book Stores, Inc. v. City of Raleigh, 53 N.C. App. 753, 281 S.E.2d 761 (1981). The same rule of entitlement upon showing all standards have been met applies to subdivision-plat approvals. *See, e.g.*, William Brewster Co. v. Town of Huntersville, 161 N.C. App. 132, 588 S.E.2d 16 (2003).

37. Signorelli v. Town of Highlands, 93 N.C. App. 704, 379 S.E.2d 55 (1989); Charlotte Yacht Club, Inc. v. Cnty. of Mecklenburg, 64 N.C. App. 477, 307 S.E.2d 595 (1983).

38. Dellinger v. Lincoln Cnty. I, 248 N.C. App. 317, 832 S.E.2d 172 (2019). In *Catherine H. Barber Memorial Shelter, Inc. v. Town of North Wilkesboro*, 576 F. Supp. 3d 318 (W.D.N.C. Dec. 20, 2021), the court overturned the denial of a special use permit for a homeless shelter on this basis. After presenting sufficient competent, material, and substantive evidence that all the special use permit standards were met, the applicant was entitled to approval if there was no competent contradictory evidence. The board refused to allow the applicant to cross-examine the neighboring property owners who testified about problems at the shelter's prior location, evidence that was strongly disputed by the applicant. As the failure to allow a party to cross-examine was a clear error of law, that evidence was incompetent and could not be considered to rebut the applicant's evidence of compliance. Also, while one of the opposing neighbors was a commercial-real-estate appraiser, he offered no analysis or data to support his opinion of the shelter's harm to property values.

39. AT & T Wireless PCS, Inc. v. Winston-Salem Zoning Bd. of Adjustment, 172 F.3d 307 (4th Cir. 1999).

40. 299 N.C. 211, 219, 261 S.E.2d 882, 887–88 (1980). In this case, the Town of Nags Head denied a special use permit for a planned-unit development with thirty-two multifamily-dwelling units, a sewage-treatment facility, and recreational facilities. The town conceded that the application met all of the specific requirements of the ordinance. The denial was based on a concern that firefighting capacity may be inadequate, but no evidence was in the record to support that finding. The city also had conceded that the concern over adequate firefighting capacity would exist regardless of the type of use or development of the property involved. A second ground for denial related to odors from the proposed wastewater-treatment facility, but the applicant presented expert testimony that the facility would not create odors, and the neighboring opponents offered only unsubstantiated opinions that it may be problematic.

41. *See, e.g.*, Innovative 55, LLC v. Robeson Cnty., 253 N.C. App. 714, 720, 801 S.E.2d 671, 676 (2017).

In *Mann Media, Inc. v. Randolph County Planning Board*,[42] the ordinance standards for a special use permit for a broadcast tower required a finding that the use "will not endanger the public health or safety." Neighbors expressed concern at the hearing about ice building up and falling from the tower or its support cables. The petitioner acknowledged that he could not guarantee ice would not travel off-site in the event of a storm, though such was unlikely. The court upheld the permit denial based on a failure of the petitioner to meet the burden of proof on this general standard.

Similarly, in *Butler v. City Council of Clinton*,[43] the court held that evidence that a proposed crematory "likely would not" endanger the public health, safety, and general welfare was insufficient to meet an ordinance requirement for a finding that the proposed use "will not" harm these interests. By contrast, if the ordinance says the permit *shall be issued* unless the board finds a standard is violated, the permit must be issued in the absence of evidence that a standard is violated.[44]

It is increasingly common for zoning ordinances to explicitly state the allocation of the burden of production or burden of persuasion. For example, the Nash County development ordinance provides:

> The burden of persuasion on the issue of whether the development, if completed as proposed, will comply with the requirements of this Ordinance remains at all times on the applicant. The burden of persuasion on the issue of whether the application should be turned down for any of the reasons set forth in Subsection (I) [standards related to endangering the public health and safety, injury to neighboring property values, harmony with the neighborhood] rests on the party or parties urging that the requested permit should be denied.[45]

Even so, although an ordinance may specify that the applicant must show, for example, that the project will not harm neighboring property values or create a traffic problem, if the applicant presents uncontroverted substantial evidence that the standard is met, this constitutes a prima facie showing of entitlement to the approval. When substantial expert testimony is presented that the standards are met, a board may not make a lay determination, unsupported by substantial evidence, that the expert methodology used was inadequate or that it simply does not believe the proffered evidence.[46]

Adequacy of Evidence

When special use permits are contentious, they often involve disputes as to the effect of the project on the character of the neighborhood and on neighboring property values. A 2005 survey of all North Carolina cities and counties with zoning indicated that these were the most difficult standards for decision-making boards to apply. When asked if there was any one standard that posed more difficulty

---

42. 356 N.C. 1, 565 S.E.2d 9 (2002). *See also* Harding v. Bd. of Adjustment, 170 N.C. App. 392, 612 S.E.2d 431 (2005) (where ordinance required board to find project "will not adversely affect the health or safety" of neighbors, board properly placed burdens of production and proof on applicant). *But see* PHG Asheville, LLC v. City of Asheville, 374 N.C. 133, 839 S.E.2d 755 (2020) (when applicant presents prima facie case for a special use permit and there is no contrary evidence presented, the applicant is entitled to approval even if the standards are phrased as in *Mann*).

43. 160 N.C. App. 68, 72, 584 S.E.2d 103, 106 (2003). *See also* SBA, Inc. v. City of Asheville, 141 N.C. App. 19, 539 S.E.2d 18 (2000).

44. *See, e.g.*, Coleman v. Town of Hillsborough, 173 N.C. App. 560, 619 S.E.2d 555 (2005).

45. Nash County, N.C., Unified Development Ordinance § 4-7.5(J) (2022). This provision is discussed *in* Hopkins v. Nash Cnty., 149 N.C. App. 446, 450, 560 S.E.2d 592, 595 (2002).

46. *PHG Asheville*, 374 N.C. 133, 839 S.E.2d 755 (2020). The court also expressed doubt that the manner in which an ordinance is couched has any effect on the question of law as to whether a prima facie case has been established for a special use permit. *Id.* at 153 n.5, 839 S.E.2d at 768 n.5.

Table 16.1 Special Use Permit Standards Deemed Most Difficult to Apply

Standard	% of Respondents
Not substantially injure the value of adjoining property or be a public necessity	30
Be in harmony with the area or compatible with neighborhood	25
Meet all required conditions and specifications	17
Be in general conformity with comprehensive plan	14
Not materially endanger public health or safety	11
Other specific standards	5

than others for their boards, nearly a third identified property-value impacts and a quarter identified neighborhood compatibility.[47] These responses are summarized in Table 16.1.

The question of the quality of evidence necessary to support findings relative to the general standards for special use permits is evolving.[48] More-recent cases emphasize the need for a stronger foundation and greater detail in the evidence presented. A brief review of the holdings relative to these typical general standards follows.

Endangering the Public Health or Safety

Several North Carolina cases involving special use permits for broadcast and telecommunication towers illustrate the quantity and quality of evidence needed to address public-health and safety standards.

The first dealt with the potential hazard of ice falling from tower supports. In *Mann*,[49] an application for a special use permit to construct a 1500-foot broadcast tower was denied on several grounds, including that the applicant had not met the burden of showing "that the use will not materially endanger the public health or safety if located where proposed and developed according to the plan as submitted and approved."[50] The court held that the evidence presented by tower opponents (ice in a cooler and anecdotal hearsay) was not competent to establish a public-safety hazard. However, the ordinance placed the burden of establishing that the use would not pose a safety hazard on the applicant. Here the applicant testified that while he believed ice on the wires would not pose a safety problem, he could not state with certainty that falling ice in a storm would not pose a risk to the permanent structures located in close proximity to the towers. The court upheld the denial, concluding the board's finding that the applicant failed to establish that a lack of hazards was "neither whimsical, nor patently in bad faith, and it is not indicative of a lack of any course of reasoning or exercise of judgment."[51]

Two other special use permit cases involving broadcast towers dealt with the potential hazards presented to aircraft and illustrate the importance of quantitative evidence as well as personal observations. In *Cumulus Broadcasting, LLC v. Hoke County Board of Commissioners*,[52] the county denied a special use permit for a proposed 499-foot radio tower in a residential-agricultural zoning district. Several pilots and the owner of a nearby private airstrip testified that, based on their personal knowledge and

---

47. OWENS, *supra* note 12, at 14.
48. Also see Chapter 15 for a general discussion of presentation of evidence in quasi-judicial matters.
49. 356 N.C. 1, 565 S.E.2d 9 (2002).
50. *Id.* at 11, 565 S.E.2d at 16 (quoting the governing ordinance).
51. *Id.* at 17, 565 S.E.2d at 20.
52. 180 N.C. App. 424, 638 S.E.2d 12 (2006).

observations, the tower posed a hazard to air navigation. However, none of the witnesses rebutted the applicant's quantitative data and other evidence in support of the application. The court held that there was insufficient evidence to rebut the applicant's prima facie entitlement to the permit. A contrasting result obtained in *Davidson County Broadcasting, Inc. v. Rowan County*.[53] The plaintiffs applied for a special use permit to construct a 1350-foot radio broadcast tower. The key issue was whether the proposed tower violated the ordinance standard prohibiting creation of "hazardous safety conditions" with respect to users of a private airport located within five miles of the proposed tower. At the hearing, the applicant presented a letter from the Federal Aviation Administration making a "Determination of No Hazard" resulting from the tower. The evidence presented in opposition included testimony from a representative of the state Department of Transportation, numerous pilots who used the nearby private airport, and aviation experts, all of whom testified that the tower would pose a safety hazard given its proximity to the private airport. The court held that this was sufficient evidence to support a finding that the tower would pose a safety hazard.

The courts have on several occasions invalidated special use permit denials based on a generalized fear that the proposed project would increase crime rates and thus be a hazard to public safety.

In *Sun Suites Holdings, LLC v. Board of Aldermen*, the court invalidated a town council's denial of a special use permit for an extended-stay hotel on the grounds that the project would materially endanger public safety. The court held that a whole-record review established that this finding was not supported by substantial evidence. General expressions of a fear of potential increases in crime in the vicinity of any hotel are insufficient to establish a threat to public safety. Similarly, a recitation of crime statistics with reference to another extended-stay hotel in the town, without any foundation as to how those relate to the subject project, was held inadequate to support a denial.[54]

Clark v. City of Asheboro involved a special use permit for a proposed manufactured-home park in the Asheboro extraterritorial area. The applicants presented detailed evidence at the hearing to support the application. Six neighbors appeared and presented testimony in opposition, generally contending that the project would be "an eyesore" and would bring increased crime and traffic to the area. The court held that the permit was improperly denied, as the evidence in opposition was characterized as being generalized fears that park residents would be low-income individuals who would constitute a danger to the neighborhood, concerns unsupported by competent evidence.[55]

The courts have also addressed evidence on public-safety impacts in a variety of other contexts.

Several cases have held the applicant's evidence sufficient to establish compliance, while the opponents' contrary evidence was insufficient to rebut the showing of compliance.

In *Blair Investments, LLC v. Roanoke Rapids City Council*,[56] the court invalidated the denial of a special use permit for a telecommunication tower where the denial was based on unsubstantiated neighbor "concerns" and objections about the health impacts of a preexisting, unrelated building on the site.

---

53. 186 N.C. App. 81, 649 S.E.2d 904 (2007), *review denied*, 362 N.C. 470, 666 S.E.2d 186 (2008).

54. Sun Suites Holdings, LLC v. Board of Aldermen, 139 N.C. App. 269, 533 S.E.2d 525, *review denied*, 353 N.C. 280, 546 S.E.2d 397 (2000). *See also* Weaverville Partners, LLC v. Town of Weaverville Zoning Bd. of Adjustment, 188 N.C. App. 55, 66, 654 S.E.2d 784, 792 (2008) (general reports of crime rates with multifamily housing constitutes speculative opinion and generalized fear).

55. *Clark v. City of Asheboro*, 136 N.C. App. 114, 524 S.E.2d 46 (1999) (the project was an eighty-six-unit manufactured-home park on a twenty-six-acre parcel). Similarly, in *Cox v. Hancock*, 160 N.C. App. 473, 586 S.E.2d 500 (2003), the court upheld issuance of a special use permit for an apartment building where the applicant presented testimony on traffic control, positive impacts on surrounding property values, stormwater drainage, and compatibility with the surrounding neighborhood, and the neighbors had only generalized objections.

56. 231 N.C. App. 318, 752 S.E.2d 524 (2013).

Potential environmental harms were addressed in *Little River, LLC v. Lee County*.[57] The applicant for a special use permit for a rock quarry showed that all required state and federal permits pertaining to blasting, air quality, and water quality would be secured prior to operation. To address traffic concerns, the applicant presented testimony and offered permit conditions regarding noise, dust suppression, and road improvements. Neighbors of the property expressed concerns that the state and federal permits had not been secured yet. The court held that the applicant had met the burden of producing evidence to establish a prima facie showing of no harm to public health and safety, and that the neighbors' concerns did not rebut this prima facie showing. *Ecoplexus Inc. v. County of Currituck*[58] addressed issues of wind damage and potential runoff from stormwater and herbicides. The applicant presented testimony from engineers regarding the safety of materials to be used on-site, the stormwater-management plan to be subsequently approved by environmental officials, and the wind-load design for the proposed solar arrays. The court found the board wholly ignored this evidence, which made a prima facie showing of compliance with the health-and-safety standard, and instead improperly relied on "generalized fears" of opposing witnesses.

Similarly, in *Ward v. Inscoe*,[59] the court held that presentation of evidence on landscaping buffers, removal of undergrowth, consideration of traffic counts provided by the state Department of Transportation, modification of existing streets, installation of a traffic light, improvements to storm drainage, and relocation of a fire hydrant adequately supported a finding that the proposed bank would not hinder public safety.

Other cases have held the contrary evidence presented by opponents to a special use permit to be sufficient to justify a permit denial.

In *Butler*, the court upheld denial of a special use permit for a crematory. The ordinance required a finding that the use "will not be detrimental to or endanger the public health, safety, morals, or general welfare."[60] Neighboring residents testified about concerns of learning disabilities and cancer caused by the emissions, and the psychological effects on children in the neighborhood. A doctor testified about potential health impacts of mercury and dioxin emissions. The court held in a whole-record review that this was sufficient evidence to support a finding that the use could endanger the public welfare.

In *Wolbarsht v. Board of Adjustment of Durham*,[61] the petitioner requested a special use permit to replace an existing four-foot-high fence in the front yard with a six-foot-high chain-link fence so that his dog could roam in the front yard as well as in the back (where there was already a six-foot-high fence). The court upheld a denial on the grounds that the project would be inconsistent with the public health, safety, and welfare based on testimony from neighbors on the negative visual impacts of the fence and the danger of allowing the dog so close to passersby.

In *Signorelli v. Town of Highlands*,[62] the court held that although the applicant had submitted sufficient information to establish a prima facie entitlement to a special use permit for a game room in a donut shop, the lack of specificity in the application as to hours of operation, number of machines, and methods of supervision justified the board of adjustment's finding that it was unable to conclude that the use would not endanger the public health or safety.

---

57. 257 N.C. App. 55, 809 S.E.2d 42 (2017).

58. 257 N.C. App. 9, 809 S.E.2d 148 (2017).

59. 166 N.C. App. 586, 603 S.E.2d 393 (2004).

60. Butler v. City Council of Clinton, 160 N.C. App. 68, 71, 584 S.E.2d 103, 106 (quoting Standards of the Clinton, N.C., Zoning Ordinance § 10.7(1)).

61. 116 N.C. App. 638, 448 S.E.2d 858 (1994), *review denied*, 338 N.C. 671, 453 S.E.2d 186 (1995).

62. 93 N.C. App. 704, 379 S.E.2d 55 (1989).

Harmony with the Area

An ordinance's inclusion of a particular use as a special use establishes a rebuttable presumption that the use is compatible with the surrounding area. The harmony standard often produces generalized objections from neighbors.[63] It is not uncommon for boards to hear testimony from objecting neighbors that the proposal is simply a bad project that does not fit where it is proposed.

In *Woodhouse*, the court noted that "inclusion of the particular use in the ordinance as one which is permitted under certain conditions, is equivalent to a legislative finding that the prescribed use is one which is in harmony with the other uses permitted in the district."[64] Similarly, in *Harts Book Stores v. City of Raleigh*,[65] the court held that it was improper to deny a special use permit for an adult bookstore on the grounds that it would be incompatible with surrounding buildings, since its inclusion as a special use by the zoning regulation was conclusive on the policy question of use compatibility.

These statements, if literally applied, would make a permit standard of harmony or compatibility superfluous. Cases applying this rule have more precisely noted that inclusion of a use as a permissible special use within a district establishes a prima facie showing or a rebuttable presumption of harmony with the surrounding area rather than a conclusive finding of harmony. For example, in *American Towers, Inc. v. Town of Morrisville*,[66] the court noted that inclusion of telecommunication towers as a potential special use in an industrial zoning district itself established a prima facie case of harmony with the surrounding area, which was conclusive absent presentation of substantial evidence to rebut that presumption. Inclusion as a possible special use in the district means that it is not inherently incompatible, but a detailed review is needed to assure that the particular location and design proposed will in fact be compatible with the immediate surroundings. Therefore, the burden is on the challengers to rebut the presumption of harmony with specific reasons the project as proposed is inharmonious rather than simply objecting to the location of the use in their neighborhood. A number of North Carolina cases illustrate the evidence required to establish that a proposed special use is *not* in harmony with the surrounding area.

In *Davidson County Broadcasting Co. v. Iredell County*, the court upheld denial of a special use permit for a 1130-foot radio broadcast tower in a residential-agricultural zoning district. The court found evidence submitted by the opposing neighbors was sufficient to rebut the presumption of harmony. The evidence included photographs; diagrams of the height of the tower in relation to its surroundings; testimony regarding the height, appearance, and lighting of the tower; and testimony on the impact of construction.[67]

---

63. When queried as to the source of evidence presented on neighborhood compatibility, North Carolina cities and counties reported that such evidence was most typically presented by neighbors (74 percent), followed in order of frequency by testimony from the owner or developer (68 percent), reference to consistency with adopted plans (64 percent), and testimony from professional planners (41 percent). OWENS, *supra* note 12, at 15.

64. 299 N.C. 211, 216, 261 S.E.2d 882, 886 (1980) (quoting 3 ARDEN H. RATHKOPF, THE LAW OF ZONING AND PLANNING 54–55 (1979)).

65. 53 N.C. App. 753, 281 S.E.2d 761 (1981).

66. 222 N.C. App. 638, 731 S.E.2d 698 (2012), *review denied*, 743 S.E.2d 189 (2013). *See also PHG Asheville, LLC v. City of Asheville*, 374 N.C. 133, 839 S.E.2d 755 (2020) (unrebutted expert testimony on project's harmony with surroundings is conclusive).

67. 248 N.C. App. 305, 790 S.E.2d 663 (2016), *review denied*, 369 N.C. 530 (2017). The plaintiffs argued that it was an error of law for the board not to apply a conclusive presumption of harmony based on inclusion of this use as a possible special use in the district. The court, in a de novo review, held inclusion only created a presumption that could be rebutted by substantial evidence to the contrary.

In *Hopkins v. Nash County*,[68] the court upheld the denial of a special use permit for a land-clearing and inert-debris landfill (or, as the court began its opinion, "This is the case of a stump dump denied."). The evidence presented by neighbors who objected to the landfill was that the area, which was zoned A-1 Agricultural, was previously agricultural in nature, the site of a long-standing crossroads community, and now primarily single-family residential, and that the thirty to forty trucks per day that would use the landfill would bring disruptive traffic, noise, and dust into the residential area. The court held this to be sufficient evidence to rebut the presumption of harmony with the surrounding area.[69]

In *SBA, Inc. v. City of Asheville*,[70] the court upheld the denial of a special use permit for a 175-foot telecommunication tower. There was uncontroverted evidence that the tower would be four times taller than existing buildings in the neighborhood. Twelve witnesses testified that the tower would be an eyesore. The court held that the applicant's own evidence, a computer-generated photograph superimposing the tower, corroborated the proposed tower's visibility and predominance over existing buildings and showed that it would be "in sharp contrast" to its surroundings. The court held this to be sufficient to establish that this particular tower would not be compatible with the neighborhood.

In *Vulcan Materials Co. v. Guilford County Board of County Commissioners*,[71] the board of county commissioners denied a special use permit for a proposed rock quarry on the grounds that there was insufficient credible evidence to find that the use would be compatible with the surrounding land uses. The court held that the record showed all uses within two miles of the quarry were residential, which was sufficient evidence for this finding.

In *Petersilie v. Boone Board of Adjustment*,[72] the court upheld the denial of a special use permit for an apartment building in a neighborhood of single-family homes. The court ruled that although the applicant submitted sufficient evidence to support the issuance of the permit, there had also been competent evidence before the board of adjustment regarding problems of noise, traffic congestion, crime, vandalism, and effects on property values to justify the denial of the permit.

By contrast, the courts have on a number of occasions found there to be *insufficient evidence* in the record to support a conclusion that a proposed special use is not in harmony with its surrounding area. In these cases, the courts concluded that the evidence presented was insufficient to rebut a prima facie showing of harmony.

In *Ecoplexus*, neighbors opposed a solar farm proposed for a defunct golf course adjacent to farmland and a residential neighborhood. The applicant's evidence stressed the large vegetated buffers, screening, and limited traffic to show harmony, while the neighbors offered unsubstantiated fears of stormwater runoff and the undesirability of solar energy.[73]

In *McDonald v. City of Concord*,[74] neighbors challenged a special use permit issued by the city to Cabarrus County for a law-enforcement center located along the edge of downtown Concord. The permit

---

68. 149 N.C. App. 446, 560 S.E.2d 592 (2002).

69. A similar ruling, which does not have precedential value, is *Templeton Properties, LP v. Town of Boone*, 234 N.C. App. 303, 759 S.E.2d 311 (2014), *aff'd per curiam by equally divided court*, 368 N.C. 82, 772 S.E.2d 239 (2015). The court of appeals had held that the issue of harmony was a mixed question of fact and law, and the board's findings regarding the size of the building, amount of parking, lighting, and anticipated traffic volume relative to the surrounding residential area were properly considered to rebut the presumption of harmony.

70. 141 N.C. App. 19, 539 S.E.2d 18 (2000). In *Mann*, the court noted in dicta that inclusion in the controlling ordinance of a use as a special use in a particular district established a prima facie case that the use was in harmony with the general zoning plan, but that presumption might be rebutted in the hearing. Mann Media, Inc. v. Randolph Cnty. Planning Bd., 356 N.C. 1, 19, 565 S.E.2d 9, 20 (2002).

71. 115 N.C. App. 319, 444 S.E.2d 639, *review denied*, 337 N.C. 807, 449 S.E.2d 758 (1994).

72. 94 N.C. App. 764, 381 S.E.2d 349 (1989).

73. Ecoplexus Inc. v. Cnty. of Currituck, 257 N.C. App. 9, 809 S.E.2d 148 (2017).

74. 188 N.C. App. 278, 655 S.E.2d 455 (2008).

authorized construction of three buildings on a ten-acre site: a sheriff's office, an annex, and a jail. The center would be located adjacent to the existing jail, on the portion of the site zoned "central city." The remainder of the site (which was not proposed for development) was zoned "residential compact" and adjoined the plaintiffs' residential neighborhood. The permit standard at issue was that the project had to conform "to the character of the neighborhood, considering the location, type, and height of buildings or structures and the type and extent of landscaping and screening on the site."[75] The court concluded that the decision to issue the permit was supported by competent, substantial, and material evidence. The ordinance directed that *Webster's Third New International Dictionary* be used to define its terms. Applying those definitions, as well as the specific items listed in the standard to address neighborhood compatibility, the court concluded that the proposed buildings were sufficiently similar to historical uses in this portion of downtown; that the bulk, height, style, and appearance of the proposed buildings was similar to the neighboring governmental and business buildings in the central-city district; and that these governmental uses had always been adjacent to residential areas. The court noted that the permit contained conditions for a fifty-foot vegetated buffer for the portion of the site contiguous to residential areas. While there was contrary evidence presented, the court cannot substitute its judgment between two reasonably conflicting views so long as the board's conclusion on harmony was supported by the evidence.

In *Little River*, the court held that generalized fears and speculation by opponents to a rock quarry were insufficient to rebut a presumption of harmony.[76] In *Habitat for Humanity of Moore County, Inc. v. Board of Commissioners of Pinebluff*,[77] the court found the testimony in opposition to the permit to be both very general and likely applicable to virtually any development of the site. In *Humane Society of Moore County, Inc. v. Town of Southern Pines*,[78] the court overturned the denial of a special use permit for an animal shelter. The court found testimony of landscape architects as to noise and odor impacts to be speculative. The court noted that witnesses had also either ignored the fact that ministorage warehouses, an airport, and another animal hospital were already located in the area or had conceded that the proposed use was in harmony with them. In *Ward*, involving a special use permit for a bank with four drive-through windows, the court found that presentation of evidence regarding the mix of existing uses in the area, along with conditions imposed relative to street parking, lighting, tree removal, and vegetative buffers, sufficiently supported a finding that the project would not substantially injure adjoining properties.[79] In *MCC Outdoor, LLC v. Town of Franklinton*,[80] involving an application for a special use permit to erect billboards, the court held that the neighbors' ability to see a billboard from their property was insufficient to support a finding that the signs would be incompatible with the neighborhood, given the presence of other businesses, signs, and an active rail line in the immediate area.

The zoning-enabling statute also includes a specific limit on the use of a neighborhood-harmony standard. In 2021, the General Assembly prohibited the use of a harmony standard when applied to projects providing affordable housing. G.S. 160D-703(b1)[81] provides that if a parcel is in a zoning district

---

75. *Id.* at 279, 655 S.E.2d at 456–57 (quoting City of Concord, N.C., Unified Development Ordinance § 6.2.7).

76. Little River, LLC v. Lee Cnty., 257 N.C. App. 55, 809 S.E.2d 42 (2017).

77. Habitat for Humanity of Moore Cnty., Inc. v. Bd. of Comm'rs of Pinebluff, 187 N.C. App. 764, 653 S.E.2d 886 (2007).

78. Humane Soc'y of Moore Cnty., Inc. v. Town of S. Pines, 161 N.C. App. 625, 589 S.E.2d 162 (2003).

79. Ward v. Inscoe, 166 N.C. App. 586, 603 S.E.2d 393 (2004).

80. MCC Outdoor, LLC v. Town of Franklinton, 169 N.C. App. 809, 610 S.E.2d 794 (2005).

81. This provision was created by S.L. 2021-180, § 5.16(a).

where multifamily structures are "an allowable use," a harmony requirement may not be required for permit approval if the development contains affordable housing units.[82]

Injure Value of Adjoining Property

North Carolina cities and counties report that the question of a proposed special use permit project's impact on adjoining property values is the single most difficult standard for their boards to apply.[83]

A significant portion of this difficulty is that evidence on property-value impacts is frequently offered by lay witnesses. When asked how evidence is typically presented on property-value impacts, North Carolina cities and counties report that testimony from neighbors and the owner or developer of the property are by far the most common sources of this evidence.[84] This in large part explains the amendment to the zoning statutes in 2009 that limits the use of opinion evidence from nonexpert witnesses on the issue of property-value impacts.[85]

Where expert testimony is offered to establish property-value impacts, it is important that the witness be properly qualified as an expert and that an adequate foundation be established for expert opinions that are offered. In *Mann*, the court noted that a rigorous standard is necessary to establish a foundation for opinion testimony regarding property-value impacts. The applicant's witness on property-value impacts was a professional appraiser; the objecting neighbors presented testimony from a contractor and a real-estate agent. The court noted that all three witnesses offered only speculative opinions about values without supporting facts or examples and ruled that such evidence cannot be the foundation of a finding of adverse impacts.[86] Similarly, in *Humane Society*, the court held that testimony by an appraiser as to the property-value impacts of a proposed animal shelter was based on speculative opinions rather than facts and could not be the basis of a finding on value impacts.[87] In *Dellinger v. Lincoln County II*, the court held that testimony from two appraisers could not be used to make a determination about property-value impacts of a solar farm because the first used as a comparable a solar farm without similar setback, landscaping, and buffering being imposed on the proposed farm and the second appraiser offered only a personal opinion unsupported by quantitative analysis.[88]

---

82. For purposes of this restriction, affordable housing units are defined as those for families or individuals with incomes below 80 percent of the area median income. While use of the term "allowable use" is not a defined term, nor is it typical zoning nomenclature, it would apparently be applicable to any zoning district where multifamily use is either a permitted use or a use allowed by special use permit. It would not include a single-family residential zoning district where multifamily uses are not allowed by right or with a special use permit. This limit on the use of a harmony standard would also apply to a quasi-judicial review of a site plan for a multifamily project with affordable housing. Most site-plan reviews use only objective standards, which would not include a harmony standard. But if such a standard is included in a site plan or other permitting review, this limitation would be applicable.

83. OWENS, *supra* note 12, at 14.

84. Sixty-four percent of jurisdictions responding to a 2005 survey reported that testimony from neighbors was typically offered to establish property-value impacts in special use permit hearings. Fifty-nine percent of the jurisdictions reported testimony from the owner or developer was typically offered on this point, 39 percent reported evidence was typically presented from a real-estate appraiser, and 24 percent reported testimony from real-estate agents. OWENS, *supra* note 12, at 15.

85. G.S. 160A-393(k)(3).

86. Mann Media, Inc. v. Randolph Cnty. Planning Bd., 356 N.C. 1, 565 S.E.2d 9 (2002).

87. Humane Soc'y of Moore Cnty. v. Town of S. Pines, 161 N.C. App. 625, 589 S.E.2d 162 (2003). The appraiser testified that data on impacts of comparable facilities were not available and had based his testimony on seven case studies based on inquiries of appraisers, assessors, brokers, developers, and landowners near other objectionable land uses.

88. 266 N.C. App. 275, 832 S.E.2d 172 (2019). The case was subsequently remanded for reconsideration in light of *PHG Asheville*. 374 N.C. 430 (2020).

By contrast, the court in *Leftwich v. Gaines*, a case for damages resulting from the improper actions of a zoning official, allowed testimony from a plaintiff with experience in real-estate matters to be used as a foundation for setting property values in the context of assessing damages.[89]

Conclusory statements and speculative comments by neighbors cannot properly be the basis of findings relative to property-value impacts. In *Sun Suites*, a case involving a special use permit to build an extended-stay hotel, speculative comments by a neighbor and a real-estate agent about property-value impacts were held to be insubstantial evidence on the effects of the hotel project on surrounding property values.[90]

When credible quantitative evidence on property-value impacts is presented, that evidence cannot be rebutted by generalized contradictory testimony, be it from opposing experts, lay witnesses, or the board itself. In *PHG Asheville, LLC v. City of Asheville*,[91] the applicant presented uncontroverted expert testimony regarding property-value impacts. The court held the board could not find the expert's methodology inadequate based on only its own lay opinion. In *Ecoplexus*, the applicant presented expert testimony on the absence of adverse property-value impacts to neighbors of a proposed solar farm, while the neighbors' expert on property-value impact testified only to his opinion of the "highest and best" use of the property, which was not a permit standard (and he offered no supporting studies).[92] In *Little River*, the applicant presented expert appraisal testimony on property-value impacts, and the opponents' expert addressed potential impacts more broadly than the ordinance standard, which only addressed impacts on "adjoining and abutting" properties.[93] In *Innovative 55, LLC v. Robeson County*, the court held that once an applicant presented expert testimony on the absence of adverse property-value impacts, speculative lay opinion and a neighborhood petition were not sufficient evidence to deny a special use permit for a solar farm.[94] In *Dellinger v. Lincoln County I*, the plaintiffs presented expert testimony from two qualified real-estate appraisers that a solar farm as proposed would not have an impact on neighboring property values. The court held that this established a prima facie entitlement to approval absent contrary substantial, material evidence.[95] In *Weaverville Partners, LLC v. Town of Weaverville Zoning Board of Adjustment*,[96] the plaintiff challenged the denial of a special use permit for an apartment complex. The plaintiff's properly qualified real-estate appraiser testified that he had conducted a market analysis of similarly situated neighborhoods in the town, reviewed sales history around the site over the previous ten years, conducted interviews with nearby purchasers, and reviewed the architectural plans. The opposing testimony addressed two factors: (1) countywide data regarding the effect of apartments in depressing rates of property-value appreciation and (2) whether nearby sales were less than the asking price. The court held neither established a violation of the ordinance standard of substantial depreciation of value. Likewise, testimony regarding the incongruity of the project design

89. 134 N.C. App. 502, 511, 521 S.E.2d 717, 724–25 (1999), *review denied*, 351 N.C. 357, 541 S.E.2d 714 (2000). *See also* Huff v. Thornton, 287 N.C. 1, 213 S.E.2d 198 (1975); Zagaroli v. Pollock, 94 N.C. App. 46, 379 S.E.2d 653, *review denied*, 325 N.C. 437, 384 S.E.2d 548 (1989) (allowing real-estate-developer testimony relative to property value).

90. Sun Suites Holdings, LLC v. Board of Aldermen, 139 N.C. App. 269, 533 S.E.2d 525, *review denied*, 353 N.C. 280, 546 S.E.2d 397 (2000).

91. 374 N.C. 133, 839 S.E.2d 755 (2020).

92. Ecoplexus Inc. v. Cnty. of Currituck, 257 N.C. App. 9, 809 S.E.2d 148 (2017).

93. Little River, LLC v. Lee Cnty., 257 N.C. App. 55, 809 S.E.2d 42 (2017).

94. Innovative 55, LLC v. Robeson Cnty., 253 N.C. App. 714, 801 S.E.2d 671 (2017). The court reached the same conclusion for the same reasons on evidence regarding traffic impacts on public safety.

95. Dellinger v. Lincoln Cnty. I, 248 N.C. App. 317, 789 S.E.2d 21, *review denied*, 369 N.C. 190, 794 S.E.2d 324 (2016). The court subsequently addressed the property-value evidence to the contrary and found it insufficient. 266 N.C. App. 275, 832 S.E.2d 172 (2019). This second case was then remanded for reconsideration in light of *PHG Asheville*. 374 N.C. 430 (2020).

96. 188 N.C. App. 55, 654 S.E.2d 784 (2008). The site was across the street from an apartment building and adjacent to a commercial strip on one side with single-family residential development on the other sides.

with neighboring properties was based solely on personal observations and had no quantitative link to a substantial depreciation in property values.

The fact that evidence of property-value impacts is available and not presented can seriously undermine the case of the party with the burden of establishing (or contesting) that fact. In *SBA*,[97] the plaintiffs appealed the city council's denial of a special use permit for a telecommunication tower. The Asheville ordinance required a conclusion that the project would not substantially injure the value of adjoining or abutting property. The plaintiffs presented a property-value impact study to demonstrate compliance with this standard, but the city staff expressed concern that the study addressed other towers and neighborhoods, not the neighborhood in question. The court was particularly concerned with the plaintiffs' failure to address the property-value impacts of an existing telecommunication tower a short distance from the proposed site that potentially affected the same neighborhoods. The court thus held that the plaintiffs "simply did not meet their burden of demonstrating the absence of harm" to neighboring property values.[98] Similarly, in *American Towers*, the ordinance required the applicant to show the project would not substantially harm neighboring property values. The court upheld denial of the permit based in part on the board's finding that the appraisal information submitted by the applicant failed to address potential impacts in settings similar to the case at hand.[99] By contrast, the court in *PHG Asheville* found that the board could not reject substantial evidence from expert testimony in the record based on its own assessment of that testimony's adequacy.[100]

On occasion, a zoning regulation will include a standard regarding property-value impacts that is similar to the standards discussed above but different in some critical aspects. In one example, *Dismas Charities v. City of Fayetteville*,[101] the standard employed was that the use "allows for the protection of property values." The court held that this was not the equivalent of the typical standard that the use "not substantially injure the value of adjoining or abutting property" for two reasons. First, it was not limited to impacts on adjoining or abutting properties. Second, *allowing* for "the protection of property values" is not the same as substantially injuring adjoining property values. The court held that this standard only required that the applicant show it has incorporated "reasonable" elements in its plans that provide for the benefit of the protection of property values generally as opposed to showing adjacent property values would not be harmed.[102]

---

97. SBA, Inc. v. City of Asheville, 141 N.C. App. 19, 539 S.E.2d 18 (2000).

98. *Id.* at 27, 539 S.E.2d at 23.

99. Am. Towers, Inc. v. Town of Morrisville, 222 N.C. App. 638, 731 S.E.2d 698 (2012), *review denied*, 743 S.E.2d 189 (2013). The board had found the appraisal information insufficient for several reasons. In reviewing impacts on neighboring subdivisions, the submitted study had only looked at subdivisions built after the adjacent telecommunication tower was present, while in this case the adjacent subdivisions were already in existence. (The study also failed to consider potential loss in value due to reduced "curb appeal.")

100. PHG Asheville, LLC v. City of Asheville, 374 N.C. 133, 839 S.E.2d 755 (2020). Here, the board was not resolving conflicting evidence since there was no evidence presented to the contrary; it did have concerns, however, about the reliability of the expert testimony.

101. 282 N.C. App. 29, 870 S.E.2d 144 (2022). The plaintiff applied for a special use permit to construct a halfway house for prisoners transitioning into society. The property was a vacant lot in the downtown area.

102. The court found that the record included evidence that showed the proposed use incorporated elements to protect property values generally, and the attractive, commercial-grade building would have high-maintenance standards. As no contrary competent, material, and substantial evidence was presented, the plaintiff was entitled to permit issuance.

Traffic Impacts

As with the property-value standard, boards must often deal with cases where there is both technical evidence on traffic impacts presented by experts and evidence offered by lay neighbors concerned about traffic that would be generated by proposed new development.

The cases clearly indicate that speculative objections from lay witnesses about traffic effects, like lay opinions on property value, are insufficient to rebut quantified evidence from properly qualified experts.[103] In *Weaverville Partners*, the applicant for a special use permit for an apartment complex presented testimony from a traffic engineer that the project and its access road would not create traffic problems for pedestrians and vehicles. The engineer produced trip-generation data, related the project to the town road plans, and described measures for minimizing congestion. The opposing testimony from neighbors was characterized as speculative lay opinion, unsupported by mathematical studies or a factual basis and thus insufficient to rebut the credible quantitative evidence of the applicant.[104]

Several cases illustrate the evidence needed to support a finding that a proposed special use permit would create adverse traffic impacts. In *Howard v. City of Kinston*,[105] the court upheld a finding that significant adverse impacts on traffic would endanger public health and safety. The findings were based on testimony from city planning staff that specified trip-generation projections and from a neighbor who testified as to the number of children in the area and past experience in this particular area with the safety of walkers and cyclists. In *Ghidorzi Construction, Inc. v. Town of Chapel Hill*,[106] the court ruled that the council's denial of a special use permit because of effects on traffic safety was supported by substantial, material, and competent evidence, given the traffic studies and reports submitted by the petitioner and the town staff. The town council was not required to consider possible future road improvements in making its judgment. In *In re Goforth Properties, Inc.*,[107] the court held that evidence in the record regarding increased traffic counts and their effects on traffic safety at a nearby intersection, and for nearby schools and fire stations, constituted competent, material, and substantial evidence to support the council's finding that the proposed development would not maintain public health and safety.

By contrast, in *Triple E Associates v. Town of Matthews*, the court held that the board may not rely on speculative traffic projections to make a finding regarding traffic congestion.[108] The court reached a similar conclusion in a case involving preliminary plat approval, holding that speculative comments about the impact of traffic on children playing in the street was an inadequate basis for plat denial.[109] The fact that state transportation officials have not objected and that permit conditions were imposed to address traffic issues has also been important in finding no harms to safety based on traffic impacts.[110]

---

103. As with property-value impacts, the statute was amended in 2009 to expressly limit the use of opinion evidence from nonexpert witnesses on the issue of public-safety impacts of traffic. G.S. 160D-1402(j)(3).

104. 188 N.C. App. 55, 654 S.E.2d 784 (2008). *See also* Blue Ridge Co. v. Town of Pineville, 188 N.C. App. 466, 655 S.E.2d 843, 848–49, *review denied*, 362 N.C. 679, 669 S.E.2d 742 (2008) (noting expert testimony that the substantial increase in traffic generated would not create an undue safety problem cannot be rebutted by lay testimony that offers no mathematical studies but only speculative and generalized concerns).

105. 148 N.C. App. 238, 558 S.E.2d 221 (2002).

106. 80 N.C. App. 438, 342 S.E.2d 545, *review denied*, 317 N.C. 703, 347 S.E.2d 41 (1986). The application was for a ninety-one-unit development on a 15.2-acre tract.

107. 76 N.C. App. 231, 332 S.E.2d 503, *review denied*, 315 N.C. 183, 337 S.E.2d 857 (1985).

108. 105 N.C. App. 354, 413 S.E.2d 305, *review denied*, 332 N.C. 150, 419 S.E.2d 578 (1992). *See also* PHG Asheville, LLC v. City of Asheville, 374 N.C. 133, 839 S.E.2d 755 (2020) (uncontroverted expert testimony regarding traffic impacts cannot be rejected based only on the board's own lay opinion of study's adequacy).

109. Guilford Fin. Servs., LLC v. City of Brevard, 356 N.C. 655, 576 S.E.2d 325 (2003), *per curiam, adopting dissent in* 150 N.C. App. 1, 563 S.E.2d 27 (2002).

110. Little River, LLC v. Lee County, 257 N.C. App. 55, 809 S.E.2d 42 (2017) (reversing denial of special use permit for a rock quarry).

Conformity with the Comprehensive Plan

Plan consistency was made a mandatory consideration in legislative rezoning decisions in 2005.[111] This factor has, however, long been a standard for special use permits in many zoning regulations. In spite of the fact that many plans are general in nature (or perhaps because of this), plan conformance has rarely arisen in North Carolina litigation on special use permits.

In *Davidson County Broadcasting Co. v. Iredell County*, the court affirmed it was permissible to include plan consistency as a special use permit standard and to use the adopted plan as a guide to determine harmony with the area.[112] In *Vulcan*, the board of county commissioners denied a special use permit for a proposed rock quarry on the grounds that there was insufficient credible evidence to find that the use would be in conformity with the land use plan. The court of appeals held that evidence in the record showing that the land use plan reserved the area for residential use was sufficient to support the decision to deny the permit.[113] By contrast, in *American Towers*, the court held that a suggestion in the plan that the subject property may in the future be rezoned from industrial to residential was not sufficient to find plan inconsistency prior to any such rezoning.[114]

Public Necessity

In *SBA*, the plaintiff appealed the city council's denial of a special use permit for a 175-foot telecommunication tower. Lack of evidence presented by the applicant regarding the feasibility of alternate sites or stealth technology (and that significant coverage gaps would remain even with this tower) supported a conclusion that it had not been established that the use was reasonably necessary.[115]

Scope of Permissible Conditions

G.S. 160D-705(c) provides that "reasonable and appropriate conditions and safeguards" may be imposed on any special use permit.

---

111. For a discussion of the mandatory plan-consistency review in legislative zoning decisions, see Chapter 22.

112. Davidson Cnty. Broad. Co. v. Iredell Cnty., 248 N.C. App. 305, 790 S.E.2d 663 (2016), *review denied*, 369 N.C. 530 (2017). The plaintiffs argued that it was an error of law for the board not to apply a conclusive presumption of harmony based on inclusion of this use as a possible special use in the district. The court, in a de novo review, held inclusion only created a presumption that could be rebutted by substantial evidence to the contrary.

113. Vulcan Materials Co. v. Guilford Cnty. Bd. of Cnty. Comm'rs, 115 N.C. App. 319, 444 S.E.2d 639, *review denied*, 337 N.C. 807, 449 S.E.2d 758 (1994). *See also* Schooldev East, LLC v. Town of Wake Forest, 284 N.C. App. 434, 876 S.E.2d 607 (2022) (while community-plan policy by itself is advisory only, provisions in a unified development ordinance can make it a standard for regulatory decisions); Piney Mountain Neighborhood Ass'n v. Town of Chapel Hill, 63 N.C. App. 244, 251, 304 S.E.2d 251, 255 (1983) (even though plan is advisory, proper to consider as a factor in special use permit decision). For a case addressing this in the context of a subdivision-plat-approval decision, see *Blue Ridge Co. v. Town of Pineville*, 188 N.C. App. 466, 655 S.E.2d 843, *review denied*, 362 N.C. 679, 669 S.E.2d 742 (2008). The town denied approval of a plat in part based on a conclusion that the project failed to meet a requirement that it be consistent with adopted public plans for public facilities, including schools. The court held there was insufficient evidence in the record to support a conclusion that the project would lead to school overcrowding in a way that violated town plans and policies. The court noted it was uncertain that there was in fact an adopted plan or policy specifically addressing this point. The ordinance did not require a school-impact analysis, and in any event, the overcrowding existed even without this subdivision.

114. Am. Towers v. Town of Morrisville, 222 N.C. App. 638, 731 S.E.2d 698 (2012), *review denied*, 743 S.E.2d 189 (2013). In *Ecoplexus Inc. v. County of Currituck*, 257 N.C. App. 9, 809 S.E.2d 148 (2017), the court held that the plan policies cited to justify denial of a special use permit for a solar farm applied to offshore-energy development, not solar farms.

115. SBA, Inc. v. City of Asheville, 141 N.C. App. 19, 539 S.E.2d 18 (2000).

The statute goes on, however, to provide that special use permits cannot be subject to conditions that the local government does not have statutory authority to regulate or that the courts have held to be unenforceable if imposed as a direct regulation.[116]

Any condition imposed must be related to standards for the permit that are in the ordinance.[117] Each condition that is imposed must be supported by adequate evidence in the record.[118]

---

116. G.S. 160D-705(c). This provision was added to the statutes by S.L. 2015-286, § 1.8. This provision was amended in 2019 to list examples of impermissible conditions, including unauthorized taxes, impact fees, building-design standards, and excess driveway-related improvements. S.L. 2019-111, § 1.12.

117. Hewett v. Cnty. of Brunswick, 155 N.C. App. 138, 573 S.E.2d 688 (2002); Overton v. Camden Cnty., 155 N.C. App. 100, 574 S.E.2d 150 (2002).

118. Nw. Prop. Grp., LLC v. Town of Carrboro, 201 N.C. App. 449, 687 S.E.2d 1 (2009). The court invalidated a permit condition that limited use of a side-street access to a commercial project to emergency vehicles only. Although neighbors had expressed concerns about traffic impacts at the hearing, the board made no findings justifying the imposition of such a condition. Also see the discussion of the necessity for supporting evidence for a condition in *Ward*, 166 N.C. App. 586, 603 S.E.2d 393 (2004).

CHAPTER 17

Variances

The legal concept of providing administrative relief to detailed governmental regulations in exceptional individual cases has a considerable lineage.[1]

The model for the zoning variance was the building code established for New York City in 1862. It provided the Department of Buildings with the power to "modify or vary any of the several provisions of [the] act to meet the requirements of special cases, where the same do not conflict with public safety and the public good, so that substantial justice may be done."[2] In 1916, New York incorporated a similar provision for variation from the strict application of regulations in the nation's initial comprehensive-zoning regulation.[3]

The city acknowledged that its brief zoning ordinance could not fully anticipate all of the variations in particular parcels of land, individual land uses, and peculiar situations that would arise with zoning implementation. Situations would invariably crop up where it would be neither fair nor desirable to apply the general standards in the ordinance to a particular case. So the initial rationale for the variance power was to provide a tool to perfect a crude regulatory instrument.[4] The variance was also deemed to be a constitutional necessity to prevent what would otherwise be an inflexible, unreasonable, arbitrary application of zoning ordinances[5]—to be, in effect, a safety valve for circumstances not anticipated at the time of zoning-ordinance adoption. This notion of the variance being limited to unanticipated and peculiar circumstances continues to be a factor in variance law.

Those supporting zoning also based the zoning variance on pragmatic and tactical considerations. In the first decades of zoning application, they deemed it advisable to limit exposure to courts that might invalidate the entire zoning enterprise.[6] They also felt frequent amendment by the governing board would

---

1. "The term 'dispensing power' is used in the history of English constitutional law with reference to the alleged royal prerogative to suspend in favor of particular individuals or cases the operation of a general law—a power, the exercise of which by the Crown was finally declared illegal in the seventeenth century . . . ." ERNST FREUND, ADMINISTRATIVE POWERS OVER PERSONS AND PROPERTY: A COMPARATIVE STUDY 128 (1928).

2. 1862 N.Y. Laws, ch. 356, p. 591.

3. NEW YORK CITY, N.Y., BUILDING ZONE RESOLUTION § 20 (1916). This initial zoning ordinance was rudimentary at best, with only about seven pages of text. New York at the time had a population of over 5 million persons and an area of nearly 300 square miles.

4. Ernst Freund referred to the zoning board of appeals as "that original and ingenious institution devised to cover a multitude of sins." Ernst Freund, *Some Inadequately Discussed Problems of the Law of City Planning and Zoning*, 24 ILL. L. REV. 135, 144 (1929).

5. In zoning's infancy the principal constitutional concern was avoidance of a due-process challenge. Robert A. Williams Jr., *Euclid's Lochnerian Legacy, in* ZONING AND THE AMERICAN DREAM: PROMISES STILL TO KEEP 278 (Charles M. Haar & Jerold S. Kayden eds., 1989). In its second zoning opinion, the U.S. Supreme Court invalidated a residential zoning classification as applied to a lot located between residential and commercial/industrial areas. Nectow v. City of Cambridge, 277 U.S. 183 (1928). In the modern era, the variance has come to be seen as a protection against takings claims.

6. Newman F. Baker, *The Zoning Board of Appeals*, 10 MINN. L. REV. 277, 280–83 (1926). Baker quotes Edward Bassett, "[I]n many cities there is no doubt that the courts would have punched holes through every zoning plan unless the city had a Board of Appeals . . . to inject a sensible amount of adaptation in exceptional cases." *Id.* at 282.

be undesirable.[7] The variance was thus seen as a pragmatic means of taking individual disputes out of the political and judicial realms that might be less hospitable to effective zoning practices.

Statutory Authority for Variances

The variance power was included in the Standard State Zoning Enabling Act promulgated by the U.S. Department of Commerce in 1922,[8] which largely followed the New York City model. Most states incorporated similar language into their statutes. The North Carolina zoning statutes generally follow the original provisions in the Standard State Zoning Enabling Act.

Chapter 160D, Section 705(d) of the North Carolina General Statutes (hereinafter G.S.) is the statutory authorization for zoning variances.[9] The enabling statute in North Carolina, as in most states, requires a four-fifths supermajority vote of the decision-making board to grant a variance.[10]

Specific provisions for variances, often substantially similar to the zoning variance, are included in various other development-regulation statutes, including those for housing codes, floodplain zoning, airport zoning, water-supply-watershed protection, and the Coastal Area Management Act.[11] With the enactment of Chapter 160D in 2019, the standards and procedures for variances in most of these separate statutes were harmonized with the zoning-variance standards and procedures.

Some authorizations for development regulations, such as the subdivision-enabling statute, have no specific provisions authorizing variances. Variances can be allowed for these regulations by individual local ordinances. G.S. 160D-705(b) authorizes use of the variance power in "any other ordinance that regulates land use or development," provided that it is done consistently with the provisions of the zoning variance. As a result, for example, some subdivision ordinances allow petitions for variances. If

---

7. As was common with the progressive-movement principles underlying zoning adoption in the 1920s, this notion of having a board of experts (rather than politicians on the governing board) making adjustments was a popular justification for the board of adjustment's variance power. *See, e.g., id.* at 280.

8. STANDARD STATE ZONING ENABLING ACT, § 7 (1926), *reprinted in* ROBERT M. ANDERSON & BRUCE B. ROSWIG, PLANNING, ZONING & SUBDIVISION: A SUMMARY OF STATUTORY LAW IN THE 50 STATES 178 (1966). The Standard State Zoning Enabling Act used only the term *unnecessary hardship*, while the New York City ordinance on which it was based also included *practical difficulties* as a basis for a variance. About half of the states, including North Carolina, incorporated both terms in their enabling acts. See generally AMERICAN LAW OF ZONING §§ 13:10, 13:11 (5th ed. Dec. 2022 Update).

9. Chapter 160D, Section 705(d) of the North Carolina General Statutes (hereinafter G.S.). These provisions were updated in 2005. S.L. 2005-418, §§ 8(a), (b). The provisions were further revised in 2013, codifying much of the case law discussed below on the definition of *unnecessary hardship* and deleting *practical difficulties* from the language. S.L. 2013-126. The provision regarding reasonable accommodation for persons with disabilities was added by S.L. 2019-111.

10. The requirement for a supermajority was initially imposed on the board of appeals in the original New York City zoning ordinance that served as the national model for zoning in the United States. There the requirement was for a five-sevenths vote to grant a variance. The draftsman of that ordinance noted, "[I]t was considered that inasmuch as the grant of a variance permit allowed the applicant to do something that his neighbors could not do under the strict application of the law, the favorable vote of the board should be greater than a mere majority." EDWARD M. BASSETT, ZONING: THE LAWS, ADMINISTRATION, AND COURT DECISIONS DURING THE FIRST TWENTY YEARS 119 (1940). For more details on voting and calculating the supermajority, see Chapter 15 on quasi-judicial procedures.

The North Carolina statute was amended in 2005 to clarify that vacant positions and members excused from voting due to a conflict of interest are not counted in computing the supermajority. S.L. 2005-418, §§ 8(a), (b), amending G.S. 160D-406(i).

11. *See* G.S. 160D-1208(b) (housing appeals board may "adapt the application of the ordinance to the necessities of the case" upon finding unnecessary hardships); G.S. 63-32(b) (airport zoning); G.S. 113A-113A-120.1 (Coastal Area Management Act); G.S. 143-214.5(b) (state approval of local variances under water-supply-watershed-protection ordinances); G.S. 143-215.54A(b) (authority and standards for variances in floodplain zoning, including use variances).

this is the case, the standards and procedures set forth for variances in the subdivision regulation must mirror the zoning statute.[12]

The North Carolina statutes assign the variance decision-making responsibility to the board of adjustment but allow cities and counties to alternatively designate the planning board or governing board to perform this function.[13] The vast majority of North Carolina cities and counties have chosen to leave this responsibility with the board of adjustment.[14]

A variance is not a personal right but is tied to the specific parcel of property for which it is issued. As G.S. 160D-104 provides, all development approvals made under Chapter 160D "attach to and run with the land." The duration of a variance is not set by statute, but G.S. 160D-403(c) provides that local "development approvals" expire after one year if work has not substantially commenced. G.S. 160D-102(13) defines "development approvals" to include variances.

Requests for variances are not unusual. In a 2002 survey, North Carolina cities and counties reported receiving over 1800 variance petitions in the previous year. Many of these requests are approved, as that survey reported 72 percent of the requests were granted.[15]

Standards

Those drafting the original zoning scheme acknowledged that the statutory standards for granting variances were "rather vague, elusive, and elastic."[16] Several early zoning cases held that these standards were so general as to constitute an unlawful delegation of legislative discretion,[17] particularly in the absence of procedural-due-process protections such as a hearing and written findings of fact supported by adequate evidence.

---

12. Before G.S. 160D-705(d) was amended to make its provisions applicable to all local development regulations, *Hemphill-Nolan v. Town of Weddington*, 153 N.C. App. 144, 568 S.E.2d 887 (2002), distinguished the process permissible in a subdivision ordinance from the zoning process. This case involved denial of a variance for a cul-de-sac-length limit in a subdivision ordinance. The court held that the provisions then in G.S. 160A-388 setting time limits for appeals of zoning variances applied only to ordinances adopted pursuant to Part 3 of Article 19 of G.S. 160A (which authorized zoning ordinances), and that since Part 2 of the article (which authorized subdivision ordinances) was at the time silent on this point, appeals of those decisions must be brought within a reasonable time established by common law rather than the thirty days specified for zoning-variance appeals.

13. G.S. 160D-302(b).

14. A 2002 survey indicated that 83 percent of North Carolina cities and counties assign variance decision-making to boards of adjustment, 11 percent to the governing board, and 5 percent to the planning board. DAVID OWENS & ADAM BRUEGGEMANN, A SURVEY OF EXPERIENCE WITH ZONING VARIANCES 10 (UNC School of Government, Special Series No. 18, Feb. 2004).

15. *Id.* at 17. Other national studies indicate that an approval rate of 70 to 80 percent is common. David Owens, *The Zoning Variance: Reappraisal and Recommendations for Reform of a Much-Maligned Tool*, 29 COLUM. J. ENVTL. L. 279, 295–96 (2004).

16. EDWARD M. BASSETT ET AL., MODEL LAWS FOR PLANNING CITIES, COUNTIES, AND STATES 64 (1935). The general nature of the standard was intentional:

> [T]he Standard Zoning Act . . . grants in broad terms to boards of appeals the power of variance for practical difficulty and unnecessary hardship. Of this breadth there has been considerable criticism. We believe that in any narrowing of this power there is the risk that cases of hardship and injustice will arise for which no practicable remedy is provided, with the result that the community will be injured, as it is in all cases of injustice, and the constitutionality of the law imperiled.

Id. at 13.

17. *Welton v. Hamilton*, 344 Ill. 82, 91, 176 N.E. 333, 337 (Ill. 1931) (variance had been granted for a twenty-story apartment building in a Chicago zoning district with a height limit of seventy-two feet); Jack Lewis, Inc. v. Mayor of Baltimore, 164 Md. 146, 149, 164 A. 220, 222 (1933); Sugar v. N. Balt. Methodist Protestant Church, 164 Md. 487, 494, 165 A. 703, 705–06 (Md. 1933) (variance was for confectionary and delicatessen in a residential zoning district).

Historically, it was not uncommon for individual zoning ordinances to provide more detailed standards elaborating on these basic provisions—in particular, additional guidance about what constitutes an unnecessary hardship that would justify a variance. The standards for variances in state law are mandatory, and local governments are preempted from adopting standards contrary to those of their states.[18] Supplementary standards that provide additional guidance and elaboration of state standards have generally been held to be permissible in this context,[19] but given the specificity on the definition of *unnecessary hardship* added to the North Carolina statute in 2013, most local elaboration in this state is likely preempted.

The standards and limits for variances are set out in G.S. 160D-705(d). That statute provides:

When unnecessary hardships would result from carrying out the strict letter of a zoning regulation, the board of adjustment shall vary any of the provisions of the zoning regulation upon a showing of all of the following:

(1) Unnecessary hardship would result from the strict application of the regulation. It shall not be necessary to demonstrate that, in the absence of the variance, no reasonable use can be made of the property.

(2) The hardship results from conditions that are peculiar to the property, such as location, size, or topography. Hardships resulting from personal circumstances, as well as hardships resulting from conditions that are common to the neighborhood or the general public, may not be the basis for granting a variance. A variance may be granted when necessary and appropriate to make a reasonable accommodation under the Federal Fair Housing Act for a person with a disability.

(3) The hardship did not result from actions taken by the applicant or the property owner. The act of purchasing property with knowledge that circumstances exist that may justify the granting of a variance is not a self-created hardship.

(4) The requested variance is consistent with the spirit, purpose, and intent of the regulation, such that public safety is secured and substantial justice is achieved.

Notably, this statute establishes an entitlement to a variance upon showing the standards are met. It states that the local government "shall vary" the regulations upon a showing that "all" of the standards are met.

A substantial judicial gloss has been applied to the statutory standards for zoning variances over the past eighty years.[20] Courts around the country have established detailed interpretations of the statutory requirements a petitioner must meet to qualify for a zoning variance and have, to a lesser extent, elaborated on the negative community impacts that variances must avoid. While the precise tests vary from state to state, the common tenor set very early was that the "power of variation is to be sparingly

---

18. *See, e.g.,* Nelson v. Donaldson, 255 Ala. 76, 84, 50 So. 2d 244, 251 (1951) (municipality must adhere to state standards if considering variance); Celentano v. Bd. of Zoning Appeals, 149 Conn. 671, 677, 184 A.2d 49, 52 (1962) (board has no power to enlarge or limit statutory variance provisions); Cohen v. Bd. of Appeals, 100 N.Y.2d 395, 402, 764 N.Y.S.2d 64, 68–69, 795 N.E.2d 619, 623–24 (2003) (state statute on area variances preempts local ordinance); Coderre v. Zoning Bd. of Review, 102 R.I. 327, 330, 230 A.2d 247, 249 (1967).

19. *See, e.g.,* Gould v. Santa Fe Cnty., 131 N.M. 405, 411, 37 P.3d 122, 128 (Ct. App. 2001) (overturning density variance and holding local ordinance may contain more restrictive or detailed standards provided they do not conflict with state variance standards). *But see* Perkins v. Town of Ogunquit, 709 A.2d 106, 110–11 (Me. 1998) (overturning frontage variance and holding zoning statute implicitly preempts local waiver or relief from ordinance based on lesser standards than in statute); Cole v. Bd. of Zoning Appeals, 39 Ohio App. 2d 177, 181, 317 N.E.2d 65, 68 (1973) (upholding denial of use variance and holding local standards cannot be more stringent nor more liberal than state-statute criteria for variances); Lincourt v. Zoning Bd. of Review, 98 R.I. 305, 309, 201 A.2d 482, 485 (1964) (local standards may provide neither more nor less than the state standard).

20. For a comprehensive collection of the case law interpreting the limits of the variance power in the first quarter century of zoning in the United States, see Philip P. Green, Jr., *The Power of the Zoning Board of Adjustment to Grant Variances from the Zoning Ordinance,* 29 N.C. L. Rev. 245 (1951).

exercised and only in rare instances and under exceptional circumstances peculiar in their nature, and with due regard to the main purpose of a zoning ordinance to preserve the property rights of others."[21]

These statutory and judicial standards require that the person seeking a variance show that a substantial and unnecessary hardship would result from a strict application of the regulation and granting relief would not harm neighbors or the community.

Degree of Hardship

As historically interpreted by the courts, the most significant limitation on the variance power is the requirement that a petitioner establish that compliance with the strict terms of the ordinance would cause *unnecessary* hardship.

There is broad legal consensus that to be "unnecessary," this requisite burden must be substantial. Inherent in any regulatory scheme is the understanding that some burdens shared by all do not rise to the level of qualifying the owner for variance consideration. The courts have held with near uniformity that even though more profitable uses are available or that the cost of compliance increases the cost of development, these factors do not constitute undue hardship.[22] However, what constitutes the minimum reasonable use that must be allowed or when the additional costs imposed to develop in strict compliance with zoning standards become unduly excessive are the most difficult issues of judgment and discretion to be determined in variance decisions.

The most stringent application of the hardship test nationally requires an owner to show that strict compliance with the zoning would prevent any reasonable use of the property.[23] Such a rigorous application of this standard allows the variance to be used as a constitutional safety valve to avoid what might otherwise be unlawful takings.[24] When strictly applied, this requirement substantially limits the range

---

21. Hammond v. Bd. of Appeal, 257 Mass. 446, 448, 154 N.E. 82, 83 (1926) (upholding variance granted to allow retail store in residential district, despite several unsuccessful rezoning requests, upon showing inability to rent structure as residence). *See also* Norcross v. Bd. of Appeal, 255 Mass. 177, 183, 150 N.E. 887, 890 (1926) (upholding height variance).

22. *See, e.g.*, MacLean v. Zoning Bd. of Adjustment, 409 Pa. 82, 87, 185 A.2d 533, 536 (1962) (showing of greater financial gain if gas station were allowed in a residential zoning district is insufficient to justify variance); Natrella v. Bd. of Zoning Appeals, 231 Va. 451, 458, 345 S.E.2d 295, 300 (1986) (affirming dimensional variance for nonconforming structure, holding that while financial loss alone is insufficient to justify a finding of undue hardship, it is a factor to be taken into account); State v. Winnebago Cnty., 196 Wis. 2d 836, 844, 540 N.W.2d 6, 9–10 (Wis. Ct. App. 1995) (invalidating variance that would have allowed more intensive shoreland development). *But see* Bouley v. City of Nashua, 205 A.2d 38 (N.H. 1964) (restriction in use resulting in reduction of sales price of lot from $17,500 to $3000 is unnecessary hardship absent injury to adjoining property or public interest). *See also* Bassett, *supra* note 16, at 124.

23. A leading early case noted that the record must establish that "the land in question cannot yield a reasonable return" without the variance. Otto v. Steinhilber, 282 N.Y. 71, 76, 24 N.E.2d 851, 853 (1939) (overturning variance issued to construct a skating rink on a parcel that was primarily zoned residential). Some states have incorporated such a definition of *undue unnecessary hardship* into their zoning statutes. *See, e.g.*, 65 Ill. Comp. Stat. 5 / 11-13-4 (requires showing that property "cannot yield a reasonable return" without a variance); Vt. Stat. Ann. tit. 24, § 4469 (requires that variance is "necessary to enable the reasonable use of the property"). When the issue is the additional costs imposed, the petitioner must establish that development or use without a variance would be cost prohibitive. *See, e.g.*, Gemma v. Zoning Bd. of Review, 93 R.I. 440, 445, 176 A.2d 722, 725 (1962) (to constitute unnecessary hardship the cost of site preparation must be so great as to take the property out of the market for permitted purposes).

24. A land use regulation that deprives the owner of all economically beneficial or productive use is, with limited exceptions, an unconstitutional taking. Lucas v. S.C. Coastal Council, 505 U.S. 1003, 1015 (1992). This strict test of unnecessary hardship for a variance is similar, though some courts have noted that it is not quite as restrictive. *See, e.g.*, Belvoir Farms Homeowners Ass'n v. North, 355 Md. 259, 281, 734 A.2d 227, 240 (1999). See Chapter 24 for a discussion of regulatory-takings law.

of discretion available to boards making variance decisions. It is the rare variance request that meets such a strict test of hardship, and the fact that variances are routinely approved without meeting it has long been a principal judicial and academic criticism of variance practice.[25]

The first major North Carolina case on zoning variances, *Lee v. Board of Adjustment*,[26] involved a request to build a grocery store/service station in Rocky Mount in a district zoned exclusively for residential use. This case addressed the "undue" hardship required to qualify for variance consideration. Because the applicant only held an option to purchase the land, the court ruled, he would suffer no undue hardship.[27] The court noted that the applicant could simply not execute the option, thereby avoiding any hardship at all. The court also noted that there was no hardship based on the contention that the proposed use would be more profitable:

> It is erroneous to base a conclusion that the denial of an application would work an unnecessary hardship because the applicant could earn a better income from the type of building proposed.
>
> The financial situation or pecuniary hardship of a single owner affords no adequate grounds for putting forth this extraordinary power affecting other property owners as well as the public.[28]

The court in *Williams v. North Carolina Department of Environment & Natural Resources* further explored the requirement for unnecessary hardship.[29] It held that the owner's possession of other devel-

---

25. Two judicial alternatives to this strict test evolved in other states to increase the potential availability of variances. The first, which appeared in the 1950s, was to apply the "no reasonable use" test only to use variances and to apply a less-stringent test for dimensional variances. The rationale for this distinction is that dimensional variances pose less of a potential harm to neighbors and thus warrant less-stringent judicial oversight. While this distinction may reflect a good-faith effort by the courts to better align variance law with variance practice, there is no statutory basis in most states for it. The leading case making this distinction was *Village of Bronxville v. Francis*, 1 A.D.2d 236, 239, 150 N.Y.S.2d 906, 909 (App. Div.), *aff'd*, 153 N.Y.S.2d 220, 135 N.E.2d 724 (N.Y. 1956). New York statutes now use a multipart formula for deciding dimensional variances. N.Y. Town Law § 267-b(3)(b). This standard balances impacts on the petitioner and the community, and it does not require a showing of practical difficulties. Kaiser v. Town of Islip Zoning Bd. of Appeals, 74 A.D.3d 1203, 1205, 904 N.Y.S.2d 166, 168–69 (App. Div. 2010); Sasso v. Osgood, 86 N.Y.2d 374, 383, 633 N.Y.S.2d 259, 263–64, 657 N.E.2d 254, 258–59 (1995). *See also In re* Stadsvold, 754 N.W.2d 323 (Minn. 2008) (applying "practical difficulty" standard to dimensional variances and "particular hardship" standard to use variances); State *ex rel*. Ziervogel v. Washington Cnty. Bd. of Adjustment, 676 N.W.2d 401 (Wis. 2004). *But see* City & Borough of Juneau v. Thibodeau, 595 P.2d 626, 634 (Alaska 1979); Cochran v. Fairfax Cnty. Bd. of Zoning Appeals, 267 Va. 756, 766, 594 S.E.2d 571, 577 (2004). Some states have incorporated differential hardship standards for dimensional and use variances into their zoning-enabling statutes. *See, e.g.*, Me. Rev. Stat. Ann. tit. 30-A, § 4353(4) (authorizing local limits on use variances); R.I. Gen. Laws § 45-24-41(d). A second alternative is to consider the degree of impairment the regulation causes to reasonable use and the extent of the costs it imposes as factors in determining whether the hardship is sufficient to justify a variance. Simplex Techs., Inc. v. Town of Newington, 145 N.H. 727, 731–32, 766 A.2d 713, 717 (2001) (replacing no-reasonable-use test for unnecessary hardship with three-factor test for the requisite hardship: (1) ordinance interferes with reasonable use of the property, considering its unique setting; (2) no fair and substantial relationship exists between the purpose of the ordinance and the particular restriction; and (3) variance would not injure public or private rights of others). Other states have addressed this issue legislatively. For example, in 2015 the Virginia statute on zoning variances was amended to allow a variance if strict application would "unreasonably restrict the utilization of the property." Va. Stat. § 15.2-2309.

26. 226 N.C. 107, 37 S.E.2d 128 (1946).

27. "He possesses no present right to erect a building on the lot described in his contract. To withhold from him a building permit to do what he has no present right to do cannot, in law, impose an 'undue and unnecessary hardship' upon him." *Id*. at 110, 37 S.E.2d at 131.

28. *Id*. (citations omitted).

29. 144 N.C. App. 479, 548 S.E.2d 793 (2001). The case involved judicial review of the denial of a Coastal Area Management Act variance. The terms of the variance standard in this statute are similar to those for zoning variances. This statute was amended in 2002 to delete the reference to "practical difficulties" as a variance standard, retaining only the requirement for a showing of "unnecessary hardships." S.L. 2002-68. That same amendment was later made for the zoning-variance statute. S.L. 2013-126.

opable property nearby was irrelevant, as the variance must be considered strictly in relation to the property, not the owner of the property. The critical inquiry, the court held, was whether the property could be put to some reasonable use without a variance.

The court in *Showcase Realty & Construction Co. v. City of Fayetteville Board of Adjustment* [30] likewise held that the petitioner for a variance must present substantial evidence regarding the impact of the ordinance on the owner's ability to make reasonable use of the property. The court noted that the board could not simply rely on a conclusory statement and that the financial cost of compliance alone (in this case the relocation of an improperly placed concrete slab for a building under construction) was insufficient to establish the requisite unnecessary hardship.

In contrast, the court found sufficient hardship to justify a variance in *Turik v. Town of Surf City*. [31] The town issued a building permit, and construction was under way in accordance with that permit. The adjoining property owner then objected and submitted a new survey that, if accurate, would have resulted in the pilings of the permitted building being 7.2 inches inside the mandated setback. While not explicitly addressing the degree of hardship involved, the court noted that the hardship was real (it would require demolition or substantial alteration of the existing partially completed building) and emphasized that it was not self-created, as the owner made good-faith reliance on what appeared to be a valid survey prepared by a licensed surveyor. [32]

The General Assembly clarified the zoning-variance standard in 2013 to address the issue of whether retention of any reasonable use was disqualifying for a variance. G.S. 160D-705(d)(1) was amended to explicitly provide that a showing of no reasonable use of the property without a variance is not required. [33]

Hardship Results from the Ordinance

The hardship that justifies a variance must result from the application of the ordinance itself.

---

30. 155 N.C. App. 516, 573 S.E.2d 737 (2002).

31. 182 N.C. App. 427, 642 S.E.2d 251 (2007).

32. The minimal amount of the dimensional variance sought was also of clear importance to the court, which concluded that such a small variation did not conflict with the purpose of the ordinance and would have minimal, if any, harm to the neighbor. *See also* Stealth Props., LLC v. Town of Pinebluff Bd. of Adjustment, 183 N.C. 461, 645 S.E.2d 144, *review denied*, 361 N.C. 703, 653 S.E.2d 153 (2007). This case involved a variance necessitated by a misunderstanding about which zoning district applied to the property on which the petitioner placed a modular home. The petitioner erroneously thought the property was in a zoning district that required a fifteen-foot setback. The property was actually in a district requiring a twenty-five-foot setback. The petitioner's application noted a sixteen-foot setback, but the permit (a certificate of zoning compliance) noted a twenty-five-foot setback. The petitioner built at the sixteen-foot setback, and the error was not caught until construction was complete. When the certificate of occupancy was denied, a variance was sought and denied. The court held that the variance denial was not supported by substantial, competent, and material evidence since a malfunction of the recording equipment and a disagreement about the minutes led to no transcript or detailed record of the evidence being a part of the record on appeal. The court, however, held the setback requirement to be ambiguous and ordered the variance issued on remand.

33. This provision was added by S.L. 2013-126.

The personal situation of the applicant[34] or the convenience of the owner[35] does not qualify the owner for variance consideration. This is codified in G.S. 160D-705(d)(2), which requires that the hardship not result from the personal circumstances of the applicant.

Variances requested in response to an owner's disability present a particularly difficult situation. While the courts have traditionally and consistently held that the health of the owner cannot be the basis of the hardship, some more-recent decisions allow greater flexibility to consider variances as a reasonable accommodation for persons with disabilities.[36] In recognition of this need, G.S. 160D-705(d)(2) was amended in 2019 to allow consideration of accommodation for persons with disabilities.[37]

Another dimension to this rule is that the hardship usually cannot be created by a nongovernmental restriction as opposed to by a government regulation. Courts in other states have held that a hardship caused by a restrictive covenant should not be considered in assessing hardship.[38] That said, a restrictive covenant may be a legitimate consideration in some circumstances in North Carolina. *Chapel Hill Title & Abstract Co. v. Town of Chapel Hill*[39] involved a situation where an owner could comply with a street setback imposed by restrictive covenants only if the proposed residence encroached on a stream setback at the rear of the lot required by an overlay-zoning-district requirement. The town refused to

---

34. *See, e.g.*, Garibaldi v. Zoning Bd. of Appeals, 303 A.2d 743, 745 (Conn. 1972) (invalidating variance granted from minimum-separation requirements for liquor outlets to owner whose previous store had been taken for highway construction); Crossley v. Town of Pelham, 578 A.2d 319, 320 (N.H. 1990) (invalidating dimensional variance to construct larger replacement garage on nonconforming lot); Hickox v. Griffin, 83 N.E.2d 836, 838 (N.Y. 1949) (expense of maintenance and difficulty of sale of large private estates not proper grounds for variance for location of university campus in a residential district); *In re* Kline Zoning Case, 395 Pa. 122, 124, 148 A.2d 915, 916 (1959) (respiratory ailments of resident not sufficient grounds for variance to enclose porch).

35. *See, e.g.*, Carney v. Baltimore, 201 Md. 130, 93 A.2d 74 (1952) (variance to side-yard requirement not appropriate to allow elderly owner to construct more convenient downstairs bedroom and bath).

36. The court in *Mastandrea v. North*, 361 Md. 107, 132–37, 760 A.2d 677, 691–93 (2000), upheld a variance to a buffer requirement to allow a brick pathway to a creek for access by the property owner's daughter, who used a wheelchair. The ordinance itself required reasonable accommodations to be made for persons with disabilities. *See also* Arkell v. Middle Cottonwood Bd. of Zoning Adjustment, 2007 MT 160, 338 Mont. 77, 162 P.3d 856 (allowing variance to accommodate needs of family member with disability). The Rhode Island statute on variances prohibits consideration of the personal, physical, or economic condition of the applicant, except for reasonable accommodation of physical disabilities relative to state and federal housing and disability acts. R.I. GEN. LAWS § 45-24-41(c)(1) (2002).

Challenges to the failure to grant variances for persons with disabilities may be brought as alleged failures to make the requisite "reasonable accommodation" under the federal Fair Housing Amendments Act (see Chapter 23 for additional discussion of this act). These cases tend to be highly fact-specific inquiries with varying results. *See, e.g.*, Hovsons, Inc. v. Twp. of Brick, 89 F.3d 1096 (3d Cir. 1996) (refusal of use variance to allow nursing home in residential area is a failure to make a reasonable accommodation); Brandt v. Vill. of Chebanse, 82 F.3d 172 (7th Cir. 1996) (refusal to grant variance for multiunit facility for persons with disabilities in a single-family zoning district not a violation of federal law); Judy B. v. Borough of Tioga, 889 F. Supp. 792 (M.D. Pa. 1995) (failure to issue a variance to convert a motel into a residence for disabled persons was violation of federal law); Evans v. Zoning Hearing Bd., 732 A.2d 686, 692–95 (Pa. Commw. Ct. 1999) (variance for second residential unit on lot for use by daughter with disability not required as a reasonable accommodation).

37. The provision was added by S.L. 2019-111.

38. *See, e.g.*, Brackett v. Bd. of Appeal, 311 Mass. 52, 57–58, 39 N.E.2d 956, 959–60 (1942) (hardship caused by restrictive covenant not proper grounds for variance).

39. 362 N.C. 649, 669 S.E.2d 286 (2008). The town issued a permit for a single-family residence on the lot with the house location meeting the town's twenty-eight-foot street setback. However, neighbors successfully enjoined construction because it violated a restrictive covenant (in existence prior to adoption of the zoning restriction) that required a fifty-foot street setback. The plaintiff sought a zoning variance from the town's resource-conservation-district-overlay buffering requirements that applied in the rear portion of the lot in order to shift the house location farther back from the street. The board of adjustment denied the variance on the grounds that the hardship was created by the covenants, not the town ordinances.

include the street setback required by the covenant in its consideration of a variance petition submitted regarding the zoning-buffer requirement. The court held that the terms of the zoning ordinance compelled the board of adjustment to consider the effect of the restrictive covenant in its evaluation of the variance petition. The ordinance specifically directed that the board "shall consider the uses available to the owner of the entire zoning lot" in making its determination.[40] As the restrictive covenant prevented the owner from constructing a home outside the zoning buffers, the court held that factor should have been considered in a determination of the "uses available" to the owner.[41]

Peculiar to Property Affected

Another qualification holds that the hardship must be related to the specific property involved.[42] The classic justification for a variance is that the unique physical conditions of the property involved—such as a steep slope or the presence of wetlands—make it impractical to meet the precise setbacks required by the ordinance.[43]

This qualification is incorporated into G.S. 160D-705(d)(2), which requires that "the hardship results from conditions that are peculiar to the property, such as location, size, or topography." A closely related restriction, also incorporated into G.S. 160D-705(d)(2), is that the hardship cannot result "from conditions that are common to the neighborhood or the general public." The reasoning here is that if the hardship is common to a number of properties, a zoning amendment, not a variance, is the proper remedy.

The fact that the owner of the parcel subject to the variance petition owns other developable property nearby is irrelevant, as the variance must be considered strictly in relation to the property, not the owner of the property.[44]

Not Self-Created

The substantial hardship that justifies a variance cannot be self-induced or self-created.[45] This qualification is incorporated into G.S. 160D-705(d)(3).

The hardship cannot be the result of the applicant's own actions, such as an unintentional violation, buying the property for an unpermitted purpose and then seeking a variance,[46] or selling part of a parcel

---

40. Chapel Hill, N.C., Land Use Management Ordinance art. 3.6.3(j)(2)(A) (2004).

41. *Chapel Hill Title & Abstract*, 362 N.C. at 652; 669 S.E.2d at 288. The court remanded the case with an order that the variance be issued.

42. *See, e.g.,* Young Women's Hebrew Ass'n v. Bd. of Standards & Appeals, 266 N.Y. 270, 275, 194 N.E. 751, 752 (1935) (convenience of passing motorists not proper grounds for variance for gasoline station).

43. *See, e.g.,* Husnander v. Town of Barnstead, 139 N.H. 476, 479, 660 A.2d 477, 479 (1995) (odd shape of buildable area left after application of setbacks along lakefront lot would not allow construction of functional residence); Lang v. Zoning Bd. of Adjustment, 160 N.J. 41, 733 A.2d 464 (1999) (allowing variance for replacement of above-ground pool with in-ground pool on narrow lot); Rodenstein v. Bd. of Appeal, 337 Mass. 333, 334–37, 149 N.E.2d 382, 383–84 (1958) (presence of subsurface stone on lot justified variance to allow property in residential district to be used as a parking lot); Ferry v. Kownacki, 396 Pa. 283, 152 A.2d 456 (1959) (presence of ravine, gully, and septic lines on lot justify variance for location of gasoline station in residential district).

44. Williams v. N.C. Dep't of Env't & Nat. Res., 144 N.C. App. 479, 548 S.E.2d 793 (2001).

45. For a collection of cases on this point, see Richard Gutekunst, Comment, *The Self-Inflicted Hardship Rule in Pennsylvania Variance Law*, 27 Vill. L. Rev. 156 (1981); Osborne M. Reynolds, Jr., *Self-Induced Hardship in Zoning Variances: Does a Purchaser Have No One but Himself to Blame?* 20 Urb. Law. 1 (1988).

46. *See, e.g.,* Josephson v. Autry, 96 So. 2d 784, 789 (Fla. 1957) (invalidating variance granted to allow gas station in area zoned for motels). There is a split of authority on this test nationally. Some states follow the rule that purchase with knowledge of zoning restrictions is a self-imposed hardship that bars a variance, others reject that

and seeking a variance to develop the remainder.[47] Several states allow variances when there has been a good-faith mistake by the owner,[48] but if there is any negligence or bad faith involved, the variance generally will be denied.[49]

The North Carolina statute specifically provides that purchase of the property with knowledge that circumstances exist that may warrant granting a variance is not a self-created hardship. In essence, a purchaser can step into the shoes of the seller and if the seller could qualify for a variance, so may the purchaser.

Consistent with Intent and Purpose of the Regulation

While much of the variance litigation focuses on the hardship threshold for variance consideration, the potential impact of variances on community interests is also an important factor limiting local government authority to issue variances.[50]

G.S. 160D-705(d) requires that variances be consistent with the spirit and intent of the zoning ordinance.[51] The requirement that variances promote the public safety and welfare and that substantial justice is served requires the board to find that the variance would promote (or at least not harm) the interests of the community as a whole.

In instances where the regulation expresses a clear intent, a variance that authorizes contrary action is impermissible, as such is tantamount to an ordinance amendment.[52] A number of courts have used this rationale to hold all use variances illegal.[53]

---

test, and still others hold that this is one factor to consider but is not determinative in itself. Richard Roeser Prof'l Builder, Inc. v. Anne Arundel Cnty., 368 Md. 294, 299–319, 793 A.2d 545, 549–60 (2002) (rejecting purchase with knowledge as a factor); Ifrah v. Utschig, 98 N.Y.2d 304, 746 N.Y.S.2d 667, 774 N.E.2d 732 (2002) (purchase with knowledge of limitation is one factor to consider). *See generally* DANIEL R. MANDELKER, LAND USE LAW § 6.47 (6th ed. 2018).

47. *See, e.g.*, Bd. of Zoning Appeals v. Waskelo, 240 Ind. 594, 168 N.E.2d 72 (1960) (where owner sells part of conforming lot, variance may not be granted to allow construction on undersized remainder); Olsen v. City of Hopkins, 288 Minn. 25, 27–28, 178 N.W.2d 719, 721 (1970) (overturning variance for commercial use of remainder parcel in residential district); Leimann v. Bd. of Adjustment, 9 N.J. 336, 88 A.2d 337 (1952) (irregularly shaped parcel assembled after zoning enactment does not qualify for variance).

48. *See, e.g.*, Moyerman v. Glanzberg, 391 Pa. 387, 398, 138 A.2d 681, 687 (1958) (upholding side-yard variance when mistake as to lot width discovered after construction); DeFelice v. Zoning Bd. of Review, 96 R.I. 99, 103, 189 A.2d 685, 687–88 (1963) (upholding front-yard-setback variance for addition constructed in good faith before error in setback measurement discovered).

49. *See, e.g.*, Misuk v. Zoning Bd. of Appeals, 138 Conn. 477, 481, 86 A.2d 180, 182–83 (1952) (variance for side-yard encroachment inappropriate where owner's reckless conduct—no building permit obtained or survey conducted prior to initiation of construction—created the need for a variance).

50. Courts have also used the question of consistency with the purpose of the regulation as a critical factor in determining whether a hardship is unreasonable. *See, e.g.*, State v. Kenosha Cnty. Bd. of Adjustment, 218 Wis. 396, 413, 577 N.W.2d 813, 821 (1998).

51. G.S. 160D-705(d)(4).

52. Where an area variance would substantially alter a dimensional requirement, a zoning amendment rather than a variance is the appropriate relief. One Meridian Partners, LLP v. Zoning Bd. of Adjustment, 867 A.2d 706 (Pa. Commw. 2005) (invalidating Philadelphia variance that would have allowed a 300 percent increase in floor area, along with a substantial increase in building height and lot coverage); *In re* Schrader, 1983 OK 19, 660 P.2d 135, 139 (variance for a carport that would effectively eliminate the entire required side-yard setback is inconsistent with intent of ordinance).

53. *See, e.g.*, Bradley v. Zoning Bd. of Appeals, 165 Conn. 389, 393, 334 A.2d 914, 915–16 (1973) (even if hardship shown, board has no authority to issue variance for multifamily elderly-housing project in single-family district); Stice v. Gribben-Allen Motors, Inc., 216 Kan. 744, 756, 534 P.2d 1267, 1276 (1975) (invalidating variance for commercial-automobile sales lot in residential district, holding substantial departure from zoning not within spirit

In *Lee*, the court specifically held that use variances are illegal in North Carolina, finding that allowing a use not permitted by the ordinance cannot be within the purpose and intent of the ordinance:

> "Unnecessary hardship" as used in the statute does not embrace the restriction of the desire to perform an act which would abrogate the very intent and purpose of the ordinance, amend, if not partially repeal, an act regularly adopted by the local Legislature, and create a means by which the entire ordinance could be frustrated at will by limitless exceptions.
>
> . . . In the exercise of its discretion, however, it [the board of adjustment] is not left free to make any determination whatever that appeals to its sense of justice. It must abide by and comply with the rules of conduct provided by its charter—the local ordinance enacted in accord with and by permission of the State zoning law.
>
> . . . .
>
> Thus the power to "determine and vary" is limited to such variations and modifications as are in harmony with the general purpose and intent of the ordinance and do no violence to its spirit.
>
> . . . .
>
> . . . [T]he Board of Adjustment is not a law-making body. The Statute . . . cedes it no legislative authority. Hence it has no power to amend the ordinance under which it functions.
>
> No power to convert a residential section into a business district or to permit business establishments to invade a residential section is conferred. Therefore it cannot permit a type of business or building prohibited by the ordinance, for to do so would be an amendment of the law and not a variance of its regulations.[54]

The court in *Sherrill v. Town of Wrightsville Beach*[55] likewise ruled that a variance could not be granted for a duplex in an area zoned for single-family use. Such a substantial departure from the terms of the ordinance would violate the spirit and purpose of the ordinance. "A nonconforming building or use that conflicts with the general purpose or spirit of the zoning ordinance can only be authorized by the board of aldermen acting in their legislative capacity to rezone, not under the guise of a variance permit."[56] The court ruled that even though the duplex was also a residential use and there were already other duplexes in the neighborhood as nonconforming uses, the ordinance specifically limited density by allowing only single-family residences. If that was to be changed, it had to be done through an ordinance amendment, not by a variance. Similarly, in *Robertson v. Zoning Board of Adjustment*,[57] the court upheld denial of a variance by the Charlotte board of adjustment for a fence that exceeded the height limit set in the zoning ordinance. Substantial portions of the fence were eight feet high while the ordinance only allowed fences five feet above grade. The court agreed that such a substantial height

---

and intent of ordinance); Banks v. City of Bethany, 1975 OK 128, 541 P.2d 178, 181 (variance to allow extension of commercial use into residentially zoned portion of lot would be contrary to comprehensive plan and inconsistent with intent of ordinance). *But see* Clarke v. Morgan, 327 So. 2d 769 (Fla. 1976) (upholding statute allowing City of Tampa to issue use variances where adequate guiding standards provided, such as no new construction on unimproved lots and mandatory planning-board review); Matthew v. Smith, 707 S.W.2d 411, 414 (Mo. 1986) (overruling prior decision that held use variances prohibited).

54. 226 N.C. 107, 110–12, 37 S.E.2d 128, 131–32 (1946) (citations omitted). *Cf. James v. Sutton*, 229 N.C. 515, 50 S.E.2d 300 (1948), where the court distinguished a situation that allowed a board of adjustment to approve an otherwise prohibited use in an area upon finding that it was not injurious to adjacent properties from an illegal use variance. The former was allowed and is analogous to a conditional or special use, not a use variance. Courts in other states have also emphasized that use variances risk crossing the line between a permissible adjustment of the policies in the ordinance and an impermissible legislative amendment of the ordinance. *See, e.g.*, Topanga Ass'n for a Scenic Cmty. v. Cnty. of L.A., 522 P.2d 12 (Cal. 1974) (invalidating variance to allow mobile-home park).

55. 76 N.C. App. 646, 334 S.E.2d 103 (1985).

56. *Id.* at 648, 334 S.E.2d at 104.

57. 167 N.C. App. 531, 605 S.E.2d 723 (2004), *review denied*, 359 N.C. 322, 611 S.E.2d 417 (2005).

variance (60 percent in the front yard and 33 percent in the side yard) would be contrary to the purpose of the ordinance and thus impermissible.[58]

The General Assembly in 2005 incorporated this prohibition against use variances into the enabling statutes. G.S. 160D-705(d) provides that "[n]o change in permitted uses may be authorized by variance."[59] Since the board of adjustment has no legal authority to issue a use variance, there is no necessity to make findings on the merits of such a petition, so it may be summarily denied.[60]

Courts have likewise held that a nonconforming use may not be extended by variance[61] and that it is not permissible to adjust zoning-district boundaries through a variance.[62] Courts have also held that variances are only appropriate when the variance will not alter the "essential character" of the adjoining neighborhood.[63] These limitations help distinguish when a zoning amendment rather than a variance is the appropriate relief to be sought.

There are also situations where a variance that is otherwise justified can be denied because of the harm it would generate. For example, if it is found that a variance would create a nuisance, harm neighboring property values, cause environmental harm,[64] create undue traffic hazards,[65] or cause more harm to neighbors than benefit to the applicant,[66] it may be denied. The fact that the variance would be inconsistent with an adopted comprehensive plan may also justify variance denial.[67]

---

58. The court applied a de novo review to the alleged error of law regarding interpretation of the hardship required to qualify for a variance. The court also noted the board's conclusions that the alleged hardship was self-created, personal in nature (arising from a dispute with a neighbor), and would create a nuisance.

59. Other states also have statutory prohibitions on use variances. *See, e.g.,* CAL. GOV'T CODE § 65906 (prohibiting use variances).

60. Donnelly v. Bd. of Adjustment, 99 N.C. App. 702, 708, 394 S.E.2d 246, 250 (1990); *Sherrill,* 76 N.C. App. at 648, 334 S.E.2d at 104.

61. *See, e.g.,* Colati v. Jirout, 186 Md. 652, 659, 47 A.2d 613, 616 (1946) (no authority for variance to allow substantial enlargement of building housing a nonconforming commercial use in a residential zone); Rexon v. Bd. of Adjustment, 10 N.J. 1, 9, 89 A.2d 233, 236 (1952) (variance may not be issued to allow industrial use in commercial zone even though adjacent land is in industrial use and zone); *In re* Crossroads Recreation, Inc. v. Broz, 4 N.Y.2d 39, 46, 172 N.Y.S.2d 129, 133–34, 149 N.E.2d 65, 68 (1958) (inability to replace nonconforming gasoline station with modern facility is not undue hardship); Griffin v. Zoning Bd. of Review, 98 R.I. 233, 237, 200 A.2d 700, 702–03 (1964) (variance may not be issued to expand nonconforming cafe).

62. *See, e.g.,* Real Props., Inc. v. Bd. of Appeal, 319 Mass. 180, 184, 65 N.E.2d 199, 201 (1946) (inappropriate to extend commercial area into adjacent residential zone by variance).

63. *See, e.g.,* Commons v. Westwood Zoning Bd. of Adjustment, 81 N.J. 597, 610, 410 A.2d 1138, 1145 (1980) (appropriate to deny variance if it would adversely affect character of neighborhood); Otto v. Steinhilber, 282 N.Y. 71, 76, 24 N.E.2d 851, 853 (1939).

64. Town of Beverly Shores v. Bagnall, 590 N.E.2d 1059, 1063 (Ind. 1992) (upholding denial of variance for residence construction in manner that would have obliterated a protected sand dune); Grey Rocks Land Trust v. Town of Hebron, 136 N.H. 239, 614 A.2d 1048 (1992) (variance to expand nonconforming marina invalid as it would substantially impair natural scenic, recreational, and environmental values sought to be protected by zoning district); Biggs v. Town of Sandwich, 124 N.H. 421, 428, 470 A.2d 928, 932 (1975) (upholding denial of variance for structure that would use septic system constructed within wetland setback because such created an unacceptable risk of pollution); Saturley v. Town of Hollis, 129 N.H. 757, 762, 533 A.2d 29, 32 (1987) (upholding variance denial for residence and septic tank within wetland setback based on potential threat of septic system failure and runoff posed to public water supply).

65. *See, e.g.,* Bell Sav. & Loan Ass'n v. Zoning Hearing Bd., 8 Pa. Commw. 335, 338, 301 A.2d 436, 437 (1973) (upholding denial of dimensional variance for drive-in bank that would create traffic hazard).

66. *See, e.g.,* Planning Bd. v. Zoning Bd. of Appeals, 5 Mass. App. Ct. 789, 790, 360 N.E.2d 677, 678 (1977) (impact of variance on other property within the zoning district is a mandatory factor that must be considered). Many of the cases on this point have dealt with use variances.

67. For a collection of cases regarding variances and comprehensive-plan consistency, see Erwin S. Barbre, Annotation, *Requirement That Zoning Variances or Exceptions Be Made in Accordance with Comprehensive Plan,* 40 A.L.R.3d 372 (1982).

The requirement that variances be consistent with the spirit of the ordinance is not limited to use variances. This point is emphasized in *Chambers v. Zoning Board of Adjustment*.[68] Here the court ruled that the Winston-Salem board of adjustment could not grant a variance for a housing project that only had on-street parking when the zoning ordinance specifically required garages or other on-site parking. The court ruled as follows:

> The wording of the ordinance leaves little or no doubt as to its meaning, and to approve the plan on the present showing would be to eliminate [the parking requirement] in its entirety. If the provision is to be removed, it should be done by the authority that ordained it—the city council.
>
> It is plain from the record that we are dealing with a highly controversial project. In passing on the legality of [the parking requirement], we must assume the city council said what it meant and meant what it said.[69]

Similarly, in *Donnelly v. Board of Adjustment*,[70] the court held that where a zoning ordinance, read as a whole, expresses a clear intent to exclude tall privacy fences from visible locations, the board of adjustment is without authority to grant a variance, as such would be directly contrary to the ordinance. By contrast, in *Premier Plastic Surgery Center, PLLC v. Board of Adjustment*, the court held that a variance for a second monument sign to identify a business within a multibusiness complex was not inherently inconsistent with the ordinance's limit of one sign for a multitenant business property. As the sign was at a second entrance to the business complex, the court concluded that the variance should be viewed as an area variance to the sign-size limit rather than a use variance for a second sign.[71]

The statutory provision that "substantial justice" be done[72] with variances also allows a board to consider the impacts of a proposed variance on the community. In *Cary Creek Ltd. Partnership v. Town of Cary*, the court held that this factor allows a board to consider whether it would be fair to other developers to grant a variance to a particular petitioner.[73]

As in all aspects of quasi-judicial decision-making, evidence must be submitted to document why a particular variance proposal is or is not consistent with the spirit, purpose, and intent of the ordinance.[74] Specific, focused language in the ordinance is the best evidence of intent. Legislative history (such as minutes of the deliberation at the time of adoption, staff reports relative to the language chosen, examples of the problems before the jurisdiction that led to adoption, and the like) may also be helpful.

---

68. 250 N.C. 194, 108 S.E.2d 211 (1959).

69. *Id.* at 198, 108 S.E.2d at 214.

70. 99 N.C. App. 702, 394 S.E.2d 246 (1990).

71. 213 N.C. App. 364, 713 S.E.2d 511 (2011). As the court found the findings made to support the variance denial were insufficient, the case was remanded for further proceedings.

72. G.S. 160D-705(d)(4).

73. 207 N.C. App. 339, 700 S.E.2d 80 (2010). One of the board members had expressed reservations about granting a variance to allow development in a riparian buffer given that prior developers had been required to respect similar buffer requirements.

74. See *Williams v. North Carolina Department of Environment & Natural Resources*, 144 N.C. App. 479, 548 S.E.2d 793 (2001), where the court held that inadequate evidence had been presented regarding the purpose and intent of the regulation. The rule involved did not specifically address the issue (redevelopment of a vacant but previously developed site where coastal wetlands had reemerged), and other rules allowed some degree of reconstruction of nonconformities. *See also* 321 News & Video, Inc. v. Zoning Bd. of Adjustment, 174 N.C. App. 186, 619 S.E.2d 885 (2005) (evidence supported finding that alternate buffers to adult use were not present).

Conditions on Variances

Conditions may be imposed on a variance, provided they are reasonably related to the condition or circumstance that gave rise to the need for the variance.[75] Many zoning ordinances specifically direct the board to impose such conditions where warranted.

If an applicant accepts and acts on a variance with conditions, those conditions are binding and may not be subsequently challenged. In *Franklin Road Properties v. City of Raleigh*,[76] the plaintiff filed a site plan and requested that it be approved with a variance to allow parking and driveways to be placed within the highway-setback area. The governing board approved the plan and the variance. The plaintiff subsequently brought a declaratory-judgment action contesting the validity of an additional requirement to expand the adjacent roadway prior to building-permit issuance. The court noted that the variance conditions could not be challenged in this fashion.[77]

If amendment to variance conditions is sought, that application must generally be treated in much the same manner as the original variance request. It is subject to the same application, hearing, and board-action requirements as the original application. Further, since res judicata applies to variance decisions, any request for modification of the variance or its conditions must be based on a modification to the proposed project, changed conditions, or changes in the ordinance.[78]

Like other zoning approvals, variances run with the land.[79] Therefore, any condition on a variance applies to subsequent owners as well.[80] For this reason an increasing number of local governments require that variances be recorded in the chain of title for the property to ensure that future owners are aware of any conditions on the variance.[81] This is sometimes enforced by adding a condition to the variance that it is not effective until it is recorded.

---

75. G.S. 160D-705(d). The North Carolina statutes also specifically mention "appropriate conditions and safeguards" being imposed on special use permits. G.S. 160D-705(c). "Although the Standard Zoning Act and most state zoning acts do not expressly authorize the board of adjustment to attach conditions to variances, the power to do so is recognized as inherent in the statutory power to grant variances." DANIEL R. MANDELKER, *supra* note 46, § 6.48. *See, e.g.*, Town of Burlington v. Jencik, 168 Conn. 506, 509, 362 A.2d 1338, 1339–40 (1975) (express authority not required for imposition of reasonable conditions on variance); Robinson v. Town of Hudson, 154 N.H. 563, 568–69, 914 A.2d 239, 243–44 (2006) (board has inherent authority to impose reasonable conditions).

76. 94 N.C. App. 731, 381 S.E.2d 487 (1989).

77. "[P]laintiff has clearly requested, obtained and accepted the benefits of a variance . . . . Plaintiff is therefore precluded from attacking the validity of this zoning ordinance . . . through its complaint seeking declaratory judgment." *Id.* at 735, 381 S.E.2d at 490.

78. *See, e.g.*, Cohen v. Borough of Fair Lawn, 85 N.J. Super. 234, 204 A.2d 375 (Super. Ct. App. Div. 1964).

79. *See, e.g.*, Reid v. Zoning Bd. of Appeals, 235 Conn. 850, 670 A.2d 1271 (1996) (holding that a variance condition limiting its use to the lifetime of the petitioner was personal and thus invalid, but given the statutory provision that severs invalid conditions from variances, the variance survives and could be used by subsequent purchaser); Stop & Shop Supermarket Co. v. Bd. of Adjustment, 162 N.J. 418, 432–33, 744 A.2d 1169, 1177–78 (2000) (use variance to allow residentially zoned property to be used as parking can be used forty years later by commercial-use successor).

80. *See, e.g.*, Goldberg v. Milwaukee Bd. of Zoning Appeals, 115 Wis. 2d 517, 340 N.W.2d 558 (Ct. App. 1983).

81. G.S. 160D-705(c) specifically authorizes a local zoning regulation to require that a special use permit be recorded in the chain of title. The statute does not include a similar provision for variances, but it is generally assumed that this is within the scope of authority for zoning administration.

CHAPTER 18

Appeals of Administrative Decisions, Staff Determinations, and Ordinance Interpretations

Administrative decisions on land use regulatory matters made by city or county staff members are generally subject to an administrative appeal. For example, a decision by a zoning administrator that a particular land use is not permitted on a site, a ruling on how a setback is measured, or a determination that a zoning violation exists may be appealed to the board of adjustment.[1]

Appeals to the board of adjustment prior to judicial review have long been required by the zoning-enabling statute. The 1923 North Carolina zoning-enabling act provided that the governing board could appoint a board of adjustment to "hear and decide appeals from and review any order, requirement, decision or determination made by an administrative official charged" with zoning enforcement.[2]

One of the state's first zoning cases, *Harden v. City of Raleigh*,[3] confirmed that a zoning ordinance can assign appeals of staff decisions to a board of adjustment and that such appeals are quasi-judicial in nature. Many other local land use development regulations have also incorporated similar administrative appeals.[4]

The provision for appeals of all administrative decisions made under development regulations is now codified at Chapter 160D, Section 405 of the North Carolina General Statutes (hereinafter G.S.).[5]

These administrative appeals cannot be used to challenge the constitutionality of an ordinance provision. The statutes allow appeals directly to superior court on questions of law, such as vested-rights claims, scope of statutory authority, and constitutional issues.

In *Dobo v. Zoning Board of Adjustment*, the court held that a petitioner cannot raise a constitutional challenge in the course of appealing a zoning officer's interpretation of an ordinance.[6] In these instances the board of adjustment has no authority to rule on the constitutionality of the ordinance, and the superior court is limited to review of whether the board properly affirmed or overruled the officer's

---

1. Local ordinances can also provide for appeals of determinations of ancillary officers involved with development regulations. Fantasy World, Inc. v. Greensboro Bd. of Adjustment, 162 N.C. App. 603, 592 S.E.2d 205, *review denied*, 358 N.C. 543, 599 S.E.2d 43 (2004) (upholding ordinance requirement that decision of city tax collector to deny privilege license to business based on zoning noncompliance must be appealed to board of adjustment).

2. S.L. 1923-250, § 7.

3. 192 N.C. 395, 135 S.E. 151 (1926).

4. A 2012 survey of North Carolina local governments reported 170 appeals to boards of adjustment in the previous year. Most of the appeals (88 percent) were brought by the owner of the affected property. David W. Owens & Dayne Batten, *2012 Zoning Survey Report: Zoning Adoption, Administration, and Provisions for Design Standards and Alternative Energy Facilities*, PLAN. & ZONING L. BULL. No. 20 (UNC School of Government, July 2012).

5. Chapter 160D, Section 1114 of the North Carolina General Statutes (hereinafter G.S.) also provides that appeals of stop-work orders are made to the board of adjustment under G.S. 160D-405, and G.S. 160D-1403(b) does the same for appeals of administrative decisions under subdivision regulations.

6. 149 N.C. App. 701, 706, 562 S.E.2d 108, 111–12 (2002), *rev'd on other grounds*, 356 N.C. 656, 576 S.E.2d 324 (2003).

determination.[7] Where an administrative appeal is possible, it is generally a mandatory prerequisite to judicial review.[8]

Final Decision Required

G.S. 160D-405(a)[9] provides that decisions made by the staff under Chapter 160D are subject to appeal to the board of adjustment.[10]

The administrative decisions that are subject to appeal are defined by G.S. 160D-102(1) to be "[d]ecisions made in the implementation, administration, or enforcement of development regulations that involve the determination of facts and the application of objective standards . . . ." This includes staff determinations, defined by G.S. 160D-102(10) to be "written, final, and binding order[s], requirement[s], or determination[s] regarding an administrative decision." The ordinance may assign appeals of decisions on other development regulations to the board of adjustment but is not required to.

The board does not have jurisdiction to render advisory interpretations. There must be an actual controversy and a final decision or formal determination in order for the board of adjustment to have subject-matter jurisdiction. *Ashe County v. Ashe County Planning Board* involved an application for a permit for an asphalt plant under the county's Polluting Industries Development Ordinance.[11] The ordinance required buffers for regulated uses from commercial uses, schools, and health-care facilities. It also mandated that all required state permits be obtained before the county permit could be issued. While a state air-quality permit was pending, the county planning director sent a letter in response to a request from the applicant stating that the application met the requirements of the county ordinance and that he would make a "favorable recommendation" to issue the county permit once the state permit was obtained and final inspections were made.[12] The court held that the planning director's letter was not a "final determination" that could have been appealed to the board of adjustment. It was not determinative as it explicitly stated that there was no authority to issue the county permit until all mandated conditions had been met and that those conditions had not in fact been met. As such, it was only a recommendation provided at a preliminary stage of the review. The court noted that allowing an appeal of a staff comment on one aspect of the standards, in this case compliance with setback requirements, prior to a final administrative decision would invite multiple, piecemeal interlocutory appeals.[13]

---

7. *See also* Batch v. Town of Chapel Hill, 326 N.C. 1, 11, 387 S.E.2d 655, 661–62 (1989), *cert. denied*, 496 U.S. 931 (1990). Issues related to the scope and form of judicial review are discussed in Chapter 29.

8. See the discussion of exhaustion of administrative remedies in Chapter 29.

9. G.S. 160D-405 and -406 were substantially amended in 2013 to codify and clarify the law on administrative appeals. S.L. 2013-126. This update eliminated the provision in prior law for the board of adjustment to pass upon disputed lot lines. The rationale is that the board has no particular expertise in surveying or property-boundary issues, and these issues are best resolved judicially if need be. Since the location of zoning-district boundaries is an interpretation of the ordinance, a staff determination of those lines can be appealed to the board.

10. While the default board to hear appeals of final staff decisions is the board of adjustment, this statute provides flexibility by allowing a different board to hear the appeal if so designated by statute or by local ordinance. Appeals of decisions on erosion and sedimentation control, stormwater, and housing-code violations do not automatically go to the board of adjustment.

11. 376 N.C. 1, 852 S.E.2d 69 (2020).

12. After the planning director's letter was issued and while the state permit was still pending, the county enacted a temporary moratorium on these permits. The county then denied the permit application based on the moratorium. The case is discussed in the context of the permit-choice rule in Chapter 19.

13. The remaining issues on appeal, including the completeness of the application and the effect of the moratorium that was adopted while the application was pending, were remanded to the court of appeals for reconsideration in light of the holding on the lack of binding effect of the planning director's letter.

Tate v. Board of Adjustment also illustrates this rule.[14] This case involved a dispute in Asheville over the use of a swimming pool. The pool had been constructed at a residence that was also used as a nonconforming day-care center. The application stated that the pool was for personal use, but neighbors subsequently complained that the children in day care were using it. The city staff asked the board of adjustment for a ruling on whether this constituted a zoning violation, and the board ruled that it did. On appeal, the court held that the board was without jurisdiction to hear this matter, as it had only appellate, not original, jurisdiction.[15] The proper procedure was for the staff to make a ruling on whether the ordinance had been violated and then have an affected person who disagreed with that determination appeal it to the board of adjustment.

It is also necessary that there be an official staff decision that directly affects the legal rights of the party making the appeal. *In re Appeal of the Society for the Preservation of Historic Oakwood*[16] provides an example of this rule. Here the underlying issue was whether a shelter proposed by the Raleigh Rescue Mission should be considered multifamily housing, which was permitted in the applicable zoning district, or transitional housing, which was not. When the plaintiff neighbors raised objections to the proposed facility, the deputy city attorney asked the zoning administrator for an opinion on this issue. The zoning administrator issued a memorandum in response, stating that the structure proposed was permitted but the proposed use might not be. The neighbors appealed this determination to the board of adjustment. The court held that the zoning administrator's decision was not an "order, requirement, decision, or determination" that could be appealed to the board because the memorandum was merely advisory. The order "must have some binding force or effect for there to be a right of appeal. . . . Where the decision has no binding effect, or is not authoritative or a conclusion as to future action, it is merely the view, opinion, or belief of the administrative official."[17]

A letter from the zoning administrator interpreting the ordinance was held to be an appealable final determination in *Meier v. City of Charlotte*. When the plaintiff questioned compliance with a building-height limit for a residence being constructed next door, the zoning staff met on-site with representatives of the builder and the plaintiff to review the work and discuss how the height limit would be applied. The zoning administrator then mailed a letter to the plaintiff's attorney and the builder stating his interpretation of the height limit and how it applied to this project. The letter concluded that the height involved, with the proposed setback additions, would comply with the zoning ordinance. The court held the letter was a final determination on interpretation of the ordinance that could be appealed to the board of adjustment. It was written at the request of affected persons by the person authorized to make official interpretations. It explained how the ordinance would be interpreted and concluded that the project would comply with the ordinance if it was built in accordance with the plans submitted. The letter was definitive, authoritative, and thus appealable.[18]

---

14. 83 N.C. App. 512, 350 S.E.2d 873 (1986). This is a standard requirement in most states. *See, e.g.,* Franco v. Wheelock, 750 A.2d 957 (R.I. 2000) (zoning board of review has no authority to issue advisory opinions).

15. *Tate,* 83 N.C. 512, 350 S.E.2d 873.

16. 153 N.C. App. 737, 571 S.E.2d 588 (2002).

17. *Id.* at 742–43, 571 S.E.2d at 591 (citations and internal quotations omitted). In an analogous situation in a vested-rights case, the court held that an owner could not rely on staff assurances that a waiver would be granted in the future, as that was not a binding decision. Wilson v. City of Mebane Bd. of Adjustment, 212 N.C. App. 176, 710 S.E.2d 403 (2011).

18. 206 N.C. App. 471, 698 S.E.2d 704 (2010). The letter also required that a sealed survey be submitted prior to issuance of a certificate of occupancy. The plaintiff contended the determination was not final until receipt and review of the survey. The court held the as-built survey was required only to demonstrate compliance with the interpretation and was not in itself an interpretation of the ordinance.

Similarly, in *S.T. Wooten Corp. v. Board of Adjustment*, the court addressed a letter sent by a zoning administrator that determined whether a particular use was permitted within a zoning district.[19] The court held that the letter was a binding final interpretation, noting that the writing was from the person authorized to make a formal interpretation, it addressed a specific question of interpretation, and the ordinance specified an explicit route of appeal from determinations by the zoning administrator. The fact that the letter included superfluous advice (that a site plan and building permit would be required prior to construction) did not render the interpretation any less binding on the question of whether the proposed use was permitted. As the town did not appeal this determination, the court held that the town was bound by it. By contrast, failure to respond to an email from a landowner that states the landowner's interpretation of the ordinance is not a binding decision that can be appealed.[20]

Process for Appeals

G.S. 160D-405 includes various additional procedural considerations regarding these administrative appeals. Appeals are initiated by a person with standing to appeal. A notice of appeal is to be filed with the city or county clerk. The notice must state the grounds for the appeal. New issues may be raised at the hearing, but if doing so would unduly prejudice a party, the board must continue the hearing to allow time for an adequate response.

This statute also sets a uniform time to make appeals to the board. An appeal must be filed within thirty days of receiving notice of a final, binding administrative decision.[21] G.S. 160D-405(b) provides that a determination by the zoning administrator is to be provided in writing and delivered to the person requesting it by personal delivery, electronic mail, or first-class mail. The recipient then has thirty days from receipt of the decision to make the appeal.

Any other person with standing, such as a neighbor who is affected, has thirty days from receipt of actual or constructive notice of the decision to file an appeal. An example of actual notice would be a written copy of the decision, comparable to what the person requesting the decision received. Constructive notice can be provided by activity on the site, such as grading, surveying, or other clearly visible indicators that a regulatory determination has been made. Constructive notice can, however, be nebulous. For example, if the determination addressed building height or a particular land use, the construction or activity on-site would have to proceed far enough for the implications of the determination to become visible to a neighbor. G.S. 160D-405(b) provides an alternative for those owners who want a more definitive point for determining that constructive notice has been provided. It gives the landowner the option of posting notice of the determination on the site to provide constructive notice to those who may appeal that determination to the board of adjustment. This posted notice can be provided for zoning or subdivision determinations. Such a posting is the responsibility of the owner, not the local government. It is not mandatory unless required by the local ordinance. If a sign is posted, it must be prominently posted, include contact information for the local official making the decision, and remain on the site for at least ten days. The owner is to verify the posting to the local government. If a

---

19. 210 N.C. App. 633, 711 S.E.2d 158 (2011). The interpretation involved here was whether an asphalt plant proposed for a heavy-industrial zoning district in Zebulon was a permitted use or required a special use permit. The use was not explicitly mentioned in the ordinance. The zoning administrator ruled that the use was permitted. Some eight years later, a subsequent zoning administrator ruled that a special use permit was required. The court found the initial letter to be binding on the town.

20. Am. Entertainers, LLC v. City of Rocky Mount, 2016 WL 4728077 (No. 5:14-CV-438-D, E.D.N.C., Sept. 8, 2016).

21. Prior to amendment of this statute in 2013, the law allowed each individual ordinance to set a time for making an appeal.

posting is made, the constructive notice that starts the thirty-day period to appeal begins to run from the date the notice is first posted.

Once an appeal is made, the official who made the decision being appealed is to compile all of the documents and exhibits on the matter and transmit this record to the board. A copy of this administrative record is also to be provided to the person making the appeal (and to the landowner if that is not the person making the appeal).

An appeal of an enforcement action stays the enforcement unless there is imminent peril to life or property, or the violation is transitory in nature. In those instances where enforcement is not stayed, the appellant may request an expedited hearing. If that request is made, the board must meet within fifteen days to hear the appeal.[22] An appeal does not stay further processing of permit applications, but the appellant may request a stay of a final decision or issuance of building permits pending resolution of the appeal. This does not occur automatically; it must be requested by the appellant.

Officials whose determinations are appealed are required to appear as witnesses at the appeal hearing.[23]

The statute confirms that when the board of adjustment hears an appeal from another board, it does not take any new evidence but rather reviews the record made by the other board's hearing. The primary example of this would be the review of a decision on a certificate of appropriateness made by a historic-preservation commission. In these instances, the board of adjustment acts as an appeals court and does not conduct a new hearing.

The law also expressly authorizes the parties to agree to voluntary alternative-dispute resolution of appeals (such as mediation).[24] The zoning ordinance may set up procedures to facilitate and manage that.

Rules of Interpretation

When appeals are made contesting the interpretation of local development regulations or the terms of individual development approvals,[25] the general rules of statutory construction apply for both the board hearing the administrative appeal and for courts hearing a subsequent judicial appeal.[26]

In addition to these rules of interpretation, an ordinance may also provide other guides to the intentions of the adopting body. It may include not only definitions but also specific rules of construction. These directions are also considered in the appeals.[27]

---

22. G.S. 160D-405(f).

23. G.S. 160D-406(e).

24. G.S. 160D-405(g).

25. The terms used in an individual permit do not necessarily have the same meaning as the terms used in the ordinance.

> Definitions found in conditional use zoning permits can be different from those found for the same terms in general ordinances because conditional use permits are necessarily more specific in application and restriction than general provisions. Conditional use permit "inconsistencies" with more general ordinances are normally contemplated as an acceptable means to require more restrictive uses in a given specific area or location.

Westminster Homes, Inc. v. Town of Cary Zoning Bd. of Adjustment, 354 N.C. 298, 305–06, 554 S.E.2d 634, 639 (2001).

26. George v. Town of Edenton, 294 N.C. 679, 242 S.E.2d 877 (1978); *In re* O'Neal, 243 N.C. 714, 92 S.E.2d 189 (1956). *See also* Cogdell v. Taylor, 264 N.C. 424, 142 S.E.2d 36 (1965) (rules applicable to construction of statutes also apply to construction of municipal ordinances); Perrell v. Beaty Serv. Co., 248 N.C. 153, 160, 102 S.E.2d 785, 790 (1958). *See generally* 3 NORMAN J. SINGER, SUTHERLAND STATUTES AND STATUTORY CONSTRUCTION §§ 58–65 (7th ed., Nov. 2022 Update).

27. *See, e.g., Westminster Homes*, 354 N.C. at 305, 554 S.E.2d at 639 (noting that the ordinance provisions titled "General Rules of Construction" specify that in the event of any conflict between requirements or standards, the more restrictive provision shall apply).

A review of the interpretation of a development regulation is a question of law that is subject to de novo review on both administrative and judicial appeal.[28]

Deference

A zoning administrator or other expert agency's interpretation is entitled to due consideration, but the meaning of terms in the ordinance is a legal question that must be examined de novo by both the board of adjustment and a reviewing court.[29]

G.S. 160D-1402(j)(2) provides that on judicial review, "The court shall consider the interpretation of the decision-making board, but is not bound by that interpretation, and may freely substitute its judgment as appropriate."[30] It is likely this directive should also be applied to boards hearing appeals of staff administrative decisions and determinations.

Basic Rules of Construction

The principal consideration in interpretation is to give effect to the intent of the legislative body that enacted the provision, considering the purpose of the ordinance and problems it attempts to address.[31] Amendments to a regulation that clarify its intent, rather than making a substantial alteration of its meaning, are considered in interpreting the provision even if the amendment is made after the contested decision.[32]

---

28. Ayers v. Bd. of Adjustment, 113 N.C. App. 528, 439 S.E.2d 199, *review denied*, 336 N.C. 71, 445 S.E.2d 28 (1994).

29. *In re* Broad & Gales Creek Cmty. Ass'n, 300 N.C. 267, 275, 266 S.E.2d 645, 651 (1980) (interpretations of statute by agency with expertise in administering it are entitled to due consideration). The courts are to "accord considerable weight" to an agency's determination and will defer to that interpretation if it is based on a permissible construction of the statute. Cnty. of Durham v. N.C. Dep't of Env't & Nat. Res., 131 N.C. App. 395, 396–97, 507 S.E.2d 310, 311–12 (1998), *review denied*, 350 N.C. 92, 528 S.E.2d 361 (1999). However, while the court gives "great weight" to an agency's interpretation, that interpretation is not binding and an agency interpretation that conflicts with the clear intent of the statute is not followed. High Rock Lake Partners, LLC v. N.C. Dep't of Transp., 366 N.C. 315, 319, 735 S.E.2d 300, 303 (2012). *See also* Faizan v. Grain Dealers Mut. Ins., 254 N.C. 47, 118 S.E.2d 303 (1961) (such interpretation given due consideration); Shealy v. Associated Transp., Inc., 252 N.C. 738, 114 S.E.2d 702 (1960) (such interpretation strongly persuasive); Gill v. Bd. of Comm'rs, 160 N.C. 176, 76 S.E. 203 (1912) (such interpretation given great consideration); Darbo v. Old Keller Farm Prop. Owners' Ass'n, 174 N.C. App. 591, 621 S.E.2d 281 (2005) (planning-board interpretation entitled to deference).

30. See the discussion of judicial deference to agency interpretations when making a de novo review in Chapter 29.

31. "It is a cardinal principle that in construing statutes, the courts should always give effect to the legislative intent." State v. Tew, 326 N.C. 732, 738–39, 392 S.E.2d 603, 607 (1990). The "basic rule is to ascertain and effectuate the intent of the legislative body." Coastal Ready-Mix Concrete Co. v. Bd. of Comm'rs, 299 N.C. 620, 629, 265 S.E.2d 379, 385 (1980); Bryan v. Wilson, 259 N.C. 107, 110, 130 S.E.2d 68, 70 (1963). "[U]nder the maxim 'Ut res magis valeat quam pereat,' it becomes the duty of the court by proper construction to determine and declare its meaning if that may be ascertained with reasonable clearness and certainty." State v. Humphries, 210 N.C. 406, 409, 186 S.E.2d 473, 475 (1936).

32. Ray v. N.C. Dep't of Transp., 366 N.C. 1, 9, 727 S.E.2d 675, 682 (2012); Jeffries v. Cnty. of Harnett, 259 N.C. App. 473, 817 S.E.2d 36, 48 (2018).

Where clear, plain, and unambiguous language is used, it controls.[33] The common and ordinary meanings of nontechnical words should be applied[34] unless the ordinance specifically defines a term, in which case the specified meaning must be applied.[35] Also, the meaning of a questionable word may be ascertained by reference to associated surrounding words—*noscitur a sociis*.[36]

All terms within a provision[37] and all provisions within an ordinance must be considered,[38] and all should be considered as a whole.[39] For example, in *85° & Sunny, LLC v. Currituck County*, the court held that a specific provision regarding nonconforming campgrounds and a general provision applicable to all nonconformities should be interpreted as general and specific provisions on the same subject that "should be read together and harmonized" where possible.[40]

The ordinance should be interpreted in a manner that avoids absurd consequences.[41]

---

33. JVC Enterprises, LLC v. City of Concord, 376 N.C. 782, 855 S.E.2d 158 (2021) (local act clearly transferred authority of Board of Light and Water to assess utility fees to the city, so without ambiguity there is no need to apply rules of construction); *High Rock Lake Partners*, 366 N.C. at 322, 735 S.E. 2d at 305; Williams v. Williams, 299 N.C. 174, 180, 261 S.E.2d 849, 854 (1980). If the legislative intent is clear in the language used, there is no need for judicial refinement of the language. *See also* Schroeder v. City of Wilmington, 282 N.C. App. 558, 872 S.E.2d 58 (2022) (when statute is unambiguous, its placement within the statutes is less probative of legislative intent than the language itself).

34. Utils. Comm'n v. Edmisten, 291 N.C. 451, 465, 232 S.E.2d 184, 192 (1976). *See also* State v. Raines, 319 N.C. 258, 262, 354 S.E.2d 486, 489 (1987); Penny v. City of Durham, 249 N.C. 596, 600, 107 S.E.2d 72, 76 (1959) (addressing the meaning of *directly opposite* in context of protest petitions); O'Neal, 243 N.C. 714, 92 S.E.2d 189; *In re* W.P. Rose Supply Co., 202 N.C. 496, 163 S.E.2d 462 (1932); Schooldev East, LLC v. Town of Wake Forest, 284 N.C. App. 434, 876 S.E.2d 607 (2022) (addressing meaning of "street," "sidewalks," "improvements," and "ingress and egress" relative to statute limiting city regulation of school-driveway improvements); Greene Citizens for Responsible Growth, Inc. v. Greene Cnty., 143 N.C. App. 702, 547 S.E.2d 480, *review denied*, 553 S.E.2d 413 (2001) (addressing the requirement to "consider alternative sites" in landfill-siting decisions); Kirkpatrick v. Vill. Council of Pinehurst, 138 N.C. App. 79, 86, 530 S.E.2d 338, 343 (2000) (addressing meaning of *enlargement* in nonconformity limitations); Rice Assocs. v. Town of Weaverville Bd. of Adjustment, 108 N.C. App. 346, 348, 423 S.E.2d 519, 520 (1992) (addressing ordinance requirement for two points of ingress and egress for a development); Donnelly v. Bd. of Adjustment, 99 N.C. App. 702, 707, 394 S.E.2d 246, 250 (1990) (addressing definition of "picket" and "stockade" fences).

35. Carter v. Carter, 232 N.C. 614, 616, 61 S.E.2d 711, 713 (1950).

36. Morecock v. Hood, 202 N.C. 321, 323, 162 S.E.2d 730, 731 (1932).

37. *Penny*, 249 N.C. at 600, 107 S.E.2d at 76 (in interpreting the term *directly opposite*, each word must be given meaning rather than treating the modifier *directly* as a mere redundancy); Nash–Rocky Mount Bd. of Educ. v. Rocky Mount Bd. of Adjustment, 169 N.C. App. 587, 610 S.E.2d 255 (2005) (holding grant of zoning jurisdiction to "erection, construction, and use of buildings" does not include coverage of construction of a gravel parking lot).

38. Duke Power Co. v. City of High Point, 69 N.C. App. 378, 387, 317 S.E.2d 701, 706, *review denied*, 312 N.C. 82, 321 S.E.2d 895 (1984) (no part of a statute should be considered mere surplusage).

39. State v. Fox, 262 N.C. 193, 194, 136 S.E.2d 761, 762 (1964). The ordinance should also be read in relation to other ordinances adopted by the same jurisdiction on the same subject—*in pari materia. See, e.g.*, Town of Spruce Pine v. Avery Cnty., 346 N.C. 787, 488 S.E.2d 144 (1997) (appropriate to consider all state water-quality-protection statutes in determining the scope and purposes of the water-supply-watershed-protection statute); Fairway Outdoor Advert., LLC v. Town of Cary, 225 N.C. App. 676, 739 S.E.2d 579 (2013) (consider all sections of ordinance related to process for appealing staff decisions); *In re* Request for Declaratory Ruling by the Envtl. Mgmt. Comm'n, 155 N.C. App. 408, 573 S.E.2d 732 (2002), *review denied*, 357 N.C. 62, 579 S.E.2d 392 (2003) (in determining that the agency could include wetlands as "waters" as defined by the statutes, it is appropriate to consider the language and spirit of the statutes and their purposes and similar long-standing federal interpretations of "waters of the United States"); Dev. Assocs. v. Wake Cnty. Bd. of Adjustment, 48 N.C. App. 541, 269 S.E.2d 700 (1980), *review denied*, 301 N.C. 719, 274 S.E.2d 227 (1981) (appropriate to examine other statutes defining *agriculture* in reviewing scope of bona fide "farm" exemption from county zoning).

40. 279 N.C. App. 1, 15, 864 S.E.2d 742, 751, *review denied*, ___ N.C. ___, 865 S.E.2d 858 (2021).

41. "In construing statutes courts normally adopt an interpretation which will avoid absurd or bizarre consequences, the presumption being that the legislature acted in accordance with reason and common sense and did not intend untoward results." State *ex rel.* Comm'r of Ins. v. N.C. Auto. Rate Admin. Office, 294 N.C. 60, 68, 241 S.E.2d 324, 329 (1978); Young v. Whitehall Co., 229 N.C. 360, 367, 49 S.E.2d 797, 802 (1948).

If possible, an interpretation should be made that reconciles conflicts between sections.[42] When a provision has two reasonable interpretations, if one avoids a serious constitutional question, it should be applied. If reconciliation of conflicting sections is not possible, the more recently enacted provision generally prevails,[43] and a more specific provision controls over a more general one.[44] In *Visible Properties, LLC v. Village of Clemmons*, multiple sections of the ordinance regulated off-premises signs in a conflicting manner—the applicable general-zoning district, an overlay zoning district, and specific sign regulations.[45] The court noted that where a reasonable interpretation can avoid a conflict between provisions, it should be adopted. It therefore held that the specific sign regulation superseded the more general base- and overlay-district regulations.

When the ordinance restricts property rights, restrictions not clearly included within the ordinance should not be implied. In *Visible Properties*, the court held that the regulation was ambiguous as to whether digital billboards were included within the definition of prohibited "moving and flashing signs" and "electronic message boards." Given two reasonable interpretations, that they were or were not prohibited, the ambiguity was resolved in favor of the interpretation permitting the free use of property.[46]

The North Carolina cases applying these principles to the interpretation of development regulations have been relatively straightforward.[47]

Plain Meaning

When a land-development regulation has clear and unequivocal language or a specific definition, that language is controlling on boards and courts interpreting the regulation.[48] A number of cases have applied this rule in a land use law context.

In *NCJS, LLC v. City of Charlotte*, the court interpreted an ordinance provision that required preexisting dumpsters in front of a warehouse to be screened when the land and structures are "redeveloped."[49] The court held that moving the dumpsters to an alternate location along the building frontage was not enough to trigger the screening requirement because the plain meaning was that the requirement

---

42. Victory Cab Co. v. City of Charlotte, 234 N.C. 572, 576, 68 S.E.2d 433, 437 (1951). The court applied this rule in *Town of Pinebluff v. Moore County*, 374 N.C. 254, 839 S.E.2d 833 (2020). The local bill modified G.S. 160A-360(a) to grant the town up to two miles of extraterritorial jurisdiction and modified G.S. 160A-360(f) to provide that the county "shall approve" the expanded jurisdiction upon presentation of proper evidence of an annexation by the town that would allow the new jurisdiction. The court found that the amendment to G.S. 160A-360(f) did not repeal by implication the discretion granted to the county in G.S. 160A-360(d) to disapprove the extension to areas already subject to county zoning, subdivision, and building-code enforcement, noting that the statute should be read in its entirety, with each subsection harmonized and given effect if possible.

43. *Victory Cab*, at 577, 68 S.E.2d at 437.

44. State *ex rel.* Utils. Comm'n v. Lumbee River Elec. Membership Corp., 275 N.C. 250, 260, 166 S.E.2d 663, 670 (1969).

45. 284 N.C. App. 743, 876 S.E.2d 804 (2022).

46. *Id.* at 754, 876 S.E.2d at 812. *See also* Morris Commc'ns Corp. v. City of Bessemer City Zoning Bd. of Adjustment, 365 N.C. 152, 712 S.E.2d 868 (2011); Yancey v. Heafner, 268 N.C. 263, 266, 150 S.E.2d 440, 443 (1966). Also see the discussion of the interpretation of zoning limits on nonconformities in Chapter 20.

47. The exact language of the ordinance in effect at the time of the appealed decision is applied. Carolina Spirits, Inc. v. City of Raleigh, 127 N.C. App. 745, 493 S.E.2d 283 (1997), *review denied*, 347 N.C. 574, 498 S.E.2d 380 (1998).

48. For examples of the application of the plain-meaning rule in the interpretation of related statutes, see *Town of Boone v. State*, 369 N.C. 126, 134, 794 S.E.2d 710, 716 (2016) (authority of legislature to set municipal corporate limits and extraterritorial jurisdiction); *Quality Built Homes Inc. v. Town of Carthage*, 369 N.C. 15, 19–20, 789 S.E.2d 454, 457–58 (2016) (authority for public-enterprise impact fees); *Smith Chapel Baptist Church v. City of Durham*, 350 N.C. 805, 811, 517 S.E.2d 874, 878 (1999) (authority to impose stormwater fees).

49. NCJS, LLC v. City of Charlotte, 255 N.C. App. 72, 80, 803 S.E.2d 684, 690–91 (2017) (quoting CITY OF CHARLOTTE, N.C., CHARLOTTE ZONING ORDINANCE § 12.303).

was triggered only by redevelopment of the land and the warehouse building, not just relocating the dumpsters.

In *Long v. Currituck County*, the court interpreted the ordinance definition of a single-family detached dwelling as "a building" not attached to any other "principal structure" to prohibit a project with one main building and two wing buildings.[50]

In *Fehrenbacher v. City of Durham*, the court held that a requirement that a cell tower not be "readily identifiable" as a cell tower did not mean that it not be visible, but that steps be taken to camouflage its function.[51] The cell tower, designed as a "giant fake pine tree," was twice the height of nearby pine trees but was otherwise "authentic looking," and from some views it blended into the surrounding rural residential setting.[52]

In *Fort v. County of Cumberland (Fort II)*, the court considered the plain and ordinary meaning of the term *vocational school* to mean a facility that qualifies people for jobs, a purpose that did not include a shooting range that allowed people to practice an existing skill.[53]

In *Lipinski v. Town of Summerfield*, the zoning officer interpreted attachment of tarps to a permitted chain-link fence six months after original construction as a prohibited fence "constructed in whole or in part of readily flammable material such as paper, cloth or canvas."[54] The court held that the plain meaning of the permitted and prohibited materials applied to the fence as originally constructed, not to subsequent screening attached to the fence.[55]

In *Busik v. N.C. Coastal Resources Commission*, the regulation required one setback from the ocean for "a structure" of 5000 square feet or less and a greater setback for larger structures. A neighbor contended that a project with four separate structures, totaling over 5000 square feet, should have been subject to the larger setback requirement. The court disagreed, holding that the plain meaning of the regulation entailed the requirement's application to a single structure, not an entire development or collection of structures.[56]

---

50. Long v. Currituck Cnty., 248 N.C. App. 55, 787 S.E.2d 835, *review dismissed as moot*, 369 N.C. 74, 793 S.E.2d 222 (2016). The main building and each of the wings were 5000 square feet, with the two wings connected to the main building with conditioned hallways. Given the three buildings were the same size and all were used for residential purposes, none of the buildings could be considered accessory to the others, so each must be considered a principal structure, and only one principal structure was allowed on a single lot. While the State Building Code Council in 2015 ruled that the structure was subject to the one- and two-family building code rather than the commercial building code, the court held the Council's determination was applicable to the state building code but not to the county unified development ordinance. In a subsequent case regarding the same project, the court upheld the constitutionality and statutory authority of the county to enact and enforce this ordinance. LeTendre v. Currituck Cnty., 259 N.C. App. 512, 817 S.E.2d 73 (2018), *review denied*, 372 N.C. 54, 822 S.E.2d 641 (2019). Apparently in response to these rulings, in 2019 the General Assembly amended G.S. 153A-346 to prohibit a county from using a definition of a "building" that differs from the definitions in state statutes or in rules adopted by the State Building Code Council. S.L. 2019-111. In *Currituck County v. LeTendre*, 2020 WL 6750429 (No. 2-19-CV-27-BO, E.D.N.C., Nov. 17, 2020), the federal district court held that this 2019 legislation was a "clarification" rather than a substantial alteration of the statute. For that reason, the court ruled that the 2019 legislation requires the county's definition of a building in its unified development ordinance to be consistent with the State Building Code Council's interpretation that it was in fact a single building for local regulatory purposes.

51. Fehrenbacher v. City of Durham, 239 N.C. App. 141, 768 S.E.2d 186 (2015).

52. *Id.* at 151–53, 768 S.E.2d at 194–95.

53. Fort v. Cnty. of Cumberland (*Fort II*), 235 N.C. App. 541, 761 S.E.2d 744, *review denied*, 367 N.C. 798 (2014).

54. Lipinski v. Town of Summerfield, 230 N.C. App. 305, 306, 750 S.E.2d 46, 48 (2013) (quoting TOWN OF SUMMERFIELD, N.C., DEVELOPMENT ORDINANCE § 6-5.3 (2010)).

55. *Lipinski*, 230 N.C. App. 305, 750 S.E.2d 46.

56. Busik v. N.C. Coastal Res. Comm'n, 230 N.C. App. 148, 753 S.E.2d 326 (2013), *review denied*, 367 N.C. 502 (2014).

In *MNC Holdings, LLC v. Town of Matthews*, the court held that a provision allowing nonconforming structures to be modified when required by law or an order of the building inspector allowed an alteration in either situation, not just the latter one.[57]

In *Four Seasons Management Services, Inc. v. Town of Wrightsville Beach*, the court held that an ordinance provision on "accessory uses" was inapplicable to "accessory structures" where the ordinance expressly defined both and applied differential treatment to them.[58] The court also noted it was significant that all other sections of the ordinance applied greater review to proposed structures and major construction, buttressing the intent to distinguish "accessory structures" and "accessory buildings" from "accessory uses."

In *Lambeth v. Town of Kure Beach*, the court held that where the zoning ordinance specifically regulated the width of "driveways," the town could not interpret that to include all impervious surfaces (driveways and sidewalks in this case).[59]

In *Capital Outdoor, Inc. v. Guilford County Board of Adjustment*, the zoning ordinance prohibited billboards located within 300 feet of "any residentially zoned property."[60] The ordinance had two residential zoning districts, one for single-family and one for multifamily. The county staff interpreted this restriction to also apply to the agricultural district because residences were a permitted use in that district. The court held otherwise, that the language in the ordinance was unambiguous and that the restriction should apply only to areas zoned residential. It also noted that, according to the ordinance, the agricultural district was "primarily intended to accommodate uses of an agricultural nature."[61]

In *Procter v. City of Raleigh Board of Adjustment*, the court held that the staff and board of adjustment may not interpret an ordinance to impose a maximum setback (sometimes referred to as a "build to" line) where the terms of the ordinance clearly impose only a minimum setback.[62]

In *Harry v. Mecklenburg County*, the court held that where an ordinance clearly specifies that a pier is an accessory use, it is error for the zoning administrator to allow the pier to be considered a principal use in the absence of other structures on the lot.[63]

In *R.L. Coleman & Co. v. City of Asheville*, the permit for a shopping-center expansion included a condition that the center's internal driveways have a T connection with the adjacent road. While street standards allowed an intersection of between 60 and 90 degrees, the court held that the specific permit condition was unambiguous in that a T intersection required a 90-degree connection.[64]

In *Robinhood Trails Neighbors v. Winston-Salem Zoning Board of Adjustment*, the court held that it was inappropriate to use property-tax maps to define the term *lots* when the ordinance specifically defined "Lot, Zoning" differently.[65]

57. MNC Holdings, LLC v. Town of Matthews, 223 N.C. App. 442, 735 S.E.2d 364 (2012).

58. Four Seasons Mgmt. Servs., Inc. v. Town of Wrightsville Beach, 205 N.C. App. 65, 695 S.E.2d 456 (2010).

59. Lambeth v. Town of Kure Beach, 157 N.C. App. 349, 578 S.E.2d 688 (2003).

60. Capital Outdoor, Inc. v. Guilford Cnty. Bd. of Adjustment, 152 N.C. App. 474, 567 S.E.2d 440, *review denied*, 356 N.C. 611, 574 S.E.2d 676 (2002).

61. *Id.* at 476, 567 S.E.2d at 442. *See also* E. Outdoor, Inc. v. Bd. of Adjustment, 150 N.C. App. 516, 564 S.E.2d 78 (2002), (upholding interpretation of Johnston County zoning provision that billboards not permitted in the AR/R-40 zoning district).

62. Procter v. City of Raleigh Bd. of Adjustment, 140 N.C. App. 784, 538 S.E.2d 621 (2000).

63. Harry v. Mecklenburg Cnty., 136 N.C. App. 200, 523 S.E.2d 135 (1999).

64. R.L. Coleman & Co. v. City of Asheville, 98 N.C. App. 648, 392 S.E.2d 107, *review denied*, 327 N.C. 432, 395 S.E.2d 689 (1990).

65. Robinhood Trails Neighbors v. Winston-Salem Zoning Bd. of Adjustment, 44 N.C. App. 539, 261 S.E.2d 520, *review denied*, 299 N.C. 737, 267 S.E.2d 663 (1980).

In *Woodhouse v. Board of Commissioners*, the court concluded that "additional uses" cited in the ordinance in the section on planned-unit developments included any type of residential use, not just the single-family uses allowed in the underlying zoning district.[66]

In *James v. Sutton*, the Charlotte zoning ordinance allowed as a permitted use in the business zoning district those businesses used "in whole or in part" for retail sales. The court held that this, by its express terms, allowed a candy factory where some 15 to 20 percent of candy produced was sold through an on-site retail store.[67]

Common Definitions

A number of cases stress the importance of using the common meanings of terms that are not defined in the ordinance.[68]

In *PBK Holdings, LLC v. County of Rockingham*, the court consulted a dictionary to interpret the undefined terms *local* and *regional* as applied to differential zoning regulation of landfills.[69]

In *Morris Communications Corp. v. City of Bessemer City Zoning Board of Adjustment*, the court held that where the ordinance does not define the term *work* in requiring work to be commenced under its regulations to prevent expiration of a permit, the term should be given its ordinary meaning. Since the dictionary definition of *work* includes mental as well as physical efforts, it was unreasonable, the court found, to interpret the term to require physical work on the site in addition to efforts expended in working with state transportation officials and the landowner to establish a site for a relocated sign.[70]

In *Morris Communications Corp. v. Board of Adjustment*, the court held it was reasonable to interpret *sign structure* to include all of the materials that made up the sign.[71]

In *Malloy v. Zoning Board of Adjustment*, the ordinance limited nonconforming "structures" and defined the term *structure* to mean "that which is built or constructed."[72] The court looked to the dictionary definitions of *built* and *constructed* and concluded that a storage tank affixed to a concrete pad was a structure covered by the ordinance provision.

In *In re Appeal of the Society for the Preservation of Historic Oakwood*, the court looked to the dictionary definitions of *decision* and *determination* for aid in deciding that an advisory memorandum without binding effect was not an appealable decision or determination.[73]

In *Tucker v. Mecklenburg County Zoning Board of Adjustment*, the court looked to dictionary definitions of *sales* and *gifts* to determine whether a kennel holding abandoned animals awaiting potential

---

66. Woodhouse v. Bd. of Comm'rs, 299 N.C. 211, 261 S.E.2d 882 (1980).

67. James v. Sutton, 229 N.C. 515, 50 S.E.2d 300 (1948). *See also* Kinney v. Sutton, 230 N.C. 404, 53 S.E.2d 306 (1949) (commercial dining room operated by resident of structure is a commercial use not within permitted residential uses).

68. The same standard applies to interpretation of administrative rules. *See, e.g.,* Capital Outdoor, Inc. v. Tolson, 159 N.C. App. 55, 582 S.E.2d 717, *review denied*, 357 N.C. 504, 587 S.E.2d 662 (2003) (interpreting the terms *height* and *sign structure* in rules on billboards in accordance with their common or ordinary meanings).

69. PBK Holdings, LLC v. Cnty. of Rockingham, 233 N.C. App. 133, 756 S.E.2d 821, *appeal dismissed*, 367 N.C. 788 (2014).

70. Morris Commc'ns Corp. v. City of Bessemer City Zoning Bd. of Adjustment, 365 N.C. 152, 712 S.E.2d 868 (2011).

71. Morris Commc'ns Corp. v. Bd. of Adjustment, 159 N.C. App. 598, 603, 583 S.E.2d 419, 422 (2003), *appeal dismissed*, 357 N.C. 658, 590 S.E.2d 269 (2003). The court went on, however, to hold that the ordinance could not prohibit replacement of the sign-face frame as that was specifically allowed by state regulations.

72. Malloy v. Zoning Bd. of Adjustment, 155 N.C. App. 628, 631, 573 S.E.2d 760, 762 (2002).

73. *In re* Soc'y for the Pres. of Historic Oakwood, 153 N.C. App. 737, 571 S.E.2d 588 (2002).

adoption was a "commercial kennel."[74] The court held that since a donation was only requested but not required prior to adoption of rescued animals, the board of adjustment's determination that the kennel was not commercial in nature was reasonable.

In *County of Durham v. Roberts*, the court held that horses must be considered to be included within the term *livestock*, given standard dictionary definitions as well as their inclusion in a wide variety of statutes dealing with livestock.[75]

In *BellSouth Carolinas PCS, L.P. v. Henderson County Zoning Board of Adjustment*, the court considered dictionary definitions, a legal dictionary, and state regulatory statutes in concluding that a cellular telephone tower was a "public utility station."[76]

In *MMR Holdings, LLC v. City of Charlotte*, the court applied the dictionary's first and more literal definition of *façade* rather than a second definition that was more metaphoric.[77]

In *Ball v. Randolph County Board of Adjustment*, the court held that remediation of petroleum-contaminated soil cannot be considered an agricultural use, even though the soil is spread on a field, tilled, and planted with a ground cover.[78]

In *Ayers v. Board of Adjustment*, the court ruled that forestry uses do not include timber-industry activities, noting that all other uses permitted in the district were low-density, noncommercial uses and that allowing timber processing would be inconsistent with the plain and ordinary meaning of the term *forestry*.[79]

In *Moore v. Board of Adjustment*, the court concluded that an open-air flea market is not a permitted use in a zoning district that allows "stores and shops conducting retail business."[80]

The court in *Cardwell v. Town of Madison Board of Adjustment*[81] held that it was inappropriate for the zoning administrator to rely on the State Building Code's definition of a building; rather, the administrator should rely on the definition in the zoning code and, if undefined there, on the customary dictionary definition of *building*.[82] Similarly, in *Riggs v. Zoning Board of Adjustment*,[83] the court held that the zoning

74. Tucker v. Mecklenburg Cnty. Zoning Bd. of Adjustment, 148 N.C. App. 52, 557 S.E.2d 631 (2001), *aff'd in part*, 356 N.C. 658, 576 S.E.2d 324 (2003). In a similar ruling, the court in *Dobo* held that the actual use of property, not its potential use, must be considered in determining whether a use is in fact "accessory." Here a large sawmill was being operated in the rear yard of a residence. Although the saw was large enough for commercial use, the fact that the evidence submitted indicated it had been used only for noncommercial purposes precluded a finding that it was a commercial or industrial use. Dobo v. Zoning Bd. of Adjustment, 149 N.C. App. 701, 710–13, 562 S.E.2d 108, 114–16 (2002), *dissenting opinion adopted per curiam in* 356 N.C. 656, 576 S.E.2d 324 (2003). *See also* Jirtle v. Bd. of Adjustment, 175 N.C. App. 178, 622 S.E.2d 713 (2005) (holding food pantry an accessory use to a church).

75. Cnty. of Durham v. Roberts, 145 N.C. App. 665, 551 S.E.2d 494 (2001).

76. BellSouth Carolinas PCS, L.P. v. Henderson Cnty. Zoning Bd. of Adjustment, 174 N.C. App. 574, 621 S.E.2d 270 (2005).

77. MMR Holdings, LLC v. City of Charlotte, 174 N.C. App. 540, 621 S.E.2d 210 (2005).

78. Ball v. Randolph Cnty. Bd. of Adjustment, 129 N.C. App. 300, 498 S.E.2d 833, *appeal dismissed*, 349 N.C. 348, 507 S.E.2d 272 (1998). For additional cases interpreting the statutory exemption for bona-fide-farm uses in county zoning, see Chapter 22.

79. Ayers v. Bd. of Adjustment, 113 N.C. App. 528, 439 S.E.2d 199, *review denied*, 336 N.C. 71, 445 S.E.2d 28 (1994).

80. Moore v. Bd. of Adjustment, 113 N.C. App. 181, 182, 437 S.E.2d 536, 537 (1993).

81. 102 N.C. App. 546, 402 S.E.2d 866 (1991).

82. Similarly, in the context of interpreting a private restrictive covenant that allowed residences and garages on a lot, the court used dictionaries to determine the ordinary meaning of *garage* in concluding that the meaning included a detached covered carport. Sanford v. Williams, 221 N.C. App. 107, 727 S.E.2d 362, *review denied*, 366 N.C. 246, 731 S.E.2d 144 (2012). In 2019, the General Assembly amended the zoning statutes to prohibit a county from using any definition of "building" that differs from the definitions in state statutes or in rules adopted by the State Building Code Council. S.L. 2019-111.

83. 101 N.C. App. 422, 399 S.E.2d 149 (1991).

administrator and the board of adjustment had erred in considering a stormwater system (consisting of a parking area, swales, and in-ground piping) not to be a "structure," ruling that in the absence of a more precise definition in the ordinance, the definition that should have been applied was the natural and recognized meaning of the term, which here included any piece of work composed of parts joined together in some definite manner.

In *Raleigh Place Associates v. City of Raleigh Board of Adjustment*, the court used common meanings to distinguish a roof sign (for which a sign permit was required) from a canopy sign (for which no permit was required).[84]

In *Town of Southern Pines v. Mohr*, the court held that a treatment facility for emotionally disturbed children operated under the direct control of the state Department of Human Resources was a governmental function permissible in a district that allowed public buildings, hospitals, and sanitariums.[85]

In *Coastal Ready-Mix Concrete Co. v. Board of Commissioners*, the court interpreted *appurtenances* as used in the ordinance to be something physically secondary to a primary part that served a useful or necessary function in connection with the primary part. Thus, a forty-five-foot-tall cement-mixing bin was held not to be a "mechanical appurtenance" to the conveyor belt taking materials to its top.[86]

In *Yancey v. Heafner*, the court held that a lighted football field with bleachers seating 4000 people was a usual and necessary part of the adjacent permitted school.[87] In *In re Couch*, the court ruled that a car wash was included within the permitted use of an automobile service station when that use was defined by the ordinance to include minor repairs and gas stations customarily offered car washes.[88]

In *Penny v. City of Durham*, the court held that use of the phrase *directly opposite* for determining the validity of a protest petition must be read to mean opposite the portion of the land being rezoned, not opposite the entire parcel.[89]

Intent

Several cases look to the intent of the ordinance to help define unclear terms. Intent is determined by examining the language used, the spirit of the regulation, and the goal of the regulation.[90] A court does not, however, consider testimony from staff or a board member on the original intent of the text.[91]

In *MNC Holdings, LLC v. Town of Matthews*, the court held that a provision allowing nonconforming structures to be modified when required by law or an order of the building inspector allowed an alteration required to come into compliance with state environmental regulations (not just for building safety), given the intent of allowing owners flexibility when necessary to comply with state and federal mandates.[92]

---

84. Raleigh Place Assocs. v. City of Raleigh Bd. of Adjustment, 95 N.C. App. 217, 382 S.E.2d 441 (1989).

85. Town of Southern Pines v. Mohr, 30 N.C. App. 342, 226 S.E.2d 865 (1976).

86. Coastal Ready-Mix Concrete Co. v. Bd. of Comm'rs, 299 N.C. 620, 265 S.E.2d 379 (1980).

87. Yancey v. Heafner, 268 N.C. 263, 150 S.E.2d 440 (1966).

88. *In re* Couch, 258 N.C. 345, 128 S.E.2d 409 (1962). *See also* Cnty. of Durham v. Maddry & Co., 315 N.C. 296, 337 S.E.2d 576 (1985).

89. Penny v. City of Durham, 249 N.C. 596, 107 S.E.2d 72 (1959).

90. Westminster Homes, Inc. v. Town of Cary Zoning Bd. of Adjustment, 354 N.C. 298, 303–04, 554 S.E.2d 634, 638 (2001).

91. Fort v. Cnty. of Cumberland (*Fort I*), 218 N.C. App. 401, 408, 721 S.E.2d 350, 356, *review denied*, 366 N.C. 401 (2012). *See also* State v. Nat'l Food Stores, Inc., 270 N.C. 323, 332–33, 154 S.E.2d 548, 555 (1967).

92. 223 N.C. App. 442, 735 S.E.2d 364 (2012). The court also noted the regulation should be liberally construed in favor of the owner of regulated property.

In *Fort v. County of Cumberland (Fort I)*, the court examined the statement of intent in the definition of a zoning district, as well as the title of the district, in interpreting the scope of permitted uses.[93]

In *Cambridge Southport, LLC v. Southeast Brunswick Sanitary District*, the court looked to the purpose of a law extending development approvals during the 2008 recession in interpreting "development approvals" to apply to utility-capacity allocations.[94]

In *Westminster Homes, Inc. v. Town of Cary Zoning Board of Adjustment*, the court considered the language of a permit condition, the "clear desire" for privacy, and a wide, undisturbed buffer in interpreting a fence requirement to preclude individual gates in a fence along the rear of a subdivision.[95]

In *Hayes v. Fowler*, the applicable zoning district permitted residences but not commercial uses or guesthouses. The court held that the plaintiffs' proposed bed-and-breakfast was not an accessory use to the permitted residential use of the structure and that the intent of the ordinance clearly was to prohibit uses similar to the proposed bed-and-breakfast.[96]

In *Rauseo v. New Hanover County*, the court held that it was reasonable for a county board of commissioners to conclude that a fire station is included within "government offices and buildings" and allowed by the ordinance in question as a special use.[97]

In *Capricorn Equity Corp. v. Town of Chapel Hill Board of Adjustment*, the court held that a structure consisting of two halves, each half comprising six bedrooms with three connecting baths but only one kitchen and a single living room, was a duplex (a permitted use) rather than a rooming house (a use requiring a site plan prior to approval).[98]

In *Allen v. City of Burlington Board of Adjustment*, the court held that it was inappropriate to consider a community kitchen primarily serving transients as "similar" to a permitted rooming house, which serves guests residing on-site for some fixed period.[99] The court held it permissible to consider an adult day-care facility as equivalent to a rooming house and to allow offices as incidental to permitted uses.

In *Donnelly v. Board of Adjustment*, the court, considering the language of the Pinehurst zoning ordinance and its purpose of preserving the appearance of a resort town, ruled that a lot fronted by a city street and bounded by a restricted-access highway on the rear was a "through lot."[100] The court also ruled that, absent definition by the ordinance, the ordinary meaning should be given to the term *picket fence*.

In *P.A.W. v. Town of Boone Board of Adjustment*, the court upheld a determination that a required 100-foot buffer between a high-density planned-unit development and an adjacent low-density residential district had to be located entirely within the high-density zoning district.[101] The applicant had

---

93. *Fort I*, 218 N.C. App. 401, 721 S.E.2d 350. In a second case involving the same facility, the court noted that the zoning ordinance was amended in 2011 to shift from a general provision that "[a]ll uses of property are prohibited except those that are permitted" to "[a]ll uses of property are allowed as a use by right except where this ordinance specifies otherwise," evidencing an intent to "broaden the spectrum of permissible uses." Fort v. Cnty. of Cumberland (*Fort II*), 235 N.C. App. 541, 549, 761 S.E.2d 744, 749–50, *review denied*, 367 N.C. 798 (2014). *See also* Fehrenbacher v. City of Durham, 239 N.C. App. 141, 768 S.E.2d 186 (2015) (noting the intent of the ordinance to protect natural beauty while meeting needs for wireless-communication services when interpreting the requirement for stealth cell towers).

94. Cambridge Southport, LLC v. Se. Brunswick Sanitary Dist., 218 N.C. App. 287, 721 S.E.2d 736 (2012).

95. *Westminster Homes*, 354 N.C. 298, 554 S.E.2d 634.

96. Hayes v. Fowler, 123 N.C. App. 400, 473 S.E.2d 442 (1996).

97. Rauseo v. New Hanover Cnty., 118 N.C. App. 286, 289, 454 S.E.2d 698, 700 (1995). *See also* Carter v. Stanly Cnty., 125 N.C. App. 628, 635, 482 S.E.2d 9, 13, *review denied*, 346 N.C. 276, 487 S.E.2d 540 (1997) (holding notice of hearing regarding "government owned buildings, facilities, and institutions" was broad enough to include state prisons).

98. Capricorn Equity Corp. v. Town of Chapel Hill Bd. of Adjustment, 334 N.C. 132, 431 S.E.2d 183 (1993).

99. Allen v. City of Burlington Bd. of Adjustment, 100 N.C. App. 615, 397 S.E.2d 657 (1990).

100. Donnelly v. Bd. of Adjustment, 99 N.C. App. 702, 394 S.E.2d 246 (1990).

101. P.A.W. v. Town of Boone Bd. of Adjustment, 95 N.C. App. 110, 382 S.E.2d 443 (1989).

contended that the buffer only had to be between building sites and therefore could in part be within the adjacent zoning district.

In *Atkins v. Zoning Board of Adjustment,* the court noted that the interpretation of restrictions on nonconformities should take account of the policy of eventually eliminating nonconformities.[102]

In *MacPherson v. City of Asheville,* the court held that a person holding a binding contract to purchase was an "owner" within the intent of the provision requiring the owner or the owner's agent to apply for site-plan approval.[103]

In *Myers Park Homeowners Ass'n v. City of Charlotte,* the court held that the ordinance definition of a dormitory as a structure intended to be occupied as a dwelling showed an intent to treat a dormitory as a residential use.[104]

In *85° & Sunny, LLC v. Currituck County,*[105] the court noted that an interpretation of restrictions on nonconformities should consider the intention of limiting the continued existence of a nonconforming RV park. As for the scope of allowed improvements, the court must consider both the specific provision in the ordinance regarding nonconforming campgrounds and the general-ordinance provisions applicable to all nonconformities. The provisions should be interpreted as general and specific provisions on the same subject to be read together and harmonized where possible. To apply only the specific campground provision (not permitting additional campsites or land area devoted to campgrounds) and not apply the general limitation (not enlarging, expanding, or intensifying the nonconforming use) would be contrary to the stated purpose of the regulation to limit the continued existence of nonconformities by allowing indefinite extension of their lifespan through regular upgrading with new amenities.

Specialized Rules of Construction

On occasion the court has employed additional specialized rules of construction to address particular interpretations.

The doctrine of *ejusdem generis* provides that when an enumeration of specific words is followed by general words or terms, the general term shall be held to refer to the same classification as the specific terms.

The court applied this doctrine in *Chambers v. Zoning Board of Adjustment* to hold that where the ordinance required that a "garage or other satisfactory automobile storage space" equal to one space per unit be provided on the premises, on-street parking could not be used to meet the requirement (reasoning that the "other" storage in this context must be similar in nature to an off-street garage).[106] However, this rule must only be applied if in fact the court determines that the specific words in the list are part of a related series.

In *Bryan v. Wilson,* the Greenville zoning ordinance's list of permitted uses included "schools, institutions of an educational or philanthropic nature, [and] public buildings."[107] The court held that each of these was a separate, independent use and thus that a building to be leased for use as a post office was permissible, as the permissible public buildings were not limited to schools and philanthropic entities.

---

102. Atkins v. Zoning Bd. of Adjustment, 53 N.C. App. 723, 281 S.E.2d 756 (1981).

103. MacPherson v. City of Asheville, 283 N.C. 299, 196 S.E.2d 200 (1973).

104. Myers Park Homeowners Ass'n v. City of Charlotte, 229 N.C. App. 204, 747 S.E.2d 338 (2013).

105. 279 N.C. App. 1, 864 S.E.2d 742, *review denied,* ___ N.C. ___, 865 S.E.2d 858 (2021).

106. 250 N.C. 194, 198, 108 S.E.2d 211, 214 (1959).

107. 259 N.C. 107, 108, 130 S.E.2d 68, 69 (1963). Philip Green noted that the court had "the dubious assistance of conflicting testimony from two university English professors." PHILIP P. GREEN, JR., LEGAL RESPONSIBILITIES OF THE LOCAL ZONING ADMINISTRATOR IN NORTH CAROLINA 47 (2d ed. 1987).

In *South Boulevard Video & News, Inc. v. Charlotte Zoning Board of Adjustment*,[108] the court was faced with the question of whether sexually explicit videotapes fell within "publications, books, magazines, and other periodicals which are distinguished or characterized by their emphasis on matter depicting, describing, or relating to specified sexual activities or specified anatomical areas," a standard set out in a statute covering "adult bookstores."[109] The court considered the context of the words in the statute and other statutes on the same subject matter and concluded that "publications" was intended to include videotapes.[110]

Another well-established rule of construction is *expressio unius est exclusio alterius*: the mention of an express item implies the exclusion of others.[111] If, however, such a mention is prefaced by terminology such as *including* or *including, but not limited to*, that phrasing is deemed by the courts to express a legislative intent *not* to exclude other items from the list.[112] This canon applies, however, only when the items listed are an associated group or series, justifying an inference that unlisted items were intentionally rather than inadvertently omitted.[113]

In *Appalachian Materials, LLC v. Watauga County*,[114] the court held that a definition of *educational facility* listing specific types of schools was intended to exclude other types of facilities, such as a school district's administrative offices.

In *Fort I*, the ordinance listed "SCHOOLS, public, private, elementary or secondary" as a permitted use.[115] The court rejected the plaintiff's contention that this included all types of private or public schools, including its firearms-training facility. The court ruled that only elementary and secondary schools were included, as the ordinance specifically prohibited vocational and trade schools in this district. The court noted that an interpretation should presume that no part of the ordinance is surplusage, and it noted that an interpretation of the ordinance as including all types of public or private school would render the qualifier regarding elementary and secondary schools meaningless.[116]

This rule was also applied to resolve the interpretation of a minimum-separation requirement in the Raleigh zoning code's adult-business-siting standards.[117] The ordinance required adult businesses to be located at least 2000 feet from various specified sensitive land uses, including "specialty schools." An issue in the special use permit hearing was the calculation of the separation from a karate school located within rented space in a building housing several other uses. The ordinance included several detailed directions for computing this minimum distance, including a requirement to consider the "entire property" of the adult business, particularly including the parking area for off-street parking.

108. 129 N.C. App. 282, 498 S.E.2d 623, *review denied*, 348 N.C. 501, 510 S.E.2d 656 (1998).

109. *Id*. at 284, 498 S.E.2d at 624 (quoting G.S. 14-202.10(2)).

110. *See also* Hemphill-Nolan v. Town of Weddington, 153 N.C. App. 144, 146–47, 568 S.E.2d 887, 889–90 (2002). The court held that the provisions in G.S. 160A-388 relating to appeals of variances must be read in context and that it was inappropriate to apply individual phrases out of context. The town argued that use of the terms "any ordinance" and "any matter" made the provisions of the section applicable to subdivision ordinances, but the court pointed out that this statute was clearly intended to apply only to zoning ordinances when read as a whole.

111. *See, e.g.*, Baker v. Martin, 330 N.C. 331, 410 S.E.2d 887 (1991); Campbell v. First Baptist Church, 298 N.C. 476, 259 S.E.2d 558 (1979); Bd. of Drainage Comm'rs v. Credle, 182 N.C. 442, 109 S.E. 88 (1921).

112. N.C. Tpk. Auth. v. Pine Island, Inc., 265 N.C. 109, 120, 143 S.E.2d 319, 327 (1965). Several commentators have concluded that the negative implication of the *expressio unius* rule is not often factually justified. *See, e.g.*, Frederick Reed Dickerson, The Interpretation and Application of Statutes 234–35 (1975).

113. Patmore v. Town of Chapel Hill, 233 N.C. App. 133, 142, 757 S.E.2d 302, 307 (2014).

114. 262 N.C. App. 156, 822 S.E.2d 57 (2018).

115. 218 N.C. App. 401, 721 S.E.2d 350, *review denied*, 366 N.C. 401, 735 S.E.2d 180 (2012). The plaintiffs contended this definition included their firearms-training facility for military, law-enforcement, and security personnel. In addition to classrooms, the facility included multiple firing ranges.

116. *Id.*, 218 N.C. App. 401, 721 S.E.2d 350.

117. Mangum v. Raleigh Bd. of Adjustment, 196 N.C. App. 249, 255, 674 S.E.2d 742, 747–48 (2009).

The court reasoned that, as the ordinance specifically included the parking area for the adult use but only included "a place of regular sessions" in the school definition, the ordinance should be interpreted to apply the inclusion of the parking area only for the adult use.[118]

A closely related rule is *noscitur a sociis*: associated words explain and limit each other. The court applied this rule in *Jeffries v. County of Harnett*,[119] finding that where the statute listed rural activities as examples of agritourism, which was exempt from county zoning, other activities must be similar to the listed items.

---

118. *Id.* at 254, 674 S.E.2d 747.
119. 259 N.C. App. 473, 817 S.E.2d 36, 50 (2018), *review denied*, 372 N.C. 297, 826 S.E.2d 710 (2019).

Application and Enforcement of Regulations

PART 5

CHAPTER 19

Vested Rights

When development regulations are adopted or amended, projects that are either underway or already in existence may be inconsistent with the new requirements. An issue then arises—must the development conform to the preexisting or the new regulation?

This problem involves two closely related issues. The first is whether a landowner has a statutory or constitutional right to complete work or continue a land use that is contrary to newly adopted standards. That issue is one of vested rights and is the subject of this chapter. The second issue is what local governments can do through the ordinance itself to allow, restrict, or terminate situations that do not conform to new ordinance requirements. This issue, regarding limits on nonconformities, is discussed in Chapter 20.

Defining the point at which a development secures legal protection from changes in ordinance requirements has been subject to substantial litigation and legislation in North Carolina. There are three methods to establish a vested right to continue development even though requirements change.

The first is to qualify for a statutory vested right. The legislature has created several statutory vested rights. These are secured by obtaining a building permit, a local development approval, a site-specific vesting plan, a multiphase-development approval, or a development agreement. Related to these statutory vested rights, North Carolina statutes also provide that if a development regulation changes between the time an application is filed and a permit decision is made, the applicant can choose which regulation is to be applied.

The second method of continuing development after a change in requirements is to secure a judicially established common law vested right by making substantial expenditures in good-faith reliance on a valid government approval, with substantial detriment if compliance with the current law is mandated.[1]

The third method for establishing a vested right to ongoing development amid changed mandates is for the ordinance itself to expressly state that development may continue under previous requirements. This is accomplished with language indicating that amendments to the ordinance shall apply prospectively.

These vested rights, like all other land use regulatory approvals, run with the land.[2] They are not a personal or contractual right of the landowner or occupant that can be shifted to some other parcel

---

1. For a review of North Carolina case law before the creation of the statutory vested right, see PHILIP P. GREEN, JR., THE DOCTRINE OF "VESTED RIGHTS" IN NORTH CAROLINA ZONING LAW 3–4 (1986). For a national overview, see CHARLES L. SIEMON ET AL., VESTED RIGHTS: BALANCING PUBLIC AND PRIVATE DEVELOPMENT EXPECTATIONS (1982).

2. Chapter 160D, Section 102 of the North Carolina General Statutes (hereinafter G.S.). In addition to this general provision, several statutes address it directly in a vested-rights context. G.S. 160D-108(i) provides that statutory vested rights attach to and run with the land rather than being a personal right of the landowner, with the exception of N.C. Department of Transportation sign permits issued under G.S. 136-131.1 and -131.2, where the vested rights belong to the permittee. G.S. 160D-1011 requires that development agreements be recorded in the county where the affected property is located and that the burdens and benefits of such agreements be binding on and inure to all successors in interest to the original parties to the agreement. Nationally, the general rule is that vested rights are a personal right and do not run with the land. AMERICAN LAW OF ZONING § 32:8 (Dec. 2022 Update). *See, e.g.,* BBC Land & Dev., Inc. v. Butts Cnty., 281 Ga. 472, 640 S.E.2d 33 (2007) (as vested rights require substantial expenditures

of land.[3] Rather, the right is attached to the parcel for which the right or permit is secured and may be exercised by subsequent owners of that parcel.

Statutory Vested Rights

To provide a clear and simple alternative to the frequently contentious common law vested right, the legislature has adopted statutory means for vested rights to be secured. These methods do not replace but rather supplement the common law vested right.[4]

A statutory vested right precludes any action by the local government "that would change, alter, impair, prevent, diminish, or otherwise delay the development or use of the property allowed by the applicable land development regulation or regulations."[5] The individual statutory vested rights, each of which is discussed below, and their durations are:

1. a building permit (six months);
2. a local development approval (one year or as otherwise specified by the local development regulation) or other state or local development permit;[6]
3. a site-specific vesting plan (two years, but this may be extended to five years by local development regulation);
4. a multiphase-development plan (seven years); and
5. a development agreement (indefinite and set by individual agreement).

Establishment of one type of statutory vested right does not preclude establishment of a vested right under another provision of the statute. They are not mutually exclusive. Also, once development is substantially underway under a statutory vested right, that right can become a common law vested right that extends beyond the statutory period.

The permit-choice rule, also described below, allows an applicant for a development permit to choose coverage by the original rules or the amended rules if the rules change after an application is submitted but before a permit decision is made. If a development application is approved, the statutory vested rights described below relate back to the time of the original permit application.[7]

Statutory vesting does not apply if the owner consents in writing to the application of the amended regulation.[8] In addition, a site-specific vesting plan includes several additional exceptions that are discussed below.

Once work is commenced under any statutory vested right, the statutory vesting expires if work is intentionally and voluntarily discontinued for twenty-four months unless the statute provides a longer

---

by person claiming the right, since subsequent purchasers have made no such expenditures, they have no vested rights). Some other states similarly provide by statute that a vested right runs with the land. *See, e.g.,* Colo. Rev. Stat. § 24-68-103 (2022).

3. Griffin v. Town of Unionville, No. 3:05-cv-514-RJC, 2008 WL 697634 (W.D.N.C. Mar. 11, 2008).

4. This is specifically provided for in G.S. 160D-108(c) and (i).

5. G.S. 160D-108. This provision was added by S.L. 2019-111, § 1.3.

6. For the purposes of statutory vested rights, G.S. 160D-108(j) provides that the definition of a "development permit" as used in the permit-choice statute is applicable. That definition, in G.S. 143-755(e)(2), is broader than the definition of a "development approval" in G.S. 160D-102(13). In addition to the administrative and quasi-judicial approvals under Chapter 160D, it also includes state agency permits for development, driveway permits, erosion- and sedimentation-control permits, and sign permits.

7. G.S. 160D-108(d). This provision was added by S.L. 2019-111, § 1.3.

8. G.S.160D-108.

vesting period.[9] The twenty-four-month period is tolled for proceedings at the board of adjustment or in court relating to the development.

After approval of a statutory vested right, the local government may make subsequent inspections and reviews to ensure compliance with the rules in effect at the time of the original application.[10]

A person claiming a statutory or common law vested right may submit information to the zoning administrator or other designated officer for a determination for the existence of a vested right.[11] That determination may be appealed to the board of adjustment, which reviews the question of vested rights de novo. In lieu of appealing to the board of adjustment, the person claiming vested rights may bring a civil action.[12] Courts are required to award attorney's fees and costs to the appealing party if the local government "took action inconsistent with, or in violation of," the permit-choice and vested rights statutes.[13]

Permit Extension

In addition to these ongoing statutory provisions for vested rights, temporary measures have in the past been adopted that extend the period in which permitted development must be initiated.

In 2009, the General Assembly adopted legislation extending most state and local development approvals for a three-year period.[14] This law, enacted in response to the major economic recession in 2008–2009, suspended the running of the period of "development approvals"[15] valid at any time between January 1, 2008, and December 31, 2010. In 2010, the General Assembly further refined this permit-extension law

---

9. G.S. 160D-108(d). This rule creates some ambiguity when applied to a vested right that has a shorter duration, such as the six months for a building permit or the one-year default period for a local development approval, if a different time is not set by the local regulation.

10. G.S. 160D-108(g).

11. G.S. 160D-108(h). The failure to raise a statutory vested rights claim during the consideration of a special use permit when that was a material issue for the permit precludes production of findings by the board on that issue. Given that, the court held in *Jubilee Carolina, LLC v. Town of Carolina Beach*, 268 N.C. App. 90, 834 S.E.2d 665 (2019), that a vested rights claim could not be raised for the first time in a certiorari review of the quasi-judicial permit decision.

12. G.S. 160D-108(h). Judicial review of a vested-rights claim is discussed in Chapter 29.

13. G.S. 6-21.7. This provision was added by S.L. 2019-111, § 1.11.

14. S.L. 2009-406. This uncodified act was subsequently amended by S.L. 2009-484, § 5.1 and S.L. 2009-572. The law was closely modeled on a New Jersey statute first adopted in 1992 and extended in 2008. N.J. STAT. ANN. §§ 40:55D-136.1 to .6. Other states took similar action during the 2008–10 recession. *See, e.g.,* 2010 MASS. ACTS ch. 240, § 173 (tolling many development approvals for the period from Aug. 15, 2008, to Aug. 15, 2010).

In *Cambridge Southport, LLC v. Southeast Brunswick Sanitary District*, 218 N.C. App. 287, 721 S.E.2d 736 (2012), a landowner secured a capacity allocation from the defendant utility authority and paid impact fees related to it. The agreement provided that the developer had three years to complete the project, or the allocation would expire. The project was started but then put on hold and foreclosed during the 2008 recession. The plaintiff, a real-estate developer, acquired the foreclosed project and sought to restart it. Even though four years had elapsed, the court held that the law extending permits tolled the expiration of the utility allocation, so no fees were forfeited.

15. The law specifies a number of state and local regulatory approvals that are expressly included: city and county approvals of sketch plans, preliminary plats, subdivision plats, site-specific and phased-development plans, development permits, development agreements, and building permits. It defines *development* broadly to include land subdivision; site preparation (grading, excavation, filling, etc.); the construction, reconstruction, conversion, structural alteration, relocation, or enlargement of any building or other structure or facility; and any use, change in use, or extension of use of land, building, or structure. The amendment made by S.L. 2009-572 provides that the law does not reactivate any utility allocation associated with development approvals that expired between January 1, 2008, and August 5, 2009, if the water or sewer capacity was reallocated to other development projects based on the expiration of the prior allocation and there is insufficient supply to accommodate both projects.

and extended the time period within which development approvals were tolled to December 31, 2011.[16] Local governments were given the option of opting out of the additional extension.

A decade later, a second permit-extension period was enacted in response to the COVID-19 pandemic.[17] This law, adopted in 2020, provided that the period of any development approval and any associated statutory vested right for any development approval that was current and valid between March 10 and April 28, 2020, was extended until 150 days from the rescission of the COVID-19 state of emergency. The COVID-19 state of emergency ended on August 15, 2022. The development approvals included in this extension were building permits, development approvals, preliminary and final plats, site-specific and multiphase-development plans, certificates of appropriateness, development agreements, and erosion- and sedimentation-control plans.

Permit-Choice Rule

Both statutory and common law vested rights are based on reliance on a valid governmental approval. A related but different question arises when regulations are amended while a development application is pending. No vested right exists because there has not yet been any governmental approval of a proposed development. Still, the applicant has often spent considerable time, effort, and money preparing an application based on the development standards then in effect.

The legislature in 2014 determined that it would not be reasonable or equitable to mandate that pending applications be amended to comply with newly adopted regulations. Chapter 143, Section 755 of the North Carolina General Statutes (hereinafter G.S.),[18] applicable to state and local approvals for any type of development, provides that if a rule or ordinance changes between the time an application is filed and a permit decision is made, the applicant may choose which version of the rule or ordinance shall be applied to the application. Once the applicant makes that choice, a permit decision is made and then the statutory and common law vested-right provisions discussed below become applicable if the application is approved.

G.S. 143-755(a) provides that if the applicant chooses the old rule, the local government may not require the applicant to wait for action on the proposed rule change prior to action on the permit application.

If it is determined that an application was wrongfully denied or an illegal condition was imposed on a permit, and if the applicable rules were changed after the wrongful denial or illegal condition, then the applicant may choose which of the rules will apply to the permit and use. But if the applicant chooses

---

16. S.L. 2010-177. In addition to adding a fourth year to the tolling period, this law clarified that it does not change any contract obligations, including bonds, and that a new water or sewer tap fee may not be assessed if the fee was previously paid in full for a project. It added provisions that continuing compliance with the original terms of approval is required, that any mandated performance guarantees must be maintained for the full extended period of approval, and that infrastructure must be provided to allow certificates of occupancy for allowed development. If any conditions are not met, the permit-approval extension may be terminated. If the extension is to be terminated, written notice of the termination and the reason for doing so must be mailed to the last known address of the original holder of the development approval. Local government terminations can be appealed to the board of adjustment.

17. S.L. 2020-3, § 4.40. The state of emergency was set by Executive Order 116 (Gov. Roy Cooper, Declaration of a State of Emergency to Coordinate Response and Protective Actions to Prevent the Spread of COVID-19, March 10, 2020). The period of permit extension was lengthened by S.L. 2020-97, § 321 and again by S.L. 2021-3, § 2.21.

18. S.L. 2014-120, § 6. G.S. 160D-108(b) explicitly makes the statute applicable to local government development-regulation decisions. The permit-choice rule initially did not apply to zoning decisions. The zoning exception to the rule was repealed by S.L. 2015-246, § 5. The permit-choice rule was further amended in 2019 by S.L. 2019-111, § 1.1. These amendments also added definitions of "development," "development permit," and "land development regulations." G.S. 143-755(e) and 160D-108(j). These definitions are generally consistent with the definitions in G.S. 160D-102.

to have the old rules apply, any provisions determined to be illegal are unenforceable without written consent from the applicant.

G.S. 143-755(b1) provides that the permit-choice rule no longer applies if an applicant puts a permit application on hold for six consecutive months or fails to respond to the government's requests for additional information for more than six consecutive months. If the permit application is resumed in these situations, it is to be reviewed under the rules in effect at that time.

G.S. 143-755(d) provides that any person aggrieved by a state agency or local government failure to comply with the permit-choice rule can seek a court order compelling compliance. The court is directed to set such an action for immediate hearing, and subsequent proceedings are to get priority from both the trial and appellate courts.

G.S. 160D-108(e) addresses the issue of multiple local development approvals that may be required for a single project.[19] If an applicant applies for and obtains one local development permit (the initial development permit), that permit triggers permit choice for subsequent local development permits under the rules applicable at the time of application for the initial development permit.[20] All rules in other local development regulations applicable at the time the application for initial permit approval is submitted may, at the election of the applicant, be applied to the decision for approvals under other local development regulations. That protection continues for eighteen months after the approval of the initial development permit.[21] The applicant must be actively pursuing that original application to maintain the permit-choice rights for other development regulations.

G.S. 160D-107(c) provides that the permit-choice rule applies at the expiration of a development moratorium if a complete application was submitted prior to the effective date of the moratorium.[22] In *Ashe County v. Ashe County Planning Board*,[23] the court held that an application for an asphalt plant submitted prior to the adoption of a moratorium (and subsequent adoption of more stringent regulations) was not "complete" and thus did not trigger the permit-choice rule. The application submitted under the then-effective ordinance did not include a state air-quality permit that was required before the local permit could be approved. Because the court held that the application was not complete without the state permit approval, this application was not exempt from the moratorium, and the permit-choice rule did not apply when permit review resumed upon expiration of the moratorium.

Building Permits

The first general statutory vested right was enacted in 1985.[24] It created G.S. 160D-108(d)(1) to provide that as long as there is a valid outstanding building permit, any zoning-regulation changes (including "amendments, modifications, supplements, repeal or other changes in zoning regulation and restrictions and zone boundaries") do not apply to the permitted project unless the owner consents.

---

19. This provision was added by S.L. 2019-111, § 1.3.

20. Sign permits, erosion-control permits, and sedimentation-control permits are not considered "initial development permit applications" for the purposes of this expanded permit-choice rule.

21. The provision was amended by S.L. 2021-168, § 1 to clarify that this eighteen-month period for subsequent permit applications electing to use the permit-choice rule does not limit the duration of a statutory vested right.

22. This provision was added by S.L. 2019-111.

23. 284 N.C. App. 563, 876 S.E.2d 687 (2022).

24. S.L. 1985-540. The law was effective October 1, 1985, and does not have retroactive application. Appeal of CAMA Permit No. 82-0010 v. Town of Bath, 82 N.C. App. 32, 345 S.E.2d 699 (1986). A limited statutory provision on vested rights had previously been adopted to address shifts in zoning jurisdiction between cities and counties. S.L. 1973-525. It did not create a new vested right; rather, it provided that when a vested right has been acquired under an approval issued by a city or a county, the right survives any transfer of jurisdiction over land use regulation to another unit of government.

The building permit is not a generic approval for building. It only applies to a permit required under the State Building Code.[25] A project built without a required building permit has no vested rights under this statute. One constructed with a building permit has a vested right to be maintained as originally constructed.[26] In *Simpson v. City of Charlotte*, the court confirmed that other local permits, such as quarry permits or certificates of zoning compliance, may not be used to establish this statutory vested right (although they may form the basis for a common law vested right if substantial expenditures are subsequently made in good-faith reliance on such other permits).[27]

If the building permit expires, the vested right in zoning also expires. State law provides that the building permit automatically expires in six months if work is not commenced or if work is started but then discontinued for twelve months.[28] Also, if the building permit is revoked, the vested right expires. Building permits are revoked for any substantial departure from the approved plans, failure to comply with any applicable state or local law (not just the State Building Code and the zoning regulation), or any misrepresentations made in securing the permit. Mistakenly issued building permits may be revoked.[29]

These statutory provisions allow landowners to secure a vested right earlier than is allowed under common law. Prior case law explicitly held that a permit itself, without any expenditures based upon its approval, created no vested right. The statutory vested right does not require substantial expenditures in reliance on the permit, just the issuance of a valid building permit.

The statutes are by their terms limited to land uses that require a building permit. They do not address a change in use that involves no new structures, nor do they address uses that can be substantially undertaken without the need of a structure (e.g., some mines, landfills, open-storage uses, or surface-parking lots).

Local Development Permits

G.S. 160D-108(d) sets the general rule that vested rights for a building, use of a building, use of land, or subdivision of land that are established upon approval of a local development permit are effective as long as the permit remains valid. The vesting for approved permits relates back to the date of the permit application.

A local development permit is valid for one year, unless otherwise specified by statute.[30] A local development regulation can set a longer period, allowing, for example, a two-year vesting for a special use permit. G.S. 160D-403(c) also allows a local ordinance to set a shorter duration for temporary land uses, special events, temporary signs, and similar development.

---

25. G.S. 160D-1110. In 1995, the General Assembly amended G.S. 143-215.67(a) to extend the protections that attach to a valid building permit. The law provides that the holder of a valid building permit may complete the permitted project and discharge wastes into a treatment works that is under state moratoria provided the discharge will not result in significant deterioration of the quality of receiving waters. S.L. 1995-202.

26. Thompson v. Union County, 283 N.C. App. 547, 874 S.E.2d 623 (2022). In this case, the court held that a residence presumed to have been built subject to a building permit (the permit records had been purged) has a vested right to be maintained as built, but a garage built without a building permit has no statutory vested rights.

27. 115 N.C. App. 51, 57, 443 S.E.2d 772, 776 (1994). Courts in other states have similarly held that where a statute creates a vested right based on a specified permit or permit application, only that specific permit or application can create the right. For example, the court in *Abbey Road Group, LLC v. City of Bonney Lake*, 167 Wash. 2d 242, 218 P.3d 180 (2009), held that where a statute created a vested right based on a building-permit application, a site-plan application without an accompanying building-permit application does not create a vested right.

28. G.S. 160D-1111. See the discussion of *Sandy Mush Properties, Inc. v. Rutherford County* below regarding the impact of litigation on the expiration of building permits.

29. G.S. 160D-1115.

30. G.S. 160D-108(d) and -403(c) provide that unless a different vesting period is set by state law, a local development approval expires one year after issuance unless work has substantially commenced.

If the applicant fails to substantially commence authorized work while a local development permit is valid, the development permit and vesting expire. With the substantial commencement of authorized work under a valid permit, vesting continues. If, after beginning, the work on a project is "intentionally and voluntarily discontinued" for a period of twenty-four consecutive months, this vesting expires.[31]

Site-Specific Vesting Plans

In 1990, the legislature broadened the statutory vested right to provide for vested rights based on site-specific vesting plans approved by local governments.[32]

The law created G.S. 160D-108.1 to define these rights.[33] The provisions establish a vested right for a minimum of two years and, at the city's or county's discretion, a maximum of five years for the type and the intensity of use allowed by the zoning in effect at the time of plan approval. Aspects of the development beyond the type and intensity of the development have, at most, a limited vesting.[34] If local governments do not amend their ordinances to define and establish a process for approving site-specific vesting plans, an owner may go to court to establish this vested right based on any zoning approval.

Each local government is to define by ordinance what constitutes a site-specific vesting plan in its jurisdiction. The statute offers some guidance on this definition by providing that a site-specific vesting plan must describe with "reasonable certainty the type and intensity of use for a specified parcel" of land that is proposed for development. It must include site boundaries and natural features and the approximate location and dimensions of buildings and improvements. The document that constitutes a site-specific vesting plan must be identified as such at the time of issuance. Other locally required land use approvals may be used for this purpose, including special use permits, site plans, and subdivision plats.[35] Sketch plans and variances generally do not qualify.[36]

Once a local ordinance defines what constitutes a site-specific vesting plan and sets the term of this statutory vested right, those provisions are binding. For example, in *Michael Weinman Associates*

---

31. G.S. 160D-108(d). The twenty-four-month period is tolled during the pendency of appeals regarding the development approval to the board of adjustment or to the courts.

32. S.L. 1989-996. This law became effective October 1, 1991. It was originally codified as G.S. 153A-344.1 and 160A-385.1.

33. The provisions for site-specific vesting plans were incorporated into G.S. 160D-108 along with other statutory vested rights in the version of that law as originally enacted in 2019. S.L. 2019-111, pt. II. When Parts I and II of this 2019 legislation were merged in 2020, there was no consensus as to whether all of the provisions related to site-specific vesting plans should be applied to other statutory vested rights (particularly all of the exceptions to vesting), as those were not included in Part I of the 2019 legislation. As there was agreement that all of the provisions of the prior law should continue to be applicable to site-specific vesting plans, a separate statutory section, G.S. 160D-108.1, was created for this vested right. S.L. 2020-25.

34. In *Michael Weinman Associates General Partnership v. Town of Huntersville*, 147 N.C. App. 231, 555 S.E.2d 342 (2001), the court noted that the vested right in the uses allowed by the zoning did not prevent the town from imposing zoning and building-code provisions on building specifications, location of utilities, street layout, and other detailed development standards. The statute specifically provides that new overlay districts and general regulations may be applied to these projects. G.S. 160D-108.1(f)(2).

35. While not formally ruling on the point because it was not properly raised, the court in *Jubilee Carolina, LLC v. Town of Carolina Beach* noted that if the statutory vested right claim had been properly before the court, it would have held that a site-plan approval is not the same thing as a "site specific development [vesting] plan" approval. The local development regulation required the property owners wishing to establish such statutory vested rights to make their intentions known in writing to the town at the time of application, which was not done with the site plan that was approved. 268 N.C. App. 90, 834 S.E.2d 655, 670 (2019).

36. G.S. 160D-108.1(a).

General Partnership v. Town of Huntersville,[37] the zoning ordinance included five specific town approvals within the definition of a site-specific vesting plan that would provide a three-year vested right: (1) a parallel conditional use district rezoning; (2) a special use permit; (3) an overlay-district rezoning with a site plan; (4) a conditional district rezoning; and (5) an approved cluster-development plan. The court held that approval of one of the specified rezonings itself created this site-specific-development-plan vested right.

Prior to 2021, local governments could also, but were not required to, provide for a five-year vested right for more-general "phased development plans." When Chapter 160D became effective, the provision for these phased-development plans was deleted from the statutes as redundant given the creation of the multiphase-development-plan vested right in 2016.[38]

The statute sets several requirements in the process of securing local approval for site-specific vesting plans. If the approval is based on approval of another development permit or approval (such as a subdivision plat or a special use permit), whatever notice and hearing that is required for that approval is sufficient for the vesting plan approval.[39] If it is not based on another approval, the same notice and hearing as are required by G.S. 160D-602 for a rezoning must be provided. The city or the county may impose reasonable conditions on the approval of the plan. Violation of such conditions results in a forfeiture of the vested right.

The statute also contains a provision coordinating vested rights obtained by approval of site-specific vesting plans with the vested right established by issuance of a building permit.[40] If a building permit is issued during the period for which a vested right in a site-specific vesting plan exists, the normal requirement that the building permit expires if work is not commenced in six months does not apply.[41] The building permit may still be revoked for other than time-related reasons.

G.S. 160D-108.1(f)(1) provides several exceptions to vesting under a site-specific vesting plan. These include: (1) with the written consent of the owner; (2) hazards are discovered that pose a serious threat to the public health, safety, or welfare (which requires findings to this effect after a properly noticed evidentiary hearing); (3) if the owner is compensated; (4) there were material misrepresentations in the application and approval process (which also requires an evidentiary hearing); or (5) state or federal laws or regulations preclude the development as originally contemplated.

Also, G.S. 160D-108.1(f)(2) provides that the vested right in a site-specific vesting plan does not preclude the later imposition of overlay zones and regulations that are applicable city- or countywide, such as building, fire, plumbing, electrical, and mechanical codes.

Multiphase-Development Plans

An additional statutory vested right was created in 2016 for multiphase developments.[42]

G.S. 160D-108(f) provides vesting for a "multi-phased development." To qualify, the project must contain twenty-five or more acres that are submitted for site-plan approval for construction in multiple

---

37. 147 N.C. App. 231, 555 S.E.2d 342. The town had rezoned a 168-acre tract to a highway-commercial district, a parallel conditional use district.

38. The provision was deleted by S.L. 2019-111.

39. G.S. 160D-108.1(c).

40. G.S. 160D-108(d)(3)(b).

41. The North Carolina Council of Code Officials (COCO) has suggested that approval of development plans include a condition that the developer build according to the building-code provisions in effect at the time construction commences in order to avoid vesting construction standards as well as zoning-ordinance provisions. Mike Page, *Vested Rights' Effect on Building Permits*, COCO NEWSLETTER, Nov. 1991, at 1.

42. S.L. 2016-111. Subsequent modifications in the development regulations may only be applied to the project with the written consent of the landowner.

phases. Further, the project must be subject to a master development plan "with committed elements showing the type and intensity of use of each phase."[43] The vesting is automatic for any qualifying project that is approved by a city or county.

A seven-year vested right is established for all phases of the development at the time a site plan is approved for the initial phase of the development. No expenditures or investments are required for individual phases of the development.[44] The vesting applies to all provisions of the zoning regulation, the subdivision ordinance, and any other regulations included in a unified development ordinance.

Development Agreements

Beginning with California in 1979[45] and Hawaii in 1985,[46] a number of states enacted statutes that authorize cities and counties to enter into formal contractual agreements with landowners that lock in existing local ordinances affecting a project for an extended period.[47] The actual use of these statutory authorizations varies widely among the states, from widespread application in California to rare use in Hawaii.

For the most part, the courts have upheld the use of these "development agreements," especially where they are expressly authorized by statute.[48] For the purposes of this discussion, *development agreement*

---

43. This provision was modified by S.L. 2019-111, § 1.3. The definition of a qualifying multi-phase development is set by G.S. 160D-108(j)(4).

44. Under common law vesting, substantial expenditures would have to be made for the development in a particular phase of the project for that phase to get a vested right.

45. The California statute, codified at CAL. GOV'T CODE §§ 65864–65869.5 (2018), was adopted largely in reaction to the impacts of the state's common law late vesting rule on large, multiphase projects. A leading case, *Avco Community Developers, Inc. v. South Coast Regional Commission*, 17 Cal. 3d 785, 132 Cal. Rptr. 386, 553 P.2d 546 (1976), is illustrative. The landowner was developing an 8000-acre planned community. The company obtained subdivision and grading permits and had spent some $2.7 million in construction of infrastructure when the California Coastal Act became effective. The court held that the company had no vested rights as final building permits had not been issued—so there had been no detrimental reliance on the final approval—and the developer was compelled to redesign the project to comply with new permitting requirements. *See generally* Daniel J. Curtin, Jr. & Scott A. Edelstein, *Development Agreement Practice in California and Other States*, 22 STETSON L. REV. 761 (1993).

46. Hawaii case law, like California case law, had a late-vesting rule, providing that a project was not vested until the last discretionary approval had been secured. Cnty. of Kauai v. Pac. Standard Life Ins., 65 Haw. 318, 653 P.2d 766 (1982). *See generally* Kenneth R. Kupchak et al., *Arrow of Time: Vested Rights, Zoning Estoppel, and Development Agreements in Hawai'i*, 27 U. HAW. L. REV. 17 (2004).

47. ARIZ. REV. STAT. ANN. § 9-500.05; CAL. GOV'T CODE §§ 65864–65869.5; COLO. REV. STAT. ANN. §§ 24-68-101 to -106; FLA. STAT. ANN. §§ 163.3220–.3243; HAW. REV. STAT. §§ 46-121 to -132; IDAHO CODE § 67-6511A; LA. REV. STAT. ANN. §§ 33:4780.21–.33; MD. CODE ANN., LAND USE, §§ 7-301 to -306; NEV. REV. STAT. ANN. §§ 278.0201–.0207; N.J. STAT. ANN. §§ 40:55D-45.1 to -.8; OR. REV. STAT. ANN. §§ 94.504–95.528; S.C. CODE ANN. §§ 6-31-10 to -160; VA. CODE ANN. § 15.2-2303.1; WASH. REV. CODE ANN. §§ 36.70B.170–37.70B.210. Development agreements are sometimes used in some other states despite the lack of explicit statutory authorization. *See, e.g.*, Save Elkhart Lake, Inc. v. Vill. of Elkhart Lake, 181 Wis. 2d 778, 512 N.W.2d 202 (Ct. App. 1993). For a discussion of the need for a development-agreement-enabling statute for Georgia, see Michael B. Kent, Jr., *Forming a Tie that Binds: Development Agreements in Georgia and the Need for Legislative Clarity*, 30 ENVIRONS ENVTL. L. & POL'Y J. 1 (2006).

48. Courts in several states have invalidated development agreements or similar contractual arrangements where there was no explicit statutory authority for their use. *See, e.g.*, Buckhorn Ventures, LLC v. Forsyth Cnty., 262 Ga. App. 299, 585 S.E.2d 229 (2003) (invalidating settlement agreement that would limit future regulatory changes); Morgan Co. v. Orange Cnty., 818 So. 2d 640 (Fla. Dist. Ct. App. 2002) (development agreement regarding future rezoning is unlawful contract zoning).

For general background information on development agreements, see DAVID L. CALLIES ET AL., BARGAINING FOR DEVELOPMENT (2003); DAVID J. LARSEN, DEVELOPMENT AGREEMENT MANUAL (2002); MANAGING DEVELOPMENT THROUGH PUBLIC/PRIVATE NEGOTIATIONS (Rachelle L. Levitt & John J. Kirlin eds., 1985); David L. Callies, *Developers' Agreements and Planning Gain*, 17 URB. LAW. 599 (1985); Daniel J. Curtin, Jr. & Jonathan D. Witten,

refers to the contract that vests rights to develop a specific project for an extended period of time subject to the terms and conditions specified in the agreement.[49] The principal legal concern has been whether an agreement that fixes the current local development regulations in place for an extended period of time unlawfully bargains away the police power or impermissibly restricts the discretion of future elected boards to amend the ordinances. Courts have reasoned that these agreements do not do so but, rather, that they vest rights in the existing regulations applicable to a specific parcel to the mutual benefit of the landowner and the public.[50]

In 2005, the General Assembly added authorization for these agreements to the North Carolina statutes.[51] The development-agreement provisions are codified at G.S. 160D-1001 to -1017.[52]

Development agreements can only be used for projects that have a relatively detailed plan that sets out the specific land uses proposed, where buildings will be sited, how they will be designed, and the timing and financing of public facilities needed to service the development. The legal and planning costs of producing a development agreement can be substantial, further limiting its use to projects that warrant such an investment of time and money on the part of the landowner and the local government. The scale of many proposed development agreements is such that they are likely to raise considerable

---

Windfalls, Wipeouts, Givings, and Takings in Dramatic Redevelopment Projects: Bargaining for Better Zoning on Density, Views, and Public Access, 32 B.C. ENVTL. AFF. L. REV. 325 (2005); John J. Delaney, *Development Agreements: The Road from Prohibition to "Let's Make a Deal,"* 25 URB. LAW. 49 (1993); Shelby D. Green, *Development Agreements: Bargained-for Zoning That Is Neither Illegal Contract nor Conditional Zoning*, 33 CAP. U. L. REV. 383 (2004); Robert M. Kessler, *The Development Agreement and Its Use in Resolving Large Scale, Multi-Party Development Problems: A Look at the Tool and Suggestions for Its Application*, 1 J. LAND USE & ENVTL. L. 451 (1985); Barry R. Knight & Susan P. Schoettle, *Current Issues Related to Vested Rights and Development Agreements*, 25 URB. LAW. 779 (1993); Brad K. Schwartz, Note, *Development Agreements: Contracting for Vested Rights*, 28 B.C. ENVTL. AFF. L. REV. 719 (2001); Eric Sigg, *California's Development Agreement Statute*, 15 SW. U. L. REV. 695 (1985); Judith W. Wegner, *Moving Toward the Bargaining Table: Contract Zoning, Development Agreements, and the Theoretical Foundations of Government Land Use Deals*, 65 N.C. L. REV. 957 (1987).

49. There are a variety of other contractual agreements between landowners and local governments that are sometimes referred to as "development agreements." For example, it is common in some communities to enter into contractual agreements or performance guarantees for provision of public improvements or other exactions required as part of a subdivision or zoning approval. Local governments may also enter into contracts relative to construction of a joint public-private venture. See, for example, the agreements addressed in *Cheape v. Town of Chapel Hill*, 320 N.C. 549, 359 S.E.2d 792 (1987), and *Rockingham Square Shopping Center, Inc. v. Town of Madison*, 45 N.C. App. 249, 262 S.E.2d 705 (1980) (invalidating agreement by town to open road as economic-development inducement). Contractual agreements may be entered into as part of a redevelopment project or as part of an agreement to provide public subsidies for a project or a contract between a developer and a nonprofit organization or community group. For discussion of this broader type of agreement, see David A. Marcello, *Community Benefit Agreements: New Vehicle for Investment in America's Neighborhoods*, 39 URB. LAW. 657, 660–61 (2007); Laura Wolf-Powers, *Community Benefits Agreements and Local Government: A Review of Recent Evidence*, 76 J. AM. PLAN. ASS'N 141 (2010); Patricia E. Salkin & Amy Lavine, *Understanding Community Benefits Agreements: Equitable Development, Social Justice and Other Considerations for Developers, Municipalities and Community Organizations*, 26 UCLA J. ENVTL. L. & POL'Y 291 (2008). Many of these contractual obligations are sometimes also referred to as "development agreements," but they are not addressed here.

50. The California statute was upheld in *Santa Margarita Area Residents Together v. San Luis Obispo County Board of Supervisors*, 84 Cal. App. 4th 221, 100 Cal. Rptr. 2d 740 (2000). *See also* Tancas Prop. Owners Ass'n v. City of Malibu, 138 Cal. App. 4th 172, 41 Cal. Rptr. 3d 200 (2006) (agreement that does not follow statutorily mandated procedures for adoption is invalid); City of W. Hollywood v. Beverly Towers, Inc., 52 Cal. 3d 1184, 278 Cal. Rptr. 375, 805 P.2d 329 (1991) (noting use and purpose of development agreements). The Louisiana statute was upheld in *Azalea Lakes Partnership v. Parish of St. Tammany*, 859 So. 2d 57, 62 (La. Ct. App. 2003), and the Nebraska statute was upheld in *Giger v. City of Omaha*, 232 Neb. 676, 442 N.W.2d 182 (1989).

51. S.L. 2005-426, § 9.

52. For a survey of the early experience with the use of development agreements in North Carolina, see DAVID W. OWENS, THE USE OF DEVELOPMENT AGREEMENTS TO MANAGE LARGE-SCALE DEVELOPMENT: THE LAW AND PRACTICE IN NORTH CAROLINA 14–24 (UNC School of Government, Special Series No. 25, 2009).

neighborhood and public interest in the details of the agreement, thereby necessitating careful consideration of the process used to negotiate and approve the development agreement. However, even with these limitations, local governments in North Carolina have found development agreements to be a useful tool for collaboratively addressing major development proposals.

Basic Provisions Regarding Adoption

State law mandates the availability of some vested rights under local development regulations, most notably for projects with building permits, site-specific vesting plans, and multiphase developments. Unlike those earlier provisions, however, the development-agreement statute is enabling rather than mandatory.[53] Thus, a local government can choose not to use this approach at all.

If a city or county wants to use development agreements, it can adopt an ordinance specifying eligibility, local requirements and procedures, and other specifications for how these are done. Alternatively, a city or county can adopt individual development agreements without the necessity of having previously made provision for them in its development ordinances.

While development agreements closely resemble negotiated contracts in both form and substance, each individual development agreement must be approved by ordinance of the governing board.[54] In adopting that ordinance, the local government must follow the same hearing-notice process that is required for zoning-map amendments.[55] However, unlike a rezoning, the statute does not mandate referral of a proposed development agreement to the planning board for review and comment, nor does it require a plan-consistency statement. G.S. 160D-1003 requires only an advertised legislative hearing.[56] An individual local government is free to mandate planning-board referral, mailed notices, or plan-consistency statements as part of the procedures for development-agreement consideration that it sets under G.S. 160D-1003. That would, however, be a choice of the local government, not a state mandate. If there is a rezoning associated with a development agreement, and this is often the case, the rezoning must go to the planning board prior to governing-board consideration. It would be prudent in these situations to concurrently secure planning-board comment on the proposed development agreement.

The decision whether to approve a development agreement is left to the judgment and discretion of the local elected governing board. This choice is a legislative decision, much like the decision on whether to rezone a parcel of land.

While some of the procedural safeguards applicable to all land use ordinances apply (a mandatory legislative hearing with published notice), the limitations of quasi-judicial decision-making do not apply in the development-agreement context. Unlike a special use permit, the hearing on a proposed development agreement is not limited to presentation of evidence by witnesses under oath and subject to

---

53. G.S. 160D-1003(a).

54. The standard practice is for the board to adopt an ordinance authorizing the execution of a specified development agreement for a specified project. The ordinance does not include the text of the agreement but refers to a specific agreement, copies of which are available for public review at the time of the notice of the hearing. Much like any other hearing on a land use regulation, amendments may be made to the proposed agreement in response to statements and discussion at the hearing. It is likely that additional hearings are not required unless the changes made to the agreement at or after the hearing are substantial. Heaton v. City of Charlotte, 277 N.C. 506, 518, 178 S.E.2d 352, 359–60 (1971).

55. G.S. 160D-1005. The mandated published notice of the legislative hearing on a proposed development agreement comprises two newspaper advertisements, with the first at least ten but not more than twenty-five days prior to the hearing and each notice being in separate calendar weeks. The notice must specify the location of the property involved and describe the land uses proposed. The draft agreement should be complete and available for inspection at the time of publication of the notice of the hearing.

56. The hearing requirement in G.S. 160D-1005 states that the notice provisions for hearings on zoning-map amendments set in G.S. 160D-602 are to be followed.

cross-examination. Citizens are free to present their opinions on whether the proposed agreement is a good idea. Board members are not prohibited from discussing the matter outside of the hearing, but they are obligated to refrain from participating if they have a financial conflict of interest.[57] Formal findings of fact are not required. Rather, much like a rezoning, the issue is whether the proposed agreement is in the best public interest for the community.

Development agreements deal only with regulatory approval for development and cannot, in themselves, affect a local government's jurisdiction. A development agreement can only be adopted by a local government with jurisdiction for the area affected by the agreement.

In some instances the discussions about development approval will involve a shift in jurisdiction. For example, a landowner in the unincorporated area of a county may enter into negotiations with an adjacent municipality regarding extension of city utilities and city regulations to the property. It is entirely appropriate for potential annexation of the land by the city to be a part of the negotiations, but that cannot be accomplished through a development agreement. All of the usual statutory procedures for annexation would have to be completed before the city could execute a development agreement affecting that land.[58]

If multiple local governments are parties to a development agreement, the agreement must specify which local government is to be responsible for overall administration of the agreement.[59]

The parties to a development agreement are the developer of the property and the local government with land use regulatory jurisdiction for that land.[60] To qualify as a "developer" who may enter into a development agreement, the entity[61] must be one who both intends to undertake development and has a legal or equitable interest in the property. *Development* is defined very broadly for the purposes of this statute. It includes the planning for building activity, material changes in the use or appearance of structures or property, and land subdivision.[62] The local government is the city or county with land use regulatory jurisdiction.

Utility services for a development subject to a development agreement may be provided by a third party, such as a separate water or sewer utility that is not a unit of the local government that is a party to the agreement. Before 2019, there was ambiguity in the development-agreement statute as to whether utilities could be a party to a development agreement. This was resolved by the addition of a provision explicitly allowing a local or regional utility authority to be a party to a development agreement in addition to the unit of local government and the developer.[63] The local government and developer or property owner are necessary parties, while a utility may be an additional party.

---

57. While the development-agreement statutes do not include a specific conflict-of-interest standard, the same general standard applicable to governing boards and advisory boards on legislative zoning decisions would apply. G.S. 160D-109(a). See Chapter 25 for further discussion of conflicts of interest.

58. For example, the landowner could agree to seek voluntary annexation pursuant to G.S. 160A-31. That annexation would, however, have to be completed before the city would have jurisdiction to adopt a development agreement for the site. There are also separate statutes that allow two or more cities to enter agreements regarding future annexation areas. G.S. 160A-58, §§ .21 to .28. These agreements, termed *annexation agreements* by the statutes, should not be confused with development agreements. Also, cities and counties may enter into contractual agreements with developers regarding installation of public-enterprise improvements. G.S. 160A-320; 153A-320. These contracts should likewise be distinguished from the development agreements discussed in this chapter.

59. G.S. 160D-1006(c).

60. G.S. 160D-1001(b).

61. Individuals, corporations, estates, trusts, partnerships, associations, and state agencies are all "persons" who may be "developers" under this statute. G.S. 160D-102(11).

62. G.S. 160D-1002(1).

63. G.S. 160D-1006(c). The provision was added by S.L. 2019-111.

Mandatory Contents of Agreements

The mandatory contents of the development agreement are specified by statute.[64] Each agreement must contain each of these components.

The agreement must include a legal description of the property covered by the agreement and the names of its legal and equitable owners.

Each development agreement must also specify its duration. The term of an agreement can be whatever length the parties deem to be reasonable.[65] A local government and developer are authorized to enter subsequent development agreements that extend the original duration period.[66] Each such extension, however, is a separate development agreement that must be separately noticed and adopted.

The statutes also address the impact of a change in jurisdiction on the continuation of a development agreement. Where there is a change in local jurisdiction for the property subject to a development agreement (such as through annexation or extension of an extraterritorial boundary), the agreement is valid for the duration of the agreement or eight years from the date of change in jurisdiction, whichever is earlier.[67]

The development agreement must describe the proposed development of the property in some detail. It must address the types of land uses, population density, building types, intensity of uses, placement of buildings on the site, and building designs.[68] This will often involve use of exhibits or attachments, such as site plans or sample building elevations. These exhibits need to be explicitly referenced and incorporated into the agreement. Given the duration of these agreements and the reasonable likelihood that those directly involved in development-agreement approval may not be available to resolve questions in the latter stages of the development, careful attention to specificity and record keeping on this point is important for practical as well as legal reasons.

Cost sharing on infrastructure provision is often an essential aspect of the negotiations. To the extent that it is, the provisions for cost sharing must be set forth in the development agreement. The agreement must include a description of any new public facilities that will serve the development, a specification of who will provide them, and a schedule of when they will be provided so as to ensure they will be available concurrently with the impacts of the development.[69]

The statute broadly defines the "public facilities" that must be addressed. They include "major capital improvements" for transportation, water, sewer, solid waste, drainage, schools, parks and recreation, and health systems and facilities.[70]

If the local government is to provide infrastructure improvements to support the development, the agreement must specify that the delivery date of the public facilities will be tied to the successful performance of the developer.[71]

---

64. G.S. 160D-1006. These mandatory requirements apply to all development agreements adopted pursuant to this statute. Other forms of development approvals, such as site plans, special use permits, and subdivision plats often also include conditions that are negotiated between the developer or landowner and the local government. These other agreements, however, are not development agreements as defined by this statute and discussed in this chapter.

65. G.S. 160D-1004. The statute initially limited development agreements to a maximum term of twenty years. That maximum term was repealed by S.L. 2015-246, § 19.

66. G.S. 160D-1006(a)(2).

67. G.S. 160D-1010(a).

68. G.S. 160D-1006(a)(3).

69. G.S. 160D-1006(a)(4). If the agreement includes performance guarantees, 160D-804.1, which specifies the form and administration of the guarantee, is applicable. G.S. 160D-1006(f). This statute is discussed in the context of subdivision regulations in Chapter 7.

70. G.S. 160D-1002(2).

71. G.S. 160D-1006(a)(4).

If the obligation of the local government to provide infrastructure constitutes debt, the city or county must comply with all constitutional and statutory provisions regarding debts at the time of the obligation to incur the debt.[72] It is relatively rare that a development agreement itself will constitute a debt and thereby trigger this requirement. In most instances, if the agreement includes a promise of the local government to provide infrastructure and a provision of that infrastructure requires debt financing, the local government will issue the debt as a separate transaction at the time it provides the infrastructure. The development agreement can be conditioned upon the local government successfully following all legally required steps to accomplish this.

Where there are phased cost-sharing agreements, the development agreement can detail payment schedules, improvements to be installed, reimbursements for excess capacity, and similar practical issues. These provisions can also address issues such as allocation of utility capacity.

If there is to be any dedication or reservation of land for public purposes, it must be set out in the agreement.[73] Street and utility rights-of-way, park and open-space dedications, greenways, and school sites need to be addressed as applicable. Similarly, any provisions to protect environmentally sensitive lands are required to be included. This includes buffers, stormwater provisions, and the like.

The agreement must include any conditions, terms, or restrictions on the development.[74] The authority to impose conditions is broad. Conditions can be imposed if the city or county deems them necessary to protect the public health, safety, and welfare. The statute specifically mentions authority to impose provisions for preservation and restoration of historic structures.

The agreement must include a development schedule, including commencement and interim completion dates at five-year (or more frequent) intervals.[75] The agreement may also include phases for the development and other defined performance standards to be met by the developer.

If more than one local government is a party to the agreement, the agreement must specify which local government is responsible for overall administration of the agreement.[76]

Statutory Limits

When North Carolina originally authorized development agreements in 2005, there was a requirement that a project have a minimum land area of twenty-five developable acres[77] to be considered for a development agreement.[78] The minimum-acreage requirement was removed for brownfield-redevelopment projects in 2013[79] and deleted for all projects in 2015.[80]

The agreement cannot impose any tax or fee not otherwise authorized by law.[81] This limitation also specifies that an agreement does not expand local regulatory authority or authorize any local commitments other than those otherwise authorized by law. This provision was included to address concerns of the development community that local governments might use a potential development agreement as leverage to secure financial contributions or commitments for undertakings beyond those currently

---

72. G.S. 160D-1012.
73. G.S. 160D-1006(a)(5).
74. G.S. 160D-1006(a)(6).
75. G.S. 160D-1006(b). Failure to meet a commencement or completion date may not, in itself, be deemed a material breach of the agreement. Such a failure is to be judged on the "totality of the circumstances" to determine whether it constitutes a breach.
76. G.S. 160D-1006(c).
77. Wetlands, mandatory buffers, unbuildable slopes, and other portions of the property precluded from the development at the time of application were not considered in establishing the minimum acreage.
78. G.S. 160D-1004.
79. S.L. 2013-413, § 44.
80. S.L. 2015-246, § 19.
81. G.S. 160D-1006(d).

authorized by the statutes. Not surprisingly, there was a specific concern that local governments not be allowed to trade development-agreement approval for new impact fees.

A fundamental question is the impact of this limitation on matters voluntarily offered by the developer.[82] The ability to negotiate and make voluntary yet binding agreements on cost sharing for public improvements, without being bound by the limitations of formally imposed regulatory exactions,[83] is considered one of the principal reasons for the parties to use a development agreement.[84] The North Carolina development-agreement statutes note this basis for development agreements. The findings section notes that these projects "often create community impacts . . . that are difficult to accommodate within traditional zoning processes."[85]

The resolution to this dilemma is the following provision in G.S. 160D-1006(d) of the development-agreement statutes: "The development agreement also may cover any other matter . . . not inconsistent with this Chapter." This provides adequate authority to fully negotiate voluntary cost-sharing arrangements in development agreements. Voluntary payments are not a "tax or fee not authorized by law" and cooperatively addressing the costs of public improvements to deal with the impacts of approved development is consistent with the express purposes of the statute.

---

82. The question of how "voluntary" a commitment is in these negotiations is always present. In *Amward Homes, Inc. v. Town of Cary*, 206 N.C. App. 38, 698 S.E.2d 404 (2010), *aff'd per curiam by evenly divided court*, 365 N.C. 305, 716 S.E.2d 849 (2011) (stands without precedential value), the allegation that the mayor told the applicant that town-council approval of the development would not occur unless school impact fees were paid, and that the town had a custom and practice of imposing such fees, were important factors in the court's invalidation of a permit condition imposing the fee. The critical question is whether there was unlawful duress in securing the commitment. In *Meredith v. Talbot County*, 80 Md. App. 174, 560 A.2d 599 (1989), the developer of a subdivision agreed to forego development of specified lots within a proposed subdivision to protect a bald-eagle nesting area in return for prompt approval of the subdivision. The court held that the agreement was not made under duress and the owner could not subsequently challenge the condition. *See also* McClung v. City of Sumner, 548 F.3d 1219 (9th Cir. 2008) (developer's agreement to provide oversized drainage pipe in return for waiver of facilities fee upheld under state contract law, not an unconstitutional exaction). The subsequent decision in *Koontz v. St. Johns River Water Management District*, 570 U.S. 595 (2013), requires additional caution to address potential unlawful conditions, further highlighting the need to establish the voluntary nature of the condition. See Chapter 24 for a discussion of that case.

Unlike other land use regulatory provisions, a development agreement is not a permit, determination, or adjudication but is, rather, a negotiated contract with benefits and burdens for both parties. Several factors militate against undue duress in these situations. Generally, the property can be developed for some reasonable use (though perhaps less desirable or profitable for the owner) without a development agreement. Either party is free to withdraw from the negotiation for any reason at any time. The conditions must address, and payments must be devoted to, lawful public purposes. The terms of the agreement, including all conditions and payments, must be subject to a public hearing and approval by an elected governing board.

83. *See generally* David L. Callies & Julie A. Tappendorf, *Unconstitutional Land Development Conditions and the Development Agreement Solution: Bargaining for Public Facilities After* Nollan *and* Dolan, 51 CASE W. RES. L. REV. 663 (2001); Michael H. Crew, *Development Agreements After* Nollan v. California Coastal Commission, *483 U.S. 825 (1987)*, 22 URB. LAW. 23 (1990); Catherine Lockard, Note, *Gaining Access to Private Property: The Zoning Process and Development Agreements*, 79 NOTRE DAME L. REV. 765 (2004). See Chapter 24 for further discussion of exactions and the Takings Clause.

84. The California development-agreement statute was amended in 1984 to explicitly provide for inclusion of cost-sharing provisions. CAL. GOV'T CODE § 65864(c). The California statutes also expressly exempt fees set in development agreements from the landowner protections relative to development exactions in the state's Mitigation Fee Act. *See* CAL. GOV'T CODE §§ 66000, 66020. *See also* Nicolet Minerals Co. v. Town of Nashville, 2002 WI App 50, 250 Wis. 831, 641 N.W.2d 497 (agreements can include exchange of payments and permits). By contrast, the Washington statutes expressly provide that the development-agreement statutes do not authorize imposition of impact fees, inspection fees, dedications, or any other financial contribution or mitigation measure unless expressly authorized by another provision of law. WASH. REV. CODE ANN. § 36.70B.210.

85. G.S. 160D-1001. The statutory findings also note the need to integrate public capital-facilities planning and construction with the phasing of private development and the need to better structure and manage development approvals to ensure the integration of those approvals into local capital-facilities programming through flexible negotiation. *Id.*

Given the relatively common practice of developers voluntarily offering to provide more public facilities than could be mandated, this provision was clarified in 2019.[86] While retaining the prohibition on any tax or impact fee not otherwise authorized by law, the development agreement may include mutually-agreed-upon provision of public facilities and other amenities, and it may include allocations of financial responsibility for these amenities that go beyond what G.S. 160D-804 requires. These financial responsibilities must be expressly enumerated in the agreement. Any voluntary payment incorporated into a development agreement is limited to what the parties in good faith find to be mutually agreeable, in the public interest, and not contrary to express restrictions of state law.[87] This allows the local government and developer latitude to negotiate and address the full range of development issues that typically arise—traffic, utilities, neighborhood and environmental impacts—as well as issues where the traditional regulatory regime is less certain, such as affordable housing, school construction, off-site improvements, and the like.[88]

The agreement may not exempt the developer from the building code or any local housing code that is not part of the local government's development ordinances.[89]

The development agreement must be consistent with the local regulations in effect at the time of agreement approval.[90] A development agreement cannot permit a use not allowed by the applicable zoning.[91] While some states allow a development agreement to modify the underlying zoning, that is not the case in North Carolina.[92] Thus, it is important that the development described and authorized in the agreement is permissible under the local development regulations in effect at the time of adoption of the

---

86. S.L. 2019-111 added the provision to G.S. 160D-1006(d). For an example of the importance of this clarification, see *Bill Clark Homes of Raleigh, LLC v. Town of Fuquay-Varina*, 281 N.C. App. 1, 869 S.E.2d 1 (2021). The plaintiffs challenged the imposition of a capacity fee for utility services to be provided. The court remanded for consideration of whether the fee was based on ordinance requirements (not authorized) or a development agreement (which would be permissible).

87. Several courts have held that promises (and agreements to pay fees) voluntarily entered into in good faith and with consideration cannot be subsequently challenged as unconstitutional takings. *See, e.g.*, McClung v. City of Sumner, 545 F.3d 803, *modified*, 548 F.3d 1219 (9th Cir. 2008); Leroy Land Development Corp. v. Tahoe Regional Planning Agency, 939 F.2d 696, 698 (9th Cir. 1991); Xenia Rural Water Ass'n v. Dallas County, 445 N.W.2d 785 (Iowa 1989); Rischon Development Corp. v. City of Keller, 242 S.W.3d 161 (Tex. App. 2007). In *Toll Bros., Inc. v. Board of Chosen Freeholders*, 194 N.J. 223, 944 A.2d 1 (2008), the court held that development agreements were ancillary to zoning authority and thus subject to the same limits on off-site street improvements. In *Douglas County Contractors Ass'n v. Douglas County*, 112 Nev. 1452, 929 P.2d 253 (1996), the county attempted to apply an ordinance requiring payment of fees to support school construction to a subdivision that had a previously approved development agreement. The court held the fee ordinance to be a tax subject to and not permitted by the state's impact-fee legislation.

88. The parties are well-advised to explicitly discuss the implications of potential financial difficulties that may limit the ability of any party to meet their financial obligations under the agreement, including potential insolvency, bankruptcy, and similar contingencies, and to specify what the consequences of such an occurrence are to be.

89. G.S. 160D-1001(c).

90. G.S. 160D-1007. See *Walton North Carolina, LLC v. City of Concord*, 257 N.C. App. 227, 809 S.E.2d 164, 169–70 (2017), *review denied*, 371 N.C. 447, 817 S.E.2d 388 (2018), for a development agreement explicitly requiring compliance with current regulatory requirements, not a prior, expired preliminary plat.

91. *See* Neighbors in Support of Appropriate Land Use v. Cnty. of Tuolumne, 157 Cal. App. 4th 997, 68 Cal. Rptr. 3d 882 (2007). In this case a landowner sought approval to open a business hosting weddings and similar events on a vineyard located in an exclusively agricultural zoning district. The county refused to amend the text of the zoning ordinance to allow this as a permitted or conditional use in the district but did enter a development agreement allowing the use. The court affirmed a ruling that the agreement was ultra vires and void *ab initio* because it violated the statutory requirement for uniformity of regulations within a zoning district. North Carolina has a similar uniformity requirement. G.S. 160D-703(c).

92. A local government should also take care not to promise an amendment to the ordinances in return for developer concessions in the agreement. Such a quid pro quo would raise serious concern about illegal contract zoning. Morgran Co. v. Orange Cnty., 818 So. 2d 640 (Fla. Dist. Ct. App. 2002). If an ordinance amendment is needed, it must precede rather than follow a development agreement.

agreement. The statute allows a local government to negotiate with a landowner, rezone the property to a conditional zoning district, and enter into a development agreement to lock in that rezoning.[93] Though the rezoning and development agreement are legally separate actions, if they are made concurrently and in concert (albeit with the rezoning being a separate and initial vote), the practical effect is for all involved to view the legally distinct actions as a package deal.[94]

Post-Agreement Provisions

A development agreement must be recorded with the register of deeds in the county in which the property is located within fourteen days of execution of the agreement.[95] The agreement is binding on all successors in interest to the parties of the agreement, including subsequent purchasers of the land.

The local government must undertake a periodic review of the project (at least once a year) to verify compliance with the agreement.[96]

The governing statutes make provision for amendment, extension, and cancellation of the agreement. The parties may modify or cancel the agreement at any time by mutual consent.[97] Any major modification to a development agreement requires the same notice and hearing as required for initial approval.[98] The parties may enter subsequent agreements that extend the original agreement's duration period.[99]

The local ordinances in effect at the time of the agreement generally are to remain in effect for the life of the agreement. However, subsequently enacted local ordinances and ordinance amendments can be applied to the project in the same manner that is allowed for vested rights generally under G.S. 160D-108(c) or for site-specific vesting plans under G.S.160D-108.1(f).[100] G.S. 160D-108(c) allows modifications if a state or federal law mandating local enforcement that has a "fundamental and retroactive effect" on the project is changed after the project application is submitted. G.S. 160D-108.1(f) allows a broader range of changes. They include changes that have written consent of the owner, those where the landowner is made financially whole, those situations where there have been either inaccuracies or material misrepresentations in the application, and those where there are emergent serious threats to the public health, safety, and welfare.

Also, the enactment of a category of general regulations not specifically aimed at the applicable property may be applied to the project. This includes zoning rules that impose additional requirements but do not affect the type or intensity of use at the site, and the enactment of local regulations that are "general in nature and are applicable to all property subject to development regulation" by the jurisdiction.[101]

Subsequently enacted state and federal law may more readily be incorporated into a development agreement. If a state or federal law or regulation precludes the anticipated development, the local government is authorized to unilaterally modify the agreement to incorporate changes needed to secure

93. G.S. 160D-1003(b). Concurrent consideration of rezoning a parcel and a development agreement for a project on that site is a relatively common practice. *See, e.g.,* Taylor v. Canyon Cnty. Bd. of Comm'rs, 147 Idaho 424, 433–42, 210 P.3d 532, 541–49 (2009); Smith v. City of Papillion, 270 Neb. 607, 705 N.W.2d 584, 596 (2005).

94. If the property is rezoned as part of the development-agreement discussion, the parties should give some consideration to the consequences should the project authorized by the agreement fail to come to fruition. For example, the rezoning may authorize some residual uses of the property that can be undertaken without a development agreement. An alternative is to mandate initiation of a process to again rezone the property should the authorized development not be initiated within a specified time.

95. G.S. 160D-1001.

96. G.S. 160D-1008(a).

97. G.S. 160D-1009.

98. G.S. 160D-1006(e).

99. G.S. 160D-1006(a)(2).

100. G.S. 160D-1007(b).

101. G.S. 160D-108.1(f)(2).

compliance with state and federal regulatory changes. Examples would include changes needed for compliance with stormwater rules, erosion and sedimentation control, wetland protection, and the like.

In the event that a local government review indicates the developer is in material breach of the agreement, the local government must within a reasonable time provide notice of the breach (describing and documenting its nature with reasonable particularity) and provide the developer a reasonable time to cure it.[102] If the breach is not cured, the local government may unilaterally terminate or modify the agreement. The local government decision to do so may be appealed to the board of adjustment under the normal zoning-appeals provisions.[103]

The governing statutes do not specify how other appeals regarding a development agreement, such as a disagreement among the parties as to its interpretation,[104] are to be handled. In all likelihood, the appropriate process is to follow the standard approach used for zoning. That is, the local government administrator charged with implementation of the development agreement makes a formal, binding, written interpretation, which could then be appealed to the board of adjustment, and thereafter judicial review is in superior court. The statutes, however, are not explicit on this point, so whether an appeal to the board of adjustment is a necessary step to exhaust administrative remedies prior to judicial review is an open question. It would be prudent for a local government that adopts an ordinance setting procedures for development agreements to specifically address the process for administrative appeals in that ordinance.[105] It is also not uncommon for the terms of each development agreement to address the process for resolving disputes, such as inclusion of mandated mediation in the event of a disagreement regarding interpretation of the agreement.

Disputes over interpretation of agreements should, however, be distinguished from challenges to the validity of the agreement. As the decision on adoption of the agreement is legislative in nature, a board of adjustment would have no jurisdiction to hear that matter and those appeals would lie directly with the courts.[106]

As with statutes in some other states,[107] the North Carolina development-agreement statute contains provisions on mechanisms for enforcement and remedies beyond the provisions regarding a breach of the agreement. G.S. 160D-1008(d) and (e) were added to the statute in 2019.[108] They allow an ordinance setting the procedures for development agreements or an individual development agreement to specify the penalties for a breach of the agreement. They also allow either party to a development agreement, the local government or the developer, to bring suit seeking an injunction to enforce the terms of the agreement.

---

102. G.S. 160D-1008(b).

103. G.S. 160D-1008(c).

104. For an example of a dispute regarding interpretation of the terms of a development agreement, see *Building Industry Ass'n of Central California v. City of Patterson*, 171 Cal. App. 4th 886, 90 Cal. Rptr. 3d 63 (2009) (dispute regarding updated fee schedule); Sprenger, Grubb & Assocs., Inc. v. City of Hailey, 127 Idaho 576, 903 P.2d 741 (1995) (dispute as to amount of commercial development allowed by development agreement for property that was subsequently downzoned).

105. G.S. 160D-103 allows counties and cities to adopt procedures and employ organizational structures authorized by law to all aspects of their development regulations.

106. The declaratory judgment statute, G.S. 1-253 to -267, is the appropriate vehicle to challenge the constitutionality, the validity, or the construction of ordinances. As the decision to adopt a development agreement is made by ordinance, this would be the route to challenge the constitutionality or validity of an agreement. That is to be distinguished from interpretation of the terms of the agreement (which is not an ordinance).

107. *See, e.g.*, Cal. Gov't Code § 65865.4; Fla. Stat. Ann. § 163.3243; Haw. Rev. Stat. § 46-127(a); La. Rev. Stat. Ann. § 33:4780.26; Md. Code Ann., Land Use, § 7-305(h).

108. S.L. 2019-111.

Many agreements provide for specific performance and many limit monetary damages for breach. Agreements often also include express provisions regarding payment of attorney's fees in the event of a conflict.

Given the consequences for all parties, the agreement should define what constitutes a material breach and the remedies available to both parties in the event of breach.

Considering the duration of development agreements, the original parties to the agreement may be supplanted due to changes in ownership or local government jurisdiction. The landowner who negotiates and executes the agreement may well sell all or part of the property during the term of the agreement. Local jurisdiction can shift due to annexation or extension of municipal extraterritorial jurisdiction. For the most part, these changes in ownership or jurisdiction do not affect the rights or obligations contained in the agreement. The law provides that the "burdens of the development agreement are binding upon, and the benefits of the agreement shall inure to, all successors in interest to the parties to the agreement."[109]

The statutes also provide for limited modification if local government jurisdiction for the property subject to the agreement changes.[110] The government assuming jurisdiction may modify or suspend the agreement, if needed, to protect the residents of the area within the agreement or elsewhere in the jurisdiction from a condition dangerous to health or safety.

Common Law Vested Rights

The common law vested right balances two legitimate interests. On one side is the landowner's right to rely on a specific representation by a government. On the other side is the public interest in having current land use regulations uniformly applied in the community.[111]

The common law vested right is established only when each of the four following tests are met: (1) the owner has made substantial expenditures; (2) the expenditures were made in good faith; (3) the expenditures were made in reliance on valid government approval, if such was required; and (4) the owner would be harmed without a vested right.[112] The cases that establish and apply each of these tests are discussed in this section. Table 19.1 summarizes them.

Applicability

North Carolina courts have long recognized that adoption, amendment, and repeal of land use ordinances are matters within a local governing board's legislative discretion.[113] Citizens, landowners, and neighbors have no vested right to existing zoning classifications.

---

109. G.S. 160D-1011.

110. G.S. 160D-1010(f).

111. Under principles of equitable estoppel, a party is prevented "from taking unfair advantage of another when, through false language or conduct, the person to be estopped has induced another person to act a certain way, with the result that the other person has been injured in some way." *Equitable Estoppel*, BLACK'S LAW DICTIONARY (10th ed. 2014). As a general rule, estoppel does not operate against government units on zoning matters. Raleigh v. Fisher, 232 N.C. 629, 61 S.E.2d 897 (1950); Mecklenburg Cnty. v. Westbery, 32 N.C. App. 630, 233 S.E.2d 658 (1977). However, the common law vested right is conceptually similar to the doctrine of equitable estoppel.

112. Browning-Ferris Indus. of S. Atl., Inc. v. Guilford Cnty. Bd. of Adjustment, 126 N.C. App. 168, 171–72, 484 S.E.2d 411, 414 (1997).

113. See Chapter 11 regarding the discretionary nature of legislative land use regulatory decisions.

Table 19.1 Overview of Common-Law-Vested-Rights Cases in North Carolina

Case	Court	Date	Basis for Result
Vested Right Held to Exist			
Supply Co.	Sup. Ct.	1932	Commencement of work under ordinance
Hastings	Sup. Ct.	1960	Completion of project
Smith	Sup. Ct.	1969	Reliance on approval
Thomasville	Ct. App.	1973	Good-faith expenditures
Transland	Ct. App.	1973	Completion of project
Campsites	Sup. Ct.	1975	No permits required
Sunderhaus	Ct. App.	1989	Expenditure relative to total cost
Coen	Ct. App.	1990	Expenditure of labor
Cardwell	Ct. App.	1992	Reliance on approval
Woodlief	Ct. App.	2006	Prior ordinance applicable
Robins	Sup. Ct.	2007	Provisions of ordinance
Sandy Mush	Ct. App.	2007	Building permit on hold during moratorium
Morris Communications	Sup. Ct.	2011	Work to relocate sign underway
Town of Midland	Sup. Ct.	2016	Expenditures relate to entire subdivision
Vested Right Held Not to Exist			
Fisher	Sup. Ct.	1950	Improperly issued permit
Stowe	Sup. Ct.	1961	No good faith
Warner	Sup. Ct.	1964	No reliance
Tadlock	Sup. Ct.	1964	No expansion allowed
Austin	Sup. Ct.	1966	No harm to owner
Keiger	Sup. Ct.	1972	No good faith
Westbery	Ct. App.	1977	Mistakenly issued permit
Pack	Ct. App.	1988	No expansion allowed
Russell	Ct. App.	1990	No detriment
Simpson	Ct. App.	1994	Zoning permit not a "building permit"
BFI	Ct. App.	1997	Pre-permit expenditures not reliance; no detriment
Koontz	Ct. App.	1998	No good faith
Kirkpatrick	Ct. App.	2000	No good faith
PNE	Ct. App.	2001	No good faith
Huntington Properties	Ct. App.	2002	No expenditures in reliance on approval
MLC	Ct. App.	2011	No valid permit
Wilson	Ct. App.	2011	Improperly issued permit
Waste Industries	Ct. App.	2012	No reliance on permit
Walton NC	Ct. App.	2017	No good faith; no detriment

In *McKinney v. City of High Point*,[114] the court held that "[t]he adoption of a zoning ordinance does not confer upon citizens . . . any vested right to have the ordinance remain forever in force, inviolate and unchanged."[115] Similarly, the court dismissed neighbors' challenge of a Wilmington rezoning to a more intensive use, ruling that a zoning ordinance might "be repealed in its entirety, or amended as the city's legislative body determines from time to time to be in the best interests of the public."[116] An expectation that a permit may be issued is not a property right that receives due-process protection.[117] Property owners and neighbors therefore have no abstract vested right to unchanging development regulations.

When property owners take action in reliance on a government's approval of an individual project under an ordinance, they may obtain a legal right—a vested right—to complete and use a project even if it is inconsistent with newly adopted ordinance requirements. A common law vested right is not a separate property right independent of the parcel of land involved; rather, it is a right attached to the property and is a quality of the land that enhances its value.[118] The crux of the question is determining when a landowner's interest in development becomes a property right. Once it passes that threshold— once it *vests*—that interest becomes a protected right that can be restricted only within constitutional limitations.[119] Frequently, the key question in a vested-rights dispute is not whether a vested property right should be protected but, rather, precisely when such a right is created.[120]

Legal Basis

Early cases based the common law vested right on provisions of the ordinances involved. Later cases have confirmed that state and federal constitutions provide some protection from changes for projects in which parties have vested rights.

---

114. 239 N.C. 232, 79 S.E.2d 730 (1954). In this case landowners sued the city for damages when the city built a water tank on a nearby lot in a residential zoning district. Public utilities were not a permitted use in the district. One of the owners' claims was that the zoning ordinance created a vested right to that district's remaining a residential area. *See also* Allgood v. Town of Tarboro, 281 N.C. 430, 189 S.E.2d 255 (1972).

115. *McKinney*, 239 N.C. at 237, 79 S.E.2d at 734. The court continued:

> A zoning ordinance is not a contract between the municipality and its citizens. The adoption of such ordinance is a valid exercise of the police power, which is not exhausted by its use.
>
> It being a law enacted in the exercise of the police power granted the municipality, no one can acquire a vested right therein. It is subject to amendment or repeal at the will of the governing agency which created it.

Id. (citations omitted). Also, in *Marren v. Gamble*, 237 N.C. 680, 75 S.E.2d 880 (1953), the court in the previous year had noted that "a zoning ordinance does not vest in a property owner the right that the restrictions imposed by it upon his property . . . shall remain unaltered." *Id.* at 684, 75 S.E.2d at 883. These state cases are consistent with a long-standing principle in federal constitutional law that newly adopted development and land use regulations can be applied to preexisting property rights. Hadacheck v. Sebastian, 239 U.S. 394 (1915) (application of restrictions on location of brick-making operations); Reinman v. City of Little Rock, 237 U.S. 171 (1915) (application of regulations on location of livery stable); Mugler v. Kansas, 123 U.S. 623 (1887) (application of regulation on operation of a brewery). Also see the discussion of continuation of nonconformities in Chapter 20.

116. Zopfi v. City of Wilmington, 273 N.C. 430, 434, 160 S.E.2d 325, 331 (1968).

117. PNE AOA Media, LLC v. Jackson Cnty., 146 N.C. App. 470, 481, 554 S.E.2d 657, 664 (2001).

118. Town of Midland v. Wayne, 368 N.C. 55, 66, 773 S.E.2d 301, 309 (2016).

119. The court in *Adams v. Village of Wesley Chapel*, 259 F. App'x 545, 551 (4th Cir. 2007), noted that a town must recognize vested rights to develop that were established under prior county zoning and that doing so is not an equal-protection violation.

120. Another key question is how long a vested right exists once established. While statutory vested rights have explicit expiration dates, this is not the case with common law vested rights. One case has suggested that while a vested right does not have an unlimited life, the owner must be afforded a reasonable time to complete the project. Mays-Ott Co. v. Town of Nags Head, 751 F. Supp. 82, 87 (E.D.N.C. 1990).

Most of the early cases on this issue turned on provisions in the ordinance itself and are thus more nonconforming-use cases than vested-rights cases.[121] In *Stowe v. Burke*, the court acknowledged that as of 1961, a clear common law vested right had yet to be established in North Carolina jurisprudence.[122]

The first North Carolina case finding a vested right to exist apart from the nonconforming-use provisions of an ordinance was the 1964 decision *Warner v. W & O, Inc.* The court concluded that the landowner was "protected if, acting in good faith, he has made expenditures on the faith of the permit at a time when the act was lawful."[123] Although two more cases from the mid-1960s returned to the ordinance-based analysis of "completion/expansion" of a nonconforming use,[124] in 1969 the court in *Town of Hillsborough v. Smith*[125] firmly embraced the traditional common-law-vested-rights analysis. In this opinion the court rejected the concept that the vested right was based on ordinance provisions, such as those for nonconforming uses or variances in hardship situations.[126]

In *Godfrey v. Zoning Board of Adjustment*, the court noted the constitutional foundation for vested rights:

> The "vested rights" doctrine has evolved as a constitutional limitation on the state's exercise of its police power to restrict an individual's use of private property by the enactment of zoning ordinances. The doctrine is rooted in the "due process of law" and the "law of the land" clauses of the federal and state constitutions.
>
> It has been said that the solution to the "vested rights" question "has required the reconciliation of the doctrine of separation of powers with the constitutional requirements of substantive due process, a balancing of the interests of the public as a whole and those of the individual property owners, and, in many cases, the elements of good faith and bad faith and resort to equity and equitable principles."[127]

---

121. *In re W.P. Rose Builders' Supply Co.*, 202 N.C. 496, 163 S.E. 462 (1932), involved an ordinance that exempted a particular project if construction was commenced within ninety days, and the case turned on what constituted commencement. The court ruled that placement of a grease dispenser and goods to be sold constituted "starting" a gasoline filling station. The basis of the vested right was the ordinance provision itself, as the court noted: "It is deemed unnecessary to decide the constitutionality of the entire zoning ordinance . . . if, as a matter of fact, the property of plaintiffs is exempt from the operation of the ordinance by the terms thereof." *Id.* at 498, 163 S.E. at 463 (1932).

122. 255 N.C. 527, 534, 122 S.E.2d 374, 379 (1961).

123. 263 N.C. 37, 41, 138 S.E.2d 782, 785 (1964).

124. Austin v. Brunnemer, 266 N.C. 697, 147 S.E.2d 182 (1966); Town of Garner v. Weston, 263 N.C. 487, 139 S.E.2d 642 (1965).

125. 276 N.C. 48, 170 S.E.2d 904 (1969). *See also* Town of Midland v. Wayne, 368 N.C. 55, 63–64, 773 S.E.2d 301, 307–08 (2016); River Birch Assocs. v. City of Raleigh, 326 N.C. 100, 388 S.E.2d 538 (1990).

126. The court ruled:
> The defendants do not contend that, by reason of exceptional hardship, the municipal authorities should exercise a discretion granted them by ordinance. Their contention is that they have a legal right to build, which right the city cannot take from them and for which no permit is authorized by the ordinance.

Smith, 276 N.C. at 57, 170 S.E.2d at 911.

127. 317 N.C. 51, 62, 344 S.E.2d 272, 274 (1986) (citations omitted). Article I, section 19 of the North Carolina constitution mandates due process of law in the deprivation of privileges and property. Other provisions of the state constitution also support a mandatory vested right. One is the provision on ex post facto laws. N.C. CONST. art. I, § 16. In *Stanback v. Citizens National Bank*, 197 N.C. 292, 148 S.E. 313 (1929), a case involving revocation of a trust, the court held that statutes might not be retroactively applied to disturb vested, as opposed to contingent, rights. On the other hand, the provisions of the state constitution prohibiting monopolies and exclusive emoluments have been applied to limit the vesting of property rights in nonconforming uses. N.C. CONST. art. I, § 32. Burden v. Town of Ahoskie, 198 N.C. 92, 150 S.E. 808 (1929); MacRae v. City of Fayetteville, 198 N.C. 51, 150 S.E. 810 (1929); Town of Clinton v. Standard Oil Co., 193 N.C. 432, 137 S.E. 183 (1927).

In *Swan Beach Corolla, LLC v. County of Currituck*,[128] the court noted that since a claim of a common law vested right was a constitutional claim, the board of adjustment had no jurisdiction to determine the claim and thus, absent ordinance-interpretation issues, there was no requirement for quasi-judicial review prior to a judicial determination of the claim. G.S. 160D-108(h) provides that a person claiming a vested right may seek a determination on that right from the zoning administrator, but on appeal the existence of the vested right is considered de novo. This statute also provides that the person can go directly to court on this issue without first seeking a staff determination or appeal to the board of adjustment.[129]

Requirements

To establish a common law vested right in North Carolina, the landowner or the developer must have made substantial expenditures in good-faith reliance on a valid government approval, with resulting detriment if the landowner or developer is required to comply with the newly adopted requirements. Each aspect of this test must be met in order for a vested right to be established.[130]

Substantial Expenditures

The provision for substantial expenditures, sometimes phrased as "a substantial beginning of construction," is necessary to establish that the owner would suffer undue losses if required to comply with the new requirements.[131] A substantial action must have been taken to carry out an approved development project, action that involves the expenditure of money, time, or effort.

Actual construction on-site is not required to establish a substantial expenditure. In *Smith*, the defendants were in the process of instituting a dry-cleaning business when a zoning ordinance was adopted restricting the property involved to residential use. The court ruled that physical construction on the site was not required to establish a vested right: "It is not the giving of notice to the town, through a change in the appearance of the land, which creates the vested property right in the holder of the permit. The basis of his right . . . is his change of his own position in bona fide reliance upon the permit."[132] The

---

128. 234 N.C. App. 617, 760 S.E.2d 302 (2014).

129. Under this statute, if appealing directly to the court, the person making the claim may bring an original civil action as provided by G.S. 160D-1403.1.

130. In review of a Rule 12(b)(6) motion to dismiss, all of these elements of a common law vested right must be alleged, but the allegations must be assumed to be true and liberally construed when ruling on the motion to dismiss. *Swan Beach Corolla*, 234 N.C. App. 617, 760 S.E.2d 302.

131. This is similar to a required showing of a materially changed position in a traditional estoppel analysis.

132. Town of Hillsborough v. Smith, 276 N.C. 48, 54-55, 170 S.E.2d 904, 909. The detailed sequence of events was as follows: On May 3, 1968, the defendant received a building permit for the business. This case predates the 1985 legislation establishing a statutory vested right upon issuance of a building permit. There was conflicting testimony on whether the owner was advised of the pending zoning adoption at this time. Constructive notice through newspaper advertisement was apparently available, and town officials testified that actual notice was provided. The defendant denied receiving any knowledge before June 11. This knowledge is a factor in the second portion of the vested-rights test: that the expenditures be made in good faith. The jury found for the defendant on this factual question, and the court held the jury's finding to be binding. On May 22, the defendant purchased the property for $9500 and entered into a contract for construction of a $15,000 building on the site. On May 23, the corners of the proposed building were staked. On May 24, an order for dry-cleaning equipment was placed. On May 27, the zoning ordinance was adopted. On June 5 and 11, additional equipment was contracted for. On June 11, the town revoked the building permit. On July 8, work commenced with the bulldozing of an existing house on the lot. On July 11, the town instituted litigation. Despite prevailing in the litigation, the plaintiff eventually abandoned plans for a commercial structure on the lot. A brick single-family ranch house was eventually constructed on the lot. *See also* Transland Props., Inc. v. Bd. of Adjustment, 18 N.C. App. 712, 198 S.E.2d 1 (1973). By contrast, see *Sterling Homes Corp. v. Anne Arundel County*, 116 Md. App. 206, 227–28, 695 A.2d 1238, 1249 (1997) (sufficient work must be completed on-site for a member of the public to be aware of commencement of a permittable building).

expenditures and the binding contracts for the acquisition of land, construction materials, or equipment were held to be qualified expenditures. On the other hand, actual construction on the site does not automatically establish a vested right, for there must still be substantial expenditures. For example, in *Austin v. Brunnemer*,[133] the petitioner purchased a lot to establish an auto body shop and garage. The lot was graded and fenced, and a sign was erected advertising the proposed use before the adoption of a zoning ordinance prohibiting that use. The court held that a vested right had not been established as a matter of law.

The requisite level of expenditure is not an absolute amount but is proportional to the cost of the project. In *Sunderhaus v. Board of Adjustment*, the plaintiffs were installing a satellite-dish television antenna in their yard. A trench had been dug and PVC pipe installed, but the dish itself and its concrete base had not been installed when the zoning ordinance was amended to preclude placement of the dish in the proposed location. The court concluded that, given the relatively small scale of the project, the digging of the trench constituted a significant amount of the work necessary for the entire project, and a vested right had therefore been established.[134]

Substantial expenditures of time, labor, and energy as well as expenditures of money or actual construction may be considered in establishing a vested right. For example, in *Randolph County v. Coen*,[135] a landowner had formed a partnership to initiate a business to sell heavy equipment, secured the required business licenses, and fully prepared the site. Site preparation in this instance involved only clearing and grading an area for parking heavy trucks and installing a small utility building and sign. The court held that, even though a significant expenditure of money had not been made before this initial zoning of the site, a significant expenditure of labor had been made and it constituted the substantial beginning required to establish a vested right.[136]

Good Faith

The second requirement to establish a common law vested right is that the requisite substantial expenditures must have been made in good faith. A person acting with undue haste in a deliberate attempt to avoid compliance with a newly adopted zoning provision generally secures no vested rights.[137]

The leading North Carolina case on the good faith requirement is *Stowe*,[138] which involved the construction of apartment buildings in Charlotte. The plaintiffs in this case had bought their land from the

---

133. 266 N.C. 697, 147 S.E.2d 182 (1966). Three years later, the court in *Smith* distinguished *Austin* by noting that the owner had conceded that his activities before the adoption of the ordinance had not established a vested right.

134. 94 N.C. App. 324, 380 S.E.2d 132 (1989). Also see *Simpson*, where it was alleged that an expenditure of $20,000 was made after receipt of a local quarry permit. The court remanded the case to the board of adjustment, ruling, "Whether these expenditures were substantial and made in good faith are questions of fact for the Board." Simpson v. City of Charlotte, 115 N.C. App. 51, 58, 443 S.E.2d 772, 777 (1994).

135. 99 N.C. App. 746, 394 S.E.2d 256 (1990). *See also* Even v. City of Parker, 1999 SD 72, 597 N.W.2d 670 (small expenditure by person of modest means sufficient for vesting).

136. Also see *Morris Communications Corp. v. City of Bessemer City Zoning Board of Adjustment*, 365 N.C. 152, 712 S.E.2d 868 (2011), where the court held efforts to secure state approval and a new lease constituted work sufficient to establish a vested right in a billboard-relocation permit. In such instances, the court usually looks to whether there has been at least some physical activity on-site, such as land clearing and grading. *See, e.g.*, Russell v. Guilford Cnty., 100 N.C. App. 541, 397 S.E.2d 335 (1990).

137. This is similar to a provision that a person claiming the vested right meet equity's clean-hands requirement. Courts in some states also consider whether the local government has also acted in good faith. *See, e.g.*, Geisler v. City Council, 769 N.W.2d 162, 168–69 (Iowa 2009); Commercial Props. Inc. v. Peternel, 418 Pa. 304, 311, 211 A.2d 514, 518–19 (1965); State *ex rel.* Humble Oil & Refin. Co. v. Wahner, 25 Wis. 2d 1, 15–16, 130 N.W.2d 304, 311–12 (1964).

138. 255 N.C. 527, 122 S.E.2d 374 (1961). *See also* Keiger v. Winston-Salem Bd. of Adjustment (*Keiger II*), 281 N.C. 715, 190 S.E.2d 175 (1972).

In the *Stowe* case, neighbors successfully prevented a developer from constructing apartment buildings on this Charlotte site.

defendant developer, telling him that they wished to escape congestion near apartments. Their house was built near a vacant parcel of land. There was evidence that throughout the critical months of this controversy the defendant had continued to assure the plaintiffs that he would not develop apartments on this vacant parcel, even as he actively pursued plans to do just that.[139]

The court held that although the defendant had made substantial expenditures in reliance on valid building permits, no vested right had been established because the expenditures had not been made in good faith. The defendant's knowledge of both community opposition and a specific pending petition for rezoning, which if adopted would preclude the project, established the absence of good faith. His expenditures made at an extraordinary pace in a race to beat a potential rezoning were thus not considered to establish a vested right.

Godfrey, although not ruling on the question directly, reiterated the necessity of good faith on the part of the landowner seeking the vested right. In a footnote, the court reviewed the law in other states and noted that the trial court could properly conclude that application of the vested-rights doctrine was inappropriate in this case because if the owner "incurred expenses with the knowledge that a lawsuit had been filed challenging the validity of the zoning ordinance amendment under which the landowner had obtained his building permit, he proceeded at his peril and thereby acquired no vested rights . . . ."[140]

In *Kirkpatrick v. Village Council of Pinehurst*,[141] the court held that an owner of a nonconforming use did not have the good faith necessary for a vested right if that owner made expenditures related to a renovation and expansion of the nonconformity with knowledge that a subsequent rezoning, special use permit, or other approval would be necessary for that activity. Likewise, in *PNE AOA Media, LLC v.*

---

139. The chronology in the case was as follows: On April 5, 1961, the planning commission recommended that the city council adopt single-family-residential and limited-duplex zoning for the property in question. The defendant had actual notice of the proposed ordinance. Notices of the public hearing on the zoning were published on April 24 and May 1, with the hearings held on May 12 and 19. On May 11, the defendant secured a lease of forty-five years to build apartments on the property. On June 6, he formed a corporation to carry out the project. On June 7, applications were filed for building permits for ten apartment buildings to house two hundred units. On June 19, the plaintiffs, by this time no longer relying on the representations of the defendant, petitioned the city to amend the zoning to exclusively single-family use. Notice of this petition was sent to the defendant, and a hearing was set for July 17. On July 7, the final building permits were issued. Work was then carried out at "an extra-ordinary rate of speed" so that by July 17, column footings had been completed for eight buildings and were more than half complete for the remaining two buildings. Some $56,000 had been spent in this period (of an estimated total cost of $2.6 million). On July 17, the city council adopted the single-family rezoning. Construction work was halted by court order on July 18. After conclusion of the litigation, single-family homes were eventually built on the site.

140. 317 N.C. 51, 66 n.2, 344 S.E.2d 272, 280–81 n.2 (1986).

141. 138 N.C. App. 79, 88, 530 S.E.2d 338, 344 (2000).

Jackson County,[142] the court held that where a developer made expenditures prior to receiving a necessary state permit, there was a lack of the requisite good faith to be vested relative to local ordinances. In *Walton North Carolina, LLC v. City of Concord*, the court held that when an owner purchased land with knowledge that a prior regulatory approval had expired, there could be no good-faith reliance on the expired approval.[143] In *LeTendre v. Currituck County*, the court held that no vested rights were created when the substantial expenditures were made on an approval that had been appealed and was subject to reversal.[144] An owner could not elect to proceed at her own risk and then claim good-faith reliance on an approval she knew to be under appeal.

North Carolina cases have held that expenditures made between the adoption and the effective dates of a rezoning are not made in good faith. In *Warner*,[145] the court's conclusions addressed expenditures made between the adoption and the effective date of a rezoning:

> The law accords protection to non-conforming users who, relying on the authorization given them, have made substantial expenditures in an honest belief that the project would not violate declared public policy. It does not protect one who makes expenditures with knowledge that the expenditures are made for a purpose declared unlawful by duly enacted ordinance; nor does it protect one who waits until after an ordinance has been enacted forbidding the proposed use and, after the enactment, hastens to thwart the legislative act by making expenditures a few hours prior to the effective date of the ordinance.[146]

How notice of a possible change in regulations that has not yet been enacted affects the issue of good faith is less certain. In some states, the rule is that expenditures made after public notice of a specific rezoning proposal could not have been made in good faith and thus could not lead to a vested right. This is sometimes referred to as a "pending ordinance" rule.[147]

---

142. 146 N.C. App. 470, 554 S.E.2d 657 (2001).

143. 257 N.C. App. 227, 809 S.E.2d 164 (2017), *review denied*, 371 N.C. 447, 817 S.E.2d 388 (2018). The prior preliminary plat approval was based on a clustered-development option in the ordinance that had been subsequently repealed. The 2006 preliminary plat approval required a final plat submission prior to the end of 2013. However, after the 2008 recession the previous owner had gone into bankruptcy, and no final plat was submitted.

144. 259 N.C. App. 512, 817 S.E.2d 73 (2018), *review denied*, 372 N.C. 54, 822 S.E.2d 641 (2019).

145. 263 N.C. 37, 138 S.E.2d 782 (1964).

146. *Id.* at 43, 138 S.E.2d at 786–87 (citations omitted).

147. *See, e.g.*, 1350 Lake Shore Assoc. v. Healey, 861 N.E.2d 944 (Ill. 2006) (once proposed downzoning amendment is introduced, further expenditures are not in good faith); Penn Twp. v. Yecko Bros., 420 Pa. 386, 391, 217 A.2d 171, 173–74 (1966).

Knowledge of a *specific* pending change in zoning is an important factor in establishing whether the expenditures have been made in good faith.[148] In *Koontz v. Davidson County Board of Adjustment*,[149] the court found no vested rights to install manufactured housing in a newly rezoned area of Davidson County. Here the developers entered into a contract to purchase land for the purpose of developing a mobile-home community. Neighbors who opposed such a development then petitioned the county board of commissioners to rezone an area of the county (which included this site) to a zoning district that did not allow placement of manufactured housing. After notice of the public hearing on this proposed rezoning was published, the developers consulted the planning staff to determine what they needed to do to "get grandfathered." The developers subsequently proceeded to subdivide the land, record the plat, secure a zoning-compliance permit, and install roads in the subdivision prior to the vote on the rezoning. Some ten days after the rezoning was adopted, the developers began to place manufactured-housing units on the site. Upon suit by the neighbors, the court held that the developers did not have the requisite good faith and thus no vested rights:

> Because the rezoning proposal was set for hearing, developers were aware the County Commissioners were seriously considering the petition. Despite this knowledge, developers actively sought and heeded advice on how to avoid or prevent the ordinance from halting their proposed development and unilaterally proceeded with their development activities. Therefore, developers did not exercise good faith reliance on a valid permit, as a matter of law, and thus they do not have a vested right to avoid the enacted zoning changes.[150]

Knowledge of a *possible* ordinance change, however, does not, in and of itself, prevent a person from making expenditures in good faith. In *In re Campsites Unlimited, Inc.*,[151] the court held that a generalized knowledge of impending zoning, as opposed to knowledge about a specific zoning proposal, did

---

148. Justice Sharp commented in 1972:

> When, at the time a builder obtains a permit, he has knowledge of a pending ordinance which would make the authorized construction a nonconforming use and thereafter hurriedly makes expenditures in an attempt to acquire a vested right before the law can be changed, he does not act in good faith and acquires no rights under the permit.

Keiger v. Winston-Salem Bd. of Adjustment (*Keiger II*), 281 N.C. 715, 719, 190 S.E.2d 175, 178 (1972). This case involved construction of a 102-unit mobile-home park in Winston-Salem. The case went to the state supreme court twice. The first time, the court held that the board of adjustment had improperly denied a special use permit for the project but remanded the case for consideration of the effects of a subsequently adopted zoning amendment. Keiger v. Winston-Salem Bd. of Adjustment (*Keiger I*), 278 N.C. 17, 178 S.E.2d 616 (1971). In the second case, the court held that the rezoning to a district that did not allow mobile-home parks had been improperly adopted and thus did not preclude the development. *Keiger II*, 281 N.C. 715, 190 S.E.2d 175.

Adoption of the permit-choice rule by the General Assembly in 2014 and 2015 changes the calculation for land-owners. If a regulation changes between the time of a permit application and a permit decision, the applicant has a statutory right to choose to have either the original or the new regulations applied to the application.

149. 130 N.C. App. 479, 503 S.E.2d 108, *review denied*, 349 N.C. 529, 526 S.E.2d 177 (1998).

150. *Id.* at 483, 503 S.E.2d at 110. Although not addressed by the court, presumably the investment in the roads subsequent to plat approval could have been used for site-built housing as well as manufactured housing, so that there would have been no element of detriment for application of vested rights based on that expenditure.

The situation of development initiated immediately prior to the adoption of a pending ordinance amendment is a common one nationally. See, e.g., *Town of Cross Plains v. Kitt's Field of Dreams Korner, Inc.*, 321 Wis. 2d 671, 690–95, 775 N.W.2d 283, 293–96 (2009); Thompson v. Vill. of Hinsdale, 247 Ill. App. 3d 863, 876, 617 N.E.2d 1227, 1237 (1993); Glickman v. Parish of Jefferson, 224 So. 2d 141, 145 (La. Ct. App. 1969); Hanchera v. Bd. of Adjustment, 269 Neb. 623, 628–29, 694 N.W.2d 641, 646 (2005); Biggs v. Town of Sandwich, 124 N.H. 421, 426, 470 A.2d 928, 931 (1984); Clackamas Cnty. v. Holmes, 265 Or. 193, 199, 508 P.2d 190, 193 (1973); H.R.D.E., Inc. v. Zoning Officer, 189 W. Va. 283, 288, 430 S.E.2d 341, 346 (1993).

151. 287 N.C. 493, 215 S.E.2d 73 (1975).

not constitute failure to act in good faith. *Thomasville of N.C., Ltd. v. City of Thomasville*[152] illustrates this point and the balancing of equities that is inherent in vested-rights analyses. The plaintiff proposed to construct a hundred subsidized apartment units, which was allowed by the zoning. The plaintiff consulted with the city government, which subsequently sent written confirmation to the federal government that its zoning allowed this use. After the plaintiff applied for building permits, however, the city administratively delayed action on the permits and subsequently rezoned the property to allow only single-family uses. The court ruled that the plaintiff had secured a vested right. Key factors were that the plaintiff had at no time misled the city or neighbors about its intentions; there was no evidence that the plaintiff had exercised undue haste or had been engaged in a race with the city to secure a vested right before the zoning could be changed; and expenditures had been made in reliance on valid permits. Also, all required application materials had been submitted, and the building permit normally would have been issued before public notice of the rezoning. Given the strong implications that the city's approvals had purposely been delayed, the court concluded that the balance of the equities favored the plaintiff.

Reliance on Valid Approval

To establish a common law vested right, any expenditures incurred must be made in reliance on an actual, legitimate approval of an individual project.

The approval must be grounded in a site-specific review and must be a formal approval as mandated by law. Such approvals include building permits, special use permits, certificates of zoning compliance, and preliminary plat approvals.[153] Expenditures made in generalized reliance on the existing zoning or advisory letters stating current regulatory requirements, and expenditures made in order to secure government approval, are not considered.[154]

In *Waste Industries USA, Inc. v. State*,[155] the applicant for a state permit for a solid-waste landfill in Camden County undertook several mandated steps required in the state-permit-review process. The applicant secured a franchise agreement with the county and submitted site studies. While the application was pending, the General Assembly adopted a one-year moratorium on new landfills and subsequently amended the statutory standards for landfills. The court held that since a valid permit was a prerequisite to establishing a common law vested right and no permit had been secured, there were no vested rights.[156]

Particular care is warranted in terms of "certificates of zoning compliance." While some jurisdictions have a separate and distinct permit for zoning compliance, many jurisdictions incorporate zoning-compliance reviews as part of building-permit reviews and issue a single building permit that may

---

152. 17 N.C. App. 483, 195 S.E.2d 79 (1973).

153. On plats, see *River Birch Associates v. City of Raleigh*, 326 N.C. 100, 388 S.E.2d 538 (1990). The court there held that the construction of improvements pursuant to preliminary plat approval created a vested right to the completion of the project as approved. In *Browning-Ferris Industries of South Atlantic, Inc. v. Wake County*, 905 F. Supp. 312, 319 (E.D.N.C. 1995), the court found a vested right based on expenditures following approval of a site plan by the Morrisville town council. States vary as to just which forms of development approval are sufficient for vested-rights claims. *See, e.g.,* Vill., L.L.C v. Del. Agric. Lands Found. (*In re* 224.5 Acres of Land, 808 A.2d 753 (Del. 2002)) (diligent compliance with pre-permit process sufficient for vesting); Town of Largo v. Imperial Homes Corp., 309 So. 2d 571 (Fla. Dist. Ct. App. 1975) (approval of rezoning petition to allow construction of high-rise building sufficient for vesting); Metro. Dev. Comm'n v. Pinnacle Media, LLC, 846 N.E.2d 654 (Ind. 2006) (filing of building-permit application insufficient to establish vesting for billboard); Abbey Rd. Grp., LLC v. City of Bonney Lake, 167 Wash. 2d 242, 218 P.3d 180 (2009) (holding that filing of site-plan application prior to building-permit application insufficient for vested rights).

154. Philip Green long ago noted that the claim to a vested right based on reliance of a particular set of land use regulations alone is "legal nonsense." GREEN, *supra* note 1, at 5.

155. 220 N.C. App. 163, 725 S.E.2d 875, *review denied*, 366 N.C. 241, 731 S.E.2d 686 (2012).

156. *Id.* at 188, 725 S.E.2d 875 at 881–82. The permit-choice rule of G.S. 143-750 was subsequently enacted.

include a verification or certificate of zoning compliance. A regulatory approval that is mandatory before construction or other site work commences is necessary for vested-rights purposes. A letter from staff advising that a proposed use is consistent with current zoning, which is often secured by developers in the course of acquiring and financing land purchases, is not a mandated approval that authorizes a specific development project and cannot be the basis of a common law vested right.[157] Likewise, an assurance from the staff that a buffer requirement would be waived is not an "approval" that can be the basis of a vested right.[158]

The question of whether the submission of a completed application (as opposed to the issuance of a permit) can trigger a common law vested right was raised in *Robins v. Town of Hillsborough* (*Robins II*),[159] a case decided prior to enactment of the permit-choice rule. The plaintiff submitted a site plan for an asphalt plant on a site where such was a permitted use. The town, prior to acting on the site-plan-approval application, adopted a moratorium and subsequently amended the ordinance to remove asphalt plants as a permitted use. The court of appeals held that the applicant had a vested right to consideration of the application under the ordinance in effect at the time a completed application was submitted, and it reversed and remanded the matter for consideration under the terms of the ordinance in effect at the time of application.[160] The North Carolina Supreme Court, however, decided the case on narrower grounds and without expressly reaching the vested-rights question,[161] holding that the provision in the town ordinance that the board of adjustment "shall . . . [p]ass upon, decide, or determine"[162] applications for site-plan approval mandated that the board render a decision on the application. Since the board had dismissed the application without a decision upon adoption of the text amendment, the court remanded the case for decision by the board under the rules in effect at the time of application.[163]

---

157. MLC Auto., LLC v. Town of S. Pines, 207 N.C. App. 555, 702 S.E.2d 68 (2010), *review denied*, 710 S.E.2d 23. *See also* Bd. of Supervisors v. Crucible, Inc., 278 Va. 152, 677 S.E.2d 283 (2009) (vested right cannot be based on zoning-verification letter). Staff interpretations of land use regulations are discussed in more detail in Chapters 18 (defining a "final decision" and rules of interpretation) and 21 (staff interpretations).

158. Wilson v. City of Mebane Bd. of Adjustment, 212 N.C. App. 176, 710 S.E.2d 403 (2011).

159. 361 N.C. 193, 639 S.E.2d 421 (2007). While expressly noting that there was no need to decide the common law vested-right claim, in *Meares v. Town of Beaufort*, 193 N.C. App. 96, 100, 667 S.E.2d 239, 242 (2008), the court of appeals held that repeal of a contested provision in the town's historic-district guidelines while the judicial review was pending did not moot the case, as the board of adjustment had ordered a new hearing on the initial application for a certificate of appropriateness, and the applicant was entitled to a decision on the application based on the rules in effect at the time of that initial application.

160. Robins v. Town of Hillsborough (*Robins I*), 176 N.C. App. 1, 625 S.E.2d 813 (2006). The court of appeals also held that a total ban of a particular use raised constitutional issues of arbitrary and capricious action and a denial of equal protection.

161. This distinction was noted by the court of appeals in *Sandy Mush Properties, Inc. v. Rutherford County*, 181 N.C. App. 224, 638 S.E.2d 557, *remanded*, 361 N.C. 569, 651 S.E.2d 566, *aff'd*, 187 N.C. App. 809, 654 S.E.2d 253 (2007), *review dismissed*, 363 N.C. 577, 681 S.E.2d 339 (2009). When the supreme court remanded for reconsideration in light of the *Robins II* decision, the court noted that *Robins II* as decided was not a vested-rights case and thus had no impact on their prior decision regarding vested rights.

162. *Robins II*, 361 N.C. at 197, 639 S.E.2d at 423.

163. The court held that the town could not by legislative fiat dictate the outcome of this quasi-judicial process. The court pointed out that given this procedural requirement of the ordinance, it was unnecessary to address the constitutionality of the ordinance, and that portion of the court-of-appeals decision was vacated. *Id.* at 199–200, 639 S.E.2d at 425. On remand, the town heard and denied the application. The town and owner subsequently settled the case, with a reported $175,000 payment to the applicant to cover litigation costs. Emily Matchar, *Town Settles Plant Trouble*, NEWS & OBSERVER (Raleigh, N.C.), Feb. 12, 2018, at B3.

Expenditures made on a mistakenly issued permit do not establish a common law vested right. In *Mecklenburg County v. Westbery*,[164] part of the property at issue was in a residential zoning district and part was in an industrial district. The owner wanted to install a storage building that was permitted in the industrial district but not in the residential district. The building inspector mistakenly thought the site of the proposed building was in the industrial-district portion of the lot, so a building permit was issued. In reliance on that permit, the owner purchased and installed a $25,100 building.[165] The county then discovered the mistake, notified the owner that the structure was in violation of the zoning, and revoked the building permit. The court held that no vested right had been established because the use was illegal from its inception.[166] Similarly, the court in *Wilson v. City of Mebane Board of Adjustment* held that where a permit was issued without a buffer requirement mandated by the ordinance, the permit was void *ab initio* and any expenditures made pursuant to that permit could not be considered for a vested-rights analysis.[167] Also, reliance may not be made on an approval that is subject to litigation and is subsequently invalidated[168] or on a prior valid approval that has expired.[169]

Expenditures made on an illegal use do not establish a vested right even if they are made with the full knowledge of the local government. A case on zoning enforcement illustrates this point. The defendant in *City of Raleigh v. Fisher*[170] had purchased land from the city and constructed a residence on the site. The defendant operated a bakery and sandwich business from the house continuously thereafter, even though the site was in a residential zoning district. The defendant made an estimated business investment of $75,000 over the years. The city was aware of the use and collected a privilege tax on the business for nine years. At that point, however, the city directed the defendant to discontinue the business because

---

164. 32 N.C. App. 630, 233 S.E.2d 658 (1977). In an early North Carolina zoning case, the court noted that a mistakenly issued permit to bury oil storage tanks on a lot that had five months earlier been rezoned from industrial to residential did not estop the city from enforcing the correct zoning regulation. Helms v. City of Charlotte, 255 N.C. 647, 652, 122 S.E.2d 817 (1961). *See also* Premier Plastic Surgery Ctr., PLLC v. Bd. of Adjustment, 213 N.C. App. 364, 713 S.E.2d 511 (2011); E. Outdoor, Inc. v. Bd. of Adjustment, 150 N.C. App. 516, 564 S.E.2d 78 (2002). In yet another case, the court held that there were no vested rights established based on a mining permit that was subsequently revoked. The revoking agency discovered significant adverse impacts (the site would have been visible and audible from the Appalachian Trail) after permit issuance, and the court held that authority to modify the permit included authority to revoke it. Clark Stone Co. v. N.C. Dep't of Env't & Nat. Res., 164 N.C. App. 24, 594 S.E.2d 832, *review denied*, 359 N.C. 322, 603 S.E.2d 878 (2004). A prominent case from another state reaching the same result is *In re Parkview Associates v. City of New York*, 71 N.Y.2d 274, 525 N.Y.S.2d 176, 519 N.E.2d 1372 (1988). The ordinance here allowed for a nineteen-story building on the entire site at issue, but a permit was mistakenly issued that allowed a thirty-one-story building on the portion of the lot more than 100 feet from the street. The city discovered the error and revoked the permit only after the steel superstructure and most mechanical work for the taller building had been completed. The court upheld the permit revocation. A subsequent variance petition was also ultimately denied, and some eight years after construction began, the portion of the structure exceeding the actual height limit was removed.

165. The case was somewhat complicated by the fact that the permit was issued for a 40-by-60-foot storage building, and a 24-by-70-foot mobile home was actually installed for storage use.

166. *Westbery*, 212 N.C. App. 176, 233 S.E.2d 658.

167. 212 N.C. App. 176, 710 S.E.2d 403 (2011). The staff had mistakenly concluded that the ordinance in effect at the time of permit application, which allowed for waiver of the buffer, was applicable. However, a new ordinance that did not allow waiver of the buffer was adopted a year prior to the permit decision. Since the revised ordinance was applicable and the approval was inconsistent with that ordinance, the permit was void. *See also* Martel Inv. Group, LLC v. Town of Richmond, 982 A.2d 595 (R.I. 2009) (holding no vested rights established based on building permit erroneously issued without mandated development-plan review).

168. Godfrey v. Zoning Bd. of Adjustment, 317 N.C. 51, 344 S.E.2d 272 (1986). *See generally* R.P. Davis, Annotation, *Rights of Permittee Under Illegally Issued Building Permit*, 6 A.L.R.2d 960 (1949).

169. Walton N.C., LLC v. City of Concord, 257 N.C. App. 227, 809 S.E.2d 164 (2017), *review denied*, 371 N.C. 447, 817 S.E.2d 388 (2018).

170. 232 N.C. 629, 61 S.E.2d 897 (1950).

of its inconsistency with the residential zoning requirements. The court held that no vested right to the business had been established, with Justice Sam Ervin writing:

> [A] municipality can not be estopped to enforce a zoning ordinance against a violator by the conduct of its officials in encouraging or permitting such violator to violate such ordinance in times past.
>
> Undoubtedly this conclusion entails much hardship to the defendants. Nevertheless, the law must be so written; for a contrary decision would require an acceptance of the paradoxical proposition that a citizen can acquire immunity to the law of his country by habitually violating such law with the consent of unfaithful public officials charged with the duty of enforcing it.[171]

Although no vested rights can be established based on an invalid permit, it is not uncommon in these situations for the landowner to seek a variance.[172] When the cost of rectifying the mistake is high, there is no evidence of bad faith on the part of the applicant, and there is little if any harm to neighbors, it is not uncommon for such a variance petition to be granted.[173]

The requirement of reliance also means that expenditures made before approval or as part of the approval process cannot be considered to establish a vested right because they could not have been made in reliance on the permit. The leading case for this proposition is *Warner*, which involved a proposed fifty-unit apartment building in Asheville. As of the effective date of a rezoning that precluded multi-family housing, no substantial work had been done on the site, but the defendant had made substantial expenditures in securing financing and in designing the structure.[174] In ruling that no vested right had been established, the court held that the expenditures for architectural drawings needed to secure a permit "were manifestly not made in reliance on the permit thereafter issued."[175] Expenditures made in reliance on the ordinance itself,[176] on letters from staff prior to permit approval,[177] or on a preliminary "conditional" approval have all been held not to give rise to vested rights.[178] Similarly, expenditures

---

171. *Id.* at 635, 61 S.E.2d at 902 (citations omitted). *See also* LeTendre v. Currituck Cnty., 259 N.C. App. 512, 817 S.E.2d 73 (2018), *review denied*, 372 N.C. 54, 822 S.E.2d 641 (2019) (fact that county did not seek to stay construction while the permits challenged by neighbor were under appeal does not estop county from revoking permit and enforcing the ordinance if the neighbor is successful on appeal).

172. Variances are discussed in Chapter 17.

173. See, for example, *Stealth Properties, LLC v. Town of Pinebluff Board of Adjustment*, 183 N.C. App. 461, 645 S.E.2d 144, *review denied*, 361 N.C. 703, 653 S.E.2d 153 (2007). The court mandated issuance of a variance when a ten-foot mistake in the required setback was not discovered until after the permitted building was completed.

174. Warner v. W & O, Inc., 263 N.C. 37, 138 S.E.2d 782 (1964). On May 7, 1962, the defendant secured an option to purchase the site. After the defendant gave notice of exercising the option, a special proceeding was initiated on August 6 to carry out the sale (necessitated by the fact that the spouse of one of the owners was mentally incompetent). Building permits were secured on August 8. On August 9, the plaintiff, a neighboring property owner, initiated a petition to rezone the site to single-family residential use. The city council adopted the rezoning on September 13, effective September 28. Deeds conveying the property to the defendant were executed on September 26 and October 9. The proposed site of the apartment building (which the plaintiffs alleged was in fact to be a hotel) was adjacent to a single-family neighborhood along Beaver Lake in north Asheville. The site was later developed for single-family homes.

175. *Id.* at 41, 138 S.E.2d at 786.

176. "One does not acquire a vested right to build, contrary to the provisions of a subsequently enacted zoning ordinance, by the mere purchase of land in good faith with the intent of so building thereon." Town of Hillsborough v. Smith, 276 N.C. 48, 55, 170 S.E.2d 904, 909 (1969). *See also* McKinney v. City of High Point, 239 N.C. 232, 79 S.E.2d 730 (1954).

177. Wilson v. City of Mebane Bd. of Adjustment, 212 N.C. App. 176, 710 S.E.2d 403 (2011); MLC Auto., LLC v. Town of S. Pines, 207 N.C. App. 555, 702 S.E.2d 68 (2010).

178. Browning-Ferris Indus. of S. Atl., Inc. v. Guilford Cnty. Bd. of Adjustment, 126 N.C. App. 168, 172, 484 S.E.2d 411, 415 (1997).

made on engineering studies and state permit applications for expansion of use create no vested right to that expansion.[179]

There is an exception to the requirement that expenditures be made in reliance on valid government approval when no such approval is required. This exception can be an important consideration when zoning is initially adopted. In the 1975 case *Campsites Unlimited*, the petitioner secured an option to purchase unzoned lakeside property for a campground. The property was purchased in January, and engineering and design expenses were subsequently incurred. Site grading began in March. In April, initial zoning for the area was adopted by Stanly County. At that point, some $275,000 of a total esti-mated project cost of $2.7 million had been expended. Because no permit had been required for the development before April, the court allowed the January, March, and other earlier expenditures to be considered and therefore held that a vested right to the campground use had been established.[180] Such a situation is less likely to arise now because building permits have been mandatory statewide since 1985.[181] However, it remains a consideration when an area is being initially zoned and when land uses can be established without the necessity of a building or a structure.

An interesting question regarding common law vesting is raised when a project requires multiple permits and substantial expenditures are made after some but not all permits have been received.[182] For example, an improvement permit may be secured for a septic tank for a proposed commercial use of a site, and the tank may be purchased and installed. Then, before a building permit or other zoning approval has been secured for the commercial use, the site may be rezoned so that only residential use is allowed. To the extent that a common law vested right can be secured at all for a "partially" permitted project, it will apply only to the ordinances and the regulations for which permits have actually been

---

179. Griffin v. Town of Unionville, No. 3:05-cv-514-RJC, 2008 WL 697634 (W.D.N.C. Mar. 11, 2008). The plaintiff operated an inert-debris landfill with a lawfully issued special use permit. The plaintiff expended some $750,000 in applications to the state to expand the permitted wastes to include industrial solid waste. At the initial stages of the plaintiff's work, the town ordinance would have allowed industrial wastes to be added to the landfill authorized by the special use permit, but only if the operator secured an amendment to the special use permit. The town ordi-nance was amended to exclude industrial solid waste prior to the operator seeking a special use permit amendment or receiving a required franchise for an industrial-waste landfill. The court held that the plaintiff could not rely on expenditures made prior to securing required town approvals in order to establish a vested right for an industrial-waste landfill.

180. *In re* Campsites Unlimited, Inc., 287 N.C. 493, 215 S.E.2d 73 (1975). This case is discussed at some length in Michael B. Brough, The Nonconforming Use in North Carolina Zoning Law: Text and Model Ordinance (1976). The court in *MLC Automotive, LLC v. Town of Southern Pines*, 207 N.C. App. 555, 702 S.E.2d 68 (2010), emphasized that the *Campsites Unlimited* exception is generally confined to situations where there is an absence of zoning. An example is provided by *Swan Beach Corolla*, where the allegation was that substantial expen-ditures were made after subdivision approval but before zoning was applied to the land at issue. Swan Beach Corolla, LLC v. Cnty. of Currituck, 234 N.C. App. 617, 760 S.E.2d 302 (2014).

181. G.S. 160D-1110. See the discussion of statutory vested rights earlier in this chapter. Under current law, if a valid building permit is outstanding, there is a statutory vested right to complete the project. Whether a common law vested right exists is thus a moot question.

182. G.S. 160D-108(e), enacted subsequent to these cases, provides statutory options when multiple development approvals are required for a single project, as discussed earlier in this chapter.

issued.[183] In *PNE AOA Media*,[184] the court noted that where a developer makes expenditures prior to receiving a necessary state permit, there is a lack of the requisite good faith to be vested relative to local ordinances. In *Griffin Farm & Landfill, Inc. v. Town of Unionville*,[185] the plaintiffs secured a special use permit of indefinite duration for a construction-and-demolition landfill. The project also required a local government franchise and a state permit for operation, both of which had a five-year life. The court held that when the franchise and state permit expired, the owner no longer had a right to operate the landfill and could not base a vested-right claim on the special use permit alone. The vested-rights implications of multiple local permit approvals is now addressed by G.S. 160D-108(e).[186]

When a common law vested right is established based on reliance on a valid permit, it is important to note that the scope of what has been vested is limited to the scope of what was actually permitted. This limitation is illustrated by *Sandy Mush Properties, Inc. v. Rutherford County*. The dispute in this case revolved around the use of a 180-acre tract for a crushed-rock quarry. In 2001, the plaintiff applied for three building permits (a modular-office building, an office building, and a metal building) at the site of the proposed quarry. The county denied the permits based on a county-adopted moratorium on location of heavy industries near schools. While the moratorium was in litigation, the county issued building permits for these structures. Construction was initiated but later suspended. Eventually, the moratorium was declared invalid and the question arose as to the scope of vested rights secured through the building permits. The plaintiff contended that the building permit for the office building constituted a statutory or common law vesting for the use of the property as a quarry. The court held, however, that the building permit only authorized construction of an office building (which by the terms of the permit could be used as offices for various uses) and did not purport to authorize any other use of the larger site. Thus, the office-building permit did not itself constitute a statutory vesting, nor could it serve as the basis for a common law vesting for the use of the site as a quarry.[187]

183. "In those situations where multiple permits are required preliminary to the issuance of the building permit, and substantial obligations and/or expenditures are incurred in good faith reliance on the issuance of those permits, the party does acquire a vested right in those provision(s) of the ordinance or regulation pursuant to which the preliminary permit(s) was issued." *Browning-Ferris Industries*, 126 N.C. App. at 172, 484 S.E.2d at 411. *See also* Waste Indus. USA, Inc. v. State, 220 N.C. App. 163, 187, 725 S.E.2d 875, 892, *review denied*, 366 N.C. 241, 731 S.E.2d 686 (2012). This issue was also alluded to in *Town of Garner v. Weston*, 263 N.C. 487, 139 S.E.2d 642 (1965). In this case the town extended its extraterritorial zoning to an area where the defendants were installing a mobile-home park. Such use was not allowed by the town zoning. There was conflicting evidence as to how much work had actually been done at the time of the effective date of the zoning. That required water and sewer permits had not been secured was a factor in the trial court's finding that the use was not being made on the ordinance's effective date, a finding upheld by the supreme court. Also, in *Cardwell v. Smith*, 106 N.C. App. 187, 415 S.E.2d 770, *review denied*, 332 N.C. 146, 419 S.E.2d 569 (1992), expenditures to acquire other required permits after a special use permit was received were considered in establishing a vested right (as was the principal expenditure for land acquisition). The interplay of multiple permit requirements was also involved in *Martin Marietta Corp. v. Wake Stone Corp.*, 111 N.C. App. 269, 432 S.E.2d 428 (1993), *aff'd per curiam*, 338 N.C. 602 (1995), though the case was not decided on those grounds. Also, in *Meares v. Town of Beaufort*, 193 N.C. App. 49, 667 S.E.2d 244 (2008), the court noted that compliance with zoning-district dimensional standards (here a building-setback requirement) and historic-district standards were independent functions, and an inability to comply with one was irrelevant for the other decision.

184. PNE AOA Media, LLC v. Jackson Cnty., 146 N.C. App. 470, 554 S.E.2d 657 (2001).

185. No. 3:10-cv-250-RJC-DSC, 2012 W.L. 3257789 (W.D.N.C. Aug. 8, 2012).

186. This provision was added by S.L. 2019-111, § 1.3, discussed above regarding statutory vested rights.

187. 181 N.C. App. 224, 638 S.E.2d 557, *remanded*, 361 N.C. 569, 651 S.E.2d 566, *aff'd*, 187 N.C. App. 809, 654 S.E.2d 253 (2007). On appeal, the supreme court remanded this decision for reconsideration in light of the court's decision in *Robins II*. On remand, the court of appeals affirmed its prior holding. The court noted that the *Robins II* decision expressly stated it was not a vested-rights case but, rather, a question of town compliance with procedures mandated by its ordinance. Thus, the court held that *Robins II* did not affect its prior holding.

Also, if expenditures in a lawful use are limited by other regulations, the vested right will only extend to that portion of the development for which the expenditures were actually made. This is illustrated by *Huntington Properties, LLC v. Currituck County.* The plaintiff's predecessor in title had secured county approval for a 440-unit mobile-home park but only installed 140 units due to permit limits related to its wastewater-disposal system. The county subsequently amended its zoning regulation to render the park nonconforming. The court held that any vested rights of the plaintiff extended only to the 140 units actually in place.[188]

Detriment

A final element of the analysis of common law vested rights is a requirement that conformance with the new ordinance requirements must be shown to be a detriment to the landowner. If the owners can comply with the changed requirements without being harmed, they need not be treated any differently from other citizens, so the courts require detrimental reliance before validating a vested right.

Russell v. Guilford County[189] provides an example of the application of this requirement. When the plaintiff acquired the property at issue, he believed that it was all zoned for residential use. Upon learning that part of the property was zoned for commercial use, he changed his plans in order to develop that portion commercially. Those plans were "conditionally" approved. He also sought a rezoning to have the residential portion changed to commercial zoning. The county, however, did the opposite and rezoned the commercial portion to residential use. The court of appeals ruled that no vested right had been established for the commercial development because the expenditures made when the owner believed the land to be zoned entirely residential, and later expenditures that were consistent with residential zoning, could not be counted in determining whether substantial expenditures had been made. Because these expenditures could be applied to the permitted residential development, there was no harm to the owner caused by the rezoning and thus no vested right to a commercial development. A similar result was reached in *Browning-Ferris Industries of South Atlantic, Inc. v. Guilford County Board of Adjustment.* An applicant seeking approval for a solid-waste transfer station had received state permits (which subsequently were revoked) and had a site plan "conditionally" approved under the county zoning ordinance. The conditional approval was subject to twelve specific conditions and required the applicant to revise and resubmit the site plan. Prior to final approval of the site plan, the zoning regulation was amended to require a special use permit for transfer stations. The court held that the requirement itself, absent a showing that the applicant was otherwise prejudiced or harmed, was not sufficient detriment to create a vested right.[190]

Phased Developments

When phased developments are involved, the common law vested right applies only to that part of the previously approved project actually underway at the time of the ordinance change, unless the expenditures cannot be divided or allocated by phases.[191]

---

188. 153 N.C. App. 218, 226–27, 569 S.E.2d 695, 701–02 (2002).

189. 100 N.C. App. 541, 397 S.E.2d 335 (1990).

190. 126 N.C. App. 168, 172, 484 S.E.2d 411, 415 (1997). See also Walton N.C., LLC v. City of Concord, 257 N.C. App. 227, 809 S.E.2d 164 (2017), *review denied*, 371 N.C. 447, 817 S.E.2d 388 (2018) (no vested right to clustered-development option where owner concedes expenditures were needed under current zoning as well as prior zoning).

191. In *Town of Midland v. Wayne*, the court upheld a finding that a vested right had been established for all three phases on a residential subdivision based on "the unified nature" of the multiphase plan that was approved and the "benefit of the expenditures [on the first two phases of the project] to the entire subdivision." 368 N.C. 55, 64, 773 S.E.2d 301, 308 (2016). By contrast, in *PEM Entities LLC v. County of Franklin*, 57 F.4th 178, 183 (2023), the court held that there were no vested rights established in all fifteen phases to a subdivision that had received preliminary

In *In re Tadlock*,[192] the owner had begun work on a mobile-home park of seventy-five units, to be built in three stages of twenty-five units each. The first stage had been surveyed, mapped, and graded, and many of its home foundations, streets, and utilities had been installed when a Charlotte zoning regulation was adopted that did not allow mobile-home parks on the site. Fourteen units were completed. There had been no actual construction in stages two and three. The court allowed completion of the remaining eleven units in phase one of the park but held as a matter of law that the vested right did not apply to the subsequent phases, even though such use had been clearly intended by the owners and the site's value for other purposes was greatly reduced. The vested right attached only to the phase of the project that had been started when the ordinance was adopted.

The court reached the same conclusion in a case involving the expansion of an automobile junkyard in *Stokes County v. Pack.* The owners had purchased ten acres in 1979 when the area was unzoned. In 1980, they cleared five acres for an automobile garage and salvage area. In 1982, they erected and began using a building for auto repairs. In March 1983, the county zoned the site for exclusive residential and agricultural use. The court ruled that with a phased development, the vested right to the project attached only to the phase substantially underway at the time of the ordinance change. Therefore, the owners were allowed to complete the salvage yard on the five cleared acres but were not allowed to extend the business to the remaining five acres.[193] This is consistent with the general rule that a nonconforming use may be completed but not expanded.[194]

What constitutes completion of a project and what constitutes a subsequent phase is a factual inquiry that must be resolved on a case-by-case basis. Actual construction is not always the controlling factor in such a determination. For example, in *Transland Properties, Inc. v. Board of Adjustment*,[195] the petitioners had substantially begun physical construction of twelve of twenty-five planned condominium buildings when the Nags Head council amended the zoning ordinance to preclude condominium use. The town revoked the building permits for the remaining thirteen units. The court, however, held that a vested right existed for all twenty-five units because all of the land had been acquired, cleared, and graded; the streets and the sidewalks for all twenty-five units had been completed; and a water and sewer system for the entire twenty-five units was underway.[196] In a similar case, *Mays-Ott Co. v. Town of Nags Head*,[197] the court ruled that since two duplexes in a three-duplex project had been completed and most common-area improvements made, a vested right had been established for the third unit. In this instance the property was rezoned to remove cottage courts as a permissible use after the owner had secured a special use permit for the three-unit project. The owner built two units and then stopped construction for a year. The special use permit expired at the end of eighteen months, after which the town refused to renew it, even though the project met all current zoning requirements (other than the cottage-court prohibition) regarding density, setbacks, lot width, and height. The court balanced the harm to the owner of not being allowed to proceed (a loss of $256,000) against the benefit to the town of compliance and allowed the project to be completed.

---

approval but not the required final approval nor any building or construction permits. The court emphasized that expenditures made before the issuance of required approvals are not made in reliance on a valid approval. However, see the discussion in Chapter 7 regarding the binding nature of local government approval of a "preliminary" plat.

192. 261 N.C. 120, 134 S.E.2d 177 (1964). Nearly fifty years later, the mobile homes that had been placed on site as a lawful nonconformity remained, while the remainder of the site was either vacant or developed with site-built single-family homes.

193. 91 N.C. App. 616, 372 S.E.2d 726 (1988), *review denied*, 324 N.C. 117, 377 S.E.2d 246 (1989).

194. *In re* Hastings, 252 N.C. 327, 113 S.E.2d 433 (1960).

195. 18 N.C. App. 712, 198 S.E.2d 1 (1973).

196. *Id.*, 198 S.E.2d 1. An approved plan that shows sections does not in itself create a phased development unless the property is actually being developed in separate stages. *In re* Campsites Unlimited, Inc., 287 N.C. 493, 215 S.E.2d 73 (1975).

197. 751 F. Supp. 82 (E.D.N.C. 1990). In this federal-district-court opinion, state law on vested rights was applied.

Duration

There is no case law in North Carolina as to the duration of a common law vested right.

They likely do not have perpetual life, however. By analogy, most ordinances provide that nonconforming status is lost with a period of disuse,[198] and the courts have uniformly upheld those limits. If holders of vested rights do not exercise reasonable due diligence in pursuing those rights, it is likely that they eventually expire, though not at an express predetermined date as is the case with the statutory vested rights, discussed above.[199] Cases in other states have applied varying time limits for permissible reliance on common law vested rights, ranging from a few months to decades.[200]

Ordinance Provisions

A land use ordinance can provide by its own terms that an amendment applies prospectively. This can be done by stipulating an effective date sometime after the amendment is adopted or by stipulating that the amendment applies only to applications received after a certain date.[201]

Northwestern Financial Group, Inc. v. County of Gaston provides an example of this situation.[202] Gaston County adopted a mobile-home-park ordinance effective July 1986. An updated version of the ordinance was adopted effective September 1987. Under the updated ordinance, plans submitted before the effective date of the new ordinance were to be considered under the old ordinance. The court held that a plan submitted before the effective date of the amendments must be considered under the old ordinance, a right that was not waived by the subsequent submittal of plan revisions made in response to or at the request of regulatory review agencies.

A similar rule may be established by local custom even when it is not explicitly stated in the ordinance. In *Woodlief v. Mecklenburg County*,[203] the county issued a floodlands-development permit, discovered a mistake had been made in the permit review, revoked the permit, and required the owner to submit a revised application with a new flood study. The county advised the owner that the revision would be considered under the terms of the ordinance in effect at the time of the original application, not the revised ordinance adopted in the period between the original decision and submission of the revised application. A neighbor challenged this determination. The court held that the county's longstanding practice of considering permit revisions under the original ordinance unless the ordinance specifically provides otherwise applied.

---

198. Termination of a nonconformity due to abandonment, discontinuance, or cessation of use is discussed in Chapter 20. Also, once work is commenced under a statutory vested right, the statutory vesting expires if work is intentionally and voluntarily discontinued for twenty-four months unless the statute provides a longer vesting period. G.S. 160D-108(d).

199. The court in *Mays-Ott Co. v. Town of Nags Head*, 751 F. Supp. 82, 87 (E.D.N.C. 1990), suggested that the owner must be afforded a reasonable amount of time to complete a project.

200. *See, e.g.*, Whitehead Oil Co. v. City of Lincoln, 245 Neb. 660, 515 N.W.2d 390 (1994) (vested right retained after eighteen years of inactivity when subsequent zoning amendment is arbitrary); AWL Power, Inc. v. City of Rochester, 148 N.H. 603, 608–09, 813 A.2d 517, 523 (2002) (rights permanently vested when development was substantially completed but then delayed due to economic downturn); Fountain Vill. Dev. Co. v. Multnomah Cnty., 176 Or. App. 213, 221, 31 P.3d 458, 462 (2001) (upholding treatment of vested right same as nonconformity under county ordinance and thus subject to being lost upon two years of inactivity).

201. As a practical matter, the permit-choice rule discussed above now largely resolves most similar situations.

202. 329 N.C. 180, 405 S.E.2d 138 (1991).

203. 176 N.C. App. 205, 625 S.E.2d 904, *review denied*, 360 N.C. 492, 632 S.E.2d 775 (2006).

It is also not uncommon for local ordinances to include an expiration period for development approvals. State law provides that if work is not commenced under a building permit within six months, the permit expires. A number of local governments have similar provisions for various local approvals, particularly special use permits. G.S. 160D-403(c) now provides that local approvals have a one-year duration unless a different time is specified by statute or ordinance. Compliance with the terms of those limitations (such as commencing work within the mandated period) is required to secure a vested right under those permits.

CHAPTER 20

Nonconformities

Nonconformities are those land uses, structures, or lots that were legal when established but do not conform to the requirements of subsequently adopted or amended land use regulations. An action that is initiated in violation of an ordinance does not enjoy nonconforming status. A violation of the ordinance does not ripen into a lawful nonconformity with the passage of time.[1]

While not required by state statute,[2] from the outset most zoning regulations contained provisions to allow for the continuance of nonconformities.[3] Such provisions are also relatively common in other land-development regulations.

A use is not always required to be in operation to acquire nonconforming status. For example, in *Randolph County v. Coen*,[4] the court noted that before the effective date of the ordinance, the owners had formed a partnership for the business; cleared the site; installed a small utility building, mailbox, and sign at the site; and secured the required business licenses and some vehicles for sale; therefore, they had established a lawful nonconforming heavy-equipment-sales use even though no actual on-site sales had been made. This case illustrates also the rather gray boundary between vested-rights cases and nonconforming-use cases.

Whether or not a use was in existence before an ordinance was passed is a factual matter to be determined on a case-by-case basis. The initial determination is made by the zoning administrator,

---

1. *See, e.g.*, Overton v. Camden Cnty., 155 N.C. App. 391, 396–97, 574 S.E.2d 157, 161–62 (2002). A landowner brought in a used manufactured-housing unit without securing either a building permit or the required conditional use permit under zoning. The court held that since the use was not "otherwise lawful" when it was established, it did not have nonconforming-use status under the new ordinance.

2. Neither the Standard State Zoning Enabling Act nor the North Carolina zoning-enabling statutes have any provisions regarding nonconformities. Statutes in several other states do mandate some protection of nonconformities. *See, e.g.*, Ky. Rev. Stat. Ann. § 100.253; N.H. Rev. Stat. Ann. § 674:19; N.J. Stat. Ann. § 40:55D-68; Or. Rev. Stat. § 215.130(5). The vested rights statute (Chapter 160D, Section 108 of the North Carolina General Statutes (hereinafter G.S.) provides that "the statutory vesting period granted by this section for a nonconforming use of property shall expire if the use is intentionally and voluntarily discontinued for a period of not less than 24 consecutive months." While this provision does not directly affect limits on nonconformities in local development regulations, it may on occasion limit their application. Most existing nonconforming uses are not initiated with a statutory vested right or an application of the permit-choice rule, as development pursuant to those rights must conform to the terms of approval. However, if a zoning regulation changes the permitted uses in a way that affects a use with a statutory vested right that becomes nonconforming as a result of the change, this provision for a twenty-four-month cessation of use may apply.

3. *See, e.g., In re* W.P. Rose Builders' Supply Co., 202 N.C. 496, 163 S.E. 462 (1932). The Goldsboro zoning ordinance involved in this case exempted projects if they were already in existence or if permits had been issued for them and construction had commenced within ninety days of the effective date of the zoning ordinance. The court ruled that placement of a grease dispenser and goods to be sold constituted "starting" a gasoline filling station. Some early zoning cases held retroactive application of zoning restrictions to be invalid. *See, e.g.*, Jones v. City of L.A., 211 Cal. 304, 295 P. 14 (1930).

4. 99 N.C. App. 746, 394 S.E.2d 256 (1990).

with appeals considered in a quasi-judicial hearing by the board of adjustment.[5] The burden of proof is on the person asserting the right to maintain the nonconformity.[6]

85° & Sunny, LLC v. Currituck County[7] is illustrative of the process followed to address the factual determinations that must be made in these cases. The case involved a nonconforming RV park that had been initiated prior to the adoption of county zoning, so there was no site plan or development details submitted to secure approval prior to operation of the park. When a new owner of the park proposed to expand it and add amenities, the zoning administrator made a determination that the number of RV sites and tent campsites in existence at the time of the expansion of the nonconforming park was prohibited. The board of adjustment conducted an evidentiary hearing on the appeal of this determination and upheld the administrator's determination. The evidence presented included site plans submitted with applications for two special-event permits to hold concerts at the campground, as well as testimony from the zoning administrator who had conducted a site inspection, neighbors, previous property owners, site managers, and persons who had performed maintenance work there. The court held that there was substantial evidence in the hearing record to support the board's decision.[8]

On the other hand, whether a use was lawful under the regulations in effect at the time it was initiated or prior to the amendment that made the use unlawful is a question of law. As with interpretation of limits on nonconformities, any ambiguity on this question is resolved in favor of the free use of property. In *Frazier v. Town of Blowing Rock*,[9] for example, the plaintiff owned a property in a residential zoning district that was used for short-term rentals. Beginning in 1984, the town's zoning regulation limited "tourist homes and other temporary residences renting by the day or week" to nonresidential zoning districts. In 2019 and 2020, the regulations were amended to define "short-term rental of a dwelling unit" and to allow these only in a short-term-rental overlay district. The court held that the regulation of short-term rentals prior to 2020 was ambiguous as to whether the restrictions on the location of tourist homes included short-term rentals. The two uses are substantially similar but different. As ambiguities are to be resolved in favor of the free use of property, as a matter of law the short-term-rental use must be considered a lawful nonconformity.

Options

Given prior court cases requiring uniform treatment of existing and future land uses, the framers of early zoning ordinances were faced with a considerable dilemma. If they had required all land uses to be brought into compliance immediately, the economic costs and the political outcry might well have doomed zoning before it got started. On the other hand, if they had left nonconforming uses in place,

---

5. Ornoff v. City of Durham, 221 N.C. 457, 20 S.E.2d 380 (1942); *In re* Pine Hill Cemeteries, 219 N.C. 735, 15 S.E.2d 1 (1941). Massachusetts has a statute that addresses the sometimes-challenging evidentiary issue of establishing nonconforming status. If a structure has been erected or altered for at least ten years and no notice of zoning violation has been issued in that time, the structure is deemed to be a lawful nonconformity. MASS. GEN. LAWS ch. 40A, § 7.

6. In an enforcement case, the local government has the initial burden of showing the use or structure to be in violation of applicable regulations. Once that is done, the burden shifts to the alleged violator to establish a legal nonconforming status or other affirmative defense. Shearl v. Town of Highlands, 236 N.C. App. 113, 118, 762 S.E.2d 877, 882 (2014).

7. 279 N.C. App. 1, 864 S.E.2d 742, *review denied*, ___ N.C. ___, 865 S.E.2d 858 (2021).

8. A reviewing court applies the whole-record test to review an error of law (here, the allegation that the administrator's decision was arbitrary and capricious). Even if there is conflicting evidence presented, the court must confirm the board's findings of fact where there is substantial evidence in the record to support it. While the court must consider contradictory evidence, the reviewing court is not allowed to replace the board's judgment as between two reasonably conflicting views.

9. ___ N.C. App. ___, 882 S.E.2d 91 (2022).

they would have faced potential invalidation of the ordinance by the courts as well as an ineffectual new zoning ordinance. After all, if a city government has decided that future industries should not be located in residential areas, how can it ignore an existing factory located in a residential neighborhood?

Three main alternatives emerged to address this issue. The first required that nonconforming uses immediately be terminated or brought into compliance. For example, an industrial operation in a residential area might be required to cease operations even if that meant closing the plant. This option is not always practical or necessary, and immediate compliance can have a harsh impact on landowners who started their land use in an entirely lawful fashion. These concerns led to the second option—allowing nonconformities to continue to operate under the old rules but limiting any future expansion of that use (often referred to as "grandfathering"[10] the nonconformity).[11] This option, however, can not only leave important public interests unmet but also create inequities for landowners. For example, the proprietor of a new business that has to comply with a restrictive sign ordinance may feel at a competitive disadvantage with businesses that have older, large signs. A third option, amortization, emerged to address this situation. Under amortization, landowners are required to come into compliance with the new standards but are granted a set grace period during which they are allowed to keep their nonconformities so as to recoup much of their investment and plan for an orderly transition to the new requirements. There are other options, such as declaring nonconformities to be nuisances or using the power of eminent domain to condemn nonconformities, but these provisions are rarely used in a land use–law context.

As a general proposition, the law does not favor nonconformities,[12] for they are contrary to the general principle that if a regulation is necessary to protect the public health, safety, and welfare, it should be applied uniformly to all citizens. Therefore, the law has assumed that eventual conformance will be secured as nonconformities are gradually phased out through natural decline, decay, and abandonment. There is a tension, however, between this principle and the principle that restrictions on the use of private property should be construed to favor the free use of property. This tension has been a factor in several cases in which undefined restrictions must be interpreted, as in cases involving the resumption of nonconforming uses.

Immediate Termination

There is no absolute legal right to the continuation of a nonconformity. When public-health-and-safety considerations warrant, local regulations have long required certain noxious nonconformities to be terminated. In 1908, the North Carolina Supreme Court upheld an Edenton ordinance that required nonconforming awnings overhanging sidewalks to be removed because they were hazardous and

---

10. The term *grandfathering prior nonconformities* typically is used to describe ordinance provisions allowing the continuation of nonconformities. The term *grandfathering* originated in the former constitutional provisions adopted by southern states after the Civil War to disenfranchise African American voters while allowing illiterate white voters to remain on the rolls. The North Carolina constitution included provisions from 1868 until 1970 that made literacy a precondition to voting but exempted those who were lineal descendants of someone eligible to vote in 1867. N.C. Const. of 1868 art. VI, § 4. Thus, if a person's grandfather could have voted in 1866, that person could vote even if he or she was illiterate.

11. The local government interest in addressing the harmful impacts of continuing nonconformities is long-standing. *See, e.g.*, Am. Soc'y of Plan. Officials, *Elimination of Non-Conforming Uses* (Planning Advisory Serv. Information Report No. 2, May 1949).

12. JWL Invs., Inc. v. Guilford Cnty. Bd. of Adjustment, 133 N.C. App. 426, 430, 515 S.E.2d 715, 718 (1999), *review denied*, 251 N.C. 715, 540 S.E.2d 349 (2000); CG & T Corp. v. Bd. of Adjustment of Wilmington, 105 N.C. App. 32, 39, 411 S.E.2d 655, 659 (1992); Forsyth Cnty. v. Shelton, 74 N.C. App. 674, 676, 329 S.E.2d 730, 733, *review denied*, 314 N.C. 328, 333 S.E.2d 484 (1985); Appalachian Poster Advert. Co. v. Zoning Bd. of Adjustment, 52 N.C. App. 266, 278 S.E.2d 321 (1981).

aesthetically unpleasing.[13] In 1927, an ordinance was upheld that required existing markets selling meat or seafood in the Winston-Salem central business district to be closed, with the businesses having the option of relocating to a public market or leaving the central portion of town.[14] In these and similar situations[15] where prior lawful land uses were deemed to be public-safety problems, the courts have allowed regulations to compel that the uses be terminated or brought into conformance with the new requirements. Similar requirements in other states have been upheld by the U.S. Supreme Court. For example, the Court has upheld land use regulations that require terminating land uses when residential development of surrounding areas makes continuation of the uses harmful to neighbors.[16]

A series of five cases beginning in the late 1920s and involving gasoline filling stations raised the possibility that prohibition of nonconforming uses might be constitutionally required. In these cases, the court ruled that a general-police-power ordinance that treated existing and proposed land uses differently was illegal.

In the first case, *Town of Clinton v. Standard Oil Co.*, the contested ordinance said that "no more" filling stations could be built in the fire district, but it allowed six existing stations to remain in operation.[17] Citing the constitutional admonition regarding frequent recurrence to fundamental principles[18] and the constitutional prohibition of monopolies,[19] the court in 1927 invalidated the ordinance for failing to apply uniformly to existing and proposed businesses. Two years later, in *MacRae v. City of Fayetteville*,[20] the court invalidated an ordinance prohibiting filling stations from locating within 250 feet of a residence because the ordinance included a provision that it should "not apply to any service stations already established, and to the erection of any stations where a permit has already been issued by the city." The record showed that this exception for nonconforming uses had allowed twenty-three existing stations to remain in operation. The court therefore invalidated the ordinance for failure to be

---

13. Small v. Councilmen of Edenton, 146 N.C. 527, 60 S.E. 413 (1908). Chief Justice Walter Clark took an expansive view of the local government's police power to require the removal of nonconformities, holding that this was a policy decision for the town, not a legal issue for the courts:

> The ordinance was within the powers of the governing board of the town, and was properly held by his honor to be reasonable. If it does not meet the approval of the citizens of the town, they can secure its repeal by instructing their town council to that effect, or by electing a new board. Such local matters are properly left to the people of a self-governing community to be decided and determined by them for themselves, and not by a judge or court for them.

Id. at 528, 60 S.E. at 414.

14. Angelo v. City of Winston-Salem, 193 N.C. 207, 136 S.E. 489, *aff'd*, 274 U.S. 725 (1927).

15. *See also* State v. Perry, 151 N.C. 661, 65 S.E. 915 (1909); State v. Pendergrass, 106 N.C. 664, 10 S.E. 1002 (1890).

16. Goldblatt v. Hempstead, 369 U.S. 590 (1962) (closing mining operation); Hadacheck v. Sebastian, 239 U.S. 394 (1915) (closing brickyard); Reinman v. City of Little Rock, 237 U.S. 171 (1915) (closing livery stable). The Supreme Court has long held that regulation of preexisting businesses, as well as land uses, to prevent harm to neighbors and the public is proper and does not violate due process. Miller v. Schoene, 276 U.S. 272 (1928) (upholding destruction of diseased ornamental trees to protect neighboring apple orchards); Pierce Oil Corp. v. City of Hope, 248 U.S. 498 (1919) (upholding removal of preexisting oil-storage tanks near residences); Mugler v. Kansas, 123 U.S. 623 (1887) (upholding outlawing of use of brewery equipment after prohibition). See Chapter 24 for a discussion of the takings implications of these regulations.

17. 193 N.C. 432, 137 S.E. 183 (1927). The court had previously ruled that filling stations were not a nuisance per se. Hanes v. Carolina Cadillac Co., 176 N.C. 350, 97 S.E. 162 (1918). The court had also held that building regulations had to establish a uniform rule of action applicable to all structures, whether new, existing, or underway. State v. Tenant, 110 N.C. 609, 14 S.E. 387 (1892).

18. N.C. Const. art. I, § 35.

19. N.C. Const. art. I, § 34. The prohibition against exclusive or separate emoluments or privileges, N.C. Const. art. I, § 32, could be cited also as a limitation on disparate treatment for nonconforming uses.

20. 198 N.C. 51, 150 S.E. 810 (1929).

"uniform, fair and impartial."[21] In another 1929 case, *Burden v. Town of Ahoskie*,[22] the court invalidated a prohibition against filling stations, dance halls, pool halls, and carnivals being located within 300 feet of the town's school because the prohibition included a provision that allowed two existing nonconforming filling stations to remain for six months. The court struck the ordinance down because allowing a nonconforming use to remain even temporarily required that permits be issued for similar uses.

Rulings in two cases decided the following year upheld ordinances that addressed this problem by requiring all nonconforming filling stations to be closed. In *Town of Wake Forest v. Medlin*, the court upheld requiring a filling station that had been legally operating for twenty-five years to be closed in compliance with the new ordinance.[23] A similar result was reached in *State v. Moye*,[24] which involved an Ahoskie ordinance that prohibited any filling station within 150 feet of the town's school.

Thus, at the time that zoning ordinances were first being adopted in North Carolina in the late 1920s and early 1930s, courts were applying a principle that police-power ordinances could not exempt pre-existing uses while prohibiting similar new uses and that ordinances adopted to protect public health and safety were to be applied uniformly to both existing and future land uses of the same type. After new regulations were adopted, existing nonconformities were to be terminated if their continuation posed a significant threat to the public health and safety.

Authority to Allow Continuation

Zoning ordinances were initially being adopted in a number of North Carolina municipalities during the time when the five filling station cases were being decided, so the question naturally arose whether the provisions of zoning regulations that allowed continuation of nonconformities within limits would withstand the same constitutional scrutiny that earlier had led to the invalidation of the filling-station ordinances.

The question was resolved quickly. In *Elizabeth City v. Aydlett*,[25] the landmark 1931 case upholding zoning in North Carolina, the court distinguished a comprehensive zoning regulation from a special-purpose ordinance dealing with one use, such as filling stations, and permitted comprehensive zoning ordinances to allow retention of nonconforming uses.

In this instance the property on which the landowner wanted to locate a filling station had been placed by the city in a business zoning district that did not allow filling stations. Four existing stations

---

21. *Id.* at 55, 150 S.E. at 811.

22. 198 N.C. 92, 150 S.E. 808 (1929).

23. 199 N.C. 83, 154 S.E. 29 (1930). The ordinance in question divided the town into two parts and allowed filling stations in the business section but prohibited them in the residential section.

24. 200 N.C. 11, 156 S.E. 130 (1930), *appeal dismissed*, 283 U.S. 810 (1931).

25. 201 N.C. 602, 161 S.E. 78 (1931). After losing in the state supreme court, the landowner in this case was able to secure local legislation amending the city zoning regulation to allow his proposed filling station. S.L. 1933-263. A small station was built, initially sharing the lot with an existing residence. The gas station operated for many years with several substantial structural replacements and improvements over the decades. After the gas station closed, the structure remained in commercial use, eventually becoming a coffee shop. See DAVID W. OWENS, INTRODUCTION TO ZONING AND DEVELOPMENT REGULATION 36–39 (4th ed. 2013) for a more detailed description of the factual background of this landmark zoning case. Early zoning cases in other jurisdictions reached similar conclusions allowing differential treatment for preexisting nonconformities. *See, e.g.*, Zahn v. Bd. of Pub. Works, 195 Cal. 497, 234 P. 388 (1925), *aff'd*, 274 U.S. 325 (1927).

In 1931, in *Elizabeth City v. Aydlett*, the court upheld a zoning-ordinance prohibition against future filling stations in residential districts, but existing stations were allowed to remain. Two years later, however, the owner of this site got local legislation passed to allow the construction of the station, which was later reconstructed and operated for many years.

in that district were allowed to continue to operate as nonconforming uses. The court recognized the necessity of allowing the continuance of nonconforming uses if zoning was to work:

> Unless the theory of nonconforming uses is practically applied, it will be well-nigh impossible to zone the cities and towns of the state. It is an almost invariable rule to find a filling station in that part of a town or city which in the interest of the public welfare should, under the zoning system, be devoted to other uses. If the ordinance destroys an existing business, it is retroactive; if it cannot be enforced because such business exists, zoning as a practical matter is not possible.[26]

The court noted that as cities grew and changed, the police power had to be allowed to address changing needs: "The police power is not static. It expands to meet conditions which necessarily change as business progresses and civilization advances."[27] The court emphasized that zoning involved a consideration of the needs of the community as a whole and a balancing of the future needs of the public against the rights of the individual with a prior nonconforming use. Thus, the court allowed zoning ordinances to discriminate between existing and future uses.

Allowing nonconforming uses to continue under newly adopted zoning requirements was so well accepted by 1949 that Justice Sam Ervin Jr. dismissed in a single sentence a contention that it was unlawful discrimination: "[A nonconforming use exemption] has a sound basis and is not unreasonable."[28]

For years this authority to allow continuation of prior nonconforming land uses was allowed only for zoning regulations; the court continued to require uniformity for general-police-power ordinances.[29] The courts, however, have over time allowed land use ordinances other than zoning to provide for the continuation of nonconforming uses. In *Grace Baptist Church v. City of Oxford*,[30] the court applied a

---

26. *Aydlett*, 201 N.C. at 608, 161 S.E. at 81. *See also* Grace Baptist Church v. City of Oxford, 320 N.C. 439, 358 S.E.2d 372 (1987) (zoning ordinance could require new parking lots to be paved while allowing preexisting lots to remain unpaved).

27. *Aydlett*, 201 N.C. at 605, 161 S.E. at 79.

28. Kinney v. Sutton, 230 N.C. 404, 411, 53 S.E.2d 306, 311 (1949). *See also* CMH Mfg., Inc. v. Catawba Cnty., 994 F. Supp. 697, 701 (W.D.N.C. 1998). The court upheld without comment a zoning requirement establishing manufactured-home appearance standards that exempted mobile homes already in the county, including unsold units within the inventories of local manufactured-housing dealers.

29. For example, in 1938 an ordinance regulating the location of filling stations that was not adopted as part of the local zoning ordinance and that was not uniformly applied to existing and future uses was invalidated in *Shuford v. Town of Waynesville*, 214 N.C. 135, 198 S.E. 585 (1938).

30. 320 N.C. 439, 358 S.E.2d 372. This case involved a dispute over whether the church would have to pave its new parking lot if other churches' preexisting parking lots were allowed to remain unpaved.

standard equal-protection analysis to the nonconforming-use question, holding that because a provision of the ordinance applied with equal force to all who established a land use after the effective date of the zoning regulation, no violation of the equal-protection clause had resulted as prior nonconforming uses were differently situated. *Summey Outdoor Advertising, Inc. v. County of Henderson* followed this same line of analysis for a sign ordinance that had not been adopted as part of a comprehensive zoning ordinance.[31] In its analysis the court emphasized that judicial review of classifications of land uses for different treatment (such as different treatment of preexisting and future land uses) should be based on the reasonableness of the classification[32] and the legitimacy of the public objectives. The adult-business-location ordinance upheld in *Maynor v. Onslow County*,[33] which was adopted as a general-police-power ordinance, allowed a preexisting nonconforming business to continue for two years before coming into compliance.

These considerations, rather than the specific authority under which an ordinance was adopted (the general police power or the specific police power of zoning), are the critical factors in review of the constitutionality of provisions regarding continuation of nonconformities.

Limits on Continuation

A hallmark of early development regulations that allowed nonconformities to remain was the inclusion of restrictions designed to phase out the nonconformities through obsolescence. Several early cases regarding the repair and improvement of structures subject to fire-protection ordinances illustrate the principle. In 1894, the court upheld an ordinance prohibiting the repair of a wooden building that had been partially destroyed by fire in a district where the city of Winston's fire code would not allow new wooden buildings.[34] In 1913, the court upheld a Lincolnton ordinance prohibiting the installation of metal roofs on wooden buildings in the fire district.[35] The court acknowledged that a metal roof would provide greater protection from fire but also noted that it would prolong the life of a nonconforming wooden building and thus could be prohibited. In the court's opinion, allowing substantial repairs to a nonconforming use would defeat the object of the ordinance,

> which is not only to prohibit the building of wooden buildings within the prescribed limits, but which, though not requiring the pulling down of the wooden buildings now within the limits, prohibits their repair in order to prevent their indefinite continuance . . . . [T]his does not prohibit slight repairs, such as putting in broken windows, or hanging a shutter, or fixing up the steps. But it does prohibit such repair, as in this case, of putting on a new roof, which makes the

---

31. 96 N.C. App. 533, 386 S.E.2d 439 (1989), *review denied*, 326 N.C. 486, 392 S.E.2d 101 (1990). The ordinance regulated off-premise advertising that was larger than fifteen square feet. The applicant was denied permits for twelve new signs and had thirty-two nonconforming signs. The court noted, "[W]hile it may have been more desirable and better planning for defendant to adopt a county-wide zoning ordinance, the fact that defendant did not do so does not preclude defendant from regulating outdoor advertising" under the general police power. *Id.* at 538, 386 S.E.2d at 443. *See generally* Lathan v. Zoning Bd. of Adjustment, 69 N.C. App. 686, 317 S.E.2d 733 (1984).

32. For an example of a police-power regulation that was invalidated because it lacked a reasonable basis for such a classification, see *State v. Glidden Co.*, 228 N.C. 664, 46 S.E.2d 860 (1948). This case invalidated a state stream-protection law that allowed companies chartered before a set date to discharge deleterious substances into the water.

33. 127 N.C. App. 102, 488 S.E.2d 289, *appeal dismissed*, 347 N.C. 268, 493 S.E.2d 458, *review denied*, 347 N.C. 400, 496 S.E.2d 385 (1997).

34. State v. Johnson, 114 N.C. 846, 19 S.E. 599 (1894). The court commented on the power to prohibit new construction unless it met the fire code and continued, "[I]t is not unreasonable to require a new roof to be made of material less liable to combustion, or to forbid the repairs altogether when the damage to the building is serious." *Id.* at 849, 19 S.E. at 600.

35. State v. Lawing, 164 N.C. 492, 80 S.E. 69 (1913).

building habitable, and thereby insures its continuance. This is contrary to the spirit and the letter of the ordinance, and defeats its purpose, which is to permit only brick, concrete, or stone buildings to be erected, and contemplates the discontinuance of wooden buildings as fast as they become by decay unfit for further use or habitation.[36]

Similarly, in 1914, the court upheld a Hertford ordinance that prohibited repair of wooden buildings that had been damaged by more than one-third.[37]

Although virtually all zoning ordinances allow continuation of nonconformities, the vast majority of ordinances substantially restrict them to encourage eventual compliance with the ordinance.[38]

Typical restrictions on nonconforming uses are those prohibiting or limiting (1) their expansion or enlargement, (2) their repair or replacement, (3) changes in nonconforming uses, and (4) their resumption after being abandoned or discontinued for a specified period.[39]

The exact scope of these restrictions has proven to be particularly controversial, however, as is indicated by extensive litigation on this issue. Over the years tension has developed between the principle of eventually bringing all uses into compliance through the gradual elimination of nonconforming uses[40] and the principle of construing government restrictions on the use of private property to favor the free use of property.[41] This tension has led to increased uncertainty for both local governments and landowners about the interpretation of restrictions on continuation of nonconforming uses. The resolution is that restrictions on nonconforming uses and structures are upheld, but they must be stated clearly, and if there is any doubt about their application, they are resolved in favor of the landowner.

The scope of restrictions on nonconformities must be determined by the precise wording of the individual ordinance. As the court has noted in interpreting a nonconforming-use provision, "We must keep in mind that we are here concerned with the meaning of this particular ordinance provision, . . . not with general and divergent views as to what such exemptive provisions as to non-conforming uses in zoning ordinances should contain. Our function is to interpret . . . , not to legislate."[42] Caution must therefore be exercised in making generalizations based on these cases, as the exact wording of the restrictions involved varies.[43]

---

36. *Id.* at 496, 80 S.E. at 71.

37. State v. Shannonhouse, 166 N.C. 241, 80 S.E. 881 (1914). A few years later, the general statutes were amended specifically to authorize a prohibition against the repair of nonconforming structures in fire districts. S.L. 1917-136.

38. An early zoning text noted in this regard, "Zoning has sought to safeguard the future, in the expectation that time will repair the mistakes of the past." Edward M. Bassett, Zoning 105 (1940). Experience indicates that this optimistic expectation is often not met in practice. For a listing and analysis of the limits on nonconformities included in North Carolina zoning ordinances of the early 1950s, see Philip P. Green, Jr., Zoning in North Carolina 163–70 (1952).

39. See Michael B. Brough, The Nonconforming Use in North Carolina Zoning Law: Text and Model Ordinance 14–19 (1976), for examples of such limitations.

40. *See, e.g.,* Jirtle v. Bd. of Adjustment, 175 N.C. App. 178, 181, 622 S.E.2d 713, 715 (2005) (nonconformities not favored under state's public policy); Huntington Props., LLC v. Currituck Cnty., 153 N.C. App. 218, 223, 569 S.E.2d 695, 700 (2002) (zoning ordinances are to be strictly construed against indefinite continuation of nonconformities); Forsyth Cnty. v. Shelton, 74 N.C. App. 674, 676, 329 S.E.2d 730, 733, *review denied*, 314 N.C. 328, 333 S.E.2d 484 (1985) (zoning ordinances construed against indefinite continuation of nonconformities); Appalachian Poster Advert. Co. v. Bd. of Adjustment, 52 N.C. App. 266, 274, 278 S.E.2d 321, 326 (1981) (nonconformities not favored by the law).

41. *See, e.g.,* Atkins v. Zoning Bd. of Adjustment, 53 N.C. App. 723, 729, 281 S.E.2d 756, 759 (1981).

42. *In re* O'Neal, 243 N.C. 714, 723, 92 S.E.2d 189, 195 (1956).

43. *See, e.g.,* Four Seasons Mgmt. Servs., Inc. v. Town of Wrightsville Beach, 205 N.C. App. 65, 81–82, 695 S.E.2d 456, 466 (2010) (noting that citation to cases interpreting limitations on nonconformities is "misplaced" if there is significant difference in the language of the ordinances).

Expansion, Enlargement, and Intensification

A common restriction on nonconformities is that they not be expanded, enlarged, or intensified.[44]

Cases in this area distinguish between the completion of a valid nonconformity, which is allowed, and the expansion of a nonconformity, which is not allowed.

This distinction was first applied in *In re Hastings*.[45] The Charlotte zoning ordinance provided that nonconforming uses might "be continued, but not enlarged or extended."[46] The applicant had sixteen mobile-home sites in place when the city's zoning was first applied to the extraterritorial area in which the sites were located. The city denied approval to install additional mobile-home sites. The court held, "Whether what petitioner sought was the right to complete construction of facilities for a nonconforming use to which property had been dedicated when the ordinance took effect or was an enlargement of a subsisting nonconforming use was a question of fact to be determined by the Board of Adjustment."[47] The court went on to uphold the board's denial of permission to construct the additional sites.

In *County of Durham v. Addison*,[48] the defendant had purchased a lot and built a structure on it that served as a combination filling station, convenience store, and residence, with the intention of later building a separate structure for a residence. A well and a septic tank sufficient to serve both structures were installed. Before the second structure was built, a zoning ordinance was adopted that established minimum lot sizes and limited development to one principal use per lot. The defendant's lot was not large enough to divide and create a second lot that would meet the minimum lot size for a second structure. This suit was instituted when the defendant began construction on the second building some six and a half years after the effective date of the ordinance. The court held that denial of approval for the second structure was consistent with the ordinance limitation that allowed completion only of development that was "under construction at the time of the passage of this ordinance and the construction of which shall have been diligently prosecuted," with the entire building being completed within two years of the ordinance's effective date.[49]

The question of when the scope or size of the nonconformity may be increased without violating a prohibition on expansion of the nonconformity has been frequently litigated.

In re Tadlock[50] involved a restriction that provided, "A non-conforming open use of land shall not be enlarged to cover more land than was occupied by that use when it became nonconforming."[51] The petitioners had purchased ten acres with the intent to install a mobile-home park of seventy-five units. The construction was planned to take place in three phases of twenty-five units each. The entire site had been graded, the infrastructure for phase one had been constructed, and half of the phase-one units had been occupied when the site became subject to the zoning regulation. No construction had

---

44. "Prohibition of the expansion of a nonconforming use is lawful and consistent with good zoning practices. A county has legitimate power to regulate the extent to which nonconforming uses can be extended, expanded, and enlarged." *Huntington Props.*, 153 N.C. App. at 223, 569 S.E.2d at 699–700.

By contrast, some states have long allowed the "natural expansion" of a nonconforming commercial use so long as it is not detrimental to the public welfare, health, or safety. *See, e.g., In re* Gilfillan's Permit, 140 A. 136, 137–38 (Pa. 1927). This approach allows a business to maintain its economic viability through intensification of the use but does not allow an expansion that would constitute a substantial-enough change that it would essentially constitute a new or different use. Dipal Corp. v. Chartiers Twp. Zoning Hearing Bd., 261 A.3d 1097 (Pa. Commw. 2021) (allowing installation of seating within nonconforming convenience store).

45. 252 N.C. 327, 113 S.E.2d 433 (1960).

46. *Id.* at 328, 113 S.E.2d at 434 (quoting the Charlotte zoning ordinance).

47. *Id.* at 329, 113 S.E.2d at 434.

48. 262 N.C. 280, 136 S.E.2d 600 (1964).

49. *Id.* at 283, 136 S.E.2d at 603 (quoting the Durham zoning ordinance).

50. 261 N.C. 120, 134 S.E.2d 177 (1964). Also see the discussion of vested rights and phased developments in Chapter 19.

51. *Id.* at 123, 134 S.E.2d at 179 (quoting Charlotte zoning ordinance).

commenced on phases two and three, but they were landlocked by phase one and were of little value or use except as parts of this development. The court held that, as a matter of law, the petitioners were entitled to permits to complete phase one of the development but that nonconforming-use status did not extend to phase two or phase three.[52]

The court applied this principle of allowing completion but prohibiting expansion to an automobile salvage yard in *Stokes County v. Pack*.[53] The zoning regulation at issue here included the restriction that "[n]on-conforming uses of land shall not hereafter be enlarged or extended in any way."[54] The petitioners had purchased ten acres for an automobile salvage yard and garage. As of the effective date of the ordinance, five acres were cleared, the garage constructed, and several salvage vehicles brought onto the site. The county sought to prevent the petitioner from bringing any additional vehicles onto the site and to prevent use of the five uncleared acres for the business. The court ruled that bringing additional vehicles onto the cleared area had to be allowed as the permissible completion of a nonconforming use but that use of the additional five acres could be prohibited as an impermissible expansion of the nonconforming use.

Several cases address the issue of expansion in the context of renovations and modernization of existing nonconformities.

Kirkpatrick v. Village Council of Pinehurst[55] addressed the geographic expansion of a nonconformity in the context of "renovations" rather than initial completion or staging of a large project. The petitioner owned a nonconforming campground for recreational vehicles. The campground had some fifty sites that occupied thirteen acres within a fifty-five-acre parcel. The relevant ordinance provided that nonconforming uses must not be "enlarged or increased, nor shall any non-conforming use be extended to occupy a greater area of land" than occupied at the time it became nonconforming. The court held that this provision precluded expansion of the campground to portions of the parcel beyond the thirteen acres originally occupied and that it precluded renovations that would add additional campsites within the thirteen-acre portion of the site.

In *Huntington Properties, LLC v. Currituck County*,[56] a mobile-home park had originally been permitted for 440 rental spaces on 90 acres. However, when the park became nonconforming (and later when the plaintiff acquired title), only 140 spaces were usable due to limited wastewater-treatment capacity. The court held that only the portion of the development actually in use (the 140 spaces) constituted an existing nonconformity and that expansion beyond that number of spaces, which could be accomplished with an upgrade in the wastewater-treatment capacity, could be prohibited.

In *85° & Sunny, LLC v. Currituck County*,[57] the court reviewed a similar situation where the owner of a nonconforming RV park proposed to add RV campsites, tent camping sites, restrooms, and a pool to

52. *Id.*, 134 S.E.2d 177.

53. 91 N.C. App. 616, 372 S.E.2d 726 (1988), *review denied*, 324 N.C. 117, 377 S.E.2d 246 (1989).

54. STOKES COUNTY, N.C., ZONING ORDINANCE art. 7, § 70.1.

55. 138 N.C. App. 79, 530 S.E.2d 338 (2000). In another case, a Virginia court held that hanging an electronic message board on the front of a nonconforming billboard was an unlawful enlargement of the nonconformity. Adams Outdoor Advert., L.P. v. Bd. of Zoning Appeals, 274 Va. 189, 645 S.E.2d 271 (2007).

56. 153 N.C. App. 218, 223, 569 S.E.2d 695, 699–700 (2002).

57. 279 N.C. App. 1, 864 S.E.2d 742, *review denied*, ___ N.C. ___, 865 S.E.2d 858 (2021). As for the scope of allowed improvements, the court stated that it must consider both the specific provision in the ordinance regarding nonconforming campgrounds and the general ordinance provisions applicable to all nonconformities. The provisions should be interpreted as general and specific provisions on the same subject to be read together and harmonized where possible. To apply only the specific campground provision (not permitting additional campsites or land area devoted to campgrounds) and not apply the general limitation (not enlarging, expanding, or intensifying the nonconforming use) would be contrary to the stated purpose of the regulation to limit the continued existence of nonconformities by allowing indefinite extension of their lifespan through regular upgrading with new amenities.

a park that had been initiated prior to the adoption of county zoning. The court held that the evidence presented at the evidentiary hearing established the number of campsites in existence at the time the expansion prohibition was adopted, and that additional campsites and park amenities were prohibited.

In *Malloy v. Zoning Board of Adjustment*,[58] a nonconforming welding and gas-supply business in Asheville sought to replace a 3000-gallon aboveground liquid-oxygen-storage tank with a new 9000-gallon tank. The court held that this would constitute an unlawful expansion both because the new tank was physically larger and because it would increase the scope of the nonconforming business by allowing additional and faster service to its customers.[59] Similarly, in *APAC-Atlantic, Inc. v. City of Salisbury*,[60] the plaintiff proposed to modernize a nonconforming asphalt plant in ways that would allow a significant increase in its capacity and lower its operating costs. The court upheld a determination that this change in the scope of the use would be an impermissible enlargement of the nonconformity.

In *Land v. Village of Wesley Chapel*,[61] a nonconforming shooting range occupied two-thirds of a residential lot. The cost of improvements for construction and later reorientation of the range was $3000. The town contended that subsequent improvements in the range costing $15,000 constituted an impermissible material alteration of the nonconformity. The ordinance at the time defined "material alteration" to be a change of more than fifty percent of the replacement cost at the time of the alteration.[62] The court held that the town erred in only considering the construction costs of the shooting range and that the calculation should have included the value of the land occupied by the range.[63]

A related issue is whether the construction of new buildings associated with a nonconforming use constitutes an expansion of that use. This issue was first addressed in *In re O'Neal*,[64] a case involving a nonconforming nursing home located in a residential zoning district in Charlotte. Under the city's zoning ordinance, the lawful use of any building or land could be continued but not enlarged or extended. The ordinance allowed reconstruction of nonconforming buildings damaged by fire, explosion, flood, riot, or act of God if it was done within a year of the calamity. Because of building-code requirements for fireproofing nursing homes, the petitioners were compelled to either close the home or replace the existing frame building with a modern fireproof building. The court interpreted the ordinance as allowing reconstruction in order to comply with the building code, provided that the new building was limited to the same scale (in terms of numbers of patients served) as the structure being replaced.

Subsequent cases have limited the construction of additional or replacement buildings where that action is not mandated by law. In *Town of Newton Grove v. Sutton*,[65] the owners of a nonconforming residence in a commercial zoning district were denied approval to locate a mobile home on the site as a residence for their daughter, who had a disability. The court upheld the denial, ruling that a second residence could not be considered a "customary accessory use" and would thus be an unlawful extension

---

58. 155 N.C. App. 628, 632, 573 S.E.2d 760, 763 (2002). In *Eddins v. City of Lewiston*, 244 P.3d 174 (Idaho 2010), the ordinance allowed manufactured homes but not recreational vehicles in a manufactured-home park. The court held that the plaintiff could replace an older nonconforming vehicle with a new one as such was not a fundamental change in the use.

59. *Id.* at 632, 573 S.E.2d at 763.

60. 210 N.C. App. 668, 709 S.E.2d 390 (2011).

61. 206 N.C. App. 123, 697 S.E.2d 458 (2010).

62. VILLAGE OF WESLEY CHAPEL, N.C., LAND USE ORDINANCE § 7.3.2.

63. *Land*, 206 N.C. App. 123, 697 S.E.2d 458. Neither the frequency and duration of the use nor the net size of the shooting range increased as a result of the improvements. The estimated value of the land devoted to the shooting range was $146,000 at the time of the improvements.

64. 243 N.C. 714, 92 S.E.2d 189 (1956). *See also* Jirtle v. Bd. of Adjustment, 175 N.C. App. 178, 622 S.E.2d 713 (2005). The court held that construction of an additional building that would not increase required off-street parking was not an expansion of a nonconformity where the existing church did not meet off-street parking standards.

65. 111 N.C. App. 376, 432 S.E.2d 441, *review denied*, 335 N.C. 181, 438 S.E.2d 208 (1993).

of the nonconforming residential use. Other cases have applied this principle to limit expansion of a nonconforming private airport and a commercial agricultural business.[66] In *Four Seasons Management Services, Inc. v. Town of Wrightsville Beach*, the court held that construction of a four-story parking structure to replace a surface-parking lot at a nonconforming hotel would be an impermissible expansion of a nonconformity. The town's code expressly provided that any structural alteration or change that is voluntarily made to a nonconformity would be permissible only if the change brings the structure into complete conformity with the code.[67]

Additions to existing nonconforming buildings also may be restricted by zoning ordinances. For example, in *City of Hickory v. Machinery Co.*,[68] the defendant was not allowed to replace a nonconforming canopy with a new, larger canopy. Earlier, however, in *Clark v. Richardson*,[69] the court held that the enclosure of a porch on a nonconforming grocery store did not constitute enlargement or extension of the nonconformity. This is an area in which careful wording in a zoning ordinance is needed to clearly establish the governing board's intention. For example, if a building is nonconforming because it violates a side-yard setback, may an addition be made if the addition itself is not within the setback? Or is the addition allowed if it is within the setback but does not increase the encroachment? There is no uniform resolution to these questions in state law, so careful drafting of zoning-ordinance provisions is warranted to set forth which expansions of nonconformities are allowed.

Some ordinances explicitly prohibit the expansion of space allocated to a nonconforming use within the same building. *Fantasy World, Inc. v. Greensboro Board of Adjustment*[70] illustrates this type of restriction. Prior to enactment of restrictions on the location of adult-entertainment uses, a topless bar was operated in one portion of a building, and a restaurant was operated in another portion of the same building. After the use became nonconforming, the owner sought to use the restaurant portion of the building for lingerie sales, an adult bookstore, and an adult mini–motion picture theater. The ordinance provided that a nonconforming use could not be "enlarged, increased, or extended to occupy a greater

---

66. In *City of Brevard v. Ritter*, 14 N.C. App. 207, 188 S.E.2d 41 (1972), construction of a new pilot's lounge and airplane-storage building at a nonconforming airport in a residential district was prohibited. *Atkins v. Zoning Board of Adjustment*, 53 N.C. App. 723, 281 S.E.2d 756 (1981), involved the expansion of a commercial agricultural business. The Union County zoning ordinance at issue created two classes of nonconforming uses. Class A uses were those determined by the board of adjustment to meet several criteria, including that they did not create public health or safety threats, did not depress nearby property values, and had been lawfully established. All other uses were Class B. Less stringent restrictions were placed on the Class A uses, arguably allowing for enlargement or expansion. Class B structures and uses could not be enlarged or structurally altered. The board of adjustment granted the agricultural business Class A status and approved extra grain-drying and grain-storage facilities that had been built after the ordinance became effective but before board review (the owner had previously sought and been denied a rezoning that would have allowed the expansion). An adjacent landowner brought suit to challenge the board of adjustment's action. The court of appeals held that because the business additions had been constructed after the effective date of the ordinance, they had not been lawfully established and the board of adjustment had no authority subsequently to grant Class A status for the expansion. The court noted:

> In addition to our factual analysis, we are guided by policy considerations. That is, although zoning ordinances are "in derogation of the right of private property and provisions therein granting exemptions or permissions are to be liberally construed in favor of freedom of use," our courts have nevertheless limited the expansion of nonconforming uses with a view toward their eventual elimination.

Id. at 729, 281 S.E.2d at 759 (citation omitted). The court went on to hold that these expanded facilities could not be considered permissible accessory uses.

67. 205 N.C. App. 65, 695 S.E.2d 456 (2010). Even with the expanded parking, the hotel would still not conform with the requisite amount of off-street parking required by the ordinance. The parking structure itself did not conform to landscaping and sprinkler requirements, and the hotel had additional setback nonconformities.

68. 39 N.C. App. 236, 249 S.E.2d 851 (1978).

69. 24 N.C. App. 556, 211 S.E.2d 530 (1975).

70. 128 N.C. App. 703, 496 S.E.2d 825, *review denied*, 348 N.C. 496, 510 S.E.2d 382 (1998).

area of land or floor area than was occupied" at the time it became nonconforming.[71] Thus, the court upheld the city's denial of permission to use the remainder of the building for adult-entertainment uses.

Some ordinances distinguish between enlargement of a nonconforming use, which is generally prohibited, and intensification of the use, which may be allowed. The construction of a storage building to enclose a previously open storage area was held to be an unlawful enlargement of a nonconforming use in *Cannon v. Zoning Board of Adjustment*.[72] The Wilmington regulation at issue made it unlawful "to engage in any activity that causes an increase in the extent of nonconformity of a nonconforming situation." New structures were specifically prohibited if they would result in an "increase in the total amount of space devoted to a nonconforming use."[73] In the court's view, evidence that the previous use for open-air storage was sporadic, that it might have begun after the effective date of the ordinance, and that the site might also have been used for parking adequately supported the board of adjustment's conclusion that the enclosure would be an unlawful expansion of the nonconforming use.

A concurring opinion in *Cannon* cautioned that ordinance provisions that prohibit expansions of nonconforming uses do not automatically bar intensifications in use.[74] This point was the key issue in *Stegall v. Zoning Board of Adjustment*,[75] which directly addressed the question of when new structures become expansions rather than intensifications of nonconforming uses. The case involved a cemetery in New Hanover County that was a valid nonconforming use in a residential zoning district. The owner proposed to add an aboveground mausoleum that would entomb 180 bodies and to construct a building for administrative offices, sales, and security. At the time of the effective date of the zoning regulation, only one two-person aboveground crypt was located in the cemetery, and the sales office was off-site. The ordinance prohibited any "increase in the extent of non-conformity." However, the ordinance did allow some changes, providing that if "a non-conforming situation exists the equipment or processes may be changed if these or similar changes amount only to changes in degree of activity rather than changes in kind."[76] The court ruled that as a matter of law, aboveground burial was a fundamental aspect of a cemetery and did not constitute a change in kind of use. Therefore, the mausoleum would be not an expansion of the nonconforming use but an intensification that was allowed by the terms of the ordinance. However, the court held that construction of the office building could be prohibited as an unlawful expansion of the nonconforming use because previously there had been no sales or security office on the site.

If increases in use or intensity of use are intended to be included within the prohibited expansion of a nonconformity, the terms of the ordinance must clearly include that restriction.

---

71. Greensboro, N.C., Unified Development Ordinance § 30-4-11.2(2) (1993) (current version at Land Development Ordinance § 30-2-3.2(C) (2022)).

72. 65 N.C. App. 44, 308 S.E.2d 735 (1983).

73. Wilmington, N.C., City Zoning Ordinance §§ 13(E)(1), (5).

74. The majority rule nationally is that an increase in volume or intensity of a nonconforming use is generally not presumed to be prohibited. *See, e.g.*, DiBlasi v. Zoning Bd. of Appeals, 224 Conn. 823, 624 A.2d 372 (1993); Gordon Paving Co. v. Blaine Cnty. Bd. of Cnty. Comm'rs, 98 Idaho 730, 572 P.2d 164 (1977); Chartiers Twp. v. William M. Martin, Inc., 518 Pa. 985, 542 A.2d 985 (1988). *See generally* American Law of Zoning § 12.19(f) (5th ed., Dec. 2022 Update).

75. 87 N.C. App. 359, 361 S.E.2d 309 (1987), *review denied*, 321 N.C. 480, 364 S.E.2d 671 (1988). In *Lewis-Clark Memorial Gardens, Inc. v. City of Lewiston*, 99 Idaho 680, 587 P.2d 821 (1978), the court held that the addition of 500 aboveground crypts to a private cemetery did not constitute an enlargement of the nonconformity.

76. New Hanover County, N.C., Zoning Ordinance §§ 44-1, 44-4.

Repair and Replacement

An ordinance may limit the repair and replacement of nonconforming entities when they are substantially damaged or destroyed. Typical provisions allow repairs but prohibit replacement. A key question then becomes defining the threshold between permissible repairs and impermissible replacement. Many ordinances provide precise guidelines for this threshold, such as limiting repairs to those costing less than 50 percent of the fair-market or assessed value of a structure.

Several cases involving billboards illustrate the application of these limits. In *Appalachian Poster Advertising Co. v. Zoning Board of Adjustment*,[77] the plaintiff had two adjacent nonconforming billboards. One billboard was completely removed, and the sign face was removed from the other. After new posts were installed to replace those that had been removed, a single billboard was placed where the two smaller signs had previously been located. The Shelby zoning ordinance involved provided that nonconforming structures could be altered only when required by law, ordered by the city for safety reasons, or deemed necessary to keep the structures in sound condition. The court noted that nonconforming uses are not favored by the law and that

> [h]ere a new structure was substituted for an old one. If it is proper to do this once it will be proper to do it again and thus the life of the non-conforming structure will be indefinitely prolonged, and the whole purpose of the zoning ordinance will be defeated . . . [T]he right to make repairs has generally been limited to such as are merely routine or ordinary and which would not result in the extension of the normal life of the structure, and the replacement of a structure which has become unusable from natural deterioration has been held not permissible.[78]

A similar result obtained in *Whiteco Outdoor Advertising v. Johnston County Board of Adjustment*.[79] Here two nonconforming billboards were damaged in a windstorm, and the issue was the application of a standard prohibiting repairs to nonconformities that exceed 50 percent of their value (without specifying whether the "value" referred to original or present value). The staff denied approval for replacement based on a determination that the cost of repairs would exceed 50 percent of the original cost of erecting the signs, and the board of adjustment upheld this determination. The court affirmed, noting that, while interpretation of the ordinance is subject to de novo review on appeal, the board's interpretation of "value" was not an error of law, given the intent of the ordinance to prevent excessive repairs.[80] In *Lamar Outdoor Advertising, Inc. v. City of Hendersonville Zoning Board of Adjustment*,[81] the court upheld the board's determination that the plaintiffs had not met their burden of proof that the cost of repair was within the ordinance limits. The board properly denied approval for reconstruction in the absence of substantial evidence that the limit could be met.

A contrasting result was reached in *Appalachian Outdoor Advertising, Inc. v. Town of Boone Board of Adjustment*.[82] In this case the company had two side-by-side billboards. The structure included six

---

77. 52 N.C. App. 266, 278 S.E.2d 321 (1981).

78. *Id.* at 273–74, 278 S.E.2d at 326 (citations omitted). *See also* Pamlico Marine Co. v. N.C. Dep't of Nat. Res. & Cmty. Dev., 80 N.C. App. 201, 341 S.E.2d 108 (1986). But compare *In re Groves*, 235 N.C. 756, 71 S.E.2d 119 (1952), a per curiam opinion upholding a trial-court reversal of a board-of-adjustment decision limiting the repair of a building located in a residential area.

79. 132 N.C. App. 465, 513 S.E.2d 70 (1999).

80. *Id.* at 470–71, 513 S.E.2d at 75. The court also held that there was substantial evidence in the record to support the board's determination of the facts relative to the damage to the billboards and costs of repairs. See Chapter 15 for a more detailed discussion of evidentiary issues in quasi-judicial proceedings.

81. 155 N.C. App. 516, 522–23, 573 S.E.2d 637, 642–43 (2002). The court noted that the plaintiff's initial repair-cost estimate submitted to the town was higher than the limit allowed and that the revised submittal omitted several critical components of the cost of repair.

82. 128 N.C. App. 137, 493 S.E.2d 789 (1997), *review denied*, 347 N.C. 572, 498 S.E.2d 375 (1998).

support poles, two sign faces, and lights. A winter storm severely damaged the structure, breaking two support poles and bending one of the sign faces. The sign company proposed to replace two broken support poles and to remove, straighten, and retouch with paint the damaged sign face. The estimated cost of this work was $255; the assessed value of the signs was $2607. The town prohibited the work as "reconstruction" of a nonconforming sign. On appeal, the court ruled that since the billboard had been damaged but not destroyed, the proposed work was repair rather than reconstruction. As the ordinance allowed repair up to 50 percent of the market value of a structure, the court ruled the work permissible.

Lathan v. Zoning Board of Adjustment provides a reminder that the scope of permissible repair and replacement of nonconformities is determined by the terms of an individual ordinance rather than by general principles of law.[83] In this case a landowner proposed to replace a dilapidated building in a nonconforming lumberyard. The Union County zoning regulation allowed the board of adjustment to permit "additional structures to be built on the lot within which the nonconforming use [could] be enlarged."[84] The court held that the authority given to the board of adjustment by the zoning-enabling act to grant special exceptions[85] included the authority to allow repair and replacement of nonconforming uses.

Change in Use

Zoning ordinances may prohibit the change of one nonconforming use to a different nonconforming use.[86] As an alternative, any change in a nonconforming use may be subject to limitations enforced through a permit-review process.[87]

The provisions noted in *Forsyth County v. York* provide an example.[88] The zoning regulation allowed the board of adjustment to issue a special use permit for a change in a nonconforming use upon a finding that the new use was "less intensive in character or essentially of the same character as the original non-conforming use."[89] The defendant owned a nonconforming automobile-repair and auto-parts business in a residential zoning district. He converted it into a business selling agricultural implements. No special use permit was sought. The court held that the county was entitled to summary judgment on the facts. The defendant could not claim in this enforcement action that he qualified for a change in nonconforming use because he had not gone through the mandated permit-application process.

A variation of the change-in-use limitation is illustrated by *NCJS, LLC v. City of Charlotte*.[90] When Charlotte amended its zoning regulation to add a requirement that dumpsters be screened on three sides, existing nonconforming dumpsters were exempted until the land and structures were "redeveloped." When the owner of a warehouse in an industrially zoned area relocated two preexisting dumpsters on the street side of the building, the city contended this was "redevelopment" that triggered the screening requirement. The court found, however, that moving a dumpster is not redevelopment of the land or structure because the dumpster was an accessory use to the structure, not a nonconforming structure itself.

---

83. 69 N.C. App. 686, 317 S.E.2d 733 (1984).

84. UNION COUNTY, N.C., ZONING ORDINANCE § 70.4(3)(b).

85. Chapter 153A, Section 345(c) of the North Carolina General Statutes (hereinafter G.S.). This terminology was deleted in 2019 when this provision was updated and recodified as G.S. 160D-705(c).

86. Burton v. Zoning Bd. of Adjustment, 49 N.C. App. 439, 271 S.E.2d 550 (1980), *cert. denied*, 302 N.C. 217, 276 S.E.2d 914 (1981). Further proceedings in this case are reported at *New Hanover County v. Burton*, 65 N.C. App. 544, 310 S.E.2d 72 (1983). Some ordinances allow changes to a less intensive use or a use of a similar character.

87. See C.R. McCorkle, Annotation, *Changes, Repairs, or Replacements in Continuation of Nonconforming Use*, 87 A.L.R.2d 4 (1963).

88. 19 N.C. App. 361, 198 S.E.2d 770, *cert. denied*, 284 N.C. 253, 200 S.E.2d 653 (1973).

89. FORSYTH COUNTY, N.C., ZONING RESOLUTION § 4(a).

90. 255 N.C. App. 72, 803 S.E.2d 684 (2017).

As a general rule, a change in ownership does not affect the right to continue a nonconformity.[91] Zoning is not a personal right and thus is unconcerned with the ownership of a use or structure.[92]

Resumption and Abandonment

Zoning regulations typically provide that nonconforming-use status is lost if that use is halted for a specified period. The most commonly used time periods range from six to twenty-four months.[93] After a use has been halted for the specified period, whatever use is taken up must comply with the zoning regulations then in effect.

In most instances the nonconforming use may be resumed within the specified period. For example, in *In re Hensley*,[94] the petitioner had a nonconforming seven-unit mobile-home park in the town of Cramerton's extraterritorial zoning jurisdiction. In June, a tenant departed, moving one of the mobile homes. In July, the petitioner sought a permit to replace the unit. As specified by the regulation, "[when a] non-conforming use has been changed to a conforming use it shall not thereafter be used for any non-conforming use."[95] The town denied the permit upon a finding by the board of adjustment that the complete removal of one mobile home converted that portion of the property to a conforming use. The court of appeals reversed, noting that, also as provided by the ordinance, "[a] non-conforming use may not be reestablished after discontinuance for a period of one hundred and eighty (180) days."[96] This provision, the court ruled, implied that a nonconforming use must be allowed to be resumed within the 180-day period.

If an ordinance is precisely drafted, however, the courts will uphold a provision that does not allow resumption of use of a vacated space in a manufactured-home park. In *Williams v. Town of Spencer*,[97] the court addressed an ordinance provision that treated each lot within a park as a separate nonconforming use and explicitly provided that after a site had been vacated, another manufactured home could not be placed on that lot. Noting the policy that nonconformities are not favored, the court held that there was a legitimate governmental interest in eventually phasing out the nonconforming park.[98]

---

91. Starlites Tech Corp. v. Rockingham County, 270 N.C. App. 71, 840 S.E.2d 231 (2020) (change in ownership of a nonconforming electronic gaming business is not a change of use as a matter of law).

92. Graham Court Assocs. v. Town Council of Chapel Hill, 53 N.C. App. 543, 281 S.E.2d 418 (1981). *See generally* 2 PATRICIA E. SALKIN, AMERICAN LAW OF ZONING § 12.18(c) (5th ed. 2008); 1 KENNETH H. YOUNG, ANDERSON'S AMERICAN LAW OF ZONING § 6.40 (4th ed. 1996); C.R. McCorkle, Annotation, *Change in Ownership of Nonconforming Business or Use as Affecting Right to Continue Thereof*, 9 A.L.R.2d 1039 (1950).

93. The vested rights statute, G.S. 160D-108(d), provides that "the statutory vesting period granted by this section for a nonconforming use of property expires if the use is intentionally and voluntarily discontinued for a period of not less than 24 consecutive months." This provision does not affect most nonconforming-use limitations in local zoning regulations as those uses typically have not been initiated with a statutory vested right. However, if a zoning regulation changes the permitted uses in a way that affects a use that was established under the old rules with a statutory vested right or through exercise of the permit-choice rule, and the previously permitted use becomes non-conforming as a result of that change, then this provision for a twenty-four-month cessation of use may apply.

94. 98 N.C. App. 408, 390 S.E.2d 727 (1990).

95. CRAMERTON, N.C., ZONING ORDINANCE art. VII, § 70.2.

96. *Id.* § 70.4.

97. 129 N.C. App. 828, 500 S.E.2d 473 (1998).

98. *Id.*, 500 S.E.2d 473. The court held that there was no unconstitutional taking here because the ordinance allowed the land occupied by the nonconforming mobile-home park to be used for any of the uses allowed in an industrial zone. *See also* Cox v. City of Sasser, 300 Ga. App. 251, 684 S.E.2d 385 (2009) (upholding decision that non-conforming manufactured home could not be replaced with larger manufactured home).

The fact that an illegal attempt has been made to convert a nonconforming use to another nonconforming use has been held not to automatically preclude an owner from reestablishing the original nonconforming use within the specified period.[99]

Cases interpreting whether nonconforming status has been lost illustrate the particular care that must be given to the precise wording of zoning provisions on nonconforming uses. Different results may obtain depending upon whether the term used is *abandonment, cessation of use,* or *discontinuance.* The question is further complicated by the fact that some ordinances use several of these characterizations and apply different consequences to each. Unless more specific definitions are provided in the ordinance, the courts have interpreted *abandonment* to mean that the use has stopped and that there is no intent to restart it in the future, *cessation* of use to mean that the use is inactive but the ability to restart it remains present, and *discontinuance* to mean that the use is not active.

At issue in *Southern Equipment Co. v. Winstead*[100] was a provision in the Mount Olive zoning regulation that provided that nonconforming-use status was lost if the use "[ceased] for any reason" for six months.[101] The plaintiff owned a nonconforming concrete-mixing facility. Because of a business slump, the plant was out of operation for more than six months but was maintained throughout the period and could have resumed operation within two hours. The court held that this was not a cessation of use. The court viewed the issue as a matter of statutory interpretation, the intent of the adopting governing board being the paramount consideration. Because the regulation specified a longer period for forfeiture of nonconforming status if the use was discontinued than if it was ceased, the court held that cessation required more than failure to operate.

Similarly, in *Flowerree v. City of Concord*,[102] the ordinance provided that a nonconforming use could not be "reused after cessation of use" for three months.[103] The plaintiff owned a nonconforming duplex in a single-family zoning district. In late January, both tenants moved out. In March, advertisements to rent both units were run but were unsuccessful in attracting new tenants. Renovations were made to both units, but they were not rented until July. The city contended that because the units had not been occupied for over three months, there had been cessation of duplex use. The court held that occupancy alone could not be used to determine the use; as long as the owner was making an attempt to use the property as a duplex (as evidenced by advertisements and renovations), there was no cessation of use.[104]

A third example is provided by *MYC Klepper/Brandon Knolls LLC v. Board of Adjustment*,[105] where the court upheld a notice of violation issued after a sign that did not conform to current rules was reestablished on the site of a former sign. The ordinance provided that nonconforming signs could not be reestablished if the use was discontinued for 60 days, and the use was also deemed discontinued if not in use for 365 days regardless of any substantial good-faith effort to reestablish the sign.

By contrast, in *Dockside Discotheque, Inc. v. Board of Adjustment*,[106] the court held that nonconforming status had been lost. Under the town's zoning regulation, nonconforming status was lost if the nonconforming activity was discontinued for a consecutive period of 180 days or was discontinued for

---

99. New Hanover Cnty. v. Burton, 65 N.C. App. 544, 310 S.E.2d 72 (1983).

100. 80 N.C. App. 526, 342 S.E.2d 524 (1986).

101. Town of Mount Olive, N.C., Zoning Ordinance § 9-3-115(a)(2).

102. 93 N.C. App. 483, 378 S.E.2d 188 (1989).

103. Concord, N.C., Zoning Ordinance § 604.22.

104. *Flowerree*, 93 N.C. App. 483, 378 S.E.2d 188. *See also* Diggs v. City of Wilson, 25 N.C. App. 464, 213 S.E.2d 443 (1975). A restaurant was being operated by the plaintiff as a nonconforming use in a residential district. The plaintiff secured a building permit to remodel the restaurant, and the permit had no time limit for the work to be completed. The restaurant was closed for thirteen months while the work was underway. The court held as a matter of law that such did not constitute discontinuance of the use.

105. 238 N.C. App. 432, 767 S.E.2d 668 (2014).

106. 115 N.C. App. 303, 444 S.E.2d 451, *review denied*, 338 N.C. 309, 451 S.E.2d 635 (1994).

any period of time without a present intention of resuming that activity. The landowner had offered topless dancing on the site on an occasional basis from 1983 through 1989, the frequency ranging from once a week at times to once every two to three months. In 1990, the zoning regulation was amended to remove adult entertainment from the zoning district involved. The court held that because adult entertainment had not been offered on site for a period of eleven months at the time the restriction was enacted, no valid nonconforming use was present.

Use of the term *abandonment* in reference to the discontinuance of a nonconforming use introduces an element of intent on the part of the owner. In *Forsyth County v. Shelton*,[107] the ordinance provided that protection was lost if the use was abandoned, *abandonment* being defined as "the voluntary discontinuance of a use, when accompanied by an intent not to reestablish such use."[108] The case involved a small lake and picnic area that for twenty years had been operated as a nonconforming commercial recreation facility in a residential zoning district. After the owner became ill, it was used as a YMCA facility for an additional four years. However, this was followed by five years during which the facility was not open to the public, though it was used by family and friends of the owner for recreational purposes. The defendant contended that there had been no abandonment of the use, citing several grounds— among them, the physical facilities had remained in place even if they were not actually in commercial use, illness had made the cessation of use involuntary, some recreational use had always been made of the property, and there had always been an intent to reopen. The court of appeals agreed that the use of the term *abandonment* required an intent not to reestablish the use but found sufficient evidence to conclude that there was an intent to forego use of the property as a commercial recreation business.

CG & T Corp. v. Board of Adjustment of Wilmington[109] addressed the complex issue of whether there can be partial discontinuance of a nonconforming use or, alternatively phrased, how a limitation is to apply to a situation that presents multiple nonconformities. The plaintiff owned an industrial facility that handled oil refining, oil storage, and the sale of refined products, all lawful nonconforming uses. Oil had not been refined on-site for several years, but it was stored on-site. An occasional sale was made, and some maintenance and security work was continued. The ordinance required a special use permit to resume any nonconforming use discontinued for 365 consecutive days. The court ruled that as defined in the ordinance, the term *discontinue* was not synonymous with the term *abandon* because intent was not a factor to be considered in the discontinuance of a use. The court then upheld the zoning-enforcement officer's determination that the facility's use as an oil refinery had been discontinued, whereas its use as an oil-storage terminal (a permitted use) had been maintained.[110]

---

107. 74 N.C. App. 674, 329 S.E.2d 730, *review denied*, 314 N.C. 328, 333 S.E.2d 484 (1985).

108. *Id.* at 677, 329 S.E.2d at 732 (quoting the Forsyth County ordinance).

109. 105 N.C. App. 32, 411 S.E.2d 655 (1992).

110. *See also* Cardwell v. Town of Madison Bd. of Adjustment, 102 N.C. App. 546, 402 S.E.2d 866 (1991). This case involved a commercial warehouse being operated as a nonconforming use in a residential zoning district. The zoning administrator, relying on definitions in the State Building Code, considered the structure to be two buildings because a fire wall separated the two parts, and he ruled that nonconforming status on one half was lost because it had been unoccupied for 180 days. The court overruled this determination, holding that the administrator should have interpreted *building* as defined by the zoning code, not by the State Building Code. The court also noted the limited relevance of a definition concerning construction to a question concerning land use.

Amortization

Concept

More than eight decades of experience with land use regulation has shown that the passage of time does not invariably lead to the elimination of nonconformities. Not only do they not fade into obsolescence, but many have proven to be remarkably resilient. Some of these nonconformities have not caused problems for communities. Others, however, have endured to the substantial detriment of surrounding neighborhoods; and in the case of nonconforming commercial uses, some have obtained a monopoly position that critics have denounced as unfair.

In an effort to deal with particularly troublesome nonconformities, especially those that are less expensive to remove, local governments have turned to the practice of amortization. Amortization allows a nonconformity to remain in use for a specified grace period after a regulation has been adopted or amended so that the owner can try to recoup much of the investment; after the grace period ends, the nonconformity is to be brought into compliance or removed, even if it is still in sound operating condition.

Amortization is not a new idea. The drafters of the original 1923 Standard State Zoning Enabling Act recognized that although zoning regulations would usually be applied prospectively, occasionally there would be the need to address an existing land use problem. Therefore, they expressly declined to include a provision eliminating the possible use of termination or amortization of nonconformities.[111] Specific authority to amortize nonconforming uses was included in local legislation for Forsyth County's zoning in 1947,[112] although it is still not explicitly mentioned in the state's zoning-enabling statutes. Even so, amortization was rarely used nationally before the 1950s and came into wide use in North Carolina only in the 1980s.[113]

Across the nation as well as in North Carolina, amortization has been applied primarily to junkyards and signs.[114] It is possible, however, to apply the concept to any nonconformity. In other parts of the country, applications have covered everything from dog kennels to establishments that offer adult entertainment.

---

111. The almost universal practice is to make zoning regulations nonretroactive. However, in the Standard State Zoning Enabling Act

> it is recognized that there may arise local conditions of a peculiar character that make it necessary and desirable to deal with some isolated case by means of a retroactive provision affecting that case only. For this reason it does not seem wise to debar the local legislative body from dealing with such a situation.

U.S. Dep't of Commerce, A Standard State Zoning Enabling Act 2 (1924). For one of the earliest proposals for use of amortization in a zoning context, see Note, *Amortization of Property Uses Not Conforming to Zoning Regulations*, 9 U. Chi. L. Rev. 477 (1942). Similar to the depreciation of capital goods, the author argued that a "useful life" could be assigned to nonconforming uses based on the investment in them and the cost of coming into compliance, with compliance to be mandated at the end of that period.

112. S.L. 1947-667, § 36. For a discussion of a proposed statute specifically authorizing amortization in North Carolina, see G. Edgar Parker, Comment, *Amortization of Nonconforming Uses*, 7 Wake Forest L. Rev. 255 (1971).

113. For a review of the amortization issue in North Carolina law, see David W. Owens, *Amortization: An Old Land-Use Controversy Heats Up*, Popular Gov't, Fall 1991, at 20. *See generally* Stephen Durden, *Sign Amortization Law: Insight into Precedent, Property, and Public Policy*, 35 Cap. U. L. Rev. 891 (2007); Joseph Michaels, *Amortization and the Constitutional Methodology for Terminating Nonconforming Uses*, 41 Urb. Law. 807 (2009).

114. In a 2005 survey of North Carolina local governments by the School of Government, 28 percent of the municipalities and 32 percent of the counties reported use of amortization. The types of nonconformities most frequently amortized were off-premise advertising signs (49 percent of those employing any amortization requirement), on-premise advertising signs (42 percent), junkyards (34 percent), and adult businesses (13 percent). David W. Owens et al., Survey of North Carolina Local Governments (2005) (unpublished data) (on file with the UNC School of Government). The survey is described in David W. Owens, Special Use Permits in North Carolina Zoning 7–8 (UNC School of Government, Special Series No. 22, Apr. 2007).

After the United States Supreme Court upheld Winston-Salem's requirement for the amortization of salvage yards in *State v. Joyner*, this site was rezoned to allow continued use of the salvage yard.

Case Law

In 1929, the Louisiana Supreme Court upheld the use of amortization by the city of New Orleans in its attempt to remove commercial uses from residential neighborhoods.[115] Courts in a vast majority of the states in which amortization requirements have been challenged have held that the use of the concept is constitutional.[116]

The North Carolina courts first considered the amortization concept in a 1974 case challenging a Winston-Salem zoning regulation that required a nonconforming building-materials salvage yard to be removed within three years.[117] The salvage-yard operator challenged the amortization requirement on two grounds: (1) that it deprived him of his property without due process of law and (2) that it constituted an unconstitutional, uncompensated taking of his property. The court upheld the concept of using amortization to remove nonconforming land uses, quoting with approval a leading zoning text's statement of the rationale behind amortization: "It is reasoned that this opportunity to continue for a limited time cushions the economic shock of the restriction, dulls the edge of popular disapproval, and improves the prospects of judicial approval."[118]

As for the two specific constitutional challenges, the court upheld amortization on both counts. On the due-process issue, the key considerations were the comprehensive nature of the zoning ordinance and the city's conscious effort to balance the burdens placed on the affected individuals against the resulting

---

115. State *ex rel.* Dema Realty Co. v. McDonald, 168 La. 172, 121 So. 613 (1929). It is unlikely that the very brief grace period allowed in this case would still be upheld because it was not based on a need to protect the public health and safety.

116. Influential early cases upholding use of amortization are *City of Los Angeles v. Gage*, 127 Cal. App. 2d 442, 274 P.2d 34 (1954), and *Harbison v. City of Buffalo*, 4 N.Y.2d 553, 176 N.Y.S.2d 598, 152 N.E.2d 42 (1958). A few states have held amortization unconstitutional. *See, e.g.*, Lamar Advert. of S. Ga., Inc. v. City of Albany, 260 Ga. 46, 389 S.E.2d 216 (1990). A substantial literature on the legal issues and cases on amortization has developed nationally. *See, e.g.*, Salkin, *supra* note 92, § 12.23; Norman Williams, Jr., American Planning Law §§ 116.01–.10 (1988); Margaret Collins, *Methods of Determining Amortization Periods for Non-Conforming Uses*, 3 Wash. U. J.L. & Pol'y 215 (2000); J.F. Ghent, Annotation, *Validity of Provisions for Amortization of Nonconforming Uses*, 22 A.L.R.3d 1134 (1968).

117. State v. Joyner, 286 N.C. 366, 211 S.E.2d 320, *appeal dismissed*, 422 U.S. 1002 (1975). The case is reviewed at Allen Holt Gwyn, Case Note, *The Future of Amortization as an Effective Zoning Tool in North Carolina*, 11 Wake Forest L. Rev. 754 (1975).

118. *Joyner*, 286 N.C. at 373, 211 S.E.2d at 324 (quoting 1 Robert M. Anderson, American Law of Zoning § 6.65 (1968)).

public good. The court concluded that the amortization requirement did not violate due process because it was not unreasonable and was substantially related to valid government objectives. In considering the taking claim, the court noted the earlier filling-station cases in which nonconforming uses were required to be terminated immediately and other prior cases in which ordinances prohibiting the expansion of nonconforming uses had been approved. The court said that in essence there was no legal distinction between requiring discontinuance of a nonconforming use after a grace period and limiting its expansion or enlargement; both were valid exercises of the police power. The court joined most other states in ruling that amortization is not a taking in and of itself and is valid if the grace period is reasonable.[119]

The reasonableness of the length of the grace period is a key factor in determining the legal validity of individual amortization requirements. In North Carolina the court applies the following test for its due-process and taking analysis: (1) Are the ends sought to be achieved by the challenged regulation legitimate and the means used reasonable? (2) Is the owner left with a practical use of the property that has reasonable value?[120] In the amortization context, the length of the grace period is important in determining whether the means used by the government to bring all uses into compliance are reasonable and whether the owner of the nonconforming use or structure has been provided or left with practical use and reasonable value.

Among the detailed factors set out by the courts in determining whether a required grace period is reasonable are a consideration of the nature of the public interest being served, the economic impact on the owner, and the balance between these considerations. A detailed case-by-case analysis of an individual amortization provision is necessary to accomplish such a determination.

The first set of factors focuses on the public interest in amortization, particularly the extent of harm to the public caused by continuing the nonconformity. Attention must be given to the nature of the use and the character of the surrounding neighborhood, especially whether the nonconformity harms neighbors, poses a threat to public health or safety, significantly harms community aesthetics, and the like. If the potential harm to public interests is high enough, the local government may move beyond amortization to immediate termination of the nonconformity, even if it causes substantial harm to the individual landowner.

The second set of factors focuses on the economic impact on the individual landowner affected by the amortization requirement. In making its determination, the court examines whether the grace period allows owners to recoup a substantial portion of their investment in the nonconformity. Attention must be given to the amount of the investment in the nonconforming use or structure, the income flow that it generates, any improvements on the land, the age and the depreciation involved with improvements, the feasibility and the costs of relocation, and any salvage value. From a constitutional standpoint an amortization period need not be designed to allow owners to recoup all of their costs. However, it does need to allow enough cost recovery that an undue burden is not placed on the individual and that the individual retains some practical or economic benefit from the use of the property.

Although both sets of factors are independently important, a critical concern is that there be an appropriate balance between them. That is, as the negative effect of an amortization on the owner increases, so should the public need for the amortization.

---

119. *Joyner*, 286 N.C. 366, 211 S.E.2d 320.

120. Finch v. City of Durham, 325 N.C. 352, 384 S.E.2d 8 (1989); Responsible Citizens v. City of Asheville, 308 N.C. 255, 302 S.E.2d 204 (1983); A-S-P Assocs. v. City of Raleigh, 298 N.C. 207, 258 S.E.2d 444 (1979); Helms v. City of Charlotte, 255 N.C. 647, 122 S.E.2d 817 (1961). See Chapter 24 for a discussion of the taking issue.

A detailed case-by-case analysis of the economic effects of an amortization requirement is necessary to determine the requirement's constitutionality. In *Naegele Outdoor Advertising, Inc. v. City of Durham* (*Naegele Advertising v. Durham II*),[121] the court concluded that the taking analysis should include

> findings pertaining to every aspect of Naegele's business that will be affected by the ordinance, including the number of billboards that can be economically used for noncommercial advertising, the number that are economically useless, the terms of Naegele's leases for billboard locations, the land Naegele owns for locations and whether it has any other economic use, the cost of the billboards that cannot be used, the depreciation taken on these billboards and their actual life expectancy, the income expected during the grace period, the salvage value of billboards that cannot be used, the loss of sharing revenue, the percentage of affected signs compared to the remaining signs in Naegele's business unit, the relative value of affected and remaining signs, whether the amortization period is reasonable, and any other evidence presented by the parties that the court deems relevant.[122]

It is prudent for governments to undertake this analysis before imposing an amortization requirement. Beyond its contribution to establishing a proper legal foundation, this type of economic analysis can be useful in making policy choices on amortization requirements. The closer a grace period comes to allowing an owner to eliminate the cost of coming into compliance, the more reasonable it is to require the owner to make that contribution to the community. This analysis allows policy makers to make informed choices when balancing the economic effects on owners against the public good generated by each particular amortization requirement.

A number of North Carolina cases have addressed the application of amortization requirements. In *County of Cumberland v. Eastern Federal Corp.*,[123] the court upheld a Cumberland County zoning requirement that nonconforming signs be brought into compliance within three years, as applied to a preexisting sign with a market value of $15,000. In *R.O. Givens, Inc. v. Town of Nags Head*,[124] the court upheld a provision in the Nags Head zoning regulation that all off-premise outdoor advertising signs be removed within five and a half years of the effective date of the ordinance. In *Goodman Toyota v. City of Raleigh*,[125] the court upheld a Raleigh requirement that nonconforming windblown signs (in this case a fourteen-foot-long advertising blimp) be eliminated within ninety days. In *Summey Outdoor Advertising*,[126] the court upheld a requirement in a freestanding-sign ordinance that nonconforming signs be brought into compliance or removed within five years. In *Maynor*, a two-year amortization provision on the location of adult businesses was upheld.[127]

Similar amortization provisions have been upheld in federal court challenges to North Carolina sign ordinances. In *Major Media of the Southeast, Inc. v. City of Raleigh*, the court upheld a Raleigh ordi-

---

121. 844 F.2d 172 (4th Cir. 1988).

122. *Id.* at 178.

123. 48 N.C. App. 518, 269 S.E.2d 672, *review denied*, 301 N.C. 527, 273 S.E.2d 453 (1980).

124. 58 N.C. App. 697, 294 S.E.2d 388, *cert. denied*, 307 N.C. 127, 297 S.E.2d 400 (1982). A five-and-a-half-year amortization provision was challenged also in *Capital Outdoor Advertising, Inc. v. City of Raleigh*, 337 N.C. 150, 446 S.E.2d 289 (1994). However, the court there held that because the action had not been brought within the applicable statute of limitations, the substantive takings issue was not reached. The court arrived at the same conclusion in a challenge to a seven-year billboard-amortization requirement in *Naegele Outdoor Advertising Inc. v. City of Winston-Salem*, 340 N.C. 349, 457 S.E.2d 874 (1995) (per curiam).

125. 63 N.C. App. 660, 306 S.E.2d 192 (1983), *review denied*, 310 N.C. 477, 312 S.E.2d 884 (1984).

126. 96 N.C. App. 533, 386 S.E.2d 439 (1989), *review denied*, 326 N.C. 486, 392 S.E.2d 101 (1990).

127. 127 N.C. App. 102, 488 S.E.2d 289, *appeal dismissed*, 347 N.C. 268, 493 S.E.2d 458, *review denied*, 347 N.C. 400, 496 S.E.2d 385 (1997) (the reasonableness of the amortization provision in this general-police-power ordinance was not challenged by the plaintiff).

nance that limited the size of off-premise signs, limited their location to industrial districts, and had a five-and-one-half-year amortization period for nonconforming signs.[128] In *Naegele Outdoor Advertising, Inc. v. City of Durham* (*Naegele Advertising v. Durham I*), a similar five-and-one-half-year amortization period was upheld.[129] The federal courts have also held that the statute of limitations for challenging an amortization provision is three years, beginning on adoption of the ordinance.[130]

Amortization requirements are often applied to adult businesses. Courts in other states have upheld amortization periods of ninety days,[131] one hundred twenty days,[132] six months,[133] one year,[134] two years,[135] three years,[136] and five years.[137] As with signs, however, an individual amortization provision is invalid if it forces adult businesses to close or relocate without allowing them adequate opportunity to recoup their investments.[138]

Statutory Limits on Amortization

Industries affected by local amortization requirements have sought and obtained legislative limits on uncompensated removal of nonconformities.

The leading example of this has been limits on amortization of signs, particularly off-premise outdoor advertising. At the federal level, the Highway Beautification Act of 1965[139] provided for substantial reductions in federal highway financial grants if states did not provide monetary compensation for removal

---

128. 792 F.2d 1269 (4th Cir. 1986), *cert. denied*, 479 U.S. 1102 (1987). The court also held that the restrictions did not violate the First Amendment, as the ordinance allowed noncommercial speech on any permissible sign. *See also* Ga. Outdoor Advert., Inc. v. City of Waynesville (*Georgia Advertising I*), 833 F.2d 43 (1987) (upholding ordinance prohibiting off-premise advertising as not violative of First Amendment or due process).

129. 803 F. Supp. 1068, *aff'd*, 19 F.3d 11 (1994). The Durham ordinance prohibited all commercial off-premise advertising except along federal highways; 85 of the plaintiff's 137 billboards were nonconforming. The Durham case had previously been to the Fourth Circuit and had been remanded for a takings analysis. In that case the court directed the district court to apply a *Penn Central*–type ad hoc analysis of the impact of the regulation for takings purposes. *Naegele Advertising v. Durham II*, 844 F.2d 172, 178 (4th Cir. 1988) (referencing Penn Cent. Transp. Co. v. City of New York, 438 U.S. 104 (1978)). *See also* Ga. Outdoor Advert., Inc. v. City of Waynesville (*Georgia Advertising II*), 900 F.2d 783 (4th Cir. 1990) (remanding four-year amortization provision for outdoor advertising for findings on takings issue).

130. Nat'l Advert. Co. v. City of Raleigh, 947 F.2d 1158 (4th Cir. 1991).

131. Northend Cinema, Inc. v. City of Seattle, 90 Wash. 2d 709, 585 P.2d 1153 (1978), *cert. denied*, 441 U.S. 946 (1979) (upholding ninety-day amortization requirement that included provision for balancing public benefits and costs). *But see* PA Nw. Distribs., Inc. v. Zoning Hearing Bd., 526 Pa. 186, 584 A.2d 1372 (1991) (ninety-day amortization requirement for adult commercial enterprises unconstitutional).

132. City of Whittier v. Walnut Props., Inc., 149 Cal. App. 3d 633, 644, 197 Cal. Rptr. 127, 134 (1983).

133. Hart Book Stores, Inc. v. Edmisten, 612 F.2d 821, 830 (4th Cir. 1979), *cert. denied*, 447 U.S. 929 (1980) (upholding requirement that only one adult business could be located within a single structure, with six-month grace period for existing businesses to come into compliance).

134. T-Marc, Inc. v. Pinellas Cnty., 804 F. Supp. 1500, 1504 (M.D. Fla. 1992).

135. Maynor v. Onslow Cnty., 127 N.C. App. 102, 488 S.E.2d 289, *appeal dismissed*, 347 N.C. 268, 493 S.E.2d 458, *review denied*, 347 N.C. 400, 496 S.E.2d 385 (1997); Centaur, Inc. v. Richland Cnty., 392 S.E.2d 165, 169 (S.C. 1990).

136. Ambassador Books & Video, Inc. v. City of Little Rock, 20 F.3d 858, 865 (8th Cir. 1994), *cert. denied*, 513 U.S. 867 (1994) (business has no absolute right to continue to operate at same location and three-year amortization period is adequate).

137. Bonnell, Inc. v. Bd. of Adjustment, 791 P.2d 107, 112 (Okla. Civ. App. 1989). *See also* Town of Islip v. Caviglia, 73 N.Y.2d 544, 560, 542 N.Y.S.2d 139, 148, 540 N.E.2d 215, 224 (1989) (upholding amortization periods ranging from 1.25 years to 5.25 years, depending on the amount of capital investment in the adult business).

138. Ebel v. City of Corona, 767 F.2d 635 (9th Cir. 1985) (ninety-day amortization inadequate where adult business had five-year lease and substantial investment and ordinance allowed few if any alternative locations).

139. Pub. L. No. 89-285, 79 Stat. 1028 (1965) (codified at 23 U.S.C. §§ 101 *et seq.*).

of preexisting nonconforming signs.[140] In response, North Carolina enacted Chapter 136, Section 131.1 of the North Carolina General Statutes (hereinafter G.S.),[141] which required local governments to pay compensation for the removal of nonconforming billboards located along federal highways. In 2003, the General Assembly further limited amortization of off-premise billboards with enactment of an eighteen-month moratorium on adoption of new amortization requirements for these nonconformities.[142] In 2004, legislation was enacted to make this limitation permanent.[143] G.S. 153A-143 and 160A-199 were enacted to require monetary compensation for removal of nonconforming off-premise outdoor advertising visible from any road unless the removal was required to prevent a public nuisance, prevent a detriment to the public health or safety, relocate the sign to a comparable location so the road can be widened, or fulfill part of a relocation, reconstruction, or removal agreement with the sign owner.

G.S. 14-409.46(e) prohibits zoning ordinances from amortizing some nonconforming shooting ranges by providing that a shooting range that was lawfully in operation as of September 1, 1994, must be allowed to continue to operate, provided there has been no substantial change in the use. The law does not otherwise limit local regulatory authority regarding the location and construction of sport-shooting ranges.

By contrast, use of amortization for adult businesses was explicitly authorized in 1998.[144] This provision is codified as G.S. 160D-902(d).

G.S. 160D-1405(c1) provides that when a nonconforming use has been "grandfathered and subsequently terminated for any reason," the local government "shall bring an enforcement action within 10 years of the date of the termination of the grandfathered status, unless the violation poses an imminent hazard to health or public safety."[145] This provision requires that if a landowner does not comply with new regulations at the end of an amortization period, the local government must bring an enforcement action within ten years of the amortization's expiration. After that ten-year period of no enforcement, a noncompliant use may continue.

---

140. 23 U.S.C. § 131(g). See Chapter 23 for further discussion of this statute.

141. This section of the statutes was enacted in 1981 with a specific sunset provision. After several extensions of the sunset, S.L. 2002-11 provided that this section will expire upon the amendment to or repeal of 23 U.S.C. § 131(g). Also see G.S. 136-147 and 136-148, which authorize the use of public funds to screen or remove certain nonconforming junkyards.

142. S.L. 2003-432.

143. S.L. 2004-152.

144. S.L. 1998-46.

145. This provision was added by S.L. 2013-413. The provision was inadvertently omitted in the recodification of this section as G.S. 160D-1405. It was restored to the statutes in 2020 as G.S. 160D-1405(c1). S.L. 2020-25.

CHAPTER 21

Administration and Enforcement

Administration

Development regulations typically include a variety of administrative requirements.

Staff members administering land-development regulations have a number of duties: they process applications for development permits, explain ordinance requirements to the public, make application forms available, review applications to verify the information provided, and assess the application's compliance with the terms of the zoning ordinance. Staff officers issue routine permits; they are responsible for making inspections during and at the conclusion of the permitted work to assure that the ordinance requirements have been met. Staff officers also investigate complaints and initiate enforcement actions when violations are discovered; they are often required to make interpretations of the ordinances and issue determinations as to compliance. In addition, staff officers perform routine tasks for the planning board and board of adjustment, including preparing reports, assuring proper notice of meetings, and making reports on cases. The city or county clerk and the planning staff often share responsibility for these administrative duties.

Before the adoption of Chapter 160D, the statutes on local development regulation—Chapter 153A, Article 18, and Chapter 160A, Article 19, of the North Carolina General Statutes (hereinafter G.S.)— contained no general provisions for local administration of development regulations. These statutes only included limited administrative provisions for a few specific types of regulations, primarily for building-code and housing-code enforcement. Some of the administrative provisions for building-code enforcement were broadened over the decades to reference administration and enforcement of other development regulations.[1] However, most of the essential activities of administering development regulations—reviewing site plans, interpreting ordinances, revoking zoning permits, and issuing notices of violation—had to be drawn from implied authority or references in the building-code-enforcement statute.[2]

Chapter 160D[3] added administrative provisions applicable to all local development regulations. G.S. 160D-401(a) provides that the administrative provisions of Article 4 of Chapter 160D apply to all development regulations adopted pursuant to Chapter 160D. They also apply to any other local ordinance that substantially affects land use and development.

---

1. Chapter 153A, Section 357 and Chapter 160A, Section 417 of the North Carolina General Statutes (hereinafter G.S.) required a building permit prior to the initiation of construction, alteration, demolition, or relocation of a structure. These permits required that the work done comply with all other applicable state and local laws, including zoning requirements. G.S. 153A-363 and 160A-423 authorized issuance of "certificates of compliance" upon a final inspection of all work. Occupation of a newly constructed or altered building without such a certificate was a misdemeanor. A certificate of occupancy could be denied for inconsistency with any applicable state law or local ordinance. First Am. Fed. Sav. & Loan Ass'n v. Royall, 77 N.C. App. 131, 334 S.E.2d 792 (1985).

2. *See, e.g.,* Homebuilders Ass'n of Charlotte v. City of Charlotte, 336 N.C. 37, 442 S.E.2d 45 (1994).

3. S.L. 2019-111, pt. II.

A local government may also elect to apply these administrative provisions to any general-police-power ordinance. As was the case under prior law, local governments are expressly authorized to use any organizational structure, board, commission, or staffing arrangement authorized by Article 4 of Chapter 160D to any aspects of these other ordinances.[4] The authority to apply these provisions only extends to administration and enforcement of the regulations. It does not alter the scope of the statutory authority for those regulations.[5]

The general administrative provisions in Article 4 are supplemental to any specific administrative provisions for individual development regulations, such as building-code and housing-code enforcement. When there is difference between provisions, the more specific provision in the individual development-regulation article controls over the general provisions in Article 4.[6]

The professionalism and demeanor of zoning officers is a critical element in the successful implementation of zoning. As Philip Green noted, if the zoning administrator "is energetic, imaginative, intelligent, sensitive, and calm, he will carry out the objectives of the ordinance with a minimum of misunderstanding, contention, and bad public relations. On the other hand, inattention to detail, lack of dedication, or arrogance can ensure that he and his fellow officers remain in constant hot water."[7]

Allocation of Staff Responsibilities

G.S. 160D-402 provides the basic authorization for administrative staffing for local development regulations. It provides that local governments may appoint "administrators, inspectors, enforcement officers, planners, technicians, and other staff to develop, administer, and enforce development regulations." Potential duties of the administrative staff may include but are not limited to:

- drafting and implementing plans and development regulations;
- receiving and processing applications for development approvals;
- determining whether applications for development approvals are complete;
- providing notices of applications and hearings;
- conducting inspections;
- making decisions and determinations regarding the implementation of development regulations;[8]
- issuing or denying certificates of compliance or occupancy;[9]
- enforcing development regulations, including issuing notices of violation and orders to correct violations, and recommending bringing judicial actions against actual or threatened violations;[10]
- keeping adequate records; and
- performing any other duties that may be required in order to adequately enforce the laws and development regulations under their jurisdiction.

---

4. G.S. 160D-101(c).

5. G.S. 160D-401(b).

6. *Id.*

7. Philip P. Green, Jr., Legal Responsibilities of the Local Zoning Administrator in North Carolina 1 (2d ed. 1987). Even routine zoning administration and enforcement can subject the administrator to abuse from those subject to regulation. See, for example, *State v. Wooten*, 206 N.C. App. 494, 696 S.E.2d 570 (2010), upholding a criminal conviction for stalking against a person with a zoning issue (he had wanted to open a commercial use in a residential zoning district) who repeatedly threatened and harassed a zoning-enforcement officer.

8. G.S. 160D-403(b).

9. G.S. 160D-403(g).

10. G.S. 160D-404.

Local governments are authorized to establish interlocal agreements to handle staffing and administration of local development regulations.[11] This authority is often used, for example, by small-population municipalities that secure building-code enforcement within the city by the county inspection staff. A local government may also contract with individuals, private companies, or regional organizations to provide these administrative duties under the supervision of the local government.

Each local government is to specify which staff entity has responsibility for administration of its land-development ordinances. For example, a particular officer may be designated as the "zoning administrator" or some similar title. In the absence of a specific designation in the regulatory ordinances, the city or county manager assigns these responsibilities to a particular person or group of persons. It is typical for the administrator to also have responsibility for most local land-development regulations, though other departments or officials may administer specialized ordinances.[12]

The statutes allow substantial flexibility in just where this staff responsibility is housed. In most local governments in North Carolina, this responsibility is assigned to an inspections department or a planning department, although it can be assigned to some other department within the city or county government. Counties and cities may also establish a joint inspections and enforcement department.[13]

The administrator is a public officer[14] of the local government and, as an "officer" instead of an "employee," has certain powers, duties, and protections. The administrator should take an oath of office, swearing or affirming to support the constitution and laws and to faithfully carry out the duties of the position.[15] Some staff members working under the administrator may also have decision-making authority, and these persons similarly must take an oath of office. The oath is administered when the officer assumes the duties of the position. It should not be confused with the oath to testify truthfully that is administered each time the officer presents testimony in a hearing.

Staff Reports

One of the most common staff responsibilities is to present information to boards considering ordinance amendments and determinations of individual permits.

Surveys conducted by the School of Government in 2002, 2004, and 2006 asked what types of staff information were provided to the boards making decisions on variances, special use permits, and zoning-ordinance amendments (rezonings and text amendments). Virtually all local governments reported that a staff report containing factual information on the application or material is provided to the decision-making board, and almost all provide additional background information on the plans and ordinances involved in that decision. Nearly half also provide additional information generated by the staff about the sites involved, such as photographs or videos. Some boards ask the officers to make recommendations on individual cases, while other boards ask the staff to report only the facts of the case. (Either

---

11. G.S. 160D-402(c).

12. For example, separate offices administer septic-tank regulations.

13. Joint inspection departments are authorized by G.S. 160D-402(c). G.S. 160A-460 to -464 authorize interlocal agreements for the exercise of any governmental power or function. Several North Carolina jurisdictions use this option.

14. Pigott v. City of Wilmington, 50 N.C. App. 401, 273 S.E.2d 752, *review denied*, 303 N.C. 181, 280 S.E.2d 453 (1981). See the discussion of the officer/employee distinction relative to liability, below.

15. G.S. 160D-402(b) specifically authorizes a development regulation to require that designated staff members take an oath of office. Members of appointed boards are required to take an oath of office. G.S. 160D-309. Article VI, section 4 of North Carolina's constitution prescribes the form of the oath to be taken upon assuming elected or appointed office. G.S. 153A-26 and 160A-61 reiterate this requirement and require a copy of the oath to be filed with the city or county clerk. G.S. 14-229 prohibits acting as an officer prior to taking the oath, and G.S. 128-5 sets a $500 penalty for acting before taking the oath.

Table 21.1 Staff Reports to Boards: Percentage of Respondents Who Provide Each Type of Decision-Specific Information

Type of Information	Variances	Special Use Permits	Zoning-Ordinance Amendments
Factual information on application or petition	98%	95%	98%
Analysis of ordinance or plan involved	85%	85%	81%
Video, photo, or other site information	57%	56%	51%
Recommendation on decision	39%	60%	72%

approach is legally acceptable.) Staff recommendations on the decision are typically provided for legislative decisions. (Seventy-two percent of jurisdictions make such recommendations for proposed zoning amendments.) Staff recommendations are common, but less so, on quasi-judicial matters. (Sixty percent of jurisdictions polled make recommendations for special and conditional use permits, and 39 percent do so for variance petitions.)[16] These results are summarized in Table 21.1.

Record Keeping

The administrator is responsible for maintaining all appropriate records.[17] Files must be maintained on all applications and permit decisions. Records of enforcement actions and decisions by boards on permits, appeals, variances, and ordinance changes must be maintained. These materials are public records and must be made available for public inspection during normal business hours.[18] G.S. 160D-105(a) requires that zoning-district boundary maps be maintained for public inspection in the office of the city or county clerk (or such other office as is specified in the development regulation).[19]

---

16. David Owens & Adam Brueggemann, A Survey of Experience with Zoning Variances 14 (UNC School of Government, Special Series No. 18, 2004); David W. Owens, Special Use Permits in North Carolina Zoning 13 (UNC School of Government, Special Series No. 22, Apr. 2007); David W. Owens, Zoning Amendments in North Carolina 8 (UNC School of Government, Special Series No. 24, Feb. 2008).

17. G.S. 160D-402(b). G.S. 160D-1126 also requires inspection departments to keep complete and accurate records of applications, permits, inspections, and all other work-related materials. The court in *Shearl v. Town of Highlands*, 236 N.C. App. 113, 762 S.E.2d 877 (2014), held that the burden is on a local government to maintain an official copy of all ordinances, including the zoning map, and that this also requires retention of archival copies of ordinances and zoning maps that are no longer in effect. G.S. 132-7 requires custodians of public records to maintain said records in a safe, accessible location, normally in the building in which they are ordinarily used. *See generally* News & Observer Publ'g Co. v. State *ex rel.* Starling, 312 N.C. 276, 322 S.E.2d 133 (1984). For a more detailed review of public-records law, see David M. Lawrence, Public Records Law for North Carolina Local Governments (2d ed. 2009).

18. All "documents, papers, letters, maps, books, photographs, films, sound recordings, magnetic or other tapes, electronic data-processing records, artifacts, or other documentary material" made or received by a city or county in connection with the transaction of public business is a public record. G.S. 132-1(a). Any person may inspect these records at reasonable times and under reasonable supervision. G.S. 132-6(a). A member of the public may copy the records for free or at minimal cost. G.S. 132-1(b); 132-6(a). The person requesting inspection or copies need not disclose the purpose or motive for the request. G.S. 132-6(b). A person denied access to public records may seek a court order to compel disclosure. G.S. 132-9.

19. This provision was added by S.L. 2019-111.

The state Department of Natural and Cultural Resources establishes a schedule for record retention and disposition.[20] Records generally may not be destroyed except in accordance with this schedule.[21]

The current record-retention schedule[22] has the following requirements for materials related to planning and zoning:

- Permanent retention is required for meeting minutes of the board of adjustment, planning board, and appearance commission; the board-of-adjustment case index; subdivision records; zoning amendments; rezoning requests; adopted comprehensive plans; adopted ordinances; historic-project and major-plan reviews; variances; nonresidential zoning-compliance permits; environmental-impact studies; open-space-classification files; feasibility studies; and aerial-photography negatives. Certificates of appropriateness are to be retained for the life of the structure.
- Six years' retention is required for board-of-adjustment case files; enforcement case files; notices of violation; files on plan reviews if the recordkeeping agency is not the lead agency; files on other mandatory reviews; residential zoning-compliance permits; and temporary manufactured-housing permits.
- Three years' retention is required for files on variances and special use permits (starting at discontinuance of the use); sign permits; correspondence files; petitions concerning zoning; comprehensive-plan surveys, studies, reports, and drafts; and redevelopment and community-development-monitoring files.
- Files on special use permit applications that are not issued can be destroyed when their reference value ends.
- Local government agencies are required to retain maps, photographs, project files, and meeting packets until they are obsolete or their use ends.

Development Approvals and Determinations

The staff makes administrative decisions in the administration and implementation of development regulations. G.S. 160D-102(1) defines "administrative decisions" as those made in the implementation, administration, or enforcement of development regulations that involve "the determination of facts and the application of objective standards." These are also sometimes referred to as *ministerial decisions* or *administrative determinations*. "Development approvals" under Chapter 160D include both administrative and quasi-judicial approvals but not legislative approvals, such as a conditional rezoning.[23]

---

20. G.S. 132-8.1.
21. G.S. 132-3.
22. Detailed standards for retention of planning and development regulation and code-enforcement and inspection records are set in RECORDS RETENTION AND DISPOSITION SCHEDULE: PROGRAM RECORDS SCHEDULE: LOCAL GOVERNMENT AGENCIES (N.C. DEP'T OF NAT. AND CULTURAL RES. OCT. 1, 2021). G.S. 121-4(2) and 121-5(b) provide authority to the department for this records-management program.
23. G.S. 160D-102(13). Other "development approvals" are quasi-judicial decisions made by boards rather than by staff, including special use permits, variances, and certificates of appropriateness. "Development" is defined for purposes of Chapter 160D as including any of the following:
    (a) the construction, erection, alteration, enlargement, renovation, substantial repair, movement to another site, or demolition of any structure;
    (b) the excavation, grading, filling, clearing, or alteration of land;
    (c) the subdivision of land; or
    (d) the initiation of substantial change in use of land or the intensity of the use of land.
G.S. 160D-102(12).

The staff is generally assigned decision-making for administrative development approvals, such as zoning permits, site-plan approvals,[24] plat approvals,[25] and building permits.[26] Applications may be made by the property owner, a person leasing the property, a person with an option or contract to purchase or lease the property, or a person with an easement on the property (provided the development is within the scope of the easement).[27] Development approvals must be written but may be in print or electronic form. If electronic, the development approval must be in a format protected from further editing.[28]

Staff is also responsible for making determinations under development regulations. G.S. 160D-102(10) defines a determination as "[a] written, final, and binding order, requirement, or determination regarding an administrative decision." This includes a binding interpretation of a regulation, an affirmation or denial of nonconforming status or vested rights, a notice of violation, or some other order concerning a development regulation.

A local-development regulation may designate a staff person to make determinations under each development regulation.[29] The staff person must provide written notice of the determination to the property owner and the party seeking the determination, if different from the owner. Notice is provided by personal delivery, electronic mail, or first-class mail to the last address of the owner in county tax records and the address provided by the applicant if different from that of the owner. Additionally, an owner or applicant may post a zoning-notice sign on the affected property for ten days to establish constructive notice of the determination to neighboring parties. Unless a local ordinance requires such posted notice, it is at the option of the owner or applicant.

A development regulation may require community notice, informational meetings, or both as part of the decision-making process for administrative development approvals.[30] If these are required, the staff may be assigned responsibility for providing the notices or conducting the meetings.

A local-development regulation may authorize staff to approve minor modifications to administrative development approvals if the regulation defines those minor modifications.[31] The regulation may also exempt defined minor modifications from review and approval. Major modifications must be approved in the same manner as the original approval. In addition to minor modifications on administrative development approvals, a development regulation may authorize staff to approve minor modifications for site-specific vesting plans,[32] legislative conditional-zoning decisions,[33] and quasi-judicial special use permits.[34] For administrative modifications to legislative and quasi-judicial decisions, *minor modification* must be defined in the regulation and cannot include a change in permitted uses or the density of the overall development. Modifications that do not qualify as minor must follow the same process for approval that is required for the original approval.[35]

---

24. G.S. 160D-102(29).
25. G.S. 160D-803(b).
26. G.S. 160D-1110.
27. G.S. 160D-403(a).
28. *Id.*
29. G.S. 160D-403(b).
30. G.S. 160D-403(h).
31. G.S. 160D-403(d).
32. G.S. 160D-108(d)(3)(d).
33. G.S. 160D-703(b).
34. G.S. 160D-705(c).
35. It is likely that staff can also be authorized to administratively approve minor modifications to development agreements. G.S. 160D-1006(e) provides that a major modification to a development agreement shall follow the same procedures as initial approval. By implication, a minor modification would not have to do so.

In making staff interpretations, the administrative officer gathers information and applies the same rules of interpretation as are subsequently used by the board of adjustment and courts.[36] A final, binding staff interpretation is required before initiating a quasi-judicial appeal of the officer's determination.[37]

A question that occasionally arises is the degree to which errors in the development regulations can be "fixed" by administrative action. A great deal depends on determining the exact nature of the "error" involved.

If the error is a staff mistake in the codification of an action taken by the governing board, that is considered a scrivener's error[38] that can be immediately corrected at the staff level, as the ordinance inaccurately reflects the action actually taken by the governing board. For example, in *Laurel Valley Watch, Inc. v. Mountain Enterprises of Wolf Ridge, LLC*, the court addressed a situation where the county commissioners clearly approved a particular rezoning, but the board's minutes incorrectly specified the new zoning district for the property. Since the application, hearing notices, planning-board discussion, staff recommendation, and commissioner's discussions all clearly referenced the intended district, the court found the minutes to be a scrivener's error that could be summarily corrected.[39] Obvious typographical and formatting errors can be similarly corrected.[40]

On the other hand, if a substantive mistake is made prior to the governing-board action, and the ordinance accurately reflects what the governing board actually adopted, governing-board action is usually necessary to make the correction. In *Murdock v. Chatham County*,[41] the plaintiffs challenged (among other things) a zoning administrator's attempted fix of a zoning-map error. In 2006, a landowner approached the county about a development project that would require a rezoning. In the course of the discussions with the county staff, it was discovered that a 1974 rezoning was erroneously entered on the county's zoning map, as the area shown on the zoning map did not match the legal descriptions of the property that was supposed to have been rezoned over twenty years before. However, in 1988 the county had adopted a new zoning map, and that map adoption had incorporated the mistaken delineation from the 1970s map. The court held that even if the metes-and-bounds property description from 1974 had been incorrectly entered on the zoning map, the county commissioners in 1988 had adopted an official zoning map based on that incorrect depiction. The map with the error had therefore become the official zoning map that staff must apply until the map was amended. Since governing-board action

---

36. Rules of interpretation are discussed in Chapter 18.

37. The requirement of a final decision as a prerequisite to appellate review is discussed in Chapter 18. Also see the discussion of a formal approval as a prerequisite for a common law vested right in Chapter 19 and a review of the rules of interpretation in Chapter 18.

38. The doctrine of scrivener's error allows a court to correct a technical mistake, such as an obvious typographical error, in a document where the intended meaning is absolutely clear. *See, e.g.,* United States v. X-Citement Video, Inc., 513 U.S. 64, 82 (1994) (Scalia, A., dissenting).

39. 192 N.C. App. 391, 665 S.E.2d 561 (2008). Madison County rezoned twelve acres to accommodate a private airport adjacent to resort properties. The notice of both the planning-board hearing and the board-of-commissioners hearing on the proposed rezoning noted the proposed rezoning was to an industrial district, the only district in the county zoning ordinance that permitted an airport. The county commissioners unanimously approved the rezoning. However, the minutes of the meeting noted the property had been rezoned to a "residential-resort" district. Subsequently, when a suit was filed regarding the rezoning, the county commissioners adopted a resolution noting that a scrivener's error in the minutes incorrectly identified the zoning district adopted for this property and amended the minutes to state the property had been rezoned to an industrial district. The court held that the evidence clearly supported a conclusion that the property had in fact actually been rezoned to the industrial district.

40. Even though it is not legally necessary for the governing board to take action to fix this type of error, it is a good practice to report the fix to the board and have the correction noted in their minutes (and particularly cautious local governments may want to have the board adopt a resolution noting and approving the correction).

41. 198 N.C. App. 309, 679 S.E.2d 850 (2009), *review denied*, 363 N.C. 806, 690 S.E.2d 705 (2010).

is required to amend the zoning map, the court held that the full rezoning process must be followed if the county wanted to correct the original error.[42]

Fees

G.S. 160D-402(d) provides that reasonable fees can be required to offset the costs of administration and implementation of a development regulation.

Prior to this explicit statutory authorization, the court in *Homebuilders Ass'n of Charlotte v. City of Charlotte*[43] upheld the imposition of user fees for a variety of city services, including rezonings, special use permits, plat reviews, and building inspections, even though the city at that time had no express statutory authority to impose them. The court held that G.S. 160A-4 requires that grants of authority to cities be interpreted to include additional and supplementary powers that are expedient to execution of the city's regulatory powers. The court noted that such fees must be reasonable, generally not to exceed the cost of the regulatory program. State statutes now require that administrative fees collected for development-regulation reviews be used only for the support and administration of these programs.[44]

The amount of the fees charged varies significantly, depending on the type of approval sought and the population size of the city or county. In a 2012 survey by the School of Government, fees reported by local governments ranged from under $20 for a zoning-verification letter to over $1700 for a plat review.[45] The size and complexity of the review is generally a key factor; local governments have increasingly adjusted their fee schedules to recover more of the administrative costs of conducting development reviews.

The School's survey report also summarized typical processing times for various types of development approvals. The average processing times reported were relatively short for administrative reviews, longer for quasi-judicial decisions, and longest for legislative decisions. Zoning-verification letters were typically issued in two or three days and building permits within a week. Site-plan and preliminary plats were typically processed in four to six weeks. Variances and special use permits were typically decided in six to eight weeks, while rezonings and zoning-text amendments typically took two to three months.[46]

Development regulations also often require that additional information be provided at the applicant's expense regarding analysis of the application, such as a traffic-impact study or engineering verification of stormwater controls.

---

42. G.S. 153A-345(c) and 160A-388(c) previously authorized the board of adjustment to rule on disputed lot lines or district boundary lines, so the final decision on boundary delineations rested with the board of adjustment rather than the zoning administrator. This statutory provision was deleted by S.L. 2013-126, so these rulings and appeals to the board of adjustment are treated the same as any other ordinance interpretation.

43. 336 N.C. 37, 442 S.E.2d 45 (1994). *See also* Maready v. City of Winston-Salem, 342 N.C. 708, 467 S.E.2d 615 (1996) (upholding city use of economic-development incentives to private businesses); Moores v. Greensboro Minimum Hous. Standards Comm'n, 198 N.C. App. 384, 679 S.E.2d 480 (2009) (upholding authority to delegate hearing appeals and making final orders in housing-code appeals to housing-appeals commission). *But cf.* Bowers v. City of High Point, 339 N.C. 413, 451 S.E.2d 284 (1994) (holding that the city had no authority to pay higher retirement benefits to law-enforcement officers than amount set by statute).

44. G.S. 160D-4021(d). These provisions provide that fees collected for inspections can only be used to support the inspection department's administration and activities. This limitation was added to the statutes by S.L. 2015-145. If a court determines that a tax or fee was illegally imposed, the fee plus interest is returned to the party who made the payment. G.S. 160D-106.

45. David W. Owens and Dayne Batten, *2012 Zoning Survey Report: Zoning Adoption, Administration, and Provisions for Design Standards and Alternative Energy Facilities*, PLAN. & ZONING L. BULL. No. 20 (UNC School of Government, July 2012), at 10–11.

46. *Id.* at 12–13.

Inspections

Site inspections are a vital part of administration and enforcement of land-development regulations.

Work in progress is inspected routinely. Inspections of potential violations are often triggered by citizen complaints, but the staff may also unilaterally conduct routine inspections.[47] The authority for periodic inspections of residential structures under G.S. 160D-1207 is limited. Either the inspector must have reasonable cause to believe that unsafe, unsanitary, or hazardous conditions exist, or the property must be in a designated target area with a plan for housing improvements.[48]

The Fourth Amendment's[49] prohibition against unreasonable searches imposes important limitations on how inspections may be made. An officer may make only such reasonable initial inquiries that do not violate a person's reasonable expectation of privacy.

For residential inspections, an officer may generally approach the front door of a residence just as other members of the public do.[50] The area of a residence that is protected by the Fourth Amendment includes both the house itself and the curtilage—the area immediately surrounding the house. For example, a fenced backyard immediately adjacent to the home is within the curtilage, but an open field or a barn some distance from the house is not.[51]

The prohibition against unreasonable search and seizure applies to administrative inspection of private commercial property.[52] However, an officer may enter the customer area of a commercial establishment, purchase materials or services being offered to the general public,[53] enter any other area to which the public is invited, or view the premises from public areas.[54] However, if the officers go beyond the activities available to a normal customer, consent or a warrant is needed.[55] There is a lower expectation of privacy for commercial establishments than for residential properties, and warrantless searches of

---

47. G.S. 160D-403(e) and 160D-113 authorize inspections of work in progress. G.S. 160D-402(b) lists "conducting inspections" among the duties of staff. G.S. 160D-1117 authorizes periodic inspections for unsafe, unsanitary, or otherwise hazardous and unlawful conditions.

48. The limits on periodic inspections of residential structures were added by S.L. 2011-281. For purposes of this statute, *reasonable cause* is defined to include situations where: (1) the landlord or property owner has a history of two or more housing-code violations within a twelve-month period; (2) a complaint has been made about substandard conditions in the building or an inspection has been requested; (3) actual knowledge of an unsafe condition in the building exists; or (4) violations are visible from the exterior of the building. The exception to the reasonable-cause requirement provided for periodic inspections within targeted areas requires that the city or county first provide notice to all residents and owners in the target area, hold a public hearing on the plan for inspections, and establish a plan to assist low-income property owners with compliance with minimum-housing codes. This statute also places restrictions on local government registration and licensing programs (and the fees for such programs) related to residential-property leasing.

49. U.S. Const. amend. IV; N.C. Const. art. I, § 20. The North Carolina standards on unreasonable searches and the sufficiency of probable cause to justify searches tracks federal law. State v. Arrington, 311 N.C. 633, 319 S.E.2d 254 (1984). For an overview of state and federal law on administrative inspection warrants, see Robert L. Farb and Christopher Tyner, Arrest, Search, and Investigation in North Carolina (UNC School of Government, 6th ed. 2021).

50. State v. Tripp, 52 N.C. App. 244, 278 S.E.2d 592 (1981); State v. Prevette, 43 N.C. App. 450, 259 S.E.2d 595 (1979), *review denied*, 299 N.C. 124, 261 S.E.2d 925, *cert. denied*, 447 U.S. 906 (1980).

51. United States v. Dunn, 480 U.S. 294 (1987). In *State v. Nance*, 149 N.C. App. 734, 562 S.E.2d 557 (2002), a case involving malnourished horses and an alleged violation of an animal-cruelty ordinance, the court held that an open field is not entitled to Fourth Amendment privacy protection.

52. See v. City of Seattle, 387 U.S. 541 (1967); Donovan v. Dewey, 452 U.S. 594 (1981).

53. Maryland v. Macon, 472 U.S. 463 (1985) (upholding conviction for sale of obscene material based on detective's purchase of materials available to customers at adult bookstore).

54. Payton v. New York, 445 U.S. 573 (1980); State v. Nance, 149 N.C. App. 734, 562 S.E.2d 557 (2002) (when an officer is in a public place or other area not protected by the Fourth Amendment, knowledge gained from the officer's plain-sight observations is not a search under the Fourth Amendment).

55. Lo-Ji Sales, Inc. v. New York, 442 U.S. 319 (1979).

commercial properties may be conducted more readily if a closely regulated industry (such as alcohol sales) is involved, since there is a practice and expectation of regular inspections in those circumstances.[56]

Nonresidential areas that are not exposed to the public may also be protected.[57] For example, the North Carolina Supreme Court has held it to be impermissible to peek through the cracks in the rear of a padlocked, boarded-up commercial structure without a search warrant.[58] In addition to these constitutional protections, state criminal law prohibits any person from entering or remaining in another person's building, enclosed premises, or posted areas without authorization.[59]

The use of modern technology poses challenges as to what an officer can view that is in "plain sight" without consent or a warrant. Aerial observations are generally not considered a search under the Fourth Amendment.[60] Taking thermal images of a house from the street has, however, been held to be a search.[61]

An officer can inspect protected areas if proper consent is first obtained.[62] The person whose privacy rights are protected by the constitution must grant consent. For a dwelling, this would be an adult occupant of the dwelling. For rental properties, the tenant's consent, as opposed to that of the property owner, is required.[63] If two or more persons share a residence, any one resident may give consent to search the shared property; however, if any one of the persons sharing the space objects, there is no consent for the inspection.[64] Consent must be voluntary, but it need not be in writing, though many inspectors and enforcement officers obtain written consent for record-keeping and verification purposes. Consent may be limited in scope and may be withdrawn at any time. Some permit-application forms include a consent for inspection. Some permit conditions that are accepted also provide for inspections. In either instance, the consent may be subsequently withdrawn.[65]

If there are reasonable grounds to believe that there may be a violation, an officer can obtain an administrative-inspection warrant.[66] G.S. 15A-24.2 authorizes city and county officials and employees to obtain such a warrant from a magistrate, judge, or clerk of court (including deputy and assistant

---

56. Donovan v. Dewey, 452 U.S. 594 (1981).

57. Marshall v. Barlow's, Inc., 436 U.S. 307 (1978); Katz v. United States, 389 U.S. 347 (1967).

58. State v. Tarantino, 322 N.C. 386, 390–91, 368 S.E.2d 588, 591 (1988), *cert. denied*, 489 U.S. 1010 (1989). The court held that the general state of neglect of the closed country store in this case did not negate a reasonable expectation of privacy. *But see* Nikolas v. City of Omaha, 605 F.3d 539 (8th Cir. 2010) (peering into windows of dilapidated detached garage permissible).

59. G.S. 14, §§ 159.12 (first-degree trespass applicable to enclosed or secured areas and buildings), 159.13 (second-degree trespass applicable to posted areas), 54 (breaking and entering buildings).

60. Florida v. Riley, 488 U.S. 445 (1989) (view into greenhouse from helicopter not a search); Dow Chem. Co. v. United States, 476 U.S. 227 (1986) (use of enhanced aerial photography of industrial complex not a search); California v. Ciraolo, 476 U.S. 207 (1986) (view into fenced backyard from helicopter not a search).

61. Kyllo v. United States, 533 U.S. 27 (2001).

62. G.S. 160D-403(e) provides that inspections are authorized at "all reasonable hours" upon the presentation of proper credentials if "the appropriate consent has been given for inspection of areas that are not open to the public or [if] an appropriate inspection warrant has been secured."

63. *In re* Dwelling Owned by Double Triangle Props., Inc., 24 N.C. App. 17, 210 S.E.2d 73 (1974).

64. Georgia v. Randolph, 547 U.S. 103 (2006).

65. Crook v. City of Madison, 168 So. 3d 930 (Miss. 2015) (condition on license allowing rental-property inspection without a warrant unconstitutional). In *Bonneville v. Pierce County*, 202 P.3d 309 (Wash. Ct. App. 2008), the court upheld a warrantless-inspection-permit condition on a home-occupation approval, given that the applicant suggested the condition and the consequence of failure to allow inspection was revocation of the permit rather than criminal prosecution.

66. The federal courts have recognized an exception to the warrant requirement when the inspection involves a closely regulated business. This exception is rarely involved with zoning inspections, but it may come into play for premises used for gun or liquor sales, pawnshops, day-care centers, adult businesses, or similar businesses subject to regular and close inspection. Elks Lodge v. Bd. of Alcohol Control, 27 N.C. App. 594, 220 S.E.2d 106 (1976).

clerks).[67] An administrative-inspection warrant should be distinguished from a search warrant issued under G.S. 15A-241 (which may only be issued when there is probable cause to search for evidence of a criminal violation).

To obtain an administrative-inspection warrant, the officer must provide an affidavit to show that there is probable cause[68] that justifies the inspection (or that the inspection is part of a legally authorized program of inspection).[69] For example, one court held that there was probable cause to secure an administrative-inspection warrant when the building owner told an inspector that he intended to undertake work contrary to the zoning regulation and there was visible evidence of work taking place on-site.[70] The officer must also personally appear before the person issuing the warrant. Many inspection departments routinely seek voluntary consent to an inspection and only seek a warrant if consent is refused, but there is no requirement that consent be sought prior to securing a warrant.

Inspections conducted pursuant to an administrative-inspection warrant are subject to several statutory limitations: The warrant is valid for only twenty-four hours after its issuance, and it must be personally served on the owner or possessor of the property being searched. If the owner or possessor of the property is not present and reasonable efforts have been made to locate that person, a copy of the warrant may be posted on the property, and that has the same effect as personal service. Further, the inspection may be conducted only between 8:00 a.m. and 8:00 p.m.[71]

There is also an important limitation on evidence that may be obtained pursuant to an administrative-inspection warrant. Only evidence described in justifying the warrant may be used in subsequent enforcement actions.[72] If an officer discovers other land-development violations (or evidence of other criminal activity) during the course of the inspection, even if that evidence is in plain view, such evidence may not be used in any subsequent civil, criminal, or administrative action. If the officer has consent for the inspection, as opposed to an inspection pursuant to a warrant, evidence in plain view is not subject to this limitation.

Durham Video & News, Inc. v. Durham Board of Adjustment[73] illustrates the appropriate use of an administrative-inspection warrant. The enforcement question presented was whether the establishment operated by the plaintiff was an adult business (which was not allowed in the general-commercial zoning district in which the store was located). City zoning officers twice visited the store and briefly viewed its merchandise. Based on observations made during these visits, the officers sought and obtained an administrative-inspection warrant. Pursuant to the warrant, the officers returned to the store and

---

67. The warrant must be issued by an official whose "territorial jurisdiction encompasses the property to be inspected." G.S. 15-27.2(b). Thus, magistrates and clerks of court (and assistant and deputy clerks) may issue warrants within their county, district judges within their district, and superior-court judges statewide. The form for an administrative-inspection warrant for a particular condition or activity (and the affidavit supporting the request for the warrant) is Form AOC-CR-913M. The warrant for periodic inspections is Form AOC-CR-914M. Both forms are available online.

68. G.S. 15-27.2(c). *See also* Marshall v. Barlow's, Inc. 436 U.S. 307 (1978) (search of business without warrant unconstitutional); Camara v. Mun. Court, 387 U.S. 523 (1967) (building inspector must obtain inspection warrant when occupant objects to inspection, and probable cause is required for the warrant); See v. City of Seattle, 387 U.S. 541 (1967); Brooks v. Butler, 70 N.C. App. 681, 321 S.E.2d 440 (1984); Gooden v. Brooks, 39 N.C. App. 519, 251 S.E.2d 698 (1979).

69. G.S. 15-27.2(c).

70. Sunkler v. Town of Nags Head, No. 2:01-CV-22-H(2), 2002 WL 32395571 (E.D.N.C. May 17, 2002), *aff'd*, 50 F. App'x 116 (4th Cir. 2002).

71. G.S. 15-27.2(e).

72. G.S. 15-27.2(f).

73. 144 N.C. App. 236, 550 S.E.2d 212, *review denied*, 354 N.C. 361, 556 S.E.2d 299 (2001). *See also* S. Blvd. Video & News, Inc. v. Charlotte Zoning Bd. of Adjustment, 129 N.C. App. 282, 498 S.E.2d 623, *review denied*, 348 N.C. 501, 510 S.E.2d 656 (1998).

conducted a more thorough inspection, including recording a forty-minute video of the merchandise, viewing several videos offered for sale, and making measurements of the store. The court held that while a zoning officer can enter a commercial establishment and view everything as a normal customer would without a warrant, a more intrusive, detailed inspection can only be conducted pursuant to a valid inspection warrant. In this instance, the initial inspections were within the bounds of a warrantless inspection and in fact properly served as the basis for securing a warrant.

Staff Conflicts of Interest

G.S. 160D-109(c) prohibits staff from having financial or employment interests in any business with a financial interest in a development in the jurisdiction. An exception is provided for when a staff person is the owner of the property. This statute also more generally prohibits administrative staff from engaging in work that is inconsistent with their duties or the interest of the local government.[74]

The General Assembly clarified and strengthened the statutory conflict-of-interest standard for administrative staff with the enactment of Chapter 160D in 2019. Two additional conflict-of-interest standards for staff were incorporated into G.S. 160D-109(c).[75] First, a staff person may not make an administrative decision if the outcome would have a direct, substantial, and readily identifiable financial impact on that person.[76] Second, a staff person may not make an administrative decision if that person has a close familial, business, or other associational relationship with the applicant or another person subject to the decision.[77] In these instances, the statute directs that the decision be assigned to the staff person's supervisor or such other person as may be designated by the development regulation.

These provisions do not explicitly refer to staff recommendations (as opposed to determinations and development approvals). It would be prudent to apply the same conflict-of-interest standards as when the staff person is the decision maker, though that is not mandated by the statute.[78]

Enforcement

Notice of Violation

When an administrator determines there is a violation of a development regulation, enforcement is generally initiated with issuance of a notice of violation (often referred to as an "NOV").[79]

---

74. G.S. 160D-109(c). Many local governments also have employment and personnel policies that provide specific guidance on this issue.

75. These two standards were previously required for board members making legislative and quasi-judicial decisions. See the discussion of conflicts of interest in Chapter 25.

76. There is also a more specific prohibition on financial interests in construction businesses that is applicable to staff handling building-code enforcement. G.S. 160D-1108 prohibits staff from having a financial or employment interest in a business with a financial interest in a development in the jurisdiction.

77. G.S. 160D-109(d) defines a "close familial relationship" in this context to include a spouse, parent, child, brother, sister, grandparent, or grandchild, including the step, half, and in-law relationships.

78. By way of instructive analogy, this statute applies the same conflict of interest to recommendations made by planning boards.

79. G.S. 160D-404(a). The separate enforcement authority previously set out in the historic-preservation statutes was incorporated into the general-enforcement authority for development regulations with the enactment of Chapter 160D. G.S. 160D-404(c)(3). For properties in a local historic district or designated as local historic landmarks, the local government, the local historic-preservation commission, or a party aggrieved "may institute any appropriate action or proceedings" to prevent an unlawful demolition (by neglect or otherwise), destruction, alteration, or other illegal act. The general-enforcement authorities are also available for enforcement of historic-preservation requirements.

A written notice of violation initiates a formal enforcement action for violation of a land-development regulation.[80] This notice of violation identifies the nature of the violation and directs the owner to bring the site into compliance within a set time.[81] The burden of proving the existence of a violation is on the unit of government.[82]

A notice of violation is issued to the holder of the development approval and to the property owner if that person is not the permittee. It may also be delivered to the occupant of the property.[83] Some jurisdictions initially issue a verbal or informal request for compliance and only begin formal enforcement if compliance is not secured in a reasonable time.[84] Such an informal notice is not, however, a determination that is appealable. A notice of violation may be delivered electronically, in person, or by first-class mail to the occupant of the property or the person undertaking the work or activity.[85]

An enforcement action cannot be initiated (or a permit denied) in anticipation of a future (but not present) violation of the ordinance. In *Mitchell v. Barfield*, Durham denied a permit for a hotel, which was a permitted use in a residential zone, based on a concern that the use would be changed to a nursing home or hospital (which were not permitted uses) after construction. The court held the denial improper because there was an adequate remedy to deal with potential use changes if they actually took place.[86] Similarly, in *Thompson v. Town of White Lake*,[87] an accessory storage building under construction was modified in a way to facilitate commercial use as a multiunit storage facility rather than the permitted personal storage use. The court held that the modification in itself could not constitute the basis for finding this was a commercial use absent evidence that the building was actually put to commercial use.

---

80. An existing violation that has not been remedied constitutes an encumbrance on the property. A purchaser under a general warranty deed that does not include an exception for the violation may recover the costs of remediation from the seller, even where the purchaser has prior knowledge of the violation. War Eagle, Inc. v. Belair, 204 N.C. App. 548, 694 S.E.2d 497 (2010) (allowing purchaser to recover costs of removing building foundation placed within riparian buffer in violation of county zoning code).

81. In *Peterson v. City of Hickory*, No. 5:07-CV-00074-RLV, 2010 WL 4791901 (W.D.N.C. Nov. 17, 2010), the city issued a notice of violation regarding junk vehicles on a property as well as tenants working on a race car at night. The notice gave the plaintiff four weeks to remedy the violation or face fines. The court held that the process provided was adequate for due-process purposes (notice of violation, an opportunity to remedy, and appeal possibilities).

82. The court may not take judicial notice of the ordinance. When the applicable ordinance and the building permit are part of the record, the local government failed to meet its burden of showing a violation of the ordinance. Thompson v. Union County, 283 N.C. App. 574, 874 S.E.2d 623 (2022). *See also* Shearl v. Town of Highlands, 236 N.C. App. 113, 116–17, 762 S.E.2d 877, 881 (2014); City of Winston-Salem v. Hoots Concrete Co., 47 N.C. App. 405, 414, 267 S.E.2d 569, 575 (1980).

83. Patmore v. Town of Chapel Hill, 233 N.C. App. 133, 757 S.E.2d 302, *review denied*, 367 N.C. 519, 758 S.E.2d 874 (2014).

84. The initial notice (sometimes referred to as a "courtesy notice") seeks voluntary compliance within a set time period. If the violation has been resolved upon reinspection, the case is usually closed without further action. If the violation has not been resolved, a formal notice of violation is sent to initiate the legal enforcement process.

85. The person providing the notice of violation must certify to the local government that notice was provided, and the certificate of delivery is deemed conclusive in the absence of fraud. G.S. 160D-404(a).

86. 232 N.C. 325, 59 S.E.2d 810 (1950). In *Woodhouse v. Board of Commissioners*, 299 N.C. 211, 261 S.E.2d 882 (1980), the court ruled that future potential problems with a waste-disposal system were not valid grounds for permit denial, given the availability of permit conditions to secure proper design and adequate enforcement remedies if the system was improperly operated.

87. 252 N.C. App. 237, 797 S.E.2d 346 (2017).

Stop-Work Orders

If the officer determines that a building or structure is being constructed, reconstructed, altered, or repaired in a way that is in substantial violation of state or local law or that is dangerous, the officer can issue a formal stop-work order.[88]

A stop-work order must be in writing; it must specify the violation found; and it must tell the recipients what they must do to be able to resume work. A stop-work order must be delivered by hand, by e-mail, or by first-class mail to the person holding the development approval and the property owner. The staff member sending the order is to certify for the files the timing and content of the order and that certification is conclusive in the absence of fraud. Violation of a stop-work order is a Class 1 misdemeanor, though this criminal sanction is only applicable to violations regarding unsafe buildings.[89]

Permit Revocation

A local government has the option of revoking any permits that are being violated whether or not a stop-work order has been issued.[90] The revocation of an approval may be done in addition to issuance of a notice of violation, a stop-work order, or any other enforcement action. A permit revocation must be in writing.

The local government must follow the same process that was required for issuance of the development approval in order to revoke that approval. So an administrative approval made by a staff member may be revoked by that staff member, but a quasi-judicial approval made by a board can only be revoked by that board after an evidentiary hearing.[91]

The statutes provide that development approvals *must* be revoked in three instances: (1) when there is a substantial departure from approved plans, (2) when there is a failure to comply with the development regulation,[92] and (3) when there are false statements on the application. A permit *may* be revoked if it was mistakenly issued.

---

88. G.S. 160D-404(b). Appeals of stop-work orders are made under G.S. 160D-405.

89. Violations of development regulations were decriminalized by S.L. 2021-138, § 13, except for regulation of unsafe buildings.

90. G.S. 160D-403(f). There are separate provisions for revocation of development agreements (G.S. 160D-1008) and building permits (G.S. 160D-1115).

In a case involving a state mining permit, the court held that authority to modify the permit included authority to revoke it. Clark Stone Co. v. N.C. Dep't of Env't & Nat. Res., 164 N.C. App. 24, 594 S.E.2d 832, *review denied*, 359 N.C. 322, 603 S.E.2d 878 (2004). The agency in the case discovered significant impacts (the site would have been visible and heard from the Appalachian Trail) that would have been grounds for permit denial after a permit had been issued. The agency then revoked the permit after a public hearing on these newly discovered issues, and the court upheld the revocation.

As a general rule, a permit that is revoked creates no vested rights in the period prior to revocation. See Chapter 19 for a discussion of this issue. However, undue delay in enforcement after notice of an error can lead to a laches defense to subsequent enforcement.

91. In a case decided before the adoption of G.S. 160D-403(f), the court in *Hewett v. County of Brunswick* overturned a decision of the board of adjustment that unauthorized modification of a special use permit voided the permit, noting that neither the statutes, the ordinance, nor the permit itself provided authorization for that action. 155 N.C. App. 138, 144, 573 S.E.2d 688, 693 (2002).

92. The officer must determine that the permittee is in fact responsible for the failure to comply. See, for example, *Cain v. North Carolina Department of Transportation*, 149 N.C. App. 365, 560 S.E.2d 584 (2002). In this case, after vegetation in the right-of-way adjacent to a permitted sign was improperly destroyed in an apparent attempt to increase the visibility of the sign, the Department of Transportation revoked the sign permit. The permittee contended that the vegetative alteration was done by a sublessee without the permittee's knowledge or permission. The court held that the department must clearly identify persons who committed a violation for which revocation was permissible and must show a sufficient connection between those persons and the permittee. The trial court

Administrative Appeals

These enforcement determinations by the officer—notices of violation, stop-work orders, and permit revocations—may be appealed to the board of adjustment.[93]

The statute provides for stays of zoning-enforcement actions pending administrative appeals of a zoning officer's determination.[94] An exception is provided if the officer certifies that a stay would cause imminent peril to life or property or that the violation charged is transitory in nature and a stay would seriously interfere with enforcement. In those instances, there is no stay unless the board or a court issues a restraining order. Also, if a formal stop-work order has been issued, no further work may be undertaken during the pendency of the appeal.[95]

Occasionally, an ordinance will be amended between the time an alleged violation takes place and subsequent enforcement action. The courts have held that in this situation a board of adjustment considering appeal of a notice of violation should apply the ordinance in effect at the time of appeal.[96]

Zoning-enforcement actions may not be appealed directly to court without first going before the board of adjustment.[97] If an appeal is not made to the board of adjustment, the enforcement action may not be collaterally attacked in subsequent judicial actions. In one of the state's earliest zoning decisions, *State v. Roberson*,[98] the defendant was denied a permit to construct a store and automobile service station in a Durham residential zoning district. The board of adjustment upheld the determination that the uses were not allowed in that district. The defendant then constructed and opened the store and was charged with a zoning violation. The court held that a failure to seek judicial review of the board

---

concluded that either the sign lessee or sublessee conducted the improper vegetation removal, and it held that the lease and sublease established a sufficient connection between the permittee and these persons to warrant revocation. *See also* Outdoor E., L.P. v. Harrelson, 123 N.C. App. 685, 688, 476 S.E.2d 136, 137–38 (1996) (upholding revocation of sign company's permit based on actions by advertiser's employees); Whiteco Indus., Inc. v. Harrington, 111 N.C. App. 839, 844, 434 S.E.2d 234, 237 (1993), *review denied*, 335 N.C. 565, 441 S.E.2d 135 (1994) (upholding revocation of sign company's permit based on actions by advertiser's employees).

93. G.S. 160D-404(b). See G.S. 160D-1114 for appeals regarding building permits.

94. G.S. 160D-405(f) provides that an appeal to the board of adjustment stays all proceedings in furtherance of the action appealed from. Fines and civil penalties do not accrue during the pendency of an appeal. Town of Midland v. Harrell, 282 N.C. App. 354, 871 S.E.2d 392 (2022).

95. G.S. 160D-404(b). If the appeal involves an alleged violation of the State Building Code, the appeal is made to the state Commissioner of Insurance rather than to the board of adjustment.

96. Overton v. Camden Cnty., 155 N.C. App. 391, 395–96, 574 S.E.2d 157, 160–61 (2002). *See also* CRLP Durham, LP v. Durham City/Cnty. Bd. of Adjustment, 210 N.C. App. 203, 706 S.E.2d 317, *review denied*, 365 N.C. 348, 717 S.E.2d 744 (2011) (dismissing appeal because record not clear on whether prior or current ordinance was applicable to interpretation of conditional rezoning).

97. This would also be true for other local-development regulations that provide for administrative appeals to a board of adjustment or similar body. For a discussion of the requirement to exhaust administrative remedies prior to judicial review, see Chapter 29.

98. 198 N.C. 70, 150 S.E. 674 (1929).

of adjustment's decision precludes a collateral attack on the validity of the ordinance.[99] The exhaustion requirement does not apply to jurisdictional challenges.[100]

Sanctions and Remedies

G.S. 160D-404(c) provides that local governments may employ the same remedies for enforcement of development regulations that are available generally for city and county ordinances.[101] The provisions for enforcement of county and city ordinances are set out in G.S. 153A-123 and 160A-175.[102] Under these statutes, cities and counties have three principal tools for enforcement of ordinances: civil penalties, criminal sanctions, and injunctive relief. However, criminal sanctions are no longer available as an enforcement tool for development regulations.[103]

As a general rule, attorney's fees may not be recovered in an action to enforce a land-development-regulatory ordinance, as there is no statutory authorization for such.[104] Also, the court of appeals has

---

99. Similar holdings include: Cnty. of Durham v. Addison, 262 N.C. 280, 283–84, 136 S.E.2d 600, 603 (1964) (when board of adjustment has upheld notice of violation and denied a variance, and the decision was not appealed, defendant may not collaterally attack that decision in a subsequent county suit to enjoin construction subject to that notice of violation); Town of Pinebluff v. Marts, 195 N.C. App. 659, 673 S.E.2d 740 (2009) (when town seeks injunction to compel compliance with conditions of approval, the ordinance validity cannot be raised as a defense); Appalachian Outdoor Advert. Co. v. Town of Boone, 103 N.C. App. 504, 406 S.E.2d 297 (1991) (when board of adjustment has upheld notice of violation relative to sign placement and decision was not appealed, subsequent action seeking compensation is barred); Wil-Hol Corp. v. Marshall, 71 N.C. App. 611, 614, 322 S.E.2d 655, 657 (1984); New Hanover Cnty. v. Pleasant, 59 N.C. App. 644, 297 S.E.2d 760 (1982) (laches defense may not be raised in judicial-enforcement action where board-of-adjustment decision upholding notice of violation was not appealed); City of Elizabeth City v. LFM Enters., Inc., 48 N.C. App. 408, 269 S.E.2d 260 (1980) (when a variance has been sought and denied, and the denial has not been appealed, the zoning-ordinance provision cannot be collaterally attacked in an enforcement proceeding); City of Hickory v. Catawba Valley Mach. Co., 39 N.C. App. 236, 249 S.E.2d 851 (1978) (where the defendant fails to seek judicial review of a board-of-adjustment decision that an alleged violation was not a lawful nonconformity, the defendant cannot collaterally attack the ruling in a subsequent enforcement action). For further discussion of the exhaustion-of-administrative-remedies issue, see Chapter 29.

100. Guilford Cnty. Plan. & Dev. Dep't v. Simmons, 102 N.C. App. 325, 401 S.E.2d 659, *review denied*, 329 N.C. 496, 407 S.E.2d 533 (1991).

101. Initiation of judicial action to enforce a zoning-ordinance violation does not preclude a separate judicial action under nuisance-abatement authority. State v. Mercer, 128 N.C. App. 371, 496 S.E.2d 585 (1998).

102. A local government can also deny a privilege license for a proposed business that is not in compliance with land use regulations. Fantasy World, Inc. v. Greensboro Bd. of Adjustment, 162 N.C. App. 603, 592 S.E.2d 205, *review denied*, 358 N.C. 543, 599 S.E.2d 43 (2004). Neighbors may join a city or county's enforcement action. City of Shelby v. Lackey, 235 N.C. 343, 69 S.E.2d 607 (1952). See Chapter 29 for a discussion of parties in zoning suits. Individual cities and counties may be granted other enforcement options by local legislation. For example, S.L. 2010-62 authorizes the City of Winston-Salem to summarily abate any zoning violation that continues five days after a notice of violation, with the expense of the action to be paid by the violator. It allows a lien (with the same priority as a tax lien) to be placed on the land to recover the costs if they are not paid. A secondary lien may also be placed on any other property in the city that is owned by the violator (other than the violator's principal residence). The city can also file a notice of lis pendens with the clerk of court upon issuance of a notice of violation. With this filing, the notice of violation is thereafter binding on successors and assigns of the owner of the premises in violation. S.L. 2011-142 extended this Winston-Salem authority to allow summary action to enforce chronic zoning violations (multiple violations within a calendar year).

103. The decriminalization applies to regulations adopted under Chapter 160D of the General Statutes (except for regulation of unsafe buildings) and to local regulations on stream clearing, outdoor advertising, solar collectors, cisterns, rain barrels, and trees if adopted under authorization other than Chapter 160D. Though rarely done, a previous local ordinance could make these violations misdemeanors.

104. Thus, a county was not entitled to attorney's fees in an action to enforce junkyard-screening requirements set by county ordinance. Cnty. of Hoke v. Byrd, 107 N.C. App. 658, 668, 421 S.E.2d 800, 806 (1992). See Chapter 29 for further discussion of recovering attorney's fees in litigation.

held that city and county records prepared relative to violations of development regulations are subject to the criminal-investigations exception to the Public Records Act and may be withheld from disclosure to an alleged violator.[105]

Civil Penalties

The N.C. courts have held that the legislature may authorize state agencies and local governments to assess civil penalties of varying amounts.[106] The statutes allow an administrator to assess such a penalty if the local ordinance specifically authorizes civil penalties for violations.[107] If the ordinance includes specific procedures to be followed in assessing civil penalties, failure to follow them precludes an assessment.[108]

The maximum amount of a civil penalty must not exceed an amount that is reasonably related to the amount of harm caused by the violation and the cost to the local government of securing compliance.[109] The ordinance can provide that each day of continuing violation after notice of violation is a separate offense.[110] An evidentiary hearing is not required prior to the assessment of a civil penalty.[111]

---

105. McCormick v. Hanson Aggregates Se., Inc., 164 N.C. App. 459, 596 S.E.2d 431, *review denied*, 359 N.C. 69, 603 S.E.2d 131 (2004) (applying G.S. 132-1.4). The court further held, however, that there is not a general attorney-work-product exemption to public-records disclosure.

106. *In re* Civil Penalty, 324 N.C. 373, 379 S.E.2d 30 (1989) (upholding a penalty of $4200 for violation of the Sedimentation Pollution Control Act). The court held that civil penalties fall within the provisions of article IV, section 3 of the North Carolina constitution, which allows administrative agencies to be vested with judicial powers when they are reasonably necessary as an incident to accomplishment of the agencies' purposes. For an analysis of the case, see Farleigh Hailes Earhart, Note, *The Forty-Two Hundred Dollar Question: "May State Agencies Have Discretion in Setting Civil Penalties Under the North Carolina Constitution?,"* 68 N.C. L. REV. 1035 (1990).

107. G.S. 153A-123(c); 160A-175(c). JWL Invs., Inc. v. Guilford Cnty. Bd. of Adjustment, 133 N.C. App. 426, 515 S.E.2d 715 (1999), *review denied*, 251 N.C. 715, 540 S.E.2d 349 (2000) (affirming use of civil penalties for zoning enforcement). Civil penalties are also used to enforce other ordinances related to land use and development. *See, e.g.,* City of Charlotte v. King, 158 N.C. App. 304, 580 S.E.2d 380 (2003) (affirming a civil penalty of $5500 imposed for failure to comply with order imposed under city housing code to repair or demolish a dwelling).

108. Transylvania Cnty. v. Moody, 151 N.C. App. 389, 565 S.E.2d 720 (2002). In this sign-ordinance-enforcement case, the county failed to follow several steps required by its ordinance. The initial notices of violation did specify a reasonable time to come into compliance, and a proper compliance order was not served. Failure to follow the procedural safeguards for administration and enforcement set forth in the ordinance invalidated the civil-penalty assessment.

109. The statutes for local-development regulation do not explicitly require this. The N.C. Supreme Court in *In re Civil Penalty* noted that discretion is allowed in setting the amount of the civil penalty, provided there are adequate guiding standards (such as a range for maximum penalties and factors to be considered in determining the amount of the penalty) and procedural safeguards (such as administrative and judicial review) in place. 324 N.C. at 381–83, 379 S.E.2d at 35–36. A number of the state's natural-resource-protection statutes have specific factors that must be considered in setting the amount of civil penalties. *See, e.g.,* G.S. 113A-64(a)(3) (civil penalties under the Sedimentation Pollution Control Act are to be based on the degree and extent of harm caused, the cost of rectifying the damage, the amount the violator saved by noncompliance, whether the violation was willful, and the prior compliance record of the violator); G.S. 113A-126(d)(4) (civil penalties under the Coastal Area Management Act are to be based on the degree and extent of harm caused and the cost of rectifying the damage).

110. G.S. 153A-123(g); 160A-175(g). *See In re* N. Topsail Water & Sewer, Inc., 96 N.C. App. 468, 386 S.E.2d 92 (1989), *review denied*, 326 N.C. 364, 389 S.E.2d 810 (1990) (upholding $19,000 civil penalty assessed for a continuing violation caused by sediment from the petitioner's unpermitted ditches). This portion of the penalty was based on a failure to take corrective action after a notice of violation and an instruction to remedy the violation by constructing a dam to halt the siltation. A civil penalty can be assessed for violations taking place before the initial notice of violation. Crowell Constructors, Inc. v. N.C. Dep't of Env't, Health, & Nat. Res., 107 N.C. App. 716, 421 S.E.2d 612 (1992), *review denied*, 333 N.C. 343, 426 S.E.2d 704 (1993) (upholding $26,000 civil penalty for mining without a permit).

111. Pisgah Oil Co. v. W. N.C. Reg'l Air Pollution Control Agency, 139 N.C. App. 402, 533 S.E.2d 290, *review denied*, 353 N.C. 268, 546 S.E.2d 111 (2000) (where the record reflects that the agency had substantial evidence before it and adequately considered the statutorily mandated standards, an evidentiary hearing is not required for assessment or administrative appeal of a civil penalty).

The civil-penalty assessment can be appealed to the board of adjustment. If the notice of violation has been appealed to court and affirmed, the ordinance need not provide for a separate appeal to the board of adjustment of the civil penalties that are subsequently assessed.[112] If a civil penalty is not paid or appealed, judicial action can be initiated to collect the penalty as a debt. In such an action, the only issue is payment. The issue of whether there was a violation and any defenses that might have been raised regarding the assessment are waived by the failure to exhaust administrative remedies.[113] An exception to this exhaustion rule arises if the judicial challenge is to the constitutionality of the ordinance provision allegedly violated. In this circumstance, the court has held that if the provision is indeed illegal, the city or county has no authority to enforce it, so an administrative appeal is not required.[114]

Care must be exercised in the disposition of moneys collected as civil penalties. Fines collected as criminal penalties are required to go to the county school fund.[115] If a violation is potentially subject to criminal prosecution as well as being subject to a civil penalty (which is no longer the case for most violations of development regulations), the funds collected as civil penalties go to the school fund. If the offense involved is subject to civil penalties only and is specifically not made a crime, then the proceeds may go to a city or county fund that pays for the cost of ordinance enforcement. This consideration is of less significance after the decriminalization of development-regulation violations in 2021, though it remains relevant if unsafe-building violations are criminal offenses under a local ordinance.

---

112. Town of Midland v. Harrell, 282 N.C. App. 354, 871 S.E.2d 392 (2022). Unless required by ordinance, the governing board does not have to approve by resolution an individual civil action to collect a civil penalty.

113. Grandfather Vill. v. Worsley, 111 N.C. App. 686, 433 S.E.2d 13, *review denied*, 335 N.C. 237, 439 S.E.2d 146 (1993). This case involved an alleged violation of the zoning-regulation prohibition of portable signs. The defendant was assessed a $50 per day civil penalty after its signs were not removed in sixty days. The defendant did not make a timely appeal to the board of adjustment. In this judicial action, the defendant attempted to deny ownership of the signs. The court held that failure to appeal within the allotted period waived any right to raise defenses to the assessment in court. *See also* State *ex rel.* Cobey v. Cook, 118 N.C. App. 70, 453 S.E.2d 553, *review denied*, 340 N.C. 572, 460 S.E.2d 329 (1995) (collection action regarding $5040 civil penalty for a violation of the Sedimentation Pollution Control Act).

114. City of Wilmington v. Hill, 189 N.C. App. 173, 657 S.E.2d 670 (2008).

115. See the discussion of disposition of fines and penalties, below.

Injunctive Relief

A local government can seek an injunction or court order to compel compliance with land-development regulations.[116] Injunctions can prohibit the completion of a structure or operation of a use that violates an ordinance.[117] An injunction can compel completion of mandated improvements, such as a street.[118] A preliminary injunction may be sought to maintain the status quo during litigation, but it may only be issued if the court determines that the petitioner has shown a likelihood of both irreparable harm without the injunction and success on the merits.[119] The court may also include an order of abatement to mandate removal of an offending use, condition, or site restoration.[120] A writ of mandamus to require a local government to enforce an ordinance is, however, rarely appropriate.[121]

---

116. G.S. 153A-123(d), (e); 160A-175(d), (e); 160D-404(c)(1). Town of Midland v. Harrell, 282 N.C. App. 354, 871 S.E.2d 392 (2022); City of Raleigh v. Morand, 247 N.C. 363, 100 S.E.2d 870 (1957), *appeal dismissed*, 357 U.S. 343 (1958) (injunctive relief available for enforcement of city zoning ordinance in city's extraterritorial jurisdiction); City of Fayetteville v. Spur Distrib. Co., 216 N.C. 596, 5 S.E.2d 838 (1939) (city may seek injunction to prevent violation of zoning ordinance). An action seeking an injunction under these statutes does not require a verified complaint. Pitt Cnty. v. Dejavue, Inc., 185 N.C. App. 545, 555, 650 S.E.2d 12, 18 (2007).

117. Cnty. of Durham v. Maddry & Co., 315 N.C. 296, 337 S.E.2d 576 (1985) (use may be enjoined if it violates zoning ordinance or building code); Elizabeth City v. Aydlett, 200 N.C. 58, 156 S.E. 163 (1930). *See also* City of Asheboro v. Auman, 26 N.C. App. 87, 214 S.E.2d 621, *cert. denied*, 288 N.C. 239, 217 S.E.2d 663 (1975) (upholding injunction prohibiting continued use of improperly sited mobile home); Cnty. of Currituck v. Upton, 19 N.C. App. 45, 197 S.E.2d 883 (1973) (upholding issuance of injunction to compel the removal of a mobile home from a zoning district that did not permit freestanding mobile homes). Note, however, that mandamus will not lie against a landowner who is not a party to the suit. McDowell v. Randolph Cnty., 186 N.C. App. 17, 28, 649 S.E.2d 920, 928 (2007) (court refused to issue injunction against owner of expanded nonconforming use as only the county, not the owner, was a party to suit brought by neighbor). G.S. 1-56 provides for a ten-year statute of limitations for commencing these civil actions. In *Ocean Hill Joint Venture v. North Carolina Department of Environment, Health, and Natural Resources*, 333 N.C. 318, 426 S.E.2d 274 (1993), the court held that the one-year statute of limitations of G.S. 1-54(2) does not apply to the assessment of a civil penalty for a sedimentation violation.

118. In *Town of Midland v. Harrell*, 282 N.C. App. 354, 871 S.E.2d 392 (2022), the court held that it was appropriate for the trial court to mandate maintenance of streets until public acceptance and to make repairs necessary to return the street conditions to mandated standards. However, the court also held that the statute directs that Rule 65 of the Rules of Civil Procedure be followed, and that Rule requires that the order be specific and define in reasonable detail the acts required.

119. G.S. 1A-1, Rule 62(c). Schloss v. Jamison, 258 N.C. 271, 128 S.E.2d 590 (1962) (a temporary injunction against enforcement of a zoning ordinance while it is being challenged may be appropriate to maintain the status quo); City of New Bern v. Walker, 255 N.C. 355, 121 S.E.2d 544 (1961) (enjoining use of residentially zoned property as a commercial garage during pendency of appeal appropriate); Elizabeth City v. Aydlett, 200 N.C. 58, 156 S.E. 163 (1930) (temporary restraining orders an appropriate remedy under the zoning-enabling act). In *Walker*, the court held that the defendant was not entitled to continue the use during the pendency of the enforcement action by posting a bond. In exceptional cases, a party can also seek a temporary restraining order to require or prevent activity until a motion for a temporary injunction can be heard.

In *North Iredell Neighbors for Rural Life v. Iredell County*, 196 N.C. App. 68, 674 S.E.2d 436, *review denied*, 363 N.C. 582, 682 S.E.2d 385 (2009), the court held that the trial court did not abuse its discretion in denying a preliminary injunction to prohibit the building and operation of a biodiesel-fuel operation during litigation on the matter, as there was no indication that there was any attempt to immediately begin the project.

120. The North Carolina courts have not resolved the question of whether the trial court must balance the equities of the parties in entering injunctive relief in these situations, and courts in other jurisdictions are split on the question. Town of Pinebluff v. Marts, 195 N.C. App. 659, 665, 673 S.E.2d 740, 744 (2009).

121. David M. Lawrence, *Mandamus to Require Enforcement of Local Ordinances*, Loc. Gov't L. Bull. No. 132 (UNC School of Government, July 2013).

Unlike with civil penalties, it is not necessary for the development regulation itself to specifically authorize injunctive relief.[122] Injunctive relief is available under state law even if not specifically provided for in the ordinance.[123]

Town of Pine Knoll Shores v. Evans illustrates use of injunctive relief to compel abatement of a zoning violation. The defendant constructed an unattached deck between his house and a canal without first securing a building permit. The town cited the defendant for a zoning violation (the ordinance prohibited a separate structure on the lot, and the deck was within the minimum setback from the canal) and sought an injunction to compel removal of the deck. The court held that the deck was in fact in violation of the ordinance, upheld an order for removal, and rejected application of the doctrine of "economic waste" to justify allowing the violating structure to remain in place.[124]

Willful violation of a court order to comply subjects violators to contempt-of-court sanctions.[125] These sanctions can be severe; violators may be held in jail until compliance is secured.[126] In a contempt hearing, the burden is on defendants to purge themselves of contempt by showing compliance with court orders or securing an order's modification.[127]

Settlement

Once an enforcement action has been commenced, a local government has broad discretion to reach a settlement.[128]

---

122. If the ordinance authorizes "such other lawful action as is necessary to prevent or remedy any violation," that is broad enough to incorporate the state enabling authority to seek injunctive relief. New Hanover Cnty. v. Pleasant, 59 N.C. App. 644, 648, 297 S.E.2d 760, 762 (1982).

123. Mecklenburg Cnty. v. Westbery, 32 N.C. App. 630, 635–36, 233 S.E.2d 658, 661 (1977).

124. 331 N.C. 361, 416 S.E.2d 4 (1991). The trial court had ruled the project to be in violation of the zoning ordinance, but it ordered that the deck could remain in place upon payment of a $2000 civil penalty. The court of appeals had subsequently ruled that the trial court had had no authority to substitute a civil penalty for an order of abatement because the city's ordinance itself had to specifically provide for civil penalties pursuant to G.S. 160A-175 in order for that enforcement tool to be available (and this ordinance did not authorize civil penalties).

See also State *ex rel.* Cobey v. Simpson, 333 N.C. 81, 423 S.E.2d 759 (1992) (upholding injunctive relief to compel site restoration after a violation of the Coastal Area Management Act). The court held that the trial court erred in allowing the violator to make only partial restoration given that the state had sought full restoration. When there is no evidence that complete restoration is impractical in an environmental and engineering sense, the trial court cannot reduce the economic costs of restoration to the violator by allowing partial restoration.

125. The statutory provisions regarding civil contempt are G.S. 5A-21 to -25. Case law requires the person to be guilty of willful disobedience of the court order. *See, e.g.,* Hancock v. Hancock, 122 N.C. App. 518, 525, 471 S.E.2d 415, 419 (1996) (failure to comply must be with "knowledge and stubborn resistance").

126. McKillop v. Onslow Cnty., 139 N.C. App. 53, 532 S.E.2d 594 (2000) (upholding a finding of civil contempt and order of abatement based on the plaintiff's willful operation of an adult business in violation of the county's adult-business ordinance and previous court order to refrain from such violation); State v. Moore, 132 N.C. App. 197, 511 S.E.2d 22 (1999) (upholding finding defendant in criminal contempt for violation of a preliminary injunction prohibiting him from operating three specific adult businesses located in violation of county ordinance).

127. City of Brevard v. Ritter, 285 N.C. 576, 206 S.E.2d 151 (1974). In this case the defendant began construction of a building enlarging a private airport in violation of the zoning ordinance. The town secured a court order compelling the removal of the offending, partially completed structure. The defendant, without the town's approval and without an amendment of the court order, then began to convert the structure to another use instead of removing it.

128. This discretion is not unbounded, however. In *League of Residential Neighborhood Advocates v. City of Los Angeles*, 498 F.3d 1052 (9th Cir. 2007), the court invalidated a settlement in a federal case that allowed a congregation to operate a synagogue in a residential zoning district that required a conditional use permit for such a use. The court found that approving the use without going through the conditional use permit notice-and-hearing process violated California law and could not be done absent a finding that federal law has been violated.

If litigation has commenced, settlement usually takes the form of a consent judgment or order approved by the judge with jurisdiction over the case. All of the parties to an enforcement action must agree to a consent judgment, and any of the parties may withdraw their agreement prior to court approval and entry of a judgment.[129] If counsel represents a party, there is a presumption that the attorney has authority to act on behalf of the client, and the attorney's signature on the consent agreement is sufficient.[130]

Disposition of Fines and Penalties

The proceeds of criminal fines, and in some instances civil penalties collected, are required by the state constitution to be paid over to the school system. Article IX, section 7 of the North Carolina Constitution provides that "the clear proceeds of all penalties and forfeitures and of all fines collected in the several counties for any breach of the penal laws of the State, . . . shall be . . . used exclusively for maintaining free public schools." The voters approved a state constitutional amendment in November 2004 to provide that the General Assembly may place the clear proceeds of civil penalties, civil forfeitures, and civil fines collected by a state agency in a state fund to be used exclusively for maintaining free public schools.

Fines collected for misdemeanor criminal violations of development ordinances are included in this mandate. The inclusion of civil penalties collected is less clear, as they are imposed by local ordinance, not the "laws of the State," and arguably they are more in the nature of restitution or remediation for actual damages and the costs of securing compliance than being "penal" in nature. However, the court held in *Cauble v. City of Asheville*[131] that the clear proceeds of parking penalties collected by the city belonged to the school system. Thus, unless the land-development ordinance specifies that enforcement is through civil penalty and injunctive relief only (that is, as long as a criminal citation remains a possible enforcement tool), it is likely that the net proceeds of these civil penalties should be treated in the same manner as criminal penalties and turned over to the local school system.[132]

Enforcement of Building and Housing Codes

The statutes provide for a detailed procedure for enforcement of building and housing codes.

---

129. Milner v. Littlejohn, 126 N.C. App. 184, 187, 484 S.E.2d 453, 455, *review denied*, 347 N.C. 268, 493 S.E.2d 458 (1997).

130. Guilford Cnty. v. Eller, 146 N.C. App. 579, 553 S.E.2d 235 (2001). The person challenging the action of the attorney as unauthorized has the burden of establishing said lack of authority. In this case a husband and wife were cited for a zoning violation and the consent agreement was signed by the husband and the attorney for the husband and wife. In the absence of any evidence that the wife did not authorize the attorney's signature, the court upheld the agreement.

131. 314 N.C. 598, 336 S.E.2d 59 (1985). For an analysis of this case and a detailed review of the constitutional provision involved, see David M. Lawrence, *Fines, Penalties, and Forfeitures: An Historical and Comparative Analysis*, 65 N.C. L. Rev. 49 (1986). G.S. 153A-123(b) and 160A-175(b) provide that violation of a county or city ordinance is a criminal misdemeanor unless the governing board explicitly provides otherwise.

132. The state in 1987 adopted legislation to do this for civil penalties collected under state laws. G.S. 115C-457.2 provides that the clear proceeds from all civil penalties collected by state agencies are placed in the Civil Penalty and Forfeiture Fund. They are ultimately transferred to the State School Technology Fund and allocated to local school-administrative units. The "clear proceeds" of the fines are defined as the amount collected minus the actual costs of collection, which cannot exceed 10 percent of the amount collected. *See also* N.C. Sch. Bds. Ass'n v. Moore, 359 N.C. 474, 614 S.E.2d 504 (2005); Craven Cnty. Bd. of Educ. v. Boyles, 343 N.C. 87, 468 S.E.2d 50 (1996). This case is analyzed in Shea Riggsbee Denning, *Public School Funding in the Summer of 2005*: North Carolina School Boards Association v. Moore, Loc. Gov't L. Bull, No. 108 (UNC School of Government, Nov. 2005). *See also* DeLuca v. Smith, 261 N.C. App. 89, 820 S.E.2d 89 (2018) (remanding case for additional findings as to whether payments to settle suit regarding hog wastes was a penalty).

An enforcement officer may issue a stop-work order if work in progress is determined to be hazardous or in violation of a permit. Appeals relative to building-code issues go to the state commissioner of insurance, and appeals relative to a local ordinance go to the applicable board of adjustment.[133]

The enforcement officer may "condemn as unsafe" a building that is dangerous to life by posting a notice to that effect on the exterior of the building.[134] If prompt repairs are not made, the enforcement officer holds a hearing (after notice to the owner) on the case[135] and may thereafter order the building repaired, closed, vacated, or demolished.[136] The owner may appeal that order to the jurisdiction's governing board, which may affirm, modify, or revoke the order.[137] If the owner fails to appeal, the order is final. The court has held that these hearings and appeals constitute a quasi-judicial decision, and collateral estoppel applies to the factual determinations made after the hearing.[138] Failure to comply with the governing board's order is a misdemeanor,[139] and the jurisdiction may seek injunctive relief to secure compliance.[140]

For nonresidential buildings that are not brought into compliance, local governments also have the option of demolishing the structure and placing a lien on the property for its costs.[141]

For residential buildings in jurisdictions with a housing code, the governing board may order a building that is unfit for human habitation (or that has been abandoned) to be repaired, closed, or demolished.[142] The notice-and-hearing procedure required is generally similar to that for unsafe buildings under the State Building Code: notice to the owner; a hearing before the enforcement officer; an order to repair, close, or demolish by that officer;[143] governing-board action to confirm the order in the event

---

133. G.S. 160D-1114.

134. G.S. 160D-1119. This unsafe-building provision applies to both residential and nonresidential buildings or structures. An unsafe building is defined as one that is "especially dangerous to life because of its liability to fire or because of bad condition of walls, overloaded floors, defective construction, decay, unsafe wiring or heating system, inadequate means of egress, or other causes." G.S. 160D-1119(a). It also includes dilapidated vacant or abandoned buildings within community-development target areas. "Dilapidated" here describes buildings or structures that "cause or contribute to blight, disease, vagrancy, fire or safety hazard"; are "a danger to children"; or "tend to attract persons intent on criminal activities or other activities that would constitute a public nuisance." G.S. 160D-1119(b). A "community development target area" is defined as an area that has the characteristics of an urban-progress zone under G.S. 143B-437.09, a nonresidential redevelopment area under G.S. 160A-503(10), or a similar area deemed by the city council to be in special need of revitalization. This is not condemnation in the eminent-domain sense of acquiring title to the property.

135. G.S. 160D-1121. Notice must be by certified or registered mail or by personal service.

136. G.S. 160D-1122.

137. G.S. 160D-1123.

138. Hillsboro Partners, LLC v. City of Fayetteville, 226 N.C. App. 30, 738 S.E.2d 819, *review denied*, 367 N.C. 236, 748 S.E.2d 544 (2013).

139. G.S. 160D-1124.

140. G.S. 160D-1125.

141. G.S. 160D-1125(b) provides that if corrective action is not taken after due notice and hearing, the local government can require the building to be removed or demolished (and impose a lien for the net costs of correction).

142. G.S. 160D-1201. *See* Anita R. Brown-Graham, Affordable Housing and North Carolina Local Governments 5–8 (2006).

143. The owner must be provided a reasonable period of time to bring the structure into compliance. Horton v. Gulledge, 277 N.C. 353, 177 S.E.2d 885 (1970), *rev'd on other grounds by* State v. Jones, 305 N.C. 520, 290 S.E.2d 675 (1982) (order to demolish a dilapidated house, without option of repairing it, violates state constitution). Also, if a city-council order authorizes repair or demolition and the enforcement officer elects to allow repair, that election cannot be arbitrarily withdrawn. Wiggins v. City of Monroe, 73 N.C. App. 44, 326 S.E.2d 39 (1985).

of noncompliance;[144] the possibility of a lien on the property to cover the cost of securing compliance; and the option to initiate civil action to secure compliance.[145]

Because boarded-up buildings can have a substantial detrimental effect on neighborhoods, local governments may demolish those vacated buildings that have a blighting influence upon a neighborhood.[146] The local government must first find that the building owner has abandoned any intention of repairing or improving the structure, and the structure must have remained vacant and closed for at least one year after the city ordered code compliance. A number of local governments have secured local legislation to limit the amount of time a structure may be vacant rather than repaired or demolished.[147]

Particular care in identifying and providing proper notice to the landowner is necessary in these actions. If the jurisdiction fails to follow the statutory notice requirements, even if there is actual notice, the jurisdiction is liable to the owner for any provable damages.[148] This can be problematic with structures that have been effectively abandoned, and it can increase the costs to the jurisdiction of securing compliance, costs that often cannot realistically be recovered. But when demolition of a structure is involved, extra care and costs are necessary.[149]

---

144. Cities and counties have the option of creating a housing-appeals board to hear appeals of orders under the housing code. They may also provide for the board of adjustment to hear such appeals. G.S. 160D-305. Such a board may be authorized by ordinance to enter final orders for repair or demolition. Moores v. Greensboro Minimum Hous. Standards Comm'n, 198 N.C. App. 384, 679 S.E.2d 480 (2009). The court held that G.S. 160D-1203(5), which provides that orders for demolition or repair are not to be exercised until the "governing body" orders such, does not require action by the city council or board of county commissioners and that a housing code can delegate this authority to a housing-appeals commission.

145. G.S. 160D-1203. Occupation of a building that has been posted as unfit for human habitation is a misdemeanor. G.S. 160D-1203(4). A city must substantially comply with the requirements for posting the site and affording the owner an opportunity to be heard prior to forbidding occupation of a dwelling. Dale v. City of Morganton, 270 N.C. 567, 576, 155 S.E.2d 136, 144 (1967).

146. G.S. 160D-1203(b). Before Chapter 160D was enacted, this option was only available for cities with populations over 71,000.

147. *See, e.g.*, S.L. 2004-6 (Garner, within community-development target areas); S.L. 2003-76 (Greensboro); S.L. 2003-23 (High Point and Goldsboro, within community-development target areas); S.L. 2003-42 (Clinton, Lumberton, and Franklin, within community-development target areas); S.L. 2003-320 (Roanoke Rapids).

148. Newton v. City of Winston-Salem, 92 N.C. App. 446, 374 S.E.2d 488 (1988) (finding potential damages where the city neither served demolition order personally nor published notice when personal service could not be made and did not sell salvageable material upon demolition, both of which are statutory requirements). *See also* Farmers Bank v. City of Elizabeth City, 54 N.C. App. 110, 282 S.E.2d 580 (1981) (whether inspector used reasonable diligence to ascertain whereabouts of building owners prior to hearing and demolition was factual question precluding summary judgment). Also note that the U.S. Supreme Court has held that when an action is proposed that affects critical property rights, such as a tax sale of the property, reasonable steps must be taken to provide actual notice of the proposed action to all interested parties. Mennonite Bd. of Missions v. Adams, 462 U.S. 791 (1983). *See also* Mullane v. Cent. Hanover Bank & Trust Co., 339 U.S. 306, 314 (1950) (prior to taking action that affects a property interest protected by the Due Process Clause, government must provide "notice reasonably calculated, under all circumstances, to apprise interested parties of the pendency of the action and afford them an opportunity to present their objections").

149. An illustration is provided by *Lawyer v. City of Elizabeth City*, 199 N.C. App. 304, 681 S.E.2d 415 (2009), *review denied*, 363 N.C. 855, 694 S.E.2d 389 (2010). The plaintiffs acquired title in October 2003 to a vacant house at a tax sale. They requested that property-tax notices and bills be forwarded to them. Although a sheriff's deed was prepared at this time, the plaintiffs did not record it. In September 2004, the city inspected the house and found it to be unfit for habitation. (It had apparently been vacant since 1999.) Notices of that were sent to the previous owners, who were still listed as record owners. Upon receipt of the notice, the prior owner notified the city that the property had been sold at auction. In response, the city staff in late September made several inquiries of the county tax office and register of deeds as to ownership of this property and were informed that those records indicated the prior owners were still the owners of record. The city did not engage an attorney to conduct a title search. The city therefore continued to mail notices of its condemnation actions to the record owners. In early November, the plaintiffs recorded their tax deed. In late November 2004, the city council approved an ordinance under G.S. 160A-441,

The authority to summarily abate a situation that is a threat to public health and safety[150] may not be used to demolish a dilapidated residence without following this notice-and-hearing procedure unless the structure poses an imminent threat to public health and safety.[151]

When the governing board hears an appeal of the enforcement officer's order to repair or demolish a building, its decision is quasi-judicial, so the hearing procedures and judicial review are the same as they are for other quasi-judicial decisions.[152]

Enforcement of Subdivision Ordinances

For many years, the enforcement options for subdivision-ordinance violations were narrower than for zoning and other land-development-regulation violations. While building permits could be denied for any work inconsistent with zoning requirements,[153] G.S. 153A-334 and 160A-375 included only penal and injunctive relief for subdivision violations. In *Town of Nags Head v. Tillett*, the court held that neither the subdivision statute nor G.S. 160A-375 was broad enough to justify the denial of a building permit for an illegally subdivided lot.[154] Likewise, in *Marriott Financial Services, Inc. v. Capitol Funds, Inc.*,[155] the court ruled that the sanction for an illegal subdivision was a criminal citation, not voiding of the sale.

In 2005, the General Assembly amended these subdivision statutes to broaden the enforcement options for subdivision-ordinance violations.[156] G.S. 160D-807(a) provides that building permits may be denied for lots that are illegally subdivided and that cities and counties may institute "any appropriate action or proceedings to prevent the unlawful subdivision of land, to restrain, correct, or abate the violation, or to prevent any illegal act or conduct."

---

condemning the structure, and posted notice of that action on the site in early December. In January 2005, the city demolished the structure. The court held that reasonable persons could differ as to whether the city's actions to ascertain to whom it should send notices in its condemnation action were adequate. Therefore, it was inappropriate for the trial court to grant summary judgment for the city.

150. G.S. 153A-140; 160A-193.

151. Monroe v. City of New Bern, 158 N.C. App. 275, 580 S.E.2d 372 (2003). The court noted that summary action by the city under the nuisance-abatement statute would be permissible only in emergency situations, such as if a structure were "in such a ruinous state that it was on the verge of falling onto a sidewalk frequented by pedestrians or in a situation where the destruction of the building is necessary to stop or control a large destructive fire." *Id.* at 279, 580 S.E.2d at 375.

152. Coffey v. Town of Waynesville, 143 N.C. App. 624, 547 S.E.2d 132 (2001) (upholding order to demolish an unsafe structure after owner failed to make repairs). Allegations that proper statutory procedures were not followed and that the owner was not given a reasonable time for repair as required by the statutes are alleged errors of law, subject to de novo review. The process for securing compliance from a recalcitrant owner is often quite long. In this case, the town spent some twenty years dealing with this unoccupied building. Also see the multiyear process to secure repair or demolition of a dilapidated apartment building followed in *Knotts v. City of Sanford*, 142 N.C. App. 91, 541 S.E.2d 517 (2001).

153. G.S. 153A-357(a1) and 160A-417(a) provided for denial of building permits for work that was not consistent with the State Building Code and "all other applicable State and local laws." G.S. 160A-417(a). G.S. 153A-324 and 160A-365 provided for zoning enforcement by "any remedy" provided by G.S. 153A-123 or 160-175, respectively.

154. 314 N.C. 627, 630–31, 336 S.E.2d 394, 397 (1985). *See also* Tonter Invs., Inc. v. Pasquotank Cnty., 199 N.C. App. 579, 681 S.E.2d 536, *review denied*, 363 N.C. 663, 687 S.E.2d 296 (2009) (holding fact that project is exempt from county land-subdivision regulation does not exempt it from county zoning regulation).

155. 288 N.C. 122, 217 S.E.2d 551 (1975).

156. S.L. 2005-426, §§ 3(a), (b).

Selective Enforcement

The decision on whether to initiate an enforcement action is left to the discretion and judgment of the administrator. Officers do have a duty to make a reasonable investigation of credible complaints,[157] but there is no mandate that any particular enforcement action must result from an investigation.

Laxity of prior enforcement against others does not in itself establish a defense to an enforcement action, nor is it a constitutional violation.[158] The fact that a similar prior violation by someone else has not been prosecuted is not a valid defense on the part of a person charged with a development-regulation violation.[159]

Only in extreme instances is selective enforcement a valid defense to an alleged violation. *Brown v. City of Greensboro*[160] is illustrative. After being denied a variance, the plaintiff alleged unlawful discrimination by the city in its enforcement of off-street-parking regulations for her hair salon. The court upheld a dismissal of the claim, noting that a party alleging unlawful selective enforcement must establish a pattern of conscious and intentional discrimination done with "an evil eye and an unequal hand."[161]

Allegations of unfair enforcement against a single person can also be challenged on equal-protection grounds, but it requires particularly egregious conduct by the local government for such a claim to be successful.[162]

---

157. Midgette v. Pate, 94 N.C. App. 498, 380 S.E.2d 572 (1989). The court ruled that when a complaint alleges zoning violations and a failure of the zoning administrator to make a determination and pursue violations, it is improper for the trial court to dismiss the mandamus action brought against the town to compel enforcement. *See generally* Lawrence, *supra* note 121.

158. Grace Baptist Church v. City of Oxford, 320 N.C. 439, 358 S.E.2d 372 (1987) (to show impermissible selective enforcement, a party must establish a pattern of conscious discrimination, not mere laxity of enforcement). *See also* Karagiannopoulos v. City of Lowell, No. 3:05-cv-00401-FDW, 2008 WL 2447362 (W.D.N.C. June 13, 2008), *aff'd per curiam*, 305 F. App'x 64 (4th Cir. 2008) (longstanding noncompliance with zoning standards by previous owners does not amend the ordinance or estop the city from current enforcement action); Prewitt v. Town of Wrightsville Beach, 161 N.C. App. 481, 595 S.E.2d 442 (2003) (dismissing selective-enforcement claim regarding town setback regulations); Sherrill v. Town of Wrightsville Beach, 81 N.C. App. 369, 344 S.E.2d 357, *review denied*, 318 N.C. 417, 349 S.E.2d 600 (1986).

159. City of Gastonia v. Parrish, 271 N.C. 527, 157 S.E.2d 154 (1967). The City of Gastonia brought an action to enforce the provision of its zoning ordinance prohibiting junkyards and high fences in an extraterritorial residential zone. The court held that an allegation of unequal enforcement is no defense to an illegal act.

160. 137 N.C. App. 164, 528 S.E.2d 588 (2000). The ordinance required three off-street parking spaces per hair stylist, and the plaintiff's business had stations for ten stylists. The site, originally a retail operation, had only ten parking spaces. The plaintiff's petition for a variance that would have allowed the business to have seven stylists with the ten existing parking spaces was denied due to a lack of undue hardship, and the variance denial was not appealed.

161. *Id.* at 167, 528 S.E.2d at 590 (quoting Yick Wo v. Hopkins, 118 U.S. 356, 373–74 (1886)). *Yick Wo* is the seminal case with this holding. *See also* Bryan v. City of Madison, 213 F.3d 267 (5th Cir. 2000), *cert. denied*, 531 U.S. 1145 (2001) (rejecting selective-enforcement claim as equal-protection violation); Rouse v. Dep't of Nat. Res., 271 Ga. 726, 524 S.E.2d 455 (1999) (rejecting selective-enforcement claim). In *Wayte v. United States*, the court noted that the government has broad discretion in how it enforces criminal laws, but decisions to prosecute may not be based on an unjustifiable standard such as race, religion, or other arbitrary classification. 470 U.S. 598, 608 (1985).

162. See the discussion of *Village of Willowbrook v. Olech*, 528 U.S. 562 (2000), in Chapter 25. *See also* Karagiannopoulos, 2008 WL 2447362 (in case alleging selective enforcement of zoning restrictions, plaintiff must show differential treatment from other similarly situated persons and intentional or purposeful discrimination); Eberhart v. Gettys, 215 F. Supp. 2d 666 (M.D.N.C. 2002) (holding material issues of fact remained in denying motion to dismiss an equal-protection claim arising from alleged selective enforcement involving Town of Spencer noise ordinance).

Willful misconduct by an inspection official can, however, subject both the official and the unit of government to sanctions, such as when an inspection officer deliberately provides fraudulent information to an owner for purposes of personal gain.[163]

Time Limit to Initiate Litigation

The General Assembly in 2017 amended G.S. 1-51 and 1-49 to establish statutes of limitation for bringing legal action to enforce a development regulation.[164]

A local government has five years to bring court action, starting when "[t]he facts constituting the violation are known to the governing body, an agent, or an employee of the unit of local government" or when "[t]he violation can be determined from the public record[165] of the unit of local government." The knowledge or record must be that of the particular unit of government with the development regulation, not any local government or state agency. Additionally, the local government has seven years to bring a court action, starting when "[t]he violation is apparent from a public right-of-way" or when "[t]he violation is in plain view from a place to which the public is invited." These time limits do not apply if a condition exists that is "actually injurious or dangerous to the public health or safety."

Defenses to Enforcement

Estoppel

Under common law, an estoppel defense is generally not available for enforcement actions. A prior failure to enforce does not preclude future enforcement.[166] Also, when an applicant has received a development approval and benefited thereby, the applicant may not as a general rule later attack the validity of the ordinance. The courts apply a doctrine of quasi-estoppel to hold that the one who voluntarily proceeds under an ordinance and claims its benefits cannot later question its constitutionality in order to avoid its burdens.[167]

---

163. See the discussion of *Leftwich v. Gaines*, 134 N.C. App. 502, 521 S.E.2d 717 (1999), *review denied*, 351 N.C. 357, 541 S.E.2d 714 (2000), below.

164. S.L. 2017-10.

165. While this term is not defined in this law, G.S. 132-1 defines a "public record" and is likely instructive here. Records of public-enterprise billing records and records of criminal investigations are not defined as public records under that statute.

166. Carolina Holdings, Inc. v. Hous. Appeals Bd., 149 N.C. App. 579, 587, 561 S.E.2d 541, 546 (2002) (city is not estopped from enforcement of housing code due to the fact that the space, use, light, and ventilation violations had existed for years without citation).

167. River Birch Assocs. v. City of Raleigh, 326 N.C. 100, 388 S.E.2d 538 (1990) (when developer submits plat with more open space than the minimum ordinance requirements, accepts approval of the preliminary plat, and builds at higher densities based on it, city may refuse to modify plat to decrease open space); Convent of the Sisters of Saint Joseph v. City of Winston-Salem, 243 N.C. 316, 90 S.E.2d 879 (1956) (after applicant acts on a special use permit, subsequent purchaser may not challenge permit conditions); Wake Forest Golf & Country Club, Inc. v. Town of Wake Forest, 212 N.C. App. 632, 711 S.E.2d 816, *review denied*, 365 N.C. 359, 719 S.E.2d 21 (2011) (where plaintiff voluntarily included open space exceeding ordinance requirements in special use permit application, secured higher density, and built project, town may refuse to consider application for permit modification); Shell Island Homeowners Ass'n v. Tomlinson, 134 N.C. App. 217, 226, 517 S.E.2d 406, 413 (1999) (plaintiff may not accept variance under Coastal Area Management Act and then attack validity of rule); Franklin Rd. Props. v. City of Raleigh, 94 N.C. App. 731, 735, 381 S.E.2d 487, 490 (1989) (plaintiff may not attack validity of zoning after securing variance); Goforth Props., Inc. v. Town of Chapel Hill, 71 N.C. App. 771, 323 S.E.2d 427 (1984). In *Amward Homes, Inc. v. Town of Cary*, 206 N.C. App. 38, 698 S.E.2d 404 (2010), *aff'd per curiam by equally divided court*, 365 N.C. 305, 716 S.E.2d 849 (2011), however, the court rejected the contention that the developer's acceptance of a permit condition requiring

There are several important statutory adjustments to the common law on estoppel described below.

First, the time limits set by G.S. 1-51 and 1-49 establish statutes of limitation for bringing legal action to enforce a development regulation.

Second, the General Assembly in 2019 clarified when estoppel applies during the appeal of conditions imposed on a development permit.[168] If the applicant did not consent to the condition in writing, and the applicant is challenging the unconsented condition, then the applicant may proceed with the development and the local government may not assert the defense of estoppel against the applicant.

The landmark zoning estoppel case in North Carolina is *City of Raleigh v. Fisher*.[169] Here the defendant operated an unpermitted bakery in a Raleigh residential district. The court held that even if city personnel had known about this use, advised the defendant that it could be done, and taken no action to stop the unlawful use for a decade (and in fact had collected a business tax on the improper use for nine years), estoppel does not prevent subsequent enforcement of the zoning ordinance. The court applied the familiar rule that estoppel does not run against the government. Justice Sam Ervin concluded:

> In enacting and enforcing zoning regulations, a municipality acts as a governmental agency and exercises the police power of the State. The police power is that inherent and plenary power in the State which enables it to govern, and to prohibit things hurtful to the health, morals, safety, and welfare of society. In the very nature of things, the police power of the State can not be bartered away by contract, or lost by any other mode.
>
> This being true, a municipality cannot be estopped to enforce a zoning ordinance against a violator by the conduct of its officials in encouraging or permitting such violator to violate such ordinance in times past.[170]

The court reached a similar result in *City of Winston-Salem v. Hoots Concrete Co.*[171] In this case, initiated in 1976, the city contended that the defendant's concrete-mixing plant, constructed in 1970, was in violation of the zoning ordinance. The defense plea was that because this use was not explicitly listed in the ordinance, the city zoning officer was authorized to interpret the ordinance to determine if it was a permitted use, and that in fact the city zoning officer had interpreted the ordinance in 1970 to allow the use. The court ruled that the defendant had the burden of proving this affirmative defense and that the city was not estopped by its failure to take enforcement action.

---

payment of school impact fees and the benefits of the development approval barred a challenge to payment of fees by builders within the development. The court concluded that the benefits of the approval ran to the developer, not the plaintiff individual builders who acquired lots from the developer.

168. G.S. 160D-1403.2, created by S.L. 2019-111, § 1.10. This provision was incorporated into Chapter 160D in 2020.

169. 232 N.C. 629, 61 S.E.2d 897 (1950). The property at issue was zoned for residential use in 1923. The defendant purchased the site from the city in 1936. A residence was constructed on the site in 1938, and the defendant operated a bakery and sandwich business out of the residence from 1938 to 1949, at which point the city sued to enjoin the commercial use of the property. The defendants had invested some $75,000 in the business. *See also* Helms v. City of Charlotte, 255 N.C. 647, 652, 122 S.E.2d 817, 821 (1961) (mistakenly issued permit does not estop city from subsequent enforcement).

170. *Fisher*, 232 N.C. at 635, 61 S.E.2d at 902 (citations omitted). The court noted that a violation, no matter how long in existence, does not ripen into a permitted nonconformity. See Chapter 20 for further discussion of lawful nonconformities. *See also* LeTendre v. Currituck Cnty., 259 N.C. App. 512, 817 S.E.2d 73 (2018) (failure by neighbor or government to seek a stay while a permit is appealed does not estop future enforcement should the permit issuance be revoked on appeal).

171. 47 N.C. App. 405, 267 S.E.2d 569, *review denied*, 301 N.C. 234 (1980). The court also addressed the estoppel issue in this case earlier in *City of Winston-Salem v. Hoots Concrete Co.*, 37 N.C. App. 186, 245 S.E.2d 536, *review denied*, 295 N.C. 645, 248 S.E.2d 249 (1978).

In *Overton v. Camden County*, the court held that the county was not estopped from enforcing its ordinance based on its failure to do so at an earlier hearing,[172] and in *Town of Pine Bluff v. Marts*, the court held that the fact that an ordinance was not applicable to the first phase of a development does not estop the town from applying it to subsequent phases.[173]

Estoppel is applied in extraordinary cases. In *County of Wake v. North Carolina Dep't of Environment and Natural Resources*, the court held as a matter of law that the town was equitably estopped from withdrawing its prior approval of the county's landfill application in the state-permitting process due to its multiple acts of ratification (entering into contracts and accepting payment for wastewater treatment and approving long-range waste-disposal plans).[174]

A mistakenly issued permit does not bar future enforcement.[175] In *Mecklenburg County v. Westbery*,[176] the county mistakenly issued a building permit for installation of a mobile home for use as a storage structure in a district that did not allow mobile homes.[177] When the error was discovered, the permit was revoked and the revocation not appealed. The county then sought injunctive relief to compel removal of the offending structure. The court ruled that no vested rights accrued to an unlawfully issued permit and ordered its removal.[178] Likewise, in *Eastern Outdoor, Inc. v. Board of Adjustment*,[179] the court held that a permit can be revoked when an interpretation of the ordinance changes and it is determined that a previously issued permit was in error.

Issuance of permits for one aspect of a project does not estop the same unit of government from denying permits or enforcing regulations related to other aspects of the same project.[180]

The court in *Bailey & Associates, Inc. v. Wilmington Board of Adjustment*[181] discussed the application of judicial estoppel to a party in a zoning case. Neighborhood opponents of the project at issue

---

172. 155 N.C. App. 391, 398, 574 S.E.2d 157, 162 (2002).

173. 195 N.C. App. 659, 673 S.E.2d 740 (2009). See the discussion of application of vested rights to phased developments in Chapter 19.

174. 155 N.C. App. 225, 573 S.E.2d 572 (2002), *review denied*, 357 N.C. 62, 579 S.E.2d 386 (2003). In *Orange County v. Town of Hillsborough*, 219 N.C. App. 127, 724 S.E.2d 560 (2012), the court held that a unit of government is not subject to estoppel to the same extent as an individual or private entity, and the doctrine will not be enforced if it would impair a governmental function.

The concept of municipal estoppel is more frequently applied in land use regulatory cases in other states. For example, in *Levine v. Town of Sterling*, 300 Conn. 521, 534–40, 16 A.3d 664, 672–76 (2011), the court applied the doctrine to hold that where the town board advised a property owner that two additional residential structures could be located on his lot and that a new ordinance prohibiting such would not be applied to his project, and the owner acted on that assurance and would suffer substantial loss if required to comply with the new ordinance, estoppel precluded application of the new ordinance. *See also* Drury Displays, Inc. v. Brown, 306 Ill. App. 3d 1160, 715 N.E.2d 1230 (1999) (compelling reinstatement of permit after substantial expenditures made). In these contexts, the amplification of this concept is analogous to the common law vested-rights analysis discussed in Chapter 19.

175. Helms v. City of Charlotte, 255 N.C. 647, 122 S.E.2d 817 (1961).

176. 32 N.C. App. 630, 233 S.E.2d 658 (1977). In *MYC Klepper/Brandon Knolls LLC v. Board of Adjustment for City of Asheville*, 238 N.C. App. 432, 767 S.E.2d 668 (2014), the court noted that even if the city attorney mistakenly advised that there was no timetable for reestablishing a nonconforming sign, that would not estop the city from enforcement of a violation.

177. Part of the lot in question was zoned for industrial use, which allowed such a structure. However, part of the lot was zoned for residential use, which did not allow the structure, and the structure was located on the residentially zoned portion of the lot.

178. The court noted that injunctive relief was appropriate under the State Building Code authorization (G.S. 153A-372) irrespective of whether the zoning ordinance provided for injunctive relief.

179. 150 N.C. App. 516, 564 S.E.2d 78 (2002).

180. *See., e.g.*, N.C. Dep't of Envtl. Quality v. TRK Dev., LLC, 259 N.C. App. 597, 816 S.E.2d 232 (2018), where the court held that issuance of a sedimentation-and-erosion-control permit does not estop subsequent application of solid-waste regulations when excavation on the site unearths solid waste that must be properly disposed.

181. 202 N.C. App. 177, 194–95, 689 S.E.2d 576, 588–90 (2010).

intervened at the trial court and contended that an earlier site-development application by the plaintiff for the same site purportedly acknowledged the site to be within a conservation overlay district. They sought a determination that judicial estoppel precluded the applicant from making a contrary assertion in the current application. The court, however, held that this issue was not presented to the board of adjustment and was thus not within the record and could not be considered by the trial court.

Laches

If a local government makes affirmative assurances to a person regarding development regulations and then waits an unreasonable time after discovering that those assurances were incorrect to take action to remedy the error, and if that delay works a considerable disadvantage to the person,[182] the courts may use the equitable doctrine of laches to limit enforcement of the regulations.[183] Several cases have applied laches where the balance of equities involved was heavily weighted against enforcement.

In *Abernathy v. Town of Boone Board of Adjustment*,[184] a photo-finishing business obtained a permit for a freestanding sign from the town. Subsequently, the business considered a move from its current space to a location within an adjacent shopping center. Aware that the city sign ordinance did not allow individual freestanding signs for businesses in shopping centers, the business conditioned its purchase of the new site on approval of the city to retain the existing freestanding sign. Upon being advised by the zoning officer and building inspector that the sign could remain, the business purchased the site and relocated, incurring expenses in excess of $250,000. Some three and a half years later, in response to complaints from other businesses at the shopping center, the city advised the business that the sign was in violation of the ordinance and had to be removed. The court applied the equitable doctrine of laches and held that the substantial and unreasonable lapse of time after the city knew of the violation resulted in such a substantial change in position by the business as to make it unjust to enforce the ordinance. The court emphasized that the general rule is that laches does not apply to preclude enforcement of municipal ordinances absent both an unreasonable delay and an unreasonable disadvantage due to the delay.[185]

A similar fact pattern produced a similar result in *Town of Cameron v. Woodell*.[186] Prior to entering a contract to purchase a site to be used as a flea market and used-car lot, the defendants informed town officials of their plan and were correctly advised that the property involved was not subject to

---

182. In a rezoning context, the court noted that delay alone is insufficient to justify application of laches, as there must also be disadvantage, injury, or prejudice to the defendant as a result of the delay. Stutts v. Swaim, 30 N.C. App. 611, 228 S.E.2d 750, *review denied*, 291 N.C. 178, 229 S.E.2d 692 (1976).

183. Laches is an affirmative defense, meaning it must be pled, and the burden of proof is on the party pleading it. Taylor v. City of Raleigh, 290 N.C. 608, 622, 227 S.E.2d 576, 584 (1976); Scott Poultry Co. v. Bryan Oil Co., 272 N.C. 16, 22, 157 S.E.2d 693, 698 (1967); Peek v. Wachovia Bank & Trust Co., 242 N.C. 1, 11, 86 S.E.2d 745, 753 (1955); McDowell v. Randolph Cnty., 186 N.C. App. 17, 21, 649 S.E.2d 920, 923–24 (2007). The defense can also be raised in private actions, such as a suit to enforce private restrictive covenants. *See, e.g.,* Irby v. Freese, 206 N.C. App. 503, 696 S.E.2d 889 (2010) (holding that facts did not warrant application of laches to bar suit regarding construction within front-yard setback required by covenants).

184. 109 N.C. App. 459, 427 S.E.2d 875 (1993). The court relied on *Taylor,* 290 N.C. 608, 227 S.E.2d 576, a case applying laches to bar a challenge to enactment of a rezoning. For a discussion of laches in the context of initiating challenges to legislative and quasi-judicial decisions, see Chapter 29. *See also* Allen v. City of Burlington Bd. of Adjustment, 100 N.C. App. 615, 397 S.E.2d 657 (1990) (applying laches to bar appeal of interpretation of ordinance filed three years after contested use initiated).

185. 109 N.C. App. 459, 427 S.E.2d 875, 878–79.

186. 150 N.C. App. 174, 563 S.E.2d 198 (2002).

town zoning.[187] The defendant then opened a flea market and car lot on the site. Some three years later, the town discovered that the property was indeed inside the city's jurisdiction and issued a notice of violation.[188] The court applied the laches doctrine to preclude enforcement. The court held that the evidence supported a conclusion that the town was aware of the defendants' plans for the businesses and advised them that there was no town jurisdiction, that the defendants relied on that assurance and materially changed their condition as a result, and that the town's unreasonable delay in enforcement had substantially prejudiced the defendants.

For laches to apply, several critical requirements must be met. First, a person must obtain affirmative assurances regarding the applicability of zoning standards. Reliance on the ordinance or an absence of enforcement action is insufficient.[189] Second, the person must have made substantial detrimental reliance on that specific assurance. As with the common law vested right,[190] expenditures made prior to receiving the assurance are not considered. Third, there must have been an unreasonable delay in initiating enforcement after the government learned of the violation. Mere passage of time is insufficient.

MMR Holdings, LLC v. City of Charlotte[191] illustrates these limitations on the applicability of laches. The plaintiff automobile dealer contended that the city's delay in enforcing provisions of its sign regulations regarding balloons, pennants, and other decorations precluded enforcement action. The court noted that there was no evidence that the city ever told the plaintiff the signs were in compliance (and in fact a warning citation was issued early in the dispute) and no evidence that the plaintiff spent any money based on city assurances, so even a lengthy period between the initial city notice of violation and initiation of formal enforcement actions would not warrant application of laches.[192]

An estoppel or laches defense may not be initially raised in a judicial-enforcement action; it must be raised in the context of an appeal of the board of adjustment's decision on the notice of violation.[193]

---

187. The city actually adopted zoning for the site several weeks after this initial contact but apparently still was not aware that the site included the subject property. In the interim the defendant had executed a contract to purchase the site and had obtained necessary permits for the business from the county. The court did not address the vested-rights aspects that may have been present.

188. Upon receiving a notice of violation, the defendant applied for a conditional use permit to continue the businesses. The permit was denied. The town then brought an enforcement action to enjoin future operation of the businesses.

189. In *Fisher*, while the city knew of the violation and did not take enforcement action for an extended period, there was no assurance given that the use was legal under the zoning ordinance. The land was purchased and the business started on an understanding that the property could be used for a bakery, and the court noted that city officials "knowingly encouraged or permitted the defendants to devote the premises in question to business purposes in violation of the zoning ordinance restricting them to residential use." City of Raleigh v. Fisher, 232 N.C. 629, 634, 61 S.E.2d 897, 901 (1950). Despite this, the owner was enjoined from further using the property as a bakery.

190. For a discussion of the common law vested right, see Chapter 19.

191. 148 N.C. App. 208, 558 S.E.2d 197 (2001).

192. *See also* Capital Outdoor, Inc. v. Tolson, 159 N.C. App. 55, 64–65, 582 S.E.2d 717, 723–24, *review denied*, 357 N.C. 504, 587 S.E.2d 662 (2003). The court held that nonenforcement of a rule on billboard height limits for ten years did not warrant application of laches, as there was no showing that the billboard owners were ever given any assurance that the signs were in compliance, nor was there a showing of disadvantage due to the delay in enforcement.

193. New Hanover Cnty. v. Pleasant, 59 N.C. App. 644, 297 S.E.2d 760 (1982) (defendant cannot raise an estoppel defense at the enforcement stage, when neither the permit denial nor the board of adjustment order on the violation has been appealed).

Liability

Persons who feel they have been wrongfully harmed by land use regulatory decisions may bring suit to invalidate the individual decision. The suit may also seek payment of monetary damages to compensate for the alleged wrongdoing.[194]

A suit for damages may be brought against an officer as an individual, against the unit of government, or both. If monetary damages are sought from the government, any named individual defendants are being sued in their "official capacity," and the unit of government faces potential liability. If monetary damages are sought from individual defendants as well as (or instead of) the unit of government, each individual named as a defendant is being sued personally as an individual.[195]

Individual Liability

A member of a local board generally has absolute immunity for his or her legislative[196] and quasi-judicial[197] decisions. Elected officials and members of appointed boards making quasi-judicial zoning decisions are entitled to "legislative immunity" from suit for those actions taken within the "sphere of legislative activity."[198] In *Stephenson v. Town of Garner*, the court held that board members enjoy such immunity when exercising the discretion inherent in a special use permit decision.[199]

Administrative officials generally have qualified good-faith immunity for their administrative actions that involve some degree of discretion.[200]

---

194. For a detailed discussion of the liability issue, see Trey Allen, Local Government Immunity to Lawsuits in North Carolina (UNC School of Government, 2018); Anita R. Brown-Graham, A Practical Guide to the Liability of North Carolina Cities and Counties (UNC Institute of Government, 1999).

195. Meyer v. Walls, 347 N.C. 97, 110, 489 S.E.2d 880, 887 (1997). An action may seek both types of relief by suing an individual in both his or her official and individual capacities. *See, e.g.,* Block v. Cnty. of Person, 141 N.C. App. 273, 540 S.E.2d 415 (2000) (in case involving alleged improprieties in permitting for septic tanks, some named plaintiffs were sued only in their official capacity while others were sued in both their individual and official capacities).

196. Bogan v. Scott-Harris, 523 U.S. 44, 46 (1998) (finding absolute legislative immunity from liability for legislative activities); Lake Country Estates, Inc. v. Tahoe Reg'l Planning Agency, 440 U.S. 391 (1979); Tenney v. Brandhove, 341 U.S. 367 (1951); Bruce v. Riddle, 631 F.2d 272 (4th Cir. 1980). A project-specific action by a legislative body may be deemed as the body's having acted outside its legislative capacity. *See, e.g.,* Scott v. Greenville Cnty., 716 F.2d 1409 (4th Cir. 1983) (moratorium directed at individual building permit not a legislative action qualifying for absolute immunity).

197. *See, e.g.,* Butz v. Economou, 438 U.S. 478 (1978); Buckles v. King Cnty., 191 F.3d 1127 (9th Cir. 1999). The court applied this rule to conclude that members of a board of adjustment acting on a proceeding to decide or revoke a special or conditional use permit have absolute immunity. Davis v. Town of Holly Springs, No. 5:00-CV-368-BR(3), 2001 WL 34013440 (E.D.N.C. Apr. 25, 2001), *aff'd,* 20 F. App'x 180 (4th Cir. 2001) (dismissing claims against members of town council and board of adjustment in their individual and official capacities in litigation regarding revocation of conditional use permit). *See also* Ostrzenski v. Seigel, 177 F.3d 245, 249 (4th Cir. 1999) (absolute immunity for official performing quasi-judicial functions when adequate procedural safeguards exist).

198. Stephenson v. Town of Garner, 136 N.C. App. 444, 449, 524 S.E.2d 608, 612 (paraphrasing *Tenney,* 341 U.S. at 376), *review denied,* 352 N.C. 156, 544 S.E.2d 243 (2000).

199. 136 N.C. App. 444, 524 S.E.2d 608. *See also Bogan,* 523 U.S. 44; *Lake Country Estates,* 440 U.S. 391. To qualify for legislative immunity, the board member must be acting in a nonministerial capacity and must not be undertaking an illegal act. Vereen v. Holden, 121 N.C. App. 779, 468 S.E.2d 471, *review denied,* 347 N.C. 410, 494 S.E.2d 600 (1997).

200. For cases addressing this federal qualified immunity, see *Sullivan v. Town of Salem,* 805 F.2d 81 (2d Cir. 1986) (and cases cited therein). *See generally* Harlow v. Fitzgerald, 457 U.S. 800 (1982) (no liability for discretionary decision of administrative official unless decision violates clearly established legal rights known to a reasonable person); Eberhart v. Gettys, 215 F. Supp. 2d 666 (M.D.N.C. 2002) (discussing qualified immunity of mayor, police officer, and zoning-enforcement officer in equal-protection claim arising from alleged selective enforcement involving Town of Spencer noise ordinance); Sunkler v. Town of Nags Head, No. 2:01-CV-22-H(2), 2002 WL 32395571

An enforcement officer may be personally liable for intentional torts and for acts taken outside the scope of employment. For example, if an officer, out of personal malice toward the applicant, intentionally denies a permit that the officer knows should have been issued, the officer may have personal liability. This intentional wrongdoing is outside the scope of the officer's employment as it is not undertaken in furtherance of the employer's business.[201]

A more common situation arises when a suit alleges negligence on the part of an officer. For example, a permit is mistakenly issued and then revoked upon discovery of the mistake, with the applicant having made expenditures in the interim. In these instances, a critical issue in determining the potential individual liability is whether the person being sued is deemed an "officer" or an "employee." A public official engaged in the performance of governmental duties that involve judgment and discretion is immune from personal liability from mere negligence in the absence of malice, corruption, or actions outside the scope of employment.[202] On the other hand, an employee (and an officer performing ministerial duties) is not immune from a negligence suit.[203]

In *EEE-ZZZ Lay Drain Co. v. North Carolina Department of Human Resources*,[204] which challenged a refusal to permit use of an innovative nitrification method for an on-site waste-disposal drain field, the court held that the county health director was an "officer" and was thus shielded from liability unless corrupt or malicious acts were involved, but the engineers and supervisors within the Department of Human Resources were "employees" and subject to liability if there was negligence in the performance of their jobs. The court found no malicious or negligent acts and thus no liability.

A key question then is what distinguishes an officer from an employee for purposes of land use regulations.[205] In *Pigott v. City of Wilmington*,[206] a building inspector advised an owner that two greenhouses were not in compliance with building codes and ordered the structures to be brought up to code or demolished. After the structures were demolished at a loss of some $8000, it was discovered that one of the structures could have been brought into compliance at a relatively nominal cost and that the other

---

(E.D.N.C. May 17, 2002), *aff'd*, 50 F. App'x 116 (4th Cir. 2002) (qualified immunity for a building inspector's search of a building with a reasonably obtained administrative-inspection warrant). Also note the state "public officer" qualified immunity discussed below.

201. See the discussion of *Leftwich v. Gaines*, below.

202. Smith v. Hefner, 235 N.C. 1, 7, 68 S.E.2d 783, 787 (1952); Miller v. Jones, 224 N.C. 783, 32 S.E.2d 594 (1945). Law-enforcement officers are consistently held to be "officers." *See, e.g.*, Williams v. Holsclaw, 128 N.C. App. 205, 495 S.E.2d 166 (1998). A denial of a motion to dismiss is generally considered an interlocutory order that may not be immediately appealed. However, an order denying a motion to dismiss grounded on the defense of governmental immunity is immediately reviewable as affecting a substantial right. Derwort v. Polk Cnty., 129 N.C. App. 789, 501 S.E.2d 379 (1989); Hedrick v. Rains, 121 N.C. App. 466, 468, 466 S.E.2d 281, 283, *aff'd*, 344 N.C. 729, 477 S.E.2d 171 (1996); Clark v. Red Bird Cab Co., 114 N.C. App. 400, 442 S.E.2d 75 (1994).

203. Isenhour v. Hutto, 350 N.C. 601, 610, 517 S.E.2d 121, 128 (1999).

204. 108 N.C. App. 24, 422 S.E.2d 338 (1992). *See also* Robinette v. Barriger, 116 N.C. App. 197, 447 S.E.2d 498 (1994), *aff'd by equally divided court*, 342 N.C. 181, 463 S.E.2d 7 (1995). The federal court reached the same conclusion in *Houck & Sons, Inc. v. Transylvania County*, 852 F. Supp. 442, 448 (W.D.N.C. 1993), *aff'd*, 36 F.3d 1092 (4th Cir. 1994).

205. This situation is further complicated when a unit of government contracts with another unit of government or a private company for inspection services. G.S. 160A-413 and 153A-353 address some aspects of this issue. These statutes provide that the unit of government generally has the same potential liability that it would have if an employee of that unit of government provided the services. The statutes further provide for appropriate qualifications of the contract inspector and require nongovernmental contractors to have errors and omissions insurance coverage. The statutes do not specify whether a nongovernmental contractor is to be considered an officer of the contracting unit of government.

206. 50 N.C. App. 401, 273 S.E.2d 752, *review denied*, 303 N.C. 181, 280 S.E.2d 453 (1981). *See also Isenhour*, 350 N.C. at 610, 517 S.E.2d at 128; Meyer v. Walls, 347 N.C. 97, 113, 489 S.E.2d 880, 889 (1997); Block v. Cnty. of Person, 141 N.C. App. 273, 280–82, 540 S.E.2d 415, 420–22 (2000); Hare v. Butler, 99 N.C. App. 693, 700, 394 S.E.2d 231, 236 (1990).

structure was not even subject to the building code. The owner sued, alleging that the inspector was negligent in his interpretation of the code and enforcement order. The court applied a four-part test[207] in determining whether the chief building inspector was an officer:

1. Is the position created by the legislature? G.S. 160D-402 and -1102 authorize inspection departments and specifically mention zoning and other inspectors.
2. Does the position normally require an oath of office? Many city charters and development regulations require administrators and enforcement officers to take an oath of office.[208]
3. Does the person perform legally imposed public duties? In *Pigott*, the court cited the full range of building-inspection statutes as setting forth public duties imposed by law.
4. Is there a degree of discretion exercised? A determination whether a particular situation comports with the requirements of the development ordinances involves a sufficient degree of judgment and discretion to meet this requirement.

An enforcement officer meeting these tests who is interpreting and enforcing a land-development regulation does not have personal financial liability for good-faith mistakes made in carrying out activities within the scope of the officer's duties. Likewise, if a staff decision is made, and on appeal to the board of adjustment or the courts it is determined to have been erroneous, neither the unit of government nor the individual officer is liable in the absence of fraud or corruption.[209]

However, if the officer's action is corrupt or malicious, the officer is not immune from liability. For example, the court has held that where a city has ordered repair or demolition of a dilapidated residence and repairs have been initiated, it is corrupt, malicious, or outside the scope of employment for the city building inspector to demolish the residence.[210] Likewise, a zoning officer's intentional provision of false information about zoning requirements in order to devalue a property being acquired by a friend strips the officer of any public-officer immunity.[211]

---

207. Pigott, 50 N.C. App. at 403–04, 273 S.E.2d at 754. In *Cline v. James Bane Home Building, LLC*, 278 N.C. App. 12, 862 S.E.2d 54 (2021), a claim involving a failed septic tank, the court applied these tests and held that the sanitarian issuing the improvement permit was an employee rather than an officer.

208. G.S. 160D-402(b) provides that a development regulation may require designated staff members to take an oath of office.

209. Clinard v. City of Winston-Salem, 173 N.C. 356, 358, 91 S.E. 1039, 1040 (1917). After the inspector issued a building permit for an addition to a structure, a question arose as to whether the addition encroached on an alley subject to public use. The inspector revoked the permit until that issue could be resolved. It was eventually determined that there were no public rights to this portion of the alley. The court held that the appropriate remedy was mandamus for issuance of the permit, but there was no liability for monetary damages for the city or the inspector.

210. In *Wiggins v. City of Monroe*, 73 N.C. App. 44, 326 S.E.2d 39 (1985), the court held that an allegation that the demolition was initiated with knowledge that repairs had been started was sufficient to avoid summary judgment for the individual inspector, since if the allegation were true, there would be no public-officer immunity. In a subsequent proceeding, the court held that the plaintiff's evidence was sufficient to submit this issue to a jury rather than have a directed verdict. 85 N.C. App. 237, 354 S.E.2d 365 (1987).

211. Leftwich v. Gaines, 134 N.C. App. 502, 521 S.E.2d 717 (1999), *review denied*, 351 N.C. 357, 541 S.E.2d 714 (2000). The defendants appealed a jury verdict finding liability for fraud, negligence, and deceptive trade practices. The inspector's representation that a rezoning of the property would be illegal spot zoning, the jury concluded, was contrary to his true beliefs, was made for the purpose of deceit, was motivated by a desire to secure benefits for himself and his girlfriend, and thus constituted fraud. The court held that there was sufficient evidence to support the jury's conclusion and that, since the inspector was acting outside the scope of his duties, he was not immune from an unfair-trade-practice claim under G.S. 75-1.1. The court upheld treble damages against the individual defendant ($180,000), found the inspector jointly and severally liable for compensatory damages ($60,000), and ordered him to pay attorney's fees of $50,000.

Liability of the Unit of Government

The local government unit is generally immune from tort liability for injuries that arise during the course of its governmental activities.[212] G.S. 153A-435 and 160A-485(a), however, allow cities and counties to waive their common law governmental immunity by the purchase of liability insurance,[213] something many North Carolina cities and counties have done. The waiver is, however, limited to the amount of insurance coverage purchased by the local government.[214] Also, the waiver can be limited to those personnel and actions listed in the insurance policy.[215] Purchase of liability insurance for "law enforcement officers" does not waive sovereign immunity for building inspectors.[216]

Where immunity has been waived, the unit of government may be liable for actions taken by its employees and officers within the scope of employment. To establish liability, a plaintiff must establish proximate cause. In *Lynn v. Overlook Development*,[217] the plaintiff occupied a structure for which a building permit, but not a certificate of compliance, had been secured. After the plaintiff moved in, numerous defects were discovered, resulting in the subsequent condemnation of the unit. The court dismissed the action against the city of Asheville because the plaintiff's election to take title and assume occupancy before a final inspection or before issuance of a certificate of occupancy was an intervening, independent cause of the plaintiff's damages; thus, there was no proximate cause. Similarly, in *Eason v. Union County*,[218] the court held that where the certificate of occupancy was issued after the plaintiff purchased the house, there could be no proximate cause for a negligent-inspection claim. The court in *Eason* also noted that where the plaintiff home purchaser had knowledge of the defects prior to closing and had not taken adequate steps to assure their repair, contributory negligence would bar a negligence claim against the county. To establish a claim for negligence by an employee of the unit

---

212. Orange Cnty. v. Heath, 282 N.C. 292, 192 S.E.2d 308 (1972) (seeking a temporary restraining order that delayed a mobile-home park, the order later being held invalid, is an exercise of a government function for which there is sovereign immunity); Tabor v. Cnty. of Orange, 156 N.C. App. 88, 575 S.E.2d 540 (2003) (no liability for review of septic-tank-permit applications absent waiver of immunity); Law Bldg. of Asheboro, Inc. v. City of Asheboro, 108 N.C. App. 182, 423 S.E.2d 93 (1992), *review denied*, 333 N.C. 575, 429 S.E.2d 571 (1993) (no liability for denial of building permit); Town of Hillsborough v. Smith, 10 N.C. App. 70, 178 S.E.2d 18 (1970), *review denied*, 277 N.C. 727, 178 S.E.2d 831 (1971) (governmental immunity precludes town liability for seeking injunction to restrain alleged violation of zoning ordinance, even when it is eventually held that there was no zoning violation). *See also* Galligan v. Town of Chapel Hill, 276 N.C. 172, 171 S.E.2d 427 (1970); Moffitt v. City of Asheville, 103 N.C. 237, 9 S.E. 695 (1889). In *Hill v. Board of Aldermen*, 72 N.C. 55 (1875), the city of Charlotte was sued after the city council suspended an ordinance prohibiting firework discharges for the period between Christmas and New Year's Day, and the plaintiff's building was damaged by a fire set by firecrackers during that period. The court held that adoption and suspension of the ordinance was a legislative policy choice entrusted to the judgment and discretion of the elected officials and that governmental immunity applies to such decisions. Governmental immunity does not extend to proprietary activities of local governments, such as provision of utility service. This important distinction rarely arises in a zoning context.

213. Anita R. Brown-Graham, *Local Governments and the Public Duty Doctrine After* Wood v. Guilford County, 81 N.C. L. Rev. 2291 (2003); Patti Owen Harper, *Statutory Waiver of Municipal Immunity upon Purchase of Liability Insurance in North Carolina and the Municipal Liability Crisis*, 4 Campbell L. Rev. 41 (1981); Tamura D. Coffey, Comment, *Waiving Local Government Immunity in North Carolina: Risk Management Programs Are Insurance*, 27 Wake Forest L. Rev. 709 (1992); J. Jason Link, Note, *Searching for Limits on a Municipality's Retention of Governmental Immunity:* Lyles v. City of Charlotte, 76 N.C. L. Rev. 269 (1997).

214. G.S. 153A-435(a); 160A-485(a). Wall v. City of Raleigh, 121 N.C. App. 351, 465 S.E.2d 551 (1996).

215. Seibold v. City of Kinston, 268 N.C. 615, 151 S.E.2d 654 (1966); Doe v. Jenkins, 144 N.C. App. 131, 547 S.E.2d 124 (2001).

216. Kennedy v. Haywood Cnty., 158 N.C. App. 526, 581 S.E.2d 119 (2003) (noting that while building inspectors enforce the law and can issue stop-work orders, they have no authority to issue arrest warrants, are not certified law-enforcement officers, and are not charged with providing police protection or enforcing criminal laws).

217. 328 N.C. 689, 403 S.E.2d 469 (1991).

218. 160 N.C. App. 388, 585 S.E.2d 452 (2003).

of government, the plaintiff must also establish that the relevant standard of care has been breached. While expert testimony is usually required to establish the standard of care in professional-negligence cases, the common knowledge and experience of the jury may be sufficient in instances where there is a clear error. In *Russell v. North Carolina Department of Environment and Natural Resources*,[219] a county health-department inspector issued a septic-tank permit, but the soils reported to be on the site were not present. (They were, however, present on an adjacent lot.) The court concluded it was within the common knowledge of laypersons to find it was within the standard of care that the inspector actually inspect the right property.

Liability may also arise when the city or county fails to follow statutorily mandated procedures.[220] Governmental immunity does not protect a local government from liability for failure to follow a statute's process.

A city or county can also be held liable for managerial wrongdoing, such as failing to properly supervise an employee known to be engaged in misconduct. In *Leftwich v. Gaines*, the plaintiff alleged that Mount Airy's chief building inspector had provided her with fraudulent information regarding the adjacent property (that it could not be rezoned, that condemned structures would have to be removed at her expense, that expensive water and sewer connections would be required) in order to suppress the value of her offer for the property, thereby allowing the building inspector's girlfriend to purchase the property at a reduced price. The court held that the city was not immune from suit for negligent supervision because the city had notice of prior wrongdoing of a similar nature and had not undertaken adequate supervision to prevent a reoccurrence (he was merely asked not to do it again) and the wrongdoing took place while the inspector was on duty. In this action the city was held jointly and severally liable (with the inspector) for compensatory damages.[221]

At one point it appeared that the public-duty doctrine would further shield local governments and employees from liability. This doctrine, originally applied to law-enforcement functions,[222] states that a local government and its agents act for the benefit of the general public rather than for specific individuals, and thus there is no liability to an individual for failure to carry out those duties.[223] In a series of cases, the court of appeals extended this doctrine to apply to subdivision-plat reviews[224] and building inspections.[225] However, the state supreme court subsequently refused to extend the public-duty doc-

---

219. 227 N.C. App. 306, 742 S.E.2d 329, *review denied*, 367 N.C. 253 (2013).

220. Newton v. City of Winston-Salem, 92 N.C. App. 446, 374 S.E.2d 488 (1988) (finding city liable for damages when house was demolished under the housing code without city's having followed statutory mandates regarding notice and sale of salvage materials). *See also* Harrington v. Greenville, 159 N.C. 632, 75 S.E. 849 (1912) (city not liable for failure to abate alleged public nuisance).

221. 134 N.C. App. 502, 521 S.E.2d 717 (1999), *review denied*, 351 N.C. 357, 541 S.E.2d 714 (2000). The court held that since the inspector deliberately misled the plaintiff, this was an intentional tort rather than gross negligence. The court upheld treble damages against the individual defendant ($180,000), found the city jointly and severally liable for compensatory damages ($60,000), and ordered the individual plaintiff to pay attorney's fees.

222. Braswell v. Braswell, 330 N.C. 363, 410 S.E.2d 897 (1991); Coleman v. Cooper, 89 N.C. App. 188, 366 S.E.2d 2 (1988).

223. The cases recognized two exceptions to the public-duty doctrine: (1) where a special relationship between the individual and the local government had been established and (2) where a special duty promising protection to the individual had been created by the government, the protection was not provided, and the person suffered an injury as a result of reliance on the promise. Also, the doctrine does not apply where an employee's tort is intentional (rather than grossly negligent). *Leftwich*, 134 N.C. App. at 515, 521 S.E.2d at 727; Clark v. Red Bird Cab Co., 114 N.C. App. 400, 406, 442 S.E.2d 75, 79, *review denied*, 336 N.C. 603, 447 S.E.2d 387 (1994).

224. Derwort v. Polk Cnty., 129 N.C. App. 789, 501 S.E.2d 379 (1998).

225. Sinning v. Clark, 119 N.C. App. 515, 459 S.E.2d 71, *review denied*, 342 N.C. 194, 463 S.E.2d 242 (1995). The doctrine was also applied to animal control services in *Prevette v. Forsyth County*, 110 N.C. App. 754, 431 S.E.2d 216, *review denied*, 334 N.C. 622, 435 S.E.2d 338 (1993).

trine to local government agencies other than law enforcement.[226] The General Assembly adopted G.S. 143-299.1A in 2008 to explicitly limit application of the doctrine to alleged negligent failures of law-enforcement officers and negligent performance of health and safety inspections. The exceptions to this limit include situations where there is a special relationship or duty between the claimant and the government or where gross negligence results in the failure to perform a health or safety inspection required by statute.[227]

---

226. Thompson v. Waters, 351 N.C. 462, 526 S.E.2d 650 (2000) (public-duty doctrine not applicable to building inspection); Lovelace v. City of Shelby, 351 N.C. 458, 526 S.E.2d 652 (2000) (public-duty doctrine not applicable to emergency operators); Isenhour v. Hutto, 350 N.C. 601, 517 S.E.2d 121 (1999) (public-duty doctrine not applicable to school crossing guard); Cucina v. City of Jacksonville, 138 N.C. App. 99, 530 S.E.2d 353, *review denied*, 352 N.C. 588, 544 S.E.2d 778 (2000) (public-duty doctrine not applicable relative to alleged negligence in failing to repair stop sign); Hargrove v. Billings & Garrett, Inc., 137 N.C. App. 759, 529 S.E.2d 693 (2000) (public-duty doctrine not applicable to construction of sewer line).

227. In *Ray v. North Carolina Department of Transportation*, 366 N.C. 1, 727 S.E.2d 675 (2012), the court held that this statute clarified rather than changed the common law on the public-duty doctrine.

State and Federal Statutory and Constitutional Limits

PART 6

CHAPTER 22

State Statutory Limitations on Land Use Regulatory Discretion

The substance of local land use regulation is for the most part left to the judgment and discretion of local elected officials. Whether a parcel should be zoned for residential or business use, how much of a front-yard setback is required, what infrastructure standards should be placed in subdivision ordinances, how strict the sign regulations or limitations on nonconformities should be—all of these policy choices are made by the city council or board of county commissioners after receiving the advice of the planning board and interested citizens.

But in several circumstances the General Assembly limits the flexibility of local governments. There are instances where North Carolina statutes impose significant substantive limitations on local regulatory discretion. The statutes require that zoning be undertaken in accordance with a comprehensive or land use plan. They provide special statutory protections for agricultural uses, manufactured housing, family care homes, and hazardous-waste sites. Certain activities, such as the sale and consumption of alcohol, are regulated at the state level to the exclusion of local regulation. These and additional state-statutory limitations are discussed below.[1]

Agricultural Uses

The authority to regulate agricultural activities is one of the few significant differences between city and county authority to regulate land use in North Carolina. Cities have broad authority to regulate a wide range of agricultural activities. County authority is more limited.

Cities can regulate agricultural operations through zoning within their corporate limits but may not do so in their extraterritorial jurisdictions.[2] Cities also frequently have restrictions on keeping animals

---

1. Additional statutory limitations are discussed in other chapters. For example, statutes on environmental requirements are addressed in Chapter 10, and those on conflicts of interest are addressed in Chapter 25. Before Chapter 160D of the North Carolina General Statutes (hereinafter G.S.) was enacted, many of these state statutory limits were scattered throughout the statutes. Article 9 of Chapter 160D collects specialized statutory provisions that deal with local land-development regulation of particular land uses and particular land areas. This recodification primarily relocated these provisions, made them uniform for all cities and counties, and added minor clarifications. Section 1.5 of S.L. 2019-111 made amendments to statutes on floodplain zoning, sanitary-district zoning, water-supply-watershed regulation, and mountain-ridge-protection ordinances to align or cross-reference the procedural provisions of Chapter 160D.

2. Bona fide farms were exempt from city zoning in the extraterritorial area from 1959 to 1971, were subject to city zoning from 1971 to 2011, and exempt again after 2011.

The original municipal authorization to regulate extraterritorial planning and development exempted bona fide farms from zoning coverage because this exemption existed for county zoning. S.L. 1959-1204. The farm exemption in the extraterritorial area of cities was deleted in 1971. S.L. 1971-698. The jurisdiction of particular municipalities was then limited by local legislation. For example, S.L. 1999-57 precluded several small Guilford County municipalities (Stokesdale, Summerfield, Pleasant Garden, and Oak Ridge) from regulating agricultural land uses, and

Bona-fide-farm operations are exempt from county but not city zoning.

within the corporate limits.[3] Chapter 160D, Section 903(c) of the North Carolina General Statutes (hereinafter G.S.) allows, but does not require, cities to grant regulatory flexibility to land that is included within voluntary agricultural districts (such as allowing on-farm sales, pick-your-own operations, road signs, agritourism, and other activities incidental to farming).

When the authority to adopt zoning ordinances was extended to all counties in 1959, the legislation exempted bona fide farming from zoning regulation.[4] This exemption was later extended to farms located within municipal extraterritorial areas.

It is important to note that nonfarm uses, even if located on a bona fide farm, are not exempt from county zoning.[5] Only the farm use on a bona fide farm is exempt.

S.L. 2011-34 allowed Wake County municipalities to exempt bona fide farms from obtaining building permits for accessory buildings. The statute was amended in 2011 to exempt property used for bona-fide-farm purposes from municipal extraterritorial jurisdiction. S.L. 2011-363. The agriculture exemption from city zoning was simplified with the adoption of G.S. 160D-903(c) in 2019. The exemption more simply and directly provides that bona-fide-farm activities in the municipal extraterritorial area are exempt from city zoning to the same extent they would be exempt from county zoning. G.S. 160D-903(d) was also amended in 2019 to extend statewide the provision on municipal authority to exempt accessory farm buildings from zoning (a provision previously applicable only to specified municipalities). S.L. 2019-111.

3. G.S. 160A-186 specifically authorizes ordinances on keeping domestic animals within a city. Municipal regulation of farm animals has a long history in the state. *See, e.g.,* Town of Atl. Beach v. Young, 307 N.C. 422, 298 S.E.2d 686, *appeal dismissed,* 462 U.S. 1101 (1983) (upholding ordinance prohibiting keeping livestock, poultry, and animals other than house pets within the town); State v. Stowe, 190 N.C. 79, 128 S.E. 481 (1925) (upholding ordinance prohibiting keeping cows in Charlotte); State v. Rice, 158 N.C. 635, 74 S.E. 582 (1912) (upholding ordinance prohibiting keeping hogs within a quarter mile of Greensboro); State v. Hord, 122 N.C. 1092, 29 S.E. 952 (1898) (upholding ordinance setting minimum separations between hogpens and residences, storehouses, and wells); Rose v. Hardie, 98 N.C. 44, 4 S.E. 41 (1887) (upholding ordinance prohibiting hogs running at large). Private restrictive covenants also may restrict keeping animals on the affected property. In *Bryan v. Kittinger,* 282 N.C. App. 435, 871 S.E.2d 560 (2022), the court interpreted a covenant that provided "No animals, livestock or poultry of any kind shall be raised, bred or kept on the building site, except that dogs, cats or other household pets may be kept, provided that they are not bred or maintained for any commercial purpose." The court found that a few backyard chickens could be considered "household pets" and thus not subject to the prohibition. *See also* Steiner v. Windrow Estates Home Owners Ass'n, 213 N.C. App. 454, 713 S.E.2d 518 (2011) (holding two dwarf goats to be "household pets" rather than prohibited animals under applicable covenant).

4. S.L. 1959-1006, creating G.S. 153-266.10. The bona-fide-farm exemption is now codified at G.S. 160D-903(a).

5. G.S. 160D-903(a). *See* Ball v. Randolph Cnty. Bd. of Adjustment, 129 N.C. App. 300, 498 S.E.2d 833, *appeal dismissed,* 349 N.C. 348, 507 S.E.2d 272 (1998).

Defining Farms and Farm Uses

A critical threshold question related to the agricultural exemption from zoning is what constitutes a *bona fide farm.*

Under G.S. 160D-903(a), bona-fide-farm purposes "include the production and activities relating or incidental to the production of crops, grains, fruits, vegetables, ornamental and flowering plants, dairy, livestock, poultry, and all other forms of agriculture, as defined in G.S. 106-581.1."[6] The cross-referenced statute, G.S. 106-581.1, defines the terms *agriculture, agricultural,* and *farming* to include the following activities:

1. the cultivation of soil for production and harvesting of crops, including fruits, vegetables, sod, flowers, and ornamental plants;
2. the planting and production of timber;
3. dairying and the raising, management, care, and training of livestock, including horses, bees, poultry, deer, elk, and other animals for individual and public use, consumption, and marketing;
4. aquaculture;
5. the operation, management, conservation, improvement, and maintenance of a farm and the structures on the farm, including the repair, replacement, or expansion of such structures and construction incidental to the farming operation;[7]
6. activities incidental to the operation of a farm, including the marketing and selling of agricultural products, agritourism, the storage and use of materials for agricultural purposes (when performed on a farm), and the packing, treating, processing, sorting, storage, and other activities performed to add value to agricultural items produced on the farm;[8] and
7. a public or private grain warehouse or warehouse operation that holds grain for ten days or longer, including but not limited to all buildings, elevators, equipment, and warehouses consisting of one or more warehouse sections and considered a single delivery point with the capability to receive, load out, weigh, dry, and store grain.[9]

---

6. Also, if the property is subject to an approved conservation agreement, nonfarm products recognized by the state's Goodness Grows in North Carolina program are considered a bona-fide-farm product. G.S. 130A-291.1(g) provides that production of a crop in association with an approved nutrient-management plan that is permitted as a septage-land-application site shall be considered a bona-fide-farm purpose and thus exempt from county zoning.

7. G.S. 106-678 provides that local governments may not regulate the use, sale, distribution, storage, transportation, disposal, manufacture, or application of fertilizer. However, this statute goes on to state that "[n]othing in this section shall prohibit a county, city, or other political subdivision of the State from exercising its planning and zoning authority . . . or from exercising its fire prevention or inspection authority."

8. G.S. 160D-903(a) was amended in 2013 to expand where farming activity can take place and still allow application of the zoning exemption to marketing, selling, processing, storing, and similar activity related to farm products. That law exempted these activities for farm products produced not only on the farm property within the county's zoning jurisdiction but also those products produced on any other farm owned or leased by the farmer, wherever located. S.L. 2013-347. The provision was further liberalized in 2017 when the phrase "when conducted on the farm" was amended to read "when conducted on a farm." S.L. 2017-108, § 8.1. This provision was further extended in 2022 to include buildings and structures used solely for the storage of cotton, peanuts, or sweet potatoes (and by-products of those farm commodities) and to provide that these structures need not have the documentation required for other farm uses. S.L. 2022-55.

While not defined as "incidental" for zoning purposes, G.S. 153A-145.8 and 160A-203.2 provide that local governments may not require a permit for catering services within the county or city when the services are offered by a catering business located on a bona fide farm. The exemption addresses privilege licenses rather than development approvals.

9. S.L. 2013-347.

G.S. 160D-903(a)[10] specifies that several items shall constitute sufficient evidence that property is being used for bona-fide-farm purposes. These include: (1) a farm sales-tax exemption;[11] (2) a property-tax listing showing the property is eligible for the use-value-taxation program;[12] (3) a farm owner or operator's schedule from a federal income-tax return; or (4) a forest-management plan. This statute provides that other evidence may also be considered.[13]

"Agritourism" is included within an exempt farm use. G.S. 160D-903(a)[14] specifies what qualifies as agritourism and thus a "farm purpose" in order to be exempt from county zoning. To qualify, the land must be owned by a person who holds a qualifying farmer sales-tax exemption or is enrolled in the present-use-value property-tax program. An IRS Schedule F or a forestry-management plan still qualifies the property as a farm, but they are not sufficient to qualify agritourism as a nonfarm use exempt from zoning. The property must remain in one of the two qualifying circumstances for three years after the start of the agritourism use. If that is not done, the agritourism use becomes subject to county zoning. This statute goes on to require that the agritourism use have at least some modest farm connection by including the following:

> For purposes of this section, "agritourism" means any activity carried out on a farm or ranch that allows members of the general public, for recreational, entertainment, or educational purposes, to view or enjoy rural activities, including farming, ranching, historic, cultural, harvest-your-own activities, hunting, fishing, equestrian activities, or natural activities and attractions. A building or structure used for agritourism includes any building or structure used for public or private events, including, but not limited to, weddings, receptions, meetings, demonstrations of farm activities, meals, and other events that are taking place on the farm because of its farm or rural setting.[15]

Even if the property qualifies as a farm, farm property used for nonfarm purposes is subject to county zoning.

North Carolina cases provide additional clarification on the definition of bona fide farms and exempted farm uses.[16]

Development Associates, Inc. v. Wake County Board of Adjustment[17] involved a dog-breeding and kennel facility on a 2.5-acre tract in Wake County. The county zoning ordinance defined agricultural and

---

10. This list of items was added to the statute by S.L. 2011-363. It originally included a farm identification number issued by the U.S. Department of Agriculture, but that was deleted from the list in 2017 by S.L. 2017-108.

11. G.S. 105-164.13E requires that a person have $10,000 in annual income from farm operations in order to qualify for the sales-tax exemption. There is also a conditional exemption for new farmers.

12. G.S. 105-277.3 sets minimum acreage and farm-income levels to qualify for participation. For example, agricultural lands must have at least ten acres in actual production and at least $1000 in gross farm income, horticulture uses must have at least five acres in actual production and at least $1000 in gross income, and forestland must have at least twenty acres in actual production. Land enrolled in the federal Conservation Reserve Program is considered to be in actual production for the purposes of qualifying for use-value taxation.

13. This clarification was added to the statute by S.L. 2022-55, § 2.

14. The agritourism clarification was added to the statute by S.L. 2017-108, § 8(a).

15. G.S. 160D-903(a). Hunting, fishing, and equestrian activities were added by S.L. 2020-18.

16. Cases and statutes from other contexts also may be useful in defining *bona fide farm*. In a workers'-compensation case that also involved an agricultural exemption, the court ruled:

> Traditionally, agriculture has been defined as "the science or art of cultivating the soil and its fruits, especially in large areas or fields, and the rearing, feeding, and management of livestock thereon, including every process and step necessary and incident to the completion of products therefrom for consumption or market and the incidental turning of them to account." This traditional definition has been extended to encompass the storage and marketing of agricultural products.

Hinson v. Creech, 286 N.C. 156, 159–60, 209 S.E.2d 471, 474 (1974) (citations omitted). Also see the definitions of *agricultural land* used for use-value-property-tax purposes at G.S. 105-277.2.

17. 48 N.C. App. 541, 269 S.E.2d 700 (1980), *review denied*, 301 N.C. 719, 274 S.E.2d 227 (1981).

farming purposes to include any area of realty that either comprised forty or more acres or comprised less than forty acres but brought in an annual gross income of $500 or more from any agricultural, farming, livestock, or poultry operation, exclusive of home gardens. The court ruled that G.S. 153A-340 (now G.S. 160D-903) exempted only farming and livestock operations from zoning. Because the statute did not define the terms, the court looked to various agricultural, criminal, and negligence statutes relating to animals for guidance on what *livestock* included. The court concluded that dogs were not livestock and therefore ruled that the kennel was subject to county zoning.

Baucom's Nursery Co. v. Mecklenburg County[18] involved a nursery and greenhouse on a 19.6-acre tract in Mecklenburg County. The county had secured local legislation in 1967 explicitly authorizing it to define *bona fide farm* for the purpose of the agriculture exemption from county zoning. The county adopted the following definition:

> Any tract of land containing at least three (3) acres which is used for dairying or for the raising of agricultural products, forest products, livestock or poultry and including facilities for the sale of such products from the premises where produced provided that, a farm shall not be construed to include commercial poultry and swine production, cattle feeder lots and fur-bearing animal farms.

The court held that the nursery and greenhouse were a bona fide farm because agricultural operations included the growing of vegetables, flowers, and shrubs.

Sedman v. Rijdes[19] involved a plant- and vegetable-greenhouse operation on a 41-acre tract adjacent to the plaintiff's property in Orange County. The operation included four greenhouses, fans, a loading dock, and some sales of the plants on the premises. The court dismissed the contention that the operation was in violation of the zoning ordinance, ruling that the entire horticultural operation was exempt from zoning as a bona fide farm.

In *Ball v. Randolph County Board of Adjustment*, the court held that treatment of petroleum-contaminated soil through a process known as "land farming" was not an agricultural use. This process of soil remediation involved transporting contaminated soil to a site and treating the soil chemically with nutrients to stimulate microbial consumption of the contaminants. The process required tilling the soil to stimulate the process. The Randolph County zoning regulation did not specifically address this use. The county staff ruled that the process was a permitted use in the residential-agricultural district because of its similarity to common farming practices, a determination upheld by the board of adjustment. However, on appeal the court held that because no crops, plants, or other agricultural products were involved, it was, as a matter of law, a waste-treatment process and not an agricultural use of the land.[20]

County of Durham v. Roberts[21] addressed the question of the scope of activities that can be considered to be incidental to agricultural operations and thus within the scope of the county zoning exemption. The defendant there owned a 113-acre tract and proposed to raise horses for her family's enjoyment. The defendant improved the pastures by grading the site, removing some three feet of clay, and expanding

---

18. 62 N.C. App. 396, 303 S.E.2d 236 (1983).

19. 127 N.C. App. 700, 492 S.E.2d 620 (1997).

20. 129 N.C. App. 300, 498 S.E.2d 833, *appeal dismissed*, 349 N.C. 348, 507 S.E.2d 272 (1998). The court also noted that while soil remediation is regulated by the state, state rules do not address the location of these activities. Thus, counties can regulate the location of this state-regulated activity without being preempted by state rules. By contrast, see *Granville Farms, Inc. v. County of Granville*, 170 N.C. App. 109, 612 S.E.2d 156 (2005), where the court held that state regulation of disposal of solid wastes from wastewater-treatment plants preempted a county regulation on land application of sewage sludge. G.S. 130A-291.1(g), adopted in 2001, provides that production of a crop in accordance with an approved nutrient-management plan on land that is permitted as a septage-land-application site is a bona-fide-farm use for county zoning purposes.

21. 145 N.C. App. 665, 551 S.E.2d 494 (2001).

several ponds. The material removed was sold to an excavation contractor for use in a landfill. The county contended this constituted "resource extraction," a prohibited use in the zoning district. The court held that raising horses is the "production of livestock" within the agriculture exemption even if the horses were not commercially traded. The court further held that the pasture improvements were incidental to that operation, even if the by-products were sold for nonagricultural purposes and even if such activity is not "necessary and customary" for farming.

North Iredell Neighbors for Rural Life v. Iredell County[22] involved a proposed biodiesel operation intended to produce 500,000 gallons of fuel per year. The court held that the facility was an industrial use not covered within the bona-fide-farm exemption and that nonfarm uses of a farm were subject to county zoning. Key factors in this determination included the fact that the operation was not self-contained (some of the seeds used in production would be produced off-site) and that the facility would produce substantially more fuel than could be used for on-site agricultural activities.[23]

Hampton v. Cumberland County[24] presented the issue of whether a shooting range was agritourism and exempt from county zoning. The court noted that even though the owners had qualified the property as a farm,[25] "nonfarm uses" were still subject to zoning. The court held that having one of the qualifiers as a "farm" was "sufficient evidence" of farm use but not "conclusive evidence." However, the court found that the record before the board of adjustment did not resolve the factual determination of how the range was actually used—whether it was used occasionally by the owners and invitees for target practice or was regularly used for commercial firearms training. The court remanded the matter for findings by the board.

The court in *Jeffries v. County of Harnett* addressed whether commercial shooting activities (shooting towers, archery ranges, ranges and courses for clay pigeon shooting, rifle ranges, and pistol pits) constituted agritourism when conducted on a bona fide farm. The court noted that while hunting is a traditional rural activity, that is not the case with shooting ranges.[26] The court noted the examples of agritourism listed in the statute—"farming, ranching, historic, cultural, harvest-your-own activities, or other natural activities and attractions"—were all rural activities, and this implied that other exempt agritourism should be similar "natural" activities that could be enjoyed without alteration of the land.[27] While an outdoor shooting range may require land space that only a rural setting can provide, shoot-

22. 196 N.C. App. 68, 674 S.E.2d 436, *review denied*, 363 N.C. 582, 682 S.E.2d 385 (2009).

23. The proposed operation would produce 500,000 gallons per year while the farm operation could only use 100,000 gallons per year. The project envisioned selling the excess production to neighboring farmers. The court found this to be a commercial operation independent of the farm. The court expressly did not opine on whether production of biodiesel for use only on the farm itself would be exempt.

24. 256 N.C. App. 656, 808 S.E.2d 763 (2017), *appeal dismissed as improvidently allowed*, 373 N.C. 2, 832 S.E.2d 692 (2019).

25. The owners had secured a USDA farm identification number, which at that time was one of the listed ways to establish that the land was a farm.

26. 259 N.C. App. 473, 817 S.E.2d 36 (2018), *review denied*, 372 N.C. 297, 826 S.E.2d 710 (2019). The court considered the 2017 legislation defining *agritourism* even though the amendment was made after this litigation commenced, holding the amendment was a clarification of the bona-fide-farm exemption rather than a "substantial alteration of the law." The court concluded that the statute, even as clarified, was still ambiguous as to these shooting activities.

27. *Id.* at 489, 817 S.E.2d at 47 (quoting G.S. 99E-30(1)). Other guides to interpretation noted by the court were that the inclusion of farming and ranching, but not hunting, in the list of agricultural activities implied that shooting activities are not contemplated agritourism. Also, the listed uses of "weddings, receptions, meetings, [and] demonstrations" on a farm "because of its farm and rural setting" are all different from shooting activities. *Id.* at 493, 817 S.E.2d at 50 (quoting G.S. 153A-340(b)(2a)). The court concluded that shooting ranges shared little resemblance to the listed rural-agritourism examples or the spirit of preservation and traditionalism embodied in the statute.

ing is not purposefully performed on a farm for the aesthetic value of the farm or its rural setting. The court thus held that the shooting activities were not agritourism and were subject to county zoning.

Farmworker Housing

G.S. 160D-903(a) provides that an existing or new residence is incidental to farming and thus exempt from county zoning if it is situated on the farm, is constructed according to the residential building code, and is occupied by the owner, lessee, or operator of the farm.[28] Other buildings or structures "sheltering or supporting" the farm use and operation also are considered incidental to the farm use. Farmworker housing on the farm, including housing for temporary farm workers, is likely also exempt if it is occupied solely by persons working on that farm.[29]

The statutes also limit the use of zoning to prohibit residential incursion into agricultural areas. G.S. 160D-903(b)[30] provides that counties may not prohibit single-family detached homes on lots greater than ten acres in size in zoning districts where more than 50 percent of the land is used for agriculture or silviculture (unless the property is in a commercial or industrial zoning district allowing a broad variety of commercial or industrial uses).

Hog Farms

As the number of large-scale hog farms dramatically increased in North Carolina in the 1990s, the General Assembly took several steps to regulate the location and management of these facilities.[31] The General Assembly enacted uniform state standards for hog lots[32] but allowed no county zoning of hog farms.

The court held in *Craig v. County of Chatham* that these state statutes, along with the statutes on animal-waste-management systems, showed an intention to cover the entire field of swine-farm regulation and thus preempted both general county ordinances and local board-of-health regulation of swine farms.[33]

---

28. This clarification of the exemption was made by the 2017 Farm Bill, S.L. 2017-108.

29. Housing for migrant farm workers is broadly defined in G.S. 95-223(6). However, to be exempt from zoning it must be incidental to use of the property for farm purposes, which would generally require the workers to be engaged for work on that farm, not any farm. Other statutes and regulations have habitability standards for migrant housing. The Migrant Housing Act is codified as G.S. 95-222 to -229.1. Federal laws also impose minimum health and safety requirements for migrant agricultural workers. 29 U.S.C. § 1823.

30. This provision was added to the statutes by S.L. 2011-384 and was apparently motivated by *Tonter Investments, Inc. v. Pasquotank County*, 199 N.C. App. 579, 681 S.E.2d 536 (2009) (limiting residential use in agricultural zoning district unless lot has specified access to public water supply and to state road or its equivalent). The law provides that any ordinance provision inconsistent with its limitation is void and unenforceable as of the effective date of the law. This law also mandates a study of the extent to which counties should be able to require that lots exempt from subdivision regulation be accessible to emergency-service providers.

31. By the mid-1990s, hogs had become the leading cash-receipts farm product in North Carolina. The Smithfield Packing Company slaughterhouse in Bladen County, one of the largest such facilities in the country, has the capacity to process some 32,000 hogs per day. Several counties adopted moratoria and health-board regulations on large-scale hog farms in the early and mid-1990s. For a general overview of the state of the law on this issue in the mid-1990s, see Milton S. Heath, Jr., *Intensive Livestock Operations in North Carolina: Cases and Materials*, ENVTL. & CONSERVATION L. BULL. No. 2 (UNC Institute of Government, Mar. 1996).

32. The state enacted the Swine Farm Siting Act in 1995. S.L. 1995-420 (codified at G.S. 106-800 to -805).

33. 356 N.C. 40, 565 S.E.2d 172 (2002). *See also* Granville Farms, Inc. v. Cnty. of Granville, 170 N.C. App. 109, 612 S.E.2d 156 (2005) (state law on sludge disposal preempts county regulation of land application of biosolids).

For a time, there was an exception to the county zoning exemption for hog farms.[34] In 1997, the statute was amended to remove large swine farms from the bona-fide-farm exemption from county zoning.[35] Hog farms served by an animal-waste-management system[36] with a design capacity of 600,000 pounds steady-state live weight or greater[37] could be subjected to a county zoning regulation. A county was not permitted, however, to adopt zoning regulations that excluded such farms from the zoned area of the county, nor could it require discontinuance of large swine farms that were in existence at the time county regulations were adopted, require the amortization of such farms, or prohibit repair and replacement on those farms.[38] The zoning-exemption exception for large hog farms was, however, repealed in 2017.[39]

Farm Signs

The state statutes regarding regulation of outdoor advertising also include a modest exemption from regulation for some farm signs. G.S. 136-129(2a) exempts advertising to promote a bona fide farm that is exempt from county zoning regulation from sign regulations. The sign can be no more than three feet long on any side and must be on farm property that is owned or leased by the owner or lessee of the bona fide farm.

Other Protections for Agricultural Uses

City and county authority to regulate subdivisions in agricultural areas is also somewhat limited by the exemption of land divisions greater than ten acres from subdivision regulation (local governments may, however, establish minimum lot sizes greater than ten acres in appropriate rural-agricultural zoning districts).[40]

State legislation limits both city and county regulation of some forestry activity. G.S. 160D-921 prohibits counties and cities from regulating activities associated with growing, managing, and harvesting trees on lands subject to forestry use-value property taxation or activity being conducted in accordance with a forest-management plan.[41] These statutes provide that they do not limit local regulation of activity associated with development. A difficult situation arises when both forestry and development are involved. For example, trees may be grown on a site under a forestry-management plan until the owner

---

34. Development regulations other than zoning regulations often do not totally exempt bona-fide-farm activities. An example is a flood-hazard ordinance. G.S. 143-215.54 authorizes county flood-hazard ordinances and provides that "[g]eneral farming, pasture, outdoor plant nurseries, horticulture, forestry" and similar uses can be made in a flood-hazard area without a permit if they comply with local ordinances and other applicable laws and regulations. Also see G.S. 153A-140, which exempts bona fide farms from county public-health-nuisance abatement, but use of farm property for nonfarm purposes is not exempt.

35. S.L. 1997-458.

36. All hog farms with 250 or more swine are required to have an animal-waste-management system approved by the state. G.S. 143-215.10C.

37. The total number of animals it takes to constitute 600,000 pounds varies depending on the age and size of the animals.

38. S.L. 1997-458, § 2.2.

39. S.L. 2017-108.

40. However, G.S. 160D-903(b), discussed above, limits zoning restrictions on single-family detached homes on lots greater than ten acres in size in agricultural areas.

41. These laws explicitly provide that they do not limit local tree regulations imposed pursuant to local legislation or enacted in response to state or federal law. Cities may also regulate trees affecting their street rights-of-way. The state Department of Environment and Natural Resources has also issued administrative rules establishing forest-practice guidelines related to water-quality protection. Title 15A, Chapter 01I, Sections .0101–.0209 of the North Carolina Administrative Code (hereinafter N.C.A.C.).

determines that the site is ready for development, at which point the trees are harvested and sold and the site is subsequently converted to nonforest use. The statutes address this situation by providing that counties and cities may deny building permits, site plans, and subdivision plats in certain instances of clear-cutting the property. If the harvest results in the removal of substantially all of the trees that were protected under city or county regulation, development approval can be withheld for up to three years after the harvest (and for up to five years if the harvest was a willful violation of local ordinances). Also, G.S. 153A-123(h) and 160A-175(h) prohibit any local ordinance from regulating trees on property owned or operated by a public-airport authority.

G.S. 143-138(b4) exempts specified farm buildings outside of municipal-development-regulation jurisdiction (and greenhouses and therapeutic equine facilities inside of cities) from building code regulation.[42] Spectator seating in such buildings is subject to an annual safety inspection.

State law provides a variety of other nonregulatory protections for agricultural land uses. The state's Agricultural Development and Farmland Preservation Trust Fund[43] provides grants for purchase of agricultural conservation easements. Qualifying farmland may be assessed at its agricultural value rather than market value for property taxes.[44] Counties and cities may also establish voluntary agricultural districts that limit water and sewer assessments for farmland and require special public hearings before condemnation of farmland.[45] Property that is in active farm use may not be annexed into a city without the written consent of the owner.[46]

Private-nuisance actions against preexisting farm uses are also limited. A farmer's intentional conduct may be held to be a nuisance if it unreasonably interferes with the use and enjoyment of a neighbor's property and the gravity of the harm to the neighbor outweighs the utility of the farmer's conduct.[47]

---

42. Primitive camps and primitive farm buildings are also excluded from building code regulation by this statute.

43. G.S. 106-744. In 2001, the General Assembly appropriated $200,000 to this trust fund. Grants have been used for transactional costs in arranging donations of conservation easements and for costs for monitoring and enforcing easement agreements. The program is administered by the state Department of Agriculture, with administrative support on a contract basis from the Conservation Trust for North Carolina.

44. G.S. 105-277.2 to -277.7. G.S. 105-277.2 defines *agricultural land* as being a part of a farm unit that is actively engaged in the commercial production or growing of crops, plants, or animals. Similarly, *forestland* and *horticultural land* are defined as areas actively engaged in the commercial growing of trees and of fruits, vegetables, nursery products, or floral products, respectively. In all three instances the activity must be carried out under a sound management program and must meet size and income standards set by G.S. 105-277.3 including: (1) for agricultural lands, ten acres in actual production with an average annual gross income in the preceding three years of at least $1000; (2) for horticultural lands, at least five acres either in Christmas-tree production or with an annual gross income in the preceding three years of $1000; and (3) for forestland, at least twenty acres in actual production. There are also provisions in federal tax law that promote farmland preservation. For example, for estate-tax purposes, qualified farmland may be valued at its agricultural-use value rather than at market value. I.R.C. § 2032A.

45. G.S. 106-735 to -743.5. In 2011, the General Assembly amended G.S. 106-737 to allow property that is engaged in agriculture to be included without the necessity of being enrolled in the use-value-taxation program. In 2005, the General Assembly added "Enhanced Voluntary Agricultural Districts" to this program. S.L. 2005-390, codified at G.S. 106-743.1 to -743.5. In these districts, property that is subject to a conservation agreement may receive up to 25 percent of its gross sales from nonfarm products and still qualify as a bona fide farm for purposes of the zoning exemption. *See generally* Myrl L. Duncan, *Agriculture as a Resource: Statewide Land Use Programs for the Preservation of Farmland*, 14 Ecology L.Q. 401 (1987).

46. G.S. 160-58.54(c).

47. The basic standards for an intentional private nuisance are set forth in *Pendergrast v. Aiken*, 293 N.C. 201, 236 S.E.2d 787 (1977). It is, however, difficult for plaintiffs to prevail in nuisance actions against farm operations. *See, e.g.*, Parker v. Barefoot, 130 N.C. App. 18, 502 S.E.2d 42 (1998), *rev'd*, 351 N.C. 40, 519 S.E.2d 315 (1999). Neighbors sued the operator of an industrial hog-production facility (2880 hogs in four hog houses on a ninety-five-acre farm) that used an open-pit lagoon to deposit waste from the hogs. The plaintiffs, whose nearest residence was 650 feet from the facility, contended that the odor from the lagoons was unbearable. The jury found for the farmers. The court of appeals ordered a new trial because the trial judge refused to instruct the jury that installation of "state of

The "Right to Farm" Act, G.S. 106-701, was added to the statutes in 1979. It provides that if an agricultural or forestry operation has been in existence for one year, it shall not become a nuisance as a result of changed conditions around it unless there is a fundamental change in the farm operation.[48] The statute, as with similar legislation around the country, codifies a "coming to the nuisance" defense that protects farm operations from suits as the surrounding lands become more populated. A series of twenty-six cases in federal court were brought by some 500 neighbors of large-scale hog farms in 2013 contending the use of open waste ponds (termed hog "lagoons") and spraying the effluent on adjacent croplands constituted a nuisance, largely due to the odors.[49] The court in *In re: NC Swine Farm Nuisance Litigation* held that the right-to-farm statute did not protect the farm operation from a nuisance action brought by residents in place prior to the initiation of the swine farms.[50] A number of the cases were consolidated and the plaintiffs were awarded substantial actual and punitive damages in 2018.[51]

In 2018, the statute was amended to limit suits brought after a fundamental change in the nature of an existing farm.[52] The amendment provides that a change in the size of the farm or a change in the type of agricultural product being raised is not a "fundamental change" in the existing farm.

Protected agricultural operations include commercial production of crops, livestock, poultry, livestock products, and poultry products. Protected forestry operations include growing, managing, and harvesting trees. This statute does not limit nuisance actions where the neighboring land use was in existence prior to initiation of the agricultural use.[53] It also does not apply when the agricultural operation itself is substantially changed.[54] Attorney's fees may be awarded if the losing party made frivolous or malicious claims.

---

the art" hog-waste treatment was not a defense to a nuisance action. The supreme court reversed on the grounds that the requested instruction, while a correct statement of the law, was an insignificant aspect of the case. *See also* Elliott v. Muehlbach, 173 N.C. App. 709, 620 S.E.2d 266 (2005) (reasonable-person standard applies to alleged nuisance from operation of racetrack).

48. Cordon M. Smart, Comment, *The "Right to Commit Nuisance" in North Carolina: A Historical Analysis of the Right-to-Farm Act*, 94 N.C. L. Rev. 2097 (2016); Aaron M. McKown, Note, *Hog Farms and Nuisance Law in* Parker v. Barefoot: *Has North Carolina Become a Hog Heaven and Waste Lagoon?*, 77 N.C. L. Rev. 2355 (1999); John D. Burns, Comment, *The Eight Million Little Pigs—A Cautionary Tale: Statutory and Regulatory Responses to Concentrated Hog Farming*, 31 Wake Forest L. Rev. 851 (1996). *See generally* Jacqueline P. Hand, *Right-to-Farm Laws: Breaking New Ground in the Preservation of Farmland*, 45 U. Pitt. L. Rev. 289 (1984).

49. The lagoon and spray-field method of waste disposal was banned for new operations in 1997, but existing farms were allowed to continue the practice. S.L. 1997-458. For a review of the litigation largely from the point of view of the plaintiffs, see Corban Addison, Wastelands: The True Story of Farm Country on Trial (2022). See also D. Lee Miller and Ryke Longest, *Reconciling Environmental Justice with Climate Change Mitigation: A Case Study of NC Swine CAFOs*, 21 Vt. J. Envtl. L. 523 (2022).

50. No. 5:15-CV-00013-BR, 2017 WL 5178038 (E.D.N.C. Nov. 8, 2017).

51. The damage awards were substantial. In the four cases with punitive damage awards, the jury awarded amounts ranging from $5 million to $450 million. Those amounts were later capped at lower, but still substantial, amounts. The Fourth Circuit on appeal affirmed actual damages and remanded for recalculation of punitive damages in *McKiver v. Murphy-Brown, LLC*, 980 F.3d 937 (2020).

52. S.L. 2018-113. This bill was vetoed by Gov. Roy Cooper and became law when his veto was overridden. The constitutionality of the limits on nuisance actions in the right-to-farm statutes, G.S. 106-701 and -702, were upheld in *Rural Empowerment Ass'n for Community Help v. State*, 281 N.C. App. 52, 868 S.E.2d 645 (2021), *review denied*, ___ N.C. ___, ___ S.E.2d ___ (2022).

53. Mayes v. Tabor, 77 N.C. App. 197, 334 S.E.2d 489 (1985) (where summer camp has been in existence for sixty years, the statute does not protect adjacent hog farm that has been in existence only fifteen years).

54. Conversion of three turkey houses to a hog-production facility (consisting of two buildings and a waste-treatment lagoon) was held not to be protected by this statute on the grounds that a fundamental change in the nature of the agricultural activity removes the liability shield. Durham v. Britt, 117 N.C. App. 250, 451 S.E.2d 1 (1994), *review denied*, 340 N.C. 260, 456 S.E.2d 829 (1995).

In addition to limits on private-nuisance actions, G.S. 106-701(d) prohibits local ordinances from making agricultural operations a nuisance in a way inconsistent with these same limits, provided the agricultural operation is not operated in a "negligent or improper" manner.

Alcohol Sales

Direct state regulation of an activity may be so extensive as to preempt the field, thus effectively preventing local regulation of that activity. An example is state regulation of alcohol sales. Under North Carolina law, the state Alcoholic Beverage Control (ABC) Commission has the ultimate decision-making authority on most aspects of alcohol sales. The applicable statute, G.S. 18B-901, provides that the ABC Commission issues all ABC permits and sets forth the factors to be considered by the commission in issuing permits. These include several land use factors: the number of places already holding ABC permits within the neighborhood, parking and traffic, the kinds of businesses already in the neighborhood, the proximity of schools and churches,[55] zoning, local government recommendations, and potential detriment to the neighborhood.

The statutes require that notice be given to local governments before a decision is made on ABC permit applications.[56] The ABC Commission must consider local ordinances but is not bound by them.[57] Once a liquor merchant has secured a state ABC permit, that merchant is for the most part exempt from zoning restrictions, such as local restrictions on the location of the facility, limits on hours of operation, entertainment within the facility, and even signs advertising alcohol products.[58]

Two North Carolina cases have prohibited local governments from imposing zoning restrictions on alcohol sales over and above those applied by the state. In the first, *Staley v. City of Winston-Salem*,[59] a Winston-Salem ordinance restricting wine sales in a nonconforming restaurant in a residential zoning district was invalidated. In the second, *In re Melkonian*,[60] the town of Havelock's denial of a special use permit for a tavern that had secured an ABC license was invalidated.

State ABC licensing laws also address alcohol sales in redevelopment areas. Several cities raised concerns about convenience stores in economically depressed neighborhoods that sold large quantities of beer and wine. Some patrons had a tendency to loiter and consume the alcohol on nearby properties,

---

55. G.S. 18B-901(c)(6) specifies that the ABC Commission shall consider whether the proposed location is within fifty feet of a church or school.

56. In addition to the matter of notice of permit decisions, the statutes also address the location of ABC stores. G.S. 18B-801 prohibits a local ABC board from locating an ABC store within a city over the objection of the city's governing board. The law does allow the local ABC board to seek an override of this prohibition by the state ABC board. Also see S.L. 2009-295, which allows the ABC board to limit the location of ABC stores within 1000 feet of a school or church in Guilford County.

57. In 1994, the General Assembly amended G.S. 18B-901(c) to provide that the ABC Commission "shall consider" local zoning and related land use factors in making ABC permit decisions. S.L. 1994-749. The statute had previously read that the commission "may consider" zoning. This strengthens the consideration that must be given by the state to local zoning but stops short of mandating consistency. In 2005, this section was further amended to mandate that local governments return a Zoning and Compliance Form to the ABC Commission as part of the permit-review process. S.L. 2005-392. This act also expanded the provision relative to potential detriment to neighborhoods to specify that the commission is to consider past revocations, suspensions, and violations of ABC laws within the previous year at the location and evidence of illegal-drug activity, fighting, disorderly conduct, and other dangerous activities (both within the facility and on the associated premises).

58. An exception exists for sexually oriented businesses. G.S. 18B-904(g) allows local regulation of the location and operation of such businesses. See Chapter 26 for more details on this issue.

59. 258 N.C. 244, 128 S.E.2d 604 (1962). *See also* State v. Williams, 283 N.C. 550, 196 S.E.2d 756 (1973) (local regulation of possession of open containers of malt beverage preempted by state regulation).

60. 85 N.C. App. 351, 355 S.E.2d 503, *review denied*, 320 N.C. 631, 360 S.E.2d 91 (1987).

contributing to crime in the area and impairing neighborhood-revitalization efforts. In response, G.S. 18B-309 was adopted in 1999 to address these concerns.[61] A food business or eating establishment located in a designated urban-redevelopment area is not allowed to have alcohol sales in excess of 50 percent of its total annual sales. A city may request that the state ABC Commission conduct an audit of any such business to determine whether this maximum percentage of alcohol sales is being exceeded, but it may do so only once per year for any individual business. If a business exceeds the maximum percentage, its ABC permits are to be revoked.

State law also limits advertising of alcoholic beverages. G.S. 18B-105(b)(7) authorizes the state ABC Commission to prohibit or regulate advertising of alcoholic beverages on signs. Commission rules limit the size and text of outdoor advertising of beer, wine, and mixed beverages by permittees.[62] Industry groups may advertise beer and wine—but not liquor—on billboards.[63]

Comprehensive and Land Use Planning

Other than in the coastal area, North Carolina cities and counties are not required to adopt a comprehensive or land use plan. However, local governments that want to adopt zoning regulations must have a plan.[64]

Despite this lack of a mandate, most populous North Carolina cities and counties adopted comprehensive or land use plans well before the 2019 requirement to have a plan in order to exercise zoning went into effect. A 1998 survey reported that approximately 83 percent of the state's 100 counties, 70 percent of the cities with populations over 10,000, and 50 percent of the cities with populations under 10,000 had adopted a plan.[65] A 2008 UNC School of Government survey produced similar results: 75 percent of the cities with populations over 10,000 reported having adopted a comprehensive plan, as did 63 percent of the counties with populations over 25,000 in their unincorporated areas.[66] A 2018 School survey reported that 68 percent of responding cities (and 94 percent of cities with populations over 25,000) and 78 percent of responding counties had adopted a comprehensive plan.[67]

---

61. S.L. 1999-322.

62. 14B N.C.A.C. 15B, § .1006.

63. 14B N.C.A.C. 15B, §§ .1007–.1008.

64. G.S. 160D-501(a).

65. Ctr. for Urban and Reg'l Studies, Univ. of N.C. at Chapel Hill, Land Development Plan Guidelines for North Carolina Local Governments: Incorporating Water Quality Objectives in a Comprehensive Land Planning Framework 1 (1999).

66. David W. Owens et al., Survey of North Carolina Local Governments (2008) (unpublished data) (on file with the UNC School of Government). The survey is described in David W. Owens, Development Moratoria: The Law and Practice in North Carolina 7–8 (UNC School of Government, Special Series No. 26, 2009). Survey respondents indicated, however, that more than five years had elapsed since the adoption or updating of half of these plans. These jurisdictions also reported that a variety of other types of plans had been adopted. A majority had adopted a hazard-mitigation plan (61 percent) or a land use plan (60 percent). Other plans with high rates of adoption included a parks-and-recreation plan (45 percent), a capital-improvement plan (44 percent), and a transportation plan (40 percent). Other types of plans that had been adopted by at least 10 percent but less than 25 percent of the responding jurisdictions included small-area or neighborhood plans, corridor plans, Coastal Area Management Act plans, open-space plans, and farmland-preservation plans.

67. Owens, *supra* note 66, at 5.

Zoning to Be "In Accordance" with Plan

In North Carolina the zoning-enabling statutes have since their initial adoption provided that zoning be "in accordance with a comprehensive plan."[68] As an early California zoning decision noted, "Zoning in its best sense looks not only backward to protect districts already established but forward to aid in the development of new districts according to a comprehensive plan having as its basis the welfare of the city as a whole."[69] The fact is, though, that zoning regulations in the United States often are not based on a separate comprehensive-planning program, an actuality that led one English observer to conclude, "The most obvious defect in the whole American land use planning machinery is that the controls came before the planning."[70]

---

68. G.S. 160D-701. This requirement was included in the Standard State Zoning Enabling Act. Nearly all states still retain some variation of the requirement. 1 PATRICIA E. SALKIN, AMERICAN LAW OF ZONING §§ 5.3–.16 (5th ed., May 2019 Update).

For additional North Carolina–specific analysis of the planning-regulation relationship, see Kenneth G. Silliman, *A Practical Interpretation of North Carolina's Comprehensive Plan Requirement*, 7 CAMPBELL L. REV. 1 (1984); Mark Stanton Thomas, Comment, *Urban Planning and Land Use Regulation: The Need for Consistency*, 14 WAKE FOREST L. REV. 81 (1978). For a national perspective, see JOSEPH F. DIMENTO, THE CONSISTENCY DOCTRINE AND THE LIMITS OF PLANNING (1980); DANIEL R. MANDELKER, THE ZONING DILEMMA (1971); 1 EDWARD H. ZIEGLER JR., RATHKOPF'S THE LAW OF ZONING AND PLANNING § 12.2 (4th ed., April 2019 Update); Nathan Blackburn, Comment, *Planning Ahead: Consistency with a Comprehensive Land Use Plan Yields Consistent Results for Municipalities*, 60 OKLA. L. REV. 73 (2007); Gerald A. Fischer, *The Comprehensive Plan Is an Indispensable Compass for Navigating Mixed-Use Zoning Decisions Through the Precepts of the Due Process, Takings, and Equal Protection Clauses*, 40 URB. LAW. 831 (2008); Charles M. Haar, *"In Accordance with a Comprehensive Plan,"* 68 HARV. L. REV. 1154 (1955); Charles M. Haar, *The Master Plan: An Impermanent Constitution*, 20 LAW & CONTEMP. PROBS. 353 (1955); Laurence Kressel & Edward J. Sullivan, *Twenty Years After—Renewed Significance of the Comprehensive Plan Requirement*, 9 Urb. L. Ann. 33 (1975); Daniel R. Mandelker, *The Role of the Local Comprehensive Plan in Land Use Regulation*, 74 MICH. L. REV. 899 (1976); Stuart Meck, *The Legislative Requirement that Zoning and Land Use Controls Be Consistent with an Independently Adopted Local Comprehensive Plan: A Model Statute*, 3 WASH. U. J.L. & POL'Y 295 (2000); Richard K. Norton, *Who Decides, How, and Why? Planning for the Judicial Review of Local Legislative Zoning Decisions*, 43 URB. LAW. 1085 (2011); Charles L. Siemon, *The Paradox of "In Accordance with a Comprehensive Plan" and Post Hoc Rationalizations: The Need for Efficient and Effective Judicial Review of Land Use Regulations*, 16 STETSON L. REV. 604 (1987); Edward J. Sullivan, *The Evolving Role of the Comprehensive Plan*, 32 URB. LAW. 813 (2000).

For a basic text on land use planning, see PHILIP R. BERKE ET AL., URBAN LAND USE PLANNING (5th ed. 2006). *See also* Edward J. Kaiser & David R. Godschalk, *Twentieth Century Land Use Planning: A Stalwart Family Tree*, 61 J. AM. PLAN. ASS'N 365 (1995).

For additional information on land use planning, see JOHN M. DEGROVE WITH DEBORAH A. MINESS, THE NEW FRONTIER FOR LAND POLICY: PLANNING AND GROWTH MANAGEMENT IN THE STATES (1992); HENRY L. DIAMOND & PATRICK F. NOONAN, LAND USE IN AMERICA (1996); ERIC D. KELLY, COMMUNITY PLANNING: AN INTRODUCTION TO THE COMPREHENSIVE PLAN (2d. ed. 2000); T.J. KENT, JR., THE URBAN GENERAL PLAN (1964); INT'L CITY/ CNTY. MGT. ASS'N, LOCAL PLANNING: CONTEMPORARY PRINCIPLES AND PRACTICE (Gary Hack et al. eds., 2009).

69. Zahn v. Bd. of Pub. Works, 195 Cal. 497, 513, 234 P. 388, 395 (1925), *aff'd*, 274 U.S. 325 (1927). This sentiment was echoed in one of the earliest North Carolina guides on zoning: "Most authorities agree . . . that zoning should be approached not as a legal device complete in itself, but as one of several elements of a comprehensive city plan." PATRICK HEALY JR., A ZONING MANUAL FOR NORTH CAROLINA TOWNS AND CITIES 7 (N.C. League of Municipalities Report No. 27, July 1938). By 1935, thirty-five states had adopted enabling statutes based on the Standard State Zoning Enabling Act, while only ten had adopted statutes based on the Standard City Planning Enabling Act. Patricia E. Salkin, *The Quiet Revolution and Federalism: Into the Future*, 45 J. MARSHALL L. REV. 253, 267 (2012).

70. JOHN DELAFONS, LAND-USE CONTROLS IN THE UNITED STATES 84 (1962). An earlier critic said of zoning in 1931, "The current performance suggests planless confusion with no defined objective." Gordon Whitnall, *History of Zoning*, 155 ANNALS AM. ACAD. POL. & SOC. SCI. pt. II, at 1, 14 (1931). A 1958 legislative study commission made similar findings relative to North Carolina. "It bears emphasizing that planning must be done before these devices [zoning and subdivision regulations] are put into effect. We have found that a number of North Carolina cities and towns have zoning ordinances and subdivision ordinances without any planning program. We believe that this procedure puts the cart before the horse." N.C. GEN. ASSEMBLY, REPORT OF THE MUNICIPAL GOVERNMENT STUDY COMMISSION 10 (1958).

North Carolina courts, like many state courts,[71] did not interpret this "in accordance with a plan" requirement to mean that zoning must be compatible with a separate, formally adopted comprehensive plan. Rather, the courts required that zoning be based on a reasoned consideration of the entire jurisdiction and the full range of land use issues facing that jurisdiction. It was the thought processes underlying the planning and studies that provided the essential underpinning to establishing the reasonableness of both the original decision to adopt zoning and subsequent decisions to modify the ordinance.

One of North Carolina's earliest zoning cases confirmed the importance of comprehensive planning as the foundation for zoning, even though a formal plan document was not required at that time. The state supreme court in 1938 invalidated a purported zoning ordinance in *Shuford v. Town of Waynesville*.[72] One of several grounds for invalidation of this hastily adopted ordinance was that because it zoned only one block of the town, it was not based on a comprehensive plan and could not be sustained as a valid exercise of zoning power.

Defining a "Plan"

Cities in North Carolina were authorized to undertake planning for land use and development in 1919. That early statute did not, however, define a plan or mandate its adoption.[73]

In the 1970s, North Carolina opinions addressed the question of what exactly is the "comprehensive plan" with which zoning must be in accord. *Allred v. City of Raleigh*, a 1970 challenge to the rezoning of a 9.26-acre tract from a single-family residential district to a multifamily residential district, emphasized the necessity of applying zoning throughout the jurisdiction.[74] *A-S-P Associates v. City of Raleigh*[75]

---

71. This is the majority rule absent a specific legislative mandate for comprehensive or land use planning. *See, e.g.,* Bd. of Cnty. Comm'rs v. City of Olathe, 952 P.2d 1302 (Kan. 1998) (plan must be considered but is not binding); Rando v. Town of N. Attleborough, 692 N.E.2d 544 (Mass. App. Ct. 1998) (analysis of plan may be required, but strict accordance is not); Cnty. Council v. Zimmer Dev. Co., 120 A.3d 677 (Md. 2015); Nestle Waters N. Am., Inc. v. Town of Fryeberg, 967 A.2d 702 (Me. 2009) (plan is visionary, not regulatory); Kozesnik v. Twp. of Montgomery, 131 A.2d 1 (N.J. 1957); Apple Grp., Ltd. v. Granger Twp. Bd. of Zoning Appeals, 41 N.E.3d 1185 (Ohio 2015); Penn Street, L.P. v. E. Lampeter Twp. Zoning Hearing Bd., 84 A.3d 1114 (Pa. Commw. Ct. 2014); Hadley v. Harold Realty Co., 198 A.2d 149 (R.I. 1964); Bd. of Supervisors v. Safeco Ins. of Am., 310 S.E.2d 445 (Va. 1983). About thirty-two states now require a comprehensive plan of some description. Michael Lewyn, *The (Somewhat) False Hope of Comprehensive Planning*, 37 U. Haw. L. Rev. 39, 49 (2015). An increasing number of states require some modest degree of conformance with a separate plan. *See, e.g.,* Bridge v. Mayor of Oxford, 995 So. 2d 81 (Miss. 2008) (upholding rezoning that was debatably within comprehensive-plan policies); Riya Finnegan L.L.C. v. Twp. Council, 962 A.2d 484 (N.J. 2008) (ordinance inconsistent with plan may be adopted only if legitimate reasons for doing so are set forth); Udell v. Haas, 235 N.E.2d 897 (N.Y. 1968); Dockter v. Burleigh Cnty. Bd. of County Comm'rs, 865 N.W.2d 836 (N.D. 2015). Several states require a closer degree of plan-ordinance consistency. *See, e.g.,* Levitz v. State, 613 P.2d 1259 (Az. 1980); Foothill Cmtys. Coal. v. Cnty. of Orange, 166 Cal. Rptr. 3d 627 (Cal. Ct. App. 2014); City of Del Mar v. City of San Diego, 183 Cal. Rptr. 898, 907 (Ct. App. 1982); Durant v. D.C. Zoning Comm'n, 139 A.2d 880 (D.C. 2016); GATRI v. Blane, 962 P.2d 367 (Haw. 1998); Love v. Bd. of Cnty. Comm'rs of Bingham, 671 P.2d 471 (Idaho 1983); Howard Cnty. v. Dorsey, 438 A.2d 1339 (Md. 1982); Baker v. City of Milwaukie, 533 P.2d 772 (Or. 1975); Bell v. City of Elkhorn, 364 N.W.2d 144 (Wis. 1985). In recent decades, state legislatures have required a stronger role for plans. Among the states with statutory mandates for some degree of plan-ordinance consistency are Arizona, California, Delaware, Florida, Kentucky, Maine, Minnesota, Nebraska, New Jersey, Oregon, Rhode Island, Washington, and Wisconsin. *See, e.g.,* Cal. Gov't Code § 65860; Fla. Stat. Ann. § 163.3161(6); Ga. Code Ann. §§ 36-70-1 to -5; Haw. Rev. Stat. § 226-1; Me. Stat. tit. 30A, § 4352(2); Or. Rev. Stat. Ann. § 197.175(2); Wash. Rev. Code Ann. § 36.70A.040.

72. 214 N.C. 135, 198 S.E.2d 585 (1938).

73. S.L. 1919-23 authorized city planning boards, if appointed, "to make careful study of the resources, possibilities and needs of the city or town, particularly with respect to the conditions which may be injurious to the public welfare or otherwise injurious, and to make plans for the development of the municipality."

74. 277 N.C. 530, 544, 178 S.E.2d 432, 439–40 (1971).

75. 298 N.C. 207, 258 S.E.2d 444 (1979).

involved a challenge to the city's historic-district zoning for the Oakwood neighborhood. The court again refrained from making a precise judicial definition of a "comprehensive plan" but did provide the following as guidance:

> Absent a specific requirement in the enabling legislation, courts have generally not construed the term to require, as a condition precedent to the enactment of a zoning ordinance, the preparation and adoption of a formal master plan. . . . We do not find it necessary here to attempt an all-inclusive definition of the required comprehensive plan. What suffices as such may well vary according to the stage at which a particular city or county is in its zoning process. The evidence presented at the hearing on the motion for summary judgment showed, however, that at this late stage in its zoning process, the City of Raleigh is operating pursuant to a sufficiently comprehensive plan. The City has in effect a comprehensive set of zoning regulations which cover the entire City. The City's Planning Department has conducted comprehensive studies of the City's housing, transportation, public facilities, parks and recreation, and a wide range of other needs. Moreover, the evidence showed that before the City adopted the Oakwood Ordinance, planning studies of the area proposed to be included in the Historic District were conducted, which gave careful and comprehensive consideration to the potential effect on other ways in which the City is attempting to protect and promote the general welfare through the exercise of its zoning powers. That some inconsistencies exist among the various planning efforts engaged in by the City is not indicative of the possible absence of a comprehensive plan as so held by the Court of Appeals. A rational process of planning for a large city's varied needs inherently involves conflicts, changes, and inconsistent proposals as to how they should be met.[76]

Without mandating the contents of a comprehensive plan, the enactment of Chapter 160D in 2019 amended the statutes to set out the intent of planning, its analytical foundation, the necessity of citizen engagement in plan preparation, and the process to be followed in plan adoption. G.S. 160D-501(a1) provides:

> A comprehensive plan sets forth goals, policies, and programs intended to guide the present and future physical, social, and economic development of the jurisdiction. A land use plan uses text and maps to designate the future use or reuse of land. A comprehensive or land use plan is intended to guide coordinated, efficient, and orderly development within the planning and development regulation jurisdiction based on an analysis of present and future needs. Planning analysis may address inventories of existing conditions and assess future trends regarding demographics, economic, environmental, and cultural factors. The planning process shall include opportunities for citizen engagement in plan preparation and adoption.[77]

G.S. 160D-501(b) provides a list of topics that may be addressed in the comprehensive plan, with each local government having the discretion to address its particular needs. These topics include:

1. issues and opportunities facing the local government, including consideration of trends, values expressed by citizens, community vision, and guiding principles for growth and development;
2. the pattern of desired growth, development, and civic design, including the location, distribution, and characteristics of future land uses, urban form, utilities, and transportation networks;
3. employment opportunities, economic development, and community development;

---

76. *Id.* at 229, 258 S.E.2d at 458 (citations omitted). For further discussion of this case, see David E. Hollowell, Note, *Zoning—Historic District Zoning in North Carolina—A-S-P Associates v. City of Raleigh*, 16 WAKE FOREST L. REV. 495 (1980).

77. The sentence on land use plans was added by S.L. 2020-25.

4. acceptable levels of public services and infrastructure to support development, including water, waste disposal, utilities, emergency services, transportation, education, recreation, community facilities, and other public services, including plans and policies for provision of and financing for public infrastructure;

5. housing with a range of types and affordability to accommodate persons and households of all types and income levels;

6. recreation and open spaces;

7. mitigation of natural hazards, such as flooding, winds, wildfires, and unstable lands;

8. protection of the environment and natural resources, including agricultural resources, mineral resources, water quality, and air quality;

9. protection of significant architectural, scenic, cultural, historical, or archaeological resources; and

10. analysis and evaluation of implementation measures, including regulations, public investments, and educational programs.

Process for Plan Adoption

The statute establishes a mandatory process to be followed in plan adoption.[78] G.S. 160D-501(c) requires that a comprehensive plan or land use plan be adopted by the governing board with the advice and consultation of the planning board. Plan adoption is defined to be a legislative decision and must follow the same notice and hearing procedures that are required by G.S. 160D-601 for a zoning-text amendment.[79]

The comprehensive plan may be crafted and adopted as part of or in conjunction with other plans, such as the plans mandated by the Coastal Area Management Act. Additionally, G.S. 160D-501(a1) recognizes that local governments can and do adopt related plans, such as land use plans, small-area plans, neighborhood plans, hazard-mitigation plans, transportation plans, housing plans, and recreation-and-open-space plans.[80] If those plans are formally adopted in the same manner as the comprehensive plan, then those plans must also be considered in the consistency analysis required for zoning amendments.[81]

Plan Required for Zoning

While the adoption of a comprehensive plan or land use plan is not mandated in North Carolina,[82] in 2019 the legislature adopted a requirement for planning as a precondition of the exercise of zoning authority. G.S. 160D-501(a) states that "[a]s a condition of adopting and applying zoning regulations

---

78. As prior law did not mandate any particular process for adoption of a comprehensive plan, local governments used a variety of procedures to do so. A few adopted the plan as an ordinance, many approved it by resolution of the governing board, and some merely accepted it as a recommendation from the planning board or planning staff.

79. See Chapter 11 for details on the process for making legislative decisions. Local governments with plans adopted prior to the effective date of Chapter 160D are not required to readopt those plans. Preexisting plans remain effective even if the local government did not follow the procedures required by G.S. 160D-501. S.L. 2019-111, § 2.9(a).

80. A local government may undertake planning in coordination with other local governments, state agencies, or regional agencies. G.S. 160D-503.

81. See Chapter 11 for details on mandated plan-consistency statements required for all zoning amendments.

82. There has since 1974 been an exception to the lack of a plan mandate. The Coastal Area Management Act requires the state's twenty coastal counties to prepare comprehensive land use plans that are consistent with formal guidelines adopted by the Coastal Resources Commission. Municipalities have the option of preparing a city land use plan or being covered by the county plan. G.S. 113A, §§ 108, 109. The commission reviews and approves the plans after adoption by local governments. See the discussion of the Coastal Area Management Act in Chapter 10 for a more detailed discussion of this law. For an example of a statute that does mandate the minimum contents of a comprehensive plan, see S.C. CODE ANN. § 6-29-510.

under this Chapter, a local government shall adopt and reasonably maintain a comprehensive or land-use plan." So while a comprehensive or land use plan is not mandatory, a city or county may not exercise its zoning authority unless it has adopted and reasonably maintained a comprehensive plan.[83]

In order to adequately guide future growth, a plan must be reasonably up to date. The statute does not set a specific time frame for updating the comprehensive plan, recognizing the great variety in the state in terms of population size, growth rates, and the differing environmental, social, and economic

---

While not a plan mandate, the Land Policy Act, adopted in 1974, encouraged local land use plans. G.S. 113A-150 to -159. *See generally* LAND POLICY COUNCIL, A LAND RESOURCES PROGRAM FOR NORTH CAROLINA (1976) (recommending the development of state land policies to be used by state and local governments, a municipal and county land-classification program, a land-resources information system, and a state organizational structure to coordinate state land-related activities). The Council on State Goals and Policy also played an active role in these issues in the early 1970s. The group was reactivated by Gov. Jim Hunt in 1977 and renamed the State Goals and Policies Board. This Board took an active role in citizen surveys and policy development in the late 1970s and early 1980s (particularly with the North Carolina Tomorrow and NC 2000 initiatives). The Commission on the Future of North Carolina assumed much of this role in the early 1980s. Subsequent state "visioning" endeavors were undertaken by the Commission for a Competitive North Carolina in the mid-1990s. The North Carolina Progress Board was created in 1995 and issued its initial report on critical trends and state goals in 1997. Although the Land Policy Act has since been partially repealed, it retains a framework for state land policies and a land-classification system that may be used in local planning.

In the early 1990s, the General Assembly authorized legislative studies of both mountain-area planning and state-wide mandatory comprehensive planning. These studies, however, did not result in the enactment of legislation to do so. The reports of these studies include JOINT LEGISLATIVE COMM'N ON FUTURE STRATEGIES FOR N.C., REPORT TO THE 1991 GENERAL ASSEMBLY OF NORTH CAROLINA 9–10 (Jan. 1991) (recommending strategic-planning system for state government); MOUNTAIN AREA STUDY COMM'N, REPORT TO THE 1993 GENERAL ASSEMBLY OF NORTH CAROLINA 15–16 (Jan. 27, 1993) (recommending continued study of voluntary-planning guidelines for the mountain area); LEGISLATIVE RESEARCH COMM'N: STATEWIDE COMPREHENSIVE PLANNING COMM., REPORT TO THE 1993 GENERAL ASSEMBLY OF NORTH CAROLINA 6 (Jan. 15, 1993) (recommending creation of thirty-member Partnership for Quality Growth to conduct a thorough study of growth-and-development issues, including legislative proposals to implement coordinated and comprehensive statewide planning); LEGISLATIVE RESEARCH COMM'N: MOUNTAIN AREA STUDY COMM., REPORT TO THE 1995 GENERAL ASSEMBLY OF NORTH CAROLINA 13–14 (Jan. 11, 1995) (recommending consideration of voluntary, incentive-based model of planning- and land use–guidance systems); LEGISLATIVE RESEARCH COMM'N: COMM. ON P'SHIP FOR QUALITY GROWTH, REPORT TO THE 1995 GENERAL ASSEMBLY OF NORTH CAROLINA 6 (Jan. 11, 1995) (recommending continued study of comprehensive statewide planning systems).

A 2001 legislative study commission recommended that the state mandate comprehensive planning for all municipalities and counties. LEGISLATIVE COMM'N TO ADDRESS SMART GROWTH, GROWTH MGMT. & DEV. ISSUES, OVERARCHING GOALS AND STRATEGIES: FINAL 3–4 (Jan. 19, 2001). In 2010, a legislative study commission again recommended consideration of legislation on statewide planning principles and state-local cooperation and coordination on planning. LEGISLATIVE COMM'N ON URBAN GROWTH & INFRASTRUCTURE ISSUES, INTERIM REPORT 13 (Apr. 20, 2010). Neither resulted in enacted legislation.

Smart-growth initiatives are also discussed in Chapter 9. The General Assembly in 2010 created the Sustainable Communities Task Force to secure funding, promote regional and local planning, and develop policy recommendations in this area. Section 13.5 of the 2010 Appropriations Act, S.L. 2010-31, created G.S. 143B-344.34 to .38 to establish a sustainable-communities initiative in the state. Among the topics addressed by this initiative were better transportation choices, provision of equitable and affordable housing, enhanced economic competitiveness, support of existing communities, coordination of state policies and investments, and support of communities and neighborhoods. The law also created the Sustainable Communities Grant Fund to fund regional, city, and county planning efforts to better integrate housing and transportation decisions and to improve land use and zoning capacities. The law expired on June 30, 2016.

83. A grace period for adoption of a comprehensive plan was provided when Chapter 160D was adopted in 2019. A local government with zoning but without a comprehensive plan was required to adopt a plan by July 1, 2022, in order to continue zoning regulations. S.L. 2019-111, § 2.9(c). In 2020, this requirement was clarified to provide that adoption of either a comprehensive plan or a land use plan would suffice to retain zoning authority. S.L. 2020-25. The deadline for adoption of a comprehensive or land use plan to retain zoning authority was subsequently extended to July 1, 2023, for municipalities with populations of 1500 or less. S.L. 2022-75. In 2021, the School of Government published a guidebook for those jurisdictions that needed to update or prepare a plan to retain their authority to adopt zoning regulations. ADAM LOVELADY ET AL., PLANNC GUIDEBOOK: A PRACTITIONER'S GUIDE TO PREPARING STREAMLINED COMMUNITY PLANS (2021).

conditions affecting over 600 local governments. Rather, the mandate is that the plan must be "reasonably maintained" given the context of the individual unit of government.

The adopted plan is advisory in nature.[84] Zoning and other development regulations can be adopted and amended that are inconsistent with the adopted plan. If a zoning-map amendment is made that is inconsistent with the future land use map in an adopted plan, the zoning amendment has the effect of also amending the future land use map.[85] The plan-consistency analysis required when amending a zoning regulation ensures that the plan is consulted and considered prior to regulatory amendments.

While zoning is not required to be consistent with an adopted plan, the statutes do mandate consideration of the plan whenever zoning regulations are amended.[86] G.S. 160D-604 requires planning-board recommendations prior to initial adoption of zoning and mandate referral of proposed zoning amendments to the planning board for review and comment.[87] G.S. 160D-604(d) requires that planning-board review of zoning amendments include written comments on the consistency of the proposed amendment with the comprehensive plan and any other relevant plans (such as a small-area plan, a corridor plan, or a transportation plan) that have been adopted by the governing board. A statement from the planning board that the proposed amendment is inconsistent with a plan does not preclude the governing board from adoption of the amendment. The governing board is also required to approve a statement on plan consistency before adopting or rejecting any zoning amendment.[88] For zoning-map amendments, the governing-board statement must explain why the board believes that the action taken is reasonable and in the public interest. The statement approved by the governing board on plan consistency is not

---

84. The comprehensive plan is "advisory in nature without independent regulatory effect." G.S. 160D-501(c). See the discussion of plan-consistency statements in Chapter 11.

85. G.S. 160D-605(a). Prior to this provision's enactment, the courts had held that a plan need not be updated with each zoning amendment. In *Allgood v. Town of Tarboro*, the court considered a rezoning that was inconsistent with a land use plan that had been adopted some eight years earlier. The court noted that conditions had changed substantially after the land-development plan had been adopted and that changes in the area were documented in a detailed professional planning report. The court held that this subsequent report "furnished the Town Council with reasonable grounds and a plausible basis for adopting the amendment," even if the formal comprehensive plan itself had not been amended before the rezoning. 281 N.C. 430, 444, 189 S.E.2d 255, 264 (1972). Similarly, in *Graham v. City of Raleigh*, the court noted:

> By necessity, a comprehensive plan must undergo changes. If any zoning plan is to be comprehensive, it must be kept up to date. It would become obsolete if the council refused to recognize the changing conditions in the community. . . . Thus, the City recognized that the function of the comprehensive plan does not contemplate or require a plan which rigidly provides for or attempts to answer in minute detail every possible question regarding land utilization or restrictions or attempts to fix a zoning map in a rigid and immutable mold, but rather the plan sets out general guidelines for the guidance of zoning policy. The questioned amendment serves not merely the functions of amending the zoning ordinance, but also enunciates a change in the comprehensive plan itself, thus bringing about the necessary conformity or harmony between the amendment and the comprehensive plan.

55 N.C. App. 107, 113–14, 284 S.E.2d 742, 746–47 (1981), *review denied*, 305 N.C. 299, 290 S.E.2d 702 (1982) (citations omitted).

86. The plan-consideration requirement was added to the statutes in 2005. S.L. 2005-426, § 7; S.L. 2005-418, § 7. The initial local government implementation of this mandate is reviewed in David W. Owens, *Plan-Consistency Statements*, PLAN. & ZONING L. BULL. No. 27 (UNC School of Government, Nov. 2018). See Chapter 11 for a review of litigation on the adequacy of plan-consistency statements adopted by governing boards when making zoning amendments.

87. Prior to 2006, this was mandated for counties but not for cities, though virtually all city zoning ordinances in practice provided for such review. The governing board may proceed with consideration of zoning amendments if no planning-board comments are made within thirty days of referral and planning-board recommendations are not binding on the governing board. See Chapter 11 for a detailed discussion of the procedures that must be followed in consideration of zoning amendments.

88. G.S. 160D-605(a). The plan-consistency-statement provision was modified in 2021 to require that the statement address consistency with "an adopted comprehensive plan or land-use plan." S.L. 2021-88, § 1.(d).

subject to judicial review. The governing board is not required to approve an ordinance amendment if it is consistent with the plan or deny it if the amendment is inconsistent with the plan. Plan consistency is a factor that must explicitly be considered, but it does not control the outcome of the decision.[89]

The cases and statutes emphasize that in North Carolina, substantive, rational planning and thought, rather than a formal plan document, are vital to justify zoning and rezoning decisions. Planning studies are needed to document the public purposes being addressed and the relationship of individual zoning decisions to those purposes. Planning studies also provide technically competent analyses of the issues being considered and examine the long-term implications and the effects on other aspects of individual land use decisions.[90] In addition, planning provides for public participation, coordination of programs and decisions, and the opportunity to set forth the basic policy choices that underlie a rational program of land use regulation.[91] Documented consideration of small-area plans, traffic plans, open-space plans, redevelopment plans, and the like, as well as consideration of the comprehensive plans, provide important support to rezoning decisions both in terms of meeting the statutory requirements and the constitutional admonition to avoid arbitrary and capricious decision-making.[92]

Beyond the mandated update of a plan's future land use map, a prudent local government should make appropriate plan amendments, particularly respecting any major policy choices that may be inconsistent with a rezoning.[93] For example, if the plan calls for new commercial development to be limited to areas immediately adjacent to major intersections and a rezoning petition is being considered to allow commercial development elsewhere, a governing board should explicitly review that plan policy as part of its consideration of the proposed rezoning. The governing-board statement required by G.S. 160D-605(a) should reflect that consideration. The plan can be amended concurrently with the rezoning.[94] This can be particularly important in the judicial review of small-scale rezonings.[95]

---

89. Coucoulas/Knight Props. v. Town of Hillsborough, 198 N.C. App. 455, 683 S.E.2d 228 (2009), *aff'd per curiam*, 364 N.C. 127, 691 S.E.2d 441 (2010). In this case the court noted that a finding that a zoning amendment would be consistent with the plan does not in itself equate to a finding that the existing zoning is inconsistent with the plan. *See also* Sapp v. Yadkin Cnty., 209 N.C. App. 430, 704 S.E.2d 909 (2011) (sufficient for mandated written statement on plan consistency to be filed with the governing board prior to governing-board consideration of matter, regardless of whether a copy of the statement is attached to planning-board minutes). Other state courts have similarly held that a plan does not create a requirement or legal right that the zoning be amended to be consistent with the plan. *See, e.g.*, Martin v. Camas Cnty., 248 P.3d 1243, 1251 (Id. 2011); Hougham v. Lexington-Fayette Urban Cnty. Gov't, 29 S.W.3d 370, 373 (Ky. Ct. App. 1999).

90. Alfred Bettman, one of the principal early architects of zoning in the United States, contended that this requirement was needed to ensure that zoning decisions were based on "comprehensive and detailed" study. 1 Patricia E. Salkin, American Law of Zoning § 5.1 (5th ed., May 2019 Update).

91. See *Purser v. Mecklenburg County*, 127 N.C. App. 63, 488 S.E.2d 277 (1997), for an illustration of these points. In this case the court upheld the rezoning of a parcel from residential to business to allow for a neighborhood convenience store, pointing out that careful consideration of the development policies in the plans and how they apply to the site and the surrounding developing area are important factors in establishing the requisite reasonableness of spot zoning. See Chapter 12 regarding the role of plans in spot-zoning analysis.

92. *See, e.g.*, Summers v. City of Charlotte, 149 N.C. App. 509, 519–20, 562 S.E.2d 18, 25–26, *review denied*, 355 N.C. 758, 566 S.E.2d 482 (2002).

93. One difficulty in consideration of plans in site-specific regulatory decisions is that a plan is sometimes so general or contradictory as to provide little if any guidance. See, for example, *Mickelsen v. Warren County*, No. 5:06-CV-00360-F, 2007 WL 4245848 (E.D.N.C. Nov. 29, 2007), where the court noted that adoption of a proposed rezoning from residential to neighborhood business was consistent with the comprehensive plan's goal of encouraging commercial development, while denial would be consistent with the goal of maintaining the integrity of existing land use patterns. The court concluded that the balancing of such competing interests is the role of the legislative governing board, not a reviewing court.

94. G.S. 160D-605(a). *See also* Nelson v. City of Burlington, 80 N.C. App. 285, 341 S.E.2d 739 (1986).

95. The statement of reasonableness required by G.S. 160D-605(b) for rezonings requires attention to the factors used for a spot-zoning review. See Chapter 12 for a discussion of spot zoning. In *Godfrey v. Union County Board of*

It appears that most rezoning decisions are in fact consistent with adopted plans. In a 2008 School survey, local government planners were asked how often the rezonings in their jurisdiction were consistent with applicable adopted plans. Two-thirds replied that this was always or almost always the case.[96] In a 2018 School survey, 69 percent of responding local governments reported that zoning decisions were always or almost always consistent with adopted plans. These responses are illustrated in Figure 22.1.

There are some circumstances where the development regulation itself can elevate the plan beyond its usual advisory role. For example, it is not uncommon for special use permit standards to include a requirement that the permitted activity be consistent with the land use plan. In those instances, if evidence is presented that the project would be incompatible with the plan, the permit must be denied.[97]

Some states go beyond the provisions on planning described above to define their comprehensive plans legislatively, mandate their preparation, provide for regional and state coordination of plans, and tie their plans more directly to decisions on land use regulation.[98]

Beyond these development-regulation provisions, the legislature has also adopted incentives for land use planning.[99] In 1997, the General Assembly amended G.S. 159G-23(4) to provide that priority in

---

Commissioners, the court held:

> There is no dispute that at the time the Rape tract was rezoned Union County had in effect a comprehensive land use and development plan. While such plans may be appropriately modified after their adoption, such changes must be made consistently with the overall purposes contemplated by the adoption of the plan, and not to accommodate the needs or plans of a single property owner.

61 N.C. App. 100, 104, 300 S.E.2d 273, 275 (1983). The importance of consistency with planning policies in spot-zoning cases is discussed further in Chapter 12. Although the plan is advisory, both rezonings and individual quasi-judicial zoning-permit decisions should be reviewed in light of the adopted plan's policies before a final decision is made. In *Piney Mountain Neighborhood Ass'n v. Town of Chapel Hill*, the court noted:

> We agree with the superior court's finding that "the Comprehensive Land Use Plan does not set forth mandatory zoning requirements, but consists of general goals, standards and guidelines for the implementation of zoning policy." The Plan is, by its express terms, merely advisory . . . . A comprehensive plan "is a policy statement to be implemented by zoning regulations, and it is the latter that have the force of law." It "is generally deemed to be advisory, rather than controlling, and it may be changed at any time."

63 N.C. App. 244, 250–51, 304 S.E.2d 251, 255 (1983) (citations omitted). *See generally* Erwin S. Barbe, Annotation, *Requirement That Zoning Variances or Exceptions Be Made in Accordance with Comprehensive Plan*, 40 A.L.R.3d 372 (1982).

96. David W. Owens, Zoning Amendments in North Carolina 16 (UNC School of Government, Special Series No. 24, 2008).

97. Other states similarly allow a development regulation to mandate a plan-consistency requirement. *See, e.g.,* Board of Cnty. Comm'rs v. Condor, 927 P.2d 1339 (Colo. 1996) (while a plan is generally only advisory, subdivision regulation can mandate compliance); Laughter v. Board of Cnty. Comm'rs, 110 P.3d 875 (Wy. 2005) (ordinance can make plan compliance a mandatory standard for special use permits).

98. California first required plan consistency in 1955. Oregon required consistency with state goals in 1973. Washington, Florida, Georgia, and other states addressed the issue in the 1980s. *See, e.g.,* Cal. Gov't Code §§ 65300–65590.1; Or. Rev. Stat. Ann. § 197.175(2); Wash. Rev. Code Ann. ch. 36.70A; Fla. Stat. Ann. §§ 163.3161–.3215; Ga. Code Ann. §§ 36-70-1 to -5. *See generally* Robert C. Apgar, *Comprehensive Plans in the Twenty-First Century: Suggestions to Improve a Valuable Process*, 30 Stetson L. Rev. 965 (2001); Phillip R. Berke & Steven P. French, *The Influence of State Planning Mandates on Local Plan Quality*, 13 J. of Plan. Educ. & Res. 237 (1994); John M. DeGrove & Nancy E. Stroud, *New Developments and Future Trends in Local Government Comprehensive Planning*, 17 Stetson L. Rev. 573 (1988). *See also* Dennis E. Gale, *Eight State-Sponsored Growth Management Programs: A Comparative Analysis*, 58 J. Am. Plan. Ass'n 425 (1992). In states with mandated plan consistency, a zoning amendment that is inconsistent with the plan is invalid. *See, e.g.,* GATRI v. Blane, 962 P.2d 367 (Haw. 1998) (plan has force and effect of law, permit denial based on broad statements of policy may be arbitrary); Mikell v. Cnty. of Charleston, 386 S.C. 153, 687 S.E.2d 326 (2009).

99. State and federal grants have long been provided to local governments as incentives to undertake planning. An early and significant example was the matching-grant program for local planning established by Section 701 of the Housing Act of 1954, Pub. L. No. 83-560, 68 Stat. 590 (1954), which for several decades was the principal funding

Figure 22.1 Rezoning Consistent with Plan

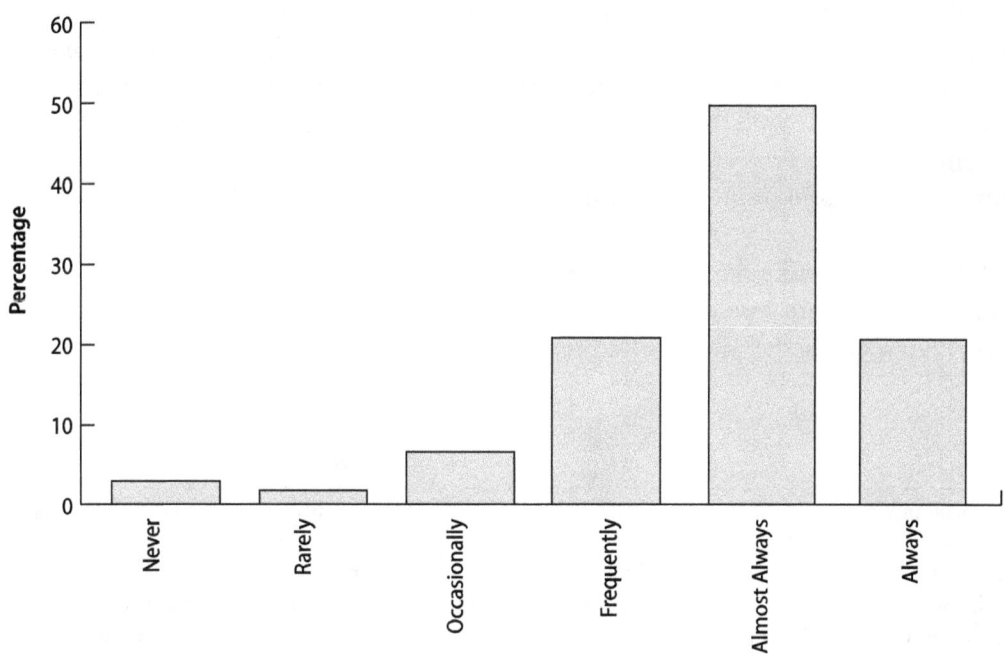

loans and grants from the state's Clean Water Revolving Loan and Grant Fund be granted to those local governments that adopt comprehensive plans containing provisions to protect existing water uses and assure compliance with water-quality standards.[100] Additional priority is to be given if the plan has provisions that exceed state minimum standards and if actions are taken to implement the plan (such as by adopting zoning).

Family Care Homes

Family care homes are facilities that provide health, counseling, or related services to a small number of persons in a family type of environment. Both state and federal laws affect zoning regulation of these facilities.[101] G.S. 160D-907, added to the statutes in 1981, provides that local ordinances must treat certain family care homes as if they were single-family homes. They cannot be prohibited in a district that

---

mechanism for much of the land use planning undertaken in North Carolina and around the country. Other focused incentives provided funding for more-specialized planning, sometimes incorporated with a provision requiring a plan as a precondition for federal funding. An example is the provision for hazard-mitigation plans in the Disaster Mitigation Act of 2000, codified at 42 U.S.C. § 5165.

100. S.L. 1997-458.

101. The tendency of local governments to use zoning to exclude treatment facilities is as old as the zoning concept. A number of ordinances in the 1920s and 1930s sought to exclude hospitals for those with infectious diseases. The drafter of the original New York City zoning ordinance noted that concerns about "the depressing effect" on the surrounding inhabitants had prompted about nineteen of the twenty municipalities in the New York area to exclude hospitals for mental illnesses. EDWARD M. BASSETT, ZONING: THE LAWS, ADMINISTRATION, AND COURT DECISIONS DURING THE FIRST TWENTY YEARS 73 (1940). Bassett recommended that the state take over the function of locating and distributing such facilities. *See generally* Brian J. Connolly & Dwight H. Merriam, *Planning and Zoning for Group Homes: Local Government Obligations and Liability Under the Fair Housing Amendments Act*, 47 URB. LAW. 225 (2015).

allows single-family residences, nor can they be subject to any special review requirements, such as a special use requirement.

To qualify for this treatment, the facility must be designed to provide room, board, and care for six or fewer disabled persons[102] in a family environment. Disabled persons include those with permanent or temporary physical, emotional, or mental disabilities[103] but not those who have been deemed dangerous to themselves or to others.[104] As with the protection for housing for persons with disabilities under the federal Fair Housing Act, these protections do not extend to homeless shelters, group homes providing services for those being released from imprisonment, and other residential facilities for those who are not disabled.

G.S. 160D-907(c) allows zoning regulations to require a half-mile separation between family care homes. Whether these minimum separations are valid under the federal Fair Housing Act is determined on a case-by-case review of whether the required separation is reasonable.[105]

In addition to development regulations, treatment facilities are also subject to substantial social-service licensing and permitting. These rules address the operation of facilities and do not preempt zoning and development regulations generally. See, for example, G.S. 131D-2.4 regarding licensing for adult care homes.

102. When G.S. 160D-907(b), which provides the definition of *family care home* for zoning purposes, was initially adopted in 1981, it included all facilities providing care, room, and board for six or fewer disabled individuals. In 1995, the legislature updated the social services statutes. As part of this update, in many instances where "domiciliary care" or "family care" homes were mentioned, the statutes were amended to change the reference to "adult care" homes. This update of the statutes related to social service regulations and licensing also inadvertently included the zoning-protection statute, amending G.S. 168-21 to add the term *adult* to the definition of *family care home* covered by the statute. As a result, some local governments amended zoning ordinances to provide single-family-residential status only to family care homes serving adult disabled persons. S.L. 2002-159 restored the language of G.S. 168-21 to its original version by removing the term "adult care" from the definition of family care homes. G.S. 168-23 voids private restrictive covenants that would preclude family care homes in areas restricted to residential use. *See also* J.T. Hobby & Son, Inc. v. Family Homes of Wake Cnty., Inc., 302 N.C. 64, 274 S.E.2d 174 (1981) (construing covenant restricting uses to single-family residential to allow family care home).

103. In *Taylor Home of Charlotte, Inc. v. City of Charlotte*, 116 N.C. App. 188, 447 S.E.2d 438 (1994), *review denied*, 338 N.C. 524, 453 S.E.2d 170 (1995), the court addressed the definition of *handicapped*. (The term *disabled* is now used by the statute.) The case involved a permit for the construction of a six-bed facility to serve AIDS patients. The court held that AIDS patients were not "handicapped persons" within G.S. 160D-907(b)(2) because they could not live within a normal residential environment. Subsequent treatment advances may well have rendered this opinion obsolete. A different case concluded that AIDS patients are clearly covered by the Federal Fair Housing Act. Support Ministries v. Vill. of Waterford, 808 F. Supp. 120 (N.D.N.Y. 1992).

In *Town of Newton Grove v. Sutton*, 111 N.C. App. 376, 432 S.E.2d 441, *review denied*, 335 N.C. 181, 438 S.E.2d 208 (1993), the owners of a nonconforming residence in a business zoning district challenged the denial of a permit to locate a mobile home on their lot for the use of their mentally ill daughter. The town concluded that placement of the unit would have been an unlawful expansion of a nonconforming use and could not be considered a customary accessory use. The court affirmed the town's decision and concluded that the state Fair Housing Act was not violated because the prohibition of mobile homes in the district applied to all property owners and was not in any way related to the defendant's child's condition. *See also* Parkwood Ass'n v. Capital Health Care Inv'rs, 133 N.C. App. 158, 514 S.E.2d 542, *review denied*, 350 N.C. 835, 539 S.E.2d 291 (1999) (holding that a temporary emergency shelter for undisciplined, delinquent, or at-risk youth is not a home serving disabled persons protected by state or federal fair-housing provisions).

104. This statute cross-references G.S. 122C-3(11)(b) for a definition of those persons with mental illnesses who are dangerous to themselves or others. This is the same definition used to qualify a person for involuntary commitment under G.S. 122C-261.

105. See discussion of this law in Chapter 23. The court in *Oxford House, Inc. v. City of Raleigh*, No. 5:98-CV-113-BO(2), 1999 WL 1940013 (E.D.N.C. Jan. 26, 1999), upheld the city's 375-yard minimum separation between "supportive housing residences," which included facilities serving disabled persons. Wilmington's half-mile separation was upheld in *Oxford House, Inc. v. City of Wilmington*, No. 7:07-CV-61-F, 2010 WL 4484523 (E.D.N.C. Oct. 28, 2010).

Historic Districts and Landmarks

Preservation of cultural resources is an important aspect of development regulation.[106] While several notable examples were in effect earlier,[107] the movement for local historic-preservation regulations expanded greatly in the 1960s. New York City's historic-preservation and landmarking law was notably upheld by the U.S. Supreme Court in 1978.[108] A substantial majority of states now have legislation for regulating historic districts and landmarks.[109]

Legislation authorizing North Carolina local governments to adopt historic-preservation regulations was enacted in 1971.[110] This statute is codified at G.S. 160D-940 to 160D-951. Many North Carolina zoning regulations provide special coverage for historic neighborhoods and for particularly important individual historic-landmark structures.[111] While such districts are relatively uncommon in very small towns, a substantial number of medium- and most large-population municipalities reported, in

---

106. *See generally* A HANDBOOK ON HISTORIC PRESERVATION LAW (Christopher Duerksen ed., 1983); JACOB H. MORRISON, HISTORIC PRESERVATION LAW (2d ed. 1965).

107. The leading national cases upholding regulation of exterior design to protect historic districts arose from challenges to New Orleans's 1937 Vieux Carré ordinance protecting the architectural character of the French Quarter. LA. CONST. of 1921, art. 14, § 22A. *See* Maher v. City of New Orleans, 516 F.2d 1051 (5th Cir. 1975); City of New Orleans v. Levy, 223 La. 14, 64 So. 2d 798 (1953); City of New Orleans v. Pergament, 198 La. 852, 5 So. 2d 129 (1941); City of New Orleans v. Impastato, 198 La. 206, 3 So. 2d 559 (1941). *See also* Op. of Justices to the Senate, 333 Mass. 773, 128 N.E.2d 557 (1955) (upholding similar regulations for Nantucket). In addition to New Orleans, other early local historic-preservation programs were in effect in: Annapolis, Maryland; Boston, Nantucket, and Salem, Massachusetts; Natchez, Mississippi; Alexandria and Williamsburg, Va.; and the Georgetown area of Washington, D.C. In 1948, Winston-Salem established one of the earliest programs of this nature in North Carolina.

108. Penn Cent. Transp. Co. v. City of New York, 438 U.S. 104 (1978). The Court had earlier accepted the legitimacy of aesthetics as a basis for governmental action. Berman v. Parker, 348 U.S. 26 (1954).

109. *See generally* Carol M. Rose, *Preservation and Community: New Directions in the Law of Historic Preservation*, 33 STAN. L. REV. 473 (1981).

110. The initial legislation authorized historic preservation districts and regulations for four local governments—Bath, Edenton, Halifax, and Winston-Salem. S.L. 1965-504. In 1967, this authority was extended to three additional jurisdictions—Hillsborough (S.L. 1967-174), Murfreesboro (S.L. 1967-303), and New Bern (S.L. 1967-1099). Wilmington was added in 1969 (S.L. 1969-246). This authority was then extended statewide to all cities and counties by S.L. 1971-884. A companion bill in 1971 added statewide local government authority for designation and protection of historic landmarks. S.L. 1971-885.

For additional background on the development of historic-preservation law and programs in the state, see *Historic Preservation Symposium*, 12 WAKE FOREST L. REV. 1 (1976); David E. Hollowell, *supra* note 76; Keith N. Morgan, *Reaffirmation of Local Initiative: North Carolina's 1979 Historic Preservation Legislation*, 11 N.C. CENT. L.J. 243 (1980); C. Thomas Ross, *Practical Aspects of Historic Preservation in North Carolina*, 12 WAKE FOREST L. REV. 9 (1976); Robert E. Stipe, *A Decade of Preservation and Preservation Law*, 11 N.C. CENT. L.J. 214 (1980); Robert E. Stipe, *Tools for Historic Preservation: Advantages and Disadvantages of Easements and Zoning*, POPULAR GOV'T, Dec. 1967, at 16.

111. See the discussion of historic preservation as a legitimate objective of governmental regulation in Chapter 25. Also see G.S. 121-4.1 regarding the North Carolina Register of Historic Places and G.S. 105-129.105 to .110 regarding state income-tax credits for rehabilitation of historic structures. There are also federal programs that promote historic-preservation efforts. The 1966 National Historic Preservation Act, codified at 16 U.S.C. §§ 470 to 470w-8, is particularly notable. Historic structures may be listed on the National Register of Historic Places. The regulations for listing are at 36 C.F.R. § 60.4. Once listed, a property receives some degree of protection from federal government activities that would affect it adversely and becomes eligible for tax credits, deductions, and other incentives for preservation and rehabilitation. Section 106 of the NHPA (16 U.S.C. § 470f) provides that before undertaking, licensing, or funding any project that might affect a National Register property, a federal agency must take into account the impact of the undertaking on the property and afford appropriate historic-preservation officials with an opportunity to comment. *See generally,* ADVISORY COUNCIL ON HISTORIC PRES., PROTECTING HISTORIC PROPERTIES: A CITIZEN'S GUIDE TO SECTION 106 REVIEW (2010); Marilyn Phelan, *A Synopsis of the Laws Protecting Our Cultural Heritage*, 28 NEW ENG. L. REV. 63 (1993); Joe P. Yeager, *Federal Preservation Law: Sites, Structures & Objects*, 8 WIDENER L. SYMP. J. 383 (2002).

Bob Stipe, an Institute of Government faculty member from 1957 to 1975, was a pioneer in the development of historic-preservation ordinances. Stipe also served as director of the state Division of Archives and History and as the State Preservation Officer.

a 2005 School survey,[112] adoption of regulations protecting these cultural resources. Fewer counties had done so (see Table 22.1). Over a hundred North Carolina local governments have established a preservation commission.

A historic-district designation is generally incorporated within a zoning regulation, often as an overlay zoning district, but may also be adopted as a separate ordinance.[113] In addition to the basic zoning requirements, any new construction, exterior alteration, or demolition within these districts must also receive a certificate of appropriateness, which is based on a determination that the proposed work is congruent with the historic character of the district.[114] Similar protections can be established for individual buildings designated as historic landmarks.[115] If a certificate of appropriateness is denied, relocation or demolition of a landmark or structure within a designated district may be delayed for a period of up to one year.[116] Regulations can also address demolition by neglect both for landmarks and

112. DAVID W. OWENS & NATHAN BRANSCOME, AN INVENTORY OF LOCAL GOVERNMENT LAND USE ORDINANCES IN NORTH CAROLINA 7 (UNC School of Government, Special Series No. 21, May 2006).

113. G.S. 160D-944. G.S. 160D, §§ 944 to 950 establishes a detailed framework for regulation of historic districts and landmarks. Adoption of a historic-district regulation must follow the standard procedures for adoption and amendment of a zoning ordinance as discussed in Chapter 11. The enactment of Chapter 160D in 2019 amended G.S. 160D-947(c) to replace the specific procedures for these decisions with a directive to follow the notice, hearing, and procedural requirements set out in G.S. 160D-406 for all quasi-judicial decisions under local-development regulations. See Unruh v. City of Asheville, 97 N.C. App. 287, 388 S.E.2d 235 (1990), review denied, 326 N.C. 487, 391 S.E.2d 813 (1990).

114. G.S. 160D-947. See generally Raynor v. Town of Chapel Hill, No. 1:18CV291, 2019 WL 503443 (M.D.N.C. Feb. 8, 2019) (rejecting constitutional challenges to application of historic-district regulation).

115. G.S. 160D, §§ 945, 946.

116. G.S. 160D-949. If the building, site, or structure has been determined by the state to be of statewide significance, approval to relocate or demolish may be denied indefinitely except where that would cause extreme hardship or would permanently deprive the owner of all beneficial use or return.

Table 22.1   Jurisdictions Adopting Historic-District or Landmark Regulations (2005)

Population	Number Responding	% of Respondents
Municipalities		
<1000	79	9
1000–4999	112	24
5000–9999	38	19
10,000–24,999	43	42
25,000–49,999	9	78
50,000+	16	88
Counties (Unincorporated Population)		
<20,000	26	12
20,000–49,999	37	14
50,000+	18	36

structures within a historic district[117] (and for contributing structures outside a historic district but within an adjacent central business district).[118]

The standards for securing a certificate of appropriateness must be set out in the regulation and must generally relate to maintenance of the particular character of that individual neighborhood.

In *Meares v. Town of Beaufort,* the court held that the standards for a historic-district certificate of appropriateness were limited to congruence with the district and could not extend to mandating congruence with the individual historic structure previously located on a particular site within a district. The court thus held that a standard in the Beaufort Historic District Guidelines restricting building height and scale of a replacement building to that of the preexisting historic structure on that parcel exceeded the town's authority.[119]

Similarly, the court in *Sanchez v. Town of Beaufort* held that since congruity must be considered contextually, the historic-commission defendant was obligated to consider the heights of all of the structures in the district in making a ruling on the plaintiff's structure, not just the heights of a few structures.[120]

For the most part, historic-district and landmark protection standards are limited to protection of the exterior features of buildings.[121] The statute, however, defines "exterior features" rather broadly, encompassing the architectural style and design of the building, including the kind and texture of

---

117. G.S. 160D-949(b).

118. G.S. 160D-950. This provision applies to downtown areas designated as Urban Progress Zones under G.S. 143B-437.09.

119. 193 N.C. App. 96, 101–02, 667 S.E.2d 239, 242–43 (2008).

120. 211 N.C. App. 574, 710 S.E.2d 350 (2011). The historic-preservation commission had limited the height of a proposed one-and-one-half-story replacement structure to twenty feet in order to preserve views, reasoning that some other one-and-one-half-story buildings in the district were twenty to twenty-two feet high. The court noted that residences closest to the subject property were twenty-six to thirty-five feet high and that this overall context had to be considered. The court also noted that the building-height condition seemed to be based on members' personal preferences rather than conformance with principles set out in state applicable commission guidelines.

121. G.S. 160D-947(a).

building materials, the size and scale of the building, and the type and style of all windows, doors, light fixtures, signs, and appurtenant features. A regulation may also address significant landscape, archaeological, and natural features of the area.

The regulations may address interior spaces in two situations. Specific interior features of architectural, artistic, or historical significance may be regulated for publicly owned landmarks and for privately owned landmarks with the owner's consent.[122]

Since the development and application of standards to preserve congruency requires some specialized expertise, the development regulation commonly provides for a historic-preservation commission[123] to develop and administer these rules. State law mandates such expertise as a prerequisite for these regulations.[124] Such a commission must have at least three members, who must have set terms of up to four years and reside within the jurisdiction. A majority of the members must have some special expertise in historic preservation. Another citizen board, such as the planning board or community appearance board, can serve as this commission if at least three of its members have the required special expertise. In addition to handling administrative responsibilities, these commissions can also acquire landmarks, restore and operate historic properties, and conduct educational programs.[125]

The statutes also set several standards for the process of considering applications for certificates of appropriateness.[126] The historic-preservation commission is required to have rules of procedure and standards for review of applications prior to initiation of regulation enforcement. Decisions on certificates of appropriateness are quasi-judicial decisions. G.S. 160D-947(c) requires the historic commission to follow the notice, hearing, and procedural requirements set out in G.S. 160D-406 for all quasi-judicial decisions made under local development regulations.[127] The statute also requires that a decision be rendered within 180 days from the date the application is filed.[128]

Before the enactment of Chapter 160D, and in a departure from the usual rule that quasi-judicial decisions are appealed directly to superior court, the statutes required that appeals of decisions of a historic-preservation commission regarding certificates of appropriateness go to the board of adjust-

---

122. If the owner's written consent is filed in the office of the register of deeds and indexed in the chain of title, that consent is binding on future owners. The consent must specify the interior features that are protected and the specific nature of that protection. G.S. 160D-947(b).

123. G.S. 160D, §§ 303, 941.

124. State law also requires expert review and comment by the state Historic Preservation Office prior to the establishment of historic districts (G.S. 160D-944(b) or designation of landmarks (G.S. 160D-945(3)).

125. G.S. 160D-303.

126. G.S. 160D-947, §§ (c), (d).

127. See Chapter 15 for a discussion of the procedures required for quasi-judicial decisions. *See generally* Butterworth v. City of Asheville, 247 N.C. App. 508, 786 S.E.2d 101 (2016) (if standards for decision require application of judgment and discretion, the decision is quasi-judicial regardless of labels applied in the development ordinance).

128. G.S. 160D-947(d). The deadline for a decision was a key factor in *Meares v. Town of Beaufort*, 193 N.C. App. 49, 667 S.E.2d 244 (2008). After the historic-preservation commission denied approval of an initial application for a certificate of appropriateness and while that denial decision was on appeal, the plaintiff owner filed a second application for an alternative structure. The ordinance required action on applications within sixty days of a final application, with the application deemed to be approved otherwise. When the commission refused to process or act upon the second application, the plaintiff sought a court order to compel issuance of the certificate of appropriateness. The court held that since it was undisputed that sixty days had passed without action on the complete application, issuance was required by the ordinance and was thus a ministerial action. The court held that there were no provisions in the ordinance or in general law that preclude an alternative application while an initial application is on appeal and that a letter from the town attorney that a second application would not be considered while the first application was on appeal, which was sent prior to the second application, cannot be considered an appealable action by the commission.

ment.[129] The board of adjustment, however, acts as an appeals court in this situation. It does not conduct a new hearing; rather, it reviews the record established by the historic-preservation commission and determines whether there was sufficient evidence to support the decision or whether it was arbitrary and capricious.[130]

G.S. 160D-947(e) was amended, as part of Chapter 160D's enactment, to allow a local government to retain this process, but it gives cities and counties the option of eliminating board-of-adjustment review and having appeals of decisions on certificates of appropriateness go directly to superior court, as is the case with appeals of all other quasi-judicial development-regulation decisions.[131] If the local regulation does not specify that the appeal goes to the board of adjustment, the appeal is made directly to superior court under G.S. 160D-1402.

Manufactured and Modular Housing

Manufactured housing is an important component in North Carolina's overall housing market and a critical component of the affordable-housing market. Mobile homes account for approximately 13 percent of the state's housing stock, about double the national share of the housing stock.[132] Despite the importance and widespread use of manufactured housing, there has been some degree of citizen antipathy toward mobile homes.[133]

Many local governments in North Carolina have long included special restrictions on manufactured housing in their development regulations.[134] By 1960, a familiar land use regulatory approach for manufactured housing had emerged: manufactured-home-park standards, floating zoning districts for

---

129. G.S. 160A-400.9(e). *See* Cherry v. Wiesner, 245 N.C. App. 339, 781 S.E.2d 871, *review denied*, 369 N.C. 33, 792 S.E.2d 779 (2016) (neighbor failed to establish standing to appeal issuance of certificate of appropriateness to the board of adjustment).

130. Appeals to the board of adjustment must be made within the times provided by G.S. 160D-405(c) for administrative appeals. In hearing these appeals, the board of adjustment is to apply the provisions of G.S. 160D-1402 for appeals in the nature of certiorari. Petitions for judicial review of the board of adjustment's decision must be made within the time periods set by G.S. 160D-1405 for appeals of quasi-judicial decisions.

131. S.L. 2019-111.

132. Am. Cmty. Survey, *Physical Housing Characteristics for Occupied Housing Units: 2011–2015 American Community Survey 5-Year Estimates* (United States Census Bureau, 2015).

In some North Carolina counties, mobile homes are nearly a third of the housing stock. In 2010, the census reported 604,286 mobile homes and a total of 4,327,528 homes (14 percent). The comparable figure in 1970 was 98,474 mobile homes and an overall total of 1,641,222 (6 percent). Estimates were that 6.5 percent of the national housing stock were manufactured units in 2011. U.S. Bureau of the Census, American Housing Survey for the United States: 2011, at 3–4 (2013).

133. Noting that there had been some improvement in attitudes toward mobile homes in the previous decade, one author reported in 1971 that, according to a national survey of planning officials, 82 percent of planning officials had a favorable view of mobile homes as housing, compared to 64 percent for planning boards, 54 percent for elected boards, and only 20 percent for the public at large. The same national survey reported that 28 percent of surveyed jurisdictions prohibited mobile-home parks, while another 13 percent limited them to industrial areas. Frederick H. Bair, *Mobile Homes Are Here to Stay*, Popular Gov't, Apr. 1971, at 20, 22.

134. *See, e.g.*, City of Raleigh v. Morand, 247 N.C. 363, 100 S.E.2d 870 (1957), *appeal dismissed*, 357 U.S. 343 (1958) (upholding ordinance prohibiting trailer parks within residential districts in the city's one-mile extraterritorial area). One of the earlier North Carolina ordinances on the subject was adopted when mobile homes were in fact mobile. The City of Durham amended its zoning ordinance in 1949 to "put an end to the indiscriminate parking of the portable dwellings within the city limits," requiring all habitable mobile units to be located in trailer parks. *Trailer Camps*, Popular Gov't, Dec. 1949, at 4.

manufactured-housing parks, special use permits for manufactured-home placement, and standards on buffers and other aspects of the design of manufactured-home parks.[135]

G.S. 160D-910[136] allows local governments to regulate the location, appearance, and dimensions of manufactured housing but prohibits the total exclusion of manufactured housing from a jurisdiction. These restrictions are generally applied to units constructed in a factory and built to the uniform national standards for manufactured homes promulgated by the U.S. Department of Housing and Urban Development.[137] Federal law preempts local construction and safety standards for manufactured housing.[138]

Many zoning ordinances establish subcategories of manufactured housing and apply differential standards to each (e.g., Class A manufactured homes are allowed in some districts, Class B in other districts).[139] Any such distinction must have a rational basis. Typical distinctions that are used are those based on the size of the units[140] or the construction standards in effect at the time of manufacture.[141]

Cities and counties may not employ factors other than appearance, dimension, and location in land use regulation of manufactured housing.

Restrictions based solely on the age of the unit are not permissible in North Carolina.[142] In *Five C's, Inc. v. County of Pasquotank*, the court invalidated an age standard used as the basis for regulation of manufactured homes. The county had adopted an ordinance under its general police power to prohibit

---

135. Philip P. Green, Jr., *Regulating Mobile Homes Through Zoning*, Popular Gov't, Mar. 1961, at 10. *See also* Michael B. Brough, *Legal Constraints upon the Regulation of Mobile Homes*, Popular Gov't, Summer 1975, at 20; Michael B. Brough, *State Laws and the Regulation of Mobile Homes*, Popular Gov't, Summer 1975, at 12.

136. This section was added to the statutes by S.L. 1987-805. G.S. 160D-910(a) directs local governments to consider allocating more land to manufactured-housing sites as a way of providing additional affordable housing in the state. In *Town of Conover v. Jolly*, 277 N.C. 439, 177 S.E.2d 879 (1970), the court invalidated an ordinance that completely barred mobile homes for residential use within the town. The court ruled that the mobile-home ordinance, which was not part of the zoning ordinance, was beyond the town's delegated police powers, for mobile homes were neither a nuisance per se nor a detriment per se to public health, morals, comfort, safety, convenience, or welfare.

137. National Manufactured Housing Construction and Safety Standards Act of 1974, 42 U.S.C. §§ 5401–5426. Federal construction and safety standards preempt the construction and safety-standard authority of states and local governments. 42 U.S.C. § 5403(d). The federal construction standards, generally referred to as the *HUD Code*, are at 42 C.F.R. § 3280.1. *See generally* Schanzenbach v. Town of Opal, 706 F.3d 1269 (10th Cir. 2013) (ten-year age limit for manufactured homes in local ordinance not preempted); Schanzenbach v. Town of La Barge, 706 F.3d 1277 (10th Cir. 2013) (ten-year age limit not preempted); Ga. Manufactured Hous. Ass'n v. Spalding Cnty., 148 F.3d 1304, 1306 (11th Cir. 1998) (roof-pitch requirement not preempted); Tex. Manufactured Hous. Ass'n v. City of Nederland, 101 F.3d 1095 (5th Cir. 1996), *cert. denied*, 521 U.S. 1112 (1997) (city restriction on location of manufactured housing not preempted); Scurlock v. City of Lynn Haven, 858 F.2d 1521 (11th Cir. 1988) (local building and electrical-code requirements preempted); Colo. Manufactured Hous. Ass'n v. Bd. of Cnty. Comm'rs, 946 F. Supp. 1539 (D. Colo. 1996), *later proceeding sub nom.* Colo. Manufactured Hous. Ass'n v. City of Salida, 977 F. Supp. 1080 (D. Colo. 1997) (ordinance requiring manufactured home to comply with building code preempted).

138. *See generally* Daniel R. Mandelker, *Zoning Barriers to Manufactured Housing*, 48 Urb. Law. 233 (2016); S. Mark White, *State and Federal Planning Legislation and Manufactured Housing: New Opportunities for Affordable, Single-Family Shelter*, 28 Urb. Law. 263 (1996).

139. See N.C. League of Municipalities et al., Manufactured Housing: Zoning Alternatives to Address North Carolina Housing Needs (1988) for an example of such classification.

140. For example, many ordinances have more restrictive locational standards for single-wide units than for double-wide units.

141. The most commonly used distinction is to have more restrictive requirements for those units constructed before the imposition of federal minimum construction standards that became effective on June 15, 1976. Housing and Urban Development (HUD) standards for wind load were substantially updated after Hurricane Andrew, with an effective date of July 13, 1994.

142. *White v. Union County*, 93 N.C. App. 148, 377 S.E.2d 93 (1989), addressed age limits for manufactured housing. The court reviewed an ordinance that limited the use of mobile homes as residences to those built after 1976 (when federal construction standards became applicable) or valued at more than $5000. The court expressed doubt about the county's statutory authority for the monetary-value requirement.

bringing manufactured homes into the county that were more than ten years old at the time of setup. The rationale offered by the county was protection of the county tax base, noting that manufactured homes rapidly decline in value and at the ten-year point have little more value than a motor vehicle, providing insufficient tax revenue to support the need for county services generated. The court held that G.S. 160D-910 limits regulation of manufactured housing to appearance and dimensional criteria and thus prohibits regulation based solely on the age or value of the unit.[143] G.S. 160D-910 was amended in 2019 to codify this restriction on exclusion of manufactured homes based on the age of the home.[144] A local government may, however, likely address age indirectly by requiring that manufactured homes be built to set federal standards in order to be permissible.[145] It is also common for local governments to have detailed standards for mobile-home parks, such as standards for road width and paving, minimum lot sizes, and provisions for waste disposal. These are sometimes incorporated into a zoning ordinance and sometimes adopted as a separate ordinance.[146]

Typical zoning requirements that have been adopted in North Carolina include limiting manufactured housing to specified zoning districts[147] or to manufactured-home parks[148] (which often can be located

---

143. 195 N.C. App. 410, 672 S.E.2d 737 (2009). The court noted that the fact that the county used its general ordinance-making power rather than the zoning power cannot be used to circumvent the clear legislative limitation on regulatory authority regarding manufactured homes.

144. S.L. 2019-111. While a restriction based on the age of the unit per se is impermissible, a local government can require that the unit be built to a particular federal standard, such as the original enactment of federal construction standards or a substantial modification of those standards. *See* note 145. Local governments often also adopt housing codes that regulate the habitability and condition of manufactured homes used as residences. These codes apply regardless of the age of the unit. Also, G.S. 130A-309.111 to .117 establishes a state grant and assistance program to assist local governments in dealing with abandoned manufactured homes.

145. A requirement that units have a HUD manufactured-housing approval, available only after 1976, is a common regulatory requirement. Some local governments require the unit to be built to the latest update of the HUD manufactured-home-building standard, particularly in areas subject to hurricanes where the wind-load standard is important. For example, the basic federal rule setting structural design standards for manufactured homes, 24 C.F.R. § 3280.305, has been updated multiple times since its original 1975 adoption. 44 Fed. Reg. 66195 (Nov. 19, 1979); 52 Fed. Reg. 4582 (Feb. 12, 1987); 58 Fed. Reg. 55006 (Oct. 25, 1993); 59 Fed. Reg. 2469 (Jan. 14, 1994); 59 Fed. Reg. 15113, 15114 (Mar. 31, 1994); 62 Fed. Reg. 54547 (Oct. 20, 1997); 70 Fed. Reg. 72043 (Nov. 30, 2005); 71 Fed. Reg. 19638 (Apr. 17, 2006); 78 Fed. Reg. 73983 (Dec. 9, 2013); 80 Fed. Reg. 53727 (Sept. 8, 2015); 86 Fed. Reg. 2520 (Jan. 12, 2021); 86 Fed. Reg. 10457 (Feb. 22, 2021). Also see the discussion of incorporation by reference in Chapter 4.

146. A 2005 survey by the School of Government indicated that 79 percent of the responding municipalities and 93 percent of the responding counties had adopted regulations on manufactured-home parks. OWENS & BRANSCOME, *supra* note 112, at 8.

147. Koontz v. Davidson Cnty. Bd. of Adjustment, 130 N.C. App. 479, 503 S.E.2d 108, *review denied*, 349 N.C. 529, 526 S.E.2d 177 (1998) (upholding zoning amendment that removed manufactured housing as a permitted use in a particular zoning district); City of Asheboro v. Auman, 26 N.C. App. 87, 214 S.E.2d 621, *cert. denied*, 288 N.C. 239, 217 S.E.2d 663 (1975) (upholding injunction to prohibit continued use of a mobile home that had been moved into a zoning district that did not allow mobile homes, even though the wheels and tongue had been removed and the unit had been placed on a permanent foundation); Town of Mount Olive v. Price, 20 N.C. App. 302, 201 S.E.2d 362 (1973) (upholding injunction compelling removal of a mobile home located in violation of the zoning ordinance).

148. Cnty. of Currituck v. Upton, 19 N.C. App. 45, 197 S.E.2d 883 (1973) (upholding an order to remove a mobile home from a zoning district that did not permit individual units outside a park); State v. Martin, 7 N.C. App. 18, 171 S.E.2d 115 (1969) (upholding conviction for violation of an Ahoskie ordinance limiting the location of mobile homes to mobile-home parks). *See also* Tex. Manufactured Hous. Ass'n v. City of Nederland, 101 F.3d 1095 (5th Cir. 1996), *cert. denied*, 521 U.S. 1112 (1997) (upholding prohibition of "trailer coaches" that meet Housing and Urban Development standards from locations outside of approved parks).

only in special overlay zoning districts).[149] Other regulations only allow units of at least a certain size to be located in specified districts.[150]

It is also common for regulations to include special provisions regarding replacement and repair of nonconforming manufactured-housing units.[151] Care is necessary in drafting the precise terms of such limitations. In a case involving the Town of Cramerton's zoning regulations, *In re Hensley*, the court ruled that where the regulation provided that a nonconforming use could not be reestablished after it had been discontinued for 180 days, a nonconforming use could be reestablished if done in less than that time. In this instance, a mobile home had been removed from a lot in a zone that did not allow mobile homes; however, the petitioner was entitled to a permit to replace the mobile home if that were done within 180 days.[152] By contrast, the court in *Williams v. Town of Spencer* upheld a regulation provision explicitly prohibiting replacement of units on vacated lots in a nonconforming manufactured-home park.[153]

Many regulations include appearance standards to integrate the units aesthetically into surrounding neighborhoods with site-built homes. These standards typically include requiring a pitched roof, requiring either skirting around the underside of the unit or location on a permanent foundation,[154] and orienting the unit to the front of the lot. Such appearance standards were upheld in *CMH Manufacturing, Inc. v. Catawba County*. The county required lap siding, minimum roof pitch, and shingled roofs for single-wide manufactured homes. Other county requirements that were not challenged included installation of a deck or porch, removal or screening of travel hitches, orientation on the lot, and brick underpinning or skirting for double-wide units. The court held that these were permissible "appearance" standards rather than "construction and safety" standards that are preempted by federal law.[155]

Regulations on manufactured housing may not be based on the ownership of the unit, for example, allowing owner-occupied but not rental manufactured housing.[156] Nor may zoning restrictions be based on the "type of people" presumed to be residing therein.[157] Only legitimate land use–related factors may be considered in framing such regulations.

---

149. The creation of a zoning district to allow location of manufactured-home parks can be challenged as unlawful spot zoning. *See* Alderman v. Chatham Cnty., 89 N.C. App. 610, 366 S.E.2d 885, *review denied*, 323 N.C. 171, 373 S.E.2d 103 (1988); Stutts v. Swaim, 30 N.C. App. 611, 228 S.E.2d 750, *review denied*, 291 N.C. 178, 229 S.E.2d 692 (1976). See Chapter 12 for a discussion of spot zoning.

150. Currituck Cnty. v. Willey, 46 N.C. App. 835, 266 S.E.2d 52, *review denied*, 301 N.C. 234, 283 S.E.2d 131 (1980). In this case the court upheld a provision prohibiting mobile homes with dimensions of less than 24' × 60' in a single-family zoning district. The court ruled that mobile homes were sufficiently different from other types of housing that a rational basis existed for differing requirements, such as this dimension standard.

151. *See, e.g.,* Forsyth Cnty. v. York, 19 N.C. App. 361, 198 S.E.2d 770, *cert. denied*, 284 N.C. 253, 200 S.E.2d 653 (1973) (upholding requirement that changes in nonconforming use and mobile-home use in certain districts be authorized by special use permits).

152. 98 N.C. App. 408, 390 S.E.2d 727 (1990).

153. 129 N.C. App. 828, 500 S.E.2d 473 (1998).

154. G.S. 160D-910(g), added to the statute in 2021, provides that the regulation cannot require a masonry curtain wall or masonry skirting for manufactured homes on land leased to the homeowner. S.L. 2021-117, § 6(a).

155. 994 F. Supp. 697 (W.D.N.C. 1998). The court further held that the challenged standards did not violate the commerce, due-process, or equal-protection clauses. *See also* Ga. Manufactured Hous. Ass'n v. Spalding Cnty., 148 F.3d 1304 (11th Cir. 1998) (holding roof-pitch requirement for manufactured housing a permissible aesthetic regulation rather than a preempted construction standard); King v. City of Bainbridge, 276 Ga. 484, 577 S.E.2d 772 (2003) (ordinance restricting location of manufactured housing not preempted); Bibco Corp. v. City of Sumter, 332 S.C. 45, 504 S.E.2d 112 (1998) (locational restricting of manufactured housing not preempted).

156. Graham Court Assocs. v. Town Council of Chapel Hill, 53 N.C. App. 543, 281 S.E.2d 418 (1981).

157. Gregory v. Cnty. of Harnett, 128 N.C. App. 161, 493 S.E.2d 786 (1997). See Chapter 25 for a discussion of legitimate objectives for development regulation.

Most zoning ordinances do not apply the requirements for manufactured housing to factory-built housing that is built to State Building Code standards.[158] The latter units are referred to as "modular" rather than "manufactured" homes. Modular units[159] are often, but not always, treated as the equivalent of site-built homes for zoning purposes.

State law does, however, set minimum design standards for modular units.[160] G.S. 143-139.1 requires modular units to meet these standards:

- The pitch of the roof must be no less than five feet of rise for every twelve feet of run for homes with a single, predominant roofline.
- The eave projections of the roof must not be less than ten inches (excluding roof gutters) unless the roof pitch is 8/12 or greater.
- The minimum height of the first-story exterior wall must be at least seven feet, six inches.
- The materials and texture of exterior materials must be compatible in composition, appearance, and durability to the exterior materials commonly used in standard residential construction.
- The modular home must be designed to require foundation supports around the perimeter.

Travel trailers and recreational vehicles (RVs) are also regulated differently than manufactured homes. They are not built to either State Building Code standards or federal manufactured-home-construction standards but are mobile vehicles or structures that can be occupied. These may not be used as a permanent dwelling unit under the State Building Code.[161] Most zoning regulations limit the location of RV parks, have standards for the parks, and prohibit extended use for occupancy outside of those permitted locations. Many zoning regulations, however, make exceptions for temporary residential use of these structures after natural disasters.

There has also been considerable litigation in the state regarding the interpretation of private-restrictive-covenant provisions related to manufactured housing.[162] However, these covenants are private

---

158. Duggins v. Town of Walnut Cove, 63 N.C. App. 684, 306 S.E.2d 186, *review denied*, 309 N.C. 819, 310 S.E.2d 348 (1983), *cert. denied*, 466 U.S. 946 (1984). The ordinance prohibited a "mobile home" in a residential zoning district but allowed "modular" and site-built homes of similar dimensions to be used. The court upheld the ordinance as validly regulating the location of various types of structures, ruling that given the presumption of validity, the city had only to establish that the ordinance was rationally related to any legitimate government objective. The protection of property values was such a legitimate objective, and the council could determine that the method of construction affected the price of homes.

159. G.S. 160D-911. G.S. 105-164.3(143) provides that a modular unit is a "factory-built structure that is designed to be used as a dwelling, is manufactured in accordance with the specifications for modular homes under the North Carolina State Residential Building Code, and bears a seal or label issued by the Department of Insurance pursuant to G.S. 143-139.1."

160. These provisions were created by S.L. 2003-400.

161. Michael J. Hamm, Recreational Park Trailers (Park Models)/Permanent Dwellings (Office of State Fire Marshal, Jan. 15, 2019). For building-code purposes, these "recreational park trailers" are defined as manufactured vehicles not larger than 400 square feet that are self-propelled or towable and designed as temporary living quarters for recreational, camping, travel, or seasonal use.

162. In *Young v. Lomax,* 122 N.C. App. 385, 470 S.E.2d 80 (1996), there were covenants prohibiting "mobile homes." The structure involved had two sections, each with a steel chassis, axles, and wheels. The axles and wheels were removed upon installation and the units were secured to concrete piers. The court held that the unit remained a mobile home as a matter of law and was distinguishable from the modular units addressed earlier in *Angel v. Truitt,* 108 N.C. App. 679, 424 S.E.2d 660 (1993), wherein the court held that placement of a modular home on a lot did not violate a restrictive covenant prohibiting mobile homes. In *Forest Oaks Homeowners Ass'n v. Isenhour,* a restrictive covenant prohibited trailers and "mobile homes" but permitted "modular or component homes or pre-built homes" if erected on a permanent foundation. 102 N.C. App. 322, 323, 410 S.E.2d 860, 861 (1991). The court applied the manufactured/modular distinction used in the State Building Code to allow a modular home to be placed on the plaintiff's lot. In *Starr v. Thompson*, the restrictive covenant at issue prohibited the use of "trailers or mobile homes." 96 N.C. App. 369, 370, 385 S.E.2d 535, 536 (1989). The court held that the restriction applied to

agreements between the property owners involved. The interpretation, administration, and enforcement of these covenants do not affect government regulations.

Preemption

The fact that a particular land use may be subject to federal, state, and local regulation is a common occurrence and does not in itself preempt local regulation. Where there is overlapping jurisdiction, however, the potential for federal or state preemption of local regulation must be considered, as the general law on preemption applies to land use regulation.

G.S. 160A-174(b) sets out the general standard for state preemption of local ordinances:[163]

A city ordinance shall be consistent with the Constitution and laws of North Carolina and of the United States. An ordinance is not consistent with State or federal law when:

1. The ordinance infringes a liberty guaranteed to the people by the State or federal Constitution;
2. The ordinance makes unlawful an act, omission or condition which is expressly made lawful by State or federal law;
3. The ordinance makes lawful an act, omission, or condition which is expressly made unlawful by State or federal law;
4. The ordinance purports to regulate a subject that cities are expressly forbidden to regulate by State or federal law;
5. The ordinance purports to regulate a field for which a State or federal statute clearly shows a legislative intent to provide a complete and integrated regulatory scheme to the exclusion of local regulation;
6. The elements of an offense defined by a city ordinance are identical to the elements of an offense defined by State or federal law.

The fact that a State or federal law, standing alone, makes a given act, omission, or condition unlawful shall not preclude city ordinances requiring a higher standard of conduct or condition.[164]

---

a factory-built modular home. The court distinguished the definitions that were applicable for zoning from those to be used in enforcing private restrictive covenants. *Starr*, 96 N.C. App. 369, 385 S.E.2d 535. In *Barber v. Dixon*, a restrictive covenant prohibited the use of a "structure of a temporary character (including house trailers)." 62 N.C. App. 455, 302 S.E.2d 915, *review denied*, 309 N.C. 191, 305 S.E.2d 732 (1983). The court held that this prohibited the use of a structure consisting of two units transported to the site, even though the wheels, tongues, and axles had been removed two days after the units had been located on the lot. *Barber*, 62 N.C. App. 455, 302 S.E.2d 915. In *Van Poole v. Messer*, a restrictive covenant prohibited temporary structures and trailers. The court held that "trailer" included a mobile home. 19 N.C. App. 70, 198 S.E.2d 106 (1973). The restrictive covenant in *Strickland v. Overman*, 11 N.C. App. 427, 181 S.E.2d 136 (1971), prohibited trailers and temporary structures, categories that the court held to include a "prefabricated modular unit."

163. The same rules have been applied under common law to counties. *See* Greene v. City of Winston-Salem, 287 N.C. 66, 75, 213 S.E.2d 231, 237 (1975) (holding State Building Code preempts local ordinance attempting to require sprinkler systems in high-rise buildings).

164. G.S. 160A-174(b). For an example of a subject that state law expressly prohibits cities from regulating, see G.S. 62-106, which provides that the North Carolina Utilities Commission may expressly preempt municipal or county development regulations in a certificate of necessity for a high-voltage transmission line. In *State ex rel. Utilities Commission v. Town of Kill Devil Hills*, 194 N.C. App. 561, 670 S.E.2d 341, *aff'd per curiam*, 363 N.C. 739, 686 S.E.2d 151 (2009), the court held that the Utilities Commission could also preempt local ordinances regarding siting of smaller transmission lines.

G.S. 160D-706(a) more specifically addresses conflicts between city and county zoning regulations and other state and local regulations. It provides that when zoning and other state or local regulations both address the size of yards or courts, the height of buildings, or a percentage of the lot that may be occupied, the more strict of the two regulations applies.

There are several provisions in state law that explicitly authorize local regulation that goes beyond state requirements for a particular activity. Examples of state minimum standards that allow more restrictive local regulation include the following: regulation of condominium projects,[165] regulation of mining if such does not directly contradict state rules,[166] location of crematoriums,[167] charter school location,[168] siting of sanitary landfills,[169] water-supply-watershed protection,[170] new nonmunicipal domestic-waste-water-discharge facilities,[171] location of air-contaminant sources,[172] housing-authority projects,[173] and veterans'-recreation-authority projects.[174] By contrast, the statutes explicitly prohibit local regulation of the state lottery, prohibit local sign restrictions that apply only to the state lottery,[175] prohibit local regulation of building-construction standards,[176] prohibit registration programs for residential rental properties,[177] and allow the state Oil and Gas Commission to override local regulations that regulate oil and gas operations.[178]

For many other topics the legislation does not explicitly address the preemption of local regulation, and the courts are left to apply the rules noted above to discern the intent of the legislature.

The courts have held in a variety of contexts that state regulation of a particular matter was not intended to occupy a field of regulation to the exclusion of local regulation. Prominent examples include regulation of billboards[179] and junkyards.[180] The courts have also frequently held that state or federal regulation of one dimension of a project does not preempt local regulation of other dimensions of the

---

165. G.S. 47A-27. See *Cary Creek Ltd. Partnership v. Town of Cary*, 203 N.C. App. 99, 690 S.E.2d 549 (2010), for an example of a case holding that state minimum standards do not preempt local regulation where the statutes explicitly provide for such.

166. G.S. 74-65.

167. G.S. 90-210.123(b) provides that a crematory may be constructed on or adjacent to any cemetery or funeral home that is located in a commercial or industrial zoning district. Crematories at other locations must comply with local zoning and environmental regulations.

168. G.S. 115C-238.29E(e).

169. G.S. 130A-294(b1)(4). The zoning must, however, have been in effect for at least ninety days prior to the state application for the landfill siting. In *PBK Holdings, LLC v. County of Rockingham*, 233 N.C. App. 353, 756 S.E.2d 821, *appeal dismissed*, 367 N.C. 788 (2014), the court upheld more stringent zoning restrictions on the location of landfills, including provisions regulating location in a floodplain or near an airport, as well as truck-entrance-location standards.

170. G.S. 143-214.5(d).

171. G.S. 143-215.1(c)(6).

172. G.S. 143-215.108(f).

173. G.S. 157-13.

174. G.S. 143B-1259.

175. G.S. 18C, §§ 170 to 171.

176. See Chapter 8 regarding State Building Code preemption. For a discussion of the impact of such a preemption on local efforts to require more sustainable development, see Sara C. Bronin, *The Quiet Revolution Revived: Sustainable Design, Land Use Regulation, and the States*, 93 MINN. L. REV. 231, 268 (2008).

177. G.S. 160D-1207(c). The scope of this prohibition is addressed in *Schroeder v. City of Wilmington*, 282 N.C. App. 558, 872 S.E.2d 58 (2022).

178. G.S. 113-415.1. Operators can petition for an override of local regulations that conflict with or are beyond state requirements. The impetus for this statute was potential hydrofracture recovery of natural gas ("fracking").

179. Lamar Outdoor Advert., Inc. v. City of Hendersonville Zoning Bd. of Adjustment, 155 N.C. App. 516, 518–21, 573 S.E.2d 637, 640–42 (2002) (state Outdoor Advertising Control Act does not preempt local sign regulation).

180. Cnty. of Hoke v. Byrd, 107 N.C. App. 658, 421 S.E.2d 800 (1992) (state Junkyard Control Act does not preempt local regulation of junkyards).

same project.[181] There are other instances, such as with local regulation of agricultural activities, discussed above, where the courts have found an intent for state rules to occupy a field to the exclusion of local regulation.[182]

When the state specifically regulates a particular aspect of an activity, a local regulation cannot be contrary to that state regulation. *Lamar OCI South Corp. v. Stanly County Zoning Board of Adjustment* is illustrative. The plaintiff owned a billboard along a state highway. The state notified the plaintiff that it planned to widen the highway and that the increased right-of-way would include the sign site, thus necessitating relocation. The plaintiff then secured N.C. Department of Transportation (NCDOT) approval to move the billboard back fifty feet from its same location along the highway. NCDOT paid for the relocation and considered the relocation to be authorized under state law and rule and to be within the billboard permit previously issued by the state. However, the billboard was nonconforming under the county zoning regulation, which had been amended after the billboard was constructed to prohibit billboards in the applicable highway-business zoning district. The county regulation prohibited the movement or replacement of nonconforming signs. The plaintiff undertook the relocation without notice to or approval from the county. The court held that the county regulation was not preempted by the state's Outdoor Advertising Control Act under G.S. 160A-174(b)(5). However, the court held that G.S. 160A-174(b)(2) was applicable since the state implementing regulations explicitly allowed relocation of a sign if it stayed within a "Sign Location/Site" that was defined by rule. The court concluded that since the state regulation and permit expressly allowed this limited relocation, that decision preempted a local relocation prohibition.[183]

---

181. In *Schooldev East, LLC v. Town of Wake Forest*, 284 N.C. App. 434, 876 S.E.2d 607 (2022), the court considered the relation between local development regulations and G.S. 160A-307.1, which prohibits cities from requiring "street improvements" for schools beyond those required for safe ingress and egress to a city street system and that are physically connected to a school driveway. The court held that the statute did not preempt the city's sidewalk connectivity requirement. As this statute did not define the terms, the court applied the ordinary meanings of "street," "improvements," and "for safe ingress and egress" to the street system. The court held that while sidewalks might be a part of a "street," they are not required for safely entering and leaving the city street system by way of school driveways. In *Davidson County Broadcasting, Inc. v. Rowan County*, 186 N.C. App. 81, 649 S.E.2d 904 (2007), *review denied*, 362 N.C. 470, 666 S.E.2d 186 (2008), the court held that federal aviation and communication law (particularly 49 U.S.C. § 41713(b)(1)) does not preempt local regulation of broadcast towers where the regulation is not in conflict with federal law. *See also* LeTendre v. Currituck Cnty., 259 N.C. App. 512, 817 S.E.2d 73 (2018), *review denied*, 372 N.C. 54, 822 S.E.2d 641 (2019) (limits on authority to regulate building-design elements in residential structures do not preclude other zoning regulations of these structures); Prewitt v. Town of Wrightsville Beach, 161 N.C. App. 481, 595 S.E.2d 442 (2003) (state legislation on building lines relative to title to artificially created beach area does not preempt local setback regulation); Huntington Props., LLC v. Currituck Cnty., 153 N.C. App. 218, 228–29, 569 S.E.2d 695, 702–03 (2002) (state permitting standards for wastewater treatment do not preempt local regulation of mobile-home-park size); Ball v. Randolph Cnty. Bd. of Adjustment, 129 N.C. App. 300, 498 S.E.2d 833, *appeal dismissed*, 349 N.C. 348, 507 S.E.2d 272 (1998) (state regulation of soil remediation does not preclude county zoning regulation of same).

182. *See* Craig v. Cnty. of Chatham, 356 N.C. 40, 565 S.E.2d 172 (2002). In *King v. Town of Chapel Hill*, 367 N.C. 400, 758 S.E.2d 364 (2014), the court invalidated an ordinance prohibiting the use of mobile phones while driving as preempted by state law. State law prohibits use of mobile phones by vehicle operators in several specific instances, limiting phone use by school-bus drivers and drivers under the age of eighteen, and limiting texting by commercial-vehicle operators. The court found these sufficient to show a legislative intent to provide a complete and integrated regulatory scheme to the exclusion of local regulation. *See also* Phillips v. Orange Cnty. Health Dep't, 237 N.C. App. 249, 765 S.E.2d 811 (2014) (state law preempts local inspection and fees for spray-irrigation wastewater systems); Granville Farms, Inc. v. Cnty. of Granville, 170 N.C. App. 109, 612 S.E.2d 156 (2005) (state law on sludge disposal preempts county regulation of land application of biosolids).

183. 186 N.C. App. 44, 650 S.E.2d 37 (2007), *aff'd per curiam*, 312 N.C. 640, 669 S.E.2d 279 (2008). *See also* Five C's, Inc. v. Cnty. of Pasquotank, 195 N.C. App. 410, 672 S.E.2d 737 (2009) (state limits on aspects of manufactured housing that can be regulated by counties apply to both zoning regulations and general-police-power regulations); State *ex rel.* Utils. Comm'n v. Town of Kill Devil Hills, 194 N.C. App. 561, 670 S.E.2d 341, *aff'd per*

Also, state statutes set forth a number of mandatory procedural requirements, particularly for legislative land use regulatory decisions.[184] These rules, such as mandates for public notice of hearings and protest petitions, preempt any local variation to the contrary.

Residential-Design Standards

G.S. 160D-702(b) limits the application of design standards for buildings subject to the N.C. Residential Code for One- and Two-Family Dwellings.[185] The restrictions do not apply to multifamily housing or to commercial, institutional, industrial, or other nonresidential buildings. The restrictions on design standards do not apply to private restrictive covenants, only to government regulation.

The law prohibits regulation of "building design elements." These features cannot be regulated directly or indirectly through a plan-consistency review. The design features that may not be regulated by zoning regulations are:

1. exterior building color;
2. type or style of exterior cladding material;
3. style or materials of roofs or porches;
4. exterior nonstructural architectural ornamentation;
5. location or architectural styling of windows and doors, including garage doors;
6. location of rooms;[186] and
7. interior layout of rooms.

The statute lists several matters as not being "building design elements." These features, which may be regulated by zoning, include the height, bulk, orientation, and location of a structure on a lot; the use of buffering or screening to minimize visual impacts, to mitigate impacts of light or noise, or to protect the privacy of neighbors; and regulations governing permitted uses of land or structures.[187]

The law creates several exceptions to the prohibition of design regulations for residential structures. Design standards that are voluntarily consented to by the owners of all the property may be applied if they are imposed as "part of and in the course of" seeking a zoning amendment or a zoning, subdivision, or other development-regulation approval.[188] Design standards developed and agreed to by the

---

curiam, 363 N.C. 739, 686 S.E.2d 151 (2009) (state Utilities Commission order directing use of new corridor for electrical transmission line preempts local regulation of same); Morris Commc'ns Corp. v. Bd. of Adjustment, 159 N.C. App. 598, 604–5, 583 S.E.2d 419, 423–24 (2003), *appeal dismissed*, 357 N.C. 658, 590 S.E.2d 269 (2003) (since NCDOT regulation specifically allows sign frame to be replaced on a permitted billboard, local sign regulation cannot prohibit replacement of frame).

184. See Chapter 11 for a review of procedural requirements relative to ordinance adoption, amendment, and repeal.

185. These provisions were added to the statutes by S.L. 2015-86. The restrictions apply to all single-family homes and duplexes. Townhouses are covered if they are built to the single-family code.

186. The prohibition of regulation of the location and layout of rooms affects zoning rules designed to limit overcrowding in residential neighborhoods. For example, regulations on the number of proposed kitchens and locations of multiple entrances were used by some local governments to limit multifamily occupancy in single-family zoning districts. The statutes allow a local government to regulate that use, but a zoning regulation cannot presume the use restriction would be violated based solely on the location, layout, or number of rooms proposed.

Also, G.S. 160D-706(b) provides that zoning ordinances may not use a definition of a "dwelling unit, bedroom, or sleeping unit" that is more expansive than a definition of these terms used in a statute or rule. This provision was added to the statutes by S.L. 2015-246.

187. A regulation that defines a "principal structure" and prohibits connecting multiple principal structures on a lot is not a prohibited regulation of building-design elements. LeTendre v. Currituck Cnty., 259 N.C. App. 512, 817 S.E.2d 73 (2018), *review denied*, 372 N.C. 54, 822 S.E.2d 641 (2019).

188. The statute does not define *voluntary* in this context. A narrow reading is that only design standards proposed by the developer are voluntary, while a broader reading is that it does not matter who proposes the standards

owners of all affected property can also be incorporated into conditional zoning, special use permits, or development agreements.

There are other specific exceptions to the prohibition listed in the law, primarily preserving historic-district regulations, where building-design elements have long been a central feature of the regulatory scheme. Building-design elements can be regulated if the regulations are directly and substantially related to safety codes, are adopted as a condition of participation in the flood-insurance program, are part of design standards for manufactured housing, or pertain to historic-preservation programs (within designated local historic districts, within historic districts on the National Register, and for designated local, state, or national landmarks).[189]

Wireless Telecommunication Facilities

Many restrictions on local land use regulation of wireless telecommunication facilities are based on federal law and are discussed in Chapter 23. However, there are state statutory restrictions as well.[190] Many of the state provisions overlap the federal statutes, but there are modest differences in the provisions.

Scope of Local Regulation

G.S. 160D-930 to -938 allows local government regulation of wireless telecommunication facilities based on "land use, public safety, and zoning considerations."[191] This expressly includes the authority to address "aesthetics, landscaping, land-use-based location priorities, structural design, setbacks, and fall zones."[192] These provisions also provide that they do not limit the provisions of local historic-district or landmark regulations.

These statutes provide that local governments may not require information on an applicant's "business decisions," specifically including information about customer demand or quality of service. This distinction poses some inherent conflict, as it is not uncommon for ordinances to allow new towers in sensitive areas (a land use consideration) only upon a showing that existing facilities are unavailable to provide adequate service (what some might consider a business decision). The statute addresses this tension by specifying the information that can be required and considered in permit reviews. A local government is allowed to consider whether an existing or previously approved structure can reasonably be used to provide service; whether residential, historic, and designated scenic areas can be served from outside the areas; and whether the proposed tower height is necessary to provide the applicant's designated service. A local government is also allowed to evaluate the reasonable feasibility of collocating new antennas and equipment on existing structures.

Local governments are prohibited from requiring that wireless facilities be located on city- or county-owned towers or facilities. They are allowed to provide expedited processing for applications for wireless facilities proposed to be located on city- or county-owned property.

Two other key issues addressed by this statute are the fees required for permit review and the construction of speculative towers. Local governments are allowed to charge an application fee that includes fees for consultants to assist in review of permit applications. These fees must be fixed in advance of the

---

(the owner, the local government, or the neighbors) as long as it is clear that the owner consents to their imposition. Simply calling a regulatory requirement "voluntary" when compliance has in fact been uniformly mandated does not make it voluntary. Lanvale Props., LLC v. Cnty. of Cabarrus, 366 N.C. 142, 731 S.E.2d 800 (2012).

189. G.S. 160D-702(b).
190. G.S. 160D, §§ 930 to 938.
191. G.S. 160D-932.
192. G.S. 160D-933(b)(1).

application and may not exceed the usual and customary costs of services provided. Local governments may add a condition to zoning approvals for new towers that building permits for the tower will not be issued until the applicant provides documentation of parties intending to locate facilities on the tower. (But the zoning permit itself may not be denied due to the lack of documentation of a committed user.) Zoning permits can require that permitted facilities be constructed within a reasonable time, provided that time is not less than twenty-four months.

Collocation

Local governments are required to provide streamlined processing for qualified collocation applications.[193] Decisions on these applications must be made within forty-five days of receipt of a completed application (and decisions on all other applications must be made within a reasonable time consistent with other land use applications). Notice of any deficiencies in a collocation application must be provided within forty-five days of submission of an application. Qualified collocation applications can be reviewed for conformance with site-plan and building-permit requirements but are not otherwise subject to zoning requirements.

Applications entitled to this streamlined review include those regarding new antennae on towers previously approved for collocation facilities if the installation is within the terms of the original permit. Other collocations entitled to this streamlined process include those that meet a set of specified conditions, including no increase in the height or width of the supporting tower, no increase in ground space for the facility, and any new equipment being within the weight limits for the structure.

Minor Modifications

Expedited review is also mandatory for minor modifications to existing towers.[194] The law sets state standards on expedited review of collocation and minor-modifications requests.

Minor modifications include:

1. adding not more than 10 percent or the height of one additional antennae array on the tower to the tower's height (with a twenty-foot separation from the nearest existing antennae),
2. adding not more than twenty feet or the width of the support structure at the level of the new appurtenance to the tower's width,
3. adding not more than 2500 square feet to the existing equipment compound.

Minor modifications (termed an "eligible facility request" by the statute) must be approved. An application is deemed complete unless the local government objects within forty-five days. Approval is required within forty-five days of an application being deemed complete. If the application is for a collocation that does not qualify as a minor modification, a decision to approve or deny must be made in the same forty-five-day period. Fees for collocation requests are capped at $1000. Such a fee may not include consultant travel costs or a consultant contingency fee.

---

193. G.S. 160D-934.

194. The provisions on minor modifications were added by S.L. 2013-185. A 2012 federal law broadened the preemption of local cell-tower regulations. It provided that state or local governments "shall approve" any eligible request to modify an existing wireless tower or base station that does not "substantially change" the tower or base station. The Federal Communications Commission in 2013 provided notice that it interpreted this law using the same standards for defining a "substantial modification" that were previously set in the context of reviewing collocation agreements and facilities in historic districts. 47 C.F.R. pt. 1., app. B, § I.C.

Small-Cell Wireless Facilities

G.S. 160D-935 establishes special requirements for permitting of small-cell wireless facilities.[195] For purposes of these regulations, a small wireless facility is one in which the antennae, whether in an enclosure or exposed, measure no more than six cubic feet.[196] All other supporting equipment (meters, switches, grounding equipment, and the like) can be no more than twenty-eight cubic feet.

The small-cell wireless facility must be placed on a pole no more than fifty feet high (plus an additional ten feet for an antenna), provided that the pole is either in a city right-of-way or is on property outside of a right-of-way that is "other than single-family residential property."[197] In areas zoned single-family residential where utilities are underground, the support pole may not exceed forty feet.[198]

The city may specify the form and content of applications for small wireless facilities. However, the city may not require the applicant to provide more information in the application than is required for communications providers that are not wireless providers. An application is deemed complete unless the city provides written notice of deficiencies within thirty days.[199] If deficiencies are identified, the applicant can cure the deficiencies and resubmit without paying an additional application fee. The application is then deemed complete upon resubmission if the deficiencies are cured. An applicant may submit a combined application for up to twenty-five separate facilities. Application fees can include the actual, direct, and reasonable costs to process and review applications, provided they do not exceed the application fee for similar activities and are capped at $100 per facility for the first five facilities and $50 per facility for each additional facility. A technical-consulting fee of up to $500 also may be charged.[200] However, statutory amendments adopted in 2018 limit fees charged for activities conducted in the public right-of-way, effectively precluding imposition of development-plan application fees on telecommunication service providers.[201]

---

195. These provisions were added to the statutes by S.L. 2017-159. In this context, "small cell" refers to the size of the area served by the facility, not the size of the equipment providing the service. Federal Communications Commission regulations on these small wireless facilities are similar, but not identical, to these state standards. *In re* Accelerating Wireless Broadband Deployment by Removing Barriers to Infrastructure Investment, 33 FCC Rcd. 9088 (Sept. 27, 2018). Also see G.S. 160A-296.1, which establishes somewhat comparable provisions for municipal review of permits for broadband providers working within city-street rights-of-way. This statute was created by S.L. 2021-180, § 38.9.

196. G.S. 160D-931(18). G.S. 160D-938(a) provides that cities may not regulate the design, engineering, construction, installation, or operation of small wireless facilities in an interior structure or on the site of an athletic stadium or facility (unless it is city owned). However, building-code provisions can be applied to these facilities. Cities may not apply their regulations for facilities in the rights-of-way of state-maintained roads, which are regulated by NCDOT. Provisions applicable to NCDOT permitting of small wireless facilities within NCDOT rights-of-way are set out in G.S. 136-18.3A. The regulatory provisions for the state are considerably less specific than those that cities may impose. The state must administer the rules in a reasonable and nondiscriminatory manner, make permit decisions in a reasonable time, and require that any new utility poles not be more than ten feet higher than nearby poles, with a maximum height of fifty feet.

197. G.S. 160D-935(c).

198. G.S. 160D-936 provides that new poles in city rights-of-way are subject to the same process of review and approval as wireless facilities. New poles are limited to a height of fifty feet, but cities have the option of allowing poles and wireless facilities exceeding this limit.

199. Federal regulations, *supra* note 194, however, require the review of the completeness of the application to be done within ten days rather than the thirty days allowed by G.S. 160A-400.54(d)(3).

200. The law also includes provisions requiring cities to allow use of their rights-of-way and to provide access to city utility poles. The city must allow access to city poles and may charge a reasonable and nondiscriminatory rate for their use, capped at $50 per pole per year. A request to collocate on a city pole may be denied if there is insufficient capacity or an engineering justification based on safety or reliability that cannot be remedied at the expense of the wireless provider. The law does not authorize location of wireless facilities on privately owned utility poles or structures without the consent of the owner.

201. S.L. 2018-145 amended G.S. 160D-935 to make G.S. 160A-296(a)(6) applicable to these fees.

A city may not establish a moratorium on filing, processing, or deciding permits for colocation of small wireless facilities. No application, permit, or fee may be required for routine maintenance, for replacement of facilities of the same or smaller size, or for "micro wireless facilities" (facilities with dimensions of no more than twenty-four inches long, fifteen inches wide, and thirteen inches high, with any exterior antennae limited to eleven inches).

City regulation can only provide for an administrative review. Approval cannot be subject to a quasi-judicial special use permit or a legislative rezoning. If the city does not act within forty-five days of receipt of a completed application, it is deemed approved.[202] Grounds for denial of a permit are limited. The standards that may be applied are:

1. the city's "applicable codes," which for the purposes of these regulations are essentially the State Building Code, including electrical, mechanical, and fire codes but not zoning or other development regulations;
2. local code provisions or regulations that concern public safety, objective design standards for decorative utility poles, city utility poles,[203] and reasonable, nondiscriminatory stealth-and-concealment requirements, including screening or landscaping for ground-mounted equipment (these requirements can be included in zoning or other ordinances and regulations);
3. public-safety and reasonable-spacing requirements concerning the location of ground-mounted equipment in a right-of-way; and
4. regulations of historic districts and landmarks.

If a permit is denied, the city must send the applicant documentation on why it was denied. The notice of denial must be sent on or before the date of denial. The applicant can then modify the application to cure the identified defects and resubmit within thirty days without paying an additional application fee. The city then has thirty days to review the resubmittal, at that point reviewing only the deficiencies cited in the denial.

The permit may not require the applicant to provide services for the city, such as reservation of fiber, conduit, or pole space. The permit may require that work commence within six months. It also may require that the facility be activated within one year of permit issuance.[204] A city can also require a work permit for work that involves excavation in the right-of-way, affects traffic patterns, or obstructs vehicular traffic. Wireless providers are required to comply with city undergrounding requirements, provided they are nondiscriminatory and have a waiver process.

Miscellaneous Additional Restrictions

Airport Zoning

In 1941, a time when no counties and very few small-population cities had zoning ordinances, the General Assembly enacted a Model Airport Zoning Act, now codified as G.S. 63, art. 4. This statute allows those cities and counties without zoning to adopt regulations pertaining to land uses and the height of

---

202. Federal regulations, *supra* note 194, require that all required permits and all administrative appeals be concluded within the applicable time limits. The time limits in the federal rules are sixty days for facilities placed on existing structures and ninety days for those on new poles. The federal rules do not provide for an automatic approval if the deadline is not met. The time limits may be extended if agreed to by the applicant.

203. Federal regulations, *supra* note 194, require aesthetic standards to be published in advance.

204. A city can require that an abandoned facility (one that has ceased to transmit a signal, unless the provider is diligently working to restore service) be removed within 180 days of abandonment. The removal requirement applies to the wireless equipment but not the pole itself. If the provider does not remove the equipment, the city can undertake the removal and recover its actual costs of doing so.

structures and trees that can affect airport operations. Several of these airport-zoning regulations are still in effect.[205]

These airport-zoning provisions were retained with the adoption of Chapter 160D in 2019. However, the procedural, enforcement, variance, and judicial-review provisions were replaced with requirements to follow the comparable provisions of Chapter 160D to ensure uniformity for all development regulations.[206]

Affordable Housing

Proponents of affordable-housing projects across the nation have long been concerned that neighborhood opposition can lead to local land use regulatory decisions limiting the siting of these projects. The result of such decisions has been the exclusion of housing opportunities for low-income persons in communities opposing them.[207] In some states there is considerable case law or statutory provisions that address this exclusionary-zoning issue. But prior to 2009, there was little legislative attention paid to this issue in North Carolina.[208]

The General Assembly in 2009 adopted G.S. 41A-4(f) to make it unlawful housing discrimination if a land use decision is based on the fact that a development includes affordable housing.[209] This statute provides, however, that a decision limiting high concentrations of affordable housing is not unlawful discrimination.[210] In 2021, the General Assembly prohibited the use of a harmony standard when applied to projects providing affordable housing. G.S. 160D-703(b1)[211] provides that if a parcel is in a zoning district where multifamily structures are an allowable use, a harmony requirement may not be required for permit approval if the development contains affordable-housing units.[212]

A prudent local government is well advised to carefully and explicitly address this concern about unlawful exclusion of affordable housing in its land use decision-making. It is not unlawful discrimination if a citizen makes a discriminatory comment in a public hearing on a project with affordable hous-

---

205. Most contemporary development regulations in those jurisdictions that have adopted zoning incorporate standards related to airports and adjacent uses into the zoning regulations rather than using a separate airport-zoning ordinance.

206. S.L. 2019-111, §§ 2.5(c)–(g).

207. See the discussion of the federal Fair Housing Act in Chapter 23 and the discussion of inclusionary zoning in Chapter 9. For a review of state-level legislation addressing the issue, see John Infranca, *The New State Zoning: Land Use Preemption Amid a Housing Crisis*, 60 B.C. L. Rev. 823 (2019); Anika Singh Lemar, *The Role of States in Liberalizing Land Use Regulations*, 97 N.C. L. Rev. 293 (2019).

208. Individual local governments have secured local legislation to modify zoning requirements to encourage provision of affordable housing. For example, S.L. 1991-119, S.L. 1991-246, and S.L. 1991-503 grant authority to Wilmington, Orange County, and the city and county of Durham, respectively, to allow zoning-density bonuses for projects providing low- and moderate-income housing.

209. S.L. 2009-533.

210. Complaints about alleged housing discrimination are made to the state Human Relations Commission and, if not resolved to the complainant's satisfaction, may thereafter be taken to court upon issuance of a right-to-sue letter by the Commission. If an action goes to court, the court has the authority under G.S. 41-7 to order injunctive relief and may award a successful plaintiff actual and punitive damages, as well as court costs and reasonable attorney's fees.

211. This provision was created by S.L. 2021-180, § 5.16(a).

212. For purposes of this restriction, affordable-housing units are defined as those for families or individuals with incomes below 80 percent of the area median income. This limitation on use of a harmony standard is likely applicable to any zoning district where multifamily use is either a permitted use or a use allowed by special use permit. It does not apply to a single-family residential zoning district where multifamily uses are not allowed by right or with a special use permit. This limit also applies to a quasi-judicial review of a site plan for a multifamily project with affordable housing. Most site plan reviews use only objective standards, which would not include a harmony standard. But if such a standard is included in a site plan or other permitting review, this limit is applicable.

ing. Still, especially in cases where such animosity is expressed or strongly implied, the staff reports and board discussion should clearly establish a legitimate, nondiscriminatory land use basis for the decision.

Amateur Radio Antennae

G.S. 160D-905 was enacted in 2007[213] to require that ordinances regulating the placement, screening, or height of amateur radio antennae and their support towers or structures "reasonably accommodate" amateur radio communications and be the "minimum practical regulation" to accomplish the city or county's purposes.[214] Cities and counties are not allowed to restrict the height of antennae or support structures to ninety feet or less unless the restriction is necessary to achieve a clearly defined health, safety, or aesthetic objective.

Bee Hives

G.S. 106-645[215] provides that county ordinances may not prohibit a person from owning or possessing five or fewer hives. Municipal regulation of hives is allowed, but the city ordinance must allow up to five hives on any parcel within the city's planning-and-development-regulation jurisdiction. The ordinance may require the hives to be placed on the ground or securely anchored, require setbacks from the property line, or otherwise regulate where the hives may be located. A city can also require removal of hives if they are not maintained or if their removal is necessary to protect the public health, safety, or welfare.

Cemeteries, Grave Sites, and Crematories

There are many state laws regarding cemeteries and grave sites but few limitations or directions regarding local land use regulation of burial sites.[216]

Most of the state statutory provisions regard protection and management of existing burial sites. State law makes it a criminal offense to deface or desecrate a gravesite.[217] State statutes require a person who discovers an unmarked burial site of human remains to contact the medical examiner and establish a process for archaeological evaluation of the site.[218] Other statutes establish procedures for relocation

---

213. S.L. 2007-147.

214. This general standard is substantially similar to the limited federal preemption approved by the Federal Communications Commission in 1985. *See In re* Federal Preemption of State & Local Regulations Pertaining to Amateur Radio Facilities (*PRB-1*), 101 F.C.C.2d 952 (Sept. 16, 1985).

215. This provision was added to the statutes by S.L. 2015-246, § 8. G.S. 160D-906 confirms that these restrictions apply to local development regulations.

216. For a general review of the land use implications on this subject, see Carlton Basmajian & Christopher Coutts, *Planning for the Disposal of the Dead*, 76 J. Am. Plan Ass'n 305 (2010). Many local governments have cemetery regulations. For example, Madison County's regulations on cemeteries require a four-foot-high fence, a minimum right-of-way connecting to a public road, and a fifty-foot setback from the property line. Madison County Land Use Ordinance § 8.1.4 (June 29, 2021).

217. G.S. 14, §§ 148, 149; State v. McLean, 121 N.C. 589, 28 S.E. 140 (1897) (unlawful for city to relocate without permission a body buried in city cemetery to pauper's section of cemetery due to nonpayment for burial lot); State v. Wilson, 94 N.C. 1015 (1886) (criminal offense for owner of land to remove monuments and plow over grave sites); State v. Sammartino, 120 N.C. App. 597, 463 S.E.2d 307 (1995) (upholding conviction of those vandalizing grave markers). Protection of grave sites under these statutes does not extend to a former grave site after the body has been removed and reinterred elsewhere. State v. Phipps, 338 N.C. 305, 449 S.E.2d 450 (1994).

218. G.S. 70, §§ 26 to 40.

of graves,[219] care of rural cemeteries,[220] operation of municipal cemeteries,[221] and regulation of non-governmental and nonreligious cemeteries.[222]

There are several state standards regarding burial sites. The Commission for Health Services is authorized to regulate location of cemeteries within public-drinking-water watersheds.[223] Rules provide that a public-water-supply well must be at least 300 feet from a burial ground.[224] Where belowground burial is involved, the top of the burial vault or other encasement must be at least eighteen inches below the ground surface.[225]

State statutes also provide that a crematory may be constructed on or adjacent to any cemetery or in or adjacent to a funeral home that is in a commercial or industrial zoning district.[226]

Construction-Fence Signs

G.S. 160D-908 exempts construction-site fence-wrap signs from zoning sign regulation.[227] Exempt signs are those affixed to perimeter fencing at a construction site. The exemption lasts until issuance of the certificate of occupancy or for twenty-four months, whichever is shorter. The only advertising that may be displayed on the fence wrap is advertising "sponsored by a person directly involved in the construction project and for which monetary compensation for the advertisement is not paid or required."[228]

Fraternities and Sororities

G.S. 160D-909 provides that a zoning or unified development ordinance may not differentiate between those fraternities and sororities that are approved or recognized by a college or university and those that are not.[229] If a development ordinance would allow a sanctioned fraternity house in a particular zoning district, it must also allow unsanctioned houses. Similarly, it is impermissible for a special use permit for a fraternity house to include a condition that the fraternity be sanctioned by a college.

---

219. G.S. 65-13 authorizes government agencies, churches, utilities, and owners of abandoned cemeteries to relocate graves in a prescribed manner. For rules regarding NCDOT removal and relocation of graves, see 19A N.C.A.C. 2B, § .0142.

220. G.S. 65-1 to -3 allow county governments to assist in maintenance of rural cemeteries and to take control of abandoned cemeteries.

221. G.S. 160A-341 to -348 authorize establishment of municipal cemeteries and set provisions for their operation and maintenance. G.S. 160A-349.1 to .15 provide for cemetery trustees to manage these cemeteries. G.S. 65-37 to -40 allow municipalities to assume possession and management of nonreligious cemeteries within the city.

222. The North Carolina Cemetery Act, G.S. 65-46 to -73. G.S. 65-69 provides that each cemetery must be no less than thirty acres. Funeral services, mutual-burial societies, and cremations are also regulated under G.S. 90-210.18 to .134, but these statutory provisions have few land use regulatory components. G.S. 90-210.130 does provide that landowner permission is necessary for disposal of cremated remains in a place other than a dedicated cemetery.

223. G.S. 130A-320.

224. 15A N.C.A.C. 18C, § .0203(2)(k).

225. G.S. 65-77.

226. G.S. 90-210.123(b).

227. These provisions were added to the statutes by S.L. 2015-246. The statute specifically refers to zoning regulations, leaving application to a separate sign ordinance uncertain.

228. While an argument can be made that this is a permissible on-site versus off-site distinction, it is unclear whether this provision would be considered content neutral under *Reed v. Town of Gilbert*, 135 S. Ct. 2218 (2015). See Chapter 28 for a discussion of the First Amendment and sign regulation.

229. These provisions were added to the statutes by S.L. 2013-413, § 6.

Government Buildings and Land Uses

Some states exempt state, municipal, and county land uses from zoning regulations.[230] That is not the case in North Carolina.

The General Assembly in 1951 adopted G.S. 160D-913.[231] This statute makes city and county zoning regulations applicable to "the erection, construction, and use of buildings by the State of North Carolina and its political subdivisions."[232] Thus, if a building is involved, zoning restrictions apply to land uses owned or operated by cities, counties, and the state.[233] The statute does provide, however, that land owned by the state may not be placed in an overlay or conditional use district without approval of the Council of State.[234]

Since a building is required to trigger application of zoning, and given that land uses per se are not covered, an open-air use of land without a building is not subject to local zoning. A landfill, parking area, or wetlands-mitigation site might fit this situation. The court of appeals held in *Nash–Rocky Mount Board of Education v. Rocky Mount Board of Adjustment*[235] that construction of a new bus parking lot

---

230. *See generally* 3 Patricia E. Salkin, American Law of Zoning §§ 18.28–.36 (5th ed., May 2019 Update); Elaine M. Tomko-DeLuca, Annotation, *Applicability of Zoning Regulations to Governmental Projects or Activities*, 53 A.L.R.5th No. 1 (1997).

231. Absent such an explicit statutory provision, the general rule is that statutes do not apply to the state and its political subdivisions. Yancey v. N.C. State Highway & Pub. Works Comm'n, 222 N.C. 106, 109, 22 S.E.2d 256, 259–60 (1942).

232. S.L. 1951-1203. These statutes only apply to local ordinances adopted pursuant to the zoning-enabling statutes. Other local land-development ordinances are not included.

There are individual exceptions to this general rule. The General Assembly in 2007 amended G.S. 143-345.5 to provide that the City of Raleigh's zoning does not apply to any state-owned building built on state-owned land located within six blocks of the state capitol without the consent of the Council of State. S.L. 2007-482. This local act was apparently enacted in response to a Raleigh ordinance requirement that the first story of parking decks in the downtown area have a storefront appearance. In 2022, the General Assembly exempted a specified parcel from Lexington's unified development ordinance for as long as the parcel is used for a public purpose. S.L. 2022-25. The site is intended to be used by Davidson County for a jail. While exempting a jail from city zoning regulations, this law provided that one city council member and one city staff member would be appointed to the Davidson County Jail Committee to participate in and vote on "matters related to the façade, exterior, sidewalks, streetscapes, and plantings of the jail."

233. A number of cases review other aspects of zoning and public buildings, all assuming the fundamental application to publicly owned buildings. *See, e.g.*, McDonald v. City of Concord, 188 N.C. App. 278, 655 S.E.2d 455, *review denied*, 362 N.C. 360, 662 S.E.2d 906 (2008) (zoning conditional use permit required for county law enforcement center); Carter v. Stanly Cnty., 125 N.C. App. 628, 482 S.E.2d 9, *review denied*, 346 N.C. 276, 487 S.E.2d 540 (1997) (upholding the adequacy of a published notice of hearing on a zoning-text amendment that added "government owned buildings, facilities, and institutions" to a list of permitted uses in the face of a challenge by neighbors objecting to the subsequent location of a state prison on the site). The court of appeals has also held that city and county ordinances adopted under the general police power can be applied on state-owned land. Slavin v. Town of Oak Island, 160 N.C. App. 57, 584 S.E.2d 100 (2003) (upholding town ordinance limiting construction of dune crosswalks over nourished beach where title to the affected area had vested in the state).

234. Since the consent of the landowner is required for all rezonings to special or conditional use districts (and conditional districts), the principal impact of this restriction is placement of state-owned properties in overlay districts such as historic-preservation districts.

235. 169 N.C. App. 587, 610 S.E.2d 255 (2005). The school board secured driveway and fence permits and then constructed a gravel lot to park additional school buses at a preexisting school. Adjacent neighbors complained about the lot's noise, dust, traffic congestion, and trash. The city then advised the school board that a special use permit would be required for continued operation of the lot. The city then denied the special use permit application. The court held that the parking lot could not be considered a "building" under the plain meaning of the statutory language; thus, the city could not require a special use permit to limit use of the parking lot. *See also* N.C. Dep't of Justice, Office of the Att'y Gen., Advisory Opinion: Applicability of Watauga County Ordinances to UNC-TV Tower in Watauga County, Op. N.C. Att'y Gen. (Sept. 20, 2000) (opining that county zoning is not applicable to

at an existing high school was not subject to city zoning jurisdiction.[236] However, when a new building is involved, zoning regulations do apply to all aspects of the construction and use of that building, including provision of mandatory off-street parking.[237]

One North Carolina case addresses the possibility that governmental functions may have some interjurisdictional zoning immunity. In *Davidson County v. City of High Point*,[238] the court of appeals ruled that a sewage-treatment plant was not a "building" under G.S. 160D-913 but rather was a "public enterprise" under G.S. 153A-274 and thus was not subject to zoning control. The state supreme court affirmed on different and narrower grounds and expressly refused to address the correctness of this rationale of the court of appeals.

The land and facilities of the federal government are not subject to local zoning.[239] The statute regarding compliance with zoning for state buildings does, however, apply to the construction and alteration of National Guard armories. While the Guard can be "federalized" and called in to service, it is still a state agency.[240]

Government Flags

G.S. 144-7.1, enacted in 2005, limits regulation of official governmental flags.[241] This statute applies to the official flags of the United States and any other nation recognized by the United States, all fifty official state flags, and the official flag of any local government in the United States or its territories. The flags that are covered must be displayed in accordance with federal law[242] and must be displayed with the approval of the owner of the land involved. Reasonable nondiscriminatory regulations can be imposed on flag size, the number of flags, their location, and the height of flagpoles.

---

state-owned television tower as such is not a "building"). See Chapter 18 for further discussion of interpretation of ordinances and statutes.

236. In 2004, the General Assembly addressed this issue by amending G.S. 160A-392 (but not the comparable county provision) to make municipal zoning applicable to the use of land as well as to the construction and use of buildings. S.L. 2004-199, § 41(e). However, in 2005 the General Assembly repealed the 2004 change so that the statute again provided that local zoning only applied to the state and local governmental entities when a building was involved. S.L. 2005-280. Also see S.L. 2005-305, § 11(a), which provides that all docks, buildings, and land under control of the State Ports Authority at Southport are fully subject to municipal zoning jurisdiction.

237. Orange Cnty. v. Town of Hillsborough, 219 N.C. App. 127, 133–34, 724 S.E.2d 560, 565 (2012). The court held that the town's zoning authority over the county's construction of a courthouse addition included the authority to regulate mandated parking for the building. Presumptively this rationale would also apply to landscaping, signage, driveways, and similar regulatory requirements associated with construction and use of a building.

238. 85 N.C. App. 26, 354 S.E.2d 280, *modified and aff'd*, 321 N.C. 252, 362 S.E.2d 553 (1987). For a review of the case, see James G. Farris, Jr., *Davidson County v. City of High Point: The North Carolina Supreme Court Solves a City-County Conflict*, 66 N.C. L. Rev. 1266 (1988). *See also* McKinney v. City of High Point, 237 N.C. 66, 74 S.E.2d 440 (1953) (holding zoning not applicable to government functions; however, case involved a water tank under construction prior to enactment of statute making government buildings subject to zoning).

239. See Chapter 23. Also see G.S. 104, where the state retains concurrent jurisdiction for certain federal lands for the service of civil and criminal process. State crimes become federal offenses on these federal lands. United States v. Raffield, 82 F.3d 611 (4th Cir.), *cert. denied*, 519 U.S. 933 (1996) (approving federal prosecution of a driving-while-impaired violation that took place on a National Forest road).

240. G.S. 127A-29 provides that the National Guard has dual status as a state militia and federal status as a reserve component of the armed services. "The National Guard functions in each state as a state agency under state authority and control, while at the same time remaining subject to regulations and orders issued by the Secretaries of the Army and Air Force, the Defense Department, and the National Guard Bureau." Culbreth v. Ingram, 389 F. Supp. 668, 674 (E.D.N.C. 2005).

241. S.L. 2005-360. It is an open question as to whether this is still a permissible content-neutral distinction under *Reed v. Town of Gilbert*, 576 U.S. 155 (2015). See Chapter 28 for a discussion of the First Amendment and sign regulation.

242. 4 U.S.C. §§ 5–10 (2005).

Gun Sales

In 1996, the General Assembly established a policy of uniform state standards for a number of local regulations on guns, including restricting local zoning control of various aspects of gun sales.[243]

Under G.S. 14-409.40, zoning regulations must treat the sale of firearms the same as any other commercial activity and must treat firearm shows the same as any other commercial show; more-restrictive regulations cannot be applied on the basis of firearm sales. The law does provide some flexibility to address safety concerns near schools. It allows zoning regulations to require a special use permit for any commercial activity within a set distance from a school as well as adoption of a permit standard that the uses must not pose a danger to the health, safety, or welfare of those attending the school.

Outdoor Advertising and Junkyards

In response to the federal Highway Beautification Act, the state in 1967 enacted detailed standards that require local regulations to address outdoor advertising and screening of junkyards that are located near federally funded highways. The state's Outdoor Advertising Control Act[244] and Junkyard Control Act[245] are discussed in Chapter 23.

Palmistry

G.S. 14-401.5 previously made it unlawful for a person to practice phrenology, palmistry, fortune telling, or clairvoyance in sixty-one specified counties.[246] This statute was repealed in 2004.[247]

Pawnshops

G.S. 91A-12 provides that local government regulations on pawnshops may not regulate the hours of operation (unless the limit applies to all businesses), the nature of the business or type of pawn transactions, or the interest, fees, or recovery charges set by the business.[248] In 1995, the General Assembly enacted local legislation allowing Raleigh to require that pawnshops secure a special use permit and to condition the permit upon a finding that the use would not be deleterious to the neighborhood in which it is located, notwithstanding the limitations of G.S. 91A-12.[249]

---

243. S.L. 1996-727. Since 1994, federal law has required applicants for federal firearms licenses to certify that "the business to be conducted under the license is not prohibited by State or local law in the place where the licensed premise is located." 18 U.S.C. § 923(d)(1)(F) (2006). Thus, this federal-licensing process for places selling firearms includes a zoning-compliance review. Also see the cases on the Second Amendment limits on gun regulations discussed in the section on shooting ranges below.

244. G.S. 136-129 to -140.1.

245. G.S. 136-144 to -155.

246. See, however, *Marks v. City of Chesapeake*, 883 F.2d 308 (4th Cir. 1989), invalidating the denial of a conditional use permit for a palmistry operation as arbitrary and capricious.

247. S.L. 2004-203, § 21.

248. State laws impose restrictions on dealers in various materials, such as requirements to maintain registers of buyers and sellers or permitting requirements. *See, e.g.,* G.S. 66-10 (covering record keeping by scrap and salvage dealers); G.S. 66-11 (regarding records for dealers in metals and secondary-metal recycling); G.S. 66-165 (as to permits for dealers in precious metals); G.S. 66-252 (relating to registration for itinerant merchants and flea markets).

249. S.L. 1995-357.

Shooting Ranges

There are both statutory and constitutional issues involved with land use regulation of shooting ranges and the location of gun sales.

The General Assembly modestly limited zoning regulation of sport-shooting ranges in 1997.[250] G.S. 14-409.46 primarily limits the applicability of noise ordinances and the liability under private-nuisance actions for the owners of sport-shooting ranges. The law also prohibits zoning regulations from amortizing some nonconforming shooting ranges by providing that a shooting range that was lawfully in operation as of September 1, 1994, must be allowed to continue to operate, provided there has been no substantial change in the use. The law does not otherwise limit local regulatory authority regarding the location and construction of sport-shooting ranges.

Highly restrictive regulations or bans on shooting ranges and the location of stores selling guns raise Second Amendment issues. The Court in *District of Columbia v. Heller*,[251] held that the Constitution protects an individual's right to bear arms. The Court noted, however that like First Amendment protection of free speech, the constitutional right to bear arms is not unlimited.[252] In *New York State Rifle & Pistol Ass'n, Inc. v. Bruen*,[253] the Court invalidated a state regulation on carrying handguns in public. The Court held that to be permissible, regulations affecting the right to bear arms "must demonstrate that the regulation is consistent with this Nation's historical tradition of firearm regulation."[254]

The application of this rationale to land use and development regulations, such as zoning restrictions on the location of shooting ranges or on places for gun sales, has produced mixed results.

In *Ezell v. City of Chicago*,[255] the court invalidated regulatory provisions that limited shooting ranges to manufacturing districts and required a minimum separation of 500 feet from residential districts, schools, places of worship, liquor retailers, libraries, hospitals, and other specified uses. This left only two percent of the city's land area potentially available and required a special use permit in those areas. In *Drummond v. Robinson Township*,[256] the court noted that restrictions on guns that were supported by "historical evidence" and "long-settled traditions" are permissible. If not in that category of regulation, intermediate scrutiny is applied to determine if the regulation serves a "significant, substantial or important" governmental interest and does not burden more conduct than reasonably necessary. The court applied that test to invalidate a limit on the types of weapons that could be used at a shooting range.

---

250. S.L. 1997-465. In addition to land use regulatory authority, G.S. 160A-186 and 153A-129 explicitly authorize cities and counties to regulate or restrict the discharge of firearms "at any time or place" (with limited exceptions). Some jurisdictions use this authority to place certain areas off-limits for the discharge of firearms (e.g., within a specified distance from a school, place of worship, or residence).

251. 554 U.S. 570 (2008). The Court invalidated a District of Columbia law making it illegal to carry an unregistered handgun.

252. "Although we do not undertake an exhaustive historical analysis today of the full scope of the Second Amendment, nothing in our opinion should be taken to cast doubt on longstanding prohibitions on the possession of firearms by felons and the mentally ill, or laws forbidding the carrying of firearms in sensitive places such as schools and government buildings, or laws imposing conditions and qualifications on the commercial sale of arms." *Id.* at 626–27. The Court noted that this list of presumptively permissible regulations was not exhaustive.

253. 142 S. Ct. 2111 (2022).

254. *Id.* at 2130.

255. 846 F.3d 888 (7th Cir. 2017). The regulation also prohibited entry to shooting ranges by those under the age of eighteen, which was upheld as minors do not have Second Amendment rights to bear arms. In *Barris v. Stroud Twp.*, 257 A.3d 209 (Pa. Commw. Ct. 2021), *review granted*, 279 A.3d 507 (Pa. 2022), the court applied this test to invalidate a ban on private target shooting unless conducted at a shooting range.

256. 9 F.4th 217 (3d Cir. 2021). The township had revised its regulations to allow only a pistol range, skeet shooting, and rim-fire rifle practice. The court found there was no historic evidence of regulations limiting training with common weapons where firearm practice was otherwise allowed.

By contrast, the court in *Teixeira v. County of Alameda*,[257] upheld minimum-separation requirements from sensitive uses applied to gun-store locations. The court noted that unlike the situation in *Ezell*, where shooting ranges were effectively prohibited, this ordinance left ample opportunities in the jurisdiction for gun sales, and there were in fact other gun stores already operational in the area.

Short-Term Rental of Residential Property

Owners of residential properties have long rented bedrooms to boarders and transient visitors. It was not unusual for zoning regulations in the 1930s and 1950s to have provisions regulating boarding and rooming houses. In later years, the use of large houses for bed-and-breakfast establishments, particularly in older neighborhoods, became commonplace in some communities. For the most part, the use of residential structures for these purposes was readily identifiable and many development regulations treated them as a lodging or commercial use rather than a residential use.[258]

While renting a home by the night or week has long been prevalent in the state's coastal and mountain resort towns,[259] doing so in non-resort areas is a newer phenomenon. With the advent of Internet marketing and booking, the use of some or all of a residential structure for short-term-rental use has become more common in recent years.[260] This widespread practice of short-term rental to transient

---

257. 873 F.3d 670 (9th Cir. 2017).

258. *See, e.g.,* Hayes v. Fowler, 123 N.C. App. 400, 473 S.E.2d 442 (1996) (use of bedrooms in a residential structure for bed-and-breakfast is not an accessory use to the residential use); Ballas v. Town of Weaverville, 121 N.C. App. 346, 465 S.E.2d 324 (1996) (upholding denial of special use permit for bed-and-breakfast in a residential zoning district given adverse impacts on surrounding neighborhood). Zoning ordinances have always, for example, regulated hotels and motels as a different use than a residential apartment building or condominium, with the difference being transient occupancy rather than permanent residence. That distinction is less clear when the short-term rental is of a single-family residential structure or a bedroom within that structure. The distinctions between a "residential structure," a "residential property," and a "residential use" are not always clear nor uniformly made by statutes and ordinances.

259. This traditional widespread use led to the 1999 adoption of the Vacation Rental Act in G.S. 42A. S.L. 1999-420. That law applies to the rental of residential property for vacation, leisure, or recreational purposes for less than ninety days by a person who has a place of permanent residence to which they intend to return. G.S. 42A-4(3). This law deals primarily with landlord-tenant and consumer-protection issues—contracts, deposits, fees, and evictions. It is not a land use regulation. In 2019, G.S. 42A-3(a) was clarified to explicitly provide that the periodic-inspection statute applies to properties covered by the Vacation Rental Act. S.L. 2019-73. The periodic-inspection statutory cross-reference in G.S. 42A-3 was updated by S.L. 2022-62 to G.S. 160D-1117, which incorporates by reference G.S. 160D-1207 for inspections of dwellings.

Rental of residential property for use as a residence, as opposed to transient occupancy, is subject to the Residential Rental Agreement law, G.S. 42-38 to -46. This law does not apply to short-term rentals and there is no common-law implied warranty of suitability imposed on the landlord of short-term rentals. Conley v. Emerald Isle Realty, Inc., 350 N.C. 293, 513 S.E.2d 556 (1999) (no liability for owner of beach cottage rented by the week where deck collapsed and injured transient occupants).

260. The advent of Airbnb, Vrbo, HomeAway, and similar online platforms facilitated widespread use of short-term rentals (STRs). Broad and unregulated use of STRs prompted concern about health and safety standards for the occupants, collection of sales and occupancy taxes, reduced supply of affordable housing, and land use impacts on neighbors. Courts in other states have held that short-term rental of a residential structure is not a "residential" land use. *See, e.g.,* Styller v. Zoning Bd. of Appeals, 169 N.E.3d 160 (Mass. 2021); Reaume v. Township of Spring Lake, 937 N.W.2d 734 (Mich. App. 2019); Bostick v. Desoto Cnty, 225 So.3d 20 (Miss. Ct. App. 2017); Working Stiff Partners, LLC v. City of Portsmouth, 232 A.3d 379 (N.H. 2019); Slice of Life, LLC v. Hamilton Twp. Zoning Hearing Bd., 207 A.3d 886 (Pa. 2019). Courts have also held that prohibition of STRs is not an unconstitutional taking. Nekrilov v. City of Jersey City, 45 F.4th 662 (3d Cir. 2022); Wallace v. Town of Grand Island, 126 N.Y.S.3d 270 (N.Y. App. Div. 4 Dep't 2020).

See generally Allyson E. Gold, *Community Consequences of Airbnb,* 94 WASH. L. REV. 1577 (2019); Marvin J. Nodiff, *Short-Term Rentals: Can Cities Get in Bed with Airbnb?,* 51 URB. LAW. 225 (2021); Dayne Lee, Note, *How*

visitors led to increased local government regulation of this use of property in residential areas.[261] Any ambiguity as to whether earlier restrictions on the location and use of "tourist homes," "boarding houses," and similar uses also apply to short-term rentals of residential properties is resolved in favor of the free use of property.[262]

In *Schroeder v. City of Wilmington*, the court addressed a regulatory program for short-term rentals of residential property.[263] The court held that G.S. 160D-1207(c) preempted the registration requirements of the regulation but not the authority to require zoning permits.[264] The court also held that this statute's permitting restriction does not apply to zoning permits or development approvals other than those for building- and housing-code enforcement. However, this provision's prohibition on requirements to "enroll" in a government program as a condition of receiving a certificate of occupancy does preclude local registration requirements for short-term rentals. As a result, the court upheld the city's regulatory provisions that restricted whole-house short-term rentals to specified zoning districts, as well as those that set parking requirements, limits on the use of properties for large gatherings, mandatory insurance, and other operational requirements. The court held that the cap on the number of short-term rentals that could be approved, the requirement for a minimum separation between short-term-rental proper-

Airbnb Short-Term Rentals Exacerbate Los Angeles's Affordable Housing Crisis: Analysis and Policy Recommendations, 10 Harv. L. & Pol'y Rev. 229 (2016); Grant Wills, *To Be or Not to Airbnb: Regulation of Short-Term Rentals in South Carolina*, 68 S.C. L. Rev. 82 (2017).

261. In North Carolina, regulations on short-term rental of residential properties were initially adopted by Asheville, Blowing Rock, Brevard, Cornelius, and Wilmington. In S.L. 2014-91, the General Assembly explicitly allowed Cornelius to use zoning to regulate the location of vacation rentals and other transient occupancy. A number of other local governments have used the general-zoning authorization to do so. For example, the Asheville UDO provides, "*Short-term vacation rental* means a dwelling unit with up to six guest rooms that is used and/or advertised through an online platform, or other media, for transient occupancy for a period of less than one month. A short-term vacation rental is considered a 'Lodging' use under this UDO." Asheville Code of Ordinances, § 7-2-5 (2019). For more on regulation of short-term rentals, see Rebecca L. Badgett & Christopher B. McLaughlin, Regulation and Taxation of Short-Term Rentals (UNC School of Government, 2019); Thomas S. Walker, Comment, *Searching for the Right Approach: Regulating Short-Term Rentals in North Carolina*, 96 N.C. L. Rev. 1821 (2018).

The court in *Nekrilov v. City of Jersey City*, 45 F.4th 662 (3d Cir. 2022), rejected claims that limits on short-term rentals violated federal constitutional requirements regarding the Takings, Due Process, or Contract clauses. The court in *HomeAway, Inc. v. City of Santa Monica*, 918 F.3d 676 (9th Cir. 2019), rejected a First Amendment challenge.

262. Frazier v. Town of Blowing Rock, ___ N.C. App. ___, 882 S.E.2d 91 (2022). Prior to 2020, the town's zoning regulation limited "tourist homes and other temporary residences renting by the day or week" to nonresidential zoning districts. In 2019 and 2020, the regulations were amended to define "short-term rental of a dwelling unit" and to allow these only in a short-term-rental overlay district. The court held that because prior to 2020 the regulations were ambiguous as to whether the restrictions on the location of tourist homes included short-term rentals, the ambiguity must be resolved in favor of the free use of property. Since the notice of violation was for a "short-term rental" use and not for a tourist home or temporary residence "renting by the day or week," the question of whether the use violated the pre-2020 regulations was not before the board of adjustment and thus could not be considered by the court.

263. 282 N.C. App. 558, 872 S.E.2d 58 (2022). The program required annual registration of properties to be offered for rent, limited their location to certain zoning districts, set various operational requirements, required a 400-foot setback from other short-term rentals, capped the overall number of short-term rentals to 2 percent of the city's residential parcels, and had a lottery system to allocate permits.

264. G.S. 160D-1207(a) authorizes periodic inspection of residential building for "unsafe, unsanitary, or otherwise hazardous or unlawful conditions." G.S. 160D-1207(c) prohibits local governments from requiring a permit under the building or housing code in order to rent residential real property absent a history of violations. For more on the periodic inspection statute, see C. Tyler Mulligan, *Residential Rental Property Inspections, Permits, and Registration: Changes for 2017*, Cmty. and Econ. Dev. Bull. No. 9 (UNC School of Government, March 2017).

ties, and the amortization requirements for nonconforming short-term rentals were so intertwined with the invalid registration requirement in this particular regulatory scheme that they were preempted.[265]

Solar Collectors

Cities and counties may not prohibit solar collectors on residences.[266] This law applies to solar collectors used for water heating, active space heating, passive heating, or electricity generation.

Ordinances may regulate the location or screening of solar collectors and may prohibit collectors that are visible from the ground if they are on the façade facing an area open to common or public access, on the roof facing down toward such an area, or are located within the area between those façades and the public area.

G.S. 22B-20 similarly restricts the use of deed restrictions and private restrictive covenants that would limit use of solar collectors.[267]

These statutes address the use of solar collectors as appurtenances or accessory uses for residences. They are not applicable where the solar collector is the primary use of the property, as with large-scale commercial solar collection arrays.[268]

Tall Structures

G.S. 143-151.70 to .77, created by the Military Lands Protection Act of 2013,[269] applies to specified major military installations, including Fort Bragg, Pope Army Airfield, Seymour Johnson Air Force Base, the Dare County Bombing Range, Camp Lejune (including New River and Cherry Point), the Elizabeth City

---

265. Separation requirements are common in zoning regulations. They are frequently applied in regulation of family care and group homes, adult businesses, places serving alcohol, and certain industrial uses. Separation requirements that do not require a registration program are presumably not preempted.

266. S.L. 2007-279. These provisions are codified at G.S. 160D-914. S.L. 2009-553 amended these statutes to extend the protection to all residential uses, not just single-family detached homes. The provision on deed restrictions is codified as G.S. 23B-20. Unlike most statutes affecting governmental land use restrictions, this statute allows a court to award costs and attorney's fees to the prevailing party in civil actions arising under these provisions. S.L. 2009-427 amends the Carrboro town charter to allow the town to prohibit private restrictive covenants that forbid conservation measures (such as clotheslines). Also see G.S. 160D-704, which authorizes cities and counties to provide density bonuses and other incentives in development regulations for developments that conserve energy. These statutes do not distinguish between traditional roof-mounted systems and freestanding solar collectors (which may be pole mounted or ground mounted) that are accessory to a residence. The issue of protection of solar access has also been addressed by several states. Troy A. Rule, *Shadows on the Cathedral: Solar Access Laws in a Different Light*, 2010 U. ILL. L. REV. 851, 874–80 (2010).

267. In *Belmont Association v. Farwig*, 381 N.C. 306, 873 S.E.2d 486 (2022), the defendants placed solar collectors on a south-facing roof that was visible from a public area. Although the applicable covenants did not expressly address solar collectors, the plaintiff's architectural review board denied approval on aesthetic grounds. The court held that G.S. 22B-20(b), which voids covenants prohibiting or having the effect of prohibiting solar collectors, was applicable. The court held that the exception to this prohibition in G.S. 22B-20(d) was not applicable because that exemption only applies to a restriction that prohibits solar collectors visible to a public area, as opposed to this restriction that had the effect of prohibiting them without expressly doing so.

268. In a 2012 School survey, only 8 percent of responding cities and counties indicated they had development regulations for commercial-scale solar facilities; only 6 percent had regulations on residential-scale solar facilities. The responses were similar regarding adoption of regulations for wind energy facilities. David W. Owens & Dayne Batten, *2012 Zoning Survey Report: Zoning Adoption, Administration, and Provisions for Design Standards and Alternative Energy Facilities*, PLAN. & ZONING L. BULL. No. 20 (UNC School of Government, July 2012), at 25. The number of local governments with these regulations later increased, given the subsequent emergence of cost-effective alternative-energy facilities and the popularity of their use in both commercial and residential settings.

269. S.L. 2013-206.

Coast Guard base, the ocean terminal at Sunny Point, the Naval Support Activity Northwest Annex (on the Virginia–North Carolina border at Chesapeake), and the radar facilities at Fort Fisher. Associated support facilities for these installations that are located in the state are also covered.

The law prohibits cities and counties from authorizing (and persons from constructing) tall structures (those over 200 feet tall) within five miles of these military bases unless the State Construction Office[270] has issued a letter of endorsement for the structure. Cities and counties may not authorize extension of electricity, telephone, water, sewer, septic, or gas utilities to any unapproved tall structure.

Those proposing a tall structure must submit a notice of intent to seek an endorsement to the affected base commander and must provide that notice and a Determination of No Hazard to Air Navigation from the Federal Aviation Administration to the Building Code Council. The council submits the application to the base for a review period of up to forty-five days and is to deny endorsement if the base determines the proposed structure would interfere with the mission, training, or operation of the military installation or if no Federal Aviation Administration determination is provided. The council is to act on the application within ninety days. Prior existing tall buildings may not be reconstructed, altered, or expanded in ways that would aggravate or intensify a violation of these requirements. Civil penalties of up to $5000 are authorized for violations.

Temporary Health-Care Structures

In 2014, the General Assembly enacted G.S. 160D-915 to mandate preferential zoning treatment for temporary health-care structures.[271] Cities and counties are required to allow qualifying structures as permitted accessory uses in all single-family residential zoning districts on any lot that allows a single-family detached home.

The statute requires that these structures be assembled off-site and temporarily located to facilitate on-site care for an impaired person. The facility cannot be more than 300 square feet in size[272] and may not be placed on a permanent foundation. Only one such structure can be located on a single lot, and it must meet all zoning setback requirements that apply to the primary structure on the lot. The caregiver must be a relative who lives on the site. If a structure qualifies, it must be permitted by right; no special use permit may be required.

Tobacco Establishments

G.S. 130A-496 prohibits smoking in enclosed areas of bars and restaurants and the common areas of lodging establishments.[273] The state interprets hookahs to be the same as pipe smoking, so a hookah bar or lounge is not permissible in an enclosed area if the establishment also sells food or alcohol.

While not a land use regulation, the statute granting local governments the authority to regulate smoking in public places has land use implications. G.S. 130A-498(b1) provides that a local government may not prohibit smoking in a tobacco shop, cigar bar,[274] or nonprofit private club if smoke from the

---

270. The review was originally assigned to the Building Code Council. The shift to the State Construction Office was made by S.L. 2014-79.

271. S.L. 2014-94. The law was modeled after a Virginia statute enacted in 2010. The local government may require an annual permit with verification that care is being provided to a person with a disability. The facility must be removed within sixty days of the time the impaired person is no longer receiving or is in need of assistance.

272. The facility must meet construction standards set by the State Building Code for modular housing. However, it is treated as tangible personal property for tax purposes.

273. Created by S.L. 2009-27, effective January 2, 2010.

274. G.S. 130A-492(2) defines a "cigar bar" and requires that it prohibit entry to persons under the age of twenty-one.

business does not migrate into an area where smoking is prohibited. For tobacco shops and cigar bars that began operation after July 1, 2009, smoking is allowed only if it is located in a freestanding structure occupied solely by that business.

Utility-Transmission Lines

In 1991, the General Assembly enacted G.S. 62-106 to allow state preemption of zoning regulations that affect large utility-transmission lines (those carrying 161 kilovolts or higher) on a case-by-case basis.[275] This statute directs a municipality or county to file with the Utilities Commission, within thirty days of its receipt of a notice of application for state approval of a transmission line, any local zoning provisions that affect the construction, operation, or maintenance of such lines. If the filing is not made, the zoning provision may not be enforced. The applicant may petition the Utilities Commission for an order preempting the ordinance, which may be granted if the commission determines that the greater public interest requires such.

In *State ex rel. Utilities Commission v. Town of Kill Devil Hills*,[276] the court rejected a contention that G.S. 62-106 divested the Utilities Commission of jurisdiction to hear disputes on the location of smaller transmission lines. The court held that there was no requirement for the utility company Dominion Power to seek a variance or other administrative relief from the town in order to construct a second transmission line, as the Utilities Commission was specifically empowered to order expansion or improvements in electrical-distribution services. As the commission found there was insufficient space in the existing utility corridor for a second line, and that an underground line or alternative route would be excessively costly, the commission had the authority to order use of the second proposed corridor, and such an order preempted local government ordinances to the contrary.

Video Poker and Electronic Gaming

Legislation prohibits location of any video poker machines in North Carolina. The ban was originally adopted in 2006[277] and expanded in 2010[278] to include video-sweepstakes and similar machines. There is an exception for machines located on tribal lands and operated under a tribal-state compact. Prior

---

275. S.L. 1991-189. The statute is codified at G.S. 62-100 to -107. Also see the Federal Power Act, 16 U.S.C. § 824, on federal permitting authority for siting power lines in congested corridors. For an analysis of the land use impacts of utility-line siting, see David R. Bolton & Kent A. Sick, *Power Lines and Property Values: The Good, the Bad, and the Ugly*, 13 URB. LAW. 331 (1999).

276. 194 N.C. App. 561, 670 S.E.2d 341, *aff'd per curiam*, 363 N.C. 739, 686 S.E.2d 151 (2009). Dominion Power owned a 115-kilovolt transmission line running along the west side (sound side) of the town. The company proposed adding a second 115-kilovolt transmission line to run in a new corridor along the main highway through the town, located on the east side of town. The town adopted an ordinance requiring aboveground transmission lines to be built in a single corridor. Dominion filed a complaint with the state Utilities Commission, seeking to preempt the ordinance and allow use of the second corridor. The commission issued an order pursuant to G.S. 62-42 directing Dominion to complete its improvements in the second corridor. The town objected, contending that since G.S. 62-106 preempts local ordinances regarding siting of transmission lines of 161 kilovolts or higher, there was by negative inference no preemption of local ordinances affecting smaller transmission lines.

277. S.L. 2006-6. The legislation gradually phased out permissible video poker machines, with all to be removed by July 1, 2007.

278. S.L. 2010-103. The law created G.S. 14-306.4 to prohibit use of electronic machines and devices for playing sweepstake games (defined as any game you enter and for which you become eligible to receive a prize). The ban includes any use of electronic machines for real or simulated video poker (and any other card game), bingo, craps, keno, lotto, pot-of-gold, eight liner, and similar games. The court in *IMT, Inc. v. City of Lumberton*, 366 N.C. 456, 738 S.E.2d 156 (2013), invalidated a local privilege-license tax on Internet-sweepstakes operators, finding an annual

to 2006, G.S. 14-306.1[279] imposed substantial state regulations on the location and operation of video poker machines.

In *Hest Technologies, Inc. v. State ex rel. Perdue*[280] the court upheld G.S. 14-306.1 as a valid regulation of conduct (not of speech), though subsequent attempts to enforce the ban have been challenging in light of the industry's continuing adjustments to the technology employed in the gaming.[281] As a result, many zoning regulations specifically regulate the location of businesses with multiple electronic-gaming stations. They are typically restricted to specified commercial zoning districts and often have separation requirements from other sensitive land uses, much like the regulations for adult businesses.

fee of $5000 per business plus $2500 per gaming machine was in effect a tax that was a violation of the just-and-equitable-taxation requirement of article V of the North Carolina constitution.

279. The video-gaming restrictions were initially created by S.L. 2000-151. The law was enacted after South Carolina outlawed video-poker gambling effective July 1, 2000, prompting concern that this might result in an influx of video-gaming machines to North Carolina. Among the regulations imposed prior to the total ban were requirements that only machines lawfully in operation and listed for taxes in the state in 2001 could be used and that any location with machines had to be at least 300 feet from another location containing machines. There were also restrictions on the age of players, hours of operation, placement of machines, and advertising. This statute specified that it did not preempt more restrictive local ordinances. Several local governments have imposed restrictions similar to those for location of adult uses on establishments with video poker machines.

280. 366 N.C. 289, 749 S.E.2d 429 (2012).

281. *See, e.g.,* Gift Surplus, LLC v. North Carolina, 380 N.C. 1, 868 S.E.2d 20 (2022) (distinguishing prohibited games conducted through the use of an entertaining display from permissible games dependent on skill or dexterity).

CHAPTER 23

Federal Statutory Limitations on Land Use Regulatory Discretion

Local ordinances and state statutes that are contrary to federal law are invalid under the Supremacy Clause of the United States Constitution. A federal statute can expressly state that it preempts local or state regulation.[1] The courts may also imply a federal preemption when the federal regulatory scheme so thoroughly occupies a field as to leave no room for supplemental state or local regulation[2] or when there is an actual conflict between federal law and local action.[3] In most instances, the fact that the federal government also regulates some aspect of an activity does not preempt local land-development regulations.[4] However, there are several notable fields where federal legislation specifically limits local regulatory action.

Also, federal civil-rights statutes provide a general ground for challenge to land use regulations alleged to deprive a person of constitutional rights. Section 1983 of the Federal Civil Rights Act of 1871[5] prohibits a person from, under color of law, depriving someone of any rights, privileges, or immunities secured by the Constitution.[6] Federal law also allows a successful party in these actions to recover attorney's and expert's fees.[7]

However, federal courts generally abstain from resolving most substantive land use–law questions. The United States Supreme Court held in *Burford v. Sun Oil Co.* that federal courts should abstain when a case presents difficult questions of state law bearing on policy problems or substantial public interest or when federal judicial intervention would be disruptive of state efforts to establish a coherent policy

---

1. *See, e.g.*, Hillsborough Cnty. v. Automated Med. Labs, Inc., 471 U.S. 707, 713 (1985). *See generally* Ashira Pelman Ostrow, *Preempting Zoning*, 36 J. Land Use & Envtl. L. 91 (2020); Kevin Perron, Note, *"Zoning Out" Climate Change: Local Land Use Power, Fossil Fuel Infrastructure, and the Fight Against Climate Change*, 45 Colum. J. Envtl. L. 573 (2020).

2. *See, e.g.*, Cipollone v. Liggett Grp., Inc., 505 U.S. 504, 516 (1992).

3. *See, e.g.*, City of Burbank v. Lockheed Air Terminal Inc., 411 U.S. 624 (1973) (city curfew on night jet flights preempted). Airport-noise restrictions are also addressed by the Airport Noise and Capacity Act of 1990, 49 U.S.C. §§ 47101–47533. *See* Jeffrey A. Berger, *Phoenix Grounded: The Impact of the Supreme Court's Changing Preemption Doctrine on State and Local Impediments to Airport Expansion*, 97 Nw. U. L. Rev. 941 (2003).

4. *See, e.g.*, S. Blasting Servs., Inc. v. Wilkes Cnty., 288 F.3d 584, 590–93 (4th Cir. 2002). The court held that Wilkes County ordinances requiring a county permit to possess, store, sell, transport, or use explosives in the county were not preempted by federal law. The federal statute, 18 U.S.C. § 848, expressly provided that the law was not intended to fully occupy the field and that more stringent local requirements did not constitute a direct and positive conflict with the federal law.

5. 42 U.S.C. § 1983.

6. Municipalities may be sued under this statute. Owen v. City of Independence, 445 U.S. 622 (1980); Monell v. Dep't of Soc. Servs., 436 U.S. 658 (1978). An allegation that a municipality hired a staff member that a citizen alleges had personal animosity toward him does not constitute municipal ratification of an alleged deprivation of constitutional rights. Orndorff v. Raley, No. 3:17-CV-00618-GCM, 2018 WL 50406090 (W.D.N.C. Oct. 17, 2018) (involving a longstanding dispute over various zoning issues between a real-estate developer and a planner for the Village of Marvin).

7. 42 U.S.C. §§ 1988(b), (c).

in these matters.[8] Federal courts may also abstain from resolving matters where such matters may be mooted by resolution in state court,[9] where there are concurrent enforcement actions underway in state court,[10] or where a losing party in state court claims the judgment violates the loser's federal rights.[11]

Federal courts are particularly deferential to state courts on questions of land use law.[12] For example, in *MLC Automotive, LLC v. Town of Southern Pines*,[13] the court held it was appropriate to stay a federal action for damages due to alleged constitutional violations pending state-court resolution of the underlying vested-rights question. Likewise, in *FC Summers Walk, LLC v. Town of Davidson*,[14] the court concluded that while state law was relatively settled regarding school impact fees, state law on adequate-public-facility requirements for public-safety and parks requirements was important and unsettled; it

---

8. 319 U.S. 315 (1943). *See also* New Orleans Pub. Serv., Inc. v. Council of New Orleans, 491 U.S. 350 (1989); Colo. River Water Conservation Dist. v. United States, 424 U.S. 800 (1976). Following this rule, federal courts have generally deferred to state-court action in all but particularly egregious violations of constitutional rights. *See, e.g.,* Front Royal & Warren Cnty. Indus. Park Corp. v. Town of Front Royal, 135 F.3d 275, 288–89 (4th Cir. 1998); Licari v. Ferruzzi, 22 F.3d 344, 349–50 (1st Cir. 1994) (only violations that shock the conscience are actionable in federal forum). However, if the unsettled area of state law is conclusively resolved while the federal case is pending, *Burford* abstention is no longer appropriate. Town of Nags Head v. Toloczko, 728 F.3d 391 (4th Cir. 2013) (state court ruled that municipalities had no public-trust-area-enforcement authority while case was on appeal). On remand the court held that the takings claim raised genuine issues of material fact regarding application of a Penn Central analysis, and thus the case was not ripe for summary judgment. Town of Nags Head v. Toloczko, No. 2:11-CV-1-D, 2014 WL 4219516 (E.D.N.C. 2014). *See also* Currituck County v. LeTendre, 2020 WL 707179 (No. 2-19-CV-27-BO, E.D.N.C., Feb. 12, 2020) (since difficult or disputed questions of state law were not raised in this enforcement action involving a disputed oceanfront structure, *Burford* abstention not appropriate).

9. R.R. Comm'n of Tex. v. Pullman Co., 312 U.S. 496 (1941). In *Mt. Airy Business Center, Inc. v. City of Kannapolis*, No. 10CV307, 2014 WL 229564 (Jan. 21, 2014), *adopted by* No. 1:10CV307, 2014 WL 975516 (M.D.N.C. Mar. 12, 2014), a challenge to the city's zoning regulation of an Internet-sweepstakes business, the court refused to apply abstention under either *Pullman* or *Burford* as any unsettled areas of state criminal law regarding these businesses did not affect the zoning regulation, and the possibility of future state-legislative action did not make this a matter of state law.

10. Younger v. Harris, 401 U.S. 37 (1971); General Auto Serv. Station LLC v. City of Chi., 319 F.3d 902 (7th Cir. 2003) (appeal of citation for violation of sign ordinance pending in state court). *See also* Mangum v. Town of Wrightsville Beach, 2019 WL 6190648 (No. 7:19-CV-29-FL, E.D.N.C., Nov. 20, 2019), *reconsideration denied*, 2020 WL 4938332 (Aug. 24, 2020), *appeal dismissed*, 2021 WL 672650 (4th Cir. Feb. 22, 2021) (dismissing federal-law claims as barred by res judicata since there was a final judgment on these same issues with the same parties in a state-court enforcement action).

11. Rooker v. Fidelity Trust Co., 263 U.S. 413 (1923); D.C. Court of Appeals v. Feldman, 460 U.S. 462, 482 (1983). The *Rooker-Feldman* doctrine is discussed and applied in *Combs v. Ashe County*, No. 5:14-CV-136, 2016 WL 3625551 (W.D.N.C. July 6, 2016), a pro se appeal regarding enforcement of the county's junkyard ordinance. *See also* May v. Morgan Cnty., 878 F.3d 1001 (11th Cir. 2017) (applying doctrine to bar federal suit challenging short-term-rental zoning regulations).

12. *See, e.g.,* MacDonald v. Vill. of Northport, 164 F.3d 964 (6th Cir. 1999); River Park, Inc. v. City of Highland Park, 23 F.3d 164, 165–67 (7th Cir. 1994) (federal courts are not zoning boards of appeals and most cases should be heard in state courts); Pomponio v. Fauquier Cnty. Bd. of Supervisors, 21 F.3d 1319, 1325 (4th Cir. 1994), *overruled in part on other grounds by* Quackenbush v. Allstate Ins., 517 U.S. 706 (1996) (interpretation of zoning and land use laws are particularly the province of state courts); Caleb Stowe Assocs., Ltd. v. Cnty. of Albemarle, 724 F.2d 1079 (4th Cir. 1984) (interpretation of scope of authority of planning bodies is a proper question of state law); Fralin & Waldron, Inc. v. City of Martinsville, 493 F.2d 481 (4th Cir. 1974) (deferring matter involving special use permits to state courts); Virdis Dev. Corp. v. Board of Supervisors, 92 F. Supp. 3d 418, 424 (E.D. Va. 2015) (virtually all zoning cases warrant *Burford* abstention); Templeton Props., LP v. Town of Boone, No. 5:07CV62-V, 2008 WL 583900 (W.D.N.C. Mar. 3, 2008) (remanding zoning case to state court); Fourth Quarter Props. IV, Inc. v. City of Concord, No. 1:02CV00908, 2004 WL 231303 (M.D.N.C. Jan. 22, 2004), *aff'd*, 127 F. App'x 648 (4th Cir. 2005) (staying federal claim pending resolution of state adjudication of claim based on alleged misapplication of zoning restrictions in airport buffer).

13. 532 F.3d 269 (4th Cir. 2008).

14. No. 3:09-CV-266-GCM, 2010 WL 4366287 (W.D.N.C. Oct. 28, 2010).

therefore held that *Burford* abstention was appropriate. Abstention, however, does not preclude a federal court from dismissing a case when there is no basis for a federal claim[15] or from deciding a case where there is a clear resolution of underlying state land use law.[16]

Increasingly, there are areas of land-development regulation where federal statutes impinge upon local discretion.[17] In addition to the statutes on fair housing, telecommunications, outdoor advertising, and junkyards discussed in this chapter, federal statutes also address religious land uses,[18] wetlands and water-quality protection,[19] and protection of endangered species' habitats;[20] they also provide incentives for action in a variety of other areas (such as coordination of land use and transportation planning).

Fair Housing

While constitutional challenges to alleged discriminatory housing practices are rarely successful,[21] plaintiffs have the additional option of basing such challenges on federal statutory protections against unlawful discrimination.[22]

---

15. *See, e.g.*, Gardner v. City of Balt. Mayor, 969 F.2d 63 (4th Cir. 1992).

16. *See, e.g.*, Ogden Fire Co. No. 1 v. Upper Chichester Twp., 504 F.3d 370 (3d Cir. 2007) (state subdivision law clear, and critical issue involved federal telecommunication law); Int'l Coll. of Surgeons v. City of Chi., 153 F.3d 356 (7th Cir. 1998) (abstention not applicable where state law on landmarks law and takings well settled and clear); Griffin v. Town of Unionville, No. 3:05-cv-514-RJC, 2008 WL 697634 (W.D.N.C. Mar. 11, 2008) (finding no vested right to expand a permitted landfill).

17. For a general discussion of federal programs affecting land-development regulations, see Peter A. Buchsbaum, *Federal Regulation of Land Use: Uncle Sam the Permit Man*, 25 Urb. Law. 589 (1993).

18. See the discussion of the Religious Land Use and Institutionalized Persons Act in Chapter 27.

19. See Chapter 10.

20. 16 U.S.C. §§ 1531–1544.

21. In *Village of Arlington Heights v. Metropolitan Housing Development Corp.*, 429 U.S. 252 (1977), an equal-protection challenge was made to a refusal to rezone a single-family site to multifamily use in order to allow a low-income-housing project. The U.S. Supreme Court held that proof of a racially discriminatory intent was necessary. A showing of disproportionate impact on minorities alone is insufficient. *See also* Cuyahoga Falls v. Buckeye Cmty. Hope Found., 538 U.S. 188 (2003). See Chapter 25 for further discussion of equal-protection issues.

Standing issues relative to those who would challenge alleged discriminatory effects of zoning are also a significant barrier to litigation on this issue. *See* Warth v. Seldin, 422 U.S. 490 (1975) (denying standing to those challenging alleged discrimination by Rochester, New York, suburb); NAACP v. City of Kyle, 626 F.3d 233 (5th Cir. 2010) (denying standing to NAACP and builders' association challenging a new requirement for masonry exteriors and an increase in minimum lot and home sizes).

22. For an overview of these issues, see David L. Callies & Derek B. Simon, *Fair Housing, Discrimination, and Inclusionary Zoning in the United States*, 49 Urb. Law. 687 (2017). See Chapter 9 for additional discussion of exclusionary and inclusionary zoning.

The Fair Housing Act[23] makes it unlawful to make a dwelling[24] unavailable to a person because of race, color, national origin, religion,[25] sex,[26] familial status, or disability.[27] The definition does not cover persons with either current illegal use of or addiction to a controlled substance, persons convicted of crimes involving the manufacture or sale of illegal drugs, or those who constitute a direct threat to the health or safety of others. Recovering substance-abuse patients are covered.[28] Persons associated or residing with individuals with defined disabilities are also covered.

Unlike with constitutional claims, a prima facie case for a statutory violation is established by showing that a policy or practice of a local government has a disparate impact on a protected class.[29] To establish

---

23. 42 U.S.C. §§ 3601–3631. As enacted in 1968, this act addressed discrimination on the basis of race, color, religion, and national origin. Sex discrimination was added in 1974. Family-status and disability discrimination were added in 1988. Also, 42 U.S.C. § 3610(g)(2)(c) provides for HUD referral to the Attorney General proceedings involving the legality of land use regulatory ordinances. *Metropolitan Housing & Development Corp. v. Village of Arlington Heights* on remand set the factors used to determine if there is actionable racial discrimination. 558 F.2d 1283 (7th Cir. 1977). *See also* Mhany Mgmt., Inc. v. Cnty. of Nassau, 819 F.3d 581 (2d Cir. 2016); Ave. 6E Invs. v. City of Yuma, 818 F.3d 493 (9th Cir. 2016); United States v. City of Black Jack, 508 F.2d 1179 (8th Cir. 1974). Also see *Parvati Corp. v. City of Oak Forest*, 709 F.3d 678 (7th Cir. 2013), where the plaintiff alleged that racial discrimination motivated a refusal to rezone property to allow conversion of a motel to a retirement facility that would largely serve African Americans. The court found no evidence of a racial basis for the decision.

24. Courts are divided as to whether a facility that only provides transient or short-term housing is a "dwelling" under this law. Intermountain Fair Hous. Council v. Boise Rescue Mission Ministries, 655 F. Supp. 2d 1150 (D. Idaho 2009) (homeless shelter not a dwelling); Woods v. Foster, 884 F. Supp. 1169, 1173–74 (N.D. Ill. 1995) (homeless shelter covered); Johnson v. Dixon, 785 F. Supp. 1, 4 (D.D.C. 1991) (doubtful that emergency overnight shelter qualifies). The term has been held not to include jails and facilities for transient guests, such as hotels, motels, or bed-and-breakfast facilities. Group homes offering treatment services are generally considered included. *See, e.g.*, Schwarz v. City of Treasure Island, 544 F.3d 1201, 1214 (11th Cir. 2008); Lakeside Resort Enters. v. Bd. of Supervisors of Palmyra Twp., 455 F.3d 154, 160 (3d Cir. 2006).

25. *See, e.g.*, LeBlanc-Sternberg v. Fletcher, 67 F.3d 412 (2d Cir. 1995) (zoning limitation on use of home for religious services).

26. *See, e.g.*, Doe v. City of Butler, 892 F.2d 3315 (3d Cir. 1989) (alleging discrimination involving group home for abused women).

27. In the Fair Housing Act, the term *handicap* is used (in contrast with many federal statutes, which favor *disability*) and is defined to include persons with physical or mental impairments that substantially limit one or more major life activities. 42 U.S.C. § 3602(h)(1). For a discussion of extension of these laws in a broader context, see William H. Grogan, *The Tension Between Local Zoning and the Development of Elderly Housing: Analyzing the Use of the Fair Housing Act and the Americans with Disabilities Act to Override Zoning Decisions*, 33 Suffolk U. L. Rev. 317 (2000).

28. Elliott v. City of Athens, 960 F.2d 975 (11th Cir. 1992); United States v. S. Mgmt. Corp., 955 F.2d 914, 923 (4th Cir. 1992); St. Paul Sober Living, LLC v. Bd. of Cnty. Comm'rs, 896 F. Supp. 2d 982 (D. Colo. 2012); McKivitz v. Twp. of Stowe, 769 F. Supp. 2d 803 (W.D. Pa. 2010); Jeffrey O. v. City of Boca Raton, 511 F. Supp. 2d 1339 (S.D. Fla. 2007). When reviewing a claim regarding a proposed facility, the court reviews the criteria for admission to the facility to determine whether there will be qualifying residents with disabilities. *McKivitz*, 769 F. Supp. 2d at 822. For example, a proposed multifamily facility for homeless veterans was held not to qualify because admission was not limited to those with post-traumatic stress disorder or some other disability. Yates Real Estate, Inc. v. Plainfield Zoning Bd. of Adjustment, 404 F. Supp. 3d 889, 924–25 (D.N.J. 2019). *See also* Bragdon v. Abbott, 524 U.S. 624 (1998) (HIV-positive person covered under comparable definition). *See generally* Brian J. Connolly & Dwight H. Merriam, *Planning and Zoning for Group Homes: Local Government Obligations and Liability Under the Fair Housing Amendments Act*, 47 Urb. Law. 225 (2015); Daniel Lauber, *A Real LULU: Zoning for Group Homes and Halfway Houses Under the Fair Housing Amendments Act of 1988*, 29 J. Marshall L. Rev. 369 (1996).

29. Proof of disparate impact is sufficient; there is no need to show a deliberate intent to discriminate. *See, e.g.*, Tex. Dep't of Hous. and Cmty. Affairs v. The Inclusive Cmtys. Project, Inc., 576 U.S. 519, 524 (2015); Reyes v. Waples Mobile Home Park Ltd. P'ship, 903 F.3d 415, 421 (4th Cir. 2018); Simms v. First Gibraltar Bank, 83 F.3d 1546 (5th Cir. 1996); Mountain Side Mobile Estates P'ship v. Secretary of Hous. & Urban Dev., 56 F.3d 1243 (10th Cir. 1995); Jackson v. Okaloosa Cnty., 21 F.3d 1531 (11th Cir. 1994); Keith v. Volpe, 858 F.2d 467 (9th Cir. 1988); Huntington Branch, NAACP v. Town of Huntington, 844 F.2d 926 (2d Cir. 1988); Betsey v. Turtle Creek Assocs., 736 F.2d 983 (4th Cir. 1984); Smith v. Town of Clarkton, 682 F.2d 1055, 1065 (4th Cir. 1972); 5-Star Athlete Development, LLC v.

a disparate-impact claim, a plaintiff must first demonstrate a causal connection between the defendant's policy and the disparate impact on a protected class. The defendant then has the burden of showing the valid interest served by the policy. If that is done, the plaintiff then has the burden of showing the defendant's interests could be served by another practice with a less discriminatory effect.

Reasonable Accommodation

Prohibited discrimination includes failure to make reasonable accommodation in rules and policies when such is necessary to afford a protected person equal opportunity to use and enjoy a dwelling.[30] The burden of establishing both the necessity and the reasonableness of the accommodation is on the plaintiff.[31] In order to be "reasonable," the accommodation must be both efficacious and proportional to its implementation cost. The determination of what is reasonable is usually a fact-specific inquiry for each claim.[32] Also, as a general rule, the plaintiff must present the information supporting the need for and reasonableness of the accommodation to the local government, not on appeal to the courts.[33]

When discrimination is alleged, a local government generally must be provided an opportunity to make a reasonable accommodation. In *United States v. Village of Palatine*, the zoning regulation at issue required a special use permit if more than three unrelated individuals were to reside in a home. Oxford House, a facility for persons recovering from substance abuse, refused to apply for a permit, contending that the public notice and hearing associated with the permit would unfairly stigmatize the facility. The court held that a claim of failure to make a reasonable accommodation was not legitimate if a permit application was never submitted and that a blanket exemption from permit requirements

---

City of Shelby, No. 1:21-CV-323-MR-WCM, 2022 WL 4287921 (W.D.N.C. May 26, 2022) (dismissing claim due to failure to allege disparate impact or disparate treatment). If a disparate-treatment claim is made, a discriminatory intent or motive must be shown.

Federal executive actions also address potential disparate impacts of federal decisions on low-income and minority neighborhoods. *See, e.g.*, Exec. Order No. 12,898, 59 Fed. Reg. 7,629 (Feb. 11, 1994), addressing environmental-justice issues. *See also* City of Cleburne v. Cleburne Living Ctr., Inc., 473 U.S. 432 (1985) (invalidating denial of special use permit for group home for the mentally disabled where ordinance did not require permit for similar group housing).

30. Fair Housing Act, 42 U.S.C. § 3604(f)(3). For additional analysis, see Robert L. Schonfeld, *"Reasonable Accommodation" Under the Federal Fair Housing Amendments Act*, 25 FORDHAM URB. L.J. 413 (1998). A reasonable-accommodation claim may be brought by the entity claiming discrimination or by the federal government. *See, e.g.*, United States v. Town of Garner, 720 F. Supp. 2d 721 (E.D.N.C. 2010) (action brought by federal government alleging failure to make reasonable accommodation for group home operated by Oxford House, with the group subsequently intervening).

31. Bryant Woods Inn, Inc. v. Howard Cnty., 124 F.3d 597, 603–04 (4th Cir. 1997). *See also* Loren v. Sasser, 309 F.3d 1296, 1302 (11th Cir. 2002); Groner v. Golden Gate Gardens Apartments, 250 F.3d 1039, 1045 (6th Cir. 2001); Elderhaven, Inc. v. City of Lubbock, 98 F.3d 175, 178 (5th Cir. 1996). *But see* Lapid-Laurel, LLC v. Zoning Bd. of Adjustment, 284 F.3d 442, 458 (3d Cir. 2002) (once plaintiff meets burden of establishing necessity, burden shifts to government to show proposed accommodation is not reasonable).

32. Since the determination is fact specific, summary judgment is usually inappropriate. *See, e.g.*, Anderson v. City of Blue Ash, 798 F.3d 338 (6th Cir. 2015) (need detailed facts to determine whether allowing miniature horse as service animal for disabled minor child would be reasonable).

33. *See, e.g.*, Yates, 404 F. Supp. 3d at 912–13.

is not reasonable.[34] However, a special permit or variance application is not required if such would be "manifestly futile."[35]

The general rule for a zoning variance is that it must be related to conditions on the property, not the personal circumstances of the occupant of the property.[36] Chapter 160D, Section 705(c) of the North Carolina General Statutes (hereinafter G.S.) creates an exception to this general rule by authorizing the issuance of a variance upon a finding that the variance is "necessary and appropriate" in order to make a reasonable accommodation under the Federal Fair Housing Act.[37] Some local development regulations also include a specific provision setting a process for a person to request that a reasonable accommodation be made.[38]

Accommodations held to be reasonable include conversion of a motel to a shelter[39] and a variance from setback requirements.[40] A total exclusion of all nursing-home facilities from a residential district has been held to be a failure to make reasonable accommodation.[41] The courts have held that when a reasonable accommodation is made, a condition can be imposed to require removal or restoration when the need for the accommodation no longer exists.[42]

There is no requirement to make accommodations that would impose an undue financial or administrative burden on the local government or require a fundamental alteration of nondiscriminatory land use policies.[43]

Reasonable accommodation has been held *not* to include the following: that part of a motel be allowed to be used as a residential treatment facility for teens with emotional or mental disabilities;[44] that multi-family housing be allowed in a single-family zoning district;[45] that "halfway houses" for recovering substance abusers be allowed in a single-family zoning district that does not allow "tourist dwellings" with frequent resident turnover;[46] that a group home be exempted from state sprinkler requirements;[47]

---

34. 37 F.3d 1230 (7th Cir. 1994). "Public input is an important aspect of municipal decision-making; we cannot impose a blanket requirement that cities waive their public notice and hearing requirements in all cases involving the handicapped." *Id.* at 1234. *See also* Tsombanidis v. W. Haven Fire Dep't, 352 F.3d 565, 578–79 (2d Cir. 2003); Oxford House, Inc. v. City of St. Louis, 77 F.3d 249 (8th Cir. 1996); Oxford House, Inc. v. City of Virginia Beach, 825 F. Supp. 1251 (E.D. Va. 1993). *But see* ARC of N.J., Inc. v. New Jersey, 950 F. Supp. 637 (D.N.J. 1996) (invalidating conditional use permit, spacing, and maximum-occupancy requirements).

35. *Id.* at 1234.

36. See Chapter 17 for a discussion of variance standards.

37. This provision was added to the mandatory standards for variances by S.L. 2019-111.

38. *See. e.g.,* Cary, N.C., Land Development Ordinance § 3.25; Winston-Salem/Forsyth County, N.C., Unified Development Ordinance § 6-1.6.

39. Judy B. v. Borough of Tioga, 889 F. Supp. 792 (M.D. Pa. 1995).

40. United States v. City of Phila., 838 F. Supp. 223 (E.D. Pa. 1993), *aff'd*, 30 F.3d 1488 (3d Cir. 1994). The court in *Trovato v. City of Manchester*, 992 F. Supp. 493 (D.N.H. 1997), required allowance of a paved parking area in the front yard as an accommodation under the Americans with Disabilities Act.

41. Hovsons, Inc. v. Twp. of Brick, 89 F.3d 1096 (3d Cir. 1996). *But see* 431 East Palisade Ave. Real Estate, LLC v. City of Englewood, 977 F.3d 277 (3d Cir. 2020) (limiting assisted-living facilities to single zoning district upheld).

42. Austin v. Town of Farmington, 826 F.3d 622 (2d Cir. 2016) (allowing variance to install an aboveground pool as an accessory use for a child with a disability is a reasonable accommodation, but town can also require reasonable restoration when child no longer resides there).

43. Erdman v. City of Fort Atkinson, 84 F.3d 960 (7th Cir. 1996).

44. Cinnamon Hills Youth Crisis Ctr., Inc. v. Saint George City, 685 F.3d 917 (10th Cir. 2012).

45. Brandt v. Vill. of Chebanse, 82 F.3d 172 (7th Cir. 1996). However, refusal to allow a variance for a group home based solely on the residents' disabled status would be a failure to make a reasonable accommodation. Tsombanidis v. W. Haven Fire Dep't, 352 F.3d 565, 580 (2d Cir. 2003).

46. Schwarz v. City of Treasure Island, 544 F.3d 1201 (11th Cir. 2008).

47. Summers v. City of Fitchburg, 940 F.3d 133 (1st Cir. 2019). *See also* Sailboat Bend Sober Living, LLC v. City of Fort Lauderdale, 46 F.4th 1268 (11th Cir. 2022) (not discrimination to refuse to exempt facility from city fire-sprinkler and state fire-prevention code).

that a disabled individual be allowed to place a carport inside a setback area;[48] that zoning density be increased to allow duplexes designed for wheelchair users;[49] or that a large care facility for the elderly be allowed on a site deemed by the town to be too small and to have traffic problems.[50]

Group Homes

The impact of the federal fair-housing law on local regulation of group homes has been a heavily litigated issue.[51] One key issue is the validity of restrictions that limit the number of unrelated[52] individuals who may reside in a single dwelling unit.[53] The U.S. Supreme Court in *City of Edmonds v. Oxford House, Inc.*[54] held that a zoning regulation limiting the number of unrelated individuals living together is not

---

48. Robinson v. City of Friendswood, 890 F. Supp. 616 (S.D. Tex. 1995). *See also* County of Sawyer Zoning Bd. v. State, 605 N.W.2d 627 (Wis. Ct. App. 1999) (refusal to grant variance to shoreland setback not discrimination under the state's fair housing law; Evans v. Zoning Hearing Bd., 732 A.2d 686 (Pa. Commw. 1999) (adding apartment above accessory building not a reasonable accommodation).

49. Hemisphere Bldg. Co. v. Vill. of Richton Park, 171 F.3d 437 (7th Cir. 1999).

50. Lapid-Laurel, LLC v. Zoning Bd. of Adjustment, 284 F.3d 442 (3d Cir. 2002).

51. For additional background on group-home regulation, see Michael J. Davis & Karen L. Gaus, *Protecting Group Homes for the Non-Handicapped: Zoning in the Post-*Edmonds *Era*, 46 Kan. L. Rev. 777 (1998); Lauber, *supra* note 28.

52. Regulation of the number of *related* individuals who live together was invalidated as an undue infringement of a fundamental right in *Moore v. City of East Cleveland*, 431 U.S. 494 (1977). The ordinance challenged in *Moore* used a complicated definition of "family" that largely limited residency in the single-family district to a nuclear family (parents and their children). The plaintiff was charged with a criminal offense because her son and two grandchildren (who were cousins rather than brothers) lived in her home. Since, under the ordinance, any number of unmarried children of whatever age would be allowed to live with parents but even a single brother and sister sharing a residence would be illegal, the Court held the regulation to be arbitrary. The Court also held this to be an unreasonable burden on familial association and, as such, a violation of substantive due process. It noted:

> The tradition of uncles, aunts, cousins, and especially grandparents sharing a household along with parents and children has roots equally venerable and equally deserving of constitutional recognition. Over the years millions of our citizens have grown up in just such an environment, and most, surely, have profited from it. Even if conditions of modern society have brought about a decline in extended family households, they have not erased the accumulated wisdom of civilization, gained over the centuries and honored throughout our history, that supports a larger conception of the family.

Id. at 504–05 (citations omitted). *See also* 42 U.S.C. § 3607(b)(2)(c) (allowing housing to be restricted to persons fifty-five years of age or older).

53. Such limitations are common and generally are enforceable. Vill. of Belle Terre v. Boraas, 416 U.S. 1 (1974) (upholding regulation restricting number of unrelated individuals who may live together). Justice Douglas concluded:

> A quiet place where yards are wide, people few, and motor vehicles restricted are legitimate guidelines in a land-use project addressed to family needs. . . . The police power is not confined to elimination of filth, stench, and unhealthy places. It is ample to lay out zones where family values, youth values, and the blessings of quiet seclusion and clean air make the area a sanctuary for people.

Id. at 9. Some states have found restrictions on the number of unrelated individuals residing together to violate state constitutional provisions. *See* City of Santa Barbara v. Adamson, 610 P.2d 436, 442 (Cal. 1980) (limit of five unrelated people who may live in single-family zone violates fundamental right to privacy under the California Constitution); Charter Twp. of Delta v. Dinolfo, 419 Mich. 253, 351 N.W.2d 831 (1984) (limit of two unrelated persons violates the due-process clause of the Michigan Constitution); State v. Baker, 405 A.2d 368, 369–70 (N.J. 1979) (limit of no more than four unrelated persons violates right to privacy and due process under the New Jersey Constitution). Other state courts have approved limits on the number of unrelated individuals who may reside within an individual single-family housing unit. *See, e.g.,* Ames Rental Prop. Ass'n v. City of Ames, 736 N.W.2d 255 (Iowa 2007) (upholding limit of no more than three unrelated individuals residing together in a single-family zoning district). Chapter 160D, Section 907, of the North Carolina General Statutes (hereinafter G.S.) limits state-law protection for family care homes to those serving six or fewer disabled individuals, but there is no explicit number in the federal legislation. See Chapter 22 for further discussion of this state law.

54. 514 U.S. 725 (1995).

exempt from the requirements of the fair-housing law.[55] However, the question of how many unrelated individuals should be allowed in a facility in order to constitute reasonable accommodation is unclear and often requires detailed fact-specific inquiries.[56]

Many land use regulations impose a minimum-separation requirement between facilities serving persons with disabilities in order to maintain the single-family, noninstitutional character of a neighborhood.[57] As with occupancy limits, the size of a separation requirement that will pass the reasonable-accommodation test is unclear. While some courts have upheld separation requirements,[58] others have invalidated substantially similar requirements.[59]

The court in *Oxford House, Inc. v. City of Raleigh* upheld the city's 375-yard minimum separation between "supportive housing residences," which included facilities serving disabled persons.[60] Wilmington's half-mile separation was upheld in *Oxford House v. City of Wilmington*.[61] If a separation provision is included in a development regulation, a prudent local government would consider including an exception to minimum-separation requirements in situations where its purpose can be otherwise met.[62]

---

55. Minimum-housing-code provisions setting minimum-square-footage requirements for each individual resident (whether or not they are related) are unaffected by this law. However, special safety requirements cannot be imposed on housing for the disabled that are not imposed on other group-living arrangements. Marbrunak, Inc. v. City of Stow, 974 F.2d 43 (6th Cir. 1992); All. for the Mentally Ill v. City of Naperville, 923 F. Supp. 1057 (N.D. Ill. 1996).

56. *See* Bryant Woods Inn, Inc. v. Howard Cnty., 124 F.3d 597 (4th Cir. 1997) (upholding occupancy limit of eight disabled persons); Smith & Lee Assocs., Inc. v. City of Taylor, 102 F.3d 781 (6th Cir. 1996) (requiring limit of no more than six disabled persons per home be raised to nine but rejecting request to raise the limit to twelve disabled persons); Oxford House–C v. City of St. Louis, 77 F.3d 249 (1996) (upholding a limit of eight unrelated individuals or three unrelated, nondisabled individuals in group homes); Swanston v. City of Plano, 557 F. Supp. 3d 781 (E.D. Tex. 2021) (limit of eight residents per sober-living facility invalidated when plaintiff showed fifteen residents was a therapeutic necessity); Oxford House, Inc. v. City of Wilmington, No. 7:07-CV-61-F, 2010 WL 4484523 (E.D.N.C. Oct. 28, 2010) (no showing that nine rather than eight residents was a necessity); Human Res. Research & Mgmt. Grp., Inc. v. Cnty. of Suffolk, 687 F. Supp. 2d 237, 263–66, (E.D.N.Y. 2010) (holding a six-person limit for those receiving treatment for drug and alcohol problems in a group home facially invalid). *See also* United States v. City of Balt., 845 F. Supp. 2d 640 (D. Md. 2012) (invalidating provision that applied standards to group homes with less than seventeen residents but not to those with more residents).

57. Several states establish separation requirements by statute to avoid what they deem to be undue concentration of family care homes. G.S. 168-22 allows a half-mile separation. This statute is discussed in Chapter 22. A number of states have similar rules. *See, e.g.*, ARIZ. REV. STAT. § 36-582H (1200-foot separation); COLO. REV. STAT. § 30-28-115(2)(b) (750-foot separation); CONN. GEN. STAT. § 8-3F (1000-foot separation). *See also* Kevin J. Zanner, *Dispersion Requirements for the Siting of Group Homes: Reconciling New York's Padavan Law with the Fair Housing Amendments Act of 1988*, 44 BUFF. L. REV. 249 (1996).

58. Familystyle of St. Paul, Inc. v. City of St. Paul, 923 F.2d 91 (8th Cir. 1991) (upholding quarter-mile separation requirement). *See also* Twp. of Plymouth v. Dep't of Soc. Servs., 198 Mich. App. 385, 501 N.W.2d 186 (1993) (upholding 1500-foot-separation requirement).

59. *See, e.g.*, Valencia v. City of Springfield, 883 F.3d 959 (7th Cir. 2018) (invalidating 600-foot separation); Oconomowoc Residential Programs, Inc. v. City of Milwaukee, 300 F.3d 775 (7th Cir. 2002) (invalidating 2500-foot spacing requirement); Larkin v. Mich. Dep't of Soc. Servs., 89 F.3d 285 (6th Cir. 1996) (invalidating 1500-foot separation requirement); Ass'n for the Advancement of the Mentally Handicapped v. City of Elizabeth, 876 F. Supp. 614 (D.N.J. 1994) (invalidating 1500-foot separation requirement); Horizon House Dev. Servs., Inc. v. Twp. of Upper Southampton, 804 F. Supp. 683 (E.D. Pa. 1992), *aff'd*, 995 F.2d 217 (3d Cir. 1993) (invalidating 1000-foot separation requirement).

60. No. 5:98-CV-113-BO(2), 1999 WL 1940013 (E.D.N.C. Jan. 26, 1999).

61. No. 7:07-CV-61-1, 2010 WL 4484523 (E.D.N.C. Oct. 28, 2010).

62. For example, see the exception to the minimum-separation requirement between adult uses discussed in *Independence News, Inc. v. City of Charlotte*, 568 F.3d 148 (4th Cir. 2008). The ordinance allowed a variance to the separation requirement upon showing manmade or natural features provided sufficient separation to prevent harmful secondary impacts.

Accommodations Under the Americans with Disabilities Act

The protections afforded persons with disabilities by the Americans with Disabilities Act (ADA) closely parallel those provided under the Fair Housing Act. Title II of the ADA provides that a person shall not be denied the benefits of services, programs, or activities of public entities or be subject to discrimination by public entities by reason of disability.[63] Planning and development regulations are generally considered programs and activities that are covered by the ADA.[64]

As with the Fair Housing Act, courts have interpreted ADA protections to prohibit intentional discrimination or disparate treatment, disparate impacts, or failure to make reasonable accommodations.[65] If a local government acts in response to community views about whether persons have disabilities, those views may be attributed to the governmental unit. Therefore, community opposition to the siting of a facility serving those regarded by the community to have disabilities can trigger the protections of the ADA.[66]

The denial of a permit or a variance to a disabled person or for a facility for disabled persons does not in itself trigger an ADA violation if there is a legitimate land use basis for the denial decision and there is no evidence of discrimination based on a disability on the face of the ordinance or in its application.[67] However, if the plaintiff presents evidence that animus against a protected group was a significant factor

---

63. 42 U.S.C.A. §§ 12131–12165. Implementing regulations are at 28 C.F.R. pt. 35. The ADA also incorporates the rights, procedures, and remedies of the Rehabilitation Act of 1973. 29 U.S.C. § 794 (prohibiting exclusion of persons with disabilities from participation in or receipt of benefits from programs or activities with federal funding.

64. *See, e.g.*, A Helping Hand, LLC v. Baltimore County, 515 F.3d 356, 361 (4th Cir. 2008) (ADA protections applicable to zoning dispute regarding siting of methadone-treatment clinic). In this case the court held that there was no showing that clinic clients were disabled under the Act as a matter of law. The ADA defines "qualified individual with a disability" as a person with a physical or mental impairment that substantially limits one or more "major life activities," someone with a record of impairment, or someone who is "regarded as" having such an impairment. Major life activities include, but are not limited to, caring for oneself, performing manual tasks, seeing, hearing, eating, sleeping, walking, standing, lifting, bending, speaking, breathing, learning, reading, concentrating, thinking, communicating, and working. 42 U.S.C.A. § 12102 (2011). Similarly, the court in *Regional Economic Community Action Program, Inc. v. City of Middletown*, 294 F.3d 35, 47–48 (2d Cir. 2002), noted that while alcoholism and drug addiction are impairments, neither is a per se disability without a showing that the condition substantially limits at least one major life activity. The court concluded that residents of a proposed halfway house did in fact have addictions that substantially limited their ability to live independently with their families. *See also* Bay Area Addiction Research v. City of Antioch, 179 F.3d 725, 730–32 (9th Cir. 1999) (applying ADA to zoning requirements).

65. *See, e.g.*, Wis. Cmty. Servs., Inc. v. City of Milwaukee, 465 F.3d 737, 753 (7th Cir. 2006); Innovative Health Sys., Inc. v. City of White Plains, 117 F.3d 37 (2d Cir. 1997), *criticized by* Zervos v. Verizon N.Y., Inc., 252 F.3d 163 (2d Cir. 2001) (invalidating denial of permit approvals for a drug-and-alcohol-rehabilitation treatment center). Many cases challenging land use restrictions on the basis of discrimination grounded in disability or a failure to make reasonable accommodation raise both Fair Housing Act and ADA claims. *See, e.g.*, Tsombanidis v. W. Haven Fire Dep't, 352 F.3d 565, 578–80 (2d Cir. 2003) (failure to treat group home as a single-family dwelling was a failure to make reasonable accommodation for group home and violated both laws).

66. *A Helping Hand*, 515 F.3d at 366.

67. An example would be denial of a permit for a nonprofit facility serving persons with disabilities in a zone reserved for commercial uses. *See, e.g.*, *Wis. Cmty. Servs.*, 465 F.3d at 754–55 (to establish ADA violation, plaintiff must show that disability of clients was cause in fact of denial of special use permit for mental health clinic); Forest City Daly Hous., Inc. v. Town of N. Hempstead, 175 F.3d 144 (2d Cir. 1999) (no ADA violation where special use permit for assisted-living facility in commercial zone would not be issued for similar home for those without disabilities); Woodward v. City of Paris, 520 F. Supp. 2d 911 (W.D. Tenn. 2007) (denial of variance for carport in side yard proper where disabled plaintiff treated the same as any other resident in the same area with a lot of similar size and shape); Robinson v. City of Friendswood, 890 F. Supp. 616 (S.D. Tex. 1995) (denial of variance for carport in side yard not a violation). The court in *Woodward* held that a requested accommodation is not reasonable if it would fundamentally alter the nature of the zoning scheme.

in the decision, that establishes a prima facie case of discrimination, and the burden then shifts to the defendant to provide a legitimate, nondiscriminatory reason for the decision.[68]

Keeping a "service animal" where development regulations would not otherwise allow such is sometimes requested as a reasonable accommodation. Whether an animal qualifies as a service animal is a two-part test. The animal must be trained to do work or perform tasks for the benefit of an individual with a disability and the tasks performed by the animal must be directly related to the individual's disability.[69] Animals that only provide emotional support, comfort, or companionship, such as a household pet, do not qualify as service animals.[70] Whether the requested accommodation is reasonable depends on the particular circumstances involved, such as whether the property is large enough to accommodate the animal without threatening legitimate safety requirements.[71]

Telecommunications

Wireless Telecommunication

Land use regulation of telecommunication towers is common. Many local ordinances limit the location of telecommunication towers to certain zoning districts, set height limits,[72] require security fencing and landscaping,[73] encourage collocation of multiple providers on a single tower, encourage use of existing structures (water towers, church steeples, tall buildings) for antenna location,[74] encourage use of camouflaging for towers (use of "stealth" designs), and include provisions for removal of abandoned towers.[75] A 2005 survey by the UNC School of Government indicated that 70 percent of the responding municipalities and 78 percent of the responding counties had adopted regulations on telecommunication towers.[76]

Both state[77] and federal laws restrict local regulation of these facilities. The Telecommunications Act of 1996 allows local regulation of the location of personal wireless services but provides for limited preemption of local ordinances in specified situations.[78] Local regulations based on the environmental

---

68. *Reg'l Econ. Cmty. Action Program*, 294 F.3d at 48–51.

69. 28 C.F.R. § 35.14. Also, 28 C.F.R. § 35.136 specifically requires reasonable modifications for miniature horses where the horse has been individually trained to do work or perform tasks for the benefit of the individual with a disability. The court in *C.L. v. Del Amo Hospital, Inc.*, 992 F.3d 901 (9th Cir. 2021), held that a formal certification of the service animal is not required.

70. Rose v. Springfield-Greene County Health Dept., 668 F. Supp. 2d 1206, 1215 (W.D. Mo. 2009) (holding plaintiff's monkey not a service animal); Pruett v. Arizona, 606 F. Supp. 2d 1065 (D. Ariz. 2009) (diabetic person's chimpanzee not a service animal).

71. *See, e.g.*, Anderson v. City of Blue Ash, 798 F.3d 338 (6th Cir. 2015) (whether resident's property was large enough to accommodate a miniature horse and whether a single miniature horse on the property would threaten public safety requires fact-specific inquiry).

72. *See, e.g.*, USCOC of Va. RSA v. Montgomery Cnty. Bd. of Supervisors, 343 F.3d 262 (4th Cir. 2003) (upholding requirement that proposed 240-foot-tall telecommunication tower's height be reduced to 195 feet to conform to zoning requirements).

73. *See, e.g.*, Davis v. SBA Towers II, LLC, 2009 ME 82, 979 A.2d 86 (interpretation of landscaping requirement).

74. *See, e.g.*, U.S. Cellular Tel. of Greater Tulsa, LLC v. City of Broken Arrow, 340 F.3d 1122 (10th Cir. 2003) (upholding denial based on evidence to demonstrate infeasibility of use of existing towers).

75. G.S. 146-29.2 allows the state to lease state-owned land for cell-tower use but requires the towers to be designed and constructed so as to allow collocation and minimize the visual impact of the towers on surrounding properties.

76. DAVID W. OWENS & NATHAN BRANSCOME, AN INVENTORY OF LOCAL GOVERNMENT LAND USE ORDINANCES IN NORTH CAROLINA 9 (UNC School of Government, Special Series No. 21, May 2006).

77. G.S. 160D-930 to -938 are discussed in Chapter 22. Note particularly the state requirements for expedited review of colocation, minor modifications, and small-cell wireless facilities.

78. 47 U.S.C. § 332(c)(7)(B). As one court noted, the law "is a deliberate compromise between two competing aims—to facilitate nationally the growth of wireless telephone service and to maintain substantial local control

health effects of radio-frequency emissions are prohibited, and the federal government exclusively deals with radio-frequency-interference issues.[79] This preemption of regulation of health effects does not, however, preclude a public agency from imposing more-stringent restrictions on emissions as part of a site-leasing agreement (versus their being imposed as a regulation).[80]

Other limitations imposed by the Telecommunications Act on land use regulation of wireless telecommunication facilities are discussed below.

Reasonable Time for Decision

Local governments are required to act on permit applications for wireless telecommunication facilities within a reasonable time.[81] In response to an industry petition for a ruling on precisely what constitutes a "reasonable time," the Federal Communications Commission (FCC) issued an order setting out "presumptively reasonable" times of 90 days to review a collocation application and 150 days to review an application for a new tower.[82]

Results have been mixed regarding the validity of moratoria on permitting these facilities. In *Sprint Spectrum, L.P. v. City of Medina*, the court upheld a six-month moratorium on issuing special use permits for towers adopted shortly after the Telecommunications Act became law, holding that this was a "necessary and *bona fide* effort to act carefully in a field with rapidly evolving technology."[83] In *Sprint Spectrum, L.P. v. Jefferson County*, the court invalidated a moratorium where the jurisdiction had previously adopted two other ninety-day moratoria and had previously adopted telecommunication-tower regulations.[84]

---

over siting of towers." Town of Amherst v. Omnipoint Commc'ns Enters., Inc., 173 F.3d 9, 13 (1st Cir. 1999). Since the Telecommunications Act contains specific enforcement provisions, actions under 42 U.S.C. § 1983 to remedy alleged violations of the act are not permitted. City of Rancho Palos Verdes v. Abrams, 544 U.S. 113 (2005).

See generally Jeffrey A. Berger, *Efficient Wireless Tower Siting: An Alternative to Section 332(c)(7) of the Telecommunications Act of 1996*, 23 TEMP. ENVTL. L. & TECH. J. 83 (2004); Steven J. Eagle, *Wireless Telecommunications, Infrastructure Security, and the NIMBY Problem*, 54 CATH. U. L. REV. 445 (2005); Sara A. Evans, *Wireless Service Providers v. Zoning Commissions: Preservation of State and Local Zoning Authority Under the Telecommunications Act of 1996*, 32 GA. L. REV. 965 (1998); Robert B. Foster, *What the Meaning of "May" May Be: Recent Developments in Judicial Review of Land Use Regulation of Cellular Telecommunications Facilities Under the Telecommunications Act of 1996*, 41 URB. LAW. 501 (2009); Robert B. Foster & Mitchell A. Carrel, *Patchwork Quilts, Bumblebees, and Scales: Cellular Networks and Land Use Under the Telecommunications Act of 1996*, 36 URB. LAW. 399 (2004).

79. 47 U.S.C. § 332(c)(7)(B)(iv); Freeman v. Burlington Broads., Inc., 204 F.3d 311, 323–24 (2d Cir. 2000) (preemption on radio-frequency-interference issue); T-Mobile Ne. LLC v. Town of Ramapo, 701 F. Supp. 2d 446, 460 (S.D.N.Y. 2009). *See also* Merrick Gables Ass'n v. Town of Hempstead, 691 F. Supp. 2d 355, 364 (E.D.N.Y. 2010) (installation not a dangerous condition under state nuisance law); AT&T Wireless Servs. of Cal. LLC v. City of Carlsbad, 308 F. Supp. 2d 1148 (S.D. Cal. 2003) (apparent real basis for denial was concern over radio-frequency emissions).

80. Sprint Spectrum, L.P. v. Mills, 283 F.3d 404 (2d Cir. 2002) (upholding more-stringent standards imposed by school district in lease for site on top of a high school); Omnipoint Commc'ns Enters., L.P. v. Twp. of Nether Providence, 232 F. Supp. 2d 430 (E.D. Pa. 2002) (town lease provisions not preempted).

81. *See* Ill. RSA No. 3, Inc. v. Cnty. of Peoria, 963 F. Supp. 732, 746 (C.D. Ill. 1997) (holding a six-month period for making a decision is not per se unreasonable).

82. *In re* Provisions of Section 332(c)(7)(B) to Ensure Timely Siting Review & to Preempt Under Section 253 State & Local Ordinances that Classify All Wireless Siting Proposals as Requiring a Variance, 24 FCC Rcd. 13994 (2009). The agency rules were upheld in *City of Arlington v. FCC*, 569 U.S. 290 (2013). In August 2010, the FCC denied a petition to reconsider these time periods and the thirty-day tolling of them to determine an application's completeness. Note that G.S. 153A-52(e) and 160A-400.52(e) each set a time of forty-five days from receipt of a complete application for collocation applications. See Chapter 22 for a discussion of this statute.

83. 924 F. Supp. 1036, 1040 (W.D. Wash. 1996).

84. 968 F. Supp. 1457 (N.D. Ala. 1997). *See also* Masterpage Commc'ns, Inc. v. Town of Olive, 418 F. Supp. 2d 66 (N.D.N.Y. 2005) (two-year moratorium and delays in scheduling hearing and vote on application constitute unreasonable delay).

Written Denials

Denials of applications for wireless telecommunication facilities must be final[85] and in writing.[86]

There was a split among federal courts as to whether a formal decision document with reasoning had to be prepared to satisfy this requirement. The Fourth Circuit upheld use of a letter of denial, holding that the Telecommunications Act does not mandate formal findings of fact analogous to those required in formal adjudications under the federal Administrative Procedure Act.[87] Other courts stressed that while formal findings are not required, a letter of denial must provide a sufficient explanation of the reasons for the permit denial to allow a reviewing court to evaluate whether the evidence in the record supporting those reasons is adequate.[88]

The Supreme Court resolved the question in *T-Mobile South, LLC v. City of Roswell*.[89] The Court held that a locality must provide reasons when it denies a siting application. While the reasons for the denial are not required to appear in the same writing as the denial,[90] they must be issued at essentially the same time as the denial.[91] The Court suggested that a local government is best served by having a separate statement of its reasons for a denial but is not required to do so by the statute. The Court emphasized,

---

85. Global Tower Assets, LLC v. Town of Rome, 810 F.3d 77 (1st Cir. 2016) (only a "final action" may be appealed under 42 U.S.C. § 332(c)(7)(B)(v).

86. The court in *Athens Cellular, Inc. v. Oconee County*, 886 F.3d 1094 (11th Cir. 2018), held that a board's denial was not effective until the board approved the written minutes for the meeting at which the denial was made. An oral decision on a permit application is not a final action that is appealable under the Telecommunications Act. T. Mobile Ne. LLC v. City of Wilmington, 913 F.3d 311, 317–23 (3d Cir. 2019). While an email regarding the decision is insufficient, the written minutes of the meeting where the action on the permit application was "indefinitely postponed" is sufficient written notice of the decision. Capital Telecom Holdings II, LLC v. Grove City, 403 F. Supp. 3d 643 (S.D. Ohio 2019).

87. AT&T Wireless PCS, Inc. v. City Council, 155 F.3d 423, 429–30 (4th Cir. 1998). The court in *Smith Communications, LLC v. Washington County*, 785 F.3d 1253 (8th Cir. 2015), held that detailed written minutes of the board's meeting were adequate to support a conditional use permit denial for a telecommunication tower). *See also* NE Colo. Cellular, Inc. v. City of N. Platte, 764 F.3d 929 (8th Cir. 2014); T-Mobile S., LLC v. City of Milton, 728 F.3d 1274 (11th Cir. 2013).

88. Helcher v. Dearborn Cnty., 595 F.3d 710, 717–23 (7th Cir. 2010) (letter of decision and detailed minutes of meeting are sufficient explanation of reasons for denial); Sprint Spectrum, L.P. v. Platte Cnty., 578 F.3d 727, 732 (8th Cir. 2009); USCOC of Greater Mo. v. City of Ferguson, 583 F.3d 1035 (8th Cir. 2009) (central concern of requirement is to enable effective judicial review); Sprint PCS Assets, LLC v. City of Palos Verdes Estates, 583 F.3d 716, 726 (9th Cir. 2009) (maps, mockups, and citizen testimony sufficient to establish towers would have adverse aesthetic impact); Omnipoint Commc'ns, Inc. v. Town of LaGrange, 658 F. Supp. 2d 539 (S.D.N.Y. 2009) (denial of variance for collocation of antennae must provide explanation of reasons for action under both state and federal law). Other courts have been more demanding, seeking specific findings linked to supporting evidence. Omnipoint Commc'ns, Inc. v. Planning & Zoning Comm'n, 83 F. Supp. 2d 306 (D. Conn. 2000); Ill. RSA No. 3, Inc. v. Cnty. of Peoria, 963 F. Supp. 732, 746 (C.D. Ill. 1997); W. PCS II Corp. v. Extraterritorial Zoning Auth., 957 F. Supp. 1230 (D.N.M. 1997) (denial of permit to locate antenna on water tower unsupported by any written findings); Smart SMR of N.Y., Inc. v. Zoning Comm'n, 995 F. Supp. 52 (D. Conn. 1998) (invalidating denial of approval to place antenna on existing windmill). In *AT&T Wireless Services of Florida, Inc. v. Orange County*, 982 F. Supp. 856 (1997), the court remanded the decision for findings, holding that a written denial without findings of fact, citations to evidence, or any explanation why the denial was made was inadequate. Also, in *Virginia Metronet, Inc. v. Board of Supervisors*, 984 F. Supp. 966, 972–73 (E.D. Va. 1998), the court held that a letter sent by staff after the meeting on the matter would not serve as the required findings, noting that the decision must come from the decision-making body).

89. 574 U.S. 293 (2015).

90. The reasons for denial can, for example, be contained in the minutes of the meeting, as was done in this case.

91. In this instance the minutes were not approved until twenty-six days after the written decision was issued, and the Court found this was not sufficiently contemporaneous. In *Cellco Partnership v. Board of Supervisors of Fairfax County*, 140 F. Supp. 3d 548 (E.D. Va. 2015), the court affirmed a written order issued three weeks after the vote on the decision, as the county made the issuance of the written order the effective date of the decision for purposes of calculating the time for appeals.

however, "that these reasons need not be elaborate or even sophisticated, but rather . . . simply clear enough to enable judicial review."[92]

Substantial Evidence

Denials of applications for wireless telecommunication facilities must be supported by substantial evidence in the hearing record.[93]

Examples of evidence found to be sufficient to justify denials include showing substantial departures from mandated setbacks;[94] failure to use mandatory camouflage measures;[95] failure to establish that required standards for a special use permit or variance would be met;[96] photo simulations, test balloons, or photographs exhibiting aesthetic impacts;[97] testimony that proposed antennae and support equipment were not well-integrated into the design of the building to which they were to be attached;[98] relevant

---

92. 574 U.S. at 302.

93. The "substantial evidence" standard is the same as the standard used in the federal Administrative Procedures Act and elsewhere in the law: less than a preponderance but more than a scintilla of evidence. It requires sufficient relevant evidence as a reasonable mind might accept to support a conclusion. Universal Camera Corp. v. NLRB, 340 U.S. 474, 477 (1951). *See, e.g.,* T-Mobile Ne. LLC v. City Council, 674 F.3d 380 (4th Cir. 2012); T-Mobile Cent., LLC v. Unified Gov't of Wyandotte Cnty., 546 F.3d 1299 (10th Cir. 2008) (substantial evidence must be in record for relevant standards in ordinance); Michael Linet, Inc. v. Vill. of Wellington, 408 F.3d 757, 762 (11th Cir. 2005); PrimeCo Personal Commc'ns, Ltd. P'ship v. City of Mequon, 352 F.3d 1147 (7th Cir. 2003) (finding insufficient evidence in record to justify permit denial); MetroPCS N.Y., LLC v. City of Mount Vernon, 739 F. Supp. 2d 409 (S.D.N.Y. 2010) (evidence in record did not support stated ground for denial); Cellco P'ship v. Franklin Cnty., 553 F. Supp. 2d 838 (E.D. Ky. 2008) (neighbor testimony regarding aesthetic impacts not substantial where higher towers already in same area); Cal. RSA No. 4 v. Madera Cnty., 332 F. Supp. 2d 1291 (E.D. Cal. 2003) (inadequate evidence in record to support denial based on plan inconsistency, aesthetic or property value, public safety, or noise impacts). *See also* AT&T Wireless PCS, Inc. v. Town of Porter, 203 F. Supp. 2d 985 (N.D. Ind. 2002) (state law can impose burden of production on applicant to establish that adverse impacts will not occur). For an analysis of this requirement, see Susan Lorde Martin, *How Much Is "Substantial Evidence" and How Big Is a "Significant Gap"? The Telecommunications Attorney Full Employment Act,* 9 WM. & MARY BUS. L. REV. 29 (2017).

94. New Cingular Wireless PCS, LLC v. Fairfax Cnty. Bd. of Supervisors, 674 F.3d 270 (4th Cir. 2012) (evidence of inconsistency with ordinance and comprehensive plan is substantial evidence); U.S. Cellular v. City of Wichita Falls, 364 F.3d 250 (5th Cir. 2004) (finding that significant departures from setback were necessary is substantial evidence); Sprint Spectrum L.P. v. Bd. of Zoning Appeals, 244 F. Supp. 2d 108 (E.D.N.Y. 2003) (noncompliance with mandated setback from property line sufficient for denial).

95. USCOC of N.H. RSA #2, Inc. v. City of Franklin, 413 F. Supp. 2d 21, 32–33 (D.N.H. 2006) (site visit and plans provided sufficient evidence of visual impacts to defeat motion for summary judgment); Omnipoint Commc'ns Enters., L.P. v. Warrington Twp., 63 F. Supp. 2d 658 (E.D. Pa. 1999).

96. Nextel Commc'ns of the Mid-Atl., Inc. v. Town of Brookline, 520 F. Supp. 2d 238 (D. Mass. 2007).

97. Smith Commc'ns, LLC v. Washington Cnty., 785 F.3d 1253 (8th Cir. 2015); Green Mountain Realty Corp. v. Leonard, 688 F.3d 40 (1st Cir. 2012); Wireless Towers, LLC v. City of Jacksonville, 712 F. Supp. 2d 1294 (M.D. Fla. 2010); Cellco P'ship v. Town of Grafton, 336 F. Supp. 2d 71 (D. Mass. 2004) (testimony and balloon test sufficient to establish adverse aesthetic impacts); *Sprint Spectrum v. Bd. of Zoning Appeals,* 244 F. Supp. 2d at 114–15 (specific and informed testimony from legislators, residents, members of civic and historical organizations, and a real-estate appraiser adequate to establish adverse aesthetic impacts on adjacent historic district); Airtouch Cellular v. City of El Cajon, 83 F. Supp. 2d 1158 (S.D. Cal. 2000) (photographs and neighbor testimony adequate to establish adverse aesthetic impact).

98. Nextel Commc'ns of the Mid-Atl., Inc. v. City of Cambridge, 246 F. Supp. 2d 118 (D. Mass. 2003).

testimony on impacts on aesthetics and property values;[99] and failure to provide requested supplemental information regarding the feasibility of colocation to meet service gaps.[100]

When the standards for approval address aesthetics and impacts on neighborhood character, there is often disagreement about what type of evidence on these issues is substantial. The Fourth Circuit has held that comments by interested citizens on aesthetics and neighborhood character can be considered as substantial evidence.[101] Other courts have been more demanding.[102] Where citizen comments alone are the basis of the decision, the Fourth Circuit has acknowledged that the citizen concerns expressed must be more than mere speculation.[103]

To the extent that a special use permit is required, compliance with the more demanding North Carolina land use law requires written findings of fact and substantial, competent, and material evidence in the record to support the decision.[104]

AT&T Wireless PCS, Inc. v. Winston-Salem Zoning Board of Adjustment illustrates application of these considerations.[105] The board there denied a special use permit for construction of a 148-foot monopole tower on property owned by the Southeastern Center for Contemporary Art in a low-density, single-family neighborhood. The applicant presented testimony from an engineer on the tower's safety and from a real-estate appraiser that the tower would not adversely affect neighboring property values. Neighborhood residents testified in opposition, largely based on aesthetic impacts. The board found for the applicant on the standards related to health and safety, required specifications, and not injuring property values but denied the permit upon finding the use was not in harmony with the area and the comprehensive plan. The court found that the mailing immediately after the vote of a notice of the

---

99. T-Mobile Ne. LLC v. Loudoun Cnty. Bd. of Supervisors, 748 F.3d 185 (4th Cir. 2014) (upholding denial based on testimony regarding aesthetic impacts and noise); Am. Tower Corp. v. City of San Diego, 763 F.3d 1035 (9th Cir. 2014) (issues regarding visual impacts associated with city design standards constitutes substantial evidence); Am. Tower LP v. City of Huntsville, 295 F.3d 1203 (11th Cir. 2002) (upholding denial based on resident testimony regarding negative aesthetic impacts and realtor testimony regarding impact on sales). T-Mobile S. LLC v. City of Jacksonville, 564 F. Supp. 2d 1337 (M.D. Fla. 2008) (upholding denial based on testimony regarding proximity of tower to neighbors and planned removal of screening trees).

100. Up State Tower Co. v. Town of Southport, 412 F. Supp. 3d 270, 288–90 (W.D.N.Y. 2019).

101. AT&T Wireless PCS, Inc. v. City Council, 155 F.3d 423, 430–31 (4th Cir. 1998). *See also* 360 Degrees Commc'ns Co. of Charlottesville v. Bd. of Supervisors, 211 F.3d 79, 85 (4th Cir. 2000) (virtually unanimous citizen opposition and plan inconsistency constitute substantial evidence); Sprint Spectrum, L.P. v. Willoth, 176 F.3d 630 (2d Cir. 1999) (record adequate to support denial of site-plan approval for three cell towers after town had concluded a single tower would be adequate).

102. T-Mobile Ne. LLC v. Incorporated Vill. of E. Hills, 779 F. Supp. 2d 256 (E.D.N.Y. 2011) (generalized aesthetic objections of neighbors and concern about property-value impacts insufficient to contradict expert testimony of applicant); Cellco P'ship v. Town Plan & Zoning Comm'n, 3 F. Supp. 2d 178 (D. Conn. 1998) (inadequate evidence in hearing record to support denial of special use permit to reconstruct a church steeple and include antennae within); AT&T Wireless Servs. of Fla., Inc. v. Orange Cnty., 994 F. Supp. 1422 (M.D. Fla. 1997) (adequate evidence in record to support denial of permit for construction of church steeple with antennae within); Century Cellunet of S. Mich., Inc., v. City of Ferrysburg, 993 F. Supp. 1072 (W.D. Mich. 1997) (adequate evidence in record to deny special use permit for tower); Ill. RSA No. 3, Inc. v. Cnty. of Peoria, 963 F. Supp. 732, 744–45 (C.D. Ill. 1997).

103. Petersburg Cellular P'ship v. Bd. of Supervisors, 205 F.3d 688, 695 (4th Cir. 2000). *See also* Ogden Fire Co. No. 1 v. Upper Chichester Twp., 504 F.3d 370, 389–90 (3d Cir. 2007) (generalized testimony about aesthetics and property-value impacts inadequate); Omnipoint Commc'ns, Inc. v. Vill. of Tarrytown Planning Bd., 302 F. Supp. 2d 205 (S.D.N.Y. 2004); Preferred Sites, LLC v. Troup Cnty., 296 F.3d 1210 (11th Cir. 2002) (citizen petitions with generalized objections inadequate basis for denial); Telespectrum, Inc. v. Pub. Serv. Comm'n, 227 F.3d 414, 424 (6th Cir. 2000); Cellular Tel. Co. v. Town of Oyster Bay, 166 F.3d 490 (2d Cir. 1999) (invalidating denial based on generalized expressions of concern); BellSouth Mobility Inc. v. Gwinnett Cnty., 944 F. Supp. 923, 928 (N.D. Ga. 1996) (generalized concerns do not constitute substantial evidence to justify a permit denial).

104. See Chapter 16 for a detailed discussion of special use permit requirements in North Carolina.

105. 172 F.3d 307 (4th Cir. 1999).

decision by the board secretary (a copy of the application with the word "Denied" written in the space indicated for disposition) satisfied the requirement for a written decision. The formal findings and a written decision relating the evidence were approved by the board several months later as part of the approval of minutes for the hearing.[106] The court held that testimony from neighbors, testimony from city staff, and letters from state agencies regarding the tower's visibility, neighborhood impacts, and impacts on a historic structure on-site constituted sufficient substantial evidence for a permit denial.

Discrimination Among Providers

Local regulations may not unreasonably discriminate among providers of functionally equivalent wireless telecommunication facilities. Regulations may not set a preference for one type of wireless technology over another.[107] They also may not favor publicly owned facilities over privately owned ones[108] or favor an initial provider of services over subsequent competitors.[109]

Granting one permit while denying another is not in itself discrimination among providers, provided there is a legitimate basis for the decisions. It is only unreasonable discrimination that is prohibited.[110] For example, a jurisdiction may permit towers in a commercial zoning district while prohibiting them in a residential district.[111]

Prohibition of Service and Significant Gaps in Service

Under Section 253 of the Telecommunications Act, local regulations may not prohibit or have the effect of prohibiting the provision of personal wireless services.[112] Prohibition includes not only a general ban on all towers in a jurisdiction[113] but also policies that "have the necessary result that all possible sites

---

106. The court rejected the district court's finding that such subsequently approved findings were pretextual or in any way improper. *AT&T Wireless v. City of Winston-Salem*, 172 F.3d at 313.

107. N.Y. SMSA Ltd. P'ship v. Town of Clarkston, 612 F.3d 97 (2d Cir. 2010). The town had established a regulatory preference for distributed-antenna systems in order to promote use of more numerous but lower and less-powerful towers.

108. Issuing permits to towers on sites leased by the town while subjecting another site to more rigorous review and denial can constitute unreasonable discrimination. Omnipoint Commc'ns, Inc. v. Common Council, 202 F. Supp. 2d 210 (S.D.N.Y. 2002). However, a preference for a publicly owned site is not in and of itself unlawful. USCOC of Greater Mo., L.L.C. v. Vill. of Marlborough, 618 F. Supp. 2d 1055, 1064–65 (E.D. Mo. 2009).

109. A denial based on a determination that one form of wireless service is already available in an area (as opposed to safety, traffic, or aesthetic concerns) improperly discriminates among providers. Sprint Spectrum, L.P. v. Town of Easton, 982 F. Supp. 47 (1997). *See also* Nextel Partners, Inc. v. Town of Amherst, 251 F. Supp. 2d 1187 (W.D.N.Y. 2003) (denial of application for antennae placement on same tower previously approved for other carrier's antennae is unreasonable discrimination where there was no plausible reason for distinction).

110. Omnipoint Commc'ns Enters., L.P. v. Zoning Hearing Bd., 331 F.3d 386, 395 (3d Cir. 2003); Nextel W. Corp. v. Unity Twp., 282 F.3d 257, 266 (3d Cir. 2002); APT Pittsburgh Ltd. P'ship v. Penn Twp., 196 F.3d 469, 480 (3d Cir. 1999).

111. Sprint Spectrum, L.P. v. Willoth, 176 F.3d 630, 639 (2d Cir. 1999) (denial of an application for collocation of antennae on an existing tower when there is no substantial evidence in the record of any significant aesthetic difference between the proposed antennae and permitted antennae violates legitimate-basis requirement); Nextel W. Corp. v. Town of Edgewood, 479 F. Supp. 2d 1219 (D.N.M. 2006).

112. 47 U.S.C. § 253 sets this standard for local ordinances. 47 U.S.C. § 332 does the same for quasi-judicial decisions. *See* Omnipoint Communications Enterprises, L.P. v. Zoning Hearing Bd., 331 F.3d 386 (upholding denial of permit for tower where other providers already present and no gaps in service established). To prevail a plaintiff must show actual or effective prohibition, not merely potential prohibition. Sprint Telephony PCS, L.P. v. Cnty. of San Diego, 490 F.3d 700 (9th Cir. 2007). *See generally* Mattaniah S. Jahn et al., *"You Want to Put That Where?" A Discussion of the Interplay between Local Zoning Control and Effective Prohibition Under the Telecom Act of 1996*, 51 STET. L. REV. 463 (2022); Andrew Erber, Note, *The Effective Prohibition Preemption in Modern Wireless Tower Siting*, 66 FED. COMM. L.J. 357 (2014).

113. AT&T Wireless PCS, Inc. v. City Council, 155 F.3d 423, 428 (4th Cir. 1998).

in a given area will be rejected."[114] The denial of an individual application does not in itself establish an "effective ban," but it can be a factor in establishing that there is such a ban if there are significant gaps in service and no reasonable alternatives for filling those gaps.[115] The carrier has the burden of establishing an effective prohibition.[116]

Significant gaps in service that cannot be closed without new facilities give rise to an effective-ban claim.[117] Federal courts were split on the question of whether a gap should be analyzed from the perspective of a consumer or a particular provider.[118] The FCC responded with a ruling that a gap in a particular provider's service is a "significant gap" under the law.[119] When a provider has made good-faith efforts to fill a significant gap, including undertaking assessments of technology and reasonable negotiations with owners of preferred alternative sites, denial of special use permits and variances for the only feasible site to fill the gap constitutes an impermissible, effective ban.[120] A local government may require that service gaps be closed in the least intrusive means available.[121]

---

114. Va. Metronet, Inc. v. Bd. of Supervisors, 984 F. Supp. 966, 971 (E.D. Va. 1998).

115. The significance of the gap is considered based on the totality of circumstances, including the physical size of the gap, number of customers affected, type of service affected, feasibility of alternate sites, evolving technology, and other factors. T-Mobile Ne. LLC v. Loudoun Cnty. Bd. of Supervisors, 748 F.3d 185 (4th Cir. 2014); T-Mobile Ne. LLC v. Fairfax Cnty. Bd. of Supervisors, 672 F.3d 259 (4th Cir. 2012); VoiceStream Minneapolis, Inc. v. St. Croix Cnty., 342 F.3d 818, 833–35 (7th Cir. 2003); Second Generation Props., L.P. v. Town of Pelham, 313 F.3d 620 (1st Cir. 2002); Nat'l Tower, LLC v. Plainville Zoning Bd. of Appeals, 297 F.3d 14 (1st Cir. 2002); 360 Degrees Commc'ns Co. of Charlottesville v. Bd. of Supervisors, 211 F.3d 79, 85 (4th Cir. 2000); *APT Pittsburgh*, 196 F.3d at 478–81; Town of Amherst v. Omnipoint Commc'ns Enters., Inc., 173 F.3d 9, 14 (1st Cir. 1999); Cellular Tel. Co. v. Zoning Bd. of Adjustment, 197 F.3d 64, 70 (3d Cir. 1999); AT&T Mobility Servs., LLC v. Village of Corrales, 127 F. Supp. 3d 1169 (D.N.M. 2015); Orange Cnty.–Poughkeepsie Ltd. P'ship v. Town of E. Fishkill, 84 F. Supp. 3d 274 (S.D.N.Y. 2015); *Nextel v. Town of Edgewood*, 479 F. Supp. 2d 1219; Omnipoint Holdings, Inc. v. Town of Westford, 206 F. Supp. 2d 166 (D. Mass. 2002).

116. T-Mobile USA, Inc. v. City of Anacortes, 572 F.3d 987, 993–95 (9th Cir. 2009); USCOC of Greater Iowa, Inc. v. Zoning Bd. of Adjustment, 465 F.3d 817, 825 (8th Cir. 2006).

117. Sprint Spectrum L.P. v. Zoning Bd. of Adjustment, 21 F. Supp. 3d 381 (D.N.J. 2014) (denial of monopole where other technological alternatives had substantial service-availability issues). Denial of a tower for improvement of indoor service where alternatives existed for meeting the need was held not to be an effective ban. Voice Stream PCS I, LLC v. City of Hillsboro, 301 F. Supp. 2d 1251, 1260–62 (D. Or. 2004).

118. *Compare* Omnipoint Commc'ns Enters., L.P. v. Zoning Hearing Bd., 331 F.3d 386 (3d Cir. 2003) (consider gaps for remote users rather than for particular providers) *with* MetroPCS, Inc. v. City & Cnty. of S.F., 400 F.3d 715 (9th Cir. 2005) (gap exists if particular provider is unable to fill its own service coverage). *See also* Omnipoint Commc'ns, Inc. v. City of White Plains, 430 F.3d 529, 536 n.3 (2d Cir. 2005) (question unsettled).

119. *In re* Provisions of Section 332(c)(7)(B) to Ensure Timely Siting Review & to Preempt Under Section 253 State & Local Ordinances that Classify All Wireless Siting Proposals as Requiring a Variance, 24 FCC Rcd. 13994, 14016 (2009).

120. T-Mobile Cent., LLC v. Charter Twp. of W. Bloomfield, 691 F.3d 794 (6th Cir. 2012); Omnipoint Holdings, Inc. v. City of Cranston, 586 F.3d 38 (1st Cir. 2009); VWI Towers, LLC v. Town of N. Andover Planning Bd., 404 F. Supp. 3d 456, 468–70 (D. Mass. 2019); T-Mobile Cent. LLC v. City of Fraser, 675 F. Supp. 2d 721 (E.D. Mich. 2009); Indus. Commc'ns & Elecs., Inc. v. O'Rourke, 582 F. Supp. 2d 103 (D. Mass. 2008) (alternative sites must be available and technically feasible to forestall effective-ban claim); USCOC of N.H. RSA No. 2, Inc. v. Town of Bow, 493 F. Supp. 2d 199 (D.N.H. 2007) (no effective ban based on denial of variance for tower proposed to be located on scenic hill where multiple alternative sites exist); Cingular Wireless, LLC v. Thurston Cnty., 425 F. Supp. 2d 1193 (W.D. Wash. 2006).

121. This requires the applicant to show a good-faith effort to identify and evaluate less intrusive alternatives, including consideration of less sensitive sites, alternative designs, and technical alternatives. Am. Tower Corp. v. City of San Diego, 763 F.3d 1035, 1056–57 (9th Cir. 2014); *MetroPCS, Inc.*, 400 F.3d at 733–35; Nextel W. Corp. v. Unity Twp., 282 F.3d 257, 265–66 (2d Cir. 2002); APT Pittsburgh Ltd. P'ship v. Penn Twp., 196 F.3d 469, 480 (3d Cir. 1999); Sprint Spectrum, L.P. v. Willoth, 176 F.3d 630 (2d Cir. 1999); Cellco P'ship v. Town of Clifton Park, 365 F. Supp. 3d 248, 263–64 (N.D.N.Y. 2019); PI Telecom Infrastructure v. City of Jacksonville, 104 F. Supp. 3d 1321 (M.D. Fla. 2015); VoiceStream Minneapolis, Inc. v. St. Croix Cnty., 212 F. Supp. 2d 914 (W.D. Wis. 2002).

Satellite Dishes

To a limited degree, FCC regulations preempt local regulations that restrict satellite dishes used to receive video programming.[122] Local regulations must have clearly defined health, safety, or aesthetic objectives and must further those objectives without unnecessarily burdening the federal interests in ensuring access to satellite services and in promoting fair and effective competition among competing providers. Regulation of satellite dishes that are two meters or less in diameter and are located in commercial or industrial districts, or those smaller than one meter in diameter in any zoning district, is presumed to be unreasonable.[123] Aggrieved persons may, after exhausting all nonfederal remedies, petition the FCC for a declaration that a local regulation is preempted.[124]

In the 1980s and early 1990s, the typical home satellite dish measured six to ten feet in diameter, a size that elicited considerable neighborhood concerns and therefore generated local regulations. A number of local regulations that prohibited rooftop installation and required rear-yard placement and substantial screening of dishes have since been held to be preempted.[125] However, height limits and screening requirements that do not unreasonably limit reception of satellite signals have been held not to be preempted.[126] Also, regulations that apply to all structures may still be applied and enforced relative to satellite dishes even if the satellite-dish regulation itself is preempted.[127] By the late 1990s, the typical dish size had shrunk to one or two feet in diameter, a size that substantially reduced neighborhood impact and thus interest in particularly restrictive regulations.

Other Radio Towers

There is an inherent conflict between amateur radio operators' desire for high towers (often located adjacent to their residences) and their neighbors and local governments' interest in limiting the aesthetic impact of towers in residential areas. Federal regulations do not preempt local height limits for these towers but do require local governments to strike a balance between these two legitimate interests.

---

122. 47 C.F.R. § 25.104(a) (1997). The rule was originally issued in 1986 and substantially revised in 1996. *See* Johnson v. City of Pleasanton, 982 F.2d 350 (9th Cir. 1992). *See generally* Christopher Neumann, *FCC Preemption of Zoning Ordinances That Restrict Satellite Dish Antenna Placement: Sound Policy or Legislative Overkill?* 71 St. John's L. Rev. 635 (1997).

123. 47 C.F.R. § 25.104(b). The presumption is rebuttable upon a showing that the regulation is necessary to accomplish the objectives and is no more burdensome than is necessary. Also see 47 C.F.R. § 1.4000, preempting local regulation of antennae for television broadcast signals, direct-broadcast satellite services, or multichannel-multipoint-distribution services if the dish is one meter or less in diameter. This preemption does not displace necessary health and safety regulations and some historic-district regulations.

124. 47 C.F.R. § 25.104(c) (1997). Nonfederal remedies include application for permits and petitions for variances but not judicial appeal of administrative determinations. Where there has been a conclusive state-court determination that a regulation is not preempted, the FCC may not overrule that determination. Town of Deerfield v. FCC, 992 F.2d 420 (2d Cir. 1993). Nor may the state determination be simply relitigated in federal court. Decker v. City of Plantation, 706 F. Supp. 851 (S.D. Fla. 1989).

125. Loschiavo v. City of Dearborn, 33 F.3d 548 (6th Cir. 1994); Kessler v. Town of Niskayuna, 774 F. Supp. 711 (N.D.N.Y. 1991); Cawley v. City of Port Jarvis, 753 F. Supp. 128 (S.D.N.Y. 1990); Vill. of Elm Grove v. Py, 724 F. Supp. 612 (E.D. Wis. 1989); Van Meter v. Twp. of Maplewood, 696 F. Supp. 1024 (D.N.J. 1988).

126. *See* Abbott v. City of Cape Canaveral, 840 F. Supp. 880 (M.D. Fla. 1994), *aff'd*, 41 F.3d 669 (11th Cir. 1994) (holding seven-foot height limit and screening requirements did not unreasonably limit reception of satellite signals). *See also Decker*, 706 F. Supp. 851 (upholding ordinance requiring rear-yard location); Brophy v. Town of Castine, 534 A.2d 663 (Me. 1987) (upholding seventy-five-foot river-setback requirement as applied to satellite-dish location).

127. Neufeld v. City of Balt., 820 F. Supp. 963 (D. Md. 1993), *aff'd*, 70 F.3d 1262 (4th Cir. 1995) (upholding application of thirty-foot front-yard setback).

In 1985, the FCC issued an order establishing limited preemption of local regulations.[128] The order requires that local regulation on placement, screening, or height of amateur radio antennae that is based on health, safety, or aesthetic considerations be crafted to accommodate reasonable amateur communications and that it be the minimum practicable regulation to accomplish the local government's purposes.[129] The FCC order preempts local regulations that preclude amateur radio-transmission towers throughout a community.[130] It does not, however, preempt reasonable height and location restrictions, provided there is evidence in the record to show that the federal interest in allowing effective amateur radio communication has been adequately considered. This generally requires a city to consider a tower application, make factual findings, and attempt to negotiate a satisfactory compromise.[131]

Commercial transmission towers are also subject to federal licensing.[132] As there is no express federal preemption of local regulation of these towers, land use regulations are routinely applied to radio- and television-tower location and design.[133] However, local regulation that is directly contrary to federal regulatory standards is preempted.[134] In the absence of direct conflicts, federal law does not preempt local land use regulations on radio-transmission towers.[135]

---

128. *In re* Fed. Preemption of State & Local Regulations Pertaining to Amateur Radio Facilities, 50 Fed. Reg. 38813-01 (Sept. 25, 1985); 47 C.F.R. § 97.15(e). *See generally* Alice J. Schwartz, Note, *Federal Preemption of Amateur Radio Antenna Height Regulation: Should the Sky Be the Limit?* 9 Cardozo L. Rev. 1501, 1526 (1988).

129. *In re Fed. Preemption,* 50 Fed. Reg. at 38816.

130. Thernes v. City of Lakeside Park, 779 F.2d 1187, 1189 (6th Cir. 1986) (total exclusion of amateur towers preempted).

131. DePolo v. Bd. of Supervisors, 835 F.3d 381 (3d Cir. 2016) (upholding a six-foot height limit); Pentel v. City of Mendota Heights, 13 F.3d 1261, 1264 (8th Cir. 1994) (denial of approval for 68-foot tower to replace ineffective 56.5-foot tower for amateur radio antenna is failure to make reasonable accommodation). *See also* Evans v. Bd. of Cnty. Comm'rs, 994 F.2d 755 (10th Cir. 1993) (county thirty-five-foot height limit for amateur radio towers not preempted); Bosscher v. Twp. of Algoma, 246 F. Supp. 2d 791 (W.D. Mich. 2003) (upholding denial of special use permit for proposed 180-foot tower for amateur radio tower); Palmer v. City of Saratoga Springs, 180 F. Supp. 2d 379 (N.D.N.Y. 2001) (failure to negotiate compromise regarding special use permit for proposed forty-seven-foot tower results in preemption of ordinance but no constitutional violations); MacMillan v. City of Rocky River, 748 F. Supp. 1241 (N.D. Ohio 1990) (city denial of thirty-foot tower for amateur radio tower to be attached to residence preempted as applied due to failure to consider federal interests); Williams v. City of Columbia, 707 F. Supp. 207 (D.S.C. 1989) (board of adjustment's denial of special exception for seventeen-foot amateur radio tower preempted due to failure to consider federal interest); Bodony v. Incorporated Vill. of Sands Point, 681 F. Supp. 1009 (E.D.N.Y. 1987) (failure to consider any possible exceptions to twenty-five-foot antenna results in ordinance preemption for failure to consider federal interests); Bulchis v. City of Edmonds, 671 F. Supp. 1270 (W.D. Wash. 1987) (denial of conditional use permit for seventy-foot-high tower preempted as applied); Zubarau v. City of Palmdale, 192 Cal. App. 4th 289, 121 Cal. Rptr. 3d 172 (2011) (allowing some restrictions on roof height, tower height, and location to stand but holding that provisions regarding radio interference preempted); Marchand v. Town of Hudson, 147 N.H. 380, 788 A.2d 250 (2001) (trial court must consider potential steps to reasonably accommodate federal interest before ordering removal of three 100-foot amateur radio towers). A successful challenger to local restrictions on height limits for amateur radio towers is generally not entitled to recover legal fees. Howard v. City of Burlingame, 937 F.2d 1376 (9th Cir. 1991).

132. 47 U.S.C. § 303. Federal regulations generally require specified painting and lighting for antennae structures or towers with heights over 200 feet. 47 C.F.R. § 17.21. These towers, as well as those near airports, are also subject to review by the Federal Aviation Administration, 47 C.F.R. § 17.7. *See generally* Phillip E. Hassman, Annotation, *Application of Zoning Regulation to Radio or Television Facilities,* 81 A.L.R.3d 1086 (1977).

133. *See, e.g.,* Carnie v. Town of Richmond, 139 N.H. 21, 648 A.2d 205 (1994) (upholding special use permit issued for antennae for cable-television receiving facility); Jasaka Co. v. City of St. Paul, 309 N.W.2d 40, 44 (Minn. 1981) (upholding revocation of permits for radio-transmission tower).

134. *See, e.g.,* Koor Commc'n, Inc. v. City of Lebanon, 148 N.H. 618, 622, 813 A.2d 418, 422 (2002) (citywide local height limit of 42 feet for new AM-radio-transmission towers preempted by federal regulation establishing a minimum height of 266 feet for such towers). The federal regulation on heights for AM stations is 47 C.F.R. § 73.189.

135. *See, e.g.,* Kroeger v. Stahl, 248 F.2d 121 (3d Cir. 1957).

Outdoor Advertising and Junkyards

The Highway Beautification Act of 1965[136] provides a strong federal incentive for states to adopt programs to control outdoor advertising and junkyards located in proximity to interstate and federally assisted primary highways. If a state fails to develop and implement a program for controlling outdoor advertising and junkyards in these areas, federal grants to those states for highway projects are to be reduced by 10 percent.[137]

For outdoor advertising,[138] states must develop regulations on billboards located within 660 feet of interstate or federally assisted primary highways. Outside of urban areas, states must regulate billboards that are more than 660 feet from the right-of-way if the sign is visible from the road and was erected for the purpose of being seen from these highways. The state regulations must restrict the location of new billboards to areas zoned for commercial or industrial use or to unzoned areas.[139] States must also limit the use of amortization[140] to remove nonconforming billboards along these federal highways.[141] These billboards can only be required to be removed upon payment of cash compensation.

In response to this federal incentive, North Carolina adopted the Outdoor Advertising Control Act in 1967.[142] G.S. 136-129 requires all billboards within 660 feet of interstate and federal primary highways to be consistent with rules adopted by the North Carolina Department of Transportation (NCDOT). G.S. 136-129.1 limits billboards located outside of urban areas that are more than 660 feet from federal highways and are visible from those roads to on-premise advertising.[143] G.S. 136-131.1[144] requires local governments to pay compensation for the removal of nonconforming billboards located along federal highways.[145] Rules adopted by NCDOT set detailed standards for billboard size and location.[146] Local governments can be assigned management control of signs in commercially and industrially zoned

---

136. Pub. L. No. 89-285, 79 Stat. 1028 (1965).

137. 23 U.S.C. §§ 131(a) (outdoor advertising), 136(b) (junkyards). For a critique, see Natalie L. Engel, Note, *Highway to the Safety Zone: Why the Highway Beautification Act Should Be Repealed and Its Federal Oversight Power Transferred to the States*, 82 OHIO ST. L.J. 1141 (2021).

138. Federal law can also limit advertising for particular products. For example, see the discussion of federal limits on tobacco advertising in *Lorillard Tobacco Co. v. Reilly*, 533 U.S. 525 (2001). Constitutional issues related to sign regulation are discussed in Chapter 28.

139. 23 U.S.C. § 131(d).

140. See the discussion of amortization in Chapter 20.

141. 23 U.S.C. § 131(g).

142. S.L. 1967-1248. *See generally* Timothy J. Fete, Jr., Comment, *Illegal Billboards: Why the General Assembly Should Revise the Outdoor Advertising Control Act to Comply with North Carolina Easement Law*, 80 N.C. L. REV. 2067 (2002).

143. G.S. 136-131.5 allows billboards that are condemned or that are obstructed by a sound barrier to be relocated on the same or an adjoining conforming parcel, subject to specified restrictions. This provision was added to the statutes by S.L. 2021-180.

144. This section of the statutes was enacted in 1981 with a specific sunset provision. After several extensions of the sunset, S.L. 2002-11 provided that this section will expire upon amendment to or repeal of 23 U.S.C. § 131(g). See G.S. 160D-912 for limits on local government regulations requiring removal or relocation of nonconforming outdoor advertising. Also see the discussion of amortization of nonconforming signs in Chapter 20.

145. In *MCC Outdoor, LLC v. Town of Wake Forest*, the plaintiff owned a billboard on leased property. When the property owner received approval of a special use permit to construct a shopping center on the site, the permit required removal of the sign at the end of the lease period. The plaintiff contended this permit condition "remove[d] or cause[d] to be removed" the sign, thus triggering this compensation statute. The court remanded for additional findings as to whether the permit requirement was the sole grounds for removal. 222 N.C. App. 70, 74, 729 S.E.2d 694, 697 (2012) (quoting G.S. 136-131.1).

146. Signs are limited to being no more than 1200 square feet in size with a 50-foot height limit. On interstates and freeways, signs must be 500 feet apart. On other federal highways, signs must be 300 feet apart outside of cities and 100 feet apart inside of cities. Title 19A, Chapter 2E, Section .0200 of the North Carolina Administrative Code (hereinafter N.C.A.C.).

areas.[147] Local governments also are required by G.S. 136-136 to provide written notice to NCDOT of all zoning changes regarding the establishment or revision of commercial or industrial zoning districts in these regulated areas. This state-regulatory scheme does not preempt local sign regulations adopted either as general ordinances or as part of a zoning regulation,[148] but the regulations must be consistent with these state standards.

Federal statutes also mandate that in order to avoid financial penalties, states must require junkyards to be removed or screened if they are within 1000 feet of an interstate or federally assisted primary highway's right-of-way or are visible from such a road.[149] For purposes of this law, the term *junkyard* includes scrapyards, automobile graveyards, garbage dumps, and landfills. Junkyards may be allowed in areas zoned for industrial use or in unzoned areas that are actually used for industrial purposes.

In response, the state in 1967 enacted the Junkyard Control Act[150] to provide for the screening or limiting of junkyards within 1000 feet of interstate and federal primary highways. G.S. 136-144 prohibits the establishment, maintenance, or operation of junkyards in these areas unless the facilities are screened from view, located in an industrially zoned area, or located in an unzoned area that is in fact used for industrial purposes. Local governments also are required by G.S. 136-153 to provide written notice to NCDOT of all zoning changes regarding the establishment or revision of industrial zoning districts in this regulated area. This statute does not preempt local regulation of junkyards adjacent to federal secondary highways or state roads.[151]

Railroad Facilities

Federal law gives the Surface Transportation Board exclusive jurisdiction over rail transportation and facilities that are part of the interstate rail system.[152] This provides substantial federal preemption of local or state regulation of railroad activities.[153] The key question for land use law is often what constitutes a rail facility that is not subject to local regulation. Rail lines are covered, but adjacent private activities are not exempt just because they have rail service.

For the most part the courts have held that facilities to load and unload freight from trains are exempt from land use regulation. The court in *Norfolk Southern Railway Co. v. City of Alexandria*[154] held that

---

147. 19A N.C.A.C. 2E, § .0204.

148. PNE AOA Media, LLC v. Jackson Cnty., 146 N.C. App. 470, 554 S.E.2d 657 (2001). See Chapter 22 for a discussion of preemption.

149. 23 U.S.C. § 136(c).

150. S.L. 1967-1198.

151. Cnty. of Hoke v. Byrd, 107 N.C. App. 658, 421 S.E.2d 800 (1992). In *State v. Jones*, 305 N.C. 520, 290 S.E.2d 675 (1982), the court upheld Buncombe County's junkyard-screening requirement. See the discussion of regulation for aesthetic purposes in Chapter 25.

152. 49 U.S.C. § 10501(b). The law provides that the Surface Transportation Board has exclusive jurisdiction over transportation by rail carriers and the construction, acquisition, operation, abandonment, or discontinuance of tracks or facilities. "Transportation" by rail includes services related to that movement, including receipt, delivery, elevation, transfer in transit, storage, and handling.

153. The preemption applies to state or local regulations that are reasonably related to "managing" or "governing" rail transport. PCS Phosphate Co. v. Norfolk S. Corp., 559 F.3d 212, 218 (4th Cir. 2009). *See generally* Carter H. Strickland, Jr., *Revitalizing the Presumption Against Preemption to Prevent Regulatory Gaps: Railroad Deregulation and Waste Transfer Stations*, 34 ECOLOGY L.Q. 1147 (2007); Matthew C. Donahue, Note, *Federal Railroad Power Versus Local Land-Use Regulation: Can Localities Stop Crude-by-Rail in Its Tracks?*, 74 WASH. & LEE L. REV. 146 (2017); Maureen E. Eldredge, Comment, *Who's Driving the Train? Railroad Regulation and Local Control*, 75 U. COLO. L. REV. 549 (2004). State and local regulation that has an incidental or remote connection to rail transportation is not preempted.

154. 608 F.3d 150 (4th Cir. 2010).

the defendant city's ordinances regulating the hauling of ethanol from a rail transloading facility were preempted. The ethanol-transloading facility handled highly flammable material and was located near residential neighborhoods and a school. The city conceded that the facility to off-load ethanol from railcars to trucks was exempt from its zoning but tried to require permits that would limit truck routes, timing of truck traffic, and the total number of trucks per day. The court held that such rules could directly impact the railroad company's ability to move goods shipped by rail and was therefore preempted because they could unduly burden rail carriage.[155]

States and local governments can impose general regulations to protect public health and safety provided they do not discriminate against rail carriers or unreasonably burden them. Requiring compliance with standard building and fire codes is often cited as an example of what is not preempted.[156] Even given these allowances, though, courts generally do not allow state or local governments to require permits or "preclearance" that could result in denials or delays in rail service. The focus is on compliance with the standards rather than the permit process.[157] Also, federal preemption does not apply to adjacent industrial or manufacturing activity beyond a transloading facility.[158]

This federal preemption also plays an important role in nonregulatory matters, particularly the acquisition of unused rail lines for greenways, bike paths, or other uses.[159]

---

155. *See also* CSX Trans., Inc. v. City of Sebree, 924 F.3d 276 (6th Cir. 2019) (ordinance requiring city approval for change in grade of railroad crossing preempted); Green Mountain R.R. v. Vt., 404 F.3d 638 (2d Cir. 2005) (rail company exempt from state land use rules that require buffer along river as applied to a transloading facility for salt, bulk cement, and steel pipe); City of Auburn v. United States, 154 F.3d 1025, 1029–31 (9th Cir. 1998) (preempting local environmental-permitting requirement for transloading facility); American Rocky Mountaineer v. Grand County, 568 F. Supp. 3d 1231 (D. Utah 2021) (county requirement for conditional use permit for temporary train station preempted); Bos. & Me. Corp. v. Town of Ayer, 191 F. Supp. 2d 257 (D. Mass. 2002) (local regulation of automobile-unloading-and-storage facility preempted); Soo Line R.R. Co. v. City of Minneapolis, 38 F. Supp. 2d 1096 (D. Minn. 1998) (city demolition permit preempted); Burlington Northern & Santa Fe Ry. Co. v. Department of Trans., 206 P.3d 261 (Or. App. 2009) (state rule setting time limit for blocking rail crossing preempted).

156. *See, e.g.,* Vill. of Ridgefield Park v. N.Y., Susquehanna & W. Ry. Corp., 750 A.2d 57, 64 (N.J. 2000); In re Vermont Railway, 769 A.2d 648 (Vt. 2000) (zoning conditions relative to salt shed used by railroad not preempted).

157. *See, e.g.,* N.Y. Susquehanna & W. Ry. Corp. v. Jackson, 500 F.3d 238 (3d Cir. 2007). The court addressed New Jersey regulations covering facilities that transferred solid waste from trucks to railcars for shipment to out-of-state landfills. Given the noise, dust, grime, and fire hazards associated with these facilities, the state adopted a number of detailed rules on their operation. The court noted that transloading is part of rail transportation, subject to federal preemption, but that reasonable health and safety rules are permitted provided they do not unreasonably burden railroading; it remanded the case for application of that standard to each particular state regulation.

158. *See, e.g.,* Hi Tech Trans, LLC v. New Jersey, 382 F.3d 295 (3d Cir. 2004) (state rules on facility to receive debris from construction sites for transfer to railcars not preempted); Fla. E. Coast Ry. Co. v. City of W. Palm Beach, 266 F.3d 1324 (11th Cir. 2001) (local zoning can be applied to yard leased by rail company where aggregate was unloaded, stockpiled, graded, and then reloaded onto trucks); CFNR Operating Co. v. City of Am. Canyon, 282 F. Supp. 2d 1114 (N.D. Cal. 2003) (bulk-transfer facility that receives pumice and cement by rail and delivers material by truck to customers not preempted from local zoning); *In re* Appeal of Vt. Ry., 171 Vt. 496, 503, 769 A.2d 648, 654–55 (2001) (local zoning of railroad's salt-shed operation not preempted as to traffic and environmental issues).

159. The preemption can preclude local condemnation of unused rail lines that have not been determined by the Surface Transportation Board to be abandoned. *See, e.g.,* City of Lincoln v. Surface Transp. Bd., 414 F.3d 858 (8th Cir. 2005). Under the National Trails System Act, 16 U.S.C. § 1247(d), the Board can approve temporary public-trail use of an unused line that is being held by the railroad for potential future rail use. The process to do so is described in SURFACE TRANSP. BD., OVERVIEW: ABANDONMENTS & ALTERNATIVES TO ABANDONMENTS (1997).

Federal Lands and Facilities

The land and facilities of the federal government are not subject to local zoning.[160]

Federal law encourages the General Services Administration to coordinate federal-agency land acquisition, use, and disposition with local zoning in urban areas. The General Services Administration is directed to carry out its work "to the greatest extent practicable," consistent with zoning and land use practices.[161] The administrator is directed to notify the local government of proposed land acquisitions and, "to the extent he determines practicable," to consider all objections and to comply with zoning in the acquisition or change in use of any real property in an urban area.[162] Privately owned land that is leased to a federal agency is, however, subject to local zoning.[163]

---

160. *See, e.g.,* Boundary Backpackers v. Boundary Cnty., 913 P.2d 1141 (Idaho 1996) (under Supremacy Clause, federal agencies not required to comply with county land use regulations). *See generally* Michael C. Blumm and James A. Fraser, *"Coordinating" with the Federal Government: Assessing County Efforts to Control Decisionmaking on Public Lands,* 38 Pub. Land & Resources L. Rev. 1 (2017).

161. 40 U.S.C. § 901.

162. 40 U.S.C. § 903.

163. Bryan v. Wilson, 259 N.C. 107, 130 S.E.2d 68 (1963) (applying zoning to privately owned building proposed to be leased for post-office use). Also see G.S. 104, where the state retains concurrent jurisdiction for specified federal lands for the service of civil and criminal process. While the state generally retains concurrent jurisdiction for crimes committed on these lands, state crimes become federal offenses on these federal lands (e.g., G.S. 104-5 regarding forest-reserve lands). United States v. Raffield, 82 F.3d 611 (4th Cir.), *cert. denied,* 519 U.S. 933 (1996) (approving federal prosecution of a driving-while-impaired violation that took place on a national-forest road).

CHAPTER 24

Takings

The Fifth Amendment to the United States Constitution includes a deceptively simple requirement: "[N]or shall private property be taken for public use, without just compensation." This is commonly known as the *Takings Clause*. Although the same language does not appear in the North Carolina constitution, the state's highest court has held that article I, section 19 of the state constitution, providing that no person shall be "deprived of his life, liberty, or property but by the law of the land," has the same functional impact as the federal Takings Clause.[1]

The compensation requirement is straightforward when the issue is seizing a private residence to quarter troops, as in the early days of the country's existence, or using private property for a public road, as in modern applications.[2] However, when a landowner alleges in an inverse-condemnation suit[3] that land use regulations are so restrictive as to be the equivalent of a seizure or a taking of property, thereby mandating compensation to the owner, the legal issues become rather complex.[4]

---

1. *See, e.g.*, Carolina Beach Fishing Pier, Inc. v. Town of Carolina Beach, 274 N.C. 362, 163 S.E.2d 363 (1968); DeBruhl v. State Highway & Pub. Works Comm'n, 247 N.C. 671, 102 S.E.2d 229 (1958).

2. Some "physical occupation" cases can present difficult issues. For example, *Long v. City of Charlotte*, 306 N.C. 187, 293 S.E.2d 101 (1982), involved a motion to dismiss an inverse-condemnation action based on aircraft over-flights brought by a plaintiff whose property was located near the end of a new runway at the municipal airport. The court ruled that the inverse-condemnation claim could proceed (noise being the "physical invasion") and that there was a taking if there was material interference with the use and enjoyment of a property so as to cause substantial diminution of its market value. *See also* Midgett v. N.C. State Highway Comm'n, 260 N.C. 241, 132 S.E.2d 599 (1963), *overruled in part on other grounds by* Lea Co. v. N.C. Bd. of Transp., 308 N.C. 603, 304 S.E.2d 164 (1983) (finding a taking where state highway caused floodwater to back up onto plaintiff's property); First Gaston Bank v. City of Hickory, 203 N.C. App. 195, 691 S.E.2d 715 (2010) (rejecting takings claim based on city approval of stormwater pipe and upland development after pipe collapsed, causing sinkhole on plaintiff's property); Smith v. City of Charlotte, 79 N.C. App. 517, 339 S.E.2d 844 (1986); Hoyle v. City of Charlotte, 276 N.C. 292, 172 S.E.2d 1 (1970).

Similarly, regulation of property adjacent to public property can raise takings issues. In *McCarran International Airport v. Sisolak*, 122 Nev. 645, 137 P.3d 1110 (2006), the Nevada court held an ordinance limiting height of structures on property adjoining an airport to be a taking.

3. Chapter 40A, Section 51 of the North Carolina General Statutes (hereinafter G.S.) provides a statutory framework for bringing an inverse-condemnation suit.

4. The British solution to this dilemma was the addition of a compensation element to the land use regulatory system. In 1947, the government created a fund to compensate those whose existing use rights could not be put to reasonably beneficial use. See Daniel R. Mandelker, *Notes from the English: Compensation in Town and Country Planning*, 49 Cal. L. Rev. 699 (1961), for a discussion of this system. For a review of the considerable literature on compensable regulations and a detailed proposed alternative, see Windfalls for Wipeouts: Land Value Capture and Compensation (Donald G. Hagman & Dean J. Misczynski eds., 1978).

Regulatory Takings

Overview of Federal Decisions

The concept that there can be a *regulatory taking*—that a land use regulation can be so restrictive as to constitute a taking of private property—was first set forth in 1922 in *Pennsylvania Coal Co. v. Mahon*.[5] The often-quoted conclusion of Justice Holmes in this case was, "while property may be regulated to a certain extent, if regulation goes too far it will be recognized as a taking."[6] The United States Supreme Court has confirmed that compensation, not just invalidation, is the appropriate remedy when there is a regulatory taking, even if the taking is temporary.[7] However, the Court has also long ruled that land use regulations preventing noxious land uses and uses that are nuisances or threats to public health and safety are not takings, even if property values are substantially reduced.[8]

At one time, the Court had also stated that a regulation that does not substantially advance a legitimate governmental objective gives rise to a takings as well as a due-process claim.[9] However, in *Lingle v. Chevron U.S.A., Inc.*, the Court held that this was not an appropriate test for a takings claim.[10]

Categorical Takings

There are two types of regulatory actions that always create takings, called *categorical takings*: regulations that authorize a physical invasion of the property and regulations that render the property worthless.[11]

---

5. 260 U.S. 393 (1922). *See also* Dellinger v. City of Charlotte, 114 N.C. App. 146, 441 S.E.2d 626 (1994), *review granted*, 336 N.C. 603, 447 S.E.2d 388, *dismissed, review improvidently granted*, 340 N.C. 105, 455 S.E.2d 159 (1995).

6. *Mahon*, 260 U.S. at 415. For further analysis of this seminal case, see Robert Brauneis, *"The Foundation of Our 'Regulatory Takings' Jurisprudence": The Myth and Meaning of Justice Holmes's Opinion in* Pennsylvania Coal Co. v. Mahon, 106 YALE L.J. 613 (1996); Carol M. Rose, Mahon *Reconstructed: Why the Takings Issue Is Still a Muddle*, 57 S. CAL. L. REV. 561 (1984); William Michael Treanor, *Jam for Justice Holmes: Reassessing the Significance of* Mahon, 86 GEO. L.J. 813 (1998).

7. First English Evangelical Lutheran Church v. County of Los Angeles, 482 U.S. 304 (1987). On remand, the California Court of Appeal ruled that the ordinance was not a taking. 210 Cal. App. 3d 1353, 258 Cal. Rptr. 893 (1989). Section 1983 of the Civil Rights Act of 1871 allows suits against entities, including local governments, who deprive persons of their constitutional rights. 42 U.S.C. § 1983.

8. Goldblatt v. Hempstead, 369 U.S. 590 (1962) (restricting quarry excavation even though preexisting mine was thereby rendered useless); Miller v. Schoene, 276 U.S. 272 (1928) (requiring destruction of diseased ornamental trees to protect apple orchards on other property); Euclid v. Ambler Realty Co., 272 U.S. 365 (1926) (limiting property to residential uses even though a 75 percent reduction in property value resulted); Pierce Oil Corp. v. City of Hope, 248 U.S. 498 (1919) (requiring removal of preexisting oil-storage tanks near residences even though it rendered existing business impractical); Hadacheck v. Sebastian, 239 U.S. 394 (1915) (requiring preexisting clay-mining and brick-manufacturing plant to be closed even though property value was reduced by more than 90 percent); Reinman v. City of Little Rock, 237 U.S. 171 (1915) (requiring preexisting livery stable to be closed when city expanded around it); Murphy v. California, 225 U.S. 623 (1912) (outlawing use of property for billiard hall); Mugler v. Kansas, 123 U.S. 623 (1887) (outlawing use of preexisting brewery equipment lawfully in use before prohibition).

9. Agins v. City of Tiburon, 447 U.S. 255 (1980). In a claim for monetary damages as the result of an alleged unconstitutional taking, a jury trial may be had on the mixed law-and-fact question of whether the permit denial was reasonably related to the justification offered by the government. City of Monterey v. Del Monte Dunes, 526 U.S. 687 (1999). The issue of whether the governmental objectives involved are legitimate and substantial is a legal question to be determined without a jury. Buckles v. King Cnty., 191 F.3d 1127, 1141–42 (9th Cir. 1999). See Chapter 25 for an additional discussion of due-process issues.

10. 544 U.S. 528 (2005) (case involved challenge to Hawaii law limiting the rent that oil companies could charge dealers leasing company-owned service stations). The decision provides a helpful overview of takings case law in the zoning area.

11. For a critique of these "bright line" tests for categorical takings, see Lynn E. Blais, *The Total Takings Myth*, 86 FORDHAM L. REV. 47 (2017).

Even modest physical invasions of property require compensation, as the right to exclude others from property is an essential attribute of property.[12] For example, in *Loretto v. Teleprompter Manhattan CATV Corp.*, the Court held that a regulation requiring an apartment-building owner to allow cable-television cables to be placed on the roof was a taking,[13] and in *Kaiser Aetna v. United States*, a requirement that members of the public be allowed access to and use of a privately owned upland pond proposed to be connected to navigable waters was held to be a taking.[14]

In order to establish a taking, the owner must be able to show that a right to exclude others existed prior to imposition of the regulation. If the public already has a right of access or use of the property, a regulation that recognizes that prior right has taken no property right from the owner. For example, in *Nies v. Town of Emerald Isle*,[15] an oceanfront property owner contended regulations restricting use of the ocean beach and allowing public driving along it constituted a taking. The court held that since the public had a legal right to use the dry-sand beach under the public-trust doctrine when the plaintiff acquired the property, the owner did not have a right to exclude the public so there was no unconstitutional taking.

Regulations that eliminate *all* economically beneficial uses of a property are also a taking. In *Lucas v. South Carolina Coastal Council*,[16] the Supreme Court held that in those rare instances where property is rendered useless by a regulation,[17] a taking has occurred regardless of the fact that a legitimate gov-

---

12. One study of federal-court litigation indicated the vast majority of takings cases in the United States in the 2000 to 2014 period involved claims of a physical taking. Dave Owen, *The Realities of Takings Litigation*, 47 B.Y.U. L. Rev. 577 (2022). *See generally* John D. Echeverria, *What Is a Physical Taking?*, 54 U.C. Davis L. Rev. 731 (2020).

13. 458 U.S. 419 (1982). In *Cedar Point Nursery v. Hassid*, 141 S. Ct. 2063 (2021), the court held that a regulation granting labor organizations temporary rights of access to agricultural employers' land to solicit support for unionization efforts constituted a physical invasion of property that was a per se regulatory taking. In *Arkansas Game & Fish Commission v. United States*, the Court held that even the temporary flooding of private property as part of a flood-control project can be a taking. 133 S. Ct. 511 (2012). The Court refused to extend this physical-invasion-takings rule to a statute restricting mobile-home-park rents and the park owner's ability to evict upon a transfer of mobile-home ownership. Yee v. City of Escondido, 503 U.S. 519 (1992). *See also* Stop the Beach Renourishment, Inc. v. Fla. Dep't of Envtl. Prot., 560 U.S. 702 (2010) (where state property law provides that avulsion does not change property lines, setting fixed property line prior to artificial beach nourishment is not a taking). In *Iowa Assurance Corp. v. City of Indianola*, 650 F.3d 1094 (8th Cir. 2011), the court held a zoning requirement that a fence be installed to enclose race cars if more than two were stored on-site is not a physical invasion under *Loretto*. The court in *Blackburn v. Dare County*, 58 F.4th 807, 811 (2023), held that a forty-five-day ban prohibiting nonresident property owners from entering the county to occupy their beach houses during the COVID-19 pandemic was not a physical appropriation for a takings analysis (and also held that it was not a taking under the Lucas or Penn Central tests).

14. 444 U.S. 164 (1979). Total removal of a core property right, such as the right of descent, can also be a taking. Hodel v. Irving, 481 U.S. 704 (1987).

15. 244 N.C. App. 81, 780 S.E.2d 187 (2015), *appeal dismissed*, 369 N.C. 484, 793 S.E.2d 699 (2016), *cert. denied*, 138 S. Ct. 75 (2017).

16. 505 U.S. 1003 (1992).

17. Carol N. Brown & Dwight H. Merriam, *On the Twenty-Fifth Anniversary of* Lucas: *Making or Breaking the Takings Claim*, 102 Iowa L. Rev. 1847 (2017) (*Lucas* plaintiffs succeed in less than 2 percent of cases). In *Cienega Gardens v. United States*, 331 F.3d 1319, 1343 (Fed. Cir. 2003), the court held that a taking occurred when a regulation effected a 96 percent loss of return on equity. In *State ex rel. Ridge Club v. Amberley Village*, 2007-Ohio-6089 (Ct. App.), *review denied*, 2008-Ohio-1635, 117 Ohio St. 3d 1460, 884 N.E.2d 68, the Court of Appeals of Ohio held that placing land in a "Park" zoning district with the only permitted uses being a golf course or park was an unconstitutional taking when the evidence supported a finding that a golf course was not a reasonable or economically viable use of the property. In a similar case involving land use restrictions limiting conversion of an existing golf course to other uses, the Supreme Court of Minnesota in *Wensmann Realty, Inc. v. City of Eagan* held that the test was "whether the city's decision leaves any reasonable, economically viable use of the property." 734 N.W.2d 623, 635 (Minn. 2007). *See also* Bettendorf v. St. Croix Cnty., 631 F.3d 421, 424–25 (7th Cir. 2011) (removal of commercial zoning from property suited for residential and agricultural uses does not render property "practically useless" and is not a taking).

ernmental objective led to the regulation. The Court held that there are limited exceptions to this rule in "total takings" situations.[18] In cases where the regulation leaves even a modest residual value in the land, courts have generally declined to apply the *Lucas* categorical-taking rule.[19] If the regulation prevents a use that would otherwise be forbidden under the state's background common law or statutory principles of nuisance and property law, there is no taking.[20]

Balancing Test

A means of determining when a taking has occurred absent the extraordinary situations of a physical invasion or a total deprivation of value has proven elusive. The courts must examine each challenged regulation on a case-by-case basis to consider the character of the governmental action and the economic impact on the landowner.[21] Justice Brennan summarized the Supreme Court's analytic framework in these situations in *Penn Central Transportation Co. v. City of New York*:

> The question of what constitutes a "taking" for purposes of the Fifth Amendment has proved to be a problem of considerable difficulty. While this Court has recognized that the "Fifth Amendment's guarantee . . . [is] designed to bar Government from forcing some people alone to bear public burdens which, in all fairness and justice, should be borne by the public as a whole," this Court, quite simply, has been unable to develop any "set formula" for determining when "justice and fairness" require that economic injuries caused by public action be compensated by the government, rather than remain disproportionately concentrated on a few persons. Indeed, we have frequently observed that whether a particular restriction will be rendered invalid by the

---

18. *Lucas*, 505 U.S. 1003. On remand, the South Carolina Supreme Court held that prohibiting construction of a habitable structure on the lot was not justified under state common law and that, therefore, the permit denial was a temporary regulatory taking. 309 S.C. 424, 424 S.E.2d 484 (1992). The state later acquired the lot for $1.5 million and resold it to developers. In the *Lucas* context, consideration of investment-backed expectations is not required. Palm Beach Isles Assocs. v. United States, 231 F.3d 1354 (Fed. Cir. 2000).

19. *See, e.g.*, Bridge Aina Le'a, LLC v. Land Use Comm'n, 950 F.3d 610 (9th Cir. 2020), *cert. denied*, 141 S. Ct. 731 (2021) (83 percent reduction in value still left substantial residual value and economically viable use of land); Cooley v. United States, 324 F.3d 1297 (Fed. Cir. 2003) (wetland regulation that reduced value by 98.8 percent not a categorical taking). However, if no economic use remains, an extremely small residual value does not preclude a *Lucas* categorical taking. Lost Tree Vill. Corp. v. United States, 787 F.3d 1111 (Fed. Cir. 2015) (wetland-permit denial resulted in loss of 99.4 percent of value). The reduction in value can also be a factor in a *Penn Central* analysis. *See, e.g.*, In re New Creek Bluebelt, Phase 4, 205 A.D.3d 808 (N.Y. App. Div. 2022) (reasonable likelihood of taking when wetland regulations reduced property value by 84 percent and use of property was effectively prohibited).

20. *See, e.g.*, Stevens v. City of Cannon Beach, 317 Or. 131, 854 P.2d 449 (1993) (upholding denial of permit for seawall, noting state law on customary use of ocean beaches is part of background principles of state property law); Machipongo Land & Coal Co. v. Commonwealth, 569 Pa. 3, 37–43, 799 A.2d 751, 771–74 (2002) (activity that pollutes state waters is a nuisance and not protected by Takings Clause); McQueen v. S.C. Coastal Council, 354 S.C. 142, 148–51, 580 S.E.2d 116, 119–20 (2003) (upholding denial of bulkhead permits along canal where lots had eroded and reverted to tidelands subject to state ownership and the public-trust doctrine, noting state property law precludes private ownership and fill of such lands). In addition to limiting nuisances, the federal navigational servitude has been held to be a background principle limiting property rights and providing a defense to a takings claim in a dredge-and-fill-permit context. Palm Beach Isles Assocs. v. United States, 208 F.3d 1374 (Fed. Cir. 2000). For a review of cases applying common-law and statutory background principles of state law to defeat regulatory-takings claims, see Michael C. Blumm and Rachel G. Wolfard, *Revisiting Background Principles in Takings Litigation*, 71 Fla. L. Rev. 1165, 1183–1203 (2019).

21. Keystone Bituminous Coal Ass'n v. DeBenedictis, 480 U.S. 470 (1987); Agins v. City of Tiburon, 447 U.S. 255 (1980); Penn Cent. Transp. Co. v. City of New York, 438 U.S. 104 (1978).

government's failure to pay for any losses proximately caused by it depends largely "upon the particular circumstances [in that] case."

    In engaging in these essentially ad hoc, factual inquiries, the Court's decisions have identified several factors that have particular significance. The economic impact of the regulation on the claimant and, particularly, the extent to which the regulation has interfered with distinct investment-backed expectations are, of course, relevant considerations. So, too, is the character of the governmental action.[22]

Where there is no physical invasion of the property and there is not a total, permanent elimination of the economically viable use of the property, this *Penn Central* framework is employed to assess whether a land use regulation constitutes a taking.

    Palazzolo v. Rhode Island illustrates the boundary between when a *Lucas* or a *Penn Central* analysis is appropriate. The case involved a denial of a proposed bulkhead and the filling of eleven acres of coastal marshland.[23] The Court held that the fact that Palazzolo took title to the property after the effective date of the state rules prohibiting wetland fill did not automatically prevent him from having a reasonable, investment-backed expectation regarding use of the property (though the existence of the regulations at the time of acquisition was one factor to consider in determining the reasonableness of development expectations).[24] The Court found that since the owner had the right to build at least one residence on the upland portion of the property, and this had an undisputed value of at least $200,000, there was no total deprivation of the economic value of the property and thus no automatic taking under the *Lucas* test. The Court remanded the case for further proceedings as to whether the case might be considered a taking under the balancing test of *Penn Central*.[25]

---

22. 438 U.S. at 123–24 (alteration in original) (citations omitted). See *Ruckelshaus v. Monsanto Co.*, 467 U.S. 986 (1984), and *Palazzolo v. Rhode Island*, 533 U.S. 606 (2001), for a discussion of what constitutes a reasonable investment-backed expectation. For an example of the character of the governmental action leading to takings, see *People ex rel. Department of Transportation v. Diversified Properties Co.*, 14 Cal. App. 4th 429, 17 Cal. Rptr. 2d 676 (1993) (regulation to depress price prior to condemnation a taking). Also see the discussion of amortization in Chapter 20.

23. 533 U.S. 606 (2001). Anthony Palazzolo bought the land in 1959 and developed and sold off most of the upland property. After a 1985 application was denied, he sought $3.15 million in damages as a taking (a calculation based on subdividing the wetland area into the seventy-four lots proposed in an early plat, although there was no town approval of such a development, and there was testimony that such density would violate town zoning and waste-disposal regulations). The Court held that the claim was ripe for judicial determination, as the state had given Palazzolo a final answer that the eleven wetland acres of the site could not be filled.

24. In a case involving denial of bulkhead and fill permits for lots along a manmade canal, the South Carolina Supreme Court held that longstanding permit requirements, coupled with a failure to seek permits in the face of ever-more-stringent regulatory requirements, indicated a lack of investment-backed development expectations. McQueen v. S.C. Coastal Council, 354 S.C. 142, 580 S.E.2d 116 (2000). The lots had eroded and reverted to wetlands. *See also* Pulte Home Corp. v. Montgomery Cnty., 909 F.3d 685, 695–97 (4th Cir. 2018) (alleged 83 percent reduction in value not a per se taking, purchase of undeveloped land without necessary infrastructure for development creates "only a hope, not a legally cognizable expectancy" of a right to develop); Rith Energy, Inc. v. United States, 247 F.3d 1355 (Fed. Cir. 2001) (regulatory regime considered in determining reasonable investment-backed expectations).

25. On remand, the Rhode Island court found the regulation was not a taking and the proposed intensive development would constitute a nuisance, thus precluding compensation. The court also found the plaintiff had no reasonable investment-backed expectation under *Penn Central* for such an intensive development. Palazzolo v. State, 2005 WL 1645974 (R.I. Super. July 5, 2005).

Property Interest Analyzed

When conducting a regulatory-takings analysis, the claimants must as a threshold matter establish that they have a property right as defined by state law. Where a rezoning or a discretionary permit (such as a special use permit) would have been necessary to undertake the development, the owner generally does not have an entitlement to the development and thus no property right that is protected by the Fifth Amendment.[26] Rights to speculative financial gains that could potentially be made in the future are not compensable.[27]

Once the claimant establishes a property right that has been affected by a regulation, the court in a takings analysis considers the property as a whole, not just the regulated portion or the time period of the regulation.[28]

In *Murr v. Wisconsin*,[29] the Supreme Court upheld a subdivision regulation that required adjacent lots in common ownership to be considered a single lot for regulatory purposes. The plaintiffs had acquired two adjacent lots along the St. Croix River. The owners proposed to relocate a cabin that was on the property to one of the lots so that the second lot could be sold and subsequently developed. The regulations required an acre of developable space for a structure, a standard the two lots together met but which neither met individually. Since the adjacent lots were nonconforming and under common ownership, the subdivision regulation required that they be treated as a single lot for regulatory purposes. The landowners contended that the takings analysis should consider the impact of the regulation on the value of the second lot only, while the government contended that the analysis should be based on the impacts of the two lots as a single unit. In determining what the unit of property should be for a takings analysis, the Court determined the relevant factors to be the treatment of the land under state

---

26. *See, e.g.*, Henry v. Jefferson Cnty., 637 F.3d 269 (4th Cir. 2011) (as owner had no entitlement to a conditional use permit for higher-density development, there was no deprivation of a property right and no taking); Griffin Farm & Landfill, Inc. v. Town of Unionville, No. 3:10-cv-250-RJC-DSC, 2012 W.L. 3257789 (W.D.N.C. Aug. 8, 2012), holding that when multiple authorizations are required and some of those have expired, the owner has no vested right to continued operation of a landfill and thus no property right upon which to base a takings claim. In *PEM Entities, LLC v. Cnty. of Franklin*, 57 F.4th 178 (2023), the plaintiff contended denial of utility service to their proposed subdivision under the county's water- and sewer-allocation ordinance constituted a taking. The court held that since under North Carolina law the plaintiff did not yet have a vested right, there could be no taking. *See also* Sunrise Corp. of Myrtle Beach v. City of Myrtle Beach, 420 F.3d 322, 330 (4th Cir. 2005) (takings analysis begins with an identification of governmental interference with an actual property right).

27. *See, e.g.*, Laurel Park Cmty., LLC v. City of Tumwater, 698 F.3d 1180 (9th Cir. 2012) (zoning mobile-home parks to limit more-lucrative future developments not a taking); Guggenheim v. City of Goleta, 638 F.3d 1111, 1120 (9th Cir. 2010) (en banc), *cert. denied*, 131 S. Ct. 2455 (2011) ("distinct investment-backed expectations" require a reasonable probability of gain, not a speculative hope of such).

28. Concrete Pipe & Prods. v. Constr. Laborers Pension Trust, 508 U.S. 602 (1993); *Machipongo Land & Coal*, 569 Pa. 3, 799 A.2d 751. *See also* Lost Tree Vill. Corp. v. United States, 707 F.3d 1286 (Fed. Cir. 2013) (single parcel owned by plaintiff is relevant parcel, not including adjacent parcel or other nearby parcels owned by plaintiff); D. Rose, Inc. v. City of Atlanta, 859 S.E.2d 514 (Ga. App. 2021) (sixty-foot setback that prevented building on part of lot not a taking, even when much of remainder of lot covered by floodplain and multiple sewer easements); Threatt v. Fulton Cnty., 266 Ga. 466, 471, 467 S.E.2d 546, 550 (1996) (requirement of fifty-foot vegetated buffer along streams not a taking absent a showing that owners have been deprived of economically viable or beneficial use of entire parcel); City of Annapolis v. Waterman, 357 Md. 484, 525–32, 745 A.2d 1000, 1022–25 (2000) (must consider entire tract when assessing regulatory-taking implications of recreational-space requirement in subdivision approval); Giovanella v. Conservation Comm'n of Ashland, 447 Mass. 720, 725–34, 857 N.E.2d 451, 456–61 (2006) (rebuttable presumption to include commonly owned contiguous property in takings analysis, subject to fact-sensitive analysis); Quirk v. Town of New Bos., 140 N.H. 124, 131, 663 A.2d 1328, 1332–33 (1995) (requirement of 200-foot buffer at boundary of campground not a taking as impact on entire parcel must be considered); Zealy v. City of Waukesha, 201 Wis. 2d 365, 374–79, 548 N.W.2d 528, 532–34 (Wis. 1996) (must consider contiguous upland portion of parcel when assessing regulatory-taking implications of zoning-ordinance wetland-conservancy requirements).

29. 137 S. Ct. 1933 (2017).

and local law, the physical characteristics of the land, and the value of the regulated portion of the land with regard to the rest of the property. Applying this analysis to the facts of the case, the Court held that the two lots were appropriately considered a single unit of property for takings analysis. The Court noted that the subdivision "merger" provision was in effect when the plaintiffs acquired the property, the topography was such that treating these two narrow lots with a common developable area was reasonable, and the merger provision added value to each individual lot. The fact that the property was adjacent to a designated wild and scenic river and was thus subject to long-standing and detailed land use regulation also factored into the reasonable expectations about the use and development of the property.

Courts similarly consider the entire parcel to be the "relevant parcel" for a regulatory-takings analysis rather than only examining the impacts on a buffer, setback area, or other portion of the property.[30]

Tahoe-Sierra Preservation Council, Inc. v. Tahoe Regional Planning Agency[31] illustrates this principle as applied to temporal segmentation. The case involved development moratoria imposed on sensitive lands adjacent to Lake Tahoe while studies, planning, and development regulations were being prepared. There were two moratoria challenged in this suit, which together prevented development in the most sensitive portions of the Lake Tahoe watershed for thirty-two months (other moratoria not involved in this litigation effectively extended the moratoria to six years). The plaintiff urged the Court to hold that all moratoria, no matter how short or long, violated the constitutional prohibition on taking private property without just compensation. The Court refused to do so. The Court held that the *Penn Central* balancing test should be applied in virtually all cases contending that a regulation was a taking. The Court found that the *Lucas* "valueless" test could not be applied to the period of the moratorium alone. Consideration of "fairness and justice" was critical, and here a careful analysis of all the factors involved led to a conclusion that there was no taking. The Court noted that temporary moratoria allowed time for necessary studies, public participation, and deliberation and that the complexity of the management issues involved with developing a complex bistate management plan justified this moratorium. While noting that moratoria lasting longer than a year may well warrant special skepticism, the Court concluded that the longer period was justified in this situation.

Ripeness

In addition to these standards defining what constitutes an unconstitutional taking, the Supreme Court has emphasized that a takings challenge may not be made before it is ripe.

Ripeness requires a final decision with respect to development of the property. At one time, many cases required a showing that the claimant had exhausted all available procedures for securing compensation prior to bringing the takings suit.[32] This often required proof that the claimant had unsuccessfully

---

30. *See, e.g.,* Blair v. Dep't of Conservation & Recreation, 457 Mass. 634, 932 N.E.2d 267 (2010) (regulation of 200-foot buffer adjacent to water-supply watershed must be reviewed in terms of impact on entire parcel, not buffer area alone).

31. 535 U.S. 302 (2002). *See also* Clayland Farm Enterprises, LLC v. Talbot Cnty., 987 F.3d 346 (4th Cir. 2021) (substantial reduction in permitted density during six-year-plan-update process not a taking); Wild River Estates, Inc. v. City of Fargo, 2005 ND 193, 705 N.W.2d 850 (twenty-one-month moratorium on building permits in floodway pending adoption of flood-hazard map not a taking). Moratoria are discussed in Chapter 9.

32. *See, e.g.,* Red Square Properties, LLC v. Town of Waynesville, 2019 WL 2420055 (No. 1:18-CV-211, W.D.N.C., May 22, 2019) (taking claim not ripe as the town had not made a final determination on the permit application but had requested additional site-stability analysis and a plan to address the unstable slope conditions; nor had the plaintiff sought relief through an inverse-condemnation action).

sought a variance, sought a rezoning, or made any available permit appeals.[33] This requirement to seek other relief is not mandatory,[34] but it is a factor in the prudential decision as to ripeness.[35]

At one time, the law required that a claimant bring an inverse-condemnation action under state law in order to have a ripe federal takings claim,[36] but that requirement was overruled in *Knick v. Township of Scott*.[37] Also, when a local government removes a takings claim to federal court, that effectively waives the requirement of seeking compensation under state law in order to have a ripe claim.[38]

North Carolina Application

The regulatory-taking issue has not been litigated much in North Carolina state courts. Only a handful of cases have addressed the issue to any substantial degree. The tests for a taking under the state constitution are consistent with the federal cases noted above.[39]

Three early decisions illustrate that the courts will uphold substantially restrictive regulations designed to protect public health and safety. In 1875, the North Carolina Supreme Court upheld a Goldsboro ordinance prohibiting wooden buildings and permitted application of the ordinance to a building already under construction,[40] ruling that no damages were due if the building was considered a nuisance because it was a fire hazard. In 1906, that same court upheld a ban on discharges into water-supply streams and noted that reasonable regulations to protect the public health, safety, and morals (including restrictions on land use and building) were not a taking.[41] In 1926, this court upheld a Winston-Salem ordinance

---

33. *See, e.g.*, CarSpa Auto., LLC v. City of Raleigh, 57 F. Supp. 3d 505 (E.D.N.C. 2014) (taking claim regarding public-access dedication); Fourth Quarter Props. IV, Inc. v. City of Concord, No. 1:02CV00908, 2004 WL 231303 (M.D.N.C. Jan. 22, 2004), *aff'd*, 127 F. App'x 648 (4th Cir. 2005) (takings claim based on alleged misapplication of zoning restrictions in airport buffer not ripe). Owners are not required to obtain a final decision, however, if the local government has used repetitive and unfair procedures to avoid issuing a final decision. Sherman v. Town of Chester, 752 F.3d 554 (2d Cir. 2014).

34. *See, e.g.*, South Grande View Dev. Co., Inc. v. City of Alabaster, 1 F.4th 1299 (11th Cir. 2021) (rezoning of plaintiff's property was a final decision, variance petition not required for ripeness).

35. *See, e.g.*, North Mill St., LLC v. City of Aspen, 6 F.4th 1216 (10th Cir. 2021) (not certain that city would deny variance, so takings claim not prudentially ripe for review).

36. Williamson Cnty. Reg'l Planning Comm'n v. Hamilton Bank of Johnson City, 473 U.S. 172 (1985).

37. 139 S. Ct. 2162 (2019). The finality requirement was not contested in this case, only the requirement to seek compensation through a state inverse-condemnation claim. *See generally* Alicia Gonzalez & Susan L. Trevarthen, *Deciding Where to Take Your Takings Case Post-*Knick, 40 Stet. L. Rev. 539 (2020).

Ripeness does not abrogate a state government's sovereign immunity. The Fourth Circuit upheld dismissal of a takings claim in federal court in *Zito v. North Carolina Coastal Resources Comm'n*, 8 F.4th 281, *cert. denied*, 142 S. Ct. 465 (2021), ruling that since state courts were open to adjudicate the taking claim, sovereign immunity precluded the federal-court claim.

38. Sansotta v. Town of Nags Head, 724 F.3d 533 (4th Cir. 2013). The court subsequently held that the prohibition of access to the property for repair work during a storm was based on grave threats to life and property and was not a taking. The town's assertion of public-trust rights in the dry-sand beach was not a physical occupation, but there were material facts in dispute regarding the application of *Penn Central* factors that rendered summary judgment inappropriate. 97 F. Supp. 3d 713 (E.D.N.C. 2014). *See also* Town of Nags Head v. Toloczko, 728 F.3d 391 (4th Cir. 2013).

39. Finch v. City of Durham, 325 N.C. 352, 371, 384 S.E.2d 8, 19 (1989) (state and federal takings claims denied "for the same reasons"); Guilford Cnty. Dep't of Emergency Servs. v. Seaboard Chem. Corp., 114 N.C. App. 1, 12, 441 S.E.2d 177, 183 (1994) (state and federal takings tests "are consistent").

40. Privett v. Whitaker, 73 N.C. 554 (1875). For a contemporary illustration of this principle, see Hillsboro Partners, LLC v. City of Fayetteville, 226 N.C. App. 30, 738 S.E.2d 819, *review denied*, 367 N.C. 236, 748 S.E.2d 544 (2013) (where dilapidated building is declared unsafe and a threat to public health and safety, the Takings Clause is not applicable to an order of demolition).

41. Durham v. Eno Cotton Mills, 141 N.C. 615, 54 S.E. 453 (1906).

prohibiting the sale of fresh meat or seafood in any location other than the city market, even when the ordinance was applied to preexisting businesses located elsewhere.[42]

In its first major review of a zoning restriction challenged as an unconstitutional taking, the state high court in 1938 examined a Greensboro setback ordinance involving the height of walls allowed on property lines. In *Appeal of Parker*, the court found no taking, though the individual project involved might cause no harm and the operation of the ordinance might seriously depreciate the property's value.[43] The court noted that an individual's right to use of the property was subordinate to the general welfare, and "incidental damage to property resulting from governmental activities or laws passed in the promotion of the public welfare [is] not a 'taking of property' for which compensation must be made."[44]

The N.C. supreme court elaborated on this point in a challenge to a Charlotte zoning requirement prohibiting a restaurant in a residential zoning district. Justice Sam Ervin wrote that "[i]f the police power is properly exercised in the zoning of a municipality, a resultant pecuniary loss to a property owner is a misfortune which he must suffer as a member of society."[45] In 1954, this court confirmed that a change in zoning did not in itself give rise to a claim for compensation by landowners whose property values were affected by the change.[46]

Helms v. City of Charlotte[47] involved two very small lots along a creek that had been rezoned from an industrial district to an exclusively residential district. The court held that reduction in value alone did not constitute a taking: "The mere fact that a zoning ordinance seriously depreciates the value of complainant's property is not enough, standing alone, to establish its invalidity."[48] The court also held, however, that to avoid a taking claim, the ordinance must not preclude all practical use of the land, thereby rendering the property "valueless." In this instance the court was clearly concerned that the city was not allowing the business or commercial use of the lots for which they were suited but had

---

42. Angelo v. Winston-Salem, 193 N.C. 207, 136 S.E. 489, *aff'd*, 274 U.S. 725 (1927).

43. 214 N.C. 51, 197 S.E. 706, *appeal dismissed sub nom.* Parker v. City of Greensboro, 305 U.S. 568 (1938). In addition to being raised when zoning affects property values, the taking issue is raised when zoning or subdivision regulations require dedication of land for roads, parks, utilities, or open space. In *River Birch Associates v. City of Raleigh*, 326 N.C. 100, 388 S.E.2d 538 (1990), the court ruled that the required conveyance of open space was not a taking because it was reasonably related to the valid purpose of preserving urban open space within a portion of the approved development. See the discussion of exactions below. The issue is raised also by the termination of noncon-forming uses, which is discussed in detail in Chapter 20.

44. *Appeal of Parker*, 214 N.C. at 57, 197 S.E. at 710.

45. Kinney v. Sutton, 230 N.C. 404, 411–12, 53 S.E.2d 306, 311 (1949). Justice Ervin's conclusion harkened back to Justice Brandeis's dissent in the Pennsylvania Coal case: "But where the police power is exercised, not to confer benefits upon property owners but to protect the public from detriment and danger, there is in my opinion, no room for considering reciprocity of advantage . . . . unless it be the advantage of living and doing business in a civilized community." Pa. Coal Co. v. Mahon, 260 U.S. 393, 422 (1922) (Brandeis, J., dissenting).

The court in *Schmidt v. City of Fayetteville* upheld the city's refusal to rezone a property zoned for single-family use to a more profitable professional-office district, noting that "[z]oning laws and land-use plans are adopted for the benefit of the citizenry as a whole. At times, that which results in an advantage to one citizen results in a disadvantage to another. This is one of the prices of living in an urban society." 568 F. Supp. 217, 221 (E.D.N.C. 1983), *aff'd*, 738 F.2d 431 (4th Cir. 1984). While the U.S. Supreme Court in *Lucas* disavowed use of a harm/benefit distinction in its takings analysis where the regulation left no viable economic value with the burdened property, the *Penn Central* balancing test acknowledges that a regulation designed "to promote the general welfare commonly burdens some more than others." Penn Cent. Transp. Co. v. City of New York, 438 U.S. 104, 133.

46. McKinney v. City of High Point, 239 N.C. 232, 79 S.E.2d 730 (1954). The court reached the same conclusion in a case challenging restrictions on signs in Charlotte's zoning ordinance. Schloss v. Jamison, 262 N.C. 108, 136 S.E.2d 691 (1964). Cases nationally support the proposition that a regulation reducing profits at a site is not a taking. *See, e.g.*, McCrothers Corp. v. City of Mandan, 2007 ND 28, 728 N.W.2d 124 (adult-entertainment restrictions that result in drop of earnings at an adult establishment are not a taking).

47. 255 N.C. 647, 122 S.E.2d 817 (1961).

48. *Id.* at 651, 122 S.E.2d at 820.

limited use to a residence; there was no evidence on the record that a small "shotgun" residence on this particular site could be sold for more than its construction cost. The court remanded the case for findings on whether the ordinance left any reasonable and practical use of the lot.[49]

The state supreme court upheld Asheville's floodplain zoning ordinance in *Responsible Citizens in Opposition to the Flood Plain Ordinance v. City of Asheville*.[50] The test articulated there for a takings analysis was (1) whether the ends sought to be achieved were within the police power and (2) whether the means by which they were obtained were reasonable. Protecting public safety was held to be a permissible objective and preventing floodway obstructions and requiring flood proofing were held to be reasonable means of accomplishing this.

In *Finch v. City of Durham*,[51] the state supreme court examined the taking issue in the context of reviewing a "downzoning" and reaffirmed the basic test for a taking: there is no taking unless the owner is deprived of practical use of the property and the property is rendered of no reasonable value. Deprivation of previously held development rights[52] and diminution of value do not in themselves constitute a taking. The *Finch* court noted that the plaintiffs had exercised an option to purchase in the knowledge that the planning board had recommended a rezoning, in essence taking a speculative risk that the rezoning would fail. The court found that the ordinance had a reasonable nexus to the legitimate public objective of maintaining the integrity of the adjacent single-family-residential neighborhood, that alternative rezonings such as clustered residential had been proposed by the city but not pursued by the owner, and that the property in any event retained practical use and reasonable value.[53]

---

49. In another taking case, *Roberson's Beverages, Inc. v. City of New Bern*, 6 N.C. App. 632, 171 S.E.2d 4 (1969), *cert. denied*, 276 N.C. 183 (1970), the court reviewed a challenge to New Bern's rezoning of a site previously used as a bottling plant (and as a warehouse for nine years) from a business-commercial zone to an office-institutional zone. The court held that depreciation of value did not render a rezoning a taking or otherwise unconstitutional. Because there was no showing that the building could not be converted to a permissible use, that it could not be razed and the property converted to a permissible use, or that the nonconforming warehouse use could not be continued, the rezoning was upheld. *See also* Blades v. City of Raleigh, 280 N.C. 531, 187 S.E.2d 35 (1972); Michael v. Guilford Cnty., 269 N.C. 515, 153 S.E.2d 106 (1967). A number of cases have also held that reasonable amortization provisions are not a taking. These cases are discussed in Chapter 20.

50. 308 N.C. 255, 302 S.E.2d 204 (1983). The court also held that regulating lands within the hazard zone, but not those outside it, did not violate the Equal Protection Clause because the distinction was a reasonable classification bearing a rational relationship to a permissible state objective.

51. 325 N.C. 352, 384 S.E.2d 8 (1989). This litigation involved the city's rezoning of a 2.6-acre undeveloped parcel adjacent to I-85 from an office-institutional zone to a residential one. The plaintiffs contended that the rezoning reduced the value of the property from $550,000 (if used for a proposed motel) to $20,000 (if used as one single-family lot). The city contended that other valuable uses were available, including use as a church, a day-care site, or additional single-family lots. The jury concluded that there had been a taking but that the plaintiffs had suffered no damages. The trial court then granted a judgment notwithstanding the verdict on damages, invalidated the rezoning, and awarded $150,937 in damages. The zoning statute was amended in 2019 to prohibit downzonings that are initiated by third parties (not initiated by the landowner or local government). G.S. 160D-601(d). S.L. 2019-111, §§ 1.4, 1.5.

52. Plaintiffs must establish that they in fact have a protected property right. In *Adams Outdoor Advertising of Charlotte v. North Carolina Department of Transportation*, the plaintiff contended that the department's planting of trees in the state right-of-way as part of a highway-beautification project obscured the visibility of eleven of its billboards and was a compensable taking under the state's inverse-condemnation statute. The state appeals court dismissed the complaint, finding no basis for a claim of a "right to be seen." 112 N.C. App. 120, 124, 434 S.E.2d 666, 668 (1993). In *Shell Island Homeowners Ass'n v. Tomlinson*, 134 N.C. App. 217, 517 S.E.2d 406 (1999), the same court held that there was no property right to protect oceanfront property from erosion with permanent hardened structures (such as bulkheads), so denial of permits to build such could not be a taking.

53. Three dissenting members of the court concluded that although the use and the value of the property after the rezoning were not such as to constitute a taking as a matter of law, they were adequate to support a jury's finding of a taking. *Finch*, 325 N.C. at 376–89, 384 S.E.2d at 21–29 (entirety of dissents). Courts in other states have applied

North Carolina's highest court again confirmed that a diminution in value resulting from a rezoning is not compensable in *Messer v. Town of Chapel Hill.*[54] In this case the plaintiffs had challenged as a taking a 150-acre rezoning to a residential zoning district that required five-acre minimum lot sizes. While their appeal was pending, the property was sold for $1.5 million. The court dismissed the takings challenge, noting that the sale "establishes beyond peradventure that the property continued to have 'a practical use and a reasonable value' following the amendment to the zoning ordinance."[55] Likewise, in *Williams v. Town of Spencer,*[56] the state court of appeals upheld an ordinance provision that did not allow vacated lots in a mobile-home park to be reoccupied by replacement manufactured-housing units. The court ruled that there was no unconstitutional taking because the ordinance allowed the land occupied by the nonconforming mobile-home park to be used for any of the uses allowed in an industrial zone. In *JWL Investments, Inc. v. Guilford County Board of Adjustment,*[57] the court of appeals rejected a claim that residential zoning with a scenic-corridor overlay was a taking, noting that the regulations did not deprive the owner of all economically beneficial or productive uses. On a related note, in *Town of Midland v. Wayne,* the court held that a common law vested right is not a separate, compensable property right for takings analysis.[58]

A federal court likewise held that a zoning amendment that results in a diminution of value does not in itself constitute an unconstitutional taking in *Adams v. Village of Wesley Chapel.*[59] The court applied the *Penn Central* balancing test, noting that the plaintiffs could make a reasonable return on their investment, just not as much as they had hoped, and that the character of the governmental action was "garden-variety zoning" intended to control growth, preserve a small-town atmosphere, and maintain a low tax rate, all legitimate governmental objectives. The takings claim was therefore dismissed.

Cases challenging the application of other land use regulations have produced similar results in the court of appeals. In *Weeks v. North Carolina Department of Natural Resources & Community Development,*[60] the court held that a limitation of permissible pier length does not deprive a riparian owner of all reasonable use of property and is thus not a taking. *King v. State*[61] involved the denial of state permits to the plaintiff, who wanted to place fill in wetlands in order to build a road and subdivide an eight-acre peninsula in Topsail Sound. The court held that the denial was not a taking because the state had established that practical development alternatives existed.[62] Likewise, in *Guilford County*

---

the *Penn Central* analysis to uphold regulations that significantly reduce but do not totally eliminate the value of property. *See, e.g.,* Animas Valley Sand & Gravel, Inc. v. Bd. of Comm'rs, 38 P.3d 59 (Colo. 2001).

54. 346 N.C. 259, 485 S.E.2d 269 (1997).

55. *Id.* at 261, 485 S.E.2d at 270 (citations to *Finch* omitted).

56. 129 N.C. App. 828, 500 S.E.2d 473 (1998).

57. 133 N.C. App. 426, 515 S.E.2d 715 (1999), *review denied,* 251 N.C. 715, 540 S.E.2d 349 (2000).

58. 368 N.C. 55, 66, 773 S.E.2d 301, 309 (2016). In this case the development was a residential subdivision approved to be developed in three phases. The project's first two phases had been developed and the court found a common law vested right existing to develop the third phase according to the approved multiphase plan. The takings claim arose when a condemnation for a natural-gas pipeline required alteration of the plans for the third phase. The court noted that the vested right was not a property interest separate from the parcel but a "unique quality of that land" that enhanced the land's value. *Id.* at 66, 773 S.E.2d at 309.

59. 259 F. App'x 545 (4th Cir. 2007). The plaintiffs acquired a 184-acre tract in Union County in 1964 for $56,500. After the area was annexed into Wesley Chapel, the town zoning reduced the maximum residential density, resulting in thirty-five fewer potential lots on the property. Although the plaintiff sold the land in 2004 for $3.7 million, it was alleged that the zoning amendment had reduced the property's value by $1.59 million.

60. 97 N.C. App. 215, 224–26, 388 S.E.2d 228, 233–35, *review denied,* 326 N.C. 601, 393 S.E.2d 890 (1990).

61. 125 N.C. App. 379, 481 S.E.2d 330, *review denied,* 346 N.C. 280, 487 S.E.2d 548 (1997).

62. The court concluded that the *Lucas* test for a taking—a deprivation of all economically beneficial or productive use of the property—was similar to the *Finch* standard of determining whether the property was left with a practical use and a reasonable value. *King,* 125 N.C. App. at 386, 481 S.E.2d at 334.

Department of Emergency Services v. Seaboard Chemical Corp.,[63] the court held that denial of a special use permit for a hazardous-waste facility in a watershed area was not a taking because many other uses of the site were permissible.[64] In *Shell Island Homeowners Ass'n v. Tomlinson*,[65] the court rejected a takings challenge to state regulations prohibiting permanent oceanfront erosion-control structures, holding there was no property right to construct such structures. The court noted that, in any event, the plaintiff was aware of this regulatory limitation prior to acquiring title or constructing the threatened hotel and condominium structure, and this prior knowledge foreclosed a taking or inverse-condemnation claim.[66] Similarly, in *Nies v. Town of Emerald Isle*, the court held that municipal regulations on driving on the dry-sand beach could not be considered a taking since the owner had no right to exclude the public from public-trust beaches.[67]

If the court determines that an action affecting the use and value of property is more properly characterized as part of the governmental property-acquisition process than a police-power regulation, compensation is also required. In some respects, this is similar to the portion of the *Penn Central* analysis that considers the purpose of the regulation. If the purpose is to reduce the cost of acquisition of land by the public, a taking may well have occurred.

This is illustrated by *Kirby v. North Carolina Department of Transportation*.[68] The Transportation Corridor Official Map Act[69] challenged in *Kirby* allowed transportation corridors to be identified on maps filed with the register of deeds by cities or the state. Once a map was filed, the law limited approval

---

63. 114 N.C. App. 1, 441 S.E.2d 177, *review denied*, 336 N.C. 604, 447 S.E.2d 390 (1994).

64. The court also held that the cost of cleaning up previous contamination at the site was not to be a factor in determining whether practical uses of the site remained, as that cost would be incurred regardless of the disposition of the special use permit.

65. 134 N.C. App. 217, 517 S.E.2d 406 (1999).

66. The court cited the holding in *Lucas* that there is no taking if a logically antecedent inquiry into the nature of the owner's estate would reveal that the proscribed uses were not part of the owner's title to begin with. Lucas v. S.C. Coastal Council, 505 U.S. 1003, 1027 (1992). *See also* Bryant v. Hogarth, 127 N.C. App. 79, 488 S.E.2d 269, *review denied*, 347 N.C. 396, 494 S.E.2d 406 (1997) (fisheries regulation prohibiting mechanical harvesting in primary nursery area not a taking of exclusive franchise to harvest shellfish in that area where rule was in place prior to issuance of franchise); Adams Outdoor Advert. of Charlotte v. N.C. Dep't of Transp., 112 N.C. App. 120, 434 S.E.2d 666 (1993) (adoption of statute authorizing planting of trees and shrubs within right-of-way prior to issuance of billboard permit precludes takings claim based on such vegetation blocking motorists' views of billboards).

67. 244 N.C. App. 81, 780 S.E.2d 187 (2015), *appeal dismissed*, 369 N.C. 484, 793 S.E.2d 699 (2016), *cert. denied*, 138 S. Ct. 75 (2017). As the public had a legal right to use the dry-sand beach under the public-trust doctrine when the plaintiff acquired the property, the owner did not have a right to exclude the public, and a regulation of how that public use takes place under the police power did not create any expanded public-use rights. Likewise, a regulation restricting the owner or the public from placing beach equipment in such a way as to obstruct access along the beach by emergency vehicles was held to be a reasonable police-power regulation and not a taking.

68. 368 N.C. 847, 786 S.E.2d 919 (2016). In *Beroth Oil Co. v. North Carolina Department of Transportation*, 256 N.C. App. 401, 808 S.E.2d 488 (2017), the court dismissed an interlocutory appeal by the state regarding claims for compensation post-*Kirby*. The court held that the state's claim of sovereign immunity was a substantial right but that it was a jurisdictional issue, and this litigation had passed the point that could be raised. Further, the General Assembly's enactment of a statutory framework for claims in inverse condemnation was an implicit waiver of sovereign immunity for these claims. The Department of Transportation's admission that it had filed an official map affecting the plaintiff's property was properly deemed an admission of a taking within the statutory framework of G.S. 136-111.

69. G.S. 136-44.50 to .54. After the *Kirby* decision, the General Assembly in 2016 amended G.S. 136-44.50 to place a moratorium on new official maps. This act also rescinded all previously adopted official maps. S.L. 2016-90, §§ 16–17. The moratorium was extended to 2019 by S.L. 2018-5, § 34.9. The Transportation Corridor Official Map Act was repealed in 2019, removing the authority of the state and local governments to adopt these future right-of-way protection measures. S.L. 2019-131.

of building permits or new subdivisions within the proposed corridor for up to three years.[70] The court found that the law gave the government the right to establish what was essentially an easement restricting the use of property as a precursor to acquisition in order to reduce the eventual cost of acquisition. Thus, the court held that the filing of the map was properly considered an exercise of eminent domain rather than the police power.

Exactions

The takings issue also arises when landowners are required to dedicate a property interest to the government as a condition of development approval. Exactions are the mandatory dedications of land, construction of facilities, or payments of funds that are imposed as a condition of development approval to address adverse public effects of development.[71] While they are not considered a regulatory taking, exactions are limited by the Takings Clause.[72]

States have traditionally imposed several different standards for how close the relationship between the exactions and the impacts of the proposed development must be. The strictest test, once applied by a minority of states, is that the impacts be uniquely and specifically attributable to the development.[73] On the other end of the spectrum, several states held that any rational relationship between the development's impacts and the exaction would suffice.[74] A majority of states used an intermediate "rational nexus" or "reasonable relationship" test.[75]

While some variation remains on the state-law aspects of this, the U.S. Supreme Court has addressed the question of exactions as takings, thereby setting a national standard based on the U.S. Constitution. These cases establish a two-prong test for the constitutionality of exactions. First, there must be a

---

70. The law allowed variances if no reasonable return could be made from the land, and it allowed landowners to petition for initiation of acquisition if the limits on development imposed an undue hardship. The plaintiffs in *Kirby* alleged that recording an official corridor map made their property unmarketable.

71. Anderson Creek Partners, L.P. v. County of Harnett, 382 N.C. 1, 14–19, 876 S.E.2d 476, 487–90 (2022). The Standard City Planning Enabling Act of 1928, the model enabling act for planning and subdivision regulation, provided that subdivision approvals could be conditioned upon provision of basic infrastructure—streets, water mains, sewer lines, or other utility structures—to serve the needs created by the subdivision. U.S. Dep't of Commerce, A Standard City Planning Enabling Act, tit. 2, § 14 (1928). Initially imposed only for on-site improvements within residential subdivisions, the concept expanded in the post–World War II development boom to include other costs generated by new development. *See generally* Timothy M. Mulvaney, *Exactions for the Future*, 64 Baylor L. Rev. 511 (2012), Ronald H. Rosenberg, *The Changing Culture of American Land Use Regulation: Paying for Growth with Impact Fees*, 59 SMU L. Rev. 177 (2006); Edward J. Sullivan & Isa Lester, *The Role of the Comprehensive Plan in Infrastructure Financing*, 37 Urb. Law. 53 (2005).

72. Statutory authority for exactions is discussed in Chapter 4 (scope of delegated authority generally) and Chapter 7 (subdivision). Impact fees are discussed in Chapter 9.

73. The leading case espousing this test was *Pioneer Trust & Savings Bank v. Village of Mount Prospect*, 22 Ill. 2d 375, 176 N.E.2d 799 (1961) (invalidating requirement of dedication of one acre for parks and schools for each sixty residential lots). *See also* Aunt Hack Ridge Estates, Inc. v. Planning Comm'n, 160 Conn. 109, 273 A.2d 880 (1970); Frank Ansuini, Inc. v. Cranston, 107 R.I. 63, 264 A.2d 910 (1970).

74. *See, e.g.*, Associated Home Builders v. City of Walnut Creek, 4 Cal. 3d 633, 94 Cal. Rptr. 630, 484 P.2d 606 (1971); Jenad, Inc. v. Vill. of Scarsdale, 18 N.Y.2d 78, 271 N.Y.S.2d 955, 218 N.E.2d 673 (1966).

75. The leading case espousing this view was *Jordan v. Village of Menomonee Falls*, 28 Wis. 2d 608, 137 N.W.2d 442 (1965). The court held that the fees charged must be for infrastructure costs that are reasonably related to the impacts of the development and the development must reasonably benefit from expenditure of the fees. *See also* Home Builders Ass'n of Cent. Ariz. v. City of Scottsdale, 187 Ariz. 479, 930 P.2d 993 (1997); Hollywood, Inc. v. Broward Cnty., 431 So. 2d 606 (Fla. Dist. Ct. App. 1983); Howard Cnty. v. JJM, Inc., 301 Md. 256, 482 A.2d 908 (1984). The Supreme Court of Utah uses the term "rough equivalence" for this principle. B.A.M. Dev., L.L.C. v. Salt Lake Cnty., 2008 UT 74, § 8, 196 P.3d 601, 603 (2008).

substantial connection between the dedication and the need for it created by the development. Second, the size of the exaction must not exceed that which is "roughly proportional" to the impacts generated by the development being approved.

In *Nollan v. California Coastal Commission*, the Court held that the exactions required are limited to those rationally related to impacts or needs generated by the proposed development.[76] For example, if a development creates the need for streets, utilities, and recreational space, it is not a taking to require that the developer bear the burden of providing them.[77]

In *Dolan v. City of Tigard*, the Court held that a mandatory exaction must not be any greater than that which is "roughly proportional" to address the impacts of the permitted development.[78] The Court noted that this is a special application of the doctrine of unconstitutional conditions, holding that "the government may not require a person to give up a constitutional right—here the right to receive just compensation when property is taken for a public use—in exchange for a discretionary benefit conferred by the government where the benefit sought has little or no relationship to the property."[79] The proportionality standard only applies in cases involving exactions, not to regulatory-takings claims generally.[80]

In *Koontz v. St. Johns River Water Management District*,[81] the Court extended the *Nollan* and *Dolan* tests to apply to proposed or discussed conditions for a regulatory approval. The landowner and water district discussed dedication of a conservation easement and other mitigation measures (retaining walls, reduction of the development footprint, and payment for off-site wetland improvements) in the context of addressing a proposed development's wetland impacts. When agreement on the mitigation conditions was not secured, the landowner accepted his permit denial and sued the district. The Court held it would be an unconstitutional condition if the government imposed demands beyond those allowed by *Nollan* and *Dolan* to address the impacts of the development. This is the case for monetary contribu-

---

76. 483 U.S. 825 (1987). *See also* Franklin Rd. Props. v. City of Raleigh, 94 N.C. App. 731, 381 S.E.2d 487 (1989).

77. River Birch Assocs. v. City of Raleigh, 326 N.C. 100, 122, 388 S.E.2d 538, 551 (1990); Town of Pinebluff v. Marts, 195 N.C. App. 659, 667–68, 673 S.E.2d 740, 745–46 (2009).

78. 512 U.S. 374 (1994). *See also* Pennell v. City of San Jose, 485 U.S. 1, 19–20 (1988). The North Carolina Court of Appeals relied on a similar test to hold that the exaction of land for a major road through a small subdivision was a taking, but the state supreme court reversed on nonconstitutional grounds. Batch v. Town of Chapel Hill, 326 N.C. 1, 387 S.E.2d 655 (1989). The court in *Anderson Creek Partners, L.P. v. County of Harnett*, 382 N.C. 1, 876 S.E.2d 476 (2022), accepted the test set out in the court of appeals' original *Batch* decision.

79. *Dolan*, 512 U.S. 374 at 385.

80. Lingle v. Chevron U.S.A., Inc., 544 U.S. 528 (2005); City of Monterey v. Del Monte Dunes at Monterey, Ltd., 526 U.S. 687, 702 (1999); McClung v. City of Sumner, 545 F.3d 803, *modified*, 548 F.3d 1219 (9th Cir. 2008) (*Nollan* and *Dolan* standards not applied to generally applicable development condition requiring installation of stormwater pipes). *See also* Yee v. City of Escondido, 503 U.S. 519, 529–32 (1992) (rent-control ordinance not a taking); *Pennell*, 485 U.S. 1. *But see* F.P. Dev., LLC v. Charter Twp. of Canton, 16 F.4th 198 (6th Cir. 2021) (*Nollan/Dolan* applied to tree-protection ordinance).

Other state courts have likewise limited the applicability of the nexus and rough-proportionality standards to exaction cases. *See, e.g.*, Greater Atlanta Homebuilders Ass'n v. Dekalb Cnty., 277 Ga. 295, 588 S.E.2d 694 (2003) (*Dolan* inapplicable to facial challenge of tree-protection ordinance); City of Annapolis v. Waterman, 357 Md. 484, 745 A.2d 1000 (2000) (*Nollan* and *Dolan* inapplicable to subdivision-approval conditions); Bonnie Briar Syndicate, Inc. v. Town of Mamaroneck, 94 N.Y.2d 96, 699 N.Y.S.2d 721, 721 N.E.2d 971 (1999) (rejecting allegation that rezoning of private golf course to open-space zone must meet *Nollan* test). California courts have held that the *Nollan* and *Dolan* tests apply to impact and development fees that are set on an individual, ad hoc–permit basis but not to general legislatively set fees. San Remo Hotel v. City & Cnty. of S.F., 27 Cal. 4th 643, 117 Cal. Rptr. 2d 269, 41 P.3d 87 (2002) (application to rent-control ordinance); Erlich v. City of Culver City, 12 Cal. 4th 854, 50 Cal. Rptr. 2d 242, 911 P.2d 429 (1996) (application to recreation, parkland, and public-art fees and dedications). California has codified its exaction standards as the Mitigation Fee Act, Cal. Gov't Code §§ 66000–66025 (2010). *See also* Action Apartment Ass'n v. City of Santa Monica, 166 Cal. App. 4th 456, 82 Cal. Rptr. 3d 722 (2008) (inapplicable to general affordable-housing requirement).

81. 570 U.S. 595 (2013).

tions (such as fees in lieu of dedications or mitigation funding) as well as exactions of land. However, the Court noted that this analysis applies to exactions, not to taxes and generally applicable utility fees.[82]

The North Carolina court addressed the distinction between exactions and user fees in *Anderson Creek Partners, L.P. v. County of Harnett*.[83] The court held that a fixed water and sewer "capacity use fee" was properly characterized as an "impact fee" and a monetary land-use exaction rather than as a "user fee." As such, the fee was held to be subject to the constitutional *Nollan/Dolan/Koontz* requirement that they be rationally related and roughly proportional to the impacts of the proposed developments. The fact that the fees were a nondiscretionary fixed amount set by a legislative body did not exempt them from this categorization, since the county had the discretion to amend and increase the fees by regulation at any time. The court expressly noted that user fees were not subject to this constitutional limit.[84]

While *Koontz* provides an important constitutional limitation on permit conditions, several courts have held that an agreement to provide land, construct facilities, or pay fees that is voluntarily entered into in good faith and with consideration cannot be subsequently challenged as an unconstitutional taking.[85]

---

82. *Id.* at 615.

83. 382 N.C. 1, 876 S.E.2d 476 (2022). The fee was required to be paid for each lot as a precondition to county concurrence in water and sewer permits issued by the state, so it met the court's definition of an exaction. The purpose of the fee was to partially recover from new customers the costs of expanding capacity of the utility services to account for future customers to be added to the system. The court concluded these were not "user fees," since they did not cover the cost of service currently provided. The fee was set by the county at $1000 for water service and $1200 for sewer service. The court held that the plaintiff's pleadings conceded the fee was rationally related to the impacts of the development but remanded for findings relative to whether it was no more than a roughly proportional amount.

84. 382 N.C. at 39, 876 S.E.2d at 503. Examples of user fees cited by the court included charges for garbage collection or provision of actual water and sewer service and costs for enforcing regulatory programs.

85. McClung v. City of Sumner, 545 F.3d 803, *modified*, 548 F.3d 1219 (9th Cir. 2008) (developer who voluntarily installed an oversized stormwater pipe in return for a waiver of certain fees cannot challenge the condition as a taking); Leroy Land Dev. Corp. v. Tahoe Reg'l Planning Agency, 939 F.2d 696, 698 (9th Cir. 1991) (developer who agreed to off-site mitigation measures cannot challenge agreed-upon condition as a taking); Xenia Rural Water Ass'n v. Dallas Cnty., 445 N.W.2d 785 (Iowa 1989) (setback requirement negotiated by the parties is not a taking); Rischon Dev. Corp. v. City of Keller, 242 S.W.3d 161 (Tex. App. 2007) (developer cannot challenge development-agreement provision as a taking). *But see* Toll Bros., v. Bd. of Chosen Freeholders, 194 N.J. 223, 944 A.2d 1 (2008) (statutory limits on exactions apply to development agreements). Also note that as a general rule a landowner cannot accept the benefits of a regulatory approval and subsequently challenge the terms of that approval. *River Birch*, 326 N.C. at 118–19, 388 S.E.2d at 548–49; Convent of the Sisters of Saint Joseph v. City of Winston-Salem, 243 N.C. 316, 90 S.E.2d 879 (1956).

CHAPTER 25

Due Process and Equal Protection

Due Process

The Due Process Clause of the Fourteenth Amendment to the United States Constitution[1] and the law-of-the-land clause[2] in article I, section 19 of the North Carolina constitution impose a *substantive* requirement that legislative land use regulatory decisions must be reasonable. These constitutional provisions also impose a rule of *procedural* fairness that is critical to quasi-judicial regulatory decisions,[3] which is discussed in Chapter 15. The two dimensions of due process are generally referred to as "substantive due process" and "procedural due process."

Substantive Due Process

A threshold inquiry in a substantive-due-process analysis is whether the right alleged to be infringed is a fundamental right.[4] If it is, the court applies a strict-scrutiny review under which a challenged regulation must serve a compelling governmental interest to survive.

If no fundamental right is involved, as is the case with the review of most development regulations, the regulation must only be rationally related to a legitimate governmental objective.[5] In this context, land-development regulatory decisions must not be arbitrary or capricious. They must address legitimate

---

1. Cleveland Bd. of Educ. v. Loudermill, 470 U.S. 532 (1985) (public employees have property right to continued employment that cannot be deprived without due process); Mullane v. Cent. Hanover Bank & Trust, 339 U.S. 306, 314–20 (1950) (in judicial settlement of trust-fund accounts, due process requires reasonable notice to apprise interested parties of the pendency of the action and afford them an opportunity to present their objections). The general constitutional requirements for quasi-judicial decisions are reviewed in Chapter 14.

2. The law-of-the-land clause in the North Carolina constitution is synonymous with the Due Process Clause of the U.S. Constitution. Rice v. Rigsby, 259 N.C. 506, 518, 131 S.E.2d 469, 477 (1963) (jury-selection method held not to be a due-process violation). The interpretations given the Due Process Clause by the United States Supreme Court are considered highly persuasive but not binding by North Carolina courts interpreting this comparable state-constitutional provision. Town of Atl. Beach v. Young, 307 N.C. 422, 428, 298 S.E.2d 686, 690–91 (1983); State v. Barnes, 264 N.C. 517, 520, 142 S.E.2d 344, 346 (1965) (ordering new trial on admissibility of confession).

3. Procedural due-process claims can also arise in the judicial review of administrative decisions. In *Nance v. City of Albemarle*, 520 F. Supp. 3d 758 (M.D.N.C. 2021), a challenge to denial of approval to convert a motel that had been cited for nuisance violations into a low-income housing facility, the court held that there was no federal due-process violation as the applicant was allowed multiple opportunities to meet with the planning director, to address the city council, and to submit multiple applications. The state constitutional and statutory procedural due-process requirements for quasi-judicial decisions are more stringent than the minimum federal standards.

4. "Fundamental" rights include those enumerated in the Constitution, such as freedom of speech, religion, and protection from unreasonable searches. It also includes rights to marital privacy.

5. *See, e.g.*, Capital Outdoor, Inc. v. Tolson, 159 N.C. App. 55, 582 S.E.2d 717, *review denied*, 357 N.C. 504, 587 S.E.2d 662 (2003) (holding right to construct outdoor advertising is not a fundamental right, so billboard regulation need only meet the rational-relationship test).

governmental objectives and use means to reach the objectives that are reasonable. Regulations must also be sufficiently precise so that a person knows what is required for compliance. These requirements are reviewed below.

To prevail on a substantive-due-process challenge of a development regulation, a plaintiff must establish that the challenged action affected a property interest possessed by the plaintiff,[6] that the government deprived the plaintiff of that interest, and that the deprivation "falls so far beyond the outer limits of legitimate governmental action that no process could cure the deficiency."[7]

In a land use context, federal courts have held that a disputed regulation must "shock the conscience" of the court for there to be a substantive-due-process violation.[8] An improper motive on the part of the local governing board will not suffice.[9] In *Siena Corp. v. Mayor of Rockville*, the Fourth Circuit court held that the action must shock the conscience in a constitutional sense, not be a routine exercise of the police power.[10] Even where the court concludes that the landowner was treated "shabbily and unfairly," the court is unlikely to hold such to be a due-process violation.[11] The governmental action must be "so

---

6. In *Sansotta v. Town of Nags Head*, 724 F.3d 533 (4th Cir. 2013), the court held that since an owner has no right to use property in a way that constitutes a nuisance, an action to abate a nuisance does not affect a property right. The court also held that assessment of a civil penalty that is not paid does not deprive a person of property. Similarly, in an action by builders and real-estate agents challenging Pinehurst's design standards, the court held that the plaintiffs had no property interest affected by the regulation containing the standards. They had no right to build houses that did not conform with zoning, no right to build a particular type or price of house, and no right to earn a specific amount of income. Quality Built Homes, Inc. v. Vill. of Pinehurst, No. 1:06CV1028, 2008 WL 3503149 (M.D.N.C. Aug. 11, 2008). In *Nance, supra* note 3, the court held that since the plaintiff did not show they had a property right to a nondiscretionary permit approval there could be no substantive-due-process violation.

Since a rezoning is a discretionary act by the local legislative body, federal courts routinely hold that plaintiffs have no protected property interest in a proposed rezoning and thus no due-process rights. *See, e.g.*, Andrews v. City of Mentor, 11 F.4th 462 (6th Cir. 2021) (denial of discretionary rezoning is not deprivation of a cognizable property interest for due-process purposes, though it may raise takings issues); EJS Props., LLC v. City of Toledo, 698 F.3d 845 (6th Cir. 2012); DC3, LLC v. Town of Geneva, 783 F. Supp. 2d 418, 422 (W.D.N.Y. 2011) (given vast discretion to change zoning designations, property owners have no cognizable property interest in the zoning designation of their property). The courts have also noted that there is no property right in the policies set out in a comprehensive plan, especially as the plan and ordinances are clearly subject to future amendment. *See, e.g.*, Pulte Home Corp. v. Montgomery Cnty., 909 F.3d 685 (4th Cir. 2018).

See generally, Brian W. Blaesser, *Substantive Due Process Protection at the Outer Margins of Municipal Behavior*, 3 Wash. U. J.L. & Pol'y, 583 (2000); Daniel R. Mandelker, *Entitlement to Substantive Due Process: Old Versus New Property in Land Use Regulation*, 3 Wash. U. J.L. & Pol'y, 61 (2000).

7. Tri-Cnty. Paving, Inc. v. Ashe Cnty., 281 F.3d 430, 440 (4th Cir. 2002) (quoting Sylvia Dev. Corp. v. Calvert Cnty., 48 F.3d 810, 827 (4th Cir. 1995)).

8. *See generally* Jane R. Bambauer and Toni M. Massaro, *Outrageous and Irrational*, 100 Minn. L. Rev. 281 (2015) (distinguishing substantiative due-process review of governmental actions that shock the conscience (the "outrageous") and those that are arbitrary and capricious (the "irrational")).

9. *See, e.g.*, Snaza v. City of Saint Paul, 548 F.3d 1178 (8th Cir. 2008); Clark v. Boscher, 514 F.3d 107 (1st Cir. 2008); Mongeau v. City of Marlborough, 492 F.3d 14 (1st Cir. 2007); United Artists Theatre Circuit, Inc. v. Twp. of Warrington, 316 F.3d 392 (3d Cir. 2003); Nestor Colon Medina & Sucesores, Inc. v. Custodio, 964 F.2d 32, 45 (1st Cir. 1992) ("truly horrendous" situation required); Chesterfield Dev. Corp. v. City of Chesterfield, 963 F.2d 1102, 1105 (8th Cir. 1992) (a bad-faith enforcement of an invalid zoning provision would not be a substantive-due-process violation).

10. 873 F.3d 456, 464 (4th Cir. 2017). The city had enacted a zoning requirement that self-storage facilities be located at least 250 feet from schools after learning of the plaintiff's plans but before any vested rights had been established. The amendment effectively prevented the proposed use of the plaintiff's site. *See also* CEnergy-Glenmore Wind Farm No. 1, LLC v. Town of Glenmore, 769 F.3d 485 (7th Cir. 2014) (upholding denial of permit based on popular opposition to project); Bettendorf v. St. Croix Cnty., 631 F.3d 421 (7th Cir. 2011) (upholding rescission of commercial zoning).

11. DLC Mgmt. Corp. v. Town of Hyde Park, 163 F.3d 124, 131 (2d Cir. 1998). In *Raynor v. Town of Chapel Hill*, No. 1:18CV291, 2019 WL 503443 (M.D.N.C. Feb. 8, 2019), the court dismissed a substantive-due-process challenge, holding that a sixteen-month protracted discussion and local appeals process was not arbitrary and irrational, nor did the process and rationales offered for denial of a certificate of appropriateness and failure to act more promptly shock the conscience of the court.

outrageously arbitrary as to constitute a gross abuse of governmental authority."[12] This reflects the federal courts' unwillingness to engage in "run of the mill" zoning disputes.[13]

Arbitrary and Capricious

A land-development regulatory decision that is arbitrary and capricious violates due process. However, given the presumption of validity accorded legislative decisions,[14] this is "a very difficult standard to meet"[15] for those challenging these decisions.

Only an action deemed by a court to be oppressive and manifestly abusive of discretion will be overturned. The challenged action must have no foundation in reason and amount to a mere arbitrary, irrational exercise with no substantial relation to legitimate public objectives.[16] If a legislative regulatory decision has a "reasonable tendency to promote the public good,"[17] "so long as there is some plausible basis for the conclusion,"[18] and absent "patently bad faith," "whimsical" decisions, or decisions made

---

12. Natale v. Town of Ridgefield, 170 F.3d 258, 259 (2d Cir. 1999). For an example of a case that fails to meet even this standard, see *Marks v. City of Chesapeake*, 883 F.2d 308 (4th Cir. 1989), where the court held that it was arbitrary and capricious to deny a conditional use permit for a palmist/fortune teller based on neighbors' religious objections rather than legitimate land use concerns.

13. Resolving the routine land-use disputes that inevitably and constantly arise among developers, local residents, and municipal officials is simply not the business of the federal courts. . . . [F]ederal courts should be extremely reluctant to upset the delicate political balance at play in local land-use disputes. Section 1983 does not empower us to sit as a super-planning commission or a zoning board of appeals, and it does not constitutionalize every "run of the mill dispute between a developer and a town planning agency." In most instances, therefore, decisions regarding the application of subdivision regulations, zoning ordinances, and other local land-use controls properly rest with the community that is ultimately—and intimately—affected.

Gardner v. City of Balt. Mayor, 969 F.2d 63, 67–68 (4th Cir. 1992) (citations omitted). *See also* Pulte Home Corp. v. Montgomery Cnty., 909 F.3d 685, 698 (4th Cir. 2018) ("Local zoning authorities must have the ability to respond to constantly changing environmental, economic, and social conditions, and we are unwilling to tie their hands . . . . To hold otherwise would be to invade the province of state law and render local officials unable to make the important decisions they were elected to make."); Henry v. Jefferson Cnty. Comm'n, 637 F.3d 269, 278 (4th Cir. 2011) ("Once again we decline the invitation to turn federal courts into clearinghouses for alleged constitutional violations that in fact are only the routine and routinely contentious disagreements arising out of local permitting decisions."); Scott v. Greenville Cnty., 716 F.2d 1409, 1419 (4th Cir. 1983). In the context of an analogous equal-protection claim, Supreme Court Justice Breyer expressed this common reluctance to federalize typical zoning disputes.

This case, however, does not directly raise the question whether the simple and common instance of a faulty zoning decision would violate the Equal Protection Clause. That is because the Court of Appeals found that in this case respondent had alleged an extra factor as well—a factor that the Court of Appeals called "vindictive action," "illegitimate animus," or "ill will." . . .

In my view, the presence of that added factor in this case is sufficient to minimize any concern about transforming run-of-the-mill zoning cases into cases of constitutional right.

Vill. of Willowbrook v. Olech, 528 U.S. 562, 565–66 (2000) (J. Breyer, concurring) (citations omitted).

14. See the discussion of the presumption of validity in judicial review of legislative decisions in Chapter 29.

15. Summers v. City of Charlotte, 149 N.C. App. 509, 518, 562 S.E.2d 18, 25, *review denied*, 355 N.C. 758, 566 S.E.2d 482 (2002).

16. Sylvia Dev. Corp. v. Calvert Cnty., 48 F.3d 810, 827 (4th Cir. 1995).

17. Marren v. Gamble, 237 N.C. 680, 686, 75 S.E.2d 880, 884 (1953).

18. Zopfi v. City of Wilmington, 273 N.C. 430, 437, 160 S.E.2d 325, 332 (1968) (citing *In re* Markham, 259 N.C. 566, 131 S.E.2d 329 (1963)); Walton North Carolina, LLC v. City of Concord, 257 N.C. App. 227, 809 S.E.2d 164 (2017), *review denied*, 371 N.C. 447, 817 S.E.2d 388 (2018) (plan inconsistency, increased traffic, negative impact on school capacity, and potential negative impact on neighboring property are plausible bases to deny rezoning); McDowell v. Randolph Cnty., 256 N.C. App. 708, 808 S.E.2d 513 (2017) (board had several plausible bases to justify its decision); Ashby v. Town of Cary, 161 N.C. App. 499, 503, 588 S.E.2d 572, 574 (2003); Graham v. City of Raleigh, 55 N.C. App. 107, 110, 284 S.E.2d 742, 744 (1981), *review denied*, 305 N.C. 299, 290 S.E.2d 702 (1982) (holding that the governing board has the primary duty and responsibility of determining whether its action is in the interest of the public health, safety, morals, or general welfare).

without "fair and careful consideration," it will not be found arbitrary and capricious.[19] This standard of review applies to both conventional rezonings and rezonings with site-specific conditions.[20]

Though only on rare occasion, courts have found that a certain legislative regulatory decision violated this standard. In *Gregory v. County of Harnett*, for example, the county denied a rezoning that effectively prohibited a manufactured-home park on the site at issue but then a few months later approved an identical rezoning request for the site.[21] The court reviewing the county's action held that where the record reflected no consideration of the character of the land, the suitability of the land for proposed uses, consistency with the county plan, or changed circumstances on the land, the rezoning was arbitrary and capricious.[22] In *Town of Green Level v. Alamance County*,[23] the county attempted to block the town's extension of extraterritorial jurisdiction by hastily adopting a "Rural Community District" zoning provision to be applied to the disputed area. The court held that the county's ordinance was arbitrary and capricious in that it was adopted to block the town's jurisdiction rather than to promote a legitimate health, safety, or welfare purpose. The record indicated that the county made no reference to a comprehensive plan in its adoption of the zoning provision, which contained no references to water-quality protection and allowed various industrial uses inconsistent with a rural community.

While mentioned by neither the *Gregory* nor the *Green Level* court, there were alleged undercurrents of potential racial and ethnic discrimination involved in both of the cases, and this factor may have prompted more searching judicial review than might otherwise have been undertaken.[24]

---

19. *Summers*, 149 N.C. App. at 519, 562 S.E.2d at 25 (internal quotations and citations omitted).

20. *Ashby*, 161 N.C. App. 499, 588 S.E.2d 572 (conditional use district rezoning decision not arbitrary and capricious if there is any plausible basis for the decision that has a foundation in reason and relation to public safety).

21. 128 N.C. App. 161, 493 S.E.2d 786 (1997). The fact that contrary results were reached in two rezoning petitions for the same parcel of land does not in itself render a decision arbitrary, even if the two decisions are close together in time. Carroll v. City of Kings Mountain, 193 N.C. App. 165, 666 S.E.2d 814 (2008).

22. *Gregory*, 128 N.C. App. at 165, 493 S.E.2d at 789. Courts in other states have also invalidated rezonings to a zoning classification that is patently unreasonable for a site. *See, e.g.*, Appeal of Realen Valley Forge Greenes Assocs., 576 Pa. 115, 838 A.2d 718 (2003) (invalidating agricultural rezoning of property in highly developed commercial area as improper "reverse spot zoning").

23. 184 N.C. App. 665, 646 S.E.2d 851, *review denied*, 361 N.C. 704, 655 S.E.2d 402 (2007).

24. In *Gregory*, hostility had been expressed by some neighbors toward Hispanic farm workers who occupied some manufactured housing in the area. In *Green Level*, some white residents of the proposed extraterritorial area had expressed concern about being subject to town regulation given a strong African American presence in town government. In neither case was racial or ethnic hostility formally established or used by the court as the basis of decision. *See* Cedar Grove Inst. for Sustainable Cmtys., Incorporation, Annexation and Extra-Territorial Jurisdiction: A Double Standard? Predominantly-Minority Towns Struggle 13–15, 23–27 (Oct. 28, 2004).

Legitimate Governmental Objectives

A governmental regulation must be reasonably related to the accomplishment of a legitimate governmental objective.[25] While the motives of individual elected officials are generally irrelevant,[26] the purpose or objective of a land use regulation is a legitimate constitutional query.

The question in zoning's infancy was whether land-development regulations could address public objectives beyond the traditional protection of public health and safety.[27] The 1923 zoning-enabling statute provided authority for regulations that address a broad range of concerns within the sphere of public-welfare protection:

> Zoning regulations shall be made in accordance with a comprehensive plan and designed to lessen congestion in the streets; to secure safety from fire, panic and other dangers; to promote health and the general welfare; to provide adequate light and air; to prevent overcrowding of land; to avoid undue concentration of population; and to facilitate the adequate provision of transportation, water, sewerage, schools, parks, and other public requirements. The regulations shall be made with reasonable consideration, among other things, as to the character of the district and its peculiar suitability for particular uses, and with a view to conserving the value of buildings and encouraging the most appropriate use of land throughout the city.[28]

The North Carolina Supreme Court noted the breadth of this range of permissible objectives and its evolving nature in the landmark case upholding zoning power, *Elizabeth City v. Aydlett*:

> The word "zoning" signifies the division of a municipal corporation into separate areas and the application to each area of regulations which generally pertain to the use of buildings or to their structural or architectural design. Such municipal action finds its authority in the police power which may be exercised, not only in the interest of the public health, morals, and safety, but for the promotion of the general welfare. This power embraces the whole system of internal regulation, and cannot be bargained away. Its nature and extent have been defined in these words: "It may be said in a general way that the police power extends to all the great public needs. It may

---

25. Town of Atl. Beach v. Young, 307 N.C. 422, 428, 298 S.E.2d 686, 690–91, *cert. denied*, 462 U.S. 1101 (1983) (upholding ordinance restricting the keeping of animals, livestock, and poultry within the city limits); Raleigh Mobile Home Sales, Inc. v. Tomlinson, 276 N.C. 661, 174 S.E.2d 542 (1970) (upholding Sunday closing ordinance); State v. Whitaker, 228 N.C. 352, 45 S.E.2d 860 (1947), *aff'd sub nom.* Lincoln Fed. Labor Union No. 19129 v. Nw. Iron & Metal Co., 335 U.S. 525 (1949) (upholding right-to-work statute).

26. For a detailed discussion of this point, see Chapter 26, which addresses motive as a factor in judicial review of adult-entertainment regulations.

27. North Carolina's general-police-power statute for cities authorizes regulation to protect "the health, safety, or welfare of its citizens and the peace and dignity of the city." Chapter 160A, Section 174 of the North Carolina General Statutes (hereinafter G.S.). G.S. 153A-121 contains the same authorization for counties.

28. G.S. 160A-383 (1923) (pertaining to cities). The current statutes contain comparable language in G.S. 160D-701. This language is substantially similar to the purposes section of the Standard State Zoning Enabling Act. A variety of other land-development-regulatory statutes include statements of purposes and objectives to be addressed. *See, e.g.*, G.S. 63-30 (airport zoning), 113A-51 (sedimentation-control regulations), 113A-102 (coastal-management regulations), 113A-207 (mountain-ridge-protection regulations), 130A-333 (regulation of on-site waste-disposal systems), 136-142 (junkyard controls), 143-214.7 (stormwater regulations), 143-215.51 (floodplain zoning), 160D-902 (regulation of adult businesses), 160A-306 (street-setback regulations), 160D-804(a) (subdivision regulation), 160D-940 (historic-district regulation), 160D-1302 (open-space protection), 160D-1201 (housing codes), 166A-2 (emergency-management programs), 168-1 (zoning affecting disabled persons).

be put forth in aid of what is sanctioned by usage, or held by the prevailing morality or strong and preponderant opinion to be greatly and immediately necessary to the public welfare."

The police power is not static. It expands to meet conditions which necessarily change as business progresses and civilization advances.[29]

This last consideration—that the scope of legitimate objectives of the police power changes with time—was noted also by the United States Supreme Court in *Village of Euclid v. Ambler Realty Co.*, a case decided some five years before *Aydlett*.[30]

The state high court wrestled with the scope of legitimate objectives for land use regulations, particularly when balanced against substantial impacts on individual liberties,[31] in a second early zoning case, *Appeal of Parker*.[32] The court there found that the rights of individuals to the use of their property are subordinate to the general welfare and such public interests as traffic control, fire safety, and aesthetics, pointing out that

> [e]ach person holds his property with the right to use the same in such manner as will not interfere with the rights of others, or the public interest or requirement. It is held in subordination to the rights of society. He may not do with it as he pleases any more than he may act in accordance with his personal desires. The interests of society justify restraints upon individual conduct and also upon the use to which the property may be devoted.[33]

---

29. 201 N.C. 602, 605, 161 S.E. 78, 79 (1931) (citations omitted).

30. The Court in *Euclid* held:

> Until recent years, urban life was comparatively simple; but, with the great increase and concentration of population, problems have developed, and constantly are developing, which require, and will continue to require, additional restrictions in respect of the use and occupation of private lands in urban communities. Regulations, the wisdom, necessity, and validity of which, as applied to existing conditions, are so apparent that they are now uniformly sustained, a century ago, or even half a century ago, probably would have been rejected as arbitrary and oppressive.

272 U.S. 365, 386–87 (1926). This view of the scope of the police power was reaffirmed in 1979 by the North Carolina Supreme Court in *A-S-P Associates v. City of Raleigh*:

> Moreover, . . . this Court must not lose sight of the fact that "[s]ince the police power of the State has not been, and by its nature cannot be, placed within fixed definitive limits, it may be extended or restricted to meet changing conditions, economic as well as social."

298 N.C. 207, 214, 258 S.E.2d 444, 449 (1979) (citation omitted).

31. The need to balance public and private interests has been a consideration of zoning from the outset. As a 1938 manual on zoning noted,

> [z]oning is the application of common sense and fairness to the public regulations governing the use of private real estate. It is a painstaking, honest effort to provide each district or neighborhood, as nearly as practicable, with *just such protection* and *just such liberty* as are sensible in *that particular district*.

Patrick Healy Jr., A Zoning Manual for North Carolina Towns and Cities 1 (N.C. League of Municipalities Report No. 27, July 1938).

32. 214 N.C. 51, 197 S.E. 706, *appeal dismissed sub nom.* Parker v. City of Greensboro, 305 U.S. 568 (1938) (upholding limits on height and character of fences built along property lines). See Chapter 24 for a discussion of the takings issue raised in this case.

33. *Appeal of Parker*, 214 N.C. at 57, 197 S.E. at 710. The dissent considered the challenged regulation to be "an unreasonable invasion of the traditional and accepted rights of property owners" and contended that zoning objectives should be limited to public necessities. *Id.* at 58, 197 S.E. at 711 (Clarkson J., dissenting). An Institute of Government commentator at the time noted the strong dissent and observed that the case marked "what may be the beginning of the end of the era of 'unlimited' police power." Dillard Gardner, *Zoning Ordinances and the Police Power*, Popular Gov't, July 1938, at 1.

A-S-P Associates v. City of Raleigh is the leading contemporary North Carolina case applying this principle to land use regulation. The court upheld adoption of a historic-district zoning classification for the Oakwood neighborhood in Raleigh, noting that

> [s]everal principles must be borne in mind when considering a due process challenge to governmental regulation of private property on grounds that it is an invalid exercise of the police power. First, is the object of the legislation within the scope of the police power? Second, considering all the surrounding circumstances and particular facts of the case is the means by which the governmental entity has chosen to regulate reasonable? This second inquiry is two-pronged: (1) Is the statute in its application reasonably necessary to promote the accomplishment of a public good and (2) is the interference with the owner's right to use his property as he deems appropriate reasonable in degree?[34]

The typical objectives of development regulations fall within the range of legitimate purposes. Performance standards for industrial uses, mandatory parking and traffic-safety requirements, and limits on building in flood-prone areas are examples of regulations directly related to the protection of public health and safety. Promotion of the general welfare of the community is a broader objective that can include a wide variety of zoning regulations. Among the specific general-welfare objectives that clearly are permissible aims for development regulation are providing for the safe, efficient, and adequate provision of public services such as water, sewer, and roads;[35] protecting public safety;[36] protecting

---

34. *A-S-P*, 298 N.C. at 214, 258 S.E.2d at 448–49 (citations omitted).

35. G.S. 160D-701 provides that zoning may be used to "facilitate the efficient and adequate provision of transportation, water, sewerage, schools, parks, and other public requirements." In *LeTendre v. Currituck County*, 259 N.C. App. 512, 817 S.E.2d 73 (2018), *review denied*, 372 N.C. 54, 822 S.E.2d 641 (2019), the court noted that the lack of infrastructure in an area justified zoning it only for very low-density residential uses. In *Tonter Investments, Inc., v. Pasquotank County*, 199 N.C. App. 579, 681 S.E.2d 536, *review denied*, 363 N.C. 663, 687 S.E.2d 296 (2009), the court held that assuring adequate roads and water service prior to construction of structures is a legitimate objective of a zoning regulation. See Chapter 9 for further discussion of adequate-public-facility ordinances.

The classic case on this objective is *Golden v. Planning Board*, 30 N.Y.2d 359, 334 N.Y.S.2d 138, 285 N.E.2d 291 (1972), *appeal dismissed*, 409 U.S. 1003 (1972). For a national review of the case law on such requirements, see John S. Herbrand, Annotation, *Validity of Municipality's Ban on Construction Until Public Facilities Comply with Specific Standards*, 92 A.L.R.3d 1073 (1980); David J. Oliveiri, Annotation, *Validity of Zoning Ordinance Deferring Residential Development Until Establishment of Public Services in Area*, 63 A.L.R.3d 1184 (1975).

36. Responsible Citizens v. City of Asheville, 308 N.C. 255, 302 S.E.2d 204 (1983).

and enhancing property values;[37] protecting residential neighborhoods;[38] providing for adequate open spaces;[39] protecting the environment and natural resources;[40] controlling drainage and preventing erosion;[41] and preventing the expansion of nonconformities.[42]

The power is not unlimited, though. The use of development regulations to exclude racial and ethnic minorities or low-income households has been a serious and continuing problem in many jurisdictions. Provisions requiring large minimum lot sizes and minimum floor areas for residential dwellings and excluding any area for multifamily housing have been used by some suburban communities to foster racial and economic segregation.[43] Given North Carolina's residential settlement patterns and annexation policies, exclusionary zoning has not heretofore been subject to extensive legislation or litigation.[44] However, in 1940 the North Carolina Supreme Court held that zoning could not be used to require

---

37. *See, e.g.*, Duggins v. Town of Walnut Cove, 63 N.C. App. 684, 306 S.E.2d 186, *review denied*, 309 N.C. 819, 310 S.E.2d 348 (1983), *cert. denied*, 466 U.S. 946 (1984). See Julian Conrad Juergensmeyer et al., Land Use Planning and Development Regulation Law § 3.14 (3d ed., Feb. 2023 Update) for a collection of national cases with the same holding.

Protection of property values has long been one of the principal grounds for public support of zoning. An entry from a 1938 manual promoting zoning in North Carolina echoes this:

> Suppose you have just bought some land in a neighborhood of homes and built a cozy little house. There are two vacant lots south of you. If your town is zoned, no one can put up a large apartment house on those lots, overshadowing your home, stealing your sunshine and spoiling the investment of 20 years' saving. Nor is anyone at liberty to erect a noisy, malodorous public garage or service station to keep you awake nights or to drive you to sell out for half of what you put into your home.
>
> If a town is zoned, property values become more stable, mortgage companies are more ready to lend money, and more houses can be built.

Patrick Healy Jr., *supra* note 31, at 1–2. As one commentator has noted, "The majority of a community is always more concerned with protecting the investment value of property than promoting its speculative value. And this was, and is, the basis of much popular support of zoning." John Delafons, Land Use Controls in the United States 82 (1962).

38. Justice William O. Douglas's opinion in *Village of Belle Terre v. Boraas* is frequently quoted:

> A quiet place where yards are wide, people few, and motor vehicles restricted are legitimate guidelines in a land-use project addressed to family needs. This goal is a permissible one . . . . The police power is not confined to elimination of filth, stench, and unhealthy places. It is ample to lay out zones where family values, youth values, and the blessings of quiet seclusion and clean air make the area a sanctuary for people.

416 U.S. 1, 9 (1974). *Cf.* Berman v. Parker, 348 U.S. 26 (1954) (upholding broad reading of police-power scope in eminent-domain case). *See also* Ames Rental Prop. Ass'n v. City of Ames, 736 N.W.2d 255 (Iowa 2007) (upholding restriction on number of unrelated individuals in a single-family dwelling). Zoning authority has been held in a number of states to be broad enough to allow local governments to establish minimum-housing-size requirements as well as minimum lot sizes. While this was done in only a few North Carolina zoning ordinances, a development regulation that sets a minimum structure size is now prohibited by G.S. 160D-702(c). That statutory restriction does not apply to private restrictive covenants, where the practice is far more prevalent.

39. River Birch Assocs. v. City of Raleigh, 326 N.C. 100, 116, 388 S.E.2d 538, 547 (1990) ("Cities may regulate open space as part of their power to provide for the physical, social, aesthetic and economic welfare of the community.").

40. *LeTendre*, 259 N.C. App. 512, 817 S.E.2d 73 (preservation of sensitive natural resources and protection of wildlife habitat).

41. Grace Baptist Church v. City of Oxford, 320 N.C. 439, 358 S.E.2d 372 (1987) (upholding requirement that off-street parking areas be paved).

42. *Grace Baptist Church*, 320 N.C. 439, 358 S.E.2d 372; State v. Joyner, 286 N.C. 366, 372, 211 S.E.2d 320, 324, *cert. denied*, 422 U.S. 1002 (1975); Huntington Props., LLC v. Currituck Cnty., 153 N.C. App. 218, 229–30, 569 S.E.2d 695, 703–04 (2002).

43. *See* Andrew H. Whittemore, *Exclusionary Zoning: Origins, Open Suburbs, and Contemporary Debates*, 87 J. Am. Plan. Ass'n. 167 (2021). An exclusionary-zoning claim was dismissed in *Quality Built Homes, Inc. v. Village of Pinehurst*, No. 1:06CV1028, 2008 WL 3503149 (M.D.N.C. Aug. 11, 2008). Also see the discussion of inclusionary zoning in Chapter 9.

44. Also see the discussion of the Fair Housing Act in Chapter 23.

residential racial segregation.[45] The challenged ordinance had set up separate residential zoning districts by race. The court had previously invalidated a general-police-power ordinance prohibiting a person from residing in a block where a majority of the houses were occupied by persons of a different race.[46]

North Carolina courts have held a variety of other purposes to be beyond the reach of land-development regulations.

Development regulations may not be used to control the ownership—as opposed to the use—of property. For example, the state appeals court has ruled that zoning cannot prevent the conversion of multifamily rental apartments to owned condominiums.[47] This court has likewise held that a zoning regulation may not provide that an "accessory" apartment is permissible only if it or the principal residence is owner-occupied.[48]

Land use regulations may not be based on the identity of the users of the property. In *Gregory*,[49] the court invalidated a rezoning that moved property from a district that allowed manufactured-home parks to one that did not. The court held that the rezoning was arbitrary after the record disclosed that it was based on undocumented concerns about crime committed by residents of manufactured-home parks and the "type of people" who reside therein, with no evidence showing any consideration of the character of the land, the suitability of the land for various uses, the provisions of the zoning plan, or changing conditions in the area.

The court has also invalidated small-scale rezonings (often referred to as spot zoning) that offer only modest public benefit but pose potential substantial harm to neighbors, holding such to be unreasonable, arbitrary, and not in the public interest.[50]

Development regulations may not be used to enforce private restrictive covenants that are not covered by the regulation itself.[51]

---

45. Clinard v. City of Winston-Salem, 217 N.C. 119, 6 S.E.2d 867 (1940).

46. State v. Darnell, 166 N.C. 300, 81 S.E. 338 (1914). In *Buchanan v. Warley*, 245 U.S. 60 (1917), the U.S. Supreme Court reached the same conclusion. *See also* Philbrook v. Chapel Hill Hous. Auth., 269 N.C. 598, 605, 153 S.E.2d 153, 159 (1967) (noting that a "zoning ordinance purporting to restrict the occupancy and use of property solely on the basis of race is unconstitutional and void"); Brown v. Town of Davidson, 113 N.C. App. 553, 439 S.E.2d 206 (1994) (allegation of racial discrimination as basis for rezoning dismissed after the forecast of proof on discriminatory intent showed only that council refused to allow commercial zoning in a developed residential area).

47. Graham Court Assocs. v. Town Council of Chapel Hill, 53 N.C. App. 543, 281 S.E.2d 418 (1981). G.S. 47C-1-106 also explicitly prohibits the use of zoning to control the condominium form of ownership. The N.C. Attorney General has opined that the use of a drug-treatment facility to provide treatment to inmates under a contract with the Department of Corrections does convert a medical facility from an "office and institutional use" to a "correctional facility use" as it is the use, not the identity of the user, that is the appropriate subject of a zoning regulation. N.C. Dep't of Justice, Office of the Att'y Gen., Advisory Opinion: Tarboro Zoning Ordinance, Op. N.C. Att'y Gen. (Mar. 2, 1995). This principle is commonly applied to limit zoning regulations. *See, e.g.*, O'Connor v. City of Moscow, 202 P.2d 401 (Idaho 1949) (holding city could not require zoning approval for a change in ownership of a pool hall, card room, or beer parlor).

48. City of Wilmington v. Hill, 189 N.C. App. 173, 657 S.E.2d 670 (2008). The city's development regulations permitted a garage apartment as an accessory use in a single-family zoning district, provided the property owner lived in either the main residence or the accessory apartment. The court held the ownership requirement unconstitutional as an impermissible regulation of ownership rather than a permissible regulation of land use. The court also held that the owner-occupant requirement was beyond the scope of delegated zoning powers. Ownership can, however, perhaps be a factor in defining a use. For example, an ordinance may allow a dog kennel for personal use, even for a nonprofit kennel, while prohibiting a commercial kennel.

49. 128 N.C. App. 161, 493 S.E.2d 786 (1997). Also see the discussion in Chapter 16 as to the application of standards regarding neighborhood harmony and public safety in making special and conditional use permit decisions.

50. *See, e.g.*, Covington v. Town of Apex, 108 N.C. App. 231, 423 S.E.2d 537 (1992). See Chapter 12 for a discussion of spot zoning.

51. See *Midgette v. Pate*, 94 N.C. App. 498, 380 S.E.2d 572 (1989), for an enforcement case that alleged both zoning violations and restrictive-covenant violations. As a general rule, the constitutional limitations on government

Courts in other states have addressed additional limitations on legitimate objectives for land-development regulations. For example, it is clear that regulations may not be used to lower land costs as a prelude to condemnation.[52] Also, it is often held that zoning may not be used to restrict commercial competition, such as by favoring a particular business or individual.[53] Regulations to limit national franchise businesses in order to protect local merchants, preserve a "local character," or prevent the sameness of "cookie cutter" development, while sometimes successful, have likewise faced substantial judicial scrutiny.[54]

The question of whether the regulation of aesthetics is a legitimate objective of land-development regulation has been a controversial topic, and one that illustrates the changing scope of the police power. For many years the courts nationally and in North Carolina held that regulations could not be based solely on aesthetics.[55] For this reason ordinances were invalidated that imposed requirements to screen junkyards[56] and regulate business signs.[57] However, in 1972 the North Carolina Supreme Court noted that there was a "growing body of authority in other jurisdictions to the effect that the police power [might] be broad enough to include reasonable regulation of property use for aesthetic reasons only."[58] Then in 1979, in the *A-S-P* case, this court stated that, although it was not yet prepared to hold that

---

regulations do not apply to private restrictive covenants, as those are agreements between private parties and not state actions. An exception to that general rule is that courts have long found that judicial enforcement of private racial restrictive covenants is state action subject to constitutional limits. Shelley v. Kraemer, 334 U.S. 1 (1948).

52. *See, e.g.*, State *ex rel.* Tingley v. Gurda, 209 Wis. 63, 243 N.W. 317 (1932); Julian Conrad Juergensmeyer et al., Land Use Planning and Development Regulation Law § 3.22 (3d ed., Feb. 2023 Update). Such an action would also be an important factor in a takings analysis. See Chapter 24 for a discussion of this issue.

53. *See* 1 Patricia E. Salkin, American Law of Zoning § 7.3 (5th ed., Dec. 2022 Update). However, ordinances designed to protect a broader area, such as a historic downtown commercial area, have been upheld. Hernandez v. City of Hanford, 159 P.3d 33 (Cal. 2007). In *City of Columbia v. Omni Outdoor Advertising*, 499 U.S. 365 (1991), an action challenging a South Carolina billboard regulation on the ground that it was anticompetitive, the Court held that the city was immune from federal antitrust laws in this type of action.

54. *See* Mark Bobrowski, *The Regulation of Formula Businesses and the Dormant Commerce Clause Doctrine*, 44 Urb. Law. 227 (2012); Jackson S. Davis, Note, *Fast Food, Zoning, and the Dormant Commerce Clause: Was It Something I Ate?* 35 B.C. Envtl. Aff. L. Rev. 259 (2008) (arguing zoning restrictions on fast-food outlets would not violate Commerce Clause); Brannon P. Denning & Rachel M. Lary, *Retail Store Size-Capping Ordinances and the Dormant Commerce Clause Doctrine*, 37 Urb. Law. 907 (2005) (reviewing regulations against "big box" stores); Patricia E. Salkin, *Municipal Regulation of Formula Businesses: Creating and Protecting Communities*, 58 Case W. Res. L. Rev. 1251 (2008); Richard C. Schragger, *The Anti-Chain Store Movement, Localist Ideology, and the Remnants of the Progressive Constitution, 1920–1940*, 90 Iowa L. Rev. 1011 (2005) (describing early efforts to protect local merchants from national-chain stores).

55. While early cases allowed aesthetic considerations to be cited as one factor underpinning an ordinance, they could not serve as the only basis for the ordinance's adoption. *See, e.g.*, Small v. Councilmen of Edenton, 146 N.C. 527, 60 S.E. 413 (1908). For a review of the law before a 1970s judicial shift, discussed in text *infra*, see H. Rutherford Turnbull, III, *Aesthetic Zoning*, 7 Wake Forest L. Rev. 230 (1971). The pre-1960s majority view nationally was that aesthetics could not be the sole or predominate basis for a regulation (but aesthetics were a permissible incidental purpose). *See, e.g.*, Thille v. Bd. of Pub. Works, 82 Cal. App. 187, 192, 255 P. 294, 296 (Ct. App. 1927); Fed. Elec. Co. v. Zoning Bd. of Appeals, 398 Ill. 142, 147, 75 N.E.2d 359, 362 (1947); 122 Main St. Corp. v. Brockton, 323 Mass. 646, 84 N.E.2d 13 (1949); Wolverine Sign Works v. City of Bloomfield Hills, 279 Mich. 205, 208, 271 N.W. 823, 825 (1937); City of Youngstown v. Kahn Bros. Bldg., 112 Ohio St. 654, 661–62, 148 N.E. 842, 844 (1925). Many of the earliest aesthetic regulations that were upheld were based on protecting the appearance of public places, such as streets and parks. *See, e.g.*, Fifth Ave. Coach Co. v. City of New York, 221 U.S. 467 (1911) (upholding ban of vehicles advertising wares on certain city streets); Chi. Park Dist. v. Canfield, 370 Ill. 447, 19 N.E.2d 376 (1939) (upholding regulation on use of boulevards within park).

56. State v. Brown, 250 N.C. 54, 108 S.E.2d 74 (1959). *See also* MacRae v. City of Fayetteville, 198 N.C. 51, 150 S.E. 810 (1929) (invalidating ordinance that prohibited gas stations within 250 feet of residences due to, among other considerations, aesthetic concerns).

57. Little Pep Delmonico Rest., Inc. v. City of Charlotte, 252 N.C. 324, 113 S.E.2d 422 (1960).

58. State v. Vestal, 281 N.C. 517, 524, 189 S.E.2d 152, 157 (1972).

the police power might justify a regulation based on aesthetics alone, it had "no difficulty" in holding that the police power encompassed the right to control the exterior appearance of private property for the objective of preserving the state's legacy of historically significant structures.[59] Finally, in a 1982 case upholding a Buncombe County junkyard-screening requirement, the court formally embraced zoning based on aesthetic concerns alone,[60] noting that this was a legitimate government objective in that it provided benefits to the general community, including "protection of property values, promotion of tourism, indirect protection of health and safety, preservation of the character and integrity of the community, and promotion of the comfort, happiness, and emotional stability of area residents."[61]

Federal cases arising in North Carolina have likewise held that protection of community aesthetics is a legitimate governmental objective. The context for this conclusion has been cases involving design standards for manufactured housing[62] and landscaping and design standards for residences in established neighborhoods.[63]

---

59. 298 N.C. 207, 216, 258 S.E.2d 444, 450 (1979). The statutory framework for local historic-district and landmark-protection programs is set out at G.S. 160D-940 to -951. For additional background on historic-preservation and land use regulations, see Chapter 22.

60. State v. Jones, 305 N.C. 520, 290 S.E.2d 675 (1982). For a case note, see Marc David Bishop, Note, *Property Law—State v. Jones: Aesthetic Regulation—From Junkyards to Residences?* 61 N.C. L. Rev. 942 (1983). Sign-regulation cases have also held aesthetics to be a legitimate governmental objective. *See, e.g.,* Transylvania Cnty. v. Moody, 151 N.C. App. 389, 565 S.E.2d 720 (2002); Cumberland Cnty. v. E. Fed. Corp., 48 N.C. App. 518, 522–24, 269 S.E.2d 672, 675–77 (1980), *review denied,* 301 N.C. 527, 273 S.E.2d 453 (1980). *See also In re* Appeal of Coastal Area Mgmt. Act Minor Dev. Permit v. Town of Bath, 82 N.C. App. 32, 345 S.E.2d 699 (1986) (holding town regulation of marinas could be based on legitimate objectives of protection of water quality, public rights of fishing and navigation, and the aesthetic characteristics of the town). For a state-by-state review of the law on this topic, see Kenneth Pearlman et al., *Beyond the Eye of the Beholder Once Again: A New Review of Aesthetic Regulation,* 38 Urb. Law. 1119 (2006). This study concludes that all states allow consideration of aesthetic objectives, among others, and nearly half allow regulations to be based on aesthetics alone.

61. *Jones,* 305 N.C. at 530, 290 S.E.2d at 681. Among the cases likewise holding that aesthetics may be the sole or predominate basis of a land use regulation are the following: Rotenberg v. City of Ft. Pierce, 202 So. 2d 782, 785–86 (Fla. Dist. Ct. App. 1967); Zimmerman v. Bd. of Comm'rs, 289 Kan. 926, 218 P.3d 400 (2009) (upholding prohibition of commercial-scale wind farm in rural area); City of Champaign v. Kroger Co., 88 Ill. App. 3d 498, 505–10, 410 N.E.2d 661, 667–70 (1980); Asselin v. Town of Conway, 137 N.H. 368, 371, 628 A.2d 247, 249–50 (1993) (upholding prohibition of internally lighted signs in a mountainous scenic municipality); Temple Baptist Church, Inc. v. Albuquerque, 98 N.M. 138, 143–44, 646 P.2d 565, 570–71 (1982); Suffolk Outdoor Advert. Co. v. Hulse, 43 N.Y.2d 483, 489, 402 N.Y.S.2d 368, 371, 373 N.E.2d 263, 265 (1977); Or. City v. Hartke, 240 Or. 35, 47, 400 P.2d 255, 261–62 (1965). *See also* Penn Cent. Transp. Co. v. City of New York, 438 U.S. 104, 129 (1978) (noting the Supreme Court "has recognized, in a number of settings, that States and cities may enact land-use restrictions or controls to enhance the quality of life by preserving the character and desirable aesthetic features of a city"). Not all states have followed this trend. *See, e.g.,* Bd. of Supervisors v. Rowe, 216 Va. 128, 145, 216 S.E.2d 199, 213 (1975).

62. CMH Mfg., Inc. v. Catawba Cnty., 994 F. Supp. 697, 711 (W.D.N.C. 1998).

63. Quality Built Homes, Inc. v. Vill. of Pinehurst, No. 1:06CV1028, 2008 WL 3503149 (M.D.N.C. Aug. 11, 2008). The court noted that the purposes of the regulations at issue included preserving the character, integrity, and ambiance of the defendant village and that the adoption process included substantial community participation and analysis of the potential financial impacts to secure compliance.

Relationship of Means to Ends

Development regulations must have a rational relationship to legitimate objectives.[64] Not only must the object of the regulation be within the police power but also the means chosen to regulate it must be reasonably necessary to accomplish that public good, and the interference with property rights must be reasonable in degree.[65]

State v. Vestal, invalidating a junkyard-screening requirement in Forsyth County, provides an example of the failure to establish such a relationship.[66] The zoning provision in this case required a six-foot-high solid wall and vegetative screen around junkyards. The county justified the ordinance on the basis of highway safety. Asserting that there "must be a reasonable basis for supposing that the restriction imposed will promote such safety,"[67] the state high court noted that in this instance the fence would be more of a visual obstruction than would the junked cars, so it found no reasonable basis for the regulation. Similarly, in *Wenco Management Co. v. Town of Carrboro*,[68] the appeals court found that a local zoning amendment effectively banning drive-in restaurants (but not other drive-in businesses or other restaurants) had no rational relationship to any legitimate government objective.

By contrast, in *State v. Jones*,[69] a case upholding a junkyard-screening requirement based on aesthetics, the state supreme court had little difficulty relating the screening requirement to an aesthetic objective, as the appearance of an appropriate fence was clearly more attractive to passing motorists than an unsightly junkyard. Even though the requisite nexus was easily established, the court went on to hold that when the regulation is addressing aesthetic objectives, the regulation must also balance the diminution in value of an individual's property against the corresponding gain to the public from the regulation in order for the regulation to be deemed reasonable. This analysis indicates that courts more readily sustain an intrusive or particularly restrictive regulation that is based on a public health or safety objective rather than one based solely on aesthetics.[70]

The requisite rational relationship can also be violated if a regulation is either overly broad or too restrictive in its application. Several land use–related ordinances in North Carolina have been invalidated because they were either too broad or not broad enough. In *Cheek v. City of Charlotte*, an ordinance prohibiting opposite-sex massages exempted hospitals, clinics, the YMCA, the YWCA, barber shops, and beauty shops from its coverage. The state supreme court held that prohibiting an act in a massage parlor that was completely legal in a barbershop was too restrictive and amounted to unlawful favoritism.[71] On the other end of the spectrum, *Treants Enterprises, Inc. v. Onslow County* provides an example of

---

64. Zoning regulation must "bear a 'substantial relation to the public health, safety, morals, or general welfare.'" Schloss v. Jamison, 262 N.C. 108, 114, 136 S.E.2d 691, 695 (1964) (quoting Vill. of Euclid v. Ambler Realty Co., 272 U.S. 365, 395 (1926).

65. Responsible Citizens v. City of Asheville, 308 N.C. 255, 261, 302 S.E.2d 204, 208 (1983).

66. 281 N.C. 517, 189 S.E.2d 152 (1972). *See also* Rose v. Guilford Cnty., 60 N.C. App. 170, 298 S.E.2d 200 (1982) (judgment on the pleadings inappropriate response to the plaintiff's allegations of arbitrary and capricious action).

67. *Vestal*, 281 N.C. at 522, 189 S.E.2d at 156.

68. 53 N.C. App. 480, 281 S.E.2d 74 (1981).

69. 305 N.C. 520, 290 S.E.2d 675 (1982). *See also* LeTendre v. Currituck Cnty., 259 N.C. App. 512, 817 S.E.2d 73 (2018), *review denied*, 372 N.C. 54, 822 S.E.2d 64 (2019) (regulation of the maximum number of principal structures on a lot is within zoning authority and reasonably related to the legitimate purposes of zoning).

70. The California courts set forth such a proposition when they upheld on remand the floodplain regulation that was the subject of *First English Evangelical Lutheran Church v. County of Los Angeles*, 210 Cal. App. 3d 1353, 258 Cal. Rptr. 893 (1989), *cert. denied*, 493 U.S. 1056 (1990), a Supreme Court taking-remedy case. *See also* McNulty v. Town of Indialantic, 727 F. Supp. 604 (M.D. Fla. 1989).

71. 273 N.C. 293, 160 S.E.2d 18 (1968). *See also* State v. Glidden Co., 228 N.C. 664, 46 S.E.2d 860 (1948) (invalidating state statute that exempted businesses chartered before certain date from prohibition on discharging hazardous materials into state waters). These cases can also be viewed as equal-protection cases, for they raise the issue of whether similarly situated persons are being treated equally.

too much breadth. In this case an ordinance regulating "companionship" businesses was invalidated. The supreme court noted that this term was "broad enough to encompass both the salubrious and the salacious" because on its face it regulated both nursing homes and escort services.[72]

Vagueness

Another aspect of the due-process requirement is that a regulation must not be unduly vague. The general test is that when read contextually, an ordinance must apprise persons of ordinary intelligence, who desire to know the law and abide by it, what is required.[73] The fact that a regulation is complicated does not make it unconstitutionally vague.[74] Where the terms of the ordinance are clear as to the application being challenged, the court will not consider potential vagueness in relation to hypothetical situations that are not presently before it.[75]

Vestal[76] provides an example of an unconstitutionally vague ordinance provision. The challenged ordinance required a junkyard fence to be located not less than fifty feet from the "edge of any public road," without defining this term.[77] It was unclear whether the required setback was to be measured from the edge of the pavement, the ditch along the road, the formal right-of-way, or some other point of reference. The court concluded that an owner would have to guess at its meaning and thereby risk a criminal violation by guessing wrong. Thus, the court held the requirement to be too vague.

Several cases address the precision required in local noise ordinances to avoid a vagueness problem. In *State v. Taylor*, the appellate court upheld an ordinance provision that prohibited keeping an animal that "habitually or repeatedly makes excessive noises that tend to annoy, disturb, or frighten [the county's] citizens."[78] The court held that since these terms have common ordinary meanings and because the defendant was given several warnings of neighbor complaints before receiving a citation for ordinance violations, his conviction was not arbitrary or subjective. In *State v. Garren*, the same court upheld an ordinance provision prohibiting sound that "annoys, disturbs, injures or endangers the comfort, health, peace or safety of reasonable persons of ordinary sensibilities" but invalidated on overbreadth grounds a provision that defined all amplified music as "loud, raucous, and disturbing" noise.[79]

---

72. 320 N.C. 776, 779, 360 S.E.2d 783, 786 (1987).

73. *See, e.g., Jones*, 305 N.C. 520, 290 S.E.2d 675. The federal standard is similar. A statute is impermissibly vague if it "fails to provide people of ordinary intelligence a reasonable opportunity to understand what conduct it prohibits" or if it authorizes or encourages arbitrary and discriminatory enforcement. Hill v. Colorado, 530 U.S. 703, 732 (2000). *See also* Broadrick v. Oklahoma, 413 U.S. 601, 608 (1973); Grayned v. City of Rockford, 408 U.S. 104, 108 (1972); Connally v. Gen. Constr. Co., 269 U.S. 385, 391 (1926) (statute unconstitutionally vague if persons of "common intelligence must necessarily guess at its meaning and differ as to its application"); CMR D.N. Corp. v. City of Phila., 703 F.3d 612 (3d Cir. 2013) (standard requiring that development be "appropriate in scale, density, character and use for the surrounding community" is not unconstitutionally vague).

74. *LeTendre*, 259 N.C. App. 512, 574, 817 S.E.2d 73, 96 (2018), *review denied*, 372 N.C. 54, 822 S.E.2d 641 (2019) ("Although the UDO provisions can be difficult to read, as many ordinances and statutes are, they are not unconstitutionally vague").

75. Town of Atl. Beach v. Young, 307 N.C. 422, 427, 298 S.E.2d 686, 690, *cert. denied*, 462 U.S. 1101 (1983) (where ordinance specifically prohibited keeping horses and goats, and defendant has admitted having two goats and a pony, court will not consider application to other animals); Bulova Watch Co. v. Brand Distribs. of N. Wilkesboro, Inc., 285 N.C. 467, 472, 206 S.E.2d 141, 145 (1974); Nicholson v. State Educ. Assistance Auth., 275 N.C. 439, 447, 168 S.E.2d 401, 406 (1969); Person v. Doughton, 186 N.C. 723, 120 S.E. 481 (1923); Comm'rs of Johnston Cnty. v. State Treasurer, 174 N.C. 141, 93 S.E. 482 (1917).

76. 281 N.C. 517, 189 S.E.2d 152 (1972).

77. *Id.* at 518, 189 S.E.2d at 153.

78. 128 N.C. App. 616, 618, 495 S.E.2d 413, 415 (1998).

79. 117 N.C. App. 393, 451 S.E.2d 315 (1994) (quoting JACKSON COUNTY, N.C., NOISE ORDINANCE art. I, §§ 1-1(a), (b)(3) (1991)).

In the context of design standards, the courts in North Carolina have upheld the use of a standard in a historic district prohibiting incongruity.[80] In those instances, there is clearly a distinctive, identifiable contextual standard to be applied. The courts have also upheld special use permit standards that require a development to be harmonious or compatible with the surrounding neighborhood.[81]

Conflicts of Interest

Persons making land use regulatory decisions have an obligation to act in the public interest. Both the Due Process Clause and statutory provisions address the question of when a conflict exists between a decision maker's personal interests and public obligations.

Many of the persons serving on boards making land use regulatory decisions are directly involved in development issues. Since the early days of zoning, it has been common for developers, builders, real-estate agents, surveyors, engineers, architects, and lawyers to be disproportionately represented on boards making legislative and quasi-judicial land use decisions.[82] More recently neighborhood activists, conservationists, and others have joined these boards. Given the strong impact development regulations have on their interests, it is hardly surprising that those most directly affected by the decisions actively seek out membership on these boards. They bring expertise and well-informed perspectives to the crafting and implementation of development regulation. But the participation in decision-making by so many persons who may be personally affected by the decisions presents the need for safeguards to assure that these decisions are being made in the public interest, not the personal interests of board members.[83]

80. A-S-P Assocs. v. City of Raleigh, 298 N.C. 207, 258 S.E.2d 444 (1979). *See generally* John J. Costonis, *Law and Aesthetics: A Critique and a Reformulation of the Dilemmas*, 80 MICH. L. REV. 355 (1982); CHRISTOPHER J. DUERKSEN & R. MATTHEW GOEBEL, AESTHETICS, COMMUNITY CHARACTER, AND THE LAW (Am. Plan. Ass'n, Plan. Advisory Serv. Report No. 489/490, 1999); Mark L. Hinshaw, DESIGN REVIEW (Am. Plan. Ass'n, Plan. Advisory Serv. Report No. 454, 1995); Jack L. Nasar & Peg Grannis, *Design Review Reviewed: Administrative Versus Discretionary Methods*, 65 J. OF THE AM. PLAN. Ass'N 424 (1999); John Nivala, *Constitutional Architecture: The First Amendment and the Single Family House*, 33 SAN DIEGO L. REV. 291 (1996); Samuel E. Poole III, *Architectural Appearance Review Regulations and the First Amendment: The Good, the Bad, and the Consensus Ugly*, 19 URB. LAW. 287 (1987); Kenneth Regan, Note, *You Can't Build That Here: The Constitutionality of Aesthetic Zoning and Architectural Review*, 58 FORDHAM L. REV. 1013 (1990); Shawn G. Rice, Comment, *Zoning Law: Architectural Appearance Ordinances and the First Amendment*, 76 MARQ. L. REV. 439 (1993). Design standards have been invalidated on vagueness grounds in several states. *See, e.g.*, City of W. Palm Beach v. State *ex rel.* Duffey, 158 Fla. 863, 30 So. 2d 491 (1947); Hanna v. City of Chi., 38 Ill. App. 3d 909, 907 N.E.2d 390 (2009) (city landmark law unduly vague and impermissible grant of discretionary power); Anderson v. City of Issaquah, 70 Wash. App. 64, 851 P.2d 744 (1993).

81. See the discussion in Chapter 16 regarding the evidence required to address this standard.

82. A 1937 national survey of planning-commission members in large cities noted that some 80 percent of commission members came from professions with a stake in the development business. ROBERT A. WALKER, THE PLANNING FUNCTION IN URBAN GOVERNMENT 150–52 (1950). This practice has been persistent over time. DON T. ALLENSWORTH, THE POLITICAL REALITIES OF URBAN PLANNING (1975). A study of the composition of planning boards and boards of adjustment concluded that a majority of members are in professions that stand to benefit from development. Jerry L. Anderson & Erin Sass, *Is the Wheel Unbalanced? A Study of Bias on Zoning Boards*, 36 URB. LAW. 447 (2004). The study recommended greater attention to members' occupations by appointing boards (as well as prohibitions against direct financial bias).

83. *See* DAVID W. OWENS, CONFLICTS OF INTEREST IN LAND-USE MANAGEMENT DECISIONS (1990). *See generally* A. FLEMING BELL, II, ETHICS, CONFLICTS, AND OFFICES: A GUIDE FOR LOCAL OFFICIALS (2d ed. 2010); Jerry L. Anderson et al., *A Study of American Zoning Board Composition and Public Attitudes Toward Zoning Issues*, 40 URB. LAW. 689 (2008); Jerry L. Anderson & Daniel Luebbering, *Zoning Bias II: A Study of Oregon's Zoning Commission Composition Restrictions*, 38 URB. LAW. 63 (2006); Mark Cordes, *Policing Bias and Conflicts of Interest in Zoning Decisionmaking*, 65 N.D. L. REV. 161 (1989); Patricia E. Salkin, Note, *Crime Doesn't Pay and Neither Do Conflicts of Interest in Land Use Decisionmaking*, 40 URB. LAW. 561 (2008).

In *County of Lancaster v. Mecklenburg County*, the North Carolina Supreme Court summarized the limitations on self-interest in land use regulatory decisions:

> Due process requires an impartial decisionmaker. An elected official with a direct and substantial financial interest in a legislative zoning decision may not participate in making that decision. Where there is a specific, substantial, and readily identifiable financial impact on a board member, nonparticipation is required. Additional considerations beyond these financial interests require nonparticipation in quasi-judicial zoning decisions. A fixed opinion that is not susceptible to change may well constitute impermissible bias, as will undisclosed *ex parte* communication or a close familial or business relationship with an applicant.[84]

Legislative decisions require policy judgment by elected officials. These officials' personal knowledge, positions on issues of importance to the community, and judgment about the preferred course for the community are important and valid components of the decision-making process. As a general rule, the individual or personal motives of governing board members are not examined in the judicial review of legislative decisions.[85] If the voters disagree with the judgment being exercised, the appropriate remedy is the ballot box. However, the judgment being exercised must be on behalf of the public interest, not the narrow self-interest of an individual board member. Thus, the courts and state statutes have imposed important conflict-of-interest limitations on land-development-regulatory policy decisions.

In addition to constitutional and common law coverage,[86] state statutes also specifically speak to the issue of conflicts of interest in legislative decisions. In 2005, the zoning statutes were amended to specifically address conflicts of interest in both legislative[87] and quasi-judicial[88] settings. Chapter 160D, Section 109, of the North Carolina General Statutes (hereinafter G.S.) codifies the standard set out in *County of Lancaster.*

For legislative decisions, the statute provides that members of city councils and county boards of commissioners "shall not vote on any zoning map or text amendment where the outcome of the matter being

---

84. 334 N.C. 496, 511, 434 S.E.2d 604, 614 (1993). *See also* Caperton v. A.T. Massey Coal Co., 556 U.S. 868 (2009) (state supreme court justice may not participate in case involving substantial contributor to his campaign); Mayberry v. Pennsylvania, 400 U.S. 455 (1971) (judge who had been repeatedly insulted by defendant was disqualified for bias in deciding criminal-contempt charge); *In re* Murchison, 349 U.S. 133 (1955) (judge who charged defendant with perjury and contempt in prior proceeding disqualified from hearing present matter).

85. In *Barger v. Smith*, 156 N.C. 323, 72 S.E. 376 (1911), the state high court held that generally the motivations behind adoption of an ordinance are irrelevant. However, the facts alleged to have been the foundation of an improper motivation can be considered in determining whether the ordinance is arbitrary.

86. In *Kendall v. Stafford*, a case in which city-council members voted on a pay raise for themselves, the court held:
> The public policy of the state, found in the statutes and judicial decisions has been pronounced against permitting one to sit in judgment on his own cause, or to act on a matter affecting the public when he has a direct pecuniary interest, and this is a principle of the common law which has existed for hundreds of years.

178 N.C. 461, 464, 101 S.E. 15, 16 (1919).

Courts in other states have held that campaign contributions to board members do not constitute an impermissible financial conflict of interest. *See, e.g.*, Breakzone Billiards v. City of Torrance, 97 Cal. Rptr. 2d 467, 81 Cal. App. 4th 1205 (Ct. App. 2000).

87. S.L. 2005-426, §§ 5(a), (b). In addition, the statutes were amended in 2009 to require all cities and counties to adopt a code of ethics. S.L. 2009-403. That provision is codified as G.S. 160A-86. *See* A. FLEMING BELL, II, A MODEL CODE OF ETHICS FOR NORTH CAROLINA LOCAL ELECTED OFFICIALS (2010). The U.S. Supreme Court upheld the constitutionality of state legislation prohibiting elected officials from voting on or advocating passage or failure of matters that would materially affect the personal interests of the official. Nev. Comm'n on Ethics v. Carrigan, 564 U.S. 117 (2011).

88. S.L. 2005-418, §§ 8(a), (b).

considered is reasonably likely to have a direct, substantial, and readily identifiable financial impact on the member."[89] The statute applies the same prohibition to advisory boards making recommendations on zoning amendments. In 2019, the General Assembly added a requirement that governing-board and planning-board members not vote on any zoning amendment if the owner of property proposed for rezoning or the applicant for a text amendment is a person with whom the member has a close family, business, or associational relationship.[90]

For quasi-judicial land use decisions, the constitutional demand for impartiality extends beyond financial conflicts to include bias, close family or associational relationships, and undisclosed ex parte communications.[91] G.S. 160D-109(d) codifies *County of Lancaster*'s heightened standard for quasi-judicial decisions, providing that members of boards making quasi-judicial land use decisions

> shall not participate in or vote on any quasi-judicial matter in a manner that would violate affected persons' constitutional rights to an impartial decision maker. Impermissible violations of due process include, but are not limited to, a member having a fixed opinion prior to hearing the matter that is not susceptible to change, undisclosed ex parte communications, a close familial, business, or other associational relationship with an affected person, or a financial interest in the outcome of the matter.

With administrative land use decisions, prior to the enactment of Chapter 160D there was not an express statutory provision on conflicts of interest, only the general provision that a staff member could not be financially interested in a firm doing regulated work within the jurisdiction and that staff members not engage in any work inconsistent with their duties.[92] G.S. 160D-109(c) extends a conflict-of-interest standard to staff making administrative decisions that is similar to that required for board members making legislative decisions. A staff member is prohibited from making a final decision on an administrative decision if the outcome would have a direct, substantial, and readily identifiable financial impact on the staff member or if the staff member has a close family, business, or associational relationship with the applicant. In these situations, the decision is to be assigned to the supervisor of the affected staff member or to such other staff person as may be designated by the development regulation.

---

89. G.S. 160D-109. Other states have similar prohibitions. For example, the Maine statute prohibits a board member from voting if they have a direct or indirect pecuniary interest in the outcome. In these instances, a board member is to disclose any pecuniary interest, abstain from voting, and make no attempt to influence the decision. Me. Rev. Stat. Ann. tit. 30-A, § 2605.

90. S.L. 2019-111, pt. II. Prior to the enactment of Chapter 160D, this restriction was only applicable for quasi-judicial decisions. G.S. 160D-109(a) and (b) extend it to legislative and advisory decisions. G.S. 160D-109(f) defines a close family relationship to be a spouse, parent, child, brother, sister, grandparent, or grandchild, including step, half, and in-law relationships. For examples of cases alleging a conflict of interest based on associational relationships, see *Global Tower Assets, LLC v. Town of Rome*, 810 F.3d 77 (1st Cir. 2016) (membership in nonprofit conservation organization); *Piscitelli v. City of Garfield Board of Adjustment*, 205 A.3d 183 (N.J. 2019) (patient-physician relationship); and *Grabowsky v. Township of Montclair*, 115 A.3d 815 (N.J. 2015) (church membership).

91. *See* Cox v. Hancock, 160 N.C. App. 473, 586 S.E.2d 500 (2003) (distant family relation not a conflict); JWL Invs., Inc. v. Guilford Cnty. Bd. of Adjustment, 133 N.C. App. 426, 515 S.E.2d 715 (1999), *review denied*, 251 N.C. 357 (2000) (participation by former county staff member on board not a per se conflict); Vulcan Materials Co. v. Guilford Cnty. Bd. of Cnty. Comm'rs, 115 N.C. App. 319, 444 S.E.2d 639, *review denied*, 337 N.C. 807, 449 S.E.2d 758 (1994) (not bias to announce intentions on decision after evidence submitted but prior to deliberation); Rice Assocs. of the S. Highlands, Inc. v. Town of Weaverville Zoning Bd. of Adjustment, 108 N.C. App. 346, 423 S.E.2d 519 (1992) (potential bias irrelevant if board has no discretion on permit outcome); *In re* City of Raleigh (Parks & Recreation Dep't) v. City of Raleigh, 107 N.C. App. 505, 421 S.E.2d 179 (1992) (governing-board decision on application by city agency not per se conflict). Also see the discussion of the requirement for impartiality of decision makers on quasi-judicial decisions in Chapter 15.

92. G.S. 160D-109.

G.S. 153A-44 and 160A-75, which address voting on legislative matters by county commissioners and city council members, respectively, were also amended in 2005 to incorporate the statutes noted above as grounds for members' abstentions.[93]

The General Assembly in 2009 mandated adoption of local codes of ethics.[94] G.S. 160A-83 requires the governing boards of cities and counties to adopt a code of ethics, and G.S. 160A-84 requires these boards to receive two hours of ethics training within a year of being elected or reelected. Even prior to this mandate, some city and county codes had ethics provisions regarding the disclosure of financial interests in matters coming before elected officials as well as requirements for nonparticipation in such matters.[95] Many of the local code provisions apply to advisory boards as well as to elected officials.

The matter of financial interests occasionally poses difficult questions in land-development-regulatory policy decisions.[96] Although board members should certainly not participate in voting on a small-scale rezoning of their own property, they must participate in adopting initial zoning for the entire jurisdiction, which affects their property. The difficult question is, at what point does the financial interest become significant enough to warrant nonparticipation? The general rule is that if a member is affected no more significantly than all other members of the community, nonparticipation is not required. However, if there is a specific, substantial, and readily identifiable financial impact on a member, nonparticipation is required even if there are others who are similarly affected.

Other forms of conflict of interest or bias can require nonparticipation in quasi-judicial decisions.[97] In the legislative arena, public policies are openly debated and resolved in decisions on zoning and rezoning. Bias, expression of opinions, and contacts with citizens about a matter before a hearing or a vote do not disqualify a member from voting on a legislative decision.[98] By contrast, the constitutional requirement for impartiality of those exercising quasi-judicial authority imposes greater demands for quasi-judicial decisions, such as decisions to grant or deny special and conditional use permits.[99] A board

---

93. S.L. 2005-426. For more details on the rules for voting on legislative decisions, see Chapter 11.

94. S.L. 2009-403.

95. For example, the Chapel Hill code provides that the mayor and members of the town council may be required to disclose their financial interests related to those applying for permits or approvals from the town and to refrain from voting where conflicts are present. CHAPEL HILL, N.C., CODE OF ORDINANCES ch. 2, §§ 2-49 to -52 (2022).

96. A 2008 UNC School of Government survey explored how often financial conflicts of interest arise in legislative zoning decisions. Responding jurisdictions reported that this was an infrequent occurrence for both the planning board and governing board. Three-quarters of the responding jurisdictions reported that a member of the planning board never or only rarely abstained or was excused from voting because of a financial conflict of interest, with a quarter of the respondents indicating this happened only occasionally. Only 2 percent of the responding jurisdictions reported that this happened frequently or more often. Financial conflicts were reported to arise even less frequently for governing board members: 81 percent of the jurisdictions surveyed reported that a city-council or county-board member either never or only rarely had to be excused from voting on a zoning-amendment matter due to a financial conflict, and 17 percent reported that this happened only occasionally. Only 2 percent of the responding jurisdictions reported that this happened frequently or more often. DAVID W. OWENS, ZONING AMENDMENTS IN NORTH CAROLINA 17 (UNC School of Government, Special Series No. 24, 2008).

97. See Chapter 15 for a more detailed discussion of quasi-judicial procedural requirements.

98. Brown v. Town of Davidson, 113 N.C. App. 553, 556, 439 S.E.2d 206, 208 (1994); Bd. of Adjustment v. Town of Swansboro, 108 N.C. App. 198, 206, 423 S.E.2d 498, 503, aff'd, 334 N.C. 421, 432 S.E.2d 310 (1993).

99. Helpful guidance is provided by Canon 3(C)(1) of the NORTH CAROLINA CODE OF JUDICIAL CONDUCT:

(1) On motion of any party, a judge shall disqualify himself/herself in a proceeding in which the judge's impartiality might reasonably be questioned, including but not limited to instances where:

(a) the judge has a personal bias or prejudice concerning a party, or personal knowledge of disputed evidentiary facts concerning the proceedings;

(b) the judge served as lawyer in the matter in controversy, or a lawyer with whom the judge previously practiced law served during such association as a lawyer concerning the matter, or the judge or such lawyer has been a material witness concerning it;

member whose opinion is fixed and not susceptible to change has an impermissible bias.[100] While even the appearance of bias must be avoided,[101] a board member simply expressing a view as to the outcome after the evidence is presented but before the board votes does not constitute impermissible bias.[102] A person contending that a board member has an impermissible bias may move for recusal of that member, and the objecting party has the burden of demonstrating that grounds for disqualification actually exist.[103] When a permit may not, as a matter of law, be issued, improper participation will not invalidate the decision.[104]

The statutes also address the procedure for resolving disputes regarding board-member participation in quasi-judicial matters. If an objection is raised to a member's participation and that member does not agree to recusal, the remaining members of the board rule on the objection by majority vote.[105]

(c) the judge knows that he/she, individually or as a fiduciary, or the judge's spouse or minor child residing in the judge's household, has a financial interest in the subject matter in controversy or in a party to the proceeding, or any other interest that could be substantially affected by the outcome of the proceeding;

(d) the judge or the judge's spouse, or a person within the third degree of relationship to either of them, or the spouse of such a person:

  (i) Is a party to the proceeding, or an officer, director, or trustee of a party;

  (ii) Is acting as a lawyer in the proceeding;

  (iii) Is known by the judge to have an interest that could be substantially affected by the outcome of the proceeding; or

  (iv) Is to the judge's knowledge likely to be a material witness in the proceeding;

N.C. RULES OF COURT, CODE OF JUDICIAL CONDUCT, Canon 3(C)(1). See Michael Crowell, *Recusal*, ADMIN. OF JUST. BULL. No. 5 (UNC School of Government, Nov. 2014) for a collection of North Carolina cases addressing this issue in the context of judicial recusal.

100. Crump v. Bd. of Educ., 326 N.C. 603, 392 S.E.2d 579 (1990); *In re* City of Raleigh (Parks & Recreation Dep't) v. City of Raleigh, 107 N.C. App. 505, 421 S.E.2d 179 (1992). *See also* Lane Constr. Corp. v. Town of Wash., 2008 ME 45, ¶ 30, 942 A.2d 1202, 1211 (personal support for project during conditional use permit review does not disqualify member absent showing of bias or predisposition). Courts in other states have generally held that past political support for a board member is not in itself a disqualifying bias. *See, e.g.*, Breakzone Billiards v. City of Torrance, 97 Cal. Rptr. 2d 467, 81 Cal. App. 4th 1205 (Ct. App. 2000) (fact that city-council members hearing conditional use permit received campaign contributions from applicant's landlord more than twelve months earlier not a conflict); Commonwealth v. Veon, 150 A.3d 435 (Pa. 2016) (intangible political gain could not constitute private pecuniary gain).

101. Ponder v. Davis, 233 N.C. 699, 706, 65 S.E.2d 356, 360 (1951) (quoting Haslam v. Morrison, 113 Utah 14, 20, 190 P.2d 520, 523 (1948). *See also* Daly v. Town Plan & Zoning Comm'n, 191 A.2d 250 (Conn. 1963) (avoid appearance of conflict to protect public confidence in integrity of zoning decisions); Haggerty v. Red Bank Borough Zoning Bd. of Adjustment, 897 A.2d 1094 (N.J. Super. Ct. App. Div. 2006) (key issue is potential for conflict, not actual conflict); *In re* Tuxedo Conservation and Taxpayers Ass'n v. Town Bd., 408 N.Y.S.2d 668 (App. Div. 1979) (apparent conflict where board member employed by advertising company that had applicant's parent company for a client); Buell v. City of Bremerton, 495 P.2d 1358 (Wash. 1972) (planning-commission members must be open-minded, objective, impartial, free of entangling influences both in fact and in appearance).

102. Vulcan Materials Co. v. Guilford Cnty. Bd. of Cnty. Comm'rs, 115 N.C. App. 319, 444 S.E.2d 639, *review denied*, 337 N.C. 807, 449 S.E.2d 758 (1994).

103. *In re* Ezzell, 113 N.C. App. 388, 394, 438 S.E.2d 482, 485 (1994). If no objection is made at the hearing and there is no showing of prejudice as a result of improper participation, appellate courts will not set aside the decision. JWL Invs., Inc. v. Guilford Cnty. Bd. of Adjustment, 133 N.C. App. 426, 515 S.E.2d 715, *review denied*, 251 N.C. 715, 540 S.E.2d 349 (2000) (upholding board member's participation in a hearing contesting a notice of violation where this board member was a former staff member in the county's planning department and had been consulted in that capacity about a rezoning of the property in question).

104. Rice Assocs. of the S. Highlands, Inc. v. Town of Weaverville Zoning Bd. of Adjustment, 108 N.C. App. 346, 423 S.E.2d 519 (1992).

105. G.S. 160D-109(e). This process of the rest of the board voting on an objection applies to legislative, quasi-judicial, and advisory decisions.

While the focus of conflict-of-interest considerations is on the decision makers, conflicts by staff members advising the decision makers can occasionally be problematic, especially for attorneys advising a board making land use decisions.[106] Surveys of North Carolina jurisdictions indicate it is very common for the city or county attorney to provide legal advice to the boards making special use permit decisions and variance decisions. In both of these types of quasi-judicial matters, some 90 percent of the jurisdictions reported that the jurisdiction's attorney provided legal representation for the decision-making board.[107] When this arrangement is used, the jurisdiction's counsel must take care to avoid playing an active role assisting staff or advocating before the board while also providing legal advice to the board.

Equal Protection

By their very nature, some land-development regulations treat citizens differently. For example, requirements imposed on property owners in one zoning district do not apply to property owners in other zoning districts. Indeed, this lack of uniformity is one of the principal features that distinguishes zoning from general-police-power regulations.[108] Yet whenever these classifications are made, the equal-protection clauses of the federal and state constitutions must be considered.[109]

Similarly Situated Persons

Since the equal-protection clauses address situations where similarly situated persons are treated differently, a critical-threshold inquiry in the land use regulatory realm involves determining when persons are in fact "similarly situated."[110]

Coucoulas/Knight Properties v. Town of Hillsborough[111] is instructive on this point. The plaintiff made an equal-protection challenge to the defendant town's denial of a petition to rezone three lots at the north end of downtown from primarily low-density residential into an "Entranceway Special Use"

---

106. In an analogous situation, Kansas's highest court held that it created an impermissible appearance of conflict for an attorney to advise the board and serve as an advocate before or on behalf of the board. Davenport Pastures, LP v. Morris Cnty. Bd. of Cnty. Comm'rs, 291 Kan. 132, 238 P.3d 731 (2010).

107. David W. Owens, Special Use Permits in North Carolina Zoning 10 (UNC School of Government, Special Series No. 22, Apr. 2007); David W. Owens & Adam Brueggemann, A Survey of Experience with Zoning Variances 13 (UNC School of Government, Special Series No. 18, Feb. 2004). Jurisdictions with large populations and a substantial case load were more likely to provide outside counsel for these boards making quasi-judicial decisions.

108. Uniformity is required for general-police-power regulations. State v. Tenant, 110 N.C. 609, 14 S.E. 387 (1892).

109. U.S. Const. amend. XIV; N.C. Const. art. I, § 19. Given the presumption of validity of local ordinances, the court will not declare the classification unconstitutional unless "it is clearly so, and every intendment will be made to sustain it." Standley v. Town of Woodfin, 186 N.C. App. 134, 140, 650 S.E.2d 618, 623 (2007).

110. The burden is on the plaintiff to submit admissible evidence that similarly situated persons were treated differently. Marsh v. Black, No. 3:10cv547, 2011 WL 4747897 (W.D.N.C. Oct. 7, 2011). The plaintiff obtained a special use permit from Union County to conduct rodeos. The county revoked the permit for conducting more events than permitted. The plaintiff contended that the county's action was based on community opposition to his predominately Hispanic clientele for the rodeos and that failure to require other similar events to secure a special use permit violated equal protection. The court granted summary judgment to the county as the allegations were unsupported by affidavits, depositions, or any admissible evidence. *See also* Harvey v. Town of Merrillville, 649 F.3d 526 (7th Cir. 2011) (dismissing equal-protection claim by subdivision whose residents contended that other subdivisions received preferential treatment when complaining about enforcement of rules on retention ponds). The residents contended that the different treatment was racially based but offered no evidence of that.

111. 199 N.C. App. 455, 683 S.E.2d 228 (2009), *aff'd per curiam*, 364 N.C. 127, 691 S.E.2d 441 (2010).

zoning district.[112] The principal basis of the plaintiff's case was that the town had rezoned property at the south end of downtown into this district and both properties were within areas designated by an adopted corridor plan as "district gateways." The court, however, held that the two parcels were not "similarly situated" as there were several critical differences between them. Primarily, the property in this case was within the town's historic district and the other rezoning was not. The court also noted that a consideration of the project's size, proposed use, density, and other factors would be necessary to determine similarity.[113]

In the zoning context, it has been held that persons within a particular zoning district are similarly situated, but persons in different districts are not.[114] Therefore, while a zoning restriction must generally apply equally to everyone within a particular zoning district,[115] it need not apply to other zoning districts. For example, provisions that address flood-hazard issues, such as preventing floodway obstructions and requiring flood proofing, may be applied only in flood-hazard zones.

The courts have also long allowed similar differences based on types of land uses, dimensional requirements, and the like.[116] In *PBK Holdings, LLC v. County of Rockingham*,[117] the court upheld a regulatory distinction between "local" and "regional" landfills, noting that even if it was assumed they were similarly situated for equal-protection purposes, there was a rational basis for differential regulation based on the differing scale of impacts of the two scales of landfills involved.

---

112. The town council approved the rezoning by a 3-2 vote, but since a valid protest petition had been filed, the rezoning failed as it did not secure the requisite three-fourths supermajority.

113. In *Sansotta v. Town of Nags Head*, 724 F.3d 533 (4th Cir. 2013), the court held that nuisance enforcement against some but not all storm-damaged structures was not an equal-protection violation. The town showed that some structures posed a greater threat to safety and public-beach use than others, and this was held to be a rational basis for differential treatment. By contrast, in a case that does not have precedential value, *Amward Homes, Inc. v. Town of Cary*, 206 N.C. App. 38, 698 S.E.2d 404 (2010), *aff'd by equally divided court*, 365 N.C. 305, 716 S.E.2d 849 (2011), the court found that similarly situated persons were being treated differently. The plaintiff builders were required to pay a school impact fee because the development involved had been approved at a time when the ordinance requiring the fee was still in effect, while builders in similar developments approved after the ordinance was repealed did not have to pay the fee. The court invalidated the school impact fee under challenge, holding that there was no rational basis for differential treatment of the builders.

114. *See, e.g.*, Quality Built Homes, Inc. v. Vill. of Pinehurst, No. 1:06CV1028, 2008 WL 3503149 (M.D.N.C. Aug. 11, 2008) (upholding regulation that applied design standards to new construction in residential zoning districts located in or near the historic core of the village without applying them in other outlying zoning districts). The same concept is applicable to other land use regulations. In a novel but unsuccessful challenge to a county regulation on the location of adult businesses, a potential patron raised an equal-protection challenge to the mandatory-separation requirement between adult businesses and residents. The court summarily dismissed the argument, noting that the requirement had equal effect on all businesses proposing to offer adult entertainment and equal effect on all those who desired to reside in close proximity to these businesses. Pitt Cnty. v. Dejavue, Inc., 185 N.C. App. 545, 564–65, 650 S.E.2d 12, 24 (2007), *review denied*, 362 N.C. 381, 661 S.E.2d 738 (2008).

115. Decker v. Coleman, 6 N.C. App. 102, 169 S.E.2d 487 (1969).

116. *See, e.g.*, Pulte Home Corp. v. Montgomery Cnty., 909 F.3d 685, 694 (4th Cir. 2018) (parcels of differing size, location, and environmental characteristics not similarly situated).

117. 233 N.C. App. 233, 756 S.E.2d 821, *appeal dismissed*, 367 N.C. 788 (2014).

Basis for Distinction

If the differential treatment burdens the exercise of a fundamental right (such as the right of free speech) or operates to the intentional[118] disadvantage of a suspect class (such as making a distinction based on race, creed, or national origin), the government must show a compelling state interest[119] to justify the distinction—a very difficult standard to meet. For example, regulation of the number of related individuals who may live together was invalidated as an undue infringement of a fundamental right in *Moore v. City of East Cleveland*.[120] North Carolina courts apply a similar two-tiered equal-protection analysis in their judicial review of ordinances—strict scrutiny for classifications involving suspect classes or impinging on fundamental rights[121] and a rational-relationship test otherwise.[122]

In these cases, however, the plaintiff must show that there was in fact some differential treatment and some evidence of purposeful discrimination. A bald assertion that ethnic discrimination was the basis for a municipality's zoning-enforcement action, coupled with no showing of disparate treatment of others who are similarly situated, is inadequate to establish an equal-protection claim.[123] In *Nance v. City of Albemarle*, the court dismissed an equal-protection challenge to the city's denial of permits to convert a motel to an assisted low-income housing facility.[124] There was no factual support for a claim that the city had a custom or policy to unlawfully limit low-income housing and the plaintiff presented no direct or indirect evidence that: (1) racial discrimination played any role in the city's permit denial; (2) there was a pattern of permit denial for affordable housing; (3) there was historical housing discrimination by the city; or (4) there were contemporaneous statements showing a reasonable inference of discrimination. However, demonstrating discriminatory intent in land development regulations is often challenging.[125]

---

118. Under the federal Constitution, some discriminatory purpose or intent, not just a differential effect, must be shown. Cuyahoga Falls v. Buckeye Cmty. Hope Found., 538 U.S. 188 (2003); Vill. of Arlington Heights v. Metro. Hous. Dev. Corp., 429 U.S. 252 (1977).

119. Mem'l Hosp. v. Maricopa Cnty., 415 U.S. 250 (1974).

120. 431 U.S. 494 (1977). For further coverage of this case and housing discrimination generally, see the discussion of the Fair Housing Act in Chapter 23.

121. The right to construct outdoor advertising signs is not a fundamental right. Transylvania Cnty. v. Moody, 151 N.C. App. 389, 397, 565 S.E.2d 720, 726 (2002).

122. Town of Atl. Beach v. Young, 307 N.C. 422, 429, 298 S.E.2d 686, 691, *cert. denied*, 462 U.S. 1101 (1983); Texfi Indus., Inc. v. City of Fayetteville, 301 N.C. 1, 10, 269 S.E.2d 142, 149 (1980).

123. In *Karagiannopoulos v. City of Lowell*, No. 3:05-cv-00401-FDW, 2008 WL 2447362 (W.D.N.C. June 13, 2008), *aff'd per curiam*, 305 F. App'x 64 (4th Cir. 2008), the plaintiff alleged that the city's zoning-enforcement action and refusal to rezone her property were based on her Hispanic ethnicity. The court dismissed the claim as she offered no evidence of an intent to discriminate on that basis other than her own assumptions (and further did not show that others who were similarly situated were being treated differently).

124. 520 F. Supp. 3d 758 (M.D.N.C. 2021).

125. *Congregation Rabbinical College of Tartikov, Inc. v. Village of Pomona*, 945 F.3d 83 (2d Cir. 2019) is illustrative. After the plaintiff acquired property formerly used as a summer camp, the town adopted several regulatory provisions that would manage future redevelopment of the property. Several years later, when rumors spread that the plaintiff was considering development of the property for an educational facility with large dormitories that would potentially more than double the village population, the village adopted additional more-restrictive zoning and wetland-protection provisions. The court found no discriminatory intent for regulatory amendments made before the town had knowledge of the plaintiff's potential plans for extensive development. However, while there was considerable discussion about traffic, environmental impacts, and other typical land-use concerns during consideration of the later more-restrictive amendments, public comments at hearings, statements by candidates for local political office, and discussion among the board members included expressions of concern about the large number of Orthodox/Hasidic Jews the potential development would bring to the village. Such statements were susceptible to an inference of religious animus and hostility that supported a finding that the village acted with discriminatory intent and purpose.

When a fundamental right or a suspect classification is not involved, the local government is required only to establish a rational basis for its differential treatment.[126] Though rare, courts on occasion find a zoning-classification action so irrational as to violate equal protection. If the distinction does not have a rational basis, it will be ruled invalid.[127] But courts will uphold a regulation if any rational basis for it can be envisioned.[128]

A zoning regulation may apply different standards to different uses within the same zoning district as long as there is a reasonable basis for the distinction. For example, in *Goforth Properties, Inc. v. Town of Chapel Hill*,[129] the court ruled that it was permissible for the town to exempt churches from off-street parking requirements because the different timing of their parking demand relative to that of businesses provided a reasonable basis for the distinction. Development regulations may also legitimately distinguish between preexisting and future uses if there is a rational basis for treating them differently.[130]

On the other hand, when there is no reasonable basis for the distinction, disparate zoning treatment is invalid. For example, the U.S. Supreme Court held in *City of Cleburne v. Cleburne Living Center, Inc.*[131] that a city may not require a group home for the developmentally disabled to secure a special use permit when it does not require other group-living facilities with a similar land use impact to do so.[132] On the other hand, a facially neutral special use permit requirement for all congregate living facilities would not violate the federal Equal Protection Clause.[133]

A land-development regulation that is neutral on its face may still be held to discriminate on the basis of race, color, nationality, or some other protected classification. This principle applies to both the express terms of the ordinance and its application. The classic formulation of this rule is *Yick Wo v.*

---

126. New Orleans v. Dukes, 427 U.S. 297 (1976); Vill. of Belle Terre v. Boraas, 416 U.S. 1 (1974); Sylvia Dev. Corp. v. Calvert Cnty., 48 F.3d 810 (4th Cir. 1995); White v. Pate, 308 N.C. 759, 766–67, 304 S.E.2d 199, 204 (1983). The party contending that the classification is irrational has the burden of establishing such. *In re* Appeals of Certain Timber Cos., 98 N.C. App. 412, 420, 391 S.E.2d 503, 507–08 (1990). *See also* PEM Entities LLC v. County of Franklin, 57 F.4th 178, 184 (2023).

127. *See, e.g.*, Lady J. Lingerie, Inc. v. City of Jacksonville, 973 F. Supp. 1428, 1448–49 (M.D. Fla. 1997) (exempting city-owned property from adult-entertainment ordinance violates equal-protection because no plausible rationale supports the exemption); Thorp v. Town of Lebanon, 2000 WI 60, 612 N.W.2d 59 (rezoning of rural parcel from "rural development" to "agricultural" alleged to be sufficiently irrational to survive motion to dismiss on equal-protection challenge).

128. Guerra v. Scruggs, 942 F.2d 270, 279 (4th Cir. 1991).

129. 71 N.C. App. 771, 323 S.E.2d 427 (1984).

130. Grace Baptist Church v. City of Oxford, 320 N.C. 439, 358 S.E.2d 372 (1987); Kinney v. Sutton, 230 N.C. 404, 53 S.E.2d 306 (1949); Elizabeth City v. Aydlett, 201 N.C. 602, 161 S.E. 78 (1931). *See also* Adams v. Vill. of Wesley Chapel, 259 F. App'x 545 (4th Cir. 2007) (differential treatment on projects with vested rights under prior ordinance not an equal-protection violation). See the discussion of nonconformities in Chapter 20.

131. 473 U.S. 432 (1985). *See also* Andrews v. City of Mentor, 11 F.4th 462 (6th Cir. 2021) (different decisions on rezoning proposals for nearly identical development on similar parcels may violate equal protection).

132. Similarly, in *Catherine H. Barber Memorial Shelter, Inc. v. Town of North Wilkesboro*, No. 5:20-CV-00163-KDB-DCK, 2021 WL 6065159 (W.D.N.C. Dec. 20, 2021), the court held that a special use permit requirement for homeless shelters violated the Equal Protection Clause as it treated similarly situated uses differently without a rational basis. The court found there were no factors relating to the intensity of the land use and the potential impact on surrounding properties that differentiated a homeless shelter from other similar uses permitted in this zoning district without a special use permit (congregate-care facilities, emergency shelters, nursing homes, hospitals, lodges, and civic/fraternal/cultural/community facilities).

133. *See, e.g.*, United States v. Vill. of Palatine, 37 F.3d 1230 (7th Cir. 1994).

Hopkins,[134] where the Supreme Court invalidated a San Francisco ordinance that effectively barred Chinese-owned laundries, holding:

> Though the law itself be fair on its face, and impartial in appearance, yet, if it is applied and administered by public authority with an evil eye and an unequal hand, so as practically to make unjust and illegal discriminations between persons in similar circumstances, material to their rights, the denial of equal justice is still within the prohibition of the constitution.[135]

Class of One

Disparate-treatment analysis can be applied even when the person raising the claim is not a member of a protected class. In *Village of Willowbrook v. Olech*,[136] the Supreme Court allowed an equal-protection challenge by a "class of one." The claim was brought by a landowner seeking damages when it was alleged that the city (in retaliation for a previous flood-damage claim brought by the landowner) attempted to require an easement double the size of the usually required easement as a condition for providing water service. However, the Court held in *Engquist v. Oregon Department of Agriculture*[137] that a class-of-one claim cannot be used to challenge discretionary decisions. This precludes challenging either legislative or quasi-judicial regulatory decisions as this type of equal-protection violation.[138]

Courts have been reluctant to extend *Olech* beyond its particular circumstances. Plaintiffs must show an extremely high degree of similarity between themselves and others alleged to have received differential treatment.[139] Courts have also generally required plaintiffs to show malice or bad faith as a foundation for the disparate treatment.[140]

---

134. 118 U.S. 356 (1886) (ordinance requiring approval of board of supervisors to operate laundry in wooden building held discriminatory as applied).

135. *Id.* at 373–74.

136. 528 U.S. 562 (2000). *See also Andrews*, 11 F.4th 462 (6th Cir. 2021) (different decisions on rezoning proposals for nearly identical development on similar parcels may violate equal protection). If successful in such a claim, reasonable attorney's fees may be awarded if there are also substantial damages. *See, e.g.*, Thorncreek Apartments III, LLC v. Mick, 886 F.3d 626 (7th Cir. 2018).

137. 553 U.S. 591 (2008).

138. Catcove Corp. v. Heaney, 685 F. Supp. 2d 328, 333 (E.D.N.Y. 2010) (dismissing claim based on a failure to approve two rezoning petitions).

139. *See, e.g.*, Freeman v. Town of Hudson, 714 F.3d 29 (1st Cir. 2013) (rejecting claim in context of alleged selective enforcement of conservation-easement restriction); Gianfrancesco v. Town of Wrentham, 712 F.3d 634 (1st Cir. 2013) (tavern owner claiming selective enforcement failed to show comparable business that was treated differently); Ruston v. Town Bd. for Skaneateles, 610 F.3d 55 (2d Cir. 2010) (similarity must be such that no rational person could regard the differences as a potential justification for differential treatment); Reget v. City of La Crosse, 595 F.3d 691 (7th Cir. 2010) (showing that other, similar automobile-salvage dealers were treated differently ruled insufficient); Cordi-Allen v. Conlon, 494 F.3d 245, 251–53 (1st Cir. 2007) (scale and timing of proposed developments used as factors for determining properties not similarly situated); Campbell v. Rainbow City, 434 F.3d 1306, 1316 (11th Cir. 2006) (degree of nonconformity with zoning used as basis for determining properties not similarly situated); 3883 Conn. LLC v. District of Columbia, 336 F.3d 1068 (D.C. Cir. 2003) (showing of disparate treatment without a rational basis required); Purze v. Vill. of Winthrop Harbor, 286 F.3d 452 (7th Cir. 2002) (showing of disparate treatment from someone who is prima facie identical in all relevant respects required).

140. *See, e.g.*, Harlen Assocs. v. Incorporated Vill. of Mineola, 273 F.3d 494 (2d Cir. 2001) (showing of malice or bad faith on the part of the government required). Without a showing of animus, there is rarely a class-of-one claim. Black Earth Meat Market, LLC v. Vill. of Black Earth, 834 F.3d 841 (7th Cir. 2016). If there is a rational basis for differential treatment, a claim does not exist. Miller v. City of Monona, 784 F.3d 1113 (7th Cir. 2015).

CHAPTER 26

Regulation of Adult Businesses

Local governments frequently impose special land use regulatory restrictions on businesses that cater to an adults-only clientele. Adult bookstores, bars with erotic dancing, and massage parlors are deemed to have potential negative effects on neighborhoods and communities, so limits on where they can be located are common. It is not unusual to also have other restrictions on the operation of these businesses. Similar restrictions are often not imposed on comparable nonadult uses, such as other bookstores, theaters, and bars.

This chapter examines the authority of local governments to impose special restrictions on adult uses in manners consistent with the First Amendment's protection of freedom of speech. Local development regulations may also address other businesses that restrict admission to adults but that do not involve protected speech, such as bars or sweepstakes parlors.[1] The limitations on local regulation based on First Amendment protections that are discussed in this chapter are not applicable to those other businesses.

Statutory Authority

Most North Carolina local governments regulate the location and operation of adult businesses under their development regulation or their general police powers.[2] Chapter 160D, Section 101(a) of the North Carolina General Statutes (hereinafter G.S.) provides that the provisions of Chapter 160D apply not

---

1. These other businesses are also sometimes subject to criminal-law restrictions as well as land use regulations, such as with unlicensed bars and "shot houses." The boundary between legal and illegal uses, such as an illegal gambling establishment and a lawful sweepstakes parlor, has been subject to considerable legislation and protracted litigation. *See, e.g.*, Gift Surplus, LLC v. North Carolina, 380 N.C. 1, 868 S.E.2d 20 (2022) (applying Chapter 14, Section 306.4 of the North Carolina General Statutes (hereinafter G.S.)). Some local land use regulations directly reference the criminal prohibitions by allowing, for example, a legal gaming use but prohibiting an illegal gambling use.

A few local development regulations also treat tattoo parlors as adult uses. It is possible these uses may have some First Amendment protection. Buehrle v. City of Key West, 813 F.3d 973 (11th Cir. 2015); Yvon v. City of Oceanside, 202 F. Supp. 3d 1147 (S.D. Cal. 2016). However, the focus of this chapter is on the more common sexually oriented business that offers some protected First Amendment speech.

2. A 2004 survey by the UNC School of Government indicated that two-thirds of responding cities and counties in North Carolina had adopted regulations on adult entertainment, with over 90 percent of the more populous jurisdictions (cities with populations over 5000 and counties with unincorporated-area populations of over 50,000) having done so. David W. Owens & Nathan Branscome, An Inventory of Local Government Land Use Ordinances in North Carolina (UNC School of Government, Special Series No. 21, May 2006). A 1997 survey indicated that twenty-three of the state's twenty-five most populous cities had adopted zoning regulations on the location of adult businesses. David W. Owens, Regulating Sexually Oriented Businesses 27–30 (UNC Institute of Government, Special Series No. 15, Jan. 1997).

In *Maynor v. Onslow County*, 127 N.C. App. 102, 488 S.E.2d 289, *appeal dismissed*, 347 N.C. 268, 493 S.E.2d 458, *review denied*, 347 N.C. 400 (1997), the court held that regulations on the location of adult businesses could be adopted as general-police-power regulations to protect the public health, safety, and welfare under G.S. 153A-121. In *Onslow County v. Moore*, 129 N.C. App. 376, 499 S.E.2d 780, *review denied*, 349 N.C. 361, 525 S.E.2d 453 (1998), the court confirmed that minimum-separation requirements for adult businesses could be adopted as either zoning requirements or as a general-police-power ordinance.

only to local development regulations, but also to "any other local ordinance that substantially affects land use and development." So the procedures set for development regulations also apply to a general-police-power ordinance on adult-business siting and operation.

G.S. 160D-902 sets out a range of specific regulatory options available to cities and counties in regulating adult businesses. The statute specifies that the regulations are to be directed toward the reduction of these businesses' secondary impacts—that is, potentially deleterious effects on property values, crime rates, and the like. Regulations can include restrictions on location and operation of the facilities, licensing requirements, and reasonable fees. These are among the specific regulatory tools authorized:

- Limits on location, including restrictions to specified zoning districts and minimum-separation requirements;
- limits on operations, including restrictions on hours of operation, requirements that all viewing booths be open and visible to managers, limits on exterior advertising and noise, restrictions on ages of patrons and employees, requirements for separations between patrons and performers, and clothing requirements for masseuses, servers, and entertainers;
- licensing, disclosure, and registration requirements, including restricting the ownership or employment of those who have criminal records for offenses reasonably related to the legal operation of a sexually oriented business;
- moratoria on new facilities or expansions while studies are conducted and ordinances debated;[3]
- amortization requirements for nonconforming adult businesses; and
- interlocal agreements whereby local governments within an interrelated geographic area can provide alternative sites for adult businesses without the necessity of each unit of government providing sites.[4]

Local governments are authorized to adopt their own detailed definitions of adult or sexually oriented businesses to precisely set the scope of local regulations.

State law generally does not preempt local regulation of adult businesses. Several older cases once held that state statutes preempted local regulation. The statute limiting adult establishments to one per structure had been held to preclude local separation requirements.[5] The statute on indecent exposure

---

3. In *Phillips v. Borough of Keyport*, 107 F.3d 164 (3d Cir. 1997), the court held that delays in issuing permits for a sexually oriented business based on an aversion to the content of the material to be sold by the business could lead to recovery on a substantive-due-process basis but that a moratorium to allow time to study secondary impacts would not. See also *Steam Heat, Inc. v. Silva*, 646 N.Y.S.2d 537 (App. Div. 1996), where the court upheld refusal to renew permits for an adult business during a one-year moratorium. In *ASF, Inc. v. City of Seattle*, 408 F. Supp. 2d 1102 (W.D. Wash. 2005), the court invalidated a seven-year moratorium on permits for adult cabarets as an unlawful prior restraint.

4. *Schad v. Borough of Mount Ephraim*, 452 U.S. 61, 75–77 (1981), indicates that this is a permissible option. In *Peterson v. City of Florence*, 727 F.3d 839 (8th Cir. 2013), the court held it was appropriate to consider sites available in the surrounding county when assessing a regulation that prohibited siting within a municipality of 0.2 square miles and a population of thirty-nine. *But see* Wolfe v. Vill. of Brice, 997 F. Supp. 939, 944–45 (S.D. Ohio 1998) (availability of potential sites in adjoining municipality does not provide adequate alternative avenues). The court in *Township of Saddle Brook v. A.B. Family Center, Inc.*, 156 N.J. 587, 597, 722 A.2d 530, 535–36 (1999), applied a multifactor analysis to define the "relevant market area," including an examination of reasonable proximity, regional marketing, transportation access, and geographic distribution of customers. The court in *Borough of Sayreville v. 35 Club*, 416 N.J. Super. 315, 3 A.3d 1268 (App. Div. 2010), however, held that it was not permissible to include jurisdictions in bordering states. *See generally* Sarah L. Swan, *Constitutional Off-Loading at the City Limits*, 135 Harv. L. Rev. 831 (2022). See the discussion below on alternative avenues of expression for more on this issue.

5. *Moore*, 129 N.C. App. at 387, 499 S.E.2d at 787–88. *See also* K. Hope, Inc. v. Onslow Cnty., 911 F. Supp. 948, 952–54 (E.D.N.C. 1995), *vacated and remanded without opinion*, 107 F.3d 866 (4th Cir. 1997).

had been held to limit regulation of topless dancers.[6] Statutes regulating alcohol sales had been held to limit local regulation of bars.[7] However, the legislature in 1998 amended the state statutes prohibiting obscenity (G.S. 14-190.1) and indecent exposure (G.S. 14-190.9), limiting adult establishments to one per structure (G.S. 14-202.11), and regulating facilities that sell alcohol (G.S. 18B-904) to specify that these statutes do not preclude local government ordinances from regulating adult businesses.[8] Each of the amended statutes states that local regulations must be consistent with constitutional protections afforded free speech.

Speech Not Covered by First Amendment Protections

As a threshold issue, to receive First Amendment protection, there must be some element of speech that is to be protected.[9] Even though adult books, films, and performances have some First Amendment protection, there are two important types of speech that do not: obscenity and public sexual conduct. Both have important implications for the regulation of adult businesses.

Obscenity

Obscenity is not protected by the First Amendment.[10] The production and dissemination (but not the mere possession in the privacy of one's home)[11] of obscene materials and the public performance of obscene acts are criminal offenses and are banned by the state. The North Carolina statutory definition of *obscenity*, which has been updated several times to conform to judicial definitions of the scope

---

6. State v. Tenore, 280 N.C. 238, 185 S.E.2d 644 (1972). The statute prohibits exposure of one's "private parts" to members of the opposite sex in a public place (which includes a private club to which the public is invited). The court here acknowledged that cities and counties can adopt "a higher standard of conduct" in their jurisdictions but held that female breasts are not "private parts" as a matter of law and that local governments cannot make an offense of identical conduct that is addressed but not proscribed by the state statute.

7. *In re* Melkonian, 85 N.C. App. 351, 355 S.E.2d 503, *review denied*, 320 N.C. 631, 360 S.E.2d 91 (1987).

8. S.L. 1998-46.

9. For example, the court in *Adam and Eve Jonesboro, LLC v. Perrin*, 933 F.3d 951, 957–58 (8th Cir. 2019), held that a store that sold lingerie, adult toys, costumes, novelties, games, massage oils, and personal lubricants, but not videos, films, books, literature, periodicals or posters, did not present a First Amendment free-speech issue. The court held that sale of sexually oriented devices is not speech or expressive conduct. In *Willis v. Town of Marshall*, 426 F.3d 251 (4th Cir. 2005), the court held that recreational dancing was not protected speech. The court upheld the town's ban of a woman from town-sponsored dances for "lewd" dancing.

10. Miller v. California, 413 U.S. 15 (1973); Paris Adult Theater I v. Slaton, 413 U.S. 49 (1973); Roth v. United States, 354 U.S. 476 (1967); Smith v. California, 361 U.S. 147 (1959). For similar state-court rulings, see *State v. Bryant*, 285 N.C. 27, 203 S.E.2d 27 (1973), and *Cinema I Video, Inc. v. Thornburg*, 83 N.C. App. 544, 351 S.E.2d 305 (1986).

There are a very limited number of narrowly defined types of expressive activity that the United States Supreme Court has ruled have no First Amendment free-speech protection. *See, as to unprotected conduct,* New York v. Ferber, 458 U.S. 747, 763 (1982) (child pornography); Va. State Bd. of Pharmacy v. Va. Citizens Consumer Council, Inc., 425 U.S. 748, 771 (1976) (fraud); Brandenburg v. Ohio, 395 U.S. 444, 447–49 (1969) (per curiam) (incitement); Beauharnais v. Illinois, 343 U.S. 250, 254–55 (1952) (defamation); Giboney v. Empire Storage & Ice Co., 336 U.S. 490, 498 (1949) (speech integral to criminal conduct); Chaplinsky v. New Hampshire, 315 U.S. 568, 572 (1942) ("the lewd and obscene, the profane, the libelous, and the insulting or 'fighting' words"). The Court has refused to add animal cruelty to this list. United States v. Stevens, 559 U.S. 460 (2010).

11. Stanley v. Georgia, 394 U.S. 557 (1969).

of First Amendment protections, applies to writings, pictures, records, films, tapes, plays, dance, and performances that match the following criteria:

1. The material depicts or describes in a patently offensive way sexual conduct specifically defined by the statute.
2. The average person applying contemporary community standards relating to the depiction or description of sexual matters would find that the material taken as a whole appeals to individuals with a prurient interest in sex.
3. The material lacks serious literary, artistic, political, or scientific value.
4. The material as used is not protected or privileged under the U.S. Constitution or the N.C. constitution.[12]

The statute makes it a felony to create, buy, or sell obscene materials and declares such to be contraband.

Several aspects of the obscenity definition are noteworthy. First, the statute specifically defines the depictions of sexual conduct covered.[13] Second, given the invocation of "community standards," the question becomes, What is the "community"? There is no requirement that a national or even a state-wide standard be applied.[14] In North Carolina it has been held appropriate to permit a jury to apply the standards of the community in which the indictment was returned and from which the jurors came.[15] However, jurors do not have unbridled discretion in determining what is patently offensive. Even though material might violate a particular community's standard of what appeals to prurient interests, the U.S. Supreme Court has ruled that only "hard-core" material can be found obscene.[16] The question of the literary, artistic, political, or scientific value of material also is determined by a national standard.[17] These factors effectively preclude a small community from adopting a highly restrictive definition of obscenity. Third, in assessing whether the material has serious literary, artistic, political, or scientific value, a jury must be instructed to consider the work as a whole and to apply a reasonable person's standard even though those qualifications are not explicitly in the North Carolina statute.[18]

Conduct

Conduct also may not be protected by the First Amendment. The boundary between conduct that is *symbolic speech* or *expressive conduct*—which is protected—and conduct that can be prohibited is sometimes difficult to discern.[19]

---

12. G.S. 14-190.1(b). The state appeals court has ruled that this definition is neither vague nor overbroad because it specifically defines the types of sexual conduct deemed obscene. Cinema I Video, Inc. v. Thornburg, 83 N.C. App. 544, 351 S.E.2d 305 (1986), *aff'd*, 320 N.C. 485, 358 S.E.2d 383 (1987).

13. G.S. 14-190.1(c).

14. Jenkins v. Georgia, 418 U.S. 153, 157 (1974) (invalidating conviction for showing film *Carnal Knowledge*).

15. State v. Mayes, 323 N.C. 159, 371 S.E.2d 476 (1988); State v. Anderson, 322 N.C. 22, 366 S.E.2d 459 (1988).

16. Although the Court has not precisely defined *hard core*, it has offered as examples representations of ultimate sex acts, masturbation, excretory functions, and lewd exhibition of the genitals. Depiction of nudity alone is insufficient to make material obscene. *Jenkins*, 418 U.S. at 160–61; Miller v. California, 413 U.S. 15, 25–27 (1973).

17. Smith v. United States, 431 U.S. 291, 301 (1977) (affirming a conviction for mailing obscene magazine and films).

18. State v. Watson, 88 N.C. App. 624, 364 S.E.2d 683 (1988).

19. For a review and critique of this distinction, see John Fee, *The Freedom of Speech-Conduct*, 109 Ky. L.J. 81 (2021).

In *United States v. O'Brien*, the U.S. Supreme Court established a four-part test to determine whether First Amendment free-speech rights are impermissibly burdened by a particular governmental regulation of "symbolic" conduct:

1. Is the regulation within the constitutional power of the government?
2. Does it further an important or substantial governmental interest?
3. Is the governmental interest unrelated to the suppression of free expression?
4. Is the restriction no greater than is essential?[20]

Public nudity in itself—outside of the context of a book, play, dance, or performance—is conduct that is not protected speech under the First Amendment.[21]

Defining Adult Businesses Subject to Regulation

Definitions of which adult-business activities are subject to regulation must be carefully drawn to ensure they are not impermissibly vague or overly broad.

A local government must determine which adult-entertainment or sexually oriented business operations are to be regulated. Most regulations address adult bookstores, adult theaters, and facilities that feature nude or topless dancing. Other ordinances regulate a broader range of businesses that do not have First Amendment protection but are restricted to an adult clientele and emphasize sexuality, such as massage parlors, adult motels, escort services, and nude-modeling studios.

To avoid being unconstitutionally vague, an ordinance regulating adult businesses must be drawn with sufficient precision so that a person of normal intelligence has fair notice of what is prohibited.[22] It must also provide enforcement officers and the courts with reasonably clear guidelines as to the scope of the regulation in order to prevent arbitrary or discriminatory enforcement.[23]

---

20. 391 U.S. 367 (1968) (upholding a draft-card-burning conviction). Courts have generally concluded that the *O'Brien* standard for review of regulations on expressive conduct are functionally interchangeable with the tests for restrictions of time, place, and manner enumerated in *City of Renton v. Playtime Theatres, Inc.*, 475 U.S. 41 (1986) (this case is discussed in detail later in this chapter). Richland Bookmart, Inc. v. Knox Cnty., 555 F.3d 512, 520–22 (6th Cir. 2009).

21. *See, e.g.,* U.S. v. Biocic, 928 F.2d 112 (4th Cir. 1991) (upholding conviction for female topless sunbather on National Wildlife Refuge property); S. Fla. Free Beaches, Inc. v. City of Miami, 734 F.2d 608, 610 (11th Cir. 1984) (holding that there is no constitutional right to sunbathe or associate in the nude); Williams v. Kleppe, 539 F.2d 803 (1st Cir. 1976) (upholding ban on nude sunbathing at national park); Eline v. Town of Ocean City, 452 F. Supp. 3d 270 (D. Md. 2020) (prohibition of female topless sunbathing not an Equal Protection violation). For a review of cases addressing the prohibition on the exposure of female breasts but not male breasts, see Max Birmingham, *The Full Monty: Analyzing the Constitutionality of Ordinances That Only Punish Women for Being Topless in Public*, 46 S. ILL. L.J. 495 (2022). *See also* Adam and Eve Jonesboro, LLC v. Perrin, 933 F.3d 951, 957 (8th Cir. 2019) (sale of sexually oriented devices is not expressive conduct with First Amendment protection). This issue of clothing restrictions for adult-business entertainers is discussed in more detail below.

22. Connally v. Gen. Constr. Co., 269 U.S. 385, 391 (1926) (statute unconstitutionally vague if persons of "common intelligence must necessarily guess at its meaning and differ as to its application"). *See also* Ashton v. Kentucky, 384 U.S. 195, 200–201 (1966) (law impacting First Amendment rights must be narrowly drawn to prevent undue constraint of those rights); Baggett v. Bullitt, 377 U.S. 360, 372 (1964) (vague laws induced individuals to avoid lawful as well as unlawful activities); Scull v. Virginia *ex rel.* Comm. on Law Reform & Racial Activities, 359 U.S. 344, 353 (1959) (vague law induced individuals to avoid lawful activity to avoid potential violation).

23. Smith v. Goguen, 415 U.S. 566, 573 (1974). The South Carolina Supreme Court held that a regulation that applied to businesses with sale of adult material as a "principal business purpose" was not sufficiently precise. City of Columbia v. Pic-A-Flick Video, Inc., 340 S.C. 278, 531 S.E.2d 518 (2000). The court in *600 Marshall Entertainment Concepts, LLC v. City of Memphis*, 705 F.3d 576, 586–87 (6th Cir. 2013) noted that confusion of zoning administrators in interpreting a regulation of a facility offering nude dancing did not in itself mean the ordinance

To avoid being unconstitutionally overly broad, the regulation must not suppress protected speech that is not connected to the secondary impacts addressed by the restrictions.[24] A key inquiry is whether the regulation proscribes a substantial amount of protected speech in addition to its legitimate sweep.[25]

In *Young v. American Mini Theatres, Inc.*, the U.S. Supreme Court held that a Detroit ordinance was sufficiently precise when it regulated exhibitions "characterized by an emphasis on" specified sexual activities or specified anatomical areas.[26] Many local ordinances simply repeat these same definitions verbatim. Other formulations that have been approved by the courts as being sufficiently precise include regulating establishments that have a "substantial or significant portion,"[27] a "preponderance,"[28] or a set percentage[29] of their merchandise or exhibitions devoted to sexually explicit material; regulating businesses having dancing that "emphasizes and seeks, through one or more dancers, to arouse or excite the patrons' sexual desires";[30] and regulating theaters that "on a regular basis" show films from which minors are excluded.[31]

In addition to holding that the use of the term *preponderance* is not unconstitutionally vague, the North Carolina courts have held that the term is not synonymous with *majority*.[32] Thus, even if less than 50 percent of the products sold are sexually explicit, if their relative location, accessibility, and display are such that they are given far greater importance and are emphasized far more than other materials, their preponderance makes the establishment a sexually oriented business. It is not necessary that

---

was unconstitutionally vague. (It also found that the ordinance provisions were straightforward.) See Chapter 25 for discussion of due-process requirements regarding vagueness.

24. *See generally* City of Chi. v. Morales, 527 U.S. 41, 52 (1999); N.Y. State Club Ass'n v. City of N.Y., 487 U.S. 1, 11 (1988); Gooding v. Wilson, 405 U.S. 518, 522 (1972); Schultz v. City of Cumberland, 228 F.3d 831, 849 (7th Cir. 2000). The courts allow a broader standing when ordinances limiting protected speech are challenged on grounds of overbreadth, reasoning that those who actually are affected are less likely to sue. Broadrick v. Oklahoma, 413 U.S. 601 (1973).

25. Virginia v. Hicks, 539 U.S. 113, 118–19 (2003) (citing *Broadrick*, 413 U.S. at 615).

26. 427 U.S. 50, 50 (1976). The Court noted that any uncertainty regarding borderline applications was readily subject to a narrowing construction by the state courts.

27. *See, e.g.*, VIP of Berlin, LLC v. Town of Berlin, 593 F.3d 179, 188–91 (2d Cir. 2009); Ill. One News, Inc. v. City of Marshall, 477 F.3d 461, 465 (7th Cir. 2007); Doctor John's, Inc. v. City of Roy, 465 F.3d 1150, 1157–60 (10th Cir. 2006); World Wide Video of Wash., Inc. v. City of Spokane, 368 F.3d 1186 (9th Cir. 2004) ("significant or substantial portion"); ILQ Invs., Inc. v. City of Rochester, 25 F.3d 1413, 1418–19 (8th Cir. 1994); 15192 Thirteen Mile Rd., Inc. v. City of Warren, 626 F. Supp. 803, 819–20 (E.D. Mich. 1985). *See also* Stansberry v. Holmes, 613 F.2d 1285, 1290 (5th Cir. 1980) (upholding as adequately specific a definition of sexually oriented commercial enterprises as those "whose major business is the offering of a service which is intended to provide sexual stimulation or sexual gratification").

28. Hart Book Stores, Inc. v. Edmisten, 612 F.2d 821, 833–34 (4th Cir. 1979) (noting that the definitions must be "reasonably specific and precise, bearing in mind that unavoidable imprecision is not fatal and celestial precision is not necessary"); S. Blvd. Video & News, Inc. v. Charlotte Zoning Bd. of Adjustment, 129 N.C. App. 282, 498 S.E.2d 623, *review denied*, 348 N.C. 501, 510 S.E.2d 656 (1998) (upholding determination that "preponderance" standard is satisfied if adult materials are given a predominant and far greater importance or emphasis in display in the store); Fantasy World, Inc. v. Greensboro Bd. of Adjustment, 128 N.C. App. 703, 496 S.E.2d 825, *review denied*, 348 N.C. 496, 510 S.E.2d 382 (1998) (the term *preponderance* is reasonably specific and sufficiently precise so as to be readily understood, thus no further definition in the ordinance is required).

29. 11126 Balt. Boulevard v. Prince George's Cnty., 886 F.2d 1415 (4th Cir. 1989), *vacated and remanded on other grounds*, 496 U.S. 901 (1990) (upholding ordinance applicable to businesses with 5 percent of stock devoted to such material).

30. KEV, Inc. v. Kitsap Cnty., 793 F.2d 1053, 1056 (9th Cir. 1986).

31. Basiardanes v. City of Galveston, 682 F.2d 1203, 1209 (5th Cir. 1982).

32. *S. Blvd. Video & News*, 129 N.C. App. at 287–88, 498 S.E.2d at 627–28; *Fantasy World*, 128 N.C. App. at 709–10, 496 S.E.2d at 829. *See also* Ent. Prods., Inc. v. Shelby Cnty., 588 F.3d 372 (6th Cir. 2009) (upholding definition based on establishment having adult entertainment as "a principal use").

the full content of all publications or films be reviewed to make this determination, as it is reasonable to base a decision that the material is adult material on examining the covers and titles of materials.[33]

Many local governments draft regulations of adult businesses to exempt mainstream businesses, such as legitimate theatrical productions or providers of therapeutic massage.[34] Exemptions for these businesses and exemptions for business with only modest adult products do not avoid First Amendment protection for those adult businesses that are regulated.[35]

Where the business involved has no on-site customers, such as a warehouse for an adult business or a site where adult activity is videotaped for distribution off-site,[36] it is generally deemed not to be an adult establishment for the purposes of regulating secondary impacts.

First Amendment Protections

Framework for Analysis

The U.S. Supreme Court first addressed the validity of a local ordinance regulating the location of adult businesses in 1976 in *Young*. The ordinance there required adult theaters to be located at least 1000 feet from any two other regulated uses and 500 feet from residential zoning districts. The city based this dispersal requirement on a finding that a concentration of adult uses "tends to attract an undesirable quantity and quality of transients, adversely affects property values, causes an increase in crime, especially prostitution, and encourages residents and business to move elsewhere."[37] The Court held that the city's interest in preventing the deterioration of urban neighborhoods justified the restriction on location of adult uses. Justice Powell's concurring opinion, which supplied the necessary fifth vote for upholding the ordinance, employed the four-part test of *O'Brien* and emphasized balancing the important and substantial governmental interest in stable neighborhoods against the incidental (and in this instance minimal) impact of the ordinance on protected speech.[38]

Ten years later, the Court revisited the issue of location limitations and upheld a more restrictive locational ordinance in *City of Renton v. Playtime Theatres, Inc.* The ordinance reviewed in *Renton* required adult theaters to be located at least 1000 feet from any residential zone, residence, church,

---

33. Durham Video & News, Inc. v. Durham Bd. of Adjustment, 144 N.C. 236, 350 S.E.2d 212, *review denied*, 354 N.C. 361, 556 S.E.2d 299 (2001).

34. A common approach is to exempt massage therapists licensed under Article 36 of G.S. 90. Some ordinances take the opposite approach and exempt all regulation of protected speech, thus avoiding First Amendment review altogether. *See, e.g.*, Stansberry v. Holmes, 613 F.2d 1285 (5th Cir. 1980) (upholding Harris County, Texas, ordinance that regulated location of massage parlors, nude-modeling studios, and the like but exempted bookstores, theaters, and businesses licensed to sell alcohol).

35. Christy v. City of Ann Arbor, 824 F.2d 489, 492 (6th Cir. 1987) (holding that First Amendment protections apply even though ordinance exempted from its coverage bookstores with less than 20 percent of their inventories devoted to sexually explicit material).

36. Voyeur Dorm, L.C. v. City of Tampa, 265 F.3d 1232 (11th Cir. 2001). While not an adult business, such an operation may constitute an unlawful business use in a residential zoning district. Flava Works, Inc. v. City of Miami, 609 F.3d 1233 (11th Cir. 2010).

37. Young v. Am. Mini Theatres, Inc., 427 U.S. 50, 55. These dispersal requirements are among the most common restrictions found in regulations for citing adult businesses. A 1996 survey of adult-business regulations in the twenty-five most populous cities found twenty-three of the twenty-four reporting cities required a minimum separation from other adult uses and from specified sensitive land uses. OWENS, *supra* note 2, 27–30. The special use permit for a topless bar at issue in *Mangum v. Raleigh Board of Adjustment* involved a separation requirement of 2000 feet. 196 N.C. App. 249, 674 S.E.2d 742 (2009).

38. *Young*, 427 U.S. at 79–80.

park, or school. The effect of this was to leave only 520 acres—amounting to roughly 5 percent of the city's land area—available for use by adult theaters.[39]

The Court held that *Renton's* ordinance should be reviewed as a content-neutral restriction on the time, place, and manner of free speech. The ordinance was deemed content neutral even though it treated theaters differently based on the type of films being shown in them. The Court reasoned that the content of the films was not the basis of the ordinance because the city council's "predominate concerns" in adopting it were the secondary effects of adult theaters on the surrounding neighborhood.[40] The Court held that the critical inquiry in determining the validity of a restriction on the location of adult uses is whether the ordinance "is designed to serve a substantial governmental interest and allows for reasonable alternative avenues of communication."[41]

The *Young* and *Renton* decisions established the following criteria for determining the validity of a local regulation for restricting the siting of adult businesses that are protected by the First Amendment. First, the regulation must not totally ban protected speech. Second, the regulation must be content neutral. If the predominate purpose of the regulation is to address the secondary impacts of adult uses, it is deemed content neutral. Third, the regulation must pass an intermediate-scrutiny review that examines the following factors:

1. Does it serve a *substantial governmental interest*? If there is an adequate foundation of study and deliberation that the governing body reasonably believes to be relevant to addressing secondary impacts in its jurisdiction, the regulation is deemed to serve a substantial governmental interest.

2. Will it allow for *reasonable alternative avenues of communication*? If the regulation provides reasonable opportunities to operate adult uses within the jurisdiction, even if the sites are not economically attractive, adequate alternative avenues have been provided.

3. Is it *narrowly tailored* to meet the substantial governmental interest?[42] If the scope of the regulation covers no more than is necessary to prevent harmful secondary impacts, it is narrowly tailored and not overly broad.

---

39. 475 U.S. 41 (1986). The *Renton* ordinance was challenged by the purchaser of two existing theaters, who proposed to convert them to adult theaters.

40. *Id.* at 47–49 (emphasis omitted). That some members of the council may have been motivated by a desire to restrict access to adult films was deemed irrelevant as long as the predominate intent was prevention of crime, protection of retail trade, maintenance of property values, and preservation of the quality of urban life.

41. *Id.* at 50. *See also* Turner Broad. Sys., Inc. v. FCC, 512 U.S. 622 (1994) (regulations unrelated to content of speech are subject to intermediate level of scrutiny).

42. Although the "narrowly tailored" test is not explicitly included in *Renton*, courts have concluded that it is implicitly there. *See, e.g.,* Richland Bookmart, Inc. v. Knox Cnty., 555 F.3d 512, 522 (6th Cir. 2009); Ben's Bar, Inc. v. Vill. of Somerset, 316 F.3d 702, 714 (7th Cir. 2003).

Content Neutrality and Motive

If a restriction on protected speech is based on the content of the speech, the courts apply strict scrutiny, and such a regulation must be narrowly drawn to accomplish a compelling governmental interest to be upheld.[43] This is a very difficult burden that is met only in extraordinary situations.[44] On the other hand, an ordinance that is content neutral can regulate the "time, place, and manner" of speech.[45]

A regulation is content neutral if it is "justified without reference to the content of the regulated speech."[46] A regulation of adult businesses is deemed by the courts to be content neutral if the predominate concern leading to its enactment is prevention of secondary impacts of the speech involved—neighborhood blight, an increase in crime, decreased property values, and the like. This test is sometimes phrased by the courts as a requirement that the regulation be "unrelated to suppression of speech."[47]

The U.S. Supreme Court has held that secondary effects do not include the reactions of those hearing the speech.[48] Secondary effects do include impacts on the viability of surrounding neighborhoods but not the potential psychological damage to the viewers of sexually explicit material.[49]

It is not unusual for the public record in the adoption of local restrictions on adult uses to contain numerous statements from members of the public, the city or county staff, and governing-board members regarding the purposes of the regulatory action. It is commonplace that many, sometimes most, of these comments focus on the content of the speech rather than on reduction of adverse secondary impacts.[50]

As a general rule, the motives of the governing board in adopting the regulation are irrelevant. Noting that it is best to eschew the guesswork inherent in determining legislative motive, the U.S. Supreme Court held in *O'Brien*, "It is a familiar principle of constitutional law that this Court will not strike down an otherwise constitutional statute on the basis of an alleged illicit legislative motive."[51] In *Mermaids, Inc. v. Currituck County Board of Commissioners*,[52] the plaintiff contended that the county had not

---

43. Sable Commc'ns of Cal. v. FCC, 492 U.S. 115 (1989) (invalidating regulation of "indecent" but nonobscene telephone communications); United States v. Grace, 461 U.S. 171 (1983).

44. For an example of the courts' sensitivity to First Amendment concerns with regulations of adult businesses, see *Y.K. Enterprises v. City of Greensboro*, No. 1:07CV0289, 2007 WL 2781706 (M.D.N.C. Sept. 21, 2007). In an action seeking to enjoin Greensboro's enforcement of an amortization provision requiring the relocation of nonconforming adult businesses, there were unresolved factual issues regarding the studies supporting the city's justification for the ordinance, the range of available alternative avenues for expression, and the rationale for differing amortization requirements for different types of adult businesses. The court refused to issue a preliminary injunction but ordered an expedited consolidated hearing. The court noted the city had voluntarily delayed enforcement during the litigation and encouraged that to continue while the case was pending.

45. Clark v. Cmty. for Creative Non-Violence, 468 U.S. 288 (1984). This test is most often applied to regulations limiting expression in a public forum. *See, e.g.,* Ward v. Rock Against Racism, 491 U.S. 781 (1989).

46. Va. State Bd. of Pharmacy v. Va. Citizens Consumer Council, Inc., 425 U.S. 748, 771 (1976).

47. United States v. O'Brien, 391 U.S. 367 (1968). Several decisions acknowledge the practical reality that many regulations on adult businesses are indeed content based (imposing more-stringent regulations solely on the basis of the types of books or videos sold or the type of entertainment provided) but conclude that adult businesses simply have a lower degree of protection than other protected speech. In *Richland Bookmart, Inc. v. Nichols*, the court termed content neutrality in these cases a "legal fiction." The court stated that rather than upholding regulations because they were content neutral, in reality the courts have simply concluded that the regulations were constitutionally valid. 137 F.3d 435, 438–41 (6th Cir. 1998).

48. Boos v. Barry, 485 U.S. 312 (1988) (invalidating an ordinance prohibiting display of signs critical of foreign governments within 500 feet of embassies).

49. *Id.* at 321.

50. *See, e.g.,* Abilene Retail No. 30, Inc. v. Bd. of Comm'rs, 492 F.3d 1164, 1173 (10th Cir. 2007) (motive of member of public that requested increased setback between adult businesses and residences in order to preclude particular store not imputed to board).

51. United States v. O'Brien, 391 U.S. 367, 383. *See also* Hart Book Stores, Inc. v. Edmisten, 612 F.2d 821, 834–35 (4th Cir. 1979).

52. 19 F. Supp. 2d 493 (E.D.N.C. 1998).

actually relied on the studies of secondary impacts it gathered and consulted before revoking its permit to operate a nightclub. The federal district court noted, "It is not for the federal courts to look behind the proffered evidence of legislative decisionmakers to discover alleged improper methods or motives."[53] Courts examine the regulation itself rather than the motive of the adopting body to determine whether the regulation serves a legitimate purpose.[54]

The critical inquiry, then, is not the motive of the adopting authority but, rather, the predominate purpose of the regulation.[55]

Thus, the government places itself at some risk of having its regulations invalidated if it does not explicitly make the predominate purpose of the restrictions an attempt to address secondary impacts.[56] This is particularly the case if the record indicates that the restrictions have been hurriedly adopted to stop a single proposed business or have a clear purpose other than dealing with secondary impacts.[57] Because these types of restrictions must be geared toward addressing secondary impacts, many courts are particularly sensitive to First Amendment infringements when the record of local consideration contains *only* expressions of moral outrage about the content of adult entertainment.

Also, if the regulation is substantially underinclusive, regulating adult businesses while not similarly regulating other businesses with similar or greater impacts on the purposes set forth, a court may find the regulations do not support a substantial government interest.[58]

---

53. *Id.* at 497.

54. SDJ, Inc. v. City of Houston, 837 F.2d 1268, 1274 (5th Cir. 1988). *See also* Ambassador Books & Video, Inc. v. City of Little Rock, 20 F.3d 858, 863–64 (8th Cir. 1994).

55. *See, e.g.,* Andy's Rest. & Lounge, Inc. v. City of Gary, 466 F.3d 550, 554–55 (7th Cir. 2006); BBL, Inc. v. City of Angola, 809 F.3d 317, 325 (7th Cir. 2015) (question is whether the adverse secondary effects invoked have a basis in reality and are likely to be reduced by the regulation); DiMa Corp. v. Town of Hallie, 185 F.3d 823, 828 (7th Cir. 1999). The court in *Zebulon Enterprises, Inc. v. DuPage Cnty.,* 43 F. Supp. 3d 881 (N.D. Ill. 2020), held that the plaintiff had stated a First Amendment claim when the ordinance preamble noted a secondary-impacts purpose, but the hearings of the ad hoc commission that developed the ordinance yielded no evidence of adverse secondary impacts.

56. A statutory or legislative preamble (or clear legislative history) may be preferable for accomplishing or enumerating such predominance, but such is not legally required, as a court can examine the face of the regulation itself, its placement in a broader regulatory scheme, and other factors contemporaneous to its adoption in order to discern its purpose. Illusions–Dallas Private Club, Inc. v. Steen, 482 F.3d 299, 310 (5th Cir. 2007) (holding Texas rule prohibiting sale of alcohol in private clubs that also offer adult entertainment to have predominate purpose other than suppression of protected speech).

57. *See* Joelner v. Vill. of Wash. Park, 508 F.3d 427 (7th Cir. 2008) (regulation prohibiting alcohol sales in future adult establishments but allowing them in existing adult businesses fails strict scrutiny, which applies because regulation is based on protecting existing businesses from competition rather than on preventing secondary impacts); Hamilton's Bogarts, Inc. v. Michigan, 501 F.3d 644 (6th Cir. 2007) (allowing preliminary injunction against enforcement of rules prohibiting nudity in establishments with alcohol license when state has not articulated what its interest is or how the rules affect it); Joelner v. Vill. of Wash. Park, 378 F.3d 613 (7th Cir. 2004) (if regulation is based on revenue concerns rather than secondary impacts, strict scrutiny applies); Phillips v. Borough of Keyport, 107 F.3d 164 (3d Cir. 1997) (ordinance must explicitly state the secondary impacts of concern); Krueger v. City of Pensacola, 759 F.2d 851, 856 (11th Cir. 1985). *See also* Avalon Cinema Corp. v. Thompson, 667 F.2d 659 (8th Cir. 1981); 754 Orange Ave., Inc. v. City of W. Haven, 761 F.2d 105, 113 (2d Cir. 1985); Keego Harbor Co. v. City of Keego Harbor, 657 F.2d 94 (6th Cir. 1981); Ent. Concepts, Inc. v. Maciejewski, 631 F.2d 497, 503–04 (7th Cir. 1980) (invalidating ordinance whose sole purpose was to regulate the showing of sexually explicit movies); People Tags, Inc. v. Jackson Cnty. Legislature, 636 F. Supp. 1345, 1354 (W.D. Mo. 1986). *But see* D.G. Rest. Corp. v. City of Myrtle Beach, 953 F.2d 140, 146 (4th Cir. 1992) (council action initiated in response to an application for a permit for a topless bar does not impute illicit motives).

58. Showtime Ent., LLC v. Town of Mendon, 769 F.3d 61 (1st Cir. 2014) (ordinance failed to regulate other business that had similar impacts on rural aesthetics and traffic, the two purposes offered to justify the ordinance).

Documenting Adverse Secondary Impacts

The courts have widely held that there are substantial governmental interests in protecting adjoining neighborhoods from blight; in preventing traffic problems, litter problems, and crime; in promoting consistency with adopted land use plans; and in maintaining property values.[59]

Once a local government establishes that the predominate concern in developing regulations for adult businesses is preventing harmful secondary impacts, it must establish a factual basis for that determination and show that the restrictions will address them.[60]

In reviewing the adequacy of evidence documenting secondary impacts and the relationship of the regulation to addressing them, courts apply a burden-shifting analysis.[61] The initial burden is on the government to provide evidence of secondary impacts.[62] Once this is done, the burden shifts to the plaintiff to rebut the evidence by showing that it does not support the rationale of the regulation or by submitting evidence that disputes the factual findings.[63] If that is done, the burden shifts back to the government to supplement the record with evidence justifying its regulation. As with the motive question, however, the courts have been fairly lenient about this requirement.[64]

A key question is the extent of the analysis that each local government must conduct in order to determine whether the specific regulation of adult businesses proposed for that community will address these legitimate concerns. In *City of Los Angeles v. Alameda Books, Inc.*,[65] the Court addressed this issue in some detail. The case involved a city regulation prohibiting more than one adult use in the same building. The ordinance also imposed minimum separations (1000 feet from other adult uses and 500

---

59. *See, e.g.*, Northend Cinema, Inc. v. City of Seattle, 585 P.2d 1153, 1158–59 (Wash. 1978) (noting "the City's great interest in protecting and preserving the quality of its neighborhoods through effective land-use planning" and zoning).

60. A content-neutral restriction on conduct, such as public nudity, is not required to be supported by evidence of impacts on a substantial government interest. City of Erie v. Pap's A.M., 529 U.S. 277, 299 (2000); Barnes v. Glen Theater, Inc., 501 U.S. 560, 567–68 (1991).

61. *Alameda Books*, 535 U.S. at 438–39.

62. *Phillips*, 107 F.3d 164; Nakatomi Invs., Inc. v. City of Schenectady, 949 F. Supp. 988 (N.D.N.Y. 1997). Plaintiff adult businesses challenging a regulation of their activities are not entitled to discovery of evidence to allow them to disprove adverse secondary impacts within the jurisdiction. Sensations, Inc. v. City of Grand Rapids, 526 F.3d 291, 297–98 (6th Cir. 2008); Deja Vu of Nashville, Inc. v. Metro. Gov't of Nashville, 466 F.3d 391, 398 (6th Cir. 2006).

63. While the initial burden on the government is light, the burden to cast doubt on those studies and their applicability is "heavier and cannot be met with unsound inference or similarly anecdotal information." Richland Bookmart, Inc. v. Knox Cnty., 555 F.3d 512, 527 (6th Cir. 2009). *See also* Alameda Books, Inc. v. City of L.A., 631 F.3d 1031, 1042–43 (9th Cir. 2011) (actual and convincing evidence that is sufficient to convincingly discredit each rationale is required in rebuttal); Imaginary Images, Inc. v. Evans, 612 F.3d 736, 747 (4th Cir. 2010).

64. In other contexts, the Court has set limits on the admissibility of scientific evidence offered by expert witnesses. Daubert v. Merrell Dow Pharm., Inc., 509 U.S. 579, 593–95 (1993) (expert scientific testimony requires an assessment of whether the reasoning or methodology underlying the testimony is scientifically valid and whether that reasoning or methodology properly can be applied to the facts in issue). Some analysts contend that few of the studies relied on for documentation of secondary impacts of adult businesses meet that rigorous standard. Bryant Paul et al., *Government Regulation of "Adult" Businesses Through Zoning and Anti-Nudity Ordinances: Debunking the Legal Myth of Negative Secondary Effects*, 6 COMM. L. & POL'Y 355 (2001). For a study showing that crime rates were actually lower near nightclubs with adult dancing, see Daniel Linz, et al., *An Examination of the Assumption That Adult Businesses Are Associated with Crime in Surrounding Areas: A Secondary Effects Study in Charlotte, North Carolina*, 38 LAW & SOC. REV. 69 (2004) (showing lower crime rates in the area surrounding the twenty adult erotic dance clubs in Charlotte in the 1998–2000 period).

The *Daubert* standard, however, has not been applied in First Amendment challenges to regulation of adult businesses. Ent. Prods., Inc. v. Shelby Cnty., 721 F.3d 729 (6th Cir. 2013); Doctor John's v. Wahlen, 542 F.3d 787, 791–94 (10th Cir. 2008) (finding adult store's rebuttal evidence on lack of secondary effects to be inadequate); Peek-A-Boo Lounge of Bradenton, Inc. v. Manatee Cnty. (*Peek-A-Boo I*), 337 F.3d 1251, 1268 (11th Cir. 2003).

65. 535 U.S. 425 (2002). *See also* Peek-A-Boo Lounge of Bradenton, Inc. v. Manatee Cnty. (*Peek-A-Boo II*), 630 F.3d 1346 (11th Cir. 2011); Sensations, Inc. v. City of Grand Rapids, 526 F.3d 291 (6th Cir. 2008).

feet from schools, parks, and religious uses). A narrowly divided Court upheld the regulation. Four justices concluded that a 1977 study of crime rates, while not looking specifically at the issue involved with this regulation, did address the impact of a concentration of adult uses and thus could be relied on to support this regulation. Those justices noted that while shoddy data or reasoning could not be used,[66] the issues studied were close enough that it was reasonable to rely on them. The critical fifth vote to uphold the regulation was Justice Kennedy's concurrence.[67] He concluded that the distinction between secondary impacts and content neutrality made here and in most adult-entertainment cases was a legal fiction, but that only intermediate rather than strict scrutiny should be applied, and the ordinance would pass that test.[68]

It is not necessary to show actual impacts of a particular adult use. It is permissible to anticipate potential impacts by reference to relevant studies of impacts elsewhere.[69]

A wide variety of studies have been found by the courts to meet the standard of "reasonably believed to be relevant."[70] Indeed, for the most part courts have deferred to local elected officials' legislative judgments in determining what studies are relevant. Some local governments have directed professional staff to study the issue and to assist in designing an ordinance that is specifically tailored to local needs.[71] A local government can also solicit analysis from local law-enforcement personnel[72] and its legal staff.[73] In a number of instances, extensive public hearings and planning-board discussions have been important in the tailoring of an ordinance to fit a particular community's needs.[74] Relying

---

66. *Alameda Books*, 535 U.S. at 438. The four dissenting justices in *Alameda Books* contended that more-rigorous studies of actual secondary impacts were needed to justify restrictions on protected speech.

67. Justice Kennedy's concurrence is controlling as the narrowest opinion joining the judgment of the Court. Ctr. for Fair Pub. Policy v. Maricopa Cnty., 336 F.3d 1153, 1161 (9th Cir. 2003).

68. Justice Kennedy's concurrence refers to content neutrality in this context as "something of a fiction." *Alameda Books*, 535 U.S. at 448. Justice Souter's dissent noted that while regulations of adult businesses are referred to as content neutral, such zoning restrictions would more aptly be termed "content correlated." *Id.* at 457.

69. *See, e.g.,* Oasis Goodtime Emporium I, Inc. v. City of Doraville, 773 S.E.2d 728, 738 (Ga. 2015).

70. For a review of the case law on establishing secondary impacts from the perspective of attorneys for the adult-entertainment industry, see Daniel R. Aaronson, et al., *The First Amendment in Chaos: How the Law of Secondary Effects Is Applied and Misapplied by the Circuit Courts*, 63 U. MIAMI L. REV. 741 (2009).

71. *See* ILQ Invs., Inc. v. City of Rochester, 25 F.3d 1413 (8th Cir. 1994) (yearlong study of secondary impacts by planning department, followed by extensive planning-board discussion and public hearings, held adequate); Holmberg v. City of Ramsey, 12 F.3d 140 (8th Cir. 1993) (hiring professional planner to investigate secondary impacts and examine other studies held adequate); Lakeland Lounge of Jackson, Inc. v. City of Jackson, 973 F.2d 1255 (5th Cir. 1992) (studies by city attorney's office and planning department, along with public hearings, held adequate even though studies not formally presented to the governing board); U.S. Partners Fin. Corp. v. Kan. City, 707 F. Supp. 1090, 1094–95 (W.D. Mo. 1989) (testimony on secondary impacts by two staff planners and two outside experts to governing-board committee held adequate to support substantial basis for regulation that is unrelated to content suppression); *Northend Cinema*, 585 P.2d at 1154–55 (holding staff study of zoning-plan requirements and surrounding land uses, followed by extensive public comment at hearings, adequate).

72. E. Brooks Books, Inc. v. City of Memphis, 48 F.3d 220, 222 (6th Cir. 1995) (report of arrest records around adult businesses and report by city vice squad held adequate); Grand Faloon Tavern, Inc. v. Wicker, 670 F.2d 943 (11th Cir. 1982) (testimony of police on extensive criminal activity at one of two topless bars in town held adequate).

73. Bonnell, Inc. v. Bd. of Adjustment, 791 P.2d 107, 112 (Okla. Civ. App. 1989) (holding detailed research and analysis by city's legal department adequate).

74. *See, e.g.,* 1995 Venture I, Inc. v. Orange Cnty., 947 F. Supp. 271 (E.D. Tex. 1996) (holding testimony and letters from concerned citizens, along with a review of a nearby jurisdiction's experience, to be an adequate basis for establishing a secondary-impacts rationale); Envy Ltd. v. City of Louisville, 734 F. Supp. 785, 786 (W.D. Ky. 1990) (series of five public hearings with testimony from law-enforcement officials, medical personnel, neighbors, real-estate professionals, city regulators, and adult-business representatives held adequate); Di Ma Corp. v. City of St. Cloud, 562 N.W.2d 312 (Minn. Ct. App. 1997) (accepting use of citizen comments, cases from other jurisdictions, and state attorney general's report to establish secondary impacts).

on local information, analysis, and debate is the best and legally safest approach to take in developing regulations on adult businesses.[75]

Since the impacts being considered are potential ones, there is no requirement to document actual impacts in the jurisdiction being regulated. In *Renton*, the U.S. Supreme Court held that an individual local government is not required "to conduct new studies or produce evidence independent of that already generated by other cities, so long as whatever evidence the city relies upon is reasonably believed to be relevant to the problem that the city addresses."[76] A local government may anticipate problems[77] by reviewing experiences elsewhere[78] and conducting a legal review of other ordinances and court decisions.[79] Courts have cautioned that local governments need to examine the studies underlying such other ordinances and not just their judicial validation.[80]

Despite this judicial deference to local legislative judgment on the relevance of studies and experiences in other locales, courts will invalidate ordinances that contain no evidence at all in the record to

---

75. In *11126 Baltimore Boulevard v. Prince George's County*, 886 F.2d 1415, 1423 (4th Cir. 1989), the court upheld a regulation restricting the location of adult bookstores, stating that local governments could assume matters of "common knowledge and experience," which the court held to include the "notorious and self-evident" secondary impacts of adult businesses. The court tempered this with the admonition that local governments should limit their consideration to the experiences of "similarly situated" or "generally comparable" communities. *Id.* at 1423. *See also* Daytona Grand, Inc. v. City of Daytona Beach, 490 F.3d 860 (11th Cir. 2007) (city may rely on reasonable anecdotal evidence as well as statistical analysis), Thames Enters., Inc. v. City of St. Louis, 851 F.2d 199, 202 (8th Cir. 1988) (holding personal observations of local elected officials carry substantial weight in establishing that there are negative secondary impacts of adult businesses).

76. 475 U.S. 41, 51–52 (1986). *See also* H & A Land Corp. v. City of Kennedale, 480 F.3d 336, 339–40 (5th Cir. 2007) (city may rely on surveys of real-estate appraisers conducted by other cities, provided the surveyed opinions address the same type of adult business); Baby Dolls Topless Saloons, Inc. v. City of Dallas, 295 F.3d 471 (5th Cir. 2002) (acceptable to rely on studies involving other adult entertainment when crafting a bikini-top requirement). Still, consideration of some evidentiary basis for secondary impacts is needed. In *MD II Entm't, Inc. v. City of Dallas*, 935 F. Supp. 1394 (N.D. Tex. 1995), the court invalidated an ordinance requiring female dancers to wear bikini tops because there was no evidence of consideration of secondary impacts as the basis for regulation).

77. "[A] city need not await deterioration in order to act." Genusa v. City of Peoria, 619 F.2d 1203, 1211 (7th Cir. 1980) (upholding zoning restrictions on location of adult businesses). *See also* Postscript Enters. v. City of Bridgeton, 905 F.2d 223, 227 (8th Cir. 1990) (holding that a small town need not conduct independent health studies to justify ordinance requiring open booths in adult establishments).

78. *See, e.g.*, Ways v. City of Lincoln, 331 F.3d 596 (8th Cir. 2003); Cricket Store 17, LLC v. City of Columbia, 97 F. Supp. 3d 737 (D.S.C. 2015) (evidence of secondary impacts at regulated site not required as city may rely on evidence from elsewhere that is reasonably believed to be relevant); Oasis Goodtime Emporium I, Inc. v. City of Doraville, 773 S.E.2d 728, 738 (Ga. 2015). Studies cited as being reviewed by others include those from Austin, Boston, Cleveland, Detroit, Indianapolis, Los Angeles, New York, Oklahoma City, Phoenix, and Seattle.

79. *See* Ben Rich Trading, Inc. v. City of Vineland, 126 F.3d 155 (3d Cir. 1997) (holding that consideration of testimony before state legislative committees and from other states considering similar restrictions was sufficient); Ambassador Books & Video, Inc. v. City of Little Rock, 20 F.3d 858 (8th Cir. 1994) (study of other ordinances by city attorney staff, followed by consultation with planning staff, held adequate); Int'l Eateries of Am., Inc. v. Broward Cnty., 941 F.2d 1157, 1162–63 (11th Cir. 1991) (reliance on Detroit ordinance upheld in *Young* ruled sufficient); Centerfold Club, Inc. v. City of St. Petersburg, 969 F. Supp. 1288 (M.D. Fla. 1997) (holding that consideration of studies from other cities, along with reports from city staff and citizens, established an adequate basis of studies); Tee & Bee, Inc. v. City of W. Allis, 936 F. Supp. 1479 (E.D. Wis. 1996) (consideration of studies from elsewhere in the country held adequate); Quetgles v. City of Columbus, 268 Ga. 619, 491 S.E.2d 778 (1997) (holding that consideration of other cities' studies on secondary impacts was sufficient).

80. *See, e.g.*, H & A Land Corp. v. City of Kennedale, 480 F.3d 336, 339 (5th Cir. 2007) (noting need to segregate studies regarding impacts of establishments offering only off-site consumption of adult materials from studies examining on-site consumption). Still, a good deal of latitude is allowed in this respect as well. *See, e.g.*, LLEH, Inc. v. Wichita Cnty., 289 F.3d 358 (5th Cir. 2002) (allowing rural area to rely on secondary-impact studies from urban areas).

justify a concern about secondary impacts.[81] Where there is uncontradicted, specific evidence of a lack of secondary impacts, the local government cannot ignore the evidence and legitimately contend that the restrictions are aimed at secondary impacts.[82] This is particularly the case if existing adult businesses in the jurisdiction have not created secondary impacts.[83] Also, if the studies and cases cited all deal with impacts in contexts other than the subject of the regulation, the court may find them not to be germane.[84]

---

81. *See* Illusions–Dallas Private Club, Inc. v. Steen, 482 F.3d 299, 312–15 (5th Cir. 2007) (judicial citations and common sense alone are insufficient evidence to support regulation of alcohol sales in clubs with adult entertainment); R.V.S., L.L.C. v. City of Rockford, 361 F.3d 402, 411–13 (7th Cir. 2004) (invalidating regulation of clothed erotic dancing due to lack of evidence of adverse secondary impacts); Ranch House, Inc. v. Amerson, 238 F.3d 1273 (11th Cir. 2001) (remanding a challenge to an Alabama statute prohibiting businesses from exhibiting nudity for entertainment purposes due to no evidence on record regarding secondary impacts); 754 Orange Ave., Inc. v. City of W. Haven, 761 F.2d 105, 112 (2d Cir. 1985) (invalidating ordinance on adult bookstores where there was "no evidence whatsoever" relating potential impacts to legitimate public interests); CLR Corp. v. Henline, 702 F.2d 637, 639 (6th Cir. 1983) (invalidating ordinance restricting location of adult bookstores where there was a complete failure to assert a factual justification, compelling or otherwise, for restriction); Books, Inc. v. Pottawattamie Cnty., 978 F. Supp. 1247, 1256 (S.D. Iowa 1997) (where record is "totally devoid of any purported justification whatsoever" regarding secondary impacts, ordinance is invalid); *Nakatomi Investments*, 949 F. Supp. 988 (invalidating ban on topless dancing as based on moral concerns rather than the amelioration of secondary impacts); Steverson v. City of Vicksburg, 900 F. Supp. 1 (S.D. Miss. 1994) (invalidating total ban on topless dancing in part due to lack of documentation of secondary impacts); N. St. Book Shoppe, Inc. v. Vill. of Endicott, 582 F. Supp. 1428, 1435 (N.D.N.Y. 1984) (invalidating ordinance absent "some showing of some factual basis for the purported governmental interest"); E & B Enters. v. City of Univ. Park, 449 F. Supp. 695, 697 (N.D. Tex. 1977) (invalidating restriction on adult theater where there was no evidence of secondary impacts, noting that if "the neighborhood preservation justification is a mere mask to cover an attempt to run out of town a theater whose fare some citizens do not approve," the restriction must fall); Secret Desires Lingerie, Inc. v. City of Atlanta, 470 S.E.2d 879 (Ga. 1996) (no evidence of secondary impacts regarding modeling studios); Chambers v. Peach Cnty., 266 Ga. 318, 321, 467 S.E.2d 519, 523 (Ga. 1996) (invalidating restrictions on nude dancing where no evidence of adverse secondary impacts was presented to the governing board at the time of adoption of the restriction); T & D Video, Inc. v. City of Revere, 670 N.E.2d 162 (Mass. 1996).

82. *Peek-A-Boo I*, 337 F.3d 1251 (11th Cir. 2003); Flanigan's Enters., Inc. of Ga. v. Fulton Cnty. (*Flanigan's I*), 242 F.3d 976 (11th Cir. 2001). Subsequent to the initial *Peek-A-Boo* decision, the county gathered voluminous evidence and conducted lengthy public hearings in the process of crafting and adopting a new set of restrictions. The revised regulations were upheld in *Peek-A-Boo II*, 630 F.3d 1346 (11th Cir. 2011). In *Flanigan's I*, the challenged regulation prohibited sale of alcohol at adult establishments. However, a study by the county police documented that adult establishments with alcohol had a lower crime rate and fewer service calls than similar nonadult establishments. A study commissioned by the adult businesses showed no detrimental economic impact on nearby properties, a result confirmed by the county tax assessor.

83. *See* Ebel v. City of Corona, 767 F.2d 635, 638 (9th Cir. 1985) (application of restriction on adult-bookstore location invalid when applied to existing bookstore, and city failed to link the business to any of the cited secondary impacts); Krueger v. City of Pensacola, 759 F.2d 851 (11th Cir. 1985) (where there is no evidence of crime problems at existing topless bars, mere speculation as to potential problems is inadequate to establish a legitimate purpose for ban on topless bars). *See also* Janra Enters., Inc. v. City of Reno, 818 F. Supp. 1361, 1364 (D. Nev. 1993) (invalidating restriction on adult-business location where there was no evidence presented to support assumption that regulation would prevent secondary harms).

84. In *Annex Books, Inc. v. City of Indianapolis*, 581 F.3d 460, 462–67 (7th Cir. 2009), the challenged regulation limited hours of operation of adult bookstores and was applied to stores that had no live entertainment and no private-viewing booths. None of the studies relied on by the city addressed these types of businesses. The plaintiff produced evidence that these types of regulated stores did not have adverse secondary impacts. The court therefore remanded the case for a further review of the city's justification for the regulation. On remand the court found the additional evidence submitted by the city insufficient to justify a denial of a preliminary injunction against enforcement of the ordinance. 624 F.3d 368 (7th Cir. 2010). The Seventh Circuit also applied this reasoning to remand a restriction that limited the location of an adult bookstore that offered no live entertainment or on-site viewing (the regulation required a 1000-foot separation from places of worship and residences). New Albany DVD, LLC v. City of New Albany, 581 F.3d 556 (7th Cir. 2009).

Since it is permissible to design a regulation to prevent future problems, a local government is under no obligation to make a post-enactment study of actual impacts at particular locations.[85]

Local governments should ensure that the studies used are in fact related to the type of sexually oriented business being regulated. Several ordinances have been invalidated due to insupportable inferences about the scope of potential secondary impacts, especially when the regulation was aimed at businesses of a different character from those studied.[86] Similarly, some courts have been reluctant to sanction the use of a study on the impacts of one type of adult business, such as a theater that presents live peep shows, in a case involving a totally different type of business, such as one that only rents videos.[87]

Care should be taken also to prepare the necessary information in the course of actually considering the adoption of restrictions rather than afterward in response to litigation. Courts generally allow the use of studies conducted after adoption of a regulation only if the studies supplement information that was available prior to adoption.[88] While it is not necessary that the elected officials personally review all of the studies, they should be aware of their existence and have the opportunity to review them prior to adoption if desired.[89]

Likewise, in *Abilene Retail No. 30, Inc. v. Board of Commissioners*, 492 F.3d 1164 (10th Cir. 2007), the county cited studies from urban areas to justify restrictions on a single adult bookstore located at an interstate interchange in a rural area. The court held that the county must do more than cite an existing body of prepackaged secondary-impacts studies from other jurisdictions as a justification for regulating an adult business without regard to its type or setting.

85. Independence News, Inc. v. City of Charlotte, 568 F.3d 148 (4th Cir.), *cert. denied*, 558 U.S. 992 (2009). The city adopted an eight-year-amortization provision for nonconforming adult-business locations. The court rejected the plaintiff's contention that a showing of no adverse secondary impacts at this location during the amortization period invalidated the amortization requirement.

86. Tollis, Inc. v. San Bernardino Cnty., 827 F.2d 1329, 1332–33 (9th Cir. 1987). *See also* Christy v. City of Ann Arbor, 824 F.2d 489, 493 (6th Cir. 1987) ("some relevant evidence" required to establish a link to secondary impacts); Avalon Cinema Corp. v. Thompson, 667 F.2d 659, 661–62 (8th Cir. 1981) (no substantial government interest in regulation absent some empirical evidence that a single theater would cause secondary impacts).

87. Wolff v. City of Monticello, 803 F. Supp. 1568, 1572–73 (D. Minn. 1992) (holding that an ordinance based on studies of adult entertainment as principal use is not narrowly drawn if applied to uses where adult aspects are an accessory use); World Wide Video v. City of Tukwila, 816 P.2d 18, 21 (Wash. 1991) (city cannot rely on studies of impact of peep-show businesses to justify regulation as to location of adult video store with only "take-home" fare). *But see* T-Marc, Inc. v. Pinellas Cnty., 804 F. Supp. 1500, 1503 (M.D. Fla. 1992) (holding that *Renton* does not mandate comparisons between different types of adult uses if the same secondary effects are being addressed).

88. White River Amusement Pub, Inc. v. Town of Hartford, 481 F.3d 163, 171 (2d Cir. 2007) (government must have some evidence of secondary impacts prior to enactment of regulation); *Peek-A-Boo I*, 337 F.3d 1251, 1268 (11th Cir. 2003); SOB, Inc. v. Cnty. of Benton, 317 F.3d 856, 862–63 (8th Cir. 2003) (upholding ban on totally nude dancing where relevant studies considered prior to enactment); D.H.L. Assocs., Inc. v. O'Gorman, 199 F.3d 50, 57–58 (1st Cir. 1999); Z.J. Gifts D-2, L.L.C. v. City of Aurora, 136 F.3d 683, 690 (10th Cir. 1998); 11126 Balt. Boulevard v. Prince George's Cnty., 886 F.2d 1415, 1425 (4th Cir. 1989), *vacated and remanded on other grounds*, 496 U.S. 901 (1990) (trial testimony and supplemental evidence cannot sustain regulation if there is no evidence in the preenactment legislative record, but such proof can be used to explain stated interests); SDJ, Inc. v. City of Houston, 837 F.2d 1268, 1274 (5th Cir. 1988); 15192 Thirteen Mile Rd., Inc. v. City of Warren, 626 F. Supp. 803, 825 (E.D. Mich. 1985) (post hoc justifications should be considered suspect in order to ensure that the proffered justification is not pretextual but may be considered to supplement the record); Chambers v. Peach Cnty., 266 Ga. 318, 321, 467 S.E.2d 519, 523 (1996) (affidavit on other studies prepared for litigation held inadequate if there is no evidence that the studies were considered prior to adoption). *But see* BGHA, LLC v. City of Universal City, 340 F.3d 295, 299 (5th Cir. 2003) (city may develop evidence of secondary impacts prior to enactment or by adducing such evidence at trial); DiMa Corp. v. Town of Hallie, 185 F.3d 823, 829–30 (7th Cir. 1999).

89. Pitt Cnty. v. Dejavue, Inc., 185 N.C. App. 545, 650 S.E.2d 12, 21–22 (2007), *review denied*, 362 N.C. 381, 661 S.E.2d 738 (2008) (noting that staff compiled reports, staff orally summarized reports, and reports were available to the elected officials for questions); Lakeland Lounge of Jackson, Inc. v. City of Jackson, 973 F.2d 1255, 1258 (5th Cir. 1992) (city council can rely on staff and planning-board review of studies).

Reasonable Alternative Avenues for Expression

A regulation of adult businesses may not totally preclude location of a business offering constitutionally protected speech from the entire jurisdiction.[90] A permissible reasonable limitation on the location of adult businesses cannot actually be a de facto exclusion of all such businesses. Many local governments have attempted to come as close to exclusion as possible, so defining the bounds of permissible restrictions is frequently litigated.

A number of courts have upheld restrictions that generally fall close to the facts presented in *Renton*[91]—limiting adult uses to about 5 percent of the jurisdiction's area.[92] On the other hand, courts

---

90. *See, e.g.,* Incubus Invs., L.L.C. v. City of Garland, No. Civ.A. 303CV2039-K, 2003 WL 23095680 (N.D. Tex. Dec. 17, 2003) (granting injunction for adult bookstore where ordinance prohibited any business whose primary purpose was offering sexually explicit materials). It may be possible to consider availability of sites in nearby jurisdictions that are part of an integrated real-estate market. Schad v. Borough of Mount Ephraim, 452 U.S. 61, 75–77 (1981); G.S. 160A-181.1(e). *See, e.g.,* Twp. of Saddle Brook v. A.B. Family Ctr., Inc., 156 N.J. 587, 722 A.2d 530 (1999). *But see* Wolfe v. Vill. of Brice, 997 F. Supp. 939, 944–45 (S.D. Ohio 1998); Borough of Sayreville v. 35 Club, 416 N.J. Super. 315, 3 A.3d 1268 (App. Div. 2010) (not permissible to include jurisdictions in bordering states). *See generally* Sarah L. Swan, *Constitutional Off-Loading at the City Limits,* 135 Harv. L. Rev. 831 (2022).

91. 475 U.S. 41 (1986). This case is discussed in greater detail in the text above. *See supra* text accompanying notes 39–42.

92. *See, e.g., Dejavue,* 185 N.C. App. at 561, 650 S.E.2d at 21–22 (upholding restrictions that left 19 percent of county's land area available). *See also* Blue Canary Corp. v. City of Milwaukee, 270 F.3d 1156 (7th Cir. 2001) (upholding restriction on location of alcohol-free adult burlesque theater); *Z.J. Gifts,* 136 F.3d 683 (upholding ordinance that left 11 percent of city's land area available); Woodall v. City of El Paso, 49 F.3d 1120, 1124–27 (5th Cir. 1995) (holding that at least fifty alternative sites for twenty-two existing adult businesses were adequate to justify upholding regulation); Grand Brittain, Inc. v. City of Amarillo, 27 F.3d 1068, 1069–70 (5th Cir. 1994) (upholding restriction that left sixty-three potential sites for relocation of amortized adult uses, even though most sites did not have water and sewer or available buildings for lease); Ambassador Books & Video, Inc. v. City of Little Rock, 20 F.3d 858, 864–65 (8th Cir. 1994) (upholding limiting adult businesses to 6.75 percent of city's land area; ninety-seven potential sites for relocation of amortized existing uses were available); Holmberg v. City of Ramsey, 12 F.3d 140, 144 (8th Cir. 1993) (upholding restriction that allowed relocation of amortized uses to 35 percent of city's commercial zones, noting high relocation costs irrelevant); Int'l Eateries of Am., Inc. v. Broward Cnty., 941 F.2d 1157, 1165 (11th Cir. 1991) (upholding restriction that left at least twenty-six alternative sites for location of adult establishments); Alexander v. City of Minneapolis, 928 F.2d 278, 283–84 (8th Cir. 1991) (upholding restriction that left 6.6 percent of city's commercial area available, noting that some owners had successfully relocated); *SDJ,* 837 F.2d at 1276–77 (upholding restriction where a study found at least forty potential alternative sites in the 20 percent of the city area studied); Specialty Malls of Tampa v. City of Tampa, 916 F. Supp. 1222, 1230–31 (M.D. Fla. 1996) (upholding restriction to 7.5 percent of city area); O'Malley v. City of Syracuse, 813 F. Supp. 133, 146–47 (N.D.N.Y. 1993) (upholding requirement limiting strip clubs to 4 percent of city area); *T-Marc,* 804 F. Supp. at 1504–05 (M.D. Fla. 1992) (upholding restriction that left at least 123 alternative sites available); S. Ent. Co. of Fla. v. City of Boynton Beach, 736 F. Supp. 1094, 1101 (S.D. Fla. 1990) (upholding restriction limiting location of adult business to eleven potential sites in a city with a population of 45,000); Function Junction, Inc. v. City of Daytona Beach, 705 F. Supp. 544, 552 (M.D. Fla. 1987) (holding twelve alternate locations as reasonable alternatives); S & G News, Inc. v. City of Southgate, 638 F. Supp. 1060, 1066 (E.D. Mich. 1986) (upholding restriction limiting adult uses to a commercial zone comprising 2.3 percent of city jurisdiction); DiRaimo v. City of Providence, 714 A.2d 554 (R.I. 1998); Centaur, Inc. v. Richland Cnty., 301 S.C. 374, 380, 392 S.E.2d 165, 168–69 (1990) (holding sixteen alternative sites adequate); Condor, Inc. v. Bd. of Zoning Appeals, 328 S.C. 173, 493 S.E.2d 342 (1997) (twenty-one alternate sites adequate).

have invalidated restrictions that effectively leave no alternate sites available.[93] Cases on the borderline, such as those allowing only 1 percent of the city's area for this type of use, have gone both ways.[94]

The test that is often applied requires a case-by-case analysis of the detailed facts of each situation, with the critical inquiry being whether the application of the regulation leaves realistic sites available within the jurisdiction's commercial-real-estate market for uses that are protected adult speech.[95] In *Topanga Press, Inc. v. City of Los Angeles*,[96] the court set forth the following guidelines to aid in determining

---

93. *See, e.g.,* Woodall v. City of El Paso, 959 F.2d 1305, 1306 (5th Cir. 1992) (per curiam) (an ordinance that only makes available land that is physically or legally unsuitable for adult businesses has effectively suppressed protected speech); Ebel v. City of Corona, 767 F.2d 635, 638–39 (9th Cir. 1985) (ordinance invalid if there are no practically effective alternative locations for amortized adult businesses); CLR Corp. v. Henline, 702 F.2d 637 (6th Cir. 1983) (two to four potential sites for adult uses in a city with a population of 60,000 inadequate); Basiardanes v. City of Galveston, 682 F.2d 1203, 1214 (5th Cir. 1982) (ordinance that banned adult uses from 90 percent of city and severely restricted location in remainder, rendering it all but impossible to locate an adult theater in city, ruled invalid); Keego Harbor Co. v. City of Keego Harbor, 657 F.2d 94, 98–99 (6th Cir. 1981) (total ban of adult uses in very small jurisdiction not invalid per se but need and reasonable nearby alternatives must be established); Janra Enters., Inc. v. City of Reno, 818 F. Supp. 1361, 1364 (D. Nev. 1993) (three potential sites for adult business in a city of fifty-five square miles held inadequate alternative avenues); Purple Onion, Inc. v. Jackson, 511 F. Supp. 1207, 1224 (N.D. Ga. 1981) (Atlanta ordinance invalid as it leaves "very few feasible sites" available); Bayside Enters., Inc. v. Carson, 450 F. Supp. 696, 702 (M.D. Fla. 1978) (Jacksonville ordinance invalid as application of separation requirements results in a total ban for all practical purposes of adult bookstores and theaters); A.F.M., Ltd. v. City of Medford, 428 Mass. 1020, 704 N.E.2d 184 (1999) (invalidating ordinance limiting adult businesses to one small city block that was completely occupied). For a comparison of various judicial tests for adequacy of available sites, see Ashley C. Phillips, Comment, *A Matter of Arithmetic: Using Supply and Demand to Determine the Constitutionality of Adult Entertainment Zoning Ordinances*, 51 EMORY L.J. 319 (2002).

The regulation upheld by the federal district court in *Mermaids, Inc. v. Currituck County Board of Commissioners* limited adult businesses to the county's heavy-manufacturing zoning districts and required a 1000-foot separation from a variety of sensitive land uses. The court noted that this was not a complete bar to these uses and was thus a reasonable alternative for location of protected speech, even if not commercially desirable for such. 19 F. Supp. 2d 493, 498 (E.D.N.C. 1998).

94. *Compare Lakeland Lounge*, 973 F.2d at 1259–60 (upholding ordinance limiting adult businesses to 1.2 percent of city land area as adequate for relocation of five to six adult uses required by amortization provision to move) *and* D.G. Rest. Corp. v. City of Myrtle Beach, 953 F.2d 140, 147 (4th Cir. 1992) (upholding ordinance limiting topless dancing to "a few poorly lit sites in industrial areas") *with* Walnut Props., Inc. v. City of Whittier, 861 F.2d 1102, 1108–09 (9th Cir. 1988) (invalidating ordinance leaving 1.4 percent of city's land available for adult uses, as the paucity of alternatives would make a mockery of First Amendment protections). *See also* Christy v. City of Ann Arbor, 824 F.2d 489, 492 (6th Cir. 1987) (remanding ordinance restricting stores with more than 20 percent of business devoted to adult material to a 0.23 percent area of city to determine adequacy of alternatives); Int'l Food & Beverage Sys. v. City of Fort Lauderdale, 794 F.2d 1520, 1526–27 (11th Cir. 1986) (remanding ordinance limiting topless bars to twenty-two potential sites for review of adequacy in light of *Renton*).

95. *See, e.g.,* Stardust, 3007 LLC v. City of Brookhaven, 899 F.3d 1164 (11th Cir. 2018) (upholding ordinance where seventy-three potential sites identified); BBL, Inc. v. City of Angola, 809 F.3d 317 (7th Cir. 2015) (forty-one sites identified by city sufficient to avoid preliminary injunction); MJJG Rest. LLC v. Horry Cnty., 102 F. Supp. 3d 770 (D.S.C. 2015) (upholding ordinance where seventy-nine potential sites available).

96. 989 F.2d 1524 (9th Cir. 1993) (invalidating ordinance due to lack of suitable alternative sites for relocation of amortized adult businesses). *See also* Lund v. City of Fall River, 714 F.3d 65 (1st Cir. 2013) (eight sites available); Big Dipper Ent., L.L.C. v. City of Warren, 641 F.3d 715 (6th Cir. 2011) (twenty-seven potential sites and two applications in previous five years); Exec. Arts Studio, Inc. v. City of Grand Rapids, 391 F.3d 783, 797 (6th Cir. 2005) (invalidating ordinance that left only "around a half dozen" sites available in a city with over 2500 commercially usable parcels); Isbell v. City of San Diego, 258 F.3d 1108 (9th Cir. 2001) (application of *Topanga Press* analysis); David Vincent, Inc. v. Broward Cnty., 200 F.3d 1325, 1334–35 (11th Cir. 2000) (noting factors to consider in determining commercial viability of potential sites); 725 Eatery Corp. v. City of New York, 408 F. Supp. 3d 424 (S.D.N.Y. 2019) (having only thirteen potential sites in Manhattan denies adequate alternative channels).

whether property should be considered part of the relevant commercial-real-estate market (and thus available as a potential reasonable alternative avenue for conveying protected speech):[97]

1. Is it reasonable to believe the property would ever become available for any commercial use?[98]
2. Is the property reasonably accessible to the general public, particularly if the sites are in manufacturing or industrial areas?
3. Do the sites in manufacturing zones have proper infrastructure for commercial uses, such as sidewalks, roads, and lighting?[99]
4. Do the sites suit some generic commercial venture?[100]

There is not a need to show that adult uses could be profitably operated at such alternative sites, but if the costs of improvements necessary to make the site suitable for any commercial use are so high as to be prohibitive, the site cannot realistically be considered part of the commercial-real-estate market.[101] Similarly, if the land is permanently dedicated to other uses (such as a municipal airport or landfill), the fact that it is technically "available" under the ordinance is irrelevant because that land is not part of the commercial-real-estate market.[102]

An important aspect of the alternative-sites inquiry is whether the potential supply of sites is reasonably related to the history of demand for such in the particular locality.[103] For example, in a small town

---

97. *Topanga Press*, 989 F.2d at 1531.

98. The fact that other commercial uses occupy the space and restrictive leases limit adult uses does not remove the sites from consideration. Lim v. City of Long Beach, 217 F.3d 1050 (9th Cir. 2000).

99. In *Tollis Inc. v. County of San Diego*, 505 F.3d 935, 941–42 (9th Cir. 2007), the court upheld an ordinance restricting adult businesses to industrial zoning districts that did not allow other commercial uses, noting that the industrial area at issue was "reasonably accessible" and had sufficient infrastructure. In *Daytona Grand, Inc. v. City of Daytona Beach*, 490 F.3d 860 (11th Cir. 2007), the court found that sites in an unimproved heavy-industrial park could be considered as reasonable alternatives. Twenty-four of the potential twenty-five sites in the city were located in this one site, which was owned by a single entity apparently uninterested in leases or sales to adult businesses. The court held that it was sufficient if the sites were potentially developable. *See also Lund*, 714 F.3d 65 (appropriate to consider governmental restrictions on use and development of potential sites, but not appropriate to consider private economic factors such as existing leases).

100. K. Hope, Inc. v. Onslow Cnty., 911 F. Supp. 948, 959 (E.D.N.C. 1995) ("If the land remaining to adult establishments post-zoning would not normally be considered a potential site for *any* business, it is not available under *Renton*."). On appeal, this decision was vacated as the court concluded a *Pullman* abstention was appropriate given the uncertain state law on authority to adopt the ordinance. 107 F.3d 866 (4th Cir. 1997).

101. Sidewalks and streetlights are not necessarily required if other commercial enterprises located at the site would not necessarily need such amenities. Diamond v. City of Taft, 215 F.3d 1052 (9th Cir. 2000). *See also* Centerfold Club, Inc. v. City of St. Petersburg, 969 F. Supp. 1288, 1302–04 (M.D. Fla. 1997).

102. It may not be necessary, however, for alternative sites to actually be on the market. S. Ent. Co. of Fla., Inc. v. City of Boynton Beach, 736 F. Supp. 1094, 1101 (S.D. Fla. 1990) (alternative sites may be considered even where the owner has indicated an unwillingness to lease to adult businesses).

103. In *Buzzetti v. City of New York*, 140 F.3d 134, 140–41 (2d Cir. 1998), the court noted that allowing for approximately 500 potential sites in a city in which approximately 177 adult businesses were in operation (this use constituting some 11 percent of the city land area) was sufficient. The New York state courts reached the same conclusion. Stringfellow's of N.Y., Ltd. v. City of New York, 91 N.Y.2d 382, 671 N.Y.S.2d 406, 694 N.E.2d 407 (1998). *See also* Hickerson v. City of N.Y., 146 F.3d 99, 107–08 (2d Cir. 1998). In *North Avenue Novelties, Inc. v. City of Chicago*, 88 F.3d 441 (7th Cir. 1996), the court held that the number of potential locations available relative to the number of existing facilities was a critical inquiry. It ruled that adequate alternatives were available given that twenty-two to fifty-six potential sites had been identified, thirty-five uses currently were in operation, and the city was receiving only four or five new inquiries each year. In *Cricket Store 17, LLC v. City of Columbia*, 97 F. Supp. 3d 737 (D.S.C. 2015), the court held that forty-six potential sites provided adequate alternative avenues. In *Fly Fish, Inc. v. City of Cocoa Beach*, 337 F.3d 1301 (11th Cir. 2003), the court invalidated locational restrictions that effectively precluded relocation of existing adult businesses.

that has not previously had an adult business, the court held that four potential sites were sufficient.[104] Another court held that twenty-five potential sites were adequate in a jurisdiction with ten operating adult businesses.[105] As a general rule, remaining nonconforming sites where an adult business continues in operation can be considered in determining the number of total sites available within a community.[106] While it is important for a local government to carefully consider the range of alternate sites that would be available under various regulatory schemes as it considers adoption of adult-business regulations, it is not necessary that the government map potential locations prior to adoption of the ordinance.[107]

If the regulatory scheme allows opponents of adult businesses to effectively block pending applications for siting approval, the court may well find alternative avenues of expression to be unreasonably limited.[108]

The issue of when the adequacy of alternative sites should be assessed has also been litigated. One court has held that the critical inquiry involves determining what sites are available at the time the regulation is challenged—more specifically, as close to the time a judgment is issued as is feasible—rather than only assessing availability at the time of the restriction's enactment.[109]

---

104. *Diamond*, 215 F.3d 1052. *See also* D.H.L. Assocs., Inc. v. O'Gorman, 199 F.3d 50 (1st Cir. 1999). In *3570 East Foothill Blvd., Inc. v. City of Pasadena*, 912 F. Supp. 1257 (C.D. Cal. 1995), the court held that, in light of the predominantly residential character of the city and the fact that only one adult business was located there, a jury could find that eleven to twenty-six individual sites was an ample number of available alternatives. In a subsequent proceeding, the court held that eleven to sixteen sites available for simultaneous operation would be adequate, given that only one adult business was operating in the city and that the plaintiff was the only person in ten years to have applied to operate an additional facility. 980 F. Supp. 329, 337–43 (C.D. Cal. 1997).

105. Red-Eyed Jack, Inc. v. City of Daytona Beach, 322 F. Supp. 2d 1361 (M.D. Fla. 2004). In *Big Dipper Entertainment, L.L.C. v. City of Warren*, 641 F.3d 715 (6th Cir. 2011), the court upheld an ordinance where there were at least twenty-seven potential sites available, only one existing adult business in the city, and only two applications for new such businesses within the previous five years. In *ATL Corp. v. City of Seattle*, 758 F. Supp. 2d 1147 (W.D. Wash. 2011), the court upheld a dispersal requirement that left space for at least seventy-five new adult cabarets in a city with four operating cabarets and six additional applications in the previous six years.

106. Boss Capital, Inc. v. City of Casselberry, 187 F.3d 1251, 1254 (11th Cir. 1999).

107. Pitt Cnty. v. Dejavue, Inc., 185 N.C. App. 545, 563–64, 650 S.E.2d 12, 23 (2007), *review denied*, 362 N.C. 381, 661 S.E.2d 738 (2008). It is also useful to include a variance or exception process for mandatory-separation requirements when those are not necessary to effectuate the purpose of the restriction. For example, in *Independence News, Inc. v. City of Charlotte*, 568 F.3d 148 (4th Cir. 2009), the ordinance allowed a variance to the separation requirement upon a showing that manmade or natural features provided sufficient separation to prevent harmful secondary impacts.

108. Young v. City of Simi Valley, 216 F.3d 807 (9th Cir. 2000). The ordinance here required a minimum separation from sensitive uses and applied the requirement even if such a use secured administrative zoning approval while the adult-business application was pending.

109. TJS of N.Y., Inc. v. Town of Smithtown, 598 F.3d 17 (2d Cir. 2010). *But see* Bigg Wolf Discount Video Movie Sales, Inc. v. Montgomery Cnty., 256 F. Supp. 2d 385 (D. Md. 2003) (must consider site availability at time of adoption of ordinance).

Narrowly Tailored Restrictions

A regulation that restricts adult businesses must be narrowly tailored to meet the legitimate objective of preventing secondary impacts. A closely related requirement is that the regulation not be overly broad.[110] "Narrowly tailored," however, is not the same as "the least restrictive possible." Local governments are allowed considerable discretion in formulating the details of these regulations.[111]

A challenge based on lack of narrow tailoring most frequently arises when a restriction is drafted so tightly as to preclude even a single showing or rental of an adult film or performance or to include the sale of even a single publication that includes adult materials. An ordinance that is drafted to cover any and all sexually explicit material, including a single magazine, performance, or film showing, faces significant legal problems if challenged. Examples of ordinances invalidated on this basis include an ordinance that banned any female topless appearance in any public place;[112] one that applied to any theater even temporarily used for presentation of adult films;[113] one that applied to any depiction of specified sexual activity, no matter how brief;[114] one that purportedly addressed traffic problems but only applied to one topless bar and not twenty other nearby bars without adult entertainment;[115] and one that prohibited any exhibition of nudity.[116]

Ordinances that based a separation requirement on the presence of any residence (e.g., ones requiring the adult use to be 500 feet from any residence as opposed to 500 feet from a residential zoning district) have also been invalidated, with courts reasoning that such a restriction is not narrowly tailored because the residence may be an isolated dwelling with no surrounding neighborhood to protect, and there may be no children living there.[117]

Finally, regulations applicable to establishments that only sell videos for off-premises viewing have been held not to be narrowly tailored.[118]

---

110. *See, e.g.*, Cheshire Bridge Holdings, LLC v. City of Atlanta, 15 F.4th 1362 (11th Cir. 2021) (adult business regulation not overly broad); J.L. Spoons, Inc. v. Dragani, 538 F.3d 379, 383–86 (6th Cir. 2008) (state rule prohibiting nudity and topless dancing in establishments with alcohol licenses not overly broad); Giovani Carandola, Ltd. v. Bason, 303 F.3d 507 (4th Cir. 2002) (regulation of dancers at clubs with ABC licenses overly broad as the regulation included serious artistic performances as well as adult clubs).

111. New Albany DVD, LLC v. City of New Albany, 581 F.3d 556, 559 (7th Cir. 2009) (addressing size of mandatory separation between adult businesses and places of worship).

112. Doran v. Salem Inn, Inc., 422 U.S. 922, 933–34 (1975).

113. Tollis, Inc. v. San Bernadino Cnty., 827 F.2d 1328, 1333 (9th Cir. 1987). *But see* BZAPS, Inc. v. City of Mankato, 268 F.3d 603 (8th Cir. 2001) (upholding ordinance prohibiting one-time nude performance at a bar that did not regularly feature adult entertainment).

114. Avalon Cinema Corp. v. Thompson, 667 F.2d 659, 663 (8th Cir. 1981).

115. Keego Harbor Co. v. City of Keego Harbor, 657 F.2d 94, 98 (6th Cir. 1981) (noting that less intrusive measures were available, such as ticketing parking violators).

116. Purple Onion, Inc. v. Jackson, 511 F. Supp. 1207, 1219–22 (N.D. Ga. 1981). The Atlanta ordinance invalidated in this case defined adult bookstores to include any building that contained a magazine characterized by an emphasis on the depiction of specified anatomical parts, leading the court to observe, "The many Atlanta subscribers to Playboy and other similar magazines would be amazed to find that their homes are considered to be adult book stores and subject to the zoning restrictions under the ordinance." *Id.* at 1220. *See also* Exec. Arts Studio, Inc. v. City of Grand Rapids, 391 F.3d 783, 796–97 (6th Cir. 2005) (invalidating adult-bookstore regulation that also applied to "mainstream bookstores" that have an "adult segment or section"); Triplett Grille, Inc. v. City of Akron, 40 F.3d 129, 134–35 (6th Cir. 1994) (invalidating total ban on all nudity, including theatrical performances as well as in adult establishments, as overly broad). *But cf.* O'Malley v. City of Syracuse, 813 F. Supp. 133, 141–43 (N.D.N.Y. 1993) (upholding total ban on nudity).

117. Amico v. New Castle Cnty., 571 F. Supp. 160, 169–70 (D. Del. 1983). The district court in *Young v. American Mini Theatres, Inc.*, discussed in greater detail in the text above, reached this same conclusion, a result that was not challenged in the Supreme Court. Nortown Theatre, Inc. v. Gribbs, 373 F. Supp. 363, 369–70 (E.D. Mich. 1974), *rev'd on other grounds sub nom.* Am. Mini Theatres v. Gribbs, 518 F.2d 1014 (6th Cir. 1975), *rev'd sub nom.* Young v. American Mini Theatres, Inc., 427 U.S. 50 (1976).

118. Carico Invs., Inc. v. Tex. Alcoholic Beverage Comm'n, 439 F. Supp. 2d 733, 750 (S.D. Tex. 2006); Encore Videos, Inc. v. City of San Antonio, 330 F.3d 288, 295 (5th Cir. 2003).

Restrictions on Alcohol in Adult Establishments

The presence of alcoholic beverages does not affect the scope of First Amendment protections. The U.S. Supreme Court had implied in *California v. LaRue* that additional restrictions on adult entertainment may be imposed on the authority of the Twenty-first Amendment's grant of power to regulate alcohol sales.[119] However, in striking down restrictions on advertising retail prices of alcoholic beverages, the Court, in *44 Liquormart, Inc. v. Rhode Island*,[120] held that although the Twenty-first Amendment grants states the authority to regulate commerce, it in no way reduces the protections afforded by the First Amendment. The Court noted that "the States' inherent police powers provide ample authority to restrict the kind of 'bacchanalian revelries' described in the *LaRue* opinion regardless of whether alcoholic beverages are involved. . . . Without questioning the holding in *LaRue*, we now disavow its reasoning insofar as it relied on the Twenty-first Amendment."[121]

A number of jurisdictions have enacted regulations to prohibit alcohol sales in establishments featuring adult entertainment.[122] Many courts have upheld such restrictions as reasonable content-neutral restrictions to reduce secondary impacts.[123] As with locational restrictions, the adopting jurisdiction must establish that the regulation is content neutral, is based on relevant studies of secondary impacts, leaves reasonable alternative avenues for expression of protected speech, and is narrowly tailored to

---

119. 409 U.S. 109 (1972). *See also* N.Y. State Liquor Auth. v. Bellanca, 452 U.S. 714, 717 (1981) (state authority to ban alcohol sales includes authority to ban sales in adult establishments); City of Newport v. Iacobucci, 479 U.S. 92, 95 (1986) (upholding ordinance prohibiting nude and nearly nude dancing in establishment with on-premises alcohol sales); Doran v. Salem Inn, Inc., 422 U.S. 922, 932–33 (1975) (alcohol licensing can include ban on adult entertainment); City of Kenosha v. Bruno, 412 U.S. 507, 515 (1973) (alcohol ban in adult establishments facially constitutional).

120. 517 U.S. 484 (1996). *See* Ben's Bar, Inc. v. Vill. of Somerset, 316 F.3d 702, 709–13 (discussing interplay of *LaRue, 44 Liquormart, American Mini Theaters,* and *Barnes*); BZAPS, Inc. v. City of Mankato, 268 F.3d 603, 608 (8th Cir. 2001) (continued reliance on *LaRue* for regulation of alcohol at adult establishments).

121. *44 Liquormart,* 517 U.S. at 515–16. The concurring opinion adds, "The Twenty-first Amendment does not trump First Amendment rights or add a presumption of validity to a regulation that cannot otherwise satisfy First Amendment requirements." *Id.* at 533.

That an establishment contains materials protected by the First Amendment does not exempt it from other legitimate police regulations. See, for example, *Arcara v. Cloud Books, Inc.,* 478 U.S. 697 (1986), which upheld a New York statute allowing the closure of premises found to be used as places of prostitution as applied to an adult bookstore.

122. See the discussion above on the constitutional issues regarding the interplay of the First and Twenty-first Amendments.

123. Foxxxy Ladyz Adult World, Inc. v. Vill. of Dix, 779 F.3d 706 (7th Cir. 2015); Imaginary Images, Inc. v. Evans, 612 F.3d 736 (4th Cir. 2010) (upholding Virginia statutes and ABC rules that allow adult-entertainment establishments to sell beer and wine but not mixed drinks); E. Brooks Books, Inc. v. Shelby Cnty., 588 F.3d 360, 366–68 (6th Cir. 2009) (upholding Tennessee statute that prohibited sale of alcohol by adult businesses); Richland Bookmart, Inc. v. Knox Cnty., 555 F.3d 512, 532 (6th Cir. 2009) (upholding prohibition of alcohol sales on premises of adult-entertainment facilities); Daytona Grand, Inc. v. City of Daytona Beach, 490 F.3d 860 (11th Cir. 2007) (upholding minimum separation between alcohol sales and adult entertainment); 181 S. Inc. v. Fischer, 454 F.3d 228 (3d Cir. 2006) (upholding state rule prohibiting erotic dancing at facilities with alcohol licenses); G.M. Enters., Inc. v. Town of St. Joseph, 350 F.3d 631 (7th Cir. 2003); Artistic Ent., Inc. v. City of Warner Robins, 331 F.3d 1196 (11th Cir. 2003) (upholding ordinance banning alcohol sales in adult establishments); Ben's Bar, Inc. v. Vill. of Somerset, 316 F.3d 702, 728 (7th Cir. 2003) (upholding prohibition of sale or consumption of alcohol in establishments with adult entertainment); Wise Enters., Inc. v. Unified Gov't of Athens–Clarke Cnty., 217 F.3d 1360 (11th Cir. 2000); Sammy's of Mobile, Ltd. v. City of Mobile, 140 F.3d 993, 997 (11th Cir. 1998) (noting that this was the least restrictive means of "controlling the combustible mixture of alcohol and nudity"); Pancakes, Biscuits & More, LLC v. Pendleton Cnty. Comm'n, 996 F. Supp. 2d 438 (N.D. W. Va. 2014); DFW Vending, Inc. v. Jefferson Cnty., 991 F. Supp. 578, 597–99 (E.D. Tex. 1998) (holding that prohibiting the sale of alcohol at establishments with adult entertainment did not violate equal protection); Ranch House, Inc. v. City of Anniston, 678 So. 2d 745 (Ala. 1996); Oasis Goodtime Emporium I, Inc. v. DeKalb Cnty., 272 Ga. 887, 536 S.E.2d 520 (2000); Goldrush II v. City of Marietta, 267 Ga. 683, 482 S.E.2d 347 (1997); El Marocco Club, Inc. v. Richardson, 746 A.2d 1228 (R.I. 2000); Robinson v. City of Longview, 936 S.W.2d 413 (Tex. App. 1996). *See also* J.L. Spoons, Inc. v. Dragani, 538 F.3d 379, 383–86 (6th Cir. 2008) (state rule prohibiting nudity and topless dancing in establishments with alcohol licenses not overly broad).

address prevention of secondary impacts. The experience of Fulton County, Georgia, is instructive in this respect. The court struck down the county's initial restriction of alcohol in adult businesses because the county had ignored all of the relevant local evidence (three empirical studies) in adopting it.[124] The county reenacted a ban after conducting additional studies that did show a relationship to secondary impacts, reviewing additional studies from other jurisdictions, and receiving additional anecdotal testimony at a local hearing. The court upheld the second ban.[125]

North Carolina law prohibits the depiction of sex acts or "bottomless" dancing in facilities with ABC licenses.[126] This law was amended in 2003[127] to clarify the state's authority to regulate sexually explicit performances at facilities with ABC licenses.[128] The amendment codified the regulatory prohibition against performers in facilities with ABC licenses exposing their genitals or simulating sexual acts, clarified that the intent is to prevent secondary impacts, and provided an exception for serious literary, artistic, scientific, or political expressions.[129]

Clothing Restrictions

Erotic dancing per se has some First Amendment protection, though this protection is not unassailable. An issue that frequently arises is whether minimum-clothing or coverage requirements can be imposed on performers providing adult entertainment.

The U.S. Supreme Court has on three occasions addressed the constitutionality of laws banning topless or totally nude dancing, debating just how much First Amendment protection should be provided to commercial, sexually explicit speech.[130] While there is a split on the Court as to the test to be used and how rigorously a favored test is to be applied, it is not disputed that erotic dancing deserves some degree of constitutional protection.[131] Even so, regulations that impose minimal costume requirements in order to mitigate secondary impacts have been upheld.

---

124. *Flanigan's I*, 242 F.3d 976 (11th Cir. 2001).

125. Flanigan's Enters. Inc. of Ga. v. Fulton Cnty. (*Flanigan's II*), 596 F.3d 1265 (11th Cir. 2010). *See also* Trop, Inc. v. City of Brookhaven, 764 S.E.2d 398 (Ga. 2014).

126. G.S. 18B-1005.1(a).

127. S.L. 2003-382, creating G.S. 18B-1005.1.

128. The legislative action was prompted by litigation that invalidated enforcement regulations implementing the prior statute. In *Giovani Carandola, Ltd. v. Bason*, 147 F. Supp. 2d 383 (M.D.N.C. 2001), a case involving topless dancers at Christie's Cabaret in Greensboro, the court ruled that regulations covering dancers at clubs with ABC licenses were unconstitutional as they amounted to content-based restrictions on free speech and were not narrowly drawn to address a compelling governmental interest. On appeal the court issued a narrower ruling but still upheld an injunction against enforcement because the regulations were too broad in that they included serious artistic performances as well as adult clubs. 303 F.3d 507 (4th Cir. 2002). Courts typically hold that inclusion of legitimate theater performances renders adult-establishment regulation impermissibly overbroad. *See, e.g.*, Legend Night Club v. Miller, 637 F.3d 291 (4th Cir. 2011) (invalidating as overly broad a Maryland statute prohibiting nudity and adult entertainment in facilities with licenses to sell alcoholic beverages); Odle v. Decatur Cnty., 421 F.3d 386, 395–99 (6th Cir. 2005); Triplett Grille, Inc. v. City of Akron, 40 F.3d 129, 136 (6th Cir. 1994); Conchatta Inc. v. Miller, 458 F.3d 258, 266 (3d Cir. 2006); Ways v. City of Lincoln, 274 F.3d 514, 519 (8th Cir. 2001); Norfolk 302, LLC v. Vassar, 524 F. Supp. 2d 728, 733 (E.D. Va. 2007) (invalidating as overly broad and vague a statute "strikingly similar" to the North Carolina statute invalidated in *Carandola*). *But see* SOB, Inc. v. Cnty. of Benton, 317 F.3d 856, 864–65 (8th Cir. 2003) (overbreadth not fatal where there are no artistic or literary venues that would be affected).

129. The amended statute was upheld in *Giovani Carandola, Ltd. v. Fox*, 470 F.3d 1074 (4th Cir. 2006). *See also* Nico Enters., Inc. v. Prince George's Cnty., 186 F. Supp. 3d 489 (D. Md. 2016) (intent clause limited definition in manner to prevent overbreadth).

130. The Court has implied that commercial sexually oriented speech is entitled to less protection than political speech, noting that we would not "march our sons and daughters off to war" to protect it. *Young*, 427 U.S. at 70.

131. The Court has stated that nude dancing is entitled to the "barest minimum" of protection. Doran v. Salem Inn, Inc., 422 U.S. 922, 932 (1975). The Court has also noted that erotic dancing is "only marginally" of First

Broader restrictions may not pass muster. In *Schad v. Borough of Mt. Ephraim*, for example, the Court held that a Philadelphia suburban community's total ban on commercial live entertainment, a measure that had been adopted to close a "peep show" in an adult bookstore, was unconstitutional. The Court held that the borough had not established any justification for a total ban and that it had failed to provide adequate alternative avenues for the presentation of speech protected by the First Amendment, including nonobscene nude dancing.[132]

By contrast, in *Barnes v. Glen Theatre, Inc.*, the Court upheld an Indiana statute prohibiting totally nude dancing.[133] As has been the situation in a number of First Amendment cases, *Barnes* produced a fractured Court—in this instance there were four separate opinions—that supported regulation rather than a total ban on dancing. The plurality opinion held that nude dancing was on the periphery of protected speech and that the requirement that dancers wear minimal costumes was a narrowly tailored response to the important governmental interest of protecting public morals. Under this rationale, for a state or a local government to ban topless dancing in a manner that is consistent with the *Barnes* decision, it would have to establish (or at least cite) secondary impacts from topless bars as opposed to simply prohibiting topless dancing per se.

A divided Court again upheld an ordinance imposing a requirement of minimal costumes for erotic dancers in *City of Erie v. Pap's A.M.*[134] The plurality opinion held that the ordinance was a content-neutral measure designed to address secondary impacts and that the *de minimis* intrusion on expression involved did not render the ordinance content-based. The Court applied the *O'Brien* tests and upheld the regulation.

Several subsequent cases have explored just how much clothing can be required without violating the minimal First Amendment protection for erotic performances.

A number of cases have upheld regulations prohibiting totally nude dancing.[135] Courts have been more cautious when the clothing restrictions have been broadly applied to venues beyond adult businesses or have been a total ban of a class of expression.[136] Courts have upheld ordinances that impose "bikini top"

Amendment value and is within the "outer perimeters" of the First Amendment. Barnes v. Glen Theatre, Inc., 501 U.S. 560, 566 (1991). The Fourth Circuit Court of Appeals held that erotic dancing is removed from the core concerns of the First Amendment, noting that "activities that have little to do with advocacy, deliberation, or the exposition of ideas have correspondingly little to do with the First Amendment." Imaginary Images, Inc. v. Evans, 612 F.3d 736, 743 (4th Cir. 2010) (citations omitted).

132. 452 U.S. 61 (1981). *See also Doran*, 422 U.S. 922 (invalidating a Long Island town's ordinance banning topless dancing, upholding a district-court conclusion that an ordinance prohibiting any female from appearing in any public place with uncovered breasts was overly broad); Erznoznik v. City of Jacksonville, 422 U.S. 205 (1975) (invalidating an ordinance that prohibited the display of any nudity on an outdoor movie screen).

133. 501 U.S. 560 (1991) (upholding an Indiana statute requiring dancers to wear pasties and a G-string in order to prevent harmful secondary effects). Local ordinances similar to this Indiana statute have been upheld in several cases. *See* SBC Enters., Inc. v. City of S. Burlington, 892 F. Supp. 578 (D. Vt. 1995); Pap's A.M. v. City of Erie, 674 A.2d 338 (Pa. Commw. Ct. 1996).

134. 529 U.S. 277 (2000). The ordinance required erotic dancers to wear pasties and G-strings. Justice Souter again agreed that *O'Brien* provided the proper test for review of the ordinance, but he would have remanded to allow a greater record on the question of whether there were facts to support the claim that the ordinance was designed to address real secondary impacts rather than speculative ones.

135. *See, e.g.*, G.M. Enters., Inc. v. Town of St. Joseph, 350 F.3d 631 (7th Cir. 2003); Fly Fish, Inc. v. City of Cocoa Beach, 337 F.3d 1301, 1308–09 (11th Cir. 2003). *But see* Dream Palace v. Cnty. of Maricopa, 384 F.3d 990, 1017–21 (9th Cir. 2004) (prohibition of nude dancing, seminude dancing, and "simulated sex acts" overly broad).

136. *See, e.g.*, Chase v. Davelaar, 645 F.2d 735, 737 (9th Cir. 1981) (invalidating ban on the display of female breasts at any place serving food or beverages as overly broad); Steverson v. City of Vicksburg, 900 F. Supp. 1 (S.D. Miss. 1994) (invalidating total ban of topless dancing). *See also* Conner v. Town of Hilton Head Island, 314 S.C. 251, 254, 442 S.E.2d 608, 610 (1994) (total ban on nude and seminude dancing violates the First Amendment); Pel Asso, Inc. v. Joseph, 262 Ga. 904, 427 S.E.2d 264 (1993) (invalidating ordinance that prohibited "total nude dancing" and

requirements using the rationale enumerated in *Barnes*.[137] However, where the proper constitutional foundation has not been established, such requirements have been invalidated.[138]

Under common law in North Carolina, public nakedness has always been conduct that amounts to a criminal offense.[139] G.S. 14-190.9 codifies the common law rule and makes indecent exposure a misdemeanor. *Indecent exposure*, as defined by this statute, occurs when one willfully exposes one's private parts "in any public place and in the presence of any other person or persons, . . . or aids or abets in any such act, or . . . procures another to perform such act."[140] In *State v. Jones*, a topless dancer was charged with violation of this statute. The court held that "private parts" are male and female genitalia and do not include female breasts.[141] In *State v. Fly*,[142] the court considered legislative amendments after *Jones*, concluding that the statute also prohibited total exposure of the buttocks but not the wearing of minimal clothing, such as a thong or G-string. A "public place" in the context of this statute includes any area open to the public. In upholding a conviction for indecent exposure in a nightclub, the state supreme court held that "there is nothing whatsoever in the present or former indecent exposure statutes that in any way requires the viewers of the exposure of one's private parts to be unwilling observers."[143]

restricted "partial nude dancing" as overly broad and vague). The Georgia court subsequently upheld an ordinance that applied only to live entertainment featuring topless or bottomless dancing in facilities serving alcohol. S.J.T., Inc. v. Richmond Cnty., 263 Ga. 267, 430 S.E.2d 726 (1993).

137. *See, e.g.*, Greenville Bistro, LLC v. Greenville Cnty., 435 S.C. 146, 866 S.E.2d 562 (2021) (upholding regulation of "semi-nude" dancing); Cafe 207, Inc. v. St. Johns Cnty., 856 F. Supp. 641 (M.D. Fla. 1994) (upholding ordinance requiring that costumes not expose more than three-fourths of the breasts or more than two-thirds of the buttocks); SBC Enters., Inc. v. City of S. Burlington, 892 F. Supp. 578 (D. Vt. 1995); Bright Lights, Inc. v. City of Newport, 830 F. Supp. 378 (E.D. Ky. 1993) (noting that Newport's position as a de facto adult-entertainment "combat zone" for neighboring Cincinnati justified the requirement).

138. MD II Ent., Inc. v. City of Dallas, 935 F. Supp. 1394 (N.D. Tex. 1995). The city had amended its ordinance to require female dancers to wear bikini tops rather than pasties to avoid regulation as adult entertainment. The court found the regulation to be content based because there was no evidence of consideration of secondary impacts as the basis for regulation. Likewise in *Steverson v. City of Vicksburg*, 900 F. Supp. 1 (S.D. Miss. 1994), the court invalidated an ordinance that completely prohibited topless dancing throughout the city. As there was a total ban of topless performers in adult establishments, the court found the *Renton* standard for adequate alternative avenues of expression to be violated (*see* City of Renton v. Playtime Theatres, Inc., 475 U.S. 41 (1986) (discussed *supra* in the text accompanying notes 39–42)). The court also found in respect to the ban that the city had not presented evidence of secondary impacts or evidence that the ordinance was narrowly drawn. *Steverson*, 900 F. Supp. 1.

139. State v. Roper, 18 N.C. 208 (1835) (upholding a conviction for exposing one's private parts while on a public highway). For more on distinguishing regulated conduct from protected speech, see *supra* text accompanying note 19.

140. G.S. 14-190.9(a).

141. 7 N.C. App. 166, 171 S.E.2d 468 (1970). A conviction of the dancers and nightclub owner under this statute for "bottomless" dancing was upheld in *State v. King*, 285 N.C. 305, 204 S.E.2d 667 (1974).

142. 348 N.C. 556, 561, 501 S.E.2d 656, 659 (1997).

143. *King*, 285 N.C. at 311, 204 S.E.2d at 671. In a case involving public drunkenness, the court defined a public place as one "which in point of fact is public as distinguished from private, but not necessarily a place devoted solely to the uses of the public, a place that is visited by many persons and to which the neighboring public may have resort, a place which is accessible to the public and visited by many persons." State v. Fenner, 263 N.C. 694, 698, 140 S.E.2d 349, 352 (1965).

Other Operational Regulations

In order to reduce exposure to minors[144] and to protect surrounding businesses, ordinances may limit exterior advertising.[145] However, a total ban on all outside advertising has been invalidated as too broad.[146]

In order to reduce disease and illegal activity, many ordinances covering live performances require individual viewing booths to be open and constantly visible to the business operator. These requirements are constitutionally permissible.[147]

Other specific restrictions upheld by the courts include requiring dancers to be physically separate from patrons,[148] requiring entertainers to be over a specified age,[149] requiring owners and permittees to

144. *See* Crawford v. Lungren, 96 F.3d 380 (9th Cir. 1996) (upholding ban of adult materials in news racks to prevent access by minors).

145. Excalibur Grp., Inc. v. City of Minneapolis, 116 F.3d 1216 (8th Cir. 1997) (upholding size-limit requirement that only flat wall signs be used); Basiardanes v. City of Galveston, 682 F.2d 1203, 1218–20 (5th Cir. 1982) (holding provocative posters can be banned but prohibition of sign with legend "Adult Theater" is too broad); Hamilton Amusement Ctr., Inc. v. Verniero, 156 N.J. 254, 716 A.2d 1137 (1998) (upholding statute that limited adult businesses to two exterior signs, including a single identification sign of no more than forty square feet); State v. Holmberg, 545 N.W.2d 65, 70–71 (Minn. Ct. App. 1996) (upholding Minneapolis ordinance limiting signs in windows and requiring that no merchandise or entertainment be visible from the exterior of a building).

146. Wolff v. City of Monticello, 803 F. Supp. 1568, 1575 (D. Minn. 1992) (total ban on interior and exterior advertising is not narrowly tailored). *See also* Pleasureland Museum, Inc. v. Beutter, 288 F.3d 988 (7th Cir. 2002) (limitation to display of name of enterprise only invalid); MD II Ent., Inc. v. City of Dallas, 28 F.3d 492, 496–97 (5th Cir. 1994) (invalidating restriction of any term in advertising that is calculated to attract patrons with nudity, seminudity, or simulated nudity).

147. *See, e.g.*, Fantasy Land Video, Inc. v. Cnty. of San Diego, 505 F.3d 996, 1002–04 (9th Cir. 2007) (upholding open-booth requirement and limits on hours of operation); *Pleasureland Museum*, 288 F.3d at 1003–04; Ben Rich Trading, Inc. v. City of Vineland, 126 F.3d 155 (3d Cir. 1997) (may not ban booths but may require them to be open); Matney v. Cnty. of Kenosha, 86 F.3d 692 (7th Cir. 1996) (upholding open-booth requirement); Spokane Arcade, Inc. v. City of Spokane, 75 F.3d 663, 666–67 (9th Cir. 1996) (upholding open-booth requirement); Mitchell v. Comm'n on Adult Ent. Establishments, 10 F.3d 123, 139–44 (3d Cir. 1993) (upholding open-booth requirement); Bamon Corp. v. City of Dayton, 923 F.2d 470, 473–74 (6th Cir. 1991); Doe v. City of Minneapolis, 898 F.2d 612, 615–20 (8th Cir. 1990) (upholding open-booth ordinance); Berg v. Health & Hosp. Corp., 865 F.2d 797 (7th Cir. 1989) (upholding open-booth ordinance); Wall Distribs., Inc. v. City of Newport News, 782 F.2d 1165, 1168–70 (4th Cir. 1986) (upholding open-booth requirement); Ellwest Stereo Theaters, Inc. v. Wenner, 681 F.2d 1243, 1247–48 (9th Cir. 1982) (upholding open-booth ordinance, noting right of privacy does not extend to public places such as theaters).

148. *See, e.g.*, Ent. Prods., Inc. v. Shelby Cnty., 588 F.3d 372 (6th Cir. 2009) (upholding limits on physical contact and requirement that dancers be at least eighteen inches above and six feet away from patrons); Fantasy Ranch Inc. v. City of Arlington, 459 F.3d 546 (5th Cir. 2006) (upholding requirement of performers being on stage of at least eighteen inches height and six feet from customers unless separated by solid glass wall); Gammoh v. City of La Habra, 395 F.3d 1114 (9th Cir. 2005) (upholding requirement for two-foot minimum separation between adult-cabaret performers and patrons); G.M. Enters., Inc. v. Town of St. Joseph, 350 F.3d 631 (7th Cir. 2003) (upholding requirement that dancers be at least eighteen inches above and five feet away from patrons); Deja Vu of Nashville, Inc. v. Metro. Gov't of Nashville & Davidson Cnty., 274 F.3d 377 (6th Cir. 2001) (upholding eighteen-inch stage-height requirement); Colacurcio v. City of Kent, 163 F.3d 545 (9th Cir. 1998) (upholding minimum ten-foot separation between dancers and patrons); DLS, Inc. v. City of Chattanooga, 107 F.3d 403 (6th Cir. 1997) (upholding minimum six-foot separation between dancers and patrons); Hang On, Inc. v. City of Arlington, 65 F.3d 1248 (5th Cir. 1995); Kev, Inc. v. Kitsap Cnty., 793 F.2d 1053, 1061–62 (9th Cir. 1986) (upholding requirements that exotic dancing be conducted at least ten feet away from patrons and on a stage raised at least two feet above the floor as reasonable to prevent drug trafficking or bargaining for sexual favors); T-Marc, Inc. v. Pinellas Cnty., 804 F. Supp. 1500, 1506–07 (M.D. Fla. 1992) (upholding requirement of minimum three-foot separation between exhibitors and patrons); State v. Bouye, 325 S.C. 260, 484 S.E.2d 461 (1997).

149. *See, e.g.*, Club Madonna, Inc. v. City of Miami Beach, 42 F.4th 1231 (11th Cir. 2022) (upholding ordinance requiring record-keeping and identification requirements to ensure performers are over eighteen years of age); DC Operating, LLC v. Paxton, 586 F. Supp. 3d 554 (W.D. Tex. 2022) (refusing to enjoin statute raising age limit for employees of adult businesses from eighteen to twenty-one); Valdez v. Paxton, 553 F. Supp. 3d 387 (W.D. Tex. 2021) (upholding prohibition of "all working relationships" between persons age eighteen to twenty and sexually oriented businesses); Doe I v. Landry, 909 F.3d 99 (5th Cir. 2018) (upholding requirement that entertainers be at least twenty-one years old).

be over a specified age,[150] limiting the hours of operation of adult businesses,[151] requiring adult materials to be in sealed wrappers with any sexually explicit covers being opaquely covered,[152] requiring employees of massage parlors to remain fully clothed at all times,[153] and establishing minimum room sizes.[154]

A limitation on the types of erotic dance movements that can be performed was invalidated as unduly burdening protected expression.[155] However, a prohibition against performing simulated sex acts or fondling specified anatomical areas has been upheld.[156]

Another management technique frequently used by local governments is to require the owners and employees of adult establishments to be licensed. Licensing requirements address the important issues of how the adult use is operated and managed. They differ from land use regulations, which apply to the physical property involved irrespective of the owners or operators, in that they focus management attention on the operators of the use.

It has been held permissible to require disclosure of the names of the owners, operators, and employees of adult establishments in order to check criminal records.[157] However, requirements for the disclosure

---

150. *See, e.g.,* American Entertainers, L.L.C. v. City of Rocky Mount, 888 F.3d 707, 720–22 (4th Cir. 2018) (upholding provision that applicant and business principals be at least twenty-one years old).

151. *See, e.g.,* Ctr. for Fair Pub. Policy v. Maricopa Cnty., 336 F.3d 1153 (9th Cir. 2003) (upholding requirement that adult businesses close at 1:00 a.m.); Schultz v. City of Cumberland, 228 F.3d 831 (7th Cir. 2000) (upholding limitation of hours of operation to 10:00 a.m. to midnight, Monday through Saturday); DiMa Corp. v. Town of Hallie, 185 F.3d 823, 829–30 (7th Cir. 1999) (upholding required closing from 2:00 a.m. to 8:00 a.m. on weekdays and from 3:00 a.m. to 8:00 a.m. on weekends); Lady J. Lingerie, Ltd. v. City of Jacksonville, 176 F.3d 1358 (11th Cir. 1999) (upholding required closing from 2:00 a.m. to noon); *Ben Rich Trading,* 126 F.3d 155 (upholding limitation of hours of operation to 8:00 a.m. to 10:00 p.m.); *Mitchell,* 10 F.3d at 132–39 (upholding requirement limiting hours of operation to 10:00 a.m. to 10:00 p.m., Monday through Saturday); Star Satellite, Inc. v. City of Biloxi, 779 F.2d 1074, 1079–80 (5th Cir. 1986) (upholding requirement limiting hours of operation to 10:00 a.m. to midnight, Monday through Saturday); Envy Ltd. v. City of Louisville, 734 F. Supp. 785, 790 (W.D. Ky. 1990) (upholding a limit on operation between 12:00 a.m. and 6:00 a.m. as reasonable to prevent noise and crime problems). *But see* Faraone v. City of E. Providence, 935 F. Supp. 82 (D.R.I. 1996) (invalidating provision prohibiting sale or rental of adult videos on Sundays and holidays). Note that in North Carolina, state regulations set maximum hours of operation for establishments with ABC licenses, and this may preempt stricter local regulation. *In re* Melkonian, 85 N.C. App. 351, 355 S.E.2d 503, *review denied,* 320 N.C. 631, 360 S.E.2d 91 (1987).

152. Upper Midwest Booksellers Ass'n v. City of Minneapolis, 780 F.2d 1389 (8th Cir. 1985).

153. Mini Spas, Inc. v. S. Salt Lake City Corp., 810 F.2d 939 (10th Cir. 1987).

154. *Lady J. Lingerie,* 176 F.3d 1358 (upholding 1000-square-foot minimum room size). *But see* U.S. Sound & Serv., Inc. v. Twp. of Brick, 126 F.3d 555 (3d Cir. 1997). The town justified a regulation that required a video store to limit its adult material to 10 percent of the structure's floor area on the basis of preventing exposure of adult materials to minors. The court termed this a direct rather than a secondary impact and applied a strict-scrutiny analysis to invalidate the requirement.

155. *Schultz,* 228 F.3d at 847–48. *See also* Dream Palace v. Cnty. of Maricopa, 384 F.3d 990, 1017–21 (9th Cir. 2004) (prohibition of "simulated sex acts" overly broad).

156. Giovani Carandola, Ltd. v. Fox, 470 F.3d 1074 (4th Cir. 2006) (upholding G.S. 18B-1005.1, which prohibits simulation that gives a realistic impression of specified sex acts or fondling specified erogenous zones in facilities with ABC licenses). *See also* New York v. Ferber, 458 U.S. 747, 765 (1982); Farkas v. Miller, 151 F.3d 900 (8th Cir. 1998) (upholding statute that prohibited actual or simulated public performance of sex acts); KEV, Inc. v. Kitsap Cnty., 793 F.2d 1053, 1057–58 (9th Cir. 1986).

157. TK's Video, Inc. v. Denton Cnty., 24 F.3d 705, 709 (5th Cir. 1994) (upholding requirement to disclose names of owners, directors, partners, employees, and clerks); T-Marc, Inc. v. Pinellas Cnty., 804 F. Supp. 1500, 1505–06 (M.D. Fla. 1992) (upholding requirement that adult-use establishments disclose employees' names, aliases, and dates of birth but prohibiting requirements for more extensive information); Envy Ltd. v. City of Louisville, 734 F. Supp. 785, 790 (W.D. Ky. 1990); Broadway Books, Inc. v. Roberts, 642 F. Supp. 486, 492–93 (E.D. Tenn. 1986) (substantial record of criminal violations justifies disclosure requirement). *See also* Am. Library Ass'n v. Reno, 33 F.3d 78 (D.C. Cir. 1994) (upholding some but not all record-keeping and disclosure requirements of the federal Child Protection and Obscenity Enforcement Act).

of past aliases have been invalidated, as have requirements to disclose all shareholders[158] or to allow local law enforcement to verify the work status of employees.[159] It is not permissible to require that a log be kept of the names of customers, as this would unduly impinge on the right of association.[160]

Any regulatory fees charged must be reasonably related to the costs of administering and enforcing the particular ordinance.[161]

Prior Restraint

Many regulations of adult entertainment require that governmental approval be secured prior to the initiation of activity. Such an approach can raise First Amendment issues regarding potential unlawful prior restraint of protected speech.

A prior restraint—a government regulation that restricts speech before it is made—has a heavy presumption of invalidity because of the risk of censorship.[162] The courts have held that any prior restraint must have clear and definite standards for decisions and must have adequate procedural safeguards to ensure prompt decisions and prompt judicial review.[163] In the context of a content-neutral regulation of

---

158. E. Brooks Books, Inc. v. City of Memphis, 48 F.3d 220, 226 (6th Cir. 1995) (invalidating requirement that all shareholders be disclosed, noting that disclosure requirement must be limited to those with a controlling interest and those with operational responsibilities); Acorn Invs., Inc. v. City of Seattle, 887 F.2d 219, 224–26 (9th Cir. 1989); Genusa v. City of Peoria, 619 F.2d 1203, 1217 (7th Cir. 1980).

159. Wacko's Too, Inc. v. City of Jacksonville, 522 F. Supp. 3d 1132 (M.D. Fla. 2021) (holding verification of work status preempted by federal immigration laws).

160. *See, e.g.*, Treants Enters., Inc. v. Onslow Cnty., 94 N.C. App. 453, 380 S.E.2d 602 (1989). The court held that a client record-keeping requirement patently interfered with social relationships and thus was subject to strict scrutiny. The court found that less intrusive means of preventing prostitution, such as surveillance, informants, and undercover agents, were available. *Id.* at 458–61, S.E.2d at 605–06.

161. Acorn Invs., Inc. v. City of Seattle, 887 F.2d 219, 224–26 (9th Cir. 1989) (invalidating licensing fee for operators of adult peep shows of $650 per year plus $25 per month per machine; finding asserted additional policing costs of $65,068 were unrelated to activities of these businesses). *See also E. Brooks Books*, 48 F.3d at 223 (application fee of $5000 invalidated by district court; city reduced fee to $500, which was not challenged on appeal); *TK's Video*, 24 F.3d at 710 (holding a $500 fee for businesses and $50 fee for individuals to be reasonable); Tee & Bee, Inc. v. City of W. Allis, 936 F. Supp. 1479 (E.D. Wis. 1996) (upholding $500 application fee); Bright Lights, Inc. v. City of Newport, 830 F. Supp. 378 (E.D. Ky. 1993) (upholding $5000 application fee); Movie & Video World, Inc. v. Bd. of Cnty. Comm'rs, 723 F. Supp. 695 (S.D. Fla. 1989) (upholding annual licensing fee of $800 plus $40 per booth for adult video booths); *Broadway Books*, 642 F. Supp. at 493 (upholding a refundable $500 application fee); Bayside Enters., Inc. v. Carson, 450 F. Supp. 696, 704–06 (M.D. Fla. 1978) (holding a $500 licensing fee unreasonable); City of Great Falls v. M.K. Enters., Inc., 732 P.2d 413 (Mont. 1987) (upholding a $300-per-video-booth fee as reasonably related to the cost of regulation where estimated first-year cost was $13,000 and the fee would generate $17,700). For a review of an analogous question of the First Amendment and fees, see W. McConnell, *The Constitutionality of Assessing Parade-Permit Fees*, Loc. Gov't L. Bull. No. 62 (UNC Institute of Government, Oct. 1994).

162. Bantam Books, Inc. v. Sullivan, 372 U.S. 58, 70 (1963).

163. A prompt judicial decision, as well as prompt access to the courts, is required. City of Littleton v. Z.J. Gifts D-4, L.L.C., 541 U.S. 774 (2004). In this case the Supreme Court held that the state's ordinary judicial-review periods were adequate to meet this requirement as long as the courts were sensitive to the need for prompt review in First Amendment cases. *See also* FW/PBS, Inc. v. City of Dallas, 493 U.S. 215 (1990) (invalidating ordinance regulating adult businesses due to failure to provide time limitation within which a decision must be made); Se. Promotions, Ltd. v. Conrad, 420 U.S. 546, 560 (1975) (procedural safeguards mandatory for prior restraints); Freedman v. Maryland, 380 U.S. 51 (1965) (licensing schemes that are a prior restraint on protected speech must contain adequate procedural safeguards).

the time, place, and manner of speech, there must be adequate standards to guide regulatory decisions and render them subject to effective judicial review.[164]

The potential for an impermissible prior restraint arises in the context of licensing schemes for adult businesses, their owners, and their performers.[165] A license requirement that does not have clear and definite standards for decisions as well as adequate procedural safeguards to ensure prompt decisions and judicial review is an unlawful prior restraint.[166]

Licensing and permit standards that have been invalidated as too broad include requirements that the operator be "of good moral character,"[167] that operators be local residents,[168] that the business be operated "in a peaceful and law-abiding manner,"[169] that licensees not possess or display "immoral, indecent, lewd, or profane" materials,[170] and that the proposed business comply with "all applicable laws."[171] Standards that are redundant to the point of harassment have been invalidated as well.[172]

The mere fact that an adult business is required to obtain a privilege license before operations commence is not an unlawful prior restraint.[173] Similarly, a nondiscretionary site-plan review that is also required of all comparable development proposals is not a prior restraint.[174]

Any regulation imposing a prior restraint must provide for a brief review of license applications and must make provision for prompt judicial review[175] of any denials. In *City of Littleton v. Z.J. Gifts D-4 L.L.C.*, the Supreme Court held that the state's ordinary judicial-review periods were adequate

164. Thomas v. Chi. Park Dist., 534 U.S. 316, 323 (2002) (upholding licensing and permit requirements for activities in a public park). *See also* HH-Indianapolis, LLC v. Consolidated City of Indianapolis & County of Marion, 889 F.3d 432 (7th Cir. 2018) (content-neutral regulation of location of store selling adult merchandise not an unlawful prior restraint).

165. A prior restraint has been defined as "a governmental restriction on speech or publication before its actual expression." *Prior restraint*, BLACK'S LAW DICTIONARY (10th ed. 2014). *See, e.g.*, Artistic Ent., Inc. v. City of Warner Robbins, 223 F.3d 1306 (11th Cir. 2000) (invalidating licensing requirement for adult businesses due to lack of provision allowing operation if city fails to act on application in a brief, fixed time).

166. *See, e.g.*, Fly Fish, Inc. v. City of Cocoa Beach, 337 F.3d 1301 (11th Cir. 2003) (invalidating license provisions for adult business based on unfettered discretion in decisions on licenses, lack of maximum time period for city action, and fee unrelated to administrative costs). A requirement that the business comply with all applicable laws has been held permissible as it grants the reviewer almost no discretion. Am. Entertainers, L.L.C. v. City of Rocky Mount, No. 5:14-CV-438-D, 2016 WL 4728077 (E.D.N.C. Sept. 8, 2016).

167. Genusa v. City of Peoria, 619 F.2d 1203, 1217 (7th Cir. 1980); Broadway Books, Inc. v. Roberts, 642 F. Supp. 486, 494–95 (E.D. Tenn. 1986) (holding that a license requirement that the applicant have good moral character is "an amorphous standard requiring the licensing authority to exercise unguided subjective judgment"); Bayside Enters., Inc. v. Carson, 450 F. Supp. 696, 706–07 (M.D. Fla. 1978); Clark v. City of Fremont, 377 F. Supp. 327 (D. Neb. 1974).

168. *Broadway Books*, 642 F. Supp. at 494 (invalidating thirty-day local-residency requirement as violation of equal protection); *Bayside Enters.*, 450 F. Supp. at 699.

169. Bronco's Ent., Ltd. v. Charter Twp. of Van Buren, 421 F.3d 440, 449 (6th Cir. 2005); E. Brooks Books, Inc. v. City of Memphis, 48 F.3d 220, 227 (6th Cir. 1995).

170. Carico Invs., Inc. v. Tex. Alcoholic Beverage Comm'n, 439 F. Supp. 2d 733, 745–49 (S.D. Tex. 2006).

171. American Entertainers, L.L.C. v. City of Rocky Mount, 888 F.3d 707, 720–22 (4th Cir. 2018). The court noted that mandating compliance with building codes, zoning regulations, and health and safety rules was acceptable, but as phrased the ordinance allowed case-by-case consideration of any other local, state, or federal law or regulation to be the basis for denial and this was too broad and left too much discretion with the city police chief.

172. Pleasureland Museum, Inc. v. Beutter, 288 F.3d 988 (7th Cir. 2002); Schultz v. City of Cumberland, 228 F.3d 831, 852 (7th Cir. 2000).

173. Fantasy World, Inc. v. Greensboro Bd. of Adjustment, 162 N.C. App. 603, 592 S.E.2d 205, *review denied*, 358 N.C. 543, 599 S.E.2d 43 (2004). *See also* MJJG Rest. LLC v. Horry Cnty., 102 F. Supp. 3d 770 (D.S.C. 2015).

174. *Bronco's*, 421 F.3d at 445.

175. Deja Vu of Nashville, Inc. v. Metro. Gov't of Nashville & Davidson Cnty., 274 F.3d 377 (6th Cir. 2001) (invalidating licensing ordinance where judicial review is through discretionary writ of certiorari); *E. Brooks Books*, 48 F.3d at 224–45 (6th Cir. 1995) (holding a potential delay of five months for judicial review inadequate). *See also* Deja Vu of Cincinnati, L.L.C. v. Union Twp. Bd. of Trs., 411 F.3d 777 (6th Cir. 2005).

to meet this requirement as long as the courts were sensitive to the need for prompt review in First Amendment cases.[176]

Use of special use permits to review proposed adult-entertainment facilities poses a particular prior-restraint concern. Some courts have held that a special use permit requirement that applies to all similar uses (for example, all bars or retail establishments, not just topless bars or adult bookstores) is a content-neutral land use rule that is not subject to a prior-restraint analysis.[177] Other courts have applied a prior-restraint analysis,[178] and the prudent local government should incorporate these considerations if a special use process is a part of that governing body's regulatory scheme for adult businesses.

The principal problem with employing a special use process to regulate adult businesses is the discretionary nature of the standards to be used. If the standards to be applied are objective, there is no need to require a special use permit.[179] If the standards involve judgment and discretion, they may well be invalid if the special use permit requirement is considered a prior restraint.[180]

Standards that have been invalidated as too broad include these requirements: the use must be "essential or desirable" and not "detrimental";[181] the use must be consistent with the purpose of the ordinance, with its appearance not having an adverse effect on adjacent properties and its use being reasonably related to existing land uses;[182] and the site must be adequate in size, must not adversely affect a place of worship or park, must be sufficiently buffered from residential uses, must not have an exterior inconsistent with nearby commercial uses, must be consistent with the comprehensive plan and other city plans, and must be adequately served by public services, including highways of sufficient width.[183]

---

176. 541 U.S. 774 (2004). Prior to this decision, the Fourth Circuit Court of Appeals invalidated an ordinance that allowed up to 150 days to make an initial decision on an application for an adult-business license, with a period of at least 103 days for a subsequent judicial review, ruling that this was not a "brief period" for decisions on applications and that it did not provide the requisite "prompt" judicial review. 11126 Balt. Boulevard v. Prince George's Cnty., 58 F.3d 988, 996, 1101 (4th Cir. 1995).

177. Marty's Adult World of Enfield, Inc. v. Town of Enfield, 20 F.3d 512, 515 (2d Cir. 1994) (holding as valid a special use permit review required for all businesses). *See also* Arcara v. Cloud Books, Inc., 478 U.S. 697 (1986) (upholding a New York statute that allowed closure of premises found to be used as a place of prostitution as applied to an adult bookstore, ruling that establishments that include protected First Amendment speech are not exempt from other legitimate police regulations).

178. *See, e.g.*, Bickers v. Saavedra, 502 F. Supp. 3d 1354 (S.D. Ind. 2020) (holding special use permit requirement for adult cabaret an overly broad prior restraint). This concern with the discretionary standards inherent in a special use permit review can also be an unlawful prior restraint for expressive conduct other than adult entertainment. A special use permit requirement for a spiritual center in an agriculturally zoned area was held to be an unlawful prior restraint in *Spirit of Aloha Temple v. County of Maui*, 49 F.4th 1180 (9th Cir. 2022).

179. Mom N Pops, Inc. v. City of Charlotte, 979 F. Supp. 372 (W.D.N.C. 1997). Adult uses were permitted by right in several zoning districts if specified minimum-separation and objective operational standards were met. The court held that this was not a prior restraint as neither the zoning administrator nor the privilege-license issuer exercised any discretion in review of applications. *Accord* Santa Fe Springs Realty Corp. v. City of Westminster, 906 F. Supp. 1341 (C.D. Cal. 1995).

180. *See, e.g.*, Green Valley Invs., LLC v. Winnebago Cnty., 794 F.3d 864 (7th Cir. 2015); Lady J. Lingerie, Inc. v. City of Jacksonville, 176 F.3d 1358, 1362 (11th Cir. 1999); ATM Express, Inc. v. City of Montgomery, 376 F. Supp. 2d 1310 (M.D. Ala. 2005) (invalidating license requirement for adult video stores that included a "community standards" criterion). *See also* Blue Moon Ent., LLC v. City of Bates City, 441 F.3d 561 (8th Cir. 2006) (adult business may make facial challenge of conditional use permit requirement as an unlawful prior restraint).

181. CR of Rialto, Inc. v. City of Rialto, 975 F. Supp. 1254 (C.D. Cal. 1997); *See also* Amico v. New Castle Cnty., 571 F. Supp. 160, 172–73 (D. Del. 1983).

182. Bukaka, Inc. v. Cnty. of Benton, 852 F. Supp. 807 (D. Minn. 1993). *See also* Franklin Equities, L.L.C. v. City of Evanston, 967 F. Supp. 1233 (D. Wyo. 1997) (requirement that use be compatible with surrounding uses held invalid).

183. *Santa Fe Springs Realty Corp.*, 906 F. Supp. 1341; Dease v. City of Anaheim, 826 F. Supp. 336 (C.D. Cal. 1993).

Examples of standards that have been upheld include these requirements: the adult use must not unreasonably increase pedestrian traffic, noise, or disruptive conduct,[184] and it must be operated in compliance with the ordinance's regulations for design and use.[185] In *Steakhouse, Inc. v. City of Raleigh*,[186] the federal circuit court upheld the city's requirement of a special use permit for adult establishments, noting that these uses may have differing parking and safety concerns than otherwise similar commercial establishments would have. The court held that the standards for permit issuance—effects on parking, traffic, police protection, noise, light, stormwater runoff, pedestrian circulation, and safety—forced the board to focus on "concrete topics that generate palpable effects on the surrounding neighborhood" rather than allowing consideration of "malleable concepts [such] as local welfare, decency, and good order."[187]

In addition to definite standards, a regulation that is a prior restraint must provide for both prompt decisions[188] and prompt judicial review, which often cannot be assured with a special use process.

An alternative that may hold some promise for local governments that propose to use a special use review would be to allow protected speech in some geographic areas or in certain circumstances by right and by special use in other situations. For example, New Haven, Connecticut, adopted an ordinance that required all adult cabarets to obtain a special-exception permit but allowed topless dancing as a use by right in other adult establishments that did not also provide food or drink. In a challenge to that ordinance, the court held that because the expressive speech involved (topless dancing) was allowed without a special-exception permit in part of the jurisdiction, requiring a special-exception permit in other parts of the city constituted a content-neutral time-place-and-manner regulation, and therefore a prior-restraint analysis would be inappropriate.[189]

184. Fantasy Book Shop, Inc. v. City of Bos., 652 F.2d 1115, 1122–23 (1st Cir. 1981) (upholding application of cited standards but disallowing as too subjective standard that use not harm "legitimate protectable interests of the affected citizens." *Id.* at 1119.).

185. *Santa Fe Springs Realty Corp.*, 906 F. Supp. 1341.

186. 166 F.3d 634 (4th Cir. 1999).

187. *Id.* at 639.

188. Bronco's Ent., Ltd. v. Charter Twp. of Van Buren, 421 F.3d 440, 445 (6th Cir. 2005) (135-day maximum period for decision is timely); ATL Corp. v. City of Seattle, 758 F. Supp. 2d 1147 (W.D. Wash. 2011) (where licensing requirement for adult cabarets has no time period for decisions, adoption of policy to make decisions within thirty days is inadequate, so regulation is an invalid prior restraint); Specialty Malls of Tampa v. City of Tampa, 916 F. Supp. 1222 (M.D. Fla. 1996) (adequate procedural safeguards exist where initial decision always made within thirty days and city-council action on appeal of denials always made within forty-five days); Books, Inc. v. Pottawattamie Cnty., 978 F. Supp. 1247 (S.D. Iowa 1997) (licensing scheme for adult businesses is an invalid prior restraint when it has no time period for rendering a final decision); CR of Rialto, Inc. v. City of Rialto, 975 F. Supp. 1254 (C.D. Cal. 1997) (conditional-development permit is invalid prior restraint if no time limit for decision is imposed); Franklin Equities, L.L.C. v. City of Evanston, 967 F. Supp. 1233, 1238 (D. Wyo. 1997) (required decision within forty-five days of "closing of the record" ruled an inadequate time limitation); Bukaka, Inc. v. Cnty. of Benton, 852 F. Supp. 807 (D. Minn. 1993) (no time period for decisions presents likely unlawful prior restraint). *See also* Ino Ino, Inc. v. City of Bellevue, 132 Wash. 2d 103, 937 P.2d 154 (1997) (provision allowing topless dancing only in the presence of a licensed manager held invalid as an unlawful prior restraint due to lack of temporary licensing during the fourteen-day license-processing period). By contrast, in *Florida Video Xpress, Inc. v. Orange County*, 983 F. Supp. 1091 (M.D. Fla. 1997), the court upheld a licensing requirement for adult businesses as meeting the requirements imposed on prior restraints in that it mandated a decision on license applications within thirty days and provided for immediate judicial review by right.

189. Crown St. Enters., Inc. v. City of New Haven, 989 F. Supp. 420 (D. Conn. 1997).

CHAPTER 27

Regulation of Religious Land Uses

Many religious activities and venues can be affected to some degree by land use regulations. Zoning districts define the uses that can be located on a particular site, and they may exclude houses of worship as well as other uses sponsored by religious bodies, such as schools, day-care facilities, homeless shelters, and food banks. Dimensional requirements may establish setbacks or height limits that affect religious structures. Parking, landscaping, noise, and sign regulations also may limit options open to religious groups.

A number of state courts in the 1950s invalidated local government attempts to use zoning to limit religious uses in residential areas of the nation's burgeoning suburbs,[1] but the more recent trend has been to subject religious uses to the same generally applicable standards as comparable secular uses.[2]

In North Carolina many local governments have traditionally applied all of their land use regulations to religious uses. The courts have supported this.[3] For the most part, however, religious uses are treated sympathetically, and the restrictions applied have been modest.[4] Houses of worship are either favored

---

1. *See, e.g.*, State *ex rel.* Lake Shore Drive Baptist Church v. Vill. of Bayside Bd. of Trs., 12 Wis. 2d 585, 108 N.W.2d 288 (1961) (upholding exclusion of church from residential district as being arbitrary and capricious). For a collection of these cases, see R.P. Davis, Annotation, *Zoning Regulations as Affecting Churches*, 74 A.L.R.2d 377 (1960). Many of these state court decisions were based on substantive-due-process grounds, holding there was no rational basis for an exclusion or for treating religious uses differently from secular uses with comparable land use impacts. Laurie Reynolds, *Zoning the Church: The Police Power Versus the First Amendment*, 64 B.U. L. Rev. 767, 777–83 (1985) (contending that the Free Exercise Clause does not mandate an exemption for religious uses). Some states still hold that local governments do not have authority to regulate religious uses. *See, e.g.*, Vill. Lutheran Church v. City of Ladue, 935 S.W.2d 720, 722 (Mo. Ct. App. 1996) (authority to regulate buildings and land used for "trade, industry, residence or other purposes" (Mo. Ann. Stat. § 89.020) does not include the authority to regulate religious uses for other than public-safety impacts). Other states have long held that land use restrictions need not make special provisions or exceptions for religious uses. *See, e.g.*, Corp. of Presiding Bishop of Church of Jesus Christ of Latter-Day Saints v. City of Porterville, 90 Cal. App. 2d 656, 203 P.2d 823 (1949) (upholding exclusion of churches from single-family residential zone).

2. Most states have allowed the application of general zoning regulations to religious uses, including restrictions on off-street parking, wetlands, signs, size limits, setbacks, and special or conditional use permit procedures.

3. *See* Grace Baptist Church v. City of Oxford, 320 N.C. 439, 358 S.E.2d 372 (1987) (application of paving requirement for off-street parking to church upheld, though the court expressly noted that the church had not raised First Amendment or state religious-liberty-clause issues in its complaint); Convent of Sisters of Saint Joseph v. City of Winston-Salem, 243 N.C. 316, 90 S.E.2d 879 (1956) (application of zoning to parochial school upheld); Jirtle v. Bd. of Adjustment, 175 N.C. App. 178, 622 S.E.2d 713 (2005) (application of zoning to a church-related food pantry); Allen v. City of Burlington Bd. of Adjustment, 100 N.C. App. 615, 397 S.E.2d 657 (1990) (application of zoning to a community kitchen operated by a religious group upheld).

4. A 1997 review of zoning treatment of religious land uses in North Carolina municipalities indicated that places of worship are allowed as a permitted use in most zoning districts. The most common restrictions were limits on the location of places of worship in specialized zoning districts (such as conservation overlay districts) and special use permit requirements for large-scale religious uses in residential areas. Building setbacks and off-street parking requirements were typically applied. Height-limit exemptions for steeples or belfries were also common. Accessory uses (such as shelters, schools, or recreation facilities) were often subject to the same restrictions as comparable secular uses.

or considered relatively benign from a land use–impact perspective, so they usually are allowed in most zoning districts, though more-stringent standards are sometimes applied to facilities that serve large numbers of people.

Overview of First Amendment Issues

The First Amendment[5] both prohibits the establishment of a state religion and protects individuals in their free exercise of religion. The North Carolina Constitution also contains protection for freedom of religion.[6]

---

5. The U.S. Constitution also forbids religious tests for federal offices. U.S. CONST. art. VI, cl. 3. *See* McDaniel v. Paty, 435 U.S. 618 (1978) (invalidating state prohibition on ministers running for public office).

6. One of North Carolina's earliest governance schemes, traditionally said to have been drafted by John Locke and adopted by the Lords Proprietors in 1669 before the area became a royal colony, guaranteed absolute freedom to all religious bodies. WILLIAM S. POWELL, THE CAROLINA CHARTER OF 1663 19 (1954). The current state constitution provides, "All persons have a natural and inalienable right to worship Almighty God according to the dictates of their own consciences, and no human authority shall, in any case whatever, control or interfere with the rights of conscience." N.C. CONST. art. I, § 13. The North Carolina Supreme Court has held that the state constitution both guarantees freedom of religious profession and worship and firmly establishes a separation of religion and government. Heritage Vill. Church & Missionary Fellowship, Inc. v. State, 299 N.C. 399, 263 S.E.2d 726 (1980).

The state guarantee of religious freedom has never been absolute. The N.C. Constitution of 1776 prohibited a "clergyman, or preacher of the gospel, of any denomination" from serving in the legislature or council of state. N.C. CONST. art. XXXI (1776). It further provided that "no person, who shall deny the being of God or the truth of the Protestant religion, or the divine authority either of the Old or New Testaments, or who shall hold religious principles incompatible with the freedom and safety of the State, shall be capable of holding any office or place of trust or profit in the civil department within this state." N.C. CONST. art. XXXII (1776). John Culpepper of Anson County was expelled from the state House of Commons on December 19, 1801, because he was continuing to preach while in office. In 1809, the right to membership in the state House of Commons of a Jewish member, Jacob Henry of Carteret County, was challenged, and the House refused to unseat him. For an analysis of the various issues at play with the vote on unseating Henry, see Seth B. Tillman, *A Religious Test in America? The 1809 Motion to Vacate Jacob Henry's North Carolina State Legislative Seat—A Reevaluation of the Primary Sources*, 98 N.C. HIST. REV. 1 (2021). William Gaston, a Catholic from New Bern, was one of the more prominent and well-respected early officeholders in North Carolina, serving in the state House of Commons from 1807 to 1809 (as speaker in 1808), the state Senate in 1812, and the U.S. Congress from 1812 to 1817. Gaston was elected by the legislature to the state supreme court, where he served with distinction from 1833 until his death in 1844. Gaston argued for deletion of the religious test at the 1835 constitutional convention, contending, "I trust that we shall act up to the axiom proclaimed in our Bill of Rights, and permit no man to suffer inconvenience or to incur incapacity, because of religion, whether he be Jew or Gentile, Christian or Infidel, Heretic or Orthodox." WILLIAM GASTON, SPEECH OF THE HONORABLE JUDGE GASTON, DELIVERED IN THE RECENT STATE CONVENTION OF NORTH CAROLINA ASSEMBLED FOR THE PURPOSE OF REVISING THE CONSTITUTION 36 (1835). While not abolished, the religious test was amended in 1835 to change the requirement for "Protestant" belief to "Christian" belief and was further amended in 1868 to simply require a belief in God. It continues in that form in the current constitution, albeit unenforceably so. *See* Torcaso v. Watkins, 367 U.S. 488 (1961) (invalidating similar Maryland provision). Of the forty persons serving on the state supreme court up to 1919, there were twenty-three Episcopalians, seven Presbyterians, four Methodists, three Catholics, two Baptists, and one Freethinker (members were elected by the legislature prior to 1868 and popularly elected thereafter). Walter Clark, HISTORY OF THE SUPREME COURT OF NORTH CAROLINA, 27 (1919). *See generally* Kemp P. Battle, AN ADDRESS ON THE HISTORY OF THE SUPREME COURT, 103 N.C. 339, 371 (1883); R.D.W. CONNOR, WILLIAM GASTON: A SOUTHERN FEDERALIST OF THE OLD SCHOOL AND HIS YANKEE FRIENDS, 1778–1844 43 (1934); JOHN V. ORTH, THE NORTH CAROLINA STATE CONSTITUTION: A REFERENCE GUIDE 137 (1993).

Several aspects of constitutional jurisprudence on religious freedom are clear. Government may not regulate religious beliefs.[7] Intentional discrimination on the basis of religion violates both Equal Protection and the Free Exercise clauses of the constitution.[8]

Constitutional protection of the free exercise of religion also extends beyond beliefs to many physical acts based on those beliefs, such as assembling for worship and partaking of sacraments.[9] For example, a regulation designed specifically to prohibit animal sacrifice by followers of the Santería religion (as opposed to a uniformly applicable law on animal slaughter) was invalidated in *Church of the Lukumi Babalu Aye, Inc. v. City of Hialeah.*[10] A regulation that requires prior approval for the exercise of religion that includes highly discretionary standards can be an unlawful prior restraint.[11]

However, the U.S. Supreme Court has held that generally applicable regulations that are neutrally applied can restrict even religiously justified conduct. The difficulty is at the intersection of these two considerations: the freedom of individuals to believe (and so behave) as they wish on religious matters and the authority of states to regulate behavior uniformly for the public good.

The initial landmark case that addressed this conflict and established strong judicial protection of free-exercise rights is *Sherbert v. Verner.*[12] Adell Sherbert was a Seventh-Day Adventist who lost her job in a South Carolina textile mill for refusing to work on Saturdays after the mill expanded from a five- to a six-day workweek. The Court announced a "strict scrutiny" test for government regulations that significantly burden religious practices: the regulation is invalid unless the government is both addressing

_____

7. Employment Division, Department of Human Resources v. Smith:

> The free exercise of religion means, first and foremost, the right to believe and profess whatever religious doctrine one desires. . . . [G]overnment may not compel affirmation of religious belief, punish the expression of religious doctrines it believes to be false, impose special disabilities on the basis of religious views or religious status, or lend its power to one or the other side in controversies over religious authority or dogma.

494 U.S. 872, 877 (1990) (citations omitted). In many respects this requirement that regulations not be directed toward the substance of religious beliefs is similar to the requirement that restrictions on constitutionally protected speech be content neutral. *See* Heffron v. Int'l Soc'y for Krishna Consciousness, Inc., 452 U.S. 640 (1981). "The Free Exercise Clause commits government itself to religious tolerance, and upon even slight suspicion that proposals for state intervention stem from animosity to religion or distrust of its practices, all officials must pause to remember their own high duty to the Constitution and to the rights it secures." Church of the Lukumi Babalu Aye, Inc. v. City of Hialeah, 508 U.S. 520, 547 (1993). *See also* Locke v. Davey, 540 U.S. 712, 725 (2004) (upholding statute providing college scholarships but excepting those pursuing degrees in devotional theology as there was no showing of an animus toward religion).

8. *See, e.g.,* Congregation Rabbinical College of Tartikov, Inc. v. Village of Pomona, 945 F.3d 83 (2d Cir. 2019).

9. *Smith,* 494 U.S. at 877.

10. *Lukumi Babalu Aye,* 508 U.S. 520. The Court unanimously concluded that the ordinance in question was specifically designed to stop a house of worship, school, cultural center, and museum planned by the plaintiff.

11. Spirit of Aloha Temple v. County of Maui, 49 F.4th 1180 (9th Cir. 2022) (special use permit requirement for a spiritual center in an agriculturally zoned area an unlawful prior restraint).

12. 374 U.S. 398 (1963). The test enumerated in *Sherbert,* known as the "substantial-burden test" and discussed in the text below, was reaffirmed in *Wisconsin v. Yoder,* 406 U.S. 205 (1972), where the Court invalidated a state law mandating school attendance for Amish children. Subsequent case law has defined the substantial-burden test. *See* Hernandez v. Comm'r, 490 U.S. 680 (1989) (disallowing charitable-contribution tax deduction for "audit" sessions in Scientologist training classes not a substantial burden); Lyng v. Nw. Indian Cemetery Protective Ass'n, 485 U.S. 439, 450–51 (1988) (a substantial burden is one that coerces persons into acting contrary to their religious beliefs); Hobbie v. Unemployment Appeals Comm'n, 480 U.S. 136 (1987) (denial of unemployment benefits for Seventh-Day Adventist fired for not working on Saturdays a substantial burden); Thomas v. Review Bd. of the Ind. Emp't Sec. Div., 450 U.S. 707, 718 (1981) (a substantial burden is more than an incidental effect that makes religious practice more difficult). In *Moore-King v. County of Chesterfield,* 708 F.3d 560 (4th Cir. 2013), the court upheld a "fortune-teller" ordinance in a challenge by a "spiritual counselor," ruling her activity was more a way of life based on personal and philosophical choices, not religious belief.

a compelling state interest[13] and has chosen a narrowly tailored method of regulation. However, in *Employment Division, Department of Human Resources v. Smith* (*Smith*),[14] the Court in 1990 retreated from this strict judicial scrutiny. Two Oregon counselors, members of the Native American Church, were fired from a private drug-rehabilitation firm because of their use of peyote. It was undisputed that the ingestion of hallucinogenic peyote was one of their religious sacraments. After the counselors were denied unemployment benefits on the ground that they had been dismissed for misconduct—peyote use was a criminal offense in Oregon at that time[15]—they challenged the determination. The Oregon Supreme Court applied the *Sherbert* test and ruled that the counselors were entitled to unemployment compensation because preserving the financial integrity of the compensation fund was not a sufficiently compelling governmental interest to justify substantially burdening the counselors' religious expression.[16] However, on appeal the U.S. Supreme Court ruled that if the regulation is a valid and neutral law of general applicability,[17] the Constitution does not mandate that the legislature provide a religion-based exemption. The Court concluded, "To make an individual's obligation to obey such a law contingent upon the law's coincidence with his religious beliefs, except where the State's interest is 'compelling' . . . contradicts both constitutional tradition and common sense."[18]

---

13. The Court noted that regulation of religiously based conduct upheld in the past addressed conduct that "invariably posed some substantial threat to public safety, peace or order." *Sherbert*, 374 U.S. at 403. Prohibition of religiously motivated but dangerous activity, such as handling poisonous snakes, has long been allowed. State v. Massey, 229 N.C. 734, 51 S.E.2d 179, *appeal dismissed*, 336 U.S. 942 (1949). *See also* Bob Jones Univ. v. United States, 461 U.S. 574, 604 (1983) (upholding revocation of tax-exempt status because compelling governmental interest in eradicating racial discrimination in education justified substantial burden on religious belief against interracial relationships).

14. 494 U.S. 872 (1990). *See also* United States v. Lee, 455 U.S. 252 (1982) (government may require payment of social security taxes by those with religious objection).

15. A number of states exempt peyote use in religious ceremonies from criminal sanction. Not long after the *Smith* decision, Oregon joined their ranks. OR. REV. STAT. ANN. § 475.992(5) (Supp. 1996). Section 2(b)(1) of the American Indian Religious Freedom Act Amendments of 1994, 42 U.S.C. § 1996a(b)(1), created a national exemption. The key issue from a free-exercise standpoint, though, is not whether the government could make such an exemption but whether the Constitution requires it to do so.

16. Smith v. Emp't Div., Dep't of Human Resources, 721 P.2d 445, 449–50 (Or. 1986).

17. Most courts have concluded that the potential for seeking a variance does not remove the typical land use regulation from the category of a "generally applicable" law. Lighthouse Inst. for Evangelism, Inc. v. City of Long Branch, 510 F.3d 253, 276–77 (3d Cir. 2007); Grace United Methodist Church v. City of Cheyenne, 451 F.3d 643, 651 (10th Cir. 2006).

18. *Smith*, 494 U.S. at 885 (citations omitted). A regulation that applies only to conduct motivated by religious beliefs is not "generally applicable" and so would have to be supported by a compelling governmental interest. "A law that targets religious conduct for distinctive treatment or advances legitimate governmental interests only against conduct with a religious motivation will survive strict scrutiny only in rare cases." Church of the Lukumi Babalu Aye, Inc. v. City of Hialeah, 508 U.S. 520, 546 (1993).

Particular care is important when individualized conditions are being imposed, such as a condition on a special use permit for a religiously sponsored homeless shelter. As the court concluded in *Lukumi Babalu Aye*, "The Free Exercise Clause commits government itself to religious tolerance, and upon even slight suspicion that proposals for state intervention stem from animosity to religion or distrust of its practices, all officials must pause to remember their own high duty to the Constitution and to the rights it secures." *Id.* at 547. Also, the Court noted in *Smith* that a heightened scrutiny of even neutral laws of general application may be warranted when the law burdens both free exercise of religious views and other protected First Amendment rights. 494 U.S. at 881–82 (noting "hybrid" claims had received heightened scrutiny). Free-expression claims are often closely related to free-speech and freedom-of-association claims.

In *Fulton v. City of Philadelphia*, 141 S. Ct. 1868 (2021), the Court held that a regulation prohibiting foster-care-placement agencies that contracted with the city from discriminating on the basis of sexual orientation that allowed individual exceptions but not a religious-based exception is not a rule of general application subject to *Smith. See also* Mast v. Fillmore Cnty., 141 S. Ct. 2430 (2021) (remanding in light of *Fulton* enforcement of county regulation requiring wastewater treatment for "gray water"—water used for household laundry, dishwashing, and the like—as applied to Amish community).

The North Carolina Supreme Court reached a similar result. A person convicted of peyote and marijuana use contended that his consumption was a sacramental practice of the Neo-American Church, of which he was a member. The court noted that the Free Exercise Clause "permits a citizen complete freedom of religion. He may belong to any church or to no church and may believe whatever he will, however fantastic, illogical, or unreasonable, but nowhere does it authorize him in the exercise of his religion to commit acts which constitute threats to the public safety, morals, peace and order."[19]

The *Smith* analysis was soon applied in the land use area.[20] One early case rejected a contention that *Smith* was limited to criminal statutes and held that a Salvation Army shelter was not exempt from state regulations on rooming houses and boardinghouses.[21] A second case, *Rector of St. Bartholomew's Church v. City of New York*,[22] upheld application of a historic-preservation ordinance to a church. The court applied the *Smith* analysis and concluded that the New York Landmark Law was a neutral law of general application. Although the law substantially limited the church's options for using its real-estate holdings to raise revenue,[23] the court found that it did not prevent the church from carrying out its religious and charitable missions in its current building. The court also held that because there was no showing of a discriminatory motive in the law's application, and no coercion related to the religious practice involved, the law did not violate the Free Exercise Clause.[24] State court decisions on the application of historic-district and landmark restrictions on places of worship have been mixed.[25]

---

19. State v. Bullard, 267 N.C. 599, 603, 148 S.E.2d 565, 568 (1966).

20. Subsequent to the 2000 adoption of the Religious Land Use and Institutionalized Persons Act, much of the litigation in this area has involved both constitutional and statutory claims. Most of these contemporary cases are reviewed in the discussion of that statute below.

21. Salvation Army v. Dep't of Cmty. Affairs, 919 F.2d 183 (3d Cir. 1990) (holding that even though operation of shelters is a sacrament for the Salvation Army, *Smith* requires application of neutral, generally applicable regulations on boardinghouses).

22. 914 F.2d 348 (2d Cir. 1990). *See also* Daytona Rescue Mission, Inc. v. City of Daytona Beach, 885 F. Supp. 1554 (M.D. Fla. 1995). *But see* Mount St. Scholastica, Inc. v. City of Atchison, 482 F. Supp. 2d 1281 (D. Kan. 2007) (since state historic-preservation statute allowed city council to overrule order denying demolition upon finding no feasible and prudent alternatives are available, law is not one of general application, and strict scrutiny under the First Amendment applies).

23. The church proposed to replace its seven-story Community House, built in 1928, with a forty-seven-story commercial office tower.

24. *See also* Mount Elliott Cemetery Ass'n v. City of Troy, 171 F.3d 398, 405 (6th Cir. 1999) (upholding refusal to rezone single-family area for religious cemetery, noting locational restriction was a neutral law of general applicability).

25. The Washington state court, in several post-*Smith* decisions, has applied the *Sherbert* analysis to invalidate landmark-protection ordinances. That court has found ordinances not to be neutral and has ruled that the economic burden inherent in historic-district restrictions creates a substantial impediment to religious expression and, in addition, that landmark preservation is not a sufficiently compelling governmental interest to justify such a burden. First Covenant Church v. City of Seattle, 120 Wash. 2d 203, 840 P.2d 174 (1992). The Washington court has concluded also that such restrictions violate the state constitution's religious-freedom provisions. In *Munns v. Martin*, 131 Wash. 2d 192, 930 P.2d 318 (1997), the court invalidated a potential fourteen-month delay imposed on church demolition of a school to construct a pastoral center. In *First United Methodist Church v. Hearing Examiner for the Seattle Landmarks Preservation Board*, 129 Wash. 2d 238, 916 P.2d 374 (1996), the court held that landmark designation would reduce the resale value of the church, thus reducing the potential revenues available for its religious mission and substantially burdening the church without a compelling justification. The court noted that the designation was not unconstitutional per se but failed here on an "as applied" analysis. *Id.* at 252, 916 P.2d at 381.

The Massachusetts Supreme Judicial Court invalidated a Boston landmark regulation of the interior of church space as unduly infringing on the religious liberties guaranteed by the state constitution. Soc'y of Jesus of New Eng. v. Bos. Landmarks Comm'n, 409 Mass. 38, 564 N.E.2d 571 (1990). The court had previously upheld landmark regulation of the exterior of religious buildings that are visible from a public way. Opinion of the Justices to the Senate, 333 Mass. 783, 128 N.E.2d 563 (1955). *See also* Soc'y for Ethical Culture in the City of N.Y. v. Spatt, 51 N.Y.2d 449, 434 N.Y.S.2d 932, 415 N.E.2d 922 (1980) (upholding landmark designation).

Statutory Protection of Religious Land Uses

Religious Freedom Restoration Act

In response to a perceived weakening of the protection of religious freedom resulting from the *Smith* decision,[26] Congress in 1993 enacted the Religious Freedom Restoration Act (RFRA),[27] the key provisions of which established a "strict scrutiny" test for any government regulations that significantly burden religious freedom. The law provided that "government shall not substantially burden a person's exercise of religion even if the burden results from a rule of general applicability."[28] Exceptions were allowed only if there was a "compelling governmental interest" and if the government had chosen the "least restrictive means" of furthering that interest.[29] The express intent of Congress in enacting the law was to overturn the *Smith* decision and return to the *Sherbert* strict-scrutiny standard for reviewing substantial governmental infringement on religious liberty.[30]

In *City of Boerne v. Flores*,[31] the high Court ruled that Congress had exceeded its authority in adopting the RFRA and declared the act unconstitutional. The Court held that although Congress can enact legislation to remedy violations of constitutional protections, it cannot enact laws that change the scope of those rights.[32] In addition, the Court held that the historic-preservation ordinance involved did not violate the *Smith* standard:

> It is a reality of the modern regulatory state that numerous state laws, such as the zoning regulations at issue here, impose a substantial burden on a large class of individuals. When the exercise of religion has been burdened in an incidental way by a law of general application, it does not follow that the persons affected have been burdened any more than other citizens, let alone burdened because of their religious beliefs.[33]

---

26. Where there is a marked pattern of unconstitutional discrimination, as with the action of southern states prior to enactment of the Voting Rights Act of 1965, remedial action has been upheld. South Carolina v. Katzenbach, 383 U.S. 301 (1966). Whether there is in fact the requisite widespread pattern or practice of discrimination against religious land uses to justify remedial action is contested in the literature. *See* Mark Chaves & William Tsitsos, *Are Congregations Constrained by Government? Empirical Results from the National Congregations Study*, 42 J. CHURCH & ST. 335 (2000) (finding denial of approvals extraordinarily uncommon). For examples of those making the case that discrimination is widespread, see Von G. Keetch & Matthew K. Richards, *The Need for Legislation to Enshrine Free Exercise in the Land Use Context*, 32 U.C. DAVIS L. REV. 725 (1999); Douglas Laycock, *State RFRAs and Land Use Regulation*, 32 U.C. DAVIS L. REV. 755 (1999); Roman P. Storzer & Anthony R. Picarello, Jr., *The Religious Land Use and Institutionalized Persons Act of 2000: A Constitutional Response to Unconstitutional Zoning Practices*, 9 GEO. MASON L. REV. 929 (2001). For those making the case that there is not widespread discrimination, see Caroline R. Adams, Note, *The Constitutional Validity of the Religious Land Use and Institutionalized Persons Act of 2000: Will RLUIPA's Strict Scrutiny Survive the Supreme Court's Strict Scrutiny?*, 70 FORDHAM L. REV. 2361 (2002); Stephen Clowney, Comment, *An Empirical Look at Churches in the Zoning Process*, 116 YALE L.J. 859 (2007); Ariel Graff, *Calibrating the Balance of Free Exercise, Religious Establishment, and Land Use Regulation: Is RLUIPA an Unconstitutional Response to an Overstated Problem?*, 53 UCLA L. REV. 485 (2005); Marci A. Hamilton, *Federalism and the Public Good: The True Story Behind the Religious Land Use and Institutionalized Persons Act*, 78 IND. L.J. 311 (2003). *See also* Daniel P. Lennington, *Thou Shalt Not Zone: The Overbroad Applications and Troubling Implications of RLUIPA's Land Use Provisions*, 29 SEATTLE U. L. REV. 805 (2006).

27. 42 U.S.C. §§ 2000bb to 2000bb-4 (1994). Several states, including Florida, Illinois, and Rhode Island, have adopted comparable state-level legislation.

28. *See id.* § 2000bb-1(a). For a collection of cases applying the substantial-burden test under this act, see *Hicks v. Garner*, 69 F.3d 22, 26 n.22 (5th Cir. 1995).

29. *See* 42 U.S.C. § 2000bb-1(b).

30. *See id.* § 2000bb(b)(1).

31. 521 U.S. 507 (1997).

32. The Court also invalidated aspects of the Americans with Disabilities Act on similar grounds of Congress exceeding the remedial authorization of the Fourteenth Amendment. Bd. of Trustees v. Garrett, 531 U.S. 356 (2001).

33. *Boerne*, 521 U.S. at 535.

Religious Land Use and Institutionalized Persons Act

Congress responded to the *Boerne* decision by adopting the Religious Land Use and Institutionalized Persons Act of 2000 (RLUIPA).[34] To overcome the constitutional infirmity identified in *Boerne*, the proponents of the law contend that it is a remedial action authorized by Section 5 of the Fourteenth Amendment and is further justified under the Commerce Clause.[35] Judicial challenges to the constitutionality of RLUIPA have been unsuccessful.[36]

RLUIPA essentially codifies the *Sherbert* and *Lukumi Babalu Aye* rules.[37] It establishes a general rule that land use regulations[38] shall not impose a substantial burden on religious exercise (including religious assembly)[39] unless this is in furtherance of a compelling governmental interest and is the least restrictive means of furthering that interest. The statute goes beyond these previous constitutional provisions. The law also mandates that land use regulations must not treat religious assemblies on "less than equal terms" with nonreligious uses and must not discriminate on the basis of religion or religious denomination.[40] It also provides that a jurisdiction shall not totally exclude or unreasonably limit religious assemblies or structures.[41]

If a plaintiff produces prima facie evidence to support a violation of the general rule of RLUIPA, the government bears the burden of persuasion on any element of the claim (except that the plaintiff bears the burden on whether the restriction substantially burdens exercise of religion).[42] A prevailing party

---

34. Pub. L. No. 106-274 (codified at 42 U.S.C. §§ 2000cc to 2000cc-5). The law was effective September 22, 2000. Also see the American Indian Religious Freedom Act, Pub. L. No. 95-341, codified in part at 42 U.S.C. § 1996. *See generally* Lucien J. Dhooge, *A Case Law Survey of the Impact of RLUIPA on Land Use Regulation*, 102 Marq. L. Rev. 985 (2019).

35. 42 U.S.C. § 2000cc(a)(2)(B).

36. The section of RLUIPA addressing institutionalized persons was held not to be a facial violation of the Establishment Clause in *Cutter v. Wilkinson*, 544 U.S. 709 (2005). The act was held facially valid under the U.S. Constitution in *Freedom Baptist Church v. Township of Middletown*, 204 F. Supp. 2d 857 (E.D. Pa. 2002) (denying motion to dismiss challenge to town regulations applicable to religious land uses). *See also* Mayweathers v. Newland, 314 F.3d 1062, 1066 (9th Cir. 2002) (holding RLUIPA constitutional exercise of congressional spending power in a case involving prison inmates).

37. World Outreach Conference Ctr. v. City of Chi., 591 F.3d 531, 534 (7th Cir. 2009); Sts. Constantine & Helen Greek Orthodox Church, Inc. v. City of New Berlin, 396 F.3d 895, 897 (7th Cir. 2005); Midrash Sephardi, Inc. v. Town of Surfside, 366 F.3d 1214, 1232 (11th Cir. 2004).

38. The law applies to a "zoning or landmarking law" that "limits or restricts a claimant's use or development of land." 42 U.S.C. § 2000cc-5(5). The law applies to governmental land use regulations if the "program or activity" receives federal financial assistance, affects interstate commerce, or is part of a system of individualized determinations of the proposed use of the property (such as requiring a special use permit for places of worship). 42 U.S.C. § 2000cc(a)(2). As typical land uses by a religious entity might not in themselves constitute the "exercise of religion" in a free-exercise context and RLUIPA covers any exercise regardless of it being compelled by or central to a system of religious beliefs, the statute is broader than a free-exercise claim. Lighthouse Inst. for Evangelism, Inc. v. City of Long Branch, 510 F.3d 253, 273–74 (3d Cir. 2007); Cambodian Buddhist Soc'y of Conn., Inc. v. Planning & Zoning Comm'n, 285 Conn. 381, 411, 941 A.2d 868, 888–89 (2008).

39. 42 U.S.C. § 2000cc(a)(1). The law specifically states that the "use, building, or conversion of real property for the purpose of religious exercise shall be considered to be religious exercise." 42 U.S.C. § 2000cc-5(7)(B).

40. 42 U.S.C. § 2000cc(b)(1). See, for example, a RFRA and free-exercise case, *Brown v. Borough of Mahaffey*, 35 F.3d 846 (3d Cir. 1994), which involved the town blocking access through a park to land being used for a tent revival. The court noted that if the action constituted intentional discrimination against the religious use, that action could serve no legitimate governmental purpose. Opposition and animus toward the particular religion involved that is expressed at hearings on the application can establish improper religious animus. *See, e.g.*, Jesus Christ Is the Answer Ministries, Inc. v. Baltimore County, 915 F.3d 256, 263–65 (4th Cir. 2019).

41. 42 U.S.C. § 2000cc(b)(3).

42. *Id.* § 2000cc-2(b).

making a successful RLUIPA challenge is entitled to reasonable attorney's fees.[43] The statute of limitations for bringing a RLUIPA claim begins to run when the challenged decision is formally made (such as on the date of signing of an order denying a permit).[44]

While most RLUIPA claims are brought by religious entities contending that there has been a violation of the law, claims are sometimes brought by landowners who contend that the land use regulation has prevented sale or lease to a religious entity. This raises the question whether a landowner whose personal religious expression has not been affected has standing for a RLUIPA claim in this circumstance. In *Dixon v. Town of Coats*,[45] the plaintiff owned a building in a six-block downtown area that was placed in a mixed-use zoning district that did not allow places of religious assembly. When a lessee was denied permission to use the building for a church, the court held that the landowner had standing to bring a RLUIPA challenge.

Scope of RLUIPA Coverage

RLUIPA does not apply to all governmental decisions. It is applicable only for land use regulations and the treatment of institutionalized persons. While most of the challenged regulations involve traditional zoning requirements (such as rezonings, special use permits, and variances), courts have also found closely related regulations (such as off-street parking requirements) to be covered.[46] In *Redeemed Christian Church of God (Victory Temple) Bowie v. Prince George's County*, the court held that an individualized decision on whether to change a property's water and sewer classification was a land use regulation subject to RLUIPA.[47]

---

43. In *World Outreach Conference Center v. City of Chicago*, 896 F.3d 779 (7th Cir. 2018), the court awarded $467,973.45 in attorney's fees and damages of $40,001.00 in a long-running RLUIPA litigation. In *DiLaura v. Township of Ann Arbor*, 471 F.3d 666 (6th Cir. 2006), the court upheld an attorney's-fee award of $178,535.61 in a case involving a bed-and-breakfast providing complimentary food and accommodations for guests staying for religious prayer and contemplation.

44. United States v. Maui Cnty., 298 F. Supp. 2d 1010 (D. Haw. 2003).

45. No. 5:08-CV-489-BR, 2010 WL 2347506 (E.D.N.C. June 9, 2010). *See also* Berry v. Jefferson Parish, 326 F. App'x 748 (5th Cir. 2009) (dismissing claim by owners who wished to sell the land to "Christian-affiliated developer"); DiLaura v. Ann Arbor Charter Twp., 30 F. App'x 501 (6th Cir. 2002) (owner proposing to donate land to religious entity for religious use had standing); Moxley v. Town of Walkersville, 601 F. Supp. 2d 648 (D. Md. 2009) (owner losing contract to sell to religious entity has standing).

46. *See, e.g.*, Bethel World Outreach Ministries v. Montgomery Cnty. Council, 706 F.3d 548 (4th Cir. 2013) (applicable to water and sewer regulation); Fortress Bible Church v. Feiner, 694 F.3d 208 (2d Cir. 2012) (applicable to environmental-impact analysis associated with land-development approval); Pass-A-Grille Beach Community Church, Inc. v. City of St. Pete Beach, 515 F. Supp. 3d 1226 (M.D. Fla. 2021) (applicable to city regulation of use of church parking lot); United States v. Cnty. of Culpeper, 245 F. Supp. 3d 758 (W.D. Va. 2017) (applicable to septic "pump and haul" permit for mosque); Summit Church v. Randolph Cnty. Dev. Auth., No. 2:15-CV-82, 2016 WL 865302 (N.D. W.Va. Mar. 2, 2016) (applicable to deed restriction imposed by redevelopment authority). *See* Shelley Ross Saxer, *Assessing RLUIPA's Application to Building Codes and Aesthetic Land Use Regulation*, 2 Alb. Gov't L. Rev. 623 (2009) (arguing for broad application of law).

A plaintiff must exhaust any local land use appeals in order to have a ripe RLUIPA claim. Miles Christi Religious Order v. Twp. of Northville, 629 F.3d 533 (6th Cir. 2010). The plaintiffs owned a residence zoned for single-family use. In addition to housing brothers of the religious order, the residence was used for religious services. Neighbors complained about parking on the front lawn in violation of town ordinances. The town cited the plaintiff and required that a site plan be submitted to show adequate off-street parking. The court held that failure to submit the site plan or request a variance rendered an RLUIPA claim not ripe.

47. 17 F.4th 497 (4th Cir. 2021). Property purchased by the plaintiff for construction of a new church was within the county's urban-growth area but was also in a water-and-sewer classification area designated for future water service. In order to apply for development approvals, the plaintiff had unsuccessfully petitioned for the property to be reclassified as a community-service area. The court noted that federal law governed statutory construction of the term "zoning" in RLUIPA, not state definitions. The court concluded: "In any event, it is not the label that a

Nonregulatory decisions do not come within the purview of potential protection under this statute. Given this fact, a variety of nonregulatory governmental actions that have land use impacts have been held not to be subject to this law, including involuntary annexation,[48] use of eminent domain,[49] and road-closing decisions.[50]

For the most part, only those activities of a religious entity that can be characterized as "exercises of religion" qualify for statutory or constitutional protection. This clearly includes use of land and buildings for worship and the necessary accessory uses[51] for that worship, such as regulations on parking lots and signs.[52] Ancillary and accessory uses that are part of a religious entity's ministry are also generally covered.[53] These uses include church-sponsored monasteries, rectories, schools, day cares,[54] family-life centers,[55] student centers,[56] counseling centers, homeless shelters,[57] soup kitchens, food pantries,[58] and the like. Protection does not extend to land uses and activities that may be owned by a religious entity but are put to nonreligious uses, such as meeting spaces for other groups,[59] investment property leased for commercial purposes, campgrounds,[60] housing for the disabled and elderly,[61] portions of church premises rented for a secular school,[62] or even sometimes church office space.[63]

government puts on its regulation that determines whether RLUIPA applies, but rather how the regulation actually functions. If a regulation divides a community into zones, restricting or limiting how land can be used within each zone, the regulation is a zoning law subject to RLUIPA." *Id.* at 509.

48. Vision Church v. Vill. of Long Grove, 468 F.3d 975, 997–98 (7th Cir. 2006) (RLUIPA is not applicable to involuntary-annexation decision).

49. St. John's United Church of Christ v. City of Chi., 502 F.3d 616 (7th Cir. 2007) (condemnation of cemetery not a land use regulation); Faith Temple Church v. Town of Brighton, 405 F. Supp. 2d 250, 254 (W.D.N.Y. 2005) (use of eminent domain to acquire a site for parkland that was desired by the adjacent church for expansion purposes not subject to RLUIPA).

50. Prater v. City of Burnside, 289 F.3d 417, 434 (6th Cir. 2002) (RLUIPA not applicable to decision on opening or closing a roadway).

51. Accessory uses are generally those that are incidental to and customarily a part of the principal use. Most zoning regulations allow accessory uses to be located with their principal permitted use.

52. Trinity Assembly of God of Balt. City, Inc. v. People's Counsel for Balt. Cnty., 407 Md. 53, 962 A.2d 404 (2008) (regulating size of on-site signs).

53. *See generally*, Sara C. Galvan, Note, *Beyond Worship: The Religious Land Use and Institutionalized Persons Act of 2000 and Religious Institutions' Auxiliary Uses*, 24 YALE L. & POL'Y REV. 207 (2006); Shelley Ross Saxer, *Faith in Action: Religious Accessory Uses and Land Use Regulation*, 2008 UTAH L. REV. 593 (2008).

54. City of Richmond Heights v. Richmond Heights Presbyterian Church, 764 S.W.2d 647 (Mo. 1989). *But see* Ridley Park United Methodist Church v. Zoning Hearing Bd., 920 A.2d 953 (Pa. Commw. Ct. 2007) (refusal to allow church to operate day-care center on site had a *de minimis* impact on religious exercise).

55. Mintz v. Roman Catholic Bishop of Springfield, 424 F. Supp. 2d 309 (D. Mass. 2006) (parish center with social hall, kitchen, and offices).

56. Episcopal Student Found. v. City of Ann Arbor, 341 F. Supp. 2d 691 (E.D. Mich. 2004).

57. Stuart Circle Parish v. Bd. of Zoning Appeals, 946 F. Supp. 1225 (E.D. Va. 1996); Jesus Ctr. v. Farmington Hills Zoning Bd. of Appeals, 215 Mich. App. 54, 544 N.W.2d 698 (1996).

58. Jirtle v. Bd. of Adjustment, 175 N.C. App. 178, 622 S.E.2d 713 (2005).

59. Glenside Ctr., Inc. v. Abington Twp. Zoning Hearing Bd., 973 A.2d 10 (Pa. Commw. Ct. 2009) (use of space for meetings of Alcoholics Anonymous not a use for religious purposes).

60. City of Hope v. Sadsbury Twp. Zoning Hearing Bd., 890 A.2d 1137 (Pa. Commw. Ct. 2006) (campground for use by nondenominational ministry).

61. Greater Bible Way Temple of Jackson v. City of Jackson, 478 Mich. 373, 733 N.W.2d 734 (2007) (apartments across street from church to be used by elderly and disabled).

62. Calvary Christian Ctr. v. City of Fredericksburg, 832 F. Supp. 2d 635 (E.D. Va. 2011). The court reached the same conclusion at the preliminary-injunction phase of this litigation. 800 F. Supp. 2d 760 (E.D. Va. 2011).

63. Cathedral Church of the Intercessor v. Incorporated Vill. of Malverne, 353 F. Supp. 2d 375, 390–91 (E.D.N.Y. 2005) (expansion for administrative-office use by church); N. Pac. Union Conference Ass'n of the Seventh-Day Adventists v. Clark Cnty., 118 Wash. App. 22, 74 P.3d 140 (2003) (denial of permit for church office building in an agricultural district not a substantial burden).

RLUIPA also includes a "safe harbor" provision. A government charged with a RLUIPA violation may avoid the force of the law by changing the policy or practice to remove the substantial burden it imposed.[64]

Defining a "Substantial Burden"

In many respects the critical question in assessing a RLUIPA or First Amendment claim is the threshold inquiry of whether the challenged regulation substantially burdens the free exercise of religion.[65] If the burden imposed is not substantial, there is no potential constitutional or statutory violation.[66] Under RLUIPA, the substantial-burden test is applicable in three situations: where federal funding is being used for a program, where interstate commerce is affected, or when individualized land use determinations are being made.[67]

The initial question is how burdensome a restriction must be in order to be "substantial." Neither the First Amendment nor RLUIPA purport to exempt religious activity from land use regulations. Religious entities are only protected when the burden becomes substantial.[68] Several formulations of a test for defining how substantial the burden must be to trigger some legal protection have been used.

In *Bethel World Outreach Ministries v. Montgomery County Council*, the court held that in the land use context it is a substantial burden if the regulation puts "substantial pressure" on the religious entity to modify its behavior.[69]

In *Midrash Sephardi, Inc. v. Town of Surfside*, the court held that the burden must be more than an "inconvenience" on religious exercise. To be impermissible, the burden must be "akin to significant

---

64. 42 U.S.C. § 2000cc-3(e). *See* Riverside Church v. City of St. Michael, 205 F. Supp. 3d 1014 (D. Minn. 2016); Grace Church of Roaring Fork Valley v. Bd. of Cnty. Comm'rs, 742 F. Supp. 2d 1156 (D. Colo. 2010).

65. For general case law defining the substantial-burden test in a First Amendment context, see *Lyng v. Northwest Indian Cemetery Protective Ass'n*, 485 U.S. 439, 450–51 (1988) (a substantial burden is one that coerces persons into acting contrary to their religious beliefs), and *Thomas v. Review Board of the Indiana Employment Security Division*, 450 U.S. 707, 718 (1981) (a substantial burden is more than an incidental effect that makes religious practice more difficult). *See generally* Ira C. Lupu, *Where Rights Begin: The Problem of Burdens on the Free Exercise of Religion*, 102 HARV. L. REV. 933 (1989).

66. Given the similarity of the tests involved on this issue in First Amendment, RFRA, and RLUIPA cases, there is a fair amount of case law on it. Courts have applied the pre-*Smith* case law defining a *substantial burden* regarding the application of RLUIPA and RFRA. Marria v. Broaddus, 200 F. Supp. 2d 280, 298 (S.D.N.Y. 2002). For a collection of cases applying the substantial-burden test under RFRA, see *Hicks v. Garner*, 69 F.3d 22, 26 n.22 (5th Cir. 1995). There are, however, modest but potentially important differences in the two statutory and the constitutional provisions. RFRA defines "exercise of religion" with reference to the constitutional law while RLUIPA focuses on land uses for religious exercise and expressly does not require that it be compelled by or be central to a system of religious belief. *See* Navajo Nation v. U.S. Forest Serv., 479 F.3d 1024, 1033 (9th Cir. 2007), *aff'd*, 535 F.3d 1058 (9th Cir. 2008).

67. 42 U.S.C. § 2000cc(a)(2). For a discussion of the individualized determination trigger, see *Cambodian Buddhist Society of Connecticut, Inc. v. Planning & Zoning Commission of Newtown*, 285 Conn. 381, 415–20, 941 A.2d 868, 890–93 (2008). RLUIPA also prohibits a land use regulation that "unreasonably limits" religious assemblies, institutions, or structures within a jurisdiction. 42 U.S.C. § 2000cc(b)(3)(B). This limitation is often addressed concurrently with the substantial-burden limitation.

68. "[T]he adjective 'substantial' must be taken seriously lest RLUIPA be interpreted to grant churches a blanket immunity from land-use regulation." World Outreach Conference Ctr. v. City of Chi., 591 F.3d 531, 539 (7th Cir. 2009).

69. 706 F.3d 548, 556 (4th Cir. 2013). The court also noted it is not necessary to show the regulation "targeted" the religious entity. The church sought to build a larger facility and had bought land in a "rural density transfer zone" where churches were a permitted use at the time of purchase. *Id.* at 553.

pressure which directly coerces the religious adherent to conform his or her behavior accordingly" or to "force adherents to forego religious precepts."[70]

In *Civil Liberties for Urban Believers (CLUB) v. City of Chicago*, the court held that to constitute a substantial burden, the restriction must "bear[] direct, primary, and fundamental responsibility for rendering religious exercise—including the use of real property for the purpose thereof within the regulated jurisdiction generally—effectively impracticable."[71] This test was later relaxed to whether the regulation "seriously violates" religious exercise.[72]

In *Guru Nanak Sikh Society of Yuba City v. County of Sutter*, the court held that the regulation must be "oppressive," imposing a significant restriction on religious exercise.[73]

In *Roman Catholic Bishop of Springfield v. City of Springfield*, the court reviewed various tests for a substantial burden and adopted a functional approach that examined relevant factors such as whether the regulation targeted a particular group because of hostility to the religion, whether the regulation was designed to reach a predetermined outcome, or whether it was arbitrarily and capriciously applied.[74]

In *Livingston Christian Schools v. Genoa Charter Township*, the court held that the burden must have "some degree of severity" to be considered substantial and identified these relevant factors in making that determination: (1) whether feasible alternative locations were available; (2) whether there would be substantial delay, uncertainty, or expense imposed; and (3) whether any burden was self-imposed.[75]

By contrast, courts have held that a facially neutral land use regulation adopted for legitimate purposes unrelated to religion is considered an incidental rather than a substantial burden.[76]

---

70. 366 F.3d 1214, 1227 (11th Cir. 2004). *See also* Grace United Methodist Church v. City of Cheyenne, 451 F.3d 643 (10th Cir. 2006) (not a substantial burden if regulation makes it more difficult to exercise religion but has no tendency to coerce action contrary to religious belief); San Jose Christian Coll. v. City of Morgan Hill, 360 F.1024, 1034 (9th Cir. 2004). In *Lakewood, Ohio Congregation of Jehovah's Witnesses, Inc. v. City of Lakewood*, 699 F.2d 303 (6th Cir. 1983), the court applied the following two-step inquiry to determine whether there was a substantial burden: (1) What is the nature of the religious observance at stake (with "fundamental tenets" and "cardinal principles" receiving greater protection)? and (2) What is the nature of the burden (with indirect economic impacts being permissible)?

71. 342 F.3d 752, 761 (7th Cir. 2003). In *Cornerstone Bible Church v. City of Hastings*, 948 F.2d 464 (8th Cir. 1991), the challenged regulation excluded churches as incompatible with the revitalization of a central business district. The court remanded the case for additional findings under a traditional analytic framework of content-neutral time-place-and-manner regulation of speech (e.g., adequacy of studies relative to adverse secondary impacts of church location in the commercial district). *See also* Love Church v. City of Evanston, 896 F.2d 1082 (7th Cir. 1990); Int'l Church of the Foursquare Gospel v. City of Chi. Heights, 955 F. Supp. 878 (N.D. Ill. 1996) (denial of special use permit to locate a church in a vacant commercial building did not constitute a substantial burden because churches were a permitted use in more than 60 percent of the city); Stuart Circle Parish v. Bd. of Zoning Appeals, 946 F. Supp. 1225 (E.D. Va. 1996); *San Jose Christian College*, 360 F.3d at 1033–36.

72. Schlemm v. Wall, 784 F.3d 362, 364-65 (7th Cir. 2015). The "effectively impractical" test was deemed to be too stringent in light of the decisions in *Burwell v. Hobby Lobby Stores, Inc.*, 573 U.S. 682 (2014), and *Holt v. Hobbs*, 574 U.S. 352 (2015). The court in *Immanuel Baptist Church v. City of Chicago*, 473 F. Supp. 3d 813 (N.D. Ill. 2020), found an off-street parking requirement a substantial burden.

73. 456 F.3d 978, 988 (9th Cir. 2006). *See also* Int'l Church of the Foursquare Gospel v. City of San Leandro, 634 F.3d 1037 (9th Cir. 2011) (exclusion of church from industrial district, where there is testimony that no ready alternatives are available, is substantial burden). The city later settled this case with a payment of $2.3 million to the church.

74. 724 F.3d 78, 95–97 (1st Cir. 2013).

75. 858 F.3d 996, 1003–05 (6th Cir. 2017). The court found that an alternate school location twelve miles away meant there was not a substantial burden. The court also noted that evidence of discriminatory intent was appropriately considered in assessing whether the regulation was narrowly tailored but is not a factor in assessing the substantial-burden issue.

76. Lighthouse Inst. for Evangelism, Inc. v. City of Long Branch, 510 F.3d 253, 275–76 (3d Cir. 2007).

No Substantial Burden Found

Routine land use regulations are usually found not to impose a substantial burden on the exercise of religion.[77]

A typical restriction is to limit the location of places of worship in residential areas.[78] The court in *Midrash Sephardi* held that "reasonable 'run of the mill' zoning considerations" (such as locating places of assembly outside of residential areas and addressing the size, congruity with existing nearby uses, and parking availability for a proposed land use) are not a substantial burden.[79] The court in *Grace United Methodist Church v. City of Cheyenne* similarly upheld the city's refusal to grant a variance for the church's proposed 100-child day-care center in a low-density residential neighborhood.[80] In a pre-RLUIPA case, *Lakewood, Ohio Congregation of Jehovah's Witnesses, Inc. v. City of Lakewood*, the court upheld an ordinance that prohibited the construction of churches in most of the city's residential zoning districts. Churches were allowed only in some multifamily residential and business districts, which comprised some 10 percent of the city land area. The court held that there was not a substantial

---

77. *See, e.g.*, Wesleyan Methodist Church of Canisteo v. Vill. of Canisteo, 792 F. Supp. 2d 667 (W.D.N.Y. 2011) (prohibition of expansion of nonconforming church in industrial zoning district not a substantial burden). In *Chabad of Nova, Inc. v. City of Cooper City*, the parties used an analysis of the availability of reasonable alternative avenues for expression similar to that used in adult-business-siting cases. 575 F. Supp. 2d 1280, 1289 (S.D. Fla. 2008).

78. The alleged substantial burden can be on a private religious use as well as a public one. Anselmo v. Cnty. of San Diego, 873 F. Supp. 2d 1247 (E.D. Cal. 2012) (applicable to private chapel proposed for personal use on ranch in an agricultural zoning district).

79. 366 F.3d 1214, 1227 (11th Cir. 2004). In *Thai Meditation Ass'n of Ala. v. City of Mobile*, 980 F.3d 821, 829–33 (11th Cir. 2020), the court remanded a case challenging a zoning regulation that prohibited construction of a meditation and retreat center in a residential district. Among the factors to be considered for the substantial-burden test was whether the regulation "effectively deprives the plaintiffs of any viable means by which to engage in protected religious exercise." *See also* Roman Catholic Archdiocese of Kansas City v. City of Mission Woods, 337 F. Supp. 3d 1122, 1134–41 (D. Kan. 2018) (provision prohibiting use of single-family residence as church meeting house not invalid at summary-judgment stage of proceeding); Hollywood Cmty. Synagogue, Inc. v. City of Hollywood, 430 F. Supp. 2d 1296, 1317–19 (S.D. Fla. 2006) (prohibition on holding services in residentially zoned areas where there are other areas suitably zoned is not a substantial burden under RLUIPA, but showing of substantial burden not required if unequal treatment is established); Corp. of the Presiding Bishop of the Church of Jesus Christ of Latter-Day Saints v. City of W. Linn, 338 Or. 453, 111 P.3d 1123 (2005) (requirement that conditional use permit application be revised to provide larger buffers between proposed meetinghouse and adjacent single-family residential area not a substantial burden under RLUIPA). In *Hollywood Community Synagogue, Inc. v. City of Hollywood*, 436 F. Supp. 2d 1325 (S.D. Fla. 2006), the plaintiff did secure relief on constitutional grounds. *See also* First Vagabonds Church of God v. City of Orlando, 610 F.3d 1274 (11th Cir. 2010) (upholding ordinance regulating large-scale feeding operations in public park under state RLUIPA-like law); Tran v. Gwinn, 262 Va. 572, 580, 554 S.E.2d 63, 67 (2001) (requirement of special use permit for places of worship in a residential conservation zone is only a minimal and incidental burden on free exercise of religion); Open Door Baptist Church v. Clark Cnty., 140 Wash. 2d 143, 995 P.2d 33 (2000) (requiring a church in a rural-estate zoning district to obtain a conditional use permit is a permissible incidental burden on free exercise of religion).

80. 451 F.3d 643 (10th Cir. 2006). The proposed day-care center would have operated eighteen hours per day, seven days per week, and would have been open to the public regardless of religious affiliation. The zoning ordinance limited day-care facilities in this zone to those serving twelve or fewer children. *See also* Redwood Christian Sch. v. Cnty. of Alameda, No. C-01-4282 SC., 2007 WL 781794 (N.D. Cal. Mar. 8, 2007) (denial of conditional use permit for a 650-student school held to not be an unreasonable limitation under RLUIPA where denial based solely on impacts on the land and neighborhood, without consideration of religious orientation of school and other sites, existed within jurisdiction for school siting). A zoning provision that closed a homeless shelter being operated as an accessory use by a church was upheld on the basis that the burden on the church to move the shelter to an appropriate zoning district was less than the burden on the county if it were forced to allow the shelter to operate in violation of the ordinance. First Assembly of God of Naples, Fla., Inc. v. Collier Cnty., 27 F.3d 526 (11th Cir. 1994). For examples of other cases applying a similar balancing analysis, see *Daytona Rescue Mission, Inc. v. City of Daytona Beach*, 885 F. Supp. 1554 (M.D. Fla. 1995) and *Church of Jesus Christ of Latter-Day Saints v. Jefferson County*, 741 F. Supp. 1522 (N.D. Ala. 1990).

burden on religious practices because the ordinance did not prohibit construction but only restricted the particular sites available to the congregation.[81]

A somewhat more difficult analysis arises when a person proposes to conduct religious services or prayer groups in a residence. In *Grosz v. City of Miami Beach*, a leading pre-*Smith* case, the court upheld a zoning-enforcement action taken to prohibit an elderly rabbi from conducting religious services in a converted garage adjacent to his house. The property was in a single-family zoning district. Churches were prohibited in that district but allowed as permitted uses in all other zoning districts. The court found that the interest in protecting residential neighborhoods from the impacts of institutional uses was important and that the burden on the petitioner to move his religious services to an appropriate zoning district was not substantial, since half the city (including an area only four blocks away from the plaintiff's house) freely allowed religious institutions.[82] By contrast, the court in *LeBlanc-Sternberg v. Fletcher* invalidated a zoning regulation that prohibited rabbis from conducting services in their home after a jury had found the regulation was adopted with an intent and purpose of religious discrimination.[83]

In other instances, the land use regulations limit noncommercial uses, including religious uses, in commercial or industrial areas in order to promote economic development. The court in *CLUB* held that Chicago's land use restrictions for places of worship did not violate RLUIPA or the Constitution. The challenged zoning ordinance allowed places of worship by right in all residential districts (which included the majority of land available for development) but required a special use permit in commercial districts and a rezoning in manufacturing districts.[84] The court in *San Jose Christian College v. City of Morgan Hill* held that restriction of places of worship to particular zoning districts and refusals to rezone property for religious uses did not impose an impermissible substantial burden on religious exercise.[85] In *Petra Presbyterian Church v. Village of Northbrook*, the court upheld a prohibition that kept churches and secular membership organizations from locating in an industrial zoning district.[86] The court in *New Harvest Christian Fellowship v. City of Salinas* addressed a regulation designed to promote commercial

---

81. 699 F.2d 303 (6th Cir. 1983). The court applied a two-step inquiry to determine whether there was a substantial burden: (1) What is the nature of the religious observance at stake (with "fundamental tenets" and "cardinal principles" receiving greater protection)? And (2) What is the nature of the burden (with indirect economic impacts being permissible)? *See also* Johnson v. Caudill, 475 F.3d 645 (4th Cir. 2007) (noting wide range of other zoning districts within which church could operate day-care facility).

82. 721 F.2d 729 (11th Cir. 1983). *See also* Christian Gospel Church, Inc. v. City & Cnty. of S.F., 896 F.2d 1221 (9th Cir. 1990); Messiah Baptist Church v. Cnty. of Jefferson, 859 F.2d 820 (10th Cir. 1988) (upholding denial of approval to build a church in an agricultural zone).

83. 67 F.3d 412 (2d Cir. 1995). The record showed that large numbers of Hasidic Jews had moved to the area in part because the township rules in the unincorporated area allowed religious services in homes. The village (Airmont) incorporated and adopted more restrictive zoning to prohibit "home synagogues" partially in reaction to this influx. Also see *Murphy v. Zoning Commission*, 402 F.3d 342 (2d Cir. 2005), discussed below at note 121.

84. *See also* Berry v. Jefferson Parish, 326 F. App'x 748 (5th Cir. 2009) (dismissing claim by owners who wished to sell the land to "Christian-affiliated developer"); DiLaura v. Ann Arbor Charter Twp., 30 F. App'x 501 (6th Cir. 2002) (owner proposing to donate land to religious entity for religious use had standing); Moxley v. Town of Walkersville, 601 F. Supp. 2d 648 (D. Md. 2009) (owner losing contract to sell to religious entity has standing).

85. 360 F.3d 1024, 1033–36 (9th Cir. 2004) (denial of rezoning for religious-education use not a substantial burden where alternative sites within city were available). *But cf.* Int'l Church of the Foursquare Gospel v. City of San Leandro, 634 F.3d 1037 (9th Cir. 2011) (exclusion of places of worship from industrial zones creates triable issue of fact regarding substantial burden).

86. 489 F.3d 846 (7th Cir. 2007). The court noted that "[w]hen there is plenty of land on which religious organizations can build churches (or, as is common nowadays, convert to churches buildings previously intended for some other use) in a community, the fact that they are not permitted to build everywhere does not create a substantial burden." *Id.* at 851. The court held that to establish a substantial burden, the religious entity would have to establish that exclusion from the industrial zone left such a paucity of other potential sites that a substantial burden was created. *See also* Truth Found. Ministries, NFP v. Village of Romeoville, 387 F. Supp. 3d 896 (N.D. Ill. 2016) (upholding exclusion of churches from manufacturing and industrial zoning districts).

development in a three-block downtown area.[87] The zoning restriction prohibited clubs, lodges, places of religious assembly, and similar assembly uses from operating on the ground floor of buildings facing Main Street. The court held that this was not a substantial burden for three reasons. First, the regulation did not prohibit religious use of the building since the first floor could have been reconfigured to place the assembly area away from the street front or the second floor could have been used for assemblies.[88] Second, there were many other sites in the city available and the city had a demonstrated record of approving applications for similar religious uses elsewhere. Third, the plaintiff purchased the building with knowledge of the restrictions on assembly use of the first-floor street front.

Other nondiscriminatory land use regulations on religious uses are typically upheld. Examples include the following routine land use restrictions: limitations on the size and height of buildings used for religious uses;[89] compliance with building codes and building permits[90] and building safety codes;[91] limits on the height and size of signs;[92] limits on outdoor lighting;[93] a requirement confining religiously sponsored multifamily housing to a zoning district that allows multifamily housing;[94] a requirement that all nonagricultural, nonresidential uses in a rural-agricultural district be separated from existing agricultural and residential uses by at least 1000 feet;[95] routine historic-preservation standards, especially where the regulations do not totally frustrate religious exercise;[96] a requirement that places of worship

---

87. 29 F.4th 596 (9th Cir. 2022). While not finding a substantial burden, the court did find an equal treatment violation, discussed below at note 140.

88. The court also noted that the city offered several alternative approaches to accommodate the religious use, all of which were rejected by the plaintiff. This stark contrast to the situation of a religious use facing multiple denials and noncooperation from the city was a factor in finding the lack of a substantial burden.

89. *See, e.g.,* Living Water Church of God v. Charter Twp. of Meridian, 258 F. App'x 729 (6th Cir. 2007) (25,000-square-foot limit on buildings in residential district not a substantial burden as applied to special use permit for school adjacent to church); Vision Church v. Vill. of Long Grove, 468 F.3d 975, 999–1000 (7th Cir. 2006) (55,000-square-foot size limit on church not a substantial burden); Cathedral Church of the Intercessor v. Incorporated Vill. of Malverne, 353 F. Supp. 2d 375, 390 (E.D.N.Y. 2005) (limits on size of expansion and off-street parking requirements not a substantial burden); Korean Buddhist Dae Won Sa Temple of Haw. v. Sullivan, 87 Haw. 217, 953 P.2d 1315 (1998) (height limit on temple not a substantial burden). *See also Love Church,* 896 F.2d at 1086.

90. *See, e.g.,* St. Paul's Foundation v. Ives, 29 F.4th 32 (1st Cir. 2022) (compliance with approved building plans for building permit not a substantial burden).

91. *See, e.g.,* Temple of 1001 Buddhahs v. City of Freemont, 562 F. Supp. 3d 408 (N.D. Cal. 2021) (compliance with fire safety, earthquake, electrical, waste-disposal, and structural-integrity codes not a substantial burden).

92. Trinity Assembly of God of Balt. City, Inc. v. People's Counsel for Balt. Cnty., 407 Md. 53, 96–97, 962 A.2d 404, 429–31 (2008) (upholding sign size limit of twenty-five square feet and six-foot height as applied to proposed church sign of 250 square feet and twenty-five-foot height with changeable copy). In *Osborne v. Power,* 318 Ark. 858, 890 S.W.2d 570 (1994), the court held that a large light-and-sound Christmas display at a residence could be enjoined as a nuisance. In *Signs for Jesus v. Town of Pembroke,* 977 F.3d 93 (1st Cir. 2020), the court held that a regulation prohibiting electronic changing signs in the zoning district in which the church was located was not a substantial burden. In *Cities4Life, Inc. v. City of Charlotte,* 2019 WL 4127295 (No. 3:17-cv-670-KDB-DSC, July 26, 2019), *report and recommendation adopted,* 2019 WL 4121998 (W.D.N.C, Aug. 29, 2019), the court held that the city's preexisting ban on portable signs did not impose a substantial burden on the religious-exercise rights of those protesting at a women's health clinic.

93. Marianist Province of U.S. v. City of Kirkwood, 944 F.3d 996 (8th Cir. 2019) (not substantial burden to comply with city regulations on outdoor lighting and noise, applied to denial of lighting for baseball field at all-boys religious school); Edgewater High School of the Sacred Heart v. City of Madison, 601 F. Supp. 2d 413 (W.D. Wis. 2022) (not substantial burden to deny adding lighting and sound system for athletic field).

94. Greater Bible Way Temple of Jackson v. City of Jackson, 478 Mich. 373, 733 N.W.2d 734 (2007) (construction of apartment complex not religious exercise, but even if it were, requirement to build in appropriate zoning district is not a substantial burden).

95. Primera Iglesia Bautista Hispana of Boca Raton, Inc. v. Broward Cnty., 450 F.3d 1295 (11th Cir. 2006).

96. World Outreach Conference Ctr. v. City of Chi., 591 F.3d 531, 538–39 (7th Cir. 2009) (holding that refusal to allow demolition of landmarked building in order to build a church family-life center is not a substantial burden when church has sufficient vacant land on site to construct the center). Also see the discussion on applying

be harmonious with the general character of a rural area in order to secure a special use permit;[97] and a limit on providing medical services (pregnancy tests and ultrasounds) at a pregnancy resource center where prayer meetings, counseling, and Bible studies could be conducted.[98]

The costs and procedural difficulties inherent in securing special use permits and other regulatory approvals have been held not to impose a substantial burden.[99] In *CLUB*, the court noted that the additional costs of securing special use permits or rezonings did not make locating places of worship in the city impractical, and thus there was not a substantial burden on religious exercise under the act.[100] However, imposition of a requirement to obtain permits that are not in fact required, especially when imposed on a small religious organization with limited resources, can be a substantial burden.[101]

Substantial Burden Found

Several cases have found land use regulations to impose a substantial burden or to be an unreasonable limitation on free exercise.

In *Jesus Christ Is the Answer Ministries, Inc. v. Baltimore County*,[102] the court held that the zoning setback and parking requirements related to conversion of a prior residence to a church substantially

---

historic-preservation standards in *St. Bartholomew's Church*, 914 F.2d 348, 354–57 (2d Cir. 1990). Whether the religious entity reasonably believed the use to be permitted as opposed to requiring a special use permit can be a factor in whether a substantial burden was created. Liberty Temple Full Gospel Church, Inc. v. Vill. of Bolingbrook, 868 F. Supp. 2d 765 (N.D. Ill. 2012).

97. Cambodian Buddhist Soc'y of Conn., Inc. v. Planning & Zoning Comm'n of Newtown, 285 Conn. 381, 941 A.2d 868 (2008). *See also* Alive Church of the Nazarene, Inc. v. Prince William Cnty., 59 F.4th 92, 106–07 (4th Cir. 2023) (requirement to obtain special use permit or farm winery ABC permit not a substantial burden when property was acquired with knowledge of those requirements).

98. A Hand of Hope Pregnancy Resource Center v. City of Raleigh, 386 F. Supp. 3d 618 (E.D.N.C. 2019). In rejecting the substantial-burden claim, the court noted that the overwhelming majority of the Center's religious exercise was allowed at the site and that the medical tests could be performed at the Center's other appropriately zoned facility. Such an inconvenience was held not to amount to a substantial burden.

99. Vision Church v. Vill. of Long Grove, 468 F.3d 975, 990–91 (7th Cir. 2006) (requirement that church secure a special use permit does not in itself unreasonably limit religious assembly); Konikov v. Orange Cnty., 410 F.3d 1317, 1323–24 (11th Cir. 2005) (requirement to obtain a special use permit before operating a "religious organization" in a residential zoning district is not a substantial burden); Christian Assembly Rios de Agua Viva v. City of Burbank, 237 F. Supp. 3d 781 (N.D. Ill. 2017) (delay, uncertainty, and expense associated with requirement to obtain special use permit not a substantial burden, but regulation violated RLUIPA equal-terms requirement). Sisters of St. Francis Health Servs., Inc. v. Morgan Cnty., 397 F. Supp. 2d 1032, 1050–51 (S.D. Ind. 2005) (requirement that proposed hospital expansion submit permit applications not a substantial burden under RLUIPA); Hale O Kaula Church v. Maui Planning Comm'n, 229 F. Supp. 2d 1056 (D. Haw. 2002) (requiring religious uses to obtain a special use permit is not a facial violation of RLUIPA); Cnty. of L.A. v. Sahag-Mesrob Armenian Christian Sch., 188 Cal. App. 4th 851, 116 Cal. Rptr. 3d 61 (2010) (requirement to secure conditional use permit prior to opening 800-student school not a substantial burden); Ridley Park United Methodist Church v. Zoning Hearing Bd., 920 A.2d 953 (Pa. Commw. Ct. 2007) (refusal to allow church to operate day-care center on site had a *de minimis* impact on religious exercise); Tran v. Gwinn, 262 Va. 572, 554 S.E.2d 63 (2001) (upholding ordinance requiring special use permit for places of worship in residential zoning district). *See also* Guatay Christian Fellowship v. Cnty. of San Diego, 670 F.3d 957 (9th Cir. 2011) (RLUIPA claim not ripe if no application made for required use permit).

100. Civil Liberties for Urban Believers v. City of Chi., 342 F.3d 752, 761–62 (7th Cir. 2003).

101. *World Outreach Conference Center*, 591 F.3d at 537–38. The court noted that the resources of the religious institution must be considered because "burden is relative to the weakness of the burdened." *Id.* at 538. In this case the religious institution was seeking to continue use of a former YMCA building and rent its rooms to victims of Hurricane Katrina, while the city alderman for that site had sought to have the building used for commercial purposes by a developer who was one of his substantial financial backers.

102. 915 F.3d 256 (4th Cir. 2019). A church was a permitted use in the zoning district, but it was subject to specified dimensional requirements. The court noted it was significant that the applicant submitted a revised site plan

burdened religious exercise. The organization acquired the property with a reasonable expectation that it could be used for a church but was prevented from doing so by the application of the regulation. In this instance, the court found the proposed use would serve an unmet religious need, the restriction was absolute rather than conditional, and as a result the organization would need to acquire a different property.

A substantial burden has also been found when the religious use is a permitted use under zoning, but denial of a waste-disposal permit has precluded construction.[103]

One of the more common instances of an impermissible substantial burden being found occurs when there have been multiple denials of land use approvals for a particular applicant or the grounds for denial seem arbitrary. In cases finding a substantial burden, it is notable that often the applicant made efforts to comply with land use regulations and concerns but suffered multiple rebuffs. In several instances the professional planning staff and planning board recommended approval but elected officials denied the application. The applicants often agreed to mitigation conditions. By contrast, challenges under RLUIPA are much less likely to be successful where there is evidence that the local government attempted to work with the applicant, and it is the applicant who initiates litigation prior to exhausting reasonable efforts to secure approval.[104]

In *Sts. Constantine & Helen Greek Orthodox Church, Inc. v. City of New Berlin*, the court found that the city's refusal to rezone (based in large part on a concern that other institutional uses might locate on the site if the church's plans for construction were unsuccessful) posed a substantial burden under RLUIPA. The church had submitted multiple applications and modified its proposal to address municipal concerns, yet the court found the city had engaged in deliberate and unjustified delay.[105]

---

to address concerns raised about the setbacks and parking in the denial of its initial site plan. The county, however, dismissed the second plan on res judicata grounds even though it was substantially different from the first plan.

103. United States v. Cnty. of Culpeper, 245 F. Supp. 3d 758 (W.D. Va. 2017) (denial of septic "pump and haul" permit for mosque).

104. *Westgate Tabernacle, Inc. v. Palm Beach County*, 14 So. 3d 1027 (Fla. Dist. Ct. App. 2009), illustrates the point. This case involved continued operation of a homeless shelter in a zoning district that required a conditional use permit for such a use. The shelter opened without seeking the required permit. After a notice of violation, a permit application was submitted but then withdrawn, even though the county had offered assistance in seeking the permit. The court held that the requirement to apply for a special exception was not a substantial burden (nor was the requirement to find a location in an appropriately zoned area or to secure the proper permits).

105. 396 F.3d 895 (7th Cir. 2005). The court noted that this was an as-applied challenge as opposed to the facial challenge in the earlier *CLUB* case. It did not help the city's case that a Protestant church was already located on one adjoining tract and another had been approved for the other side of the site. *See also* Rocky Mountain Christian Church v. Bd. of County Comm'rs, 613 F.3d 1229 (10th Cir. 2010) (denial of most aspects of special use permit application for expansion of church complex in rural area).

A substantial burden has been found to exist in several federal-district court cases. *See* Reaching Hearts Int'l, Inc. v. Prince George's Cnty., 584 F. Supp. 2d 766 (D. Md. 2008) (county's actions, including denial of land-classification change in water and sewer plan, increase in impervious-surface limits, and denial of subdivision, improperly precluded church construction on vacant parcel); Chabad of Nova, Inc. v. City of Cooper City, 575 F. Supp. 2d 1280 (S.D. Fla. 2008) (invalidating exclusion of religious assemblies from suburban business district); Mintz v. Roman Catholic Bishop of Springfield, 424 F. Supp. 2d 309 (D. Mass. 2006) (denial of permit to construct parish center with social hall, kitchen, and offices adjacent to existing church and rectory due to lot-coverage limits improper); Elsinore Christian Ctr. v. City of Lake Elsinore, 291 F. Supp. 2d 1083, 1088–96 (C.D. Cal. 2003) (denial of a conditional use permit for relocation of a church in a downtown district unlawful); Cottonwood Christian Ctr. v. Cypress Redevelopment Agency, 218 F. Supp. 2d 1203 (C.D. Cal. 2002) (enjoining city action to acquire vacant parcel for commercial redevelopment after denial of conditional use permit for a 4700-seat church facility on the site); Alpine Christian Fellowship v. Cnty. Comm'rs, 870 F. Supp. 991 (D. Colo. 1994) (restricting establishment of a religious school within an existing permitted church building due to traffic concerns and neighborhood compatibility not compelling grounds for denial). *See also* Bikur Cholim, Inc. v. Vill. of Suffern, 664 F. Supp. 2d 267 (S.D.N.Y. 2009) (motion to dismiss denied, as denial of variance could be a substantial burden for communal home that provides

Likewise, in *Guru Nanak*, the court held that the denial of the initial application for a conditional use permit for a temple on a small tract within the city and denial of a second conditional use permit application for a rural site zoned for agricultural use constituted a substantial burden without compelling governmental interests.[106] The court concluded that the history of denials, coupled with the city's broad and inconsistent reasons for denial, showed that the county was likely to deny approval for almost any location, thus constituting a substantial burden.

A third example is *Westchester Day School v. Village of Mamaroneck.* This protracted dispute resulted from the denial of a permit for a new classroom and renovations of an existing building at a religious day school. The court noted that the local government's decision-making was conducted with "an arbitrary blindness to the facts." Considering that the district court had found grounds for the denial to be arbitrary and capricious under state land use law, that the school had no financially viable alternatives, and that their application was denied outright rather than approved with conditions, the appeals court determined the denial to be a substantial burden.[107]

Also, applications with a high degree of discretion, as is the case with a petition for a rezoning, have a greater potential for masking religious discrimination than do special use permits with clearly bounded discretion and the requirement for evidence and findings to support the decision.[108] In these situations it is incumbent upon the jurisdiction denying approval to clearly establish a legitimate, nondiscriminatory land use basis for its decision.

---

temporary housing near hospital for Jews whose beliefs prohibit travel on the Sabbath, which is a question for the jury); Shepherd Montessori Ctr. Milan v. Ann Arbor Charter Twp., 259 Mich. App. 315, 675 N.W.2d 271 (2003) (remanding appeal of denial of special use permit for religious elementary school for findings).

In *Westchester Day School v. Village of Mamaroneck*, 386 F.3d 183 (2d Cir. 2004), the court noted that a denial of some aspects of a project is not equivalent to a total denial of the use and that the protection afforded by RLUIPA to the religious aspects of a use do not extend to the secular portions of the use.

106. 456 F.3d 978 (9th Cir. 2006). Applying this standard, the court in *Grace Church of North County v. City of San Diego*, 555 F. Supp. 2d 1126 (S.D. Cal. 2008), held that a conditional use permit for a religious use in an industrial park that was issued for a five-year term rather than the requested ten-year term (and with no reasonable expectation that an extension would be granted) constituted a substantial burden. The court noted that considerable hostility was expressed in the permitting process toward any religious use of this industrial area. In *Harbor Missionary Church Corp. v. City of San Buenaventura*, 642 Fed. App'x. 726 (9th Cir. 2016), the court held that requiring a special use permit and then refusing to permit continuation of a church's homeless-outreach mission at its current location would be a substantial burden. *See also* Riverside Church v. City of St. Michael, 260 F. Supp. 3d 1122 (D. Minn. 2017) (holding zoning restriction prohibiting church use of a movie theater in a commercial district violated the First Amendment because it was not narrowly tailored).

107. 504 F.3d 338, 351–52 (2d Cir. 2007). The litigation proved costly for the village. In addition to over $900,000 in its own legal fees, a newly elected village council settled this litigation with an agreement to issue the regulatory approvals and payment of $4.75 million in damages and legal fees for the plaintiff. In *Fortress Bible Church v. Feiner*, 734 F. Supp. 2d 409 (S.D.N.Y. 2010), the court held that a denial of permission to construct a church was a substantial burden where the denial was motivated by bad faith—here a reaction to the church's failure to make a significant donation to the town—and an improper purpose. The court characterized the town's concerns about legitimate land use issues—traffic, parking, and safety—as unsupported if not wholly fabricated. On appeal, the court of appeals found no rational basis for the town's denial. 694 F.3d 208 (2d Cir. 2012).

108. For a discussion of these factors, see *Timberline Baptist Church v. Washington County*, 211 Or. App. 437, 154 P.3d 759 (2007) (finding denial of special use permit for parochial school proposed to be adjacent to permitted church and day care but outside urban-growth boundary did not impose substantial burden under RLUIPA).

Defining a Compelling State Interest

Most land use regulations of religious uses have a legitimate secular basis[109] and are routinely upheld as such. Examples include concerns about traffic and parking impacts, property-value impacts, land use compatibility,[110] adequacy of utilities, revitalization of commercial areas,[111] health and safety concerns,[112] or preservation of historic and aesthetic attributes of a community.[113] Documentation of the secular rationale for the regulation can be in the form of staff analysis or planning studies, consideration of studies conducted in other communities, or comments received during the public participation and hearings leading to adoption of the regulation. This information should be developed and considered during the process of adoption of the regulation, not prepared as a rationalization after the fact.

If the regulation is found to impose a substantial burden, a more exacting compelling interest must be established under a strict-scrutiny analysis. RLUIPA requires that a substantial burden be justified only by a compelling governmental interest and the use of the least restrictive means of addressing that interest.[114] The government must also show that pursuit of the compelling interest was the actual reason for taking the challenged action.[115]

As for a compelling interest, regulations of religiously based conduct that have been upheld have generally addressed actions that "invariably posed some substantial threat to public safety, peace or order."[116] For example, a prohibition of religiously motivated but dangerous activity, such as handling poisonous snakes, has long been allowed.[117] In the context of land use regulation, building regulations on fire safety and similar concerns are compelling interests.[118]

More routine land use concerns such as traffic congestion (as opposed to traffic safety) and neighborhood or plan compatibility rarely rise to the level of a compelling governmental interest.[119]

---

109. In *First Assembly of God v. City of Alexandria*, 739 F.2d 942 (4th Cir. 1984), the court upheld conditions in a special use permit that limited enrollment in a church day school to preschool through ninth grade, required erection of a fence, and required a landscaped buffer between the school and the surrounding neighborhood, finding that these restrictions had a strictly secular purpose.

110. *See, e.g.*, Christian Gospel Church, Inc. v. City & Cnty. of S.F., 896 F.2d 1221 (9th Cir. 1990) (upholding denial of a conditional use permit for a church in a residential zoning district); Messiah Baptist Church v. Cnty. of Jefferson, 859 F.2d 820 (10th Cir. 1988) (upholding prohibition of substantial church complex in a rural area). In *Andon, LLC v. City of Newport News*, 813 F.3d 510 (4th Cir. 2016), the court did not find a substantial burden where the religious user entered a lease for an office building to relocate, but the lease was contingent on obtaining city approval, and that approval was denied based on failure to meet a setback requirement.

111. *See, e.g.*, Int'l Church of the Foursquare Gospel v. City of Chi. Heights, 955 F. Supp. 878 (N.D. Ill. 1996) (upholding the denial of a permit to locate a church in a vacant department store based on the city's need to preserve the area for commercial revitalization).

112. *See, e.g.*, Congregation Beth Yitzchok of Rockland, Inc. v. Town of Ramapo, 593 F. Supp. 655 (S.D.N.Y. 1984) (upholding a Ramapo, N.Y., requirement for zoning compliance as applied to a religious nursery school being operated by a synagogue). The court applied a balancing test and concluded that public fire-safety regulations justified even a substantial burden on religious practices. Allegations that restriction is necessary to support a compelling interest must be factually supported. *See, e.g.*, Reaching Hearts Int'l, Inc. v. Prince George's Cnty., 584 F. Supp. 2d 766, 788 (D. Md. 2008) (no evidence in record to factually support assertion that land use restriction needed to protect adjacent water-supply reservoir).

113. *See, e.g.*, Rector of St. Bartholomew's Church v. City of N.Y., 914 F.2d 348 (2d Cir. 1990).

114. 42 U.S.C. § 2000cc(a).

115. Shaw v. Hunt, 517 U.S. 899, 908 (1996) (holding congressional redistricting plan not narrowly drawn).

116. Sherbert v. Verner, 374 U.S. 398, 403 (1963).

117. *See, e.g.*, State v. Massey, 229 N.C. 734, 51 S.E.2d 179, *appeal dismissed*, 336 U.S. 942 (1949).

118. *See, e.g.*, Peace Lutheran Church & Acad. v. Vill. of Sussex, 2001 WI App 139, 631 N.W.2d 229 (upholding requirement for a fire-sprinkler system in a church building challenged under state constitutional provision on free exercise).

119. *See, e.g.*, Int'l Church of the Foursquare Gospel v. City of San Leandro, 634 F.3d 1037 (9th Cir. 2011) (expressing doubt that preservation of land for industrial development is a compelling interest); Westchester Day Sch. v.

Narrowly Tailored and Least Restrictive Means

When a land use regulation substantially burdens exercise of religion, it must be narrowly tailored to address a compelling government interest and the least restrictive means to address that governmental interest must be used.

The court in *Murphy v. Zoning Commission*[120] held an order limiting attendance at prayer meetings in a residence to be unlawful. The town had issued a cease-and-desist order under its zoning ordinance to prohibit attendance by more than twenty-five persons who were not family members at regularly scheduled prayer meetings in a residence. The trial court held that the order violated both RLUIPA and the Free Exercise Clause. The lower court also noted that the restriction could have been more narrowly tailored to specifically address parking and traffic concerns. However, the court of appeals subsequently held that the case was not ripe, as the homeowners had not sought a variance, which would have stayed all enforcement actions until a decision was made on the variance petition.[121]

In *Pass-A-Grille Beach Community Church, Inc. v. City of St. Pete Beach*,[122] the city cited the church for violation of its parking regulations. The church, which was located across the street from a popular beach area, opened its parking lot to the public for free, contending that this was not a lot subject to city regulations for commercial parking lots (though the church often sought donations and contributions from the people who parked there). The city attempted to require that only patrons of the church could use the lot for "legitimate church purposes" as determined by the city. The court held that this was not an "incidental" burden or mere "inconvenience" in light of the church's sincere belief of using the parking as a means of outreach and hospitality.

Particular attention should be given to the question of whether regulation leaves available reasonable alternative avenues for religious expression. For example, a zoning-regulation ordinance that prohibits all places of worship throughout the entire jurisdiction would almost certainly be invalid. On the other hand, a more carefully crafted zoning restriction (for example, one that restricted places of worship seating more than 200 persons to particular zoning districts or to sites fronting adequate roads) would likely be acceptable.

Another consideration is whether the contested decision is the appropriate or only time available for the local government to address the asserted governmental interest. In *Redeemed Christian Church of God (Victory Temple) Bowie v. Prince George's County*, the court held that while consideration of traffic safety may be a compelling interest, under the county's regulatory scheme it was more appropriately addressed at the later subdivision-approval stage of development review rather than in a decision on the property's water and sewer classification.[123] Allowing the project to proceed to a later stage of review was deemed to be a less restrictive means of addressing the asserted interest.

Vill. of Mamaroneck, 504 F.3d 338, 353 (2d Cir. 2007) (denial based on "undue deference to the opposition of a small group of neighbors" is not a compelling interest); Mintz v. Roman Catholic Bishop of Springfield, 424 F. Supp. 2d 309, 323–24 (D. Mass. 2006) (setback and lot-coverage limits not a compelling interest). In *Grace Church of North County v. City of San Diego*, 555 F. Supp. 2d 1126 (S.D. Cal. 2008), the court held that preservation of land within an industrial park for industrial uses could not be considered a compelling interest when the regulation allowed religious uses with a conditional use permit, allowed office uses, and granted a conditional use permit for five years rather than the requested ten-year permit. In *Redeemed Christian Church of God (Victory Temple) Bowie v. Prince George's County*, 17 F.4th 497 (4th Cir. 2021), the court assumed, without deciding, that traffic concerns could be a compelling interest.

120. 289 F. Supp. 2d 87 (D. Conn. 2003).
121. Murphy v. New Milford Zoning Comm'n, 402 F.3d 342 (2d Cir. 2005).
122. 515 F. Supp. 3d 1226 (M.D. Fla. 2021).
123. 17 F.4th 497, 511–12 (4th Cir. 2021).

Nondiscrimination and Treating Religious Land Uses on Equal Terms

Land use regulations affecting religious uses must not discriminate because of the religion involved and must be equally applied to secular land uses with similar land use impacts. For example, a zoning restriction that prohibits a religiously sponsored soup kitchen while permitting an adjacent commercial restaurant would raise serious questions about whether there was in fact a legitimate secular purpose for the restriction.[124] A discriminatory regulation would also raise due-process[125] and equal-protection[126] objections. That similar secular uses are not being similarly regulated would certainly undercut an argument that there is a compelling need for the regulation.

A local government must avoid disproportionate impacts among different religions.[127] If one religion is singled out for favorable treatment, the regulation may well violate the Establishment Clause. But if the regulation is tailored to prevent a particular religious practice, such as Santería animal slaughter in the *Lukumi Babalu Aye* case, the regulation violates the Free Exercise Clause. It is critical therefore that a land use regulation be applied uniformly across the board to all religious uses with similar impacts. Toward this end it is advisable to use objective land use standards where possible, thereby avoiding discretionary standards that heighten the risk of discriminatory application to those religious uses not favored by a particular community.

A case illustrating this principle, *Islamic Center of Mississippi, Inc. v. City of Starkville*,[128] invalidated the denial of approval to use an existing house in a residential zone for a mosque. Considerable circumstantial evidence of religious discrimination was at play in this case, as the city had routinely approved all similar requests made by Christian entities. Yet the city council denied the approval for the Islamic center on the basis of a neighbor's complaint about congestion, parking, and traffic problems. The court applied a *Sherbert*-like analysis, concluding that this application of the zoning ordinance substantially burdened religious practices by allowing no sites for worship within walking distance of a local campus and that it was not narrowly drawn in support of a substantial governmental interest. Similarly, in *Islamic Society of Basking Ridge v. Township of Bernards*,[129] the court held that application of a more demanding off-street parking requirement for a mosque than was applicable to a Christian church was impermissible discrimination under RLUIPA.

---

124. In addition to the equal-terms provision, the RLUIPA also expressly prohibits discrimination on the basis of religion or religious denomination. This provision is rarely litigated as it requires intentional or purposeful discrimination. Alive Church of the Nazarene, Inc. v. Prince William Cnty., 59 F.4th 92, 104–06 (4th Cir. 2023). *See also* Chabad Lubavitch of Litchfield Cnty., Inc. v. Litchfield Historic Dist. Comm'n, 768 F.3d 183, 198 (2d Cir. 2014).

125. *See, e.g.*, Catholic Bishop of Chi. v. Kingery, 371 Ill. 257, 20 N.E.2d 583 (1939) (prohibition of parochial school in zoning district that allows public schools is capricious and invalid).

126. Congregation Rabbinical College of Tartikov, Inc. v. Village of Pomona, 945 F.3d 83 (2d Cir. 2019); Reaching Hearts Int'l, Inc. v. Prince George's Cnty., 584 F. Supp. 2d 766, 781–84 (D. Md. 2008) (actions to prevent church use of rural land while allowing others to use land in this way, when accompanied by statements indicating intentional religious discrimination, violate Equal Protection Clause); Open Homes Fellowship, Inc. v. Orange Cnty., 325 F. Supp. 2d 1349 (M.D. Fla. 2004) (denial of permit for group home housing faith-based substance-abuse program, while allowing other group homes by right in same zoning district, has no rational basis and violates both due process and equal protection); Vineyard Christian Fellowship v. City of Evanston, 250 F. Supp. 2d 961, 975–79 (N.D. Ill. 2003) (ordinance prohibiting religious institutions from conducting services in zoning district while allowing cultural and membership organizations violates Equal Protection Clause).

127. Facial neutrality of the ordinance is inadequate. Consideration must also be given to the neutrality of the ordinance as applied. *Lukumi Babalu Aye*, 508 U.S. 520, 534.

128. 840 F.2d 293 (5th Cir. 1988). See also *Church of Jesus Christ of Latter-Day Saints v. Jefferson County*, 741 F. Supp. 1522 (N.D. Ala. 1990), where the court held that a refusal to rezone to allow construction of a church on an eleven-acre tract in a low-density residential area of the county impermissibly burdened free expression of religion.

129. 226 F. Supp. 3d 320 (D.N.J. 2016).

The religious beliefs of a person or a group are beyond the scope of governmental regulation. A land use regulation aimed at religious activities alone, at a particular religion, or even at a particular religious land use would violate both the Constitution and RLUIPA. It is impermissible for a regulation to be targeted at minority or unpopular religious uses while exempting mainstream religious uses with similar land use impacts.[130] Regulating a particular land use activity out of disdain for the religious beliefs underlying that conduct or based on the type of people practicing those beliefs is impermissible.

RLUIPA requires that land use regulations not be imposed "in a manner that treats a religious assembly or institution on less than equal terms with a nonreligious assembly or institution."[131] This section of RLUIPA does not include the qualifications included in the law's general rule. It does not reference a substantial burden, a similarly situated secular use, or a compelling governmental interest. Courts have therefore held that no showing of a substantial burden is required if there is a violation of the equal-terms provision. In *Lighthouse Institute for Evangelism, Inc. v. City of Long Branch*,[132] the court noted that the statute includes the substantial-burden test in one section but not in this section, indicating an intent not to require such a showing. (And the court noted that free-exercise jurisprudence does not require such a showing where religious discrimination is involved.) The court, however, did not read this section to create strict liability for any disparate treatment, as only differential treatment of a similarly situated use constitutes treatment on less than the requisite equal terms. The equal-terms provision only applies to religious entities. It does not extend to use of property by a nonreligious entity for purposes such as weddings.[133]

Several tests have emerged for determining whether the contested regulation violates RLUIPA's equal-terms provision.

The *Lighthouse Institute* court held that the critical inquiry is whether there is differential treatment of an analogous secular use[134] that has a similar impact on the aims of the regulation.[135] With this

---

130. "[T]he First Amendment forbids an official purpose to disapprove of a particular religion or of religion in general." Church of the Lukumi Babalu Aye, Inc. v. City of Hialeah, 508 U.S. 520, 532 (1993) (citations omitted). Several cases illustrate the prejudicial impacts of religious animus expressed during consideration of an application leading to a finding of a constitutional or statutory violation. *See, e.g.*, Congregation Rabbinical College of Tartikov, Inc. v. Village of Pomona, 945 F.3d 83 (2d Cir. 2019); Jesus Christ Is the Answer Ministries, Inc. v. Baltimore Cnty., 915 F.3d 256, 263–65 (4th Cir. 2019).

131. 42 U.S.C. § 2000cc(b)(1). Some of the cases also approach land use–regulatory distinctions between comparable religious and secular uses as an "unreasonable limitation" under 42 U.S.C. § 2000cc(b)(3). *See, e.g.*, Chabad of Nova, Inc. v. City of Cooper City, 575 F. Supp. 2d 1280 (S.D. Fla. 2008). *See generally* Sarah Keeton Campbell, Note, *Restoring RLUIPA's Equal Terms Provision*, 58 DUKE L.J. 1071 (2009) (arguing for strict implementation of the plain text of the provision).

132. 510 F.3d 253, 262–64 (3d Cir. 2007). *See also* Summit Church v. Randolph Cnty. Dev. Auth., No. 2:15-CV-82, 2016 WL 865302 (N.D. W.Va. Mar. 2, 2016) (violates equal terms to prohibit religious services in building where theater performances are allowed); Hope Rising Cmty. Church v. Municipality of Penn Hills, Civil Action No. 15-1165, 2015 WL 7720380 (W.D. Pa. Oct. 28, 2015) (church should be treated equally to other places of assembly, including parks, playgrounds, and educational institutions); Hollywood Cmty. Synagogue, Inc. v. City of Hollywood, 430 F. Supp. 2d 1296, 1317–19 (S.D. Fla. 2006) (showing of substantial burden not required if unequal treatment is established).

133. Epona, LLC v. Cnty. of Ventura, 876 F.3d 1214, 1226 (9th Cir. 2017).

134. Identification of a comparable secular use may be difficult in that it should have comparable scale and land use impacts. For example, in *Irshad Learning Center v. County of Dupage*, 937 F. Supp. 2d 910 (N.D. Ill. 2013), the plaintiff Islamic learning center contended that conditional use permits were routinely issued for secular schools in the relevant area, but the court found the offered secular counterparts did not have similar zoning and land use impacts. In *Covenant Christian Ministries, Inc. v. City of Marietta*, 654 F.3d 1231 (11th Cir. 2011), the court held that parks, playgrounds, and neighborhood recreation centers were similar secular places of assembly for the purposes of equal-terms analysis.

135. *Lighthouse Institute for Evangelism, Inc. v. City of Long Branch*, 510 F.3d 253, 266 (3d Cir. 2007). In *Opulent Life Church v. City of Holly Springs*, 697 F.3d 279 (5th Cir. 2012), the court held that the test requires an examination of the regulatory purpose of the regulation and whether the religious use is treated as well as every nonreligious use

formulation of the test, an examination of the purposes of the regulation and a principled rationale for any differential treatment are important parts of this inquiry.

A variation of this test inquires whether the comparable uses are similarly situated in regard to the "accepted zoning criteria" involved. For example, in *River of Life Kingdom Ministries v. Village of Hazel Crest*,[136] the court inquired into the regulatory criteria being employed, such as addressing traffic impacts, promoting uses that generate shopping opportunities and sales-tax revenues, and the effect on demand for public services. The court upheld the exclusion of churches, community centers, and schools from a relatively small downtown commercial district.

A third approach has looked to functional intent and purposes of the regulation, particularly in facial challenges.[137] A critical inquiry in this regard is whether a similarly situated nonreligious comparator received or could receive differential treatment under the challenged regulation.[138] This test is applied in the Fourth Circuit.[139]

Using these tests, it has been held to be a RLUIPA violation to prohibit places of worship in a commercial district that allows other nonprofit uses, such as private clubs and lodges;[140] to prohibit religious assembly where comparable secular civic assembly is allowed;[141] to require a special use permit when

---

that is similarly situated relative to that purpose. *See also* Calvary Chapel Bible Fellowship v. County of Riverside, 948 F.3d 1172 (9th Cir. 2020) (where both religious and secular assemblies were allowed if they are "special occasion facilities," which required that the facilities be used for a specific period of time in return for compensation, there is no unequal treatment); Tree of Life Christian Sch. v. City of Upper Arlington, 905 F.3d 357 (6th Cir. 2018) (no evidence religious school treated any differently from secular school).

136. 611 F.3d 367 (7th Cir. 2010). *See also* Word Seed Church v. Village of Hazel Crest, 533 F. Supp. 3d 637 (N.D. Ill. 2021) (no evidence of unequal treatment). A federal court reviewing an RLUIPA challenge to a Raleigh regulation restricting the location of an abortion-counselling clinic that used medical-ultrasound tests was reviewed using this test. A Hand of Hope Pregnancy Res. Ctr. v. City of Raleigh, 332 F. Supp. 3d 983 (E.D.N.C. 2018) (denying plaintiff's motion for summary judgment on equal-terms claim).

137. Midrash Sephardi, Inc. v. Town of Surfside, 366 F.3d 1214, 1230–31 (11th Cir. 2004). In *Thai Meditation Ass'n of Ala. v. City of Mobile*, 980 F.3d 821, 829–33 (11th Cir. 2020), the court held that allowing a long-standing fishing and hunting club to repair storm damage and expand was not a valid comparator to a proposed new meditation and retreat center.

138. Primera Iglesia Bautista Hispana of Boca Raton, Inc. v. Broward Cnty., 450 F.3d 1295, 1311 (11th Cir. 2006). *See also* Tree of Life Christian Sch. v. City of Upper Arlington, 905 F.3d 357, 368 (6th Cir. 2018); Centro Familiar Cristiano Buenas Nuevas v. City of Yuma, 651 F.3d 1163, 1173 (9th Cir. 2011); Elijah Grp., Inc. v. City of Leon Valley, 643 F.3d 419, 424 (5th Cir. 2011); River of Life Kingdom Ministries v. Vill. of Hazel Crest, 611 F.3d 367, 371 (7th Cir. 2010).

139. Alive Church of the Nazarene, Inc. v. Prince William Cnty., 59 F.4th 92, 102 (4th Cir. 2023).

140. *Midrash Sephardi*, 366 F.3d 1214. *See also* Elijah Grp., Inc. v. City of Leon Valley, 643 F.3d 419 (5th Cir. 2011) (violation of equal-terms provision where ordinance prohibited churches from business district but allowed nonretail, nonreligious private clubs by special use permit); Christian Fellowship Ctrs. of N.Y., Inc. v. Vill. of Canton, 377 F. Supp. 3d 146 (N.D.N.Y. 2019) (prohibition of religious use in commercial district where other nonprofit places of assembly are allowed likely violates equal-treatment standard under any of the various tests); Vietnamese Buddhism Study Temple in Am. v. City of Garden Grove, 460 F. Supp. 2d 1165, 1174 (C.D. Cal. 2006) (preliminary injunction halting ordinance enforcement appropriate under RLUIPA where ordinance allows private clubs and other secular assemblies by right but requires religious assemblies to secure conditional use permit).

141. In *New Harvest Christian Fellowship v. City of Salinas*, 29 F.4th 596 (9th Cir. 2022), the court held that an express distinction between "[c]lubs, lodges, and places of religious assembly, and similar assembly uses" and all other nonreligious assemblies with regard to permitted first-floor uses in the small downtown commercial district is a prima facie case of unequal treatment. It allowed a nonreligious place of assembly, such as a movie theater, but not a religious one, and the city produced no acceptable zoning criterion to support such a distinction. *See also* Konikov v. Orange Cnty., 410 F.3d 1317, 1327–29 (11th Cir. 2005) (cannot prohibit religious meetings in home where family, social, and civic gatherings of same size and frequency would be allowed); Hollywood Cmty. Synagogue, Inc. v. City of Hollywood, 430 F. Supp. 2d 1296, 1319–21 (S.D. Fla. 2006) (RLUIPA violated if comparable nonreligious assemblies and institutions are allowed in a residential district while religious assembly is prohibited or if there is discrimination between religious affiliations).

comparable secular uses are allowed as by-right permitted uses,[142] to deny a special use permit for expansion of a nonconforming church and religious school where a permit has previously been issued for a somewhat similar expansion of a school in the same agricultural zoning district;[143] to require shorter light poles at a parochial school than is allowed at a comparable public school;[144] or to single out for zoning enforcement a halfway house sponsored by a religious group in a way not done for comparable secular group homes.[145] On the other hand, it has been held that a water-and-sewer-availability decision for a secular museum subject to a different plan in another part of the county is not unequal treatment.[146] Similarly, a requirement that a place of worship obtain a special use permit to locate in an agricultural zoning district while allowing farm wineries (an agritourism use) to operate there by right has been held not to be unequal treatment.[147]

The law has also been applied in a zoning-enforcement context, with a court holding that it violates RLUIPA to revoke a church's accessory-use approval for a catering operation by a for-profit lessee while allowing neighboring nonreligious uses to conduct identical uses.[148] However, exclusion of all institutional uses, including both places of worship and schools, from an industrial zoning district is acceptable.[149]

It may be possible in narrow circumstances to treat a religious use more strictly than comparable secular uses. Courts have allowed ordinances to distinguish commercial from noncommercial places of assembly, though considerable caution should be exercised in these situations.[150] If places of religious assembly are being treated differently from some other secular places of assembly, it is incumbent on

---

142. Omar Islamic Center, Inc. v. City of Meriden, No. 3:19-CV-00488, 2022 WL 4599150 (D. Conn. Sept. 30, 2022). The applicable zoning district allowed offices, hotels, convention centers, shops and stores and service establishments (such as bakeries, barberies, restaurants, and theaters), and institutional, public, and municipal buildings by right but required a special use permit for places of worship. The zoning regulation was amended while this litigation was pending to remove the special use permit requirement. The court held that this mooted the request for injunctive relief but not the claim for damages incurred while the regulation was in place.

143. Rocky Mountain Christian Church v. Bd. of Cnty. Comm'rs, 613 F.3d 1229 (10th Cir. 2010). *Cf.* Grace Church of Roaring Fork Valley v. Bd. of Cnty. Comm'rs, 742 F. Supp. 2d 1156 (D. Colo. 2010) (distinguishing church use from schools and clubhouses for which county had no regulatory review, uses in other areas of the county, and substantially smaller uses).

144. Corp. of the Catholic Archbishop of Seattle v. City of Seattle, 28 F. Supp. 3d 1163 (W.D. Wash. 2014).

145. Holy Ghost Revival Ministries v. City of Marysville, 98 F. Supp. 3d 1153 (W.D. Wash. 2015).

146. Canaan Christian Church v. Montgomery Cnty., 29 F.4th 182 (4th Cir. 2022).

147. Alive Church of the Nazarene, Inc. v. Prince William Cnty., 59 F.4th 92, 103–04 (4th Cir. 2023). The court held that since the stated purpose of the zoning district was to protect agricultural uses, an agritourism use and a religious use are not comparable relative to the purpose of the regulation.

148. Third Church of Christ, Scientist v. City of N.Y., 626 F.3d 667 (2d Cir. 2010).

149. Petra Presbyterian Church v. Vill. of Northbrook, 489 F.3d 846 (7th Cir. 2007).

150. Exclusion of places of worship from a commercial-redevelopment area was upheld in *Lighthouse Institute for Evangelism, Inc. v. City of Long Branch*, 510 F.3d 253, 270 (3d Cir. 2007). By contrast, the court found the exclusion of places of worship included in an ordinance in effect *prior to* adoption of the redevelopment plan was a violation of the equal-terms provision. The plan's purpose was not clearly identified, and it allowed secular noncommercial uses, such as government service and municipal building, whose land use impacts were similar to those of the excluded religious noncommercial uses.

Other courts have been less sympathetic to such commercial-protection rationales for differential treatment of religious uses. The court in *Digrugilliers v. Consolidated City of Indianapolis*, 506 F.3d 612, 616–17 (7th Cir. 2007), was not sympathetic to a rationale for excluding religious uses from one zoning-district classification that allowed comparable secular uses: State law prohibited establishments from selling liquor or pornography within 200 or 500 feet of a church, respectively. Therefore, a district classification that allowed such establishments could prohibit religious uses to prevent them from interfering with the location of those establishments. The court approved a preliminary injunction to stay an order that a small church in an industrial area be vacated or obtain a variance. *See also* Centro Familiar Cristiano Buenas Nuevas v. City of Yuma, 651 F.3d 1163 (9th Cir. 2011).

the local government to establish that this treatment addresses legitimate differential land use impacts and is undertaken without any religious animus.[151]

Another question presented by a standard of uniform application of regulations is how far a local government can go in exempting religious uses from otherwise uniform regulations, such as exempting a church message board from sign regulations. A degree of accommodation of religious practices by way of exemption is permissible.[152] For example, the federal government exempted sacramental use of wine from the general ban on alcohol use during Prohibition. In *Smith*, Justice Scalia noted that the Oregon legislature could choose to exempt sacramental use of peyote from state criminal sanctions.[153] However, an exemption that is overly broad may well raise a question as to the legitimacy of the avowed secular purpose of the regulation. Local governments should establish a record that an exemption will not significantly undermine the secular purposes of the regulation.

Special care is warranted if individualized exemptions are possible or if individualized conditions are being imposed. In these instances there is a reasonable possibility that the *Sherbert* rule will still apply: If there would be a substantial burden on religious practice, relief must be granted unless there is a compelling governmental interest not to do so and the least restrictive regulation has been employed.[154] The Court has noted also that precision in findings justifying a restriction on constitutionally protected rights is necessary when individualized land use determinations are made (such as with special or conditional use permits and variances).[155]

Exemptions come with an additional concern: Do they violate the Establishment Clause by improperly favoring a religious use over a secular use with similar land use impacts?[156] For the most part, though, Establishment Clause challenges of exemptions have been unsuccessful.[157] *Goforth Properties, Inc. v. Town of Chapel Hill* is a typical result. The court held that a zoning provision exempting churches in the central business district from off-street parking requirements was reasonable given differences between churches and businesses relative to the times they generate peak parking demands.[158] However, an exemption based solely on religious grounds rather than on differential secular impacts would be suspect.

---

151. In *Signs for Jesus v. Town of Pembroke*, 230 F. Supp. 3d 49 (D.N.H. 2017), the court held that it was not an equal-terms violation for a prohibition of "electronic-changing signs" to be applied to a church sign but not a legally nonconforming sign at a commercial use or a governmental sign at a public school.

152. Ehlers-Renzi v. Connelly Sch. of the Holy Child, Inc., 224 F.3d 283 (4th Cir. 2000) (upholding ordinance that exempted parochial schools from special use permit requirements); Boyajian v. Gatzunis, 212 F.3d 1 (1st Cir. 2000), *cert. denied*, 531 U.S. 1070 (2001) (upholding Massachusetts statute that forbade municipal zoning from excluding religious and educational uses from any zoning district). These cases generally employ the Establishment Clause analysis of *Lemon v. Kurtzman* to find that the exemptions serve a secular purpose rather than advancing or endorsing religion. 403 U.S. 602 (1971). However, the Court in *Kennedy v. Bremerton School Dist.*, 142 S. Ct. 2407 (2022), largely abandoned the *Lemon* test in favor of a review of historical practices and understandings. *See also* Larkin v. Grendel's Den, Inc., 459 U.S. 116 (1982) (invalidating on Establishment Clause grounds a Massachusetts statute giving churches veto power over liquor-license applications for facilities within 500 feet of churches). *See generally* Walz v. Tax Comm'n of N.Y., 397 U.S. 664 (1970) (upholding property-tax exemption for religious organizations).

153. "But to say that a nondiscriminatory religious-practice exemption is permitted, or even that it is desirable, is not to say that it is constitutionally required." Emp't Div., Dep't of Human Res. v. Smith, 494 U.S. 872, 890 (1990).

154. "The *Sherbert* test, it must be recalled, was developed in a context that lent itself to individualized governmental assessment of the reasons for the relevant conduct." *Id.* at 884.

155. Dolan v. City of Tigard, 512 U.S. 374, 395–96 (1994).

156. Justice Stevens's concurring opinion in *Boerne* expressed the view that exemption of a religious use from a historic-preservation ordinance, but not a similar secular use, would violate the Establishment Clause. City of Boerne v. Flores, 521 U.S. 507, 536–37 (1997).

157. *See, e.g.*, United States v. Maui Cnty., 298 F. Supp. 2d 1010, 1015 (D. Haw. 2003).

158. 71 N.C. App. 771, 323 S.E.2d 427 (1984). *See also* Cohen v. City of Des Plaines, 8 F.3d 484 (7th Cir. 1993) (upholding day-care-regulation exception for church nursery schools). Accepting the city's contention that the purpose of the exemption was to reduce governmental interference with religious organizations, the court held that this was an adequate secular purpose that did not endorse religious activities. *Id.*

CHAPTER 28

Regulation of Signs

Most businesses have signs on their premises to draw attention to their locations and activities. Billboards are widely used to promote commercial products.[1] Noncommercial signs are used to promote causes, nonprofit organizations, and political candidates. Many cities even erect their own promotional signs welcoming visitors.

While signs have considerable commercial and social value, they can impair traffic safety and significantly affect community aesthetics. Most jurisdictions regulate signs.[2] In North Carolina, sign regulations may be adopted as part of a zoning regulation or as separate police-power regulations.[3]

Sign regulations, however, burden speech and are therefore subject to constitutional review.[4] While sign bans are possible in areas that do not qualify as public forums, most signs are proposed for areas that face First Amendment scrutiny.[5]

Particular care is necessary when regulating signs containing political speech, when regulating highly personal speech (such as yard signs), or when applying discretionary standards in sign regulation.

As a general rule, First Amendment limits on government regulations do not apply to private restrictive covenants, such as a prohibition on yard signs or flags. These are agreements between private parties and not state actions.[6]

---

1. The industry's national trade association estimated that $8 billion was spent on outdoor advertising in 2018. Out of Home Advertising Association of America, Inc., *Historical Revenue*, https://oaaa.org/AboutOOH/Factsamp;Figures/HistoricalRevenue.aspx (last accessed Jan. 30, 2023).

2. State and local regulation of billboards began soon after the initial appearance of this form of advertising. *See* St. Louis Gunning Advert. Co. v. City of St. Louis, 235 Mo. 99, 146, 137 S.W. 929, 942 (1911) (upholding authority to regulate billboards).

3. *See* PNE AOA Media, LLC v. Jackson Cnty., 146 N.C. App. 470, 554 S.E.2d 657 (2001); Summey Outdoor Advert., Inc. v. Cnty. of Henderson, 96 N.C. App. 533, 386 S.E.2d 439 (1989), *review denied*, 326 N.C. 486, 392 S.E.2d 101 (1990). The state also has a regulatory program for signs along state highways as provided in Chapter 136, Sections 126 through 140 in the North Carolina General Statutes (hereinafter G.S.). See Chapter 23 for a discussion of sign legislation. State legislation also regulates signs in particular areas. *See, e.g.*, S.L. 1993-559 (limiting billboards near Pilot Mountain State Park).

4. *See, e.g.*, Am. Legion Post 7 v. City of Durham, 239 F.3d 601, 606–07 (2001) (limit on maximum size of flag burdens free speech).

5. Due process also requires that sign regulations be designed to address legitimate governmental objectives. See Chapter 25 for discussion of this issue. Use of sign amortization is also limited by takings considerations and statutory limits discussed in Chapters 20 and 24.

6. An exception is that courts have long found judicial enforcement of private racially restrictive covenants is state action subject to constitutional limits. Shelley v. Kraemer, 334 U.S. 1 (1948). That concept has generally not been extended to judicial enforcement of other restrictions. *See, e.g.*, Loren v. Sasser, 309 F.3d 1296 (11th Cir. 2002) (judicial enforcement of deed restriction prohibiting For Sale sign on residential lot not state action); Linn Valley Lakes Property Owners Ass'n v. Brockway, 250 Kan. 169, 824 P.2d 948 (1992) (enforcement of covenant prohibiting signs not state action).

First Amendment Principles

Test for Symbolic Speech

While not directly applicable to sign regulation, the tests developed to review regulation of symbolic speech have influenced the First Amendment analysis of sign regulations. The basic test in this area was set out in *United States v. O'Brien*,[7] where the U.S. Supreme Court applied the following four-part test to determine whether First Amendment free-speech rights are impermissibly burdened by a particular governmental regulation of symbolic conduct:

1. Is the regulation within the constitutional power of the government?
2. Does it further an important or substantial governmental interest?
3. Is the governmental interest unrelated to the suppression of free expression?
4. Is the restriction no greater than is essential?

Test for Commercial Speech

Commercial speech is that which is related solely to the economic interest of the speaker and audience. It is deemed "commercial" if it is an advertisement, it refers to a specific product or service, and the speaker has an economic motivation for the speech.[8] Sometimes the boundary between commercial and noncommercial speech is blurred. For example, murals that do not promote a product, service, or business are generally treated as art rather than commercial speech, though distinguishing the two can be difficult.[9] But a sign that also includes photos or art does not remove it from the commercial-speech category if it is designed to attract customers.[10]

Commercial speech possesses some First Amendment free-speech protection,[11] however, it is subject to a lesser degree of scrutiny than noncommercial speech.[12] The general standard for regulation of commercial speech—an intermediate level of judicial scrutiny—is similar to the test for symbolic speech and is set forth in *Central Hudson Gas & Electric Corp. v. Public Service Commission*.[13] *Central Hudson* established the following four-part test for assessing restrictions on commercial speech:

1. To be protected, the speech must concern lawful activity and not be misleading. While misleading or deceptive advertisements may be prohibited, a variety of regulations attempting to restrict advertising of lawful and constitutionally protected activities have been invalidated.[14]

---

7. 391 U.S. 367, 377 (1968) (upholding conviction for burning a draft card).

8. Greater Baltimore Ctr. for Pregnancy Concerns, Inc. v. Mayor & City Council of Baltimore, 721 F.3d 264, 285 (4th Cir. 2013).

9. *See, e.g.*, Morris v. City of New Orleans, 399 F. Supp. 3d 624 (E.D. La. 2019) (invalidating regulation that distinguished commercial signs from noncommercial murals). *See generally* Christina C. Orlando, Note, *Art or Signage? The Regulation of Outdoor Murals and the First Amendment*, 35 Cardozo L. Rev. 867 (2013).

10. *See, e.g.*, Wag More Dogs, LLC v. Cozart, 680 F.3d 359, 370 (2012) (mural on wall of doggie day care held to be commercial speech).

11. Va. State Bd. of Pharmacy v. Va. Citizens Consumer Council, 425 U.S. 748, 771 (1976). Prior to the 1970s, commercial speech was generally considered not to have First Amendment protection. *See, e.g.*, Valentine v. Chrestensen, 316 U.S. 52 (1942).

12. Ohralik v. Ohio State Bar Ass'n, 436 U.S. 447, 456 (1978) (upholding ban on lawyer solicitation of clients in person). *See* Francesca L. Procaccini, *Equal Speech Protection*, 108 Va. L. Rev. 353 (2022) (arguing for dismantling the concept of a hierarchy of speech protections).

13. 447 U.S. 557 (1980) (invalidating a total ban of promotional advertising by electric utilities). This basic test was reaffirmed in the context of invalidating some of the restrictions imposed on tobacco advertisement and sales by Massachusetts. Lorillard Tobacco Co. v. Reilly, 533 U.S. 525 (2001).

14. *In re* R.M.J., 455 U.S. 191, 203 (1982) (invalidating limitation on lawyer advertisement); Bates v. State Bar of Ariz., 433 U.S. 350 (1977) (price advertisement for routine legal services); Carey v. Population Servs. Int'l, 431 U.S.

2. The asserted governmental interest in the restriction must be substantial (rather than compelling). The government has the burden of justifying its restrictions by showing that the harms it seeks to prevent are real.[15]

3. The regulation must directly advance the governmental interest. The government must have more than mere speculation that the interest will be advanced; it must demonstrate that the harms are real, and that the regulation will in fact alleviate them to a material degree.[16] Detailed empirical studies are not, however, required.[17]

4. The regulation must be no more extensive than necessary. The regulation does not have to be the least restrictive means of regulation, but there must be a "reasonable fit" between means and ends.[18]

Content and Viewpoint Neutrality

Regulations based on the content or viewpoint of speech face strict and demanding First Amendment scrutiny. If the regulation of speech is based on content, the regulation must be the least restrictive means available to address a compelling governmental interest.[19] The compelling-interest test is difficult but not impossible to satisfy. Courts have noted, for example, that while there are compelling government interests in public safety,[20] general considerations of aesthetics and traffic safety are substantial but not compelling government interests.[21]

A regulation is content neutral if it is justified without reference to the content of the regulated speech.[22] This test is sometimes phrased as a requirement that the regulation be substantially

---

678 (1977) (regarding contraceptives); Bigelow v. Virginia, 421 U.S. 809 (1975) (regarding abortions). In North Carolina, the court rejected an argument that regulation of video-gaming devices was a restriction on speech (because it regulated devices that used "entertaining displays" to reveal winnings), holding that the law regulated conduct, not speech. Hest Techs., Inc. v. State *ex rel.* Perdue, 366 N.C. 289, 749 S.E.2d 429 (2012).

15. Edenfield v. Fane, 507 U.S. 761, 770–73 (1993) (invalidating ban on all personal solicitations by CPAs); Zauderer v. Office of Disciplinary Counsel of the Supreme Court of Ohio, 471 U.S. 626, 647 (1985) (invalidating restriction on lawyer advertisement); Bolger v. Youngs Drug Prods. Corp., 463 U.S. 60 (1983) (invalidating ban on objectionable direct-mail advertisements for contraceptives). It is not necessary that the ordinance itself explicitly specify the governmental interest in sign regulation. Allison Outdoor Advert., LP v. Town of Canton, No. 1:11cv58, 2012 WL 4061510 (W.D.N.C. Sept. 14, 2012).

16. Greater New Orleans Broad. Ass'n v. United States, 527 U.S. 173, 188 (1999) (invalidating prohibition of broadcast advertisement for lawful casino gambling).

17. Fla. Bar v. Went for It, Inc., 515 U.S. 618, 627–28 (1995) (upholding regulation prohibiting lawyer direct-mail solicitations of personal-injury or wrongful-death clients within thirty days of accident).

18. Bd. of Trs. of the State Univ. of N.Y. v. Fox, 492 U.S. 469, 480 (1989) (upholding university regulation prohibiting commercial demonstrations, such as "Tupperware parties," in dormitories).

19. Sable Commc'ns of Cal. v. FCC, 492 U.S. 115, 126 (1989) (invalidating regulation of "indecent" but nonobscene telephone communications); United States v. Grace, 461 U.S. 171 (1983) (invalidating statute prohibiting display of signs or leafleting on Supreme Court grounds).

20. Foti v. City of Menlo Park, 146 F.3d 629, 637 (9th Cir. 1998) (invalidating some restrictions on signs carried by anti-abortion protestors and attached to their parked car, but upholding limits on sign size and number).

21. In *Central Radio Co. v. City of Norfolk*, 811 F.3d 625 (4th Cir. 2016), the court held that "[a]lthough interests in aesthetics and traffic safety may be 'substantial government goals,' neither we nor the Supreme Court have ever held that they constitute compelling government interests." *Id.* at 633. *See also* Neighborhood Enters., Inc. v. City of St. Louis, 644 F.3d 728, 738 (8th Cir. 2011). By contrast, the court in *Fanning v. City of Shavano Park*, 429 F. Supp. 3d 320 (W.D. Tex. 2019), held that protection of community aesthetics could be a compelling interest for prohibiting yard banners in a small city that has "a central focus on its appearance, beauty, and charm." *Id.* at 333. This case was, however, vacated and remanded for reconsideration in light of ordinance amendments and *Reagan National Advertising.* 853 F. App'x 951 (5th Cir. 2021).

22. Va. State Bd. of Pharmacy v. Va. Citizens Consumer Council, 425 U.S. 748, 771 (1976).

unrelated to suppression of speech.[23] Regulations that make distinctions based on the content of speech are generally not considered content neutral.[24]

Courts have, however, allowed the content of speech to be considered while still finding a regulation to be content neutral. A regulation is content neutral if the predominate concern leading to its enactment relates to the secondary impacts of the speech and not the content of the speech itself. Secondary impacts include effects on community aesthetics and the surrounding neighborhoods, effects on traffic safety, and the like. Secondary impacts do not include effects such as the reactions of those hearing the speech.[25] The actual motives of board members are generally not considered in determining the content neutrality of regulations.[26]

The principal area of litigation addressing content neutrality and secondary impacts involves cases authorizing regulation of adult entertainment.[27] In *Young v. American Mini Theatres, Inc.*, the Supreme Court held that the city's interest in preventing the deterioration of urban neighborhoods justified restrictions on location of adult uses.[28] In *City of Renton v. Playtime Theatres, Inc.*, the Court again upheld location restrictions imposed on adult-entertainment facilities. The ordinance in *Renton* was deemed content neutral even though it treated theaters differently based on the type of films being shown therein. The Court reasoned that the content of the films was not the basis of the ordinance because the city council's "predominate concern" in adopting it was ameliorating the secondary effects of adult theaters on surrounding neighborhoods (enhancing prevention of crime, protection of retail trade, maintenance of property values, and preservation of the quality of urban life). When secondary impacts form the basis of regulation of protected speech, local governments can rely on evidence and studies from other jurisdictions to support the regulation.[29]

When the speech is indiscriminately available to minors, as is the case with most exterior signs, there is a governmental interest in protecting children from sexually explicit and vulgar advertisements that can justify additional restrictions. This has been held to be a substantial governmental justification for restricting commercial speech.[30]

Any prior restraint on speech—a government regulation that restricts speech before it is made— must have clear and definite standards for decisions and must have adequate procedural safeguards to

---

23. Reno v. Am. Civil Liberties Union, 521 U.S. 844 (1997) (invalidating restrictions on transmittal of indecent material over the Internet); United States v. O'Brien, 391 U.S. 367 (1968).

24. R.A.V. v. City of St. Paul, 505 U.S. 377 (1992) (imposing additional penalties on fighting words that provoke violence based on race, color, creed, or gender is subject to strict scrutiny); Police Dep't of Chi. v. Mosley, 408 U.S. 92, 99 (1972) (ordinance allowing peaceful labor picketing but banning all other picketing near schools is not content neutral).

25. Boos v. Barry, 485 U.S. 312 (1988) (invalidating an ordinance prohibiting display of signs critical of foreign governments within 500 feet of embassies).

26. *See, e.g.*, Cleveland Area Bd. of Realtors v. City of Euclid, 88 F.3d 382, 387–88 (6th Cir. 1996). The court noted that whether the city council here was motivated by a desire to prevent "white flight" when restricting residential For Sale signs was not relevant when a legitimate aesthetic objective for the regulation existed (though the regulation was invalidated on other grounds).

27. These cases are discussed in detail in Chapter 26.

28. 427 U.S. 50 (1976).

29. City of Renton v. Playtime Theatres, Inc., 475 U.S. 41, 50–52 (1986). *See also* City of Erie v. Pap's A.M., 529 U.S. 277, 296 (2000); Barnes v. Glen Theater, Inc., 501 U.S. 560, 583–84 (1991).

30. In *FCC v. Pacifica Foundation*, 438 U.S. 726 (1978), the Court upheld a rule prohibiting a radio broadcast of "indecent" language in the afternoon when it would be accessible to children (the broadcast, George Carlin's "Filthy Words" monologue, featured frequent use of the prohibited language). The Court noted that language that might be protected in one context, such as political speech, could be prohibited when used in a context readily accessible to children. The Court noted a compelling interest in the protection of minors in *Sable Communications of Cal. v. Federal Communications Comm'n*, 492 U.S. 115, 126 (1989).

ensure prompt decisions and judicial review.[31] Some courts have held that a regulation that applies to all similar uses (for example, all bars or retail establishments, not just topless bars or adult bookstores) is a content-neutral land use rule that is not subject to a prior-restraint analysis.[32]

Application to Sign Regulations

Public Forum

The standard of review applied to regulations affecting protected speech depends in part on whether the speech is taking place in a public forum.[33] Content-based restrictions of speech in a public forum are subject to strict judicial scrutiny. Content-neutral restrictions in a public forum receive intermediate scrutiny.

By contrast, if the speech is not in a public forum, signs can be banned or regulated with only a reasonableness standard applied in judicial review.[34] Speech regulations in nonpublic forums do need to be viewpoint neutral.[35]

The most significant of the nonpublic-forum areas for sign purposes is the public-street right-of-way. A local government may completely ban all signs located on public property, provided it has not designated the area a public forum for speech purposes.[36] The U.S. Supreme Court has held that a sidewalk leading from a parking area to a post office is also not a public forum if it is not part of the regular pedestrian-circulation system.[37]

Relation to Substantial Governmental Interests

A key aspect of applying the *Central Hudson* test is determining what constitutes a substantial governmental interest and what a local government must do to document the relationship of the regulation to that interest.

---

31. FW/PBS, Inc. v. City of Dallas, 493 U.S. 215 (1990) (invalidating ordinance regulating sexually oriented businesses due to failure to provide time limitation within which a decision must be made); Freedman v. Maryland, 380 U.S. 51 (1965) (licensing schemes that are a prior restraint on protected speech must contain adequate procedural safeguards).

32. *See, e.g.,* Marty's Adult World of Enfield, Inc. v. Town of Enfield, 20 F.3d 512, 515 (2d Cir. 1994) (holding special use permit review required for all businesses valid). Regulation of adult businesses is discussed in Chapter 26.

33. Traditional public forums are public places historically associated with the free exercise of expressive activities. United States v. Grace, 461 U.S. 171, 177 (1983). *See, e.g.,* Clatterbuck v. City of Charlottesville, 708 F.3d 549, 555 (4th Cir. 2013) (city's downtown pedestrian mall is a "quintessential public forum").

34. A nonpublic forum includes public property that is not by tradition or designation a forum for public communication, and the government has wider latitude to limit speech in these areas. Perry Educ. Ass'n v. Perry Loc. Educators' Ass'n, 460 U.S. 37, 46 (1983) (upholding restriction on rival union's use of teacher mailboxes as the mailboxes were not a public forum).

35. Int'l Soc'y for Krishna Consciousness, Inc. v. Lee, 505 U.S. 672, 679 (1992). A prohibition of all "political" advertising on buses, though a nonpublic forum, constitutes impermissible viewpoint discrimination (and also is incapable of "reasonable" application). White Coat Waste Project v. Greater Richmond Transit Co., 35 F.4th 179 (4th Cir. 2022); American Freedom Defense Initiative v. Suburban Mobility Auth., 978 F.3d 481 (6th Cir. 2020); Young Israel of Tampa, Inc. v. Hillsborough Area Regional Transit Auth., 582 F. Supp. 3d 1159 (M.D. Fla. 2022) (invalidating ban on all religious advertisements on buses).

36. City Council of L.A. v. Taxpayers for Vincent, 466 U.S. 789 (1984) (upholding ban of flyers placed on telephone poles within the public-street right-of-way). North Carolina prohibits all advertising signs within state-highway rights-of-way. Title 19A, Chapter 2E, Section .0415 of the North Carolina Administrative Code.

37. United States v. Kokinda, 497 U.S. 720 (1990) (upholding viewpoint-neutral federal regulation prohibiting soliciting on postal premises). *But see* Rappa v. New Castle Cnty., 18 F.3d 1043, 1070–71 (3d Cir. 1994) (noting streets and sidewalks are in many instances traditional public forums).

The governmental interest supporting most sign regulations is protection of community aesthetic values and promoting traffic safety.[38] Safeguarding aesthetics and community character has long been recognized as a legitimate governmental interest.[39] In the leading case on billboard regulations, *Metromedia, Inc. v. City of San Diego*, a plurality of the Supreme Court held that there are substantial state interests in traffic safety and aesthetics and that sign regulations are a legitimate means of serving those objectives.[40] Also, aesthetics alone may serve as a sufficient justification for sign regulation.[41]

A sign regulation must directly advance the government's substantial interests and be no more extensive than necessary. Courts have been willing to accept an adequate relationship between regulations and these objectives without individualized study or documentation.[42] Once these objectives are set out in the ordinance, courts are highly deferential in accepting such justifications.[43] It is thus important that a sign ordinance specify the governmental interests it is designed to address, as courts may well not imply a valid objective.[44]

Courts are also deferential to the precise framing of sign regulations limiting commercial speech, noting that the fit between the regulation and its purposes must be reasonable as opposed to using the least restrictive means. A sign regulation may address some, but not all, signs that affect the governmental interest being addressed. For example, sign regulations have been upheld that prohibit off-premise billboards but allow signs on public property,[45] allow signs on public-transit stops,[46] or exempt noncommercial signs.[47] Courts have noted that distinctions between types of signs need to be meaningful and must not defeat the purpose of the regulation under challenge.

---

38. *See, e.g.*, E.B. Elliott Advert. Co. v. Metro. Dade Cnty., 425 F.2d 1141 (5th Cir. 1970); Transylvania Cnty. v. Moody, 151 N.C. App. 389, 396–97, 565 S.E.2d 720, 725 (2002).

39. Vill. of Belle Terre v. Boraas, 416 U.S. 1 (1974); Berman v. Parker, 348 U.S. 26, 33 (1954).

40. 453 U.S. 490 (1981).

41. Nat'l Advert. Co. v. City of Raleigh, 947 F.2d 1158, 1168 (4th Cir. 1991); Naegele Outdoor Advert., Inc. v. City of Durham, 844 F.2d 172, 174 (4th Cir. 1988); Ga. Outdoor Advert., Inc. v. City of Waynesville, 833 F.2d 43, 46 (4th Cir. 1987); Major Media of the Se., Inc. v. City of Raleigh, 792 F.2d 1269, 1272 (4th Cir. 1986). See the discussion of aesthetics as a legitimate objective for government regulation in Chapter 25.

42. Ackerley Commc'ns of the Nw., Inc. v. Krochalis, 108 F.3d 1095 (9th Cir. 1997) (upholding Seattle limitations on billboards without the necessity of "detailed proof" that the regulation in fact advances city's interests in aesthetics and traffic safety).

43. Outdoor Sys., Inc. v. City of Lenexa, 67 F. Supp. 2d 1231, 1238–39 (D. Kan. 1999). However, there must be some indication that the regulation advances the asserted interest in some direct and material way. Pagan v. Fruchey, 492 F.3d 766, 772–73 (6th Cir. 2007) (invalidating restriction on For Sale signs on vehicles parked on public streets, as no evidence that regulation advanced interest of preventing people coming into the roadway for nontraffic purposes was offered).

44. Desert Outdoor Advert., Inc. v. City of Moreno Valley, 103 F.3d 814, 819 (9th Cir. 1996); Nat'l Advert. Co. v. Town of Babylon, 900 F.2d 551, 555–56 (2d Cir. 1990) (sign regulation must identify the particular government interests sought to be advanced).

45. Clear Channel Outdoor, Inc. v. City of N.Y., 594 F.3d 94, 106–07 (2d Cir. 2010). *See also* Interstate Outdoor Advert., L.P. v. Zoning Bd., 706 F.3d 527 (3d Cir. 2013) (upholding ban on all billboards).

46. Metro Lights, L.L.C. v. City of L.A., 551 F.3d 898, 900 (9th Cir. 2009).

47. RTM Media, L.L.C. v. City of Houston, 584 F.3d 220, 226–27 (5th Cir. 2009) (noting the vast majority of signs in the city were commercial messages, so focusing regulation on them was a reasonable fit with the city's aesthetic and traffic-safety objectives). The commercial/noncommercial distinction is discussed in greater detail in the text below.

Typical Time-Place-and-Manner Restrictions

A local government may impose content-neutral time-place-and-manner regulations on signs.[48] These regulations must, however, be designed to serve a substantial governmental interest while allowing reasonable alternative avenues of expression, and they must be narrowly tailored to meet the governmental interest involved. Reasonable content-neutral limitations on sign size, color, lighting, height, and spacing generally are legally acceptable. Though no formal study is required to justify these limitations, it is useful for any such regulation to contain an explicit statement of purpose to aid in assessing the reasonableness of its restrictions.[49]

A regulation can ban all signs in defined areas, such as historic districts or redevelopment areas.[50] Many jurisdictions prohibit commercial signs and billboards in residential areas.[51]

---

48. The principles for time-place-and-manner restrictions are set forth in a series of cases addressing a variety of issues involving the limitation of public speech. *See* Hill v. Colorado, 530 U.S. 703 (2000) (upholding statute requiring protestors handing out leaflets and handbills, displaying signs, and engaging in other like behavior to maintain eight-foot separation from persons entering health-care facilities); Ward v. Rock Against Racism, 491 U.S. 781, 791 (1989) (upholding regulations on the volume of musical performances in Central Park); Clark v. Cmty. for Creative Non-Violence, 468 U.S. 288, 293 (1984) (upholding regulation of use of tent cities on the Washington Mall by protest groups); Heffron v. Int'l Soc'y for Krishna Consciousness, Inc., 452 U.S. 640 (1981) (upholding content-neutral regulation that all persons selling, exhibiting, or distributing material at state fair do so only from a fixed location). *See also* Turner Broad. Sys., Inc. v. FCC, 512 U.S. 622, 641–43 (1994); R.A.V. v. City of St. Paul, 505 U.S. 377, 382 (1992) (invalidating ordinance prohibiting display of symbols that arouse anger, alarm, or resentment on the basis of race, color, creed, religion, or gender as not content neutral and failing a strict-scrutiny review) .

49. *See, e.g.*, Salib v. City of Mesa, 212 Ariz. 446, 133 P.3d 756 (Ct. App. 2006) (upholding regulation prohibiting businesses from covering more than 30 percent of their windows with signs).

50. *See, e.g.*, Messer v. City of Douglasville, 975 F.2d 1505 (11th Cir. 1992) (upholding ban of signs in historic district); Donnelly Advert. Co. v. City of Balt., 279 Md. 660, 370 A.2d 1127 (1977) (upholding ban of signs in urban-renewal area). *See also* Burke v. City of Charleston, 893 F. Supp. 589 (D.S.C. 1995), *vacated and remanded*, 139 F.3d 401 (4th Cir. 1998) (upholding restriction on painting murals on exterior walls of buildings in a historic district). Such locational restrictions have a long history. New York City, for example, in 1940 banned off-premises commercial advertising signs located within 200 feet of and visible from major highways. Infinity Outdoor, Inc. v. City of N.Y., 165 F. Supp. 2d 403, 406 (E.D.N.Y. 2001). The ban was apparently rarely enforced prior to enactment of the Federal Highway Beautification Act of 1965. Also see the discussion of amortization of nonconforming signs in Chapter 20.

51. *See, e.g.*, Naegele Outdoor Advert. Co. of Minn. v. Vill. of Minnetonka, 162 N.W.2d 206 (Minn. 1968) (upholding ban of billboards in residential area). A 1999 informal survey by Scenic North Carolina indicated that some sixty-one cities in the state prohibited new off-premises billboards altogether. In a 2012 School of Government survey, 46 percent of responding North Carolina cities and counties reported that they completely prohibited off-premises commercial advertising signs. David W. Owens & Dayne Batten, *2012 Zoning Survey Report: Zoning Adoption, Administration, and Provisions for Design Standards and Alternative Energy Facilities*, PLAN. & ZONING L. BULL. No. 20 (UNC School of Government, July 2012), at 20–21.

Most sign regulations limit sign size, particularly square footage and height.[52] Other common limits include those on illumination of signs, duration of display, spacing between signs,[53] and the number of signs at a particular location.[54]

Regulations can limit particular types of signs. Typical limitations that have been upheld include those that prohibit portable signs,[55] flashing or blinking signs,[56] electronic changeable-copy signs,[57] digital signs,[58] or pole signs;[59] those that ban moving parts on signs;[60] and those that bar the advertising of vehicles and watercraft.[61]

---

52. Sign size and height limits are routinely approved by the courts. A 250-square-foot size limit for all off-premise signs was upheld in *Covenant Media of North Carolina, L.L.C. v. City of Monroe*, 285 F. App'x 30 (4th Cir. 2008). *See also* Leibundguth Storage & Van Serv., Inc. v. Vill. of Downers Grove, 939 F.3d 859 (7th Cir. 2019) (upholding size limit of 1.5 square feet per linear foot of building frontage for signs painted on walls); Get Outdoors II, LLC v. City of San Diego, 506 F.3d 886, 893–94 (9th Cir. 2007) (upholding variable size and height limits based on width of adjacent right-of-way and speed limits); Prime Media, Inc. v. City of Brentwood, 398 F.3d 814 (6th Cir. 2005) (upholding ordinance restricting billboards to 6-foot height and 120-square-foot size); Wilson v. City of Louisville, 957 F. Supp. 948 (W.D. Ky. 1997) (upholding requirement that freestanding signs be reduced from a maximum size of thirty-two square feet to no more than eight square feet and limiting their display to the hours of operation of the activity on site); Donrey Commc'ns Co. v. City of Fayetteville, 280 Ark. 408, 660 S.W.2d 900 (1983) (upholding seventy-five-square-foot size limit). *See also* Foti v. City of Menlo Park, 146 F.3d 629, 640–43 (9th Cir. 1998) (upholding size limit of three square feet for picket signs and a limit of one sign per picketer). *But see* Clear Channel Outdoor, Inc. v. City of St. Paul, 618 F.3d 851 (8th Cir. 2010) (invalidating prohibition of billboard extensions—graphics or words that extend above or off the sides of the rectangular face of a sign—because city failed to meet state law requirement that it articulate in writing the rationale for its decision).

53. Hucul Advertising, LLC v. Charter Twp. of Gaines, 748 F.3d 273 (6th Cir. 2014) (upholding 4000-foot spacing requirement between digital billboards).

54. Long Island Bd. of Realtors v. Incorporated Vill. of Massapequa Park, 277 F.3d 622 (2d Cir. 2002) (upholding limit on number of signs posted and regulating height, size, and duration of display); Vosse v. City of N.Y., 144 F. Supp. 3d 627 (S.D.N.Y. 2015) (upholding regulation prohibiting illuminated signs in certain districts if at a height of more than forty feet above curb level); Asselin v. Town of Conway, 137 N.H. 368, 628 A.2d 247 (1993) (upholding limit on internal illumination of signs).

55. *See, e.g.*, Don's Porta Signs, Inc. v. City of Clearwater, 829 F.2d 1051 (11th Cir. 1987) (regulations effectively banned these types of signs); Lindsay v. City of San Antonio, 821 F.2d 1103 (5th Cir. 1987) (generally deferring to legislative judgment on aesthetic issues); Harnish v. Manatee Cnty., 783 F.2d 1535 (11th Cir. 1986). However, the court in *LaCroix v. Town of Fort Meyers Beach*, 38 F.4th 942 (11th Cir. 2022), invalidated a regulation that banned all portable signs as applied to handheld portable signs. The court concluded that the total prohibition, much like the prohibition of small political yard/window signs in *Ladue* (see note 139), unduly foreclosed alternative means of communication. The court distinguished this impermissible total ban from a more focused permissible ban on commercial portable signs.

56. *See, e.g.*, La Tour v. City of Fayetteville, 442 F.3d 1094, 1095 (8th Cir. 2006). The court upheld a ban on "any sign which flashes, blinks, or is animated" as applied to a changeable-copy sign posted in the window of an accountant. The court also held that an exemption for time and temperature signs was permissible.

57. *See, e.g.*, Naser Jewelers, Inc. v. City of Concord, 513 F.3d 27 (1st Cir. 2008); Carlson's Chrysler v. City of Concord, 938 A.2d 69 (N.H. 2007).

58. In *Fairway Outdoor Advertising, LLC v. City of High Point*, No. 1:21-CV-00867, 2022 WL 17975990 (M.D.N.C. Dec. 28, 2022), the court upheld the denial of applications for new digital billboards and the replacement of an existing vinyl billboard with a digital billboard. The city zoning regulation allowed new billboards only in the heavy industrial zoning district; digital signs, however, were not allowed in that district, which effectively banned digital billboards citywide. *See also* Adams Outdoor Advert. Ltd. P'ship v. City of Madison, 56 F.4th 1111 (7th Cir. 2023) (upholding an on/off-premises distinction and finding a prohibition of digital billboards advanced significant interests in aesthetics and traffic safety).

59. *See, e.g.*, G.K. Ltd. Travel v. City of Lake Oswego, 436 F.3d 1064 (9th Cir. 2006).

60. *See, e.g.*, State v. Dahl, 676 N.W.2d 305 (Minn. Ct. App. 2004).

61. Lone Star Security and Video, Inc. v. City of Los Angeles, 827 F.3d 1192 (9th Cir. 2016) (upholding content-neutral ban on mobile billboards); Supersign of Boca Raton, Inc. v. City of Fort Lauderdale, 766 F.2d 1528 (11th Cir. 1985) (noting that *Central Hudson* requirement (see *supra*, note 13) that restriction directly advance asserted governmental interest does not require that all problems related to aesthetics be solved, and partial solutions may

A regulation may limit the number and height of flagpoles and the number and maximum size of flags, even as applied to U.S. flags.[62] In 2005, the legislature enacted limits on the regulation of official government flags. Chapter 144, Section 7.1 of the North Carolina General Statutes (hereinafter G.S.) allows reasonable nondiscriminatory regulations on flag size, the number of flags, their location, and the height of flagpoles. A flag on governmental property and used by the government is governmental speech that is not subject to First Amendment limitations.[63]

This is not to say, however, that all content-neutral time-place-and-manner restrictions are valid. One federal court invalidated a nearly total ban of all commercial and noncommercial yard signs as failing to be narrowly tailored and failing to provide alternative channels of communication.[64] Another invalidated an ordinance prohibiting street graphics with "any statement, word, character or illustration of an obscene, indecent or immoral nature" as overly broad and impermissibly vague.[65] A regulation allowing two fifteen-day displays per year on portable signs was invalidated, with the court there noting that periodic removal of such signs exacerbated their distracting quality, so the regulation did not directly advance the traffic-safety or aesthetic objectives of the city.[66]

Prior-Restraint Considerations

In general, prior restraints of protected speech are only allowed if they are imposed for a short time period and provide a process for adequate and swift judicial appeal.[67]

Content-neutral time-place-and-manner regulations of the use of a public forum do not amount to a prior restraint,[68] but even these regulations must avoid placing unbridled discretion in the hands of government officials.[69]

The requirement that a permit be obtained for a sign does not in itself raise prior-restraint issues.[70] Still, when a sign ordinance includes discretionary standards for decision (typically by requiring a special use permit for the sign rather than making it a permitted use subject to objective standards), prior-

---

be advanced). In *Boyer v. City of Simi Valley*, 978 F.3d 618 (9th Cir. 2020), the court held that a prohibition on mobile billboards that exempted emergency, construction, repair, and maintenance vehicles was not content neutral and remanded the case for evaluation under a strict-scrutiny test.

62. Am. Legion Post 7 v. City of Durham, 239 F.3d 601, 606–07 (4th Cir. 2001). In nonresidential districts, flagpoles were limited to a maximum height of 70 feet and flags to 216 square feet. In residential districts, the limits were 25 feet for flagpoles and 40 square feet for flags. There was also a limit of three flagpoles per property and two flags per flagpole, as well as setback requirements.

63. *See* Walker v. Texas Div., Sons of Confederate Veterans, Inc., 576 U.S. 200 (2015) (license plates are governmental speech); Pleasant Grove City v. Summum, 555 U.S. 460, 467–469 (2009) (display of monument in public park is governmental speech). However, if the government allows private parties to display flags on the governmental flagpole, that is speech subject to First Amendment protection. Shurtleff v. City of Boston, 142 S. Ct. 1583 (2022) (restriction on use of city flagpole for religious flags when other private flags are allowed is impermissible content discrimination).

64. Cleveland Area Bd. of Realtors v. City of Euclid, 88 F.3d 382, 387–88 (6th Cir. 1996).

65. Solomon v. City of Gainesville, 763 F.2d 1212, 1213 (11th Cir. 1985). The plaintiff operated Leonardo's Pizza and had a sign with a modified version of a Leonardo da Vinci drawing that the city deemed indecent.

66. Dills v. City of Marietta, 674 F.2d 1377 (11th Cir. 1982). On the other hand, in *Mobile Signs, Inc. v. Town of Brookhaven*, 670 F. Supp. 68 (E.D.N.Y. 1987), the court upheld a requirement that display of temporary commercial signs on the same premises be limited to a maximum of six months per year.

67. Freedman v. Maryland, 380 U.S. 51, 57–59 (1965). Justice Blackmun, in *Virginia State Board of Pharmacy v. Virginia Citizens Consumer Council*, expressed some question as to whether prior-restraint consideration was applicable to commercial speech. 425 U.S. 748, 771 n.24 (1976).

68. Thomas v. Chi. Park Dist., 534 U.S. 316, 322 (2002).

69. FW/PBS, Inc. v. City of Dallas, 493 U.S. 215, 225–26 (1990).

70. Infinity Outdoor, Inc. v. City of N.Y., 165 F. Supp. 2d 403, 425–30 (E.D.N.Y. 2001).

restraint considerations may arise.[71] For example, a sign ordinance that allowed an administrator to deny a permit for signs deemed harmful to the city's health, welfare, or aesthetic quality was invalidated because it gave staff unbridled discretion.[72] Note that in North Carolina the type of "unbridled discretion" that would render a sign ordinance an unlawful prior restraint[73] would also violate the general zoning standards that require special use permits to have adequate guiding standards.[74]

The failure to include a time limit for making a decision on a sign-permit application can constitute an unlawful prior restraint.[75] However, the negligent handling of a sign-permit application that results in long delays has been held to not be an unlawful prior restraint. In *Covenant Media of South Carolina, LLC v. City of North Charleston*,[76] the permit application was apparently lost, but the applicant made no inquiries as to its status during the period and the court found no unlawful prior restraint.

Content Neutrality

Many sign ordinances make content-related distinctions. They may have differential standards for on-site and off-site signs or distinguish between commercial and noncommercial signs. Sign regulations may contain exemptions or standards that vary based on the sign's message. Indeed, even the tests to

---

71. If the standards are objective, there is no prior-restraint issue. Mom N Pops, Inc. v. City of Charlotte, 979 F. Supp. 372 (W.D.N.C. 1997). Adult uses were permitted by right in several zoning districts provided specified minimum-separation and objective operational standards were met. The court held that this was not a prior restraint as neither the zoning administrator nor the privilege-license issuer exercised any discretion in review of applications.

72. Desert Outdoor Advert., Inc. v. City of Moreno Valley, 103 F.3d 814, 818–19 (9th Cir. 1996). In *GEFT Outdoor, LLC v. Monroe Cnty.*, 62 F.4th 321 (7th Cir. 2023), the court held that the county's procedures for considering a variance petition for a digital billboard that did not comply with content-neutral standards was not an unlawful prior restraint. In *International Outdoor, Inc. v. City of Troy*, 974 F.3d 690 (6th Cir. 2020), the court held that the zoning-variance standards in the ordinance prior to its amendment constituted an unlawful prior restraint. The corrective ordinance amendment removed content-based restrictions, clarified the variance standards, and made issuance mandatory upon finding the criteria were met. The amendment also limited the size of ground signs and provided that no variance would be granted for signs exceeding the size and height limitations by more than twenty-five percent. In *North Olmstead Chamber of Commerce v. City of North Olmstead*, 86 F. Supp. 2d 755, 775–78 (N.D. Ohio 2000), the court invalidated a sign ordinance as an invalid prior restraint when it provided that the reviewing official "may" issue permits, allowed the reviewing official to consider "facts and circumstances" that were not specified, and had no time period for final decisions. In *Outdoor Systems, Inc. v. City of Merriam*, 67 F. Supp. 2d 1258, 1271–73 (D. Kan. 1999), the court invalidated an ordinance because it sent sign permits to the community-development committee of the city council for approval and provided no set standards or maximum time period for decision. The court also found the ordinance invalid because it allowed the administrator to remove "unattractive" signs and those that the administrator deemed a "menace to the community," required signs to conform "to the aesthetics of the immediate area," and prohibited "obscene, indecent or immoral matter" on signs (all without further definition). In *Abel v. Town of Orangetown*, 759 F. Supp. 161 (S.D.N.Y. 1991), the court invalidated a sign regulation as an unlawful prior restraint because it gave unbridled discretion to decision makers. The regulation required a permit for signs but contained no standards by which the permits were to be decided.

73. *See, e.g.*, G.K. Ltd. Travel v. City of Lake Oswego, 436 F.3d 1064, 1082 (9th Cir. 2006). This does not, however, preclude use of appropriately bounded design standards. *See, e.g.*, Outdoor Media Grp., Inc. v. City of Beaumont, 506 F.3d 895, 904–05 (9th Cir. 2007). In *World Wide Rush, LLC v. City of Los Angeles*, 606 F.3d 676 (9th Cir. 2010), the court upheld an ordinance that banned "supergraphic" signs but contained an exemption for signs approved pursuant to a special plan, supplemental use district, or development agreement.

74. See Chapter 16.

75. Adams Outdoor Advert. Ltd. P'ship v. Penn. Dep't of Transp., 930 F.3d 199, 208 (3d Cir. 2019) (sign regulation with no time limit for decision invalid as a failure to provide the strict administrative time limit for decision required by *City of Littleton v. Z.J. Gifts D-4, L.L.C.*, 541 U.S. 774 (2004)). *See also* Solantic, LLC v. City of Neptune Beach, 410 F.3d 1250 (11th Cir. 2005) (absence of a time limit is invalid prior-restraint grounds); Roma Outdoor Creations, Inc. v. City of Cumming, 599 F. Supp. 2d 1332 (N.D. Ga. 2009).

76. 493 F.3d 421, 430–35 (4th Cir. 2007).

be employed by a reviewing court vary to a degree depending on the content of the speech being regulated: commercial speech receives less protection than noncommercial speech, speech related to adult entertainment gets less protection than other commercial speech, and political speech receives more protection than other noncommercial speech.

Some content-related distinctions in sign regulations are legally permissible, but the distinctions must be carefully crafted to avoid constitutional infirmity. These distinctions raise a variety of issues. Do the distinctions remove the content neutrality of the ordinance, thereby triggering strict scrutiny?[77] Do the distinctions so undermine the purposes of the ordinance that it no longer directly advances legitimate objectives? Do the distinctions render the ordinance unduly underinclusive? Or does the lack of distinctions render it unduly overinclusive?

The U.S. Supreme Court addressed the content neutrality of sign regulations in *Reed v. Town of Gilbert*, invalidating a regulation that had different size and duration limits for different categories of noncommercial signs. Political signs, ideological signs, and temporary directional signs were treated differently. The Court found this to be a content-based distinction that did not pass a strict-scrutiny review.[78] Thus, distinction in sign regulations that treat differing types of noncommercial messages differently[79] (e.g., allowing political signs but not ideological signs) or distinguishing between types of commercial messages (e.g., allowing temporary directional signs for real-estate open houses but not other temporary commercial signs) is almost certainly invalid.

On-Site/Off-Site Distinctions

In *Metromedia*, the Supreme Court applied the *Central Hudson* test and held that while a sign regulation may not favor an on-site commercial message over a noncommercial message, it could permit on-site commercial signs while prohibiting off-site commercial signs.[80]

---

77. Content-neutral regulations, on the other hand, are reviewed under an intermediate-scrutiny test.

78. 576 U.S. 155 (2015). Even though the regulation was viewpoint neutral, the Court found the differential treatment of the noncommercial signs to be clearly content based. While the Court was unanimous in its judgment, it splintered into three groups on the rationale for the decision. Three justices joined the majority with a strict reading of content neutrality, three joined a concurring opinion noting a number of potential non-content-based permissible distinctions between types of signs, and three concurred in the result only. For commentary, see Enrique Armijo, Reed v. Town of Gilbert: *Relax, Everybody*, 58 B.C. L. Rev. 65 (2017); Ashutosh Bhagwat, *In Defense of Content Regulation*, 102 Iowa L. Rev. 1427 (2017); Note, *Free Speech Doctrine After* Reed v. Town of Gilbert, 129 Harv. L. Rev. 1981 (2016).

79. *See, e.g.*, Willson v. City of Bel-Nor, 924 F.3d 995 (8th Cir. 2019) (invalidating ordinance that distinguished between types of flags); GEFT Outdoor LLC v. Consolidated City of Indianapolis & Cnty. of Marion, 187 F. Supp. 3d 1002, 1014 (S.D. Ind. 2016) (exemption for noncommercial opinion signs facially invalid); Marin v. Town of Southeast, 136 F. Supp. 3d 548 (S.D.N.Y. 2015) (invalidating ordinance that exempted political signs).

80. 453 U.S. 490, 508 (1981). In *Rappa v. New Castle County*, 18 F.3d 1043, 1065 (3d Cir. 1994), the court concluded that where there is a "significant relationship" between the content of speech and a specific location, exemptions from a general ban on signs for those signs that have such a relationship are permissible, provided that there is no attempt to limit viewpoints, there is no attempt to limit subject matter, the regulation is substantially related to an important state interest, and the exception is narrowly drawn and no broader than necessary. The court found that an on-site/off-site distinction generally meets this test.

Courts have upheld sign regulations that banned[81] or strictly limited off-site commercial signs from particular zoning districts or even jurisdiction-wide, while allowing on-site commercial signs.[82] Regulations that were more stringent for off-premise signs than for on-premise signs in the same area were likewise upheld.[83] While the Court in *Reed* held that distinguishing between different types of noncommercial signs was not content-neutral regulation, the question was left as to whether these distinctions between types of commercial signs—on-site versus off-site—would continue to be held to be content-neutral.

The Court answered this question in *City of Austin v. Reagan National Advertising of Austin, LLC,*[84] ruling that the differential treatment of on-premises/off-premises signs is still content neutral in time, place, and manner for the purpose of First Amendment review. The ordinance that was upheld prohibited new off-premises signs but allowed existing off-premises signs to remain as lawful nonconformities. The ordinance also allowed on-premises signs, but not off-premises ones, to be digitized.

A variation of the on-site/off-site distinction includes regulations that allow identification signs but prohibit advertising signs. For example, such a distinction often allows a wall or monument sign that contains the name of a building for identification purposes but would not allow a commercial advertisement at the same location. *Melrose, Inc. v. City of Pittsburgh* addressed the question whether such a distinction is permissible and how it can be applied to signs that have both aspects, such as when a commercial entity buys the naming rights to a building and proposes to use its corporate name or product as the building name. The court applied a "context-sensitive" analysis and upheld the distinction, noting that it was substantially related to an important public interest (associating a name with a particular location to assist the public in recognizing and finding it) and that the exception to the ban on commercial advertising was narrowly drawn.[85]

The on-site/off-site distinction has also been allowed for noncommercial signs. A historic-district regulation was upheld that allowed on-site noncommercial messages while prohibiting off-site non-

---

81. *See, e.g.,* Rzadkowolski v. Vill. of Lake Orion, 845 F.2d 653 (6th Cir. 1988) (upholding regulation that allowed only on-site signs, even when application of standards allowed only one billboard in small village); Naegele Outdoor Advert., Inc. v. City of Durham, 844 F.2d 172, 173–74 (4th Cir. 1988); Ga. Outdoor Advert., Inc. v. City of Waynesville, 833 F.2d 43, 46 (4th Cir. 1987); Wheeler v. Comm'r of Highways, 822 F.2d 586 (6th Cir. 1987) (upholding regulation banning off-site signs in defined area but allowing signs containing commercial or noncommercial messages related to activity on-site or sale of products on-site); Major Media of the Se., Inc. v. City of Raleigh, 792 F.2d 1269, 1272 (4th Cir. 1986). *See also* Schloss v. Jamison, 262 N.C. 108, 136 S.E.2d 691 (1964); Summey Outdoor Advert., Inc. v. Cnty. of Henderson, 96 N.C. App. 533, 386 S.E.2d 439 (1989), *review denied,* 326 N.C. 486, 392 S.E.2d 101 (1990); R.O. Givens, Inc. v. Town of Nags Head, 58 N.C. App. 697, 294 S.E.2d 388, *cert. denied,* 307 N.C. 127, 297 S.E.2d 400 (1982).

82. *See, e.g.,* Contest Promotions, LLC v. City & Cnty. of S.F., 874 F.3d 597 (9th Cir. 2017) (on-site/off-site distinction for commercial advertising allowed under *Reed* and *Central Hudson* test applies); Lavey v. City of Two Rivers, 171 F.3d 1110 (7th Cir. 1999).

83. *See, e.g.,* Nat'l Advert. Co. v. City & Cnty. of Denver, 912 F.2d 405 (10th Cir. 1990) (upholding regulation prohibiting off-site signs within 660 feet of a freeway while allowing on-site commercial signs and noncommercial signs in same area); Nat'l Advert. Co. v. City of Orange, 861 F.2d 246, 250 (9th Cir. 1988) (upholding on-site/off-site distinction for commercial signs but not for noncommercial signs); Infinity Outdoor, Inc. v. City of N.Y., 165 F. Supp. 2d 403 (E.D.N.Y. 2001) (upholding prohibition of off-site commercial signs in areas within 200 feet of major streets and parks and within residential and some commercial zones while allowing on-site commercial signs in the same areas).

84. 142 S. Ct. 1464 (2022). *See also* GEFT Outdoor, LLC v. City of Westfield, 39 F.4th 821 (7th Cir. 2022); Suffolk Outdoor Advertising Co. v. Hulse, 439 U.S. 808 (1978).

85. 613 F.3d 380 (3d Cir. 2010). The court approved the following four criteria used by the city to distinguish a permissible identification sign from an impermissible advertising sign: (1) whether the sign's purpose was to identify a destination point at a specific location; (2) whether the established location is important to a material segment of the public; (3) the intended longevity of the sign; and (4) whether the owner or principal user of the building was in control of the sign.

commercial messages.[86] The on-site/off-site distinction is not, however, uniformly upheld.[87] In *Ackerley Communications of Massachusetts, Inc. v. City of Cambridge*,[88] for example, the court addressed a sign regulation requiring amortization of nonconforming signs. The local ordinance made no distinction between commercial versus noncommercial or on-site versus off-site signs. However, state law allowed amortization provisions to be applied only to off-site signs. All of the plaintiff's advertising signs had been converted to noncommercial messages during the litigation, but all were categorized as off-site noncommercial. Thus, the effect of the ordinance was to allow nonconforming on-site noncommercial (and commercial) signs to be maintained while amortizing off-site noncommercial signs. The court found no aesthetic basis for the differential treatment of on-site and off-site noncommercial signs, and it was concerned that such a rule gave unfair access to billboards displaying noncommercial messages to a single group: the owners of on-site commercial signs could in the future display noncommercial messages on their signs, but the owners of off-site commercial billboards could not. The relief granted was, however, not what the sign company sought—it won only the right to continue displaying noncommercial messages on its nonconforming billboards.

Commercial/Noncommercial Distinctions

The courts for the most part have held that a commercial/noncommercial distinction does not negate the content-neutral basis of a sign regulation.[89] However, the question of the degree to which sign regulations may (or even must) treat commercial and noncommercial signs differently has proven particularly vexing.

A sign regulation may not treat noncommercial speech more restrictively than commercial speech.[90] In *Metromedia*, the U.S. Supreme Court held that a regulation allowing commercial messages at a particular site cannot prohibit noncommercial messages at the same site,[91] and this rule has been uniformly applied.[92] Many ordinances address this concern with a "substitution provision" allowing a

---

86. Messer v. City of Douglasville, 975 F.2d 1505, 1509–11 (11th Cir. 1992) (upholding a viewpoint-neutral regulation that banned all off-site signs in the historic district). In *Southlake Property Associates, Ltd. v. City of Morrow*, 112 F.3d 1114, 1118 (11th Cir. 1997), the court did away with any problem in distinguishing on-site/off-site noncommercial messages by defining all noncommercial messages to be "onsite."

87. In *National Advertising Co. v. City of Orange*, 861 F.2d 246 (9th Cir. 1988), a regulation that prohibited all off-site signs was held valid as applied to commercial signs but invalid as applied to noncommercial signs.

88. 88 F.3d 33 (1st Cir. 1996). *See also* Ackerley Commc'ns of Mass., Inc. v. City of Somerville, 878 F.2d 513 (1st Cir. 1989).

89. Lavey v. City of Two Rivers, 171 F.3d 1110, 1116 (7th Cir. 1999) (allowing exemption of construction and governmental signs as "common-sense exceptions"); Am. Legion Post 7 v. City of Durham, 239 F.3d 601, 608–09 (2001). *See also* Gen. Auto Serv. Station v. City of Chi., 526 F.3d 991, 1007–08 (7th Cir. 2008) (exemption for prior nonconforming signs is content neutral). The use of this distinction while retaining content neutrality is implicitly approved by *City of Austin v. Reagan National Advertising of Austin, LLC*, 142 S. Ct. 1464 (2022).

90. *See, e.g.*, G.K. Ltd. Travel v. City of Lake Oswego, 436 F.3d 1064, 1081 (9th Cir. 2006); Nat'l Advert. Co. v. City of Orange, 861 F.2d 246, 248 (9th Cir. 1988).

91. Metromedia, Inc. v. City of San Diego, 453 U.S. 490, 513 (1981).

92. Café Erotica of Fla., Inc. v. St. Johns Cnty., 360 F.3d 1274 (11th Cir. 2004) (impermissible to limit political-message signs to 32 square feet where commercial signs can be 560 square feet); Desert Outdoor Advert., Inc. v. City of Moreno Valley, 103 F.3d 814 (9th Cir. 1996) (1997) (regulation may not allow on-site commercial messages while restricting noncommercial messages to off-site signs); Matthews v. Town of Needham, 764 F.2d 58 (1st Cir. 1985) (regulation prohibiting political signs but allowing on-site commercial signs is facially invalid); John Donnelly & Sons v. Campbell, 639 F.2d 6, 15–16 (1st Cir. 1980), *aff'd*, 453 U.S. 916 (1981) (while statute's restrictions on commercial advertisements could likely be justified under the First Amendment, statute cannot restrict noncommercial speech more stringently than commercial speech); Infinity Outdoor, Inc. v. City of N.Y., 165 F. Supp. 2d 403 (E.D.N.Y. 2001) (upholding ordinance that prohibited off-site commercial signs while allowing off-site noncommercial signs on the same sites); Fla. Outdoor Advert., LLC v. City of Boynton Beach, 182 F. Supp. 2d 1201 (S.D. Fla. 2001) (holding that ordinance that failed to allow noncommercial messages where commercial messages

noncommercial message to be displayed anywhere a commercial message may be displayed.[93] Such a clause should not impose additional procedural hurdles (such as a permit or fee) that make obtaining approval for a noncommercial substitution more expensive or time-consuming than securing approval for the commercial message.[94]

Local governments must also consider the converse of this distinction: allowing a noncommercial message but prohibiting a commercial message at the same site. Under the rationale that commercial speech is afforded less First Amendment protection than noncommercial speech, many jurisdictions apply more stringent regulations to commercial signs than to signs with noncommercial messages (often by exempting or providing less stringent restrictions on noncommercial signs).[95] *City of Cincinnati v. Discovery Network, Inc.*[96] raises a cautionary note regarding such an approach. The high Court there invalidated a regulation that banned only news racks containing advertising flyers, holding that such a content-based distinction is unconstitutional unless the government entity involved establishes a close fit between the regulation and its purposes. The city's asserted purpose in *Discovery Network* was to address aesthetic and safety concerns. Whether the news rack contained commercial advertisements or newspapers had no bearing on the impact of the news rack relative to those objectives. Thus, the Court held such a distinction to be invalidly underinclusive. As *Lorillard Tobacco Co. v. Reilly*[97] confirmed, however, a commercial/noncommercial distinction is not per se invalid, but it does raise concerns about the fit between the regulation and its purposes. Therefore, a sign ordinance making such a distinction should be carefully supported by a justifying rationale.[98]

---

were permitted was facially invalid, and that subsequent amendments to cure this problem will not moot the case as sign applications were pending prior to amendment); Outdoor Sys., Inc. v. City of Merriam, 67 F. Supp. 2d 1258 (D. Kan. 1999) (invalidating a regulation based on the differential treatment provided on-site commercial and on-site noncommercial messages, finding that the challenged ordinance, for example, allowed political signs such as "Vote for Joe" to be up for only thirty days while on-site commercial signs such as "Eat at Joe's" could remain in place indefinitely); Metromedia, Inc. v. Mayor of Balt., 538 F. Supp. 1183 (D. Md. 1982) (ordinance may restrict commercial billboards in an urban-renewal area but may not prohibit noncommercial messages where commercial messages are allowed).

93. The Fourth Circuit has consistently upheld such substitution provisions. Ga. Outdoor Advert., Inc. v. City of Waynesville, 833 F.2d 43, 46 (4th Cir. 1987); Major Media of the Se., Inc. v. City of Raleigh, 792 F.2d 1269, 1273 (4th Cir. 1986). Similar holdings in other circuits include *Outdoor Systems, Inc. v. City of Mesa*, 997 F.2d 604 (1993) (upholding ordinance distinguishing off-site/on-site commercial signs but allowing all permitted signs to carry a noncommercial message), and *National Advertising Co. v. Town of Babylon*, 900 F.2d 551, 557 (2d Cir. 1990).

94. Beaulieu v. City of Alabaster, 454 F.3d 1219 (11th Cir. 2006) (invalidating provision that permitted commercial signs by right and without permits in commercial zoning district but required permit to substitute political sign).

95. *See, e.g.*, Maldonado v. Morales, 556 F.3d 1037 (9th Cir. 2009) (upholding California Outdoor Advertising Act provisions banning off-site commercial advertisement but allowing noncommercial messages).

96. 507 U.S. 410 (1993).

97. 533 U.S. 525 (2001).

98. RTM Media, L.L.C. v. City of Houston, 584 F.3d 220 (5th Cir. 2009); G.K. Ltd. Travel v. City of Lake Oswego, 436 F.3d 1064 (9th Cir. 2006) (upholding pole-sign ban that allowed a limited number of noncommercial exceptions for public signs, hospital signs, railroad signs, and danger signs); Infinity Outdoor, Inc. v. City of N.Y., 165 F. Supp. 2d 403, 421–22 (E.D.N.Y. 2001) (upholding ordinance that distinguished off-site commercial signs from on-site commercial and noncommercial signs).

Crafting the definitions that distinguish commercial from noncommercial messages is also challenging. For example, when is a mural on the side of a building art as opposed to an advertisement? *Compare* Wag More Dogs, Ltd. Liability Corp. v. Cozart, 680 F.3d 359 (4th Cir. 2012) (mural of dogs playing on side of a pet day care is an advertisement) *with* Complete Angler, LLC v. City of Clearwater, 607 F. Supp. 2d 1326 (M.D. Fla. 2009) (mural of fish on side of a tackle shop is not an advertisement).

Some courts have applied *Reed* to find that sign regulations for murals that exempt public art and noncommercial messages remove content neutrality and thus trigger strict scrutiny of the regulation.[99]

Regulating Noncommercial Content

It is not uncommon for sign regulations to make content-related distinctions among signs. With noncommercial signs, this often takes the form of exemptions from regulations for specified signs: directional signs, historic markers, signs at places of worship, temporary banners for nonprofit organizations, and the like.

A carefully limited number of noncommercial exemptions generally does not pose a significant First Amendment problem. For example, the court in *Messer v. City of Douglasville*[100] upheld exemptions for directional traffic signs and one bulletin board per site, noting that the regulation made no preference for different types of noncommercial messages. Similarly, the court in *Adams Outdoor Advertising Ltd. Partnership v. Pennsylvania Department of Transportation* held that an exemption for official signs is not a content-based restriction.[101]

Still, the U.S. Supreme Court expressed serious reservations in *Metromedia* about allowing some noncommercial messages while prohibiting others.[102] A number of courts have found any distinctions based on the content of noncommercial signs to be invalid.[103] In *Bowden v. Town of Cary*, the plaintiff

---

99. Cent. Radio Co. v. City of Norfolk, 811 F.3d 625 (4th Cir. 2016) (sign ordinance that exempts "works of art" not content neutral); Neighborhood Enters., Inc. v. City of St. Louis, 644 F.3d 728 (8th Cir. 2011) (ordinance regulating commercial advertising but exempting flags and civic crests not content neutral); Morris v. City of New Orleans, 399 F. Supp. 3d 624, 636–37 (E.D. La. 2019) (regulation distinguishing murals with a commercial message from those that are noncommercial public art is a content-based regulation). The court upheld an ordinance that applied to all "painted wall signs" in Leibundguth Storage & Van Serv., Inc. v. Vill. of Downers Grove, 939 F.3d 859 (7th Cir. 2019). In a decision that predates *Reed*, the Fourth Circuit held that a Cary ordinance limiting the size of signs in residential areas was content neutral even though it exempted public art and holiday displays. Brown v. Town of Cary, 706 F.3d 294 (4th Cir. 2013) (applied to a sign painted across the front of a house protesting the town's actions in improving the adjacent road to the alleged harm of the homeowner). *See also* Hellbender, Inc. v. Town of Boone, No. 5:12CV45-RLV, 2013 WL 1349286 (W.D.N.C. Mar. 31, 2013) (noise ordinance that contained exception for high-school, college, and nonrecurring community events was still content neutral).

100. 975 F.2d 1505, 1512–13 (11th Cir. 1992). *See also* Carpenter v. City of Snohomish, No. C06-0755-JCC, 2007 WL 1742161 (W.D. Wash. June 13, 2007). The court held that a requirement that wall murals in a historic district be "sympathetic to historical context" and consistent with the visual landscape of the 1880s–1930s era was content neutral as it regulated the manner of speech rather than the message communicated.

101. 930 F.3d 199, 206 (3d Cir. 2019). The court held this to be a permissible exemption for government speech. In *Signs for Jesus v. Town of Pembroke*, 977 F.3d 93 (1st Cir. 2020), the court held that an electronic-sign ban that included exemptions for government signs and prior nonconforming signs was not a content-based distinction. The regulation was upheld under intermediate scrutiny, based on a conclusion that it was narrowly tailored to address significant governmental interests in aesthetic protection and traffic safety. The court also dismissed equal-protection, free-exercise, and RLUIPA claims.

102. 453 U.S. 490, 514–15 (1981).

103. Solantic, LLC v. City of Neptune Beach, 410 F.3d 1250 (11th Cir. 2005) (invalidating ordinance exempting a number of governmental and other signs from restrictions on illumination and changeable copy); Desert Outdoor Advert., Inc. v. City of Moreno Valley, 103 F.3d 814 (9th Cir. 1996) (holding that distinguishing permissible noncommercial messages based on content is invalid without a compelling justification); Dimmitt v. City of Clearwater, 985 F.2d 1565, 1569–70 (11th Cir. 1993) (holding regulation allowing government flags but not other noncommercial flags is a content-based restriction that must be supported by a compelling state interest); Nat'l Advert. Co. v. Town of Niagara, 942 F.2d 145 (2d Cir. 1991) (invalidating ordinance that allowed on-site commercial and some, but not all, noncommercial messages, holding that severance clause could not save the ordinance); Nat'l Advert. Co. v. Town of Babylon, 900 F.2d 551, 557 (2d Cir.), *cert. denied*, 498 U.S. 852 (1990) (holding that exemptions for temporary political signs and signs for parades, festivals, and fund drives impermissibly discriminate among types of noncommercial signs based on content); National Advert. Co. v. City of Orange, 861 F.2d 246 (9th Cir. 1988) (invalidating

and city engaged in an extended dispute after the city widened a street adjacent to his home. In response the plaintiff had "Screwed by the Town of Cary" painted in large letters across the front of his home. The city cited him for a violation of its sign ordinance. The relevant regulation exempted several types of signs, including holiday decorations, public art, and temporary signs advertising town-recognized events. The court noted that even though there was no intent on the part of the town to suppress any particular content and that the town's objectives (aesthetics and traffic safety) were content neutral, the ordinance required a "searching inquiry" to determine if a particular sign was regulated. The court therefore held that the exemptions rendered the ordinance content based rather than content neutral.[104]

Regulating Commercial Content

With commercial signs, local governments are often requested to make exceptions for some signs (e.g., For Sale signs, signs advertising local businesses, or time/temperature displays).[105] There may be an interest in imposing more-restrictive regulations for commercial signs advertising certain products or businesses (e.g., tobacco, alcohol, adult use, or gambling). Since such distinctions insert content sensitivity into the regulations, there are significant First Amendment restrictions on the extent to which this can be done.

Some limited commercial-content distinctions are acceptable. *Metromedia* allows distinctions based on whether the commercial activity being advertised on a sign is taking place on-site.[106] *Central Hudson* allows a ban on advertisement of illegal products or activities.[107]

Courts are, however, very sensitive to regulations whose terms vary based on the content of the advertisement. In *Discovery Network*, the Supreme Court invalidated a regulation that distinguished among the types of papers inside of regulated news racks.[108] In *Consolidated Edison Co. of New York v. Public Service Commission*,[109] the Court invalidated as impermissible content-based discrimination a regulation prohibiting electric-bill inserts promoting nuclear power while allowing other inserts. The fact that an advertisement is offensive to many does not remove its First Amendment protection.[110]

---

a regulation that prohibited most off-site noncommercial messages but allowed some exceptions based on content, holding that content-based distinctions must be supported by a compelling justification); N. Olmstead Chamber of Commerce v. City of N. Olmstead, 86 F. Supp. 2d 755, 764–69 (N.D. Ohio 2000) (invalidating ordinance that provided different treatment to noncommercial messages depending on "use type" of sign, where ordinance categorized signs as project sign, organizational sign, identification sign, etc.); Outdoor Sys., Inc. v. City of Merriam, 67 F. Supp. 2d 1258 (D. Kan. 1999) (invalidating an ordinance that allowed some off-site noncommercial signs—memorial signs; bulletin-board signs; temporary signs of a civic, political, or religious nature; certain flags; and holiday decorations— while prohibiting all others); Outdoor Sys., Inc. v. City of Atlanta, 885 F. Supp. 1572 (N.D. Ga. 1995) (holding that it is impermissible content-based discrimination for sign regulations to temporarily allow Olympic-related signs, which could include up to 20 percent commercial content, where other noncommercial and commercial signs would be prohibited). *See also* Perry v. L.A. Police Dep't, 121 F.3d 1365 (9th Cir. 1997) (impermissible content discrimination for ordinance to limit sales along sidewalks to nonprofit organizations selling merchandise with an ideological, political, religious, or philosophical message).

104. 754 F. Supp. 2d 794 (E.D.N.C. 2010). The principal violation here was that the sign at issue was approximately forty-eight square feet, while the ordinance limited noncommercial signs in this residential zoning district to five square feet. After finding the ordinance was not content neutral, the court applied strict scrutiny and invalidated the regulation as not supporting compelling governmental interests and not being narrowly drawn.

105. G.K. Ltd. Travel v. City of Lake Oswego, 436 F.3d 1064 (9th Cir. 2006).

106. Metromedia, Inc. v. City of San Diego, 453 U.S. 490 (1981).

107. Cent. Hudson Gas & Elec. Corp. v. Pub. Serv. Comm'n, 447 U.S. 557 (1980).

108. City of Cincinnati v. Discovery Network, Inc., 507 U.S. 410 (1993).

109. 447 U.S. 530 (1980).

110. Sambo's, Inc. v. City Council, 466 F. Supp. 177, 180 (N.D. Ohio 1979) (holding that even distasteful advertising that could connote racial prejudice has First Amendment protection).

One approach local governments have taken is to argue that the content can be considered in order to prevent adverse secondary impacts, much as is the case with regulation restricting the location of adult entertainment. An example of the application of this rationale is *Excalibur Group, Inc. v. City of Minneapolis*, where the court upheld limitations on the signs that could be displayed by an adult establishment. The ordinance prohibited signs displaying pictures of products or entertainment offered in the establishment, prohibited opaque windows and signs in windows, and allowed only a one-square-foot sign noting hours of operation and admittance of adults only. The court allowed these sign restrictions, which applied only to commercial establishments that offered adult entertainment, as a narrowly tailored means of reducing adverse secondary impacts.[111] On the other hand, the court in *Passions Video, Inc. v. Nixon*[112] invalidated a Missouri statute that prohibited all off-premises billboards for adult businesses if the billboard was within a mile of a state highway. The law also strictly limited the content of allowed on-premises advertising signs. The court held that both regulations were not narrowly tailored.

Such arguments are, however, rarely successful outside of the adult-entertainment area. A leading example is provided by *Linmark Associates, Inc. v. Township of Willingboro*. There the Supreme Court invalidated a sign regulation that prohibited placement of For Sale signs in residential areas. The local government justified the restriction on prevention of secondary impacts, arguing that it was designed to promote stable, integrated neighborhoods and to prevent panic sales and "white flight." The Court held that this could not justify content-based restrictions on commercial speech.[113] Another example is provided by *Sandhills Ass'n of Realtors v. Village of Pinehurst*.[114] The village adopted regulations on temporary signs that had differing size and content rules depending on the type of sign.[115] The rules limited the size of real-estate signs, the colors that could be used, the duration a sign could be displayed, and the content that could be included on the sign. The court held this to be a content-based restriction that failed both as a reasonable time-place-and-manner restriction and as a commercial-speech regulation under *Central Hudson*.[116]

---

111. 116 F.3d 1216 (8th Cir. 1997). *See also* SDJ, Inc. v. City of Houston, 837 F.2d 1268 (5th Cir. 1988). In *Basiardanes v. City of Galveston*, 682 F.2d 1203 (5th Cir. 1982), the court held that the city could prohibit display of provocative, lurid, or sexually explicit posters by an adult theater as a narrowly tailored means of reducing adverse secondary impacts.

112. 458 F.3d 837 (8th Cir. 2006). Similarly, the court in *Pleasureland Museum, Inc. v. Beutter*, 288 F.3d 988 (7th Cir. 2002), noted the prevention of adverse secondary impacts justified much of the city's regulation of adult businesses, but the court invalidated a restriction that limited adult-business signs to including only the name of the business.

113. 431 U.S. 85 (1977). Cases with similar conclusions include *Cleveland Area Board of Realtors v. City of Euclid*, 88 F.3d 382, 388 (6th Cir. 1996) (invalidating total ban on residential yard signs), and *Rappa v. New Castle County*, 18 F.3d 1043, 1069–70 (3d Cir. 1994) (expressing doubt that the secondary-impacts analysis should be applied to regulations affecting political speech and holding that for said analysis to apply, speech that is prohibited must produce greater secondary impacts than that which is permitted).

114. No. 1:98CV00303, 1999 WL 1129624 (M.D.N.C. Nov. 8, 1999). *See also* Citizens for Free Speech II v. Long Beach Twp. Bd. of Comm'rs, 802 F. Supp. 1223 (D.N.J. 1992) (distinction between For Sale and For Rent yard signs is content-based regulation).

115. The regulations applied to both noncommercial signs (political signs, those for church functions, holiday decorations, and the like) and commercial signs (real-estate For Sale, construction, yard sales, special business events, etc.).

116. The court noted that while aesthetic concerns were a substantial governmental interest, they were not a compelling interest and the regulation was not narrowly tailored. The fact that different rules were applied to different types of temporary signs was also a significant issue. The court pointed out that aesthetic concerns could potentially justify uniform regulations but stated that singling out particular commercial messages for more-restrictive regulation is a content-based regulation that casts doubt on the alleged governmental interest supporting the regulation. *See* Gold Coast Publ'ns, Inc. v. Corrigan, 42 F.3d 1336 (11th Cir. 1994), *cert. denied*, 516 U.S. 931 (1995) (upholding uniform regulation on color and size of lettering on all news racks).

Some local governments propose limitations on signs advertising alcoholic beverages. The Supreme Court implied in *California v. LaRue*[117] that additional restrictions on adult entertainment might be imposed on the authority of the Twenty-First Amendment's grant of authority to regulate alcohol sales. However, in *44 Liquormart, Inc. v. Rhode Island*,[118] the Court held that although the Twenty-First Amendment grants states the authority to regulate commerce, it in no way reduces the protections afforded by the First Amendment. Thus, restrictions on signs related to alcohol are analyzed under the same rules applicable to other commercial speech.

The Court has on several occasions reviewed sign and advertising limitations regarding gambling. Two early cases upheld restrictions, but the most recent case invalidated the restriction.

In *Posadas de Puerto Rico Associates v. Tourism Co. of Puerto Rico*,[119] the Court applied the *Central Hudson* analysis to uphold a statute restricting casino advertisement to tourists (banning signs and other advertisement directed toward Puerto Rico residents). The Court noted that if the state could ban casino gambling altogether, it could take the lesser step of limiting its advertisement. This notion was subsequently disavowed in *44 Liquormart* and *Rubin v. Coors Brewing Co.*[120] In *United States v. Edge Broadcasting Co.*,[121] the Court again applied the *Central Hudson* analysis to uphold a statute prohibiting radio stations in nonlottery states from broadcasting lottery advertisements. (The station involved was licensed in North Carolina, located just inside the state, and the vast majority of its audience was in Tidewater, Virginia. At the time, North Carolina did not have a state lottery.)

However, in *Greater New Orleans Broadcasting Ass'n v. United States*,[122] the Court invalidated restrictions on advertisements for lawful casino gambling placed on stations in Louisiana, where such casinos are lawful. The Court again applied the *Central Hudson* analysis. The Court noted that casino gaming was lawful in Louisiana and that while there were substantial state interests in limiting the social costs of gambling, federal and state policies on allowing or limiting such gambling were "now decidedly equivocal," thus making it more difficult to establish the contention that limits on this commercial speech advanced a substantial state interest. Given the various exemptions allowed (such as for gaming in Native American casinos and other forms of gambling) and alternatives for addressing social costs (controls on admissions, location restrictions, licensing requirements, credit limits, and the like), the Court held that there was an insufficient fit between the regulation and its purpose: it neither directly advanced those objectives nor was it any more restrictive than necessary.

Application of the *Central Hudson* requirements that restrictions on commercial speech be no more extensive than necessary led the Supreme Court to invalidate Massachusetts restrictions on tobacco advertisements in *Lorillard Tobacco*. The Court there invalidated a prohibition of billboards advertising smokeless tobacco and cigars within 1000 feet of schools and playgrounds. Similar restrictions on cigarette billboards were held preempted by federal law on tobacco advertising. The Court found that while preventing underage tobacco use was a substantial governmental interest and restrictions on targeted advertisements were substantially related to that interest, the regulation was not sufficiently tailored. The government must carefully calculate the costs and benefits associated with the burden on free speech, and here that calculation was not done. The Court noted that in urban areas the challenged setback amounted to a near-total ban and that a ban on signs of all sizes rather than only large

117. 409 U.S. 109 (1972).

118. 517 U.S. 484 (1996) (striking down restrictions on advertising retail prices of alcoholic beverages).

119. 478 U.S. 328, 340–44 (1986).

120. 44 Liquormart, Inc. v. Rhode Island, 517 U.S. 484 (1996); Rubin v. Coors Brewing Co., 514 U.S. 476 (1995) (invalidating regulations prohibiting the advertising of the alcohol content of beer).

121. 509 U.S. 418 (1993).

122. 527 U.S. 173 (1999). In *WV Ass'n of Club Owners and Fraternal Services, Inc. v. Musgrave*, 553 F.3d 292 (4th Cir. 2009), the court upheld some exterior-advertising restrictions for legalized video lottery machines.

billboards—including, for example, a small sign in a store window saying cigars are sold inside—was overly broad.[123]

While courts are sympathetic to protection of minors, regulations cannot "reduce the adult population . . . to reading only what is fit for children."[124] Such restrictions must be narrowly tailored; otherwise, an overly broad restriction is invalid. As Justice Frankfurter memorably put it, "Surely, this is to burn the house to roast the pig."[125] The Supreme Court applied strict scrutiny to a statute restricting cable television that made content-based distinctions, noting that "the objective of shielding children does not suffice to support a blanket ban if the protection can be obtained by a less restrictive alternative."[126]

Still, when the speech is indiscriminately available to minors, as is the case with most signs, some restrictions are permissible.[127] Restrictions on outdoor advertisements carefully targeted at the protection of minors have been upheld. The Fourth Circuit has been particularly receptive to these considerations. In *Anheuser-Busch, Inc. v. Schmoke*,[128] the court upheld a Baltimore ordinance prohibiting alcohol advertising near schools as a reasonable time-place-and-manner restriction that satisfied the four-part test of *Central Hudson*. On reconsideration on remand in light of *44 Liquormart*, the Fourth Circuit again upheld the ordinance.[129]

Special Considerations Regarding Political Signs

Very careful judicial scrutiny is applied to regulating signs expressing political views.[130] This includes both political campaign signs[131] and signs expressing a view on a public-policy issue.[132] Protection of political speech is a core component of First Amendment law. Whether it involves flag burning,[133] flag alteration,[134] campaign contributions,[135] or offensive words,[136] the U.S. Supreme Court has been especially

---

123. 533 U.S. 525 (2001).

124. Butler v. Michigan, 352 U.S. 380, 383 (1957) (overturning conviction for selling books that tend to incite minors to violent, depraved, or immoral acts).

125. *Id.* at 383.

126. United States v. Playboy Entm't Grp., Inc., 529 U.S. 803, 814 (2000) (invalidating regulation imposing time restrictions on cable broadcast of sexually explicit material).

127. The Court has approved restrictions on radio broadcast of "indecent" material. FCC v. Pacifica Found., 438 U.S. 726 (1978) (the case involved the late George Carlin's seven words you cannot say on the radio). *See also* Coyote Publ'g, Inc. v. Miller, 598 F.3d 592 (9th Cir. 2010) (upholding limits on advertisements in theaters and on public streets for brothels in the Nevada counties where prostitution is legal).

128. 63 F.3d 1305 (4th Cir. 1995).

129. Anheuser-Busch, Inc. v. Schmoke, 101 F.3d 325 (4th Cir. 1996). *But see* Khademi v. S. Orange Cnty. Cmty. Coll. Dist., 194 F. Supp. 2d 1011, 1028–29 (C.D. Cal. 2002) (while college can limit advertisements for illegal products, ban of all advertisements for alcohol, tobacco, and guns is overly broad).

130. The Court has long recognized the importance of protecting "uninhibited, robust, and wide-open" debate on public issues. New York Times Co. v. Sullivan, 376 U.S. 254, 270 (1964).

131. Political campaign speech has the fullest and most urgent First Amendment protection. McIntyre v. Ohio Elections Comm'n, 514 U.S. 334, 346 (1995); Eu v. S.F. Cnty. Democratic Cent. Comm., 489 U.S. 214, 219 (1989).

132. These are sometimes referred to as "cause" signs as distinguished from "campaign" signs. Both have First Amendment protection. *See, e.g.,* Savago v. Vill. of New Paltz, 214 F. Supp. 2d 252 (N.D.N.Y. 2002) (sign regarding terrorists); Knoeffler v. Town of Mamakating, 87 F. Supp. 2d 322 (S.D.N.Y. 2000) (invalidating ordinance that permitted some on-site commercial signs but prohibited most noncommercial signs); Pica v. Sarno, 907 F. Supp. 795 (D.N.J. 1995) (invalidating ordinance regulating window and yard signs applied to prevent a homeowner's complaint about a developer); State *ex rel.* Dep't of Transp. v. Pile, 1979 OK 152, 603 P.2d 337 (sign opposing United Nations).

133. Texas v. Johnson, 491 U.S. 397 (1989).

134. Spence v. Washington, 418 U.S. 405 (1974).

135. Buckley v. Valeo, 424 U.S. 1 (1976).

136. Cohen v. California, 403 U.S. 15 (1971) ("F*** the Draft" printed on back of jacket worn in courthouse is protected speech); Hess v. State of Indiana, 414 U.S. 105 (1973) (profanity used in speech at rally is protected speech). In

wary of regulation of political speech or speech on matters of public concern.[137] Attempts to regulate the content of political messages are particularly suspect.[138]

Many local governments have restrictive rules on signs in residential areas in order to protect and enhance the quiet, noncommercial aesthetic of neighborhoods.[139] Attempts to ban all signs, including political messages, are difficult to justify. In *City of Ladue v. Gilleo*, the Court invalidated a ban on yard and window signs, holding that the plaintiff's small signs were political speech (the signs protested the Gulf War) and that a ban precluded a traditional and important means of conveying political messages.[140] Many local governments thus attempt to balance legitimate public interests in aesthetics, safety, and litter control with the rights to post political signs by regulating rather than banning political signs.

Durational restrictions on display of political signs are very common, particularly for campaign signs. The notion is that since the signs are related to a particular election, regulations that limit their display to some reasonable proximity to the election do not infringe on free-speech rights. Many jurisdictions attempt to balance political expression and aesthetic impacts by setting limits on how long before an election a campaign sign can be posted and how soon after the election the signs can remain posted. In North Carolina, regulations prohibiting posting of the signs more than sixty or ninety days before an election are common, as are requirements to remove the signs seven to ten days after the election.[141]

State statutes have a specific time limit for permissible campaign signs in the rights-of-way of state roads, allowing them to be displayed from thirty days before the beginning of early voting to ten days after the election.[142] Courts around the country have strictly reviewed similar time limits to ensure they are narrowly tailored and not unduly restrictive.[143] For the most part, restrictions that do not allow

---

Snyder v. Phelps, 562 U.S. 443 (2011), the Court held that "outrageous" language on picket signs displayed near the funeral of a soldier killed in the Iraq War that caused emotional distress was protected speech.

Cases have upheld the use of profanity and offensive language as protected speech in a variety of contexts. *See, e.g.*, Wood v. Eubanks, 25 F.4th 414 (6th Cir. 2022) ("F*** the Police" on shirt at county fair is protected speech); Survivors Network of Those Abused by Priests, Inc. v. Joyce, 779 F.3d 785 (8th Cir. 2015) (offensive language on protest signs is protected speech); Payne v. Pauley, 337 F.3d 767 (7th Cir. 2003) (profanity directed at police is protected speech). *See generally* Alexandra B. Bachman, Note, *WTF? First Amendment Implications of Policing Profanity*, 17 First Amend. L. Rev. 65 (2018).

137. Connick v. Myers, 461 U.S. 138, 145 (1983). This includes matters of political, social, or other concern to the community. San Diego v. Roe, 543 U.S. 77, 83–84 (2004).

138. Lebron v. Wash. Metro. Area Transit Auth., 749 F.2d 893 (D.C. Cir. 1984) (restriction on "deceptive" or "distorted" political signs invalid).

139. Sign regulations imposed by a private homeowners' association are generally not affected by these restrictions on government regulation of signs. *See, e.g.*, Comm. for a Better Twin Rivers v. Twin Rivers Homeowners' Ass'n, 192 N.J. 344, 929 A.2d 1060 (2007).

140. 512 U.S. 43 (1994). *See also* Peltz v. City of S. Euclid, 11 Ohio St. 2d 128, 228 N.E.2d 320 (1967) (invalidating a citywide ban on political signs). Some courts countenance regulations of all temporary or noncommercial signs that include political signs. *See, e.g.*, G.K. Ltd. Travel v. City of Lake Oswego, 436 F.3d 1064, 1077 (9th Cir. 2006); Ross v. Goshi, 351 F. Supp. 949 (D. Haw. 1972).

141. In a 2012 School of Government survey on the regulation of political signs, 73 percent of responding cities and counties reported that they regulated the time for display of political signs. Seventy percent reported that they had size limits, 47 percent reported that they had height limits and limits in sight triangles, 31 percent reported a limit on the maximum number of signs that could be displayed, and 13 percent had spacing requirements. Owens & Batten, *supra* note 51, at 21.

142. G.S. 136-32(b) (enacted in 2011). The statute also has dimensional restrictions (no higher than 42 inches and no larger than 864 square inches) and locations restrictions (no closer than three feet from the pavement of the road, not within a controlled-access road right-of-way, no obstruction of visibility at an intersection, no obstruction of another sign).

143. An additional consideration is that a regulation that sets different durational limits for different types of signs, as in allowing campaign signs to be posted for longer periods than other noncommercial yard signs, is likely no longer content neutral under *Reed*, thereby subjecting the regulation to strict scrutiny. Ficker v. Talbot Cnty., 553 F. Supp. 3d 278, 283 (D. Md. 2021) (different size and durational limits for different types of noncommercial signs is not content neutral).

posting of campaign signs at least sixty days before an election have been invalidated.[144] Requirements for post-election removal of campaign signs are more frequently upheld.[145]

A limit on the size of political signs is another common restriction. Some regulations limit the size of individual signs, while others place a limit on the total size of all signs on a lot. Reasonable size limits are typically upheld, but limits that render the signs ineffective as a means of communicating the political message are invalidated.[146] Reasonable related regulations, such as a prohibition of illuminated signs, are permissible, but not if other, nonpolitical signs are not subject to the same limitations.[147]

Limits on the number of political signs that can be posted on a single lot are another common restriction. The Fourth Circuit Court of Appeals addressed this question in *Arlington County Republican Committee v. Arlington County*.[148] The court invalidated a limit of two political signs per yard. While the court was willing to assume that the regulation was a content-neutral time-place-and-manner restriction,

---

144. Whitton v. City of Gladstone, 54 F.3d 1400, 1403–04 (8th Cir. 1995) (invalidating regulation limiting political signs to thirty days before and seven days after an election, noting appearance and maintenance concerns could be addressed more narrowly, such as by limiting any temporary sign to a ninety-day display period); John Donnelly & Sons v. Campbell, 639 F.2d 6 (1st Cir. 1980) (three-week display period insufficient); Knoeffler v. Town of Mamakating, 87 F. Supp. 2d 322 (S.D.N.Y. 2000); Outdoor Sys., Inc. v. City of Merriam, 67 F. Supp. 2d 1258 (D. Kan. 1999) (invalidating thirty-day limit on political signs); Outdoor Sys., Inc. v. City of Lenexa, 67 F. Supp. 2d 1231 (D. Kan. 1999) (invalidating requirement that political campaign signs be removed within seven days of election); Curry v. Prince George's Cnty., 33 F. Supp. 2d 447, 454–55 (D. Md. 1999) (invalidating ordinance limiting campaign signs to forty-five days before election through ten days of election, with a thirty-day limit for posting other "public interest" signs); Dimas v. City of Warren, 939 F. Supp. 554 (E.D. Mich. 1996) (invalidating requirements that election signs be posted no more than forty-five days before election, removed within seven days after election); McCormack v. Twp. of Clinton, 872 F. Supp. 1320 (D.N.J. 1994) (invalidating requirement that political signs be displayed no more than ten days before or three days after event); City of Antioch v. Candidates' Outdoor Graphic Serv., 557 F. Supp. 52 (N.D. Cal. 1982) (invalidating ordinance requirement limiting posting of election signs to sixty days before election); Orazio v. Town of N. Hempstead, 426 F. Supp. 1144 (E.D.N.Y. 1977) (invalidating ordinance provision prohibiting posting political wall signs more than six weeks before election, noting there was no similar time limit on commercial on-site wall signs); McFadden v. City of Bridgeport, 422 F. Supp. 2d 659 (N.D. W. Va. 2006) (invalidating requirement that campaign signs be posted no more than thirty days before and two days after election); City of Painesville Bldg. Dep't v. Dworken & Bernstein Co., 89 Ohio St. 3d 564, 733 N.E.2d 1152 (2000); Collier v. City of Tacoma, 121 Wash. 2d 737, 854 P.2d 1046 (1993) (sixty-day limit not narrowly tailored); City of Lakewood v. Colfax Unlimited Ass'n, 634 P.2d 52, 63 (Colo. 1981) (sixty days inadequate). *See generally* Jules B. Gerard, *Election Signs and Time Limits*, 3 WASH. U. J.L. & POL'Y, 379 (2000).

145. *See, e.g., Collier*, 121 Wash. 2d 737, 854 P.2d 1046 (upholding requirement that campaign signs be removed within seven days of election). To avoid potential problems with the regulation being deemed content based rather than content neutral, some jurisdictions apply these durational limits to all temporary signs, not just political signs associated with a particular election.

146. Cases upholding political-yard-sign size and number limits include *Baldwin v. Redwood City*, 540 F.2d 1360 (9th Cir. 1976), upholding size restrictions on campaign signs (sixteen square feet per sign and eighty square feet per parcel, and *Kolbe v. Balt. Cnty.*, 730 F. Supp. 2d 478 (D. Md. 2010), upholding eight-square-foot size limit for temporary signs as applied to political sign. On the other hand, the court in *Verrilli v. City of Concord*, 548 F.2d 262 (9th Cir. 1977), invalidated a four-square-foot size limit of political signs and limit of one sign per lot. More recently, the court in *Willson v. City of Bel-Nor*, 470 F. Supp. 3d 994 (E.D. Mo. 2022), held that a limit of one yard sign (with two faces allowed) and one governmental flag (but other flags counted as the one allowed "sign" per lot) was far too broad given the asserted governmental interest in aesthetics and traffic safety. The differential treatment of types of flags was also deemed to render the regulation not content neutral.

147. Whitton v. City of Gladstone, 54 F.3d 1400 (8th Cir. 1995).

148. 983 F.2d 587 (4th Cir. 1993). The restriction here was a limit of not more than one temporary noncommercial sign per principal dwelling unit in residential zoning districts, plus one For Sale or Lease sign upon which a political message could be substituted. *See also* Fehribach v. City of Troy, 412 F. Supp. 2d 639 (E.D. Mich. 2006) (invalidating limit of two signs per lot); *Dimas*, 939 F. Supp. 554 (invalidating limit of one sign per candidate or issue); Brayton v. City of New Brighton, 519 N.W.2d 243 (Minn. Ct. App. 1994) (upholding limit of one noncommercial opinion sign allowed year-round, plus one sign per ballot issue and per candidate during election season).

it held that it was not sufficiently narrowly tailored (limits on the design and condition of signs, setbacks from streets, and duration limits could address legitimate aesthetic concerns while allowing greater political expression, the court noted) and left inadequate alternative means of political expression.

A limit on sign location is another common regulation of political signs.[149] The Supreme Court upheld a ban of all political signs within 100 feet of polling places in *Burson v. Freeman*,[150] and the fact that signs to be placed on utility poles in a public right-of-way were political ads did not invalidate their prohibition in *Members of the City Council v. Taxpayers for Vincent*.[151] G.S. 163-166.4(a) requires a buffer around North Carolina polling places within which signs may not be posted. Where practical the buffer is to be fifty feet from the door of the polling place, but in no case is it to be less than twenty-five feet.

While the use of profane or offensive language is generally protected political speech,[152] its use on signs visible to the general public may be subject to regulation.[153] The use of profane language on a residential yard sign could be considered directed toward a "captive audience" and thus subject to greater regulation.[154] The exposure to unwilling and captive residential neighbors and their children is an entirely different context than seeing and hearing that language at a political rally or public event one chooses to attend. Also, courts have held that commercial speech that is readily available to minors can be regulated to protect children from sexually explicit and vulgar advertisements.[155] If permissible, the regulation must be narrowly tailored and use the least restrictive option for shielding children.[156] It is not clear, however, whether this rationale would also apply to highly protected political speech.

---

149. Beaulieu v. City of Alabaster, 454 F.3d 1219 (11th Cir. 2006) (invalidating regulation allowing temporary real-estate signs but prohibiting political signs in commercial zoning district); Rappa v. New Castle Cnty., 18 F.3d 1043 (3d Cir. 1994) (invalidating restrictions on signs within twenty-five feet of public right-of-way due to lack of content neutrality); Matthews v. Town of Needham, 764 F.2d 58 (1st Cir. 1985) (regulation prohibiting political signs but allowing on-site commercial signs held facially invalid).

150. 504 U.S. 191 (1992). *See also* Anderson v. Spear, 356 F.3d 651, 662 (6th Cir. 2004) (collection of cases on mandated buffer zones for signs near polling places).

151. 466 U.S. 789 (1984).

152. See cases cited above at note 135.

153. The court in *Cohen* noted that while profanity is protected political speech, "government may properly act in many situations to prohibit intrusion into the privacy of the home of unwelcome views and ideas which cannot be totally banned from the public dialogue . . . upon a showing that substantial privacy interests are being invaded in an essentially intolerable manner." 403 U.S. at 21 (citations omitted).

154. While invalidating an ordinance that prohibited showing any nudity at a drive-in theater that might be visible from a public area, the Court noted selective restrictions on speech could be upheld where "the degree of captivity makes it impractical for the unwilling viewer . . . to avoid exposure." Erznoznik v. City of Jacksonville, 422 U.S. 205, 209 (1975). Based on that rationale, the Court in *Frisby v. Schultz*, 487 U.S. 474 (1988), upheld a content-neutral prohibition of picketing individual residences as a narrowly tailored restriction on speech to prevent intrusion on residential privacy while allowing ample alternative channels available for communication.

155. FCC v. Pacifica Foundation, 438 U.S. 726 (1978) (upholding a rule prohibiting broadcast of "indecent" language aired in the afternoon); Sable Communications of Cal. v. Federal Communications Comm'n, 492 U.S. 115, 126 (1989) (protection of minors is a compelling interest for speech regulation). Restrictions on outdoor advertising signs have been upheld on this rationale. Anheuser-Busch, Inc. v. Schmoke II, 101 F.3d 325 (4th Cir. 1996) (upholding ordinance prohibiting alcohol advertising near schools). *See also* Bethel School Dist. v. Fraser, 478 U.S. 675 (1986) (*Cohen* protection of profanity as speech is not applicable to the speech rights of children in a public school).

156. U.S. v. Playboy Entertainment Group, 529 U.S. 803 (2000). The necessity of careful tailoring in this context is provided by *Flying Dog Brewery v. North Carolina Alcoholic Beverage Control Commission*, 603 F. Supp. 3d 257 (E.D.N.C. 2022). The plaintiff appealed the denial of their right to include a nude cartoon figure standing by a campfire on a beer-bottle label. The rule justifying the denial prohibited depiction of advertising images deemed by the ABC Commission to be "undignified, immodest, or in bad taste." The court held that this rule was too broad to withstand constitutional scrutiny. The standard in the rule prohibited far more speech than that necessary to protect minors. The court noted, however, that it may have been permissible if the rule were drawn more narrowly to prohibit "vulgar words or images of a sexual, violent, or illegal nature." *Id.* at 264.

Fees for placement of political signs are also sometimes charged to cover the costs of implementation and enforcement of regulations. Reasonable content-neutral fees will generally be upheld, but care must be taken to limit the costs for review of covered signs and ensure that no exemptions exist for similar signs.[157]

---

157. Forsyth Cnty. v. Nationalist Movement, 505 U.S. 123, 130–33 (1992) (fee for parade permit must include narrowly drawn, reasonable, objective standards for setting fee); Cox v. New Hampshire, 312 U.S. 569, 576–78 (1941) (allowing fees for parade permits where amount of fee is designed to meet administrative expenses and maintain order in the streets); Baldwin v. Redwood City, 540 F.2d 1360 (9th Cir. 1976) (invalidating fees for campaign-sign permits); Sugarman v. Vill. of Chester, 192 F. Supp. 2d 282 (S.D.N.Y. 2002) (applying rule to several sign ordinances, upholding those that were uniform and invalidating those that were not). *See also* Riel v. City of Bradford, 485 F.3d 736 (3d Cir. 2007) (upholding fee exemption for all temporary signs in a historic district).

Judicial Review

PART 7

CHAPTER 29

Judicial Review

The overwhelming majority of land use decisions by local governments are not challenged in court. Several surveys conducted by the School of Government indicate that judicial review is sought for only a handful of variance, special use permit, or zoning-amendment decisions. Table 29.1 summarizes these reported judicial-appeal rates.[1] Still, given the volume of decisions made, the courts are called upon to review a sizable number of land use regulatory decisions each year, and it is typically the most controversial and complicated cases that come before the courts.

Table 29.1   Frequency of Judicial Review Sought

Type of Approval (Year Surveyed)	Total Number Sought	% Appealed to Court
Variance Petitions (2002)	1806	2.5
Special Use Permit Applications (2004)	2207	1.6
Zoning-Map Amendments (rezonings) (2006)	3029	0.9

Form of Action

While the occasional case is appropriate for federal courts,[2] most litigation on land use regulatory ordinances takes place in state courts.

G.S. 160D-1401 confirms that challenges to legislative land use regulatory decisions are brought under Chapter 1, Sections 253 to 267 of the North Carolina General Statutes (hereinafter G.S.), the state's declaratory-judgment statute. These provisions may be used to address disputes regarding the constitutionality, validity, or construction of ordinances and for original civil actions claiming a vested

---

1. David W. Owens, Zoning Amendments in North Carolina 18 (UNC School of Government, Special Series No. 24, Feb. 2008). A 2017–18 survey of all local governments in North Carolina confirmed that these trends continue. Cities and counties responding reported that only 83 cases were initiated in the previous year regarding their development regulations. Of these, 60 percent were brought by the landowner or applicant, 30 percent by a neighbor, and 10 percent by the local government. Appeals of staff interpretations of the ordinance were the most frequent subject of litigation, with approximately 25 percent of the cases. Appeals regarding special use permits, enforcement actions, site-plan approvals, and rezonings were the next most frequent subjects of litigation, each with 10 to 15 percent of the cases. Decisions on variances, certificates of appropriateness, text amendments, and plat approvals were all litigated, but each with less than 10 percent of the cases. David W. Owens, *2018 Survey Report: Adoption and Administration of Local Development Regulations, Conditional Zoning, and Subdivision Administration*, Plan. and Zoning L. Bull. No. 30 (UNC School of Government, Dec. 2020), at 15–16.

2. See Chapter 23 regarding federal statutory claims. Chapters 24 to 28 also discuss federal constitutional claims that may serve as the foundation for litigation in federal courts.

right.[3] However, they do not allow for advisory opinions or judgments before a genuine controversy arises. A legislative regulatory decision is not reviewable upon a writ of certiorari.[4]

G.S. 160D-1403.1 further provides that a person may also bring "an original civil action seeking declaratory relief, injunctive relief, damages, or any other remedies provided by law or equity" to establish a vested right, to assert a claim that a regulation is unconstitutional on its face or as applied, that the regulation is preempted or in excess of statutory authority, or that it constitutes an unconstitutional taking of private property.[5]

Appeals of quasi-judicial land use regulatory decisions are reviewed by the superior court in proceedings in the nature of certiorari.[6] In most instances, judicial appeals of administrative land use decisions will also be in the nature of certiorari because the initial appeal generally goes to the board of adjustment, and that board's decision is the subject of the judicial review.[7]

G.S. 160D-1402(b) sets the requirements for a petition for writ of certiorari. The petition must contain the basic facts that establish standing, the grounds of the alleged error, the facts that support any alleged conflict of interest,[8] and the relief the person seeks from the court. G.S. 160D-1402(e) provides that upon filing the petition, petitioners shall submit to the clerk of superior court a proposed writ. The

---

3. Taylor v. City of Raleigh, 290 N.C. 608, 620, 227 S.E.2d 576, 583 (1976); Blades v. City of Raleigh, 280 N.C. 531, 544, 187 S.E.2d 35, 42 (1972); Vill. Creek Prop. Owners' Ass'n v. Town of Edenton, 135 N.C. App. 482, 520 S.E.2d 793 (1999).

4. *In re* Markham, 259 N.C. 566, 569, 131 S.E.2d 329, 332, *cert. denied*, 375 U.S. 931 (1963); Massey v. City of Charlotte, 145 N.C. App. 345, 355, 550 S.E.2d 838, 845, *review denied*, 354 N.C. 219, 554 S.E.2d 342 (2001).

5. This provision was added to the statutes by S.L. 2019-111, § 1.7.

6. In 2009, the General Assembly codified most of the provisions for judicial review of quasi-judicial zoning decisions as Chapter 160D, Section 1402 of the North Carolina General Statutes (hereinafter G.S.). An appeal of a decision not to consider an application for a quasi-judicial permit due to an incomplete application must also be made in the nature of certiorari. Northfield Dev. Co. v. City of Burlington, 165 N.C. App. 885, 599 S.E.2d 921, *review denied*, 359 N.C. 191, 607 S.E.2d 278 (2004). Appeals of quasi-judicial decisions made under other development ordinances (such as subdivision regulations) are reviewed in the same manner. G.S. 160D-1403. In *Hemphill-Nolan v. Town of Weddington*, 153 N.C. App. 144, 568 S.E.2d 887 (2002), which involved denial of a variance for a cul-de-sac length limit in a subdivision ordinance, the court held that the superior court has discretion to grant a writ of certiorari "in proper cases" and that this was such a case.

7. Administrative decisions under zoning ordinances are appealed first to the board of adjustment, and the board's decision can subsequently be appealed to superior court in the nature of certiorari. G.S. 160D, §§ 405(a), (k); G.S. 160D-1402. Prior to enactment of Chapter 160D, there was some uncertainty regarding administrative land use regulatory decisions that were made under ordinances other than zoning where the ordinance involved did not provide for an appeal to the board of adjustment. It is likely that such an appeal would also be a "proper case," as the court held in *Hemphill-Nolan*, 153 N.C. App. at 148, 568 S.E.2d at 889–90. G.S. 160D-405(a) now provides that all administrative decisions made by staff under Chapter 160D are made to the board of adjustment unless other statutes or ordinances expressly direct the appeals to a different board.

One exception to this rule involves administrative decisions on subdivision plats. While staff or a staff committee usually makes these administrative decisions, some local ordinances assign these decisions to the governing board (typically when the decision also includes acceptance of dedications of land or improvements) or to the planning board. G.S. 160D-1403(b) provides that if the administrative decision on plat approval or implementation of subdivision regulations is made by the governing board or planning board, the appeal is made to superior court for declaratory or equitable relief. These appeals must be made within thirty days from receipt of written notice of the decision.

8. An allegation of improper conflict of interest must be made in a timely fashion. In *McMillan v. Town of Tryon*, 200 N.C. App. 228, 683 S.E.2d 747 (2009), the appellate court upheld the trial court's decision not to allow a complaint to be amended to add a conflict-of-interest allegation when the motion to amend was filed nearly a year after the initial complaint and a week after the defendants' motion for summary judgment with supporting affidavits. The court noted that even if the defendants' motion added new information about the details of the case, the plaintiff's failure to undertake any discovery until that point should not burden the defendants. Thus, the court held that the trial court did not abuse its discretion in denying the motion to amend the complaint. G.S. 160D-1402(i)(2) does allow the record on appeal to be supplemented with evidence regarding an alleged conflict of interest.

proposed writ must include a direction to the responding local government to prepare and certify to the court by a specified date the record of the board's proceedings on the matter. The petition is filed with the clerk of superior court in the county in which the matter arose. The clerk then issues the writ ordering the city or county to prepare and certify to the court the record. Petitioners must serve the writ upon all respondents, following the same rules for service of a complaint in a civil suit.[9] No summons is to be issued. While not expressly addressed by G.S. 160D-1402, prior case law provides that the petition need not be verified.[10] The clerk is directed to issue the writ without notice to the respondents if the petition is properly filed and is in proper form.

Respondents may file a response to the petition but are not required to. The common practice in North Carolina is not to file such a response. Rather, the record of the quasi-judicial proceeding is submitted, and the parties deal with the merits of the matter through motions to dismiss or at trial. However, a response must be filed to contest standing, and that response must be served on all petitioners at least thirty days before the hearing on the petition.[11] If the response is not served within that time period, the matter may be continued to allow the petitioners time to respond.

In general, it is inappropriate to challenge a legislative decision as part of judicial review of a quasi-judicial or administrative decision applying the ordinance.[12] In *Simpson v. City of Charlotte*, a neighbor appealed to the board of adjustment the zoning administrator's decision to issue a permit for expansion of a quarry. The board upheld the decision to issue the permit, and that decision was then appealed to superior court. The trial court held the ordinance provision at issue to be invalid. The court of appeals overturned that determination, holding that the board of adjustment had the authority only to grant or deny the permit and that the trial court, through its derivative appellate jurisdiction, could therefore not go beyond that issue to address the validity of the ordinance.[13]

The constitutionality of an ordinance provision likewise cannot be challenged in a certiorari review of a board of adjustment's decision. In *Batch v. Town of Chapel Hill*, the court held that it was an error to join a complaint alleging constitutional causes of action (a taking and denial of equal protection) with a petition for writ of certiorari seeking review of denial of subdivision approval under the city's development ordinance.[14] When an applicant has received a permit and benefited thereby, the applicant

9. G.S. 160D-1402(e) directs that the service of petition on the respondents is to be made in the same manner as service of a complaint under G.S. 1A-1, Rule 4(j).

10. Garrity v. Morrisville Zoning Bd. of Adjustment, 115 N.C. App. 273, 444 S.E.2d 653, *review denied*, 337 N.C. 692, 448 S.E.2d 523 (1994) (petition for writ of certiorari need not be verified); Little v. City of Locust, 83 N.C. App. 224, 349 S.E.2d 627 (1986), *review denied*, 319 N.C. 105, 353 S.E.2d 111 (1987).

11. G.S. 160D-1402(f). Answers may also be used to challenge jurisdiction prior to submittal of the record.

12. Some cases have allowed challenges to the validity of a zoning requirement when the ordinance is applied. See, for example, *White v. Union County*, 93 N.C. App. 148, 377 S.E.2d 93 (1989), a case challenging the denial of a special use permit to establish electrical power to a mobile home. The court concluded that the plaintiff could directly challenge the validity of the ordinance requirement in the suit, provided the action was brought within the appropriate statute of limitations for legislative zoning decisions.

13. 115 N.C. App. 51, 443 S.E.2d 772 (1994). The court has held that the General Assembly may, by local legislation, specifically authorize legislative zoning decisions in an individual jurisdiction to be reviewed in a petition for certiorari. Gossett v. City of Wilmington, 124 N.C. App. 777, 478 S.E.2d 648 (1996).

14. 326 N.C. 1, 11, 387 S.E.2d 655, 661–62, *cert. denied*, 496 U.S. 931 (1990). Grounds for review in the nature of certiorari include reviewing for errors in law and for arbitrary and capricious decisions, so some overlap in issues raised is possible. *See also Guilford County Department of Emergency Services v. Seaboard Chemical Corp.*, 114 N.C. App. 1, 10–11, 441 S.E.2d 177, 182, *review denied*, 336 N.C. 604, 447 S.E.2d 390 (1994) (where the court held that the superior court would not have jurisdiction to adjudicate a takings claim in a certiorari review but would have jurisdiction in an original action). There is also the issue of exhaustion of administrative remedies through application for permits and pursuit of available administrative appeals prior to making a constitutional challenge of an ordinance.

may not later attack the validity of the ordinance.[15] In *Dobo v. Zoning Board of Adjustment*, the court held that a petitioner cannot raise a constitutional challenge in the course of appealing a zoning officer's interpretation of the ordinance. In these cases, the board of adjustment has no authority to rule on the constitutionality of the ordinance, and the superior court is limited to review of whether the board properly affirmed or overruled the officer's determination.[16]

Because of these limitations, it is appropriate for a plaintiff to bring two separate actions when challenging the validity of an ordinance as well as seeking review of an individual decision under that ordinance. For example, in *Cary Creek Ltd. Partnership v. Town of Cary*,[17] the town's development ordinance included a riparian-buffer requirement. After the plaintiffs were denied a variance from the buffer requirements, they brought a declaratory-judgment action challenging the validity of the ordinance. The court held that the plaintiffs' separate certiorari proceeding challenging the variance denial did not deprive the court of subject-matter jurisdiction to hear this declaratory-judgment action as these two legal actions must be brought separately.

The statutes were amended in 2019 to allow joinder of an original civil action to challenge the constitutionality or statutory authority for a local government action with a petition for writ of certiorari.[18]

There are also substantial limits on the ability to challenge the validity of an ordinance in the judicial review of an enforcement action. The time to challenge a permit decision or its conditions arises at the time of permit decision, not when it is enforced.[19] If an appeal challenges whether there was a violation or whether the particular enforcement remedy is appropriate, an initial appeal must be made to the board of adjustment. The enforcement action may not be collaterally attacked in subsequent judicial actions.[20]

---

15. River Birch Assocs. v. City of Raleigh, 326 N.C. 100, 388 S.E.2d 538 (1990); Convent of the Sisters of Saint Joseph v. City of Winston-Salem, 243 N.C. 316, 90 S.E.2d 879 (1956); Wake Forest Golf & Country Club, Inc. v. Town of Wake Forest, 212 N.C. App. 632, 711 S.E.2d 816, *review denied*, 365 N.C. 359, 719 S.E.2d 21 (2011); Shell Island Homeowners Ass'n v. Tomlinson, 134 N.C. App. 217, 226, 517 S.E.2d 406, 413 (1999); Franklin Rd. Props. v. City of Raleigh, 94 N.C. App. 731, 735, 381 S.E.2d 487, 490 (1989); Goforth Props., Inc. v. Town of Chapel Hill, 71 N.C. App. 771, 323 S.E.2d 427 (1984). If, however, a permit was not actually required, then the permittee can subsequently challenge the enforceability of conditions on that permit. Stegall v. Zoning Bd. of Adjustment, 87 N.C. App. 359, 361 S.E.2d 309 (1987), *review denied*, 321 N.C. 480, 364 S.E.2d 679 (1988). *See also* Quality Built Homes Inc. v. Town of Carthage, 371 N.C. 60, 813 S.E.2d 218 (2018) (plaintiffs not estopped from challenging a water-and-sewer availability fee on the basis of an acceptance of benefits because the plaintiffs received no benefit to which they would not otherwise have been entitled); Buckland v. Town of Haw River, 141 N.C. App. 460, 541 S.E.2d 497 (2000) (authority to impose off-site conditions on subdivision-plat approval).

16. 149 N.C. App. 701, 706, 562 S.E.2d 108, 111–12 (2002), *rev'd on other grounds*, 356 N.C. 656, 576 S.E.2d 324 (2003). *See also* 321 News & Video, Inc. v. Zoning Bd. of Adjustment, 174 N.C. App. 186, 619 S.E.2d 885 (2005).

17. 203 N.C. App. 99, 690 S.E.2d 549, *review denied*, 364 N.C. 600, 703 S.E.2d 441 (2010).

18. Codified at G.S. 160D-1403.1(d), created by S.L. 2019-111, § 1.7. If joined, both actions may be decided in the same proceeding. The record for the decision being reviewed in the petition for certiorari may not be supplemented unless otherwise allowed for the civil action.

19. *See, e.g.,* Town of Pinebluff v. Marts, 195 N.C. App. 659, 663, 673 S.E.2d 740, 743 (2009); Forsyth Cnty. v. York, 19 N.C. App. 361, 364–65, 198 S.E.2d 770, 772, *cert. denied*, 284 N.C. 253, 200 S.E.2d 653 (1973).

20. Cnty. of Durham v. Addison, 262 N.C. 280, 283–84, 136 S.E.2d 600, 603 (1964); State v. Roberson, 198 N.C. 70, 150 S.E. 674 (1929); Appalachian Outdoor Advert. Co. v. Town of Boone, 103 N.C. App. 504, 406 S.E.2d 297 (1991); New Hanover Cnty. v. Pleasant, 59 N.C. App. 644, 297 S.E.2d 760 (1982); City of Elizabeth City v. LFM Enters., Inc., 48 N.C. App. 408, 269 S.E.2d 260 (1980); City of Hickory v. Catawba Valley Mach. Co., 39 N.C. App. 236, 249 S.E.2d 851 (1978). See the discussion of the requirement to exhaust administrative remedies below. Also see the discussion of enforcement in Chapter 21.

In relatively rare instances, a writ of mandamus is the appropriate form of action.[21] In *Morningstar Marinas/Eaton Ferry, LLC v. Warren County*,[22] the zoning administrator ruled that the plaintiff did not have standing to make an appeal on an ordinance interpretation to the board of adjustment. The court held that this determination must be made by the board itself and issued a writ of mandamus ordering the administrator to carry out the ministerial act of placing the matter on the board agenda.

Parties

Care must be exercised in identifying the proper governmental party in a suit challenging a land development regulatory decision.[23]

For a legislative decision, the governmental unit itself, not the governing board or its individual members, is the proper party if the decision is being challenged.[24] If monetary damages are being sought, board members may be sued in their individual as well as their official capacities.[25]

For quasi-judicial decisions, G.S. 160D-1402(d) provides that the respondent to the petition for writ of certiorari is the local government, not the individual board making the decision.[26] A petition that

---

21. The necessary elements for a writ of mandamus are that: (1) the party has a clear legal right to the act requested; (2) the officer has a clear legal duty to perform the act; (3) the act is ministerial, without the exercise of discretion; (4) the officer has neglected or refused to perform the duty; and (5) there is no alternative legally adequate remedy available. *In re* T.H.T., 362 N.C. 446, 453–54, 665 S.E.2d 54, 59 (2008). For a summary of the law on mandamus in North Carolina in this context, see David M. Lawrence, *Mandamus to Require Enforcement of Local Ordinances*, Loc. Gov't. L. Bull. No. 132 (UNC School of Government, July 2013).

22. 368 N.C. 360, 777 S.E.2d 733 (2015).

23. For the general provisions on parties in civil actions, see G.S. 1, §§ 57 to 72.3.

24. G.S. 160D-1401 expressly provides that the governmental unit shall be named as a party in these declaratory-judgment actions. In an action challenging a rezoning, the court noted, "Undoubtedly, the real party in interest in this case is Hertford County, not the Board of Commissioners." Piland v. Hertford Cnty. Bd. of Comm'rs, 141 N.C. App. 293, 296, 539 S.E.2d 669, 671 (2000). G.S. 153A-11 and 160A-11 provide that the county and city are corporate entities to sue and be sued in their own names, and the courts have long held that the governmental entity itself is the proper party rather than its officers. Lenoir Cnty. v. Crabtree, 158 N.C. 357, 74 S.E. 105 (1912) (county must sue and be sued in its own name); Young v. Barden, 90 N.C. 424 (1884) (city must be sued in its corporate name). G.S. 1-260 also requires that the N.C. Attorney General be served with a copy of the proceedings in any action alleging the unconstitutionality of an ordinance. *See also* Macon Cnty. v. Town of Highlands, 187 N.C. App. 752, 654 S.E.2d 17 (2007) (holding that neither the county nor individual commissioners were proper parties entitled to challenge the town's methods of computing the number of extraterritorial members to be appointed to the town planning board and board of adjustment).

In federal actions, suit against individuals in their official capacity is equivalent to suit against the governmental entity. Kentucky v. Graham, 473 U.S. 159, 165–67 (1985). Therefore, individuals named in their official capacity will be dismissed as parties.

25. See Chapter 21 for a discussion of liability of the governmental unit and individual board members or employees for monetary damages.

26. Prior to the 2009 addition to the statutes of this explicit provision regarding respondents, courts had held that the board making a quasi-judicial decision (as opposed to the jurisdiction itself or the individual board members) was a necessary party in a judicial appeal of a quasi-judicial decision. In *Mize v. County of Mecklenburg*, 80 N.C. App. 279, 341 S.E.2d 767 (1986), which involved an action challenging a zoning officer's interpretation, the court held that the board of adjustment is an independent body, not an agent of the county commissioners, and is hence a necessary party. Likewise, in *City of Raleigh v. Hudson Belk Co.*, 114 N.C. App. 815, 443 S.E.2d 112 (1994), involving an appeal by the city of the board of adjustment's reversal of the zoning officer's interpretation of sign limitations, the city failed to join the board of adjustment as a necessary party, and the action was therefore dismissed. *See also In re* Appeal of Harris, 273 N.C. 20, 159 S.E.2d 539 (1968) (statutes providing for judicial review of administrative decisions should be liberally construed to preserve the right of appeal).

Similarly, since it is the unit of government that is the party, the governing board has the authority to settle litigation regarding appeals of quasi-judicial decisions even if it was not the decision-making body. G.S. 160D-406(k).

names the board of adjustment rather than the unit of government is a failure to name a necessary party and must be dismissed.[27] An exception to this rule arises if the unit of government participates in the litigation, waiving the failure to join the unit itself.[28] If the petition for review is brought by the unit of government itself, the respondent is to be the decision-making board. If the petitioner is not the applicant for the decision being contested, the applicant must also be named as a respondent. A petitioner may also name as a respondent any owner or lessee of the property subject to the application if that person participated in the hearing or was the applicant.[29]

When an error is made in identifying proper parties, a complaint may be amended to add the proper parties. However, in *City of Raleigh v. Hudson Belk Co.*, the N.C. Court of Appeals held that the trial court has no responsibility to add a necessary party on its own motion. If the petitioner did not name the proper board as a party and made no request of the judge to do so, the trial court may properly dismiss the case.[30] Also, a motion to amend the complaint must be made in a timely fashion. In *Piland v. Hertford County Board of Commissioners*,[31] an action challenging a rezoning, the complaint improperly named the board of commissioners rather than the county itself as a defendant. The court held that while the trial court may grant a motion to amend the complaint to amend the name of the proper parties, such an amendment does not relate back to the original filing. Thus, if a necessary party is not included prior to the running of the applicable statute of limitations, the suit will be time-barred, and this cannot be corrected by the motion to amend.[32]

When the government brings the action, as with an enforcement action, it must also take care to identify and name the real party in interest.[33]

---

27. Azar v. Town of Indian Trail Bd. of Adjustment, 257 N.C. App. 1, 809 S.E.2d 17 (2017). The plaintiff had challenged the denial of a special use permit application. The court also held that an amended petition to add a party does not relate back to the original filing, so if the amendment is not filed within the time period for filing the petition, the petition is properly dismissed for failure to name a necessary party.

28. MYC Klepper/Brandon Knolls L.L.C. v. Bd. of Adjustment for Asheville, 238 N.C. App. 432, 767 S.E.2d 668 (2014). The court held that a failure to join the city itself as a necessary party did not deprive the court of subject-matter jurisdiction and the city's participation in the proceedings cured this procedural defect. *See also* Phillips v. Orange Cnty. Health Dep't, 237 N.C. App. 249, 765 S.E.2d 811 (2014) (allowing action to proceed when county board of health rather than the county was the named defendant).

29. In an enforcement action seeking injunctive relief regarding an alleged violation of a sedimentation- and erosion-control ordinance, the court held that the landowner was a necessary party. Durham Cnty. v. Graham, 191 N.C. App. 600, 663 S.E.2d 467 (2008). The defendant secured a land-disturbance permit for a landfill. The county issued a notice of violation alleging that more than an acre had been disturbed, the fill had extended into a floodplain, and the sediment had not been contained on-site. The county sought an injunction to compel restoration and compliance with the terms of the permit. Subsequent to the permit and notice of violation, the property changed hands and went into foreclosure. The title was transferred to the lender. The court held that the current owners of the property were necessary parties as their rights to use the property would be affected by an injunction. The court held that lien holders were not necessary parties, nor was the city (which would have had to permit the remedial actions being sought).

30. 114 N.C. App. 815, 443 S.E.2d 112 (1994).

31. 141 N.C. App. 293, 539 S.E.2d 669 (2000). The basic rule on relation back is set forth in *Crossman v. Moore*, 341 N.C. 185, 459 S.E.2d 715 (1995).

32. Hirschman v. Chatham Cnty., 250 N.C. App. 349, 792 S.E.2d 211 (2016). This challenge to issuance of a conditional use permit named only the county as the respondent, neglecting to name the applicant as is required by G.S. 160D-1402(d). The court ruled that the statute makes the applicant a necessary party, a failure to name a necessary party deprives the superior court of jurisdiction, and an appeal cannot be amended to add a necessary party after the time period to file the appeal has run.

33. *See, e.g.*, State v. Nance, 266 N.C. App. 353, 831 S.E.2d 605, *review denied*, 838 S.E.2d 182 (2020). In this public-nuisance case, the court held that it was improper to name the former manager of the motel that was the subject of the complaint as a party. Although she at one time oversaw day-to-day operations of the motel, she was no longer employed when the claim was brought, so the complaint against her was properly dismissed. An enforcement

Standing

Individual Standing

A suit challenging a land-development regulatory decision must be brought by a party with standing, that is, one whose legal rights are affected by the decision.[34] If the plaintiff in a suit challenging a decision does not establish standing, the superior court has no subject-matter jurisdiction to hear the case.

Since standing is a jurisdictional requirement, it must be alleged when the action is brought.[35] Thus, a petition for a writ of certiorari or a claim for a declaratory judgment must contain allegations to support the standing of the entity filing the action. The burden of establishing standing is on the party bringing the action.[36] When making a standing determination, the court views the allegations as true and the record in the light most favorable to the nonmoving party.[37]

If standing is challenged, evidence must be presented to support standing in order to survive a motion to dismiss or a motion for summary judgment. *Cherry Community Organization v. City of Charlotte* illustrates how the level of detail and evidentiary support for an allegation of special damages becomes more demanding as a case proceeds. The plaintiff nonprofit organization challenged the rezoning. The court held that while the plaintiff's pleadings contained an allegation of special damages sufficient to defeat a motion to dismiss, the failure to produce any evidence to support the allegation of special damages warranted summary judgment for the city.[38]

The United States Supreme Court in *Lujan v. Defenders of Wildlife* held that the "irreducible constitutional minimum" of standing contains three elements:

1. "injury in fact," an invasion of a legally protected interest that is (a) concrete and particularized and (b) actual or imminent rather than conjectural or hypothetical;
2. the injury is fairly traceable to the challenged action of the defendant; and
3. it is likely, as opposed to merely speculative, that the injury will be redressed by a favorable decision.[39]

---

action under a development regulation may name the property owner, the occupant of the property, or both. Patmore v. Town of Chapel Hill, 233 N.C. App. 133, 757 S.E.2d 302, *review denied*, 367 N.C. 519, 758 S.E.2d 874 (2014).

34. "The gist of the question of standing is whether the party seeking relief has alleged such a personal stake in the outcome of the controversy as to assure that concrete adverseness which sharpens the presentation of issues upon which the court so largely depends for illumination of difficult constitutional questions." Stanley v. Dep't of Conservation & Dev., 284 N.C. 15, 28, 199 S.E.2d 641, 650 (1973) (quoting Flast v. Cohen, 392 U.S. 83, 99 (1968) (internal quotations omitted)). For general reviews of the law of standing for land use cases, see John D. Ayer, *The Primitive Law of Standing in Land Use Disputes: Some Notes from a Dark Continent*, 55 Iowa L. Rev. 344 (1969); Robert A. Hendel, Note, *The "Aggrieved Person" Requirement in Zoning*, 8 Wm. & Mary L. Rev. 294 (1967).

35. Where all parties are represented by counsel and no objection to standing is made at either the quasi-judicial hearing or the superior court's review of a petition for certiorari, the question of standing will not be considered on appeal. Little River, LLC v. Lee Cnty., 257 N.C. App. 55, 61, 809 S.E.2d 42, 47, *review denied*, 818 S.E.2d 692 (2017).

36. Thrash Ltd. P'ship v. Cnty. of Buncombe (*Thrash I*), 195 N.C. App. 678, 680, 673 S.E.2d 706, 708 (2009); Neuse River Found. v. Smithfield Foods, 155 N.C. App. 110, 113, 574 S.E.2d 48, 51 (2002), *review denied*, 356 N.C. 675, 577 S.E.2d 628 (2003). If standing is contested in a quasi-judicial matter, the board making the decision, not the zoning administrator, is charged with making the initial determination on standing. Morningstar Marinas/Eaton Ferry, LLC v. Warren Cnty., 368 N.C. 360, 777 S.E.2d 733 (2015).

37. Mangum v. Raleigh Bd. of Adjustment, 362 N.C. 640, 644, 669 S.E.2d 279, 283 (2008).

38. 257 N.C. App. 579, 809 S.E.2d 397, *review denied*, 371 N.C. 114, 812 S.E.2d 850 (2018). The court held that a party may not rest on mere allegations in their pleadings but must, by affidavits or other means, set forth specific facts to support those assertions. A concurring opinion would have upheld the summary judgment because the plaintiff failed to forecast competent evidence to support a finding of special damages, which is a justiciable issue, rather than because they had not established they were an aggrieved party.

39. 504 U.S. 555, 560–61 (1992). *See also* Massachusetts v. Envtl. Prot. Agency, 549 U.S. 497, 517 (2007). Federal courts also consider prudential standing, asking whether the claim is sufficiently individualized to ensure effective

For years, North Carolina courts generally applied this basic test.[40] However, in *Committee to Elect Dan Forest v. Employees Political Action Committee*, the court conducted an extensive survey of standing rules from the state constitution, English common law, and the federal tests up to and including the *Lujan* standard.[41] The court concluded that since the state constitution does not contain a "case or controversy" provision similar to that in the federal Constitution, under state law an injury in fact is not required when a statutory or common law right is at issue because "injury" is deemed to be the infringement of a legal right rather than factual harm. The court concluded "the 'concrete adverseness' rationale undergirding our standing doctrine is grounded on prudential principles of self-restraint in exercise of our power of judicial review for constitutionality, which is itself only an incident of our exercise of the judicial power to determine the law in particular cases."[42] While "injury in fact" is not required, a "direct injury" to a legal right is required.[43]

Although originally the cases applied slightly different tests for standing to review legislative zoning decisions, quasi-judicial decisions, and other development regulations, as discussed below, the courts now view these standards as analogous.[44]

Legislative Decisions

The basic rule for standing to challenge legislative decisions in state court in North Carolina is set forth in *Taylor v. City of Raleigh*.[45] The court there ruled that challenges to legislative zoning decisions could be brought only "by a person who [had] a specific personal and legal interest in the subject matter affected by the zoning ordinance and who [was] directly and adversely affected thereby."[46] A citizen or taxpayer may not file a lawsuit as a member of the general public to bring a conceptual challenge to a legislative

---

judicial review. Elk Grove Unified Sch. Dist. v. Newdow, 542 U.S. 1, 11 (2004). In federal court, standing must be established for each particular claim raised, as standing to raise one claim does not open the door to raise any claim. *See, e.g.*, Covenant Media of S.C., LLC v. City of N. Charleston, 493 F.3d 421, 429 (4th Cir. 2007) (standing to challenge lack of time period for decision in sign ordinance does not confer standing to challenge other substantive provisions in sign ordinance).

40. Morgan v. Nash Cnty., 224 N.C. App. 60, 65, 735 S.E.2d 615, 619 (2012), *review denied*, 366 N.C. 561, 738 S.E.2d 379 (2013); Marriott v. Chatham Cnty., 187 N.C. App. 491, 494, 654 S.E.2d 13, 16 (2007); Neuse River Found., Inc. v. Smithfield Foods, Inc., 155 N.C. App. 110, 114, 574 S.E.2d 48, 51–52 (2002).

41. 376 N.C. 558, 853 S.E.2d 698 (2021).

42. *Id.* at 595, 853 S.E.2d at 725.

43. *See* United Daughters of the Confederacy, N.C. Div., Inc. v. City of Winston-Salem, ___ N.C. ___, 881 S.E.2d 32 (2022); The Society for the Hist. Pres. of the Twenty-Sixth N.C. Troops, Inc. v. City of Asheville, 282 N.C. App. 700, 872 S.E.2d 134, *review allowed*, 880 S.E.2d 679 (2022).

44. *See, e.g.*, *Cherry*, 257 N.C. App. 579, 809 S.E.2d 397, *review denied*, 371 N.C. 114, 812 S.E.2d 850 (2018).

45. 290 N.C. 608, 227 S.E.2d 576 (1976). This case involved a challenge to Raleigh's annexation and rezoning of a 39.89-acre tract. For additional statements of the standing test for legislative zoning decisions, see *Grace Baptist Church v. City of Oxford*, 320 N.C. 439, 444, 358 S.E.2d 372, 375 (1987) (holding that a plaintiff must "produce evidence that he has sustained an injury or is in immediate danger of sustaining an injury as a result of enforcement" of the ordinance in order to have standing to challenge the constitutionality of a zoning-ordinance provision); *Godfrey v. Zoning Board of Adjustment*, 317 N.C. 51, 344 S.E.2d 272 (1986); *Blades v. City of Raleigh*, 280 N.C. 531, 544, 187 S.E.2d 35, 42 (1972) ("owners of property in the adjoining area affected by the ordinance" have standing); *Zopfi v. City of Wilmington*, 273 N.C. 430, 160 S.E.2d 325 (1968); *Templeton v. Town of Boone*, 208 N.C. App. 50, 701 S.E.2d 709 (2010); *Musi v. Town of Shallotte*, 200 N.C. App. 379, 684 S.E.2d 892 (2009); and *Village Creek Property Owners' Ass'n v. Town of Edenton*, 135 N.C. App. 482, 520 S.E.2d 793 (1999).

46. *Taylor*, 290 N.C. at 620, 227 S.E.2d at 583. *See also* City of Shelby v. Lackey, 236 N.C. 369, 72 S.E.2d 757 (1952) (holding that if complaint failed to show how neighbor would be affected by zoning decision (e.g., whether neighbor was town citizen or property owner or what nature of injury was), then neighbor should not be accepted as party plaintiff); Budd v. Davie Cnty., 116 N.C. App. 168, 171, 447 S.E.2d 449, 451, *review denied*, 338 N.C. 667, 453 S.E.2d 174 (1994) (adjacent and nearby property owner who has easement interest in part of the land being rezoned has standing to challenge rezoning).

decision.[47] In *Taylor*, the challenge was brought not by adjoining landowners but by neighbors separated from the rezoned area by a forty-five-acre buffer area that was not rezoned. The court held that the plaintiffs lacked standing given the minimal effect of the rezoning on them. In reaching this conclusion, the court considered (1) the modest additional uses allowed in the new district (the change was from R-4 to R-6, which allowed for increased density but not a substantial change in the type of uses); (2) the distance of the rezoned property from the plaintiffs' property (none of the challengers owned adjacent property; the closest lot was one-half mile from the rezoned property); and (3) the manner in which the plaintiffs had participated in the city's consideration of the matter (they had not protested before the lawsuit).[48]

A number of North Carolina cases have applied this rule that a party must show a specific personal and legal interest that would be directly and adversely affected in order to have standing to challenge a legislative zoning decision.

In *Davis v. City of Archdale*, the court ruled that the alleged diminution of property values due to increased traffic and increased demands on overburdened utilities did not result in "special damages" distinct from those incurred by the rest of the community. Therefore, the plaintiff had no standing to challenge the rezoning.[49] The use of the special-damages test in the *Davis* case was taken from the cases on standing to challenge quasi-judicial zoning decisions.

Thrash Ltd. Partnership v. County of Buncombe (*Thrash II*) involved a facial challenge to the validity of an ordinance that established different standards for multifamily dwellings, depending on the elevation of the property involved. The court held that the plaintiffs, who had not filed an application to develop, had standing to challenge the procedures by which the ordinance was adopted. The court noted that the fact that the plaintiffs owned land that was subject to the regulations was sufficient for a facial challenge. The court distinguished such a facial challenge to the process of ordinance adoption from a challenge based on a claim that the ordinance was arbitrary or violated a constitutional principle.[50] In the latter situations, known as "as applied" challenges, a particular application of the ordinance would be needed to assert a claim.[51] The court applied this same standing analysis in a companion case to *Thrash II*, which challenged the process by which the county initially amended its zoning ordinance to extend it from partial-county zoning to countywide coverage.[52]

47. For example, the state supreme court dismissed a challenge to Durham County's initial zoning ordinance brought by a group of citizens before enforcement of that ordinance. Fox v. Bd. of Comm'rs, 244 N.C. 497, 94 S.E.2d 482 (1956). The court ruled that, rather than going forward with building and then challenging the denial, the applicant had to follow procedures for appealing a permit denial to the board of adjustment and then make subsequent judicial appeal. The court found that "[p]laintiffs cannot present an abstract question and obtain an adjudication in the nature of an advisory opinion." *Id.* at 500, 94 S.E.2d at 485. Enactment of the ordinance can be enough in itself to create a genuine controversy for standing purposes, as, for example, when an amortization provision is adopted requiring removal of an existing land use.

48. Other states also use multiple factors in assessing standing in this context. *See, e.g.,* Reynolds v. Dittmer, 312 N.W.2d 75 (Iowa Ct. App. 1981) (consider proximity, character of neighborhood, type of zoning change, and statutory rights of notice of hearing).

49. 81 N.C. App. 505, 344 S.E.2d 369 (1986). The court of appeals has noted in dicta that status as an adjoining or nearby owner, even without an allegation of a reduction in property value, might be sufficient to confer standing in a challenge to a legislative zoning decision in a declaratory-judgment action. Concerned Citizens of Downtown Asheville v. Bd. of Adjustment, 94 N.C. App. 364, 366, 380 S.E.2d 130, 132 (1989).

50. 195 N.C. App. 727, 673 S.E.2d 689 (2009). The rules at issue here limited density, parking standards, building heights, road construction, and the area of land disturbance. The ordinance was adopted using the procedures for a general-police-power ordinance rather than those required for a zoning ordinance.

51. Andrews v. Alamance Cnty., 132 N.C. App. 811, 513 S.E.2d 349 (1999) (holding that a landowner had no standing to challenge the constitutionality of a mobile-home-park ordinance where no site plan or subdivision plat had been filed, no steps had been taken to develop the property, and no permits of any kind had been applied for or denied).

52. *Thrash I*, 195 N.C. App. 678, 673 S.E.2d 706 (2009).

In *Templeton v. Town of Boone*,[53] the court distinguished standing for constitutional challenges from standing for statutory challenges of legislative decisions. For a constitutional challenge, the court held that a plaintiff must show an injury in fact or an immediate danger of injury as a result of enforcement of the challenged ordinance. For a statutory challenge, establishing ownership of land affected by the challenged ordinance was held to be sufficient for standing. However, subsequent rulings have held that an injury in fact is not required when a statutory or common law right is at issue.[54]

In *Morgan v. Nash County*,[55] neighbors and the City of Wilson challenged the county's rezoning of a rural parcel to accommodate construction of a potential chicken-processing plant. If the plant had been constructed, it would have used a spray field located several miles away for disposal of the facility's treated wastewater. A spray field was already a permitted use of that tract, so it was not a part of the contested rezoning. The city asserted that since its water supply was in the same watershed as the proposed spray field, the potential contamination occasioned by that location of the spray fields was sufficient potential injury to invoke standing. The court disagreed, noting that this parcel could already be used as a spray field by the chicken-processing plant or some other party. Since invalidation of the contested rezoning would not prevent that potential use as a spray field, the alleged injury would not be redressed by a favorable decision, and thus the city did not have standing under the *Lujan* standard nor would this constitute a direct injury under the *Taylor* standard.[56] The court also noted that since a spray field would be subject to state and federal effluent standards and monitoring, the alleged injury was conjectural rather than actual or imminent.

In *Ring v. Moore County*,[57] the court reached a similar conclusion in application of the *Taylor* standard to find a lack of standing. Owners of a chicken farm challenged a rezoning that would have doubled the permissible residential density on neighboring land. The court held that the plaintiffs had failed to show an actual or imminent, concrete, particularized injury, noting the rezoning did not change permitted uses and the allegation of future neighbor conflicts was only conjecture.[58] The court distinguished *Thrash II*, noting that the plaintiffs in *Thrash II* owned land that would be subject to the challenged regulation as opposed to the neighboring land owned by the plaintiffs in *Ring*.

In *Byron v. Synco Properties, Inc.*,[59] neighbors challenging a rezoning raised facial constitutional challenges and a statutory-interpretation issue regarding the General Assembly's repeal of the protest petition. However, none of the plaintiffs owned property sufficiently close to the rezoned property to have been eligible to file a protest petition if it had not been repealed. Because they had no interest pro-

---

53. 208 N.C. App. 50, 701 S.E.2d 709 (2010). An opinion in this case that concurred in part would have held that an allegation of actual or threatened enforcement is only required for an as-applied constitutional challenge but not for a facial constitutional challenge. *See also* PEM Entities LLC v. County of Franklin, 57 F.4th 178, 182 (2023) (holding a determination that a proposed development cannot receive water and sewer service on the terms to which it claims to be entitled is an injury in fact that confers standing for constitutional claims).

54. United Daughters of the Confederacy, N.C. Div., Inc. v. City of Winston-Salem, ___ N.C. ___, 881 S.E.2d 32 (2022) (the complaint alleged no proprietary or contractual interest in the monument by the plaintiff, so without a legal right affected there it had no standing to challenge the monument's removal); Comm. to Elect Dan Forest v. Emps. Pol. Action Comm., 376 N.C. 558, 853 S.E.2d 698 (2021).

55. 224 N.C. App. 60, 735 S.E.2d 615 (2012), *review denied*, 366 N.C. 561, 738 S.E.2d 379 (2013).

56. The court also noted that while adjoining-property status is not essential to standing, proximity is a factor. In this case the city's property was three and one-half miles from the rezoned property, which the court deemed too remote to support a claim of standing. The standing of the neighboring property owners who were also plaintiffs was upheld by the trial court and not challenged on appeal.

57. 257 N.C. App. 168, 809 S.E.2d 11 (2017).

58. The plaintiffs had alleged that the increased residential density would increase traffic, noise, light pollution, and the "virtual certainty" of complaints about the odors, dust, and feathers from the plaintiffs' adjacent poultry farm.

59. 258 N.C. App. 372, 813 S.E.2d 455 (2018).

tected by that statute, they were not "directly and adversely affected" by the repeal or interpretation of the statute and thus had no standing to challenge its repeal or interpretation.[60]

In *Violette v. Town of Cornelius*,[61] adjacent property owners challenged a conditional rezoning that would allow construction of an amenity center for a subdivision. The court held that the property owner's opinion regarding diminution of value is not competent evidence to show a substantial reduction in property value that would have established the neighbor's standing.[62]

A specific provision was added to the statutes in 2019 to codify the rules on standing for bringing a civil action to establish a vested right, to assert a claim that a regulation is unconstitutional on its face or as applied, or to assert that the regulation is preempted, exceeds statutory authority, or constitutes an unconstitutional taking of private property. The statute provides that the permit applicant has standing to bring these claims, as does any person who owns, leases, has an easement in, or has an option or contract to purchase the land subject to the decision being challenged.[63]

Quasi-Judicial Decisions

The basic rule for standing to challenge quasi-judicial decisions is similar to the one applicable to legislative decisions, discussed in the preceding subsection, though it has a statutory dimension.

G.S. 160D-1402(c) defines who can file a petition for writ of certiorari to review a quasi-judicial land use regulatory decision.[64] This section specifies three categories of entities with standing to bring these judicial appeals. The first category covers those who applied for approval or who have a property interest in the project or property subject to the application.[65] This includes all persons with a legally

---

60. *Id.* at 378, 813 S.E.2d at 457. As they could not have availed themselves of the protest-petition statute and it was not their property being rezoned, the court held that the plaintiffs also had no constitutionally protected interests affected by the challenged rezoning process, only a generalized grievance. With no immediate danger of a direct injury to a constitutionally protected right, they had no standing to raise a constitutional challenge. *See also* Grace Baptist Church v. City of Oxford, 320 N.C. 439, 444, 358 S.E.2d 372, 375 (1987); Coventry Woods Neighborhood Ass'n v. City of Charlotte, 202 N.C. App. 247, 257, 688 S.E.2d 538, 545 (2010).

61. 283 N.C. App. 565, 874 S.E.2d 217 (2022). The court noted that the *Taylor* standard for standing—allegations of a specific personal and legal interest that would be directly and adversely affected—is no longer sufficient to establish standing in a declaratory-judgment action. A showing of "special damages," citing the quasi-judicial cases noted below, is required, thereby confirming the conflation of standing standards for legislative and quasi-judicial appeals.

62. The court noted that under prior law the opinion of a property owner was presumptively competent evidence of its value. Gillis v. Arringdale, 135 N.C. 295, 302, 47 S.E. 429, 432 (1904). However, that rule was overturned in United Community Bank (Georgia) v. Wolfe, 369 N.C. 555, 559–60, 799 S.E.2d 269, 272 (2017).

63. G.S. 160D-1403.1(b), created by S.L. 2019-111, § 1.7.

64. G.S. 160D-405(b) cross-references the statute for standing for judicial review, G.S. 160D-1402(c), so as to have a single standing standard for both appeal to the board of adjustment and appeals from the board. Prior to the adoption of G.S. 160D-1402, the court held that the provision granting the county the authority to appeal to the board of adjustment also provided standing for judicial appeals. Cook v. Union Cnty. Zoning Bd. of Adjustment, 185 N.C. App. 582, 588–89, 649 S.E.2d 458, 464–65 (2007). Also see G.S. 160A-400.9(e), which provides that an "aggrieved party" has standing to appeal a historic-preservation commission's decision on a certificate of appropriateness to the board of adjustment and subsequently on to superior court.

Section 7 of the Standard State Zoning Enabling Act, on which the North Carolina zoning-enabling act was modeled, provided that judicial review of quasi-judicial decisions could be made not only by "persons aggrieved" and the unit of government but also by any taxpayer. U.S. DEP'T OF COMMERCE, A STANDARD STATE ZONING ENABLING ACT (1924). A minority of states included that broad authorization of standing. North Carolina was not among them.

65. Prior to adoption of this section in 2009, the law was not entirely clear on how far this category extended beyond the owner of the fee interest in the property. The court held in *Humble Oil & Refining Co. v. Board of Aldermen*, 284 N.C. 458, 202 S.E.2d 129 (1974), that an option holder who had exercised an option to develop the property, subject to the necessary zoning permits being obtained, had standing to participate in a review of those permits. In *Habitat for Humanity of Moore County, Inc. v. Board of Commissioners*, 187 N.C. App. 764, 653 S.E.2d 886 (2007),

defined interest in the property, including not only an ownership interest but also a leasehold interest, an option to purchase the property, or an interest created by an easement, restriction, or covenant. The second category is the local government whose board made the decision being appealed. The third category includes other persons who will suffer special damages as a result of the decision. This category includes both qualifying associations and individuals (such as neighbors who contend that the decision will adversely affect their property).

In a challenge of a special exception granted by Guilford County for a mobile-home park, the N.C. Supreme Court, in *Jackson v. Guilford County Board of Adjustment*, stated that the following test was to be used for assessing standing in state court for quasi-judicial zoning decisions:

> The mere fact that one's proposed lawful use of his own land will diminish the value of adjoining or nearby lands of another does not give to such other person a standing to maintain an action, or other legal proceeding, to prevent such use. If, however, the proposed use is unlawful, as where it is prohibited by a valid zoning ordinance, the owner of adjoining or nearby lands, who will sustain special damage from the proposed use through a reduction in the value of his own property, does have a standing to maintain such proceeding.
>
> . . . . If, however, that which purports to be an amendment permitting a use of property forbidden by the original ordinance is, itself, invalid, the prohibition upon the use remains in effect. In that event, the owner of other land, who will be specially damaged by such proposed use, has standing to maintain a proceeding in the courts to prevent it.[66]

In a series of cases applying this special-damages test for standing to appeal quasi-judicial zoning decisions, the courts have held that appellants must present evidence both that they are owners of affected property[67] and that they will suffer special damages distinct from the rest of the community.[68]

Mere proximity of land ownership is insufficient.[69] In *Smith v. Forsyth County Board of Adjustment*, an adjacent owner sought to challenge an ordinance interpretation allowing a new church and associated

---

the ordinance specifically allowed special use permit applications and subdivision plats to be submitted by landowners, their agents, or persons who had contracted to purchase the property. The plaintiff organization's director testified at the permit hearing that his group had an option to purchase, and the council found the application to be complete. The court held that this was sufficient to establish standing for the plaintiff to file the application and pursue the appeal. *See also* Cox v. Hancock, 160 N.C. App. 473, 586 S.E.2d 500 (2003) ("prospective vendee" is real party in interest in special use permit application and litigation). Similarly, the state court of appeals had held that a person bound by contract to purchase the land in question also has standing. Deffet Rentals, Inc. v. City of Burlington, 27 N.C. App. 361, 219 S.E.2d 223 (1975). By contrast, the N.C. Supreme Court had held that a mere optionee did not have standing. Lee v. Bd. of Adjustment, 226 N.C. 107, 37 S.E.2d 128 (1946). Also, in *Wil-Hol Corp. v. Marshall*, 71 N.C. App. 611, 322 S.E.2d 655 (1984), the appeals court ruled that the estranged wife of a month-to-month lessee whose lease had been terminated had no interest in property sufficient to confer standing to challenge the applicability of a zoning ordinance.

66. 275 N.C. 155, 161, 166 S.E.2d 78, 82–83 (1969) (citations omitted). The opinion implies use of the same standing standard for legislative matters. *See also Lee*, 226 N.C. 107, 37 S.E.2d 128.

67. Pigford v. Bd. of Adjustment, 49 N.C. App. 181, 270 S.E.2d 535 (1980), *review denied*, 301 N.C. 722, 274 S.E.2d 230 (1981).

68. Cook v. Union Cnty. Zoning Bd. of Adjustment, 185 N.C. App. 582, 649 S.E.2d 458 (2007) (evidence in record showed residents of subdivision adjacent to proposed Wal-Mart would suffer special damages to their property that are unique in character and quantity and are distinct from those inflicted on the community at large).

69. Casper v. Chatham Cnty., 186 N.C. App. 456, 651 S.E.2d 299 (2007) (neighboring landowners sought to challenge a conditional use permit for a retail use). Other states split on the question of whether proximity in itself is sufficient for standing. *See, e.g.*, Anundson v. City of Chi., 44 Ill. 2d 491, 496, 256 N.E.2d 1, 3–4 (1970) (any adjoining owner has standing); Anderson v. Swanson, 534 A.2d 1286, 1288 (Me. 1987) (abutters with some other allegation of injury have standing); Bryniarski v. Montgomery Cnty. Bd. of Appeals, 247 Md. 137, 145, 230 A.2d 289, 294 (1967) (adjoining and nearby property owners have prima facie special damages); Marashlian v. Zoning Bd. of Appeals, 421 Mass. 719, 721, 660 N.E.2d 369, 372 (1996) (abutters required to receive notice of hearing have a rebuttable

athletic fields. The court held that the plaintiff had failed to establish that she was a person aggrieved with standing to appeal to the board of adjustment because an allegation of mere proximity, absent an allegation of special damages distinct from the community, is insufficient to establish standing.[70]

The most common way of establishing standing is a credible allegation that the activity, if approved, would diminish the value of the property of the person claiming standing. The harm, however, must be property specific. An alleged diminution of property values in the neighborhood or larger community is insufficient to confer standing.[71] The requirement to use only competent, expert testimony to show property-value impacts that applies to evidentiary findings relative to meeting the standards of the ordinance does not apply to an allegation of property-value impacts for standing purposes.[72]

It is not necessary, however, to show a negative property-value impact in order to establish special damages. In *Mangum v. Raleigh Board of Adjustment*, two adjacent owners and an additional neighboring business owner challenged a special use permit issued for an adult-entertainment establishment. The court found that allegations of parking, stormwater, and crime problems were sufficient to establish "special damages" and, contrary to suggestions in earlier cases, that a plaintiff was not required to also show that property values would have been reduced as a result of the special use permit.[73] Other cases have allowed alleged harms based on traffic and noise to be considered without explicit reference to property-value impacts.[74] Increased noise from an adjacent shooting range and the loss of waterfront views from construction of a contested structure have also been held sufficient to establish standing.[75]

The potential for special damages may be established by affidavits or testimony. In *Murdock v. Chatham County*,[76] the plaintiffs alleged in their complaint that they owned land adjoining the larger

---

presumption that they are persons aggrieved); Kalakowski v. John A. Russell Corp., 137 Vt. 219, 222, 401 A.2d 906, 908 (1979) (statute provides standing for those "in the immediate neighborhood").

70. 186 N.C. App. 651, 652 S.E.2d 355 (2007). *See also* Heery v. Town of Highlands Zoning Bd. of Adjustment, 61 N.C. App. 612, 300 S.E.2d 869 (1983) (showing of special damages distinct from those incurred by the rest of the community required for neighbors' standing to appeal the granting of special use permit for multifamily housing); Sarda v. City/Cnty. of Durham Bd. of Adjustment, 156 N.C. App. 213, 575 S.E.2d 829 (2003) (allegation that petitioner resides 400 yards away from paintball playing field that received special use permit is insufficient alone to establish standing absent allegation of special damages); Lloyd v. Town of Chapel Hill, 127 N.C. App. 347, 489 S.E.2d 898 (1997).

71. Cherry v. Wiesner, 245 N.C. App. 339, 781 S.E.2d 871, *review denied*, 369 N.C. 33, 792 S.E.2d 779 (2016).

72. Fort v. Cnty. of Cumberland, 218 N.C. App. 401, 405, 721 S.E.2d 352, 354, *review denied*, 366 N.C. 401 (2012). The court noted that the limitation on competent evidence for a substantive finding of fact is in G.S. 160D-1402(j), not in the subsection on standing, G.S. 160D-1402(c).

73. 362 N.C. 640, 669 S.E.2d 279 (2008). *See also* Bailey & Assocs., Inc. v. Wilmington Bd. of Adjustment, 202 N.C. App. 177, 689 S.E.2d 576 (2010) (allowing neighbors standing to intervene on similar grounds).

74. *See* Taylor Home of Charlotte, Inc. v. City of Charlotte, 116 N.C. App. 188, 447 S.E.2d 438 (1994); Kentallen, Inc. v. Town of Hillsborough, 110 N.C. App. 767, 431 S.E.2d 231 (1993) (allegation that plaintiff is owner of adjoining property is insufficient to confer standing without allegation relating to whether and in what respect that land would be adversely affected). *But see* Piney Mountain Neighborhood Ass'n v. Town of Chapel Hill, 63 N.C. App. 244, 304 S.E.2d 251 (1983) (allegation that members live in affected area and will potentially suffer injury sufficient to confer standing).

75. *Fort*, 218 N.C. App. 401, 721 S.E.2d 350 (allegation of increased noise, threat to groundwater quality, threat to personal safety, and adverse property-value impacts sufficient to confer standing to neighbors challenging interpretation allowing shooting range); Sanchez v. Town of Beaufort, 211 N.C. App. 574, 710 S.E.2d 350, *review denied*, 365 N.C. 349, 718 S.E.2d 152 (2011) (neighbor directly across the street from property seeking a certificate of appropriateness from historical commission had special damages based on alleged violation of historic guidelines, loss of waterfront views, and depreciated property value).

76. 198 N.C. App. 309, 679 S.E.2d 850 (2009), *review denied*, 363 N.C. 806, 690 S.E.2d 705 (2010). The plaintiffs also submitted affidavits from an appraiser and a real-estate agent stating that the project would make the neighboring properties less attractive to potential purchasers. *See also* McMillan v. Town of Tryon, 200 N.C. App. 228, 287–88, 683 S.E.2d 743, 746–47 (2009) (neighbor's testimony at hearing regarding children walking in the street, impacts of increased stormwater, noise, and traffic were sufficient to establish standing to challenge conditional use permit).

tract at issue in the case and presented evidence about the adverse impacts on their property from the site's lights, noise, and stormwater runoff should the proposed project be built. The court held that this was sufficient to establish the requisite special damages.[77] Expert testimony about the inappropriateness of a proposed use is also adequate to establish the requisite special damages.

The court applies a de novo review on a motion to dismiss for lack of standing. In this context the court views the allegations as true and in the light most favorable to the nonmoving party.[78]

It is not necessary for those seeking judicial review to have formally intervened in the quasi-judicial hearing.[79]

Courts have applied a similar but more general standing test outside of the zoning arena. In *Marriott v. Chatham County*, the county approved several large developments on tracts adjacent to parcels owned by the plaintiffs without requiring an environmental-impact statement. The court held that in order to have standing to challenge the decision on requiring an impact statement, the plaintiffs had to show: (1) injury in fact, (2) that the injury was fairly traceable to the challenged action, and (3) that it was likely the injury would be redressed by a favorable decision.[80]

Courts apply similar rules on standing in challenges to permits under the highly analogous Administrative Procedure Act. In *Neuse River Foundation, Inc. v. Smithfield Foods, Inc.*, the state appeals court held that the plaintiff had to allege (1) injury in fact to a protected interest that could not be considered merged in the general public right, (2) causation, and (3) a proper or individualized form of relief. The court found that injury to aesthetic or recreational interests alone cannot confer standing on an environmental plaintiff as this is within the general public right.[81] The requirement for injury in fact was, however, subsequently held not to be required when a purely statutory or common law right is at issue.[82]

---

77. *See also* Allen v. City of Burlington Bd. of Adjustment, 100 N.C. App. 615, 397 S.E.2d 657 (1990). In this case a Burlington property owner who objected to a community kitchen and a homeless shelter in his neighborhood was held to have established sufficient special damages through his own testimony.

78. *Mangum*, 362 N.C. at 644, 669 S.E.2d at 283; *McMillan*, 200 N.C. App. at 287–88, 683 S.E.2d at 746–47.

79. Cook v. Union Cnty. Zoning Bd. of Adjustment, 185 N.C. App. 582, 591, 649 S.E.2d 458, 466 (2007).

80. 187 N.C. App. 491, 493, 654 S.E.2d 13, 15 (2007), *review denied*, 362 N.C. 472, 666 S.E.2d 122 (2008). Note, however, that subsequent decisions limit the requirement for a showing of an injury in fact. Comm. to Elect Dan Forest v. Emps. Pol. Action Comm., 376 N.C. 558, 853 S.E.2d 698 (2021).

The county's subdivision ordinance contained a provision that allowed the planning board to require an environmental-impact statement if the development exceeded two acres and the board deemed the statement "necessary for responsible review" due to the nature of the land or peculiarities in the proposed layout of the development. The plaintiffs sought to enjoin development of the property until the county amended its ordinance to provide minimum criteria for when an impact statement would be required, and they sought a writ of mandamus to compel the county to make these amendments. The court noted that an ordinance allowing an impact statement but providing no minimum criteria for when a statement is required is invalid. Since the ordinance as written was invalid and the court had no authority to order the ordinance amended, there was no likelihood the plaintiff's injury could be redressed by a favorable decision. Therefore, the court held that the trial court properly dismissed the action for lack of standing.

Other statutes affecting development may contain particular standing provisions. See, for example, G.S. 113A-66, which provides a private cause of action for a person damaged by a violation of the Sedimentation Pollution Control Act. The court has held that issuing a notice of violation of act is necessary to trigger this standing. Applewood Props., LLC v. New S. Props., LLC, 366 N.C. 518, 742 S.E.2d 776 (2013).

81. 155 N.C. App. 110, 574 S.E.2d 48 (2002), *review denied*, 356 N.C. 675, 577 S.E.2d 628 (2003). In *County of Wake v. North Carolina Department of Environment & Natural Resources*, 155 N.C. App. 225, 573 S.E.2d 572 (2002), *review denied*, 357 N.C. 62, 579 S.E.2d 386 (2003), the court held that the individual neighbors who initiated the appeal of the permit issuance were aggrieved persons with standing to challenge the permit (they had alleged noise, pollution, landscape changes, and other negative environmental consequences that would interfere with the use and enjoyment of their property), as was the town (due to the impacts on its tax base and planning jurisdiction).

82. Comm. to Elect Dan Forest v. Emps. Pol. Action Comm., 376 N.C. 558, 853 S.E.2d 698 (2021).

The North Carolina statutes do not explicitly address the effect of jurisdictional boundaries on standing. In *Good Neighbors of South Davidson v. Town of Denton*, the state supreme court took special note of the fact that those complaining of improper spot zoning were located outside of the jurisdiction of the offending town and had no political recourse regarding the challenged legislative zoning decisions.[83] In the quasi-judicial context, the fact that affected property is outside of the jurisdiction of the decision-making jurisdiction has no bearing on whether the property will suffer special damages.

A plaintiff may, with good cause, be allowed to amend a defective petition for judicial review to add requisite allegations regarding standing. In *Darnell v. Town of Franklin*,[84] the plaintiff had appeared before the town's board of adjustment and town council (which had final decision-making authority for variances under the town's zoning ordinance) to object to a setback variance for an adjoining property owner. Upon issuance of the variance, the plaintiff filed a petition for writ of certiorari seeking judicial review of the variance decision. The petition stated that the plaintiff was an adversely affected property owner but contained no allegations specifying how the plaintiff was aggrieved by the decision. The town moved to dismiss for lack of subject-matter jurisdiction. While that motion was under advisement, the plaintiff sought to amend her pleadings to add specific allegations of harm. The court held that while the initial petition was deficient, the plaintiff had clearly established by her participation in the matter before the town boards that she was affected by the action in a manner distinct from the rest of the community. Therefore, the trial court should have allowed her to amend the petition under G.S. 1A-1, Rule 15(a).

As for appellate judicial review, only actual parties to litigation may appeal a trial court's decision. In *Duke Power Co. v. Salisbury Board of Adjustment*,[85] the appeals court held that the fact that neighbors were affected by a zoning decision, appeared at the board of adjustment's hearing on a variance, and attended the trial-court hearing on the matter did not confer on them a right to appeal the trial court's decision absent their formal intervention in the judicial proceeding.[86]

Associational Standing

It is relatively common for a group, such as a neighborhood association, to seek to initiate or intervene as a party in a judicial challenge to a land use regulatory decision. This scenario presents the question of when the group itself, as distinct from its individual members, can be a party in zoning litigation.[87]

In some situations it is clear that there is no standing for a particular group. An association seeking standing must as a threshold matter establish its legal existence. If the group has been formally

---

83. 355 N.C. 254, 559 S.E.2d 768 (2002). Most other states take the view that being in a neighboring jurisdiction does not affect standing. *See, e.g.*, Scott v. City of Indian Wells, 492 P.2d 1137 (Cal. 1972); Moore v. City of Middleton, 975 N.E.2d 977 (Ohio 2012). Out-of-state neighbors were found to have standing in *Abel v. Planning & Zoning Comm'n of New Canaan*, 998 A.2d 1149 (Conn. 2010).

84. 131 N.C. App. 846, 508 S.E.2d 841 (1998).

85. 20 N.C. App. 730, 202 S.E.2d 607, *review denied*, 285 N.C. 235, 204 S.E.2d 22 (1974).

86. See, however, *Procter v. City of Raleigh*, 133 N.C. App. 181, 514 S.E.2d 745 (1999), in the discussion of permissive intervention, below. Rule 38 of the Rules of Appellate Procedure governs substitution of a party during appellate review. In *Weishaupt-Smith v. Town of Banner Elk*, 264 N.C. App. 618, 826 S.E.2d 734 (2019), the court applied this rule to prevent another neighbor who had not participated in the superior-court case from stepping into the shoes of a litigant that sold its property during the pendency of the appeal. The court held that substitution was permissible only upon the death of a party while the appeal is pending. As the party had not died nor was she otherwise unable to continue to litigate, the neighbor seeking substitution had no standing.

87. Daniel Mandelker notes that though the case law on this point is mixed nationally, the trend is toward granting organizations standing in a representational capacity. DANIEL R. MANDELKER AND MICHAEL ALLAN WOLF, LAND USE LAW § 8.06 (6th ed. 2018). *See, e.g.*, Tri-Cnty. Concerned Citizens, Inc. v. Bd. of Cnty. Comm'rs, 32 Kan. App. 2d 1168, 95 P.3d 1012 (2004); Douglaston Civic Ass'n v. Galvin, 36 N.Y.2d 1, 364 N.Y.S.2d 830, 324 N.E.2d 317 (1974).

incorporated, such as by securing legal status as a nonprofit corporation, it must state that in its complaint.[88] If the group is an unincorporated nonprofit association, it may assert a claim in its name on behalf of its members

> if one or more of them have standing to assert a claim in their own right, the interests the nonprofit association seeks to protect are germane to its purposes, and neither the claim asserted nor the relief requested requires the participation of a member or a person referred to as a "member" by the nonprofit association.[89]

If the unincorporated group is not a nonprofit association, it must have recorded a certificate of its activities with the county register of deeds in the county where it operates.[90] Failure to establish the legal existence of the group will result in dismissal of the group as a party.[91]

Also, if none of the individual members of a group have standing, the group does not have standing. Some member of the group must show actual harm in order to be aggrieved.[92]

A variety of zoning cases in North Carolina—some involving legislative zoning decisions and others quasi-judicial decisions—have allowed a group standing if some of its individual members had standing. For example, in *River Birch Associates v. City of Raleigh*, the court noted that to have standing, the "complaining association or *one* of its members must suffer some immediate or threatened injury."[93] The court stated the general rule for associational standing as follows:

> An association has standing to bring suit on behalf of its members when: (a) its members would otherwise have standing to sue in their own right; (b) the interests it seeks to protect are germane to the organization's purpose; and (c) neither the claim asserted nor the relief requested requires the participation of individual members in the lawsuit.[94]

---

88. "Any party not a natural person shall make an affirmative averment showing its legal existence and capacity to sue." G.S. 1A, Rule 9(a).

89. G.S. 59B-8(b). *See also* G.S. 1-69.1.

90. G.S. 66-68. G.S. 1-69.1(a)(3) requires that the specific location of the recordation of this certificate must be included in the complaint of such an unincorporated association.

91. N. Iredell Neighbors for Rural Life v. Iredell Cnty., 196 N.C. App. 68, 674 S.E.2d 436, *review denied*, 363 N.C. 582, 682 S.E.2d 385 (2009).

92. Concerned Citizens of Downtown Asheville v. Bd. of Adjustment, 94 N.C. App. 364, 380 S.E.2d 130 (1989). By analogy, the Administrative Procedure Act allows a contested case to be initiated by persons whose rights are "substantially prejudiced." G.S. 150B-23(a). In *Sound Rivers, Inc. v. N.C. Department of Environmental Quality*, 271 N.C. App. 674, 845 S.E.2d 802 (2020), *review allowed*, 856 S.E.2d 99 (2021), the court held that the plaintiff group had standing to challenge a water-discharge permit for a quarry based on the allegation that discharge would degrade water quality in the creek if the applicable water-quality standards were not met. Members of the plaintiff group owned homes and businesses along a creek that would receive twelve million gallons per day of wastewater. *See also* Friends of Lincoln Lake v. Town of Lincoln, 2010 ME 78, 2 A.3d 284 (group has no standing to appeal permit for wind-power project where no showing of particularized injury to member of group has been made).

93. 326 N.C. 100, 130, 388 S.E.2d 538, 555 (1990) (emphasis added). *See also* C.C. & J. Enters., Inc. v. City of Asheville, 132 N.C. App. 550, 512 S.E.2d 766, *review dismissed as improvidently granted*, 351 N.C. 97, 521 S.E.2d 117 (1999) (proper to allow an adjoining neighborhood association to intervene, as it had alleged special damages (reduced property values) to qualify as an aggrieved party); Piney Mountain Neighborhood Ass'n v. Town of Chapel Hill, 63 N.C. App. 244, 304 S.E.2d 251 (1983). *See generally* Creek Pointe Homeowners' Ass'n v. Happ, 146 N.C. App. 159, 552 S.E.2d 220 (2001), *review denied*, 356 N.C. 161, 568 S.E.2d 191 (2002).

94. *River Birch Associates*, 326 N.C. at 130, 388 S.E.2d at 555. The N.C. Supreme Court took this standard from *Hunt v. Washington State Apple Advertising Commission*, 432 U.S. 333, 343 (1977), and cited with approval *Warth v. Seldin*, 422 U.S. 490 (1975) (while holding no standing for plaintiffs challenging alleged exclusionary zoning of suburb, Court noted that standing of one member confers standing on associational group). *See also* Sierra Club v. Morton, 405 U.S. 727 (1972) (if a member of the group suffers harm, the group has associational standing). The standard for associational standing is also discussed, but not decided, in *Wake Cares, Inc. v. Wake County Board of Education*, 190 N.C. App. 1, 9–10, 660 S.E.2d 217, 222–23 (2008), where the court held that the plaintiff association did not attempt to meet any of the standards for associational standing.

The court reaffirmed the use of this analytic approach to associational standing in *Willowmere Community Association v. City of Charlotte*,[95] where the court found that neighboring homeowners' associations had standing to challenge a rezoning to allow multifamily housing on land adjoining the neighborhoods.

However, in a case challenging a rezoning, *Northeast Concerned Citizens, Inc. v. City of Hickory*,[96] the state court of appeals held that, contrary to the general rules on associational standing, a corporation does not have standing in a zoning case unless every member or shareholder has a specific, personal legal interest in the subject matter, or the corporation itself has such an interest, because that is the requirement for a person to have standing in a zoning case. Since the record in the case indicated that at most only twelve of the plaintiff nonprofit corporation's 114 members had such an interest, the court held that the plaintiff had no standing. The majority distinguished *River Birch Associates* as setting a general rule on associational standing and applying it to that suit's element of unfair or deceptive trade practices while contending that zoning cases have a more demanding standard for determining standing.[97] However, the *River Birch Associates* decision involved application of development-ordinance requirements (the authority to require transfers of required open space to a homeowners' association, the effect of preliminary plat approval on dedications and vested rights, and the dedication of open space as a regulatory taking), and the standing of the association was assumed but not discussed by the court.[98] In contrast, the decision concluded with a holding that the association did not have standing to prosecute the fraud and unfair-trade-practice claims.[99] The *Northeast Concerned Citizens* concurrence would not have required each member of the association to have individual standing. It suggested using the following factors to determine whether an association should have standing:

> (1) the capacity of the organization to assume an adversary position, (2) the size and composition of the organization as reflecting a position fairly representative of the community or interests which it seeks to protect[,] (3) the adverse effect of the decision sought to be reviewed on the group represented by the organization as within the zone of interests sought to be protected[, and (4) whether full participating membership in the representative organization [is] open to all residents and property owners in the relevant neighborhood.[100]

The N.C. Supreme Court has indicated sympathy with this latter view. In *State Employees Ass'n of North Carolina v. State*,[101] the court of appeals denied associational standing where not all members of the group had standing. The dissent, largely relying on *River Birch Associates*, would have allowed

---

95. 370 N.C. 553, 809 S.E.2d 558 (2018). The court of appeals had found no standing due to the association's failure to strictly adhere to its own bylaws regarding the process to authorize its boards to initiate litigation. The supreme court held that a corporate litigant is not required to affirmatively plead or prove its compliance with its internal rules and bylaws relating to the decision to bring suit.

96. 143 N.C. App. 272, 545 S.E.2d 768, *review denied*, 353 N.C. 526, 549 S.E.2d 220 (2001). *See also* Landfall Grp. Against Paid Transferability v. Landfall Club, Inc., 117 N.C. App. 270, 450 S.E.2d 513 (1994).

97. The *Northeast Concerned Citizens* court concluded in a footnote that the standing requirements laid out in *Taylor v. City of Raleigh* (290 N.C. 608, 227 S.E.2d 576 (1976))—a specific and personal interest in the matter with a direct, adverse effect on a person—were different from and more stringent than more-general standards for associational standing in other contexts. *Northeast Concerned Citizens*, 143 N.C. App. at 277 n.1, 545 S.E.2d at 772 n.1. See the discussion of *Taylor* in the text above at note 45.

98. *River Birch Associates*, 326 N.C. at 128, 388 S.E.2d at 554.

99. *Id.* at 129–30, 388 S.E.2d at 555–56.

100. *Northeast Concerned Citizens*, 143 N.C. App. at 280, 545 S.E.2d at 774 (alteration in original) (quoting Douglaston Civic Ass'n v. Galvin, 324 N.E.2d 317, 321 (N.Y. 1974)). The concurring opinion contended that the majority view is contrary to the law on associational standing in other jurisdictions and may have the practical effect of "drastically curtail[ing] North Carolina citizens' ability to challenge zoning changes." *Northeast Concerned Citizens*, 143 N.C. App. at 280, 545 S.E.2d at 774.

101. 154 N.C. App. 207, 573 S.E.2d 525 (2002).

standing for the association where a member had standing. In a per curiam opinion, the supreme court approved the views set forth in the dissent.[102]

The question of associational standing in appeals of quasi-judicial decisions was clarified in 2009 by the enactment of G.S. 160D-1402(c)(3). It provides that neighborhood associations and associations organized to protect and foster the interests of the neighborhood or local area have standing, provided at least one of the members of the association would have individual standing and the association was not created in response to the particular development that is the subject of the appeal.

Intervention

The rules for intervention in a judicial challenge to a quasi-judicial decision are set by G.S. 160D-1402(g). The statute provides that Rule 24 of the Rules of Civil Procedure is to be applied if the applicant and persons with a property interest in the subject property can intervene as a matter of right. Others must demonstrate that they would have had standing to initiate the proceeding.

Rule 24 generally provides that, to intervene by right, a person must either show a statutory right to do so or show (1) an interest in the property or transaction involved; (2) that disposition of the matter will as a practical matter affect that interest; and (3) that the person's interest is not adequately represented by the existing parties.[103]

Rule 24 also provides for permissive intervention. In *Procter*, neighbors had participated in a board of adjustment case, and the board had upheld the staff interpretation of the ordinance favored by the neighbors. Given the city's defense of the board decision in the trial court, the neighbors did not seek to intervene. But when the city decided not to appeal an adverse trial-court ruling, the neighbors sought to intervene to pursue appellate-court review. The trial court rejected the motion to intervene as not timely. The court of appeals reversed, concluding that the extraordinary and unusual circumstances of the case made intervention timely under Rule 24(a)(2). The court found that the neighbors had an interest in the transaction, an alleged practical impairment of that interest, and inadequate representation

---

102. State Emps. Ass'n of N.C. v. State, 357 N.C. 239, 580 S.E.2d 693 (2003). *See also* N.C. Forestry Ass'n v. N.C. Dep't of Env't & Nat. Res., 357 N.C. 640, 588 S.E.2d 880 (2003) (holding trade association had standing to appeal a determination that new or expanding wood-chip mills were excluded from coverage under a general timber-products industry permit).

103. Bailey & Assocs., Inc. v. Wilmington Bd. of Adjustment, 202 N.C. App. 177, 689 S.E.2d 576 (2010) (allowing intervention by neighbors who alleged that impacts from increased traffic, light, and noise would adversely affect the use and enjoyment of their property and adjacent protected waterways). *See generally* Holly Ridge Assocs., LLC v. N.C. Dep't of Env't & Nat. Res., 361 N.C. 531, 648 S.E.2d 830 (2007); High Rock Lake Partners, LLC v. N.C. Dep't of Transp., 204 N.C. App. 55, 693 S.E.2d 361, *review denied*, 364 N.C. 325, 700 S.E.2d 753 (2010) (owner of property must be allowed to intervene as real party in interest in challenge to conditions imposed on a driveway-permit application made by previous owner, who subsequently assigned all rights to the landowner).

In a case decided before G.S. 160D-1402 was adopted in 2009, the plaintiff filed suit challenging the denial of a conditional use permit for a single-family development. Neighbors sought to intervene in support of the board's denial, alleging that significant traffic increases as a result of a conditional use permit issuance would adversely affect their property values. The neighbors also alleged that the applicant and board intended to settle the suit by issuing the permit and sought a stay to prevent such action, pending the outcome of the appeal. The trial court denied the motion to intervene on the basis that the neighbors did not have standing under the special-damages test, discussed in the text above beginning at note 49 (and on the same day entered a consent judgment reversing the permit denial and remanding the case for further board proceedings). The court held that appellate review was not mooted by the settlement between the plaintiff and the board and that Rule 24 (rather than the special-damages or aggrieved-person standard) governs intervention in all civil actions. Councill v. Town of Boone Bd. of Adjustment, 146 N.C. App. 103, 551 S.E.2d 907 (2001). In *Lloyd v. Town of Chapel Hill*, 127 N.C. App. 347, 489 S.E.2d 898 (1997), the court applied the special-damages test rather than Rule 24 to determine whether a party could intervene.

by the existing parties (and that the city's appeal to superior court had been adequate representation prior to the city's decision not to appeal the trial court's adverse ruling).[104]

Statutes of Limitation

The requirement for timely filing of an action is jurisdictional. If an appeal is not made within the appropriate period, the action must be dismissed.[105]

Legislative Decisions

In the absence of a statute setting a time limit for challenging the validity of a legislative land use regulatory decision, a provision not included in the original zoning-enabling act, courts applied the doctrine of laches from common law.[106] This doctrine holds that if a person negligently fails to bring a claim within a reasonable amount of time, the claim will not be allowed if the lapse of time and other circumstances would serve to prejudice the rights of the party against whom the claim is made. Three decisions in the late 1970s applied this doctrine to judicial challenges of legislative zoning decisions made from two to six years earlier. Two of these cases resulted in the challenges being dismissed, but the third allowed the challenge of a six-year-old rezoning.[107]

To resolve the uncertainty generated by these cases, the General Assembly established statutory timelines for bringing these challenges and has made several modifications to those periods. In 1981, the legislature first added an explicit nine-month statute of limitations for challenges of legislative zoning decisions to the zoning-enabling statutes. This time period was shortened to two months in 1996.[108] In 2011, the time period to challenge legislative decisions other than zoning-map amendments was extended to one year in many instances and as much as three years in others.[109]

The statutes of limitation for legislative zoning decisions are codified in the civil-procedure portions of the statutes. G.S. 1-54(10) sets the general rule of a one-year statute of limitations to contest the

---

104. 133 N.C. App. 181, 514 S.E.2d 745 (1999).

105. *See, e.g.,* Shearin v. Lloyd, 246 N.C. 363, 98 S.E.2d 508 (1957); McCrann v. Vill. of Pinehurst, 216 N.C. App. 291, 716 S.E.2d 667 (2011) (dismissing special use permit appeal filed one day late); Congleton v. City of Asheboro, 8 N.C. App. 571, 174 S.E.2d 870 (1970).

106. Also see the discussion of laches and estoppel in the context of enforcement actions in Chapter 21.

107. In *Taylor v. City of Raleigh*, 290 N.C. 608, 227 S.E.2d 576 (1976), the court ruled that the challenge was barred by laches because it was filed more than two years after the rezoning, during which time both the city and the landowner had made substantial expenditures in reliance on the rezoning. Similarly, in *Capps v. City of Raleigh*, 35 N.C. App. 290, 241 S.E.2d 527 (1978), the court dismissed a suit initiated in 1975 to challenge the 1969 rezoning of an area from single-family residential to a district that allowed multifamily housing. The defendants had spent more than $600,000 and had otherwise materially changed their position in reliance on the rezoning. Therefore, the court of appeals held that the suit was barred by laches. By contrast, in *Stutts v. Swaim*, 30 N.C. App. 611, 228 S.E.2d 750, *review denied*, 291 N.C. 178, 229 S.E.2d 692 (1976), a suit initiated in June 1974 to challenge, as illegal spot zoning, the November 1968 rezoning of a four-acre tract in the town of Randleman's extraterritorial area from single-family residential to a mobile-home district was allowed. The court of appeals held that the challenge was not barred by laches because delay in bringing the action was alone insufficient to establish laches. Rather, there had to be an affirmative showing that the delay worked to the disadvantage, the injury, or the prejudice of the defendant. For a discussion of laches in enforcement cases, see Chapter 21.

108. S.L. 1996-746. In *Reunion Land Co. v. Village of Marvin*, 129 N.C. App. 249, 497 S.E.2d 446 (1998), the court held that when the statute of limitations changes, plaintiffs must file their actions within a reasonable time, but in no event can they file beyond the new statute of limitations (here, within two months of the effective date of this legislative change, October 1, 1996).

109. S.L. 2011-384.

validity of a zoning or unified development ordinance other than some rezonings. The action accrues when the party bringing it first has standing to do so, provided any challenge to the adoption process is brought within three years of the challenged adoption. G.S. 1-54.1 sets a two-month statute of limitations for legislative zoning decisions that involve adopting or amending a zoning map or approving a request for a rezoning to a conditional district, with such action accruing upon adoption of the ordinance or amendment.

The planning-and-development-regulation statutes, G.S. 160D-1405, restate these statutes of limitation and provide that they do not prohibit a party in a zoning-enforcement action or persons appealing a notice of violation from raising the invalidity of the ordinance as a defense, but any challenge to the adoption process must be brought within three years of the challenged adoption.[110]

In a series of cases, the courts have applied this statute to dismiss challenges to the validity of legislative zoning decisions.[111] The municipal provision was first applied in *Sherrill v. Town of Wrightsville Beach*, in which the court held that G.S. 160D-1405 prohibited a challenge to the validity of a zoning amendment brought more than nine months after the rezoning (in this instance, a text amendment deleting duplexes as a permitted use).[112] Similarly, in *Appeal of CAMA Permit No. 82-0010 v. Town of Bath*, a challenge to a zoning amendment by the town of Bath preventing additional marinas in town waters, the court held that allegations of procedural irregularities regarding public notice and hearings on rezonings had to be brought within nine months of the adoption of the amendment.[113] In *Thompson v. Town of Warsaw*, the court of appeals applied this statute of limitations to bar a challenge to a "variance" issued by the town council that the plaintiffs contended was a de facto rezoning.[114] In *Laurel Valley Watch, Inc. v. Mountain Enterprises of Wolf Ridge, LLC*, the appeals court again applied this statute of limitations to litigation that raised the question of whether the zoning map accurately reflected the actual zoning amendment made by the county commissioners.[115] In *Schwarz Properties, LLC v. Town of Franklinville*, the court applied this statute of limitations once again to prevent a challenge to zoning restrictions limiting the age of manufactured housing proposed to be located in the town.[116] In *Templeton*, the court applied this statute to a challenge of the procedures followed in adopting steep-slope and viewshed-protection ordinances incorporated into the town's unified development ordinance.[117]

---

110. G.S. 160D-1405(b).

111. The burden is on the defendant to plead an affirmative defense, including a statute of limitations. G.S. 1A, Rule 8(c). If the statute of limitations is raised as a defense, the long-standing and somewhat atypical rule in North Carolina is that the burden is then on the plaintiff to show that the claim is not time-barred. Lea Co. v. N.C. Bd. of Transp., 308 N.C. 603, 629, 304 S.E.2d 164, 181 (1983); Hooper v. Carr Lumber Co., 215 N.C. 308, 311, 1 S.E.2d 818, 820 (1939); Moore v. Westbrook, 156 N.C. 482, 492, 72 S.E. 842, 847 (1911); Ga.-Pac. Corp. v. Bondurant, 81 N.C. App. 362, 363–64, 344 S.E.2d 302, 304 (1986).

112. 81 N.C. App. 369, 344 S.E.2d 357, *review denied*, 318 N.C. 417, 349 S.E.2d 600 (1986).

113. 82 N.C. App. 32, 345 S.E.2d 699 (1986).

114. 120 N.C. App. 471, 462 S.E.2d 691 (1995).

115. 192 N.C. App. 391, 665 S.E.2d 561 (2008). In August 2005, the county commissioners met and unanimously approved a rezoning to an industrial zoning district to accommodate a proposed private airport. However, the minutes of the meeting noted that the property had been rezoned to a "residential-resort" district. The plaintiff filed this action in March 2006. The court held that since the evidence clearly supported a conclusion that the property had actually been rezoned to the industrial district in August 2005 and that there was a scrivener's error in the minutes, the two-month statute of limitations to challenge the rezoning ran from August 2005. The court found no evidence that the plaintiff had made any detrimental reliance on the scrivener's error.

116. 204 N.C. App. 344, 693 S.E.2d 271 (2010). The town on January 8, 2008, adopted a zoning provision precluding issuance of permits for location of manufactured homes more than ten years old. In February 2009, the state supreme court issued its decision in *Five C's, Inc. v. County of Pasquotank*, 195 N.C. App. 410, 672 S.E.2d 737 (2009), which invalidated a similar ten-year limitation on manufactured housing. This suit was filed in April 2009. The court held that it was time-barred, however, as it should have been filed no later than March 8, 2008.

117. 208 N.C. App. 50, 701 S.E.2d 709 (2010).

The county limitations provision was applied in *Baucom's Nursery Co. v. Mecklenburg County*. The court there ruled that an action brought in 1987 to challenge a zoning amendment adopted in 1982 was barred by the nine-month statute of limitations established in G.S. 160D-1405.[118]

The municipal statute was applied to extraterritorial zoning in *In re Raynor*,[119] which involved the original adoption of zoning by the town of Garner for part of its extraterritorial jurisdiction in 1982 and a subsequent refusal to rezone the property at issue to a lower-intensity residential district in 1987. The court ruled that the statute of limitations in G.S. 160D-1405 precluded a challenge to the zoning five years after the action was taken.

For the most part, the two-month statute of limitations does not apply to land use ordinances that are not zoning ordinances. In *Lanvale Properties, LLC v. County of Cabarrus*,[120] the court held that even though a contested school-impact-fee provision was included within a zoning ordinance, the provision was not a "zoning ordinance" since it was not authorized by the zoning-enabling statute; therefore, the statute of limitations applicable to contesting the validity of a zoning ordinance was inapplicable. In *Coventry Woods Neighborhood Ass'n v. City of Charlotte*, the court refused to apply the two-month statute of limitations to a challenge of a subdivision ordinance. The court distinguished zoning ordinances from subdivision ordinances and applied the more general three-year statute of limitations in G.S. 1-52 to the subdivision ordinance.[121]

An exemption apparently exists for challenges to the adoption of an extraterritorial-boundary ordinance under G.S. 160D-202. Although such an ordinance is within Chapter 160D, it is not a zoning ordinance per se, though a zoning-map amendment to zone the extraterritorial area is often considered concurrently with the extraterritorial-boundary map. In *Pinehurst Area Realty, Inc. v. Village of Pinehurst*,[122] a challenge was brought, two years after the fact, based on alleged procedural irregularities in the adoption of an extraterritorial-boundary extension and application of zoning to the area. The court held that the then-applicable nine-month statute of limitations barred the challenge. In similar fashion, the court in *Potter v. City of Hamlet* applied the two-month statute of limitations to dismiss a challenge brought four years after adoption of an extraterritorial-boundary ordinance.[123]

118. 89 N.C. App. 542, 366 S.E.2d 558, *review denied*, 322 N.C. 834, 371 S.E.2d 274 (1988). The court also ruled that to bring an action for actual damages, a plaintiff had to show that the county's government immunity had been waived by the purchase of liability insurance (which was not shown here). The court further ruled that punitive damages were allowed only if authorized by statute, and no such statute existed in respect to counties in North Carolina. *See also* White v. Union Cnty., 93 N.C. App. 148, 377 S.E.2d 93 (1989) (challenge to mobile-home provision in zoning ordinance must be brought within nine months of adoption of regulation).

119. 94 N.C. App. 91, 379 S.E.2d 880, *review denied*, 325 N.C. 707, 388 S.E.2d 448 (1989).

120. 366 N.C. 142, 731 S.E.2d 800 (2012).

121. 202 N.C. App. 247, 688 S.E.2d 538, *review denied*, 364 N.C. 128, 695 S.E.2d 757 (2010). The federal court in *FC Summers Walk, LLC v. Town of Davidson*, No. 3:09-CV-266-GCM, 2010 WL 4366287 (W.D.N.C. Oct. 28, 2010), also held that an adequate-public-facilities ordinance incorporated into a unified development ordinance may be a "development regulation ordinance" as distinct from a "zoning ordinance" subject to the two-month statute of limitations.

122. 100 N.C. App. 77, 394 S.E.2d 251 (1990), *review denied*, 328 N.C. 92, 402 S.E.2d 417 (1991).

123. 141 N.C. App. 714, 541 S.E.2d 233, *review denied*, 353 N.C. 379, 547 S.E.2d 814 (2001). The plaintiff purchased a nonconforming small grocery store in the city's extraterritorial area. After failing to get an ABC permit for off-premise beer sales (denied as an unlawful expansion of a nonconformity) and failing to secure a rezoning, the plaintiff challenged the adoption of extraterritorial jurisdiction some four years earlier on the grounds that the boundary map had not been filed with the county register of deeds. While noting that the city had substantially complied with the notice requirements, the court held that G.S. 160D-1405 barred the action.

Apart from a legislative zoning decision, the court has applied the three-year statute of limitations for a liability created by statute to an allegation that a utility impact fee was imposed in excess of the statutory authority for public-enterprise fees.[124]

Quasi-Judicial Decisions

The time period to initiate a judicial challenge of a quasi-judicial zoning decision is set by G.S. 160D-1405(d).[125] The statute provides that appeals to superior court must be made within thirty days of the later of (1) the effective date of the decision, which is when the written decision is filed with the clerk to the board or to an official designated by the ordinance[126] or (2) after a written copy of the decision is provided to the property owner, the applicant, and any person who has submitted a written request for a copy before the effective date of the decision.[127] If the quasi-judicial decision is mailed but a copy is not filed with the clerk to the board, the period does not begin to run.[128]

The time period for filing a petition of certiorari is strictly enforced. In *McCrann v. Village of Pinehurst*,[129] the town council issued a special use permit. The day after the vote, but before the written decision was filed, opposing neighbors requested by voicemail a copy of the decision. The written decision was filed, and a copy was sent to the neighbors. The court held that the thirty-day period to appeal must be measured from the date the decision was filed, not the date a verbal request for the decision was made.[130] Because this appeal was filed thirty-one days after the decision was filed, it was not timely and the court had no jurisdiction to hear it.

Enforcement Actions

In most North Carolina cities and counties, development-regulation violations are investigated and cited on a complaint basis. Enforcement officers do not tend to initiate independent investigations of violations absent the filing of a complaint. Statutes of limitation enacted in 2017, however, limit the authority of

---

124. Quality Built Homes Inc. v. Town of Carthage, 371 N.C. 60, 813 S.E.2d 218 (2018); Bill Clark Homes of Raleigh, LLC v. Town of Fuquay-Varina, 281 N.C. App. 1, 869 S.E.2d 1 (2021). The court in *Quality Built Homes* held that the statute began to run when the fees were paid, not when the fee ordinance was adopted. The court also held that the plaintiffs' acceptance of benefits did not estop them from challenging the fees because the payments were involuntary and the plaintiffs received no additional benefits from them.

125. This statute applies to all quasi-judicial decisions made under Chapter 160D regulations. G.S. 160D-406(k) expressly provides that judicial review of quasi-judicial decisions are governed by G.S. 160D-1402 and must be filed within the times specified by G.S. 160D-1405(d).

126. The statute specifically states that it is the "decision of the board" that must be filed and served on the parties. Since the decision must include sufficient findings of fact and conclusions (see Chapter 15 for a further discussion of these requirements), a letter simply noting the outcome of the vote is inadequate. If the formal written decision is not adopted until the minutes of the board meeting are approved, it is likely that this time period does not begin to run until a copy of the minutes is mailed to the parties.

127. When first-class mail is used to deliver the decision, three days is added to the time to file a petition for review. G.S. 160D-110(c). This statute further provides that delivery by electronic mail shall be deemed to be received on the date sent.

128. Ad/Mor v. Town of S. Pines, 88 N.C. App. 400, 363 S.E.2d 220 (1988).

129. 216 N.C. App. 291, 716 S.E.2d 667 (2011).

130. As the statute at the time of this case required a written request for the decision made at the hearing, the verbal request did not affect the running of the statute of limitations. The town's "professional and courteous conduct" in responding to the oral request did not constitute grounds for extending the time period. The court concluded, "We decline to hold that attorneys must take care not to be too cooperative, cordial, or professional in dealing with opposing counsel lest they inadvertently waive their clients' statutory rights or protections." *Id.* at 296, 716 S.E.2d at 671.

a city or county to pursue a violation if it has been known to the local government, or could have been known to it, and no enforcement action has been initiated.[131]

G.S. 1-51 provides that a suit against a landowner for violation of any land use regulation or permit must be initiated within five years. The five-year period starts to run when the facts of the violation are known to the governing board, when they are known to any agent or employee of the local government, or when the violation can be determined from the public records of the local government.[132]

G.S. 1-49 sets a seven-year period to bring suit for a land use violation running from the time the violation is "apparent from a public right of way" or is in "plain view from a place to which the public is invited."

In both instances, an action for an injunction can be brought later to address "conditions that are actually injurious or dangerous to the public health or safety."[133]

Constitutional Claims

If an owner alleges that the application of a development regulation has violated a constitutional right,[134] the owner generally may bring suit within three years on that issue alone. In several cases, however, the state court of appeals has concluded that the much shorter nine-month (now two-month) statute of limitations in G.S. 160D-1405 applies to those claims as well.[135] By contrast, the Fourth Circuit has applied the three-year statute of limitations of G.S. 1-52(5) for constitutional challenges[136] and has held that there is no statute of limitations for facial challenges.[137] In *Capital Outdoor Advertising, Inc. v.*

---

131. S.L. 2017-10. This may provide some incentive for local governments to cite known violations even if no complaint has been filed.

132. Apparently, any public record triggers the running of this period, including a filing with a utility department, a tax listing, or a filing with the planning-and-inspections department.

133. G.S. 1-49; G.S. 1-51.

134. There is no federal statute of limitations for actions alleging a violation of the United States Constitution. In these cases, the federal courts apply the relevant state's personal-injury statute of limitations. Wilson v. Garcia, 471 U.S. 261 (1985); Bireline v. Seagondollar, 567 F.2d 260 (4th Cir. 1977).

135. Naegele Outdoor Advert., Inc. v. City of Winston-Salem, 113 N.C. App. 758, 762, 440 S.E.2d 842, 844 (1994), *aff'd*, 340 N.C. 349, 457 S.E.2d 874 (1995); Pinehurst Area Realty, Inc. v. Vill. of Pinehurst 100 N.C. App. 77, 81, 394 S.E.2d 251, 253–54 (1990), *review denied*, 328 N.C. 92, 402 S.E.2d 417 (1991); Sherrill v. Town of Wrightsville Beach, 81 N.C. App. 369, 344 S.E.2d 357, *review denied*, 318 N.C. 417, 349 S.E.2d 600 (1986). Note, however, that in *Frizzelle v. Harnett County*, 106 N.C. App. 234, 416 S.E.2d 421, *review denied*, 332 N.C. 147, 419 S.E.2d 571 (1992), the court held that the county had waived the nine-month statute of limitations because it was not raised in the county's answer nor had the county given notice of it to the plaintiff when it was raised in response to a summary-judgment motion.

136. Nat'l Advert. Co. v. City of Raleigh, 947 F.2d 1158, 1162 (4th Cir. 1991), *cert. denied*, 504 U.S. 931 (1992). See also *Franks v. Ross*, 313 F.3d 184, 194 (4th Cir. 2002), applying the three-year statute of limitations in G.S. 1-52(16) to an environmental-justice claim regarding the siting of a Wake County landfill. In *Epcon Homestead, LLC v. Town of Chapel Hill*, 62 F.4th 882 (4th Cir. 2023), the plaintiff challenged a requirement that they contribute $803,250 to an affordable-housing trust fund as a condition of approval of a special use permit for a sixty-three-unit housing development. The claims were a lack of state statutory authority, violation of substantive due process, and an unconstitutional taking. The court dismissed the case, applying the three-year statute of limitations for personal injury actions, running from the time the plaintiff knows or has reason to know of his or her injury. At that point, the constitutional claim is complete and present. The court concluded that the plaintiff in this case knew of the injury when it began purchasing the land that was already subject to the challenged condition of the special use permit. Once the condition was imposed, the Takings Clause claim became cognizable under *Koontz* and *Knick*, so the statute of limitations began to run when the plaintiff knew of that condition, not when the initial or final payment was made. *Id.* at 888–89.

137. *National Advertising*, 947 F.2d at 1162, 1168. *See also* Frye v. City of Kannapolis, 109 F. Supp. 2d 436 (M.D.N.C. 1999) (no statute of limitations for facial First Amendment challenge to adult-establishment-siting regulations).

City of Raleigh,[138] the state supreme court reviewed these conflicting results on applied challenges and observed that the state court-of-appeals decisions seemed to be "the better reasoned decisions" given the specificity of the statute of limitations explicitly related to legislative zoning decisions. However, since neither the nine-month nor the three-year provision had been met in that case, the court declined to resolve the matter.[139] Thus, where the same governmental action may be characterized in several ways, it is unclear which of these statutes will control.

In 2019, the statutes were amended to authorize an original civil action to challenge an administrative decision on the grounds that it is unconstitutional or lacks statutory authority. The action must be brought within one year of the date the written notice of the final decision is delivered to the aggrieved party.[140]

Others

In some instances the enabling statutes do not specify a particular time for appeals.[141] In *Point South Properties, LLC v. Cape Fear Public Utility Authority*, the court applied the ten-year statute of limitations for actions not otherwise specifically addressed by the statutes to a claim that utility impact fees were imposed in excess of the statutory authority for such fees.[142]

Also, the state inverse-condemnation statute, G.S. 40A-51, has a two-year period within which to file a claim.[143] G.S. 1-52 further provides for a general three-year statute of limitations on claims based on liabilities created by statute (unless a particular statute sets a different period) and claims for damages related to the construction or repair of improvements to real property.[144] These different periods are summarized in Table 29.2.

---

138. 337 N.C. 150, 446 S.E.2d 289 (1994).

139. *Id.* at 162, 446 S.E.2d at 296–97.

140. G.S. 160D-1403.1, created by S.L. 2019-111, § 1.7. This statute also allows a civil action to claim a vested right.

141. The statutes have been amended over time to specify statutes of limitation for many typical land use regulatory decisions, obviating the need to rely on this general provision. For example, in 2009, G.S. 153A-336 and 160A-377 were adopted to specify times for appeals of subdivision-plat decisions. S.L. 2009-421. Earlier cases applied a "reasonable time" standard for many of these. White Oak Props., Inc. v. Town of Carrboro, 313 N.C. 306, 327 S.E.2d 882 (1985); Allen v. City of Burlington Bd. of Adjustment, 100 N.C. App. 615, 397 S.E.2d 657 (1990); *In re* Greene, 29 N.C. App. 749, 225 S.E.2d 647, *review denied*, 290 N.C. 661, 228 S.E.2d 451 (1976). The rule requiring appeals to be filed within a reasonable time was applied to an appeal of a subdivision-variance denial in *Hemphill-Nolan v. Town of Weddington*, 153 N.C. App. 144, 568 S.E.2d 887, 889–90 (2002), and to historic-district regulations in *Meares v. Town of Beaufort*, 193 N.C. App. 96, 104, 667 S.E.2d 239, 244 (2008).

142. 243 N.C. App. 508, 778 S.E.2d 284 (2015). The court held that since the fees were ultra vires because the property was in an unserved area, the three-year statute of limitations for liabilities created by statute was not applicable, nor was the two-year statute of limitations for liabilities arising out of a contract as there were no services provided and no contract for services. In a federal-court action involving this same issue against the same utility, the court found that the plaintiff's federal claim was subject to the three-year statute of limitations of G.S. 1-52(5) for personal-injury actions, but the state-law claims were timely under this *Point South Properties* rationale. Tommy Davis Constr., Inc. v. Cape Fear Pub. Util. Auth., 807 F.3d 62 (4th Cir. 2015).

143. See, for example, *Robertson v. City of High Point*, 129 N.C. App. 88, 497 S.E.2d 300 (1998), where the court ruled that an inverse-condemnation suit alleging damages from an adjacent landfill was barred by this two-year statute of limitations when the damage commenced in October 1993 and the suit was not filed until December 1996. (The court also held that the general three-year statute of limitations also barred claims based on nuisance, negligence, and trespass.)

144. In *Dawson v. North Carolina Department of Environment & Natural Resources*, 204 N.C. App. 524, 694 S.E.2d 427 (2010), the court refused to apply the three-year statute of limitations regarding negligent construction of improvements to a claim regarding a faulty inspection of land for suitability for septic tanks; the inspection related to the land rather than any improvement that had been constructed. In *Town of Black Mountain v. Lexon Insurance*, 238 N.C. App. 180, 768 S.E.2d 302 (2014), *review denied*, 368 N.C. 249, 771 S.E.2d 307 (2015), involving enforcement of a subdivision performance guarantee, the court noted that this three-year limit does not apply to a city or county exercising a governmental function.

Table 29.2 Summary of Statutes of Limitation for Land Use Actions

Time Period	General Statute	Coverage
10 years	1-56	Actions for relief not otherwise limited by statute
6 years	1-50(a)(3)	Actions to enforce private restrictive covenants
3 years	1-52	Liability created by statute; damages related to construction of improvements; personal-injury suits
2 years	40A-51	Inverse-condemnation claims
1 year	1-54(10) 160D-1405(b)	Validity of ordinance (running from acquisition of standing, with three-year maximum for allegation of procedural defect in adoption); vested-right claim (running from notice of determination)
60 days	1-54.1 160D-1403(a), -1405(a)	Challenges to validity of rezoning
30 days	160D-1403, -1405(d)	Challenges to quasi-judicial zoning decisions (variances, special use permits, interpretations, quasi-judicial plat approvals); challenges to administrative plat approvals

Initiation of Time

When statutes of limitation begin to run is a critical issue. This issue often arises in the context of whether the period begins to run when the contested regulation is adopted or when it is enforced.

In *National Advertising Co. v. City of Raleigh*,[145] a challenge to a five-and-a-half-year amortization provision in Raleigh's zoning ordinance, the Fourth Circuit held that the time limit for bringing the lawsuit (three years, under G.S. 1-52(2), discussed in the text above) commenced with the adoption of the ordinance requirement, rejecting the plaintiff company's contentions that the amortization requirement was a continuing constitutional violation or that the limitations period started to run only at the expiration of the amortization period.[146] State courts have reached the same conclusion in sign-amortization cases.[147] However, in *Coventry Woods*, a case challenging the validity of a subdivision ordinance, the court held that the limitations period began to run when the plaintiffs learned of the plat-approval decision that gave rise to the challenge.[148]

145. 947 F.2d 1158 (1991), *cert. denied*, 504 U.S. 931 (1992). See Chapter 20 for a discussion of amortization.

146. G.S. 1-52(2) has also been held to bar a takings claim based on a septic-tank ban to protect water quality. Ocean Acres Ltd. P'ship v. Dare Cnty. Bd. of Health, 707 F.2d 103 (4th Cir. 1983). However, this statute of limitations has been held not to bar an inverse-condemnation action based on continuing overflights of property near a municipal airport. Hoyle v. City of Charlotte, 276 N.C. 292, 172 S.E.2d 1 (1970).

147. *See, e.g.*, Capital Outdoor Advert. Co. v. City of Raleigh, 337 N.C. 150, 163–64, 446 S.E.2d 289, 297 (1994).

148. 202 N.C. App. 247, 688 S.E.2d 538, *review denied*, 364 N.C. 128, 695 S.E.2d 757 (2010). The challenged ordinance allowed preliminary plat approval to be made without a hearing and notice to the neighbors. The neighbors contended that adoption of an ordinance without these violated their due-process rights. Although the plaintiffs prevailed on the limitations issue, the court held that no property rights had been violated. In *South Shell Island Investment v. Town of Wrightsville Beach*, 703 F. Supp. 1192, 1195 (E.D.N.C. 1988), the court also applied the three-year statute of limitations to claims alleging improper impact and tap fees. On the continuing-wrong doctrine generally, see *Williams v. Blue Cross Blue Shield of North Carolina*, 357 N.C. 170, 178–81, 581 S.E.2d 415, 423–24 (2003) and *Faulkenbury v. Teachers' & State Employees' Retirement System of North Carolina*, 345 N.C. 683, 694–95, 483 S.E.2d 422, 429–30 (1997).

Ripeness

As with all litigation, only a final action that has legal consequences may be reviewed by the courts.

Fleischhauer v. Town of Topsail Beach[149] illustrates this principle as applied to review of development-regulation decisions. The plaintiffs owned soundfront lots on a narrow portion of Topsail Beach. After the town repealed its dune-protection ordinance, the plaintiffs sought a declaratory judgment that development of oceanfront lots adjacent to their property would violate town and federal laws, and they sought an injunction to prevent the town from issuing permits for any excavation of dunes or development on these lots. No permits to develop the oceanfront lots had been submitted. The court held that the matter was not ripe for adjudication. A speculative possibility that development might proceed in a manner inconsistent with the law is not a justiciable case or controversy. A final determination of what development, if any, the town would permit is required before the matter is ripe for adjudication.

Exhaustion of Administrative Remedies

A person must seek any available administrative appeal of a zoning decision as a prerequisite to judicial review.[150] Failure to seek quasi-judicial review of an administrative decision (such as a permit denial or a determination regarding nonconformity) precludes judicial review of that decision.[151] The local govern-

---

149. No. COA-17915, 2018 WL 1162817 (N.C. Ct. App. Mar. 6, 2018) (originally unpublished, published by petition). *See also* Ballantyne Village Parking, LLC v. City of Charlotte, 818 F. App'x, 198, 2020 WL 3265007 (No. 19-1213, 4th Cir. June 17, 2020) (due-process claim regarding development permit not ripe for judicial review due to the lack of finality on an unresolved easement dispute and a pending board of adjustment decision on an appeal regarding the permit); CarSpa Auto., LLC v. City of Raleigh, 57 F. Supp. 3d 505 (E.D.N.C. 2014) (takings claim not ripe where plaintiff failed to apply to variance regarding exaction for public-access right-of-way).

150. Sanford v. Williams, 221 N.C. App. 107, 116–19, 727 S.E.2d 362, 368–70, *review denied*, 366 N.C. 246, 731 S.E.2d 144 (2012) (where zoning officer's determination regarding application of side-yard setback for a carport is not appealed to the board of adjustment, court has no subject-matter jurisdiction to hear appeal); Laurel Valley Watch, Inc. v. Mountain Enters. of Wolf Ridge, LLC, 192 N.C. App. 391, 665 S.E.2d 561 (2008) (court was without subject-matter jurisdiction to hear complaint against developers for a zoning violation because plaintiff failed to seek zoning administrator's ruling on zoning compliance and then to appeal that determination to designated board before initiating judicial review); Northfield Dev. Co. v. City of Burlington, 165 N.C. App. 885, 599 S.E.2d 921, *review denied*, 359 N.C. 191, 607 S.E.2d 278 (2004) (where plaintiff's application for a special use permit was rejected due to an incomplete application, superior court has no subject-matter jurisdiction to consider action for damages or for mandamus to compel permit issuance); Town of Garner v. Weston, 263 N.C. 487, 139 S.E.2d 642 (1965); Potter v. City of Hamlet, 141 N.C. App. 714, 541 S.E.2d 233, *review denied*, 353 N.C. 379, 547 S.E.2d 814 (2001) (failure to seek judicial review of board of adjustment's finding regarding expansion of nonconformity precludes subsequent collateral attack of that determination); Midgette v. Pate, 94 N.C. App. 498, 380 S.E.2d 572 (1989) (neighbor challenging lack of enforcement of zoning requirement must first secure ruling from administrator and appeal that ruling to the board of adjustment before seeking judicial intervention). *See also* Sunkler v. Town of Nags Head, No. 2:01-CV-22-H(2), 2002 WL 32395571 (E.D.N.C. May 17, 2002), *aff'd*, 50 F. App'x 116 (4th Cir. 2002) (failure to appeal zoning-enforcement decision to board of adjustment precludes suit alleging negligence of town officials). *See generally* Note, *Exhaustion of Remedies in Zoning Cases*, 1964 Wash. U. L.Q. 368; Donald C. Scriven, Comment, *Exhausting Administrative and Legislative Remedies in Zoning Cases*, 48 Tul. L. Rev. 665 (1974).

Granting the approval sought renders judicial review of claims arising under that action moot. Shell Island Homeowners Ass'n v. Tomlinson, 134 N.C. App. 286, 291, 517 S.E.2d 401, 404 (1999).

151. State v. Roberson, 198 N.C. 70, 150 S.E. 674 (1929); Ward v. New Hanover Cnty., 175 N.C. App. 671, 625 S.E.2d 598 (2006) (interpretation of terms of permit must be appealed to board of adjustment as prerequisite to judicial review); Grandfather Vill. v. Worsley, 111 N.C. App. 686, 689, 433 S.E.2d 13, 15, *review denied*, 335 N.C. 237, 439 S.E.2d 146 (1993) (failure to appeal notice of violation and civil-penalty assessment to board of adjustment waives any right to raise in superior court any defenses to the assessment); Appalachian Outdoor Advert. Co. v. Town of Boone, 103 N.C. App. 504, 406 S.E.2d 297 (1991); Wil-Hol Corp. v. Marshall, 71 N.C. App. 611, 322 S.E.2d 655 (1984); Quadrant Corp. v. City of Kinston, 22 N.C. App. 31, 205 S.E.2d 324 (1974). Also see the discussion of enforcement

ment must have made a final decision and all administrative appeals must have been exhausted before judicial review can be initiated. Interlocutory appeals are not allowed.[152]

A person who fails to seek judicial review of a board of adjustment's decision cannot collaterally attack the ruling in a subsequent enforcement action.[153] A minimum-housing code may provide that a person who fails to appeal to the housing-appeals board or board of adjustment an order to repair, vacate, or demolish a residence deemed unfit for habitation has failed to exhaust administrative remedies and may not collaterally attack the order in court.[154]

There are several situations when an administrative appeal is not required. These are situations where there is no jurisdiction to grant the relief sought at the administrative level. If the constitutionality of a regulation is challenged, administrative remedies are inadequate because the administrative board has no jurisdiction to grant the relief sought; therefore, a futile administrative appeal is not required.[155]

---

actions in Chapter 21. Also, G.S. 160D-947 provides an option to local governments regarding appeals of decisions on certificates of appropriateness under a historic-preservation regulation. The regulation may require that those decisions are appealed to the board of adjustment or that they go directly to superior court.

A number of cases involving appeals under the Administrative Procedure Act have held that a failure to exhaust administrative appeals deprives the courts of subject-matter jurisdiction and that judicial appeals are properly dismissed under Rule 12(b)(1). Citizens for Responsible Roadways v. N.C. Dep't of Transp., 145 N.C. App. 497, 550 S.E.2d 253 (2001), *review denied*, 355 N.C. 210, 559 S.E.2d 798 (2002) (failure to seek Administrative Procedure Act review of finding of no significant impact that obviates need for environmental-impact statement bars judicial review); Presnell v. Pell, 298 N.C. 715, 721, 260 S.E.2d 611, 615 (1979); Bryant v. Hogarth, 127 N.C. App. 79, 83, 488 S.E.2d 269, 271, *review denied*, 347 N.C. 396, 494 S.E.2d 406 (1997); Flowers v. Blackbeard Sailing Club, Ltd., 115 N.C. App. 349, 444 S.E.2d 636 (1994); Leeuwenburg v. Waterway Inv. Ltd. P'ship, 115 N.C. App. 541, 545, 445 S.E.2d 614, 617 (1994); N. Buncombe Ass'n of Concerned Citizens v. Rhodes, 100 N.C. App. 24, 394 S.E.2d 462 (1990); Porter v. N.C. Dep't of Ins., 40 N.C. App. 376, 253 S.E.2d 44, *review denied*, 297 N.C. 455, 256 S.E.2d 808 (1979). *See also* Barris v. Town of Long Beach, 208 N.C. App. 718, 704 S.E.2d 285 (2010) (trial court has no jurisdiction to hear dispute regarding town improvements within nonexclusive street right-of-way since Coastal Area Management Act permit application was made (and not yet decided or appealed) and administrative appeal under that act is exclusive remedy).

152. However, when multiple claims are raised, if the trial court enters a final judgment as to a claim and certifies that there is no just reason for delay, then that judgment is subject to judicial review. Martin Marietta Techs., Inc. v. Brunswick Cnty., 348 N.C. 698, 500 S.E.2d 665 (1998) (citing DKH Corp. v. Rankin-Patterson Oil Co., 348 N.C. 583, 500 S.E.2d 666 (1998)).

153. Town of Pinebluff v. Marts, 195 N.C. App. 659, 673 S.E.2d 740 (2009); New Hanover Cnty. v. Pleasant, 59 N.C. App. 644, 297 S.E.2d 760 (1982); City of Elizabeth City v. LFM Enters., Inc., 48 N.C. App. 408, 269 S.E.2d 260 (1980); City of Hickory v. Catawba Valley Mach. Co., 39 N.C. App. 236, 249 S.E.2d 851 (1978). To the extent that multiple issues are presented in a subsequent action, collateral estoppel only acts to bar relitigation of issues that were actually before the board or court previously and were both critical and necessary to the decision. *See, e.g.*, United States v. Town of Garner, 720 F. Supp. 2d 721 (E.D.N.C. 2010) (in case alleging failure to make reasonable accommodation for a group home, court found that collateral estoppel applies only to the parties in the prior matter and only to the issues actually addressed by the board of adjustment).

154. Cheatham v. Town of Taylortown, 254 N.C. App. 613, 803 S.E.2d 658 (2017) (applying G.S. 160D-1208 provision for appeals of orders adopted under a minimum-housing code).

155. In *Swan Beach Corolla, L.L.C. v. County of Currituck*, 234 N.C. App. 617, 760 S.E.2d 302 (2014), the court held that a claim of a common law vested right presents a constitutional question that is outside the jurisdiction of a board of adjustment, so if there is no interpretation of the ordinance involved, there is no exhaustion requirement for an appeal to the board of adjustment. *See also* City of Wilmington v. Hill, 189 N.C. App. 173, 657 S.E.2d 670 (2008) (defendant not required to appeal civil penalty to board of adjustment before bringing action challenging the constitutionality of the ordinance provision allegedly violated); Meads v. N.C. Dep't of Agric., 349 N.C. 656, 670, 509 S.E.2d 165, 174 (1998); Shell Island Homeowners Ass'n v. Tomlinson, 134 N.C. App. 217, 224, 517 S.E.2d 406, 412 (1999). However, if an adequate remedy is available through administrative appeals and judicial review of a determination, failure to pursue that remedy bars a subsequent constitutional challenge. Askew v. City of Kinston, ___ N.C. App. ___, 883 S.E.2d 85 (2022). The court found that the right to appeal unsafe building condemnation orders to the city council or superior court provided an adequate statutory remedy to address the plaintiff's claims. As a general rule, one may not voluntarily proceed under a statute or ordinance, accept its benefits, and then challenge its

This concept was codified in 2019, as G.S. 160D-1403.1 was created to provide that a person may bring an original civil action to establish a vested right, to assert a claim that a regulation is unconstitutional on its face or as applied, that the regulation is preempted or in excess of statutory authority, or that it constitutes an unconstitutional taking of private property. However, this statute also provides that if the issue being challenged is the interpretation of the regulation by a local enforcement officer, that claim must first be submitted to the board of adjustment.[156]

If the defendant can establish that the property involved is in fact outside of the geographic jurisdiction of the government purporting to regulate it, then there is no jurisdiction for the board of adjustment, and thus no appeal to it is necessary.[157] If no provision for an administrative appeal is made by a particular ordinance, such an appeal is not available and application for it need not be made.[158] Finally, if the jurisdiction refuses to issue a decision that can be appealed to the board of adjustment, judicial review is appropriate.[159]

Stays

The statutes specifically provide for stays of enforcement actions pending administrative appeals. G.S. 160D-405(f) provides that if an appeal is made *to* the board of adjustment, all proceedings in furtherance of the action appealed from are stayed once the appeal is filed. The statute provides two exceptions to this rule. If the zoning officer certifies either that a stay would cause imminent peril to life or property or that the violation charged is transitory and a stay would seriously interfere with enforcement, then there is no stay unless the board or a court issues a restraining order. If enforcement is not stayed, due to one of these two circumstances, the person appealing can request an expedited hearing, which then triggers a requirement that the board meet to hear the appeal within fifteen days of the request.

---

constitutionality to avoid its burdens. However, G.S. 160D-1403.2 provides that a local government may not assert an estoppel claim in a proceeding before a board of adjustment or in a civil action if the landowner or permit applicant is challenging conditions of approval that were not consented to in writing. See the discussion in Chapter 21 regarding estoppel and enforcement.

156. G.S. 160D-1403.1, created by S.L. 2019-111, § 1.7.

157. Guilford Cnty. Planning & Dev. Dep't v. Simmons, 102 N.C. App. 325, 401 S.E.2d 659, *review denied*, 329 N.C. 496, 407 S.E.2d 533 (1991). The defendant was denied a permit to construct two chicken houses and subsequently denied a variance for the same, and the variance decision was not appealed. After the defendant began construction, the county commenced an enforcement action. The court held that an allegation that the property was not in the county's jurisdiction could be raised as a defense to the enforcement action; however, if the property were found to be in the county, the defendant could not collaterally attack the unappealed board-of-adjustment decision. In a subsequent proceeding after remand, the court upheld the trial court's determination that the property was not in fact within the county, thus depriving the board of adjustment and the court of subject-matter jurisdiction. *See* Guilford County Planning & Development Department v. Simmons, 115 N.C. App. 87, 443 S.E.2d 765 (1994).

158. Ornoff v. City of Durham, 221 N.C. 457, 20 S.E.2d 380 (1942); State v. Roberson, 198 N.C. 70, 150 S.E. 674 (1929). In *Town of Kenansville v. Summerlin*, 70 N.C. App. 601, 320 S.E.2d 428 (1984), a case involving a permit decision, the court ruled that it was inappropriate to dismiss the defendant's appeal for having failed to make the usually requisite administrative appeal because the town had not appointed a board of adjustment or designated a body to serve as such. However, because the defendant had produced no evidence to support issuance of the permit and had not applied for a variance, the court held that it was proper to find the defendant in violation of the zoning ordinance. Occasionally, there is simply a lack of clarity in the ordinance as to whether appeals are or are not allowed or required. See, for example, *FC Summers Walk, LLC v. Town of Davidson*, No. 3:09-CV-266-GCM, 2010 WL 4366287 (W.D.N.C. Oct. 28, 2010), where the town staff made several determinations about the application of an adequate-public-facility requirement to different aspects of the plaintiff's development, some of which were appealed to the town council while others were not.

159. Meares v. Town of Beaufort, 193 N.C. App. 49, 62, 667 S.E.2d 244, 253 (2008).

The rules are different for quasi-judicial appeals to the board of adjustment for matters other than an enforcement action. G.S. 160D-405(f) provides that the appeal of a decision granting a permit or affirming that a use is permitted does not stay further review of an application or permission to use the property. In these situations, the appellant may request a stay of a final permit decision or issuance of building permits, and the board may grant it, but it is not automatically provided. Without a stay, permittees are free to proceed at their own risk while appeals are pending.[160]

A party desiring to preserve the status quo during the pendency of litigation may seek a judicial order to stay action during this period if that is not automatically applied with an enforcement appeal.[161] G.S. 160D-1402(e) provides that after filing a petition for writ of certiorari, a party may request a stay pending superior-court review. The court may grant the stay in its discretion and may require security for the adverse party (but no bond or other security may be required for a stay issued in favor of a local government). Similarly, G.S. 160D-1402(n) provides that filing a petition for judicial review of a quasi-judicial decision invokes stays as provided for in G.S. 160D-405.

If appellate judicial review is sought, there is an automatic stay of the trial court's order, but only until the expiration of time for giving notice of appeal.[162] Voluntary compliance with the trial court's order is permissible even in this period unless one of the parties secures an injunction to prohibit action. In *Estates, Inc. v. Town of Chapel Hill*, the denial of a special use permit was appealed, and the trial court subsequently ordered the permit issued. Neighbors who had intervened appealed to the court of appeals, but the town did not join the appeal and issued the permit while the matter was pending before the court of appeals. The court ruled that the town was not compelled to issue the permit during the period of the automatic stay, but it could voluntarily do so if the intervenors did not secure an injunction to prohibit it from doing so. Once the permit was issued, the intervenors' appeal was moot.[163]

Rules of Civil Procedure

As a general proposition, the Rules of Civil Procedure govern trial-court judicial review of development-regulation decisions.[164] For example, in *Darnell*, the court held that Rule 15, which allows amendment of a pleading once before a responsive pleading is filed, applied to a petition for a writ of certiorari.[165]

However, the court has held that rules do not apply when they are not relevant or applicable to a particular review. This issue most frequently arises with judicial review of a quasi-judicial decision. Since this form of action is essentially an appellate review, some of the rules of procedure have been held to be inapplicable. For example, having a trial by jury under Rule 38(b) does not apply because the court is reviewing the factual findings already made by the board making the quasi-judicial decision.[166] Similarly, Rule 41(a), regarding a voluntary dismissal of an action without prejudice and subsequent refiling within a year, does not apply because the petition for a writ of certiorari is requesting judicial review of a prior

---

160. Godfrey v. Zoning Bd. of Adjustment, 317 N.C. 51, 64 n.2, 344 S.E.2d 272, 280 n.2 (1986).

161. On appellate review of a trial court's refusal to issue a stay, the standard of review is abuse of discretion. *Meares*, 193 N.C. App. at 63, 667 S.E.2d at 254 (affirming refusal to grant stay).

162. G.S. 1A, Rule 62.

163. 130 N.C. App. 664, 504 S.E.2d 296 (1998), *review denied*, 350 N.C. 93, 527 S.E.2d 664 (1999). See below for further discussion of mootness.

164. The rules apply in all actions of a civil nature except where a differing procedure is prescribed by statute. This includes review of a quasi-judicial decision by writ of certiorari as well as original civil actions. G.S. 160D-1402 sets a number of specific rules for judicial review of quasi-judicial decisions.

165. 131 N.C. App. 846, 849, 508 S.E.2d 841, 844 (1998). Also see *Mize v. County of Mecklenburg*, 80 N.C. App. 279, 341 S.E.2d 767 (1986), reviewing the discretion of the court to allow an amendment to a petition for writ of certiorari to add a necessary party.

166. Henderson v. Cnty. of Onslow, 245 N.C. App. 151, 154–55, 782 S.E.2d 57, 59–60 (2016).

decision rather than initiating a new action.[167] Rule 52(a)(1), requiring a trial court to make findings of fact, is inapplicable to review of quasi-judicial decisions since the trial court is conducting an appellate review of the board's findings.[168] The court has held that when conducting a review in the nature of certiorari, a motion for summary judgment under Rule 62, regarding stay of proceedings pending appeals, does not apply.[169] On the other hand, Rule 62 has been held to be applicable to these proceedings.[170]

Briefs on appeal must meet all standard requirements, including setting out a complete summary of the facts, a statement of the questions for review, and an argument addressing each question separately, with pertinent assignments of error and appropriate references to the record on appeal.[171]

Interlocutory Appeals

For appellate review to be in order, the trial court must certify the case for appeal[172] or have entered an order that would both deprive the appellant of a substantial right and result in that right being lost absent appellate judicial review before final disposition of the case.[173]

Several cases have addressed the issue of interlocutory appeals in the context of land-development regulation.

In *Coates v. Durham County*, neighbors challenged the county's issuance of a special use permit to construct a school. The superior court reversed the issuance of the permit and remanded the matter with an order to advertise and conduct a new hearing on the application. The contractor who would build

---

167. *Henderson*, 245 N.C. App. at 158, 782 S.E.2d at 61. The court noted that the proceeding is initiated by the initial quasi-judicial decision—issuing a notice of violation, deciding a special use permit, or deciding a variance—not the filing of a petition for judicial review of that decision.

168. Thompson v. Union County, 283 N.C. App. 547, 874 S.E.2d 623 (2022); Myers Park Homeowners Ass'n, Inc. v. City of Charlotte, 229 N.C. App. 204, 214, 747 S.E.2d 338, 346 (2013). Rather than findings of fact, the trial court in these cases must only set forth sufficient information in its order to allow a reviewing court to determine the scope of review used and the application of that review by the court.

169. Batch v. Town of Chapel Hill, 326 N.C. 1, 11, 387 S.E.2d 655, 662 (1990).

170. Estates, Inc. v. Town of Chapel Hill, 130 N.C. App. 664, 667, 504 S.E.2d 296, 299 (1998).

171. Northwood Homeowners Ass'n v. Town of Chapel Hill, 112 N.C. App. 630, 436 S.E.2d 282 (1993). In *Walsh v. Town of Wrightsville Beach Board of Alderman*, 361 N.C. 348, 644 S.E.2d 224 (2007) (per curiam), the town had issued building permits for two single-family beach cottages on an adjacent lot formerly owned by the plaintiff. The plaintiff appealed the staff determination (which had been upheld by the board of adjustment) that the property contained two buildable lots rather than one. The court of appeals, 179 N.C. App. 97, 632 S.E.2d 271 (2006), upheld the trial court's dismissal for failure to include clear references in the record or transcript for the assignment of error and a failure of the appellate brief to reference a clear assignment of error for each question presented. The supreme court reversed and remanded for reconsideration in light of new directions for rules for applying sanctions and discretion in applying rules of appellate procedure. On remand, in an unpublished opinion, the court of appeals again upheld the trial court's dismissal, noting that even though the plaintiff owned adjoining property, there had been no allegation of the requisite special damages, and thus the plaintiff had not established standing. Walsh v. Town of Wrightsville Beach Bd. of Alderman, No. COA05-1478-2, 2007 WL 3256669 (N.C. Ct. App. Nov. 6, 2007), *appeal dismissed*, 657 S.E.2d 891 (N.C. 2008).

172. G.S. 1A, Rule 54(b).

173. G.S. 1-277(a); G.S. 7A-27(b)(3). Goldston v. Am. Motors Corp., 326 N.C. 723, 726, 392 S.E.2d 735, 736 (1990); State v. Fayetteville St. Christian Sch., 299 N.C. 351, 261 S.E.2d 908, *appeal dismissed*, 449 U.S. 807 (1980). In *High Rock Lake Partners, LLC v. North Carolina Department of Transportation*, 204 N.C. App. 55, 693 S.E.2d 361, *review denied*, 364 N.C. 325, 700 S.E.2d 753 (2010), the court held that an interlocutory order denying a landowner's right to intervene in a suit contesting conditions imposed on a driveway permit could be immediately appealed where the original permit applicant had withdrawn from the project and assigned all its rights to the landowner.

the school under the permit appealed the order remanding the case. The court held that avoidance of a rehearing is not a substantial right, so the appeal of the remand order was interlocutory and premature.[174]

In *LeTendre v. Currituck County*,[175] the plaintiff sought a preliminary injunction to enjoin enforcement of a zoning ordinance after losing a case regarding interpretation of the ordinance. The court held that the county's right to enforce its ordinance is a substantial right that would be impaired if delayed by the litigation, so the trial court's grant of a preliminary injunction could be immediately appealed.

In *Royal Oak Concerned Citizens Ass'n v. Brunswick County*,[176] the plaintiffs sought to depose the former county manager and a former county commissioner in a case alleging a pattern and practice of racial discrimination in rezonings for a landfill expansion. The county objected, claiming a privilege based on legislative and quasi-judicial immunity. The trial court entered orders allowing the depositions, subject to some limits on testimony from the county commissioner. The county appealed the order, but the court dismissed the appeal as interlocutory. While the claim of a privilege is a substantial right, the trial court's order did not preclude objections at the deposition based on an asserted privilege; thus, there was no right to an immediate appeal.

In *Hyatt v. Town of Lake Lure*, the plaintiff sued the state and town regarding the town's lake-structure regulations. The trial court granted summary judgment in favor of the town but did not rule on the claims against the state. The court noted that at common law there was no appeal of right from a decision of a trial court, and thus an appellant must strictly comply with the statutory provisions setting forth an avenue of appeal. Here, a grant of partial summary judgment did not completely dispose of the case, so the court held it to be an interlocutory order that was not subject to appeal.[177]

Two cases address appeals regarding preliminary injunctions. In *Bessemer City Express, Inc. v. City of Kings Mountain*,[178] the city adopted a zoning amendment restricting the location, design, and use of video-gaming machines, requiring a special use permit for them and amortizing nonconforming operations after a six-month grace period. The plaintiff operators of video-game arcades filed a declaratory-judgment action contesting the validity of the regulation and sought a preliminary injunction to enjoin enforcement, which they were denied. The court held that an appeal of the denial of a preliminary injunction did not affect a substantial right (at the time of appeal, the ordinance requiring removal had not taken effect), and in any event their overall business could continue in operation, pending resolution of the case on the merits. Similarly, in *City of Fayetteville v. E & J Enterprises*,[179] the court held that the appeal of the denial of a preliminary injunction to prevent city enforcement of a regulation that prohibited topless dancing at a rebuilt nightclub (the original nonconforming topless club had been destroyed in a fire) should be dismissed as interlocutory. The business could operate (and offer non-topless dancing) during the pendency of the case, so the court held that the owner's substantial rights were not affected in a way that would escape review before final judgment in the case.

In *Jennewein v. City Council*,[180] the court held that it was premature to seek appellate review of a trial court's order remanding a special use permit decision for a de novo administrative hearing.

---

174. 266 N.C. App. 271, 831 S.E.2d 392 (2019). The court noted the remand was not with an order to issue or deny the permit, but rather to conduct a new, properly advertised hearing.

175. 259 N.C. App. 512, 817 S.E.2d 73 (2018), *review denied*, 372 N.C. 54, 822 S.E.2d 641 (2019).

176. 233 N.C. App. 145, 756 S.E.2d 833 (2014).

177. 191 N.C. App. 386, 663 S.E.2d 320 (2008). There was no Rule 54(b) certification in the record.

178. 155 N.C. App. 637, 573 S.E.2d 712 (2002).

179. 90 N.C. App. 268, 368 S.E.2d 20 (1988). The case involved Rick's Lounge in downtown Fayetteville.

180. 46 N.C. App. 324, 264 S.E.2d 802 (1980).

Standard of Judicial Review

Legislative Decisions

Courts nationally and in North Carolina give substantial deference to the judgment of elected officials making legislative land use regulatory decisions.

In one of the earliest zoning cases in North Carolina, the court held in *Appeal of Parker* that a zoning ordinance is presumed to be valid and that a court must defer to the city council's legislative judgment unless it is clearly unreasonable or abusive of discretion. A zoning ordinance is not invalid unless it clearly "has no foundation in reason and is a mere arbitrary or irrational exercise of power having no substantial relation to the public health, the public morals, the public safety or the public welfare in its proper sense."[181] The court further held the following:

> When the most that can be said against such ordinances is that whether it was an unreasonable, arbitrary or unequal exercise of power is fairly debatable, the courts will not interfere. In such circumstances the settled rule seems to be that the court will not substitute its judgment for that of the legislative body charged with the primary duty and responsibility of determining whether its action is in the interest of the public health, safety, morals or general welfare.[182]

In a more recent zoning case, the court similarly observed, "In reviewing an ordinance to determine whether the police power has been exercised within constitutional limitations, this Court does not analyze the wisdom of a legislative enactment."[183]

Only an action deemed by the court to be oppressive and manifestly abusive of discretion will be overturned. If the action had a "reasonable tendency to promote the public good, it [will be deemed to have represented] a valid exercise of [the state's police] power, and [it will be] entitled to implicit obedience."[184] When reviewing rezonings, courts "are not free to substitute their opinion for that of the legislative body so long as there is some plausible basis for the conclusion reached by that body."[185] A governing board's decision not to zone or to rezone a parcel has the same presumption of validity. Such a decision is a policy choice that is left by the courts to the discretion of locally elected officials.[186]

---

181. 214 N.C. 51, 55, 197 S.E. 706, 709 (citations omitted), *appeal dismissed*, 305 U.S. 568 (1938). *See also* Vill. of Euclid v. Ambler Realty Co., 272 U.S. 365, 388 (1926).

182. *Appeal of Parker*, 214 N.C. at 55, 197 S.E. at 709. For an earlier case that reached the same result, see *Small v. Councilmen of Edenton*, 146 N.C. 527, 60 S.E. 413 (1908). *See generally* 1 Edward H. Ziegler Jr., Rathkopf's The Law of Zoning and Planning § 5:2 (4th ed., Oct. 2019 Update).

183. Grace Baptist Church v. City of Oxford, 320 N.C. 439, 443, 358 S.E.2d 372, 374 (1987) (upholding regulation requiring off-street paved parking). *See also* Town of Atl. Beach v. Young, 307 N.C. 422, 298 S.E.2d 686, *cert. denied*, 462 U.S. 1101 (1983).

184. Marren v. Gamble, 237 N.C. 680, 686, 75 S.E.2d 880, 884 (1953). In a decision upholding a Walnut Cove zoning regulation that prohibited locating mobile homes in certain zoning districts, the court held that "[i]f the enactment and enforcement of the zoning ordinance is rationally related to a legitimate governmental objective," the presumption of validity applies. Duggins v. Town of Walnut Cove, 63 N.C. App. 684, 688, 306 S.E.2d 186, 189, *review denied*, 309 N.C. 819, 310 S.E.2d 348 (1983), *cert. denied*, 466 U.S. 946 (1984). *See also* Currituck Cnty. v. Willey, 46 N.C. App. 835, 266 S.E.2d 52, *review denied*, 301 N.C. 234, 283 S.E.2d 131 (1980).

185. Zopfi v. City of Wilmington, 273 N.C. 430, 437, 160 S.E.2d 325, 332 (1968). A whole-record review is conducted to determine whether there is a reasonable basis for the action taken. Good Neighbors of Oregon Hill Protecting Prop. Rights v. Cnty. of Rockingham, 242 N.C. App. 280, 774 S.E.2d 902, *review denied*, 368 N.C. 429, 778 S.E.2d 78 (2015) (remanding a challenged rezoning for a new summary-judgment hearing where trial court substituted its own findings of fact for those of the decision-making board).

186. *See, e.g.,* Ashby v. Town of Cary, 161 N.C. App. 499, 588 S.E.2d 572 (2003). The plaintiffs challenged a refusal by the town of Cary to rezone a parcel in an existing commercial area from low-density residential to a business conditional use district. The court affirmed that a conditional use district rezoning decision is a purely legislative decision; it is to be overturned only if the record before the town council at the time of the decision demonstrates that the decision had no foundation in reason and bore no substantial relationship to the public health, safety, morals, or

The fact that some other formulation of an ordinance could have been adopted and may have also been a reasonable approach to address the issue at hand does not render an ordinance arbitrary or capricious.[187]

The burden is on a challenger to establish the invalidity of a legislative regulatory decision.[188] The courts employ a whole-record review to allegations that a legislative decision is arbitrary and capricious.[189] The reviewing court must base its decision on the record before the board rather than taking additional evidence to make a de novo ruling.[190]

In a legislative decision, unlike quasi-judicial decisions, there is not a formal "record" of evidence because there is a public hearing on the matter rather than an evidentiary hearing. Some of the confusion on this point is semantic in that courts are applying the same whole-record test to allegations that the decision was arbitrary and capricious, and there is some tendency to cite and quote cases involving quasi-judicial decisions in cases addressing legislative decisions. The record for a legislative decision will primarily be the minutes of the hearing and board-member discussions in the meeting in which the decision was made.[191]

A limited exception to the presumption of validity of legislative regulatory decisions exists for spot-zoning cases.[192] In these cases the burden is on the government to establish a reasonable basis for the rezoning decision.[193]

---

welfare. If there is any plausible justification for the decision that has a basis in reason and a relation to public safety, the decision must be affirmed.

187. *See., e.g.*, State v. Maynard, 195 N.C. App. 757, 673 S.E.2d 877 (2009). The court upheld an ordinance adopted by Nashville limiting the number of dogs kept on premises within the city. The ordinance limit was two dogs over the age of five months for lots of 30,000 square feet or less, with an additional dog allowed for lots of at least 37,000 square feet. The fact that the town could have chosen to base the regulation on the size or breed of dog did not render its choice irrational.

188. *Young*, 307 N.C. 422, 426, 298 S.E.2d 686, 690; Kinney v. Sutton, 230 N.C. 404, 53 S.E.2d 306 (1949); *Maynard*, 195 N.C. App. at 759, 673 S.E.2d at 879; Nelson v. City of Burlington, 80 N.C. App. 285, 288, 341 S.E.2d 739, 741 (1986).

189. Coucoulas/Knight Props., LLC v. Town of Hillsborough, 199 N.C. App. 455, 457–58, 683 S.E.2d 228, 230 (2009), *aff'd per curiam*, 364 N.C. 127, 691 S.E.2d 411 (2010); Summers v. City of Charlotte, 149 N.C. App. 509, 562 S.E.2d 18, *review denied*, 355 N.C. 758, 566 S.E.2d 482 (2002); Teague v. W. Carolina Univ., 108 N.C. App. 689, 692, 424 S.E.2d 684, 684, *review denied*, 333 N.C. 466, 427 S.E.2d 627 (1993). The courts likewise apply a whole-record review to allegations that a quasi-judicial decision was arbitrary and capricious.

190. Kerik v. Davidson Cnty., 145 N.C. App. 222, 551 S.E.2d 186 (2001).

191. Required statements of rationale that must be adopted for all legislative zoning decisions are discussed in Chapter 11. These statements should provide a starting point in a review of whether a contested decision was arbitrary and capricious. *See. e.g.*, Clear Channel Outdoor, Inc. v. City of St. Paul, 618 F.3d 851 (8th Cir. 2010) (examining a similar required statement in determining a ban on billboard "extensions" or appendages was arbitrary and capricious).

192. See Chapter 12 for a complete discussion of spot zoning.

193. Federal courts apply heightened scrutiny to land use regulations that significantly impact private-property rights. *See* Dolan v. City of Tigard, 512 U.S. 374 (1994); Lucas v. S.C. Coastal Council, 505 U.S. 1003 (1992); Nollan v. Cal. Coastal Comm'n, 483 U.S. 825 (1987); First English Evangelical Lutheran Church v. County of Los Angeles, 482 U.S. 304 (1987). Substantial academic comment has been made on whether a shift in the presumption of validity has taken place as well as on the circumstances under which a shift *should* take place. *See, e.g.*, Robert J. Hopperton, *The Presumption of Validity in American Land-Use Law: A Substitute for Analysis, a Source of Significant Confusion*, 23 B.C. Envtl. Aff. L. Rev. 301 (1996); Daniel R. Mandelker & A. Dan Tarlock, *Shifting the Presumption of Constitutionality in Land-Use Law*, 24 Urb. Law. 1 (1992).

Quasi-Judicial Decisions

The courts apply a different, though often also deferential, review to quasi-judicial land use regulatory decisions. This standard for review applies to administrative or ministerial regulatory decisions as well.[194]

In *Harden v. City of Raleigh*,[195] one of the state's first zoning cases, the city staff's denial of a permit for a gasoline filling station in a neighborhood-business district was appealed to the board of adjustment and upheld. The court ruled that the board of adjustment's decision of the appeal was quasi-judicial. As such, the decision was not to be overturned by the court unless it was shown to be arbitrary.[196]

The statute provides that appeals of quasi-judicial decisions are subject to review by the superior court by proceedings in the nature of certiorari.[197] As the North Carolina Supreme Court has noted, in hearing such an appeal, the trial-court judge is sitting in an appellate capacity:

> In reviewing the sufficiency and competency of the evidence at the appellate level, the question is not whether the evidence before the superior court supported that court's order but whether the evidence before the town board was supportive of its action. In proceedings of this nature, the superior court is not the trier of fact. Such is the function of the town board. The trial court, reviewing the decision of a town board on a conditional use permit application, sits in the posture of an appellate court. The trial court does not review the sufficiency of evidence presented to it but reviews that evidence presented to the town board.[198]

The trial court is therefore bound by the facts found by the decision-making board that are supported by competent, substantial evidence.[199] The trial court may not make new findings of fact or conduct a de novo review of the evidence because it is the sole province of the decision-making board to weigh the evidence and make determinations of credibility.[200] The trial court may recite, summarize, or synthesize the evidence that was before the decision-making board.[201]

---

194. *See, e.g.*, Nazziola v. Landcraft Props., Inc., 143 N.C. App. 564, 545 S.E.2d 801 (2001) (applying whole-record review to ministerial subdivision-plat decision alleged to be arbitrary and capricious). In most instances such decisions will reach the court only as quasi-judicial decisions because an initial administrative appeal of the ministerial decision to the board of adjustment is necessary to exhaust administrative remedies (with subsequent judicial review of the board's decision).

195. 192 N.C. 395, 135 S.E. 151 (1926).

196. "Quasi judicial functions, when exercised, not arbitrarily, but in subordination to a uniform rule prescribed by statute, ordinarily are not subject to judicial control. It is only in extreme cases, those which are arbitrary, oppressive, or attended with manifest abuse, that the courts will interfere." *Id.* at 397, 135 S.E. at 152–53.

197. G.S. 160D-1402.

198. Coastal Ready-Mix Concrete Co. v. Bd. of Comm'rs, 299 N.C. 620, 626–27, 265 S.E.2d 379, 383 (1980). *See also* Powell v. N.C. Dep't of Transp., 347 N.C. 614, 624, 499 S.E.2d 180, 185 (1998).

199. In judicial review of a quasi-judicial decision, collateral estoppel applies, and an issue of fact that has been litigated and determined is conclusive in judicial review. *See, e.g.*, Hillsboro Partners, LLC v. City of Fayetteville, 226 N.C. App. 30, 738 S.E.2d 819, *review denied*, 367 N.C. 236, 748 S.E.2d 544 (2013) (factual determination that building is unsafe is binding on review).

200. Mangum v. Raleigh Bd. of Adjustment, 196 N.C. App. 249, 260, 674 S.E.2d 742, 750–51 (2009); Thompson v. Town of White Lake, 252 N.C. App. 237, 797 S.E.2d 346, 352–53 (2017); Ghidorzi Constr., Inc. v. Town of Chapel Hill, 80 N.C. App. 438, 440, 342 S.E.2d 545, 547 (1986); Deffet Rentals, Inc. v. City of Burlington, 27 N.C. App. 361, 363–64, 219 S.E.2d 223, 226 (1975). The superior court's review is "limited to errors alleged to have occurred before the local board." Tate Terrace Realty Inv'rs, Inc. v. Currituck Cnty., 127 N.C. App. 212, 218, 488 S.E.2d 845, 848, *review denied*, 347 N.C. 409, 496 S.E.2d 394 (1997).

201. Cary Creek Ltd. P'ship v. Town of Cary, 207 N.C. App. 339, 700 S.E.2d 80 (2010); Cannon v. Zoning Bd. of Adjustment, 65 N.C. App. 44, 47, 308 S.E.2d 735, 737 (1983). "Summarizing" the facts by the trial court cannot, however, resolve disputed facts that were not resolved by the board below. Hampton v. Cumberland Cnty., 256 N.C. App. 656, 808 S.E.2d 763 (2017), *cert. improvidently granted*, 373 N.C. 2, 832 S.E.2d 692 (2019).

The trial judge is authorized to review questions of law and legal inference arising on the record. The broad discretionary powers normally vested in a trial judge are absent.[202]

Judicial review sometimes presents a mixed question of law and fact. For example, interpretation of a term in the ordinance or statute is a question of law, but whether the actions of a landowner or applicant fall within that interpretation is a question of fact.

The basic standard for judicial review of quasi-judicial decisions is set forth in *Coastal Ready-Mix Concrete Co. v. Board of Commissioners* and is codified at G.S. 160D-1402(j). Courts reviewing quasi-judicial decisions examine the following five questions:

1. Were there errors in law?
2. Were proper statutory and ordinance procedures followed, and was the decision within statutorily delegated authority?
3. Were due-process rights secured (including rights to offer evidence, cross-examine witnesses, and inspect documents)?
4. Was competent, material, and substantial evidence in the record to support the decision?[203]
5. Was the decision arbitrary and capricious?[204]

The court, depending on which of these issues is being reviewed, applies one of two standards of review.

A *de novo review* is made when there are alleged errors of law.[205] Whether the record contains competent, material, and substantial evidence is a conclusion of law subject to de novo review.[206] In these reviews, the court is not bound by findings made by the decision-making board. Instead, the court considers the matter anew, as if not considered or decided by the board.[207] This is true both for trial-court review and for appellate-court review.[208]

If a trial court fails to properly make a de novo review, the appellate court can apply a de novo review rather than remand the case. However, this can only be done if the record on appeal is complete enough to provide the requisite information for the review (all of the relevant ordinance provisions, for example).[209] With appellate review of alleged errors of law, since the appellate court is making a de novo review as well, the standard of review used by the trial court is irrelevant.[210]

A *whole-record review* is conducted of allegations that a decision was not supported by the evidence or that the decision was arbitrary and capricious.[211] In these reviews, the board's findings of fact are

---

202. *In re* Pine Hill Cemeteries, Inc., 219 N.C. 735, 738, 15 S.E.2d 1, 3 (1941). *See also* Humble Oil & Refin. Co. v. Bd. of Aldermen, 284 N.C. 458, 202 S.E.2d 129 (1974); Jamison v. Kyles, 271 N.C. 722, 157 S.E.2d 550 (1967); Jarrell v. Bd. of Adjustment, 258 N.C. 476, 128 S.E.2d 879 (1963); Mize v. Cnty. of Mecklenburg, 80 N.C. App. 279, 284, 341 S.E.2d 767, 770 (1986).

203. G.S. 160D-1405(j)(3), as amended by S.L. 2019-111, § 1.9, provides that opinion testimony from lay witnesses is not considered competent evidence on specified issues even if no objection was made to that testimony at the evidentiary hearing.

204. *Coastal Ready-Mix*, 299 N.C. at 626, 265 S.E.2d at 383.

205. G.S. 160D-1402(j)(2).

206. *Id. See also* PHG Asheville, LLC v. City of Asheville, 374 N.C. 133, 150–51, 839 S.E.2d 755, 766–67 (2020); Schooldev East, LLC v. Town of Wake Forest, 284 N.C. App. 434, 876 S.E.2d 607 (2022); Clark v. City of Asheboro, 136 N.C. App. 114, 119, 524 S.E.2d 46, 50 (1999).

207. Amanini v. N.C. Dep't of Human Res., 114 N.C. App. 668, 674, 443 S.E.2d 114, 118 (1994). However, a degree of deference is applied in some circumstances. See the discussion of deference in de novo reviews, below.

208. *In re* Appeal of Willis, 129 N.C. App. 499, 501–02, 500 S.E.2d 723, 726 (1998).

209. Welter v. Rowan Cnty. Bd. of Comm'rs, 160 N.C. App. 358, 585 S.E.2d 472 (2003).

210. Capital Outdoor, Inc. v. Guilford Cnty. Bd. of Adjustment, 355 N.C. 269, 559 S.E.2d 547 (2002), *per curiam, rev'g*, 146 N.C. App. 388, 552 S.E.2d 265 (2001).

211. Powell v. N.C. Dep't of Transp., 347 N.C. 614, 623, 499 S.E.2d 180, 185 (1998); ACT-UP Triangle v. Comm'n for Health Servs., 345 N.C. 699, 706, 483 S.E.2d 388, 392 (1997); Associated Mech. Contractors, Inc. v. Payne, 342 N.C. 825, 832, 467 S.E.2d 398, 401 (1996); Thompson v. Wake Cnty. Bd. of Educ., 292 N.C. 406, 410, 233 S.E.2d 538,

binding on the reviewing court if they are supported by substantial, competent evidence.[212] Similarly, federal courts "must accord a zoning board's fact finding the same preclusive effect to which it [would have been entitled] in the state courts when the agency acted in a judicial capacity and the parties had an adequate opportunity to litigate."[213]

If both types of allegations are made, the trial court must delineate which standard was applied to which issue (and apply more than one standard if the issues so require).[214] In *Myers Park Homeowners Ass'n v. City of Charlotte*, the court noted that although an interpretation of the ordinance is a question of law subject to de novo review, the sufficiency of the evidence before the board to make its interpretation is reviewed under the whole-record test.[215] In *Fort v. County of Cumberland*, the court applied this rule while reviewing an interpretation of the ordinance and noted that, though the court cannot substitute its judgment for that of the decision-making board, the decision must have a rational basis in the evidence.[216] In *Mount Ulla Historical Preservation Society, Inc. v. Rowan County*, the court held that whether res judicata applies to a second quasi-judicial decision involving the same subject matter is a question of law, but whether there was a material change in the application is a factual question subject to a whole-record review.[217]

While fundamental fairness is required, the strict rules of evidence and procedure can be relaxed, and harmless errors will generally not result in a remand on appeal. Several cases illustrate this rule. In *Durham Video & News, Inc. v. Durham Board of Adjustment*,[218] the board of adjustment failed to comply with a city rule requiring that a copy of the planning department's staff report be provided to the petitioner ten days before the hearing. The court of appeals held that this did not prejudice the plaintiff because the staff report included only information that was already a matter of public record or otherwise available to the plaintiff. In *Dockside Discotheque, Inc. v. Board of Adjustment*,[219] the court held that a board's action of conducting an improper closed session to deliberate after all of the evidence had been received was not a reversible error.

---

541 (1977); *In re* Appeal of Willis, 129 N.C. App. 499, 500 S.E.2d 723 (1998); Ballas v. Town of Weaverville, 121 N.C. App. 346, 465 S.E.2d 324 (1996).

212. Capricorn Equity Corp. v. Town of Chapel Hill Bd. of Adjustment, 334 N.C. 132, 431 S.E.2d 183 (1993); *In re* Appeal of Hastings, 252 N.C. 327, 113 S.E.2d 433 (1960); *In re* Pine Hill Cemeteries, Inc., 219 N.C. 735, 15 S.E.2d 1 (1941); Tate Terrace Realty Inv'rs, Inc. v. Currituck Cnty., 127 N.C. App. 212, 218, 488 S.E.2d 845, 849, *review denied*, 347 N.C. 409, 496 S.E.2d 394 (1997). *See also* Meads v. N.C. Dep't of Agric., 349 N.C. 656, 663, 509 S.E.2d 165, 170 (1998).

213. AT&T Wireless PCS, Inc. v. Winston-Salem Zoning Bd. of Adjustment, 172 F.3d 307, 314 (4th Cir. 1999).

214. Mann Media, Inc. v. Randolph Cnty. Planning Bd., 356 N.C. 1, 14, 565 S.E.2d 9, 18 (2002); McMillan v. Town of Tryon, 200 N.C. App. 228, 683 S.E.2d 747 (2009); Friends of Mt. Vernon Springs, Inc. v. Town of Siler City, 190 N.C. App. 633, 660 S.E.2d 657 (2008); Sun Suites Holdings, LLC v. Bd. of Aldermen, 139 N.C. App. 269, 273, 533 S.E.2d 525, 528, *review denied*, 353 N.C. 280, 546 S.E.2d 397 (2000); Vill. Creek Prop. Owners' Ass'n v. Town of Edenton, 135 N.C. App. 482, 520 S.E.2d 793 (1999); *In re* Appeal of Willis, 129 N.C. App. 499, 502, 500 S.E.2d 723, 726 (1998).

215. 229 N.C. App. 204, 747 S.E.2d 338 (2013).

216. 235 N.C. App. 541, 761 S.E.2d 744, review denied, 367 N.C. 798 (2014). The court upheld a determination that a shooting range (which was not listed as a use in the zoning ordinance) was most nearly similar in its impacts to a recreation/amusement use based on the testimony of the planning director as to the similarity of impacts regulated. In *Hampton v. Cumberland County*, 256 N.C. App. 656, 808 S.E.2d 763 (2017), *cert. improvidently granted*, 373 N.C. 2, 832 S.E.2d 692 (2019), another shooting-range case, the court applied this rule and determined that the trial court improperly made its own findings and that the board below had not made sufficient factual findings to apply the statute. The court remanded the case for adoption of sufficient factual findings.

217. 232 N.C. App. 436, 754 S.E.2d 237 (2014).

218. 144 N.C. App. 236, 550 S.E.2d 212, *review denied*, 354 N.C. 361, 556 S.E.2d 299 (2001).

219. 115 N.C. App. 303, 444 S.E.2d 451, *review denied*, 338 N.C. 309, 451 S.E.2d 634 (1994). *See also* Charlotte Yacht Club, Inc. v. Cnty. of Mecklenburg, 64 N.C. App. 477, 307 S.E.2d 595 (1983).

If the subject of a zoning-enforcement action seeks judicial intervention to enjoin enforcement, the appellate court conducts a de novo review of the trial court's order.[220]

Deference in De Novo Reviews

A court is not bound by a board's interpretation of the terms of an ordinance, as these are questions of law subject to a de novo review.[221] G.S. 160D-1402(j)(2), enacted in 2009, provides that the court making a de novo review of a board interpretation "shall consider the interpretation of the decision-making board, but is not bound by that interpretation, and may freely substitute its judgment as appropriate."[222]

Case law provides some guidance as to the degree of consideration given and the circumstances in which it is appropriate for the court to substitute its judgment. As stated in *MacPherson v. City of Ashville*, "Where an issue of statutory construction arises, the construction adopted by those who execute and administer the law in question is relevant and may be considered. Such construction is entitled to 'great consideration.'"[223] The degree of deference accorded is related to the thoroughness with which the issue was considered by the board, the validity of its reasoning, and the consistency with which it has been applied.[224]

A number of cases, many decided before the amendment to G.S. 160D-1402(j) noted above, applied some judicial deference to staff and board interpretations of land-development regulations.[225] In *P.A.W. v. Town of Boone Board of Adjustment*, the court noted that because the board is "vested with reason-

220. LeTendre v. Currituck Cnty., 259 N.C. App. 512, 817 S.E.2d 73 (2018), *review denied*, 372 N.C. 54, 822 S.E.2d 64 (2019). The appellate court presumes a trial court's ruling granting or denying a preliminary injunction to be correct, but it is not bound by the trial court's findings and may review, weigh, and find facts for itself.

221. "Under de novo review a reviewing court considers the case anew and may freely substitute its own interpretation of an ordinance for a board of adjustment's conclusions of law." Morris Commc'ns Corp. v. City of Bessemer City Bd. of Adjustment, 365 N.C. 152, 156, 712 S.E.2d 868, 871 (2011) (reversing interpretation of "work" required to be commenced to avoid expiration of sign permit). Ayers v. Bd. of Adjustment, 113 N.C. App. 528, 439 S.E.2d 199 (1994). *See also* High Rock Lake Partners, LLC v. N.C. Dep't of Trans., 366 N.C. 315, 319, 735 S.E. 2d 300, 303 (2012) (deference accorded agency determination, but only if it is not contrary to express terms and intent of ordinance or statute).

222. This statute was further amended in 2019 to clarify that the question of whether the record contains competent, material, and substantial evidence is a conclusion of law subject to de novo review. S.L. 2019-111, § 1.9.

223. 283 N.C. 299, 307, 196 S.E.2d 200, 206 (1973) (citation omitted) (upholding city's determination that applicant for site-plan approval was an "owner" within the intent of the ordinance). *See also* Hensley v. N.C. Dep't of Env't & Nat. Res., 364 N.C. 285, 698 S.E.2d 41 (2010) (deference to Division of Land Resources, the agency responsible for administering statute, in interpretation of Sedimentation Pollution Control Act); Darbo v. Old Keller Farm Prop. Owners' Ass'n, 174 N.C. App. 591, 621 S.E.2d 281 (2005) (planning board's long-standing interpretation of ordinance entitled to considerable deference); MW Clearing & Grading, Inc. v. N.C. Dep't of Env't & Nat. Res., 171 N.C. App. 170, 614 S.E.2d 568 (2005) (deference accorded Environmental Management Commission's interpretation of controlling statutes), *rev'd in part*, 360 N.C. 392, 628 S.E.2d 379 (2006); Britt v. N.C. Sheriffs' Educ. & Training Standards Comm'n, 348 N.C. 573, 576, 501 S.E.2d 75, 77 (1998).

224. Brooks v. McWhirter Grading Co., 303 N.C. 573, 581, 281 S.E.2d 24, 29 (1981).

225. For a review of case law interpreting various provisions of North Carolina zoning ordinances, see Chapter 18. The courts also apply this rule in de novo reviews of statutory and administrative rule interpretation under the Administrative Procedure Act. *In re* Broad & Gales Creek Cmty. Ass'n, 300 N.C. 267, 275, 266 S.E.2d 645, 651 (1980) (deference accorded expertise of agency administering a law). In *County of Durham v. North Carolina Department of Environment & Natural Resources*, 131 N.C. App. 395, 507 S.E.2d 310 (1998), *review denied*, 350 N.C. 92, 528 S.E.2d 361 (1999), the court upheld the agency's interpretation of the statutes to distinguish inert-debris landfills from sanitary landfills. The court noted the long-standing judicial tradition of deferring to a specialized agency's interpretation of a statute it administers so long as the interpretation is reasonable and is based on a permissible construction of the law. A similar federal rule is set forth in *Chevron U.S.A. v. Natural Resources Defense Council*, 467 U.S. 837 (1984).

able discretion in determining the intended meaning of an ordinance, a court may not substitute its judgment for the board's in the absence of error of law, or arbitrary, oppressive, or manifest abuse of authority."[226] Similar rulings include cases involving board interpretation of the terms "abandon" and "discontinue" as related to nonconformities,[227] interpretation of when renovation constitutes expansion of a nonconforming use,[228] interpretation of what constitutes a group home,[229] interpretation of what uses were included within the term "government offices and buildings,"[230] interpretation of the term "value" as applied to a damaged nonconforming sign,[231] and interpretation of what constituted a private or commercial kennel under the terms of the zoning ordinance.[232]

There are limits to what a court will accept. In *Harry v. Mecklenburg County*, the court noted that although a zoning administrator's interpretation is entitled to some deference, this should not occur if the interpretation is contrary to the express purpose of the ordinance.[233] Similarly, where the terms of an ordinance are clear, it is improper for either the board or the staff to go beyond those terms in interpreting the ordinance.[234] There are also cases where courts accorded no deference at all to board interpretation.[235]

It should be noted that although the court may not give deference to the board's interpretation of the ordinance, the board's findings of fact are binding if supported by the evidence. This can be an important distinction, particularly when mixed questions of fact and law are presented.

---

226. 95 N.C. App. 110, 113, 382 S.E.2d 443, 444–45 (1989).

227. CG & T Corp. v. Bd. of Adjustment, 105 N.C. App. 32, 39, 411 S.E.2d 655, 659 (1992) (upholding interpretation that element of intent not required for discontinuance of nonconformity).

228. APAC-Atl., Inc. v. City of Salisbury, 210 N.C. App. 668, 709 S.E.2d 390 (2011).

229. Taylor Home of Charlotte Inc. v. City of Charlotte, 116 N.C. App. 188, 193, 447 S.E.2d 438, 442, *review denied*, 338 N.C. 524, 453 S.E.2d 170 (1994) (upholding interpretation that some element of rehabilitation was required for qualification as a group home).

230. Rauseo v. New Hanover Cnty., 118 N.C. App. 286, 454 S.E.2d 698 (1995) (upholding interpretation that a volunteer fire station was a government building).

231. Whiteco Outdoor Advert. v. Johnston Cnty. Bd. of Adjustment, 132 N.C. App. 465, 513 S.E.2d 70 (1999) (upholding interpretation that "value" of signs meant their initial value).

232. Tucker v. Mecklenburg Cnty. Zoning Bd. of Adjustment, 148 N.C. App. 52, 557 S.E.2d 631 (2001) (upholding interpretation that without breeding, selling, training, or boarding, a kennel for rescued dogs was not a commercial kennel).

233. 136 N.C. App. 200, 523 S.E.2d 135 (1999). The court found that the administrator's determination that a pier could be a principal use rather than an accessory use if it were the only structure on the lot was contrary to the "only logical construction of the Ordinance." *Id.* at 203, 523 S.E.2d at 138. *See also* Koontz v. Davidson Cnty. Bd. of Adjustment, 130 N.C. App. 479, 503 S.E.2d 108, *review denied*, 349 N.C. 529, 526 S.E.2d 177 (1998) (overturning board of adjustment's determination that vested rights existed); Ball v. Randolph Cnty. Bd. of Adjustment, 129 N.C. App. 300, 498 S.E.2d 833 (1998) (overturning board's determination that remediation of petroleum-contaminated soil was an agricultural use).

234. Procter v. City of Raleigh Bd. of Adjustment, 140 N.C. App. 784, 538 S.E.2d 621 (2000) (if there is no ambiguity in ordinance, it is error for board of adjustment to look beyond the language of the ordinance in making its interpretation); Ayers v. Bd. of Adjustment, 113 N.C. App. 528, 439 S.E.2d 199, *review denied*, 336 N.C. 71, 445 S.E.2d 28 (1994) (apply plain and ordinary meaning of words in interpreting ordinance); Cardwell v. Town of Madison Bd. of Adjustment, 102 N.C. App. 546, 402 S.E.2d 866 (1991) (improper for administrator and board of adjustment to use technical definition of *building* from the building code rather than relying on the zoning code); Riggs v. Zoning Bd. of Adjustment, 101 N.C. App. 422, 399 S.E.2d 149 (1991) (holding zoning administrator and board of adjustment erred in not considering a stormwater system a structure, ruling that the definition of *structure* that should be applied (in the absence of a more precise definition in the ordinance) was the natural and recognized meaning of the term).

235. Hayes v. Fowler, 123 N.C. App. 400, 473 S.E.2d 442 (1996) (interpretation of the ordinance is a question of law subject to de novo review by the trial court wherein the court may freely substitute its judgment for that of the board of adjustment).

Record on Appeal

If there is an allegation that the evidence did not support a board's decision or that the decision was arbitrary and capricious, the court is limited to reviewing the whole record before the decision-making board to determine whether the record supports the board's conclusions. For alleged errors of law, the court undertakes a de novo review.[236]

In either event, the superior court is acting in an appellate-review capacity and does not take additional evidence.[237] The writ of certiorari does not lie to review questions of fact to be determined outside the record.[238]

The statutory timetables for serving and filing the record on appeal are mandatory and have to be met unless extensions of time are granted.[239] Absent service of the case on appeal, only the record proper is reviewed on appeal.[240]

G.S. 160D-1402(h) specifies the content of the record on appeal of quasi-judicial decisions. It provides that the record includes all documents and exhibits submitted to the decision-making board and the minutes of the meetings at which the matter was heard. Any party may request that the record include an audiotape or videotape of the meeting if that is available. Any party may also include a verbatim transcript of the meeting, with the cost of preparation of the transcript being the responsibility of the party choosing to include it. The record must be bound, paginated, and served on all petitioners by the local government within three days of filing it with the court. The court may allow the record to be supplemented with affidavits or testimony regarding standing, alleged impermissible conflicts of interest, and the legal issues of constitutionality or statutory authority for the decision (as these legal issues are beyond the scope of issues that could have been addressed by the original decision-making board). The parties may agree, or the court may direct, that matters unnecessary for judicial review be excluded from the record or that other matters be included.[241]

G.S. 160D-1402(i) requires the trial court to take new evidence in very limited circumstances. These include where the record is not adequate to allow an appropriate determination of standing, alleged conflicts of interest, constitutional violations, or a lack of statutory authority.[242]

---

236. *In re* Appeal of Willis, 129 N.C. App. 499, 500 S.E.2d 723 (1998).

237. Capricorn Equity Corp. v. Town of Chapel Hill, 334 N.C. 132, 431 S.E.2d 183 (1993) (superior court must base review on record presented and may not make additional findings of fact when reviewing board of adjustment's decision); Jamison v. Kyles, 271 N.C. 722, 157 S.E.2d 550 (1967) (where there were sufficient facts on the record to support the board of adjustment's findings, the trial court erred in overruling those findings); *In re* Appeal of Hastings, 252 N.C. 327, 113 S.E.2d 433 (1960) (board of adjustment's findings of fact may not be overturned on judicial review if supported by adequate evidence in the record); Lamar OCI S. Corp. v. Stanly Cnty. Zoning Bd. of Adjustment, 186 N.C. App. 44, 650 S.E.2d 37 (2007), *aff'd per curiam*, 362 N.C. 670, 669 S.E.2d 322 (2008) (trial court properly denied county's motion to supplement the record with affidavits because in quasi-judicial matters, the court may not consider evidence not before the board of adjustment).

238. *In re* Pine Hill Cemeteries, Inc., 219 N.C. 735, 15 S.E.2d 1 (1941).

239. City of Hickory v. Catawba Valley Mach. Co., 38 N.C. App. 387, 248 S.E.2d 71 (1978).

240. Thurston v. Salisbury Zoning Bd. of Adjustment, 24 N.C. App. 288, 210 S.E.2d 275 (1974).

241. In *Fehrenbacher v. City of Durham*, 239 N.C. App. 141, 768 S.E.2d 186 (2015), the court held that this provision also allows a judge to include additional material to be reviewed as part of the record when the court is conducting a de novo review of the interpretation of the ordinance. This material must have been submitted as part of an original application but not introduced as evidence in the board hearing. (In this instance, the court was allowed to include a photo simulation of a stealth cellular tower that was submitted by the applicant to the zoning administrator but not presented to the board of adjustment.)

242. Prior to 2019, the court had discretion as to whether to allow the record to be supplemented. S.L. 2019-111, § 1.9, amended the statute to make this mandatory. The Rules of Civil Procedure regarding discovery are to be followed if the record is supplemented on these issues. G.S. 1A, Rule 59(4), allows motions for a new hearing if newly discovered material evidence is found that the party making the motion could not have discovered with due diligence. Rule

It is also important to include the relevant portions of the development regulation in the record. The court may not take judicial notice of a municipal or county ordinance.[243]

Mootness

If an ordinance is amended while litigation is pending, the case becomes moot, and the appeal is dismissed if the amendment provides the plaintiff the relief sought in the litigation.[244] However, if the amendment does not provide the relief sought by litigation, the claim remains valid and the case is not moot.

For example, in *Lambeth v. Town of Kure Beach*, the town denied a permit to widen a driveway based on a long-standing but unwritten interpretation of its ordinance. While litigation on the denial was pending, the town amended the ordinance to clearly prohibit the proposed activity. The court held that this did not moot the appeal because the applicant was challenging the propriety of the denial, and the language of the ordinance at the time of the denial was the legal issue before the court (rather than the amended language).[245] In *Wilson v. City of Mebane Board of Adjustment*,[246] the court held that subsequent amendment of the development ordinance in a way that may have made a project permittable does not moot a challenge to a permit based on the prior ordinance when the only permits that were issued were based on the prior ordinance.

The fact that a successful petitioner or applicant abandons a project after securing a rezoning or zoning permit does not moot an action brought by a neighboring third party to challenge the rezoning

60(b)(2) allows a judgment to be set aside on the same grounds. However, in *Bailey & Associates, Inc. v. Wilmington Board of Adjustment*, 202 N.C. App. 177, 193, 689 S.E.2d 576, 588 (2010), the court indicated that this motion needs to be made and decided by the board making the decision as otherwise the trial court would have no record on the issue on appeal.

243. High Point Surplus Co. v. Pleasants, 263 N.C. 587, 591, 139 S.E.2d 892, 895–96 (1965); McEwen Funeral Serv. v. Charlotte City Coach Lines, Inc., 248 N.C. 146, 150–51, 102 S.E.2d 816, 820 (1958). These cases were decided long before local ordinances became commonly available online. Still, unless introduced into evidence, there is no certainty that the terms of the ordinance that is readily available on the Internet were in effect at the time of the challenged action, so the applicable ordinance must be introduced into evidence. Thompson v. Union County, 252 N.C. App. 237, 874 S.E.2d 623 (2022).

The court in *Anderson Creek Partners, LP v. Harnett County*, 275 N.C. App. 423, 854 S.E.2d 1 (2020), took judicial notice of interlocal agreements that had been entered into by the county and utility districts. The court held these to be "important public documents" that could be noticed under *State ex rel. Utils. Comm'n v. S. Bell Tel. & Tel. Co.*, 289 N.C. 286, 221 S.E.2d 322 (1976). Also see G.S. 8C-1, Rule 201(b) on judicial notice of adjudicative facts. It allows notice of a fact that is "not subject to reasonable dispute in that it is either (1) generally known within the territorial jurisdiction of the trial court or (2) capable of accurate and ready determination by resort to sources whose accuracy cannot reasonably be questioned."

244. Davis v. Zoning Bd. of Adjustment, 41 N.C. App. 579, 255 S.E.2d 444 (1979). *See generally* State v. McCluney, 280 N.C. 404, 407, 185 S.E.2d 870, 872 (1972); Prop. Rights Advocacy Grp. v. Town of Long Beach, 173 N.C. App. 180, 182–83, 617 S.E.2d 715, 717–18 (2005).

245. 157 N.C. App. 349, 578 S.E.2d 688 (2003). In *Meares v. Town of Beaufort*, 193 N.C. App. 96, 100, 667 S.E.2d 239, 241–42 (2008), the court held that repeal of a contested provision in the town's historic-district guidelines while judicial review was pending did not moot the case because the board of adjustment had ordered a new hearing on the initial application for a certificate of appropriateness, and the applicant was entitled to a decision on the application based on the rules in effect at the time of that initial application. In *Bailey & Associates, Inc. v. Wilmington Board of Adjustment*, 202 N.C. App. 177, 689 S.E.2d 576 (2010), the court noted that the express terms of an ordinance-amendment adoption can also provide that the amendment applies prospectively only.

246. 212 N.C. App. 176, 710 S.E.2d 403 (2011).

or permit issuance.[247] A case brought by the applicant for development permits is not rendered moot because a planned operator of the development abandons the project.[248]

On the other hand, if a permit denial is being appealed and the permit is issued while the matter is still on appeal, that action moots the appeal.[249] Similarly, if a special use permit is issued after remand from a court hearing an appeal and no injunction prevents that issuance, the statute provides that any appeal of the remand order or the subsequently issued permit is moot.[250]

The statute was amended in 2019 to provide that action in the nature of certiorari to challenge a quasi-judicial decision and original civil actions to challenge the constitutionality or statutory authority for an action are not rendered moot if the aggrieved person loses the applicable property as a result of the action being challenged.[251]

---

247. Friends of Mt. Vernon Springs, Inc. v. Town of Siler City, 190 N.C. App. 633, 660 S.E.2d 657 (2008). The court noted that abandonment of the project by the applicant does not provide the relief sought—here invalidation of the rezoning and revocation of the permit. In *Adams v. Village of Wesley Chapel*, 259 F. App'x 545 (4th Cir. 2007), the court held that the plaintiff's sale of the land that was the basis of a constitutional challenge to land use restrictions on the property did not moot the case.

248. Schooldev East, LLC v. Town of Wake Forest, 284 N.C. App. 434, 876 S.E.2d 607 (2022). The plaintiff was denied a major site-plan and major subdivision-plan approval for development of a school site. A separate entity had planned to operate a charter school at the site. The town contended that since that separate entity had withdrawn its application for state approval to operate the school, this permit denial challenge was moot. The court ruled that approval to develop the site is a separate legal question from authority to operate a school on that site, so withdrawal by the potential school operator has no impact on the standing of the proposed developer's suit regarding the development permit decisions.

249. Carolina Marina & Yacht Club, LLC v. New Hanover Cnty. Bd. of Comm'rs, 207 N.C. App. 250, 699 S.E.2d 646 (2010), *review denied*, 365 N.C. 89, 706 S.E.2d 253 (2011). The plaintiff applied for a special use permit to modify an existing commercial marina. The county denied the special use permit, but on appeal the superior court overturned that decision and ordered the permit issued. A neighbor who opposed the project and had intervened in the judicial review appealed that decision to the court of appeals. The county did not join in the appeal. The neighbor unsuccessfully sought a stay of the trial court's order and an injunction to prohibit permit issuance while she pursued the appeal. The county subsequently issued the special use permit. The court held that since the only issue on appeal was the validity of the county's permit denial, subsequent issuance of the permit resolved that matter and made the appeal moot. The same result obtained in *Estates, Inc. v. Town of Chapel Hill*, 130 N.C. App. 664, 504 S.E.2d 296 (1998), *review denied*, 350 N.C. 93, 527 S.E.2d 664 (1999). The denial of a special use permit was appealed, and the trial court subsequently ordered the permit issued. Neighbors who had intervened appealed to the court of appeals, but the town did not join the appeal and issued the permit while the matter was pending before the court of appeals. The court ruled that although the town was not compelled to issue the permit during the period of the automatic stay, it could voluntarily do so unless the intervenors secured an injunction to prohibit it from doing so. Once issued, the intervenors' appeal was moot. For a situation where the court held that judicial review was not made moot by a subsequent permit issuance, see *Councill v. Town of Boone Board of Adjustment*, 146 N.C. App. 103, 551 S.E.2d 907, *review denied*, 354 N.C. 360, 560 S.E.2d 130 (2001). The intervenors had alleged that a settlement of the case was illegal and that the permit was issued pursuant to that consent judgment, so the issue originally raised was still at issue.

250. G.S. 160D-1402(l1). This provision was added by S.L. 2021-168, § 4.

251. G.S. 160D-1402(i), added by S.L. 2019-111, §§ 1.7 and 1.9. This is, however, expressly made subject to limitations in state and federal constitutional law and case law, presumably related to requirements for a case or controversy under Article III of the U.S. Constitution and article 1, section 18 of the North Carolina constitution.

Disposition

If a court invalidates a legislative land use regulatory decision, the challenged action is void *ab initio*.[252] However, even if the legislative action is invalidated, additional remedies on the landowner may not be imposed unless the landowner (as well as the unit of government involved) was a party to the suit.[253]

G.S. 160D-1402(k) addresses the remedies available for consideration by courts in review of quasi-judicial decisions. It provides that a court may affirm or reverse the original decision made by the local government board or may remand it with either instructions or a direction for further proceedings.[254] A remand can be made to correct a procedural record or to make findings of fact based on the existing record. If the court finds the board's decision is not supported by substantial, competent evidence in the record or has an error of law, the remand may include an order to issue the approval (subject to reasonable and appropriate conditions) or to revoke the approval.[255] The relief can also include appropriate injunctive orders.

If there is competent, material, and substantial evidence in the record to support findings that all relevant standards have been met and no competent evidence to the contrary, the trial court may order the permit issued without further hearing on remand (conversely, it can order the permit revoked if it is determined it was wrongfully issued).[256] If a permit contains conditions deemed to be improper, and it is clear that the reissuance of a corrected permit is the only possible result on remand, the court may order the offending conditions struck and a corrected permit reissued with any conditions expressly consented to by the applicant as part of the permit application, during the board hearing, or during

---

252. Keiger v. Winston-Salem Bd. of Adjustment, 281 N.C. 715, 721, 190 S.E.2d 175, 179 (1972).

253. McDowell v. Randolph Cnty., 186 N.C. App. 17, 649 S.E.2d 920 (2007).

254. Under prior case law, the usual course of action if the court determined the record was insufficient to support the findings was a remand of the case for further hearing by the board. *See, e.g.,* Deffet Rentals, Inc. v. City of Burlington, 27 N.C. App. 361, 219 S.E.2d 223 (1975); Long v. Winston-Salem Bd. of Adjustment, 22 N.C. App. 191, 205 S.E.2d 807 (1974) (remanding case for de novo board proceeding to secure competent evidence). The trial court must rely solely on the grounds for action set forth by the board making the quasi-judicial decision; it is error for the court to substitute or supplement the findings or conclusions made in the administrative proceeding. Godfrey v. Zoning Bd. of Adjustment, 317 N.C. 51, 63–64, 344 S.E.2d 272, 279–80 (1986) (quoting Secs. & Exch. Comm'n v. Chenery Corp., 332 U.S. 194, 196 (1947)); Ballenger Paving Co. v. N.C. State Highway Comm'n, 258 N.C. 691, 695, 129 S.E.2d 245, 248 (1963); Guilford Fin. Servs., LLC v. City of Brevard, 356 N.C. 655, 576 S.E.2d 325 (2003), *per curiam, adopting dissent in* 150 N.C. App. 1, 563 S.E.2d 27 (2002).

255. The exact terms of a judicial order overturning a decision is important. In *Appalachian Materials, LLC v. Watauga County*, 283 N.C. App. 117, 872 S.E.2d 591 (2022), the plaintiff appealed a permit denial that was based on several grounds. The court of appeals overturned the denial, ruling that one of the grounds for denial was based on a misinterpretation of the regulation. On remand, the county again denied the permit, citing the other grounds for denial. The court of appeals in this case held that the initial order on appeal reversed the original decision rather than vacating it. It therefore held its mandate on the initial appeal and directed the trial court to order issuance of the permit. Although the county was not required to raise these other issues in the original appeal, by failing to ask for reconsideration of the initial broad mandate or to appeal that to the supreme court, the original broad mandate is the law of the case.

256. G.S. 160A-393(l)(3). *See also* Stealth Props., LLC v. Town of Pinebluff Bd. of Adjustment, 183 N.C. App. 461, 645 S.E.2d 144, *review denied*, 361 N.C. 703, 653 S.E.2d 163 (2007) (where there is insufficient evidence in the record to support a variance denial and there is evidence to support its issuance, proper course is to remand with instructions to issue the variance); Cumulus Broad., LLC v. Hoke Cnty. Bd. of Comm'rs, 180 N.C. App. 424, 638 S.E.2d 12 (2006); Humane Soc'y of Moore Cnty., Inc. v. Town of S. Pines, 161 N.C. App. 625, 589 S.E.2d 162 (2003); Sun Suites Holdings, LLC v. Bd. of Aldermen, 139 N.C. App. 269, 533 S.E.2d 525, *review denied*, 353 N.C. 280, 546 S.E.2d 397 (2000); Clark v. City of Asheboro, 136 N.C. App. 114, 524 S.E.2d (1999); *Estates*, 130 N.C. App. 664, 504 S.E.2d 296.

the judicial review.[257] If the court finds a decision upholding a zoning-enforcement action to be unsupported by substantial, competent, and material evidence, the court is directed to reverse the decision.[258]

Once remanded, appellate judicial review is premature pending resolution of the case on remand.[259]

Since interpretation of the ordinance or statute is a question of law subject to de novo review, in most instances the appropriate judicial disposition of such a matter is an order mandating issuance or denial of the challenged permit. The same is true for an appeal of a ministerial decision that does not involve contested facts.[260]

Default Judgment

Under G.S. 1A, Rule 55(a), if a party fails to make a pleading, the opposing party may seek a default judgment. Once a judgment by default is entered, under Rule 55(d) the court may set it aside for good cause.

The court applied these Rules of Procedure in a long-running dispute regarding vested rights to commercial development on the Currituck Outer Banks. The landowner claimed a common law vested right and violation of various constitutional rights when the county denied that the vested right existed. After the trial court dismissed the claims, the court of appeals upheld dismissal of some claims and remanded for consideration of the remaining claims.[261] The attorneys for the parties immediately began discussions about discovery and settlement. While those discussions were underway, the plaintiffs sought and obtained a default judgment in the amount of $39 million. The plaintiffs contended that the defendants were required to file responsive pleadings within thirty days of the mandate being issued for the appellate court's remand decision. The defendants contended that an answer was not required until the trial court entered an order reinstating the vested rights claim it had originally dismissed, but they filed a response some six days after the thirty-day deadline.[262] The court of appeals held that the proper standard to be applied in consideration of the motion to set aside the default judgment was (1) Was the moving party diligent in pursuit of the matter? (2) Did the nonmoving party suffer harm by virtue of the delay? and (3) Would the moving party suffer a grave injustice by being unable to defend the action? The court applied these tests and found that the trial court abused its discretion by not setting aside the default judgment.[263] Given a colorable argument that a response was not required, the absence of any

---

257. The express provision regarding conditions that may be imposed was added to the statute by S.L. 2019-111, § 1.9. *Overton v. Camden Cnty.*, 155 N.C. App. 100, 109, 574 S.E.2d 150, 156 (2002). The court cited cases from several other jurisdictions with similar holdings. These include *Belvoir Farms Homeowners Ass'n v. North*, 355 Md. 259, 268, 734 A.2d 227, 232–33 (1999), and *Parish of St. Andrew's Protestant Episcopal Church v. Zoning Board of Appeals*, 155 Conn. 350, 354, 232 A.2d 916, 919 (1967).

258. The provision regarding enforcement actions was added to the statute by S.L. 2019-111, § 1.9.

259. *Jennewein v. City Council*, 46 N.C. App. 324, 264 S.E.2d 802 (1980).

260. *Clinard v. City of Winston-Salem*, 173 N.C. 356, 358, 91 S.E. 1039, 1040 (1917). In this case, after the inspector issued a building permit for an addition to a structure, a question arose as to whether the addition encroached on an alley subject to public use. The inspector revoked the permit until that issue could be resolved. It was eventually determined that there were no public rights to this portion of the alley. The court held that the appropriate remedy was mandamus for issuance of the permit but that there was no liability for monetary damages for the city or the inspector.

261. *Swan Beach Corolla, L.L.C. v. Cnty. of Currituck*, 234 N.C. App. 617, 760 S.E.2d 302 (2014).

262. In an initial appeal regarding the default judgment, the court, in an unpublished opinion, dismissed the appeal as interlocutory because it was filed before the default judgment was entered. *Swan Beach Corolla, L.L.C. v. Cnty. of Currituck*, No. COA15-293, 2015 WL 8747777 (N.C. Ct. App. Dec. 15, 2015).

263. *Swan Beach Corolla, L.L.C. v. Cnty. of Currituck*, 255 N.C. App. 837, 805 S.E.2d 743 (2017), *aff'd per curiam*, 371 N.C. 110, 813 S.E.2d 217 (2018). The court noted three factors supporting setting aside the default judgment. First, both parties were diligently pursuing the matters, scheduling meetings regarding settlement during the thirty-day period. Second, there was no showing of harm to the plaintiff occasioned by a six-day delay in filing in the context of litigation that had been underway for two years. Third, given the size of the damage award, the inability to defend against the substance of the vested rights claim worked a grave injustice against the defendant.

dilatory action by the defendant, and the lack of harm occasioned by the modest delay, the failure to set aside the entry of a default judgment for good cause was an abuse of discretion.

Attorney's Fees

Successful litigants may not recover attorney's fees as costs or damages unless that is expressly authorized by statute.[264]

Among the statutes allowing for recovery of attorney's fees are G.S. 6-19.1, if the court finds that a state agency has acted without substantial justification;[265] G.S. 6-21.5, if the court finds that the losing party raised no justiciable issue of either law or fact;[266] G.S. 6-21.7, if a city or county has acted outside the scope of its legal authority (and awarding attorney's fees is required if the court finds that the action was also an abuse of discretion);[267] G.S. 19-8, for nuisance-abatement actions; G.S. 41A-7, for enforcement actions under the state Fair Housing Act; G.S. 106-701(f), if frivolous or malicious claims are

---

264. Stillwell Enters., Inc. v. Interstate Equip. Co., 300 N.C. 286, 289, 266 S.E.2d 812, 814 (1980). *See also* Buckhannon Bd. & Care Home, Inc. v. W. Va. Dep't of Health & Human Res., 532 U.S. 598, 602 (2001); Cnty. of Hoke v. Byrd, 107 N.C. App. 658, 668, 421 S.E.2d 800, 806 (1992) (county not entitled to attorney's fees in an action to enforce junkyard-screening ordinance). In *Swaps, LLC v. ASL Properties, Inc.*, 250 N.C. App. 264, 791 S.E.2d 711 (2016), a dispute between adjoining landowners regarding use of an easement, the court held that attorney's fees were not costs that could be awarded under the Uniform Declaratory Judgment Act.

265. The award is at the discretion of the trial court. High Rock Lake Partners, LLC v. N.C. Dep't of Transp., 234 N.C. App. 336, 760 S.E.2d 750 (2014). In *Batson v. Coastal Resources Commission*, 282 N.C. App. 1, 871 S.E.2d 120 (2022), the court remanded the case to determine if the defendant knowingly applied an incorrect standard for review of a third-party appeal request. If so, the action would be without substantial justification and attorney's fees could be awarded.

G.S. 6-19.1 is only applicable when successfully challenging a state-agency decision. It does not apply to challenges of local government decisions. Izydore v. City of Durham, 228 N.C. App. 397, 746 S.E.2d 324, *review denied*, 367 N.C. 261, 749 S.E.2d 851 (2013). The court held that because G.S. 6-21.7 specifically addresses attorney's fees when cities and counties act outside the scope of their authority, this supports an interpretation that G.S. 6-19.1 is applicable only to state agencies.

266. In *Morgan v. Nash County*, 224 N.C. App. 60, 735 S.E.2d 615 (2012), *review denied*, 336 N.C. 561, 738 S.E.2d 379 (2013), the court vacated an award of attorney's fees and expenses under this provision. While the appeal of the trial court's judgment was pending, the plaintiffs challenging a rezoning filed a Rule 60(b) motion for relief from the judgment based on newly discovered evidence. The trial court denied that motion and awarded the defendant attorney's fees and expenses incurred in responding to the plaintiff's motion. On appeal, that award was vacated because the court found that the subject matter of the issues raised in the motion for relief were the same as those pending in the appeal, so the trial court had no jurisdiction after the notice of appeal.

267. This statute was amended in 2019 to require awarding of attorney's fees if the local government violates a law setting "unambiguous limits" on its authority or if the local government takes action inconsistent with the permit-choice rule. In this context, the statute defines "unambiguous" to mean "the limits of authority are not reasonably susceptible to multiple constructions." S.L. 2019-111, § 1.11.

In *Etheridge v. County of Currituck*, 235 N.C. App. 469, 481, 762 S.E.2d 289, 298 (2014), the court held that because the purported adoption of an illegal spot zoning was outside of the county's statutory authority, it would only constitute an abuse of discretion if the action taken could not have been the result of a reasoned decision. Attorney's fees are at the discretion of the court if the action is outside the scope of authority but not so egregious as to constitute an abuse of discretion. In *Phillips v. Orange County Health Dep't*, 237 N.C. App. 249, 765 S.E.2d 811 (2014), the court upheld an award of attorney's fees where the county attempted to require local inspection of spray-irrigation wastewater systems permitted by the state. In *Tommy Davis Construction, Inc. v. Cape Fear Public Utility Authority*, 807 F.3d 62 (4th Cir. 2015), the court upheld an award of attorney's fees as within the discretion of the trial court where unauthorized impact fees were imposed. In *Town of Midland v. Harrell*, 282 N.C. App. 354, 871 S.E.2d 392 (2022), the court upheld an award of attorney's fees for an action to recover civil penalties imposed during the pendency of an appeal. In *TAC Stafford, LLC v. Town of Mooresville*, 282 N.C. App. 686, 872 S.E.2d 95 (2022), the court held that attorney's fees must be paid by the town because the challenged fees that were paid for off-site transportation improvements exceeded unambiguous limits on its statutory authority.

made by a losing party in an agricultural-nuisance case; G.S. 106-804, for enforcement of the Swine Farm Siting Act; G.S. 132-9, for securing disclosure of unlawfully withheld public records or for making a bad-faith or frivolous claim regarding public records;[268] and G.S. 143-318.16B, for enforcement of the open-meetings law.[269] As there is no statutory authority for such, attorney's fees are generally not available in land use litigation.

G.S. 1A, Rule 65(e) does allow an award of damages upon dissolving a temporary restraining order or preliminary injunction. The court in *Schwarz Properties, LLC v. Town of Franklinville* noted that a showing of malice or want of probable cause for the preliminary-injunctive relief is not a prerequisite to the award of costs in this context.[270]

When a plaintiff brings a successful action under Section 1983 of U.S. Code Title 42 regarding a violation of constitutional rights, Section 1988 under the same title allows the prevailing plaintiff to recover attorney's fees.[271] If, however, the plaintiff in such an action prevails on statutory grounds and the constitutional issues are not addressed, no attorney's fees are available.[272] If some of the claims made are successful and others fail, attorney's fees are only awarded for the time devoted to the successful claims.[273]

---

268. In *Quality Built Homes, Inc. v. Village of Pinehurst*, No. 1:06CV1028, 2008 WL 3503149 (M.D.N.C. Aug. 11, 2008), the village was awarded attorney's fees for defending a frivolous public-records claim. The plaintiffs requested certified copies of the zoning amendments and council minutes on the last working day before the Christmas holiday. The records were made available on the first working day after the Christmas holiday (the plaintiffs contended they were not available until the day after the New Year's holiday). The court held that there is no legal right to immediate production and the records were clearly provided in a reasonable time period.

269. For an example of a case awarding attorney's fees under such a statutory authorization, see *Table Rock Chapter of Trout Unlimited v. Environmental Management Commission*, 191 N.C. App. 362, 663 S.E.2d 333 (2008) (allowing attorney's fees pursuant to G.S. 6-19.1 when state agency's decision not to reclassify waters was successfully challenged as being without substantial justification and there were no special circumstances that would make the award unjust). In *Williams v. North Carolina Department of Environment & Natural Resources*, 166 N.C. App. 86, 601 S.E.2d 231 (2004), the court held that it is improper to award attorney's fees where a regulatory decision is ultimately overturned by the court but there was conflicting evidence and a difficult factual determination at issue (in this case, determining whether the property included coastal wetlands). The court noted that when a reasonable person could have agreed with the agency, their decision could not be characterized as "without substantial justification."

270. 204 N.C. App. 344, 693 S.E.2d 271 (2010). The plaintiff had sued to invalidate an age restriction in a mobile-home regulation and had secured a temporary restraining order precluding denial of permits for location of manufactured homes during the litigation. Following a hearing, the trial court dissolved the order, allowed the town to revoke permits issued while it was in effect, dismissed the plaintiff's claims, and awarded damages to the town for the costs of defending the matter. The court of appeals upheld the award of costs (equal to the town's liability-insurance deductible).

271. *See, e.g.*, Amward Homes, Inc. v. Town of Cary, 206 N.C. App. 38, 698 S.E.2d 404 (2010), *aff'd by equally divided court*, 365 N.C. 305, 716 S.E.2d 849 (2011). The plaintiffs successfully contended that the collection of school impact fees that were not statutorily authorized violated substantive due process, thus entitling recovery of attorney's fees and costs ($368,000 in this case) in addition to a refund of the fees collected. *See also Phillips*, 237 N.C. App. 249, 765 S.E.2d 811 (awarding attorney's fees when plaintiff successfully challenged county authority to inspect and charge inspection fees for spray-irrigation wastewater-treatment system when county authority preempted by state).

272. In *Giovanni Carandola, Ltd. v. City of Greensboro*, No. 1:05CV1166, 2007 WL 703333 (M.D.N.C. Mar. 1, 2007), *aff'd per curiam*, 258 F. App'x 512 (4th Cir. 2007), the plaintiffs challenged the city's adult-entertainment regulations. The plaintiffs' challenge of the ordinance consisted of two constitutional claims and a third claim contending that the city's interpretation of the ordinance was incorrect as a matter of law. The court granted summary judgment for the plaintiffs on the statutory-interpretation claim (finding that they were grandfathered by the terms of the ordinance). The court held that since the plaintiffs had not prevailed on the two constitutional claims, however, attorney's-fee awards were not permissible.

273. See, for example, *Cities4Life, Inc. v. City of Charlotte*, No. 3:17-CV-00670-KDB-DSC, 2021 WL 724609 (4th Cir. Feb. 24, 2021), where those picketing an abortion clinic settled a suit that alleged violations of their constitutional rights through enforcement of zoning restrictions, sign regulations, and picketing rules. The zoning claim was dismissed, and the sign claim resolved, so the settlement addressed the terms of enforcement of the picketing restrictions. Only attorney's fees related to the picketing settlement were warranted.

APPENDIX A

Land Use Litigation in North Carolina: Case Digests

This appendix contains digests of North Carolina cases on land use. The cases are presented chronologically, as reported, with those heard by the supreme court coming first, those by the court of appeals second, and selected federal court cases arising in North Carolina third. Cases decided through April 2023 are included. Each digest is accompanied by one or more descriptors that identify the main subjects of the litigation. A list of cases by subject follows the three groups of case digests.

Supreme Court

Attorney General v. Blount, 11 N.C. 384 (1826)
Injunctions; Nuisances

Residents of Tarboro sought an injunction to prohibit construction of a mill. A pond on the site of a former mill was alleged to have been noxious and unhealthy for the town's residents. The court ruled that an injunction to prevent the use was appropriate before construction because there was an adequate showing that public harm would follow.

Attorney General *ex rel.* City of Raleigh v. Hunter, 16 N.C. 12 (1826)
Injunctions; Nuisances

This case involved a request for an injunction against an existing millpond in Raleigh. The court ruled that an injunction was proper, noting that the millpond was a nuisance in the seat of government, where its officers were compelled to reside. The court reasoned that individual private-property rights have to yield to the rights and welfare of the public.

Attorney General *ex rel.* Eason v. Perkins, 17 N.C. 38 (1831)
Injunctions

This case was brought by an adjacent landowner to prohibit reconstruction of a millpond in Pitt County. The court ruled that injunctive relief was not appropriate (although damages would be) because there was a showing of harm to one landowner only, not to the general public, and there was a showing of public need and benefit from the mill.

State v. Mathews, 19 N.C. 424 (1837)
Nuisances

The owner of a house in a rural area twice invited persons attending nearby horse races to his home. He sold liquor and food to these persons, who engaged in card playing, drinking, and several fights. The court held that the occasional provision of lodging and food did not make the owner an innkeeper, so he could not be charged with allowing gambling in a public house, and gaming in a private house was not illegal.

Attorney General *ex rel.* Bradsher v. Lea's Heirs, 38 N.C. 301 (1844)
Injunctions; Nuisances

In an action to enjoin construction of a millpond, the court ruled that an injunction would not issue unless there was harm to the general public or considerable disparity between the private harm and the public convenience.

Dargan v. Waddill, 31 N.C. 244 (1848)
Nuisances

An adjacent landowner brought suit for damages caused by the erection, three feet from his property line, of a fifty-horse stable with wooden floors that served an adjacent hotel. The properties were located on the courthouse square in Wadesboro. The court ruled that although a stable was not a nuisance per se and was a necessary accessory use for the hotel, it had to be designed and operated so as not to cause "unnecessary damage" to neighbors. In this case, the noise from the wooden floors was sufficient to warrant damages.

Simpson v. Justice, 43 N.C. 115 (1851)
Injunctions; Nuisances

This action was brought by a resident of New Bern to enjoin the construction of a distillery across the street from his residence. The court ruled that an injunction should not issue until more certain damages were proven.

Wilder v. Strickland, 55 N.C. 386 (1856)
Injunctions; Nuisances

In an action to enjoin construction of a millpond on the Tar River in Nash County, the court ruled that injunctions were not warranted when the potential injury was "slight or doubtful" and that if actual injury to health or property eventually resulted after construction, the remedy of damages would be available.

Ellison v. Commissioners of Washington, 58 N.C. 57 (1859)
Cemeteries; Injunctions; Nuisances

This case was an action to enjoin the city of Washington from using land adjacent to the plaintiff's residence as a cemetery. The court ruled that when a nuisance is dubious or contingent, injunctions are not appropriate but damages at law might be. In this instance, cemeteries were judged to be of great public benefit and not a nuisance when properly carried out. Also, because the plaintiff had acquired the residence after the city had purchased the adjoining property and with knowledge of its intended use, the equities were balanced against an injunction.

Hyatt v. Myers, 71 N.C. 271 (1874)
Injunctions; Nuisances

In this case to enjoin operation of a cotton mill in Washington, the court ruled that when a jury had concluded that a mill was a nuisance to neighbors, it was appropriate to order the nuisance abated (in this case, to order a higher smokestack).

Hyatt v. Myers, 73 N.C. 232 (1875)
Injunctions; Nuisances

This case involved a continuing effort to enjoin operation of a cotton and grist mill on the waterfront in Washington. The court ruled that those living in an urban area by that choice had to accept the inconveniences of noise, smoke, dust, flies, and rats; they could not legally complain of their neighbors' land uses as long as those uses were carried out for reasonable purposes and were undertaken with prudent precautions to avoid annoying neighbors.

Privett v. Whitaker, 73 N.C. 554 (1875)

Nonconformities; Takings; Vested rights

The town of Goldsboro passed an ordinance prohibiting wooden buildings in certain areas. The day before adoption, the plaintiff had begun construction of such a building. The court held that it was within the town's authority to declare such buildings a nuisance and prevent their construction. The mayor was not liable for damages in halting construction of a nonconforming building or in removing one. Also, no compensation was due from the town if the building was or had become a nuisance, but damages might be appropriate if it was a nuisance by ordinance only.

Dorsey v. Allen, 85 N.C. 358 (1881)

Nuisances

In this action to enjoin completion of a planing mill and cotton gin, the court ruled that a possibility of future damage is insufficient to warrant injunctive relief, especially when the public benefits of the use were likely to outweigh the private inconvenience.

State v. Black, 94 N.C. 810 (1886)

Nuisances

The defendant rented a two-room, second-floor apartment in Charlotte. In addition to sleeping there, the defendant frequently ran poker games in the apartment (with the defendant serving as a banker, selling and cashing poker chips). The court upheld a conviction of running an illegal common gaming house, which is a public nuisance. The fact that the rooms were also used as a residence was irrelevant.

State v. Tenant, 110 N.C. 609, 14 S.E. 387 (1892)

Uniformity of standards; Vested rights

An Asheville ordinance that prohibited all buildings unless a permit was first secured from the city council (with no standards as to types of uses or building materials set forth in the ordinance) was held to be invalid because it failed to furnish a uniform rule of action and left matters to the arbitrary will of the aldermen. An implementing ordinance was also held invalid as applied to a building whose construction had already commenced.

State v. Johnson, 114 N.C. 846, 19 S.E. 599 (1894)

Nonconformities; Use restrictions; Vested rights

A Winston ordinance establishing "fire limits" and prohibiting the erection of wooden buildings within those limits was upheld, even though it might cause suspension of previously contracted work.

State v. Hord, 122 N.C. 1092, 29 S.E. 952 (1898)

Nuisances; Use restrictions

The town of King's Mountain adopted an ordinance prohibiting the keeping of hog pens within one hundred yards of another person's dwelling, storehouse, or well. The court upheld the ordinance, ruling it permissible to have a separation requirement that did not apply to the owner's dwelling, storehouse, or well. The court reasoned that the owner could protect his or her own residence and the ordinance could properly focus on preventing harmful impacts on neighbors.

Duffy v. E.H. & J.A. Meadows Co., 131 N.C. 31, 42 S.E. 460 (1902)

Nuisances

A guano factory near New Bern was ruled not to be a nuisance per se, even though the odors emitted could be smelled at a great distance and were unpleasant and objectionable. The court noted, however, that a similar use in a thickly populated area might be deemed a nuisance.

Redd v. Edna Cotton Mills, 136 N.C. 342, 48 S.E. 761 (1904)

Nuisances

In this case, the court ruled that the early morning blowing of a factory whistle was not a nuisance per se but might subsequently be established as a nuisance by evidence that would convince a jury that the plaintiff's health and home had been impaired.

City of Durham v. Eno Cotton Mills, 141 N.C. 615, 54 S.E. 453 (1906)

Takings; Use restrictions

The city of Durham brought this action to halt the discharge of pollutants into the Eno River seventeen miles above the city's water-supply intake. In upholding a statute prohibiting discharges into water-supply streams, the court discussed the police power at length, noting that reasonable regulations to protect the public health, safety, and morals (including restrictions on land use and building) did not amount to a taking.

Hickory v. Southern Railroad, 143 N.C. 451, 55 S.E. 840 (1906)

Nuisances; Remedies

In this case, to enjoin the expansion of a rail-freight yard that a jury had found to be a public nuisance, the court ruled that an order requiring the erection of crossing gates, rather than an order enjoining the use completely, was appropriate.

Small v. Councilmen of Edenton, 146 N.C. 527, 60 S.E. 413 (1908)

Nonconformities; Purposes; Use restrictions

An Edenton ordinance forbidding the construction of awnings that overhung sidewalks and compelling the removal of nonconforming awnings was upheld. Fire safety, aesthetics, and similar factors were held to be within the legitimate purposes for which the council's legislative discretion might be exercised.

Cherry v. Williams, 147 N.C. 452, 61 S.E. 267 (1908)

Injunctions; Nuisances

A neighbor brought this action to enjoin the use of adjoining property in a thickly settled portion of Greensboro as a hospital to treat tuberculosis. The court ruled that injunctive relief against such a use was appropriate pending a full trial on the issue. The court did note that the defendant might take the risk of proceeding with construction because the injunction was against the use rather than against the building.

State v. Whitlock, 149 N.C. 542, 63 S.E. 123 (1908)

Aesthetics; Setbacks; Signs

This case involved an Asheville ordinance requiring billboards to be secure and to meet a minimum setback from the sidewalk. The court ruled the setback requirement to be invalid as beyond the police power because it was based on aesthetic concerns rather than on public-safety considerations. [Note: *State v. Jones*, 305 N.C. 520, 290 S.E.2d 675 (1982), overruled this decision.]

Barger v. Barringer, 151 N.C. 433, 66 S.E. 439 (1909)

Nuisances

A property owner constructed a "very rude, unsightly board fence" that was eight feet, six inches high on the property line, four feet away from the neighbor's windows. The fence cut off the neighbor's view, air, and light. The fence was constructed after the neighbor complained of the filthy condition of the owner's stables. The court found that the malice of the owner was a substantial factor in the judgment, as the fence substantially harmed the neighbor with no corresponding benefit to the owner. The court held this to be a private nuisance.

Berger v. Smith, 156 N.C. 323, 72 S.E. 376 (1911)
Motives; Nuisances; Use restrictions

The town of Pikeville passed an ordinance prohibiting the erection or operation of sawmills in a certain part of town. The defendant had a mill under construction in that area; he alleged that a similar mill was in operation in the center of town and that its owner had secured adoption of this ordinance to prevent competition. The court held that the mill was not a nuisance per se. It also ruled that although the motives of the governing board are generally not to be considered, the presence of another unregulated mill could be a factor in determining whether the ordinance was arbitrary. Finally, the court concluded that the disputed facts should be submitted to a jury.

State v. Staples, 157 N.C. 637, 73 S.E. 112 (1911)
Signs

The court upheld an Asheville ordinance requiring all billboards to be located at least twenty-four inches off the ground, finding that it was a reasonable exercise of the police power to prevent fires and unsanitary accumulation of debris.

State v. Rice, 158 N.C. 635, 74 S.E. 582 (1912)
Extraterritorial jurisdiction; Use restrictions

A Greensboro ordinance uniformly prohibiting the keeping of hogs within one-fourth of a mile from the city limits was held to be valid as within the police power, for sanitary purposes.

Berger v. Smith, 160 N.C. 205, 75 S.E. 1098 (1912)
Nuisances

A neighbor brought this action to prevent construction of a sawmill. The court ruled that when a land use is not a nuisance per se, and a sawmill is not, injunctive relief before its construction is not appropriate, especially when the public benefits of the use outweigh its harm to a private party. If the use is operated in a way to injure neighbors, action might be brought at that time. An ordinance may not by its adoption make a use a nuisance that in fact was not a nuisance.

State v. Lawing, 164 N.C. 492, 80 S.E. 69 (1913)
Amortization; Nonconformities

A Lincolnton ordinance prohibiting the construction or repair of wooden buildings was upheld. The ordinance prohibited the repair of metal roofs on existing wooden buildings. Prohibiting the improvement of roofs was allowed as a way of gradually phasing out a nonconformity.

State v. Shannonhouse, 166 N.C. 241, 80 S.E. 881 (1914)
Amortization; Nonconformities

A Hertford ordinance requiring a permit before any construction of, addition to, or repair of wooden buildings within a designated fire district was upheld. The ordinance included a prohibition on repair when more than one-third of a structure was damaged.

State v. Darnell, 166 N.C. 300, 81 S.E. 338 (1914)
Interpretation; Purposes; Use restrictions

A Winston ordinance prohibiting a person of one race from residing on a block where the houses were occupied by a majority of persons of another race was held to be invalid as beyond the police power delegated to municipalities. The court ruled that authority of such broad scope, lacking precedent in the state and affecting such a basic right as selling or leasing one's property, cannot be inferred to be granted by the words conferring authority to enact ordinances for the general welfare.

Jones v. Lassiter, 169 N.C. 750, 86 S.E. 710 (1915)
Injunctions; Nuisances

This case was brought to enjoin operation of an asphalt-mixing plant near a residence in Raleigh. The court ruled that important public works and improvements should generally not be halted by injunctions. Further, it held that any damages to the plaintiff's property should be addressed through monetary compensation.

State v. Wilkes, 170 N.C. 735, 87 S.E. 48 (1915)
Nuisances

The court held that a jury may find a stable located four feet from a dwelling to be a nuisance where the odor is such that the neighbors are occasionally prevented from eating their meals.

State v. Bass, 171 N.C. 780, 87 S.E. 972 (1916)
Uniformity of standards; Use restrictions

A Nashville ordinance prohibiting the construction of stables closer to neighbors than to owners was held to be invalid because it was not uniform in application and did not protect the public health. It gave an owner the power to annoy neighbors at will if he or she was willing to endure the same annoyance.

Clinard v. City of Winston-Salem, 173 N.C. 356, 91 S.E. 1039 (1917)
Liability

The city denied a building permit for an addition to a building because there was a pending dispute as to the width of an adjacent alley. It was subsequently determined that the alley had not been widened and the permit was improperly denied. However, the court held that the power to grant or deny building permits was a governmental function and that the city had no liability in an action for damages in the absence of proof that the application was corruptly or oppressively refused.

Lawrence v. Nissen, 173 N.C. 359, 91 S.E. 1036 (1917)
Use restrictions

A Winston-Salem ordinance prohibiting for-profit hospitals from locating within 100 feet of a residence was upheld as a valid exercise of the police power to prevent, or to reduce the possibility of the spread of, infectious diseases.

Hanes v. Carolina Cadillac Co., 176 N.C. 350, 97 S.E. 162 (1918)
Use restrictions

In this action by a neighbor for an injunction to prevent establishment of a gasoline storage area, it was held that automobile garages and filling stations were a public convenience and were not a nuisance per se even in residential neighborhoods.

Gulf Refining Co. v. McKernan, 179 N.C. 314, 102 S.E. 505 (1920)
Use restrictions

A Sanford ordinance prohibiting aboveground storage of gasoline for sale within 1000 feet of any dwelling was upheld as a valid police-power regulation.

Brunswick-Balke-Collender Co. v. Mecklenburg County, 181 N.C. 386, 107 S.E. 317 (1921)
Use restrictions

In this license-fee case, the court held that regulating billiard halls was within the police power in order to prevent disorder and demoralization. An ordinance requiring a public hearing (with notice) and sound discretion in approving a location was held to be warranted, as was a distinction in standards between urban and rural areas.

State v. Vanhook, 182 N.C. 831, 109 S.E. 65 (1921)
Use restrictions

A Durham ordinance that prohibited the maintenance of a dance hall without the consent of the town council was upheld as a valid police power regulation.

Turner v. City of New Bern, 187 N.C. 541, 122 S.E. 469 (1924)
Aesthetics; Use restrictions

An ordinance forbidding erection of lumberyards, loading docks, and wharves within a long-established residential area along the Neuse River was held to be within the town's police powers and valid unless there was a showing that this discretionary power had been abused. Aesthetics was found to be a valid ground for regulation when considered along with public health and safety (though not as an exclusive factor, absent compensation).

Bizzell v. Board of Aldermen (*Bizzell I*), 192 N.C. 348, 135 S.E. 50 (1926)
Use restrictions

A Goldsboro ordinance forbidding construction of a filling station without the approval of the town council was held to be invalid. Subjecting a legitimate business (as opposed to a poolroom or a dance hall) to the arbitrary judgment of the council was deemed unlawful.

Bizzell v. Board of Aldermen (*Bizzell II*), 192 N.C. 364, 135 S.E. 58 (1926)
Adoption

To be valid, a zoning ordinance must follow all required procedures for adoption. In this case, no notice had been given nor public hearings held (the planning commission was at work on an initial plan and ordinance), so the ordinance was invalidated.

Harden v. City of Raleigh, 192 N.C. 395, 135 S.E. 151 (1926)
Board of adjustment; Judicial review; Quasi-judicial

Raleigh's denial of a permit for a filling station in a neighborhood-business district was upheld. The court ruled that the board of adjustment might determine what uses were noxious or offensive and that such a decision was a quasi-judicial one, not to be overturned by the court unless it was shown to be arbitrary, oppressive, or manifestly abusive.

Angelo v. City of Winston-Salem, 193 N.C. 207, 136 S.E. 489, *aff'd*, 274 U.S. 725 (1927)
Takings; Nonconformities

Winston-Salem adopted an ordinance that prohibited the sale of fresh meat or seafood at any location in the central portion of town other than a city-owned market. The court upheld the ordinance as within the police power to protect public health and enforce sanitary regulations. Persons with preexisting business interests were adequately protected in that they could either rent space in the public market or relocate to an area outside the central business district.

Town of Clinton v. Standard Oil Co., 193 N.C. 432, 137 S.E. 183 (1927)
Uniformity of standards; Use restrictions

An ordinance prohibiting new filling stations within Clinton's fire district while allowing six existing stations to remain was held to be invalid.

Anderson v. City of Asheville, 194 N.C. 117, 138 S.E. 715 (1927)
Taxes

The court held that a city may not establish differential property-tax rates for different zones of the city.

Little v. Board of Adjustment, 195 N.C. 793, 143 S.E. 827 (1928)
Board of adjustment; Quasi-judicial; Reapplication

The court found that the board of adjustment had improperly reopened and reheard a case presented upon the identical facts of a previously decided matter. The court reasoned that because the board of adjustment was a quasi-judicial body, the doctrine of res judicata applied to it.

MacRae v. City of Fayetteville, 198 N.C. 51, 150 S.E. 810 (1929)
Uniformity of standards; Use restrictions

A Fayetteville ordinance prohibiting the erection of new filling stations within 250 feet of a residence, but not applying to existing stations, was held to be invalid as nonuniform in application and confiscatory of property.

State v. Roberson, 198 N.C. 70, 150 S.E. 674 (1929)
Appeals; Exhaustion

The court dismissed a challenge to Durham's zoning ordinance. It ruled that the applicant had to follow procedures for appeal of permit denial to the board of adjustment and seek subsequent judicial appeal; the applicant could not simply go forward with building and then challenge the denial.

Burden v. Town of Ahoskie, 198 N.C. 92, 150 S.E. 808 (1929)
Uniformity of standards; Use restrictions

An Ahoskie ordinance prohibiting gas stations (and several other uses) within 300 feet of a public school, but allowing an existing station to remain, was invalidated as nonuniform in application. The fact that an ordinance had subsequently been adopted to bar the existing stations at a future date did not influence the disposition of this case, for the plaintiff was entitled to a judgment based on then-current facts and ordinances.

Elizabeth City v. Aydlett, 198 N.C. 585, 152 S.E. 681 (1930)
Enforcement; Injunctions

An action was initiated to enforce the provisions of an ordinance restricting the location of filling stations. The ordinance had been adopted under the city's general ordinance-making powers (rather than under a zoning-enabling statute). The court held that no injunctive relief was warranted.

Town of Wake Forest v. Medlin, 199 N.C. 83, 154 S.E. 29 (1930)
Use restrictions

A Wake Forest ordinance restricted gas stations to the nonresidential, business side of town. The court upheld the ordinance because it operated in like fashion on all within the affected area. Declaration of the stations as a nuisance in fact was permissible as long as the council acted reasonably (not arbitrarily or with unjust discrimination), and nonconforming uses might be required to move.

State v. Moye, 200 N.C. 11, 156 S.E. 130 (1930), *appeal dismissed*, 283 U.S. 810 (1931)
Use restrictions

This case involved the prohibition by the town of Ahoskie of any filling station within 150 feet of the town's school. The ordinance was upheld because no discrimination was shown.

Elizabeth City v. Aydlett, 200 N.C. 58, 156 S.E. 163 (1930)
Enforcement

The court ruled that under the zoning-enabling act, any appropriate action to restrain, abate, or prevent illegal building was authorized. Therefore, a suit for an injunction to prohibit the completion of construction or the operation of an illegal structure was permissible.

Elizabeth City v. Aydlett, 200 N.C. 796, 156 S.E. 163 (1930)
Enforcement

Temporary restraining orders were ruled to be an appropriate remedy under the zoning-enabling act.

City of Goldsboro v. W.P. Rose Builders' Supply Co., 200 N.C. 405, 157 S.E. 58 (1931)
Appellate procedures

The court ruled that when an injunction had been continued on other grounds, a city could not appeal a holding that a zoning ordinance was void until a final review of the entire case had been undertaken.

Elizabeth City v. Aydlett, 201 N.C. 602, 161 S.E. 78 (1931)
Nonconformities; Purposes; Uniformity of standards

This is the basic case upholding zoning as a legitimate exercise of the police power in North Carolina. The court held that a properly adopted zoning ordinance is a permissible exercise of the police power. The ordinance can completely prohibit uses in certain districts, even though a special-purpose ordinance cannot, and such prohibitions are not considered takings. Allowing prior nonconforming uses to continue is not unlawful discrimination.

Holton v. Northwestern Oil Co., 201 N.C. 744, 161 S.E. 391 (1931)
Nuisances

This case was an action by neighbors to seek damages and to abate the alleged nuisance of an adjacent gas station. The court ruled that a gas station is not a nuisance per se, that occasional gasoline odors are a de minimis injury, and that the rowdiness of station occupants and customers could be remedied by calling the police. Therefore, no damages or injunctive relief was awarded.

In re W.P. Rose Builders' Supply Co., 202 N.C. 496, 163 S.E.2d 462 (1932)
Nonconformities

This case involved the operation of a filling station in a converted Goldsboro bus station. The zoning ordinance by its terms did not apply to uses that existed or had been permitted, provided that construction began within ninety days of the ordinance's effective date. The court held that placement of a grease dispenser and merchandise on the premises three days before the expiration of the period constituted commencement of the use. It also held that the factual dispute over whether work on the installation of gas pumps had started was for the jury to decide.

State v. Everhardt, 203 N.C. 610, 166 S.E. 738 (1932)
Nuisances

Defendant operated a dance hall, in a rural area just outside of Landis, where large numbers gathered to dance, drink, and generally act in a boisterous fashion, to the detriment of surrounding homes and the passing public. The court upheld her conviction for maintaining a common nuisance.

King v. Ward, 207 N.C. 782, 178 S.E. 577 (1935)
Nuisances

In this case, a cotton gin opposite the plaintiff's property was found to be a nuisance and damages were awarded. The court held that although the business itself might be a lawful use of the property, if it was operated in a negligent and unreasonable fashion, it might be declared a nuisance.

In re Broughton Estate, 210 N.C. 62, 185 S.E. 434 (1936)
Reapplication

Three years after an initial permit denial, Raleigh's board of adjustment approved a permit for a filling station. The court held that the prior denial was not res judicata on the grounds that the board had found traffic conditions at the site had materially changed.

Appeal of Parker, 214 N.C. 51, 197 S.E. 706, *appeal dismissed*, 305 U.S. 568 (1938)
Presumption of validity; Setbacks; Takings

The defendant constructed a wall along his rear- and side-yard property lines. The wall exceeded the height limit in the zoning ordinance. The court upheld Greensboro's setback provisions, ruling that a zoning ordinance was presumed valid and the courts are to defer to the city council's legislative judgment unless it was clearly unreasonable or abusive of discretion. The fact that individual projects may not cause harm or that enforcement may seriously depreciate a property's value does not invalidate the ordinance. An individual's right to the use of property is subordinate to the general welfare and to public interests such as traffic control, fire safety, and aesthetics.

Shuford v. Town of Waynesville, 214 N.C. 135, 198 S.E. 585 (1938)
Adoption; Comprehensive plan; Interim ordinances; Uniformity of standards

The city adopted a zoning ordinance without going through the requisite statutory procedures, so the court declared the ordinance invalid. No public hearing had been held, no planning agency created, and no comprehensive plan completed. Although the town might adopt regulations on building under its general ordinance-making power if due-process and equal-protection standards were met, if this approach is used all uses must be treated uniformly. In this case, a specific ordinance prohibiting new filling stations on a single block while a zoning ordinance was being prepared was invalidated because it allowed existing stations in the same area to continue, thus tending to create a monopoly. The ordinance was also invalidated because it zoned only a single part of the city and was therefore not in accord with a comprehensive plan for the city.

Aydlett v. Carolina By-Products Co., 215 N.C. 700, 2 S.E.2d 881 (1939)
Nuisances

The plaintiff owned three residences adjacent to the defendant's rendering plant, located just outside of Greensboro. The plaintiff contended that the odors from the plant substantially reduced the enjoyment and value of his residential property. The court upheld a jury award of monetary damages for reduction of the plaintiff's property values.

Eldridge v. Mangum, 216 N.C. 532, 5 S.E.2d 721 (1939)
Consistency with enabling statute; Preemption

The court ruled that when the zoning-enabling statute and a local ordinance conflict, the state statute controls. Specifically, Raleigh could not by ordinance convert to a simple-majority vote the three-fourths vote required when a protest petition had been filed.

City of Fayetteville v. Spur Distributing Co., 216 N.C. 596, 5 S.E.2d 838 (1939)
Injunctions; Use restrictions

A Fayetteville ordinance prohibited the storage of more than 4500 gallons of gasoline within the fire district of the city. The court ruled that cities have the power to seek injunctions to prevent violations of zoning ordinances and that protection of the public safety through this type of regulation (without having to wait for the use to become an actual nuisance) is within the police power.

Clinard v. City of Winston-Salem, 217 N.C. 119, 6 S.E.2d 867 (1940)
Purposes

A Winston-Salem zoning ordinance creating separate residential districts based on race was invalidated. The court held that use restrictions based on race are beyond the police power and unconstitutionally restrict the right to sell property.

In re Pine Hill Cemeteries, Inc., 219 N.C. 735, 15 S.E.2d 1 (1941)
Board of adjustment; Judicial review; Nonconformities; Quasi-judicial

The Durham zoning administrator ruled that a cemetery in Durham had been established as a prior nonconforming use. After a hearing, the board of adjustment ruled the same way. The trial court remanded the matter to the board for additional fact-finding. The supreme court ruled that the board of adjustment was a quasi-judicial body and that its decisions were final. Judicial review is limited to errors of law, and cases may not be remanded for the finding of additional facts.

State v. Brown, 221 N.C. 301, 20 S.E. 286 (1942)
Nuisances

The court upheld a conviction for operating a parlor for horse-race betting in Greensboro.

Ornoff v. City of Durham, 221 N.C. 457, 20 S.E.2d 380 (1942)

Board of adjustment; Judicial review; Nonconformities; Procedures

The court ruled that whether a nonconforming junkyard was in existence on a site when the zoning ordinance was adopted was a question of fact to which the parties have a right to trial by jury. Because the ordinance did not give the board of adjustment any authority regarding nonconforming uses, the court held it proper for this appeal to go directly to the courts.

Lee v. Board of Adjustment, 226 N.C. 107, 37 S.E.2d 128 (1946)

Applicants; Quasi-judicial; Variances

An option holder requested a variance to build a grocery store/service station in an area zoned for exclusive residential use by the Rocky Mount zoning ordinance. The court held that (1) because only an option was held, there was no present legal right to build, and therefore there could be no "undue hardship"; (2) financial loss occasioned by inability to construct a nonconforming use is not "undue hardship"; and (3) as a quasi-judicial rather than a legislative body, the board of adjustment has to act within the spirit and the intent of the ordinance and cannot effectively "amend" it by granting a use variance that would create a nonconforming use.

Kass v. Hedgpeth, 226 N.C. 405, 38 S.E.2d 164 (1946)

Adoption; Use restrictions

Zoning procedures were not followed in adoption of a Lumberton ordinance regulating tobacco warehouses, so it was held not to be valid as a zoning ordinance. Further, it was judged not to be justified under the general ordinance-making power. Because tobacco warehouses are not a nuisance per se and because a valid building permit had been issued, an action by a neighbor to enjoin construction had to be denied.

Town of Clinton v. Ross, 226 N.C. 682, 40 S.E.2d 593 (1946)

Adoption; Nuisances

An action by a neighbor to enforce an ordinance restricting the location of a tobacco warehouse in Clinton was not allowed. The court ruled that such a warehouse is not a nuisance per se, even though it generated substantial traffic, because it was located in an industrial area.

James v. Sutton, 229 N.C. 515, 50 S.E.2d 300 (1948)

Board of adjustment; Nonconformities; Variances

This case involved the location of an establishment that manufactured and sold candy in a Charlotte area zoned for business. The court ruled that although the board of adjustment cannot authorize a nonconforming use, this particular use might be allowed because the ordinance permitted uses that "in whole or in part" involved retail sales. As to whether the use met the ordinance standard that it not be injurious to neighboring property because of smoke, odor, or noise, the court held that this was a factual finding for the board of adjustment.

Kinney v. Sutton, 230 N.C. 404, 53 S.E.2d 306 (1949)

Presumption of validity; Use restrictions

Charlotte's prohibition of restaurants in residential districts was upheld. The court ruled that the burden is on the challenger to show that the ordinance bears no substantial relation to the health, the safety, the morals, or the general welfare of the community.

Pake v. Morris, 230 N.C. 424, 53 S.E.2d 300 (1949)

Nuisances

In this private-nuisance action, the court ruled that a fish-processing plant was not a nuisance per se. However, if it should be operated in the future in a manner that causes substantial annoyance, material physical discomfort, or injury to the health or the property of neighbors, it might be declared a nuisance in fact.

Barrier v. Troutman, 231 N.C. 47, 55 S.E.2d 923 (1949)
Nuisances

In this private-nuisance action, the plaintiff's medical clinic was located 400 yards from the end of the defendant's runway, and airplanes frequently flew over the property at an altitude of 100 feet. The court ruled that even though the enterprise was lawful, the plaintiff did suffer to the extent that he was deprived of the comfort and the enjoyment of his property; that damages were an inadequate remedy; and that an injunction was appropriate.

Mitchell v. Barfield, 232 N.C. 325, 59 S.E.2d 810 (1950)
Change in use; Enforcement

The Durham City Council denied a permit for a hotel, which was a permitted use in a residential zone, based on a concern that the use would be changed after construction. The court held the denial improper because there was an adequate remedy to deal with potential use changes if and when they actually took place.

City of Raleigh v. Fisher, 232 N.C. 629, 61 S.E.2d 897 (1950)
Enforcement; Estoppel; Mistakes

The city initiated a zoning-enforcement action to close a bakery that was being operated as a nonconforming use in a Raleigh residential district. The fact that city personnel had known about this use and done nothing to stop it (and in fact had collected a business tax on the improper use for nine years) did not prevent subsequent enforcement of the zoning ordinance. An injunction to require cessation of the illegal use was found to be appropriate.

City of Shelby v. Lackey, 235 N.C. 343, 69 S.E.2d 607 (1952)
Standing

The court allowed neighbors to join a city's suit to enforce a zoning ordinance.

In re Groves, 235 N.C. 756, 71 S.E.2d 119 (1952)
Nonconformities; Repairs

The court upheld the trial court's reversal of the building inspector and board of adjustment's refusal to issue a permit for repair of a nonconforming structure.

Wilcher v. Sharpe, 236 N.C. 308, 72 S.E.2d 662 (1952)
Delegation; Nuisances

Neighbors sought to enjoin operation of a feed mill in Elm City. The court denied the injunction, noting that for a legitimate business such as this, the apprehension of injury was insufficient to warrant judicial intervention and that remedies existed should the operation of the mill become a nuisance in fact. Further, an ordinance prohibiting a mill without the consent of all owners within 300 feet was found to be an invalid delegation of legislative power to private parties.

Vance S. Harrington & Co. v. Renner, 236 N.C. 321, 72 S.E.2d 838 (1952)
Adoption

An ordinance was developed by a special zoning commission created by the General Assembly for the rural area around the Cherry Point military base. The court invalidated the ordinance, holding that zoning was a government power that cannot be exercised by such a public-private group (the commission had military and local members), even though the county board had given final approval to the ordinance and sat as the board of adjustment.

City of Shelby v. Lackey, 236 N.C. 369, 72 S.E.2d 757 (1952)
Standing

The court ruled that if a complaint fails to show how "neighbors" would be affected by a zoning decision (e.g., whether they were town citizens or property owners or what the nature of their injury was), they should not be accepted as party plaintiffs.

McKinney v. City of High Point, 237 N.C. 66, 74 S.E.2d 440 (1953)
Government uses

The High Point zoning ordinance required the board of adjustment's approval for utility uses. The town built a water tower in a residential area without following this procedure. The court held that the construction met a government purpose and therefore was not subject to the zoning ordinance. [Note: G.S. 160D-913, which was subsequently enacted, makes construction and use of buildings by the state and local governments subject to zoning.]

Marren v. Gamble, 237 N.C. 680, 75 S.E.2d 880 (1953)
Presumption of validity

This case was brought by a Charlotte landowner to compel rezoning of his corner lot to the same classification that existed on the other corners of the intersection, as required by the zoning-enabling statute. [Note: The four-corners provision of the statute was subsequently repealed.] The court noted that the legislature can set conditions on how cities apply their zoning powers and that a standard that has a reasonable tendency to promote the public good is a valid exercise of the police power.

McKinney v. City of High Point, 239 N.C. 232, 79 S.E.2d 730 (1954)
Takings; Vested rights

Neighbors sought damages resulting from the construction of a water tank by High Point. The court held that the residents had no vested right to current zoning: an exercise of the police power is always subject to amendment or repeal at the will of the government. The court held further that it was appropriate for the courts to consider damages caused by glare from the tank but not damages related to the tank's inconsistency with the zoning ordinance.

Robbins v. City of Charlotte, 241 N.C. 197, 84 S.E.2d 814 (1954)
Interpretation

This case involved interpretation of the four-corners provision of the zoning-enabling act. [Note: This provision was subsequently repealed.] The court ruled that where there was a "T" intersection, the rule did not apply to the land across from the intersection because it was not a "corner."

State v. Owen, 242 N.C. 525, 88 S.E.2d 832 (1955)
Extraterritorial jurisdiction

A criminal action to enforce the zoning ordinance of Winston-Salem in the city's extraterritorial area was not allowed because there was no explicit legislative authorization for the city to exercise its powers outside its boundaries. [Note: G.S. 160A-360 now authorizes municipal extraterritorial zoning statewide.]

Convent of Sisters of St. Joseph v. City of Winston-Salem, 243 N.C. 316, 90 S.E.2d 879 (1956)
Enforcement; Special uses

The court ruled that when the conditions and the benefits of a special use permit have been accepted, the permit holder cannot subsequently challenge the validity of the conditions. The conditions were held also to apply to a subsequent purchaser who acquired the property with knowledge of the conditions and who was under the general supervision of the original permit holder.

Wilson Realty Co. v. City & County Planning Board, 243 N.C. 648, 92 S.E.2d 82 (1956)
Exactions; Subdivisions

The Winston-Salem/Forsyth County planning board attempted to require reservation of a six-acre tract in a seventy-acre subdivision for the proposed Silas Creek Parkway, a divided four-lane road. The court remanded the case on procedural grounds (in mandamus proceedings, the court is limited to facts in evidence) but expressed serious doubts about the authority of the local government to require the reservation as a condition of approval.

In re O'Neal, 243 N.C. 714, 92 S.E.2d 189 (1956)

Nonconformities; Variances

A structure being put to a nonconforming use may be replaced with a modern building when that is required by the state's building code as long as the nonconforming use is not intensified. In this instance, a small nursing home in a residential district in Charlotte was allowed to be replaced with a new building as long as the number of patients was not increased. Conditions on the use of the new building were permissible.

Bryan v. Sanford, 244 N.C. 30, 92 S.E.2d 420 (1956)

Interpretation

This case involved consideration of whether the four-corners provision of the zoning-enabling act applied to streets that had been platted but not yet opened. The court ruled that when the streets had been dedicated and accepted, a corner legally existed, even though it had not yet been built. [Note: This statutory provision was subsequently repealed.]

Fox v. Board of Commissioners, 244 N.C. 497, 94 S.E.2d 482 (1956)

Agricultural uses; Standing

The court ruled that a zoning ordinance's validity could not be challenged in the abstract; challengers have to show some personal, direct, and irreparable injury to bring suit. The trial court had ruled that Durham County's more detailed definition of "bona fide farm" (setting acreage and farm-income standards) was an impermissible construction of the statutory agricultural exemption from county zoning that was contained in the local bill authorizing this ordinance.

City of Raleigh v. Morand, 247 N.C. 363, 100 S.E.2d 870 (1957), *appeal dismissed*, 357 U.S. 343 (1958)

Extraterritorial jurisdiction; Manufactured housing

A Raleigh ordinance prohibiting trailer parks within residential districts in the city's one-mile extraterritorial area was upheld. The court ruled that injunctive power to enforce the ordinance is available.

Penny v. City of Durham, 249 N.C. 596, 107 S.E.2d 72 (1959)

Protest petitions

Setting up a 150-foot buffer on shopping-center property between the street and a portion of the property that was to be rezoned was held to be sufficient to avoid application of the protest-petition provisions of the zoning-enabling statute. "Directly opposite" was held to mean opposite the portion of the land being rezoned, not opposite the entire parcel.

State v. Brown, 250 N.C. 54, 108 S.E.2d 74 (1959)

Aesthetics; Junkyards

This case involved a criminal citation under the state statute (G.S. 14-399) prohibiting junkyards within 150 feet of a paved highway unless screened from view. The court ruled that the statute was based solely on aesthetic grounds and was therefore unconstitutional and invalid. [Note: See *State v. Jones*, 305 N.C. 520, 290 S.E.2d 675 (1982), discussed below, upholding aesthetics as a legitimate objective.]

Chambers v. Zoning Board of Adjustment, 250 N.C. 194, 108 S.E.2d 211 (1959)

Parking; Variances

The Winston-Salem board of adjustment's approval of a low-income-housing project that provided for on-street parking only was invalidated in light of an ordinance requirement that "garage or other satisfactory automobile storage space" equal to one space per unit be provided on the premises. The court ruled that the city council might amend this requirement, but the board of adjustment could not do so by variance.

Rhyne v. Town of Mount Holly, 251 N.C. 521, 112 S.E.2d 40 (1960)
Enforcement; Nuisances

Plaintiff had an overgrown vacant lot that was in violation of the town's nuisance-lot ordinance. The town used earth-moving and other equipment to clean up the lot. In the course of doing so, about 100 small oak trees (each at twelve to fifteen feet high) were removed. The court held that while the town is not liable for damages incident to abatement of the nuisance, it is liable for damages for acts not necessary to remove or abate the nuisance.

Little Pep Delmonico Restaurant, Inc. v. City of Charlotte, 252 N.C. 324, 113 S.E.2d 422 (1960)
Aesthetics

The plaintiff challenged a Charlotte ordinance limiting business signs over the sidewalk in Charlotte's central business district. The court ruled that an ordinance based on aesthetics alone was invalid and that it was appropriate for those subject to the ordinance to seek injunctive relief against its enforcement rather than wait for criminal enforcement to challenge the ordinance. [Note: See *State v. Jones*, 305 N.C. 520, 290 S.E.2d 675 (1982), discussed below, upholding aesthetics as a legitimate objective.]

In re Hasting, 252 N.C. 327, 113 S.E.2d 433 (1960)
Nonconformities; Vested rights

This action involved a proposed expansion of a mobile-home park in a Charlotte extraterritorial area zoned for rural use. The court held that whether the addition of twenty-nine manufactured-home sites to a sixteen-site project was the "completion" (allowed) or the "expansion" (not allowed) of a nonconforming use was a question of fact to be determined by the board of adjustment, whose finding would not be overturned by the court if there was sufficient evidence to support it.

Pharr v. Garibaldi, 252 N.C. 803, 115 S.E.2d 18 (1960)
Government uses; Nuisances

A neighbor sued to enjoin the expansion of a state prison on the outskirts of Raleigh as a nuisance and as an expansion of a nonconforming use under the city's zoning ordinance. The court held that insufficient facts were pleaded (e.g., whether the area was in compliance with the residential zone and whether the ordinance prohibited the use) to challenge compliance with the ordinance. Also, the prison was ruled to be an essential government function, not a nuisance per se.

Walker v. Town of Elkin, 254 N.C. 85, 118 S.E.2d 1 (1961)
Notice; Spot zoning

Elkin rezoned a 3.56-acre parcel and amended the zoning text to allow a new use of right within a district. The court held that the published notice provided had been adequate. Also, no improper spot zoning was found, for the council had acted in good faith with a thorough analysis of the suitability of the site for its uses and the compatibility of surrounding land uses.

City of New Bern v. Walker, 255 N.C. 355, 121 S.E.2d 544 (1961)
Enforcement

The city sought to enforce its zoning restrictions by enjoining the defendants from using residentially zoned property as a commercial garage. The court held that the defendant was not entitled to continue the use during the pendency of the enforcement action by posting a bond. A temporary injunction was a proper remedy, and the record was held to be sufficient to support one here.

Stowe v. Burke, 255 N.C. 527, 122 S.E.2d 374 (1961)
Vested rights

Neighbors sued to enjoin the construction of an apartment complex in Charlotte. After receiving notice of a proposed rezoning to limit the use of the property to single-family homes, and after receiving notice of the opposition of neighbors, the defendant proceeded to lease the property and start construction before the adoption of the rezoning. The action involved the expenditure of over $60,000 and the completion of foundations for eight of ten proposed buildings. The court held that no vested rights had been established because the expenditures had not been made in good faith; the defendant had moved forward with construction at an extraordinary pace in an attempt to establish a vested right before rezoning.

Helms v. City of Charlotte, 255 N.C. 647, 122 S.E.2d 817 (1961)
Downzoning; Mistakes; Notice; Takings

This suit involved several small lots in Charlotte rezoned from an industrial to a residential district. The court held that newspaper notice according to the enabling statute had been adequate; that due process did not require individual notice; that a mistakenly issued building permit does not estop the city from subsequent enforcement; and that zoning districts do not have to follow property lines. To avoid a taking claim, some practical, reasonable use has to be left, and such has to be supported by definite, sufficient findings. Because the trial court had not made sufficient findings as to whether the lots had any practical and reasonable value for residential purposes (e.g., whether houses could be sold for an amount greater than their construction cost), the case was remanded for additional evidentiary findings.

In re Couch, 258 N.C. 345, 128 S.E.2d 409 (1962)
Interpretation

In interpreting Durham's zoning ordinance, the court ruled that a car wash was included within the permitted use of "automobile service station" when that term was defined by the ordinance to include minor repairs and when gas stations in the area involved normally offered car washes.

Schloss v. Jamison, 258 N.C. 271, 128 S.E.2d 590 (1962)
Enforcement

The court ruled that a temporary injunction against enforcement of a zoning ordinance while it was being challenged was appropriate to maintain the status quo.

Staley v. City of Winston-Salem, 258 N.C. 244, 128 S.E.2d 604 (1962)
Alcohol sales; Preemption

A Winston-Salem ordinance was invalidated insofar as it purported to restrict the sale of wine in a nonconforming restaurant in a residential zone. The court held that state statutes controlling alcoholic beverages preempt the field regarding where wine could be sold.

Jarrell v. Board of Adjustment, 258 N.C. 476, 128 S.E.2d 879 (1963)
Board of adjustment; Evidence; Oaths; Quasi-judicial

In a review of a High Point board of adjustment's determination on whether a nonconforming use was in effect at the time of adoption of the zoning ordinance, the court ruled that such a finding of fact had to be supported by competent and substantial evidence. Although some informality is acceptable, the board can dispense with no essential element of a fair trial. Also, the testimony before the board has to be under oath.

Bryan v. Wilson, 259 N.C. 107, 130 S.E.2d 68 (1963)
Government uses; Interpretation

The Greenville zoning ordinance's list of permitted uses in a particular zone read "schools, institutions of an educational or philanthropic nature, public buildings." The court interpreted this phrase to be three separate types of uses and held a post office to be permitted.

In re Markham, 259 N.C. 566, 131 S.E.2d 329, *cert. denied*, 375 U.S. 931 (1963)
Amendments

In a challenge to the Durham City Council's refusal to rezone a parcel from residential to commercial use, the court held that amendment of the zoning ordinance is a legislative decision of the council. It is within the council's discretion to rezone a property or not, and such a decision is not subject to judicial review on certiorari.

Brannock v. Zoning Board of Adjustment, 260 N.C. 426, 132 S.E.2d 758 (1963)
Board of adjustment; Special uses; Voting

In reviewing a special use permit for a parking lot in a Winston-Salem residential zone, the court held that a change in the membership of the board of adjustment between the original hearing and the vote on the matter is acceptable if the new members have ample access to the minutes and the records.

In re Tadlock, 261 N.C. 120, 134 S.E.2d 177 (1964)
Nonconformities; Phased development; Vested rights

This case involved the completion of a nonconforming mobile-home park in a Charlotte residential zone. The court held that when eleven of twenty-five units in phase one of the project had been completed, with all the necessary infrastructure for the entire phase having been completed at the time of the ordinance's effective date, there is a right to complete phase one. However, phases two and three were not covered because planning a development, per se, is not enough to create a vested right to continue; therefore, their construction can be prohibited as the expansion of a nonconforming use.

Schloss v. Jamison, 262 N.C. 108, 136 S.E.2d 691 (1964)
Signs

Charlotte prohibited off-premise advertising signs in the central business district. The regulation was upheld as a legitimate part of the comprehensive zoning ordinance. The court found that the ordinance was not based exclusively on aesthetic grounds and was related to the valid purpose of establishing a "first class business and commercial district in the heart of the downtown area." Allowing on-premise signs was held not to be unlawful discrimination.

County of Durham v. Addison, 262 N.C. 280, 136 S.E.2d 600 (1964)
Nonconformities

This case involved construction on a lot that was too small to conform to the Durham County zoning ordinance. The lot was purchased in 1954, a store was built on part of the lot in 1955, zoning was adopted effective in 1956, and an attempt was made to construct a second structure in 1962. The court held that although the second structure would have been legal before the zoning, and although all the infrastructure was in place, the second building would be nonconforming and could be prohibited.

Warner v. W & O, Inc., 263 N.C. 37, 138 S.E.2d 782 (1964)
Vested rights

A neighbor challenged the construction of an apartment building in Asheville. The site had been changed to a single-family zone after the defendant had secured an option for purchase, obtained a building permit, and completed initial site preparation. The court held that the permit itself created a right to work, not a vested right to complete the work. Only substantial expenditures in good-faith reliance on the approval created a vested right. Funds spent to secure approval are not "in reliance," and funds spent after knowledge of an ordinance change are not "in good faith." [Note: G.S. 160A-385(b), which was subsequently enacted, creates a vested right based on building permits per se.]

Town of Garner v. Weston, 263 N.C. 487, 139 S.E.2d 642 (1965)
Manufactured housing; Nonconformities; Vested rights

This case involved the completion of a mobile-home park in Garner's extraterritorial area. The court ruled that the trial judge's finding that the use had not been in existence on the effective date of the ordinance was permissible, given conflicting evidence. Further, the ordinance provided for appeal to the board of adjustment and no appeal had been made, so there was a failure to exhaust administrative remedies.

Armstrong v. McInnis, 264 N.C. 616, 142 S.E.2d 670 (1965)
Amendments; Protest petitions

High Point rezoned a 200-acre tract from residential use to use as a planned industrial park. The court ruled that a jury trial was not in order because the facts as found by the planning board and the city council were controlling. Although an earlier rezoning proposal had been subject to a protest petition, this was a modified proposal that left a 101-foot buffer not rezoned, so the protest petition provisions were inapplicable.

Austin v. Brunnemer, 266 N.C. 697, 147 S.E.2d 182 (1966)
Variances; Vested rights

This was an action challenging the denial of a variance for an automobile body shop in Gaston County neighborhood and highway districts. The court held that even though the property had been purchased, graded, and fenced, and a sign had been erected, all before the effective date of zoning, there was no vested right to construct. Whether a variance should be granted for the project was a matter for the discretion of the board of adjustment.

Craver v. Board of Adjustment, 267 N.C. 40, 147 S.E.2d 599 (1966)
Board of adjustment; Evidence; Oaths; Special uses

The Winston-Salem board of adjustment denied a variance for a special use permit for a mobile home on a lot with an existing residence. The court held that witnesses before the board do not have to be sworn when the applicant is present, his or her own testimony is not sworn, and a full and open discussion ensues.

Joyner v. Zoning Board of Adjustment, 267 N.C. 44, 147 S.E.2d 602 (1966)
Board of adjustment; Evidence; Oaths

The court held that witnesses before the board of adjustment do not have to be sworn when the applicant is present, his or her own testimony is not sworn, and a full and open discussion ensues.

Yancey v. Heafner, 268 N.C. 263, 150 S.E.2d 440 (1966)
Government uses; Interpretation

The court held that a lighted football field with bleachers for seating 4000 people was a usual and necessary part of the adjacent school and was an appropriate use in a zoning district permitting schools.

Michael v. Guilford County, 269 N.C. 515, 153 S.E.2d 106 (1967)
Airports; Statements of reasonableness

A property owner at the end of a runway brought this action to have the Guilford County zoning ordinance declared invalid for his property on the grounds that increased airport use had rendered the property unsuitable for its zoned residential and agricultural uses. The court held that the owner could bring an inverse-condemnation action against the airport authority or request a variance from the board of adjustment but could not have the ordinance ruled invalid in this manner.

City of Gastonia v. Parrish, 271 N.C. 527, 157 S.E.2d 154 (1967)
Enforcement; Evidence; Junkyards

The City of Gastonia brought an action to enforce the provision of its zoning ordinance prohibiting junkyards and high fences in an extraterritorial residential zone. The court held that a copy of the original lost zoning map could be used to establish that the property was zoned residential. An allegation of unequal enforcement was no defense to an illegal act.

Jamison v. Kyles, 271 N.C. 722, 157 S.E.2d 550 (1967)
Board of adjustment; Home occupation; Judicial review

This case involved the question of whether the operation of a beauty parlor in the owner's residence was a "customary home occupation" under the Charlotte zoning ordinance. The zoning administrator and the board of adjustment concluded that it was not. The court held that there were sufficient facts on the record to support the board of adjustment's findings and that the trial court had overruled those findings in error.

In re Rea Construction Co., 272 N.C. 715, 158 S.E.2d 887 (1968)
Board of adjustment; Permitted uses

Neighbors challenged the construction of an asphalt-mixing plant in a Statesville industrial district. The court held that the board of adjustment was without authority to revoke the permit because this use was explicitly listed as permitted in the applicable district.

Taylor v. Bowen, 272 N.C. 726, 158 S.E.2d 837 (1968)
Jurisdiction

In an action involving the Methodist College area of Fayetteville, the court ruled that when the area had been annexed by the city, the city's zoning superseded the prior zoning enacted by the county.

Zopfi v. City of Wilmington, 273 N.C. 430, 160 S.E.2d 325 (1968)
Purposes; Spot zoning

The city rezoned a sixty-acre triangular tract formed by two major roads. Most of the land had originally been zoned for single-family residential use. The change put the 27.5 acres at the point of the triangle in a commercial district and the next 12 acres in a multifamily residential district; it left the remaining 20.5 acres in a single-family residential district. Neighbors in the adjacent single-family district challenged the rezoning as spot zoning. The court upheld the rezoning, noting that neighbors have no vested right to the existing zoning. The basic tests of validity were (1) whether the council acted in good faith; (2) whether the act was arbitrary or capricious; and (3) whether it contributed to a legitimate purpose of the enabling legislation. In this case, there was an ample showing of legitimate and rational grounds for rezoning forty acres bounded by heavily traveled highways and leaving a twenty-acre low-density buffer between existing residential uses.

Freeland v. Orange County, 273 N.C. 452, 160 S.E.2d 282 (1968)
Adoption; Hearings

Opponents challenged Orange County's adoption of zoning in Chapel Hill township. Five hundred people attended the mandated public hearing. One hour each was allotted to proponents and opponents of the adoption, with each side getting an additional fifteen minutes for rebuttal. Some thirty-one persons spoke, evenly balanced between sides. The commissioners entertained no questions. Some 200 additional people indicated that they would have spoken if given the opportunity. In upholding the adoption, the court held that orderly and fair public-hearing procedures can be employed and that not all those present have to be allowed to speak.

Jackson v. Guilford County Board of Adjustment, 275 N.C. 155, 166 S.E.2d 78 (1969)
Board of adjustment; Quasi-judicial; Special uses; Standing

Neighbors challenged the board of adjustment's granting of a special use permit for a mobile-home park in a Guilford County agricultural district. The court upheld the General Assembly's delegation of zoning authority to counties. It also upheld the delegation of decision-making on special use permits to the board of adjustment, provided that the board is limited to determining whether factors set forth in the ordinance have been met. The board may not, however, make legislative findings (e.g., whether the proposed use is "in the public interest").

Town of Hillsborough v. Smith, 276 N.C. 48, 170 S.E.2d 904 (1969)
Vested rights

This case involved construction of a proposed dry-cleaning business in downtown Hillsborough. After the issuance of a building permit but before zoning was enacted that made dry cleaning an impermissible use, the permit holder had bought the land and had entered into construction and equipment contracts. The court ruled that although the building permit itself does not confer vested rights, substantial expenditures in good faith reliance on it do (actual construction is not required, only substantial expenditures). When there is conflicting evidence on knowledge of the pending zoning change, and hence on the requisite good faith, the jury finding will not be disturbed. [Note: G.S. 160D-108(c) subsequently enacted, creates a vested right based on the building permit alone.]

State v. McBane, 276 N.C. 60, 170 S.E.2d 913 (1969)
Enforcement; Subdivisions

The defendant was charged with selling lots in an unapproved subdivision in Guilford County. The court dismissed the charge because the warrant did not include all the essential elements of a misdemeanor (e.g., that the land was within the county's jurisdiction).

Horton v. Gulledge, 277 N.C. 353, 177 S.E.2d 885 (1970)
Demolition; Housing code

Greensboro determined that a rental residential building owned by the plaintiff was unfit for human habitation and that it could not be repaired at a cost of less than 60 percent of its present value. The city ordered the building demolished. The house was located in an urban-renewal area. The court held that while the city could order that the house not be occupied while it remained in a dilapidated condition, it could not order it demolished for aesthetic reasons alone. The court further held that the city cannot order demolition without giving the owner reasonable opportunity to bring the building into compliance with the housing code.

In re Ellis, 277 N.C. 419, 178 S.E.2d 77 (1970)
Special uses

This case involved the same application that was addressed in *Jackson v. Guilford County Board of Adjustment,* 275 N.C. 155, 166 S.E.2d 78 (1969), discussed above. The court ruled that the board of commissioners, like the board of adjustment, could not deny special use permits in its unguided discretion (or based on a very general standard such as a finding that granting the permit would "adversely affect the public interest").

Town of Conover v. Jolly, 277 N.C. 439, 177 S.E.2d 879 (1970)
Manufactured housing

The court ruled that an ordinance completely barring mobile homes for residential use within the entire town is invalid. The ordinance, which was not part of the zoning ordinance, was held to be beyond the town's delegated police powers, for mobile homes are not a nuisance per se nor a detriment per se to public health, morals, comfort, safety, convenience, and welfare. [Note: G.S. 160D-910 was subsequently enacted to codify portions of this ruling.]

Allred v. City of Raleigh, 277 N.C. 530, 178 S.E.2d 432 (1971)
Contract zoning; Spot zoning

The city rezoned a 9.26-acre tract adjacent to the Raleigh beltline (but without access to the beltline) from low-density residential to multifamily residential use. The planning board had recommended denial. Several previous attempts to rezone the site to commercial use had been subject to protest petitions and had failed. The court held this rezoning to be invalid as contract and spot zoning. On the contract zoning question, the applicable test was whether all of the uses permitted in the new zone (not just the proposed project) were appropriate for the site, given its location and the surrounding circumstances.

Heaton v. City of Charlotte, 277 N.C. 506, 178 S.E.2d 352 (1971)
Notice; Protest petitions

Neighbors contested the rezoning of 40.3 acres of a 111.8-acre tract from residential to shopping-center and multi-family residential use. The court upheld the rezoning. The public notice of the hearing had been for a larger portion of the property to be rezoned but also contained a statement that the area and the classification might be adjusted. The court ruled that a published notice is adequate unless the action ultimately taken is substantially different (and less favorable to the complaining party) and the initial notice does not indicate a possibility of substantial changes. For the requirement of an extraordinary vote to be triggered by a protest petition, the protesters have to own 20 percent or more of the area extending 100 feet from the rezoned portion of the tract. The 100-foot area is measured from the zoning district boundary, not the property boundary.

Keiger v. Winston-Salem Board of Adjustment, 278 N.C. 17, 178 S.E.2d 616 (1971)
Board of adjustment; Quasi-judicial; Special uses

The board of adjustment denied a special use permit for a mobile-home park on a 14.5-acre site in a highway business district. The court ruled that when an ordinance sets forth specific standards for a special use permit, the board of adjustment cannot deny a permit on the grounds of inconsistency with the ordinance's "purpose and intent" because that would be exercising legislative powers reserved to the council (and is the equivalent of an impermissible "public interest" review by a board of adjustment).

Orange County v. Heath, 278 N.C. 688, 180 S.E.2d 810 (1971)
Repeal; Spot zoning

Orange County rezoned fifteen acres from a residential district to a mobile-home-park district, the tract being adjacent to a five-acre mobile-home park that predated the zoning ordinance. A week later, without additional notice, the rezoning was rescinded. The court ruled that the original rezoning was not spot zoning and that the attempted repeal was not effective in that the same procedure (notice and a hearing) has to be followed to rescind an action as to adopt or amend the zoning ordinance.

Blades v. City of Raleigh, 280 N.C. 531, 187 S.E.2d 35 (1972)
Contract zoning; Spot zoning

The Raleigh city council rezoned a five-acre tract from a single-family residential district to one allowing multifamily residences, rest homes, hospitals, and other uses. The court ruled the rezoning invalid because there was no showing of unanticipated changed conditions (a finding required by the ordinance provision on rezonings). Also, given the lack of any showing of facts distinguishing this tract from the surrounding area, which was zoned single-family residential, the action was invalid spot zoning. Further, because only a particular use, rather than all the permitted uses in the new district, had been considered by the city council, the action was invalid contract zoning.

Allgood v. Town of Tarboro, 281 N.C. 430, 189 S.E.2d 255 (1972)
Spot zoning

The town rezoned a twenty-five-acre tract from a residential to a shopping-center district. The court noted changed conditions in the eight years between the original zoning and the rezoning (including road, water, and sewer extensions and the development of additional housing), finding that the rezoned classification would have been justified at the time of original zoning if the same conditions had existed then. Therefore, the action was held not to be spot zoning.

Keiger v. Winston-Salem Board of Adjustment, 281 N.C. 715, 190 S.E.2d 175 (1972)
Notice

This case involved the rezoning of part of a 14.5-acre tract, on the petition of neighbors, to limit its use as a proposed mobile-home park. The court ruled that the public-notice requirements for the zoning amendment had not been followed, so the rezoning was invalid, the original zoning was still in effect, and the previously improperly denied permit should issue.

State v. Vestal, 281 N.C. 517, 189 S.E.2d 152 (1972)

Junkyards; Vagueness

Forsyth County amended its zoning ordinance to require a fence around junkyards. The court ruled the provision void for vagueness because it required a fence not less than fifty feet from the "edge of any public road" without defining the term. The court also noted that the county had not established public-safety grounds for such a requirement in a rural area away from intersections.

Orange County v. Heath, 282 N.C. 292, 192 S.E.2d 308 (1972)

Damages; Enforcement

The court ruled that the county could not be sued for damages as a result of securing a temporary restraining order that delayed a mobile-home park, the order later being held invalid. Seeking the order was an exercise of a government function for which there was sovereign immunity.

MacPherson v. City of Asheville, 283 N.C. 299, 196 S.E.2d 200 (1973)

Applicants; Interpretation

This case involved an interpretation of a provision in the Asheville ordinance requiring the "owner" or his or her agent to apply for site-plan approval for a group development. The court held that a person holding a binding contract to purchase was an owner within the intent of the ordinance.

Humble Oil & Refining Co. v. Board of Aldermen, 284 N.C. 458, 202 S.E.2d 129 (1974)

Applicants; Board of adjustment; Procedures; Quasi-judicial; Special uses; Standing

The Chapel Hill town council denied a special use permit for a filling station in the central business district. The court held that an option holder who had exercised the option subject to the necessary permits being obtained to develop the property had standing to participate in the review of the decision. When an ordinance has a process for mandatory referral to the planning board before council action, that procedure cannot be ignored by the council; thus, the application here was remanded for consideration de novo. In the reconsideration, the board of adjustment (and/or the council) has to act in its quasi-judicial capacity, basing its decision on competent, material, and substantial evidence according to all essential elements of a fair trial, including the right to offer evidence, cross-examine witnesses, have sworn testimony, and offer rebuttal.

City of Brevard v. Ritter, 285 N.C. 576, 206 S.E.2d 151 (1974)

Enforcement

The defendant began construction of a building enlarging a private airport in violation of the Brevard zoning ordinance. The town secured a court order compelling the removal of the offending partially completed structure. The defendant, without the town's approval and without an amendment of the court order, then began to convert the structure to another use instead of removing it. The court ruled that in a contempt hearing, the burden is on the defendant to purge himself of contempt by showing compliance with the court order or by securing its modification.

Humble Oil & Refining Co. v. Board of Aldermen, 286 N.C. 170, 209 S.E.2d 447 (1974)

Special uses

The Chapel Hill town council denied a special use permit on the basis of information received after the public hearing and not considered by the planning board. The court ruled the denial invalid and remanded the application for de novo consideration.

State v. Joyner, 286 N.C. 366, 211 S.E.2d 320, *appeal dismissed*, 422 U.S. 1002 (1975)

Amortization; Nonconformities

The defendant challenged a Winston-Salem zoning-ordinance provision that required a nonconforming building materials salvage yard to be removed within three years of the ordinance's adoption. The court held that amortization requirements are valid if reasonable. This particular provision was upheld as being neither a violation of due process nor an unconstitutional taking.

In re Campsites Unlimited, Inc., 287 N.C. 493, 215 S.E.2d 73 (1975)
Vested rights

This case involved a 155-acre campground in Stanly County. The court ruled that when $275,000 had been spent toward a $2.7 million project for a use that was legal before initial zoning, a vested right to the use was established. In overruling the board of adjustment's finding that the applicant had knowledge of the pending zoning and therefore did not have the requisite good faith for a vested right, the court found that acting on knowledge of a general plan to zone an entire area (as opposed to a specific pending proposal affecting an individual site) did not constitute bad faith. The court also noted a legitimate business need for the expedited construction involved.

Marriott Financial Services, Inc. v. Capitol Funds, Inc., 288 N.C. 122, 217 S.E.2d 551 (1975)
Remedies; Subdivisions

The buyer of property that had not been legally subdivided sought reconveyance and the return of the purchase price when the city of Raleigh denied the buyer a driveway permit for the illegal lot. The court ruled that although illegal subdivision was a criminal act, the sanction was the criminal penalty set out in the statute, not the voiding of the sale (unless the legislature clearly evidenced an intent that a sale be voided).

Taylor v. City of Raleigh, 290 N.C. 608, 227 S.E.2d 576 (1976)
Laches; Standing

This case involved a challenge to Raleigh's annexation and rezoning of a 39.89-acre tract. The court ruled that the plaintiffs had no standing to challenge the annexation because they were neither residents of the city nor residents of the area being annexed. Further, the court ruled that the challenge to the rezoning was barred by laches because it had been filed over two years after the rezoning, and both the city and the landowner had made substantial expenditures in reliance on the rezoning.

George v. Town of Edenton, 294 N.C. 679, 242 S.E.2d 877 (1978)
Procedures; Reapplication

Edenton rezoned a ten-acre tract from a residential to a shopping-center district. The court ruled the rezoning invalid because it had been made within three months of the denial of a rezoning petition for the same site and the local ordinance mandated a six-month minimum period before reconsideration. The court noted that this provision applied to amendments by either individual-parcel rezoning or comprehensive revision of the ordinance.

Adams v. North Carolina Department of Natural & Economic Resources, 295 N.C. 683, 249 S.E.2d 402 (1978)
Coastal Area Management Act; Delegation

This case upheld the constitutionality of the Coastal Area Management Act. The court ruled that the coastal counties constituted a valid legislative class and that the Coastal Area Management Act was therefore not an invalid local act. There was not an unlawful delegation of legislative authority because adequate guiding standards (as specific as the circumstances permitted) and procedural safeguards were provided. Taking and unlawful search claims were dismissed as premature.

A-S-P Associates v. City of Raleigh, 298 N.C. 207, 258 S.E.2d 444 (1979)
Comprehensive plan; Historic preservation

The plaintiff challenged the validity of a ninety-eight-acre historic-district overlay zone adopted by the City of Raleigh for the Oakwood neighborhood. The court ruled that the regulation of exterior structural alterations for historic-district preservation is within the police power and promotes the general welfare by providing education on the past, stimulating economic revitalization, fostering architectural creativity, and generating tourism. Such regulation might be applied to an entire district, not just to existing historic structures. The court also ruled that there was no impermissible delegation of legislative authority, given the adequacy of standards and a provision for appeal to the board of adjustment; that exclusion from the district of part of a block with an existing modern structure does not violate the Equal Protection Clause; that Raleigh's citywide zoning, plans, and historic-district study constitute a "comprehensive plan" within the meaning of the enabling statute; and that an overlay district does not violate the uniformity-of-districts provision.

Woodhouse v. Board of Commissioners, 299 N.C. 211, 261 S.E.2d 882 (1980)
Enforcement; Planned-unit developments; Special uses

The Nags Head council denied a special use permit for a planned-unit development on a 5.5-acre site in a residential district. The court reversed the denial, ruling that grounds for denial have to be based on competent, substantial evidence related to specific standards. In interpreting the phrase "additional uses" in the section of the ordinance on planned-unit developments, the court ruled that it included any type of residential use, not just the single-family uses allowed in the underlying zoning district. The court also ruled that future potential problems with the waste-disposal system were not valid grounds for denial, given the availability of permit conditions to secure proper design and adequate enforcement remedies if the system was improperly operated.

Coastal Ready-Mix Concrete Co. v. Board of Commissioners, 299 N.C. 620, 265 S.E.2d 379, *reh'g denied*, 300 N.C. 562, 270 S.E.2d 106 (1980)
Interpretation; Judicial review; Special uses

The Nags Head town council denied a special use permit for a cement plant in a commercial zoning district. The court upheld the denial, noting that the scope of judicial review on appeal included (1) reviewing for errors in law; (2) ensuring that proper procedures in both statute and ordinance had been followed; (3) ensuring that due-process rights had been secured (including rights to offer evidence, cross-examine witnesses, and inspect documents); (4) ensuring that competent, material, and substantial evidence supported the decision; and (5) ensuring that decisions were not arbitrary and capricious. The court interpreted "appurtenances" as used in the ordinance to be something physically secondary to a primary part that served a useful or necessary function in connection with the primary part (in ruling that a forty-five-foot-tall cement-mixing bin was not a "mechanical appurtenance" to the conveyor belt taking materials to its top).

In re Broad & Gales Creek Community Ass'n, 300 N.C. 267, 266 S.E.2d 645 (1980)
Delegation; Secondary impacts; Wetlands

The applicant was denied a dredge-and-fill permit for the construction of a boat ramp on Broad Creek in Carteret County. The court held that the dredge-and-fill statute is not an unlawful delegation of legislative authority and that the burden of proof in administrative appeals can be placed on the party making the appeal. The court further held that protection of the use and enjoyment of adjoining properties is within the police power and that the county, in reviewing a permit application, might properly consider the full range of impacts that would flow from a permitted activity.

State v. Jones, 305 N.C. 520, 290 S.E.2d 675 (1982)

Aesthetics; Junkyards

Buncombe County adopted an ordinance requiring fencing to screen junkyards from view in residential areas. The court ruled that regulations could be based on aesthetics alone, with the diminution in value of individual property being balanced against the corresponding gain to the public from the regulation. The court also ruled that an ordinance is not void for vagueness if, when read contextually by persons of ordinary intelligence, it apprises them of what is required to abide by the law.

Long v. City of Charlotte, 306 N.C. 187, 293 S.E.2d 101 (1982)

Airports; Takings

This case involved an action for inverse condemnation due to aircraft overflights, brought by a landowner located one mile north of the end of a new runway at Douglas Municipal Airport. The court ruled that there is a taking if there is material interference with the use and enjoyment of a property so as to cause substantial diminution of its market value. The amount of compensation is the diminution in value. The court dismissed trespass and nuisance claims, as well as claims for punitive damages and special damages for physical distress or mental anguish.

Responsible Citizens v. City of Asheville, 308 N.C. 255, 302 S.E.2d 204 (1983)

Floodplain zoning and insurance; Takings

The plaintiffs challenged Asheville's floodplain zoning ordinance on the grounds that it constituted a taking. The court upheld the ordinance. The test articulated for takings analyses was (1) whether the ends sought to be achieved were within the police power and (2) whether the means by which they were obtained were reasonable. Protecting public safety is a permissible objective, and preventing floodway obstructions and requiring flood proofing are reasonable means of accomplishing this objective. Regulating lands within the hazard zone, but not those outside it, was held not to violate the Equal Protection Clause because the distinction between hazardous and nonhazardous areas is a reasonable classification that bears a rational relationship to a permissible state objective.

White Oak Properties, Inc. v. Town of Carrboro, 313 N.C. 306, 327 S.E.2d 882 (1985)

Appeals; Timeliness

The Carrboro town council denied a special use permit for a townhouse project. The petition for certiorari was filed forty-seven days after the notice of denial. The court ruled that the thirty-day time limit for filing appeals applies to the board of adjustment's decisions but not to the council's decisions because it was set forth in the statutory procedures applying to the former but not to the latter. In the absence of an explicit statutory time period for filing appeals, the court looks to filing within a "reasonable time" considering all the circumstances. [Note: G.S. 160D-1405(d) now sets a thirty-day time limit for filing a judicial appeal of all quasi-judicial decisions. On remand, the court of appeals in White Oak Properties held that there had been no error in the trial court's decision ordering the town to issue the special use permit. (74 N.C. App. 605, 328 S.E.2d 907)]

Town of Nags Head v. Tillett, 314 N.C. 627, 336 S.E.2d 394 (1985)

Enforcement; Subdivisions

This case involved the purchase of a lot in a subdivision that had not received local subdivision approval, with subsequent town denial of a building permit on the grounds of failure to comply with the subdivision ordinance and nonconformance with the zoning ordinance. The court ruled that since the enforcement provisions of the subdivision statute included only penal and injunctive relief for future violations, they were not broad enough to justify the denial of a building permit for an illegal lot. However, the zoning-enforcement provision did allow such a denial. [Note: G.S. 160D-807(a) now allows denial of building permits for illegally subdivided lots.] The court further ruled that the sales contract called for no "governmental regulation that would prevent the reasonable use of the property for residential purposes," that denial of the building permit was such, and therefore that the purchaser was entitled to rescission of the instruments of conveyance and restitution.

County of Durham v. Maddry & Co., 315 N.C. 296, 337 S.E.2d 576 (1985)

Change in use; Interpretation; Permitted uses

Durham County sought to enjoin the operation of an automobile repair shop in a building permitted as a "farm building," which was located in a zoning district that did not allow automobile repair shops. The court ruled that the use could be enjoined on the grounds that the change in use violated the State Building Code (an inspection and a permit were required for a change in use) and the zoning-ordinance provision on automobile storage. An additional question on interpretation of the zoning-ordinance provisions on permitted uses was remanded for further fact-finding [whether this use was included in "repair, replacement or adjustment to vehicles . . . limited to minor accessory parts," allowed for gasoline service stations].

Farr v. Board of Adjustment, 315 N.C. 309, 337 S.E.2d 581 (1985)

Judicial review

Because the issue of prior nonconforming use was not raised in this case (judicial decisions may be based only on the issues raised and briefed by the parties and supported by the record), the case was remanded.

Godfrey v. Zoning Board of Adjustment, 317 N.C. 51, 344 S.E.2d 272 (1986)

Nonconformities; Vested rights

Union County rezoned a 17.45-acre tract from residential to heavy industrial to allow the construction of a grain storage facility. While a challenge to the rezoning was pending in superior court, the facility was built. After construction was completed, the trial court ruled that the rezoning was invalid spot zoning. On appeal, the court of appeals upheld the invalidation of the rezoning. The board of adjustment then ruled that the use had become nonconforming as a result of the judicial invalidation (the rezoning still being valid at the time of construction). On a second review, the court of appeals ruled that the expenditure of $400,000 in reliance on the then-valid building permit had created a vested right to continue the use. The supreme court, however, ruled that the use was not nonconforming under the ordinance because it was not in existence at the time of the original zoning and that the judicial invalidation of the rezoning was not in itself a "rezone" (rather, the original zoning was reinstated). The supreme court further ruled that because the vested-rights issue had not been before the board of adjustment, consideration of it by the court of appeals had been improper. In a footnote, the court strongly suggested that because a lawsuit had been filed to challenge the rezoning, any expenditures made in reliance on the building permit were not in good faith, and the owner was proceeding at his own risk. The court also held that the rezoning could properly be challenged through a declaratory-judgment action and that the plaintiffs were not required to seek an injunction to prevent construction while the lawsuit was underway.

Farr v. Board of Adjustment, 318 N.C. 493, 349 S.E.2d 576 (1986)

Accessory buildings and uses

A detached building behind the petitioner's residence was used as a residence for her son and his family. The structures were located in a residential zone of Rocky Mount restricted to single-family residential use. The court ruled that the zoning ordinance did not prohibit this use because it allowed the use of an accessory building as a residence by the owners. The court deemed the "owners" to include the title holder's son and his family. Further, the ordinance's prohibition against more than one main building per lot was not violated because the second building was an accessory building.

Grace Baptist Church v. City of Oxford, 320 N.C. 439, 358 S.E.2d 372 (1987)

Enforcement; Nonconformities; Parking

The plaintiff church challenged a zoning requirement that it pave off-street parking and limit sign sizes, though such restrictions were not imposed on churches and businesses in place prior to the adoption of this ordinance requirement. The court upheld the paving requirement as reasonably related to legitimate public objectives regarding drainage, erosion, and appearance. Allowing previously existing unpaved parking lots to continue as nonconforming uses is not unlawful discrimination, as preexisting uses are not similarly situated. To show impermissible selective enforcement, a party must establish a pattern of conscious discrimination, not mere laxity of enforcement.

Cheape v. Town of Chapel Hill, 320 N.C. 549, 359 S.E.2d 792 (1987)

Economic development

The plaintiff challenged legislation allowing Chapel Hill to participate in an economic development venture encompassing parking, hotel, and commercial facilities, known as Rosemary Square. The court ruled that the legislation was valid (not an impermissible regulation of trade or an improper joint venture) and that the town has the power to convey air rights above the property.

Davidson County v. City of High Point, 321 N.C. 252, 362 S.E.2d 553 (1987)

Conditions; Government uses; Jurisdiction; Special uses; Utilities

This case involved the application of a condition imposed in a special use permit issued by the county to the city for the city's sewage-treatment plant, to be built outside the city in the county's jurisdiction. The condition required county approval of sewer service extensions. The court ruled that county approval was not required in subsequently annexed areas. The court further ruled that acceptance of the permit did not preclude a subsequent challenge of its interpretation (as opposed to its validity), nor did failure to immediately pursue administrative remedies upon issuance, because the city had been unaware of this differing interpretation until the dispute actually arose.

Chrismon v. Guilford County, 322 N.C. 611, 370 S.E.2d 579 (1988)

Contract zoning; Spot zoning

Guilford County rezoned a 5.06-acre tract (along with a 3.18-acre tract across a small dirt road that was being used for a related, valid nonconforming use) from an agricultural to a "conditional use industrial" district. The rezoning was invalidated by the court of appeals as both illegal spot zoning and illegal contract zoning. The supreme court overruled on both grounds and upheld the rezoning. The court ruled that the concept of conditional use district zoning is valid as long as the zoning is reasonable, is neither arbitrary nor unduly discriminatory, and is in the public interest. It does not have to allow all of the uses in the corresponding general-use district. Spot zoning per se is not invalid but must be justified by a reasonable basis. Factors to be applied in a case-by-case analysis of its reasonableness include the size of the tract; the compatibility with the existing comprehensive zoning plan; the benefits and the detriments for the owner, the neighbors, and the community; and the relationship between the old and the new permitted uses. Contract zoning, which is invalid, involves the petitioner and the local government undertaking reciprocal obligations in the context of a bilateral contract. Permissible conditional use district zoning involves a unilateral promise from landowners about their intended use of the land, with the local zoning authority retaining its independent decision-making authority.

Hall v. City of Durham, 323 N.C. 293, 372 S.E.2d 564 (1988)
Contract zoning

The city rezoned a 12.9-acre tract from single-family residential and neighborhood-commercial use to "heavy commercial with development plan." A detailed site design, an offer to donate adjacent land to a nonprofit group, and a deed restriction in the nature of a reverter clause donating the property to a nonprofit group or the city if the use for which the developer was applying was ever abandoned were also submitted. The court ruled that this was not invalid contract zoning because there was no evidence that the city had undertaken to obligate itself. However, the court invalidated the rezoning because when the council was rezoning from one general-use district to another, it had to consider all permissible uses in the new zone, not just the one offered by the owner. Local legislation authorizing the city to require the submission of development plans with rezoning requests did not alter this basic responsibility.

In re Civil Penalty, 324 N.C. 373, 379 S.E.2d 30 (1989)
Enforcement; Sedimentation

The court upheld the constitutionality of an administrative agency's assessing civil penalties when they are reasonably necessary to accomplish the agency's purposes. The court ruled that article IV, section 3, of the North Carolina constitution allows an agency to exercise discretion in setting the amount of the penalty, provided that the legislature authorizes a range for the penalties and sets guiding standards. The court upheld a penalty of $4200 for violation of the Sedimentation Pollution Control Act that had been assessed for violations resulting from grading 2.5 acres for a street in an eighteen-acre subdivision in Caldwell County.

Finch v. City of Durham, 325 N.C. 352, 384 S.E.2d 8 (1989)
Downzoning; Takings

This case involved the city's rezoning of a 2.6-acre parcel adjacent to I-85 from an office-institutional to a residential district. The property was originally zoned for residential use, was rezoned for office use in 1979, and was rezoned back to residential use in 1985. The plaintiff contended that the 1985 rezoning had reduced the value of the property from $550,000 (if used for a proposed motel) to $20,000 (if used as one single-family lot). The city contended that other valuable uses were also available, including a church, a day-care site, or additional single-family lots. A jury found a taking but awarded no damages. The trial court then granted a judgment notwithstanding the verdict as to damages, invalidated the rezoning, and awarded $150,937 in damages. The supreme court reaffirmed the test that there is no taking unless the owner is deprived of all practical use of the property and the property is rendered of no reasonable value. Deprivation of previously held property rights and diminution of value do not in and of themselves constitute a taking. The court found that the ordinance had a reasonable nexus to a legitimate public objective, that alternative rezonings such as clustered residential had been proposed by the city but not pursued by the owner, and that the property in any event retained practical use and reasonable value.

State *ex rel.* Rhodes v. Gaskill, 325 N.C. 424, 383 S.E.2d 923 (1989)
Coastal Area Management Act; Enforcement; Mootness

A consent judgment providing for restoration of an excavated pond in wetlands and a civil penalty was reached while the case was pending before the supreme court. Therefore, on its own motion the court dismissed the case as moot.

State *ex rel.* Rhodes v. Simpson, 325 N.C. 514, 385 S.E.2d 329 (1989)
Coastal Area Management Act; Enforcement; Jury trial

The court held that the defendant did not have a right to trial by jury in an enforcement action brought under the Coastal Area Management Act and the dredge-and-fill statute. The right to a jury trial applies only to actions respecting property for which the right existed either by common law or by statute as of the 1868 adoption of the state constitution (or had been subsequently created by statute).

Batch v. Town of Chapel Hill, 326 N.C. 1, 387 S.E.2d 655, *cert. denied*, 496 U.S. 931 (1990)
Exactions; Subdivisions

The town denied approval for an eleven-lot, twenty-acre subdivision. The grounds for the denial included failure to accommodate a proposed major parkway included in the town's adopted thoroughfare plan that ran through the property. The trial court and the court of appeals ruled that the denial was based on a demand for an unconstitutional taking. The supreme court first ruled that the trial court had improperly made additional findings of fact, noting that, as an appellate body making a review of the town's quasi-judicial plat approval, it can only review whether the town board's findings were supported by competent evidence in the record. The court held that there was sufficient evidence in the record to support a finding that the development had not taken into account present and future road plans as set forth in the adopted thoroughfare plan. A requirement to coordinate plans was within the statutory power of the town and was not tantamount to a compulsory dedication. If there was a single valid ground for denial, it was unnecessary to review the other grounds. Because the court ruled that there had been a valid permit denial on adequate and independent state grounds, it also dismissed the federal statutory and constitutional claims.

River Birch Associates v. City of Raleigh, 326 N.C. 100, 388 S.E.2d 538 (1990)
Exactions; Open space; Subdivisions

The city denied approval of a plat for a twenty-four-unit townhouse development on a three-acre parcel. The denial was based on a finding that the site had previously been shown as open space on a preliminary plat approved for a larger development that included this site. The rest of the site had previously been developed in accordance with the preliminary plat. The court ruled that the city's statutory authority to require the dedication or the reservation of open space included the authority to compel conveyance of the open space to a homeowners' association. The court ruled that preliminary plat approval had given the developers substantial rights, including the right to construct improvements and the vested right to complete the project once substantial expenditures had been made in good-faith reliance on the approval. Once the developers exercised those rights, they were bound by the preliminary plat even if it exceeded the minimum requirements of the city, and they could not revert to the minimum standards unless a plan amendment was approved by the city. The required conveyance of open space was held not to be a taking because it was reasonably related to the valid purpose of preserving urban open space.

Sofran Corp. v. City of Greensboro, 327 N.C. 125, 393 S.E.2d 767 (1990)
Amendments; Notice

The city rezoned an eighteen-acre tract from industrial and residential to commercial use. The zoning amendment was initially adopted on April 17. The city council reconsidered the adoption and again voted for the rezoning on May 15. The city charter allowed petitions to be filed to mandate repeal or referenda on certain ordinances, including rezoning. Such petitions were required to be filed within thirty days of the adoption of the ordinance. In this instance, the petition was filed fifty-eight days after the April 17 vote but within thirty days of the May 15 vote. The council voted to rescind the rezoning on August 7. The court ruled that the referendum petition had not been filed on time because the thirty days had to run from the amendment's initial adoption. The court also ruled that the August 7 repeal was invalid because the requirements of public notice and a hearing for zoning actions had not been followed.

Lynn v. Overlook Development, 328 N.C. 689, 403 S.E.2d 469 (1991)
Building permits and inspection; Certificate of compliance; Enforcement

The plaintiff occupied a structure for which a building permit, but not a certificate of compliance, had been secured. After the plaintiff moved in, numerous defects were discovered, resulting in the subsequent condemnation of the unit. The court dismissed the action against the city of Asheville because the plaintiff's election to take title and assume occupancy before a final inspection or before issuance of a certificate of occupancy was an intervening, independent cause of the plaintiff's damages; thus, there was no proximate cause for a negligence claim against the city.

Concerned Citizens of Brunswick County Taxpayers Ass'n v. Holden Beach Enterprises, Inc., 329 N.C. 37, 404 S.E.2d 677 (1991)

Easements

The plaintiffs claimed a prescriptive easement to secure access to Shallotte Inlet in the town of Holden Beach. Some 3700 feet of the 5400-foot sandy trail involved had been paved and closed to the public as a private subdivision road. The court held that a prescriptive easement over a dynamic area of windswept sands subject to ocean flooding might be established even if the exact path used changed over time. The requirement is that there must be substantial identity of the location of the trail. The court also held that seasonal use of the accessway and ineffective attempts by the owners to halt public use had not disrupted the continuous use required for a prescriptive easement.

Northwestern Financial Group, Inc. v. County of Gaston, 329 N.C. 180, 405 S.E.2d 138 (1991)

Manufactured housing; Vested rights

Gaston County adopted a mobile-home-park ordinance effective July 1986. An updated version of the ordinance was adopted effective September 1987. The updated ordinance provided that plans submitted before the effective date of the new ordinance would be considered under the old ordinance. The court held that when a plan had been submitted before the effective date of the amendments, it had to be considered under the old ordinance, and that right was not waived by the subsequent submittal of plan revisions when the revisions were made in response to or at the request of regulatory review agencies. The court further held that when a project meets all of the objective standards in the ordinance, it cannot be denied on a general finding that it is a hazard to the public welfare.

Town of Pine Knoll Shores v. Evans, 331 N.C. 361, 416 S.E.2d 4 (1991)

Enforcement

The defendant constructed an unattached deck between his house and a canal without first securing a building permit. The town contended that the deck violated zoning provisions prohibiting a separate structure on the lot and the minimum setback from the canal. The trial court ruled the project to be in violation of the zoning ordinance but ordered that the deck could remain in place upon payment of a $2000 civil penalty. The court held that the ordinance prohibited buildings and decks in the setback area and rejected application of the doctrine of "economic waste" to justify allowing the violating structure to remain in place. Also, the court of appeals had held that the trial court had had no authority to substitute a civil penalty for an order of abatement because the city's ordinance itself had specifically to provide for civil penalties pursuant to G.S. 160A-175 in order for that enforcement tool to be available (and this ordinance did not authorize civil penalties). This latter issue was not appealed to the supreme court.

State *ex rel.* Cobey v. Simpson, 333 N.C. 81, 423 S.E.2d 759 (1992)

Coastal Area Management Act; Enforcement

Administrative rules adopted under the Coastal Area Management Act required violations to be corrected by restoring a site to its predevelopment condition. The act also authorized the enforcing agency to seek injunctive relief in the judicial system and authorized such other relief as the court deemed proper. The court held that the trial court erred in allowing the violator to make only partial restoration, given that the state had sought full restoration. When there was no evidence that complete restoration was impractical in an environmental and engineering sense, the trial court cannot reduce the economic costs of restoration to the violator by allowing partial restoration.

Ocean Hill Joint Venture v. North Carolina Department of Environment, Health, & Natural Resources, 333 N.C. 318, 426 S.E.2d 274 (1993)

Sedimentation; Statutes of limitation

The court held that the one-year statute of limitations (G.S. 1-54(2)) does not apply to the assessment of a civil penalty for a sedimentation violation.

Capricorn Equity Corp. v. Town of Chapel Hill, 334 N.C. 132, 431 S.E.2d 183 (1993)
Findings; Interpretation; Judicial review

The issue presented was whether a particular structure should be considered a "duplex" (a permitted use) or a "rooming house" (a use requiring a site plan prior to approval) under the town zoning ordinance. Each half of the structure had six bedrooms with three connecting baths, a single kitchen, and a single living room. The town staff ruled it was not a duplex and denied the permit application. The board of adjustment affirmed the staff decision, but the trial court reversed. The supreme court ruled that the superior court may not make additional findings of fact but must base its review on the record presented. The court then interpreted the ordinance, considering its language, spirit, and goals, to find the structure was a duplex as a matter of law.

Board of Adjustment v. Town of Swansboro, 334 N.C. 421, 432 S.E.2d 310 (1993)
Board of adjustment

The governing board amended the zoning ordinance to abolish the board of adjustment and then immediately reestablished a reconstituted board. The members of the original board sued, contending this action illegally shortened their terms of office. The court held that while the statutes require that a board of adjustment have three-year terms, the existence of a board of adjustment is not mandated and thus the governing board retains the option of abolishing the board at any time, provided all of the statutory procedures for zoning amendments are followed. Therefore, the governing-board action was upheld.

County of Lancaster v. Mecklenburg County, 334 N.C. 496, 434 S.E.2d 604 (1993)
Conflicts of interest; Quasi-judicial; Special uses

Adjoining counties challenged a permit for a landfill issued to Mecklenburg County by the Charlotte-Mecklenburg Building Standards Department. The court noted that special use permits may not be delegated to staff but must be determined by a board of adjustment (or other board acting as a board of adjustment) following an evidentiary hearing. The court held that staff might make findings and decide an application involving objective, nondiscretionary standards and that this permit was in the latter class. On conflicts of interest, the court noted that due process requires nonparticipation in legislative zoning decisions if a board member has a direct and substantial financial interest and also requires nonparticipation in quasi-judicial zoning decisions if the member has a financial interest, a close relationship with the parties, or a bias. Absent a showing of undue influence, administrative zoning decisions can be made by a staff member of an employing unit of government. [Note: This conflict-of-interest standard was subsequently codified as G.S. 160D-109(a).]

Homebuilders Ass'n of Charlotte v. City of Charlotte, 336 N.C. 37, 442 S.E.2d 45 (1994)
Delegation; Fees

The plaintiff challenged Charlotte's authority to impose user fees for a variety of city services, including rezonings, special use permits, plat reviews, and building inspections. The court upheld imposition of the fees even though the city had no express statutory authority to impose them, ruling that G.S. 160A-4 requires that grants of authority to cities be interpreted broadly to include additional and supplementary powers that are expedient to execution of the city's regulatory powers. The court noted that such fees must be reasonable, generally not to exceed the cost of the regulatory program. [Note: This fee authorization was subsequently codified as G.S. 160D-402(d).]

Naegele Outdoor Advertising, Inc. v. Harrelson, 336 N.C. 66, 442 S.E.2d 32 (1994), *per curiam, reversing and adopting dissent in* 112 N.C. App. 98, 434 S.E.2d 244 (1993)
Signs

The question presented was whether the temporary visibility of a junkyard during highway construction renders an unzoned area a "commercial area" so as to allow placement of outdoor advertising. The Department of Transportation (DOT) denied applications for billboards in the area at issue, contending that commercial activities were not visible prior to construction and that screening of the site was planned at the conclusion of the construction. The trial court ruled for the sign company, and the court of appeals affirmed. In a per curiam opinion, the court reversed the court of appeals, adopting the dissent as the rationale for the decision. The dissent in the court of appeals had noted that the department had an obligation to screen the junkyard that was made visible by the road construction and that the department's rules provide that temporary visibility during construction does not render a site commercial or industrial for purposes of the Outdoor Advertising Control Act.

Capital Outdoor Advertising, Inc. v. City of Raleigh, 337 N.C. 150, 446 S.E.2d 289 (1994)
Amortization

The plaintiff sign companies owned fifty-six off-premise signs subject to the city's October 1983 ordinance that restricted the size of signs, mandated minimum separation between signs, and limited their location to industrial zoning districts. The ordinance required nonconforming signs to be brought into compliance within a five-and-a-half-year amortization period. This suit challenging the constitutionality of the ordinance was filed in April 1989, more than three years after the ordinance took effect. The court held that the cause of action accrued as of the date of enactment of the ordinance, as this was when a concrete injury to the plaintiffs occurred. As to the appropriate statute of limitations to apply, the court noted that cases applying the nine-month limitations period for challenging legislative zoning decisions seemed better reasoned than those applying the three-year personal-injury statute; however, since this action met neither time period, the issue was not decided.

Empire Power Co. v. North Carolina Department of Environment, Health, & Natural Resources, 337 N.C. 569, 447 S.E.2d 768 (1994)
Appeals

This case addressed the issue of whether the Administrative Procedure Act provides for a contested-case review for third parties if the substantive act involved is silent on this issue. The court held that the Administrative Procedure Act confers upon any "person aggrieved" the right to commence a contested-case appeal (in this instance, an appeal to the Environmental Management Commission challenging issuance of an air-quality permit).

North Buncombe Association of Concerned Citizens v. North Carolina Department of Environment, Health, & Natural Resources, 338 N.C. 302, 449 S.E.2d 451 (1994)
Appeals

A citizens group appealed a mining permit issued to Vulcan Materials, Inc., for a quarry in Buncombe County. The trial court ruled the permit invalid because the state had not complied with a Buncombe County provision requiring an environmental-impact statement. The court of appeals reversed because the petitioner had not first pursued a contested case through the Office of Administrative Hearings. The petitioner then filed an appeal with the Office of Administrative Hearings, which allowed the appeal and then dismissed it as not being filed in a timely manner. On this second appeal, the court of appeals held that there was no right to an administrative hearing before the office. On appeal, the court held that the Administrative Procedure Act allows for third-party contested-case reviews of mining-permit decisions. The case was again remanded to superior court for a hearing as to whether the filing of the petition for review was timely.

Naegele Outdoor Advertising, Inc. v. City of Winston-Salem, 340 N.C. 349, 457 S.E.2d 874 (1995) (per curiam)
Amortization; Signs

The city adopted a seven-year amortization requirement for non-conforming off-premise signs. The amortization requirement was adopted in 1985 and this action was filed in 1992, shortly after the amortization period expired. The court held that the statute of limitations for an action challenging this requirement began to run upon adoption of the amortization provision. The court expressed no opinion as to whether the appropriate statute to apply was the nine-month zoning statute of limitation or the two-year provision of G.S. § 40A-51, as neither was met in this case.

Save Our Rivers, Inc. v. Town of Highlands, 341 N.C. 635, 461 S.E.2d 333 (1995)
Appellate procedures; Standing

The court ruled that a petition for judicial review under the Administrative Procedure Act must explicitly state the exceptions taken and the relief requested. The court held that where proposed new evidence is cumulative and not materially different from that offered in the original hearing, it is inappropriate to remand for taking the additional evidence.

Gwathmey v. State, 342 N.C. 287, 464 S.E.2d 674 (1996)
Public-trust doctrine; Wetlands

This case involved disputed title to regularly flooded marshlands in New Hanover County. The State Board of Education between 1926 and 1945 had conveyed title to the areas to private parties. The state contended that lands between high and low tides were subject to the public-trust doctrine and could not have been conveyed in fee simple. The court held that "navigability" is determined not by an ebb-and-flow test (whether the waters are subject to lunar tides) but, rather, by whether the waters are navigable in fact by pleasure or commercial watercraft, even if those waters have not been used for such purposes. The court held that the General Assembly could by special act convey fee title to submerged lands subject to the public-trust doctrine, though there was a rebuttable presumption that it had not done so. However, such a grant free of public-trust restrictions must be made in clear and express terms. The court held that the authority delegated to the State Board of Education to convey marsh and swampland did not include an express provision allowing sale free of public-trust rights. The court remanded the case for further findings as to whether the waters and marshland involved were navigable in fact.

Appalachian Poster Advertising Co. v. Harrington, 343 N.C. 303, 469 S.E.2d 554 (1996), *per curiam, reversing and adopting dissent in* 120 N.C. App. 72, 460 S.E.2d 887 (1995)
Delegation; Signs

The plaintiff had a billboard adjacent to Interstate 40 in McDowell County that was lawfully in existence prior to the enactment of the Outdoor Advertising Control Act. The state Department of Transportation (DOT) revoked the sign permit when the company replaced the sign face, sign poles, and cross bracing. In this per curiam decision, the court reversed the court of appeals' decision below and adopted that court's dissent. That opinion held that the DOT had authority under G.S. 136-130 and 136-133 to regulate replacement or repair of lawful nonconforming signs as well as the erection of new signs. The opinion also held that the plaintiff's sign had been substantially changed, that a requirement that the sign not be "substantially" changed was not unduly vague, and that the policies in the Outdoor Advertising Control Act provided adequate guiding standards for the DOT Secretary in administering the law.

Three Guys Real Estate v. Harnett County, 345 N.C. 468, 480 S.E.2d 681 (1997)
Subdivisions; Interpretation

The owner of a 231.37-acre parcel proposed to divide the land into twenty-three lots and proposed no street rights-of-way or other access to the lots. A revised plat was filed after suit showing access to each lot by a series of private-driveway easements. The owner contended that the subdivision was exempt from county regulation in that each proposed lot was greater than ten acres and no public rights-of-way were proposed. The county refused to approve the plat filing, contending that the subdivision did not qualify for exemption. The trial court agreed, finding that the private driveways would be open for public use and the county could regulate the division under its subdivision authority. The court of appeals reversed the findings that the private easements constituted a street right-of-way but held that county approval could be withheld if the development posed a danger to the public health, safety, and welfare. The court reversed. The court concluded that the statutory exemption is clear and unambiguous: if all lots created by a subdivision exceed ten acres and there is no public-right-of-way dedication involved, the subdivision is exempt from any and all county subdivision regulation.

Messer v. Town of Chapel Hill, 346 N.C. 259, 485 S.E.2d 269 (1997)
Mootness; Takings

The owners of a 150-acre tract brought this action to challenge a rezoning that reduced the allowed residential density from three units per acre to one unit per five acres. The owners contended that the value of the property was $3 million prior to the rezoning and that after the rezoning the development costs would exceed the sales value of the five-acre lots. The court of appeals upheld dismissal of the takings and due-process claims on ripeness grounds, noting that the owners had not filed a development plan nor sought a variance. While on appeal the owners sold the property for $1.5 million. The court ruled that this sale rendered the suit moot, as the plaintiffs no longer had any development interests in the property and the receipt of $1.5 million "establishes beyond peradventure" that the property had a practical use and a reasonable value, and a mere diminution in value, even if severe, is not an unconstitutional taking.

Cates v. Department of Justice, 346 N.C. 781, 487 S.E.2d 723 (1997)
Liability

The court held that the state is not required to defend a sanitarian alleged to have conducted negligent preliminary site evaluations for septic tank suitability. In this instance, a Durham County sanitarian provided a preliminary evaluation of a site and determined that forty-nine lots were suitable for on-site septic tanks. Based on this, a developer purchased the tract and marketed lots. It was later determined that twenty of the forty-nine lots were not suitable. The sanitarian sought state-provided counsel under G.S. 130A-4(b). The state refused to provide counsel for the sanitarian on the grounds that in performing a preliminary soil evaluation, the sanitarian was not enforcing state rules. The court held that since there are no provisions for preliminary evaluations under state law or rules, and since this was done strictly as a local service, the state had no obligation to provide counsel.

Town of Spruce Pine v. Avery County, 346 N.C. 787, 488 S.E.2d 144 (1997)

Delegation; Watershed protection

This suit was brought by the Town of Spruce Pine (which is in Mitchell County) against neighboring Avery County and involved a dispute over the city's proposed location of a new water-supply intake in the North Toe River (which would trigger a requirement that Avery County adopt a watershed-protection ordinance). In 1988, the city asked the Environmental Management Commission (EMC) to reclassify the North Toe for water supply purposes. The EMC agreed. In 1993, the county denied the city's building-permit application for a water-supply intake, prompting the city to file this suit against the county. The county countersued, contending that the watershed act is unconstitutional. The city prevailed at the trial court level in 1994. The legislature passed a bill in 1995 that required the EMC to place the watershed in a less restrictive WS-IV class, and this was done. The county also agreed to allow the intake to be constructed. But the litigation on the constitutionality of the state law requiring local watershed-protection ordinances continued. The court of appeals held that the level of guidance the General Assembly provided to the EMC for its rulemaking was inadequate and was thus an unlawful delegation of legislative authority to the executive branch of state government.

The court reversed and upheld the water-supply-protection statute. The court noted that the legislative standards need only be as specific as the circumstances permit and that procedural safeguards can be used to assure adherence to legislative standards where precise standards are not appropriate. The court recognized the complexity of watershed classification and management, the general goals for water quality standards in G.S. 143-211, the direction in G.S. 143-214.5 to use density limits and/or performance standards to regulate watershed development to protect water quality, and the detailed rulemaking-hearing requirements of G.S. Chapter 150B as adequate for legislative guidance on the exercise of this delegated power. The parties in this case agreed that subsequent legislation that exempted a single watershed from the coverage of the state watershed-protection program was adopted without a rational basis. The court noted that while this may well make the legislation making that exemption unconstitutional, it does not invalidate the basic watershed-protection statute.

Martin Marietta Technologies, Inc. v. Brunswick County, 348 N.C. 688, 500 S.E.2d 665 (1998)

Appeals; Preemption; Vested rights

Brunswick County adopted an ordinance prohibiting the use of explosives and dewatering in any mining operation located within five miles of the Brunswick nuclear plant or the Sunny Point military ammunition depot. The ordinance would have precluded a Martin Marietta open-pit limestone mine proposed to be located in these areas. The trial court held that Martin Marietta had established vested rights, that state law preempted the county ordinance, and that the ordinance was void due to failure of the county to follow appropriate notice procedures. The court of appeals ruled that the county's appeal of this judgment was interlocutory and must be dismissed and that a state mining-permit decision, which had not yet been made, was necessary to determine whether there was any conflict between the state and local regulatory provisions. The court reversed and remanded for a decision on the merits of the case.

Beechridge Development Co., LLC v. Dahners, 350 N.C. 583, 516 S.E.2d 592 (1999)

Easements; Subdivisions

A Chapel Hill subdivision platted in 1966 had two easements running along its outer boundary. The easement along the southern boundary was denominated a "public easement" on the plat, while the easement on the northern boundary was labeled a "sanitary sewer easement." In 1997, the adjacent property owner sought a declaratory judgment that the southern easement could be used by the local water-and-sewer authority for the installation of a sanitary sewer to serve development of the adjacent property.

The trial court used extrinsic evidence (primarily public records related to city approval of the subdivision) to find that the "public easement" could be used for a sanitary sewer. The court of appeals reversed, ruling that it was improper for the court to consider extrinsic evidence when the terms on the plat were not ambiguous (and holding that the term "public easement" did not include a sewer easement to serve an adjacent private development). The court reversed in a per curiam opinion, ruling that while the term "public easement" was indeed not ambiguous, it encompasses a wide variety of uses, including a sanitary-sewer line.

Smith Chapel Baptist Church v. City of Durham, 350 N.C. 805, 517 S.E.2d 874 (1999), *superseding* 348 N.C. 632, 502 S.E.2d 364 (1998)

Delegation

As part of its stormwater-management program, the city assessed fees on all developed property, with the fees based on the impervious area of the assessed land.

In its original 1998 opinion, the court upheld the authority of the city to impose fees to operate its program. The court held that while the public-enterprise statutes did not give the city authority to impose these fees, the authority could be based on the state constitutional provision (article XIV, section 5) establishing protection of the environment as a proper function of local governments and G.S. 160A-4, which gives cities the supplementary power to impose reasonable fees to put the program into implementation.

After a rehearing, the court issued a new opinion, holding that the plain language of G.S. 160A-314(a1) provides that city stormwater utility fees are limited to the costs of providing a stormwater and drainage system (rather than the full cost of maintaining a comprehensive stormwater-quality-management program). The court found that costs associated with educational programs, guidance manuals, used-oil recycling, household-hazardous-waste collection, and litter-enforcement programs could not be funded through use of these fees (though they could be funded through the general fund). The court upheld basing the amount of stormwater fees on the amount of impervious area of the property as rational, reasonable, and within the statutory authority of G.S. 160A-314.

Parker v. Barefoot, 351 N.C. 40, 519 S.E.2d 315 (1999), *per curiam, reversing and adopting dissent in* 130 N.C. App. 18, 502 S.E.2d 42 (1998)

Nuisances

The defendant operated a hog farm adjacent to the plaintiff's lands. The ninety-five-acre hog facility had four hog houses, 2880 hogs, and an open lagoon for waste disposal. This action alleged that noxious odors from the facility constituted a nuisance. At trial, the jury found for the defendant. The majority opinion of the court of appeals ordered a new trial because the trial judge had refused to issue an instruction to the jury that installation of state-of-the-art technology was not a defense to a nuisance claim. The dissent, adopted by the court, affirmed the trial court on the grounds that the proposed instruction, while legally accurate, was not warranted by the facts and had played little if any role in the jury's decision.

Northfield Development Co., Inc. v. City of Burlington, 352 N.C. 671, 535 S.E.2d 32 (2000)

Evidence; Manufactured housing; Standing

The plaintiff company unsuccessfully sought the rezoning of two tracts to a manufactured-home overlay district. This district was "permitted by right" in three specified residential zoning districts. One of the tracts was sold by the plaintiff prior to the instant litigation, with a provision in the sales contract that the price of the land would be increased a specified amount if the rezoning was approved by a specified date.

The court of appeals held that the plaintiff had standing to challenge the rezoning, as the additional sales price constituted the requisite specific personal and legal interest in the matter that directly and adversely affected the plaintiff. The court held that the rezoning denial did not violate the mandate of G.S. 160D-910 that municipalities not exclude manufactured housing from the jurisdiction, as two other manufactured-housing overlay districts had been approved by the city. The statute does not create a mandate for a "substantial presence" of manufactured homes, the court found; rather, it prohibits a total exclusion. The court held that the decision to create the overlay district was most analogous to a quasi-judicial decision and that the mayor was thus entitled to a quasi-judicial testimonial privilege and could not be deposed regarding his actions, intentions, or motives regarding the decision. The case was remanded on the question of whether the decisions made pertaining to the denial were arbitrary and capricious.

On appeal, the court affirmed in a per curiam opinion the court of appeals' majority opinion on the statutory-interpretation issue and dismissed other aspects of the appeal as improvidently allowed.

Westminster Homes, Inc. v. Town of Cary Zoning Board of Adjustment, 354 N.C. 298, 554 S.E.2d 634 (2001)
Interpretation

Plaintiffs applied for and were granted a conditional use rezoning and concurrent special use permit for a single-family residential development at a density higher than allowed by the previous zoning. One permit condition required construction of a seven-foot-high fence located forty-five feet off the property line. The permit required a fifty-foot natural and undisturbed buffer along the property line and included detailed specifications for the fence, with a deed disclosure to purchasers regarding the placement, integrity, and maintenance of the fence. The town issued notices of violation when home purchasers in the development subsequently installed gates in this fence. The board of adjustment upheld the zoning officer's determination that the permit provisions did not allow construction of gates in this fence.

The court affirmed. The court noted that the more specific terms of a special use permit can be and typically are used to place additional project-specific restrictions, and here a close and careful reading of the permit indicated an intention to have a fence without gates to provide privacy and a wide, comprehensive buffer. The court noted that the petitioners voluntarily agreed to the buffer and could not subsequently attack it as a taking.

Good Neighbors of South Davidson v. Town of Denton, 355 N.C. 254, 559 S.E.2d 768 (2002)
Spot zoning

Piedmont Chemical Industries owned fifty acres in Davidson County on which they operated a chemical-storage facility. Upon adoption of county zoning for the property, the property was placed in a rural agricultural district and the facility became a nonconforming use. After two unsuccessful attempts to have the county rezone the property to industrial use, the company sought satellite annexation from the Town of Denton (the principal corporate limits were over two miles away). Shortly after the 1998 satellite annexation, the town zoned ten acres of the site as light industry and forty acres as heavy industry.

The court held this to be illegal spot zoning. The court confirmed that unlike regular rezoning, spot zoning does not enjoy a presumption of validity; a clearly established reasonable basis must support it. The court applied the spot zoning reasonableness analysis it had enumerated in *Chrismon v. Guilford County*, 322 N.C. 611, 370 S.E.2d 579 (1988), finding the following factors to be persuasive: (1) the property had been reclassified from the county's most restrictive to the town's least restrictive district; (2) there was no evidence that the town rezoning was consistent with a comprehensive plan; (3) while there were benefits of the rezoning for the owner, there were no corresponding benefits for neighbors or the surrounding community and substantial potential negative impacts on the neighbors. Further, the court held that the analysis of relative benefits and detriments of the spot zoning must include analysis of the area and persons actually affected, not just those within the rezoning government's jurisdiction. The fact that this property was a satellite annexation and the town was politically insulated from the neighbors' concerns led the court to be particularly sensitive to this balancing of benefits and detriments.

Capital Outdoor, Inc. v. Guilford County Board of Adjustment, 355 N.C. 269, 559 S.E.2d 547 (2002), *per curiam, reversing* 146 N.C. App. 388, 552 S.E.2d 265 (2001)
Interpretation; Signs

The Guilford County zoning ordinance prohibited billboards within 300 feet of "any residentially zoned property." The plaintiff applied for a permit for a sign within 300 feet of an "agricultural" zoning district, a district primarily intended to accommodate agricultural uses but which allowed residences as a use of right. The staff denied the permit. The board of adjustment affirmed that interpretation of the ordinance and denied a variance.

A divided court of appeals remanded because it could not determine which standard of review the court had applied to which portions of its judgment. The majority noted that a de novo review is proper for alleged errors of law, while a whole-record review is appropriate for allegations that the decision was unsupported by the evidence or was arbitrary and capricious. The dissent contended that since the appellate court was reviewing for errors of law (the interpretation of the terms of the ordinance), it did not matter what standard of review the trial court had employed.

On appeal, the court in a per curiam opinion adopted the dissenting opinion as to the standard of review and remanded for consideration of the proper interpretation of the ordinance.

Mann Media, Inc. v. Randolph County Planning Board, 356 N.C. 1, 565 S.E.2d 9 (2002)
Evidence; Special uses; Telecommunication towers

The plaintiff applied for a special use permit to construct a 1500-foot telecommunication tower. The zoning-ordinance standards for special use permits required the planning board to find that the use would not materially endanger the public health or safety, that it would not substantially injure adjoining- and abutting-property values, and that the location and character of the use would be in harmony with the area proposed for siting.

The court upheld the permit denial, noting that the central issue presented was whether there was competent, substantial, and material evidence in the record to support a permit denial. The planning board's finding relative to public safety was based on a conclusion that ice forming and falling from a tower at the proposed location would endanger the public safety due to the number and density of adjoining residences. The court held that under a whole-record review, this conclusion must stand unless it is arbitrary and capricious. On this point, the court held that anecdotal hearsay offered by opponents was not competent to establish a hazard but that the applicant had failed to carry his burden that the ice would not pose a safety risk (citing testimony by the applicant stating that while danger from falling ice was not likely, he could not guarantee it was not a risk). Because the applicant failed to show that the public-safety standard would be met, the applicant had not established a prima facie case necessary to compel competing evidence to support a denial.

The court also noted that since the applicant's witness on property-value impacts failed to specifically address impacts on properties adjoining or abutting telecommunication towers, his testimony did not establish that the project would not harm such properties' value. The court was skeptical about the use of testimony regarding property values from both the opponents (who offered testimony from a real-estate agent and a contractor) and the applicant (who offered the professional appraiser), as neither had data from comparable properties adjacent to a tower.

On the question of whether the proposed tower was in harmony with the surrounding area, the court agreed that a de novo review of this question was appropriate (since such an interpretation question is an alleged error of law) and that inclusion of a use as a special use in a zoning district establishes a prima facie case that it is harmonious. However, since other standards for the permit were not met, the court declined to address the sufficiency of evidence on this particular finding.

Craig v. County of Chatham, 356 N.C. 40, 565 S.E.2d 172 (2002)
Agricultural uses; Preemption

The plaintiff challenged the county's authority to adopt three ordinances regulating swine farms: (1) a swine ordinance adopted under the general police powers of the county; (2) an identical ordinance adopted as a board-of-health rule; and (3) zoning regulations on large hog farms. The swine ordinance and the board-of-health rule established setback distances and buffers for swine farms and waste-disposal spray fields for those farms with 250 or more pigs. These requirements were more stringent than state regulations. The ordinances also required a financial guarantee for waste-lagoon cleanup and violation remediation.

The court held that the state laws on hog farms provide a complete and integrated system of regulation that evidences an intent to occupy the entire field to the exclusion of local regulation. The court examined the statements of intent and purpose in the state legislation and considered the burden on farmers that would be occasioned by dual state and local regulation. Statements of purpose in the law regarding the need for a coordinated state-management program that minimizes burdens on farmers were important in establishing legislative intent, as was the breadth and scope of state regulation. The court held that more-stringent board-of-health regulations could only be imposed if there are specific reasons clearly related to a local health need, and in this case no such need beyond state Environmental Management Commission rules had been established. The court noted that counties had been delegated authority to regulate some large-scale hog farms through zoning and that a restriction of such operations to specified zoning districts is acceptable. However, since the challenged zoning ordinance made compliance with the preempted swine ordinance a precondition of zoning approval, it was also invalid.

Morris Communications Corp. v. City of Asheville, 356 N.C. 103, 565 S.E.2d 70 (2002)
Protest petitions; Signs

The city council unanimously adopted a requirement that off-premise signs be limited to six square feet. The council then, by a four-to-three vote, adopted a seven-year amortization requirement for all nonconforming signs. The plaintiff, who owned "a vast majority" of the signs required to be amortized, had filed a protest petition objecting to this zoning-text amendment.

To be valid, a protest petition must be signed by the owners of 20 percent of the "area of the lots included in a proposed change." The issue in this case was the proper delineation of this area. The city determined that there were existing off-premise signs on 244 acres, there were 4928 acres in the city zoned to allow off-premise signs, and the entire city zoning jurisdiction was 32,700 acres. The plaintiff contended that the 20 percent calculation should be based on 244 acres; the city contended that 32,700 acres was the proper denominator for the calculation.

The court held for the plaintiff, reasoning that in this narrow circumstance the only immediate and actual effect of the amendment was the eventual removal of existing nonconforming signs, so these are the only lot owners who should be considered "included in a proposed change." Since the city failed to apply this calculation, it failed to meet its affirmative obligation to calculate the sufficiency of the protest petitions. Therefore, the court held that since there was not a three-fourths majority in favor of the amendment, its enactment was invalid. [Note: The protest-petition provisions were subsequently repealed.]

Guilford Financial Services, LLC v. City of Brevard, 356 N.C. 655, 576 S.E.2d 325 (2003), *per curiam, adopting dissent in* 150 N.C. App. 1, 563 S.E.2d 27 (2002)
Evidence; Quasi-judicial; Subdivisions

The petitioner sought approval of a project to place a twenty-eight-unit affordable-housing project on a five-acre site. The proposal involved a preliminary plat. The city's technical advisory committee recommended approval. The planning board met twice to consider the plat. Neighbors appeared and objected, raising concerns about traffic, safety, and consistency with the land use plan and subdivision ordinance. The planning board eventually recommended approval of a revised plat. The town council then held two hearings on the plat, with considerable neighborhood opposition being raised. A third revised plat was submitted in response to concerns raised, but ultimately the council denied plat approval, citing concerns about impacts on consistency with zoning requirements regarding concentration of two-family dwellings and impacts on public health and safety.

The majority opinion in the court of appeals held that since the subdivision ordinance included discretionary standards, this preliminary plat approval was a quasi-judicial decision. The majority would have remanded for a hearing and findings consistent with the due-process requirements. The dissent agreed that the decision was quasi-judicial in nature but held that a remand was unnecessary. The court noted that both parties were represented by counsel and had ample opportunity to present evidence. Since neither party requested that witnesses be under oath or be cross-examined, and neither requested an opportunity to present rebuttal evidence, those rights were deemed waived. The dissent held that the evidence relied upon by the council to support its denial was inadequate in that (1) evidence on traffic impact showed an imperceptible impact, not a threat to public safety; (2) as a matter of law, when duplexes are allowed by right in a zoning district, a statement in the "Purposes" section of the ordinance that duplexes be "unconcentrated" cannot be the basis of a denial of approval when the specific density standards for the zoning district are not violated; and (3) generalized opinions about traffic safety for children or impacts on neighbors cannot be the basis for a finding. Since the applicant made a prima facie case for approval and there was no substantial evidence supporting denial, the appropriate resolution was an order directing plat approval rather than a remand.

The court adopted the dissent in a per curiam opinion.

Dobo v. Zoning Board of Adjustment, 356 N.C. 656, 576 S.E.2d 324 (2003), *per curiam, adopting dissent in* 149 N.C. App. 701, 562 S.E.2d 108 (2002)

Accessory buildings and uses; Appellate procedures; Evidence

In 1996, the petitioners bought and installed a sawmill in their backyard. The sawmill was used to produce lumber to construct outbuildings and walkways on the property and to make furniture. Some lumber was given away to friends and relatives, but none was sold. In 1999, the property was annexed by Wilmington. The city cited the petitioners for a zoning violation, contending the sawmill was not a lawful accessory use. The board of adjustment upheld that determination.

The court of appeals held that the board of adjustment and the trial court correctly refused to consider the petitioners' constitutional claims. In making a quasi-judicial review of the zoning officer's interpretation of the ordinance, the board of adjustment could only reverse, affirm, or modify the decision; it had no authority to address challenges to the validity of the ordinance. A constitutional challenge to the validity of the ordinance could only be considered in a separate civil action, not a certiorari review of a zoning official's determination. The court also held that if there is sufficient competent, substantial, and material evidence in the whole record to support the board's findings, the presence of other arguably incompetent evidence does not deprive the petitioners of a fair hearing.

The court of appeals, however, split on the question of whether the board's decision should be upheld. The majority opinion was that there was substantial, competent, and material evidence in the record to support the board's decision that a sawmill of this size is not customarily incidental and subordinate to the primary residential use of the property, regardless of whether there were commercial sales of its products. The dissent contended that the actual use of the sawmill was the critical inquiry rather than its size and potential use. In this respect, since all of the evidence was that no actual commercial or industrial use had been made, the sawmill was a legitimate accessory use.

The court adopted the position of the dissent in a per curiam opinion.

North Carolina Forestry Ass'n v. North Carolina Department of Environment & Natural Resources, 357 N.C. 640, 588 S.E.2d 880 (2003)

Standing

In 1998, the defendant department issued a general permit for stormwater discharges associated with industrial activities. Unlike a previous general permit, this general permit excluded new or expanding wood-chip mills from its coverage, requiring these entities to undergo a lengthier individual permit review. The plaintiff nonprofit trade association, whose members operate wood-chip mills, petitioned for a contested-case hearing to challenge this determination. While an administrative-law judge recommended finding that the plaintiff had standing as a "person aggrieved," the final order adopted by the Environmental Management Commission held that the association did not have standing. The trial court ruled that the group did have standing, but the court of appeals reversed.

The court held that while neither the association nor any of its members had applied for a permit, the decision to exclude wood-chip mills from the general permit adversely affected the plaintiff and its members as a result of the change in required permitting processes. Therefore, the plaintiff was a "person aggrieved" with standing to bring a contested-case hearing.

Robins v. Town of Hillsborough, 361 N.C. 193, 639 S.E.2d 421 (2007)

Moratoria; Vested rights

The plaintiff contracted to purchase a parcel in the Hillsborough extraterritorial area and submitted a site plan for an asphalt plant on the site (this use being a permitted use subject to site-plan approval). The town board of adjustment held three hearings on the site-plan application. Prior to the fourth hearing, the town board adopted a moratorium on permitting for asphalt plants and other similar manufacturing operations. Prior to termination of the moratorium, the town council amended the zoning ordinance to prohibit asphalt plants throughout the town and the extraterritorial area. The board of adjustment thereafter terminated consideration of the plaintiff's application. The trial court upheld the town action, ruling that the moratorium was properly adopted and that the ordinance amendment prohibited approval of the plant. The court of appeals reversed, holding that the applicant had a vested right to consideration of the application under the ordinance in effect at the time a completed application was submitted. The court of appeals also held that a total ban of a particular use raised constitutional issues of arbitrary and capricious action and a denial of equal protection.

The court found that the provision in the town ordinance that the board of adjustment "*shall* pass upon, decide, or determine" applications for site-plan approval required the board to render a decision on the application and that, therefore, the termination of consideration of the application here was improper. The court held that the town could not by legislative fiat dictate the outcome of this quasi-judicial process and thus remanded the case for decision by the board under the rules in effect at the time of application. The court concluded that given this procedural requirement of the ordinance, it was unnecessary to address the constitutionality of the ordinance and that portion of the court of appeals decision was vacated. [Note: The permit-choice statute was subsequently enacted.]

Holly Ridge Associates, LLC v. North Carolina Department of Environment & Natural Resources, 361 N.C. 331, 648 S.E.2d 830 (2007)

Civil penalties; Sedimentation; Standing

The plaintiff owned a large tract in Onslow County adjacent to Stump Sound that was being developed as a resort residential community. In 1998, the plaintiff undertook a substantial ditch-excavation project (seventeen major ditches of eight miles in length over a thirty-four-acre area). In 1999, the defendant department cited the plaintiff for violations of the Sedimentation Pollution Control Act and then, following the plaintiff's failure to take corrective action, assessed a $32,100 civil penalty. In 2000, following continued failure to take corrective action, additional civil penalties totaling $118,000 were assessed. In its contested-case appeal of the penalty, the plaintiff for the first time asserted a forestry exemption for its work on the site.

The court of appeals held that allowing intervention in the contested-case appeal by the Shellfish Growers Association and the Coastal Federation was proper. Both groups adequately showed in their motions to intervene that the rights of their members may be directly affected by the outcome of the matter. The court held that admission of the department's supplemental discovery submittal and the failure of the administrative-law judge to grant a continuance were not an abuse of discretion. The court found that the administrative-law judge and trial court properly interpreted the forestry exemption to be inapplicable, as it applies only to those activities specifically undertaken for the production and harvesting of timber and not to drainage activities for other purposes.

The court reversed, holding that Rule 24 of the Rules of Civil Procedure, G.S. 1A-1, controls the issue of whether intervention as a full party should be allowed. The court found that while the groups seeking to intervene had an interest in the underlying dispute (whether the ditching activity was within the forestry exemption), they had no interest in the property in dispute here (the civil penalty imposed), so there could be no intervention by right under Rule 24(a). The court also held that permissive intervention under Rule 24(b) was inappropriate given the burden to the petitioners of an extra round of discovery. The court noted that the groups had alternative means of participation available, such as participation as amici curiae in the contested case, filing a separate state case, or intervention as less than a full party under Rule 23(d). [Note: The groups seeking to intervene successfully brought a federal action contending that the underlying activities in the Holly Ridge Associates case constituted a violation of the Clean Water Act. See *N.C. Shellfish Growers Ass'n v. Holly Ridge Assocs.*, 278 F. Supp. 2d 654 (E.D.N.C. 2003). A consent decree was subsequently entered in that case.]

Walsh v. Town of Wrightsville Beach, 361 N.C. 348, 644 S.E.2d 224 (2007) (per curiam)
Appellate procedures; Standing

The defendant town issued building permits for two single-family beach cottages on property adjacent to the plaintiff's property. The plaintiff appealed the permit issuance to the board of adjustment, which denied the appeal. The trial court dismissed the appeal for lack of standing and subject-matter jurisdiction. The court of appeals dismissed the appeal for failure to include clear record or transcript references for the assignment of error and failure by the appellate brief to reference a clear assignment of error for each question presented. The court reversed and remanded for reconsideration in light of new directions for rules for application of sanctions and discretion in application of rules of appellate procedure.

Chapel Hill Title & Abstract Co. v. Town of Chapel Hill, 362 N.C. 649, 669 S.E.2d 286 (2008)
Restrictive covenants; Variances

The plaintiffs owned a lot in Chapel Hill that was subject to both conventional zoning setbacks and further setbacks based on a resource-conservation-district (RCD) overlay. The defendant town issued a permit in 2002 for a single-family residence on the lot, with the house location meeting the town's twenty-eight-foot street-setback requirement. However, neighbors successfully enjoined construction because it violated a 1959 private restrictive covenant that required a fifty-foot street setback and set minimum lot sizes. The plaintiff acquired additional land to meet the lot size issue. However, since compliance with the restrictive covenant would push the building site back into the RCD setbacks, the plaintiff sought a zoning variance from the town. The board of adjustment denied the variance on the grounds that the hardship was created by the covenants, not the town ordinances. The trial court reversed, ruling that since the covenants were existing when the RCD provisions were adopted, it was the ordinance that effectively precluded building on the site. The court of appeals held that the board of adjustment correctly considered only the application of the ordinance in determining whether there was undue hardship to qualify for a variance.

The court held that the terms of the zoning ordinance itself compelled the board of adjustment to consider the effect of the restrictive covenant in evaluation of the variance petition. The ordinance specifically directed that the board "shall consider the uses available to the owner of the entire zoning lot" in making its determination. As the restrictive covenant prevented the owner from constructing a home outside the RCD, the owner had no reasonable use of the property outside the RCD, and the board had to consider that in its determination of the "uses available" to the owner. The court thus remanded with instructions that the variance be issued.

Mangum v. Raleigh Board of Adjustment, 362 N.C. 640, 669 S.E.2d 279 (2008)
Standing

The board of adjustment issued a special use permit for an adult establishment near the Raleigh-Durham Airport. The plaintiff adjacent-property owners filed for judicial review of the permit. Two of the three plaintiffs alleged that they were adjacent property owners and the third that she owned a nearby business that would be adversely affected. The trial court reversed the decision to grant the permit. The court of appeals, however, found that the plaintiffs did not have standing for judicial review.

The court held that while an allegation of proximity is relevant, it alone is insufficient to confer standing. A credible allegation of special damages is necessary to establish standing. The court held that allegations of parking problems, stormwater problems, and crime problems were sufficient to establish "special damages" and that evidence of property-value harm is not required for standing. The court remanded the case for a decision on the merits of the permit issuance.

Hensley v. North Carolina Department of Environment & Natural Resources, 364 N.C. 285, 698 S.E.2d 41 (2010)

Sedimentation

Plaintiffs challenged an erosion-and-sedimentation-control variance granted to allow the expansion of a golf course adjacent to a trout stream at a development in Burnsville. The defendant Department had approved construction of fairways and cart paths that involved removing the tree canopy above about a half-mile of the stream and enclosing about a third-mile of the stream with pipes and culverts. The approval included strict conditions to minimize sedimentation during the construction process. The law allowed land-disturbing activities in the trout-stream buffer that are "temporary" and "minimal." The court held that the purpose of the law was to prevent harmful sedimentation during construction, not to control land use within the buffer. As the construction process itself was temporary and the sedimentation controls imposed would ensure minimal sedimentation, the court upheld the approval.

Morris Communications Corp. v. City of Bessemer City Zoning Board of Adjustment, 365 N.C. 152, 712 S.E.2d 868 (2011)

Interpretation; Nonconformities; Vested rights

In July 2005, the state condemned for a road-widening project a portion of the property on which the plaintiff had a lawful billboard. In August 2005, the plaintiff secured a sign permit from the city for a relocated billboard, and in November 2005 secured a building permit from the county for that work. Each permit required "work" to commence within six months. In June 2006, the county renewed the building permit. Later in June 2006, the city amended its ordinance to ban billboards. In December 2006, the plaintiff relocated the billboard, which was apparently the initial physical construction on site. The city contended that the plaintiff's sign permit had expired after six months (in February 2006) because there was no work on site, so the county's renewal of the building permit was in error and the city's June 2006 billboard ban precluded issuance of a permit for the relocation. On appeal of the city's notice of a violation of the city ordinance, the board of adjustment, trial court, and court of appeals upheld the city's interpretation of the law.

The court reversed, noting that interpretation of the ordinance is a de novo question of law. The term "work" was not defined by the ordinance or the permit. The court held that the zoning administrator and board of adjustment's conclusion that some physical work of the nature authorized by the permit on site was required to constitute "work" under the terms of the ordinance was unreasonable. Governmental restrictions on the use of land are to be strictly construed in favor of free use of real property. Thus, this "narrow and unduly restrictive interpretation" of an undefined and ambiguous term was inappropriate. The court relied on several factors to conclude that "work" had commenced within the permit period. The dictionary definition of "work" includes mental efforts to achieve an objective, and the record established that the plaintiff had engaged in active negotiations with the N.C. Department of Transportation and the landowner in this period. The state's common law has also long included work beyond physical alterations on site to be considered in vested-rights analysis. Further, the board of adjustment should act to prevent errors or abuse by zoning administrators and to achieve just results. Given the fact that this was an involuntary relocation of a sign to accommodate road widening, plus the town's acknowledged hostility toward billboards, the "overly restrictive" interpretation of a vague ordinance should have been reversed.

Wally v. City of Kannapolis, 365 N.C. 449, 722 S.E.2d 481 (2012)
Amendments; Statements of reasonableness

Neighbors challenged a conditional rezoning that allowed office, light-industrial, and retail uses. The city's zoning commission had recommended approval. At the city council's public hearing on the rezoning, a staff report was presented that included an analysis of plan consistency and other factors, including impacts on safety, traffic, parking, the environment, and public facilities.

The court invalidated the rezoning for failure to comply with the requirement of G.S. 160D-605 that the governing board adopt a statement on plan consistency and briefly explain why the action taken is reasonable. While the substance of a statement that was adopted is not subject to judicial review, whether or not it existed is reviewable. Here the court found that the city council failed to adopt any statement as required by the statute. The fact that a staff report addressing these matters was presented to the council was irrelevant, as the report only expressed the staff's views on the matter, and the statute requires a statement of the governing board's rationale.

Lanvale Properties, LLC v. County of Cabarrus, 366 N.C. 142, 731 S.E.2d 800 (2012)
Adequate public facilities; Impact fees

The plaintiff proposed a residential development in the city of Locust. The county refused to issue building permits unless the plaintiff complied with adequate-public-facility requirements in the county zoning ordinance. The county had initially adopted adequate-public-facility requirements in 1998 as part of its subdivision ordinance. The provisions prohibited approval of residential subdivisions if there was inadequate school capacity for the projected development, but the proposed subdivision could be approved upon entering a consent agreement to pay a fee to be used for capital costs of providing additional school capacity. In 2004, the county secured local legislation to allow application of the "school adequacy review" in the county subdivision ordinance within municipalities as well as the county. In 2007, the county substantially modified the adequate-public-facility-review process and moved the requirements to the county zoning ordinance. If available student capacity was inadequate, the provisions provided for denial of the application or imposition of conditions to mitigate impacts, including deferring or phasing final approval until school capacity became available, reducing density, or entering a consent agreement to provide financial payments to address needed school capacity.

The court held that the county lacked statutory authority under the county's zoning authority to impose a voluntary mitigation fee to remedy inadequate school capacity. The court noted that the purposes of zoning ordinances include facilitating the "efficient and adequate provision" of specified public facilities, including schools. However, the grant-of-powers section of the zoning-enabling statute specifies the regulations that can be imposed to address those purposes. These include regulation of building size, lots, setbacks, density, and the use of land and buildings. The court found the ordinance to be a "carefully crafted revenue generation mechanism" rather than a use of those tools. The court noted that subdivision regulations can address some aspects of the provision of public facilities in the land-subdivision-approval process, but it held the scope of the zoning authority to be distinct from the scope of authority under subdivision ordinances. The court further held there was no implied authority for the provisions, ruling G.S. 153A-4 on broad construction to be inapplicable, as the provision is a rule of statutory construction only to be applied in the interpretation of ambiguous statutes. The court held that the scope of the zoning authority in this situation was not ambiguous. The court held that the local legislation secured by the county did not confer authority to adopt these provisions. The court also held that because the contested provisions were not a zoning ordinance, the statute of limitations applicable to contesting the validity of a zoning ordinance or amendment was inapplicable.

Hest Technologies, Inc. v. State, 366 N.C. 289, 749 S.E.2d 429 (2012)
Video gaming

The court upheld G.S. 14-306.4, which banned the operation of electronic machines that use "entertaining displays" to reveal sweepstakes winnings. The court ruled that the law regulates conduct, not protected speech.

High Rock Lake Partners, LLC v. North Carolina Department of Transportation, 366 N.C. 315, 735 S.E.2d 300 (2012)

Driveway permits

The plaintiff proposed a subdivision on a peninsula that extended into High Rock Lake. A state road extended down the peninsula, crossing a railroad near the top of the peninsula. A preliminary plat for the development was submitted to Davidson County for approval, which was denied by the planning board but approved on appeal by the board of commissioners. The plaintiff applied for a driveway permit from the N.C. Department of Transportation to connect to the state road below the railroad crossing. The department issued the permit, conditioned upon (1) expanding the state road at the rail crossing to a width sufficient to accommodate two lanes of traffic, rail-crossing gates, and flashers and (2) securing required licenses and approvals from the owning and the operating railroads to install required crossing improvements so as to retain the "sealed corridor" level of safety. The railroad then concluded that any crossing was unacceptable unless it included a grade separation.

The court held that the department had exceeded the scope of its authority. G.S. 136-18(29) addresses the design of driveway connections to state roads, balancing the public interest in a safe highway system with an owner's property right of access to the highway. While the statute authorizes regulation of the size, location, design, and construction of driveway improvements, it does not authorize requirements to make off-site improvements or to obtain another property owner's approval.

Applewood Properties, LLC v. New South Properties, LLC, 366 N.C. 518, 742 S.E.2d 776 (2013)

Interpretation; Sedimentation; Standing

The plaintiffs owned and operated a golf course adjacent to the defendant's residential development. During construction the defendant was issued a notice of noncompliance with the Sedimentation Pollution Control Act (SPCA) and ordered to take corrective action. Subsequent inspections showed that the corrective actions had been taken, but additional corrective actions were ordered. The next month a dam on the project failed, and the plaintiffs' property was flooded and damaged as a result. Additional notices of noncompliance were issued after the dam failure, but no notice of violation was issued. The plaintiffs claimed negligence, nuisance, trespass, intentional misconduct, and a violation of the SPCA. The trial court dismissed the SPCA claim. The jury awarded the plaintiffs $675,000 in damages on the nuisance claim. The plaintiffs appealed the dismissal, which was affirmed by a divided court of appeals.

The court noted that G.S. 113A-66 provides for a private civil action when there has been a violation of the SPCA, a relevant ordinance or order, or a sedimentation-control plan. The court interpreted this provision to allow a private cause of action only when a defendant has been cited for a violation of the statute. A "notice of noncompliance" is insufficient to confer standing, as this specific defendant was not cited with a notice of violation. The only formal notice of violation was issued after the suit was filed and was issued to a different party than the defendant in this action.

King v. Town of Chapel Hill, 367 N.C. 400, 758 S.E.2d 364 (2014)

Preemption; Scope of authority

Plaintiff towing company brought a declaratory-judgment action, seeking to invalidate two ordinances regulating the towing of cars parked without permission in private parking areas. The towing ordinance specified the size and content of warning notices to be posted in parking lots, set vehicle-release requirements, and set maximum fees to be charged. The second ordinance prohibited the use of mobile phones while operating a motor vehicle.

The court noted that where enabling legislation is clear and unambiguous, there is no room for judicial construction, and the plain and definite meaning of the statute must be applied. The rule of broad construction provided in G.S. 160A-4 is only applicable when the grant of authority is ambiguous. Here, the authority is the general police power of G.S. 160A-174, authorizing regulations to protect or promote public health, safety, and general welfare. This grant of authority is "by its very nature ambiguous." Therefore, it is given a broad construction, tempered by the mandate that it be exercised within constitutional limits. This requires a rational, real, substantial relation to the protection of public health, safety, and general welfare. The court found that the warning-sign requirements met that standard. However, the town does not have the authority to create a fee schedule for the towing without express statutory authority. The court held that the ordinance provision requiring tow operators to accept credit or debit cards for payment of towing fees was reasonably related to citizen safety and welfare in allowing owners to have quick and easy access to their towed vehicles. However, as with towing fees, the town does not have the authority to cap the towing fee by not allowing towers to pass debit and credit-card charges on to those who illegally parked.

The court invalidated the mobile-phone ban as preempted by state law. State law prohibits the use of mobile phones by vehicle operators in several specific instances—limiting phone use by drivers under the age of eighteen, phone use by school-bus drivers, and texting by commercial-vehicle operators. The court found these prohibitions sufficient to show a legislative intent to provide a complete and integrated regulatory scheme to the exclusion of local regulation.

Town of Midland v. Wayne, 368 N.C. 55, 773 S.E.2d 301 (2015)
Condemnation; Vested rights

Cabarrus County in 1997 approved a development plan for a largely residential development on a 250-acre tract. Two phases of the development were substantially developed and sold. The parcel involved in this litigation was in the undeveloped portion of the project. The defendant owned the undeveloped tract, and a limited-liability company controlled by the defendant owned the developed portion of the approved development. Installation of a pipeline precluded completion of the development in the same manner originally approved, allegedly rendering the property unsuitable for the approved development. The plaintiff alleged an inverse condemnation based on loss of the vested right to complete the overall project as originally permitted.

The court affirmed the trial court's finding of a vested right to develop the parcel. The multiphase residential-development plan that was approved for the overall project was consistent with the inherent nature of residential development, and the defendant reasonably and in good faith relied on that approval. The defendant made substantial expenditures of money, time, and labor based on this approval, which never lapsed. In order for the contiguous properties to be considered as a whole for the takings analysis, the factors to be considered were (1) unity of ownership, (2) unity of use, and (3) physical unity. Here, the parcels were adjacent, satisfying physical unity. Being subject to a single approved development plan that led to a vested right for the overall project satisfied the unity of use. Given the joint vested right and the controlling interest in the defendant's company, the "modicum of unity of ownership" was also met. The court held that the vested right is not a separate property interest for takings analysis. However, the vested right provides a unique quality to the land to which it is attached that enhances its value and must be considered in assessing the precondemnation value of the property.

Morningstar Marinas/Eaton Ferry, LLC v. Warren County, 368 N.C. 360, 777 S.E.2d 733 (2015)
Appeals; Standing

The plaintiff operated a commercial marina on Lake Gaston. The owner of another marina across a small cove from the plaintiff's property proposed to build townhouses on a residentially zoned tract and use part of the site as a driveway to an adjacent commercially zoned parcel that included a dry-stack boat-storage facility. The plaintiff asked for a formal ruling on whether the drive connecting a boat launch on the residential area to the commercial boat-storage facility could be located in a residential zoning district. The zoning administrator determined that the drive issue was not regulated by county zoning. The plaintiff appealed this determination to the board of adjustment, but the county attorney and zoning administrator determined that the plaintiff did not have standing and refused to place the appeal on the board's agenda. The plaintiff sought a writ of mandamus to compel the question be heard by the board.

The court held that mandamus was a proper writ in this instance because the zoning administrator has a ministerial duty to place appeals on the board of adjustment's agenda. The question of standing to make the appeal is a legal question for the board, and it is not within the power of the administrator to rule on standing. Once the appeal is on the agenda, the board should rule on whether the plaintiff has standing.

Byrd v. Franklin County, 368 N.C. 409, 778 S.E.2d 268 (2015), *per curiam, adopting dissent in* 237 N.C. App. 192, 765 S.E.2d 805 (2014)
Interpretation; Shooting ranges; Unlisted uses

The plaintiffs proposed to locate a shooting range on their property. The zoning provisions in the county's unified development ordinance provided that any use not specifically included in the table of permitted uses was prohibited. The ordinance did not list shooting ranges, so the plaintiffs were advised that the use was prohibited, and it was suggested they seek a text amendment to include shooting ranges in the table of uses. The majority opinion in the court of appeals held that because this was not a listed use, the ordinance unambiguously prohibited it. The dissent contended that *Land v. Village of Wesley Chapel*, 206 N.C. App. 123, 697 S.E.2d 458 (2010), rejected the concept that a zoning ordinance may prohibit uses that are not explicitly allowed. Given that the law favors the uninhibited free use of land, such an automatic disallowance of a use because the ordinance failed to identify it is invalid. In a per curiam opinion, the court adopted this dissenting opinion.

Kirby v. N.C. Department of Transportation, 368 N.C. 847, 786 S.E.2d 919 (2016)
Condemnation; Takings

The Transportation Corridor Official Map Act, G.S. 136-44.50 to -44.54, allowed transportation corridors to be identified on maps filed with the register of deeds. Once the maps were filed, the law limited approval of building permits or new subdivisions within the corridors for up to three years. The law also allowed for variances to be granted if no reasonable return could be made from the land, and it allowed landowners to petition for initiation of acquisition if the limits on development imposed an undue hardship. The plaintiffs owned property affected by a 1997 official map designation for a proposed loop road around northern Winston-Salem. They alleged that the act made their property unmarketable and was an unconstitutional taking of their property.

The court held that filing a corridor-protection map under the Official Map Act is an exercise of the power of eminent domain rather than an exercise of the police power, thus necessitating compensation. While the law uses regulatory authority for building permits and plat approvals, the court found that the law gives the N.C. Department of Transportation the right to establish what is essentially an easement restricting the use of property as a precursor to acquisition and is thus an exercise of eminent domain.

Quality Built Homes Inc. v. Town of Carthage, 369 N.C. 15, 789 S.E.2d 454 (2016)
Impact fees; Interpretation; Scope of authority

Carthage adopted water and sewer impact fees to be assessed upon final plat approval and due either when a tap fee was paid to access the utility systems or when a development permit was secured. The fees were to be used to cover the costs of expanding the water and sewer systems. These fees were in addition to tap fees to access the systems and regular monthly charges for water and sewer customers. The impact fees were assessed regardless of the property owner's actual use of the systems or whether the town actually expanded the system.

The court held that the authority to establish fees and charges for use of services provided by public enterprises was inadequate to authorize this type of impact fee. While the county-public-enterprise statutes authorize fees for "services furnished or to be furnished," the municipal statute only authorizes fees for "services furnished," omitting the "to be furnished" authorization. As the plain meaning of the statute is unambiguous, a broad construction to resolve ambiguity is not warranted. The court further noted that the city had not secured local legislation to authorize impact fees, as several other local governments had done. Under the statute in effect at the time of the assessment of these fees, a city could only impose fees and charges for the contemporaneous use of water and sewer services, and it was not authorized to collect fees for future discretionary spending.

Town of Boone v. State, 369 N.C. 126, 794 S.E.2d 710 (2016)
Extraterritorial jurisdiction

When extraterritorial planning-and-development jurisdiction was authorized for cities in 1959, local legislation provided that Boone did not have such power. In 1961, this authority was extended to Boone, but the town did not exercise it until 1981. In 2014, the General Assembly enacted local legislation again withdrawing extraterritorial-jurisdiction authority from Boone and returning jurisdiction to the county. The town challenged the withdrawal of authority as a facially unconstitutional local act on the grounds that it would remove the town's authority to regulate on the basis of health, sanitation, and the abatement of nuisances.

The court held that local governments are creatures of the state and that the General Assembly has plenary power to create, organize, and abolish cities. The state constitution grants the state authority to provide for "the organization and government and the fixing of boundaries" of local governments. The court held the plain meaning of this provision to allow setting corporate limits and extraterritorial-jurisdiction boundaries (if any). The General Assembly is allowed to meet the needs of differing communities by local act. The limitation on local legislation affecting health and sanitation applies to the powers and duties conferred upon local governments, as distinct from setting the boundaries within which those powers may be exercised.

Willowmere Community Ass'n v. City of Charlotte, 370 N.C. 553, 809 S.E.2d 558 (2018)
Standing

Two neighboring homeowners' associations sought to challenge the rezoning of a seven-acre parcel to allow development of a seventy-unit multifamily project proposed by the Charlotte-Mecklenburg Housing Partnership. At the hearing, neither party raised standing as an issue, but the trial court issued summary judgment for the defendants, finding that both plaintiff groups lacked standing because neither followed the process required by their bylaws regarding initiation of litigation.

The court held that the standing issue could be raised by either party or by the court on its own motion. The court found that while neither association might have complied with their bylaws' notice and meeting requirements necessary to initiate litigation, this had not resulted in a lack of standing to bring this action. Compliance with their internal bylaw procedures was a nonjurisdictional technicality.

Quality Built Homes Inc. v. Town of Carthage, 371 N.C. 60, 813 S.E.2d 218 (2018)
Estoppel; Statutes of limitation

The court held that the time to challenge unlawful fees imposed for the future provision of water and sewer services begins to run when the fees are paid, not when the fee ordinance is adopted. The court held the applicable statute of limitations was the three-year statute of limitations for a liability created by statute (here, a fee in excess of that authorized by the public-enterprise statutes). The court also held that the plaintiffs were not estopped from challenging the fee on the basis of an acceptance of benefits for two reasons. First, the payment was not voluntary but was required in order to get water and sewer services. Second, the plaintiffs received no benefit from payment of the fee to which they would not otherwise have been entitled.

PHG Asheville, LLC v. City of Asheville, 374 N.C. 133, 839 S.E.2d 755 (2020)
Evidence; Special uses

The plaintiff, a developer, appealed the city council's denial of a special use permit for a hotel and associated parking structure in downtown Asheville. At the evidentiary hearing before the city council, PHG presented three expert witnesses, including an appraiser who testified on property-value impacts and a professional engineer who testified on traffic impacts. Three citizens spoke in favor of the project and several others asked questions of the applicant's witnesses, but none offered evidence to show the permit standards were not met. The council, however, concluded that the applicant had not submitted sufficient evidence to make a prima facie case that the standards were met and denied the permit.

The court held that whether a prima facie case had been made is a question of law subject to de novo review, while the question of whether substantial evidence was in the record to support the board's factual finding is subject to a whole-record review. In this instance, the permit applicant presented substantial evidence that the standards were met and no contrary evidence was presented. Once the applicant's burden of production is met, the burden shifts to opponents to produce substantial evidence to the contrary. While council members asked questions about the impact of other planned hotels on property values and raised several questions about how the traffic-impact analysis was conducted, no contrary evidence was presented at the hearing. The applicant is not required to rebut potential issues raised by board members that are not within the range of issues and data required by the relevant standards in the ordinance. Thus, as a matter of law, the applicant was entitled to permit approval as their evidence was unchallenged and unrebutted.

The court noted that board members can rely upon their special knowledge, provided those facts are disclosed at the hearing and are relevant to the applicable standards. When an expert witness offers evidence based on studies conducted in accordance with industry standards using standard data and methods, if no contradictory evidence is offered, the council may not rebut that study with its lay opinion as to the adequacy of the study methods.

Town of Pinebluff v. Moore County, 374 N.C. 254, 839 S.E.2d 833 (2020)

Extraterritorial jurisdiction; Interpretation

The town secured local legislation to extend its potential extraterritorial planning and development regulation by two miles. The local legislation included a provision that the county "shall adopt a resolution" authorizing town jurisdiction upon presentation by the town of proper evidence that the annexation had extended the potential extraterritorial jurisdiction (ETJ) area. The county contended this did not remove the requirement for discretionary county approval if the county was exercising zoning and subdivision controls in the affected area. The court applied the rules of statutory construction that disfavor an interpretation that repeals a statutory requirement by implication, that reads the statute as a whole, and that gives effect to each section of a statute. The court held that the local legislation amended the state statute limiting the city to a one-mile ETJ but did not repeal the provision requiring county approval of an ETJ beyond one mile if the county had applied its zoning and subdivision regulations there.

Ashe County v. Ashe County Planning Board, 376 N.C. 1, 852 S.E. 2d 69 (2020)

Determinations

Appalachian Materials applied for a permit for an asphalt plant under the county Polluting Industries Development Ordinance (PIDO). The PIDO required buffers separating regulated uses from commercial uses, schools, and health-care facilities. The ordinance also mandated that all required state permits be obtained before the county permit could be issued. The permit application stated that the required state air-quality permit was pending. In response to a request from the applicant, the county planning director sent a letter stating that the application met the requirements of the county ordinance and that he would make a "favorable recommendation" to issue the county permit once the state permit was obtained and final inspections were made. The county board of commissioners subsequently enacted a moratorium on asphalt plants. While the moratorium was in effect, the applicant submitted the state air-quality permit. The planning director denied the application, in part based on the moratorium. The applicant appealed the denial to the planning board, which was sitting as the board of adjustment. While the appeal was pending, the county board lifted the moratorium and replaced the PIDO with a new ordinance creating additional standards for the regulated uses. The planning board reversed the planning director's decision, and the county appealed that decision.

The court held that the planning director's letter was not a "final determination" that could have been appealed to the board of adjustment. It was neither "determinative" nor was it "authoritative" as it explicitly stated that there was no authority to issue a permit until all mandated conditions had been met and that those conditions had not in fact been met. As such, it was nothing more than a recommendation provided at a preliminary stage of the review. Allowing an appeal of a comment on one aspect of the standards, in this case compliance with setback requirements, prior to a final decision would invite multiple, piecemeal interlocutory appeals. The remaining issues, including the completeness of the application and the effect of the moratorium, were remanded to the court of appeals for reconsideration in light of the holding on the lack of binding effect of the planning director's letter.

JVC Enterprises, LLC v. City of Concord, 376 N.C. 782, 855 S.E.2d 158 (2021)
Impact fees; Interpretation

The plaintiff challenged water- and wastewater-capacity fees imposed as a condition of development approval. The city contended its charter and local acts granted the authority to impose fees for services to be furnished in the future.

The court applied a de novo review to the question of statutory interpretation as to the scope of the city's authority and held that these statutes unambiguously gave the city this authority. The original local act provided authority to the Board of Light and Water Commissioners to impose fees for services to be provided (as distinguished from the general public-enterprise statute that did not provide that authority). A subsequent legislative act dissolved that board and transferred all its powers and duties to the city. Given this plain and definite meaning of the two local acts, there is no need to rely on canons of statutory interpretation to ascertain whether the repeal and transfer of powers included this specific authority.

Cheryl Lloyd Humphrey Land Investment Co. v. Resco Products, Inc., 377 N.C. 384, 858 S.E.2d 795 (2021)
Hearings; First Amendment

Plaintiff entered negotiations to sell forty-five acres near Hillsborough to a purchaser who planned a 118-unit townhouse development on the property. Part of the property was adjacent to a quarry owned by the defendant. When the town held a hearing on the annexation and rezoning of the property, the defendant opposed the rezoning, contending that there was explosive blasting on the site and future residents would be endangered by flying rocks, air blasts, and ground vibrations. The defendant later conceded that there had been no violations of their mining permit and that they could conduct activities on the site without endangering future residents on the plaintiff's land. After the town rezoned the property, the purchaser excluded the area adjacent to the quarry from the purchase, citing the dangers raised by the defendant in the rezoning hearing. The plaintiff brought this action, contending the intentional and malicious misrepresentations made by the defendant at the rezoning hearing constituted tortious interference with the plaintiff's economic advantage by inducing the purchaser to exclude this area from their purchase of the townhouse site.

The court held that the defendant's statements at the rezoning hearing were protected First Amendment speech as part of their right to petition the government. The right to attempt to influence the legislative choice of the town council exists regardless of the defendant's motives and protects selfish or misleading speech. Neither the maliciousness nor the falsity of the speech has any bearing on its protected status.

C Investments 2, LLC v. Auger, 383 N.C. 1, 881 S.E.2d 270 (2022)
Restrictive covenants; Interpretation

The court interpreted a provision in the Real Property Marketable Title Act that when an owner has a thirty-year unbroken chain of title, any restrictive covenants that are not mentioned in the chain of title, other than those that restrict the property to residential use, are extinguished. In this instance, covenants for a 1952 subdivision limited the property to residential use; they also restricted additional development of the lots. The court held that the plain and unambiguous language of G.S. 47B-3(13) provides that where the subdivision has covenants applicable to a general or uniform scheme of development restricting the property to residential use only, the covenant is not extinguished. However, the other covenants—limiting the size, number, location, and design of structures on the lots, as well as the future subdivision of the lots—were all extinguished after thirty years.

Belmont Association v. Farwig, 381 N.C. 306, 873 S.E.2d 486 (2022)
Restrictive covenants

The defendants placed solar collectors on the roof of their home in Belmont. The collectors were visible from a public area. Although the applicable covenants did not expressly address solar collectors, the plaintiff's architectural-review board denied approval on aesthetic grounds. The court held that G.S. 22B-20(b), which voids covenants prohibiting or having the effect of prohibiting solar collectors, was applicable. The exception to this prohibition in G.S. 22B-20(d) was not applicable, the court held, because it only concerned the prohibition of solar collectors visible from a public area, as opposed to the aesthetic restriction that in effect prohibited solar collectors without expressly doing so.

Anderson Creek Partners, LP v. County of Harnett, 382 N.C. 1, 876 S.E.2d 476 (2022)
Impact fees; Takings

Plaintiff developers challenged a county "capacity use fee" for sewer service. The purpose of the fee was to partially recover from new customers the costs of expanding capacity of the utility services to account for future customers that would be added to the system. The fee was required to be paid for each lot as a precondition to county concurrence in water and sewer permits issued by the state.

The court concluded the fees were not "user fees" to cover the cost of any service currently provided. They were properly characterized as an "impact fee" and a monetary land-use exaction because they were required to be paid prior to county approval to develop a particular parcel of land. The fact that the fees were a non-discretionary fixed amount set by a legislative body did not exempt them from this categorization since the county had the discretion to amend and increase the fees by regulation at any time. As such, the fee was subject to the constitutional *Nollan/Dolan/Koontz* requirement that they be rationally related and roughly proportional to the impacts of the proposed developments. The court held that the plaintiff's pleadings conceded the fee was rationally related to the impacts of the development but remanded for findings relative to whether it was no more than a roughly proportional amount.

United Daughters of the Confederacy, N.C. Div., Inc. v. City of Winston-Salem, ___ N.C. ___, 881 S.E.2d 32 (2022)
Standing; Monuments

The plaintiffs challenged the city's decision to remove a Confederate monument located in front of the former county courthouse. The court held that since the plaintiffs' complaint did not allege that the group had any ownership or contractual interest in the monument, it had no legal rights under common law, state statutes, or the constitution that would be affected by its removal. Without such a proprietary or contractual interest, it had no standing to challenge the city's action. As there was no identification of individual members of the organization and no allegations related to their standing, the group could not have associational standing based on the standing of a member of the organization. The court held that the action should have been dismissed without prejudice since, without standing, the trial court could not review the substance of the claim to determine if it should be dismissed with prejudice.

Duke Energy Carolinas, LLC v. Kiser, ___ N.C. ___, ___ S.E.2d ___ (2023)
Riparian access; Public trust doctrine

The defendants owned an island in Lake Norman. Their predecessor in title had granted a flowage easement to the plaintiffs for land that was submerged when Lake Norman was created and a flood easement for the area immediately adjacent to the lake that was normally on high ground but would be subject to periodic flooding. At issue was the right of the defendant to bulkhead and backfill an area within the flood easement and the right of the plaintiff to permit construction of a dock and piers within the flowage easement to neighboring third-party property owners. The court held that two easements not only gave Duke Energy the right to submerge the land for a lake and prohibit unauthorized fill but also gave Duke Energy "absolute water rights" to treat the servient estate "in any manner deemed necessary or desirable." Thus, the plain, broad, and unambiguous language of the easement allows Duke Energy to allow third-party homeowners to build docks, piers, and other structures along the shoreline and to use the waters of Lake Norman for recreation. This dock and pier permitting program is consistent with Duke Energy's federal licensing obligations for this hydroelectric lake and is consistent Duke Energy's long-standing permit plan for homeowners' lake access facilities.

Court of Appeals

Decker v. Coleman, 6 N.C. App. 102, 169 S.E.2d 487 (1969)
Conditions; Uniformity of standards

Neighbors brought an action to enforce a fifty-foot buffer requirement imposed by the Asheville city council as a condition of a rezoning. The court ruled that the buffer requirement was invalid in that it applied only to a rezoning affecting one property rather than to all similar zoning districts in the city. Individualized conditions on a rezoning are not enforceable as they violate the requirement that zoning standards be uniform within a particular zoning district.

Roberson's Beverages, Inc. v. City of New Bern, 6 N.C. App. 632, 171 S.E.2d 4 (1969), *cert. denied*, 276 N.C. 183 (1970)
Downzoning; Takings

New Bern rezoned a site previously used as a bottling plant (and used as a warehouse for nine years) from a business-commercial zone to an office-institutional zone. The court held that depreciation of value does not render a rezoning a taking. Because there was no showing that the building could not be converted to a permissible use, that the building could not be razed and the property converted to a permissible use, or that the nonconforming warehouse use could not be continued, the rezoning was upheld.

State v. Martin, 7 N.C. App. 18, 171 S.E.2d 115 (1969), *cert. denied*, 276 N.C. 184 (1970)
Manufactured housing

The defendant appealed his conviction for parking a mobile home in Ahoskie in violation of an ordinance limiting the location of mobile homes to mobile-home parks. The court upheld the ordinance and the conviction.

State v. Flynt, 8 N.C. App. 323, 174 S.E.2d 120 (1970), *cert. denied*, 277 N.C. 115 (1970)
Appellate procedures

In this criminal case alleging violation of a Winston-Salem zoning ordinance, the court ruled that the defendant did not have a right to appeal a superior court order denying a writ of certiorari for a review of the district court's judgment because the superior court's order was not a final judgment.

Town of Hillsborough v. Smith, 10 N.C. App. 70, 178 S.E.2d 18 (1970), *cert. denied*, 277 N.C. 727, 178 S.E.2d 831 (1971)
Appeals; Bonds; Damages

The town had posted a bond when seeking an injunction to restrain an alleged violation of the zoning ordinance. The supreme court eventually ruled that the town was not entitled to restrain the activity. In this case, the appeals court ruled that the town had government immunity and was not liable for damages in seeking an injunction. The purchase of a bond was ultra vires and did not serve to waive that immunity. However, because the surety company voluntarily undertook its obligation for a premium, it was not relieved by a vicarious extension of sovereign immunity.

In re Coleman, 11 N.C. App. 124, 180 S.E.2d 439 (1971)
Appeals; Standing

This case was brought by "neighbors" challenging the expansion of a privately owned building leased to the postal service that was partially located in a residential zone. The court ruled that the plaintiffs had not established standing to bring the action because there was no showing of their identity, their proximity to the building, or the nature of their aggrievement.

Strickland v. Overman, 11 N.C. App. 427, 181 S.E.2d 136 (1971)
Manufactured housing; Restrictive covenants

The restrictive covenant in this case prohibited trailers and temporary structures, and those categories were held to include a "prefabricated modular unit."

Kenan v. Board of Adjustment, 13 N.C. App. 688, 187 S.E.2d 496, *cert. denied*, 281 N.C. 314, 188 S.E.2d 897 (1972)
Special uses

The Chapel Hill board of adjustment denied a special use permit for a self-service filling station in the central business district. The court ruled that the four general standards set forth in the ordinance provided sufficient guidance for the board's discretion and that the burden was on the petitioner to present evidence to the board that it met the conditions of the ordinance. The four standards relied upon required a showing that the use would (1) not materially endanger the public health or safety; (2) meet all required conditions and specifications; (3) not substantially injure the value of adjoining property or be a public nuisance; and (4) be in harmony with the area in which it is located and be in general conformity with the comprehensive plan.

Carter v. Town of Chapel Hill, 14 N.C. App. 93, 187 S.E.2d 588, *cert. denied*, 281 N.C. 314, 188 S.E.2d 897 (1972)
Evidence; Special uses

The court ruled that a board acting on a special use permit could consider unsworn testimony and otherwise depart from the rules of evidence as long as the hearing was conducted in a fair and orderly manner and all parties were accorded due process of law.

City of Brevard v. Ritter, 14 N.C. App. 207, 188 S.E.2d 41 (1972)
Nonconformities

The court ruled that construction of a new 3000-square-foot building for a pilots' lounge and an auxiliary hangar was an expansion of a nonconforming use not allowed by the zoning ordinance.

Thomasville of North Carolina, Ltd. v. City of Thomasville, 17 N.C. App. 483, 195 S.E.2d 79 (1973)
Vested rights

The developer of a 100-unit apartment complex for a subsidized-housing project in Thomasville consulted with the city government, was advised that zoning permitted the development, secured an option to purchase, and submitted detailed building plans for the permit application. Neighbors then petitioned for a downzoning to a single-family district. After administrative delay by the city, the developer secured a court order mandating the issuance of the building permits and spent substantial sums on site preparation and construction contracts. The town then rezoned the property. The court held that a vested right had been established. Good faith was a question of fact for the jury or the trial judge in the absence of a jury. The record supported a finding of good faith in that the developer had made no misrepresentation of his plans to the city or to neighbors, the entire development project had been conducted without extraordinary haste for the purpose of thwarting the zoning ordinance, and substantial expenditures had been made after valid building permits had been granted.

Transland Properties, Inc. v. Board of Adjustment, 18 N.C. App. 712, 198 S.E.2d 1 (1973)
Vested rights

The town of Nags Head attempted to revoke building permits for the uncompleted portion of a condominium project. Twelve of the permitted twenty-five buildings had been completed at the time of a rezoning that prohibited condominiums on this site. The court ruled that the developer had a vested right to complete the entire project. Actual construction under the valid building permits was not required; substantial expenditures for acquisition of land, purchase of equipment, and building contracts qualified.

County of Currituck v. Upton, 19 N.C. App. 45, 197 S.E.2d 883 (1973)
Enforcement; Manufactured housing

The court upheld the issuance of an injunction to compel the removal of a mobile home from a zoning district that did not permit freestanding mobile homes.

Van Poole v. Messer, 19 N.C. App. 70, 198 S.E.2d 106 (1973)
Manufactured housing; Restrictive covenants

A restrictive covenant prohibited temporary structures and trailers. The court held that the term *trailer* included a mobile home, and it remanded the case on an estoppel question.

Forsyth County v. York, 19 N.C. App. 361, 198 S.E.2d 770, *cert. denied*, 284 N.C. 253, 200 S.E.2d 653 (1973)
Enforcement; Manufactured housing; Nonconformities; Special uses

The court upheld a requirement of the Forsyth County zoning ordinance that changes in nonconforming uses and mobile homes in certain districts be authorized by special use permits. The fact that permits for a mobile home at the site at issue had previously been denied did not establish the futility of applications when no judicial review of the denials had been sought.

Town of Mount Olive v. Price, 20 N.C. App. 302, 201 S.E.2d 362 (1973)
Enforcement; Manufactured housing

The town had secured an injunction compelling the removal of a mobile home located in the town in violation of the zoning ordinance. The court ruled that the statute requiring the recording of the ordinance in the office of the county register of deeds was not in effect at the time of adoption of this ordinance and therefore was not relevant in this case.

Duke Power Co. v. Salisbury Board of Adjustment, 20 N.C. App. 730, 202 S.E.2d 607, *cert. denied*, 285 N.C. 235, 204 S.E.2d 22 (1974)
Standing

The court ruled that the fact that neighbors were affected by a zoning decision, appeared at the board of adjustment's hearing on a variance, and attended the trial court's hearing on the matter did not confer upon them a right to appeal the trial court's decision (absent their intervening in the judicial proceeding). Only actual parties to litigation may appeal a trial court's decision.

Williamson v. Avant, 21 N.C. App. 211, 203 S.E.2d 634, *cert. denied*, 285 N.C. 596, 205 S.E.2d 727 (1974)
Subdivisions

The court ruled that a division of land for the purpose of dividing an estate among the heirs was not a subdivision under the statutory definition, so a failure to obtain approval under the subdivision ordinance was not a defect of title.

Quadrant Corp. v. City of Kinston, 22 N.C. App. 31, 205 S.E.2d 324 (1974)
Appeals; Discretion

The court ruled that when a landowner applied for a building permit and complied with the zoning ordinance, the building inspector had no discretion to deny the application. When no timely appeal had been made of a board of adjustment's decision, subsequent judicial challenge of the decision was improper.

Long v. Winston-Salem Board of Adjustment, 22 N.C. App. 191, 205 S.E.2d 807 (1974)
Board of adjustment; Evidence; Judicial review; Special uses

The court ruled that in reviewing applications for special use permits, the board of adjustment has to base its decision on substantial, competent evidence. When no such evidence is in the record, it is improper for the board to deny an application, and it is improper for the trial court to order its issuance. The present case was remanded to the board of adjustment for de novo consideration based on competent evidence.

Thurston v. Salisbury Zoning Board of Adjustment, 24 N.C. App. 288, 210 S.E.2d 275 (1974)
Appellate procedures

The court ruled that absent service of the case on appeal pursuant to G.S. 1-282, the review on appeal would be on the record proper alone.

Clark v. Richardson, 24 N.C. App. 556, 211 S.E.2d 530 (1975)

Nonconformities

The court held that the enclosure of a porch on a nonconforming grocery store in Mayodan did not constitute an enlargement or an extension of the nonconformity.

Diggs v. City of Wilson, 25 N.C. App. 464, 213 S.E.2d 443 (1975)

Nonconformities

A restaurant was operated by the plaintiff as a nonconforming use in a residential district. The plaintiff secured a building permit to remodel the restaurant. The permit had had no time limit for the work to be completed. The restaurant was closed for thirteen months while the work was underway. The court held as a matter of law that such a suspension of operations during the construction work does not constitute "discontinuance" of the use.

City of Asheboro v. Auman, 26 N.C. App. 87, 214 S.E.2d 621, *cert. denied*, 288 N.C. 239, 217 S.E.2d 663 (1975)

Enforcement; Manufactured housing

The city sought an injunction to prohibit the defendants from the continued use of a mobile home that had been moved into a zoning district that did not allow mobile homes. The court upheld the issuance of the injunction, even though the defendants had removed the wheels and the tongue of the mobile home and had erected a foundation for it.

Deffet Rentals, Inc. v. City of Burlington, 27 N.C. App. 361, 219 S.E.2d 223 (1975)

Appellate procedures; Vested rights

A property owner secured an option to purchase unzoned property within the city's extraterritorial-zoning area for the purpose of constructing an apartment complex. After the owner consulted with the city and was asked to delay submission of plans, the city zoned the area for single-family use. The court ruled that it was error for the trial court to make new findings of fact because the board of adjustment's findings are final if they are supported by the evidence and are not arbitrary, oppressive, or manifestly abusive of authority. Although the court implied some sympathy with the vested-rights contention, it remanded the case to the board of adjustment for a determination on competent, substantial evidence.

Freewood Associates, Ltd. v. Davie County Zoning Board of Adjustment, 28 N.C. App. 717, 222 S.E.2d 910, *review denied*, 290 N.C. 94, 225 S.E.2d 323 (1976)

Nonconformities; Special uses

The applicant proposed a nudist camp in a residential-agricultural zoning district in rural Davie County. The court upheld a denial of a special use permit and a nonconforming use permit. It concluded that the applicant had failed to establish the requisite good faith for expenditures to create a valid nonconforming use (and had failed to provide the requisite notice for the application for the permit) because all applications and discussions with the county had referred to a "family campground" rather than a "nudist camp" in a deliberate attempt to conceal the true use of the property.

In re Greene, 29 N.C. App. 749, 225 S.E.2d 647, *review denied*, 290 N.C. 661, 228 S.E.2d 451 (1976)

Appeals; Timeliness

Neighbors challenged the modernization of a nonconforming cement plant in a residential zone in Boone. The court ruled that appeals of the issuance of a building permit have to be made within a reasonable time to the board of adjustment. Further, because the work had already been completed, revocation of the building permit would have had no practical effect.

Town of Southern Pines v. Mohr, 30 N.C. App. 342, 226 S.E.2d 865 (1976)

Group homes; Interpretation

The court ruled that a center for the treatment of emotionally disturbed children, which was operated by a regional mental health center (a subunit of the state Department of Human Resources), was a "public building," which was a permitted use under the town zoning ordinance.

Stutts v. Swaim, 30 N.C. App. 611, 228 S.E.2d 750, *review denied*, 291 N.C. 178, 229 S.E.2d 692 (1976)

Laches; Manufactured housing; Spot zoning

This action, initiated in June 1974, challenged the November 1968 rezoning of a four-acre tract in Randleman's extraterritorial area from a single-family residential district to a mobile-home district. The court held that because there was no showing of a reasonable basis for the action, the rezoning constituted illegal spot zoning. The court further held that the challenge to the rezoning was not barred by laches because a delay in bringing the action was alone insufficient to establish laches. Rather, there has to be an affirmative showing that the delay has worked to the disadvantage, the injury, or the prejudice of the defendant. [Note: G.S. 160D-1405(a), which was subsequently enacted, establishes a sixty-day statute of limitations for challenging zoning-map amendments.]

Gardner Homes, Inc. v. Gaither, 31 N.C. App. 118, 228 S.E.2d 525, *review denied*, 291 N.C. 323, 230 S.E.2d 675 (1976)

Mistakes; Sales contracts

In this action to rescind a contract to purchase a hotel for conversion to apartments in Elizabeth City, the court ruled that when there was a mistake by both parties about a fact critical to a contract, the contract may be rescinded. Here, both parties to a land-sale contract had believed that the local zoning would allow the intended use, when in fact it did not.

Mecklenburg County v. Westbery, 32 N.C. App. 630, 233 S.E.2d 658 (1977)

Enforcement; Mistakes; Vested rights

The county mistakenly issued a building permit for a mobile storage structure on a lot in a zoning district that did not permit such structures. When the mistake was discovered, the permit was revoked and the revocation not appealed. The court ruled that no vested rights accrued to an unlawfully issued permit. The court noted that injunctive relief was appropriate under the State Building Code authorization provision (G.S. 160D-1125) irrespective of whether the zoning ordinance provided for injunctive relief.

Sellers v. City of Asheville, 33 N.C. App. 544, 236 S.E.2d 283 (1977)

Extraterritorial jurisdiction; Notice

The city attempted to extend its zoning to an area one mile beyond its city limits. The court ruled that the published notice was inadequate because it did not refer to extraterritorial zoning (which was being initially imposed) and did not fairly and sufficiently apprise those whose rights might be affected of the nature and the character of the action proposed. Also, the map was inadequate in that G.S. 160D-202(e) required a description adequate to allow landowners to know whether or not they were covered. A blanket one-mile standard does not meet the definitiveness mandated by statute.

Sampson v. City of Greensboro, 35 N.C. App. 148, 240 S.E.2d 502 (1978)

Exactions; Subdivisions

The owners of an industrial park that had been platted and approved under the city's subdivision ordinance sought to prevent the city from constructing a sanitary sewer along a dedicated easement in the park. The court ruled that once the dedication had been offered by tendering the plat and had been accepted by the city, it could not be withdrawn. Because the ordinance explicitly allowed the city to use the easement for any public purpose, the owner could not restrict it to one particular use.

Capps v. City of Raleigh, 35 N.C. App. 290, 241 S.E.2d 527 (1978)

Amendments; Laches; Notice

This case involved a challenge initiated in 1975 to a 1969 rezoning of an area from a single-family residential district to a district that allowed multifamily housing. The court ruled that actual notice to landowners was not required and that a newspaper notice, the posting of signs in the area, and news coverage constituted adequate constructive notice. Since the defendants had spent over $600,000 and had otherwise materially changed their position in reliance on the rezoning, the court held that the suit was barred by laches. [Note: G.S. 160D-1405(a), which was subsequently enacted, establishes a sixty-day statute of limitations for challenging zoning-map amendments.]

Washington Park Neighborhood Ass'n v. Winston-Salem Board of Adjustment, 35 N.C. App. 449, 241 S.E.2d 872, *review denied*, 295 N.C. 91, 244 S.E.2d 263 (1978)

Board of adjustment; Hearings; Minutes; Special uses

The Winston-Salem board of adjustment granted a special use permit for a parking lot in a residential zone, and neighbors challenged the action. In upholding the issuance of the permit, the court ruled that board of adjustment's hearings do not have to be sound-recorded if adequate written minutes are kept. Findings have to be based on competent, material, and substantial evidence. It was ruled to be permissible to read each of the required findings into the record at the beginning of a hearing and to allow motions on individual permits that the findings had been met and were incorporated into the motion by reference.

Johnson v. Town of Longview, 37 N.C. App. 61, 245 S.E.2d 516, *review denied*, 295 N.C. 550, 248 S.E.2d 727 (1978)

Amendments; Notice

This case involved a challenge to the denial of a permit to expand a hosiery mill into a residential zoning district. The court upheld the denial, ruling that the ordinance had been properly codified and that the public hearings required by the statutes then in effect had been conducted.

City of Winston-Salem v. Hoots Concrete Co., 37 N.C. App. 186, 245 S.E.2d 536, *review denied*, 295 N.C. 645, 248 S.E.2d 249 (1978)

Estoppel; Interpretation

The city attempted to enjoin the continued operation of a concrete-mixing plant in a limited-industrial district. The defendant contended that the zoning officer had approved the use and had allowed it to continue for five years. This particular use was not listed among the permitted ones, and the ordinance directed that the zoning officer in reviewing the application apply the most similar listed use. The court ruled that if the city officer, in exercising the discretion to interpret the ordinance that was specifically granted by the ordinance, had in fact approved the use, the city would be estopped from subsequently enjoining the use.

City of Hickory v. Catawba Valley Machinery Co., 38 N.C. App. 387, 48 S.E.2d 71 (1978)

Appellate procedures

The court ruled that statutory timetables for serving and filing the record on appeal have to be met unless extensions of time are granted.

City of Hickory v. Catawba Valley Machinery Co., 39 N.C. App. 236, 249 S.E.2d 851 (1978)

Appeals; Enforcement; Nonconformities

The city sought to compel the removal of a canopy extending into a front-yard setback in violation of the zoning ordinance. The defendant contended that this was a valid nonconforming use, whereas the city contended that it was an enlargement of the previous use without a building permit. The court ruled that because the defendant had failed to seek judicial review of the board of adjustment's findings, it could not collaterally attack the ruling in this subsequent enforcement action.

Davis v. Zoning Board of Adjustment, 41 N.C. App. 579, 255 S.E.2d 444 (1979)
Mootness

This case involved the alleged violation of a provision of the Union County zoning ordinance limiting animals in certain residential districts to two per household. While the appeal was pending, the ordinance was amended to allow the use in question. Therefore, the court dismissed the appeal.

In re Milliken, 43 N.C. App. 382, 258 S.E.2d 856 (1979)
Wetlands

The petitioner had completed construction of a causeway that filled some three acres of coastal wetlands and had started construction of a bridge across Little Shallotte Creek in Brunswick County without first obtaining the dredge-and-fill permit that was required under G.S. 113-229. The court held that this statute could not be used to address work already completed, that its effect was prospective only. Therefore, an after-the-fact permit application could not be considered.

City of Wilmington v. Camera's Eye, Inc., 43 N.C. App. 558, 259 S.E.2d 589 (1979)
Mootness

The city brought an action to enforce the use restrictions of Wilmington's historic-district ordinance. While the case was on appeal, the defendant, a bookstore, lost its lease and vacated the premises. The court dismissed the appeal as moot.

Robinhood Trails Neighbors v. Winston-Salem Board of Adjustment, 44 N.C. App. 539, 261 S.E.2d 520, cert. denied, 299 N.C. 737, 267 S.E.2d 663 (1980)
Evidence; Interpretation; Special uses

A neighborhood association challenged a special use permit issued by Winston-Salem's board of adjustment for a parking lot adjacent to a grocery store. The store's attorney testified as a witness at the board hearing. The court ruled that although an attorney should generally not appear as a witness in a case that he or she is trying, such an appearance is not absolutely prohibited in local administrative board hearings. The court also interpreted the zoning ordinance's definition of "lot" to be an area under common ownership being devoted to a use; it did not rely on the meaning of the term as set out in the tax map.

Lee v. Simpson, 44 N.C. App. 611, 261 S.E.2d 295, review denied, 299 N.C. 737, 267 S.E.2d 662 (1980)
Amendments; Notice

The court invalidated a Union County rezoning because the county failed to follow the process for notifying adjacent landowners that was set forth in the zoning ordinance.

Yates v. City of Raleigh, 46 N.C. App. 221, 264 S.E.2d 798 (1980)
Nuisances

The city cited the plaintiff for maintaining a public nuisance. The plaintiff alleged that the city then improperly entered the property and removed tools and equipment in the process of cleaning the lot. The court held that it was inappropriate to grant a motion to dismiss the claim. Even if the lot was in fact a nuisance, the city can only remove or destroy private property on that lot to the extent necessary to remove or abate the nuisance. Here, an issue of fact existed as to whether the equipment removed was a part of the nuisance condition.

Jennewein v. City Council of Wilmington, 46 N.C. App. 324, 264 S.E.2d 802 (1980)
Appellate procedures

The plaintiff appealed the denial of a special use permit, and the trial court remanded the matter for a de novo hearing before the council. The court held that appellate review was premature pending the remanded hearing and decision.

Currituck County v. Willey, 46 N.C. App. 835, 266 S.E.2d 52, *review denied*, 301 N.C. 234, 283 S.E.2d 131 (1980)

Manufactured housing

The court upheld a provision of the Currituck County zoning ordinance prohibiting mobile homes with dimensions of less than twenty-four feet by sixty feet in a single-family district. The court ruled that mobile homes are sufficiently different from other types of housing that a rational basis exists for differing requirements, such as this dimension standard.

Lathan v. Union County Board of Commissioners, 47 N.C. App. 357, 267 S.E.2d 30, *review denied*, 301 N.C. 92, 273 S.E.2d 298 (1980)

Spot zoning

The court ruled that a Union County rezoning of an 11.412-acre tract from residential to light-industrial use was illegal spot zoning. The lack of major transportation access, the lack of public water and sewer services, and the incompatible surrounding land uses were factors in this finding, for the court found no evidence in the record to establish a reasonable basis for the rezoning.

City of Winston-Salem v. Hoots Concrete Co., 47 N.C. App. 405, 267 S.E.2d 569, *review denied*, 301 N.C. 234 (1980)

Enforcement; Estoppel; Interpretation

In this case, initiated in 1976, the city contended that the defendant's concrete-mixing plant, constructed in 1970, was in violation of the zoning ordinance. The defense plea was that because this use was not explicitly listed in the ordinance, the city zoning officer was authorized to interpret the ordinance to determine if it was a permitted use, and that in fact the city zoning officer had interpreted the ordinance in 1970 to allow the use. The court ruled that the defendant had the burden of proving this affirmative defense, that the city was not estopped by its failure to take enforcement action, that evidence of other permissible uses and the cost of the defendant's investments should have been allowed in evidence as relevant to a determination of whether the purported 1970 approval had in fact been given, and that the estoppel instruction was confusing enough to warrant a new trial.

Springdale Estates Ass'n v. Wake County, 47 N.C. App. 462, 267 S.E.2d 415 (1980)

Subdivisions

The court ruled that the county violated the provision of its subdivision ordinance prohibiting the use of subdivision names that "duplicate[d] or closely approximate[d]" the names of existing subdivisions when it had approved "Springdale Woods" and "Springdale Gardens" after previously approving "Springdale Estates." A recombination of lots is not exempt from subdivision approval unless a finding is made that the resultant lots meet or exceed current subdivision standards.

National Advertising Co. v. Bradshaw, 48 N.C. App. 10, 268 S.E.2d 816 (1980)

Enforcement; Nonconformities; Signs

The plaintiff had a nonconforming sign with a Department of Transportation (DOT) permit. After the sign was damaged in a storm, DOT revoked the permit because it determined that the sign was damaged by more than 50 percent. The court held that neither the state Administrative Procedure Act nor due-process principles entitled the plaintiff to a hearing before the secretary on its permit revocation. The court upheld the revocation.

City of Elizabeth City v. LFM Enterprises, Inc., 48 N.C. App. 408, 269 S.E.2d 260 (1980)

Appellate procedures; Enforcement

The city sought a mandatory injunction to enforce compliance with a zoning requirement for a front and side yard planting strip. The court ruled that when a variance has been sought and denied and the denial has not been appealed, the zoning-ordinance provision cannot be collaterally attacked in an enforcement proceeding.

County of Cumberland v. Eastern Federal Corp., 48 N.C. App. 518, 269 S.E.2d 672, *review denied*, 301 N.C. 527, 273 S.E.2d 453 (1980)

Aesthetics; Amortization; Jurisdiction; Nonconformities; Signs

The court upheld enforcement of the county sign ordinance against two preexisting signs that exceeded the size allowed by the ordinance. The court upheld a three-year amortization period and dismissed a First Amendment claim. Further, the court ruled that the ordinance can lawfully be based on aesthetic concerns and that its lack of application within city boundaries does not violate the Equal Protection Clause.

Development Associates v. Wake County Board of Adjustment, 48 N.C. App. 541, 269 S.E.2d 700 (1980), *review denied*, 301 N.C. 719, 274 S.E.2d 227 (1981)

Agricultural uses; Interpretation

The court overruled a board of adjustment's determination that a dog-breeding and kennel facility on a 2.5-acre parcel was exempt from zoning coverage as a bona fide farm. The court concluded that G.S. 160D-903 exempts only farming and livestock from county zoning and that dogs are not livestock within the meaning of the statute.

Pigford v. Board of Adjustment, 49 N.C. App. 181, 270 S.E.2d 535 (1980), *review denied and appeal dismissed*, 301 N.C. 722, 274 S.E.2d 230 (1981)

Standing

The court ruled that because the record did not establish that the petitioner was the owner of affected property or an aggrieved party, it had been error for the trial court to review this decision of Lenoir County's board of adjustment.

Emanuelson v. Gibbs, 49 N.C. App. 417, 271 S.E.2d 557 (1980)

Exactions; Subdivisions

The defendants placed posts along a lane that was on the boundary of the plaintiff's property and the defendant's subdivision. The county had approved the subdivision plat showing the lane as a right-of-way with a notation expressly accepting the road dedication but assuming no responsibility for the maintenance of the road until the county determined it to be in the public interest. The court held that this acceptance was sufficient to establish a completed dedication.

Burton v. New Hanover County Zoning Board of Adjustment, 49 N.C. App. 439, 271 S.E.2d 550 (1980), *review denied*, 302 N.C. 217, 276 S.E.2d 914 (1981)

Board of adjustment; Evidence; Hearings; Minutes; Nonconformities; Oaths

This case involved an appeal of a finding that the petitioner had illegally extended a nonconforming use in New Hanover County. The court ruled that when adequate minutes were available for two hearings and a transcript was available for a third, an adequate record existed for judicial review. Further, when witnesses for neither side had been sworn but the petitioner had been present and had had the right to offer evidence and cross-examine witnesses, the petitioner's right to insist on sworn testimony was deemed to have been waived.

Pigott v. City of Wilmington, 50 N.C. App. 401, 272 S.E.2d 752 (1981)

Liability

The city building inspector notified the plaintiff that two small greenhouses he had constructed violated the building code and would have to be brought to code standards or demolished. After the greenhouses were removed, the city determined that one of them was exempt from code requirements and could have remained. The court held that the building inspector was a "public official" engaged in governmental functions because (1) the position was created by statute, (2) the official was required to take an oath of office, (3) the official performed public functions prescribed by law, and (4) the inspector was vested with a measure of discretion. Because the inspector was such a public official engaged in the performance of governmental duties, there could be no liability for the city unless the actions were corrupt, malicious, or outside the scope of the official's duties.

Appalachian Poster Advertising Co. v. Zoning Board of Adjustment, 52 N.C. App. 266, 278 S.E.2d 321 (1981)

Amortization; Nonconformities; Signs

In this case from Shelby, two immediately adjacent, unlighted, 12-by-24-foot billboards, which were a non-conforming use in a residential zone, were replaced with a single, lighted, 12-by-48-foot billboard. The court upheld the board of adjustment's finding that this action was an illegal expansion of a nonconforming use because the ordinance did not allow for structural alterations or improvements beyond routine maintenance and repair. The court noted that nonconforming uses are not favored by the law and that it is permissible for zoning ordinances to provide for their gradual phasing out by amortization, attrition, or otherwise.

Wenco Management Co. v. Town of Carrboro, 53 N.C. App. 480, 281 S.E.2d 74 (1981)

Amendments; Downzoning; Purposes

The court invalidated a rezoning by Carrboro that had the effect of prohibiting restaurants with drive-in windows (but not all restaurants or all businesses with drive-in windows) from locating within the town and that had clearly appeared to be directed at a single business. The court ruled that the record failed to demonstrate any rational relationship of the amendment to a legitimate police-power objective. However, the court upheld a simultaneously adopted ordinance prohibiting left turns into and out of the restaurant as a valid way of dealing with potentially hazardous traffic congestion.

Graham Court Associates v. Town Council of Chapel Hill, 53 N.C. App. 543, 281 S.E.2d 418 (1981)

Ownership

The town attempted to regulate the conversion of an existing apartment complex to condominiums through the zoning ordinance. The court held that the zoning-enabling statutes authorize the regulation of land use but not the regulation of land ownership, so the town was without authority to require a special use permit for a conversion in the form of ownership.

Atkins v. Zoning Board of Adjustment, 53 N.C. App. 723, 281 S.E.2d 756 (1981)

Accessory buildings and uses; Interpretation; Nonconformities

The court ruled that the portion of the nonconforming agricultural-services business in Union County constructed after the adoption of the zoning ordinance did not qualify as nonconforming. The court noted a policy consideration to limit the expansion of nonconforming uses with a view toward their eventual elimination. The court further held that the addition of facilities to store and transport sand, gravel, and lumber could not be considered an accessory use to the business of hauling grain, lime, and fertilizer.

Harts Book Stores, Inc. v. City of Raleigh, 53 N.C. App. 753, 281 S.E.2d 761 (1981)

Adult uses; Special uses

The board of adjustment denied a special use permit for an adult bookstore although the proposed bookstore met all of the objective standards set out in the ordinance (parking, a sign, and separation from other adult entertainment and residential districts). The court ruled the denial improper, holding that when an applicant produces competent, substantial, and material evidence that all of the standards established by the ordinance are met, and when no contrary evidence has been produced, the permit has to be issued. A finding that the use would be a "detriment to the neighborhood" as grounds for denial is an improper delegation of legislative power to the board, and such unguided discretion is unlawful.

Graham v. City of Raleigh, 55 N.C. App. 107, 284 S.E.2d 742 (1981), *review denied*, 305 N.C. 299, 290 S.E.2d 702 (1982)

Contract zoning; Spot zoning

The city rezoned a 19.3-acre tract in Raleigh from residential to various uses, including office and institutional. The court ruled that a rezoning is presumed valid if there are reasonable grounds to conclude that it advances a legitimate public purpose. The court found that the record documented thorough council consideration of growth, traffic, and neighborhood factors. The council had considered all permitted uses within the new district and the comprehensive plan. Further, the council had not relied on a specific development proposal.

R.O. Givens, Inc. v. Town of Nags Head, 58 N.C. App. 697, 294 S.E.2d 388, *cert. denied*, 307 N.C. 127, 297 S.E.2d 400 (1982)

Amortization; Nonconformities; Signs

The plaintiff challenged a Nags Head requirement that off-premise commercial billboards be removed after a five-and-a-half-year amortization period. The court upheld the ordinance. It ruled that federal and state law does not preempt local regulation in commercial and industrial areas and that legislation requiring compensation for the removal of signs had been enacted after these signs were required to be removed. The court rejected a First Amendment challenge, upheld the reasonableness of the amortization period, and rejected an equal-protection claim regarding lack of application to on-premise advertising.

New Hanover County v. Pleasant, 59 N.C. App. 644, 297 S.E.2d 760 (1982)

Appeals; Enforcement

New Hanover County attempted to secure an injunction requiring defendants to cease operation of a commercial business in a residential district and compelling removal of certain structures via an order of abatement. The offending structures had been built after the denial of a building permit for noncompliance with the zoning ordinance, after a notice of violation upon commencement of construction, and after a board of adjustment's finding that the structure was in violation of the zoning ordinance, which had not been appealed to the courts. The court ruled that an ordinance provision authorizing any lawful action to prevent or remedy any violation was broad enough to invoke the statutory authority for injunctive relief provided generally for enforcement of county ordinances. Further, the court ruled that the defendant could not raise an estoppel defense at the enforcement stage when neither the permit denial nor the board of adjustment's order had been appealed.

Messer v. Town of Chapel Hill, 59 N.C. App. 692, 297 S.E.2d 632 (1982), *review denied*, 307 N.C. 697, 301 S.E.2d 390 (1983)

Exactions; Subdivisions

The court upheld Chapel Hill's relocation of a two-acre open-space area required to be dedicated to public use as a condition of approval of a forty-lot, twenty-nine-acre subdivision. The court ruled that the city has the authority to set the location of the recreation area as a condition of approval and that use of the site does not have to be restricted to subdivision residents.

Rose v. Guilford County, 60 N.C. App. 170, 298 S.E.2d 200 (1982)

Judicial review

The plaintiff challenged a rezoning of a 100-acre tract that had the effect of prohibiting the location of any additional mobile homes on the plaintiff's property. The court ruled that a judgment on the pleadings was inappropriate in that the plaintiff had alleged arbitrary and capricious action by the county.

National Advertising Co. v. Bradshaw, 60 N.C. App. 745, 299 S.E.2d 817 (1983)

Enforcement; Evidence; Signs

The state Department of Transportation (DOT) revoked the plaintiff company's billboard permit due to unpermitted removal of vegetation in front of the sign. The company denied responsibility for cutting the vegetation. A DOT employee testified that the vegetation was removed contemporaneously with a change of advertising on the sign. Absent any further evidence as to the identity of those responsible, the court held this was inadequate evidence to support a conclusion that the defendant was responsible.

Godfrey v. Union County Board of Commissioners, 61 N.C. App. 100, 300 S.E.2d 273 (1983)
Contract zoning; Spot zoning

Neighbors challenged the rezoning of a 17.45-acre tract from a low-density residential district to a heavy-industrial one. The court found the rezoning to be illegal spot zoning, given that all the surrounding land use was low-density residential and the property rezoned had no characteristics to distinguish it from the adjoining property. The court noted that although the property might well have been suitable for the rezoned category, its indistinguishable character relative to surrounding property and zoning was deemed controlling. Also, reliance by the county on a specific planned use of the property after the rezoning was invalid as contract zoning.

Heery v. Town of Highlands Zoning Board of Adjustment, 61 N.C. App. 612, 300 S.E.2d 869 (1983)
Special uses; Standing

Neighbors challenged the granting of a special use permit by the town of Highlands. The court ruled that the plaintiffs lacked standing to challenge this decision because they were not "aggrieved parties" under G.S. 160D-1402(c); that is, they had not established that they would suffer any "special" damages distinct from those incurred by the rest of the community. Also, a challenge to the ordinance provision allowing the board of adjustment to issue permits on a three-fifths vote (rather than on the four-fifths majority required by statute) was dismissed because the board acted unanimously in this instance.

Jennewein v. City Council of Wilmington, 62 N.C. App. 89, 302 S.E.2d 7, *review denied*, 309 N.C. 461, 307 S.E.2d 365 (1983)
Evidence; Historic preservation; Special uses

The court upheld the denial of a special use permit for an antique shop in the city's historic district. The court held that there was competent, material, and substantial evidence in the record to support the council's finding that increased traffic and use of flammable solvents in occasional furniture refinishing would "materially endanger the public health and safety," given the neighborhood of old wooden buildings located very close together.

Baucom's Nursery Co. v. Mecklenburg County, 62 N.C. App. 396, 303 S.E.2d 236 (1983)
Agricultural uses

The court held that a 19.6-acre tract used as a plant nursery and greenhouse was a bona fide farm within the definition of G.S. 160D-903 and within the definition of such a farm in the county zoning ordinance (such definition being explicitly allowed by local legislation). The agricultural products raised and sold on the property included vegetables, flowers, and shrubs.

Barber v. Dixon, 62 N.C. App. 455, 302 S.E.2d 915, *review denied*, 309 N.C. 191, 305 S.E.2d 732 (1983)
Manufactured housing; Restrictive covenants

A subdivision restrictive covenant prohibited the use of a "structure of a temporary character (including house trailers)." The court held that this covenant prohibited use of a structure comprising two units transported to the site, even though the wheels, the tongues, and the axles had been removed two days after the units had been located on the lot.

City of Sanford v. Dandy Signs, Inc., 62 N.C. App. 568, 303 S.E.2d 228 (1983)
Nonconformities; Signs

The defendant had erected the posts and the framing for a billboard before the effective date of a zoning-ordinance provision prohibiting such a sign but had not actually installed the sign itself. The court ruled that the sign was a permissible nonconforming use under the prior zoning.

Piney Mountain Neighborhood Ass'n v. Town of Chapel Hill, 63 N.C. App. 244, 304 S.E.2d 251 (1983)
Comprehensive plan; Special uses; Standing

Neighbors appealed the town council's issuance of a special use permit for a subsidized-housing project. The court ruled that the neighborhood association had standing to sue based on the property interests of its members. In upholding the issuance of the permit, the court ruled that the comprehensive plan was by its own terms advisory and general and that the evidence supported a finding that the project would conform to the plan, would not harm neighboring property values, and was a public necessity. The court further ruled that due process is not violated by the fact that neither the minutes nor a transcript of the public hearing before the council had been completed when the council voted on the matter a week following the hearing. Finally, the court ruled that the findings made by the council in issuing the permit could simply repeat the requisite findings in the ordinance.

Lewis v. City of Washington, 63 N.C. App. 552, 305 S.E.2d 752 (1983)
Mistakes; Sales contracts

The plaintiff had contracted to lease property from the city to construct and rent boat slips. After payment of $500 to the city, both parties had discovered that the proposed use would be inconsistent with city zoning. The court ruled that the lease contract was ultra vires because the city could not enter into a contract that "disadvantageously affect[ed]" its government powers, including zoning. Therefore, the plaintiff was entitled to neither specific performance nor damages. [Note: The supreme court reversed the judgment on the matter of recovery of the $500 rental but otherwise upheld the decision. 309 N.C. 818, 310 S.E.2d 610.]

Goodman Toyota, Inc. v. City of Raleigh, 63 N.C. App. 660, 306 S.E.2d 192 (1983), *review denied*, 310 N.C. 477, 312 S.E.2d 884 (1984)
Amortization; Nonconformities; Signs

The court upheld application of the city's sign ordinance to an advertising blimp used by the plaintiff. The court ruled that the ordinance was designed to address legitimate public purposes (aesthetics and traffic safety) and did so by reasonable means (the benefits to the legitimate purpose outweighing the burden on the plaintiff). The court further ruled that the ninety-day amortization period for windblown signs was adequate and that the provision of the ordinance allowing such signs during special events was clear enough to permit those affected to know that they were so situated and was therefore not void for vagueness.

Duggins v. Town of Walnut Cove, 63 N.C. App. 684, 306 S.E.2d 186, *review denied*, 309 N.C. 819, 310 S.E.2d 348 (1983), *cert. denied*, 466 U.S. 946 (1984)
Manufactured housing; Presumption of validity

A landowner challenged a town ordinance that prohibited a "mobile home" in a residential zoning district but allowed "modular" and site-built homes of similar dimensions to be used. The court upheld the ordinance as validly regulating the location of various types of structures. Also, the court ruled that given the presumption of validity, the city only had to establish that the ordinance was rationally related to any legitimate government objective. The protection of property values is such a legitimate objective. The council could determine that the method of construction was a factor in affecting the price of homes.

Charlotte Yacht Club, Inc. v. County of Mecklenburg, 64 N.C. App. 477, 307 S.E.2d 595 (1983)
Special uses

The county board of commissioners denied a special use permit for a bathhouse and a campground adjacent to Lake Wylie. The court ruled that the trial court had improperly overturned the county commission's decision. When an applicant fails to produce sufficient evidence for the commission to make its requisite finding, the permit has to be denied.

Roberts v. City of Brevard, 64 N.C. App. 542, 307 S.E.2d 781 (1983)
Planned-unit developments

Neighbors challenged a project to build eleven duplexes on a 3.29-acre tract in Brevard. The proposed development was a permitted use in the applicable zoning district and met all dimensional standards. It also met the definition of planned-unit development in the ordinance, which allowed for exceptions to certain standards following a special approval procedure. The court ruled that the planned-unit development process was optional and had to be followed only if exemption from applicable standards was being sought.

Cannon v. Zoning Board of Adjustment, 65 N.C. App. 44, 308 S.E.2d 735 (1983)
Nonconformities

The plaintiff proposed construction of a storage shed on property being put to a nonconforming use in a residential district in Wilmington. The court ruled that the evidence supported the board of adjustment's finding that such construction would be an unlawful expansion of a nonconforming use, even if the area in question had previously been sporadically used for open-air storage or as a stable.

Martin Marietta Corp. v. Forsyth County Board of Adjustment, 65 N.C. App. 316, 309 S.E.2d 523 (1983)
Appellate procedures

After the board of adjustment denied a special use permit for a quarry, the trial court dismissed the matter "without prejudice" for failure to properly serve the respondent. The petitioner appealed the dismissal, the respondent appealed the "without prejudice" portion, and the petitioner then dropped the appeal. The court ruled for the respondent, noting that once the trial court had dismissed the matter, it was without personal jurisdiction and was therefore without power to grant any relief.

New Hanover County v. Burton, 65 N.C. App. 544, 310 S.E.2d 72 (1983)
Nonconformities

The county sought to prohibit the defendant from engaging in any nonconforming use of a property following a judicial determination that the defendant had illegally converted one nonconforming use to another. The ordinance allowed a nonconforming use to continue unless it had been discontinued for two years, and the board in this instance had made no finding relative to a period of discontinuance of the original nonconforming use. The court upheld a trial court order prohibiting the new unapproved nonconforming use but allowing resumption of the previous permissible nonconforming use.

Lee v. Union County Board of Commissioners, 65 N.C. App. 810, 310 S.E.2d 122 (1984)
Reapplication

The county rezoned a ten-acre tract in Union County from one residential district to another. A previous application had been invalidated by the courts for failure to properly follow procedures for notice to neighbors. The court ruled that the ordinance provision prohibiting the reconsideration of a rezoning petition within one year of a denial does not apply to a judicial invalidation.

Clark v. City of Charlotte, 66 N.C. App. 437, 311 S.E.2d 71 (1984)
Reapplication

The court upheld a provision of the Charlotte zoning ordinance requiring a two-year wait following the denial of a petition for a rezoning for any petition that involved the same classification that had been denied or that involved a higher classification.

Lathan v. Zoning Board of Adjustment, 69 N.C. App. 686, 317 S.E.2d 733 (1984)
Nonconformities

The Union County board of adjustment allowed a dilapidated nonconforming building to be razed and a new structure built. The ordinance explicitly allowed nonconforming uses to be enlarged with new structures, upon approval by the board of adjustment. The court held that this action was within the authority for boards to allow exceptions. [Note: G.S. 160D-705(c) was subsequently amended to delete provisions for "special exceptions."]

Town of Kenansville v. Summerlin, 70 N.C. App. 601, 320 S.E.2d 428 (1984)
Appeals; Board of adjustment; Principal use

The defendant attempted to build a second structure on a lot in violation of the town's zoning ordinance, which restricted development to one principal use per lot. The court ruled that the town must follow statutory procedures for zoning, including appointing a board of adjustment or designating an appropriate body to serve as such. Because that had not been done here, the court ruled that it was inappropriate to dismiss the defendant's appeal for failure to make the usually requisite administrative appeal. However, the court then ruled that the defendant had produced no evidence to support the issuance of a permit and had not applied for a variance, so the trial court had been proper in finding the defendant in violation of the zoning ordinance and ordering compliance.

Wil-Hol Corp. v. Marshall, 71 N.C. App. 611, 322 S.E.2d 655 (1984)
Exhaustion; Standing

The defendant challenged an eviction from a mobile-home park in Wake Forest, alleged to have been based on a request from the town to the plaintiff to close the park for noncompliance with the zoning ordinance. The court ruled that the estranged wife of a month-to-month lessee whose lease had been terminated had no interest in property sufficient to confer standing to challenge either the eviction or the applicability of the zoning ordinance. Further, because no appeal of the zoning had been made to the board of adjustment, judicial review was not authorized.

Goforth Properties, Inc. v. Town of Chapel Hill, 71 N.C. App. 771, 323 S.E.2d 427 (1984)
Appeals; Discrimination; Estoppel; Parking

The plaintiff challenged the town's requirement that off-street parking be provided or that, in lieu thereof, payment be made to a special parking fund. The plaintiff had secured a permit for a restaurant that required such payment, had made the payment, had constructed the restaurant, and then had initiated this challenge. The court ruled that having accepted the benefits of a permit, a plaintiff is estopped from subsequently challenging the fee requirement. The court also ruled that it is permissible for the town to exempt churches from this requirement (a reasonable basis for the distinction being the different timing of their parking demand) and to hold the money in a fund for later expenditure.

Wiggins v. City of Monroe, 73 N.C. App. 44, 326 S.E.2d 39 (1985)
Demolition; Housing code; Liability

The city found a house owned by the plaintiff to be unfit for habitation and dilapidated. The city's building inspector ordered the house vacated, repaired, or demolished within ten days. Upon no action or appeal by the plaintiff, the city council a month later affirmed the order and the council action was also not appealed. The inspector then ordered repairs, and in an order issued nearly a year later directed the work to commence within ten days and be completed within sixty days. Nine days after this order the town commenced demolition. The court held that the city council order authorized repair or demolition and that once the officer elected to allow repair, that election could not be arbitrarily withdrawn. The court also held that the enforcement officer had potential liability as an officer, as there was an allegation of corrupt and malicious conduct, and that the city had potential liability given its purchase of liability insurance.

Forsyth County v. Shelton, 74 N.C. App. 674, 329 S.E.2d 730, *review denied*, 314 N.C. 328, 333 S.E.2d 484 (1985)
Nonconformities

The property at issue had been put to a nonconforming use by the defendant as a commercial swimming lake, picnic area, and amusement area. Following an illness of the owner, the property was initially leased to others for a similar use and then used by family members for noncommercial purposes for at least four years. The ordinance defined abandonment of a nonconforming use to be voluntary discontinuance with an intent not to reestablish such use. The court ruled that whether discontinuance is voluntary is a question of fact to be determined given all the circumstances present, including illness. The court ruled that there was sufficient evidence for the trier of fact reasonably to find that there had been voluntary abandonment.

In re Goforth Properties, Inc., 76 N.C. App. 231, 332 S.E.2d 503, *review denied*, 315 N.C. 183, 337 S.E.2d 857 (1985)
Special uses

The applicant appealed the denial of a special use permit for a 180-unit apartment complex in Chapel Hill. The court ruled that the evidence in the record regarding increased traffic counts and their effects on traffic safety at a nearby intersection and for nearby schools and fire stations constituted competent, material, and substantial evidence to support the council's finding that the proposed development would not maintain public health and safety.

Sherrill v. Town of Wrightsville Beach, 76 N.C. App. 646, 334 S.E.2d 103 (1985)
Judicial review; Variances

The applicant unsuccessfully sought a variance to construct a duplex in a single-family zoning district. The court ruled that as a matter of law the city was without authority to grant a variance because a substantial departure from the ordinance would violate its spirit and could be accomplished only through a rezoning. The single-family designation explicitly limited density and a duplex would increase density. Therefore, a duplex could not be a proper subject for a variance, even though it was also a residential use and even though there might be other duplexes in the area as nonconforming uses.

First American Federal Savings & Loan Ass'n v. Royall, 77 N.C. App. 131, 334 S.E.2d 792 (1985)
Subdivisions

This case involved a dispute between the plaintiff, a lot purchaser, and the defendant, a developer, over who had the responsibility to pay for a $12,569 water-line extension required by the city of Raleigh before it would grant a certificate of occupancy for the plaintiff's building. Because the developers had contracted in the sale to provide water and sewer service and to convey the property free and clear of all encumbrances, and because the city's approval of the subdivision required the water line that was the subject of this litigation, the court upheld a summary judgment for the plaintiff.

Mayes v. Tabor, 77 N.C. App. 197, 334 S.E.2d 489 (1985)
Nuisances

The plaintiffs operated a summer camp near Brevard. The defendant subsequently located a hog farm on adjacent property. The plaintiff brought a nuisance action, alleging that keeping 300 to 500 hogs in pens as close as ten feet from the property line unreasonably harmed the plaintiff's land. The court held that since the defendant had not engaged in negligent operation of the farm, the standard for injunctive relief was whether the defendant's intentional action caused an unreasonable interference with the use and enjoyment of the plaintiff's land. The reasonableness of the defendant's activity is to be determined by weighing the gravity of the harm to the plaintiff against the utility of the defendant's conduct. The court held that the nuisance protection for agricultural uses provided by G.S. 106-701 was inapplicable in this case as the plaintiff's camp use long predated establishment of the agricultural use.

Willis v. Union County, 77 N.C. App. 407, 335 S.E.2d 76 (1985)
Comprehensive plan; Contract zoning

Neighbors challenged a rezoning. The court ruled that summary judgment for the county had been improperly granted in that there were genuine issues of material facts: (1) there was no evidence in the record of the geographic scope of the county zoning ordinance nor of studies that had been done to develop the comprehensive plan and (2) there was evidence in the record that specific plans for the property had been considered, raising the issue of contract zoning.

Pamlico Marine Co. v. North Carolina Department of Natural Resources & Community Development, 80 N.C. App. 201, 341 S.E.2d 108 (1986)
Coastal Area Management Act; Interpretation

The plaintiff appealed a $250 civil penalty assessed for replacing the decking around a marina in Back Creek in Bath without the permit required under the Coastal Area Management Act. The court held that the replacement of decking that had been removed ten years earlier was new development and was thus subject to permit requirements. The court further held that it was not "repair or replacement" because the old decking no longer existed; rather, it was an "accessory" use as defined by Coastal Area Management Act regulations. The court interpreted the ambiguously worded regulation that set the criteria for permit exemptions for "minor" work. The text of the exemption stated that "all of the following criteria" must be met, but the six listed criteria were connected with the word "or." The court held that the intent of the regulation was that each of the six criteria had to be met.

Mize v. County of Mecklenburg, 80 N.C. App. 279, 341 S.E.2d 767 (1986)
Appellate procedures; Enforcement; Jury trial

The zoning administrator ordered the plaintiff to stop using land for an airport. That order was upheld by the board of adjustment. The court of appeals ruled that the board of adjustment (as distinct from the county per se) was a necessary party for lawsuit purposes. However, if a timely petition for review naming the county as a defendant had been filed, the trial court should have allowed a motion to amend the petition to join the board of adjustment. But the trial court had not been the trier of fact, so a jury trial had not been appropriate in this matter. No stays were provided for in the statute during an appeal from the board to the courts, so it had not been error for the trial court to enjoin operation of the airport.

Nelson v. City of Burlington, 80 N.C. App. 285, 341 S.E.2d 739 (1986)
Contract zoning; Reapplication; Spot zoning

The court ruled that when property immediately across the street has been zoned for business, rezoning a small parcel from single-family and multifamily residential to business use is not arbitrary, capricious, or implausible. The court further ruled that an ordinance could prohibit a reapplication for rezoning from citizens for twelve months without applying the same limitation to rezonings initiated by the council or the planning board. Finally, the court held that when there is evidence that the council considered a specific development proposal rather than all permissible uses under the new zoning category, it is inappropriate to grant summary judgment on a contract-zoning issue.

Ghidorzi Construction, Inc. v. Town of Chapel Hill, 80 N.C. App. 438, 342 S.E.2d 545, *review denied*, 317 N.C. 703, 347 S.E.2d 41 (1986)
Special uses

The court ruled that the council's denial of a special use permit for a ninety-one-unit development on a 15.2-acre tract because of effects on traffic safety was supported by substantial, material, and competent evidence, given the traffic studies and reports submitted by the petitioner and the town staff. The town council is not required to consider possible future road improvements in making its judgment.

Southern Equipment Co. v. Winstead, 80 N.C. App. 526, 342 S.E.2d 524 (1986)

Nonconformities

The petitioner had not actually operated a nonconforming concrete-mixing plant in Mount Olive for more than six months but had maintained the plant, the equipment, the inventories, and the utilities during this period. In interpreting the ordinance, the court ruled that this was not "ceasing" the use (which would lead to a forfeiture of nonconforming status in six months) but was more similar to "discontinuing" the use (which would lead to forfeiture of nonconforming status in twelve months).

Brummer v. Board of Adjustment, 81 N.C. App. 307, 343 S.E.2d 603, *review denied*, 318 N.C. 413, 349 S.E.2d 590 (1986)

Board of adjustment; Evidence

The Asheville board of adjustment issued a variance to a front-yard setback and included a condition on the height of the structure. The owner and neighbors disagreed on how the height should be measured and secured an interpretive ruling from the board. The court ruled that the board's finding of fact on this matter had no evidentiary support and therefore could not stand.

Sherrill v. Town of Wrightsville Beach, 81 N.C. App. 369, 344 S.E.2d 357, *review denied*, 318 N.C. 417, 349 S.E.2d 600 (1986)

Amendments; Enforcement; Statutes of limitation

The court held that the statute of limitations prohibited a challenge to the validity of a zoning amendment (in this instance a text amendment deleting duplexes as a permitted use) brought more than nine months after the rezoning. To have a refusal to rezone set aside, the plaintiff has to meet an extraordinarily high burden of showing that the governing board could have had no legitimate reason for its decision. Laxity of enforcement per se does not establish a constitutional violation. The plaintiff was simply unable to make the required showing. Also, there was no showing of a taking or a violation of the Equal Protection Clause.

Davis v. City of Archdale, 81 N.C. App. 505, 344 S.E.2d 369 (1986)

Standing

In this challenge to a rezoning, the court ruled that an alleged diminution of property values due to increased traffic and increased demands on overburdened utilities does not rise to the level of special damages distinct from those incurred by the rest of the community, a prerequisite for standing. Therefore, the plaintiff had no standing to challenge the rezoning.

Appeal of CAMA Minor Development Permit No. 82-0010 v. Town of Bath, 82 N.C. App. 32, 345 S.E.2d 699 (1986)

Coastal Area Management Act; Notice; Purposes; Vested rights

The petitioner challenged the adoption of a zoning ordinance by the town of Bath that prohibited the wet or dry storage of boats at marinas. The court upheld the ordinance as being based on legitimate objectives (protection of the water quality, the rights of fishing and navigation, and the aesthetic characteristics of the town) and achieved by reasonable means (the public good achieved outweighing the interference with the property owners' rights, given the extensive uses to which the property could still be lawfully put). The court held that the public notice and the planning-board referral had been adequate, even though substantial changes were made, because the original notice had been sufficiently broad to indicate the possibility of substantial change and the changes had been within the fundamental character of the matter noticed and discussed at the hearings. The court further ruled the statute creating a statutory vested right upon the issuance of a building permit did not apply retroactively to this project.

Lyerly v. Malpass, 82 N.C. App. 224, 346 S.E.2d 254 (1986), *review denied*, 318 N.C. 695, 351 S.E.2d 748 (1987)
Subdivisions

This case involved a dispute over the construction of a boat basin and a road pavement for a subdivision in New Hanover County. The court ruled that even though no written document had expressly promised that these improvements would be made, the recorded plats, the restrictive covenants, and the oral representations had created an implied promise. There was an affirmative obligation to complete the amenities that had served as an inducement for those buying in the subdivision. The court further ruled that it was within the trial court's discretion to award specific performance rather than monetary damages.

Little v. City of Locust, 83 N.C. App. 224, 349 S.E.2d 627 (1986), *review denied*, 319 N.C. 105, 353 S.E.2d 111 (1987)
Appellate procedures

The court held that petitions for certiorari for superior-court review of decisions by the board of adjustment are not the equivalent of a beginning of an action. Therefore, they do not have to be verified, and there is no need for a summons in these proceedings.

Tate v. Board of Adjustment, 83 N.C. App. 512, 350 S.E.2d 873 (1986)
Board of adjustment; Jurisdiction

A question arose as to whether a swimming pool at a residence that was also used as a nonconforming day care center might be used by those participating in the day-care program. The Asheville city staff asked the board of adjustment for an interpretation of the ordinance. The court ruled that the board was without jurisdiction to provide the interpretation because it is an appellate body and could not offer advisory opinions. The staff must make an initial ruling, which an affected party might appeal to the board.

Town & Country Civic Organization v. Winston-Salem Board of Adjustment, 83 N.C. App. 516, 350 S.E.2d 893 (1986), *review denied*, 319 N.C. 410, 354 S.E.2d 729 (1987)
Appeals; Notice

The plaintiff organization appealed a permit issued for the construction of six radio towers to the board of adjustment. The court ruled that the board should have dismissed the appeal because it had not been made within the thirty days allowed by the ordinance. Even if the notice of the decision had not been posted as required, more than thirty days had elapsed between the delivery of the towers on the site and the appeal, so there was no prejudice to the petitioners because of the lack of posting.

Whiteco Metrocom, Inc. v. Roberson, 84 N.C. App. 305, 352 S.E.2d 277 (1987)
Enforcement; Signs

The court upheld a state Department of Transportation revocation of a billboard permit when the appellant's agents improperly serviced the sign via access from the interstate highway. The fact that the workers were unsupervised, uncontrolled, independent subcontractors did not absolve the permittee of responsibility, as a duty to comply with the law cannot be delegated.

Wiggins v. City of Monroe, 85 N.C. App. 237, 354 S.E.2d 365, *review denied*, 320 N.C. 178, 358 S.E.2d 72 (1987)
Demolition; Housing code; Liability

The plaintiffs contended that the city's building inspector "willfully, wantonly, and maliciously" ordered demolition of a dilapidated house they owned rather than allowing previously ordered repairs to be undertaken. After a jury trial on the matter, the trial court issued a directed verdict for the defendant. The court held that the issue should have been submitted to the jury.

***In re* Melkonian, 85 N.C. App. 351, 355 S.E.2d 503,** *review denied*, **320 N.C. 631, 360 S.E.2d 91 (1987)**
Alcohol sales; Preemption

Havelock denied a special use permit for a tavern that had been issued an alcoholic beverage control (ABC) permit by the state ABC commission. The court ruled that G.S. 18B-901 preempted the field as to both the fitness of the applicant and the place of alcohol sales. Although the ABC commission expressly "may consider" parking, zoning, and local government recommendations, it has sole discretion in permitting ABC facilities. The trial court's order requiring the issuance of the city permits was upheld.

Town of Lake Waccamaw v. Savage, 86 N.C. App. 211, 356 S.E.2d 810, *review denied*, **320 N.C. 797, 361 S.E.2d 89 (1987)**
Extraterritorial jurisdiction

The town brought an action to enforce its sign ordinance. The court ruled that the extraterritorial ordinance was invalid for failure to adequately describe the area pursuant to G.S. 160D-202(e). The map used had sweeping curves, no scale, and did not coincide with any geographic features.

Stegall v. Zoning Board of Adjustment, 87 N.C. App. 359, 361 S.E.2d 309 (1987), *review denied*, **321 N.C. 480, 364 S.E.2d 679 (1988)**
Cemeteries; Nonconformities; Special uses

The petitioner proposed installation of aboveground crypts and a sales office at a nonconforming cemetery in New Hanover County. Even though the petitioner had, at the building inspector's insistence, secured a special use permit that included a condition prohibiting aboveground crypts and the petitioner had not appealed that permit, the court ruled that aboveground burial was a fundamental aspect of cemeteries, not a change in kind of activity, and was therefore not an unlawful expansion of a nonconforming use. The court noted that the ordinance did not prohibit an intensification of nonconforming uses. The sales/security office was deemed to be a prohibited expansion. The court ruled that the petitioner was not bound by limitations in the special use permit condition because it only authorized what the petitioner already had a legal right to do, so the petitioner had secured no benefit via the permit.

Cardwell v. Forsyth County Zoning Board of Adjustment, 88 N.C. App. 244, 362 S.E.2d 843, *review denied*, **321 N.C. 742, 366 S.E.2d 858 (1987)**
Board of adjustment; Procedures; Special uses

In this case challenging the issuance of a special use permit for a quarry, the court ruled that local legislation allowed the board of adjustment to make determinations by a simple-majority vote. However, the board was required to follow its own procedures. The record failed to state in detail the facts supporting the findings that had been made, and the required summary of the evidence by the chair, with opportunities for the parties to make objections or corrections, had not been made. Therefore, the court remanded the case to the board for adherence to its procedures.

Ad/Mor v. Town of Southern Pines, 88 N.C. App. 400, 363 S.E.2d 220 (1988)
Appeals

The board of adjustment ruled that the petitioner's sign violated the defendant town's sign ordinance. G.S. 160D-1405(d) provides that appeals to superior court must be made within thirty days of the later of (1) the receipt by aggrieved parties of the notice of decision or (2) the filing of the decision in an office designated by the ordinance. The record showed only that the petitioner had not filed the judicial appeal within thirty days of receipt; there were no findings by the trial court with respect to the date of filing in an office. Therefore, the court ruled that it had been improper for the trial court to dismiss the appeal. The case was remanded for a finding on the filing date.

Webb v. City of Raleigh, 88 N.C. App. 480, 363 S.E.2d 681 (1988)
Signs

The court ruled that a banner containing a political message, which was attached to the side of a building, was not covered by Raleigh's sign ordinance because the ordinance did not prohibit noncommercial signs.

Baucom's Nursery Co. v. Mecklenburg County, 89 N.C. App. 542, 366 S.E.2d 558, *review denied*, 322 N.C. 834, 371 S.E.2d 274 (1988)
Damages; Statutes of limitation; Timeliness

The court ruled that an action brought in 1987 to challenge a zoning amendment adopted in 1982 was barred by the nine-month statute of limitations for challenging text amendments that was in effect at that time. The court further ruled that to bring an action for actual damages, a plaintiff must show that a county's governmental immunity had been waived by the purchase of liability insurance (which the plaintiff here had not shown) and that punitive damages were allowed only if authorized by statute (and no such statute existed in respect to counties in North Carolina).

Alderman v. Chatham County, 89 N.C. App. 610, 366 S.E.2d 885, *review denied*, 323 N.C. 171, 373 S.E.2d 103 (1988)
Contract zoning; Manufactured housing; Spot zoning

The county rezoned a 14.2-acre tract from an agricultural to a mobile-home district. The court ruled the rezoning invalid as impermissible spot and contract zoning. The county had considered and rejected five previous rezoning requests for a larger parcel that included the area under dispute. The rezoned parcel was in the midst of a 500-acre area zoned for agricultural uses but was adjacent to a 16-acre parcel already zoned for mobile homes. The court found no "clear showing of a reasonable basis" for the rezoning, which was required for the spot zoning, considering (1) changed conditions, (2) particular characteristics of the area being rezoned, and (3) the classification and the development of nearby land. Because the proposal had been approved only on the basis of a reduction in the density of the project, and there had been no determination that the site was suitable for all uses permitted in the proposed zoning classification, the court concluded that the rezoning was also improper contract zoning.

Teen Challenge Training Center, Inc. v. Board of Adjustment, 90 N.C. App. 452, 368 S.E.2d 661 (1988)
Appeals; Vested rights

Neighbors challenged a certificate of zoning compliance issued by Moore County for use of a 30.9-acre parcel in a residential-agricultural district. The certificate was issued on August 20, 1985. An appeal was made to the board of adjustment on July 8, 1986, which subsequently revoked the certificate of compliance. The applicant had spent some $30,000 on the project in reliance on the certificate. The court held that appeals had to be made to the board within a "reasonable time," and because the ordinance did not set a specific time, reasonableness depended upon the circumstances. In this case the neighbors had learned of the project no later than April 14, 1986, and no evidence had been presented to justify the delay in appealing, so the court ruled that the appeal to the board should have been dismissed as not being timely. [Note: G.S. 160D-405(d), which sets a thirty-day time limit to appeal to the board of adjustment, was subsequently enacted.]

Stokes County v. Pack, 91 N.C. App. 616, 372 S.E.2d 726 (1988), *review denied*, 324 N.C. 117, 377 S.E.2d 246 (1989)
Nonconformities; Phased development; Vested rights

The petitioner purchased a ten-acre site for a garage and automobile-salvage business. Five acres had been cleared and were in use as a garage and a junkyard at the time of adoption of a zoning ordinance that prohibited these uses. The court ruled that when there was a phased development, nonconforming-use status is applied only to the phases actually underway at the time they became nonconforming, because completion of a nonconforming use is permissible but expansion of one is not. Therefore, the petitioner was allowed to add additional salvage vehicles to the five-acre portion of the site underway but was not allowed to expand the use into the uncleared five-acre portion.

Newton v. City of Winston-Salem, 92 N.C. App. 446, 374 S.E.2d 488 (1989)
Demolition

The plaintiff, an owner of rental property, had been served in 1982 with an order to repair the dwelling. However, four certified-mail letters sent to the plaintiff in 1984–85 regarding a demolition order had been returned marked "unclaimed." A notice of impending demolition had then been posted on the site. After the building had been demolished, the plaintiff brought this action for damages. The court held the city liable because of a failure to strictly follow the notice provisions of G.S. 160D-1203, ruling that reasonable diligence in securing actual notice does not excuse a failure to secure personal service or notice by publication. The court also ruled that the city was required to sell the salvageable materials and credit the receipts against the costs of demolition.

Cardwell v. Smith, 92 N.C. App. 505, 364 S.E.2d 625, *review denied*, 324 N.C. 334, 378 S.E.2d 790 (1989)
Appeals

Neighbors challenged a special use permit issued for a rock quarry in Forsyth County. While one appeal of the permit decision was pending, the zoning ordinance had been amended, and this action had been brought. The court held that before it could rule on the applicability of the amendment to this project, the validity of the original permit had to be determined, and that matter was still in litigation. Therefore, the court ruled that it had been improper for the trial court to enter summary judgment in this case; it should have been dismissed as not ripe for determination.

White v. Union County, 93 N.C. App. 148, 377 S.E.2d 93 (1989)
Manufactured housing; Special uses

The county denied a special use permit to establish electrical power for a pre-1976 mobile home. The ordinance limited the use of mobile homes as residences to those built after 1976 or valued at more than $5000. The court ruled that the applicant could secure judicial review of the denial. The court expressed some doubt about the county's statutory authority for the monetary-value requirement.

Blackwell v. Dorosko, 93 N.C. App. 310, 377 S.E.2d 814, *withdrawn in part*, 95 N.C. App. 637, 383 S.E.2d 670 (1989)
Erosion; Misrepresentation

The plaintiffs, purchasers from Michigan, had bought a condominium at Kure Beach. Subsequent erosion had damaged decks, led to special assessments for sandbags, and endangered the structure. At an initial hearing, the court dismissed the plaintiffs' allegations of fraud and misrepresentation brought against the real-estate agent on the grounds that the agent had made only general representations about the rate of erosion and had volunteered to secure additional information, an offer the plaintiffs had declined. On rehearing, the court ruled that the evidence on whether the agent had in fact offered to secure the additional information was controverted and that summary judgment was therefore inappropriate. Further, the court noted that a practice did not have to be calculated to deceive in order to constitute a deceptive trade practice but only had to have the capacity or the tendency to deceive.

Flowerree v. City of Concord, 93 N.C. App. 483, 378 S.E.2d 188 (1989)
Nonconformities

A duplex apartment was being put to a nonconforming use in a single-family zoning district. Both units were vacated in February, and one was then re-rented in July. The city denied a certificate of occupancy for the second unit on the grounds that the ordinance provided that a cessation of use for three months constituted an abandonment of the nonconforming use. The court ruled that there had been no cessation of use, noting that the ordinance should have been interpreted to balance the interest of the city in phasing out nonconforming uses against the rights of the property owner. Because the owner had advertised the property, had listed it with a real-estate agent, and had undertaken renovations to improve its marketability, there had been no intent to abandon the nonconforming use.

Signorelli v. Town of Highlands, 93 N.C. App. 704, 379 S.E.2d 55 (1989)
Evidence; Special uses

The town denied a special use permit to establish a game room in a donut shop. The court held that although the applicant had submitted sufficient information to establish a prima facie entitlement to the permit, the lack of specificity in the application as to hours of operation, number of machines, and methods of supervision justified the board of adjustment's finding that it was unable to conclude that the use would not endanger the public health or safety.

In re Raynor, 94 N.C. App. 91, 379 S.E.2d 880, *review denied*, 325 N.C. 707, 388 S.E.2d 448 (1989)
Extraterritorial jurisdiction; Notice; Timeliness

Garner adopted zoning in 1982 for part of its extraterritorial jurisdiction. In 1987, the town refused to rezone the property at issue here to a lower-intensity residential district. The court ruled that the original published and mailed notices of the public hearing on the zoning had been adequate and that further notice of the planning board and the town council's consideration of the matter had not been required because the subsequent amendments to the proposal as submitted to the hearing had not been substantial. The court ruled that the statute of limitations precluded a challenge to the rezoning five years after the action was taken.

In re Raynor, 94 N.C. App. 173, 379 S.E.2d 884, *review denied*, 325 N.C. 546, 385 S.E.2d 495 (1989)
Hearings; Special uses

The applicant appeared before the town board subsequent to its hearing on his application for a special use permit and offered additional permit conditions in response to concerns raised at the hearing. The plaintiffs, neighbors challenging the issuance of the permit, complained that they had no notice of the board meeting at which the additional conditions were offered. The court upheld the issuance of the permit, noting that the town ordinance explicitly allowed applicants an opportunity to amend their applications in response to comments made at the required public hearing. The court also pointed out that the additional conditions offered by the applicant here were not tantamount to the introduction of evidence.

Sunderhaus v. Board of Adjustment, 94 N.C. App. 324, 380 S.E.2d 132 (1989)
Satellite dishes; Vested rights

The Town of Biltmore Forest sought to prohibit the completion of the installation of a satellite dish in the plaintiff's front yard. Before the adoption of an ordinance regulating dishes, the plaintiff had excavated a trench and laid PVC pipe for the wiring to run from the proposed dish to his residence. The court ruled that when substantial work has been completed on a lawful project, a vested right exists to complete the project. The court also held that a satellite dish was not a "building or structure" requiring a permit under the prior ordinance; it fell within the "usual private and domestic outbuildings and uses" exempted from permit requirements.

Concerned Citizens of Downtown Asheville v. Board of Adjustment, 94 N.C. App. 364, 380 S.E.2d 130 (1989)
Standing

No standing was found for the plaintiff, an unincorporated association, to challenge a zoning permit for a shelter for the homeless in Asheville. The court ruled that the plaintiff's members were not aggrieved persons because there had been no showing of special damages (amounting to a reduction in the value of their property) distinct from those incurred by the community at large.

Midgette v. Pate, 94 N.C. App. 498, 380 S.E.2d 572 (1989)

Enforcement; Restrictive covenants

A neighboring-property owner brought an action to compel enforcement of the town of Snow Hill's zoning ordinance. The neighbor contended that a pool, bathhouse, and fence violated zoning setback provisions and that memberships were being sold for pool use, making it an illegal commercial use in a residential zoning district. The court ruled that when a complaint alleges zoning violations and a failure of the zoning administrator to make a determination and pursue violations, it is improper for the trial court to dismiss a mandamus action brought against the town to compel enforcement. The court also ruled that a claim had been stated here regarding violation of restrictive covenants but that appeal of administrative permits issued by the town had to be made to the board of adjustment rather than directly to the court.

Franklin Road Properties v. City of Raleigh, 94 N.C. App. 731, 381 S.E.2d 487 (1989)

Exactions; Variances

The plaintiff secured a variance to allow parking and driveways within a road-setback area, as measured from the right-of-way as it would exist after a proposed road expansion. The plaintiff challenged the requirement to measure from the proposed right-of-way and the requirement that the road be widened as a precondition to securing a permit to develop the proposed office condominium. The court ruled that having accepted the benefits of the variance, the plaintiff was precluded from attacking the validity of that ordinance requirement. The court remanded the required exaction for road widening to the trial court for findings on whether there was a rational nexus between the exaction and the effects of the development.

Petersilie v. Boone Board of Adjustment, 94 N.C. App. 764, 381 S.E.2d 349 (1989)

Evidence; Special uses

The court upheld the denial of a special use permit for an apartment building in a neighborhood of single-family homes. The court ruled that although the applicant submitted sufficient evidence to support the issuance of the permit, there had also been competent evidence before the board of adjustment regarding problems of noise, traffic congestion, crime, vandalism, and effects on property values to justify the denial of the permit.

P.A.W. v. Boone Board of Adjustment, 95 N.C. App. 110, 382 S.E.2d 443 (1989)

Buffer zones; Interpretation

The board of adjustment interpreted a provision of the zoning ordinance requiring a 100-foot buffer between a high-density planned-unit development and an adjacent low-density residential district. The board ruled that the buffer had to be located entirely within the high-density zoning district, whereas the applicant contended that the buffer only had to be between building sites and could therefore be in part in the adjacent zoning district. The court upheld the board's ruling, holding that in ascertaining the intent of the governing board in adopting the ordinance, the language of the ordinance, its spirit, and its goals should be examined, and the board of adjustment's determination should not be overturned unless it was arbitrary, oppressive, or manifestly abusive of discretion.

Westminster Co. v. Union Mutual Stock Life Insurance Co., 95 N.C. App. 117, 381 S.E.2d 857 (1989)

Interpretation; Restrictive covenants

A restrictive covenant limited the use of property to "wholesale and retail as permitted under applicable zoning ordinances." A bowling center was proposed for the site. The court held a bowling center to be a "retail" business because in common usage the term included the sale of services as well as the sale of tangible goods.

In re J.H. Carter Builder, Inc., 95 N.C. App. 182, 381 S.E.2d 889, *review denied*, 325 N.C. 707, 388 S.E.2d 458 (1989)
Board of adjustment; Reapplication

The Raleigh board of adjustment granted a lot-size variance six weeks after originally denying the variance petition. The Raleigh code required a rehearing to be denied if there had been no substantial change in the facts, the evidence, or the conditions in the case. The court ruled that a board of adjustment has to follow its own procedural rules; because no changes had been demonstrated, the board could not take up the rehearing. The court considered "rehearing" and "reconsideration" to be synonymous.

Raleigh Place Associates v. City of Raleigh Board of Adjustment, 95 N.C. App. 217, 382 S.E.2d 441 (1989)
Interpretation; Signs

The court held that the board of adjustment had properly ruled that a sign on a structure covering two lanes for drive-through teller windows was a "roof sign," for which a sign permit was required, rather than a "canopy sign," for which a permit was not required. Because the ordinance did not define roof or canopy, the words were to be construed in accordance with their ordinary and common meaning.

Town of Knightdale v. Vaughn, 95 N.C. App. 649, 383 S.E.2d 460 (1989)
Enforcement; Injunctions

The court ruled that a preliminary order enjoining the defendant from operating a used car lot in violation of the zoning ordinance had been improperly issued. Even though injunctive relief might ultimately be the appropriate remedy, a preliminary injunction has to be supported by a clear showing of specific facts of irreparable harm. This showing had not been made.

Price v. Walker, 95 N.C. App. 712, 383 S.E.2d 686 (1989)
Easements; Exactions

The plaintiffs sought to close a pathway across their property. The deeds of both the plaintiffs and the defendant referred to this "road" and referenced a recorded plat map that also showed the road. The court ruled that although there had been no formal dedication to or acceptance by a public agency, the parties had acquired an easement of ingress and egress upon purchase of the lots.

Rice v. Randolph, 96 N.C. App. 112, 96 S.E.2d 295 (1989)
Subdivisions

In this case between two lot owners regarding use rights to a right-of-way in a subdivision, the court ruled that the grantor and the other record owners of lots in the subdivision were necessary parties because the grantor retained the underlying fee interest and the other lot owners had use rights to an easement dedicated by plat.

Town of Swansboro v. Odum, 96 N.C. App. 115, 384 S.E.2d 302 (1989)
Adoption; Extraterritorial jurisdiction; Notice

The court invalidated the town's adoption of extraterritorial zoning because of its failure to follow the statutorily mandated procedures for adoption. The public notice had failed to describe the nature and the character of the proposed action (it had said only that the hearing would be for the purpose of discussing extraterritorial jurisdiction); it had not described in any way the area affected; it had not been published in successive weeks (there had been ten days between the two notices); the adoption had occurred eight months after the hearing (without further notice or hearing); and the boundary description had never been filed with the register of deeds as required by G.S. 160D-202(e).

Starr v. Thompson, 96 N.C. App. 369, 385 S.E.2d 535 (1989)

Manufactured housing; Restrictive covenants

A restrictive covenant prohibited the use of "trailers or mobile homes." The court held that the restriction applied to a factory-built modular home consisting of two eight-by-forty-foot sections that had been delivered to the site with a permanent chassis with removable axles. The wheels, the axles, and the tongue had been removed, and the units placed on footings on the site. The court distinguished the definitions that were applicable for zoning from those to be used in enforcing private restrictive covenants.

In re North Topsail Water & Sewer, Inc., 96 N.C. App. 468, 386 S.E.2d 92 (1989), *review denied,* 326 N.C. 364, 389 S.E.2d 810 (1990)

Enforcement

The court upheld a $19,000 civil penalty assessed for a continuing violation caused by sediment from the petitioner's unpermitted ditches entering and filling Mill Creek in Onslow County. This portion of the penalty was based on a failure to take corrective action after a notice of violation and instruction to remedy the violation by constructing a dam to halt the siltation. The court held that there was substantial evidence in the record to support a determination that the petitioner's pattern of intentional resistance had amounted to willful noncompliance.

Summey Outdoor Advertising, Inc. v. County of Henderson, 96 N.C. App. 533, 386 S.E.2d 439 (1989), *review denied,* 326 N.C. 486, 392 S.E.2d 101 (1990)

Amortization; Nonconformities; Signs

The plaintiff challenged an ordinance setting maximum dimensions, setbacks, and minimum separations for off-premise signs larger than fifteen square feet. Nonconforming signs were required to come into conformance or be removed within five years. The court ruled that the county had statutory authority for this ordinance under its general police powers (G.S. 153A-121), that the ordinance did not violate the equal-protection clause by distinguishing between on- and off-premise signs, that it served legitimate public purposes, and that it used reasonable means to carry out those purposes. Further, the ordinance did not constitute a taking because it allowed reasonable use of the property and employed a reasonable amortization period.

Weeks v. North Carolina Department of Natural Resources & Community Development, 97 N.C. App. 215, 388 S.E.2d 228, *review denied,* 326 N.C. 601, 393 S.E.2d 890 (1990)

Coastal Area Management Act; Judicial review; Public-trust doctrine

The court affirmed summary judgment for the state, upholding the denial of a Coastal Area Management Act permit for a 900-foot-long pier in Bogue Sound. The denial was based primarily on interference with the public's use rights in the sound. The court held that when judicial review of a board's findings of fact in a quasi-judicial hearing has not been sought, the facts established by the board are binding in subsequent litigation on the matter. The court further ruled that the denial did not constitute a taking of private property without compensation.

Unruh v. City of Asheville, 97 N.C. App. 287, 388 S.E.2d 235, *review denied,* 326 N.C. 487, 391 S.E.2d 813 (1990)

Historic preservation; Procedures; Protest petitions

The plaintiffs filed a protest petition regarding a rezoning creating a historic district. The rezoning had been adopted by a 4–3 vote. The court invalidated the rezoning, holding that when protest petitions are filed, the city has an affirmative duty to determine whether the three-fourths vote requirement has been triggered. Because the city had not ruled on the adequacy of the petitions, the ordinance amendment was voided. The court further ruled that no appeal to the board of adjustment is required to exhaust administrative remedies when a challenge to an ordinance's validity is made under the Declaratory Judgment Act by a person who has a specific personal and legal interest and is adversely affected by the ordinance. [Note: The statute allowing protest petitions was subsequently repealed.]

In re Hensley, 98 N.C. App. 408, 390 S.E.2d 727 (1990)

Manufactured housing; Nonconformities

The court ruled that when the Town of Cramerton's zoning ordinance provided that a nonconforming use could not be reestablished after it had been discontinued for 180 days, a nonconforming use could be reestablished if done so in less than that time. In this instance, a mobile home had been removed from a lot in a zone that did not allow mobile homes; however, the petitioner had sought to replace the mobile home with another unit within 180 days and was thus entitled to a permit for it.

R.L. Coleman & Co. v. City of Asheville, 98 N.C. App. 648, 392 S.E.2d 107, *review denied*, 327 N.C. 432, 395 S.E.2d 689 (1990)

Interpretation; Parking

The plaintiff's permit for a shopping-center expansion was conditioned upon construction of a "T" intersection built according to city standards for an internal road's connection with the adjacent public highway. City standards allowed an intersection of between sixty and ninety degrees. The court held that the permit condition was unambiguous in that a "T" intersection required a ninety-degree connection. The court further held that a minor realignment of the directional orientation of parking spaces reasonably met the parking requirements of the approved site plan.

Mahaffey v. Forsyth County, 99 N.C. App. 676, 394 S.E.2d 203 (1990), *review denied*, 327 N.C. 636, 399 S.E.2d 327, *aff'd*, 328 N.C. 323, 401 S.E.2d 365 (1991)

Spot zoning; Statutes of limitation

The court ruled that the nine-month statute of limitations for challenging zoning-ordinance amendments (1) applied to all defendants even if plead by only one defendant; (2) was not overcome by an allegation that the rezoning constituted an ongoing constitutional violation; (3) was not affected by the actual use of the property; and (4) was not affected by a judicial invalidation of a subsequent rezoning of part of the same property. The court invalidated the subsequent rezoning of a 0.576-acre parcel as illegal spot zoning. The court found the zoning for highway business to be (1) inconsistent with the surrounding residential zoning; (2) inconsistent with the county's comprehensive plan; (3) detrimental to the community (citing traffic and aesthetic concerns resulting from commercial strip development), with only marginal benefits (there were other readily available sources for the automobile parts to be sold at the proposed store); and (4) a substantial departure from the preexisting zoning.

Donnelly v. Board of Adjustment of the Village of Pinehurst, 99 N.C. App. 702, 394 S.E.2d 246 (1990)

Interpretation; Variances

The court ruled that a lot fronted by a city street and bounded by a restricted-access highway on the rear was a "through lot" as defined by the Pinehurst zoning ordinance, considering the language of the ordinance and its purpose of preserving the appearance of a resort town. The court ruled that absent definition by the ordinance, the ordinary meaning should be given to the term "picket fence." When a variance is directly contrary to the zoning ordinance (in this case a six-foot-tall privacy fence constructed on a one-to-two-foot earthen berm on a site where the ordinance allowed only a three-foot, six-inch picket fence), the board of adjustment has no authority to grant the variance and consequently has no duty to make findings and conclusions on the merits of the request.

Randolph County v. Coen, 99 N.C. App. 746, 394 S.E.2d 256 (1990)

Nonconformities; Vested rights

Before the effective date of a zoning ordinance, the defendant formed a partnership to sell heavy equipment; cleared a site; installed a small utility building, a mailbox, and a sign at the site; obtained the required dealer's licenses; and secured vehicles for sale. The court ruled that the defendant had established a lawful nonconforming use. This constituted the expenditure of substantial labor and energy required to create a vested right to this use. The court noted that, in general, nonconforming uses cannot be expanded and the underlying policy is for their eventual abolishment.

North Buncombe Ass'n of Concerned Citizens, Inc. v. Rhodes, 100 N.C. App. 24, 394 S.E.2d 462 (1990)
Appeals

A citizens' group challenged the issuance of a mining permit for a quarry expansion near Weaverville. The plaintiffs alleged that (1) the Mining Act was unconstitutional on its face and as applied; (2) the provisions of the Act were violated by the permit; (3) the state had erred in failing to require an environmental-impact statement as stipulated by a Buncombe County ordinance that was adopted during the pendency of the permit application; (4) the permit approval violated due process; and (5) the project was a nuisance. The trial court granted summary judgment for the plaintiff on the environmental-impact statement count and summary judgment for the defendant on the constitutional and statutory challenges; it stayed trial on the nuisance count. The court of appeals, however, held that because the plaintiff had not sought contested-case review of the mining-permit decision under the Administrative Procedure Act and had thus failed to exhaust administrative remedies, the superior court had no subject-matter jurisdiction on the first three claims.

Pinehurst Area Realty, Inc. v. Village of Pinehurst, 100 N.C. App. 77, 394 S.E.2d 251 (1990), *review denied*, 328 N.C. 92, 402 S.E.2d 417, *cert. denied*, 501 U.S. 1251 (1991)
Notice; Statutes of limitation

The court upheld the dismissal of a challenge to a zoning ordinance filed after the nine-month period in the statute of limitations had run. The court ruled that a rezoning to a classification that was more restrictive than requested but less restrictive than the prior zoning as a matter of law caused no damage to the landowner and that a suit based thereon had been properly dismissed for failure to state a claim.

Coulter v. City of Newton, 100 N.C. App. 523, 397 S.E.2d 244 (1990)
Open meetings; Special uses

This case involved an ordinance standard that required approved plans for water and sewer systems as a precondition to a special use permit. The court ruled that this requirement was met when the permit itself contained terms and conditions specifying an agreement for the city to extend a water line and for the applicant to extend a sewer line to the site. The court dismissed a challenge to the validity of this agreement based on a violation of G.S. 143-318.11, ruling that open-meeting law challenges have to be brought within forty-five days of the initial disclosure of the action allegedly taken at a closed meeting; in this case, the plaintiffs had learned of the agreement more than sixty days before initiating litigation.

Russell v. Guilford County, 100 N.C. App. 541, 397 S.E.2d 335 (1990)
Vested rights

The plaintiff claimed a vested right based on substantial expenditures in good-faith reliance on a prior approval. The court held that no vested right had been established, noting these factors: the original purchase had not been based on the prior zoning; the proceeds from a loan on the property had been used for other projects, for work necessary to secure approval to develop, and for work consistent with the prior zoning; and there had been no substantial expenditure of time or labor on the project (no site preparation). Therefore, the court held that "substantial expenditures" had not been made.

Allen v. City of Burlington Board of Adjustment, 100 N.C. App. 615, 397 S.E.2d 657 (1990)

Accessory buildings and uses; Appeals; Interpretation; Laches; Standing

A property owner who objected to a community kitchen and a homeless shelter in his neighborhood was held to have alleged sufficient special damages distinct from those incurred by the community at large to have standing as an aggrieved party to challenge a zoning-ordinance interpretation. An appeal of the interpretation that a homeless shelter was a permissible use was barred by laches and the ordinance (which provided that appeals had to be brought within a "reasonable time"); the appellant had constructive notice of the ongoing use in 1986 and the appeal had been brought in 1989. The permissibility of the use was unaffected by a proposed expansion of the shelter. However, an appeal regarding the use of the facility as a community kitchen was timely because such a use should not have been considered the equivalent of a "boarding house." The adult day care and allied church offices that were included were within the range of uses that could have been deemed permitted.

Dale v. Town of Columbus, 101 N.C. App. 335, 399 S.E.2d 350 (1991)

Contract zoning; Spot zoning

This action challenged the rezoning of a 4.99-acre tract from a single-family residential district to a highway-commercial district. The court held that this was not spot zoning because the property had been bounded on two sides by commercial or institutional zones before the rezoning (the court also noted that there was community benefit in the rezoning). The court further held that this was not contract zoning, even though the applicant had noted a specific use for the property, because the governing board had explicitly considered all permissible uses in the new zone and had understood that the owner was not limited to the use mentioned (and there had been no reciprocal agreement between the town and the owner).

Riggs v. Zoning Board of Adjustment, 101 N.C. App. 422, 399 S.E.2d 149 (1991)

Interpretation; Structures

The Carteret County zoning ordinance provided that the maximum coverage of a "structure and parking area" was 65 percent. The owner's building covered 52.4 percent of the total acreage and did not provide for parking; however, a stormwater-collection system consisting of asphalt coverage, concrete swales, and in-ground piping occupied much of the rest of the lot. The court held that the zoning administrator and the board of adjustment erred in not considering the stormwater system a "structure," ruling that the definition that should be applied (in the absence of a more precise definition in the ordinance) was the natural and recognized meaning: any piece of work artificially built up or composed of parts joined together in some definite manner.

Cramer Mountain Country Club & Properties, Inc. v. North Carolina Department of Natural Resources & Community Development, 102 N.C. App. 286, 401 S.E.2d 851 (1991)

Sedimentation

The Department of Natural Resources and Community Development assessed a $6600 civil penalty (a continuing violation that was assessed at $100 per day for sixty-six days) for failure to file a sedimentation plan, provide a buffer, plant the buffer, or build sedimentation basins. The administrative-law judge recommended a reduction in the penalty, but the agency upheld the full amount. The trial court reversed the agency's decision. The court of appeals reinstated the full penalty, concluding that there was substantial evidence in the whole record to support the agency's decision.

Forest Oaks Homeowners Ass'n v. Isenhour, 102 N.C. App. 322, 401 S.E.2d 860 (1991)

Manufactured housing; Restrictive covenants

The restrictive covenant in this case prohibited trailers and "mobile homes," but it permitted "modular or component homes or pre-built homes" if erected on a permanent foundation. The court applied the manufactured/modular distinction used in the state building and zoning code to rule that a modular home could be placed on the lot in question.

Guilford County Planning & Development Department v. Simmons, 102 N.C. App. 325, 401 S.E.2d 659, *review denied*, 329 N.C. 496, 407 S.E.2d 533 (1991)

Enforcement; Jurisdiction; Procedures

The defendant was denied a permit to construct two chicken houses. He was subsequently denied a variance for the same, and the variance decision was not appealed. The defendant then began construction, and when the county commenced this enforcement action, he defended with a contention that the chicken houses were not in the county's jurisdiction. The trial court held for the defendant on the grounds that the property was not shown on the zoning map. The court of appeals remanded the case to secure a finding on whether the property was within the county. If not, the enforcement action had to be dismissed for lack of jurisdiction. If so, the defendant could not collaterally attack jurisdiction; such an action can only be raised in an appeal of the variance denial.

Conservation Council of North Carolina v. Haste, 102 N.C. App. 411, 402 S.E.2d 447 (1991)

Appeals; Coastal Area Management Act

A Coastal Area Management Act permit was issued to the North Carolina Department of Transportation to construct a stone revetment and groin for the protection of the southern end of the Oregon Inlet bridge. The permit was issued under a temporary rule that allowed such a project. The plaintiff requested a hearing to contest the issuance of the permit. When the request was denied, the plaintiff appealed. The court held that the allegation that the act's provisions for notice and comment on rule amendments had not been followed was a sufficient basis to grant a hearing. The petitioner was not required to use the exact language of the statute ("arbitrary and capricious" or "abuse of discretion") as long as the substance of the merits of the claim was clear. The court did note that a permanent rule that had subsequently been properly adopted might well allow the project.

Cardwell v. Town of Madison Board of Adjustment, 102 N.C. App. 546, 402 S.E.2d 866 (1991)

Interpretation; Nonconformities

A commercial warehouse was operated as a nonconforming use in a residential zoning district. The zoning administrator, relying on definitions in the state building code, considered the structure two buildings because of a fire wall separating the two parts and ruled that nonconforming status on one half had been lost because it had been unoccupied for 180 days. The court overruled this determination, holding that the administrator's interpretation should have been based on the definition in the zoning code, not the building code (the court also noted the limited relevance of a definition concerning construction to a land use question).

Webb v. North Carolina Department of Environment, Health & Natural Resources, 102 N.C. App. 767, 404 S.E.2d 29 (1991)

Coastal Area Management Act

An adjacent landowner challenged the location permitted for a bulkhead on his neighbor's lot on Banks Channel in Wrightsville Beach. An administrative-law judge recommended that the permit be revoked. However, the Coastal Resources Commission upheld the permit as issued. The court of appeals affirmed the commission's decision, holding that the decision did not have to include a point-by-point refutation of the administrative-law judge's findings and conclusions as long as the reasons for the commission's decision were specific and clearly stated. The court ruled that because the Coastal Area Management Act regulations did not specify how the "mean high water" line was to be determined, the approximate location of the line by expert staff using physical indicators on site was adequate.

Pamlico Tar River Foundation, Inc. v. Coastal Resources Commission, 103 N.C. App. 24, 404 S.E.2d 167 (1991)
Appeals; Coastal Area Management Act; Evidence

The plaintiff's request for an administrative hearing to contest the issuance of a Coastal Area Management Act permit for a 302-slip marina proposed for Chocowinity Bay in Beaufort County was denied. The court held that to be entitled to a hearing under G.S. 113A-121.1, a petitioner has to present relevant evidence to show that a substantive standard of the law would be violated by the project and the petitioner had failed to do so. An affidavit supporting an alleged violation of standards had been offered after the decision to deny the hearing request had been made. The court ruled that this evidence was material, not merely cumulative, and remanded the case to the trial court to determine whether it could reasonably have been presented before or during the consideration of the plaintiff's petition for a hearing as required by G.S. 150B-49.

Appalachian Outdoor Advertising Co. v. Town of Boone, 103 N.C. App. 504, 406 S.E.2d 297 (1991)
Appeals; Signs

The town found that a sign constructed by the plaintiff was in violation of the zoning ordinance because it blocked an adjacent sign. The board of adjustment upheld the zoning administrator's determination that the sign was in violation, and the plaintiff did not appeal that decision within the thirty days provided by G.S. 160D-1405(d). The court upheld the dismissal of this later judicial appeal for compensation on the grounds that the issue could have been and was raised in the unappealed decision of the board of adjustment and thus could not be collaterally attacked in a subsequent proceeding.

Vulcan Materials Co., Inc. v. Iredell County, 103 N.C. App. 779, 407 S.E.2d 283 (1991)
Adoption; Interim ordinances; Moratoria

The county adopted an ordinance putting a sixty-day moratorium on the issuance of any building permits for uses that would be contrary to the county's land use plan, pending its consideration of a zoning ordinance. The court ruled that this was a land use ordinance and that therefore the public-notice and hearing requirements of G.S. 160D-601 had to be met for it to be valid (which had not been done in this case). Therefore, the plaintiff was entitled to a mandatory injunction directing the issuance of a building permit for the proposed quarry.

CG & T Corp. v. Board of Adjustment of Wilmington, 105 N.C. App. 32, 411 S.E.2d 655 (1992)
Nonconformities

The plaintiff challenged a city finding that nonconforming status had been lost for its nonconforming oil refinery in Wilmington. The zoning administrator ruled that nonconforming status was lost because of cessation of use. The plaintiff contended that although oil was not being refined on site, the facility was being used for oil storage and being maintained for future reuse as a refinery. The ordinance provided that when a nonconforming use was "discontinued" for 365 days, its nonconforming status was lost. The court rejected the plaintiff's contention that an intent not to resume was required, as would have been the case had the ordinance used the term "abandoned," and upheld the board of adjustment's conclusion that nonconforming status had been lost as adequately supported by competent, substantial, and material evidence based on the whole record. The court also held that the decision had not been arbitrary or capricious and that a motion to reopen the hearing for additional evidence had been properly denied by the board.

Triple E Associates v. Town of Matthews, 105 N.C. App. 354, 413 S.E.2d 305, *review denied*, 332 N.C. 150, 419 S.E.2d 578 (1992)

Evidence; Special uses

The town denied a special use permit for a day-care center, determining that the application met none of the three requisite findings of the ordinance (that a proposed project be consistent with the plan, that it be compatible with the general characteristics of the area, and that it not worsen traffic congestion). The court held that the permit must be issued if the applicant presented uncontroverted competent, substantial, and material evidence that the standards had been met. The court ruled that on the first two points there was inadequate contravening evidence and that on the third point the town had improperly considered speculative traffic projections. The matter was remanded for a de novo hearing on the traffic condition only.

City of High Shoals v. Vulcan Materials Co., 105 N.C. App. 424, 413 S.E.2d 294, *review denied*, 332 N.C. 343, 421 S.E.2d 145 (1992)

Adoption; Vested rights

The defendant attempted to construct a rock quarry and applied for and received county building, well installation, and improvement permits in July 1989. It applied for a state mining permit in September 1989, which was issued in March 1990. The city had informed the defendant in July 1989 that part of the site was in the city, that the part had since 1973 been zoned for residential use, and that the city was considering adopting extraterritorial zoning for the remainder of the site. The extraterritorial zoning was enacted in December 1989. At trial, the city failed to produce a copy of its 1973 ordinance but had produced two affidavits from city officials and certified county records as to the ordinance's existence. The court of appeals held that it had been improper for the trial court to grant summary judgment for the plaintiff on the basis of the nonexistence of the ordinance. The court of appeals did not therefore reach the issue of whether any vested rights had been established before the December 1989 adoption of extraterritorial zoning.

Cardwell v. Smith, 106 N.C. App. 187, 415 S.E.2d 770, *review denied*, 332 N.C. 146, 419 S.E.2d 569 (1992)

Vested rights

Neighbors brought an action to enjoin operation of a quarry. The court held that there was uncontroverted evidence that the defendant had spent over $1 million in reliance on a special use permit issued pursuant to the Forsyth County zoning ordinance before the amendment of the ordinance to remove quarries from the permitted uses in this zoning district. Therefore, summary judgment that a vested right had been established was appropriate. The common law vested right did not depend on the issuance of a building permit.

Frizzelle v. Harnett County, 106 N.C. App. 234, 416 S.E.2d 421, *review denied*, 332 N.C. 147, 419 S.E.2d 571 (1992)

Adoption; Notice

The court held that the notices of public hearings on the extension of zoning to the southern portion of Harnett County were inadequate. The mailed-notice provisions then in effect did not apply unless there were tax maps available for the area (there were not), but the ordinance itself required mailing a notice and posting one, which had not been done. These ordinance requirements applied to initial adoption as well as to rezonings. The court also held that because the county had failed to raise the nine-month statute of limitations in its answer or to give notice of it to the plaintiff when it was raised in response to a summary-judgment motion, it had been waived.

Stepp v. Summey Outdoor Advertising, Inc., 106 N.C. App. 621, 417 S.E.2d 848 (1992)

Signs

This action involved a controversy between the lessee and the lessor of a site for an outdoor advertising sign. The court interpreted the lease to require that the defendant conform his sign to the Hendersonville zoning ordinance (which did not allow a separate structure on the lot if the sign was nonconforming).

Shear v. Stevens Building Co., 107 N.C. App. 154, 418 S.E.2d 841 (1992)
Subdivisions

The court held that when a recorded subdivision plat depicted a lake and a surrounding undeveloped area, an easement to that area was created for lot purchasers. Representations at sale and subsequent actions by the seller might further define the scope of the easement. In this case, it was held that the purchasers had secured by implied dedication an easement to the lake in the Cardinal Hills subdivision in Raleigh. The court further held that the lot owners benefited by the easement should pay the costs of maintaining the dam and the easement.

Ford v. North Carolina Department of Environment, Health, & Natural Resources, 107 N.C. App. 192, 419 S.E.2d 204 (1992)
Sedimentation

The plaintiff was assessed $17,240 in civil penalties for violations of the Sedimentation Pollution Control Act. After a hearing the administrative-law judge made findings of fact and recommended that no penalty be assessed. The secretary of the Department of Environment, Health, and Natural Resources accepted some of the factual findings and made a final agency decision assessing an $8620 civil penalty. The trial court reversed the decision for failure to state specific reasons for not accepting the administrative-law judge's findings. The court of appeals overruled, concluding that G.S. 150B-36 and -51 allowed the body making the final decision to make an independent assessment of the evidence in the record and enter its own conclusions based thereon.

In re Raleigh (Parks & Recreation Department), 107 N.C. App. 505, 421 S.E.2d 179 (1992)
Bias; Evidence; Special uses

Neighbors challenged a special use permit issued by the Raleigh City Council to the Raleigh Parks and Recreation Department for the construction of the Walnut Creek outdoor amphitheater. The court concluded that there was sufficient evidence in the record to support findings that the nearby properties would be protected from sound amplification and light, that there would not be a substantial adverse impact on surrounding properties, and that property values in the surrounding neighborhood would not be substantially reduced. The court noted that use of a summary of the evidence presented, rather than a verbatim transcript, was permissible but made appellate review difficult. The court held that due process was not violated by the fact that city council members had previously participated in planning for this municipal venture and were generally enthusiastic about the project because there was no evidence of impermissible bias (a fixed opinion that was not susceptible to change before the hearing).

County of Hoke v. Byrd, 107 N.C. App. 658, 421 S.E.2d 800 (1992)
Junkyards

The court upheld a county ordinance requiring that automobile junkyards or repair shops located within 300 feet of the center line of a public road, within one-half mile of any school or church, within 300 feet of a housing unit, or within any residential area be surrounded by fencing and vegetated screening. The court ruled that such an ordinance was within the general police power, that it did not violate the Equal Protection Clause, and that G.S. 136-141 to 155 did not preempt the ordinance because this junkyard was not within 1000 feet of an interstate or primary highway.

Crowell Constructors, Inc. v. North Carolina Department of Environment, Health, & Natural Resources, 107 N.C. App. 716, 421 S.E.2d 612 (1992), *review denied*, 333 N.C. 343, 426 S.E.2d 704 (1993)
Enforcement; Mining

The court upheld a $26,000 civil penalty for mining without a permit. The court found that penalties could be assessed for violations that occurred before receipt of a notice of violation, provided that the notice was made before the assessment. The court also upheld initial use of "pacing" off the area to determine the size of the cleared portion.

EEE-ZZZ Lay Drain Co. v. North Carolina Department of Human Resources, 108 N.C. App. 24, 422 S.E.2d 338 (1992)

Liability

This case involved a challenge to a refusal to permit use of an innovative nitrification method for on-site waste-disposal drain fields. The court held that state departments and the county health department had government immunity from suit, that the county health director was an "officer" and thus shielded from liability unless corrupt or malicious acts were involved, and that engineers and supervisors within the Department of Human Resources were "employees" and subject to liability if there was negligence in the performance of their jobs. The court found no malicious or negligent acts and thus no liability.

Law Building of Asheboro, Inc. v. City of Asheboro, 108 N.C. App. 182, 423 S.E.2d 93 (1992), *review denied*, 333 N.C. 575 (1993)

Building permits and inspection

The court ruled that there was no authority to bring a lawsuit for damages for the denial of a building permit.

Covington v. Town of Apex, 108 N.C. App. 231, 423 S.E.2d 537 (1992), *review denied*, 333 N.C. 462 (1993)

Special uses; Spot zoning

Neighbors challenged the rezoning of a single lot containing a former post office from an office and institutional district to a conditional use district that would allow an electronic assembly business. The court upheld summary judgment for the challengers. It ruled that the plaintiffs had made an adequate showing of minimal benefits to the community, which was not sufficiently controverted by the city, and had made an adequate showing that the rezoning decision was unreasonable, arbitrary, and not in the public interest. Further, the court held that the rezoning was unreasonable spot zoning given the small size of the rezoning, its inconsistency with the town's comprehensive plan, the modest benefit to the owners, the considerable opposition by neighbors, and the incompatibility of the proposed new use with surrounding uses.

Ballance v. North Carolina Coastal Resources Commission, 108 N.C. App. 288, 423 S.E.2d 815 (1992), *review denied*, 333 N.C. 536 (1993)

Coastal Area Management Act

The petitioners requested a contested-case hearing to appeal a Coastal Area Management Act permit issued to extend a pier and to construct docking facilities in Pamlico Sound off Ocracoke Island. The petition was denied on the basis of a conclusion that the petitioners had failed to put forth a prima facie case that permit standards had been violated. The trial court ruled that the denial of the request for a hearing was improper and revoked the permit. The court held that the denial of the request for a hearing was a final agency decision both on the question whether a hearing should be held and on the merits of the appeal. The court further held that uncontradicted evidence in the whole record supported the trial court's conclusion that the permit violated permit standards.

Rice Associates of the Southern Highlands, Inc. v. Town of Weaverville Zoning Board of Adjustment, 108 N.C. App. 346, 423 S.E.2d 519 (1992)

Bias; Special uses

The board of adjustment denied a special use permit for a unified housing development. A board member who had previously expressed bias against the petitioner fully participated in the hearing. The denial was based on failure to provide more than one ingress and egress to the project, as was required by the ordinance. The court upheld the denial, ruling that the petitioner was not entitled to the permit under any circumstances because the project failed to meet an objective standard in the ordinance that involved no discretion. Therefore, the bias of the member could not have affected the outcome of the decision.

Angel v. Truitt, 108 N.C. App. 679, 424 S.E.2d 660 (1993)
Manufactured housing

The court held that placement of a modular home on a lot did not violate a restrictive covenant prohibiting "mobile homes." The court applied the customary definition of "mobile homes" at the time the covenant was executed (1981), using the dictionary definition of a mobile home to mean a house trailer that is hauled by a truck. Since the modular unit involved here had no permanent chassis or axles and was placed on a permanent foundation, it was ruled not to be covered by the prohibition.

Abernathy v. Town of Boone Board of Adjustment, 109 N.C. App. 459, 427 S.E.2d 875 (1993)
Enforcement; Laches; Signs

Owners of a photo-finishing business obtained a permit for a freestanding sign from the town. Subsequently, they considered a move from their leased space to an adjacent shopping center. Aware that the city sign ordinance did not allow freestanding signs for businesses in shopping centers, they conditioned their purchase of the new site on approval of the city to retain their existing freestanding sign. Upon being advised by the zoning officer and building inspector that the sign could remain, they purchased the site and relocated. Some three and a half years later, in response to complaints from other businesses at the shopping center, the city advised the business that the sign was in violation of the ordinance and had to be removed. The court held that the substantial lapse of time after the city knew of the violation resulted in such a change in position by the business as to make it unjust to enforce the ordinance. For laches to run against a city, both the delay on the part of the city and the disadvantage to the party must be unreasonable.

Gaskill v. State *ex rel.* Cobey, 109 N.C. App. 656, 428 S.E.2d 474, *review denied*, 334 N.C. 163, 432 S.E.2d 359 (1993)
Appeals; Coastal Area Management Act; Procedures

A petition was filed with the Office of Administrative Hearings to contest a civil penalty and restoration order assessed for illegal fill of a salt marsh. However, the original filing did not include an affidavit verifying that the contents of the petition were true, but the petitioner and his attorney signed the petition. A verification was subsequently filed but after the twenty-day period for filing had passed. Because a verified petition for review was not filed within the statutory period allowed, the court held that the petition was properly dismissed for lack of subject-matter jurisdiction.

Kentallen, Inc. v. Town of Hillsborough, 110 N.C. App. 767, 431 S.E.2d 231 (1993)
Standing

The town issued a special use permit for the expansion of a nonconforming metal storage building. An adjacent property owner challenged the permit on the grounds that the addition would have a negative impact on its property and would not be visually attractive. The trial court allowed the challenge but upheld the issuance of the permit by the board of adjustment. On appeal, the court held that the petition should have been dismissed for lack of standing. Even though the petitioner was an adjoining owner, there was no allegation of the manner in which the value or enjoyment of the property would be adversely affected by the permitted expansion (and the allegations that were made were too general to support a finding of pecuniary loss).

Martin-Marietta Corp. v. Wake Stone Corp., 111 N.C. App. 269, 432 S.E.2d 428 (1993), *review denied,* **335 N.C. 770, 442 S.E.2d 517 (1994),** *aff'd per curiam,* **338 N.C. 602 (1995)**
Libel; Rezoning

The plaintiff Martin-Marietta proposed a quarry in Nash County. It then obtained a mining permit for the quarry, with said permit being conditioned on subsequent receipt of air and water permits. A county land use permit was then issued (though the property was not yet zoned). Wake Stone, which already had a quarry in the county, complained of what they considered special treatment that had been given to Martin-Marietta in obtaining the mining permit and urged the county to place the property in an agricultural zoning district that did not allow a quarry. The county subsequently did so and revoked the previously issued land use permit. Martin-Marietta alleged that material submitted to the county board of commissioners by Wake Stone during this debate was libelous. The court held that the material was not such that as a matter of law it tended to disgrace, degrade, or hold the plaintiff up to public hatred, contempt, or ridicule and was thus not so obviously defamatory as to be libelous. The court held that there were sufficient allegations of unfair trade practices to send that issue to trial.

Town of Newton Grove v. Sutton, 111 N.C. App. 376, 432 S.E.2d 441, *review denied,* **335 N.C. 181, 438 S.E.2d 208 (1993)**
Manufactured housing

Defendant owners of a nonconforming residence in a business zoning district were denied a permit to locate a mobile home on their lot for the use of their mentally ill daughter. The court held that the town properly concluded that placement of the unit would have been an unlawful expansion of a nonconforming use and could not be considered a customary accessory use. The court held that the state Fair Housing Act was not violated because the prohibition of a mobile home in this district applied to all property owners and was not in any way related to the defendants' child's disabling condition.

Grandfather Village v. Worsley, 111 N.C. App. 686, 433 S.E.2d 13, *review denied,* **335 N.C. 237, 439 S.E.2d 146 (1993)**
Appeals; Enforcement; Signs

The defendant was requested to remove portable signs that violated the village's zoning ordinance and advised of a $50 per day civil penalty if the signs were not removed in sixty days. After the period for removal had run, a citation was issued along with a $50 assessment. The defendant was again notified when the daily penalty had reached $700 and advised that any appeal had to be filed with the board of adjustment within thirty days, as required by the ordinance. An appeal was filed, but it was after the thirty-day period. The court held that failure to appeal within the allotted period waives any right to raise defenses to the assessment in court.

Whiteco Industries, Inc. v. Harrelson, 111 N.C. App. 815, 434 S.E.2d 229 (1993), *review denied,* **335 N.C. 566 (1994)**
Signs

The court held that the state Department of Transportation has the authority to revoke an outdoor advertising permit based on the actions of an advertiser's employees. In this case, the revocation was due to the fact that employees had cut down ten trees on the highway right-of-way in front of the advertiser's sign.

Walker v. North Carolina Department of Environment, Health, & Natural Resources, 111 N.C. App. 851, 433 S.E.2d 767, *review denied,* **335 N.C. 243, 439 S.E.2d 164 (1993)**
Marinas; Public-trust doctrine

The court held that construction of a 148-slip commercial marina occupying six acres of public-trust waters in Oriental required an easement from the state Department of Administration.

Adams Outdoor Advertising of Charlotte v. North Carolina Department of Transportation, 112 N.C. App. 120, 434 S.E.2d 666 (1993)
Signs; Takings

The plaintiff contended that the Department of Transportation's planting of trees in the state right-of-way as part of a highway beautification project obscured the visibility of eleven of its billboards in Mecklenburg County and was a compensable taking under the state's inverse-condemnation statute. The court dismissed the complaint, finding no basis for a claim of a "right to be seen."

Northwood Homeowners Ass'n v. Town of Chapel Hill, 112 N.C. App. 630, 436 S.E.2d 282 (1993)
Appeals; Procedures

This challenge to the issuance of a special use permit was dismissed because the appellant's brief failed to set out a full and complete statement of the facts, failed to set out each argument, and failed to state each question separately with pertinent assignments of error and appropriate references to the record on appeal.

Moore v. Board of Adjustment of City of Kinston, 113 N.C. App. 181, 437 S.E.2d 536 (1993)
Interpretation

The court upheld the city's conclusion that an open-air flea market was not a permitted use in a zoning district that allowed "stores and shops conducting retail business."

Ayers v. Board of Adjustment for Robersonville, 113 N.C. App. 528, 439 S.E.2d 199 (1994), *review denied*, 336 N.C. 71, 445 S.E.2d 28 (1994)
Interpretation

The plaintiff began operating a wood yard in a residential zoning district in the town's extraterritorial area. On this site, cut timber was unloaded, weighed, graded, and reloaded for sale. "Forestry" is a permitted use in this district. The zoning officer and board of adjustment concluded that "forestry" does not include ancillary timber-industry activities, but the trial court ruled that the use was "forestry" up to the point of processing. The court of appeals reversed, noting that all other uses permitted in this district were low-density, noncommercial and that allowing timber processing was inconsistent with the plain and ordinary meaning of the term "forestry."

King v. North Carolina Environmental Management Commission, 112 N.C. App. 813, 436 S.E.2d 865 (1994)
Wetlands

The court ruled that where there is substantial evidence in the record that filling a two-acre interior wetland will result in a loss of its uses as a nutrient and sediment filter, the denial of a Section 401 water-quality certification by the Environmental Management Commission must be upheld.

Brown v. Town of Davidson, 113 N.C. App. 553, 439 S.E.2d 206 (1994)
Amendments; Motives; Rezoning

The plaintiff challenged a refusal to rezone property from a residential district to a commercial district. The first allegation was of racial discrimination, as the residential property involved was predominately owned by African Americans and petitions for rezoning of undeveloped white-owned property on the other end of the street had been rezoned. The court held that there was no forecast of proof of a racially discriminatory intent or purpose, so this claim was properly dismissed. The second allegation was a due-process violation due to lack of an impartial decision maker, as several board members stated prior to the public hearing that they opposed the rezoning. The court held that since rezoning is a legislative rather than a quasi-judicial decision, a predisposition on the matter is not a due-process violation.

Guilford County Department of Emergency Services v. Seaboard Chemical Co., 114 N.C. App. 1, 441 S.E.2d 177, *review denied*, 336 N.C. 604, 447 S.E.2d 390 (1994)

Hazardous waste; Takings

The county denied a special use permit for the continued operation of a hazardous- and toxic-waste facility because it was in a watershed; it had resulted in releases of hazardous substances; it had failed to comply with state, federal, and county regulations; and it violated several zoning provisions. The defendant alleged that other uses of the property were not possible due in large part to the cleanup costs at the site. The court held that the defendant could raise claims of a taking in an independent action rather than in a certiorari review of the permit decision. However, the court held that the denial of a permit did not constitute a regulatory taking. The ordinance left many possible uses of the property, and the costs of cleaning up the site should not be considered because the cleanup was required whether or not the use as a waste facility continued.

Dellinger v. City of Charlotte, 114 N.C. App. 146, 441 S.E.2d 626, *review granted*, 336 N.C. 603, 447 S.E.2d 388 (1994), *dismissed, review improvidently granted*, 340 N.C. 105, 455 S.E.2d 159 (1995)

Exactions; Subdivisions

The city denied site-plan approval for an apartment complex that was located in the right-of-way of a proposed thoroughfare. The proposed development was to be comprised of 240 apartments in fifteen buildings on 15.51 acres. Of these fifteen buildings, nine were within the proposed seventy-foot right-of-way or forty-foot setback for the proposed road. The court held that the city had failed to follow the procedures required by the city ordinance (which mandated a finding that a required dedication (1) would not result in the deprivation of reasonable use of the property and (2) was reasonably related to the traffic generated by the proposed development or the impact of the dedication was mitigated).

City of Raleigh v. Hudson Belk Co., 114 N.C. App. 815, 443 S.E.2d 112 (1994)

Appeals; Parties

The city zoning inspector ruled that the city's sign ordinance only allowed one wall sign per building, while Hudson Belk contended that the limitation only set a maximum size per sign. The board of adjustment ruled for the company, and the city sought judicial review of that determination. The court upheld the trial court's dismissal of suit because the city failed to join the board of adjustment as a necessary party.

Simpson v. City of Charlotte, 115 N.C. App. 51, 443 S.E.2d 772 (1994)

Appeals; Quarries; Vested rights

A landowner who lived across the street from a quarry challenged a permit issued for a 112-acre expansion of the quarry. At the time of the permit decision, quarries were allowed in all zoning districts subject to specified findings, but the ordinance was amended shortly after the permit was issued to limit quarries to certain zoning districts. The trial court ruled that this was contrary to the requirement of G.S. 160D-701 that zoning should promote the public health, safety, and welfare. The court reversed, holding that only the validity of the permit, not the validity of the ordinance, had been properly before the trial court. The court held that there was insufficient information before the board to determine whether a vested right had been established prior to ordinance amendment. The court ruled that a zoning permit for the quarry was not a "building permit" that created a statutory vested right under the statutes then in effect but remanded to determine whether the $20,000 spent after receipt of the quarry permit was substantial and made in good faith. The court affirmed the conclusion that noise and vibration requirements in the ordinance apply to operation of the use, not its initial approval.

Guilford County Planning & Development Department v. Simmons, 115 N.C. App. 87, 443 S.E.2d 765 (1994)
Jurisdiction

This case involved whether the site of two proposed chicken houses was in the county and thus subject to county zoning. The trial court held that the site of the buildings was in Alamance County. The court held that failure of the defendant to file a judicial appeal of the board of adjustment's decision that the property was in Guilford County did not waive the fundamental question of whether the board had subject-matter jurisdiction. The court held that where there was conflicting information as to the location of the county line (the tax map showed it to be in Guilford but earlier zoning maps showed it to be in Alamance), the finding of fact by the trial court that the property was outside the county will not be disturbed if it is supported by competent evidence. Given the finding that the Guilford County board of adjustment never properly had subject-matter jurisdiction, res judicata cannot apply to their prior ruling.

Town of Cary v. Franklin-Sloan V.F.W. Post 7383, 115 N.C. App. 113, 443 S.E.2d 791 (1994)
Exactions; Special uses

The town approved a special use permit for construction of a VFW post on a five-acre tract in 1979. The site plan had two parallel dashed lines with the notation "80 foot proposed thoroughfare" between them, but there were no distances, bearings, or other attempts to locate the right-of-way precisely on the site. In 1989, the city filed a suit contending that an eighty-foot right-of-way had been dedicated and seeking to condemn an additional twenty feet. VFW testified that they intended to keep a potential right-of-way open but never intended to make an uncompensated dedication of the land to the city. The court held that there had been no dedication because there was not an adequate description of the street.

Garrity v. Morrisville Board of Adjustment, 115 N.C. App. 273, 444 S.E.2d 653, *review denied*, 337 N.C. 692, 448 S.E.2d 523 (1994)
Appeals; Board of adjustment; Jurisdiction

The town governing board approved a site plan for a regional solid-waste facility. Neighbors then petitioned the board of adjustment for an "interpretation and administrative review" of the governing-board approval, and the board of adjustment reversed the approval. The court held that the board of adjustment had no jurisdiction to review the governing-board decision. G.S. 160D-405 allows appeals to the board of adjustment of decisions by administrative officials, and the governing board is not an "administrative official." The court also held that the petition for writ of certiorari to the superior court challenging the board of adjustment's action need not be verified.

Dockside Discotheque, Inc. v. Board of Adjustment, 115 N.C. App. 303, 444 S.E.2d 451, *review denied*, 338 N.C. 309, 451 S.E.2d 635 (1994)
Findings; Nonconformities; Open meetings

The petitioners operated a topless bar in a Southern Pines central business zoning district. After the ordinance was amended to restrict topless bars to other zoning districts, no topless entertainment was offered for a sixteen-month period. The zoning administrator ruled that the bar's nonconforming status had been lost. On appeal of this determination, the board of adjustment heard evidence then entered into a thirty-minute executive session to discuss the case, subsequently upholding the zoning administrator's decision. The court held that while the executive session may have violated the open-meetings statute, it was not an abuse of the trial court's discretion to refuse to vacate the board's decision since the session had "little effect" on the decision. The court held that the board's failure to make any findings did not necessitate a remand because there was no dispute as to material facts and the record presented a full understanding of the issues. The court held that since the use was not in operation when the ordinance restriction was adopted, there could be no nonconforming status for the bar.

Vulcan Materials Co. v. Guilford County Board of Commissioners, 115 N.C. App. 319, 444 S.E.2d 639, *review denied*, 337 N.C. 807, 449 S.E.2d 758 (1994)

Bias; Quarries; Special uses

The board of county commissioners denied a special use permit for a proposed rock quarry on the grounds that there was insufficient credible evidence to find that the use would be compatible with the surrounding land uses, would not endanger public health and safety, would not substantially injure the value of adjoining property, and would be in conformity with the land use plan. The trial court ruled that there was not substantial, competent, and material evidence to support this conclusion. The court reversed, holding that the record showed all uses within two miles of the quarry were residential and that the land use plan reserved the area for residential use. The court held that there was no showing of bias because the announcement by some board members that they intended to vote against the permit came after the evidence had been presented in the hearing and there was no showing that members had a fixed decision prior to the hearing.

Flowers v. Blackbeard Sailing Club, 115 N.C. App. 349, 445 S.E.2d 614, *review granted*, 337 N.C. 691, 448 S.E.2d 522 (1994), *dismissed, review improvidently granted*, 340 N.C. 357, 457 S.E.2d 599 (1995)

Coastal Area Management Act; Remedies

An adjacent riparian owner filed this trespass action on the grounds that the defendant's pier obstructed the plaintiff's riparian access rights. The plaintiff had objected to a permit application filed to authorize the pier under the Coastal Area Management Act. However, when the permit was issued, the plaintiff did not appeal the permit issuance but instead brought this trespass action some twenty-two months later. The court noted that the statutes provided a clear administrative-appeal route to a specialized agency with the expertise and ability to address the precise issues raised by the plaintiff. The court therefore held that the superior court lacked subject-matter jurisdiction because of the plaintiff's failure to pursue this administrative remedy.

Leeuwenburg v. Waterway Investment Ltd. Partnership, 115 N.C. App. 541, 445 S.E.2d 614 (1994)

Coastal Area Management Act; Remedies

This case was a declaratory-judgment action seeking to invalidate a Coastal Area Management Act permit issued to the defendant for a pier located over wetlands to which the plaintiff claimed title. The court held that failure to appeal a Coastal Area Management Act permit decision regarding the pier's location was failure to exhaust administrative remedies, and therefore the plaintiff was not entitled to judicial review.

Coastal Ready-Mix Concrete Co. v. North Carolina Coastal Resources Commission, 116 N.C. App. 119, 446 S.E.2d 823, *review denied*, 337 N.C. 800, 449 S.E.2d 566 (1994)

Appellate procedures; Coastal Area Management Act

A landowner in the Jockey's Ridge area of environmental concern contended that a regulation's restrictions on sand mining constituted a taking. The trial court affirmed the permit denial at issue in the case but denied the state's motion for summary judgment on the taking issue and ordered that issue put on the trial docket. The court held that the state could not immediately appeal the taking issue as that would be an interlocutory appeal.

Budd v. Davie County, 116 N.C. App. 168, 447 S.E.2d 449, *review denied*, 338 N.C. 667, 453 S.E.2d 174 (1994)
Spot zoning

The court invalidated a rezoning of two tracts from residential-agricultural to industrial-special use. The rezoning was requested for a sand-mining operation along the Yadkin River. The tracts rezoned were a fourteen-acre tract along the river and a sixty-foot-wide, half-mile-long strip across an adjoining eighty-one-acre tract. All of the land along a four-to-five-mile route that trucks would use to haul sand away from this site was zoned residential or agricultural. The court held that this was spot zoning and that it had no reasonable basis. The comprehensive plan showed no industrial uses for this area; there was no evidence of benefit to the county from the mining; there was evidence of traffic and safety problems; and there was evidence that the use was incompatible with surrounding land uses. The court held that the adjoining landowner had standing to bring this declaratory-judgment action challenging the rezoning (and noted that ownership alone in the adjoining area affected by a legislative zoning decision may be sufficient to confer standing, as contrasted with the more demanding standard for affected parties challenging a quasi-judicial zoning decision).

Taylor Home of Charlotte, Inc. v. City of Charlotte, 116 N.C. App. 188, 447 S.E.2d 438 (1994), *review denied*, 338 N.C. 524, 453 S.E.2d 170 (1995)
Group homes

The city issued a permit for the construction of a six-bed facility to serve AIDS patients, finding it to be a "family care home" under G.S. 160D-907 and a permitted "group home" under the Charlotte ordinance. On appeal by neighbors, the board of adjustment reversed. The trial court and court of appeals affirmed this reversal. The appeals court held that (1) the facility was not a "group home" under the ordinance because that term was defined as providing for "rehabilitation" and AIDS patients could not be restored to live normal lives and (2) that patients with full-blown AIDS were not "handicapped persons" within G.S. 160D-907(b)(2) because they could not live within a normal residential environment (this term has since been changed in the statute to "persons with disabilities"). [Note: The city subsequently agreed to allow these facilities as part of a settlement agreement in a case brought by the federal government under the Fair Housing Act.]

Robinette v. Barriger, 116 N.C. App. 197, 447 S.E.2d 498 (1994), *aff'd by equally divided court*, 342 N.C. 181, 463 S.E.2d 7 (1995)
Liability

After an Alexander County sanitarian informed the plaintiff that a tract was "provisionally suitable" for on-site waste disposal, the plaintiff purchased the site in order to develop a lakeside subdivision. The health-department staff approved a map indicating the number of lots and septic-tank locations. After a final plat was recorded, a state soil scientist examined the lots and concluded conventional septic tanks could not be placed on nine of the ten proposed lots; however, another state official concluded that permits for an alternative system could be issued if properly conditioned. The county officer subsequently issued the permits without such conditions. After consultation with state officials, the county sanitarian revoked the improvements permits. Following rule amendments, permits were later issued for all but one lot. The owner sued the county (the health department), a state officer at the Department of Environment, Health, and Natural Resources, and the sanitarian individually for damages resulting from the delay. The court held there was no liability for any of the defendants. The local health department is an agent of the state, and claims against it must be filed with the N.C. Industrial Commission. The state officer was not acting in a malicious, wanton, or reckless fashion so as to justify a finding of liability. Finally, the county sanitarian was acting in an official capacity and could not be sued in an individual capacity.

Wolbarsht v. Board of Adjustment of Durham, 116 N.C. App. 638, 448 S.E.2d 858 (1994), *review denied,*
338 N.C. 671, 453 S.E.2d 186 (1995)
Evidence; Special uses

After a dog bite resulted in serious injury to a passerby, the city directed the petitioner to restrain his large dog. The petitioner then requested a special use permit to replace an existing four-foot-high fence in the front yard with a six-foot-high chain-link fence so that the dog could roam in the front yard as well as in the back (where there was already a six-foot-high fence). The board of adjustment unanimously denied the permit based on testimony from neighbors on the negative visual impacts of the fence and on allowing the petitioner's multiple dogs to come so close to passersby. The court held that the denial was supported by competent, substantial, and material evidence and was not arbitrary or capricious.

Durham v. Britt, 117 N.C. App. 250, 451 S.E.2d 1 (1994), *review denied,* **340 N.C. 260, 456 S.E.2d 829 (1995)**
Agricultural uses

The court held that conversion of three turkey houses to a hog-production facility (consisting of two buildings and a waste-treatment lagoon) is not protected by G.S. 106-701, known as the "right to farm" statute, which limits nuisance claims against agricultural operations. The court held that if there is a fundamental change in the nature of the agricultural activity, there is no liability shield.

State v. Garren, 117 N.C. App. 393, 451 S.E.2d 315 (1994)
Noise; Vagueness

Defendants challenged a Jackson County noise ordinance that prohibited "loud, raucous and disturbing noise." The defendants were cited for playing a stereo too loud and for having a live band playing outside a residence. The court found the portion of the ordinance prohibiting the loud playing of amplified sound to be overly broad and therefore an unconstitutional limitation on First Amendment rights of free speech. However, it upheld the section of the ordinance prohibiting any sound that "annoys, disturbs, injures or endangers the comfort, health, peace or safety of reasonable persons of ordinary sensibilities" as neither overly broad nor unduly vague, noting that objective evidence would be necessary to support a conviction, such as testimony that a person could not hear ordinary conversation or that windows and furniture in adjacent buildings were being rattled.

Friends of Hatteras Island National Historic Maritime Forest Land Trust for Preservation, Inc. v. Coastal Resources Commission, 117 N.C. App. 556, 452 S.E.2d 337 (1995)
Coastal Area Management Act; Interpretation

The plaintiff organization challenged a Coastal Area Management Act major-development permit issued to the Cape Hatteras Water Association by the Coastal Resources Commission for construction of nine water-supply wells in the Buxton Woods State Coastal Reserve. A trial court revoked the permit on the grounds that substantial evidence did not support its issuance and because it was arbitrary and capricious under the Coastal Area Management Act. The appeals court upheld the permit revocation, holding that the wells were not a "public use" as contemplated by the statute, which provides that the reserve is to include undeveloped coastal lands for research and education, with other compatible public uses such as fishing, hunting, navigation, and recreation. The court concluded that the level of development required for installing and monitoring the wells was inconsistent with the legislative intent that the lands remain essentially "undeveloped." The court also held that judicial review of Coastal Area Management Act permit decisions could be filed either in Wake County or in the county in which the dispute arises.

State *ex rel.* Cobey v. Cook, 118 N.C. App. 70, 453 S.E.2d 553, *review denied*, 340 N.C. 572, 460 S.E.2d 329 (1995)

Enforcement; Sedimentation

The state assessed a $5040 civil penalty for a violation of the Sedimentation Pollution Control Act. The defendant did not appeal the assessment to the Office of Administrative Hearings but refused to pay the penalty. The state brought a collection action. The court upheld the assessment, holding that civil penalties are not an unlawful delegation of judicial power as they are reasonably necessary to the enforcement of the Act (even after the state had secured authority to issue stop-work orders).

Rauseo v. New Hanover County, 118 N.C. App. 286, 454 S.E.2d 698 (1995)

Interpretation; Special uses

The New Hanover County Board of Commissioners issued a special use permit to the Ogden Volunteer Fire Department for a fire station. The board held three hearings on this matter, with the applicant being asked after each of the first two hearings to further consider alternative sites and to examine ways to address the concerns of neighboring opponents. After the third hearing, the permit was issued. The court ruled that it was reasonable to interpret the ordinance to include a fire station within its "government offices and buildings" permitted special use. The court noted that the board's decision was entitled to deference, and it found that the decision that the project met the standards in the ordinance was supported by substantial evidence in the record. The court further held that there is no requirement for a board to adopt its findings of fact at the close of the hearing unless there is a specific requirement for immediate adoption of findings in the local ordinance.

Dare County Board of Education v. Sakaria, 118 N.C. App. 609, 456 S.E.2d 842 (1995), *aff'd*, 342 N.C. 648, 466 S.E.2d 717, *cert. denied*, 519 U.S. 976 (1996)

Mitigation; Wetlands

The court held that the county board of education had the authority to condemn lots adjacent to the Cape Hatteras School for use as fill material and wetlands mitigation (as part of a project to expand the school's athletic fields). Previous applications to develop the site with either no mitigation or with off-site mitigation had been denied by state and federal environmental agencies. The court found that the board had broad discretion in determining what constituted a "suitable site" and what land is "necessary" for school facilities and that the decision to acquire these lots was not an abuse of discretion.

Buie v. High Point Associates, Ltd., 119 N.C. App. 155, 458 S.E.2d 212, *review denied*, 341 N.C. 419, 461 S.E.2d 755 (1995)

Restrictive covenants

The court held that the use of property for a drainage system for adjacent commercial development violated a restrictive covenant that the property be limited to "residential purposes only." The fact that the system also benefited the residential uses was immaterial. The court upheld issuance of a mandatory injunction to compel removal of the offending drainage system.

Shoney's of Enka, Inc. v. Board of Adjustment, 119 N.C. App. 420, 458 S.E.2d 510 (1995)

Findings; Variances

The Asheville board of adjustment denied a variance for a new sign. The board voted three to two to grant the variance, with the motion failing due to lack of the requisite four-fifths vote. The court reversed and remanded, holding that the board must adopt basic findings with sufficient specificity to inform the parties and the court as to what induced the decision. In this instance, only a preprinted form supported the variance denial, with no case-specific information added. The court held that conclusory findings alone are insufficient for either the granting or the denial of a variance.

Rusher v. Tomlinson, 119 N.C. App. 458, 459 S.E.2d 285 (1995)
Coastal Area Management Act

A neighboring owner appealed issuance of a Coastal Area Management Act permit for berthing two large vessels in the Cape Fear River in Wilmington. The court ruled that the third-party request for a contested-case hearing had been properly denied, as there is no requirement that an easement be secured for a berthing facility as it involved no structures over water.

Sinning v. Clark, 119 N.C. App. 515, 459 S.E.2d 71, *review denied*, 342 N.C. 194 (1995)
Building permits and inspection; Public-duty doctrine

The court held that a building inspector (and a city) were not liable to a home purchaser for negligence where a building inspection failed to discover structural defects and code violations that rendered the purchaser's residence unfit for occupation. The only way liability may be imposed in such situations is through the creation of a special relationship between the injured party and the city.

Thompson v. Town of Warsaw, 120 N.C. App. 471, 462 S.E.2d 691 (1995)
Statutes of limitation; Variances

The town board in 1988 authorized a landowner to construct an industrial garage in a residential zoning district. The town termed this a "variance" and did not follow any of the statutory-notice provisions for a rezoning. This suit was filed in 1993 challenging the action as an illegal rezoning. The court held that the nine-month statute of limitations barred the suit and upheld its dismissal.

Naegele Outdoor Advertising, Inc. v. Hunt, 121 N.C. App. 205, 465 S.E.2d 549 (1995), *review denied*, 342 N.C. 895, 467 S.E.2d 904 (1996)
Signs; Spot zoning

The state Department of Transportation attempted to revoke permits issued for three billboards along Interstate 85 in Davidson County on the grounds that the site of the signs had been improperly spot zoned from Rural Agricultural to Highway Commercial. The court rejected the spot-zoning challenge, holding that the record supported a conclusion that the zoning was in accordance with state law and consistent with a comprehensive plan.

Ballas v. Town of Weaverville, 121 N.C. App. 346, 465 S.E.2d 324 (1996)
Evidence; Findings; Special uses

The plaintiffs were denied a special use permit for a bed-and-breakfast in a rehabilitated house in a residential district on the basis of negative impacts on neighboring property values and inadequate roads and utilities. The court held that there was adequate evidence in the record to support a finding on either side of the property-values impact issue (the plaintiffs had submitted evidence that the use would be "an attribute to the community," and the opponents had submitted testimony from a real-estate appraiser that surrounding property values would be reduced), but evidence submitted after the hearing by the town regarding acceptance of the infrastructure improvements could not be considered. Since the board of adjustment had not adopted findings indicating the basis of their decision, the case was remanded for proper findings.

Young v. Lomax, 122 N.C. App. 385, 470 S.E.2d 80 (1996)
Manufactured housing; Restrictive covenants

The issue in this case was the interpretation of private restrictive covenants for a subdivision in Cabarrus County. The covenants prohibited "mobile homes." The structure involved had two sections, each with a steel chassis, axles, and wheels. The axles and wheels were removed upon installation and the units were secured to concrete piers. The court held that the unit remained a "mobile home" as a matter of law and was distinguishable from the modular units secured to permanent foundations.

Hayes v. Fowler, 123 N.C. App. 400, 473 S.E.2d 442 (1996)
Accessory buildings and uses; Interpretation

The plaintiffs contracted to purchase a historic home, Maryhurst, in Pinehurst. The seller was the Catholic Diocese and the structure had been used as a meeting place for religious and secular groups by a church located a block and a half away. The applicable zoning district permitted residences and churches but not commercial uses or guest houses. The court held that the plaintiffs' proposed use of four of the structure's eleven bedrooms for a bed-and-breakfast was not an accessory use to the permitted residential use of the structure. However, the court held that the church's previous use of the structure for classes, meetings, retreats, and social activities was not use as a "church" as defined by the ordinance but rather was use as a nonconforming community center. Thus, a secular purchaser would be allowed to continue (but not expand) the nonconforming use of the structure as a meeting center and site for social events.

Midway Grading Co. v. North Carolina Department of Environment, Health, & Natural Resources, 123 N.C. App. 501, 473 S.E.2d 20 (1996)
Enforcement; Sedimentation

The court held that an erosion-and-sedimentation-control plan is required whenever a person uncovers or disturbs a tract greater than one acre; there is no requirement that this person own the land being disturbed. The court further held that service of the notice of violation of the Sedimentation Pollution Control Act by certified mail to an officer of the corporation alleged to be in violation was adequate under the state Administrative Code and that the formal provisions of G.S. 1-75.10 regarding proof of service of process are not applicable.

Outdoor East, LP v. Harrelson, 123 N.C. App. 685, 476 S.E.2d 136 (1996)
Signs

The court upheld state Department of Transportation authority to revoke the sign permit for a nonconforming billboard in a noncommercial/nonindustrial area based on the illegal conduct of an advertiser's employees.

Walker v. Coastal Resources Commission, 124 N.C. App. 1, 476 S.E.2d 138 (1996), *review denied*, 346 N.C. 185, 486 S.E.2d 220 (1997)
Attorney's fees

The court awarded attorney's fees to the plaintiff who had prevailed in a previous suit challenging the issuance of a Coastal Area Management Act permit for a marina in the absence of an easement from the state for use of the public-trust waters. The court held that there was no "substantial justification" for the agency's original decision (even though it had been initially upheld by the trial court), and thus attorney's fees could be awarded pursuant to G.S. 6-19.1. The court did not allow recovery of attorney's fees and costs for the administrative hearing, however, only for the subsequent judicial appeal.

City of Roanoke Rapids v. Peedin, 124 N.C. App. 578, 478 S.E.2d 528 (1996)
Delegation

The Halifax County Board of Health adopted regulations on smoking in public places. The court held that because the regulations set different rules for different facilities (e.g., requiring restaurants with over thirty seats to provide a nonsmoking area but not imposing the same mandate on smaller restaurants), the board had improperly engaged in making legislative policy choices involving factors other than public health (such as balancing economic costs and health impacts).

Gossett v. City of Wilmington, 124 N.C. App. 777, 478 S.E.2d 648 (1996)
Amendments; Judicial review; Procedures

The petitioners sought rezoning from a single-family residential district to a multifamily conditional use district in order to construct forty condominium units. The city council denied the rezoning and the petitioner sought judicial review by filing a writ of certiorari. The court held that it was appropriate to challenge this particular rezoning as a quasi-judicial decision because the Wilmington city charter specifically provided that the city's conditional use district zoning proceeding was quasi-judicial in nature. [Note: The statutory authorization for conditional use district zoning was subsequently repealed.]

March v. Town of Kill Devil Hills, 125 N.C. App. 151, 479 S.E.2d 252 (1997)
Parking; Streets

The plat for a subdivision in Kill Devil Hills showed a 100-foot right-of-way between the bypass and the beach road. The town had accepted the right-of-way dedication, but this portion of the road had not been paved or opened. The town proposed to construct two travel lanes and forty-four parking places in the median. Neighbors challenged the parking, contending this was a "parking lot" rather than a street. The court upheld inclusion of the parking area within the right-of-way, holding that provision of on-street parking was within the town's discretion and was consistent with the use of the dedicated area as a street.

King v. State, 125 N.C. App. 379, 481 S.E.2d 330, *review denied*, 346 N.C. 280, 487 S.E.2d 548 (1997)
Coastal Area Management Act; Takings

The plaintiff's Coastal Area Management Act permit application to develop an eight-acre peninsula in Topsail Sound was denied. The development proposal was for a road down the center of the property, a bulkhead around the perimeter of the peninsula, and a fifty-lot subdivision along the road. The application was modified to delete the subdivision. Since the proposed road crossed wetlands in the interior of the property, a federal wetland permit was required under Section 404 of the federal Clean Water Act. The state denied a water-quality certification necessary for the federal permit and also denied the state Coastal Area Management Act permit. On appeal to the Coastal Resources Commission, the state permit was issued, but the permit was subject to receiving a water-quality certification. However, the denial of the certification was subsequently upheld by the Environmental Management Commission and affirmed by the courts. The court held that the determination of the facts of the case in the administrative hearings was binding for subsequent judicial review. The court further held that since practical alternatives to the plaintiff's proposed development scheme were established in the hearings (such as relocating the road and building houses on pilings), there had not been a regulatory taking. Owners are not entitled to maximizing their profits, only to some practical use of their properties with reasonable value.

Carter v. Stanly County, 125 N.C. App. 628, 482 S.E.2d 9, *review denied*, 346 N.C. 276, 487 S.E.2d 540 (1997)
Amendments; Notice; Rezoning

In this challenge to the county's authority to acquire land to be given to the state for a prison site, the court addressed the adequacy of the notice of the hearing on a rezoning of the site. The notice of the public hearing stated that the proposed text amendment would allow "government owned buildings, facilities, and institutions" as permitted uses in the affected zoning districts. The court held that this fairly and sufficiently notified the public as to the character of the proposed action and that the complaint that the notice should have been more precise or have mentioned a potential prison siting was a political rather than a legal complaint.

Wade v. Town of Ayden, 125 N.C. App. 650, 482 S.E.2d 44 (1997)
Application; Special uses

The court invalidated issuance of a special use permit for a multifamily-housing project. The Ayden zoning ordinance required submission of "complete final plans" before final approval could be granted. The applicant had submitted a "sketch plan" that did not include utility, street, and other engineering data. The court held that the ordinance requirements for the application were binding on the town and that the town had no authority to consider an incomplete application.

Pine Knoll Ass'n v. Cardon, 126 N.C. App. 155, 484 S.E.2d 446, *review denied*, 347 N.C. 138, 492 S.E.2d 26 (1997)
Coastal Area Management Act; Riparian access

Adjacent property owners, both with piers, disputed riparian rights along a navigable canal in Pine Knoll Shores. The court held that where there is an irregular shoreline (here the canal frontage made a right angle at or near the property boundary), a reasonable-use test should be employed to allow both owners access to the water.

Browning-Ferris Industries (BFI) of South Atlantic, Inc. v. Guilford County Board of Adjustment, 126 N.C. App. 168, 484 S.E.2d 411 (1997)
Vested rights

In the period between the time the plaintiff initiated the process of securing approval for operating a waste-transfer site and the time building permits were secured, the zoning ordinance was amended to require a special use permit (a waste-transfer station previously being a permitted use in the heavy industrial zone applicable to the site). BFI obtained a letter from the county planner stating that a waste-transfer station was a permitted use at a particular site and it had submitted a site-development plan to the county prior to acquiring the site. The site plan was "conditionally approved" by a staff technical-review committee nine days prior to the ordinance amendment, but neither final approval nor a building permit had been secured when the special use permit requirement was imposed. The court held that no vested rights had been established, finding that expenditures based on the pre-amended ordinance, the planner's letter, or the conditional approval were not made in reliance on a valid final approval. Further, the court noted that there had been no showing of any detriment or prejudice to the applicant as a result of having to apply for a special use permit for the transfer station.

Baker v. Town of Rose Hill, 126 N.C. App. 338, 485 S.E.2d 78 (1997)
Evidence; Special uses

The town board issued a special use permit for a soybean-meal transfer facility. The court upheld the board's approval of the permit. Evidence held to support the findings included testimony and site plans regarding the location of houses, other industrial uses, rail lines, and highways relative to the proposed facility, as well as evidence on impacts of dust, truck traffic, potential freight spills, and pedestrian safety. The court also held that the board's vote was not invalidated by the change in membership of one member between the time of the hearing and the second vote, noting that the new member had previously served on the planning board and had been furnished a copy of the full record prior to the vote and that since four of the five board members had voted to approve the permit, the petitioners had failed to show a harm to their interests.

Simmons v. City of Hickory, 126 N.C. App. 821, 487 S.E.2d 583 (1997)
Building permits and inspection; Public-duty doctrine

A city conducting building inspections in its extraterritorial jurisdiction has not created a "special relationship" with the owner of the structure being inspected. Thus, under the public-duty doctrine, the city and its inspectors are not liable to a home purchaser for negligence even if an inspection they conducted failed to discover structural defects and code violations.

Purser v. Mecklenburg County, 127 N.C. App. 63, 488 S.E.2d 277 (1997)
Comprehensive plan; Spot zoning

A neighbor challenged Mecklenburg County's rezoning of a 14.9-acre tract from residential to a commercial conditional use district as illegal spot zoning. The court held that the county had established a reasonable basis for the rezoning. The court found the site met all of the standards for the proposed neighborhood convenience center established in the General Development Policies District Plan and the East District Plan (both components of the county's comprehensive plan) regarding size, density, buffers, traffic flow, and distance from other commercial centers. The court found that the required site plan would integrate the center into the neighborhood and ensure that the development was in harmony with the surrounding residential uses.

Maynor v. Onslow County, 127 N.C. App. 102, 488 S.E.2d 289, *appeal dismissed*, 347 N.C. 268, 493 S.E.2d 458, *review denied*, 347 N.C. 400, 496 S.E.2d 385 (1997)
Adult uses; Amortization

Onslow County, which did not have a countywide zoning ordinance, adopted a general-police-power ordinance restricting the location of adult businesses (the ordinance established a minimum requirement of a 1000-foot separation between an adult business and any residence, place of worship, school, day-care facility, playground, or other adult business) and establishing a two-year amortization requirement for preexisting nonconforming adult businesses. A nonconforming adult business challenged the ordinance. The court held that this was a valid regulation to protect the public health, safety, and welfare under G.S. 153A-121 and dismissed constitutional challenges that the ordinance was vague or overly broad.

Tate Terrace Realty Investors, Inc. v. Currituck County, 127 N.C. App. 212, 488 S.E.2d 845 (1997), *review denied*, 347 N.C. 409, 496 S.E.2d 394 (1997)
Adequate public facilities; Evidence; Special uses

The plaintiff applied for a special use permit and sketch-plan approval for a 601-lot subdivision. The county denied the permit, finding that the proposed development would violate the standard that a project not "exceed the county's ability to provide adequate facilities, including, but not limited to schools, fire and rescue, law enforcement, and other county facilities." At the initial hearing on the matter, the planning director testified under oath about comments received on the project, including a written comment from the school superintendent, and the petitioner estimated that the project would increase the county's school enrollment by 10 percent. At a continued hearing in which the petitioner did not participate (the petitioner had requested a "continuance" the day prior to the hearing), a letter from the superintendent on long-range needs of the school system was presented. At its final meeting to decide the application, the board received a staff analysis recommending denial based on inadequate school facilities to support the development, and the board of commissioners made its denial on that basis.

The court held that the whole record included adequate competent, substantial, and material evidence to support the denial. Failure to participate in the duly advertised continued hearing waived any right to object to the competency of the testimony from an unsworn witness at that hearing. Also, since claims regarding vested rights, the authority to enact moratoria, and the county's duty to provide school facilities were not raised as cross-assignments of error, the petitioner had waived those matters on appeal. Finally, the court imposed double costs on the petitioner's counsel for filing an appeal brief 40 percent longer than court rules allowed.

Lloyd v. Town of Chapel Hill, 127 N.C. App. 347, 489 S.E.2d 898 (1997)
Standing; Variances

The petitioner sought variances to construct ten single-family residences on preexisting lots located within the Bolin Creek floodplain and within the town's Resource Conservation District. The town planning staff recommended approval, and intervening neighbors objected. The board of adjustment voted six to four to grant the variances, thus ultimately denying the variance as the requisite four-fifths majority was not secured. The court held that the intervenors did not have standing. Their affidavits in support of standing merely indicated they were nearby property owners and did not allege (nor did the record support the conclusion) that they would suffer any special damages distinct from the rest of the community.

Onslow County v. Moore, 127 N.C. App. 546, 491 S.E.2d 670 (1997), *vacated and remanded for consideration on the merits*, 347 N.C. 672, 500 S.E.2d 88 (1998)
Adult uses; Appellate procedures

This case consolidated three cases involving enforcement of the county's adult-business regulations. The trial court upheld the constitutionality of the ordinance but ruled it partially preempted by state law, prompting appeals by both the county and proprietors of regulated businesses. The court dismissed all appeals for failure to make timely filings of the record on appeal. [Note: For the case on remand, see *Onslow County v. Moore*, 129 N.C. App. 376, 499 S.E.2d 780, *review denied*, 349 N.C. 361, 525 S.E.2d 453 (1998), discussed below.]

Sedman v. Rijdes, 127 N.C. App. 700, 492 S.E.2d 620 (1997)

Agricultural uses

The defendants operated a plant and vegetable greenhouse operation on a forty-one-acre tract adjacent to the plaintiff's property. The operation included four greenhouses, fans, a loading dock, and some sales of the plants on the premises. The court dismissed the contention that the operation was in violation of the Orange County zoning ordinance, ruling that the entire horticultural operation was exempt from zoning as a bona fide farm under G.S. 160D-903.

Everhart & Associates, Inc. v. Department of Environment, Health, & Natural Resources, 127 N.C. App. 693, 493 S.E.2d 66 (1997), *review denied*, 347 N.C. 575, 502 S.E.2d 590 (1998)

Coastal Area Management Act; Comprehensive plan; Wetlands

The plaintiffs were denied a Coastal Area Management Act permit to place septic tanks and houses on Tolson's Island in Hyde County on the basis of inconsistency with the county land use plan and wetland fill. The plan prohibited development of estuarine islands within one mile of Ocracoke Island. The court upheld the Coastal Resource Commission's determination that the proposal was inconsistent with the plan (overruling an administrative-law judge's conclusion that the area was a "peninsula" rather than an "island"). The state had offered testimony at the administrative hearing on the issue of whether the land was an island, but the hearing officer ruled that the determination must be made on the map in the plan alone. The court held that it was proper for the commission to consider offers of proof made at the administrative hearing as they are part of the whole record before the body.

Wooten v. Town of Topsail Beach, 127 N.C. App. 739, 493 S.E.2d 285 (1997), *review denied*, 348 N.C. 78, 505 S.E.2d 888 (1998)

Parking; Streets

A portion of a dedicated street right-of-way had not been improved but had been used for access to Banks Channel, for parking boats and trailers, and for access to a private residence. The court held that the town could not block vehicular traffic and convert the right-of-way to a park without complying with the applicable statutes for closing a dedicated street.

Carolina Spirits, Inc. v. City of Raleigh, 127 N.C. App. 745, 493 S.E.2d 283 (1997), *review denied*, 347 N.C. 574, 498 S.E.2d 380 (1998)

Adult uses; Interpretation

The plaintiff operated a nightclub featuring female impersonators and contended that the zoning restrictions related to adult uses should not be applied to this business. The court held that the parties were disputing the definition of "adult establishments" set forth in the 1977 zoning ordinance, which had been subsequently amended. The court dismissed the action as moot (there being no real controversy as to the prior definition).

Appalachian Outdoor Advertising Co., Inc. v. Town of Boone Board of Adjustment, 128 N.C. App. 137, 493 S.E.2d 789 (1997), *review denied*, 347 N.C. 572, 498 S.E.2d 375 (1998)

Nonconformities; Signs

The plaintiff had a nonconforming billboard that was damaged in a storm. The structure consisted of two sign faces, six supporting poles, and lights. The damage necessitated replacement of two of the support poles and removal, straightening, and repainting of one sign face. The town staff sought to prohibit the work as "reconstruction" of a nonconformity, and the board of adjustment upheld this determination. The court held that the work was permissible "repair," noting that the sign had been damaged, not destroyed, and that the cost of the work was $255 while the tax value of the billboard was $2607 (well below the 50 percent of market value allowed by the ordinance for repair of nonconforming structures).

Gregory v. County of Harnett, 128 N.C. App. 161, 493 S.E.2d 786 (1997)
Amendments; Rezoning

The plaintiff owned a seventy-three-acre tract zoned to allow manufactured-home parks as a permitted use. A fourteen-lot park had been constructed on the property. Neighbors sought to have a 324-acre area that included the plaintiff's property rezoned to a district that prohibited manufactured-home parks but allowed manufactured homes as a special use on individual lots. The county board of commissioners denied the rezoning petition. Another neighbor filed a virtually identical rezoning petition three days after the initial denial. After additional public hearings, the second petition was approved three months later. The court invalidated the rezoning as arbitrary and capricious, finding that it was based on concerns about alleged crime problems generated by residents of mobile-home parks and that the record was devoid of any consideration of consistency with the character of the land, the suitability of the land for this use, consistency with the comprehensive plan, or the existence of any changed circumstances since the original zoning had been adopted.

State v. Mercer, 128 N.C. App. 371, 496 S.E.2d 585 (1998)
Adult uses; Appellate procedures; Nuisances

The operators of adult businesses in Onslow County sought to have a nuisance action brought by the state pursuant to Chapter 19 of the General Statutes dismissed because cases involving the same defendants were pending alleging violations of the county's adult-business ordinance. The court held that the nuisance action violation involved different subject matter, issues, and potential relief, and was thus not precluded by the pending litigation regarding local ordinance violations.

State v. Taylor, 128 N.C. App. 616, 495 S.E.2d 413 (1998)
Noise; Vagueness

The court upheld a conviction for violation of the county's animal control ordinance provisions related to excessive noise by dogs. Neighbors complained that the defendant's walker hounds' barking was relentless, incessant, and lasted almost twenty-four hours per day. The ordinance made it unlawful to keep an animal that "habitually or repeatedly makes excessive noises that tend to annoy, disturb, or frighten citizens." The court held that these terms had commonly accepted meanings and were sufficiently certain so as not to be impermissibly vague.

Fantasy World, Inc. v. Greensboro Board of Adjustment, 128 N.C. App. 703, 496 S.E.2d 825, *review denied*, 348 N.C. 496, 510 S.E.2d 382 (1998)
Adult uses; Nonconformities

The court ruled that expansion of the floor space devoted to a nonconforming adult business was a violation of the zoning ordinance. A portion of the structure at issue had been lawfully operated as a topless bar and the remainder operated as a restaurant. After adoption of separation requirements for adult businesses that rendered the use nonconforming, the restaurant closed. After a period of inactivity, the owner sought to use the former restaurant portion of the building for an adult bookstore and/or adult mini–motion picture theater. The ordinance explicitly prohibited increasing the floor area devoted to nonconformities, which the court held prohibited the expansion. The court also upheld use of a "preponderance" of matter being devoted to sexually explicit materials as sufficiently precise and ruled that there was sufficient evidence in the record to support a finding that the area was being used as an adult mini–motion picture theater.

Reunion Land Co. v. Village of Marvin, 129 N.C. App. 249, 497 S.E.2d 446 (1998)
Statutes of limitation

After the defendant village amended its zoning ordinance, the statute of limitations in G.S. 1-54.1 to challenge legislative zoning decisions was changed from nine months to two months. The court held that when the legislature shortens a statute of limitations, a plaintiff must file suit within a reasonable time but in no event can he or she file beyond the new statute of limitations. Thus, actions challenging legislative zoning decisions had to have been filed within two months of the effective date of the statutory amendment. Since this case was filed within nine months of a zoning decision by the village but not within two months of the effective date of the legislative amendment, the suit was held to have been properly dismissed.

South Blvd. Video & News, Inc. v. Charlotte Zoning Board of Adjustment, 129 N.C. App. 282, 498 S.E.2d 623, *review denied*, 348 N.C. 301, 510 S.E.2d 656 (1998)
Adult uses; Interpretation

The question presented here was whether the petitioner's facility was an adult establishment. The ordinance defined the term to include bookstores where a "preponderance of its publications" were "books, magazines, and other periodicals" devoted to adult materials. The court found that the use of the term "preponderance" was not unconstitutionally vague. It also held that "preponderance" did not mean that more than 50 percent of the materials in a facility had to be devoted to adult material but, rather, that adult materials were given a predominant and far greater emphasis in display within a store and in importance to the store's overall business. The court held that videotapes could be considered within the "publications" subject to this definition. Finally, the court also upheld a contempt citation based on efforts to circumvent court orders regarding the business.

Ball v. Randolph County Board of Adjustment, 129 N.C. App. 300, 498 S.E.2d 833, *appeal dismissed*, 349 N.C. 348, 507 S.E.2d 272 (1998)
Agricultural uses; Interpretation

The question presented here was whether remediation of petroleum-contaminated soil could be considered an agricultural use of land. The ordinance did not explicitly address this use. The zoning administrator concluded that since the state regulated this activity, the use occurred on open agrarian land, and open land and soil tilling were involved, it could be carried out in a residential-agricultural zoning district. The board of adjustment upheld this determination. The court reversed, holding as a matter of law that soil remediation is a waste-treatment process, not an agricultural use.

Onslow County v. Moore, 129 N.C. App. 376, 499 S.E.2d 780, *review denied*, 349 N.C. 361, 525 S.E.2d 453 (1998)
Adult uses; Preemption

The court upheld Onslow County's ordinance that established minimum-separation requirements for adult businesses, holding that these requirements could be adopted as either zoning requirements or as a general-police-power ordinance. The court held that the state's indecent-exposure statute does not preempt the regulations but that the state's law limiting adult businesses to one per structure (G.S. 14-202.11) does preempt a separation requirement between adult uses. [Note: The statute was subsequently amended to remove any preemption.]

In re Willis & City of Southport Board of Adjustment, 129 N.C. App. 499, 500 S.E.2d 723 (1998)
Board of adjustment; Judicial review

The court held that a superior court hearing an appeal of a board of adjustment's decision must, depending on the type of issue being reviewed, apply one of two standards of review. For alleged errors of law, the court undertakes a de novo review. If the allegation is that the evidence did not support the decision or that the decision was arbitrary and capricious, the court is limited to reviewing the whole record before the board of adjustment to determine if it supports the board's conclusions. Since both types of allegations were made in this case and the trial court did delineate which standard was applied to which issue, the court remanded the case for a new order specifying application of the appropriate scope of review for each allegation.

Derwort v. Polk County, 129 N.C. App. 789, 501 S.E.2d 379 (1998)

Public-duty doctrine; Subdivisions

The county approved a subdivision plat submitted by the plaintiffs. The plat was recorded, the site graded, roads and a water line installed, and lots were sold with guarantees that septic-tank approval could be obtained. It was subsequently determined that none of the lots were suitable for septic tanks. The court held that the county could not be held liable for damages under the public-duty doctrine. Since the county owed no legal duty to the plaintiffs, there could be no liability even if there was negligence in subdivision approval.

Williams v. Town of Spencer, 129 N.C. App. 828, 500 S.E.2d 473 (1998)

Manufactured housing; Nonconformities; Takings

The court upheld an ordinance provision that allowed nonconforming manufactured-housing parks to remain but explicitly prohibited bringing in a new unit when a leased mobile-home lot was vacated. The court found that such a policy is rationally related to a legitimate governmental objective of eventually phasing out non-conformities and held that a provision like the one challenged here is not a taking since the land can be used for any of the uses allowed in the industrial zone, and thus the owner is not deprived of all economically beneficial or productive use of the land.

Koontz v. Davidson County Board of Adjustment, 130 N.C. App. 479, 503 S.E.2d 108, *review denied*, 349 N.C. 529, 526 S.E.2d 177 (1998)

Manufactured housing; Vested rights

Shortly after developers entered into a contract to purchase a 6.78-acre site for the purpose of developing a mobile-home community, the plaintiffs petitioned the county to rezone the site to exclude mobile homes as a permissible use from an area that included this site. After the notice of the hearing on the proposed zoning amendment was published but before the zoning change was adopted, the developer applied for and received subdivision approval and commenced work on streets and landscaping. However, no mobile homes were located within the subdivision until some ten days after the zoning change was adopted. The zoning administrator, the board of adjustment, and the trial court held that the developers had a vested right to place mobile homes on the site. The court reversed. The developers knew the proposed specific zoning amendment had been set for public hearing before making substantial expenditures and they had actively sought and acted upon advice on how to circumvent the proposed amendment. The court thus held that the developers had not proceeded in good faith.

Estates, Inc. v. Town of Chapel Hill, 130 N.C. App. 664, 504 S.E.2d 296 (1998), *review denied*, 350 N.C. 93, 527 S.E.2d 664 (1999)

Appellate procedures

The town council denied a special use permit for an apartment complex and single-family development proposed for a thirty-four-acre parcel. The applicant appealed and neighbors opposed to the project intervened. The trial court reversed the denial and ordered the town to issue the permit. The intervenors filed notice of appeal to the court of appeals but did not apply for a stay of the trial court's order. The town did not appeal. While the case was on appeal, the town council issued the special use permit for the project. The court held that Rule 62 of the Rules of Civil Procedure provides an automatic stay of the trial court's judgment but does not prevent the town from voluntarily complying with the trial court's judgment. To maintain the status quo, the intervenors must obtain an injunction prohibiting the issuance of the permit during the pendency of the appeal. Once the town issued the permit, the appeal became moot.

County of Durham v. North Carolina Department of Environment & Natural Resources, 131 N.C. App. 395, 507 S.E.2d 310 (1998), *review denied*, 350 N.C. 92, 528 S.E.2d 361 (1999)
Interpretation

The court held that the state Department of Environmental Quality had correctly interpreted the statutes to distinguish "land clearing and inert debris" landfills from "sanitary landfills." The court noted that while a de novo review is made on statutory-interpretation questions, the court also accords considerable weight to the agency's interpretation and will not disturb such if it is based on a permissible interpretation of the statute. The court further held that since the requirements for notice to the county of a proposed site only apply to sanitary landfills, there is no requirement to provide such notice regarding land-clearing and inert-debris landfills.

Crist v. City of Jacksonville, 131 N.C. App. 404, 507 S.E.2d 899 (1998)
Findings; Variances

The plaintiff constructed a replica of a church on his residential lot. The structure was located within the required five-foot side-yard setback line for the zoning district involved. The city staff ruled that this was an impermissible location of an accessory building. The board of adjustment denied a variance to allow the structure to be located on the lot but failed to make any findings of fact. The court ruled that the issue of whether this structure was an "accessory building" was not presented to the trial court and thus could not be raised on appeal. The court rejected the city's contentions that findings are not required for denial of a variance and remanded the case to the board of adjustment to make appropriate findings of fact to support their decision.

Water Tower Office Associates v. Town of Cary Board of Adjustment, 131 N.C. App. 696, 507 S.E.2d 589 (1998)
Appellate procedures

The plaintiff contended that its property was zoned for commercial use. However, the city staff ruled the property was zoned for residential use. Upon inquiry from the plaintiff, the city advised the plaintiff that the ruling could be appealed to the board of adjustment, but the city made no mention of the time period for making such an appeal. The Cary zoning ordinance required that appeals to the board of adjustment be made within thirty days of the contested decision. The plaintiff did not appeal until after the thirty-day period had run. The board heard the case and upheld the staff determination. The court held that the appeal was properly dismissed for failure to make a timely appeal to the board of adjustment, noting that the ordinance provisions on appeals are binding on the board as well as on the appellant. Since the appeal was not made within the requisite thirty-day period, the board was without subject-matter jurisdiction to hear the case. The fact that the board actually heard the case was irrelevant, as the board could not waive its lack of subject-matter jurisdiction; the city was entitled to raise the defense for the first time on judicial appeal. The court also noted that the city had no obligation to notify persons of the thirty-day period at the time of decision.

Darnell v. Town of Franklin, 131 N.C. App. 846, 508 S.E.2d 841 (1998)
Appellate procedures; Standing

The plaintiff appeared before the town's board of adjustment and town council (which had final decision-making authority for variances under the town's zoning ordinance) to object to a setback variance for an adjoining property owner. Upon issuance of the variance, the plaintiff filed a petition for writ of certiorari seeking judicial review of the variance decision. The petition stated that the plaintiff was an adversely affected property owner but contained no allegations specifying how the plaintiff was aggrieved by the decision. The town moved to dismiss for lack of subject-matter jurisdiction. While that motion was under advisement, the plaintiff sought to amend her pleadings to add specific allegations of harm. The court held that while the initial petition was deficient, the plaintiff had clearly established by her participation in the matter before the town boards that she was affected by the action in a manner distinct from the rest of the community. Therefore, the trial court should have allowed her to amend the petition under G.S. § 1A-1, Rule 15(a).

State v. Moore, 132 N.C. App. 197, 511 S.E.2d 22 (1999)
Adult uses; Enforcement

The court upheld a finding that the defendant was in criminal contempt for violating a preliminary injunction prohibiting him from operating three specific adult businesses located in violation of a county ordinance requiring a 1000-foot separation from residences. The court held the ordinance to be within the constitutional power of the county and not unduly vague.

Whiteco Outdoor Advertising v. Johnston County Board of Adjustment, 132 N.C. App. 465, 513 S.E.2d 70 (1999)
Amortization; Evidence; Interpretation; Signs

The plaintiff managed two nonconforming billboards along I-95 in Johnston County. Both signs were greatly damaged in a windstorm. The zoning ordinance allowed repair but prohibited replacement; permits were required before repairs deemed substantial could be made, however. The plaintiff replaced the signs without permits and in violation of stop-work orders. The defendant board of adjustment ordered the plaintiff to remove the signs. The plaintiff challenged this directive, arguing that it was not supported by the proof and was arbitrary and capricious. On appeal, the board of adjustment upheld the determination that the cost of repairs to the billboards exceeded 50 percent of their initial value, thus making the repairs substantial. The court concluded that there was copious competent evidence in the whole record to support the decision. The court allowed the use of a letter from the state transportation department on value, even though the author of the letter did not testify. The recipient of the letter did testify under oath, though, and was subject to cross-examination, and the applicant had ample opportunity to present evidence. The court also upheld the board's interpretation of the term "value" (of the signs) in the nonconforming section of the ordinance to mean "initial value." The court noted that while interpretation questions are a matter of law and subject to de novo review, the board's functions include interpretation of the ordinance, and its interpretation is given deference.

C.C. & J. Enterprises, Inc. v. City of Asheville, 132 N.C. App. 550, 512 S.E.2d 766, *review dismissed as improvidently granted*, 351 N.C. 97, 521 S.E.2d 117 (1999)
Special uses; Standing

The applicant appealed the denial of a special use permit for a twenty-four-unit apartment complex. The city found that the project met all of the technical requirements and development standards in the ordinance but based the denial on a general concern about impacts on health and safety (citing street conditions, topography, access, flooding potential, and proposed density). The court held that since the ordinance did not in fact list promotion of the public health, safety, and welfare as a standard for special use permit decisions (though it would have been permissible to do so), it was inappropriate for the city council to use it as a standard in reviewing the application. A general statement of intent is not a permit standard and may not be used in decision-making. The court also held that it was proper to allow an adjoining neighborhood association to intervene, as they had alleged special damages (reduced property values) to qualify as an aggrieved party.

Andrews v. Alamance County, 132 N.C. App. 811, 513 S.E.2d 349 (1999)
Manufactured housing; Standing

The county adopted a manufactured-home-park ordinance that set minimum lot sizes and frontage requirements. The plaintiff landowner filed a declaratory action challenging the constitutionality of the ordinance. The court dismissed the suit, finding that the plaintiff did not have standing. To qualify for standing, plaintiffs must show that they have already sustained injury or are in immediate danger of sustaining injury by virtue of enforcement of the ordinance. Here, there was only an allegation that the plaintiff intended to develop her land as a manufactured-home-park, with no assertions that she had developed a site plan, filed a subdivision plat, taken any steps toward development, or applied for a permit of any kind. Thus, the court held that there was no genuine controversy and no standing.

State v. Baggett, 133 N.C. App. 47, 514 S.E.2d 536 (1999)

Adult uses; Extraterritorial jurisdiction

Onslow County adopted an adult-business regulation under its general police power to be applied to all land "within the county exclusive of the jurisdiction of any incorporated municipality." The defendant operated a topless bar within one mile of the city of Jacksonville that did not comply with the minimum-separation requirements of the county ordinance. The court held that while a county general-police-power ordinance can be applied within a city's extraterritorial planning-and-zoning jurisdiction, the ordinance must plainly state its intention to do so. Where the language is ambiguous, however (as the court held the language here to be), a court will strictly construe language creating a criminal offense. Thus, the court dismissed charges against the defendant.

Procter v. City of Raleigh Board of Adjustment, 133 N.C. App. 181, 514 S.E.2d 745 (1999)

Judicial review; Standing

The petitioner contested the city's interpretation of the applicable setback before the board of adjustment. Neighbors presented information at the hearing to support the city's interpretation of the setback requirements. The board upheld the city interpretation favored by the neighbors, and the city defended that decision when the petitioner filed for judicial review. However, when the trial court reversed the board and found for the petitioner, the city decided not to appeal the decision, at which point the neighbors moved to intervene in order to continue judicial appeals. The trial court rejected the motion to intervene as not timely. The appeals court reversed, concluding that the extraordinary and unusual circumstances of the case made intervention timely under Rule 24(a)(2). The court found that the neighbors had an interest in the transaction, an alleged practical impairment of that interest, and inadequate representation by the existing parties (and the city's appeals had been adequate representation prior to the city's decision not to appeal the trial court's adverse ruling).

Parkwood Ass'n v. Capital Health Care Investors, 133 N.C. App. 158, 514 S.E.2d 542, *review denied*, 350 N.C. 835, 539 S.E.2d 291 (1999)

Group homes; Restrictive covenants

The defendant purchased a residence in Durham for use as a temporary emergency-shelter home for undisciplined, delinquent, or at-risk youth. The home served up to five youths at a time, with two supervisors in residence. The plaintiff contended that this facility violated restrictive covenants that allowed only single-family residential use (and specifically prohibited houses of detention, reform schools, and institutions of kindred character). The court pointed out that restrictive covenants are to be strictly construed and found that the use here fell within the covenants' prohibitions. The court also noted that the shelter residents were not disabled and thus were not entitled to the protections of state or federal fair-housing laws.

JWL Investments, Inc. v. Guilford County Board of Adjustment, 133 N.C. App. 426, 515 S.E.2d 715 (1999), *review denied*, 251 N.C. 715, 540 S.E.2d 349 (2000)

Conflicts of interest; Enforcement; Nonconformities; Takings

The petitioners were cited by the county for a zoning violation involving use of their property as a vehicle storage yard, a use not permitted in the residential zoning district and scenic corridor overlay districts in which the property was located. The petitioners appealed to the board of adjustment, presenting evidence that this was the continuation of a nonconforming use, while the county presented evidence that the property was previously undeveloped. The board of adjustment affirmed the county enforcement order.

The petitioners contended that there was bias on the board of adjustment due to the membership of a former employee of the county planning department. However, the court held that there was no impermissible conflict of interest in that the petitioners did not object during the hearing to the member's participation and made no showing that they were prejudiced by said participation. The court noted that the law does not favor nonconforming uses and the county's evidence of noncontinuous nonconforming status was adequate. The court held that the scenic corridor limitations were not a taking as they did not deprive the owners of all economically beneficial or productive uses of the land. The court further held that the board of adjustment had the authority to impose civil penalties.

Shell Island Homeowners Ass'n, Inc. v. Tomlinson, 134 N.C. App. 217, 517 S.E.2d 406 (1999)

Appeals; Coastal Area Management Act; Takings

The plaintiffs owned an oceanfront condominium in Wrightsville Beach. They made several Coastal Area Management Act permit applications and variance petitions to construct revetments and/or bulkheads to protect the structure from erosion and inlet migration. These applications were denied as inconsistent with state rules prohibiting hardened-erosion-control structures in inlet and ocean hazard areas. Eventually, a variance petition was granted for a smaller, temporary sandbag bulkhead immediately adjacent to the structure. The plaintiffs challenged the regulation prohibiting permanent oceanfront shoreline-erosion-control structures. The court held that the plaintiffs' nonconstitutional challenges to the rule were properly dismissed by the trial court for lack of subject-matter jurisdiction in that the plaintiffs failed to exhaust the administrative remedies provided to challenge their permit and variance. The court, however, ruled that exhaustion of administrative remedies is not required for constitutional claims.

The court found that equal-protection and due-process claims were properly dismissed because the plaintiffs had sought, accepted, and taken advantage of a variance to build a sandbag revetment. The doctrine of quasi-estoppel prevents one from voluntarily proceeding under a statute, claiming its benefits, and then questioning its constitutionality to avoid its burdens. The court further noted that even if properly before the court, the equal-protection and due-process claims were properly dismissed as there was no suspect classification, no fundamental personal constitutional rights affected, and the rule was clearly rationally related to legitimate government ends (protecting lands of environmental concern, preservation of the value and enjoyment of neighboring properties, and protection of public access to ocean beaches). The court also upheld dismissal of regulatory-taking claims urged by the plaintiffs, noting that the invasion of property and loss of value alleged here stemmed from the natural migration of the inlet, not any action of the state. Since there is no property right of riparian or littoral owners to construct hardened-erosion-control structures, no property right can be said to have been taken. Finally, the court pointed out that the rules limiting use of hardened structures were in place and known to the plaintiffs prior to the construction of their building (thus any purported right to construct a hardened-erosion-control structure was not a part of the plaintiffs' title to begin with).

Shell Island Homeowners Ass'n, Inc. v. Tomlinson, 134 N.C. App. 286, 517 S.E.2d 401 (1999)

Coastal Area Management Act; Mootness

The plaintiffs made several Coastal Area Management Act permit applications and variance petitions to construct revetments and bulkheads to protect their oceanfront condominium. These applications were denied. Eventually, a fourth variance petition was granted for a smaller, temporary sandbag bulkhead immediately adjacent to the structure. The plaintiffs challenged the denials. The court upheld the dismissal as moot, noting that the plaintiffs had failed to seek administrative review of any of the permit denials, had accepted a variance that gave them approval to build a revetment, had built that revetment, and had thus essentially received the relief originally sought (authority to construct an erosion-control device, albeit not of the same design and location as originally sought).

Leftwich v. Gaines, 134 N.C. App. 502, 521 S.E.2d 717 (1999), *review denied*, 351 N.C. 357, 541 S.E.2d 714 (2000)

Inspections; Liability

The plaintiff was interested in purchasing a tract adjacent to her land for additional access and to allow continuation/expansion of a home occupation. The plaintiff alleged that Mt. Airy's chief building inspector provided her fraudulent information regarding the adjacent property (that it could not be rezoned, that condemned structures would have to be removed at her expense, that expensive water/sewer connections would be required) in order to suppress the value of her offer for the property, thereby allowing the building inspector's girlfriend to purchase the property at a reduced price. The mayor advised the plaintiff that there had been similar previous problems with the inspector, and the town manager had asked the inspector not to purchase property within town limits.

The court found that there was sufficient evidence to support the jury's conclusion that the inspector's representation that a rezoning of the property would be illegal spot zoning was contrary to his true beliefs and was made for the purpose of deceit, that it was motivated by a desire to secure benefits for himself and his girl-friend, and that it thus constituted fraud. The court ruled that since the inspector was acting outside the scope of his duties, he was not immune from an unfair-trade-practice claim under G.S. 75-1.1. Similarly, the city was not immune from suit for negligent supervision under the public-duty doctrine for two reasons: (1) the city had notice of prior wrongdoing of a similar nature and had not undertaken adequate supervision to prevent a recurrence, plus the wrongdoing took place while the inspector was on duty, and (2) since the inspector deliberately mislead the plaintiff—an intentional tort as opposed to gross negligence—the public-duty doctrine did not apply to shield the city from liability. The court upheld treble damages against the individual defendants ($180,000), found the city jointly and severally liable for compensatory damages ($60,000), and ordered the individual defendant to pay attorney's fees of $50,000.

Village Creek Property Owners' Ass'n, Inc. v. Town of Edenton, 135 N.C. App. 482, 520 S.E.2d 793 (1999)
Judicial review; Special uses; Standing

Neighbors challenged a conditional use district rezoning and special use permit. The court noted that conditional use district rezonings involve two legally distinct decisions: the rezoning and the permit decision. The permit decision is properly challenged in the nature of certiorari, whereas the rezoning decision is properly challenged by a declaratory-judgment action. The court ruled that to establish standing, neighbors filing a declaratory-judgment action to challenge a rezoning must allege a specific personal and legal interest in the matter and that they are directly and adversely affected by the decision. They do not have to allege "special damages," as is the case for aggrieved parties seeking review of a quasi-judicial zoning decision by writ of certiorari. [Note: Statutory authority for conditional use districts with concurrent special use permits was subsequently repealed.]

Harry v. Crescent Resources, Inc., 136 N.C. App. 71, 523 S.E.2d 118 (1999)
Open space; Subdivisions

The defendant platted and recorded a five-lot subdivision adjacent to Lake Norman, and the plaintiff subsequently purchased one of the lots. The subdivision plat showed four small remnant parcels within the subdivision. The remnant parcels were unnumbered and had no purpose or use designated on the plat. The plaintiff challenged the sale of the remnant parcels to an owner who proposed to place piers on the lots. The court held that the remnant lots were not limited to open-space use. In order to be reserved for such use, the plat should have shown designation of the lots as open space, park, beach lands, or the like, or there should have been oral representations or actions on the part of the developer that reasonably led purchasers to believe the land would remain as open space. The court also refused to extend the restrictive covenants (which had been imposed on the residential lots but not the residual lots) to those residual lots under a doctrine of implied equitable servitude, as there was no evidence that the developer intended such.

Clark v. City of Asheboro, 136 N.C. App. 114, 524 S.E.2d 46 (1999)
Manufactured housing; Special uses

The petitioners were denied a special use permit by the city council for a proposed manufactured-home park. Six neighbors appeared and presented testimony in opposition. The court held that the permit was improperly denied, as there was substantial, competent, and material evidence presented to show compliance with all permit conditions. The evidence in opposition was characterized as being generalized fear that park residents would be low-income residents who would constitute a danger to the neighborhood, concerns unsupported by competent evidence. The court also held that the council had failed to make written findings of fact to support the denial and that the trial court had properly ordered the permit issued (as there was sufficient evidence in the record to support issuance and none supporting denial).

Richardson v. Union County Board of Adjustment, 136 N.C. App. 134, 523 S.E.2d 432 (1999)
Findings; Notice; Special uses

Neighbors challenged a special use permit issued for the construction of a 500-foot-tall commercial radio tower and transmitter building. The court upheld the decision, rejecting a variety of challenges. On the question of mailed notice of the hearing, the court noted that the zoning statutes require "due notice" and the zoning ordinance specified a ten-day mailed-notice requirement and specified how that period was to be computed. The court held that these requirements, rather than G.S. 1A-1, Rule 6 (the more general state law regarding computation of notice periods), control. The court also noted that it is necessary for any parties claiming inadequate notice of a hearing, in order to establish that they were prejudiced by lack of proper notice, to specify how they would have benefited from a later hearing. The court concluded that all interested persons were given an opportunity to present evidence, that the application was complete, and that all relevant permit standards were separately considered. Finally, the court held that findings to support the permit issuance need not be made simultaneously with permit approval and may be included within the subsequently issued permit.

Harry v. Mecklenburg County, 136 N.C. App. 200, 523 S.E.2d 135 (1999)
Accessory buildings and uses; Interpretation

Neighbors challenged the issuance of building permits for piers on four small lakefront lots. The lots were in an R-3 single-family residential zoning district where piers are not listed among the permitted uses. The ordinance provided that accessory uses had to be approved in conjunction with principal uses. The staff ruled that where there was no residence planned on the lot, the pier became the principal use, and they thus issued permits for the construction. The court reversed, interpreting the zoning ordinance as clearly establishing single-family housing as the primary purpose of a lot in the R-3 district, with piers being an accessory use (and thus by the terms of the ordinance not allowed in the absence of the principal use). The court noted that while the zoning administrator's interpretation is entitled to some deference, the court is not bound by that interpretation where it is contrary to the express purpose of the ordinance.

Through the Looking Glass, Inc. v. Zoning Board of Adjustment for Charlotte, 136 N.C. App. 212, 523 S.E.2d 444 (1999)
Variances

The plaintiff sought variances from the zoning ordinance requirements of a ten-foot buffer between its property and an adjacent residential use and from a five-foot side-yard setback for a driveway. Very similar variances had been granted for property directly across the street a year earlier. The board of adjustment, however, denied these variances. The court held that while the board is not bound by its previous decision, where fact situations are essentially the same, decisions should be the same. Here, the board's findings did not explain why very similar facts led to differing decisions, so the court remanded the case for additional findings in order to determine if the decision was supported by substantial evidence or was arbitrary and capricious.

Stephenson v. Town of Garner, 136 N.C. App. 444, 524 S.E.2d 608, *review denied*, 352 N.C. 156, 544 S.E.2d 243 (2000)
Liability; Special uses; Telecommunication towers

The board of aldermen denied a special use permit for a telecommunications tower. The trial court found the denial arbitrary and capricious and remanded the matter to the town for "further proceedings" in accordance with the judgment. The town held another hearing and again denied the permit. While the second denial was on appeal the town and the telecommunications company settled the suit, with the company leasing space on an alternate site (the town water tower). The owner of the site originally proposed for the tower brought this action alleging interference with contractual relations and unfair trade practices. The court found that the town had not violated the initial court order, as a second hearing was within the range of "further proceedings" mandated. The court held that cities are immune from liability for unfair-trade-practice claims. The court further held that the aldermen had legislative immunity regarding the interference with contract claim based on the special use permit denial, noting that decisions on these permits are not ministerial acts, as they involve substantial discretion. The court remanded the question of whether the water-tower lease constituted unlawful interference with a contract, noting that since governmental immunity does not extend to proprietary actions, a motion to dismiss was not properly granted.

Brown v. City of Greensboro, 137 N.C. App. 164, 528 S.E.2d 588 (2000)
Enforcement

After being denied a variance, the plaintiff alleged unlawful discrimination by the city in its enforcement of off-street parking regulations for her hair salon. The court upheld a dismissal of the claim, noting that a party alleging unlawful selective enforcement must establish a pattern of conscious and intentional discrimination done with an evil eye and an unequal hand. Neither mere laxity of enforcement nor exemptions for lawful nonconformities constitute such unlawful discrimination.

Kirkpatrick v. Village of Pinehurst, 138 N.C. App. 79, 530 S.E.2d 338 (2000)
Moratoria; Nonconformities; Vested rights

The plaintiff acquired a fifty-five-acre tract with a nonconforming fifty-unit RV campground located on a thirteen-acre portion of the site. The defendant village shortly thereafter adopted a moratorium on commercial building pending an update of the comprehensive plan and development ordinance. During the moratorium, the plaintiff acquired village permits for 112 water and sewer taps. The revised ordinance limited RV park use to 120 units and then only if a special use permit was acquired. The plaintiff then applied for such a special use permit and the permit was denied.

The court first held that the plain meaning of the ordinance did not allow the geographic area devoted to a nonconforming use to be enlarged, thus expansion of the park beyond the thirteen-acre portion of the site would be an unlawful expansion. The court then held that an increase beyond the fifty preexisting sites would constitute an enlargement of the nonconformity, not a permissible intensification of the use. Finally, the court concluded that since all expenditures by the plaintiff were made with knowledge that the use was nonconforming, there could be no finding of good faith (necessary to establish any common law vested rights to an expansion).

McKillop v. Onslow County, 139 N.C. App. 53, 532 S.E.2d 594 (2000)
Adult uses; Enforcement; Evidence

The plaintiff had previously been ordered by a court not to operate an adult business in violation of county ordinances. Upon resumption of such a business, the plaintiff was again cited for violation, and the trial court entered a finding of civil contempt and an order of abatement. The court upheld the order based on the plaintiff's willful operation of an adult business in violation of the county's adult-business ordinance. While the plaintiff's invocation of the Fifth Amendment was found to be permissible, the court noted that in a civil action such as this, the trier of fact may use that invocation to infer that truthful testimony would have been unfavorable to the plaintiff.

Sun Suites Holdings, LLC v. Town of Garner, 139 N.C. App. 269, 533 S.E.2d 525, *review denied*, 546 S.E.2d 397 (2000)
Evidence; Special uses

The town council denied the plaintiff's special use permit for an extended-stay hotel on the grounds that the project would materially endanger public safety and would substantially injure the value of adjoining property. The court held that a whole-record review established that this finding was not supported by substantial evidence. General expressions of a fear of potential increases in crime in the vicinity of any hotel are insufficient to establish a threat to public safety. Similarly, a recitation of crime statistics with reference to another extended-stay hotel in the town, without any foundation as to how those related to the subject project, was held inadequate to support a denial. Speculative comments by a neighbor and a real-estate agent about impacts on property values were likewise held insubstantial evidence on the property-value issue.

Pisgah Oil Co., Inc. v. Western North Carolina Regional Air Pollution Control Agency, 139 N.C. App. 402, 533 S.E.2d 290, *review denied*, 353 N.C. 268, 546 S.E.2d 111 (2000)
Enforcement; Hearings

The plaintiff's employee was observed by the defendant agency's inspector unloading fuel from a tanker truck into two storage tanks without using the required vapor recovery equipment. Upon being approached by the inspector, the employee acknowledged the violation and hooked up the equipment as he had just started filling the second tank. A civil penalty was assessed. The plaintiff contested the civil penalty as arbitrary and capricious. The court held that the trial court correctly applied a whole-record test in its review and upheld the penalty assessment. The court also held that the agency was not required to conduct a formal evidentiary hearing to review the penalty assessment and that enough documentation was provided in the detailed minutes of the proceedings to provide an adequate record for judicial review.

Procter v. City of Raleigh Board of Adjustment, 140 N.C. App. 784, 538 S.E.2d 621 (2000)
Interpretation

The petitioner proposed to build several duplexes with varying front-yard setbacks. The city staff interpreted the zoning ordinance to require both a minimum and a maximum setback. The court conducted a de novo review and held that the plain terms of the ordinance established only a minimum setback. The requirement for a common setback applies only when there are other buildings on the block's face, and there were no other existing buildings on this block. Given the lack of any ambiguity in the ordinance, it was error for the board of adjustment to look beyond the language of the ordinance.

SBA, Inc. v. City of Asheville, 141 N.C. App. 19, 539 S.E.2d 18 (2000)
Special uses; Telecommunication towers

The plaintiff appealed the city council's denial of a special use permit for a 175-foot telecommunications tower. While the proposal met all the technical standards of the ordinance, the court held that there was substantial evidence in the record to support conclusions that several general standards were not met. Evidence establishing that the tower would be far taller than the average building height in the area and would be clearly visible from surrounding residences addressed the standard requiring compatibility with the neighborhood. Lack of evidence presented by the applicant regarding the feasibility of alternate sites or stealth technology (and that significant coverage gaps would remain even with this tower) supported a conclusion that it had not been established that the use was reasonably necessary. The lack of data on property-value impacts in the immediate vicinity of the towers supported a conclusion that the applicant had not met its burden under the ordinance of demonstrating the absence of harm to neighboring property values. The court further held that the process used for special use permit decisions more than met the standards for permit denials under the federal Telecommunications Act (substantial evidence in the record and written findings).

Block v. County of Person, 141 N.C. App. 273, 540 S.E.2d 415 (2000)
Liability

In 1994, staff with the defendant county approved a residential building lot as suitable for a conventional septic system. The plaintiffs purchased the lot and built a house with a conventional septic system, which was approved by the county. The system failed a year later. Investigation revealed that there was no site on the lot with suitable soils for a conventional system, so the plaintiff was forced to install a low-pressure system. The county staff initially advised the plaintiff that the county would pay for the new system, but it later refused to do so. The court upheld denial of the county's motion to dismiss, holding that the environmental health specialist and the environmental health supervisor could be (and were) sued in both their individual and official capacities. The court held that these two persons were "employees" rather than "officers" because their positions were not defined or created by statute and they exercised ministerial rather than discretionary duties (reiterating that while officers cannot be held individually liable for negligence, employees can). The court further held that the public-duty doctrine was inapplicable in the case and did not bar an action against the county or the health department.

Piland v. Hertford County Board of Commissioners, 141 N.C. App. 293, 539 S.E.2d 669 (2000)
Appellate procedures; Parties; Statutes of limitation

The plaintiffs challenged the county's rezoning of 1600 acres to a heavy industry zoning district in association with a proposed steel mill and recycling facility. The complaint named the board of commissioners as the defendant. The county moved to dismiss, contending that Hertford County was the proper defendant, not the board of commissioners, and that the two-month statute of limitations had run, so the complaint could not be amended to add the county as a defendant. The plaintiffs then moved to substitute the county as defendant and both parties moved for summary judgment. The court held that the case should have been dismissed for failure to name the county as a defendant, as the motion to amend to add the county as the proper defendant (which could be granted at the trial judge's discretion) could not relate back (as this was adding a party, not just correcting a misnomer) and was thus barred by the statute of limitations.

Buckland v. Town of Haw River, 141 N.C. App. 460, 541 S.E.2d 497 (2000)
Subdivisions

The plaintiff's predecessor in title recorded a plat that included a U-shaped road within a subdivision, with both ends of the road connecting to a state highway. The right-of-way for the U-shaped road was dedicated to the state. The two prongs of the road were constructed, but the back portion (parallel to the state road) was not. The plaintiff subsequently acquired the large undeveloped lot along the back side of the unimproved road and proposed a further subdivision of that lot into eleven additional lots. The town conditioned subdivision approval upon the plaintiff's constructing the road, along with a curb and gutter, on the previously dedicated right-of-way. When the plaintiff challenged this decision, the trial court granted summary judgment to the town. The court of appeals reversed. The court interpreted the subdivision-enabling statute as only allowing requirements relative to provision of streets within the subdivision. Since the unpaved right-of-way was adjacent to rather than within the subdivision, the court held that the city had no authority to compel its improvement. The court noted that the statute allows a requirement for payment of a fee in lieu of construction for necessary roads both within and outside of the subdivision, but since the requirement here was for developer construction rather than payment of a fee, the plat denial was improper.

Davis v. Town of Stallings Board of Adjustment, 141 N.C. App. 489, 541 S.E.2d 183 (2000)
Adult uses; Evidence

The plaintiff obtained a permit to operate a video store with an adult video room. The permit contained an explicit condition that a majority of all videos must not be adult videos. Upon subsequently determining the facility was selling adult magazines and novelty items, the town concluded that the facility was an unpermitted "adult establishment." At the board of adjustment's hearing the town staff presented evidence that a substantial number of adult videos, magazines, CDs, and novelty items were present in the plaintiff's store. The plaintiff invoked the Fifth Amendment and did not testify at the hearing. The board then held that the facility violated the provisions of the permit limiting the store to trade in videos only and that it constituted an adult establishment. The court upheld the decision, finding that while the plaintiff could invoke the Fifth Amendment, the board could infer in this civil matter that failure to refute damaging evidence meant that the plaintiff was running an unlawful adult establishment.

Potter v. City of Hamlet, 141 N.C. App. 714, 541 S.E.2d 233, *review denied*, 353 N.C. 379, 547 S.E.2d 814 (2001)
Extraterritorial jurisdiction; Nonconformities; Statutes of limitation

The plaintiff purchased an existing grocery store in the Hamlet extraterritorial area and subsequently applied for an alcoholic beverage control (ABC) permit for off-premise beer sales. The city advised the state ABC Commission and the plaintiff that the store was nonconforming (it was in a heavy industry zoning district that did not allow retail uses) and that beer sales would be an unlawful expansion of the nonconformity. Rather than appeal this determination to the board of adjustment, the plaintiff sought a rezoning, which was ultimately denied. The plaintiff then brought this action, alleging that the extraterritorial-boundary ordinance was invalid, as it had not been recorded with the county register of deeds as required by G.S. 160D-202.

The court held that the plaintiff's challenge was barred by the two-month statute of limitations. When the extraterritorial-boundary ordinance was adopted, the plaintiff's predecessor in title had received mailed notice of the proposed ordinance, all published notice and hearing requirements were met, a copy of the map was filed with the city clerk, and the ordinance itself contained a metes-and-bounds description of the boundary. The court held that this constituted "substantial compliance" with the statute and gave all persons affected sufficient notice that they were covered, despite the fact that a copy of the ordinance was never filed with the register of deeds. The court also held that since the zoning officer's determination regarding the expansion of the nonconformity was not appealed to the board of adjustment, that issue could not be collaterally attacked on judicial review.

Knotts v. City of Sanford, 142 N.C. App. 91, 541 S.E.2d 517 (2001)
Demolition

After investigating a complaint and conducting the requisite hearing, the defendant city found an apartment house owned by the plaintiff to be in such a dilapidated state that it was dangerous to life, health, and other property and constituted a public nuisance. The plaintiff was ordered to repair or demolish the structure within ninety days. Upon failure of the plaintiff to comply, the city passed an ordinance directing the town to repair or demolish the structure. The plaintiff sued to block the demolition, and the parties entered a consent order requiring the plaintiff to have a contract for repair or demolition; all work was to be completed by set dates, and the city would demolish the structure if this was not done. The plaintiff again failed to comply, and the city proceeded to secure bids for demolition. The plaintiff unsuccessfully sought to have the court amend the consent order. When the city entered into a contract for demolition, the plaintiff instituted this action, alleging a taking and seeking an injunction to prevent demolition. The court upheld the dismissal of the second suit on res judicata grounds.

Grassy Creek Neighborhood Alliance, Inc. v. City of Winston-Salem, 142 N.C. App. 290, 542 S.E.2d 296 (2001)

Landfills

The plaintiff organization challenged the state utility commission's selection and the defendant city's approval of a site adjacent to an existing landfill for a proposed landfill expansion. G.S. 160A-325 requires consideration of alternative sites and socioeconomic/demographic data if a proposed site is located within one mile of an existing landfill. The court held that while expansion of a landfill into an adjacent site that requires a rezoning for such is subject to this law, this decision here was exempt under the terms of the statute because the city had approved the site, the funds for acquisition, and a lease for management of the site prior to the effective date of these statutory requirements.

Northeast Concerned Citizens v. City of Hickory, 143 N.C. App. 272, 545 S.E.2d 768, *review denied*, 253 N.C. 526, 549 S.E.2d 220 (2001)

Standing

The plaintiff citizens group challenged the defendant city's rezoning of a tract to accommodate construction of a large retail store. The developer intervened and challenged the standing of the plaintiff nonprofit corporation. The court held that a person must have a specific personal and legal interest in the subject matter to have standing to challenge a rezoning and that a corporation must either have such an interest itself or all of its members or shareholders must have such an interest. Since the record in this case indicated that at most only 12 of the plaintiff's 114 members had such an interest, the court held that the plaintiff organization had no standing.

Devaney v. City of Burlington, 143 N.C. App. 334, 545 S.E.2d 763, *review denied*, 353 N.C. 724, 550 S.E.2d 772 (2001)

Amendments; Manufactured housing; Rezoning

The court held that where a zoning ordinance's table of uses specifies that a Manufactured Housing Overlay District is "permitted by right" in a particular district, the decision on a petition to apply that district to a particular site is properly considered using quasi-judicial rather than legislative procedures. While a city council retains the discretion to approve or deny a petition, there must be a fair evidentiary hearing with appropriate findings of fact before a decision is made. Since the city council here conducted a legislative hearing with substantial attention given to citizen opinion rather than factual evidence, the court remanded the matter to the city for a quasi-judicial hearing.

Williamson v. Town of Surf City, 143 N.C. App. 539, 545 S.E.2d 798 (2001)

Streets

The defendant town obtained a state grant to construct storage and bathroom facilities on a lot it owned and used for beach-access purposes. State setbacks required that part of the construction extend into the adjacent street right-of-way. The town then followed all the provisions of G.S. 160A-299 regarding notice, hearing, and findings to close a portion of the adjacent street and to use that portion for its beach-access facility. The neighbor across the street objected and filed this challenge. The court held that all proper procedures had been followed by the town, including a finding that the plaintiff would not be deprived of reasonable access and that the closing was not contrary to the public interest. The intent of the town, and its intended subsequent use of the portion of the street closed, was irrelevant.

Nazziola v. Landcraft Properties, Inc., 143 N.C. App. 564, 545 S.E.2d 801 (2001)
Judicial review; Subdivisions

Neighbors challenged Greensboro's approval of a subdivision plat on the grounds that the decision was arbitrary and capricious. The court held that a whole-record test should be applied to determine if the decision was supported by substantial evidence. If the subdivision ordinance includes only objective, technical standards and all of these are met, plat approval must be issued. Since this is an administrative decision, no evidentiary hearing is required as part of the decision-making process, and the city staff has no authority to impose or consider factors beyond the technical standards of the ordinance.

Coffey v. Town of Waynesville, 143 N.C. App. 624, 547 S.E.2d 132 (2001)
Building permits and inspection; Demolition; Hearings

The plaintiffs owned a dilapidated building that had been a concern of the defendant town for over twenty years. A city enforcement officer inspected the property and determined it to be unsafe pursuant to G.S. 160D-1119 and so posted it. A month later, the property was reinspected, notices were reposted, and a notice of hearing was sent to the plaintiffs. A hearing was held where the plaintiffs contended they were unaware of the problems and wished to make repairs. However, it was established at the hearing that the property was listed in the tax office as having no value, and the enforcement officer noted its long state of disrepair and the plaintiffs' long-standing record of neglect. The officer thus concluded that the structure was beyond repair and entered an order of demolition. This order was appealed to the city council. The council heard the appeal, affirmed the demolition order, and set a deadline for action. The council's order was appealed to the courts, so demolition was stayed. Upon stipulation by the parties, the council held a second evidentiary hearing on the demolition appeal in order to establish a record for judicial review. The trial court affirmed the demolition order.

The appeals court held that the city council, when acting on a demolition-order appeal, sits in a quasi-judicial capacity, similar to its role in deciding a special use permit. Further, a trial court reviewing this decision sits as an appellate court. Since the plaintiffs essentially argued that an error of law had been made (they contended that improper procedures had been followed and insufficient time given for repairs), the trial court properly conducted a de novo review of the demolition order. The court concluded that all of the statutory procedures to condemn the building as unsafe had been complied with by the city. The court then held that the decision to order demolition rather than repair was supported by the evidence and that the plaintiffs had reasonable opportunities to commence repairs and had failed to do so, thus the order to demolish was not in error.

Greene Citizens for Responsible Growth, Inc. v. Greene County, 143 N.C. App. 702, 547 S.E.2d 480, *review denied*, 553 S.E.2d 413 (2001)
Landfills

The plaintiff citizen group alleged that the defendant county did not follow the requirements of G.S. 153A-136(c) when it decided to locate a new landfill on a site adjacent to an existing landfill (which was being closed). The statute requires the county to consider alternative sites and socioeconomic and demographic data prior to selecting a site within a mile of an existing landfill. The plaintiffs established that the county had secured an option on the expansion site prior to the hearing and that all alternatives listed were in areas previously deemed excluded from consideration. The court held that the plain meaning of "consider" requires a careful and thoughtful examination and "alternatives" require that there be two or more sites to choose between. The court further held that while the county is entitled to a presumption that it considered alternative sites, there was no evidence in the record to conclude that it had done so. The case was therefore remanded.

Durham Video & News, Inc. v. Durham Board of Adjustment, 144 N.C. App. 236, 550 S.E.2d 212, *review denied*, 354 N.C. 361, 556 S.E.2d 299 (2001)

Adult uses; Inspections

This case turned on whether the store operated by the plaintiff was an adult business. City zoning officers twice visited the establishment and briefly viewed its merchandise. Based on these visits, the officers sought and obtained an administrative search warrant. Pursuant to the warrant, the officers returned to the store and conducted a more thorough inspection, including recording a forty-minute video of the merchandise, viewing several videos offered for sale, and making measurements of the store.

The court held that while a zoning officer can enter a commercial establishment and view everything as a normal customer would without a warrant, a more intrusive detailed inspection must be conducted pursuant to a valid search warrant. In this instance, the initial inspections were within the bounds of a warrantless inspection and properly served as the basis for securing a warrant. The court also held that it was permissible for city staff and the board of adjustment to base a finding that a preponderance of the merchandise offered for sale was adult material on a review of titles and pictures on covers (rejecting the plaintiff's contention that the entirety of all publications and videos must be reviewed). Finally, the court held that the city's failure to comply with city rules to provide the petitioner with a copy of the written staff report being provided to the board of adjustment ten days prior to the hearing (it was provided two days in advance) did not prejudice the plaintiff, as the staff report included only information that was previously available to the plaintiff or already a matter of public record.

Williams v. North Carolina Department of Environment & Natural Resources, 144 N.C. App. 479, 548 S.E.2d 793 (2001)

Coastal Area Management Act; Variances

The petitioner was denied a Coastal Area Management Act permit to construct a freezer, storage building, and bulkhead on a canal-front lot in Engelhard. There had been two residences on the lot previously, which were removed some years prior to the application, and wetland species had reemerged on the property. The petitioner was then denied a variance to build the structures. The trial court applied the whole-record test to determine that the variance denial was unsupported by material evidence and ordered that a variance be granted. The appeals court noted that in determining whether a variance denial will produce "unnecessary hardship," the critical issue for a decision maker is whether the petitioner can make reasonable use of the property without a variance. Pecuniary loss alone does not constitute unnecessary hardship, but it is a factor to be considered. The fact that the petitioner has other lands nearby is irrelevant to the hardship determination, as the inquiry must focus on the property involved in the petition, not on the property owner. The court also found the record devoid of specific evidence regarding how peculiar or unique the situation on the petitioner's property (wetlands emerging on a previously disturbed site) was and the extent to which this situation had been considered in adopting the regulations (both being mandatory statutory standards for a Coastal Area Management Act variance). The court ruled that the trial court had no authority to issue a variance but instead should have remanded the matter for further proceedings.

Kerik v. Davidson County, 145 N.C. App. 222, 551 S.E.2d 186 (2001)

Conditions; Contract zoning

Davidson County rezoned a tract consisting of seven separate parcels to commercial, industrial, and office districts. All of the new zoning districts were general-use districts. The petitioner for the rezoning submitted a memo outlining the proposed uses of each parcel, various conditions that would be imposed on each (including buffers), and how an existing nonconformity would be relocated. The petitioner also sent a memo to each governing board member stating an intent to offer land to the county for a park and to provide sewer services to these parcels. The governing board then approved the rezoning, but it added a condition that a 100-foot buffer be added to one of the parcels.

The court held that the rezoning was a legislative decision and that the standard for judicial review was a whole-record review to determine whether the decision was arbitrary and capricious. However, rather than remand, the court addressed the merits of the contract zoning claim in the interest of judicial economy, given that the whole record was before the court. The court then upheld the rezoning, holding that there was no bilateral agreement between the county and the petitioner. The court noted that the county explicitly considered all potential uses of the proposed zoning districts, not just those proposed by the petitioner, and the planning board and governing board discussed the potential land use impacts of the rezoning (compatibility with surrounding uses, traffic concerns, and economic impacts). However, the court held that the imposition of an additional 100-foot buffer requirement violated the uniformity requirement, was separable from the balance of the rezoning, and was invalid.

Massey v. City of Charlotte, 145 N.C. App. 345, 550 S.E.2d 838, *review denied*, 354 N.C. 219, 554 S.E.2d 342 (2001)

Amendments; Conditional zoning; Contract zoning; Rezoning

Neighbors challenged a rezoning from residential to commercial in order to construct a shopping center. The petitioner submitted a site plan and list of proposed conditions for development of the site as part of the rezoning request. The city approved a conditional use district rezoning and concurrently issued a special use permit for the project but conducted the entire proceeding as a legislative rezoning. The court held that the city had authority to engage in a purely legislative conditional zoning without the necessity of an accompanying special use permit. Further, the petitioner's submission of detailed plans for site development did not constitute illegal contract zoning because this was a unilateral promise from the petitioner, not a bilateral agreement.

County of Durham v. Roberts, 145 N.C. App. 665, 551 S.E.2d 494 (2001)

Agricultural uses

The defendant owned a tract in a rural zoning district that prohibited resource extraction. The defendant operated a recreational horse farm on the site. The soil on much of the property was of negligible nutritional value and would not support a pasture for the horse farm; also, several small ponds on the site were inadequate for that proposed use. In order to address these site problems, the defendant excavated two ponds and started to excavate about three feet of clay overlay from the site (with the clay sold to the excavation contractor and removed from the site). The county, contending that this was unlawful resource extraction, issued citations to the defendant for zoning violations. The court found the activity in question to be within the G.S. 160D-903 exemption from county zoning for bona-fide-farm purposes. The court held that horses are "livestock," that breeding horses for the enjoyment of one's family is the "production" of livestock even if no commercial sales or use of the horses is involved, and that the excavation for pasturing and water purposes was incidental to this production.

Councill v. Town of Boone Board of Adjustment, 146 N.C. App. 103, 551 S.E.2d 907, *review denied*, 354 N.C. 360, 560 S.E.2d 130 (2001)

Appellate procedures; Intervention; Parties; Standing

The plaintiff was denied a special use permit by the defendant board to develop a large single-family project in Boone and appealed that denial to superior court. Neighbors who opposed the project sought to intervene, alleged that the town intended to settle the suit by issuing a permit, and sought to have the denial upheld. The trial court dismissed the motion to intervene upon finding that the neighbors did not have special damages distinct from the rest of the community. The trial court then entered a consent judgment remanding the matter to the board for issuance of the permit.

The court of appeals held that the matter was not moot due to the subsequent issuance of the permit on remand. Here, the neighbors not only appealed the denial of their motion to intervene but also contended that any settlement was illegal, and thus the issue was not moot. The court held that Rule 24 (rather than an "aggrieved" party analysis) governed the right to intervene in all civil actions. The neighbors' undisputed allegations here that dramatically increased traffic volume would affect their property values and safety were sufficient to establish that they were interested parties; the fact that the board intended to settle and issue the permit satisfied the requirements that there be a practical impairment and inadequate representation of the neighbors' interests absent intervention. The case was remanded for further proceedings on the merits of the neighbors' complaints regarding permit issuance.

PNE AOA Media, LLC v. Jackson County, 146 N.C. App. 470, 554 S.E.2d 657 (2001)
Moratoria; Signs; Vested rights

The plaintiff contacted Jackson County regarding a proposal to erect a billboard in the county and was advised that the county had no zoning and that no permits were required. The plaintiff then erected a steel monopole for the proposed billboard. Shortly thereafter the county exercised its general ordinance-making authority to adopt a sixty-day moratorium on new billboards (with no published notice and no public hearing on the moratorium ordinance). The plaintiff then applied for a state Department of Transportation (DOT) permit for the billboard, which was denied on the basis of the county moratorium.

The court held that the county had authority to adopt the moratorium and that such was not preempted by state sign regulations. The court noted that since the county explicitly used the general police power rather than zoning authority for its moratorium, the procedural requirements of notice and hearing under the zoning-enabling authority were not applicable. The court held that the plaintiff had no common law vested right to the billboard because its expenditures were not in good faith (they were made prior to securing the state/DOT permit they knew was required, which was well outside the normal business practices of the plaintiff) and not in reliance on required permits (even though no county permits were required at the time of expenditure, the state permit was). The court held that since the moratorium was not adopted under the zoning authority, the statutory site-specific development plan vesting was inapplicable. Since there was no vested property right, there was no taking and no deprivation of protected property without due process.

Guilford County v. Eller, 146 N.C. App. 579, 553 S.E.2d 235 (2001)
Enforcement

The defendant husband and wife were cited for numerous zoning violations for maintaining junked motor vehicles on several properties not zoned for such purposes. By the time of the hearing, the civil penalties involved had reached $300,000. The husband and the attorney for the husband and wife appeared at the hearing and entered a handwritten memorandum of judgment. The husband testified under oath that he understood and agreed to the consent judgment, and all persons present signed the agreement, which was later formalized by the county attorney and entered by the judge. On appeal, the defendants contended that the judgment was not effective since the wife, a named party, was not present and had not signed the consent judgment. The court held that the attorney present represented both husband and wife. There is a presumption that an attorney acts within his or her authority and with the consent of the client. Since no evidence was presented to rebut that presumption, the attorney's signature was binding on the wife.

Michael Weinman Associates General Partnership v. Town of Huntersville, 147 N.C. App. 231, 555 S.E.2d 342 (2001)
Special uses; Vested rights

The plaintiff secured a conditional use district rezoning and approval for a site-specific development plan for a mixed-use development in Mecklenburg County. The development included single-family and multifamily housing, a school, and a shopping center. The town later extended its extraterritorial-zoning jurisdiction to the property and adopted conditional use district zones that allowed all of the uses previously permitted by the county. The plaintiff sold the residential and school portions of the site and retained the commercially zoned property. The town then rezoned the commercial site to "neighborhood residential." The town zoning ordinance specifically provided that a conditional use district rezoning constitutes a site-specific development plan and vested a right to develop for three years. Thus, the court held that the plaintiff had secured a statutory vested right. The court noted, however, that the vested right did not preclude the town from enforcing newly enacted requirements regarding building specifications, location of utilities, street layout, and other details required by the town's permitting process.

Tucker v. Mecklenburg County Zoning Board of Adjustment, 148 N.C. App. 52, 557 S.E.2d 631 (2001), *aff'd in part*, 356 N.C. 658, 576 S.E.2d 324 (2003)

Accessory buildings and uses; Interpretation

The respondents operated a nonprofit kennel on their three-acre residential lot. The operation involved the rescue of stray and unwanted dogs. Ten to fifteen dogs were kept and cared for in pens adjacent to the respondents' home. Upon complaint by neighbors, the zoning staff ruled the facility a commercial kennel not permitted in this multifamily residential zoning district. The board of adjustment reversed the staff ruling, holding that the facility was a permissible private kennel. The court reviewed the alleged error of law regarding interpretation of the terms "commercial kennel," "private kennel," and the principal/accessory use distinction. The court noted that although this legal question was subject to de novo review, some deference should be given to the board of adjustment's determination, which should be overturned by a court only if the board acted arbitrarily, oppressively, manifestly abused its authority, or committed error of law. Given that there was no breeding, selling, grooming, training, or overnight boarding of animals, the court upheld the board's determination.

MMR Holdings, LLC v. City of Charlotte, 148 N.C. App. 208, 558 S.E.2d 197 (2001)

Enforcement; Laches

The plaintiff automobile dealer contended that the city's delay in enforcing provisions of its sign regulations regarding balloons, pennants, and other decorations precluded this enforcement action. The court noted that to establish a defense of laches, a plaintiff must show an unreasonable delay that worked to the plaintiff's disadvantage. Mere passage of time alone is insufficient. Here, there was no evidence that the defendant city ever told the plaintiff its signs were in compliance (and in fact a warning citation was issued early in the dispute) and no evidence that the plaintiff spent any money based on city assurances.

Howard v. City of Kinston, 148 N.C. App. 238, 558 S.E.2d 221 (2002)

Evidence; Special uses

The plaintiff's special use permit application for multifamily housing was denied by the city council. The denial followed a joint public hearing with the planning board and was based on a finding that the development would reduce property values, increase traffic, and endanger the public health and safety. The court applied a whole-record test to determine if the denial was based on substantial, competent evidence and upheld the denial. The court held that the council did not abuse its discretion by limiting the number of witnesses at the hearing. The court found that the plaintiff (who was represented by counsel) had waived rights to sworn testimony, cross-examination, and presentation of rebuttal evidence by not requesting these things at the hearing. The court also held that while letters were admitted into evidence after the hearing, there was no showing that the decision was based on them. Finally, the court concluded that the planning director's testimony about the anticipated number of trips that would be generated and a neighbor's testimony regarding personal observations about the dangers of increased traffic for children constituted substantial evidence for a finding on traffic-safety impacts.

Cain v. North Carolina Department of Transportation, 149 N.C. App. 365, 560 S.E.2d 584 (2002)

Signs

The plaintiff owned an outdoor advertising sign along Interstate 95 in Cumberland County. He leased the sign for ten years to a Florida company, which in turn subleased the sign to an adult business in Harnett County. When vegetation in the right-of-way adjacent to the sign was destroyed in an apparent attempt to increase the visibility of the sign, the state Department of Transportation (DOT) revoked the plaintiff's sign permit. The denial was appealed, with the plaintiff contending that the vegetative alteration was done by the subleasing adult business without its knowledge or permission. The court held that in order to revoke a sign permit, the DOT must clearly identify persons who committed a violation for which revocation is permissible and show a sufficient connection between those persons and the permittee. The court found that the lease and sublease established a sufficient connection between the permittee and the persons responsible for the alteration to warrant revocation.

Hopkins v. Nash County, 149 N.C. App. 446, 560 S.E.2d 592 (2002)
Special uses

The plaintiffs appealed the denial of a special use permit for a land-clearing and inert-debris landfill proposed for a clay borrow pit. The appellate court held that the trial court properly applied a whole-record review in concluding that the permit decision was adequately supported by substantial evidence. The court noted that inclusion of a use as a special use in a zoning district creates a prima facie case that the use is compatible with the surrounding area, but this can be (and in this case was) rebutted by evidence presented at the hearing. Such evidence showed that the once-rural portion of the county at issue here was now predominately residential, that many homes were close to the proposed landfill, and that extensive truck traffic would disrupt the neighborhood. The court found this to be substantial evidence that the landfill would not be in harmony with the surrounding area.

Summers v. City of Charlotte, 149 N.C. App. 509, 562 S.E.2d 18, *review denied*, 355 N.C. 758, 566 S.E.2d 482 (2002)
Amendments; Conditional zoning

Neighbors challenged two Charlotte rezonings. Both rezoning petitions included site plans, specifications of proposed uses, and proposed development guidelines. After a series of public meetings and a legislative hearing, the city adopted both rezonings. In each rezoning the council specified that the general zoning-ordinance provisions for the respective districts, the site plans, and the additional individualized proposed regulations and conditions all constituted the binding zoning regulations for each property. The court held that the adoption of a rezoning, even with individualized conditions, is a legislative rather than a quasi-judicial decision. The community meetings and legislative hearing provided in the course of the rezoning process afforded the neighbors adequate procedural due process. The court found that the rezonings were not arbitrary and capricious, as they were based on fair and careful consideration of the planning board's review, technical staff reports, and public comments. The rezonings were consistent with adopted small-area plans for the affected area, the court noted, and there was no showing of bad faith or undue discrimination. As a spot-zoning allegation was not argued on appeal, the court deemed that issue abandoned by the plaintiffs.

Carolina Holdings, Inc. v. Housing Appeals Board, 149 N.C. App. 579, 561 S.E.2d 541, *review denied*, 356 N.C. 298, 570 S.E.2d 499 (2002)
Demolition; Estoppel; Housing code

The petitioner owned an apartment complex in Charlotte and was cited for numerous housing-code violations. After a hearing, the housing inspector confirmed the violations, found the affected units could not be repaired at a cost less than 65 percent of the value of each dwelling, and ordered the structures demolished. The petitioner appealed to the city's Housing Appeals Board, which held a series of hearings on the matter. At the initial hearing the board requested that the petitioner continue recently initiated repairs and continued the appeal. At a second hearing the board ordered most of the violations to be repaired by set dates. In yet a third hearing a progress report was made on repair and there was no additional board action. The board then held a fourth hearing and, without making written findings, ordered the buildings demolished within ninety days. In a fifth hearing the board made written findings that the units were unfit for human habitation and ordered thirty-nine units to be repaired and fifteen units demolished within sixty days. The trial court affirmed the order. The appeals court found that it was not improper for the board to meet in closed session to discuss the case with its attorney (which had been done at both the fourth and fifth hearings), as the matters discussed were within the attorney-client privilege, and that all actions by the board were taken in open session. The court further held that based on a review of the whole record, the board's determination of the condition of the buildings and costs of repairs were supported by competent, substantial, and material evidence. The city was not estopped from enforcement due to the fact that the space, use, light, and ventilation violations had existed for years without citation.

State v. Nance, 149 N.C. App. 734, 562 S.E.2d 557, *review denied*, 355 N.C. 498, 563 S.E.2d 192 (2002)
Inspections

Animal control officers received a complaint regarding horses being maltreated. The officers viewed the horses (who were in a leased open pasture) from a public place on the day the complaint was received and determined that they were seriously malnourished. Three days later, they seized several of the horses in the worst condition for removal and veterinary treatment. As the horses were being removed, the defendant appeared and objected to their removal. No warrant had been obtained for the removal. The court held that an open field is not entitled to Fourth Amendment privacy protection as it is outside the home and curtilage. Observation of the horses from the public way and the neighbor's property in the open field does not require a warrant. However, seizure of the horses (which could be considered evidence of a crime) required consent or a warrant, as the horses were not on public property and there were not exigent circumstances (given the three-day delay between initial observation and seizure of the horses).

Town of Cameron v. Woodell, 150 N.C. App. 174, 563 S.E.2d 198 (2002)
Enforcement; Laches

Prior to entering a contract to purchase a site to be used as a flea market and used car lot, the defendants informed town officials of their plan and were correctly advised that the property involved was not subject to town zoning. Several weeks after the contract to purchase was executed and necessary permits for the business obtained from the county, the town adopted zoning (applicable to the site) that required a special use permit for uses such as those proposed by the defendants. The defendants then acquired title several weeks after the town's zoning of the property, subsequently secured business licenses, and opened a flea market and car lot on the site. Three years later, the town discovered the property was inside the city's jurisdiction and issued a notice of violation. The defendants then applied for a special use permit to continue the businesses, which was denied. The town sought to enjoin future operation of the businesses. The court found that laches precluded enforcement of the town ordinance as applied to both aspects of the business. The court held that the evidence supported a conclusion that the town was aware of the defendants' plans for both businesses and advised them that there was no town jurisdiction, that the defendants relied on that assurance and materially changed their condition as a result, and that the town's unreasonable delay in enforcement had prejudiced the defendants.

Eastern Outdoor, Inc. v. Board of Adjustment, 150 N.C. App. 516, 564 S.E.2d 78 (2002), *aff'd*, 357 N.C. 501, 586 S.E.2d 90 (2003)
Signs; Vested rights

Johnston County staff issued the petitioner two permits for construction of billboards in an agricultural-residential zoning district. The petitioner then began construction. However, seven weeks after issuing the permits the county revoked them on the grounds that outdoor advertising was not allowed in this zoning district. The revocations were appealed to the board of adjustment, which held that billboards were not allowed in the district, that the permits had been issued under a mistake of law, and that therefore the permits could be revoked. The court held that the dispositive issue was the interpretation of the ordinance. Since this involves an alleged error of law, a de novo review was appropriate. The court found that the terms of the ordinance were correctly interpreted as prohibiting billboards in this zoning district and that G.S. 160D-1115 provides that a mistakenly issued building permit may be revoked. The fact that the petitioner had made substantial investments in the property is immaterial if the permit is properly revoked, the court noted, as one cannot acquire a vested right to violate an ordinance.

Transylvania County v. Moody, 151 N.C. App. 389, 565 S.E.2d 720 (2002)
Enforcement; Signs

Transylvania County adopted a sign ordinance under its general ordinance-making authority. The defendant constructed two single-post sign structures without seeking a sign permit from the county. The county Inspections Department issued two stop-work orders, then a written notice of violation, and finally a suit was initiated to compel compliance. The trial court entered an order of abatement to dismantle the signs, ordered the defendant to comply with the sign ordinance in the future, and upheld a $22,300 civil penalty. The court of appeals held that the county has the option of adopting a sign ordinance under either its zoning authority or its general ordinance-making authority. The court found that the ordinance was reasonably related to the protection of legitimate governmental objectives (protection of safety and aesthetics) and that its restrictions were neither arbitrary nor unreasonable. The court likewise found no equal-protection violation. However, it did find that the county had not followed the procedures set forth in the ordinance regarding the assessment of civil penalties, so it upheld the abatement order and injunction for compliance but set aside the civil penalty.

Capital Outdoor, Inc. v. Guilford County Board of Adjustment, 152 N.C. App. 474, 567 S.E.2d 440, *review denied*, 356 N.C. 611, 574 S.E.2d 676 (2002)
Interpretation; Signs

On remand from a reversal in the supreme court, the court of appeals addressed interpretation of a zoning ordinance requirement that billboards not be located within 300 feet of "residentially zoned property." The court held that this restriction applied to "Single-Family Residential" and "Multi-Family Residential" zoning districts but not to "Agricultural" zoning districts even though residences were a permitted use in the agricultural district.

Hemphill-Nolan v. Town of Weddington, 153 N.C. App. 144, 568 S.E.2d 887 (2002)
Appeals; Subdivisions; Variances

The town's subdivision ordinance provided that permanent dead-end streets could not exceed a length of 600 feet unless necessitated by topography or property accessibility. The plaintiff sought a variance from this subdivision-ordinance requirement in order to construct a 785-foot-long cul-de-sac. Upon denial of the variance by the town council, the plaintiff sought judicial review in the nature of certiorari. The trial court dismissed the appeal because it was not filed within the thirty-day period set by the zoning statutes.

The appellate court ruled that the dismissal was improper. This statute of limitations only applied to appeals of decisions made under the zoning ordinance, and no specific time for appeals was set in the subdivision-enabling statute. The court held that while the subdivision statutes make no explicit provision for judicial review, the superior court has discretion to grant writs of certiorari "in proper cases" and that a subdivision decision is such a case. The court held that the appeal must be filed within "a reasonable time" rather than the thirty-day period set by statute for zoning appeals. The case was remanded for a determination of whether the appeal was filed within such a reasonable period and, if so, for consideration of the merits of the petition. [Note: G.S. 160D-1405(d) subsequently applied the thirty-day statute of limitations to appeals of all quasi-judicial development-regulation decisions.]

Huntington Properties, LLC v. Currituck County, 153 N.C. App. 218, 569 S.E.2d 695 (2002)

Nonconformities; Preemption; Vested rights

The plaintiffs acquired a nonconforming mobile-home park. When originally constructed, the park had 440 rental spaces. However, due to increasingly strict environmental regulations, by 1987 the park's wastewater-treatment system could only accommodate about 140 units. The county adopted a unified development ordinance in 1992 that had various limitations on the expansion of nonconformities. In 1995, the plaintiff's predecessor in interest purchased the park and hired an engineer to design, upgrade, and obtain permits for a wastewater-treatment system that would serve all of the original 440 units. The county in 1996 adopted an amendment to the nonconformities section of its ordinance to explicitly provide that improvements to water and sewer systems to increase the number of units in a mobile-home park was a prohibited expansion of a nonconformity, while improvements to better protect public health without increasing the number of units in a park were permitted.

The court noted that nonconformities are not favored by the law and held that expansion of treatment capacity to expand the number of units in the park beyond the number lawfully present when it became nonconforming was not allowed under the original ordinance or the amended version. The court held that no permits for expansion had been issued at the time the expansion became contrary to the ordinance, so there was no vested right to such. The court also held that the limitations here were legitimate zoning restrictions on the use of land and were not preempted by state regulation of wastewater-treatment facilities.

In re Appeal of the Society for the Preservation of Historic Oakwood v. Board of Adjustment, 153 N.C. App. 737, 571 S.E.2d 588 (2002)

Appeals; Jurisdiction

The Raleigh zoning ordinance allowed "multi-family housing" as a permitted use in the applicable zoning district at issue but "transitional housing" was not permitted. The Raleigh Rescue Mission proposed building a shelter, which it termed "multi-family housing." When the plaintiff neighbors objected, the deputy city attorney asked the zoning administrator for an opinion on the issue. The zoning administrator issued a memorandum in response stating that the structure proposed was permitted but the proposed use might not be. The neighbors appealed this determination to the board of adjustment (and while the appeal was pending the city council approved the project while noting the pending appeal). The court held that the zoning administrator's decision was not an "order, requirement, decision, or determination" that could be appealed to the board. The order must have some binding force or effect for there to be a right of appeal. Where the decision has no binding effect and is neither authoritative nor a conclusion as to future action, it is merely the opinion of the administrative official, and thus the board of adjustment has no jurisdiction to hear an appeal of it.

Overton v. Camden County, 155 N.C. App. 100, 574 S.E.2d 150 (2002)

Nonconformities; Special uses

The petitioners operated a nonconforming house-moving and storage business. They sought a special use permit to expand operations to a separate lot across the street from the existing business. The board of adjustment issued a permit that included the following conditions: (1) that the business on the original lot across the street be discontinued within a specified time and (2) that a previously issued permit for a third party on a neighboring lot be amended to reflect the relocation of this business.

The court acknowledged that individual conditions could be imposed on special use permits, provided those conditions are properly related to standards in the ordinance. The court held that while the county may regulate and limit lawful nonconformities, an application for a new permit pertaining to a separate lot must be reviewed on its own merits and cannot be used to impose conditions on a different lot (nor may such conditions go beyond the requirements for nonconformities set out in the ordinance). The court also held that a third party's special use permit may not be modified in the fashion undertaken here. The court found that it was proper for the trial court to order the permit reissued without the invalid conditions (rather than remanding the case to the board) because the board had already resolved and made findings on all relevant issues and the course directed by the court would be the only possible result on remand.

Neuse River Foundation, Inc. v. Smithfield Foods, Inc., 155 N.C. App. 110, 574 S.E.2d 48 (2002), *review denied*, 356 N.C. 675, 577 S.E.2d 628 (2003)

Aesthetics; Nuisances; Standing

Various plaintiffs brought an action seeking to compel the defendant to establish a fund to remediate damage allegedly caused to various rivers from swine operations and for injunctive relief prohibiting swine lagoons and spray fields. The court upheld dismissal of the action due to a lack of standing on the part of all plaintiffs. The court noted that the burden of proving the elements of standing rested with the plaintiffs and stated that the plaintiffs had to allege (1) injury in fact to a protected interest that cannot be considered merged in the general public right, (2) causation, and (3) a proper or individualized form of relief. The court held that injury to aesthetic or recreational interests alone cannot confer standing on an environmental plaintiff. Also, since the downstream riparian owners, commercial fishermen, and marina operator plaintiffs did not seek individual compensation or individualized relief, they did not have standing.

Hewett v. County of Brunswick, 155 N.C. App. 138, 573 S.E.2d 688 (2002)

Enforcement; Mining; Special uses

The plaintiff obtained a special use permit for a sand-mining operation. The permit included a condition that if any conditions of the permit were held invalid, the entire permit would be void; an accompanying letter advised the plaintiff that any changes in the permit would void the entire permit. After commencing sand mining on the affected property, the plaintiff discovered a marl deposit and secured an amendment to his state mining permit to operate a marl-mining operation on the site, with a crusher on site to process the marl. The plaintiff then applied for an electrical hookup for the crusher, which provided the county with initial notice of the proposed change in operations. Upon learning of this change, the county required the plaintiff to seek either a modification of the original special use permit or a new permit. The zoning ordinance was then amended to prohibit mines with processing on site in the zoning district in which the plaintiff's property was located. The board of adjustment then held that the original permit was void due to the change in operation and denied the application for a new permit. The court concluded that it was error for the board of adjustment to void the original permit. The court found that the ordinance in effect at the time the original permit was issued included no standards relative to project alteration and that the permit itself had no such explicit condition (and the court expressed some doubt about the statutory authority to impose such a condition). Since the applicant presented as part of his permit-modification request sufficient evidence to show that all terms of the ordinance had been met and that there was no evidence in the record to the contrary, the permit modification had to be approved.

County of Wake v. North Carolina Department of Environment & Natural Resources, 155 N.C. App. 225, 573 S.E.2d 572 (2002), *review denied*, 357 N.C. 62, 579 S.E.2d 386 (2003)

Estoppel; Landfills; Standing

Wake County obtained a state permit to expand a landfill and commenced land acquisition for it, part of which was completed. The Town of Holly Springs, in which part of the expansion was to take place, endorsed the project (which was required as part of the state-permitting process). The town and county entered interlocal agreements to finance treatment of wastewater from the landfill. Four years later, the town revoked its prior approval. The defendant state-agency staff then issued the final state permit. The court held that the individual neighbors who initiated an appeal of the permit issuance were aggrieved persons with standing to challenge the permit (they had alleged noise, pollution, landscape changes, and other negative environmental consequences that would interfere with the use and enjoyment of their property), as was the town (due to the impacts on its tax base and planning jurisdiction). The court held as a matter of law that the town was equitably estopped from withdrawing its prior approval due to its multiple acts of ratification (e.g., entering into contracts and accepting payment for wastewater treatment and approval of long-range waste-disposal plans).

Overton v. Camden County, 155 N.C. App. 391, 574 S.E.2d 157 (2002)

Enforcement; Manufactured housing; Nonconformities

The petitioner placed a mobile home on his property in 1972. The county zoning ordinance applicable to the property was effective in 1993. In 1995, the petitioner replaced the manufactured home without securing a building permit or the required special use permit. In 1998, the county zoning ordinance was replaced with a unified development ordinance. In 2000, the petitioner was cited for a zoning violation. On appeal, the board of adjustment held the petitioner in violation but allowed the manufactured home to remain in place upon payment of a fine and meeting several specified conditions (not more than one person was to reside in the home, the home was to be removed if vacated for more than sixty days, and the home was not to be a unit manufactured prior to 1976).

The court found that where there has been an ordinance amendment between the date of the alleged violation and the date of the enforcement action, the board of adjustment is to apply the ordinance in effect at the time of its decision. The court held that the manufactured home was not a lawful nonconforming use under the 1998 ordinance because appropriate permits were not secured when the unit was placed in 1995. Since the use was not lawful at the time of inception, it was not lawful under the revised ordinance. The ordinance in effect at the time of the board's decision on the enforcement appeal required a special use permit for a manufactured home on the site at issue. The conditions imposed by the board could legitimately be imposed on the requisite permit and were thus lawful here.

In re Request for Declaratory Ruling by the Environmental Management Commission, 155 N.C. App. 408, 573 S.E.2d 732 (2002), *review denied*, 357 N.C. 62, 579 S.E.2d 392 (2003)

Wetlands

The court upheld the authority of the Environmental Management Commission to regulate wetlands. The court held that wetlands were "waters" as defined by the statutes (as that term includes any "other body or accumulation of water, whether surface or underground"). Considering the language and spirit of the statutes and their purposes (and similar long-standing federal interpretations of "waters of the United States" to include wetlands), wetlands are appropriately included under state law as "waters."

Lamar Outdoor Advertising, Inc. v. City of Hendersonville Zoning Board of Adjustment, 155 N.C. App. 516, 573 S.E.2d 637 (2002)

Evidence; Nonconformities; Preemption; Signs

The plaintiff owned a nonconforming billboard that was damaged in a storm. The zoning administrator denied a permit for repair on the grounds that the cost of repairs would exceed the maximum allowed under the zoning ordinance (60 percent of the replacement cost of a comparable sign). The court held in a de novo review that as a matter of law the state Outdoor Advertising Control Act did not preempt local zoning regulation of signs, as the state statutes do not expressly do so (and in fact they recognize a local role in sign regulation), nor do the state statutes provide a complete and integrated regulatory scheme so as to justify an implied preemption. The court applied a whole-record review to conclude that the record supported the board's findings regarding the repair costs of the sign. The zoning ordinance placed upon the applicant the burden of proving that the costs of repair were within the ordinance limits. The record showed that the estimated costs of repair submitted to the board were less than the amount originally submitted to staff and that the applicant's own witness testified that the estimate omitted several essential components of reconstruction costs.

Showcase Realty & Construction Co. v. City of Fayetteville, 155 N.C. App. 548, 573 S.E.2d 737 (2002)

Evidence; Findings; Variances

The city issued a special use permit for a ministorage facility with a required front setback of fifty feet and a side setback of thirty feet. During the course of construction, a question arose as to whether the required setbacks were being observed. Construction was halted and a survey revealed that the concrete slabs for the buildings were placed with only a twenty-five-foot front setback and a twenty-nine-foot side setback. The owner then petitioned for a variance, testifying at the hearing on the matter that he thought the setback was to be measured from the road rather than the right-of-way, that he relied on the contractor and inspections staff to properly site the structure, and that he had expended all of his funds on the improperly located structure and could not afford its relocation. City staff testified that an incorrect measurement could have been made due to road construction underway at the time the structure was located on the site. The plaintiff here, the adjoining landowner, testified that if the building were completed as located it would block views of his undeveloped commercial property, reduce the value of his business, and force stormwater drainage onto his property. The board issued a variance.

The court conducted a whole-record review and invalidated the variance as unsupported by adequate evidence in the record. The ordinance amplified on the statutory language requiring a showing of "practical difficulties or unnecessary hardships" to specify that the board must find that the owner could "secure no reasonable return from, or make no reasonable use of, his property." The court held that there were only conclusory statements in the record. Financial hardship alone is insufficient to establish an "unnecessary" hardship; rather, evidence that no reasonable use or return could be made without a variance is necessary. The ordinance also required a showing that the variance would not impair an adequate supply of light and air to surrounding properties and would not impair their established property values. The court similarly found that there was a lack of evidence in the record to support findings on these standards. [Note: G.S. 160D-705(d)(1) was subsequently modified to prohibit a requirement of "no reasonable use" as a variance standard.]

Malloy v. Zoning Board of Adjustment, 155 N.C. App. 628, 573 S.E.2d 760 (2002)

Interpretation; Nonconformities

The plaintiffs operated a nonconforming welding and gas supply business in a multifamily residential district in Asheville. They replaced a 3000-gallon aboveground liquid-oxygen storage tank with a new 9000-gallon tank. Upon complaint from neighbors, the city investigated and determined this to be an unlawful expansion of a nonconforming use. The court applied a de novo review to hold as a matter of law that the storage tank was a "structure" regulated by the ordinance. The court further concluded that the new tank physically enlarged the structure and was thus a prohibited "enlargement" of the nonconformity.

Bessemer City Express, Inc. v. City of Kings Mountain, 155 N.C. App. 637, 573 S.E.2d 712 (2002), *review denied*, 357 N.C. 61, 579 S.E.2d 384 (2003)

Amortization; Appeals

The city adopted a zoning amendment restricting the location, design, and use of video-gaming machines, requiring a special use permit for them and amortizing nonconforming operations after a six-month period. The plaintiff filed a declaratory-judgment action contesting the validity of the ordinance. The plaintiffs sought and were denied a preliminary injunction to enjoin enforcement. The court held that an appeal of the denial of the preliminary injunction was an impermissible interlocutory appeal because the order did not affect a substantial right (at the time of appeal the ordinance requiring removal had not taken effect) and in any event the plaintiff's overall business could continue in operation pending resolution of the case on the merits.

Tabor v. County of Orange, 156 N.C. App. 88, 575 S.E.2d 540 (2003)
Liability

The plaintiffs applied for a septic-tank improvement permit on land they proposed to subdivide in order to place a mobile home on the property for their parents. The plaintiffs alleged that the county's environmental health specialist negligently represented that the permit would be approved (while the county contended that the specialist advised the plaintiffs that additional information was needed). After the plaintiffs constructed a road and bought a mobile home, the septic-tank permit was denied. The court held that approving or denying a septic-tank permit is a governmental function, and thus sovereign immunity bars a suit for negligence absent a waiver of immunity by the county (which was not alleged here).

Sarda v. City/County of Durham Board of Adjustment, 156 N.C. App. 213, 575 S.E.2d 829 (2003)
Special uses; Standing

The plaintiffs sought judicial review of a special use permit issued for a paintball playing field in rural Durham County. The plaintiffs, who owned a residential tract some 400 yards from the permitted site, appeared before the board of adjustment to oppose permit issuance. When the permit was issued, the plaintiffs appealed. The court held that the petitioners had merely alleged that they owned property in the immediate vicinity of the proposed project and that this was insufficient to establish that they would suffer the requisite special damages to make them aggrieved persons with standing for judicial review. Absent such an allegation, the superior court lacked subject-matter jurisdiction to hear the appeal. The court thus vacated the order and reinstated the board's permit issuance.

Monroe v. City of New Bern, 156 N.C. App. 275, 580 S.E.2d 372 (2003)
Damages; Demolition; Housing code

The plaintiff owned a seriously dilapidated abandoned residence. After it had been boarded up for three years, the town proceeded to demolish it without notice or hearing and placed a lien on the property for demolition costs. The plaintiff alleged a due-process violation and common law trespass. The court held that the city's authority to summarily demolish the house under G.S. 160A-193 (allowing summary abatement of a public nuisance) is limited to situations where the structure poses an imminent threat to public health or safety so as to constitute an emergency situation (such as being on the verge of falling on a public sidewalk or where necessary to control a large fire). In a nonemergency situation the city must follow the notice and hearing requirements of G.S. 160D-1119 to -1125. The court remanded the case for a hearing on the issue of damages.

Lambeth v. Town of Kure Beach, 157 N.C. App. 349, 578 S.E.2d 688 (2003)
Interpretation; Mootness; Vested rights

The town's zoning ordinances limited driveway width to twenty-four feet and total impervious surface coverage on a lot to 65 percent. The plaintiff had previously constructed a nineteen-foot-wide driveway and a five-foot-wide concrete sidewalk across a town right-of-way. The plaintiff sought to expand his driveway by five feet to provide easier wheelchair access for his disabled daughter. The permit was denied on the basis that the expansion would violate the twenty-four-foot limit (which was interpreted to apply to the combined width of the existing driveway and sidewalk). The board of adjustment upheld this determination. While this decision was on appeal to the superior court, the town amended and clarified the ordinance by specifying a total of twenty-four feet of impervious surface for access across a town right-of-way, and thereafter the superior court dismissed the plaintiff's action.

The court held that the case was not moot, as the ordinance in effect at the time the plaintiff's application was decided, not the subsequent amendment, was controlling. The court then found that the plain meaning of the ordinance was that a driveway width (not a driveway plus a separate sidewalk) could not exceed twenty-four feet and that, therefore, the permit denial was in error.

City of Charlotte v. King, 158 N.C. App. 304, 580 S.E.2d 380 (2003)

Enforcement; Housing code

The city imposed a civil penalty of $5500 on the defendant, a non-occupant owner of a residential structure, for failure to comply with an order to repair or demolish the structure. The ordinance exempted from civil penalties owners who occupied the structure as their principal residence. The court held that the terms of the exemption were clear and unambiguous and did not apply to the defendant.

Kennedy v. Haywood County, 158 N.C. App. 526, 581 S.E.2d 119 (2003)

Inspections; Liability

The plaintiff alleged that the county was negligent in its building inspections and issuance of a certificate of compliance for a residential structure. The court held that sovereign immunity barred such a suit against the county unless the county had waived such immunity. The county had purchased liability insurance for "law enforcement officers," an act that could underpin an allegation of waiver. However, the court found that building inspectors were not "law enforcement officers," as they have no authority to issue arrest warrants, were not certified law-enforcement officers, and were not charged with providing police protection. Further, the county insurance policy specifically excluded coverage for property damage. Given these findings, there was no waiver of immunity for building-inspection purposes.

Capital Outdoor, Inc. v. Tolson, 159 N.C. App. 55, 582 S.E.2d 717, *review denied*, 357 N.C. 504, 587 S.E.2d 662 (2003)

Due process; Interpretation; Laches; Signs

The plaintiff sign companies challenged a state administrative rule limiting the height of signs to fifty feet, measured vertically from the adjacent edge of the pavement of the main traveled way. The rule went into effect in 1990 but was not enforced by the state Department of Transportation (DOT) until 1998. In 2000, the DOT revoked the sign permits for all billboards that were more than fifty feet tall. Upon a challenge to said revocations, the court affirmed summary judgment for the state. The only issue was one of statutory interpretation. The court held that the terms "height" and "sign structure" should be assigned their common or ordinary meanings, as there was no indication that the rule intended otherwise. The DOT's interpretation that this meant that the top of a sign face could not be more than fifty feet high was deemed reasonable and correct. As for the contention that the regulation violated substantive due process, the court found that construction of billboards is not a fundamental right and that the regulation was rationally related to the governmental interests in safety and aesthetics. The court held that laches did not apply to preclude enforcement because the DOT never gave the plaintiffs any assurances that the taller signs complied with the regulation, and the plaintiffs offered no specific facts to show how they were wrongly prejudiced by the delay in enforcement.

Morris Communications Corp. v. Board of Adjustment, 159 N.C. App. 598, 583 S.E.2d 419 (2003), *appeal dismissed*, 357 N.C. 658, 590 S.E.2d 269 (2003)

Preemption; Signs

Staff for the city of Gastonia interpreted the city's sign regulations limiting replacement of sign structures to include a prohibition on changing the frame on a sign. The court held that this was a reasonable interpretation of the ordinance by the board and was entitled to deference by the courts. However, since North Carolina Department of Transportation (NCDOT) sign regulations specifically allow for repair and replacement of a sign's border and trim as well as its face, the local regulation was found to be preempted to the extent of this conflict. Since the sign here was subject to NCDOT regulations as well as to local permits, the local restriction could not be enforced on this sign.

Slavin v. Town of Oak Island, 160 N.C. App. 57, 584 S.E.2d 100, *review denied*, 357 N.C. 659, 590 S.E.2d 271 (2003)
Jurisdiction

As part of a beach-nourishment project carried out by the federal government, the town developed a program to protect sand dunes and sea turtle habitat areas that entailed depositing sand seaward of the previous high-water mark. Part of this program involved placement of sand fences along the landward side of the newly created dunes, with access points at regular intervals. Oceanfront property owners contended that the town had no authority to enact an access plan because the fences were located on state property and that each landowner had a vested right to direct, unrestricted access to the ocean that could not be limited without compensation. The court rejected both contentions, finding that while title to the renourished beach belonged to the state, this did not limit the town's general police power to enact regulations to protect a public beach within city limits. Further, the court held that while a littoral owner has a right of access to adjacent waters, it is a qualified right and is subject to reasonable regulation.

Butler v. City Council of Clinton, 160 N.C. App. 68, 584 S.E.2d 103, *review denied*, 357 N.C. 504, 587 S.E.2d 661 (2003)
Special uses

The city council denied a special use permit for location of a crematory in an office and institutional district on the grounds that the use failed to meet three of eight standards in the ordinance, including that the use will not be detrimental to the public health, safety, morals, or general welfare. The court found that there was sufficient evidence in the record to justify a denial on the public-safety ground, noting that the standard requires a finding that the use "will not" endanger public safety. The applicant's evidence showed only that the use "likely would not" harm public safety. Further, neighboring opponents presented contrary evidence of potential health impacts and adverse psychological impacts. Thus, there was sufficient competent, substantial, and material evidence in the record to support permit denial.

Welter v. Rowan County Board of Commissioners, 160 N.C. App. 358, 585 S.E.2d 472 (2003)
Judicial review; Nonconformities

The plaintiff owned a nonconforming go-cart track located in an R-A zoning district. The ordinance provided that if a nonconforming use was discontinued for a 360-day period, it could not be resumed ("discontinued" was defined as having stopped or ceased the use). The site was not leased for a summer and was later closed for repairs, and while some practice use of the track was made in this period, no events open to the public were held for over a year. Upon petition of neighbors that the property's nonconforming status had been lost, the zoning administrator ruled that since the track had discontinued its regular use as a public go-cart track for over a year, it could no longer be used as a "public speedway." The trial court upheld the zoning administrator's decision. The court of appeals concluded that the trial court should have conducted a de novo review, as interpretation of the terms of the ordinance is a question of law. However, the appellate court held that two problems precluded the lower court from doing this. First, relevant portions of the ordinance were not in the record, and second, key facts regarding the exact nature of the use that did take place on the site were not clearly resolved. The case was therefore remanded.

Eason v. Union County, 160 N.C. App. 388, 585 S.E.2d 452 (2003)
Building permits and inspection; Liability

The plaintiff bought a house in Union County. The purchase was contingent upon an independent inspection. That inspection revealed several defects. The plaintiff closed on the house with knowledge that the defects had not yet been remedied (relying on a promise from the builder that they soon would be). The defendant county issued a certificate of occupancy after closing. The builder did not subsequently correct the defects. The plaintiff then alleged negligent inspection by the county. The court held that any negligence by the county was not the proximate cause of the plaintiff's injury, as there was a closing prior to issuance of the certificate of occupancy, and thus there was no reliance on county action. Further, the plaintiff's visits to the sites and knowledge of the unrepaired defects at the time of closing constituted contributory negligence.

Cox v. Hancock, 160 N.C. App. 473, 586 S.E.2d 500 (2003)

Bias; Special uses

The defendants applied for a special use permit for construction of a 130-unit apartment building on a 13.1-acre tract in the Oxford extraterritorial area. The board of adjustment held two hearings on the application, and two members who were absent at the initial hearing attended and voted at the second hearing (and one member resigned between the two hearings). Upon approval of the application, adjacent owners appealed the issuance of the permit. The court found that a prospective vendee (as well as the record owner) could properly apply for a special use permit. The court held that an apartment building could properly be considered within the "unified housing development" allowed as a potential special use in the zoning district here. The court concluded that the application, exhibits, oral testimony presented, and extensive board discussion provided sufficient competent, substantial, and material evidence that the specific and general standards for this special use had been met. The court also ruled that there was no due-process violation created by a change in membership in the board, given that written minutes of the first hearing were available prior to the second hearing, all exhibits presented at the initial hearing were available for review in the planning office between the two hearings, and there was extensive discussion and cross-examination at the second hearing. Finally, the court held that the familial relationship of a board member (the owner of the property being sold for the development was married to the aunt of a board member) did not present a per se conflict of interest, and the burden was on the party claiming bias to show that bias existed, which was not done in this case.

William Brewster Co., Inc. v. Town of Huntersville, 161 N.C. App. 132, 588 S.E.2d 16 (2003)

Subdivisions

The plaintiff submitted a sketch plan for a 145-lot single-family subdivision. Lot sizes were proposed at approximately 6000 square feet. The tract was near another development in preliminary plat stage of development that had 20,000-square-foot lots. The plan was denied on the basis that it failed to meet two standards in the subdivision ordinance: (1) it did not conform to the most recently adopted public plans and policies for the area and (2) in an area with established development, it did not "protect and enhance the stability, environment, health, and character of neighboring areas." The plaintiff appealed. The appeals court held that the trial court properly applied a whole-record test to determine whether there was substantial, competent, and material evidence in the record to support plan denial. The court then found that the plaintiff had submitted adequate evidence that all of the zoning and subdivision requirements had been met, and thus there was an entitlement to approval absent adequate contrary evidence in the record. The court then found there was no such contrary evidence. The court of appeals concluded that there were no adopted plans and policies for any areas within a mile of the proposed development, and so the consistency requirement could not support a denial. Since the proposed nearby large lot development had not yet been built, it could not be considered "existing development," and there was no other evidence in the record that the plaintiff's proposal did not conform to surrounding conditions. The denial was accordingly overturned.

Prewitt v. Town of Wrightsville Beach, 161 N.C. App. 481, 595 S.E.2d 442 (2003)
Enforcement; Preemption

In 1998, the town issued the plaintiff a permit to build an oceanfront structure, with a required rear-yard setback of 7.5 feet from an eastern reference line established by 1939 legislation. Upon completion of the structure, the town requested a new as-built survey prior to issuing a certificate of occupancy. The new survey revealed that the structure was in fact, without any modification in plans being approved by the town, located 1.5 feet from the eastern reference line, with stairs extending past the reference line and with several other unpermitted modifications. The plaintiff appealed the denial of the certificate of occupancy to the board of adjustment and, in the event the appeal should be denied, sought a variance from the setback requirement. The board denied both. The court found that the 1939 legislation did not preempt the town's rear-yard setback regulations and that 1981 legislation amending the 1939 act to change the terminology from "building line" to "property line," along with the authorization to regulate the size of yards and location of buildings in the zoning-enabling act, provided the town valid authority to establish the rear-yard setback requirement. The court also dismissed a claim of selective enforcement, noting that the plaintiff had the burden of showing that the ordinance had been implemented with "an evil eye and uneven hand" and that the record was devoid of any evidence of conscious and intentional discrimination on the part of the town.

Ashby v. Town of Cary, 161 N.C. App. 499, 588 S.E.2d 572 (2003)
Amendments; Rezoning

The plaintiffs challenged a refusal by Cary to rezone a parcel in an existing commercial area from low-density residential to a business conditional use district. The proposed zoning was consistent with the small-area plan applicable to the area when the land was acquired, the property annexed, and the rezoning petition submitted. However, concurrent with receipt of this rezoning petition, the town received preliminary recommendations from a new corridor plan for the area. Based on concerns with traffic congestion raised in the new planning report, the town denied the rezoning. The plaintiff contended that denial was arbitrary and capricious. The court affirmed that a conditional use district rezoning decision is a purely legislative decision and is to be overturned only if the record before the town council at the time of decision demonstrates that the decision had no foundation in reason and bore no substantial relationship to the public health, safety, morals, or welfare. If there is any plausible grounding for the decision that has a basis in reason and relation to public safety, the decision must be affirmed. Here, the council's stated concern about even minimal increases in traffic in a heavily congested area met that standard of review.

Humane Society of Moore County, Inc. v. Town of Southern Pines, 161 N.C. App. 625, 589 S.E.2d 162 (2003)
Evidence; Special uses

The plaintiff proposed to build a facility in a "Planned Development" zoning district. The ordinance allowed "Veterinarian, Animal Clinic, Outside Kennel" as a special use in this district. The plaintiff's special use permit application was denied on the grounds that the use was primarily an animal shelter and adoption facility and thus not permitted, that the use would substantially injure the value of adjoining property, and that it would not be in harmony with the surrounding area. The court conducted a whole-record review and concluded that the evidence submitted established that the services to be offered included those uses common to a veterinary clinic and there was no evidence in the record to support a conclusion that adoption services would be the principal use of the facility. The court held that the evidence on property-value impacts submitted by the town's expert witness, an appraiser, was inadequate. The expert had testified that there was inadequate data regarding actual comparable value impacts of animal-care facilities on adjoining properties, so case studies of other uses and opinions of kennel operators and neighbors were used. The court held that these were speculative opinions and not a proper foundation for a finding on impacts on property values. The court found that the evidence offered on harmony with the surrounding area was similarly speculative and failed to take into consideration the proposed facility's proximity to the county airport, a mini-storage warehouse, and an existing animal hospital. Finally, the court held that the order to issue the permit on remand did not deprive the town of the opportunity to impose conditions on the permit, as the matter had been before the town board twice and the applicant had in fact consented to several modifications in the project to ameliorate its impacts.

Fantasy World, Inc. v. Greensboro Board of Adjustment, 162 N.C. App. 603, 592 S.E.2d 205, *review denied*, 358 N.C. 543, 599 S.E.2d 43 (2004)

Adult uses; Enforcement

The city tax collector denied a privilege license to the plaintiff to operate a business using a portion of a building as an adult use because another portion of the building was already in operation as a nonconforming adult use. The tax collector's decision was appealed to the board of adjustment, which upheld the denial. The court concluded that the city had authority to adopt an ordinance provision allowing the tax collector to deny a privilege license due to noncompliance with the zoning ordinance. The court held that the ordinance-enforcement provisions of G.S. 160A-175 do not limit the city's compliance powers relative to administration of the privilege-license tax. The court also ruled that the board of adjustment had jurisdiction to hear this appeal, as the tax collector is an administrative official who is charged with assessing zoning compliance (the ordinance required an assessment of regulatory compliance as part of the privilege-license review). The court further held that there was sufficient evidence presented to the board of adjustment to establish that the plaintiff was not in compliance with zoning restrictions. Finally, the court found that the city's tax and zoning requirements did not pose an unlawful prior restraint on protected speech.

Jones v. Davis, 163 N.C. App. 628, 594 S.E.2d 235, *aff'd per curiam*, 359 N.C. 314, 608 S.E.2d 754 (2004)

Manufactured housing; Subdivisions

The defendant subdivided forty-one acres in Surry County and then rented the lots to persons who placed tenant-owned manufactured homes on the lots. Neighbors challenged Surry County's approval of the subdivision plats. The court held that creation of lots for this purpose falls within the statutory and ordinance definition of a subdivision (creation of lots for the purpose of sale or building development). While zoning can regulate what use is made of the lots, the actual use is not controlling relative to plat approval. Also, the county's manufactured-home-park ordinance was not applicable to this property because by its terms it only applied to unsubdivided land.

Clark Stone Co., Inc. v. North Carolina Department of Environment & Natural Resources, 164 N.C. App. 24, 594 S.E.2d 832, *review denied*, 359 N.C. 322, 603 S.E.2d 878 (2004)

Enforcement; Mining; Vested rights

The plaintiff secured a mining permit for a tract in Avery County. When land preparation for the mine began, neighboring citizens and interest groups complained to the defendant state agency that the site was clearly visible from the Appalachian Trail and that noise from the mining operation would significantly impact users on the Trail. Neither of these considerations was known by the defendant at the time of permit issuance. After a local public hearing, the defendant issued notice of an intent to revoke the permit because of these significant adverse impacts. The plaintiff submitted landscape and screening plans, but the defendant rejected them as inadequate and revoked the mining permit.

The court applied a whole-record test to the issue of whether there was substantial evidence in the record to support the finding of significant adverse impacts and held that there was. This being the case, the court had to defer to the agency decision. The court applied a de novo standard of review to the question of statutory authority for permit revocation. Since the pertinent statute gave the defendant authority to modify the terms and conditions of a permit as it deemed appropriate, the defendant also had the authority to revoke a permit if it followed proper procedures, and it concluded here that the plaintiff mining operation would otherwise violate the requirements of the Mining Act. The court held that since the permit was mistakenly issued, the plaintiff could claim no vested rights based on it.

Sandy Mush Properties, Inc. v. Rutherford County, 164 N.C. App. 162, 595 S.E.2d 233 (2004)
Moratoria

The county published a single newspaper notice of a hearing on a proposed Polluting Industries Development Ordinance that would prohibit location of new or expanded heavy industries within 2000 feet of a church, school, or residence (the county did not have zoning). Shortly thereafter, an optionee/lessee on a tract owned by the plaintiff (which was located within 2000 feet of a school) submitted an incomplete application for a permit to locate a crushed stone quarry. The county then held the advertised hearing and adopted a 120-day moratorium on building permits for initiation of heavy industry in school zones, specifying that the moratorium was adopted pursuant to its general ordinance-making authority. The optionee then submitted a completed building-permit application. The permit was denied based on the moratorium. The county then adopted a School Zone Protective Ordinance that prohibited construction or operation of a heavy industry within 2000 feet of a school. As with the moratorium, the county specified that this ordinance was adopted pursuant to its general ordinance-making authority, although the county followed all of the notice and hearing requirements for a zoning ordinance in its consideration of this permanent ordinance.

The court held that the moratorium was improperly advertised and was thus invalid. The court reasoned that the moratorium was in effect a temporary land use plan that divided the county into two areas—a zone in which heavy industry was allowed and a smaller area where it was at least temporarily prohibited. This fact, along with the use of the building-permit system for its enforcement, led the court to conclude that the moratorium had to be adopted following the procedures for land use regulations. Since those procedures require a public hearing with two published notices and that was not done here, the moratorium was held invalid. [Note: G.S. 160D-107 was subsequently enacted to set the procedures for the adoption of moratoria.]

McCormick v. Hanson Aggregates Southeast, Inc., 164 N.C. App. 459, 596 S.E.2d 431, *review denied*, 359 N.C. 69, 603 S.E.2d 131 (2004)
Enforcement; Public records

The city of Raleigh issued a notice of zoning violation to the defendant for activities at its quarry. Prior to the board of adjustment's consideration of an appeal of this notice, the defendant sought to obtain copies of city documents relating to the matter. The city contended that these were not public records as they were related to a potential criminal investigation and were further protected by attorney-client and work product privileges.

The court held that the city attorney's office was a "public law enforcement agency" for purposes of the state Public Records Act. Since zoning violations are violations of the law, the city could invoke the Act's criminal investigation exception for closed and future investigations relative to zoning violations. The city is obligated under the law to produce the records for the judge, who will then conduct an in-camera review to determine if they are protected under this exception. The court noted, though, that the statutory protection for information protected under the Public Records Act is narrower than the traditional common law attorney-client privilege and that there is not a work product exemption to the Public Records Act.

Knight v. Town of Knightdale, 164 N.C. App. 766, 596 S.E.2d 881 (2004)
Interpretation; Manufactured housing

The plaintiffs were initially granted permits by staff of the defendant town to build a home in a certain subdivision. The staff subsequently realized that the home was modular and not manufactured, as they had assumed, which required site-plan approval by the town council. The council denied site-plan approval for the plaintiffs' modular home. The ordinance required site plans to protect other properties from "adverse effect[s] expected from the development, including without limitation, stormwater, noise, odor, on and off-street parking, dust, light, smoke, and vibration." The council's denial was based on harm to neighboring property values. The court reviewed the council's site-plan decision as a quasi-judicial decision, holding that it was not based on a permissible ground for denial under the ordinance. All of the factors listed were physical in nature, so consideration of property-value impacts was held to be beyond the scope and intent of the ordinance.

Northfield Development Co., Inc. v. City of Burlington, 165 N.C. App. 885, 599 S.E.2d 921, *review denied*, 359 N.C. 191, 607 S.E.2d 278 (2004)

Cemeteries; Judicial review; Special uses

The plaintiff applied for a special use permit for location and operation of a cemetery on a fifty-acre tract in the city's extraterritorial-zoning jurisdiction. The plaintiff refused a request by city staff to submit additional information and a site plan. The city council then denied the permit without a hearing. The plaintiff initiated this suit as a civil action to compel the city to issue the permit and sought monetary damages. After substantial discovery, the superior court granted summary judgment for the city and the plaintiff appealed. The appeals court held that the trial court had no subject-matter jurisdiction to hear this matter in this fashion. An appeal of a special use permit decision must be brought by petition for certiorari, and that was not done here. The trial court could only review the matter in an appellate capacity based on the record established in the administrative hearing and had no authority to take new evidence. Since the initial judicial appeal was not brought as a petition for certiorari, it had to be dismissed.

Williams v. North Carolina Department of Environment & Natural Resources, 166 N.C. App. 86, 601 S.E.2d 231 (2004)

Attorney's fees; Coastal Area Management Act; Costs

The plaintiff was denied a permit to fill land to construct a freezer. This decision was affirmed on a contested-case appeal by the Coastal Resources Commission, but it was ultimately overturned in court. The plaintiff then sought and was awarded attorney's fees by the trial court under G.S. 6-19.1 for the judicial review of the case and under Rule 37(c) of the Rules of Civil Procedure for the administrative portion of the case. The court of appeals held that it was improper to award attorney's fees for the judicial-review portion of the case because the state had not acted "without substantial justification" in its initial permit decision. The appellate court noted that there was conflicting evidence and a difficult factual determination at issue in the case. Even though the court eventually concluded otherwise, a reasonable person could have agreed with the defendant agency, and so their decision on the permit was not without substantial justification. The court likewise found attorney's fees for the administrative portion of the case were not warranted. An agency can only be sanctioned in this manner for a failure to admit the truth of a matter in discovery if it had no reasonable grounds to believe it might prevail on the contested factual matter. The appeals court noted that in awarding costs to the plaintiff, the trial court improperly included meals and travel expenses. Finally, the court held that the plaintiff had waived appellate consideration of the trial court's failure to grant attorney's fees for its takings claim by failing to file a cross-appeal on this issue.

Sanco of Wilmington Service Corp. v. New Hanover County, 166 N.C. App. 471, 601 S.E.2d 889 (2004)

Subdivisions

The plaintiff received preliminary plat approval from the county's Technical Review Committee (TRC) for a 427-unit condominium project. Neighbors then petitioned the county board of commissioners for a hearing on the approval. After conducting this hearing, the commissioners voted to amend the prior approval to allow only 213 units. The court invalidated the commissioners' action. By the terms of the county ordinance only the petitioner had a right to appeal the TRC decision to the county board of commissioners. Thus, the neighbors had no standing to bring an appeal and the commissioners had no jurisdiction to hear it. Also, the standards for plat approval in the county subdivision ordinance were entirely objective, so this was a ministerial decision. Once it is established by the applicant that those standards are met, the applicant is entitled to plat approval as a matter of law.

Ward v. Inscoe, 166 N.C. App. 586, 603 S.E.2d 393 (2004)
Special uses

The plaintiff neighbors challenged a special use permit issued by the city of Henderson board of adjustment. The permit was for a bank with four drive-through lanes. The trial court ruled that the board had failed to make findings, but substantial evidence in the record supported permit issuance. The court of appeals, in an earlier unpublished decision, vacated that decision and ordered a remand to the board so that the board could make the requisite findings. On remand, the board met at regularly scheduled meeting times to consider the matter, did not provide personal notice to the plaintiff neighbors, took no additional evidence, adopted findings based on the previous hearing record, and issued the permit.

The court held that this process did not violate the due-process rights of the neighbors. Since the board did not take any new evidence and only adopted findings to correct omissions from its initial consideration of the matter, notice and the right to present or rebut evidence was not required. Since there was substantial evidence in the hearing record to support the board's decision, the permit was properly issued.

Robertson v. Zoning Board of Adjustment, 167 N.C. App. 531, 605 S.E.2d 723 (2004), *review denied*, 359 N.C. 322, 611 S.E.2d 417 (2005)
Findings; Variances

The petitioners constructed a fence within the front-yard-setback area of their property that exceeded the height limit set in the Charlotte zoning ordinance. Substantial portions of the fence were eight feet high while the ordinance only allowed fences five feet above grade. The violation was discovered when city zoning inspectors visited the site in response to the petitioners' complaint about a neighbor's alleged zoning violation. The defendant zoning board granted a variance for a portion of the fence but denied the variance for the remainder. On judicial review, the trial court remanded the case for additional findings of fact. The board made said additional findings based on the evidence collected at its initial hearing of the case.

The court applied a whole-record review and found that the board's decision was not arbitrary and was based on substantial evidence. The court held that testimony, reports, photographs, and surveys in the record regarding the site topography and fence location and height sufficiently supported the board's findings on these matters as well as its conclusion that the height of the fence constituted a traffic-safety problem (among other problems). The court applied a de novo review to alleged errors of law, upholding the board's conclusion that a height variance of 60 percent in the front yard and 33 percent in the side yard would be contrary to the purpose of the ordinance and thus impermissible. The court also noted the board's conclusions that the alleged hardship was self-created, that it was personal in nature (arising from a dispute with a neighbor), and that a variance, if issued, would create a nuisance.

Nash–Rocky Mount Board of Education v. Rocky Mount Board of Adjustment, 169 N.C. App. 587, 610 S.E.2d 255 (2005)
Government uses

The plaintiff school board proposed construction of a school-bus parking lot at an existing high school. The plaintiff secured a driveway and fence permit from the city and built the lot. After complaints from adjacent neighbors, the city informed the plaintiff that a special use permit would be required for continued use of the permit. The board of adjustment then denied the special use permit. The court held that G.S. 160D-913 only extends zoning jurisdiction for governmental uses to situations involving the "erection, construction, and use of buildings" and that the plain meaning of the word "building" in this context does not include a parking lot.

[Note: In 2004, subsequent to the board of adjustment's decision in this case, G.S. 160D-913 was amended to extend zoning jurisdiction to the use of land as well as the use of buildings. The statute was again amended in 2005 to return it to its pre-2004 status. S.L. 2005-280.]

MCC Outdoor, LLC v. Town of Franklinton, 169 N.C. App. 809, 610 S.E.2d 794, *review denied*, 359 N.C. 634, 616 S.E.2d 539 (2005)
Evidence; Signs; Special uses

The plaintiff appealed the denial by the defendant board of commissioners of special use permits for two bill-boards. The court reversed the denial on multiple grounds. First, several of the findings supporting the denial stated reasons for denial unrelated to the standards for approval set forth in the ordinance. Second, there was not competent evidence in the record to support a finding that the signs would be incompatible with the surrounding neighborhood. Simple visibility for residences is insufficient support for a finding of incompatibility (given that inclusion of off-premise advertising as a special use created a presumption of compatibility). Third, rather than deny the permit based on the signs being too close to a stream under state regulations, the board should have conditioned the permit on relocation (the signs needed to be moved seven feet, and the plaintiff had agreed to do so), consistent with state regulation.

State v. Campbell, 169 N.C. App. 829, 610 S.E.2d 799 (2005)
Nuisances

The city of Salisbury brought this nuisance-abatement action against the defendants, landlords and tenants of a rental duplex, contending that alleged drug-trafficking activities and breaches of the peace at the duplex constituted a public nuisance under G.S. 19-1 and 19-1.2. The court held that three arrests of tenants for drug activity over a three-year period did not establish that the property was being leased for the purpose of illegal drug sales. The court also held that two dozen police calls to the site over the same period did not constitute a breach of the peace under the statutes, as most of the calls did not disturb the public order. (Seven were to serve warrants and six were for domestic disturbances.)

Town of Hertford v. Harris, 169 N.C. App. 838, 611 S.E.2d 194 (2005)
Nuisances

The town demolished two mobile homes being used for storage that were found to be in violation of its minimum-housing code and sought to sell the property to satisfy a lien to recover its costs. The court held there was a factual issue as to whether salvageable personal property (the homes and their contents) existed that could have offset the cost of removal or demolition, so summary judgment was not appropriate.

Granville Farms, Inc. v. County of Granville, 170 N.C. App. 109, 612 S.E.2d 156 (2005)
Preemption

The court held that state regulations on disposal of sludge from waste-treatment facilities preempt county ordinances imposing more stringent regulations on land application of biosolids (the residual sludge resulting from treatment of domestic sewage in wastewater treatment plants). The court found that the state had established a complete and integrated regulatory scheme on the disposal of these materials.

Harding v. Board of Adjustment, 170 N.C. App. 392, 612 S.E.2d 431 (2005)
Evidence; Special uses

Neighbors challenged the issuance of a special use permit for a go-cart track on a 134-acre tract in a rural portion of Davie County. The proposed track was adjacent to a nonconforming dragstrip that was also owned and operated by the permit applicant. The ordinance required the defendant board to find that the use "will not adversely affect the health or safety" of neighbors. The trial court affirmed the board's approval of the permit, citing the *Woodhouse* rule that the burden of production and persuasion is on the challenger for general permit standards. The court of appeals affirmed, holding that the board making the permit decision had in fact placed the burden for this standard on the applicant. The appellate court also held that there was substantial evidence in the record to support the board's findings relative to noise impacts. In the course of four nights of hearings on the application, a civil engineer testified for the applicant regarding expected noise levels at the property line and the impacts of mitigating features (a berm and vegetation). Although not qualified as an expert witness, the engineer submitted reports and was available for cross-examination. The neighbors did not challenge his testimony, nor did they offer any rebuttal evidence on noise.

Darbo v. Old Keller Farm Property Owners' Ass'n, 174 N.C. App. 591, 621 S.E.2d 281 (2005)
Easements; Subdivisions

The plaintiff acquired title to two lots, one within a subdivision and an adjacent 8.9-acre tract, both depicted on a prior subdivision. The subdivided lot was served by a forty-five-foot right-of-way designated as a "private drive" on the plat (this drive extended into another section of the subdivision). When the plaintiff proposed to subdivide the 8.9-acre parcel into five lots to be served by this right-of-way, the defendant association objected to plat approval. Watauga County advised the parties that it would not process the plat until the parties resolved the dispute over whether the "private right of way" could be converted to a required "county standard road."

The court held that where there were no restrictive covenants limiting use of this right-of-way to a specified number of users, and where common practice in the county was to reserve such easements for potential future road use, the trial court had properly interpreted the plat restriction to allow conversion of the easement to a broader accessway. The court also held that the planning board's long-standing interpretation of the subdivision ordinance to allow conversion of forty-five-foot private rights-of-way to improved accessways serving a larger number of lots was entitled to considerable deference.

Jirtle v. Board of Adjustment for Biscoe, 175 N.C. App. 178, 622 S.E.2d 713 (2005)
Accessory buildings and uses; Interpretation; Nonconforming use; Religious use

A church operated a food-distribution program for the poor from the basement of its education building. The church acquired an adjacent lot and proposed to construct a small building on it and to move its food-pantry program to the new building. The church was located in a residential zoning district and was nonconforming due to a lack of adequate on-site parking. The town issued a permit for the new building and a neighbor objected. The defendant board of adjustment and trial court upheld the zoning administrator's determination that the food pantry was an accessory use of the church and that it did not constitute an unlawful expansion of a nonconformity.

The appeals court agreed that this was not an unlawful expansion. The parking requirement was based on the number of seats in the largest assembly room on site. Since the sanctuary would be the largest assembly room both before and after construction of the new food pantry, there would be no change in the off-street parking requirement and thus no increase in the degree of nonconformity. The court also affirmed the holding that the food pantry was a legitimate accessory use, noting both that it was physically smaller than the principal use (1000 square feet for the pantry compared to over 9000 square feet in the existing buildings) and that the service mission of the pantry was incidental and subordinate to the church's main purpose of worship.

Ward v. New Hanover County, 175 N.C. App. 671, 625 S.E.2d 598 (2006)
Exhaustion; Special uses

In 2002, the plaintiffs sought county approval to use a forklift to move boats at their commercial marina. The county planning staff determined that this would be inconsistent with a 1971 special use permit for a boat ramp at the site. The plaintiffs in 2003 submitted a request for permit modification that would allow the forklift, withdrew that request, and in 2004 submitted a second site plan and proposed permit modification. The county planning staff then sent the plaintiffs a letter stating that they believed this would be a substantial modification of the permit requiring board approval rather than a minor modification that could be approved by staff. After meeting with the staff, the plaintiffs' attorney responded that all agreed that the county's letter was not a finding or determination subject to appeal. The plaintiffs then filed this declaratory-judgment action seeking a determination that use of the forklift was lawful.

The court held that county staff had not yet issued a formal decision on the proposed use and that the issue was subject to ongoing discussion among the parties. Since the plaintiffs had not secured a formal determination of their rights from the county staff, they failed to exhaust their administrative remedies, and this action was thus properly dismissed.

Keith v. Town of White Lake, 175 N.C. App. 789, 625 S.E.2d 587 (2006)
Adoption; Amendments; Rezoning

The town planning board recommended the rezoning of two lots owned by the plaintiff in the town's extra-territorial jurisdiction in order to bring the zoning into compliance with a newly adopted land use plan. The town's governing board, after proper notice and hearing, adopted the proposed rezoning.

The plaintiff contended that the rezoning was invalid for failure to follow the zoning-ordinance provisions setting out a procedure for "any person or organization" to petition the town board for a zoning amendment. The court held that the statutory and ordinance provisions authorizing the planning board to make recommendations for zoning text and map changes obviated the need for a formal petition when the planning board initiates a recommended amendment.

Woodlief v. Mecklenburg County, 176 N.C. App. 205, 625 S.E.2d 904, *review denied*, 360 N.C. 492, 632 S.E.2d 775 (2006)
Interpretation; Vested rights

Neighbors challenged a floodlands development permit issued for a residential subdivision. The owners secured a permit in March 2003. In May 2003, Charlotte adopted revised and more restrictive floodway regulations that affected this site. In May 2004, county staff discovered that the permit had been mistakenly issued, revoked it, and directed the owner to revise its application. A revised permit application, with a new flood study, was submitted in June 2004. The staff applied the rules in effect at the time of the original application; the neighbors contended that the updated regulations in effect at the time of "reissuance" should have been used. The board of adjustment and trial court affirmed the staff decision.

The appellate court applied a de novo review to the question of which version of the regulations was applicable vis-à-vis interpreting the ordinance. Both the original and revised ordinance were silent on this issue. However, the staff advised the owners that the matter would be considered a "revised" rather than a new application, and the staff had a long-standing prior pattern and practice of considering revisions under the rules in effect at the time of the original decision unless the regulations specifically provided otherwise. The court thus affirmed use of the original ordinance and held that it was properly applied in approving the project. [Note: The permit-choice statute allowing the applicant to choose the version of the rules to be applied was subsequently adopted.]

Broadbent v. Allison, 176 N.C. App. 359, 626 S.E.2d 758, *review denied*, 361 N.C. 350, 644 S.E.2d 4 (2006)
Airports; Nuisances

The defendant constructed an airstrip on land adjacent to the plaintiffs' property. The defendant's property had previously been farmland. The plaintiffs contended that low-flying planes over their house, barn, and riding ring (along with two plane crashes on their property) constituted a nuisance. The case began in federal court but was remanded to state court (see 155 F. Supp. 2d 520 (W.D.N.C. 2001)). The trial court upheld the jury's finding of a nuisance, upheld a compensatory damages award of $358,000, but refused to enjoin the airport use and awarded the defendant an avigation easement.

The court of appeals held that the trial court's instruction on the nuisance issue (that the plaintiffs must show substantial and unreasonable interference with the use and enjoyment of property) was correct and that the finding of a private nuisance was adequately established in the record. Because it was not clear whether the monetary damages awarded were for permanent damages, temporary damages, or both, the issues of damages and injunctive relief were remanded.

Wright v. Town of Matthews, 177 N.C. App. 1, 627 S.E.2d 650 (2006)
Interpretation; Streets

The plaintiffs challenged the defendant town's determination that the street fronting their property was a public street under the zoning ordinance. Town staff and the board of adjustment concluded that the sixty-foot right-of-way was a public street based on state maintenance of the street from about 1979 to 1985, its addition to the town street system in 1985, and town maintenance of the street subsequent to 1985, including its paving in 1991.

The court held that there was insufficient evidence to show that the contested right-of-way was a public street by express dedication. Nor was there sufficient evidence on acquisition by prescription, as the evidence of state maintenance was inconclusive and the town maintenance was just under the requisite twenty years. The court remanded the case for findings regarding an implied dedication of the right-of-way, expressly noting that the case only addressed whether the right-of-way was a "public street" for zoning purposes and not any private rights of access for the owner or adjacent owners.

Durham Land Owners Ass'n v. County of Durham, 177 N.C. App. 629, 630 S.E.2d 200, *review denied*, 360 N.C. 532, 633 S.E.2d 678 (2006)
Impact fees

The plaintiffs challenged the defendant county's statutory authority to adopt a school impact fee. The court held that the county did not have statutory authority to impose the fee. The court found that the authorization in G.S. 153A-102 to fix fees "charged by officers and employees for performing services or duties permitted or required by law" did not authorize this impact fee. The court reasoned that provision of schools is a general governmental obligation of the county itself, not a service provided by an employee. The court likewise held that while permit application and review fees were implicitly authorized by the statutory authorization of general ordinances and zoning ordinances, this does not mean that fees to fund basic governmental services such as school construction were so authorized.

Ocean Hill Joint Venture v. Currituck County, 178 N.C. App. 182, 630 S.E.2d 714, *review granted*, 360 N.C. 648, 636 S.E.2d 808 (2006), *review improvidently granted*, 361 N.C. 228, 641 S.E.2d 302 (2007)
Streets

When the plaintiff developer's residential subdivision was approved, the plat dedicated all streets to "public or private use as noted," but the plat failed to identify which streets were private and which public. The plaintiff later transferred title of the streets to a homeowners association, which paid for all road repair, maintenance, and insurance thereafter. When the plaintiff's subsequent adjacent subdivision led to increased traffic, the homeowners association petitioned the county to withdraw the plaintiff's dedication of the streets and close them to the public. The county board of commissioners approved the closure pursuant to G.S. 153A-241. The plaintiff appealed. At trial the jury concluded that the closure of the streets was contrary to the public interest. The trial court had placed on the association the burden of showing that the board was correct in ruling that the street closings were not contrary to the public interest. The association argued that this burden placement was error.

The appeals court held that G.S. 153A-241 mandates a de novo review of proposed street closings by the trial court; thus, there was no presumption in favor of the board of commissioners' decision. Further, the burden of proof at trial is to remain on the party requesting the change in the road's status (here, the property-owners association).

Koenig v. Town of Kure Beach, 178 N.C. App. 500, 631 S.E.2d 884 (2006)
Beaches; Standing

The deed to the plaintiff's oceanfront property referenced a ten-foot-wide public-access easement along the property's northern boundary. When the defendant town proposed to build a walkway and dune crossover on this easement, the plaintiff brought suit, alleging that the easement had not been dedicated to nor accepted by the town. Adjacent upland-property owners intervened in the suit, claiming a prescriptive easement over the accessway. The trial court granted summary judgment against the intervenors and the town.

The appellate court affirmed on the basis that the intervenors had not established the requisite elements for a prescriptive easement: (1) that the use is adverse or under claim of right; (2) that the use is open and notorious; (3) that the use is continuous and uninterrupted for twenty years; and (4) that there is substantial identity of the easement claimed for the requisite period. The court held that there was no evidence that the use here was without the owner's permission. Also, most of the intervenors failed to establish that they had used the accessway for more than a few years. The court further found that a court could allow permissible intervention in a case and later find the intervenors did not have standing to bring additional claims regarding a public prescriptive easement.

Litvak v. Smith, 180 N.C. App. 202, 636 S.E.2d 327 (2006), *review denied*, 362 N.C. 87, 655 S.E.2d 839 (2007)
Conflicts of interest; Sales contracts

The plaintiff contracted in May 2004 to purchase a five-acre vacant parcel in North Topsail Beach that was zoned for commercial use. The sale was conditioned on obtaining a "nonappealable final approval to rezone" the property to residential use, with the buyer to "use all reasonable diligence" in securing the rezoning. In July 2004, the plaintiff filed a petition for the rezoning, which was rejected by the town's planning board in August 2004. In September 2004, town staff recommended approval of a revised rezoning proposal. In October 2004, a valid protest petition was filed. One of the town's five council members was recused for a conflict of interest. In November 2004, the council voted 3–1 in favor of the rezoning. The town held that the rezoning had been adopted, and the defendant seller notified the plaintiff of an expected closing within sixty days. However, in December 2004, the town announced that it had reconsidered the vote calculation and decided that the recused member should have been included in the calculation of the requisite supermajority and that, therefore, the rezoning had not been approved and was void *ab initio*. Upon reconfirmation of this decision by the town council on December 20, 2004, the defendant on December 21 terminated the sales contract based on rejection of the rezoning. On December 28, the plaintiff sued the town over the rezoning vote calculation.

The court held that since the sales contract did not have a specific time limitation or a "time is of the essence" clause, the plaintiff had to be given a reasonable time to complete the rezoning contingency. The court noted that the litigation on the rezoning would likely take an indefinite but protracted time to complete and that the plaintiff had failed to waive the contingency and proceed with the purchase without the rezoning. The court held that it was thus unreasonable to require the defendant to keep the sales contract open pending resolution of uncertain and indefinite litigation. [Note: The statutes were subsequently amended to clarify that the seat of members disqualified from voting due to a conflict of interest are not counted in the computation of requisite majority votes.]

Cumulus Broadcasting, LLC v. Hoke County, 180 N.C. App. 424, 638 S.E.2d 12 (2006)
Evidence; Special uses

The plaintiff applied for a special use permit to construct a 499-foot-high radio tower. The owner of a nearby private airport and a pilot appeared at the hearing and expressed the view that the tower would interfere with aviation in the area. A letter of approval from the Federal Aviation Administration was included in the record. The defendant county denied the permit. On appeal, the trial court held that the plaintiff had presented sufficient evidence to show that permit standards were met and that the opposing evidence was "anecdotal, conclusory, and without a demonstrated factual basis." The court thus vacated the denial and remanded the matter for issuance of the permit.

The appeals court affirmed, holding that while the opposing testimony was not speculative and did not amount to mere expressions of opinion or generalized fear, it was insufficient to rebut the evidence presented by the plaintiff. The proof was based solely on personal knowledge and observations and did not rebut the quantitative data and other evidence presented in support of the plaintiff's application. Given the absence of adequate rebuttal evidence, the permit had to be issued and the remand with that directive was appropriate.

Sandy Mush Properties v. Rutherford County, 181 N.C. App. 224, 638 S.E.2d 557, *remanded by* 361 N.C. 569, 651 S.E.2d 566, *aff'd by* 187 N.C. App. 809, 654 S.E.2d 253 (2007), *review dismissed*, 363 N.C. 577, 681 S.E.2d 339 (2009)
Vested rights

The dispute in this case revolved around the use of a 180-acre tract for a crushed rock quarry.

In 2001, the plaintiff applied for three building permits (a modular office building, an office building, and a metal building) at the site of the proposed quarry. The defendant county denied the permits based on a county-adopted moratorium on location of heavy industries near schools. The plaintiff challenged the validity of the moratorium based on procedural deficiencies in its adoption. In September 2001, the trial court enjoined enforcement of the moratorium and ordered the building permits issued. The defendant appealed the trial court's determination that the moratorium was invalid but nonetheless issued the building permits. Pursuant to the permits, the plaintiff in October 2001 began construction on one of the buildings, the proposed office building. In October 2001, the contested moratorium expired and the defendant enacted an ordinance that made quarries a prohibited use at the site involved here. Construction on the office building ceased in December 2001, prior to completion of the building. In 2002, the trial court upheld the moratorium. In 2004, the court of appeals declared the moratorium invalid, and in July 2004, the plaintiff sought to resume construction of the office building. The defendant contended that the building permit had expired. The plaintiff contended that the statute providing for expiration of a building permit if construction ceased for twelve months was tolled by the appeal regarding the validity of the moratorium. The plaintiff also argued that the building permit for the office building constituted a statutory or common law vesting for the use of the property as a quarry.

Since the acknowledged use of the building was as an office for the quarry, the appellate court held that the trial court's order upholding a moratorium on the quarry operation effectively prohibited continuing construction of the office building under the building permit. The court thus held that the trial court's order and the subsequent appeal tolled the statutory period in which the plaintiff could resume construction and that there had not therefore been a twelve-month lapse in construction so as to cause the building permit to expire. However, the court held that the particular building permit only authorized construction of an office building (which by the terms of the permit could be used as offices for various uses) and did not purport to authorize any other use of the larger site. Thus, the office-building permit itself constituted neither a statutory vesting nor the basis for a common law vesting for the use of the site as a quarry.

On appeal, the court remanded this decision for reconsideration in light of its decision in *Robins v. Town of Hillsborough*, 361 N.C. 193, 639 S.E.2d 421 (2007). On remand, the court of appeals affirmed its prior holding, noting that the *Robins* decision expressly stated that it was not a vested-rights case but, rather, a question of town compliance with procedures mandated by its ordinance. Thus, the court held that *Robins* did not affect its prior holding.

Turik v. Town of Surf City, 182 N.C. App. 427, 642 S.E.2d 251 (2007)
Variances

The town issued a building permit for a duplex based on a survey submitted by the owner. A neighbor objected to the location of the duplex and submitted another survey showing the pilings for the building had been placed 7.2 inches into a 7.5-foot side-yard setback (the building itself was apparently cantilevered two feet into the setback). The defendant town issued a stop-work order, and the owner then petitioned for a variance, which was granted by the board of adjustment and affirmed by the superior court.

The appeals court upheld issuance of the variance. It noted that the applicant had relied on a licensed surveyor in establishing the building location, that the amount of the variance was minimal, and that there was no evidence of harm to the neighbor should the variance be granted.

Stealth Properties, LLC v. Town of Pinebluff Board of Adjustment, 183 N.C. App. 461, 645 S.E.2d 144, *review denied*, 361 N.C. 703, 653 S.E.2d 153 (2007)
Evidence; Records; Variances

The plaintiff petitioner mistakenly thought his property was zoned R-20, a district that mandates a sixteen-foot side-yard setback. The property was actually zoned R-30, and the correct setback was twenty-five feet. While the plaintiff's application reflected his mistaken assumption, his permit (a certificate of zoning compliance) included the correct zoning and setback information. The plaintiff proceeded to place his modular home on the lot using a sixteen-foot setback, a mistake that was not discovered during building inspections and was only identified when the town denied a certificate of occupancy. The defendant board of adjustment denied a variance petition. There was no transcript of the board hearing available due to a malfunction of the recorder. The minutes of the hearing were originally part of the record but were deleted at the petitioner's request. The trial court reversed the variance denial due to a lack of supporting evidence. The court also construed the ordinance to require the property to be zoned R-20 as it had inadequate size for a lot in the R-30 district. The trial court then issued a variance.

The appeals court ruled that the trial court properly found the variance denial to be unsupported by competent, substantial, and material evidence. The court held that the ordinance was ambiguous due to the fact that the petitioner's lot was smaller than the minimum lot size for its district. The court then found the fact that the zoning certificate issued prior to construction required a twenty-five-foot setback to be insufficient evidence to support a conclusion as to what the requisite setback was. Thus, the court upheld the trial court's ruling that there was insufficient evidence to support the variance denial. The court of appeals did hold, however, that the trial court had no authority to interpret the ordinance in this case, as that issue was not properly before the board of adjustment. The court further held that the appropriate disposition here was a remand to the board with instructions for the board to issue the variance rather than the court issuing a variance itself.

Town of Green Level v. Alamance County, 184 N.C. App. 665, 646 S.E.2d 851, *review denied*, 361 N.C. 704, 655 S.E.2d 402 (2007)
Extraterritorial jurisdiction; Objectives

The town in 2003 proposed to adopt an extraterritorial jurisdiction (ETJ) boundary ordinance to extend its zoning. The county contended that its 1997 water-supply watershed ordinance (which did not cover the physical area subject to the town's proposed ETJ) was a "zoning ordinance" and thus required the town to secure county approval of the proposed ETJ. The town disagreed and began the process to adopt an ETJ boundary ordinance. The county then quickly amended the watershed ordinance on April 19, 2004, to apply a "Rural Community District" to the disputed area. The town adopted its ETJ ordinance on April 22, 2004, and then brought a declaratory-judgment action to determine whether its ordinance was effective. The trial court held that both the 1997 and 2004 county ordinances were "zoning ordinances" that triggered the requirement in G.S. 160D-202(c) of county approval for the town ETJ ordinance.

The court reversed, holding that the watershed critical areas and balance of watershed areas depicted in the 1997 watershed area did not extend into the disputed area. Although the county ordinance spoke of "stream buffers," no streams had been mapped by the county in this area and the county had not enforced any buffer requirements in the area. Thus, the ordinance could not be considered county zoning of the area. The court found that the county's 2004 amendment to its ordinance was arbitrary and capricious in that it was adopted to block the town jurisdiction rather than to promote a legitimate health, safety, or welfare purpose. The record indicated that the county made no reference to a comprehensive plan in its adoption of the ordinance, which contained no references to water-quality protection and allowed various industrial uses inconsistent with a rural community.

Pitt County v. Dejavue, Inc., 185 N.C. App. 545, 650 S.E.2d 12 (2007), *review denied*, 362 N.C. 381, 661 S.E.2d 738 (2008)
Adult uses; Enforcement

Pitt County in 2002 adopted an adult-business ordinance that required adult businesses to meet minimum separations from each other and from sensitive land uses. The ordinance included findings regarding adverse secondary impacts and a one-year amortization requirement. Technical amendments were made to the ordinance in 2004 in conjunction with county adoption of zoning. The county brought this suit seeking a declaratory judgment that the defendants were operating adult businesses in violation of the ordinance and seeking injunctive relief to compel compliance.

The court first held that an enforcement action brought under G.S. 153A-123 does not require a verified complaint. The court found that the one-year amortization period established by the 2002 ordinance was not extended or affected by the 2004 amendments to the ordinance, nor did the amendments make the ordinance an ex post facto law.

The court also held that the ordinance did not violate the First Amendment. The county presented substantial evidence that reports and studies of adverse secondary impacts were reviewed by staff (there is no requirement that elected officials personally review studies where staff members adequately brief the board on the information and are available to answer any questions). The court further noted that the sheriff directly presented information on secondary impacts to the board. Reasonable alternative avenues of expression were maintained, noting the testimony that the ordinance left 19 percent of the county's land area available for potential adult-business location. Finally, the court dismissed the equal-protection claim of a person living within the separation area of an adult club, pointing out that he was being treated the same as all other persons living within such proximity of an adult business.

Cook v. Union County Zoning Board of Adjustment, 185 N.C. App. 582, 649 S.E.2d 458 (2007)
Hearings; Special uses; Standing

Wal-Mart applied to the defendant board of adjustment for a special use permit. The board held an evidentiary hearing that extended over five dates. The plaintiff neighboring-property owners and county staff participated fully in each hearing session. The board then closed the hearing and voted to approve the permit subject to numerous changes and submission of a revised site plan. At subsequent board meetings Wal-Mart presented several substantially revised site plans and answered questions regarding the revisions from the board. The neighbors and the county staff were not allowed to ask questions or present any evidence regarding the revised plans. The board eventually issued the permit based on a revised plan, an action that was challenged by the neighbors and the county. The trial court vacated the permit on the basis of a denial of the neighbors' due-process rights.

The court first held that both the county and the neighbors had standing to challenge the permit. The court ruled that as G.S. 160D-1402(c)(4) explicitly allows a local government to appeal as a category distinct from aggrieved persons, the county could similarly appeal from the board of adjustment. The court also held that the neighbors had shown special damages to their property unique in character and distinct from the community at large and had standing. The court found that neither the neighbors nor the county needed to make a formal motion to intervene at the board of adjustment's hearing in order to have standing for judicial review.

The court ruled that the board's refusal to allow the neighbors to present evidence or testimony or to cross-examine witnesses regarding the revised site plan violated their due-process rights and the requirements of the ordinance that persons be given the opportunity to present evidence and ask questions. The two revised site plans, while made in response to concerns raised at the evidentiary hearing, were substantively different (for example, substantially relocating the building, parking lot, and retention pond and changing the traffic pattern for the store). Therefore, the court held that the permit was properly vacated.

McDowell v. Randolph County, 186 N.C. App. 17, 649 S.E.2d 920 (2007)
Enforcement; Parties; Spot zoning

The defendant county in 2005 approved the rezoning of a 29.95-acre portion of a larger parcel (120.30 acres) from Light Industrial (LI) and Residential-Agricultural (RA) to Heavy Industry (HI). The rezoned land was the site of a lumberyard, sawmill, pallet-making operation, and other related mill works. Some portion of the mill existed when the zoning ordinance was adopted in 1987. The surrounding property was uniformly zoned Residential-Agricultural. The mill owner had between 2000 and 2004 expanded operations with appropriate permits from the county. The owner sought the rezoning when neighbors complained about the expansion, contending that it was an unlawful expansion of the industrial use of the property (as neither the LI nor the RA districts permitted sawmills). The neighbors brought this suit to (1) have the rezoning declared illegal spot zoning and (2) compel the county to enforce the ordinance provisions prohibiting the expansion of nonconformities. The trial court found the rezoning to be unlawful spot zoning but denied a mandamus request.

The court first held that the county could not plead laches as a defense. While there might be some harm to the mill owner, the county itself could show no prejudice or injury due to any delay in bringing this action. The court then applied the *Chrismon* factors (see *Chrismon v. Guilford County*, 322 N.C. 611, 370 S.E.2d 579 (1988), discussed in greater detail above) and found the rezoning to be illegal spot zoning. The court found the action to be contrary to the overall zoning plan and the county's Managed Growth Plan for the area, found the newly allowed and expanded uses were inconsistent with surrounding rural and residential uses, found inadequate support in the record for purported economic benefits to the region and county, and found substantial support for the neighbors' alleged harm due to increased noise, dust, and truck traffic. The court thus found the rezoning unreasonable. The court also held, however, that mandamus could not issue as the mill owner, who would be significantly affected, was not a party to the suit.

Childress v. Yadkin County, 186 N.C. App. 30, 650 S.E.2d 55 (2007)

Contract zoning; Findings; Spot zoning

Neighbors filed this declaratory-judgment action seeking to invalidate the rezoning of a fifty-one-acre tract from rural agricultural (RA) to restricted residential (RR). Both districts had a 30,000-square-foot minimum-lot-size requirement for residences if no public water-and-sewer supply was available and both allowed single-family residences. However, the RA district also allowed manufactured housing on individual lots, and the RR district allowed higher densities with utilities. The planning board recommended denial of the rezoning, and persons appeared both in support of and in opposition to it at the public hearing.

The court first held that this was not spot zoning. While the size of the tract was small enough to be spot zoning and most of the immediately surrounding property was zoned RA, the court noted that the two zoning districts were sufficiently similar that the rezoning did not substantially relieve or impose burdens on the rezoned property. The court went on to apply the *Chrismon* factors and concluded that even if this was spot zoning, it was reasonable. The court distinguished this modest change in zoning from a rezoning to allow commercial or industrial uses, found that the rezoning was consistent with county plans and policies, noted the benefits of county regulation of the proposed subdivision, and held that the general community impacts of the development were properly considered. The court ruled that although the landowner spoke at the hearing in some detail about the use of the property if rezoned, there was no evidence of any bilateral agreement with the county, and thus there was no contract zoning. The court also concluded that formal findings were not needed in a legislative rezoning.

Lamar OCI South Carolina v. Stanly County, 186 N.C. App. 44, 650 S.E.2d 37 (2007), *aff'd per curiam,* 362 N.C. 670, 669 S.E.2d 322 (2008)

Nonconformities; Preemption; Signs

The plaintiff company owned a billboard along a state highway. The state notified the plaintiff that it planned to widen the highway and that the increased right-of-way would include the sign site, thus necessitating relocation. The plaintiff then secured state Department of Transportation (DOT) approval to move the billboard back fifty feet from its same location along the highway. DOT paid for the relocation, considering it to be authorized under state law and rule and to be within the previously issued state billboard permit. However, the billboard was nonconforming under the county zoning ordinance, which had been amended after the billboard was constructed to prohibit billboards in the applicable Highway Business zoning district. The county ordinance prohibited the movement or replacement of nonconforming signs. The plaintiff undertook the relocation without notice to or approval from the county. The county then issued a notice of violation to the plaintiff. The board of adjustment affirmed the county's interpretation that the relocation resulted in the loss of legal nonconforming status for the billboard. The trial court upheld the board of adjustment.

The court of appeals held that the county ordinance was not preempted by the state's Outdoor Advertising Control Act under G.S. 160A-174(b)(5), which applies when the statute evidences a clear legislative intent to provide a complete and integrated regulatory scheme to the exclusion of local regulation. However, the court found that the preemption provision of G.S. 160A-174(b)(2) was applicable in this instance. That provision preempts a local regulation that makes unlawful an act expressly made lawful by state law. Here, the state implementing regulations explicitly allowed relocation of a sign if it stayed within a "Sign Location/Site" that was defined by rule. Therefore, the court concluded that since the state regulation and permit expressly allowed this limited relocation, that preempted a local relocation prohibition. The court, in a per curiam opinion, affirmed that conclusion.

Davidson County Broadcasting, Inc. v. Rowan County Board of Commissioners, 186 N.C. App. 81, 649 S.E.2d 904 (2007), *review denied*, 362 N.C. 470, 666 S.E.2d 119 (2008)
Preemption; Special uses

The plaintiffs applied for a special use permit to construct a 1350-foot radio broadcast tower. The key issue was whether the proposed tower violated the ordinance standard prohibiting creation of "hazardous safety conditions" with respect to users of a private airport located within five miles of the proposed tower. At the hearing on the application, the plaintiffs presented a letter from the Federal Aviation Administration (FAA) making a "Determination of No Hazard" resulting from the tower. A representative of the state Department of Transportation, numerous pilots who used the nearby private airport, and aviation experts testified that the tower would pose a safety hazard given its proximity to the private airport. The defendant county board of commissioners denied the application upon finding the tower would pose a safety risk. The trial court affirmed the denial.

The court first held that the ordinance was not preempted by federal law. The court noted that the FAA letter specifically noted that federal law protects only public airports, did not consider the tower's impact on the private airstrip, and explicitly noted the need for state and local government regulation to protect these airports. Thus, the court held that there was no conflict between the ordinance and the federal law. The court then found that there was substantial evidence in the record to support the board's finding that the tower would pose a safety hazard.

Casper v. Chatham County, 186 N.C. App. 456, 651 S.E.2d 299 (2007)
Special uses; Standing

The county adopted a conditional use district rezoning and approved a special use permit for a retail use on the site. Adjacent landowners challenged the issuance of the permit. The trial court dismissed the appeal for lack of standing.

The appeals court held that the plaintiff neighboring landowners did not have standing as persons aggrieved. To have standing, mere proximity of ownership is inadequate. A plaintiff must also claim special damages distinct from the rest of the community, with a particular emphasis on reduction in property value. The plaintiff also has the burden of alleging the facts on which the claim of special damages is based. Here, the plaintiffs only claimed proximity and no special damages, so they had no standing. The trial court thus had no subject-matter jurisdiction to hear their substantive claim.

Smith v. Forsyth County Board of Adjustment, 186 N.C. App. 651, 652 S.E.2d 355 (2007)
Standing

The county zoning officer issued a permit for a new church and associated athletic fields. The plaintiff neighboring-property owner appealed the officer's interpretation of several ordinance provisions to the board of adjustment. The plaintiff contended that the proposed church should have been classified as a "community church" rather than a "neighborhood church" (the ordinance distinguished the two based on seating capacities over or under 600 persons), that a buffer should have been required around the athletic field, and that grading requirements were misinterpreted. The board of adjustment upheld the zoning officer on the church definition and buffer issues and found for the plaintiff on the grading issue. The trial court dismissed the plaintiff's appeal for lack of standing.

The appellate court found that the plaintiff had failed to establish that she was a "person aggrieved" with standing to appeal to the board of adjustment. The court held that an allegation of mere proximity, absent a credible allegation of special damages distinct from the community, was insufficient to establish standing under both the state statutes and the 1947 local enabling act for Forsyth County zoning. Without standing to appeal to the board of adjustment, the question of standing for judicial review is moot.

Marriott v. Chatham County, 187 N.C. App. 491, 654 S.E.2d 13 (2007), *review denied*, 362 N.C. 472, 666 S.E.2d 122 (2008)

Environmental-impact statements; Standing

The Chatham County subdivision ordinance contained a provision that allowed the planning board to require an environmental-impact statement pursuant to Chapter 113A of the General Statutes if a development exceeded two acres in size and if the board deemed the statement "necessary for responsible review" due to the nature of the land or peculiarities in the proposed layout of the development. The plaintiffs brought this action when the county approved several large developments on tracts adjacent to parcels they owned without requiring an environmental-impact statement. The plaintiffs sought to enjoin development of the property until the county amended its ordinance to provide minimum criteria for when an impact statement would be required and sought a writ of mandamus to compel the county to make these amendments. Their efforts were halted at the trial-court level due to a lack of standing.

The court noted the requirements for standing, stating that the plaintiffs here had to show injury in fact, that the injury is fairly traceable to the challenged action, and that it is likely the injury will be redressed by a favorable decision. The court then held that it had no authority to compel the county to adopt or amend an ordinance. The court did point out, however, that G.S. 113A-8 clearly requires a local ordinance requiring environmental-impact statements to include minimum criteria to determine when statements are required. While a county has discretion as to whether to require statements and has discretion in defining minimum criteria for when statements are required, it does not have the discretion to forego minimum criteria. It was undisputed that the Chatham County ordinance had no such criteria. Thus, if the ordinance allowing an impact statement is invalid as written, and if the court has no authority to order the ordinance amended, there is no likelihood that the plaintiffs' injury could be redressed by a favorable decision. Therefore, the court held that the trial court had properly dismissed the action for lack of standing.

Macon County v. Town of Highlands, 187 N.C. App. 752, 654 S.E.2d 17 (2007)

Extraterritorial jurisdiction; Parties

The town adopted extraterritorial jurisdiction. G.S. 160D-307 provides that extraterritorial members must be appointed to the town planning board and board of adjustment, with the number of extraterritorial members being proportional to the town residents based on the respective populations of the town and its extraterritorial area. The town provided for two members of the town planning board from the Macon County portion of the extraterritorial area. The county and the members of the county board of commissioners sued, seeking to have the court declare how many members should be appointed to the town planning board.

The court determined that neither the county nor the commissioners as individuals were proper parties to the suit. The determinative issue was how the town calculated the population of the extraterritorial area in order to secure proportional representation on the planning board. As for the means of securing proportional representation, the court noted that the statute did not specify how that was to be done, so thus it is to be left largely to the judgment and discretion of the town unless its actions are "manifestly unreasonable and oppressive."

Habitat for Humanity of Moore County, Inc. v. Board of Commissioners of the Town of Pinebluff, 187 N.C. App. 764, 653 S.E.2d 886 (2007)

Special uses; Standing

The plaintiff organization applied for a special use permit to build a seventy-five-lot subdivision on property for which it had an option to purchase. The town board of commissioners found the application to be complete and concluded that the standards of the zoning district would be met, but it denied the application on the ground that it would not be harmonious with the surrounding area. On appeal, the trial court reversed the denial and remanded the matter to the town for issuance of the permit. The town appealed, arguing that the plaintiff lacked standing as it did not own the subject property and had failed to sign the application.

The court held that the plaintiff had standing to make the application for the permit. The ordinance specifically allowed special use permit applications and subdivision plats to be submitted by landowners, their agents, or persons who have contracted to purchase the property. While the ordinance provided that the zoning administrator may require the applicant to submit proof of authority to submit an application, that proof was not mandatory. In this instance, the plaintiff's director testified at the permit hearing that they had an option to purchase and the council found the application to be complete. The court found this sufficient to establish standing to file the application.

The court then noted that inclusion of a use as a special use in a district establishes a prima facie case of harmony with the area and that a finding that it is not in harmony must be supported by substantial, competent, material evidence in the record. Here, the testimony against the development was general and related to virtually any development or subdivision of the site. The court ruled this insufficient to rebut a prima facie showing of harmony.

Weaverville Partners, LLC v. Town of Weaverville Zoning Board of Adjustment, 188 N.C. App. 55, 654 S.E.2d 784 (2008)
Evidence; Judicial review; Special uses

The plaintiff challenged the denial of a special use permit for an apartment complex. The site was adjacent to a commercial strip on one side and across the street from an apartment building, with single-family residential development on the remaining sides of the site. At the hearing on the permit application, the plaintiff presented testimony from a project engineer, traffic engineer, and real-estate appraiser. Neighbors testified in opposition. The defendant board denied the permit based upon a finding that the access road for the project would create traffic problems for pedestrians and vehicles and that the project would substantially harm neighboring property values. The trial court reversed, conducting (1) a de novo review and holding that the plaintiff had submitted a prima facie case of compliance with the ordinance standards and that the evidence to the contrary was not competent, substantial, or material as a matter of law, thus concluding that the permit denial was unsupported by sufficient evidence, and (2) a whole-record review and determining that the board's findings were not supported by competent, substantial, and material evidence.

The court held that the proper standards of review had been employed and applied correctly below. The plaintiff presented credible quantitative evidence as to each standard while the rebuttal testimony was held to be largely speculative and nonexpert opinion. On the issue of traffic, the plaintiff's traffic engineer produced trip generation data, related this to the town road plans, and described measures for minimizing congestion. The opposing testimony from neighbors was characterized as speculative lay opinions unsupported by mathematical studies or a factual basis. On property values, the plaintiff's real-estate appraiser conducted a market analysis of similarly situated neighborhoods in the town, reviewed sales histories around the site, conducted interviews with nearby purchasers, and reviewed the architectural plans. The opposing testimony from neighbors looked at countywide data regarding the effect of apartments on depressing rates of property-value appreciation and whether nearby sales were less than the asking price. The court held that this did not establish violation of the ordinance standard of substantial depreciation of value. The court found that testimony presenting reports of crime rates near apartment complexes in out-of-state cities without any factual relation to this project constituted speculative opinions and generalized fears that could not support permit denial. Likewise, testimony regarding the incongruity of the project design with neighboring properties was based solely on personal observations and had no quantitative link to a substantial depreciation in property values.

Rakestraw v. Town of Knightdale, 188 N.C. App. 129, 654 S.E.2d 825, *review denied*, 362 N.C. 237, 659 S.E.2d 739 (2008)
Amendments; Notice

The plaintiff neighbors brought a declaratory-judgment action challenging the rezoning of a tract from "highway business" and "urban residential" to a "highway commercial conditional" district. The town held a public hearing on the rezoning, employing newspaper, mailed, and posted notices. The notices indicated that the rezoning would allow subdivision of the parcel and development of a shopping center–community center. The advertised hearing was continued to two additional dates. The trial court granted summary judgment for the town.

The court upheld the rezoning, finding the published notice to be legally sufficient provided there was no substantial change to the proposed ordinance as it moved toward passage and so long as interested parties were informed when additional meetings would be held. No evidence was presented to show that either of these conditions was not met. The two-by-three-foot posted sign on the site of the proposed rezoning contained the following message: "Town of Knightdale PUBLIC HEARING PROPERTY NOTICE—For more information: (phone number)." The court held that this sign was adequate to identify and locate the property and did not need to contain the level of detail found in published and mailed notices. The plaintiffs presented affidavits that not all of the mailed notices were received. However, the court held that the statute provides that if the mailer certifies the mailing of the notice, this is deemed conclusive in the absence of fraud. Here, the town made such a certification and there was no evidence of fraud presented, so there could be no issue of material fact regarding the mailing. Finally, the court held that the statutes do not preclude adoption of a conditional district with less stringent standards than the comparable conventional district, and in this instance the town ordinance explicitly allowed for such.

McDonald v. City of Concord, 188 N.C. App. 278, 655 S.E.2d 455 (2008)

Government uses; Special uses

Neighbors challenged a special use permit issued by the city to Cabarrus County for a Law Enforcement Center located along the edge of downtown Concord. The permit authorized construction of three buildings on a ten-acre site: a sheriff's office, an annex, and a jail. The Center would be located adjacent to the existing jail and would be situated on the portion of the site zoned "central city." The remainder of the site (which was not proposed for development) was zoned "residential compact" and adjoined the plaintiffs' residential neighborhood. The trial court upheld issuance of the permit.

The court applied a whole-record review and concluded that the permit decision was supported by competent, substantial, and material evidence. The permit standard at issue was that the project had to conform "to the character of the neighborhood, considering the location, type, and height of buildings or structures and the type and extent of landscaping and screening on the site." The ordinance directed that *Webster's Dictionary* be used to define its terms. Applying these definitions, as well as the specific items listed in the standard to address conformity, the court concluded that the proposed buildings were sufficiently similar to historical uses in this portion of downtown; that the bulk, height, style, and appearance of the proposed buildings was similar to the neighboring governmental and business buildings in the central city district; and that these governmental uses had always been adjacent to residential areas. The court noted that the permit contained conditions for a fifty-foot vegetated buffer for the portion of the site contiguous to residential areas. While there was contrary evidence presented, neither the trial court nor the appellate court could substitute its judgment between two reasonably conflicting views so long as the board's view was supported by the evidence.

Blue Ridge Co. v. Town of Pineville, 188 N.C. App. 466, 655 S.E.2d 843, *review denied*, 362 N.C. 679, 669 S.E.2d 742 (2008)

Evidence; Remedies; Subdivisions

The defendant town denied approval of a subdivision plat based on a conclusion by the town council that the proposal failed to meet two subdivision ordinance standards: (1) that the subdivisions be consistent with adopted public plans (including policy plans and plans for public facilities, including roads, parks, and schools) and (2) that new subdivisions be designed to "protect and enhance the stability, environment, health, and character of the neighboring area." The council based denial regarding the first standard on school overcrowding and denial regarding the second on traffic concerns. The trial court remanded for a new hearing with a directive to the town to provide the applicant with plans in effect at the time the application was filed and with the specific criteria regarding the factors to be considered by the town in determining compliance with the second standard.

The court held that there was insufficient evidence in the record to support a denial based on school overcrowding. The court noted that it was uncertain whether there was in fact an adopted plan or policy specifically addressing this point, that the ordinance did not require a school-impact analysis, and that, in any event, the overcrowding existed even without this subdivision. As for traffic impacts, the court emphasized that an expert had testified that the substantial increase in traffic that would be generated would not create an undue safety problem, while opponents offered no mathematical studies but only speculative and generalized concerns on this matter. The court held that the proposed subdivision complied with general provisions in the adopted plans calling for smaller lot sizes, connections to greenways, a mix of housing styles and densities, and size of homes. The court then upheld the remand as within the trial court's discretion to assure that the town followed the procedures in the ordinance, in this instance to provide clarification of the subjective criteria used by the town in its review.

City of Wilmington v. Hill, 189 N.C. App. 173, 657 S.E.2d 670 (2008)
Enforcement; Ownership

The city's development regulations permitted a garage apartment as an accessory use in a single-family zoning district, provided the property owner lived in either the main residence or the accessory apartment. The defendant was cited for a violation of this requirement and assessed a civil penalty. After unsuccessfully seeking an ordinance text amendment to remove the ownership requirement, the defendant refused to pay the penalty and brought this action challenging the constitutionality of said requirement.

The court held that the defendant was not required to appeal the civil penalty to the board of adjustment in order to exhaust his administrative remedies, reasoning that if the provision was indeed illegal, the city had no authority to enforce it. The court then held the ownership requirement unconstitutional as an impermissible regulation of ownership rather than a permissible regulation of land use. The court also concluded that the owner-occupant regulation was beyond the scope of delegated zoning powers.

Friends of Mt. Vernon Springs, Inc. v. Town of Siler City, 190 N.C. App. 633, 660 S.E.2d 657 (2008)
Mootness; Spot zoning

A mineral company sought a conditional use district rezoning from Agriculture-Residential to Heavy Industrial Conditional for a 1076-acre tract and a special use permit for a quarry and processing facility on the site. The town board approved both in July 2006. Neighbors filed suit against the town, challenging the rezoning and the permit issuance. At the trial court hearing, the mineral company (which had intervened in the suit) advised the court that it was no longer pursuing permits for the project and had no position on the town's motion to dismiss.

The courts held that the applicant/company's withdrawal did not render the case moot as it did not dispose of the matter in controversy, namely, the validity of the rezoning and permit issuance. The court found that given the size of the rezoning involved, it did not constitute spot zoning. The court further held that the trial court properly applied a whole-record review in (1) determining that the town's actions were not arbitrary and capricious and were supported by substantial evidence and (2) in determining that there were no errors of law in either decision.

Table Rock Chapter of Trout Unlimited v. Environmental Management Commission (EMC), 191 N.C. App. 362, 663 S.E.2d 333 (2008)
Attorney's fees

The plaintiff conservation groups petitioned the EMC to reclassify an area of the Catawba River Bridgewater Dam as "trout waters" based on uncontested information that the area supported a stocked-trout population. The EMC denied the petition and the plaintiffs brought this action challenging the decision. The trial court found that the EMC had no reasonable basis for its decision and awarded the plaintiffs attorney's fees pursuant to G.S. 6-19.1 (which allows attorney's fees in specified circumstances for those successfully challenging decisions under the state Administrative Procedure Act). The court upheld the fee award upon determining that the EMC decision was without substantial justification and there were no special circumstances that would make the award unjust.

Hyatt v. Town of Lake Lure, 191 N.C. App. 386, 663 S.E.2d 320 (2008)

Appellate procedures

The plaintiff property owner sued the State of North Carolina and the defendant town regarding the town's lake-structure regulations (following prior suits against the town in federal court). The trial court granted summary judgment in favor of the town but did not rule on the claims against the state. The plaintiff argued that this ruling amounted to a final judgment entitling her to appeal. The court held that a grant of partial summary judgment is an interlocutory order that is not subject to appeal. Accordingly, the plaintiff's appeal against the state was dismissed as premature.

Durham County v. Graham, 191 N.C. App. 600, 663 S.E.2d 467 (2008)

Enforcement; Parties; Sedimentation

The defendant secured a land-disturbance permit for a landfill. The county issued a notice of violation alleging that more than an acre had been disturbed, the fill had extended into a floodplain, and the sediment had not been contained on site. The county sought an injunction to compel restoration and compliance with the terms of the permit. Subsequent to the permit issuance and notice of violation, the subject property changed hands, went into foreclosure, and title was transferred to the lender.

The court found that the current owner of the property was a necessary party as its rights to use the property would be affected by an injunction. The court held that lien holders were not necessary parties, nor was the city (which would have to permit the remedial actions being sought).

Laurel Valley Watch, Inc. v. Mountain Enterprises of Wolf Ridge, LLC, 192 N.C. App. 391, 665 S.E.2d 561 (2008)

Amendments; Estoppel; Exhaustion

The defendants applied for a rezoning in order to construct a private airport in Madison County adjacent to resort properties they owned. The notice of both the planning board's hearing and the board of commissioners' hearing on the proposed rezoning noted that the rezoning was to be to an industrial district, the only district in the county zoning ordinance that permitted an airport. The county commissioners unanimously approved the rezoning. However, the minutes of the meeting noted that the property had been rezoned to a "residential-resort" district. The plaintiff nonprofit group filed this action alleging that the defendant developers were improperly constructing an airport in a residential-resort district and that the defendant county had improperly rezoned the land involved. The county commissioners then adopted a resolution noting that a scrivener's error had incorrectly identified the zoning district adopted for this property and amended those minutes to state that the property had been rezoned to an industrial district.

The court held that the evidence clearly supported a finding that the property had in fact actually been rezoned to the industrial district. The application, hearing notices, planning-board recommendation, affidavits of the applicant and the zoning administrator, and contemporary newspaper accounts all referred to a rezoning to the industrial district, supporting the conclusion that there was indeed a scrivener's error in the minutes. Thus, the two-month statute of limitations to challenge the rezoning ran from the initial adoption, rendering the plaintiff's challenge untimely. The court rejected an equitable estoppel argument for reliance on the mistaken minutes, as there was no evidence that the plaintiff organization or any of its principals were aware of or had relied on the mistake in the original meeting minutes. The court also noted that the trial court was without subject-matter jurisdiction to hear the complaint against the developers for a zoning violation, as the plaintiff had failed to exhaust its administrative remedies. The plaintiff should have asked the zoning administrator for a ruling on zoning compliance and appealed an adverse ruling to the designated board prior to initiating a petition for judicial review.

Meares v. Town of Beaufort, 193 N.C. App. 49, 667 S.E.2d 244 (2008)

Exhaustion; Historic preservation; Jurisdiction; Procedures

The plaintiff proposed to build a three-story commercial and residential structure within the Beaufort historic district. After the Historic Preservation Commission denied approval and while that decision was on appeal in the courts, the plaintiff filed a second application for an alternative structure. The ordinance required action on applications within sixty days of a final application, with the application deemed to be approved otherwise. When the commission refused to process or act upon the second application, this action was filed seeking mandamus to compel issuance of the certificate of appropriateness.

The court upheld the trial court's order mandating issuance of the certificate of appropriateness. Since it was undisputed that sixty days had passed without action on the complete application, the court found that issuance was required by the ordinance and was thus a ministerial action. The court held that there were no provisions in the ordinance or in general law that precluded an alternative application while an initial application was on appeal. The court noted that noncompliance with zoning setback provisions does not divest the historic commission of jurisdiction, as the historic-district requirements and zoning requirements are independent standards for review (and thus an order regarding the certificate of appropriateness does not affect the town's authority or actions under the zoning regulations). The court further held that since zoning compliance is not a predicate to the historic commission's certificate of appropriateness, and as a variance is possible from the zoning standards, potential zoning inconsistency does not render the historic commission's action moot, remove its subject-matter jurisdiction, or otherwise excuse nonaction by the commission. The court concluded that a letter from the town attorney, which was sent prior to the second application, stating that a second application would not be considered while the first application was on appeal could not be considered an appealable action by the commission. Finally, the court found that since the commission refused to act on the application, there was no decision that could be appealed to the board of adjustment, and thus there was no failure by the applicant to exhaust administrative remedies prior to initiating a court action.

Meares v. Town of Beaufort, 193 N.C. App. 96, 667 S.E.2d 239 (2008)

Historic preservation; Scope of authority; Statutes of limitation

The plaintiff proposed to build a three-story commercial and residential structure within the Beaufort historic district. After receiving preliminary plans for the structure, the Historic Preservation Commission adopted a new design guideline requiring that new buildings be consistent in height and scale with preexisting historic structures on the site at issue. The commission then, relying in part upon the new guideline, denied approval of the certificate of appropriateness for the proposed structure.

The court found the new standard to be more restrictive than allowed by the state historic-preservation statute and thus declared it to be void. The court reasoned that the design guidelines could only require congruence with the special character of the district, not with an individual historic building previously located on the site. The court held that potential inconsistency with zoning standards does not render the matter non-justiciable, as the ordinance did not require a finding of zoning compliance as a predicate to issuance of a certificate of appropriateness from the historic commission. The court also held that the two-month statute of limitations for challenging the adoption or amendment of zoning ordinances is not applicable to the challenge of design guidelines adopted by the Historic Preservation Commission.

Carroll v. City of Kings Mountain, 193 N.C. App. 165, 666 S.E.2d 814 (2008)

Amendments

In September 2005, the city, at the plaintiff's request, rezoned the plaintiff's property from residential to a general business zoning district. The following month, another resident of Kings Mountain petitioned to have the property rezoned back to a residential district. The plaintiff filed a protest petition objecting to the second rezoning. The planning board recommended approval of the second rezoning, as the town's comprehensive plan called for residential uses in this area. New city council members took office in December, and in January 2006, they rezoned the property back to residential use.

The zoning ordinance provided that petitions for amendments could only be made by those owning property or residing within the city jurisdiction. The petitioner for the second rezoning had provided a street address but had not explicitly noted that the address was within the city. The court found the petition to be adequate, noting that it was common practice before the city council not to list a city in an address unless the address was out of town. The court further noted that it could take judicial notice of the location of the given address (which was within the city).

The trial court had held that the second rezoning circumvented the process for judicial review of the first rezoning and was arbitrary and capricious given the lack of a change in circumstances between the two votes. The court held these conclusions to be erroneous, as the trial court had failed to apply a deferential review to the legislative rezoning decision, and the decision whether or not to rezone was within the legislative discretion of the city council. However, the city ordinance established a four-month waiting period between rezoning petitions for a particular parcel, and since that period was not observed, this rezoning was invalid.

State v. Town of Kill Devil Hills, 194 N.C. App. 561, 670 S.E.2d 341, *aff'd per curiam*, 363 N.C. 739, 686 S.E.2d 151 (2009)

Exhaustion; Preemption; Utilities

Dominion Power owned a transmission line running along the west side (sound side) of the defendant town. The company proposed adding a second transmission line to run in a new corridor along the main highway through the town, which is located on the east side of town. The town adopted an ordinance requiring aboveground transmission lines to be built in a single corridor. Dominion filed a complaint with the state Utilities Commission seeking to preempt the ordinance and allow use of the second corridor. The Commission issued an order pursuant to G.S. 62-42 directing Dominion to complete its improvements in the second corridor. The town objected, contending that since G.S. 62-106 preempts local ordinances regarding siting of higher-voltage transmission lines, there was by negative inference no preemption of local ordinances affecting smaller transmission lines.

The court rejected the contention that G.S. 62-106 divested the Commission of jurisdiction to hear disputes on the location of smaller transmission lines. The court held that there was no requirement for Dominion to seek a variance or other administrative relief from the town, as the Utilities Commission was specifically empowered to order expansion or improvements in electrical-distribution services. As the Commission found that there was insufficient space in the existing utility corridor for a second line and that underground lines or an alternate route around the town were excessively costly, the Commission had the authority to order use of the second proposed corridor and that order preempted town regulations to the contrary.

Five C's, Inc. v. County of Pasquotank, 195 N.C. App. 410, 672 S.E.2d 737 (2009)

Manufactured housing; Preemption

The county adopted an ordinance under its general police powers to prohibit bringing manufactured homes into the county that were more than ten years old at the time of setup. The rationale offered by the county was protection of the county tax base. More particularly, the county noted that manufactured homes rapidly decline in value and at the ten-year point have little more value than a motor vehicle, thus providing insufficient tax revenue to support the needs for county services that they generated in the first instance.

The court held that the plain meaning of G.S. 160D-910 limiting regulation of manufactured housing to appearance and dimensional criteria prohibits regulation based solely on the age or value of a unit. The fact that the county used its general ordinance-making power rather than the zoning power cannot be used to circumvent this clear legislative limitation on regulatory authority.

Town of Pinebluff v. Marts, 195 N.C. App. 659, 673 S.E.2d 740 (2009)

Enforcement; Injunctions; Takings

The town conditioned its approval of a subdivision being developed in three phases upon installation of a mini-park prior to final approval of the third phase of the development. The owner also agreed to establish a homeowners' association that would maintain the park. The owner accepted the conditions and, in order to secure final approval of the plat for the third phase prior to installation of the mini-park, posted a letter of credit to assure its construction. After the letter of credit expired and the park was still not installed, the town sought injunctive relief to compel its installation. The owner challenged the validity of the ordinance establishing the requirement and contended that the town was estopped from enforcing it, that injunctive relief was inappropriate, and that the requirement was unconstitutional as being retroactive, an unlawful impairment of contract, and a taking.

The court held that the owner could not collaterally attack the validity of the ordinance in an enforcement action. If an owner fails to challenge imposition of a condition or to seek administrative relief through a variance, the challenge may not be initiated when an enforcement action is brought. The court held that equitable estoppel cannot apply to a municipality enforcing a zoning ordinance. Injunctive relief is explicitly allowed, the court found, and while the question of whether a court must balance the equities in deciding whether to issue an injunction is an open question in this state, the only balancing questions the owner here raised related to the policy in the ordinance, not to the injunction. The court dismissed the allegation of impairment of contract, noting that approval of the first phase of the project created no contractual rights relative to subsequent phases of the development. Finally, the court held that the requirement of installation of a mini-park to serve needs created by the development was not a taking.

Thrash Ltd. Partnership v. County of Buncombe, 195 N.C. App. 678, 673 S.E.2d 706 (2009)

Amendments; Notice; Procedures; Standing

The county adopted its initial zoning ordinance in the 1970s but only applied it to two townships within the county. In 2007, the county undertook a process to extend its zoning ordinance countywide. The county ordinance required that the notice of hearing be published at least fifteen days prior to the hearing (and state law requires it to be published at ten days prior to the hearing). The initial notice was published fourteen days prior to the hearing. The proposed zoning map was submitted to the planning board for comment, but changes requested by property owners were subsequently incorporated into the map up until the day before the public hearing.

As in a companion case, discussed just below, challenging a multifamily dwelling ordinance, the court held that the plaintiff had standing even though it had not filed an application to develop. The court reasoned that in a facial challenge to the procedures by which the ordinance was adopted, ownership of land that was subject to the regulations is a sufficient basis for standing. The court then found the ordinance invalid due to a failure to meet the ordinance and state requirements for notice of the hearing. This conclusion was based on the fact that some map amendments were made after the planning board's comments were submitted. The court also noted that the maps used at the board of commissioners' hearing were not in existence, and thus not available for review and comment, at the time notice of the hearing was given.

Thrash Ltd. Partnership v. County of Buncombe, 195 N.C. App. 727, 673 S.E.2d 689 (2009)

Notice; Procedures; Standing

The county adopted an ordinance on multifamily dwellings that established differential standards depending on the elevation of the property involved. There were no requirements under the regulation for land with an elevation under 2500 feet; one set of rules for land with an elevation of between 2500 and 3000 feet; and a different set of rules for land with an elevation of more than 3000 feet. The rules (among other things) limited density, the height of buildings, parking standards, road construction, and the area of land disturbance. The county did not follow the mandatory hearing and notice provisions for zoning in adopting this ordinance, contending that it was a general-police-power ordinance.

The court found that the plaintiff, who had not filed an application to develop, had standing to bring a facial challenge to the procedures by which the ordinance was adopted. The fact that the plaintiff owned land that was subject to the regulations was sufficient for a facial challenge, while a particular application would be needed for an "as applied" challenge. The court then held the ordinance invalid on the grounds that the zoning procedures were not observed in its adoption. The court concluded that the subject matter of the ordinance addressed issues within the authority delegated to counties under its authority to adopt development regulations. As these regulations substantially affected the plaintiff's use of its property, the county could not evade the mandatory notice and hearing requirements by characterizing the ordinance as a general-police-power ordinance rather than a development regulation. [Note: G.S. 160D-101(a) was subsequently amended to clarify that the procedures for the adoption of development regulations apply to any ordinance that substantially affects land use and development.]

State v. Maynard, 195 N.C. App. 757, 673 S.E.2d 877, *review denied*, 363 N.C. 259, 677 S.E.2d 165 (2009)
Animals

The town of Nashville adopted an ordinance limiting the number of dogs that could be kept on property within town to no more than three dogs over the age of five months (and to two dogs if the lot was 30,000 square feet or less). The court held that the ordinance was reasonably related to the legitimate governmental objectives of reducing noise and odor problems in the city.

North Iredell Neighbors for Rural Life v. Iredell County, 196 N.C. App. 68, 674 S.E.2d 436, *review denied*, 363 N.C. 582, 682 S.E.2d 385 (2009)
Agricultural uses; Injunctions; Standing

An unincorporated association and several adjacent neighbors challenged the county's rezoning of a 7.88-acre portion of a 218-acre tract from a single-family residential to a heavy manufacturing conditional use district. The rezoning was done to accommodate a proposed biodiesel operation.

The court first held that the unincorporated association did not have standing, as there was not the requisite demonstration that it had proper legal existence. The group had failed to affirmatively state its location of recordation or that it was a nonprofit unincorporated association under Chapter 59B of the General Statutes.

The court next held that the proposed biodiesel production facility was an industrial use not covered within the bona-fide-farm exemption from county zoning. Key factors in this determination included the fact that the operation was not self-contained; some of the seeds used in production would be produced off-site and the operation would produce 500,000 gallons per year, while the farm operation could only use 100,000 gallons per year (with the excess being sold to neighboring farmers).

Finally, the court held that the trial court had not abused its discretion in refusing to grant a preliminary injunction pending resolution of the case. The court applied a two-step test to determine whether a preliminary injunction was appropriate, considering: (1) the likelihood of success on the merits and (2) the likelihood of irreparable harm without the injunction.

Mangum v. Raleigh Board of Adjustment, 196 N.C. App. 249, 674 S.E.2d 742 (2009)
Conditions; Evidence; Interpretation

The plaintiffs challenged the issuance of a special use permit by the board of adjustment for an adult-entertainment facility (a prior suit addressed standing for this appeal). The court first considered a 2000-foot separation requirement in the ordinance as it applied to a karate school. The court noted that the definitions in the ordinance required a measurement from the "entire property" of the adult business to the "place of regular activities" of the school. As the karate school was conducted entirely within a building and that building was more than 2000 feet from the lot line of the adult business, the court concluded that the separation requirement was met. The court found that imposition of a permit condition that the project conform to city parking and stormwater requirements was not an unlawful delegation of the board's authority, holding that there was competent substantial evidence in the record to support the board's findings that the project would comply with city standards and not adversely affect the interests enumerated in the ordinance (parking, traffic, police, noise, light, stormwater, and pedestrian circulation). Given the presence of sufficient evidence in the record, the trial court could not make a de novo review of the evidence to reach contrary findings.

Murdock v. Chatham County, 198 N.C. App. 309, 679 S.E.2d 850 (2009), *review denied*, 363 N.C. 806, 690 S.E.2d 705 (2010)

Amendments; Interpretation; Rezoning; Standing

Owners of a sixty-acre tract sought a rezoning to a conditional use district and a special use permit in order to construct a commercial complex with a home-improvement center and commercial businesses. A portion of the site had been rezoned for general business in 1974 and the residual area was zoned Residential-Agricultural. The county took three actions as a result. First, the county planning director adjusted the zoning map to increase the size of the area zoned as general business based on a conclusion that the original metes-and-bounds description of the area in the 1974 rezoning application encompassed a larger area than had been shown on the zoning map and its subsequent re-adoptions. Second, the county approved the rezoning to a conditional use district. Third, the county approved a special use permit for the project. The plaintiffs (neighboring landowners) challenged all three decisions, appealing the first and third to the board of adjustment initially.

The court first held that the plaintiffs had standing to challenge the interpretation of the zoning map. The plaintiffs alleged in their complaint that they owned adjoining land to the larger tract and presented testimony at the hearing about the adverse impacts on their property from the lights, noise, and stormwater runoff from the site should the project be built. The court held that this was sufficient to establish the requisite special damages for standing purposes.

The court then held that the zoning administrator had no authority to adjust the zoning maps to increase the area zoned as general business from twenty to thirty acres. While the board of adjustment may interpret the ordinance, such an extension of zoning district boundaries requires a zoning amendment (noting that even if there had been some original error in mapping the boundary, subsequent ordinances had adopted the boundary shown on the zoning map).

The court then invalidated the rezoning. The ordinance specifically required that there be a thirty-day period between filing an application for amendment and the public hearing on that application or petition. Since the thirty-day period before the hearing that was held fell on a Saturday, the county set a deadline of the following Monday for receipt of applications to be considered at this hearing (and this application was filed on that Monday). The court applied Rule 6(a) of the Rules of Civil Procedure to hold that if the thirty-day deadline fell on Saturday, an application would have had to be filed by the preceding Friday. As the county had no authority to waive the procedural requirements of its ordinance, the rezoning was invalid. As the rezoning to a conditional use district was invalidated, there could be no special use permit, so the court did not address that issue.

Moores v. Greensboro Minimum Housing Standards Commission, 198 N.C. App. 384, 679 S.E. 2d 480 (2009)

Enforcement; Preemption

The Greensboro code provided that appeals of a housing inspector's order to repair or demolish a dilapidated dwelling were to be made to a minimum-housing-standards commission, with that commission being delegated authority to issue a final order in the matter. The court held that G.S. 160D-1203, which provided that orders for demolition or repair are not to be exercised until the "governing body" orders such, does not require action by the city council or board of county commissioners. A housing code can delegate the authority to hear appeals and enter orders to a housing-appeals commission.

Lawyer v. City of Elizabeth City, 199 N.C. App. 304, 681 S.E.2d 415 (2009)
Enforcement; Housing code; Notice

The plaintiffs acquired title in October 2003 to a vacant house at a tax sale. The plaintiffs requested that property tax notices and bills be forwarded to them. Although a sheriff's deed was prepared at this time, the plaintiffs did not record it. In September 2004, the city inspected the house and found it to be unfit for habitation (it had apparently been vacant since 1999). Notices of that finding were sent to the previous owners, who were still listed as record owners. Upon receipt of the notice, the prior owners notified the city that the property had been sold at auction. The city subsequently made several inquiries at the county tax office and register of deeds as to ownership and was informed that those records indicated that the prior owners were still the owners of record. The city did not engage an attorney to conduct a title search and continued to mail notices of its condemnation actions to the record owners. In early November, the plaintiffs recorded their tax deed. In late November 2004, the city council approved an ordinance condemning the structure and posted notice of that action on the site in early December. In January 2005, the city demolished the structure.

The court held that reasonable persons could differ as to whether the city's actions to ascertain to whom it should send notices in its condemnation action were adequate. Therefore, it was inappropriate for the trial court to grant summary judgment for the city.

Coucoulas/Knight Properties v. Town of Hillsborough, 199 N.C. App. 455, 683 S.E.2d 228 (2009), *aff'd per curiam*, 364 N.C. 127, 691 S.E.2d 441 (2010)
Amendments; Equal protection; Plan consistency

The defendant town denied the plaintiff's petition to rezone a parcel from primarily low-density residential into an "Entranceway Special Use" district. The property was located within a historic district and within an area designated by an adopted corridor plan as a "district gateway." The town council approved the rezoning by a 3–2 vote, but since a valid protest petition had been filed, the rezoning failed as it did not secure the requisite three-fourths supermajority. The trial court held the refusal to rezone to be arbitrary and capricious and violative of equal protection because the town had placed property at the opposite end of its downtown area into this zoning district.

The court held that a whole-record review should be applied to address a claim that the decision was arbitrary and capricious. The court noted that there was no evidence, much less substantial evidence, that prior decisions of the board involved similarly situated properties as this property was within the town's historic district and other rezonings were not (and also considering the size, proposed use, density, and other factors related to entryway districts). The court pointed out that the finding that the rezoning would be consistent with the comprehensive plan did not mean that the existing zoning (which was retained, given the refusal to rezone) was inconsistent with the plan. Also, the fact that the ordinance specifically allowed denial of rezoning petitions that are deemed not to be in the public interest did not require the board to make a finding that the proposal was not in the public interest.

Tonter Investments, Inc. v. Pasquotank County, 199 N.C. App. 579, 681 S.E.2d 536, *review denied*, 363 N.C. 663, 687 S.E.2d 296 (2009)
Agriculture; Purposes; Subdivisions

The county amended its zoning ordinance to prohibit residential uses in the A-2 Agricultural zoning district and to prohibit buildings in the A-1 Agricultural zoning district unless the lot at issue has 25 feet of frontage on a state road (or road approved under the county subdivision ordinance) and is within 1000 feet of a public water supply. The plaintiffs owned three large tracts (each over twenty-five acres) that were in these two zoning districts. They alleged that these zoning amendments were ultra vires because the state subdivision-enabling statute exempts lots greater than ten acres from county subdivision regulation.

The court upheld the county ordinance, noting that the ten-acre exemption applies to subdivision ordinances, not to zoning ordinances. The court found that the county requirements of road and water access for buildable lots were reasonably related to legitimate public objectives such as provision of essential county services to residences and safety issues related to aerial spraying of pesticides in the remote and largely unpopulated A-2 zoning district (there was testimony that only five residences existed in the entire A-2 zoning district). The court also noted that while residences are allowed in many zoning districts, there is no state requirement that they be allowed in all zoning districts.

McMillan v. Town of Tryon, 200 N.C. App. 228, 683 S.E.2d 747 (2009)

Amendments; Conditional zoning; Judicial review; Procedures

The plaintiffs challenged the town's rezoning of property within a country club from open-space and single-family residential zoning districts to a residential conditional use district that would allow single-family homes, duplexes, and a tennis/swimming complex. The town ordinance required that the rezoning to the conditional use district and the accompanying special use permit be heard and decided in a single quasi-judicial hearing.

The court first upheld the trial court's denial of the plaintiffs' motion to amend their complaint a second time to add conflict of interest and bias allegations regarding one of the town council members. That motion was filed nearly a year after the initial complaint and a week after the defendant's motion for summary judgment with supporting affidavits. The court noted that even if the defendant's motion added new information about the details of the case, the plaintiffs' failure to undertake any discovery until that point should not burden the defendants. Thus, the court held that the trial court did not abuse its discretion in denying the motion to amend the complaint.

The court noted that local governments have a choice of adopting purely legislative conditional zoning or combined legislative/quasi-judicial conditional use district zoning with a concurrent conditional use permit. Here, the town chose the latter option. Therefore, the trial court had to, in addition to reviewing the legislative aspects of the decision, also conduct a review of the quasi-judicial dimension (reviewing for errors of law, proper application of required procedures, due-process protections observed, adequate evidence in the record, and arbitrary or capricious action). Since the record did not show this review, the case was remanded for imposition of the proper standard of review. [Note: The statutory authority for the adoption of conditional use district zoning with concurrent quasi-judicial permits was subsequently repealed.]

McMillan v. Town of Tryon, 200 N.C. App. 282, 683 S.E.2d 743 (2009)

Standing

The plaintiffs challenged (1) the town's rezoning of land within a country club from open-space and single-family residential zoning districts to a residential conditional use district that would allow single-family homes, duplexes, and a tennis/swimming complex and (2) the issuance of a special use permit for the project. (This case involved the permit; a companion case, discussed above, addressed the rezoning). The trial court dismissed the appeal for lack of standing.

The court conducted a de novo review of the issue of the plaintiffs' standing. All had alleged they were adjacent or nearby property owners. One had testified at the hearing on the permit about potential negative impacts of the project due to a narrow road serving as access (with children walking and biking on it), noise, stormwater-runoff increases, and an unsuitable site for septic tanks. The court held that a de novo review of standing must view the plaintiffs' allegations as true and view them in the light most favorable to them. Given that standard, the allegations of proximity to the site and the testimony regarding special damages were sufficient as a matter of law to confer standing.

Musi v. Town of Shallotte, 200 N.C. App. 379, 684 S.E.2d 892 (2009)

Contract zoning; Spot zoning; Standing

The plaintiff neighbors filed a declaratory-judgment action to challenge the rezoning of an area consisting of fifteen tracts with six different owners. The property at issue had been subject to county low-density residential zoning. The town approved a satellite annexation and rezoning to a higher density that would accommodate multifamily condominiums.

The court held that the plaintiffs had standing to challenge the rezoning. The court in a de novo review noted that the plaintiffs had alleged a specific personal and legal interest in the subject matter, which is similar to but not the same as the requirement to show special damages as an aggrieved party with a writ of certiorari.

The court found that the rezoning was not spot zoning for two reasons. First, the property was not owned by a single entity. The fact that the six owners may have been part of an extended family or had common interests did not affect this determination. Second, the area was not surrounded by a larger uniformly zoned area, as there were more than five other town and county zoning districts within a mile of the property. The court also held that the fact that the town council was aware of a specific plan to build multifamily condominiums on the site did not in and of itself indicate that the council was unaware of other uses that could be undertaken under the new zoning. The court noted that the range of uses allowed was similar to that allowed in the prior county zoning and each council member testified that they had considered the full range of permitted uses at the time of the rezoning.

Northwest Property Group, LLC v. Town of Carrboro, 201 N.C. App. 449, 687 S.E.2d 1 (2009)
Conditions; Special uses

The plaintiff applied for a special use permit to develop a grocery store and other commercial establishments. The site fronted a major street and had a side street that accessed a residential neighborhood. While a traffic-impact analysis indicated that the increase in traffic from the project would not meet N.C. Department of Transportation (NCDOT) standards for a signal or other intersection improvements, neighbors expressed concerns about traffic impacts. The plaintiff agreed to reserve land for a future roundabout at the intersection, to pay for traffic signals should NCDOT approve such, and to limit delivery-vehicle use to the side entry. The town council issued the permit but also imposed a condition that the side entrance be limited to emergency vehicles. The plaintiff contested imposition of that condition.

The ordinance was structured to require the council to make three votes on the application, determining successively that the application was complete, that it complied with all applicable portions of the ordinance, and that specified conditions were to be applied. The plaintiff contended that conditions could only be imposed if the second of these motions—that the application complied with the ordinance—failed, in that conditions could only be imposed to bring the project into compliance with the ordinance. The court held that the ordinance contemplated successive votes and that conditions consistent with the standards for conditions set out in the ordinance could be imposed even with approval of the second motion. However, the court held that the council had made no findings to support imposition of the challenged condition and therefore remanded the case to the council for reconsideration and adoption of findings to support any conditions that they might impose in that reconsideration.

Union Land Owners Ass'n v. County of Union, 201 N.C. App. 374, 689 S.E.2d 504 (2009), *review denied*, 364 N.C. 442, 703 S.E.2d 148 (2010), *review dismissed as moot*, 364 N.C. 442, 703 S.E.2d 149 (2010)
Adequate public facilities; Impact fees

Union County adopted an adequate-public-facilities ordinance (APFO) within a land use ordinance that included a calculation of a proposed development's impact on school capacity. If the development's impact would overburden school capacity, the ordinance provided several options, including reducing the scale of the proposed development, phasing its construction to match school-construction schedules, or having the developer provide funding or construction to address issues of school capacity. The county also adopted a resolution establishing a procedure to calculate the "voluntary mitigation payment" that the developer could pay to offset school-capacity deficiencies. The plaintiff developers challenged the county's authority to adopt such a regulatory scheme.

The court held that the county lacked express or implied authority to adopt this ordinance under its general-police-power, zoning, or subdivision-regulation authority. The court found that since the zoning and subdivision statutes directly addressed real-estate development, the general ordinance-making authority did not provide an independent source of authority for an adequate-public-facilities ordinance. The court noted that consideration of development impacts on the efficient and adequate provision of public services (including schools) is expressly within the permissible objectives of a zoning ordinance. However, local governments may only employ the tools provided within the statute to address this objective. The court held that the tools enumerated within the statute (size of buildings, lot sizes, setbacks, density, land uses, etc.) were not sufficiently broad to include the tools used in this APFO. Similarly, while an APFO's objectives were within those that could be addressed by a subdivision ordinance, the tools authorized therein did not include a requirement for developers to address school-facility needs by payments, land donation, or school construction. Therefore, the court held that inclusion of a "voluntary mitigation payment" and similar measures rendered the APFO beyond the scope of the county's delegated authority. The court held that this was an improper indirect attempt to impose a school impact fee.

Coventry Woods Neighborhood Ass'n v. City of Charlotte, 202 N.C. App. 247, 688 S.E.2d 538, *review denied*, 364 N.C. 128, 695 S.E.2d 757 (2010)
Due process; Notice; Statutes of limitation

Neighbors challenged the city's approval of a preliminary plat for a subdivision. The ordinance did not provide for notice to neighbors of a subdivision plat application or decision and no such notice was provided. The ordinance required appeals of subdivision decisions to be filed within ten days of the decision. Plaintiffs learned of the preliminary plat approval some six months after the decision and filed an appeal with the board of adjustment two months after learning of the decision. After a hearing, the board rejected the appeal. The plaintiffs then attempted an appeal to the planning commission, which was rejected as not being timely. The plaintiffs contended that their appeal was timely and that a preliminary plat decision made without a hearing and notice to neighbors violated their due-process rights.

The court found that the two-month statute of limitations applicable to legislative zoning decisions did not apply to a subdivision ordinance. The court held that the three-year statute of limitations of G.S. 1-52 did not begin to run on adoption of the ordinance but, rather, ran from the date the plaintiffs learned of the plat approval.

The appeals court, however, found that the plaintiffs had no property rights affected by the decision, so there could be no due-process violation. The court ruled that the plaintiffs' contentions that their rights to the use and enjoyment of their property were affected and that their property suffered a diminution in value were predicated on a reliance on an expectation of unchanged ordinances, the existing legal situation, and the current use of the tract in question, none of which are property rights protected by the constitution.

Bailey & Associates, Inc. v. Wilmington Board of Adjustment, 202 N.C. App. 177, 689 S.E.2d 576 (2010)
Estoppel; Evidence; Intervention; Mootness; Timeliness

The plaintiffs proposed to develop a tract adjacent to Motts Creek. After a concept meeting with town staff in 2005, the staff advised the plaintiff that the site was not within a conservation overlay district. When the site plan was reviewed by the city's technical-review committee in 2007, however, that committee determined that at least part of the parcel was within that overlay district and thus subject to its waterfront setback and buffer rules. The plaintiffs appealed this determination to the board of adjustment the following day. The board affirmed the determination that the parcel was within the overlay district. On appeal to superior court, neighbors were allowed to intervene, but their motion to remand the matter to the board for consideration of new evidence was denied. The trial court refused to hold that the plaintiffs' appeal to the board of adjustment was not timely. The court then reversed the board of adjustment's decision upholding the staff interpretation.

The court held that the appeal was not mooted by the city's subsequent repeal of the conservation overlay district and adoption of new conservation regulations, as that ordinance explicitly included provisions that the new rules were not applicable to pending litigation or site plans that had already been accepted for review.

The court held that contiguous- and neighboring-property owners had sufficient standing to intervene, as they had alleged specific, direct loss to their properties and their use and enjoyment of the same (having alleged increased traffic, light pollution, noise, and similar harms).

The court noted that the city ordinance required appeals to the board of adjustment regarding interpretation of the ordinance to be made within ten days after issuance of an order from the city manager. This presented a mixed question of law and fact—the interpretation of the terms "issuance" and "order" being questions of law and identifying actual dates of actions taken being a question of fact. As the board of adjustment made no findings of fact or conclusions of law on this point, it was proper for the trial court to refuse to take the issue up on appeal.

The court held that the question of whether new evidence should have been allowed under Rule 60(b)(2) was a de novo question of law for the trial court. However, since this issue was not presented to the board of adjustment and that board took no action on it, the record was devoid of anything for the trial court to review. The court held that a site-development application alleged to have been made by the plaintiffs for the same site in 2001 that purportedly acknowledged the site to be within a conservation overlay district was not presented to the board of adjustment and was thus not within the record and could not be considered by the trial court.

Cary Creek Ltd. Partnership v. Town of Cary, 203 N.C. App. 99, 690 S.E.2d 549, *review denied*, 364 N.C. 600, 703 S.E.2d 441 (2010)

Buffer zones; Jurisdiction; Preemption

The town's development ordinance included stormwater-management standards that included 100-foot riparian buffers adjacent to perennial and intermittent streams identified on U.S. Geological Survey maps and fifty-foot buffers adjacent to other surface waters. After the plaintiffs were denied a variance from the buffer requirements, they brought a declaratory-judgment action challenging the validity of said requirements and an inverse-condemnation action in the event the buffers were declared valid.

The court first held that the plaintiff's separate certiorari proceeding challenging the variance denial did not deprive the court of subject-matter jurisdiction to hear this declaratory-judgment action on the validity of the ordinance, as these two legal actions must be brought separately. However, the court found that the inverse-condemnation claim was premature and should have been dismissed, as it was dependent on the outcome of both the declaratory-judgment action and the certiorari review. The court held that the town's buffer requirements were not preempted by state watershed-protection statutes, as G.S. 143-214.5 provides for a cooperative state-local management program and explicitly allows local governments to adopt more stringent standards than the state-mandated minimum standards.

Schwarz Properties, LLC v. Town of Franklinville, 204 N.C. App. 344, 693 S.E.2d 271 (2010)

Costs; Manufactured housing; Statutes of limitation

The plaintiff sought a declaratory judgment to invalidate the town's adoption of ordinances prohibiting issuance of permits for installation of manufactured homes in the jurisdiction if the homes were more than ten years old, as well as ordinances requiring the capping of sewer lines upon removal of a structure and setting a fee for replacement of lost trash carts. The plaintiff secured a temporary restraining order (TRO) precluding denial of permits for location of manufactured homes during the litigation. Following a hearing, the trial court dissolved the TRO, allowed the town to revoke permits issued while it was in effect, dismissed the plaintiff's claims, and awarded damages to the town for the costs of defending the matter.

The court held that the two-month statute of limitations applied to the ordinance on location of manufactured homes, as it was part of the town's zoning ordinance. Since the action was filed more than a year after adoption of the restriction, the claim was time-barred and properly dismissed. Since the claims on the sewer cap and trash collection involved governmental functions, the plaintiff's failure to allege a waiver of sovereign immunity was fatal, and those claims were properly dismissed. An award of costs to the town for the expenses of defense upon dismissal of the temporary restraining order were allowed by Rule 65 of the Rules of Civil Procedure without a showing of malice or want of probable cause.

Four Seasons Management Services, Inc. v. Town of Wrightsville Beach, 205 N.C. App. 65, 695 S.E.2d 456 (2010)

Interpretation; Nonconformities; Special uses

The plaintiffs owned a multistory hotel that was a lawful nonconformity under the town zoning ordinance. The structure did not comply with various setbacks, off-street parking, and landscaping requirements. Since the hotel was built prior to the adoption of town zoning, the plaintiffs did not secure a special use permit, as is required for hotels in this zoning district. However, the plaintiffs sought and obtained a special use permit for improvements to the hotel and had twice sought and obtained amendments to that permit for additional improvements. The plaintiffs sought to construct a four-story parking structure on the site of the hotel's existing surface-parking lot without an amendment to its permit. The town contended that a permit amendment was required and that construction of the deck otherwise would be an unlawful expansion of a nonconformity. The plaintiffs argued that the deck was an "accessory use" permitted by right and that, as they were reducing the extent of the parking noncompliance, this was not an expansion of a nonconformity. The board of adjustment upheld the town's interpretation.

The court first held that construction of the parking structure required an amendment to the special use permit. The town ordinance clearly distinguished "accessory structures" and "accessory buildings" from "accessory uses." The proposed work was clearly a structure and not a use alone, so the authorization of accessory uses was not relevant to the issue of whether a permit was required under the terms of the ordinance.

The clear intent of the ordinance was to subject hotels and substantial construction in this zoning district to the "considerable scrutiny" of a special use permit process. The court also found that the proposed parking structure would be an impermissible expansion of a nonconformity as defined by the town ordinance, in that it would still have an inadequate number of parking spaces and would not comply with landscaping and sprinkler requirements. The ordinance provision allowing changes in degree but not changes in kind was inapplicable, as it was expressly limited to changes in "equipment or processes," not to this type of structural addition.

Land v. Village of Wesley Chapel, 206 N.C. App. 123, 697 S.E.2d 458 (2010)
Interpretation; Nonconformities

The plaintiff purchased a lot in Union County in 1991 and established a shooting range that occupied two-thirds of the lot. The cost of improvements for the range was $2000. In response to adjacent residential development, the plaintiff reoriented the range in 1999 at a cost of $1000. The lot was then annexed by Wesley Chapel. The town advised the plaintiff in 2007 that shooting ranges were not allowed in this residential zoning district. In 2007–08, the plaintiff improved the range at a cost of $15,000. In 2008, the town issued a notice of zoning violation, contending that the use was not lawfully established under the prior county zoning and was thus not a lawful nonconformity. Alternatively, the town contended that even if it were a lawful nonconformity, the 2008 improvements constituted an impermissible material alteration of the nonconformity. The board of adjustment upheld the zoning administrator's determination, but the trial court reversed.

The court held that the shooting range was a lawful nonconformity. The county ordinance did not specifically list "shooting ranges" as a regulated use. The ordinance provided that the list of uses should be liberally interpreted to include other uses with similar impacts and that unlisted uses that did not have similar impacts were prohibited. The town contended that the most nearly similar listed use was "privately-owned outdoor recreational facility." Since that use required a special use permit and the plaintiff did not secure such a permit from the county, the town contended that the use was not lawfully established and thus was not a lawful nonconformity. The court rejected the presumption that unlisted uses were prohibited, citing the common law principle that ambiguity should be resolved in favor of free use of property. The court held that since the ordinance did not expressly prohibit shooting ranges in this district, they should be presumed to be permitted.

The court also held that the 2007–08 improvements were not a material alteration of the shooting range. The ordinance defined "material alteration" to be a change of more than 50 percent of the replacement cost at the time of the alteration. The court held that the town erred in only considering the construction costs of the shooting range and that the calculation should have included the value of the land occupied by the range.

Amward Homes, Inc. v. Town of Cary, 206 N.C. App. 38, 698 S.E.2d 404 (2010), *aff'd by equally divided court*, 365 N.C. 305, 716 S.E.2d 849 (2011) [*stands without precedential value*]
Impact fees; Statutes of limitation

The town in 1999 adopted an adequate-public-school-facilities ordinance (APSFO). As a condition for approval of new residential developments, the ordinance required a certificate of adequate school capacity to serve the proposed development or a specified exemption from that requirement allowed for building in a low-population-density area or construction of affordable housing. The town subsequently approved several developments that included conditions requiring payment of a specified fee to the town for each building permit in order to comply with the APSFO. In 2003, the town amended the APSFO to explicitly allow payment of fees for APSFO compliance. The amended APSFO was repealed in 2004, but the repeal required continued payments within those developments approved subject to the ordinance. The plaintiff builders in one of the developments subject to the fee requirement brought this action in 2007 seeking (1) to have the APSFO declared beyond the town's delegated authority and unconstitutional, (2) a refund of the over $600,000 in fees paid out, and (3) attorney's fees and costs. The trial court held for the plaintiffs on all counts.

The court held that the imposition of the school impact fee was beyond the scope of power delegated to the town. The town had no authority to impose or accept the fees. The fact that they were imposed by a condition on permit approval rather than directly by ordinance provision was irrelevant.

On jurisdictional issues, the court held that the town's repeal of the APSFO did not moot the claims here, as the plaintiffs sought refund of fees paid and an injunction prohibiting continued fee charges. The court rejected the contention that the builders did not have standing because the fees were accepted by the developer as a condition of rezoning and subdivision approval for the development, noting that once accepted by the town the condition was imposed on the plaintiff builders. The court held that the two-month statute of limitations for challenging zoning ordinances did not apply because the APSFO was part of the subdivision ordinance rather than the zoning ordinance. The court held that the three-year statute of limitations for personal injuries applied to the claims brought under 42 U.S.C. § 1983 for alleged U.S. constitutional violations. However, the court found that this period did not begin to run until the fee was paid (rather than when the ordinance was adopted) and that each fee-payment acceptance constituted a continuing wrong by the town; the fee recovery thus could date back three years from the filing of the § 1983 claim. The court also concluded that claims for violation of the state constitution had no adequate state remedy or shorter statutory period of limitation, so the ten-year statute of limitations of G.S. 1-56 was applicable and the plaintiffs were thus entitled to recoupment of all fees paid.

The court rejected the contention that the developer's acceptance of the permit condition and the benefits of the development approval barred this challenge on estoppel grounds. The court found that the benefits of the approval ran to the developer, not the plaintiff individual builders, who acquired lots from the developer.

The court ruled that the collection of school impact fees violated substantive due process, since ultra vires acts are by definition unrelated to a valid state objective, and violated equal protection, as differential fees were applied to different developments and the plaintiffs had to continue paying fees not charged to similar developers after the ordinance was repealed. Given the constitutional violations, awarding attorney's fees was appropriate.

Meier v. City of Charlotte, 206 N.C. App. 471, 698 S.E.2d 704 (2010)
Interpretation; Statutes of limitation

The plaintiff challenged the city's interpretation of height limits and setbacks as applied to a residence being constructed on an adjacent lot. The Charlotte ordinance had a forty-foot height limit in the zoning district, specified how the height measurement was to be made, and allowed the maximum height to be exceeded if the side- and rear-yard setbacks were increased by one foot for each foot of building above forty feet. When the plaintiff questioned compliance with these regulations, the zoning staff met on site during the construction with representatives of the builder and the plaintiff to review the work and discuss how the zoning height limits would be applied. The builder provided site plans and architectural drawings for the project. The zoning administrator then mailed a letter on February 28 to the plaintiff's attorney and the builder, stating his interpretation of the height limit and how it applied to the subject project. The letter concluded that the height involved, with the proposed setback additions, would comply with the zoning ordinance. The letter also required that a sealed survey be submitted prior to issuance of a certificate of occupancy to confirm final construction compliance with the plans. The plaintiff acknowledged receipt of the letter in early March. In May, the sealed survey was submitted. The staff confirmed on May 20 that the structure was in zoning compliance. On May 23, the plaintiff appealed the interpretation to the board of adjustment. The board refused to hear the appeal, ruling that the February 28 letter was a formal determination by the staff and the ordinance required appeals to the board to be made within thirty days of receipt of that letter. The plaintiff contended that the thirty-day period did not begin to run until receipt and review of the survey.

The court found that the letter from the zoning administrator was a final determination on interpretation of the ordinance that could be appealed to the board of adjustment. It was made at the request of affected persons, made by the person authorized by the ordinance to make official interpretations, explained how the ordinance would be interpreted, and included a conclusion that if the project was built in accordance with the plans submitted, it would be in compliance with the ordinance. The letter was definitive and authoritative and was thus appealable. The as-built survey that was submitted later was to demonstrate compliance with this interpretation and was not, in and of itself, an interpretation of the ordinance. Thus, the time for appeal of the interpretation began to run upon receipt of the letter. Since the appeal was not timely under the ordinance, the board had no subject-matter jurisdiction to hear it.

Carolina Marina & Yacht Club v. New Hanover County Board of Commissioners, 207 N.C. App. 250, 699 S.E.2d 646 (2010), *review denied*, 365 N.C. 89, 706 S.E.2d 253 (N.C. 2011)
Mootness

The plaintiff applied for a special use permit to modify an existing commercial marina in a residential zoning district by adding a dry-stack storage facility. The county denied the special use permit, but on appeal the superior court overturned that decision and ordered that the permit be issued. A neighbor who opposed the project and had intervened in the judicial review appealed that decision. The county did not join in the appeal. The neighbor unsuccessfully sought a stay of the trial court's order and an injunction to prohibit permit issuance while she pursued the appeal. The county subsequently issued the special use permit. The appeals court held that the issuance of the permit mooted the appeal. Since the only issue on this appeal was the validity of the county's permit denial, subsequent issuance of the permit resolved that matter and made this appeal moot.

Cary Creek Ltd. Partnership v. Town of Cary, 207 N.C. App. 339, 700 S.E.2d 80 (2010), *review denied*, 365 N.C. 193, 707 S.E.2d 241 (2011)
Findings

The plaintiff challenged the denial of variances that would have allowed intermittent streams subject to the town's riparian-buffer requirements to be filled. The court held that while a superior court undertaking review in the nature of certiorari may not make new findings of fact, it may recite and synthesize the findings made by the decision-making board. The superior court should not review the evidence that may have supported a contrary finding, as the inquiry is limited to ascertaining whether there was substantial evidence to support the finding that was made. In this case, the court held that the findings set forth in the decision-making board's minutes (some eight paragraphs) were sufficient. Finally, as one of the standards for a variance is preserving substantial justice, it was appropriate for the board to consider the precedent that would have been established by granting a variance and to consider the fairness to those who had complied with the ordinance requirements.

MLC Automotive, LLC v. Town of Southern Pines, 207 N.C. App. 555, 702 S.E.2d 68 (2010), *review denied*, 365 N.C. 211, 710 S.E.2d 23 (N.C. 2011)
Vested rights

The plaintiffs were interested in developing an automotive sales park with multiple dealerships in the defendant town. They inquired as to the zoning of the property and were advised by the town that automobile sales were a permitted use on the property, provided all requisite permits were obtained. The plaintiffs then acquired the property, entered into a contract with an automobile company for a franchise on the site, and began to prepare site plans and applications. After the initial application (an "architectural compliance permit") was submitted, the town made comments and the plaintiff had revisions and discussions with neighbors underway. At this point citizens submitted a petition to rezone the property to a district that did not allow automobile sales as a permitted use. The plaintiff later submitted an application for an erosion-control permit and requested that the town treat a proposed site plan as a "zoning application." The town regulations and practice, however, provided for a "zoning permit" only as a unified permit approved concurrently with a building permit. Subsequently, the town approved the architectural plans but denied the erosion-control application. The town had also not acted on required water and sewer permits, driveway permits, or any site plan or building permits. At this point the town approved the rezoning petition and took no further action on pending applications as the use was no longer permitted in the newly applicable zoning district. As a result, the plaintiff's contract for the automobile dealership lapsed. The plaintiff contended that purchase of the property after receipt of letters from the town that the proposed use was permittable created a vested right. The plaintiff also argued that the town's actions leading to the loss of the automobile franchise constituted tortious interference with contract.

The court held that the plaintiffs had not established a common law vested right. The court confirmed that reliance on existing zoning is not sufficient to establish a vested right. Here, the town had zoning and a variety of specific required permits. Reliance must be on those specific approvals, not a letter from the town staff explaining the existing regulations. As none of the expenditures here were made in reliance on any of the required permits, there could be no common law vested right.

Also, there was no tortious interference with contract as there was no showing that the rezoning of the property was "without justification." The public objections to the proposed project and requested rezoning were based on the question of whether an intensive commercial use was appropriate for a site that was surrounded by residential uses on three sides and fronted a conservation area across the street on the fourth side. Consideration of the character of the district and the suitability and appropriateness of the site for particular uses is explicitly authorized as a reasonable consideration for zoning.

Templeton v. Town of Boone, 208 N.C. App. 50, 701 S.E.2d 709 (2010)
Standing; Statutes of limitation

Two property owners challenged the town's adoption of steep-slope and viewshed-protection ordinances as portions of the town's unified development ordinance. The trial court granted the town's motion to dismiss.

In order to establish standing to bring a constitutional challenge to an ordinance, a plaintiff must show an injury in fact or an immediate danger of injury as a result of enforcement of the challenged ordinance. As there was no allegation of any actual enforcement and only an allegation that property owned by the plaintiffs was affected by the ordinance, the dismissal of the constitutional claims for lack of standing was upheld.

The plaintiffs also brought a statutory claim regarding alleged improper procedures in adoption of the ordinances (including alleged changes to the map of affected areas after the notice of hearing, substantial changes in the text after the hearing, and a failure to analyze conformity with the comprehensive plan). The steep-slope provisions of the ordinance were only applicable to properties with a slope value of 30 percent or more. The complaint included no allegation that either plaintiff's property had such a slope. Therefore, those statutory challenges were also properly dismissed for lack of standing. The viewshed-protection provisions were only applicable to properties more than 100 feet above the nearest major traffic corridor and visible from such a corridor. One of the two plaintiffs did allege that their property was subject to the viewshed-protection provisions. This was sufficient to establish that the property of that plaintiff was directly and adversely affected by the ordinance, so that plaintiff had standing to make a statutory challenge of the viewshed ordinance.

The plaintiff who had standing to challenge the viewshed ordinance, however, did not join the complaint until more than two years after adoption of the ordinance. She alleged that she did not have notice that the ordinance was applicable to her until that time. The court held that the two-month statute of limitations was applicable even if the defendant failed to properly notify the plaintiff, so this complaint was properly dismissed.

Sapp v. Yadkin County, 209 N.C. App. 430, 704 S.E.2d 909 (2011)
Amendments; Conditional zoning; Discovery; Plan consistency; Recusal

The plaintiff neighbors challenged the county's rezoning of a ten-acre parcel from a Highway-Business to a Manufacturing-Industrial Conditional zoning district to allow construction of a new jail. The trial court granted a forty-five-day continuance on the county's motion for summary judgment but refused further continuances. The trial judge had also previously issued an order to the county to show cause why a writ of mandamus should not issue regarding county provision of adequate jail facilities.

The court held that there was no showing that an additional period for discovery was needed and noted that a hearing on a motion for summary judgment does not close the discovery hearing. The court found that while the trial judge had expressed an interest in prompt resolution of the jail issue, there was no evidence that he had a personal interest in the matter or any preference or opinion on the location of a new jail. Thus, there was no substantial evidence to support an allegation of bias. The court held that the facts that the planning-board minutes were not presented to the board of commissioners prior to their vote and that the planning-board minutes did not include a copy of their statement on plan consistency were irrelevant because the statutorily mandated written recommendation and statement on plan consistency from the planning board was itself before the board of county commissioners prior to their vote. Finally, the court held that a special use permit standard in the ordinance limiting correctional facilities within one mile of residential property was inapplicable as the rezoning was to a conditional zoning district that allowed this use rather than consideration of a special use permit.

CRLP Durham, LLP v. Durham City/County Board of Adjustment, 210 N.C. App. 203, 706 S.E.2d 317, *review denied*, 365 N.C. 348, 717 S.E.2d 744 (2011)

Interpretation; Records

In 2000, the county rezoned a parcel and approved its split into two parcels (one with a multifamily zoning and the other with an office-institutional zoning). The rezoning included a development plan (a mandatory part of the Durham rezoning) that included a cross-access connection provision that traffic from the office parcel be allowed to cross a portion of the multifamily parcel. The approved development plan included detailed designs for development of the multifamily parcel but only "future office development" for the second parcel. Later in 2000, the owner filed an access agreement limiting the cross-access to the second parcel to office use only. In 2005, the plaintiff purchased the multifamily parcel (including a completed apartment building); at that time the office parcel was still vacant. In 2007, the subsequent purchaser of the office parcel submitted a site plan to the county to secure approval for an apartment complex on the property. The plaintiff objected. The staff ruled that apartments were a permitted use in the applicable office zoning for this parcel and that the "office" designation on the approved development plan was suggestive of a future use but was not a binding element of the approved development plan. The staff further held that precluding cross-access to the proposed apartments pursuant to the access agreement would be inconsistent with the approved development plan. The board of adjustment upheld this staff interpretation. The trial court affirmed this decision.

The court noted that while the rezoning and development plan was approved under the ordinance in effect in 2000, that ordinance was replaced in 2006 by a unified development ordinance. While the general rule is that the board of adjustment should apply the ordinance in effect at the time of its decision, the record did not include the two ordinances and left it unclear whether the 2006 ordinance completely superseded the prior ordinance or left the prior ordinance applicable for those projects approved when it was in effect. As the record was void of evidence as to which ordinance was applicable, the court concluded that it was unable to examine the question of law as to the interpretation of the ordinance; it thus dismissed the appeal.

S.T. Wooten Corp. v. Board of Adjustment, 210 N.C. App. 633, 711 S.E.2d 158 (2011)

Interpretation

The plaintiff operated a concrete plant in Zebulon's extraterritorial jurisdiction. The defendant company wanted to add an asphalt plant at this site. The land was zoned "Heavy Industry," but the list of permitted uses for the district did not mention asphalt plants. After the defendant requested a zoning-determination letter, the zoning administrator issued a letter stating that an asphalt plant fell within the permitted uses described for the zoning district or was similar enough to be grouped with them. The defendant then secured necessary air quality, driveway, and sedimentation permits and a building permit and opened a portable asphalt plant on the site. Eight years after getting its initial zoning determination, the plaintiff notified the town that it intended to place a permanent asphalt plant on the site. The town responded that an asphalt plant was not specifically listed as a permitted use in this zoning district and that since it would have similar but greater impacts than those uses that were listed, the ordinance required a special use permit. The plaintiff contended that the town's initial determination that the use was permitted was binding and precluded a subsequent determination that a special use permit was required. The board of adjustment and the trial court held that the initial determination was not binding.

The court noted that while advisory letters are not binding, formal determinations are. The initial letter was a binding determination rather than an advisory letter, it concluded. The ordinance specially authorized the zoning administrator to make interpretations of the ordinance. The administrator's letter addressed a specific question of interpretation and included a clear interpretation that an asphalt plant was a permitted use. The fact that the letter included superfluous advice (that a site plan and building permit would be required prior to construction) did not render the interpretation any less binding on the question of whether the proposed use was permitted or not. The ordinance provided that appeals of the administrator's determinations go to the board of adjustment and specified that board appeals had to be made within thirty days of the date of the decision. The court thus concluded that the town's first determination that the asphalt plant was a permitted use was a binding and appealable zoning determination. As that determination was not appealed by the town, the town was bound by it and precluded from later making the different interpretation that a special use permit was required.

APAC-Atlantic v. City of Salisbury, 210 N.C. App. 668, 709 S.E.2d 390 (2011)

Nonconformities

The plaintiff proposed in 2007 to renovate its asphalt plant. The site of the plant had, however, been rezoned in 2001 and was nonconforming under the now-applicable zoning. The renovations involved shifting to new equipment that would allow for increased capacity, would allow for expanded use of recycled asphalt, and would reduce future operating costs. The zoning administrator denied site-plan approval for the renovation on the grounds that the renovation would be an impermissible change, enlargement, or expansion of the nonconformity. The board of adjustment upheld this determination and the trial court affirmed.

The court held that an increase in the scope, scale, or extent of a nonconforming use was an impermissible "enlargement" and that the increased plant capacity was thus a proper ground for denial of the site plan. The record also supported a conclusion that the renovation would improperly enlarge the commercial viability of the plant by reducing future operating costs. The court noted that as one of the functions of the board of adjustment is to interpret the zoning ordinance, some deference to the board's interpretation of its own code was appropriate.

Sanchez v. Town of Beaufort, 211 N.C. App. 574, 710 S.E.2d 350, *review denied*, 365 N.C. 349, 718 S.E.2d 153 (2011)

Historic preservation; Standing

A property owner in the Beaufort Historic District proposed to demolish a small cottage and replace it with a two-story residence. After several denials and mediation, the owner and the historic-preservation commission agreed to review a one-and-one-half-story structure. The plaintiff, who resided across the street, objected to the height of the proposed structure, contending it would block her views of the water and reduce her property value. The plaintiff agreed to reduce the height from the proposed twenty-nine feet to twenty-seven feet but contended that any height lower than this would not allow reasonable use of the property (considering minimum flood elevations and ceiling heights). The commission concluded that the maximum height should be twenty-four feet and therefore denied the certificate of appropriateness. On appeal, the board of adjustment determined that there was no substantial evidence in the record to support the twenty-four-foot height limit and ordered that an approval be issued. The superior court upheld the board of adjustment's decision.

The court affirmed, holding that the plaintiff had alleged sufficient special damages to have standing, as she lived directly across the street and had contended that approval would be inconsistent with historic-commission guidelines and would injure the value of her property due to the lost vista. The court held that there was insufficient evidence for the board to determine that a twenty-four-foot height limit was necessary to assure congruity with structures in the district. The commission must determine congruity contextually, the court found, considering the entire historic district. The evidence showed that residences closest to this site were twenty-six to thirty-five feet high. Further, the transcripts showed that commission members reached the twenty-four-foot requirement based on various calculations of what they considered feasible rather than upon any principle set by commission guidelines. Thus, the imposition of the twenty-four-foot height limit was arbitrary. As there was agreement that the public vista at street level would be obstructed by any structure over sixteen feet high, the applicable guideline regarding vista protection was clearly not a factor in the commission's decision and thus could not support the denial.

Wilson v. City of Mebane Board of Adjustment, 212 N.C. App. 176, 710 S.E.2d 403 (2011)
Vested rights

The plaintiff challenged the approval of a site plan and building permit for a commercial development adjacent to his residentially zoned lot, alleging that the approvals did not mandate a fifty-foot vegetated buffer as required by the city's unified development ordinance (UDO). The city and builder contended that the buffer was not required. The developer began discussions with the city about a commercial development and submitted a site plan for approval, which was subsequently amended several times. City staff advised the developer during the permit review that a waiver of the buffer requirement would be granted. However, the city adopted a new UDO prior to the plan's approval that made no provision for waiver of the buffer. The site plan and building permit were approved without a buffer requirement. The city and the developer contended that the developer had a common law vested right that did not include a buffer. The board of adjustment upheld the staff determination, as did the trial court.

The court held that the developer did not have a vested right and that the permit was void, as it did not include a requirement for the mandated buffer. To establish a common law vested right, a developer has the burden of establishing that it made substantial expenditures in good-faith reliance on a valid permit and would suffer detriment if required to comply with the amended ordinance. Here, the facts established that expenditures made prior to the adoption of the UDO were clearly made prior to site-plan approval and thus were not made in reliance on a valid approval. As the site-plan and permit approvals that were issued were in error, they were void *ab initio* and any expenditures in reliance on them could not serve as the basis of a vested right. Reliance also could not be made on city staff assurances that a waiver would be forthcoming, as such assurances do not amount to a formal determination or mandatory approval that can give rise to a vested right. The fact that the city may have subsequently amended the UDO in ways that would make the project permittable does not moot this case, as the evidence showed that the only approvals actually issued were made in error.

Wake Forest Golf & Country Club, Inc. v. Town of Wake Forest, 212 N.C. App. 632, 711 S.E.2d 816, *review denied*, 365 N.C. 359, 719 S.E.2d 21 (2011)
Estoppel; Open space

The plaintiffs owned and operated a golf course. The zoning for the tract allowed one home per acre. In 1998, the plaintiffs contracted to sell a sixteen-acre portion of the tract to a developer contingent upon approval of a planned-unit development (PUD) with thirty townhouses, six single-family homes, and a commercial area. In order to secure approval for the higher proposed density and to meet the mandated 25 percent open-space requirement for PUDs, the plaintiffs elected to designate the entire 149-acre golf course as open space in their special use permit application for PUD approval. The permit was approved with the express condition that the entire property was subject to the permit and its conditions. The townhouses were subsequently built, but the commercial area was not. Some years later the golf course experienced financial difficulties. The plaintiffs proposed converting the golf course to residential development and entered a contract for sale contingent upon approval of a development plan. Purchasers of townhouses within the PUD and neighbors sued the plaintiffs, contending that the proposal would violate promises to maintain a golf course on the site. A year after that suit was voluntarily dismissed, the plaintiffs applied for a modification to the special use permit to remove that portion of the property not required to meet the density, open-space, and other requirements of the ordinance related to the development in the PUD. The town board elected not to hear or consider the proposal to amend the special use permit. The plaintiffs brought suit to compel town action of the proposed special use permit modification. The trial court granted the town's motion for summary judgment.

The court of appeals upheld the town's refusal to consider and act upon the application. Following the rule established in *River Birch Associates v. City of Raleigh*, 326 N.C. 100, 388 S.E.2d 538 (1990), the court held that a city may refuse to consider a proposal to modify an approved permit when the permittee has taken advantage of the benefits secured by voluntarily depicting an area as open space in its plans. Here, the plaintiffs voluntarily designated the entire golf course as open space even though that substantially exceeded the ordinance's minimum open-space requirements and secured higher densities for their PUD. After building at these higher densities, the plaintiffs are estopped from attacking a condition they had proposed and the town had accepted. The town has the discretion to refuse to process an application for modification of the permit.

Premier Plastic Surgery Center, PLLC v. Board of Adjustment, 213 N.C. App. 364, 713 S.E.2d 511 (2011)
Signs; Variances; Vested rights

Plaintiff operated a medical facility in Matthews that included multiple businesses. When the lots were originally developed, there was a single drive into the property. A monument sign adjacent to the driveway listed the tenants in the development. Later a second driveway was installed some 500 feet away and around a curve from the initial drive. The plaintiff sought a permit for a second monument sign adjacent to the second drive. After being advised by the town staff that such a sign would not be permitted, the plaintiff engaged a sign contractor. The sign contractor secured a permit from the county staff, who administered the town ordinance, and erected the sign. One week after construction, the county staff revoked the permit due to inconsistency with the town ordinance. The plaintiff appealed the revocation to the town board of adjustment. The board denied the appeal and advised the plaintiff that he could appeal to superior court or seek a text amendment to allow such a second sign. The plaintiff sought a text amendment, which was denied. The plaintiff then sought a variance for the sign, which was denied.

The court held that granting a variance in this situation would not be contrary to the spirit and purpose of the ordinance. The statement of purpose of the town's sign code noted the need to protect the appearance of commercial properties, promote traffic safety, and allow for adequate and effective signage. The fact that the ordinance only allowed one sign for multitenant properties did not create a per se rule that a variance could not in any circumstances be allowed for a second sign. This variance is properly viewed as an area variance (amount of signage allowed) rather than a prohibited-use variance. The court held that the findings to support the denial were insufficient. Several were conclusory statements, and the remainder were mere conjecture unsupported by any evidence. Finally, the court held that the petitioner had no vested rights to the sign based on the initial permit. The petitioner did not appeal the determination that the permit was issued in error, so that finding was the law of the case. No vested rights can be established based on an erroneously issued permit that has been revoked, and the town was not estopped or barred by laches from the revocation.

McCrann v. Village of Pinehurst, 216 N.C. App. 291, 716 S.E.2d 667 (2011)
Special uses; Statutes of limitation

Neighbors challenged a special use permit issued for a "learning center." The town council voted to issue the permit on August 24. The following day, the neighbor left a voicemail message for the town, asking for a copy of the decision. The permit was formally issued by written order on August 30. A copy was faxed and mailed to the neighbor on that date. The neighbors filed a suit challenging the permit on September 30. The petitioner made only an informal, verbal request for a copy of the decision, which was not equivalent to a written request for a copy of the decision at the time of the hearing. The fact that the city professionally and courteously responded to the plaintiff's voicemail did not waive the statutory requirement for a timely appeal, so the deadline for filing for judicial review was thirty days from the date of filing the order. The appeal was filed thirty-one days after the order granting the permit was filed, so the court held that the appeal was not timely.

Cambridge Southport, LLC v. Southeast Brunswick Sanitary District, 218 N.C. App. 287, 721 S.E.2d 736 (2012)
Permit extension; Wastewater-capacity allocation

A developer proposed a townhouse development that would receive utility services from the defendant. In January 2006, the developer applied for a capacity allocation and paid impact fees totaling $264,000. The application stated the developer would have three years to complete the project, or the allocation would expire and the fees would be nonrefundable. The developer built the necessary infrastructure and some townhomes, but then in 2008 it went into default prior to project completion. The bank foreclosed, and the plaintiff acquired the property in late 2009. When the plaintiff sought to restart the project in 2010, it was advised that the prior utility allocation had expired, all prior payments had been forfeited, and the new allocation fee would be $648,000.

The court held that the Permit Extension Act of 2009 (S.L. 2009-406, as amended) was applicable. That law tolled the running of time periods for any development approval that was valid in the 2008–2011 period. The court rejected the contention that the utility allocation was only a contract for service and held this to be an approval covered by the statute. The court considered the express purpose of the law (facilitating completion of development projects stalled by the recession), the directive in the law for a liberal construction, and the provisions in the law directly addressing the impacts of permit extensions on utility-capacity allocations.

Fort v. County of Cumberland, 218 N.C. App. 401, 721 S.E.2d 350, *review denied*, 366 N.C. 401, 735 S.E.2d 180 (2012)

Interpretation; Schools; Standing

TigerSwan submitted a site plan for a firearms-training facility for military, law-enforcement, and security personnel. The project was proposed in a rural portion of the county. In addition to classrooms, the facility included multiple firing ranges. The property was in an agricultural zoning district that included as a permissible use "[s]chools, public, private, elementary or secondary." The zoning administrator approved the plan, classifying the business as a private school. Neighbors appealed that decision to the board of adjustment, citing environmental concerns and noting the noise from firing ranges and helicopters. The board found that the neighbors had standing and voted 3–2 to reverse the staff determination. However, given the statutory supermajority requirement in effect at the time of this decision, the staff determination was upheld.

The court first held that the neighbors had standing based on their allegation that the use was not in fact permitted by the ordinance and that the noise, potential contamination, and safety concerns would affect their property and property values. The court held that the limitation on lay testimony regarding property values set forth in G.S 160D-1402(j)(3) related to competent evidence in a quasi-judicial hearing, not the requirement for standing in G.S. 160D-1402(c). The court held that the type of facility proposed was not a permitted use. Inclusion of the terms "elementary or secondary" was intended to exclude other types of schools, particularly given the express intent of the agricultural district and the inclusion of business and commercial schools as a separate use in the ordinance. The court held the testimony of the planning director as to the original intent of the ordinance to be irrelevant, as would be testimony from a member of the board adopting the ordinance.

Town of Nags Head v. Cherry, Inc., 219 N.C. App. 66, 723 S.E.2d 156, *review denied*, 366 N.C. 386, 733 S.E.2d 85 (2012)

Beaches; Nuisances; Public-trust doctrine

As a result of storm damage, the defendant's beach cottage was disconnected from utilities and left on the ocean beach. The town sought to compel removal of the damaged structure as a public nuisance. The court held that the state government is the only body that can bring an action to enforce public-trust rights to freely use and enjoy the state's beaches. Because a principal aspect of the town's public-nuisance claim was that the damaged structure was blocking public access along the beach, only the state had standing to enforce these rights. The court also held that there were material questions of fact as to whether there was a reasonable likelihood of personal or property injury resulting from the damaged structure, so summary judgment on that issue was inappropriate. [Note: G.S. 160A-205 and 153A-145.3 were subsequently enacted to authorize cities and counties to enforce local ordinances to protect the public's right to use state ocean beaches.]

Orange County v. Town of Hillsborough, 219 N.C. App. 127, 724 S.E.2d 560 (2012)

Estoppel; Government uses; Permit conditions

The town approved the county's plans for an expansion of buildings in the courthouse complex conditioned upon submission of an acceptable plan for remote parking in order to meet the off-street parking requirements of the town's zoning ordinance. At the time of permitting, the parties envisioned a remote park-and-ride lot. At the completion of construction, the county concluded that the remote lot was not feasible and submitted an alternate parking plan, which the town rejected.

The court held that the town authority to apply zoning to the construction and use of a building includes the authority to require compliance with the parking requirements related to that building. However, the court found in a whole-record review that the county had presented an acceptable, satisfactory alternative for meeting the parking requirement, and thus the denial of the proposed modification of the parking condition was arbitrary and capricious. The court rejected the argument that the county's acceptance of the permit condition and subsequent construction estopped the county from challenging the permit condition, holding that because counties are subdivisions of the state, application of estoppel would impair mandated governmental functions and was thus inapplicable.

Templeton Properties, LP v. Town of Boone, 219 N.C. App. 266, 724 S.E.2d 604 (2012)
Quasi-judicial

The plaintiff was denied a special use permit to construct a medical clinic in a residential zoning district. The board of adjustment denied the permit. The court of appeals found that the decision had not specified the findings of fact to support the denial and remanded the case for entry of reviewable findings of fact. On remand, the board stated that it would allow oral arguments but would not accept new testimony. However, it then allowed seven citizens to speak in opposition, reiterating the facts they felt supported denial of the permit. The court held that this was, in effect, receipt of new evidence. The court held that this violated the terms of the ordinance as well as the plaintiff's due-process rights. The court again remanded the case to the board to make findings of fact based solely on the evidence presented at the original board hearings. The board of adjustment may hear legal arguments on remand but must not receive additional factual testimony or evidence.

Waste Industries USA, Inc. v. State, 220 N.C. App. 163, 725 S.E.2d 875, *review denied*, 366 N.C. 241, 731 S.E.2d 686 (2012)
Commerce Clause; Landfills; Vested rights

The state denied a permit for a regional solid-waste landfill proposed to be located in Camden County. The plaintiffs challenged G.S. 130A-295.6, adopted after a temporary moratorium on landfill permits, which established a number of specific standards for landfill siting, including height, capacity, and size limits and buffers from wildlife refuges, state game lands, and state parks. The court upheld the statute, finding there to be no discriminatory purpose against out-of-state waste and no improper incidental effect on interstate commerce. The court found that the plaintiff had no common law vested right since reliance on a valid permit is required and no state permit had been issued. The change in landfill-siting standards after a permit application had been submitted, but before any action had been taken on that application, was not a misuse of the political process that gave rise to any right to have the application considered based on the law at the time of application.

Patterson v. City of Gastonia, 220 N.C. App. 233, 725 S.E.2d 82 (2012)
Demolition; Enforcement; Hearings; Housing code; Statutes of limitation

The plaintiffs in this action were a husband, his wife, and their son. The city initiated housing-code-enforcement proceedings regarding twenty-one mobile homes owned by the husband and wife. The units were located on land leased by the parents. The city code provided that demolition could be ordered if the homes were unfit for human habitation and repairs would cost more than 50 percent of the value of the structures. The code-enforcement officer, after inspection, issued an emergency notice of violation and ordered the homes be brought into compliance within forty-eight hours. This was followed by an order directing violations to be corrected within thirty days. The plaintiffs' parents secured building permits to do so. Two months later, the city determined that repairs had not been made, served complaints on the plaintiffs, and set a hearing on the violations. After the hearing, the city issued an order to demolish all of the units unless they were brought into compliance within ten days. Upon receipt of a notice of intent to repair, the officer gave the plaintiffs thirty days to complete the repairs. Two months later, the city found the repairs had not been made, and the city council adopted resolutions ordering the homes demolished. Five months later, the city demolished six of the homes. The plaintiffs sued, alleging violation of due process and an inverse condemnation.

The court held that sovereign immunity does not apply to constitutional claims, so it was error to dismiss the due-process claim on that ground. However, this was harmless error because the plaintiffs were later allowed to amend their complaint to reassert that claim. The court held that failure to serve the son with the notices, orders, and complaints sent to the parents did not violate due process. The parents were the record owners of the units, and there was no evidence presented from the public record that the son had any ownership interests. The city had no obligation to go beyond public records to ascertain ownership.

The court held that failure to give the plaintiffs notice and an opportunity to be heard before the city council prior to passing the ordinance of demolition was not a due-process violation. The plaintiffs signed a notice of intent to repair instead of appealing the initial order of the officer to demolish the units. They chose not to appeal the supplemental order to the board of adjustment to seek additional repair time. They failed to seek injunctive relief to restrain enforcement. These statutory opportunities for administrative appeals and judicial relief provided an adequate remedy at state law to address any alleged injury, and failure to exercise those opportunities barred a constitutional claim.

The court held that the provision in G.S. 160D-1203 that an owner be given a reasonable opportunity to bring a house into code conformance does not mandate an evidentiary hearing prior to an order of demolition. Here, after the officer issued an order of demolition, the plaintiffs were given a hearing before the officer on the question of whether repairs could be made at a reasonable cost and further had the opportunity to appeal that matter to the board of adjustment. The court held that sovereign immunity barred the tort claims and that an inverse-condemnation claim for loss of the mobile homes was barred because mobile homes are considered personal property.

Fisher v. Town of Nags Head, 220 N.C. App. 478, 725 S.E.2d 99, *appeal dismissed*, 366 N.C. 244, 731 S.E.2d 166 (2012)

Beaches; Condemnation; Public-trust doctrine

As part of a ten-mile beach-nourishment project, the town sought voluntary easements from oceanfront owners and, in the same letter, notified them that if the easements were not granted, the town would condemn an easement. The letter further informed the owners that no compensation would be paid for the easement, even if condemnation was used. The plaintiff owners sought injunctive relief prior to condemnation.

The court held that the letter provided adequate notice on an intent to condemn. While not precisely meeting the statutory notice requirements, the letter clearly indicated the proposed action and cited the statutory provisions for condemnation in bold type. The general description of the dry-sand beach where the sand was to be pumped was deemed to be adequate. The court held that a monetary payment was not necessarily due, as the value added by the beach nourishment could be sufficient compensation, but it noted that the issue should be addressed in a condemnation hearing, not in this action for a preliminary injunction.

Sanford v. Williams, 221 N.C. App. 107, 727 S.E.2d 362, *review denied*, 366 N.C. 246, 731 S.E.2d 144 (2012)

Enforcement; Exhaustion; Restrictive covenants

The defendant constructed a detached carport. The building and zoning permits required a five-foot side-yard setback. When the plaintiff, the adjacent owner, complained that the carport as constructed violated the zoning ordinance, the town issued a verbal stop order and asked the defendant to submit a survey. After receiving the survey, the city took no further action. The plaintiff brought this action to enforce restrictive covenants and to compel city enforcement of the zoning setbacks.

The covenants allowed a single-family residence and a "garage" on the property. The court held that a carport was within the ordinary or customary meaning of a garage and was thus permitted. The court held that the covenant's ten-foot side-yard requirement for a "home" did not apply to a detached carport. Because the plaintiff did not appeal the issuance of the zoning permit to the board of adjustment, he failed to exhaust his administrative remedies on that issue, and thus the trial court lacked subject-matter jurisdiction to hear it.

MCC Outdoor, LLC v. Town of Wake Forest, 222 N.C. App. 70, 729 S.E.2d 694 (2012)
Appellate procedures; Signs

The plaintiff owned a billboard that had been in place for forty-five years. The sign was situated on leased property, with an annual lease renewable for up to ten years. The property was sold near the end of the ten-year period, and the new owner obtained a special use permit for a shopping center. A condition on the permit was removal of the billboard "as soon as possible with no new lease or lease extension allowed." At the termination of the lease, it was not renewed, and the plaintiff removed the sign at the owner's direction. The plaintiff sued the town for just compensation for the sign. The critical issue was whether the sign had been "removed or caused to be removed" by the town, thus triggering the compensation requirement under G.S. 136-131.1. There was conflicting evidence on whether the permit requirement was the sole reason for nonrenewal of the sign lease, so the court held the case not to be appropriate for summary judgment given a genuine issue of material fact.

American Towers, Inc. v. Town of Morrisville, 222 N.C. App. 638, 731 S.E.2d 698 (2012), *review denied,* 366 N.C. 603, 743 S.E.2d 189 (2013)
Special uses

The plaintiff applied for a special use permit to erect a telecommunication tower in an "industrial management" zoning district. The permit was denied on the grounds that it was not in harmony with the surrounding neighborhood (some of which was residential, while other portions were undeveloped), was inconsistent with the land use plan (which suggested the property may be rezoned to residential in the future), and failed to show that the project would not substantially injure neighboring property values. The court held that the first two grounds did not support permit denial. Authorization of a special use permit for a particular use in a zoning district establishes a prima facie case of harmony with the surrounding neighborhood. The proposal was consistent with the binding zoning plan by virtue of being in the industrial-management zoning district, which controls over a goal in a nonbinding land use plan. However, the applicant failed to produce a site-specific analysis demonstrating that the tower would not harm neighboring property values, so the permit denial was upheld.

Russell v. Donaldson, 222 N.C. App. 702, 731 S.E.2d 535 (2012)
Restrictive covenants

The court held that short-term rentals of single-family homes did not violate a covenant prohibiting use of the property for "business or commercial use."

MNC Holdings, LLC v. Town of Matthews, 223 N.C. App. 442, 735 S.E.2d 364 (2012)
Appellate procedures; Interpretation; Nonconformities

The plaintiff operated a medical-waste incinerator. When the town annexed the facility in 1991, it rezoned the property from an industrial to a residential zoning district, making the facility a legal nonconforming use. The plaintiff sought an approval to allow modifications to the structure in order to comply with federal and state air-quality regulations. The ordinance prohibited structural alterations for buildings housing nonconforming uses except those "required by law or an order from the [building inspector] . . . to ensure the safety of the structure." The plaintiff contended that this allowed alterations to comply with environmental laws, while the town contended that only modifications related to building safety were allowed. The court agreed that the plain reading of the provision allowed alterations "when required by law" in general. Moreover, because the plaintiff was compelled by state law to make these alterations, the provision should have been construed liberally to allow the required changes. The court also dismissed a challenge to the court of appeals' jurisdiction based on a failure to follow the rules of appellate procedure regarding service of the notice of appeal. (The notice had been provided to the plaintiff by email.) The court held that an error in service is nonjurisdictional, the plaintiff had actual notice, and the failure here was neither a gross violation nor a substantial failure.

Erthal v. May, 223 N.C. App. 373, 736 S.E.2d 514 (2012), *review denied*, 366 N.C. 421, 736 S.E.2d 761 (2013)
Restrictive covenants

The court held that boarding up to ten horses did not violate the restrictive covenants in an equine-community subdivision that limited uses to single-family residences and accessory buildings associated with pasturing horses.

Morgan v. Nash County, 224 N.C. App. 60, 735 S.E.2d 615 (2012), *review denied*, 366 N.C. 561, 738 S.E.2d 379 (2013)
Contract zoning; Plan consistency; Standing

The City of Wilson and several neighboring landowners challenged a Nash County rezoning of a 147-acre tract from a rural-commercial and residential zoning district to a general-industrial district. The property had been acquired by a not-for-profit economic-development corporation (of which the county was a member) to facilitate the recruitment of a large poultry-processing plant. The new zoning district would accommodate such a plant, along with a variety of other industrial uses. If a poultry-processing plant were to be sited on this parcel, it would also require a hatchery and land for a spray field for the processing plant's treated wastewater. The not-for-profit acquired a site two miles away that could be used as a hatchery and another site some miles away that could be used as a spray field (potential uses that could be undertaken on those sites without a rezoning).

The court held that the city did not have standing to challenge the county rezoning. The city contended the spray field proposed to be used by a poultry-processing plant was within the watershed for the town's water-supply source and would threaten the quality of its water supply. The court noted that the site for the potential spray field had not been rezoned and that such a use could be lawfully undertaken where proposed regardless of the challenged rezoning. Thus, the city's alleged injury would not be redressed by an invalidation of the rezoning. Further, given that any spray field would have to comply with state and federal effluent regulations, harm to the city's water supply was conjectural or hypothetical. While owning adjacent property is not necessary for standing, proximity is a factor, and here the city's property was 3.5 miles away from the rezoned property and too remote for standing purposes.

The county adopted a statement of plan consistency and reasonableness concurrently with the rezoning. The court held that the statutory mandate to adopt a statement "prior to" adoption of a zoning amendment allows contemporaneously adopting both the required statement and the amendment. The court held that the rezoning did not constitute illegal contract zoning. The fact that the county was recruiting a potential user of the site and that this particular use was known to all parties does not in itself constitute contract zoning. There was no bilateral or reciprocal agreement with a potential user and no obligation to sell the land to a potential user. The county was explicitly aware that a variety of other industrial uses would be authorized by the rezoning, as each board member was provided a list of all permitted uses, and the list was read aloud by staff at the rezoning hearing.

Fairway Outdoor Advertising, LLC v. Town of Cary, 225 N.C. App. 676, 739 S.E.2d 579 (2013)
Appeals; Enforcement; Interpretation; Signs

The Cary Land Development Ordinance required nonconforming pole signs to be removed at the end of an amortization period. The town staff sent the plaintiff a notice that the provision applied to a particular sign and that it must be removed. The plaintiff appealed this determination to the board of adjustment, which held that the appeal to the board was timely, but that the sign was in violation and must be removed. The board upheld the civil penalties that had been imposed.

While both the "Sign" and the "Violations and Enforcement" sections of the ordinance had specific provisions regarding administrative appeals, the ordinance provision involved in this case did not make cross-reference to those sections. Therefore, the ordinance provisions on "general appeals" was applicable, not the provisions in those more-specific sections. The general-appeals section allows appeals to the board of adjustment within thirty days of "the contested action." Because the appeal to the board was not filed until a year after receipt of official notice that the sign was in violation, the appeal was not timely. The court thus held it improper to vacate the civil penalties. The court also held that, because the ordinance provided that the planning director "may" approve an unlisted use, and there was no evidence of abuse of this discretion, it was improper for the trial court to order the sign approved as an unlisted use.

Hillsboro Partners, LLC v. City of Fayetteville, 226 N.C. App. 30, 738 S.E.2d 819, *review denied*, 367 N.C. 236, 748 S.E.2d 544 (2013)

Demolition; Enforcement; Estoppel; Takings

The plaintiff purchased property that included a building that had been damaged by a fire. The city notified the plaintiff that the building was unsafe. After a hearing, which the plaintiff did not attend, the city ordered the structure repaired or demolished. The city subsequently adopted an ordinance ordering demolition. The plaintiff then sought a permit for demolition. Some four months after adoption of the demolition ordinance, the plaintiff contended that new inspections showed the building to be safe. The city nonetheless demolished the structure.

The court held that the demolition notice, hearing, and ordinance-adoption process mandated by state law and followed by the city was quasi-judicial in nature rather than administrative. That process had resulted in a substantive decision that the structure was unsafe, and that determination had not been appealed. That determination was therefore the identical issue raised in the current appeal and had been litigated in the quasi-judicial process. The plaintiff had a full and fair opportunity to contest it at that time, and a final order that could have been appealed was made. As the underlying facts were unchanged, the plaintiff could not use its own failure to adequately inspect the property as a means to avoid the prior determination. Because the determination that the building was unsafe was binding, the building was a nuisance threatening public health and safety. Its removal was a proper exercise of the police power, and no compensation under the Takings Clause was required.

Russell v. N.C. Department of Environment and Natural Resources, 227 N.C. App. 306, 742 S.E.2d 329, *review denied*, 367 N.C. 253 (2013)

Evidence; Liability; Septic tanks

Staff from the Carteret County Health Department inspected two adjacent lots and issued permits for septic tanks on them. Several years later, a new purchaser of the lots requested issuance of a new septic-tank permit for a single residence on the combined lot. An inspector revisited the site and made a visual inspection, did not conduct new soil tests, and issued a new permit. The owners installed a modular home and septic system on the site. The system immediately failed. Despite adding fill dirt, the system continued to fail. A reinspection determined that the soil conditions on the site were inconsistent with those noted in the original inspection and were in fact unsuitable for septic systems.

The court concluded that expert testimony was not required to show that the initial inspection breached the professional standard of care in this negligence action. The evidence clearly showed that the inspector either performed the soil tests inaccurately (there was no soil of the type indicated in the report on the subject property) or that he incorrectly tested the adjacent lot, where such soil was present. This failure is within the "common knowledge of laypersons" regarding the standard of care required. The court upheld a damage award based on the cost of replacement lots less the remaining value of the current property.

The court found that the application and submissions from the applicant, along with the staff analysis and testimony, established a prima facie case that the standards for the special use permit had been met. The six neighbors who testified in opposition primarily stated concerns about the maintenance of an existing building on the lot, which was unrelated to the proposed tower. Their other concerns about health impacts were speculative and unsupported by any documentary or testimonial evidence. So the court reversed and remanded with instructions to grant the permit.

Mount Ulla Historical Preservation Society, Inc. v. Rowan County, 232 N.C. App. 436, 754 S.E.2d 237 (2014)
Reapplication

In 2005, Rowan County denied a special use permit for a 1350-foot-tall radio tower because the tower posed an unacceptable air-safety hazard to a nearby private airport. In 2010, the county granted a special use permit for a 1200-foot radio tower on the same site. The plaintiff appealed the issuance of the 2010 permit. The court held that the permit must be denied because res judicata precludes consideration of the same claim between the same parties in a quasi-judicial matter unless the specific facts or circumstances that led to the prior decision have changed to the extent that the original rationale for the decision is no longer viable and the material changes amount in essence to consideration of a new claim. Whether res judicata applies is a question of law subject to de novo review, but whether a particular application demonstrates a material change in the original application is a factual question subject to a whole-record review. Although the proposed tower in the 2010 application was 150 feet shorter, the record before the board did not indicate that this would undermine the reasoning behind the original denial. In both hearings the record produced evidence favoring and opposing the towers on air-safety grounds, and there was no evidence in the current record indicating that the grounds for the original denial were vitiated by this reduction in height.

Patmore v. Town of Chapel Hill, 233 N.C. App. 133, 757 S.E.2d 302, *review denied*, 367 N.C. 519, 758 S.E.2d 874 (2014)
Due process; Preemption; Scope of authority

The town adopted a neighborhood-conservation overlay zoning district. A major land use concern in the neighborhood was the overcrowding, noise, garbage, and traffic generated by the overcrowding of rental homes occupied by students. In addition to limits on building height and size, the zoning restrictions limited parking in the district to four cars per residential lot. The plaintiff owned rental housing in the district and was cited for excess parking.

The court held that inclusion of the parking limit was not a substantive-due-process violation because it bears a rational relationship to a legitimate governmental objective. The court found the town's evidence that the number of cars parked at a residence yielded a reasonable approximation of how many people were living at the property to provide a rational basis for its use to prevent over-occupancy of rental dwellings. Given a transient student population and landlord control of occupancy in leases, citing the owner for violations was likewise deemed reasonable. Because this was a zoning regulation addressing the land use problem of over-occupancy, the regulation was not preempted by statutes regarding regulation of parking in public vehicular areas. The court held that it was appropriate to apply the G.S. 160A-4 provisions for a broad construction of G.S. 160D-701 because the regulation was reasonably related to the statutorily approved purposes of regulating population density and traffic congestion.

Royal Oak Concerned Citizens Ass'n v. Brunswick County, 233 N.C. App. 145, 756 S.E.2d 833 (2014)

Appellate procedures; Immunity

The plaintiffs challenged a rezoning that would accommodate the expansion of a landfill in their community. The plaintiffs sought to depose the county manager and a former county commissioner. The defendant sought a protective order prohibiting the depositions, claiming legislative and quasi-judicial immunity provided a testimonial privilege. The trial court granted conditions protecting that privilege for the county commissioner, but not for the manager (reserving judgment on whether the manager could assert the privilege). That decision was appealed to the court of appeals. When the plaintiffs sought an order compelling the deposition of the manager, the trial court ordered the deposition, finding the prior ruling to be a nonappealable interlocutory order. The defendants contended that the order affected a substantial right as was immediately appealable. The court held that while assertion of legislative or quasi-judicial immunity and a resultant testamentary privilege were substantial rights, this appeal was not ripe because the trial court had not yet issued a final ruling on whether the manager could assert that privilege. The defendant is free to make good-faith objections at the deposition regarding the privilege. Until such an objection is made and the trial court rules on the scope of the legislative privilege, the issue is not properly before the court.

PBK Holdings, LLC v. County of Rockingham, 233 N.C. App. 353, 756 S.E.2d 821, *appeal dismissed*, 367 N.C. 788, 766 S.E.2d 658 (2014)

Commerce Clause; Equal protection; Landfills; Preemption

The plaintiffs challenged provisions added to the zoning section of the county's unified development ordinance that regulated "high impact" land uses. The ordinance was amended to delete requirements for special use permits for these uses and add provisions allowing the uses to be addressed through conditional zoning. The ordinance established five classes of high-impact uses, with more-intensive uses requiring greater setbacks and more-stringent reviews. "Local" landfills and "regional" landfills (the terms being undefined in the ordinance) were placed in different classes. The plaintiff contended that this distinction violated the Equal Protection Clause and the Commerce Clause and that several locational restrictions in the ordinance were preempted by state law.

The court upheld the ordinance on all counts. The court applied standard dictionary definitions to the terms *local* and *regional* and concluded there was a rational basis to consider the latter a larger and more intensive use that would have greater impacts on surrounding properties. Even if the uses were similarly situated, there was a rational basis for differential regulations. The court held that the local-regional distinction made no facial distinction between in-state and out-of-state waste generation and that more-stringent restrictions for regional landfills were based on greater impact from a more-intensive use rather than on whether the waste crossed state lines. Thus, the court found no Commerce Clause violation. The court found that restrictions on floodplain locations for landfills were not preempted because G.S. 130A-309.09C(c) expressly allows stricter local ordinances. Further, a county restriction on driveway locations is not a regulation of vehicular traffic preempted by state law.

Templeton Properties, LP v. Town of Boone, 234 N.C. App. 303, 759 S.E.2d 311 (2014), *aff'd per curiam by equally divided court*, 368 N.C. 82, 772 S.E.2d 239 (2015) [*stands without precedential value*]
Interpretation; Special uses

This case challenged the town's denial of a special use permit for a medical clinic. The site had previously been used as a small church in a mostly single-family neighborhood. The town denied the permit, concluding that the proposed clinic was not in harmony with the area, given the size of the building, the amount of parking, the lighting for parking, and the volume and timing of the traffic expected to be generated. The court held the definition of the area within which to apply the harmony standard to be a question of law subject to de novo review; however, the application of that standard to the specific facts was a factual determination subject to a whole-record review, rendering the overall determination on harmony a mixed question of law and fact. The court held that the town board properly applied a contextual definition of the term *area* that is inherently fact-specific, so the board properly considered proximity, topography, road curves, and road alignments. The court agreed that the "legislative finding" rule from *Woodhouse v. Board of Commissioners*, 299 N.C. 211, 216, 261 S.E.2d 882, 886 (1980), provides that inclusion as a potential special use establishes a prima facie showing of entitlement to the permit, but that is rebuttable by opponents producing substantial evidence that the standards are not met at a particular site. The court found there was ample evidence in this case to show a lack of harmony with the surrounding area, and the denial of the permit was upheld.

High Rock Lake Partners, LLC v. N.C. Department of Transportation, 234 N.C. App. 336, 760 S.E.2d 750 (2014)
Attorney's fees

The plaintiffs successfully challenged the imposition of conditions on a driveway permit issued in connection with a proposed subdivision near Salisbury. The courts eventually held that the Department of Transportation had exceeded its statutory authority in imposing the conditions. The plaintiffs then sought attorney's fees under G.S. 6-19.1, which allows attorney's fees to be awarded in actions against a state agency if the court finds that the agency acted without substantial justification and the award would not be unjust. The trial court denied the motion for fees. The court held the decision to award fees in these circumstances to be within the discretion of the trial court. The court noted that the trial court was not required to award fees in this situation. The court held that even if the Department of Transportation had acted without substantial justification (which the trial court did not find), there was no showing that the trial court had abused its discretion in denying an award of fees.

Swan Beach Corolla, LLC v. County of Currituck, 234 N.C. App. 617, 760 S.E.2d 302 (2014)
Exhaustion; Vested rights

The plaintiffs acquired 1400 acres in the Carova Beach area of the Currituck Outer Banks in 1966. The land at that time, and at the time of the litigation, was unserved by public roads. In 1969, the plaintiffs secured approval of a subdivision. The plat identified some 577 residential lots and 6 lots as business areas. The county had no zoning ordinance in effect at the time. Between 1968 and 1971, the plaintiffs spent $425,000 on the overall project. Zoning was adopted in 1971, with all of the plaintiffs' land placed in a residential-agricultural district that allowed only limited business uses. Similar zoning was applied in an updated ordinance adopted in 1975. In 1989, a unified development ordinance was adopted, and the property was zoned for uses that would not permit the business and commercial uses intended by the plaintiffs. In 2004, the plaintiffs made their initial application for a commercial use of the property, which was to include a convenience store, restaurant, real-estate office, and post office. The plaintiffs were advised by county staff that such uses were not permitted. The plaintiffs contended that they had a vested right to the business use. The county disagreed. No appeals were made to the board of adjustment on the matter. In 2012, this suit was filed, claiming a vested right and alleging equal-protection violations (contending that other businesses were allowed) and religious discrimination (some individual plaintiffs were Jewish).

The court held that the staff decision regarding the vested right claim did not have to be appealed to the board of adjustment. If the claim involved an interpretation of the ordinance, an appeal to the board of adjustment would be a prerequisite for judicial review. The ordinance clearly did not allow the business use, so there was no interpretation issue, only a constitutional claim to a vested right. As the board of adjustment cannot adjudicate a constitutional claim, there was no requirement for an appeal to the board and thus no failure to exhaust administrative remedies.

With a motion to dismiss under Rule 12(b)(6), the facts alleged are assumed to be true and are construed liberally. Given this, the court held that there were sufficient allegations of substantial expenditures subsequent to plat approval and prior to zoning adoption to sufficiently plead a claim for a common law vested right. Likewise, it was improper to dismiss constitutional claims regarding substantive due process and equal protection, as there is no jurisdiction for the board of adjustment regarding constitutional claims, and sovereign and governmental immunity are not defenses to these claims. The court held that it was proper to dismiss claims of nonuniform property taxation because there was no allegation of nonuniform taxation.

Atkinson v. City of Charlotte, 235 N.C. App. 1, 760 S.E.2d 395 (2014)
Amendments; Plan consistency

The city considered a text amendment to the zoning ordinance proposed by Queens College and others. The proposed amendment exempted parking decks constructed as accessories to an institutional land use from the floor-area-ratio requirements in single-family and multifamily zoning districts. The planning staff made a written statement that the amendment was consistent with the city's adopted policies, was reasonable, and was in the public interest. The planning commission's zoning committee unanimously recommended adoption, and their recommendation included a statement on plan consistency. The city council unanimously approved the statement of consistency and the proposed amendment. The plaintiff neighbor contended that the adopted statement was inadequate and that a recommendation from less than the entire planning commission was insufficient.

The court held the consistency statement adopted by the council to be inadequate. It contained only the conclusion that the proposed amendment "is found to be consistent with adopted policies and to be reasonable and in the public interest." At a minimum, the statement must include a description of plan consistency and an explanation as to why it is reasonable and in the public interest. Here, the statement adopted merely tracked the conclusory language of the statute and could not reasonably be said to include any such explanation. Accordingly, the amendment to the ordinance was void.

Osborne v. Town of Nags Head, 235 N.C. App. 121, 760 S.E.2d 766 (2014)
Procedures; Voting majority

The owner of two adjoining lots secured a variance in 1997 from the town to construct a shared driveway. (Given the topography of the lot and setbacks, the board had concluded separate driveways were not feasible.) In 2012, the plaintiff contracted to acquire one of the lots, contingent upon securing a variance for a single driveway. The plaintiff applied for a new variance for a separate driveway, which was denied on the basis that the shared driveway authorized by the 1997 variance could still be used. The owner of the adjacent lot then refused to enter a cross-easement for a shared driveway. The plaintiff then submitted a motion to reconsider denial of the variance based on this new evidence. The board voted 3–2 in favor of denying the motion to reconsider, but the board concluded that a four-fifths majority was required and thus the motion to deny reconsideration had failed. The board then heard the matter and denied the variance.

The court conducted a de novo review of the legal question of what majority was required under the statute. The court held that G.S. 160D-406(i) clearly requires a four-fifths majority to grant a variance and a simple majority to decide any other matter. Thus, only a simple majority was required to decide the motion to reconsider. As the motion to reconsider was actually denied by majority vote, the board had no jurisdiction to take up the variance.

Etheridge v. County of Currituck, 235 N.C. App. 469, 762 S.E.2d 289 (2014)

Spot zoning

Plaintiff neighbors challenged the rezoning of a parcel previously used as a granary from an agricultural to a conditional heavy-manufacturing district. The site was surrounded on three sides by land zoned for agriculture and on the fourth side by land zoned for general business. The landowner sought the rezoning to accommodate a recycling center to collect, stockpile, and sell scrap metal, rock, concrete, and dirt. The planning board recommended denial on the grounds that the rezoning was inconsistent with the current rural zoning classification and the county's comprehensive land use plan. After adoption of the rezoning, the plaintiffs contended that this was illegal spot zoning and sought attorney's fees and costs under G.S. 6-21.7.

The county conceded that this was spot zoning but contended it was reasonable. The county did not dispute that the absence of plan consistency and the small size of the parcel rezoned weighed against reasonableness, but it contended that the benefits outweighed the detriments and that the proposed uses were consistent with uses allowed on adjacent properties. The court found that the purported benefits were not supported by any evidence presented at the hearing. To the contrary, the court noted that a recycling center only provided generalized benefit with no specific connection to the surrounding rural community. The vast majority of those speaking at the hearing opposed the project, two real-estate professionals contended that the use would harm adjoining-property values, the sheriff expressed concerns that similar businesses had experienced increases in crime, and the N.C. Department of Natural and Cultural Resources expressed concern about the project's effects on two nearby historic properties. The county failed to make a clear showing that the benefits of the rezoning outweighed its detriments. The court similarly concluded that the change in districts from the least intensive to the most intensive use district, along with a lack of any indication that the project was designed to be integrated into the surrounding area, was inconsistent with the surroundings.

As for attorney's fees, G.S. 6-21.7 makes award of attorney's fees permissible in the court's discretion if the local government acts outside the scope of its authority and mandatory if the government abuses its discretion. The court held that while spot zoning is outside the scope of the county's authority, acting outside the scope of authority is not always an abuse of discretion. To be an abuse of discretion, the action must have been so arbitrary that it could not have been the result of a reasoned decision. Here, the court noted that the county board explicitly considered the *Chrismon* factors and that there was information before the board to suggest those factors were met (see *Chrismon v. Guilford County*, 322 N.C. 611, 370 S.E.2d 579 (1988)). Although the court reached a contrary conclusion, the board's action was not so unreasonable as to be an abuse of discretion.

Fort v. County of Cumberland, 235 N.C. App. 541, 761 S.E.2d 744, *review denied*, 367 N.C. 798, 766 S.E.2d 688 (2014)

Interpretation; Judicial review

Neighboring-property owners challenged the permitting of a weapons- and firearm-safety training facility. Most of the activity on the site involved outdoor gun ranges. The zoning ordinance provided that if a use was not specifically addressed in the terms of the ordinance, the standards for the land use that was "most closely related" to that use applied. As this particular use was not specifically addressed in the ordinance, the county determined the use "Recreation/Amusement Outdoor (with mechanized vehicle operations)" had the most-similar impacts. As this was a permitted use, the project was approved. Neighboring-property owners contended that the most similar use was "Schools," which was not a permitted use in this zoning district.

The court conducted a de novo review of the interpretation, noting that it must consider, but is not bound by, the board of adjustment's interpretation. The court held the intent of the adopting board to be critical and in that context noted that the ordinance expressly stated that all uses of property are allowed as a matter of right except where the ordinance specifically provided otherwise. The court held that the board of adjustment properly applied the plain and ordinary meaning of *vocational school*. Because the facility provided training to existing members of a profession to practice and refine their skill levels, with little classroom instruction, this use did not fall within the meaning of a vocational school. The court held that a whole-record review was appropriate to determine whether there was substantial evidence in the record to support a conclusion that this use was most nearly similar in impacts to an outdoor recreation activity with mechanized vehicles. Given evidence of the board's consideration of noise, traffic, and safety for neighboring properties, the board's determination was affirmed.

Shearl v. Town of Highlands, 236 N.C. App. 113, 762 S.E.2d 877 (2014)

Nonconformities; Record on appeal; Zoning maps

In 1983, the property in this litigation was zoned for commercial and residential use, with the commercial district running 230 feet from the highway centerline and the rear portion of the property zoned for residential use. The 1988 official zoning map showed the commercial-district boundary at 230 feet. In 1990, the town adopted a new zoning ordinance and map. The town contended that the 1990 map reduced the depth of the commercial zoning along the highway from 230 feet to 150 feet. The petitioner acquired the property in 1993. The plat recorded in conjunction with the petitioner's purchase reflected that revised boundary line, and the town submitted a 1996 zoning map showing the revised line. In 2009, the town issued a notice of violation for activity within the area allegedly removed from the commercial district in 1990. The board of adjustment held that the burden of proof was on the petitioner to establish that his use was a lawful nonconformity prior to 1990 and upheld the violation on that basis.

However, the 1990 official zoning map and all copies were lost, and they were not produced at trial. The court noted that state law requires the city to maintain an official copy of all ordinances, which includes the zoning map since it is a part of the zoning ordinance. While the burden is normally on a landowner to establish the existence of a valid nonconforming use, that was not possible in this case because the 1990 map was not available when the petitioner acquired the property in 1993. So the court vacated the ruling and remanded the case. The court held that on remand, the burden is on the town to establish that the 1990 ordinance moved the zoning-district line, and the petitioner can present rebuttal evidence. The plat submitted is not a zoning map and would not in itself have greater weight than the 1988 official map, which will be conclusive in the absence of new evidence regarding the 1990 amendment.

Town of Black Mountain v. Lexon Insurance Co., 238 N.C. App. 180, 768 S.E.2d 302 (2014), *review denied*, 368 N.C. 249, 771 S.E.2d 307 (2015)

Performance guarantees; Statutes of limitation; Subdivisions

Buncombe County approved several subdivisions for which the defendant issued performance bonds to guarantee completion of required infrastructure. The subdivisions were later annexed into the Town of Black Mountain. The county assigned the bonds to the town. When the companies developing the subdivisions failed and the required improvements were not completed, the town sought payment of the bonds. The defendant bond company refused to pay, contending that neither the county nor the town had standing—the county having lost jurisdiction for subdivision-ordinance enforcement upon annexation of the property and the bonds not being assignable to the town.

The court held that the county did not have jurisdiction after annexation and thus had no standing to call the bonds. However, the bonds could be and were assigned to the town, and the town could demand payment upon nonperformance. The court also held that the three-year statute of limitations on actions concerning liability under a contract did not bar the action. Since enforcement of subdivision regulations is a governmental function, the statute of limitations did not apply to the town. Even if the statute did apply, the developers had stated less than two years before commencing the action that they were committed to completing the improvements without the need of the bonds.

MYC Klepper/Brandon Knolls, LLC v. Board of Adjustment, 238 N.C. App. 432, 767 S.E.2d 668 (2014)

Estoppel; Nonconformities; Signs

The plaintiff was cited for installing a billboard in Asheville without a permit. The original billboard was erected in 1992 pursuant to a variance that required its removal in 1997, the expiration year of an amortization period then in effect. The billboard remained on site until 2007, when the sign was removed with only the poles remaining. In 2010, a new billboard was installed.

The complaint named the board of adjustment rather than the city as a party. The court held that while G.S. 160D-1402(d) requires the city to be named as the respondent, this failure did not deprive the court of subject-matter jurisdiction, and the city's participation in the proceedings cured the defect in the petition for review. The court held that since the ordinance allows reestablishment of nonconformities within sixty days, and this sign had been removed for over a year, it could not be reestablished without a permit even if it were deemed a lawful nonconformity. The court dismissed an estoppel argument based on the contention that, at the time the sign replacement was being considered for replacement, a former city attorney had advised the plaintiff that they were proceeding properly. Even if that advice was given, a mistake by a city officer would not immunize the plaintiff from liability for a zoning violation.

Six at 109, LLC v. Town of Holden Beach, 238 N.C. App. 469, 767 S.E.2d 400 (2014)
Condemnation; Demolition; Public-trust doctrine

The plaintiff owned a dilapidated four-unit oceanfront motel. The town inspector condemned the building as an unsafe structure. After a hearing at which the plaintiff presented evidence and testimony, the inspector issued an order that the structure had attracted criminal activity constituting a nuisance and was unsafe, a hazard to surrounding properties, a threat of disease, and a danger to children. The structure was ordered demolished. That order was appealed to the town council, which after notice and hearing issued an order making similar findings and upholding the order to demolish if sufficient repairs were not made.

The plaintiff contended that the town lacked subject-matter jurisdiction because the structure was in the public-trust area. The court noted that the property was condemned as unsafe under G.S. 160D-1119, an action not based on interference with public-trust rights. The court also concluded that the town council conducted a de novo review, including its own two-day hearing and site visit. The court found that there was ample evidence in the record to support the town council's conclusion that the structure was unsafe and that it met the statutory standards for mandated demolition.

Fehrenbacher v. City of Durham, 239 N.C. App. 141, 768 S.E.2d 186 (2015)
Interpretation; Records; Telecommunication towers

The city development-review board and planning director approved a 120-foot-tall telecommunication tower. The staff determined that the proposed "monopine" design of the tower complied with ordinance requirements for a "concealed wireless communication facility." The ordinance required such facilities to be aesthetically compatible with the site and its surroundings, and it gave examples of permitted concealment, including incorporation into a church steeple, bell tower, clock tower, flagpole, or tree. On appeal to the board of adjustment, neighbors testified that the monopine tower would be twice as high as the surrounding real trees.

While minutes of the board of adjustment's hearing were available, the first hour of the three-hour hearing was not recorded due to a recording malfunction. The court held that this did not result in an inadequate record for judicial review because the plaintiff's evidentiary submission of affidavits and photographs was included in the hearing record. Because the plaintiff did not identify any other competent or substantial evidence presented in the verbal testimony that was missing from the record as a result of the recording malfunction, the court held the record to be adequate for review. The court held that it was not error for the trial court to allow the tower applicant to submit photo simulations that were part of its original application but that were not presented to the board of adjustment, noting that G.S. 160D-1402(i) gives the trial court discretion to supplement the hearing record. On the de novo question of interpretation of the ordinance, the court noted that while the pole would be twice the height of existing trees, the camouflaging was such that the pole would not be "readily identifiable" to a casual observer as a cell tower and that it would be compatible with the wooded rural-residential area surrounding it.

China Grove 152, LLC v. Town of China Grove, 242 N.C. App. 1, 773 S.E.2d 566 (2015)
Impact fees

The town charged the plaintiff an "adequate public facilities fee" to ensure funding for increased public needs resulting from a residential subdivision. The court held that this was an unauthorized impact fee. While a subdivision ordinance "may provide" for a fee in lieu of recreational facilities, there is no provision in that statute that the city can condition subdivision on payment of funds to subsidize its law enforcement, fire protection, and parks. The city voluntarily returned the fee but did not pay interest. The city contended that the common law doctrine of accord and satisfaction barred the claim for interest when the plaintiff accepted the voluntary refund of the fee. The court held that the town's refund letter and its acceptance satisfied all obligations and liabilities under the adequate-public-facilities ordinance; however, it made no mention of the statutorily required interest and thus did not amount to a release of the statutory obligation to pay interest.

Good Neighbors of Oregon Hill Protecting Property Rights v. County of Rockingham, 242 N.C. App. 280, 774 S.E.2d 902, *review denied*, 368 N.C. 429, 778 S.E.2d 78 (2015)
Notice; Spot zoning; Statements of reasonableness

A father and son purchased a 102-acre parcel near Reidsville. The father then applied to rezone a two-acre portion of the property from residential agricultural to highway commercial-conditional in order to construct a kennel for a bird-dog training facility. The county rezoned the property with nine conditions, including provisions on grading, landscape buffers, lighting, and parking. Neighbors challenged the rezoning, contending that it was illegal spot zoning, that it was arbitrary and capricious, and that proper notice had not been provided for the rezoning hearing.

The court held that a rezoning can only be spot zoning if the property is owned by a single person. Because this property was owned jointly by a father and son at the time of the rezoning, it was not spot zoning. The court conducted a whole-record review on the issue of arbitrariness, with the burden on the challenger to establish invalidity. The court is not a trier of fact but reviews the whole record to assess the sufficiency of evidence presented in order to determine whether there was an error of law in this summary judgment on a declaratory-judgment proceeding. Because the court found that the trial court had mistakenly made new findings of fact, the case was remanded for a new hearing on this issue.

On the question of notice of the rezoning hearing, the court noted that the clerk to the board had made a certification of mailing of the notice, which is deemed conclusive in the absence of fraud. With no allegation of fraud, the court dismissed this claim. The court also held that pouring a concrete pad on the site prior to the rezoning for use as a personal kennel did not violate the ordinance (even if that pad could be used for a commercial kennel if the rezoning were subsequently approved).

Point South Properties, LLC v. Cape Fear Public Utility Authority, 243 N.C. App. 508, 778 S.E.2d 284 (2015)
Impact fees; Laches; Statutes of limitation

The plaintiffs proposed a subdivision in the unincorporated area of New Hanover County. Between 2003 and 2006, the plaintiffs paid required impact fees related to water and sewer services. In 2012, the plaintiffs sought a refund of the impact fees because it was undisputed that, between 2003 and 2006, the defendants provided no services in this area, had made no official decision to extend services there, and had taken no steps to provide services to these developments. The defendants contended that the claim was barred by laches and the statute of limitations.

The court held that the defendants lacked authority to impose this fee. G.S. 162A-88 allows the imposition of fees for "services furnished or to be furnished." As the defendants provided no services to the area involved and had made no commitment to provide services, the defendants had no authority to impose the fees. The court applied the ten-year statute of limitations for actions not otherwise addressed by statutes of limitation. The court held that, as an equitable defense, laches is not available for a claim that is legal rather than equitable in nature. Further, the defendant showed no harm resulting from the plaintiff's delay in bringing this action. [Note: The North Carolina Supreme Court subsequently applied a three-year statute of limitations to similar claims. Quality Built Homes Inc. v. Town of Carthage, 371 N.C. 60, 813 S.E.2d 218 (2018).]

Nies v. Town of Emerald Isle, 244 N.C. App. 81, 780 S.E.2d 187 (2015), *appeal dismissed*, 369 N.C. 484, 793 S.E.2d 699 (2016), *cert. denied*, 138 S. Ct. 75 (2017)
Beaches; Public-trust doctrine; Takings

The plaintiffs acquired an oceanfront cottage in Emerald Isle. Town ordinances allowed and regulated the driving of vehicles on the beach during specified periods of the year and prohibited placement of beach equipment within twenty feet of the oceanward base of frontal dunes in order to maintain an unimpeded travel lane for emergency services and other town personnel providing essential services on the beach. The plaintiffs contended that the vehicles driving on their property above the mean high-water line as sanctioned by the town ordinance, as well as restrictions on placement of beach equipment, constituted an unlawful taking of private property without compensation.

The parties agreed that the property boundary between state-owned and privately owned property is the mean high-water line. The court held that the public also has rights to use of the occasionally flooded portion of the beach—the "dry-sand beach"—between the mean high-tide line and the vegetation line. The court took notice that the public right of access to and use of the dry-sand beach is firmly rooted in the custom and history of North Carolina. The court held that as a matter of state property law (both in common law and recognized by statute) public-trust rights extend to the dry-sand beach as well as the wet-sand beach. As the plaintiff had no right to exclude the public from the dry-sand beach, the town regulation of beach driving in this area, even if construed as "allowing" rather than "regulating" public use, cannot be a taking. The court further held that regulation of where equipment can be placed on the beach was a legitimate use of the police power, and the means used to regulate placement of large beach equipment in order to facilitate free movement of emergency and service vehicles was a reasonable exercise of the police power.

Henderson v. County of Onslow, 245 N.C. App. 151, 782 S.E.2d 57 (2016)
Appeals; Judicial review

The plaintiffs owned a large rental house in a residential zoning district. On occasion the house was rented for weddings, family reunions, and similar events. The county cited the plaintiffs for a zoning violation, contending that use of the home for such events violated the restriction to residential use. The board of adjustment upheld the notice of violation, and a timely appeal was made to superior court. After nearly two years, the county sought to dismiss the action for failure to prosecute, which prompted the clerk of court to issue a writ of certiorari for the review of the board of adjustment's decision. At that point the plaintiff filed a notice of voluntary dismissal. Some eleven months later, the plaintiff refiled a petition for a writ of certiorari, contending that such was allowed under Rule 41(a) of the Rules of Civil Procedure.

The court held that since a writ of certiorari is a "proceeding of a civil nature," the Rules of Civil Procedure apply unless a differing procedure is prescribed by statute or when the Rules are not relevant or applicable. Rule 15 is applicable because it allows "pleadings" (which includes petitions for writs of certiorari) to be amended once as a matter of course before a responsive pleading is filed. The court held that Rule 41 on voluntary dismissals and refiling within a year is only applicable to civil "actions," and a petition for writ of certiorari is a request for judicial review of the decision of an inferior tribunal. Thus, the court held that it was proper to deny the motion to amend and refile the petition.

Cherry v. Wiesner, 245 N.C. App. 339, 781 S.E.2d 871, *review denied*, 369 N.C. 33, 792 S.E.2d 779 (2016)
Historic preservation; Standing

The Raleigh Historic Development Commission approved the plaintiffs' application for a certificate of appropriateness for construction of a "modernist" home in the Oakwood historic district. The defendant, who resided directly across the street, appealed that approval to the board of adjustment. While that appeal was pending, the plaintiff initiated and substantially completed construction of the home. The board of adjustment then held that the certificate of appropriateness was improperly issued and revoked the approval.

The court affirmed that the defendant had not established standing to challenge the certificate of appropriateness. The burden of proving the elements of standing is on the party invoking jurisdiction. The court held that proximity and diminution of property value may bear some weight on the basis for standing, but alone they are insufficient. A general allegation that property values in the general area or neighborhood will be impaired does not confer standing, as injury specific to a particular property needs to be shown to establish the requisite special damages. The court noted that the defendant's allegations of harm were either purely aesthetic or not distinct to her property. The court found that the defendant had ample opportunity to establish standing, having twice filed an application for review after retaining counsel where the application specifically asked for information to explain how the person was an aggrieved party. The court further held that the trial court did not abuse its discretion in refusing to allow the defendant to supplement the record on appeal regarding standing, given the ample opportunities to present this information earlier in the process (and the court noted that the two proffered affidavits offered little new substantive information and would not have provided a basis for standing if they had been accepted).

United States Cold Storage, Inc. v. Town of Warsaw, 246 N.C. App. 781, 784 S.E.2d 575 (2016)
Utilities

The plaintiff purchased land in 1995 from Duplin County for a large refrigerated warehouse. The purchase agreement included a provision that the county would extend utility lines to the site, that the defendant town would provide water and sewer services, and that the property would not be annexed into the town for at least eight years. The facility was built in 1997. In 2012, the General Statutes were amended to restrict involuntary annexations. In 2013, the town requested that the plaintiff voluntarily annex to the town and stated that, if that were not done, the town would cease to provide water and sewer services because the facility was outside the town's corporate limits.

The court held that the town has no legal obligation to provide water and sewer services outside its corporate limits provided it does not unfairly discriminate among similarly situated nonresidents. A municipality may provide services to nonresidents within reasonable limitations and may obligate itself by contract to provide utility services. However, unless the contract provides otherwise, these contracts are terminable at will by either party with reasonable notice to the other. This contract had no express limit on termination, and the plaintiff was on notice that the property was subject to annexation after eight years. Further, there was no showing of discrimination against the plaintiff because the town made voluntary annexation a condition of provision of service to all its commercial customers outside the town limits.

Butterworth v. City of Asheville, 247 N.C. App. 508, 786 S.E.2d 101 (2016)
Quasi-judicial

Plaintiff neighbors challenged the city's approval of a major subdivision that included a modification from the subdivision-regulation standards in order to allow narrower city streets within the subdivision. The city treated the decision to allow the modification as an administrative decision, while the plaintiffs contended that it was quasi-judicial and that their due-process rights were not applied.

The court held that case law and the statutes provide that the nature of the standards for approval determine whether the decision is administrative or quasi-judicial. If modifications can be approved following objective standards, the decision is administrative. If the standards require the exercise of judgment and discretion, the decision is quasi-judicial. The regulation allowed the modification upon showing an "unusual and unnecessary" physical hardship and allowed imposition of conditions on the modification to "ensure the purposes" of the standards waived. The court held that the decision was quasi-judicial because it entailed the application of a standard that requires exercise of judgment and discretion. The court ordered the matter remanded for a new hearing that observes the fair-trial standards required for quasi-judicial land use decisions.

Long v. Currituck County, 248 N.C. App. 55, 787 S.E.2d 835, *review dismissed as moot*, 369 N.C. 74, 793 S.E.2d 222 (2016)
Coastal Area Management Act; Interpretation

Plaintiff neighbors contended that a proposed 15,000-square-foot structure was not a "single family detached dwelling" allowed in the applicable zoning district. The zoning regulations called for "very low density residential development" in the district and allowed single-family detached dwellings but not commercial, office, or industrial uses.

The project consisted of a three-story main building with cooking, sleeping, and sanitary facilities, with a pair of two-story perpendicular wings, each with twelve bedrooms and bathrooms. A 5000-square-foot gazebo and pool were also proposed. Each of the three buildings was approximately 5000 square feet. The court noted that the oceanfront setback under the Coastal Area Management Act for large structures (those over 5000 square feet) is greater, and this project was built at a smaller-structure setback (resulting in a building location considerably oceanward of adjacent structures). The three units were originally proposed to be connected by uncovered decking, but the connectors were converted to conditioned hallways when the county determined that this was necessary to consider the project a "single principal structure" in order to comply with the zoning ordinance. The ordinance defined a permitted dwelling as one with five elements: (1) a building; (2) for residential use; (3) containing no more than one dwelling unit; (4) occupied by one family; and (5) not physically attached to any other "principal structure." County permits were issued and the entire project was constructed while this appeal was pending.

The court conducted a de novo review of the interpretation. The court noted that the prior proceedings focused on whether the use would be residential, would be a single dwelling unit, or would be used by one family. The court, however, found that the definition in the ordinance also required examination of the structure involved because the ordinance allowed only a single "principal building" on a residential lot. Even if they were functionally used together, this project had three buildings. As the three residential buildings were all the same size, none were subordinate in use, so the two wings could not be considered accessory to the main building. Each must be considered a principal structure, and a project with three principal structures on a single lot violates the ordinance. [Note: G.S. 160D-706(b), subsequently adopted, requires zoning regulations to use the same definition of *building* that appears in the State Building Code.]

Davidson County Broadcasting Co. v. Iredell County, 248 N.C. App. 305, 790 S.E.2d 663 (2016), *review denied*, 369 N.C. 530, 797 S.E.2d 13 (2017)
Evidence; Special uses

Plaintiffs appealed the denial of a special use permit for a 1130-foot radio tower proposed to be located in a residential-agricultural zoning district. The board of adjustment determined that the proposed tower was not in harmony with the surrounding area and was not consistent with the adopted land use plan.

The court held that while inclusion of a particular use as a special use within a district creates a prima facie case that the use is harmonious with the surrounding area, it can be rebutted with substantial evidence to the contrary. Evidence submitted by the opposing neighbors—photographs, diagrams of the tower's height in relation to its surroundings, testimony on the impact of its construction, and testimony on its height, appearance, and lighting—was sufficient to rebut the presumption of harmony. The adopted comprehensive plan was properly considered as a guide in determining whether the proposed use was in conformity with the area and the county's plan for development. Further, it was not a due-process violation to limit the opinion testimony on the issue of plan consistency from the plaintiff's expert witness on property-value impacts. (He had been offered as an appraisal expert, not a planning expert.) The court noted that his opinion on the plan-consistency issue was included in his written report, which was a part of the record.

Dellinger v. Lincoln County, 248 N.C. App. 317, 789 S.E.2d 21, *review denied*, 369 N.C. 190, 794 S.E.2d 324 (2016)
Evidence; Special uses

The plaintiffs applied for a special use permit to construct a solar-energy facility. The county board of commissioners denied the permit, finding that the evidence failed to establish that the project would not substantially injure neighboring property values, that it would be in harmony with the area, and that it would be in general conformity with the comprehensive plan. The trial court found it was unable to determine if the evidence supported the finding on property-value impacts and remanded that issue for new findings. When the board of commissioners heard the matter on remand, a newly elected board member stated that he had reviewed the entire record of the original hearing and voted on the matter. A second newly elected member did not participate. The board voted again to deny the permit.

The applicant had produced evidence from two expert appraisers that the project would not harm neighboring-property values, with supporting data and analysis. The court found that the plaintiff had thus submitted sufficient evidence to make a prima facie case that the property-value-impacts standard was met. One of the commissioners stated the applicant had not proved its case "beyond a doubt," and another said he found the expert testimony "unpersuasive." The court held that the board applied an improper burden of proof. Once the applicant submits competent, material, and substantial evidence that the standard is met, the burden shifts to the opponents to submit sufficient evidence to support a contrary finding.

Hirschman v. Chatham County, 250 N.C. App. 349, 792 S.E.2d 211 (2016)
Appellate procedures; Parties; Special uses

The plaintiffs appealed a special use permit for a monopole telecommunication tower. The county was the sole named respondent in the suit. The court held that G.S. 160D-1402(d) explicitly provides that when a quasi-judicial decision is challenged, the local government making the decision must be named as the respondent and, if the applicant is not the petitioner, the applicant shall also be named as a respondent. The court ruled that the statute makes the applicant a necessary party, and the failure to name a necessary party deprives the superior court of jurisdiction over reviewing the case. An appeal cannot be amended to add a necessary party after the time period to file an appeal has run.

Brookline Residential, LLC v. City of Charlotte, 251 N.C. App. 537, 796 S.E.2d 369 (2017)
Performance guarantees; Subdivisions

A previous owner of the site involved in this litigation received final plat approval in 2008 for the initial ten-lot phase of a 184-lot subdivision. A performance bond was posted for road improvements for the entire development. After building on nine of the lots and completing the roadwork for those lots, the owner ceased development. The plaintiffs acquired the property out of bankruptcy. They combined a number of the lots and secured a rezoning to build multifamily housing on the site. The city advised the plaintiffs before their purchase that the performance bond was still in effect. Later, the city advised the plaintiffs before the rezoning that the bond was for roadway improvements specified on the original subdivision plan and that the plaintiffs would be responsible for roadway improvements on a revised plan. The plaintiffs proceeded with the revised plans and rezoning, and they committed to altered road improvements. The plaintiffs requested that the city call the bond to pay for those portions of the road improvements that were within the original road plan and the altered plan. The city refused. The plaintiffs sought an order compelling the city to call the bond or to pay damages equivalent to the cost of constructing the portions of the road improvements that were common to the original and revised plans. The trial court granted summary judgment for the city.

The court held that neither the statutes nor the city ordinance created a duty on the part of the city to call the performance bond. As there was no express duty of the city to call the bond, the court would not imply such a duty. Furthermore, the court noted that the plaintiffs were not a party to the bond, were not assigned rights under the bond, and were not a third-party beneficiary of the bond. Also, the plaintiffs were expressly warned that if they sought plan revisions, they would be responsible for the improvements, and the plaintiffs agreed to construct these improvements.

Thompson v. Town of White Lake, 252 N.C. App. 237, 797 S.E.2d 346 (2017)
Accessory buildings and uses; Interpretation; Judicial review

The plaintiff secured a permit for a metal accessory-storage structure on her residentially zoned lot. During construction, the inspector found the building was being built with four doors on each side and a center dividing wall, while permit application had shown four doors, all facing away from the street. A stop-work order and notice of violation was issued, based on the structure being an unlawful commercial structure, varying from approved plans, and not being located behind the principal structure on the lot. On the allegation that the structure was commercial, the petitioner contended that the evidence did not support this, and the board's decision was thus arbitrary and capricious. This allegation required a whole-record review. Rather than remand for application of the proper standard, however, the record was clear that there was no evidence presented that the structure was being devoted to a commercial use. The fact that the structure could be converted to commercial use was not relevant to the question of its actual use. As that was the sole ground for denial by the board of adjustment, the trial court erred by substituting its own justification for the decision where the issue was the adequacy of the evidence before the board.

Innovative 55, LLC v. Robeson County, 253 N.C. App. 714, 801 S.E.2d 671 (2017)
Evidence; Special uses

The plaintiffs applied for a special use permit to construct a solar farm. Following two hearings, the board of county commissioners denied the permit on the grounds that the project would injure the use and enjoyment of neighboring properties, impede the normal and orderly development of the surrounding property, adversely affect neighboring property values, and not be in harmony with the surroundings. The court applied a whole-record review to conclude that the denial was not supported by substantial evidence. The applicants met their burden of production by submitting substantial evidence that the permit standards would be met. The opponents offered only "unsupported and highly speculative claims about their unsubstantiated fears" about traffic and property-value impacts. Further, the opponents' concerns about aesthetic impacts and harmony with the neighborhood related only to the general presence of the use, not its specific design and impact.

Cheatham v. Town of Taylortown, 254 N.C. App. 613, 803 S.E.2d 658 (2017), *review denied*, 372 N.C. 360, 828 S.E.2d 165 (2019)
Exhaustion; Housing code

The town affixed a notice of condemnation to an unoccupied house owned by the plaintiff and notified him that a hearing would be scheduled. The plaintiff filed an action to contest this action, but no hearing was scheduled, and the suit was voluntarily dismissed. The town then adopted a housing code, the plaintiff filed a second suit, and the town investigated the property again. The court held that the suit was properly dismissed with respect to claims arising after the town's adoption of the housing code. The statute and ordinance provided for an administrative hearing and appeal, which was not taken before this action was initiated. The court remanded the matter to reconsider whether dismissal of claims arising prior to the ordinance adoption was proper.

NCJS, LLC v. City of Charlotte, 255 N.C. App. 72, 803 S.E.2d 684 (2017)
Enforcement; Nonconformities

Plaintiffs owned a warehouse that was built in 1970. The warehouse included two unscreened dumpsters. The city in 1984 adopted a dumpster-screening requirement to be applied when property is developed or redeveloped. Based on photographs showing that the dumpsters had been relocated on the site, the city issued a notice of zoning violation.

The court held the interpretation of the nonconformities provisions in the ordinance to be a question of law subject to de novo review. The city staff failed to assert that any activity on the property constituted "redevelopment" so as to trigger a loss of nonconforming status for the unscreened dumpsters. As the dumpsters were permitted accessory uses to the warehouses, they were not "nonconforming structures" in themselves. The relocation of the dumpsters was not "redevelopment" of the land or structures, so the screening requirement was not triggered.

Swan Beach Corolla, LLC v. County of Currituck, 255 N.C. App. 837, 805 S.E.2d 743 (2017), *aff'd per curiam,* 371 N.C. 110, 813 S.E.2d 217 (2018)

Appellate procedures; Vested rights

This case is the third time the court of appeals heard this dispute over vested rights on the northern Currituck Banks. In the first case, the court dismissed a uniform-taxation claim but remanded the vested-rights claim. When that case was remanded, the attorneys for the parties immediately began discussions about discovery and settlement. While those discussions were underway, the plaintiffs sought and obtained a default judgment in the amount of $39 million. The plaintiffs contended that the defendants were required to file responsive pleadings within thirty days of the mandate being issued for the court of appeals' decision remanding the matter. The defendants contended that an answer was not required until the trial court entered an order reinstating the vested-rights claim it had originally dismissed, but they filed a response six days after the thirty-day deadline. The trial court refused to set aside the entry of default.

The court of appeals reversed. It held that the proper standards to be applied in consideration of the motion to set aside the default judgment were (1) whether the moving party was diligent in pursuit of the matter; (2) whether the nonmoving party suffered harm by virtue of the delay; and (3) whether the moving party would suffer a grave injustice by being unable to defend the action. The court applied these tests and found that the trial court abused its discretion by not setting aside the default judgment. First, both parties were diligently pursuing the matters, scheduling meetings regarding settlement during the thirty-day period. Second, in the context of litigation that had been underway for two years, there was no showing of harm to the plaintiff occasioned by a six-day delay. Third, given the size of the damage award, the inability to defend against the substance of the vested-rights claim worked a grave injustice against the defendant. Given a colorable argument that a response was not required, that there was no dilatory action by the defendant, and that the modest delay occasioned no harm, the failure to set aside the entry of a default judgment for good cause was an abuse of discretion.

Ring v. Moore County, 257 N.C. App. 168, 809 S.E.2d 11 (2017)

Amendments; Rezoning; Standing

Neighboring landowners challenged a rezoning, objecting to the increased residential density it would allow, alleging that it was illegal spot zoning and that there were procedural defects in its adoption. The court noted that the plaintiff has the burden of showing a specific personal and legal interest that would be directly and adversely affected by the rezoning in order to have standing. An actual, concrete, particularized injury must be shown. While the plaintiffs owned adjacent property (on which they operated a poultry farm), this rezoning did not change the permitted uses for the property rezoned (rather it allowed a greater density of single-family homes). As there was no showing of an actual or imminent injury, the plaintiffs did not have standing.

Beroth Oil Co. v. N.C. Department of Transportation, 256 N.C. App. 401, 808 S.E.2d 488 (2017)

Appellate procedures; Takings

This case involves claims for compensation due to the property restrictions imposed by the Official Map Act. The trial court issued an order finding that the plaintiff's property rights had been taken and setting forth the rules and procedures for determining the compensation due. The state filed this interlocutory appeal, contending that its substantial rights were affected and would not be fully protected by appellate review of a final decision.

The court dismissed the appeal. It held that decisions involving title and the area taken in an eminent-domain proceeding affect substantial rights, but in this instance, those were the rights of the landowners, not the condemnor. The court further held that the state's claim of sovereign immunity is a substantial right, but that is a jurisdictional issue, and this litigation has passed the point where it could be raised. Further, the General Assembly's enactment of a statutory framework for claims in inverse condemnation is an implicit waiver of sovereign immunity in an eminent-domain proceeding. The N.C. Department of Transportation's admission that it had filed an official map affecting the plaintiff's property is at this point in the litigation properly deemed to be an admission of a taking within the statutory framework of G.S. 136-111.

Hampton v. Cumberland County, 256 N.C. App. 656, 808 S.E.2d 763 (2017), *appeal dismissed, cert. improvidently granted*, 373 N.C. 2, 832 S.E.2d 692 (2019)
Agricultural uses; Shooting ranges

Plaintiffs in 2011 acquired a tract zoned as rural residential with an intent to build a home, a running trail, and firing ranges. Shortly after acquisition, the plaintiffs obtained a USDA farm identification number. In 2012, the plaintiffs built a twenty-five-yard firing range and began instructing students there. The range was expanded to forty yards in 2013. The county amended the ordinance in 2014 to set standards and require a permit for outdoor firing ranges. Among the standards was a minimum 200-acre site size. This amendment also provided that the use must be considered a principal use (not an incidental or accessory use). It contained several exemptions (occasional target practice, sighting of weapons for hunting, and temporary turkey shoots) and exempted ranges in existence as of 2005. In 2014, the plaintiffs added a 100-yard range adjacent to the initial range where additional instruction was provided. No residential or use of the property other than as a shooting range was in place. In 2015, the county issued a notice of violation and ordered the shooting ranges be razed. On appeal, the board of adjustment affirmed the finding of a zoning violation and modified the corrective action required to cease use of the firing range, as it conflicted with the ordinance.

The court held that securing a farm identification number does not as a matter of law exempt all activity on the property from county zoning. While G.S. 160D-903(a) provided that a farm number is sufficient evidence the property is being used for bona-fide-farm properties, that is not conclusive if contrary evidence is presented that nonfarm use of farm property (which is not exempt from county zoning) is taking place on the property. The court held that the board of adjustment failed to make critical findings of fact, such as whether the actual use of the property fell within any of the exempted uses of a firing range or whether commercial uses of the ranges were involved. The court noted that these are mixed questions of law and fact, and it remanded the case to the board of adjustment to make findings and in its discretion take such new evidence and arguments as it deemed appropriate. [Note: The statute was subsequently amended to remove the USDA farm identification number as proof of farm use.]

McDowell v. Randolph County, 256 N.C. App. 708, 808 S.E.2d 513 (2017)
Due process; Plan consistency; Spot zoning

Adjoining property owners challenged the county's approval of an amended site plan that had been incorporated into a prior conditional zoning. The site-plan amendment authorized the plaintiffs to relocate a chemical vat to another location on the site, to place it on a concrete pad to divert stormwater runoff to an on-site retention pond, and to add covers and screening walls for the vat. The court noted that this text amendment was presumed valid, and there was no showing that it was in bad faith, whimsical, or lacking in fair and careful consideration. The plan-consistency statement was adequate in that it cited three specific plan policies to support the action taken rather than being only a conclusory statement. Finally, as there was no change in zoning classification, this could not be deemed spot zoning.

Azar v. Town of Indian Trail Board of Adjustment, 257 N.C. App. 1, 809 S.E.2d 17 (2017)
Parties

The plaintiff secured a rezoning and special use permit to build townhouses. After twice renewing the special use permit, the board of adjustment denied the third renewal application, finding that the project would materially endanger public health and safety and would substantially injure neighboring property values. The plaintiff filed a timely petition for judicial review but named the board of adjustment rather than the town as the respondent. The board moved for dismissal on the grounds that the town had not been named as a party. The plaintiff then filed an amended petition for judicial review, naming the town as the respondent.

The court upheld dismissal of the petition. G.S. 160D-1402(d) explicitly requires that the town be named as the respondent. That was not done until the amended petition was filed, which was well outside of the thirty-day period from receipt of the board's written decision. As the town had not participated in the case or otherwise waived the failure to name it as a party, the petition was properly dismissed for failure to name a necessary party. The amended petition does not relate back to the original filing because it adds a new party rather than correcting a misnomer.

Ecoplexus Inc. v. County of Currituck, 257 N.C. App. 9, 809 S.E.2d 148 (2017)
Evidence; Interpretation; Special uses

The plaintiff applied for a special use permit for construction of a solar farm on an abandoned golf course. The county board of commissioners denied the permit on the grounds that it would endanger public health and safety due to runoff and herbicide use, was not harmonious with the surrounding area, and was not consistent with the plan.

The court found that the plaintiff's witnesses and evidence established a prima facie case of compliance with the ordinance standards. The plaintiff's witnesses testified that most existing trees would remain on the site, given the 300-foot setback required, that no hazardous materials would be used, that impervious-surface areas would be reduced and stormwater managed, and that no adverse property-value impacts would occur. Opposing witnesses objected to solar energy, the value of the existing holding ponds from the golf course that would be filled, and potential runoff issues. An opposing witness also testified that a solar farm was not the "highest and best" economic use of the property. The court found that the plaintiff had presented competent, material, and substantial lay and expert testimony that the relevant standards would be met. The court found that the board wholly ignored the plaintiff's expert testimony on water management and relied instead on lay witnesses' generalized and speculative fears. On the question of harmony and property-value impacts, the board similarly ignored expert testimony and erroneously equated harmonious use with highest and best use. Further, the board improperly applied policies in the land use plan regarding energy-production facilities such as oil wells, natural-gas wells, and associated facilities. The court noted that these facilities are distinctly different from a solar-energy farm.

Little River, LLC v. Lee County, 257 N.C. App. 55, 809 S.E.2d 42 (2017), *review denied*, 818 S.E.2d 692 (2018)
Evidence; Special uses; Standing

The plaintiff applied for a special use permit for a rock quarry. The board of adjustment denied the permit, finding that the plaintiff failed to show it would not endanger public health and safety, would meet required conditions, would not substantially injure adjoining property values, and would be in harmony with the surrounding area. The court held that the neighbors had standing to participate in this challenge to the permit denial because the plaintiff expressly consented to the neighbors' motion to intervene before the superior court. The court held that the plaintiff had submitted competent, material, and substantial evidence sufficient to make a prima facie showing of compliance with the ordinance standards, noting this to be a burden of production, not a burden of proof. The court noted that the ordinance does not require state and federal permits regarding health and safety impacts to be secured before approval of a special use permit, and since the special use permit can be conditioned upon securing those approvals, the fact that this had not yet been done was not a ground for permit denial. The court noted that the standard on property-value impacts applied to adjoining and abutting properties, which none of the intervening neighbors owned. As the intervenors had not presented substantial, competent, and material evidence to rebut the plaintiff's prima facie showing of compliance, it was an error of law to deny the permit.

Walton North Carolina, LLC v. City of Concord, 257 N.C. App. 227, 809 S.E.2d 164 (2017), *review denied*, 371 N.C. 447, 817 S.E.2d 388 (2018)

Amendments; Rezoning; Vested rights

The property subject to this litigation was zoned for low-density residential use. The zoning in 2005 allowed a higher density with an approved cluster development. The cluster-development option was repealed in 2006, but the prior owners had submitted an application before its repeal. Their application for a preliminary plat under the cluster-development option was approved. The approval was conditioned upon securing a final plat, approval of construction drawings, and approvals of water-and-sewer infrastructure by the end of 2013. Construction drawings and an infrastructure agreement were approved, but no final plat was ever submitted. Before purchasing the property in 2012, the plaintiffs received a report noting that the prior approvals had expired and a rezoning would be needed for a density greater than two units per acre. The city confirmed the expiration to the plaintiff in 2012. In 2014, the plaintiff and city entered into a development agreement regarding off-site sewer extensions to the site. The plaintiff then submitted a site plan with the originally approved higher density and clustering, which the city denied. The plaintiff sought a rezoning to a conditional district and a preliminary subdivision plat that would allow the higher density and clustering. Citing increased traffic in a congested area and negative impacts to the public-school system and to neighboring homes, the city denied the rezoning request. The plaintiff challenged this decision, contending that it had a common law right to develop under the 2006 approval, asserting that the rezoning denial was arbitrary and capricious, and seeking specific performance of the 2014 development agreement.

The court held that there were no vested rights established under the 2006 approval. Common law vesting cannot be based on the zoning ordinance itself. It requires substantial expenditures made in good-faith reliance on a valid governmental approval, resulting in the party's detriment. The 2006 approval had expired prior to the plaintiff's purchase of the property, the cluster development option had been repealed, and the plaintiff knew this at the time of acquisition. As its expenditures to date would also be needed for the lower density allowed by the current ordinance, there was also no showing of detriment. The 2014 development agreement likewise established no vested rights to the higher density because it explicitly stated that development must be consistent with current zoning requirements.

The court held that the decision to deny rezoning to a higher density was not arbitrary or capricious. The council found the proposed rezoning to be inconsistent with the current land use plan, and it noted problems with increased traffic, negative impacts on public schools, and potential harm to neighboring homes and properties. These constitute a plausible basis for the decision.

Cherry Community Organization v. City of Charlotte, 257 N.C. App. 579, 809 S.E.2d 397, *review denied*, 371 N.C. 114, 812 S.E.2d 850 (2018)

Standing

The plaintiff nonprofit organization challenged the rezoning of a parcel to a mixed-use district in order to construct a 119-foot-tall building, a parking structure, and eight attached single-family homes. The court held that although the plaintiff's pleadings contained an allegation of special damages sufficient to defeat a motion to dismiss, the failure to produce any evidence to support the allegation of special damages warranted summary judgment for the city. A party may not rest on mere allegations in its pleadings but must set forth specific facts to support those assertions. Here, showing that the plaintiff owned adjacent or nearby property was insufficient in itself to establish particularized harm.

Byron v. Synco Properties, Inc., 258 N.C. App. 372, 813 S.E.2d 455 (2018)
Standing

Plaintiff neighbors sought to challenge a Charlotte rezoning, raising facial challenges and an interpretation issue regarding statutory repeal of the protest petition. None of the plaintiffs owned property sufficiently close to the rezoned property to have been eligible to file a protest petition. As they had no interest protected by that statute, they were not "directly and adversely affected" by the repeal or interpretation of the statute, and they had no standing to challenge its repeal or interpretation. Similarly, because they could not avail themselves of the protest-petition statute, and it was not their property being rezoned, they had no constitutionally protected interests affected by the challenged rezoning process, only a generalized grievance. They alleged no immediate danger of a direct injury to a constitutionally protected right, so they likewise had no standing to raise a constitutional challenge.

Jeffries v. County of Harnett, 259 N.C. App. 473, 817 S.E.2d 36 (2018), *review denied*, 372 N.C. 297, 826 S.E.2d 710 (2019)
Agricultural uses; Shooting ranges

The court addressed whether various commercial shooting activities (shooting towers, archery ranges, clay-pigeon stations, rifle ranges, and pistol pits) constituted agritourism when conducted on a bona fide farm. An initial issue was whether the court should consider 2017 legislation defining *agritourism* that was enacted after this litigation was initiated. The court decided that because the 2017 law was a clarification of the bona-fide-farm exemption rather than a substantial alteration of the law, the 2017 law could be considered in the interpretation of the scope of the farm exemption in this case. The court concluded that the statute, even as clarified, was still ambiguous as to these shooting activities. The court noted that while hunting was a traditional rural activity, that was not the case with shooting ranges. Therefore, the court considered rules of statutory construction as an aid to ascertaining legislative intent. The court noted that the examples of agritourism listed in the statute ("farming, ranching, historic, cultural, harvest-your-own activities, or other natural activities and attractions") implied that other exempt agritourism should be similar "natural" activities that can be enjoyed without alteration of the land. Including farming and ranching in the list, but not hunting, implies that shooting activities were not contemplated as agritourism. Also, the listed uses of "weddings, receptions, meetings, [and] demonstrations" in farm buildings "because of [the property's] farm and rural setting" are all different from these shooting activities. Outdoor shooting ranges may require land space that only a rural setting can provide, but they are "not purposefully performed on a farm for the aesthetic value of the farm or its rural setting." The court concluded that shooting ranges share little resemblance to the listed rural agritourism examples or the spirit of preservation and traditionalism embodied in the statute. The court held that the shooting activities were not agritourism and were subject to county zoning.

LeTendre v. Currituck County, 259 N.C. App. 512, 817 S.E.2d 73 (2018), *review denied*, 372 N.C. 54, 822 S.E.2d 641 (2019)
Enforcement; Injunctions

The plaintiff homeowner sought an injunction to prevent the county from enforcing its zoning regulations regarding a 15,000-square-foot home built on the "roadless" area on the northern Currituck Outer Banks. The plaintiff built the structure while the county's approval was under appeal, with notice that if she did not prevail in that litigation the structures could be ordered demolished or relocated. After the structure was 95 percent complete, the court of appeals in *Long v. Currituck County*, 248 N.C. App. 55, 787 S.E.2d 835 (2016), held that the structure violated the county ordinance. In this action the plaintiff sought to enjoin the county from enforcement of the ordinance.

   The court held that the county should not be enjoined from enforcement because the plaintiff had no likelihood of success on the merits of any of her claims. The county's appeal of the preliminary injunction was interlocutory but permissible; precluding a state or local agency from enforcing the law affects a substantial right. The standard of review of a preliminary injunction is de novo, and the defendant has the burden of showing that the plaintiff does not have a likelihood of success on the merits of each claim.

The court held that the contested regulation was within the scope of the county's zoning authority. The ordinance provision in question defined single-family detached dwellings in a manner that limited residences to one "primary structure" per lot. The ordinance did not mandate any particular type of building foundation or building type, nor did it regulate building-design elements. The fact that the plaintiff constructed three attached primary structures in order to avoid increased oceanfront setbacks that would have applied to a single, larger building per the Coastal Area Management Act does not affect the validity of the county-ordinance definitions. The court then held that the ordinance as applied did not violate due process because it furthered legitimate public objectives. It allowed only low-density residential development in order to preserve natural resources, protect wildlife habitat, create service demands consistent with the very limited infrastructure, and minimize threats to life and property due to flooding and storms. The regulatory means chosen were reasonable, and the interference with private-property rights was reasonable in degree. The lot could be used as a single-family residence, and a larger structure could be built if it were located on the part of the lot farther from the ocean. There was no evidence the ordinance was applied in a discriminatory, arbitrary, or retaliatory manner. The ordinance provisions were complex and subject to interpretation, but not unconstitutionally vague. The zoning use restrictions are not preempted by State Building Code provisions because the issue here was not how the buildings were constructed but how many principal structures are allowed as a single-family detached house. Finally, no common law vested rights are created when the substantial expenditures are made on an approval that has been appealed and is subject to reversal. Owners may not elect to proceed at their own risk and then claim good-faith reliance on approvals they know to be under appeal. The fact that neither the county nor the neighbor sought to stay construction while the permits were under appeal does not estop the county from applying the ordinance once the appeal is concluded. [For further developments on this dispute, see subsequent federal court litigation below in *Currituck County v. LeTendre*, No. 2-19-CV-27-BO, 2020 WL 6750429 (E.D.N.C. Nov. 17, 2020).]

Appalachian Materials, LLC v. Watauga County, 262 N.C. App. 156, 822 S.E.2d 57 (2018)
Interpretation

The county's ordinance regulating high-impact land uses prohibited asphalt plants within 1500 feet of a public or private "educational facility," day-care facility, assisted-living facility, or nursing home. The court held that a school district's administrative office is not an educational facility as defined by the ordinance. The definition of the term in the ordinance included a list of types of schools, and it did not include administrative offices. It also included facilities owned by the listed schools and used for educational purposes, and the court noted that the school district's administrative offices were not owned by individual schools within the district.

Weishaupt-Smith v. Town of Banner Elk, 264 N.C. App. 618, 826 S.E.2d 734 (2019)
Appellate procedures; Parties

The town issued a special use permit for a telecommunication tower and a variance regarding the width of an access easement to the tower. An adjacent property owner appealed the decision. After several remands from the superior court, the town made a final decision issuing the contested permit, which was upheld by the trial court. When this petition for review of the trial court's decision was filed with the court of appeals, the adjacent property owner had sold her property. Another adjacent property owner sought to be substituted as a party under Rule 38 of the Rules of Appellate Procedure. While the person seeking to be substituted had participated in the board hearing on the permit, he had not been a party to the litigation.

The court held that substitution was not permissible. As the party had not died and was able to continue litigating, and the person seeking substitution was not a successor in interest to the property of a party, the neighbor seeking substitution had no standing to appeal the trial court's decision. The person could have filed his own petition to challenge the board's decision or intervened in the superior-court action, but substitution at this stage of the proceedings would condone an evasion of the clear jurisdictional standards for obtaining judicial review.

Coates v. Durham County, 266 N.C. App. 271, 831 S.E.2d 392 (2019)
Appeals

Neighbors challenged the county's issuance of a special use permit to construct a middle school. The superior court reversed the issuance of the permit and remanded the matter with an order to advertise and conduct a new hearing on the application. The contractor who would build the school under the permit appealed the order remanding the case. The court held appellate review to be premature because the remand by the superior court did not affect a substantial right of the contractor. Avoidance of a rehearing is not in itself a substantial right. Also, the remand did not include a directive to issue or deny the permit but rather to conduct further proceedings. Thus, this appeal is interlocutory and is properly dismissed.

Dellinger v. Lincoln County, 266 N.C. App. 275, 832 S.E.2d 172 (2019), *remanded*, 374 N.C. 430, 840 S.E.2d 778 (2020)
Conflicts of interest; Special uses

The plaintiffs leased a portion of a farm they owned for a solar farm. The county in 2013 denied a special use permit application for the farm, but on appeal the superior court remanded the case for the board to make sufficient findings. After remand, the county again denied the permit, but on judicial review the court of appeals held that the board had placed an improper burden of persuasion on the applicant and remanded the case. Before the board of county commissioners took up the case on remand, a citizen who had actively opposed the permit in 2013 had been elected to the board. This board member refused to recuse himself, contending that he could be impartial and had taken no position on the application subsequent to his election to the board.

The court held that the member had had an impermissible bias, that he should not have participated in the case on remand, and that the decision was invalid even though his vote had not been determinative of the outcome. While general expressions about renewable energy or solar farms would not have been grounds for recusal, in this instance the board member had expressed opinions and contributed funds to oppose this specific project and thus had not been impartial.

The court also held that the applicant had submitted substantial evidence to show the permit standards were met, thus establishing a prima facie case for issuance of the permit. The court found that the burden thus shifted to the opponents to show an adverse property-value impact. An appraiser's testimony on the property-value impacts from a solar farm in an unzoned county, with no setback, landscaping, or other buffering requirements, could not be used to compare to this solar farm, where landscaping and buffering were required. Another appraiser only offered a personal opinion about impacts, unsupported by quantitative analysis. The court held that this evidence was insufficient to rebut the applicant's prima facie showing of entitlement. [Note: The supreme court remanded the case for reconsideration in light of *PHG Asheville, LLC v. City of Asheville*, 374 N.C. 133, 839 S.E.2d 755 (2020).]

Jubilee Carolina, LLC v. Town of Carolina Beach, 268 N.C. App. 90, 834 S.E.2d 665 (2019)
Evidence; Special uses; Vested rights

The plaintiff secured a special use permit to construct a grocery store. The site plan showed vehicular interconnectivity with the adjacent parcel. Subsequently, the town considered a special use permit application for a different grocery store on the adjacent parcel. That applicant objected to interconnectivity. The town council found the ordinance did not require interconnectivity and issued a special use permit for the second store without that requirement. The plaintiff sued, contending that it had a vested right to interconnectivity and that there was not substantial evidence to issue the permit without an interconnectivity requirement.

The court upheld issuance of the second special use permit. The court held that there were no findings of fact on the vested-rights issue because the plaintiff had not raised the issue during the town's consideration of the second special use permit. Therefore, that issue could not have been initially raised in the permit appeal. The court also noted that because the approved site plan was not a "site specific development plan," it did not create a statutory vested right. The court found there had been substantial evidence presented that the ordinance did not require interconnectivity, and the plaintiff had not rebutted that evidence at the hearing.

State v. Nance, 266 N.C. App. 353, 831 S.E.2d 605, *review denied*, 838 S.E.2d 182 (2020)

Enforcement; Nuisances

The City of Albemarle sought to have a motel that was the site of numerous criminal complaints closed as a public nuisance. The court held the complaint against the motel manager to be properly dismissed because her employment there had ended before the complaint was filed. The court held that the city's complaint was properly dismissed because the city council had not adopted a motion to approve this particular civil action as required by the city code.

Starlites Tech Corp. v. Rockingham County, 270 N.C. App. 71, 840 S.E.2d 231 (2020)

Nonconformities

The plaintiff operated an electronics-gaming business. After the business began operation, the county adopted a regulation requiring such a business to obtain a special use permit and established minimum setbacks from residential land uses. The plaintiff business did not meet these new setbacks but contended it had been in continuous operation and was thus a lawful nonconforming use. The ownership of the business changed after its initial zoning approval. The county contended the change in ownership triggered the requirement for a special use permit and compliance with the new setbacks. The court held that a change in ownership is not a change in use and thus does not affect the plaintiff's nonconforming status. While noting this was the case as a matter of law, the court also noted that the county ordinance itself did not define a change in ownership as a change in use.

Sound Rivers, Inc. v. N.C. Department of Environmental Quality, 271 N.C. App. 674, 845 S.E.2d 802 (2020), *review allowed*, 377 N.C. 215, 856 S.E.2d 99 (2021)

Standing

The plaintiffs challenged a National Pollution Discharge Elimination System (NPDES) discharge permit for a quarry. The court held that the plaintiff environmental groups had standing to challenge the permit decision under the Administrative Procedure Act. G.S. 150B-23(a) authorizes appeals by persons whose rights are "substantially prejudiced." Members of the group owned homes and businesses along a creek that would receive twelve million gallons per day of mine wastewater and alleged that the discharge would degrade the water quality in the creek if the applicable water-quality standards were not met. On the merits of the claim, the court reviewed the decision under G.S. 150B-51, which is substantially similar to the judicial review of quasi-judicial development-regulation decisions. The court held that there was substantial evidence in the record to support the agency's decision that the applicable permit standards were met.

Hovey v. Sand Dollar Shores Homeowner's Association, Inc., 276 N.C. App. 281, 857 S.E.2d 358 (2021), *review denied*, ___ N.C. ___, 868 S.E.2d 864 (2021)

Beaches; Easements; Subdivisions

Plaintiff contended that an eight-foot-wide pedestrian easement running from a subdivision road to the oceanfront had been dedicated to the public when a forty-two-lot subdivision in Duck was platted in 1981. The certificate of dedication on the plat provided that it dedicated "all roads, alleys, walks, parks, and other sites to public or private use as noted." The court held that a transfer of property by dedication requires a clear intent to dedicate that must be unmistakable and decisive. Since this dedication expressly noted it was for both public and private use, the intent to include public use of the easement (as opposed to exclusive use by subdivision-lot owners) was ambiguous at best. As the burden to show a clear intent to dedicate is on the person propounding the existence of the dedication, that ambiguity is fatal to a claim of public dedication. The court noted this decision does not affect the rights of the plaintiff and other members of the public to use the ocean beach but only addresses the right to use this accessway across private upland property.

Cline v. James Bane Home Building, LLC, 278 N.C. App. 12, 862 S.E.2d 54 (2021)

Liability

When the plaintiffs' septic tank failed, they sued Gaston County and the county health administrator in his official and his individual capacity. The court held that the claims against the county and the staff member in his official capacity were properly dismissed given the governmental immunity of both. However, the claim against the staff member could continue as he was deemed an "employee" rather than an "officer." An officer engaged in duties that involve exercise of judgment and discretion is not personally liable for mere negligence while an employee may be liable. To qualify as an "officer," the factors to be considered are whether the position is created by the statutes, whether the position exercises sovereign power, and whether the person exercises discretion rather than performing ministerial duties. The court held that the position of "Environmental Health Administrator" was not created by statute nor do the statutes expressly authorize delegation of the duties of a statutorily created position to this person, so this person was an employee.

85° & Sunny, LLC v. Currituck County, 279 N.C. App. 1, 864 S.E.2d 742, *review denied*, ___ N.C. ___, 865 S.E.2d 858 (2021)

Nonconformities; Interpretation

The plaintiff acquired a campground that was established prior to the adoption of county zoning in 1971. The campground had continued in operation as a nonconforming use. The county development regulation prohibited enlargement, expansion in area, or intensification of the use. The nonconforming regulation included a specific provision on existing campgrounds that provided they could not be expanded to cover any additional area, nor could they exceed the total number of campsites that existed on January 1, 2013. The plaintiff's proposed site plan showed 314 RV and trailer campsites, 78 tent campsites, and various improvements including new restrooms, a swimming pool, and two dog parks. The plaintiff sought a determination as to the number of campsites allowed and the specific improvements that could be permitted. The zoning administrator determined that 234 campsites had been approved and existed as of January 1, 2013, that existing facilities could be repaired and modified, but that new improvements (bathrooms, swimming pool, and pool house among them) would be a substantial and impermissible expansion. The board of adjustment upheld the administrator's determination. The superior court reversed in part, holding that the full number of proposed campsites and bathroom facilities should be permitted, but not the new swimming pool.

The court held that there was substantial evidence in the hearing record to support the board's decision that only 234 campsites were in existence in 2013. A reviewing court applies the whole-record test to review an error of law. Even if there is conflicting evidence presented, the court must confirm the board's findings of fact where there is substantial evidence in the record to support it. Here, previously approved site plans submitted for special-event permits for concerts at the campground showed 234 campsites. While the court must consider contradictory evidence, the reviewing court is not allowed to replace the board's judgment as between two reasonably conflicting views. As for the scope of allowed improvements, the court must consider both the specific provision regarding nonconforming campgrounds and the general provisions applicable to all nonconformities. These provisions should be interpreted as general and specific provisions on the same subject to be read together and harmonized where possible. To apply only the specific campground provision (not permitting additional campsites or land area devoted to campgrounds) and not apply the general limitation (not enlarging, expanding, or intensifying the nonconforming use) would be contrary to the stated purpose of the regulation to limit the continued existence of a nonconformity by allowing an indefinite extension of its lifespan through the regular upgrading of new amenities.

Craig v. Neal, 279 N.C. App. 148, 864 S.E.2d 802 (2021)
Easements; Subdivisions

The plaintiff contended that an easement depicted on a 1952 subdivision dedicated the right-of-way to the public. The court held that since the plat simply identified the easement as an "R/W," there was no express intent to dedicate it as a public right-of-way. There was also no implied dedication, as the lot lines ran to the center of the right-of-way and the lots at the time were within Mecklenburg County (so there could have been no dedication to the City of Charlotte for a city street). Rather, the recording of the plat created a private easement to the purchaser of the lots depicted. As this right-of-way has been in continuous use, it is not extinguished by the Marketable Title Act as provided by G.S. 47B-3(3).

Bill Clark Homes of Raleigh, LLC v. Town of Fuquay-Varina, 281 N.C. App. 1, 869 S.E.2d 1 (2021)
Impact fees; Development agreements; Statutes of limitation

The plaintiff developed a subdivision in Fuquay-Varina. The parties entered into a development and infrastructure agreement. The agreement required the developer to build water and sewer lines within the development, and pay "all applicable development fees, including capacity fees"; it also required the town to extend a water line to the site and to build a sewage-pumping station on the site. The fees charged and paid included a $195,000 capacity fee. Subsequently, the supreme court held in *Quality Built Homes Inc. v. Town of Carthage*, 371 N.C. 60, 813 S.E.2d 218 (2018), that cities did not have the authority to charge capacity fees for future services to be provided. In response, the plaintiff sought a refund of the capacity fee it had paid. The town contended that since the fees were paid subject to a voluntary development agreement, they were not ultra vires.

The court held that it was improper to grant a motion to dismiss the plaintiff's claim as they alleged that the fee was charged pursuant to ordinance requirements rather than the agreement and that the fee was for future services. These claims, when reviewed most favorably to the plaintiff and taking the allegations as true, are sufficient to defeat a motion to dismiss. The court also held that the three-year statute of limitations for alleged statutory violations is applicable to this claim.

Batson v. Coastal Resources Commission, 282 N.C. App. 1, 871 S.E.2d 120 (2022) [*appeal filed*]
Attorney's fees; Coastal Area Management Act

The plaintiffs sought to appeal a Coastal Area Management Act (CAMA) permit issued to the N.C. Department of Transportation (NCDOT) for replacement of the bridge to Harkers Island. The Coastal Resources Commission (CRC) denied this third-party request to appeal, finding the one-page request for a hearing did not demonstrate that the appeal was not frivolous. The trial court reversed that decision and remanded the case for an appeal hearing. The court also awarded the plaintiff attorney's fees for the appeal of the denial of their request for a hearing.

The court held that the trial court had the authority under G.S. 6-19.1(a) to award attorney's fees for the judicial challenge of the denial of the right to file an appeal. A petition for judicial review is a "civil action" subject to this statute. G.S. 113A-121.1 provides that the CRC decision not to allow an appeal is a final agency decision subject to judicial review. The plaintiffs prevailed on the decision to allow an appeal to be made. The court noted that the CRC offered a thorough analysis of the plaintiff's claims prior to dismissing the appeal as frivolous. However, a claim is not "frivolous" simply because it does not have merit or is unlikely to succeed. Rather, it is "frivolous" only if the proponent can present no rational argument based on the evidence or the law to support it. The court remanded to the trial court for additional findings as to whether the CRC knowingly applied the wrong reading of "frivolous" (that the appeal lacked merit as opposed to having no rational argument to support it) and thus acted without substantial justification in denying the right to the appeal.

Dismas Charities, Inc. v. City of Fayetteville, 282 N.C. App. 29, 870 S.E.2d 144 (2022)
Group homes; Special uses

The plaintiff applied for a special use permit to construct a halfway house for prisoners transitioning back into society on a vacant lot in the downtown area. The site was zoned for office and institutional uses, which included hospitals, community centers, police and fire stations, fraternity houses, and motels as permitted uses. The city council denied the permit based on a finding that the applicant did not meet its burden to produce evidence on the permit standard that the project "allows for the protection of property values" and for neighboring lands to develop the uses permitted in that district. The city argued that this standard was essentially similar to the more typical standard that the use must not have a substantial adverse effect on neighboring property values.

The court applied a de novo review to the question of law as to whether the plaintiff met the burden of production for this permit standard. The court noted the standard was not whether the project would substantially harm adjoining property values but whether it would impact and protect property values generally. As the hearing record included evidence as to how the project would protect property values generally, the plaintiff's burden of production was met. As no competent evidence to the contrary was presented, the applicant was entitled to permit approval.

Town of Midland v. Harrell, 282 N.C. App. 354, 871 S.E.2d 392 (2022) *[appeal filed]*
Enforcement; Attorney's fees

The defendant in 2004 constructed a subdivision and asked the N.C. Department of Transportation (NCDOT) to assume maintenance of its streets. The NCDOT declined since the subdivision was within the newly incorporated town. The town refused to accept the streets until the defendant fixed construction damage to them. When the repairs were not made, the town cited the defendant for a zoning violation for failure to properly construct and maintain the streets. That enforcement action was upheld by the court of appeals in 2017. The town assessed civil penalties of $18,900 for the continuing violation in 2017. In this action, the town sought collection of the civil penalties, an order of abatement and a mandatory injunction to compel the road repairs, and attorney's fees. The defendant contended the civil penalties were stayed while their appeal was pending.

The court held that the town had the authority to initiate these enforcement actions, including litigation, under the terms of its ordinances without an individual resolution by the town council to do so. The court upheld the imposition of the civil penalties, noting that the defendant has unsuccessfully appealed the notice of violation. The court held that while the issue of the defendant's obligation to maintain the roads had been conclusively resolved in the prior litigation, Rule 65(d) of the Rules of Civil Procedure requires that an order granting an injunction must describe in reasonable detail the acts to be taken. Here, the order required compliance with a Proposed Repair Plan to be developed. The court remanded with a direction for the court to specify the specific NCDOT standards that had not been met and to provide a specific decree for necessary repairs. The court agreed that the civil penalties were stayed during the initial appeal of the notice of zoning violation, so the defendant's attorney's fees to contest that unauthorized action were appropriate.

Daedalus, LLC v. City of Charlotte, 282 N.C. App. 452, 872 S.E.2d 105, *review denied*, 876 S.E.2d 285 (2022)
Impact fees; Scope of authority

The city charged applicants for water and sewer services three fees: (1) a capacity fee to pay a portion of the capital costs of the system; (2) a connection/tap fee to cover the cost of connecting the property to the system; and (3) a user fee based on debt incurred for construction of the system and for its operation and maintenance expenses. The plaintiff developers contended there was no statutory authority for the capacity fee. The court held that the capacity fee charged before the 2017 statutory amendment to the public-enterprise statute authorizing system-development fees was ultra vires because these fees were not for "contemporaneous use" but were held for future discretionary spending on water and sewer expansion.

Schroeder v. City of Wilmington, 282 N.C. App. 558, 872 S.E.2d 58 (2022)

Preemption; Interpretation; Short-term rentals

The city established a regulatory program for short-term rentals of residential property. The program required annual registration of properties to be offered for rent, limited their location to certain zoning districts, set various operational requirements, required a 400-foot setback from other rentals, capped the overall number of rentals at 2 percent of the city's residential parcels, and had a lottery system to allocate permits. Existing short-term rentals that did not get permits in the lottery were given a one-year amortization period before being required to cease operations. The plaintiffs registered their townhouse for the program but were unsuccessful in the lottery. They challenged the city's authority to implement the program.

The court held that G.S. 160D-1207(c) preempted the registration program but not the authority to require zoning permits. The statute prohibited local ordinances that require: (1) "any permit or permission under Article 11 or Article 12" of Chapter 160D to lease or rent residential real property; or (2) registering rental property with the local government. The city's annual registration and lottery system was preempted by the second of these limitations. The court noted that the original 2011 statute had been amended in 2019 to add the reference to Articles 11 and 12 (the building- and housing-code articles within Chapter 160D) relative to permits and permissions that could be required. This clarified that while permit requirements under the building or housing code are preempted by the first limitation, zoning "permits and permissions" under Article 7 of Chapter 160D are not preempted. The court therefore upheld the regulatory provisions that restricted whole-house short-term rentals to specified zoning districts, as well as those that set parking requirements, limits on the use of properties for large gatherings, mandatory insurance, and other operational requirements. The court held that the provisions—the cap and separation requirements, as well as the amortization requirements—were so intertwined with the invalid registration requirement that they were also preempted.

TAC Stafford, LLC v. Town of Mooresville, 282 N.C. App. 686, 872 S.E.2d 95, *review denied*, 880 S.E.2d 696 (2022)

Attorney's fees; Exactions; Subdivisions

The plaintiff sought approval for a subdivision plat. The town approved a concept plan for the subdivision conditioned upon the completion of a traffic impact analysis (TIA) to be paid for by the developer and the completion of "any required on-site and off-site improvements." Upon completion of the TIA, the plaintiff entered into a Mitigation Measures Agreement with the town that included off-site road improvements up to 2.3 miles away from the subdivision. When the plaintiff was unable to purchase rights-of-way from the owners of some off-site properties, they requested that the town condemn those properties. The town refused to do so and denied certificates of occupancy for more than half of the subdivision lots due to the plaintiff's breach of the mitigation agreement.

The court held that the town lacked statutory authority under the subdivision-enabling statute to require off-site transportation improvements. The plaintiff had spent nearly $1 million to comply with the mitigation agreement. The court upheld the order that the town return the $101,500 paid directly to the town under this agreement, but also held that the moneys paid to other landowners for off-site rights-of-way were not an exaction paid to the government, so the town could not "return" those fees. The court remanded the question of repayment of the $155,679 cost of the TIA to determine if that amount was paid to the town or to the engineering firm. The court also held that attorney's fees must be paid by the town under G.S. 6-21.7 as the town's off-site fee charges exceeded unambiguous limits on its statutory authority.

The Society for the Historical Preservation of the Twenty-Sixth N.C. Troops, Inc. v. City of Asheville, 282 N.C. App. 700, 872 S.E.2d 134, *review allowed*, 880 S.E.2d 679 (2022)

Standing; Monuments

The plaintiffs sued to block the city's removal of the Zebulon Vance Monument from Pack Square in Asheville, contending it had a contract with the city to raise funds to restore the monument. The court held that the plaintiffs had no legal injury under the contract, as it involved only work to restore the monument, not to preserve it, and that work had been completed. The association likewise had no standing to address the city and county's compliance with the state's monument-removal statutes.

Appalachian Materials, LLC v. Watauga County, 283 N.C. App. 117, 872 S.E.2d 591 (2022)
Appeals; Judicial review

In 2015, the county denied the plaintiff's application for a permit to construct an asphalt plant because it was located too close to an educational facility and on other grounds. On appeal, the court overturned the denial, ruling that the school-office building was not an "educational facility" covered by the separation requirement. The county had not exercised an appeal under Rule 10(c) of the Rules of Appellate Procedure to have the court consider the other grounds for approval. On remand, the county again denied the permit, citing the other grounds for denial.

The court held that the initial order on appeal reversed the original decision rather than vacating it. It therefore held that its mandate on the initial appeal directed the trial court to order issuance of the permit. Although the county was not required to raise these other issues in the original appeal, by failing to ask for reconsideration of the initial broad mandate or to appeal that to the supreme court, the original broad mandate is the law of the case.

Violette v. Town of Cornelius, 283 N.C. App. 565, 874 S.E.2d 217 (2022), *review denied*, 883 S.E.2d 606 (2023)
Standing; Evidence

The plaintiff adjacent-property owners challenged a conditional rezoning that would allow construction of an amenity center in a residential subdivision for persons aged fifty-five or older. The property was zoned Rural Preservation prior to the rezoning. After the suit was filed, the town accepted a new rezoning application and again rezoned the property to correct procedural deficiencies in the original rezoning. Both rezonings were challenged in the suit.

The court held that the plaintiffs lacked standing to challenge the rezonings. The court noted that at one time allegations of a specific personal and legal interest that would be directly and adversely affected was sufficient to establish standing in a declaratory-judgment action. However, the court held that a showing of "special damages" is now required. The neighboring-property owners' opinion regarding diminution of value is not competent evidence to show the substantial reduction in property value that would have established their standing.

Thompson v. Union County, 283 N.C. App. 547, 874 S.E.2d 623 (2022)
Enforcement; Vested rights

This case involved a residence constructed in 2004 and a detached garage constructed in 2009. When the property was listed for sale in 2018, a survey showed the house encroached upon the twenty-foot side-yard setback set by the county's 2014 unified development ordinance. The garage, which had been constructed without a building permit, encroached into the setback and into a private-access easement on the property. In 2018, the plaintiffs' predecessor in title applied for an "after-the-fact" building permit for the garage and a survey that showed these encroachments. The plaintiffs' predecessor contended the garage met the pre-2014 setback requirements, but the county disagreed. The county contended the structures were "continuing violations" and issued a notice of violation regarding the setback encroachments. The plaintiffs then purchased the property "as is" with notice of the right-of-way encroachment. The county issued a new notice of violation, required an updated survey, and issued a civil penalty. The board of adjustment and superior court upheld the notice of violation.

The court noted the burden of proof to show a violation is on the county. Neither the 2014 unified development ordinance, the ordinances in effect when the structures were built, nor the original building permits were introduced as evidence in the board's hearing. A court may not take judicial notice of municipal or county ordinances. As the ordinances were not in the hearing record, the board of adjustment findings based on the terms of the ordinance were not supported by competent evidence. With no evidence of the ordinance requirements or permit conditions in the record, the county failed to meet its burden of establishing an ordinance violation regarding the residence. The court held that since the garage was admittedly built without a permit, it remanded that issue to determine consistency with the ordinance in effect at the time of construction.

The court further held that since a building permit was issued for the residence, there was a statutory vested right under G.S. 160D-108(c) to maintain the residence as constructed since there was no evidence submitted to show the construction failed to meet the terms of the original permit. As no permit had been issued for the garage, the property owners had no statutory vested rights to maintain it as built.

Schooldev East, LLC v. Town of Wake Forest, 284 N.C. App. 434, 876 S.E.2d 607 (2022), *review allowed,* 884 S.E.2d 726 (2023)
Interpretation; Comprehensive plan

The plaintiff applied for site plan and subdivision approval for a K-12 charter school in a rural-holding zoning district. The standards for quasi-judicial approval of the major site plan included plan consistency, adequate infrastructure, and that it not be detrimental to the use or development of adjacent properties or other neighborhood uses. The application was denied by the town council because it failed to meet town-plan policies regarding pedestrian and bicycle connectivity to the surrounding neighborhood.

The court held that G.S. 160A-307.1 did not preempt the city's sidewalk-connectivity requirement. That statute prohibits cities from requiring "street improvements" for schools beyond those required for safe ingress and egress to the city street system and that are physically connected to a school driveway. The court applied a de novo review of the statutory-interpretation issue. As the statute did not define the terms, the court applied the ordinary meanings of "street," "improvements," and "for ingress and egress" to the street system. The court held that while sidewalks might be a part of a "street," they are not related to the safe entering and leaving of the city street system for school driveways. When read as a whole, this statutory limit was not intended to include sidewalks. The fact that sidewalks are included within "streets" in other statutes does not affect this statute, which only addresses school-driveway connections.

The court concluded that the record included competent, material, and substantial evidence that the application was not consistent with adopted town plans and policies. The town's Community Plan included a policy that "school campuses shall be designed to allow safe, pedestrian access from adjacent neighborhoods" and its unified development ordinance required a school to achieve "walking and bicycle accessibility by schoolchildren" through off-premise sidewalks, multi-use trails or paths, or greenways connecting to existing networks. The evidence showed those policies were not met.

Ashe County v. Ashe County Planning Board, 284 N.C. App. 563, 876 S.E.2d 687 (2022) [*appeal pending*]
Interpretation; Moratoria; Permit choice

The county denied an application for approval of an asphalt plant under the county's High Impact Land Use Ordinance. The planning board (sitting as a board of adjustment) reversed the denial on appeal and the county board of commissioners appealed the planning-board decision to the court. In 2020, the supreme court held that a letter from the planning director regarding the proposed plant was not a binding determination that the permit standards had been met and remanded the case.

On remand, the court first addressed the permit-choice statutes, G.S. 143-755 and 160D-108(b). The statutes only apply if an application has been "submitted" prior to the ordinance amendments. The court held that the application submitted under the then-effective Polluting Industries Development Ordinance was not "submitted" until the state air-quality permit required before local permits could be approved had been obtained. By the time the state permit was obtained and submitted to the county, the county had adopted a moratorium on these permits. The court noted that G.S. 160D-107(c) specifically provides that the permit-choice rule only applies to developments for which "a complete application" was submitted prior to the effective date of the moratorium. Because the court held that the application was not complete without the state permit approval, this application was not exempt from the moratorium and the permit-choice rule did not apply when permit review resumed upon expiration of the moratorium.

The court then upheld the permit denial under the ordinance in effect at the time of the expiration of the moratorium. The court found the hearing record supported the staff conclusion that the proposed plant was located within 1000 feet of two commercial buildings—a barn storing hay for sale and a quarry. As the ordinance prohibited that, the application was properly denied.

Visible Properties, LLC v. Village of Clemmons, 284 N.C. App. 743, 876 S.E.2d 804 (2022)
Interpretation; Signs

The plaintiff's application to erect a digital billboard was denied as not permitted in the applicable overlay zoning district and because the sign regulation prohibited "moving and flashing signs" and "electronic message boards." The court conducted a de novo review of the interpretation of the ordinance restrictions and reversed on both grounds.

On the question of whether off-premises advertising was a permitted use on the property, the court found the ordinance ambiguous. Three sections of the ordinance addressed it differently: (1) in the applicable conventional zoning district, off-premises signs were permitted on the property; (2) in the applicable overlay zoning district, off-premises signs were not included among the permitted uses; and (3) in the specific sign regulations, off-premises signs were permitted as long as they followed certain standards. The ordinance also provided that where there was a conflict between multiple ordinance provisions, the more restrictive provision applied. The court held that where a "reasonable interpretation" can avoid a conflict between sections, it should be adopted. Here, the court reconciled these provisions to find they were not in conflict, ruling that the more specific sign regulation superseded the more general provisions of the conventional and overlay district regulations.

On the question of whether a digital billboard was permitted, the ordinance prohibited "moving and flashing signs" and "electronic message boards" without defining either term. "Digital billboards" were not addressed at all. The proposed digital billboard would not include any animation or moving images, but the static image displayed would change every six to eight seconds. The court held that while inclusion of digital billboards within the category of moving and flashing signs was a reasonable interpretation, it was also reasonable to interpret the regulation as not including a sign with static (albeit changing) images and no moving or flashing features. Similarly, it would be a reasonable interpretation to include or exclude digital billboards in the definition of an electronic message board. Given two reasonable interpretations, there is ambiguity that must be resolved in favor of the interpretation that permits the free use of property.

The court concluded that the village could have prohibited "digital billboards" or those with changeable copy. It could have clearly provided that the overlay district standards superseded the sign regulations. In the absence of that clarity, the ordinance was ambiguous and must be interpreted to allow the contested use.

Frazier v. Town of Blowing Rock, ___ N.C. App. ___, 882 S.E.2d 91 (2022)
Nonconformities

The plaintiff owned a three-unit residential property in a residential zoning district that was used for short-term rentals. Beginning in 1984, the town's zoning regulation limited "tourist homes and other temporary residences renting by the day or week" to nonresidential zoning districts. In 2019 and 2020, the regulations were amended to define "short-term rental of a dwelling unit" and to allow these only in a short-term-rental overlay district. The town cited the plaintiff for a zoning violation, contending his use violated the 1984 regulation on tourist homes and the 2020 regulation on short-term rentals.

The court held that the regulation of short-term rentals prior to 2020 was ambiguous and the 2020 amendments were adopted to clarify whether the restrictions on the location of tourist homes included short-term rentals. The two uses are substantially similar but different. Because ambiguities are to be resolved in favor of the free use of property, as a matter of law the plaintiff's use should be considered a lawful nonconformity. Since the notice of violation was for a "short-term rental" use and not for a "temporary residence renting by the day or week," the question of whether the use violated the pre-2020 regulations was not before the board of adjustment and thus cannot be considered by the court.

Askew v. City of Kinston, ___ N.C. App. ___, 883 S.E.2d 85 (2022)

Demolition; Exhaustion

The city condemned three vacant, dilapidated residential properties as unsafe buildings pursuant to G.S. 160D-1119. In each case the building inspector issued orders of abatement after an administrative hearing. The plaintiff appealed one of the orders to the city council, but not the other two. No appeals were made to superior court. An appeal was made to federal court, which dismissed the action for lack of subject-matter jurisdiction. This action was then commenced, claiming a violation of equal protection and due process under the state constitution. The right to appeal the condemnation orders to the city council or superior court provided an adequate statutory remedy to address the plaintiff's claims. As the plaintiff failed to exhaust the administrative remedies, the court lacks subject-matter jurisdiction to hear these direct constitutional claims.

Pope v. Davidson County, ___ N.C. App. ___, 885 S.E.2d 119 (2023)

Special use; Voting

The plaintiffs appealed the denial of a special use permit for a motocross training facility. At the conclusion of the evidentiary hearing, the board of adjustment voted that each of the four applicable standards had been met, but the vote to find the standard on maintaining the value of continuous property received a 3-2 affirmative vote. The board incorrectly believed that a four-fifths vote was required for each standard, so the matter was tabled until the board's next meeting. At the following meeting, the board voted to rescind their prior votes and reconsider the matter. The board then voted that the application failed to meet three of the standards. The court held that the initial affirmative vote on all four standards had the effect of issuing the permit, that reconsideration was an error of law, and that the trial court properly ordered the permit to be issued.

Selected Federal Cases Arising in North Carolina

Hart Book Stores, Inc. v. Edmisten, 612 F.2d 821 (4th Cir. 1979), *cert. denied*, 447 U.S. 929 (1980)
Adult uses

The court upheld the state statutes prohibiting a single building from housing more than one adult business. The court held this to be a content-neutral separation requirement designed to prevent adverse secondary impacts and as such a permissible time-place-and-manner restriction on speech. The court held that differential treatment of adult bookstores relative to other bookstores does not violate equal protection and that the definitions included in the law were sufficiently precise to avoid impermissible vagueness.

Ocean Acres Limited Partnership v. Dare County Board of Health, 707 F.2d 103 (4th Cir. 1983)
Moratoria; Statutes of limitation; Takings

The plaintiff proposed the use of septic tanks for a development to be located near the Fresh Pond in Nags Head. The county denied approval of the septic tanks and imposed a moratorium on permits in this area for six years, until the towns of Nags Head and Kill Devil Hills adopted regulations restricting septic tanks in the area. The court held that the septic-tank ban was not a taking, as it addressed a substantial public purpose (protection of a public water supply) and the plaintiff did make a profit on the development (albeit substantially lower than expected). The court also held that the three-year statute of limitations for bringing this action began upon adoption of the moratorium.

Schmidt v. City of Fayetteville, 568 F. Supp. 217 (E.D.N.C. 1983), *aff'd*, 738 F.2d 431 (4th Cir. 1984), *cert. denied*, 469 U.S. 1215 (1985)
Takings

The plaintiff owned a single-family residence adjacent to a four-lane road in Fayetteville. The plaintiff moved out of the home and sought a rezoning from single-family residential to a professional office district. The petition was denied, as the property was located in a large single-family district with the nearest office zoning being a mile away. A previous tenant testified that he had enjoyed living on the site and would have purchased the property for a lower sale price. The court held that while a professional office would be a more valuable use of the property, the single-family zoning did not deny all reasonable, practical, and desirable use of the property, so there was no taking.

Major Media of the Southeast, Inc. v. City of Raleigh, 792 F.2d 1269 (4th Cir. 1986), *cert. denied*, 479 U.S. 1102 (1987)
Amortization; Signs

The court upheld the city's size and locational restrictions on off-premise advertising signs. The court noted that the city could prohibit all off-premise commercial signs and that the ordinance provision allowing the substitution of a noncommercial message on any authorized commercial sign addressed potential First Amendment issues. The court held that the five-and-one-half-year amortization period allowed before nonconforming signs had to be brought into compliance allowed sufficient recoupment of sign investments, so there was no taking.

Georgia Outdoor Advertising, Inc. v. City of Waynesville, 833 F.2d 43 (4th Cir. 1987)
Aesthetics; Signs

The court upheld an ordinance prohibiting off-premise advertising signs against a First Amendment challenge, holding that aesthetics alone is a sufficient justification for the ordinance. The court remanded the takings question relative to the four-year amortization period in the ordinance.

Naegele Outdoor Advertising, Inc. v. City of Durham, 844 F.2d 172 (4th Cir. 1988)
Amortization; Signs

The court upheld summary judgment for the city on a First Amendment challenge to an ordinance prohibiting location of off-premise advertising signs along all highways except federally funded highways. The court remanded the case regarding a taking issue raised by the ordinance's five-and-one-half-year amortization provision. The court held that a full evidentiary hearing was needed on this issue, as it was by necessity an ad hoc determination of economic impact. It set out a variety of factors relevant to that inquiry, including the number of billboards that could be used for noncommercial purposes; the terms of the leases involved; the costs of billboards that could not be used; and the depreciation taken on those billboards, their life expectancy, the income they would generate in the grace period, their salvage value, and the loss of income.

South Shell Investment v. Town of Wrightsville Beach, 703 F. Supp. 1192 (E.D.N.C. 1988), aff'd, 900 F.2d 255 (4th Cir. 1990)
Equal protection; Impact fees; Statutes of limitation

The court upheld the town's utility system impact fees and water and sewer tap fees imposed on new development. The court noted that the statute of limitations applicable to claims brought under 42 U.S.C. § 1983 in North Carolina is three years, and the period runs from the initial payment of the contested fees. The court found that an increase in the challenged fees did not violate equal protection (the alleged discrimination was between previous and new users of town utilities), as the town had a rational basis for the increase. The court concluded that the town had the statutory authority to impose the fees under the public-enterprise statutes and that the fees charged were not arbitrary (noting the fees generated would be less than the cost of improvements to be made).

McCauley v. City of Jacksonville, 739 F. Supp. 278 (E.D.N.C. 1989), aff'd, 904 F.2d 700 (4th Cir. 1990)
Discrimination; Moratoria; Vested rights

The plaintiff secured a building permit for construction of an apartment complex. After sewage overflows, the state issued a water-quality notice of violation to the city and required action to prevent future sewage overflows. The city adopted a moratorium on new building permits and sewer connections. After determining that sewer lines to serve the plaintiff's property were already at capacity, the city issued a stop-work order for the plaintiff's project. The city then rezoned the property to remove multifamily residences as a permitted use in this zoning district. While the plaintiff's property could continue as a nonconforming use once sewer service became available, the plaintiff contended that the city's action made project financing infeasible. The plaintiff argued that his project would serve low-income residents and be racially integrated and that the city action denied housing opportunities on the basis of race and was also arbitrary and capricious. The district court initially dismissed the action for failure to state a claim upon which relief may be granted, but the court of appeals remanded for consideration of equal-protection and due-process issues.

On remand, the court granted summary judgment for the city, holding that the city had a legitimate, nondiscriminatory basis for preventing multifamily development at this site (the limited sewer capacity), so there was no basis for a racial motivation claim. As most of the local population would have been eligible to rent as moderate-to-low-income families, there was no showing of a disparate racial impact. Since the plaintiff had a valid building permit and had made substantial expenditures based on it, the court held that he had a vested right with due-process protection. The court held that his procedural-due-process rights were protected by the right to appeal the stop-work order to the board of adjustment and that a distinction between single-family and multifamily housing in the zoning amendment had a rational and legitimate basis.

Georgia Outdoor Advertising, Inc. v. City of Waynesville, 900 F.2d 783 (4th Cir. 1990)
Amortization; Signs

The court reversed summary judgment for the plaintiff in a challenge to the defendant city's ordinance amortization provision for nonconforming off-premise advertising signs. The court held that an amortization period does not automatically preclude a takings challenge, nor would its absence invariably render the ordinance an unconstitutional taking. It was inappropriate to hold the ordinance facially invalid, so the court remanded the matter for findings on the takings issue.

Mays-Ott Co. v. Town of Nags Head, 751 F. Supp. 82 (E.D.N.C. 1990)
Vested rights

The plaintiff developer contended that the defendant town's permit revocation for a partially completed duplex project was arbitrary and capricious and constituted a due-process violation. The plaintiff had secured a permit for a "cottage court" complex of four duplex buildings (later amended to three) with a shared pool and tennis court. The permit required that work on the project be completed in eighteen months, with provision for a twelve-month extension. After the permit was issued, the town amended its ordinances to remove cottage courts as a permissible use in this area. At the end of the eighteen-month period, the plaintiff had completed two units, installed pilings for the third, and built much of the common-area improvements. Work then paused for the summer season, and when the plaintiff sought to resume construction, the town refused to renew the permit.

The court held that the plaintiff had secured a vested right in the entire project based on substantial expenditures made in good-faith reliance on the original permit approval and the town's lack of a substantial public-policy basis for permit revocation. While the plaintiff was not entitled to an indefinite period to finish the project, here the town offered no reasonable explanation for its refusal to allow completion.

Leland v. Federal Insurance Administrator, 934 F.2d 524 (4th Cir.), *cert. denied*, 502 U.S. 957 (1991)
Floodplain zoning and insurance

The plaintiff's oceanfront structure in Topsail Beach was damaged by winter storms and declared by the town to be uninhabitable and in danger of imminent collapse. The plaintiff moved the structure across the street from its initial site and submitted a claim for relocation costs under his flood-insurance policy. The court held that the 1988 amendments to the National Flood Insurance Act (known as the Upton-Jones amendment) that provided coverage for relocation costs of imminently endangered structures was not retroactive (given no language in the statute to that effect) and thus did not cover a 1987 relocation. The fact that the relocation of the septic tank for the structure was not completed until three days after the effective date of the amendment did not serve to bring this claim within the amendment's coverage.

National Advertising Co. v. City of Raleigh, 947 F.2d 1158 (4th Cir. 1991), *cert. denied*, 504 U.S. 931 (1992)
Amortization; Signs; Statutes of limitation

The court held that the three-year statute of limitations of G.S. 1-52(5) applied to a claim that the defendant city's sign amortization period was an unconstitutional taking. The court found that the limitations period began to run upon adoption of the amortization requirement. The court also held that application of the requirement was not a continuing constitutional violation, as any resultant harm stemmed only from the initial adoption.

Naegele Outdoor Advertising, Inc. v. City of Durham, 803 F. Supp. 1068 (M.D.N.C. 1992), *aff'd*, 19 F.3d 11 (4th Cir.), *cert. denied*, 513 U.S. 928 (1994)

Amortization; Signs

The parties in this case engaged in "lengthy and exhaustive" discovery to ascertain the economic impacts of the city's five-and-one-half-year amortization requirement for off-premise advertising signs. The court found that the plaintiff's takings claim was ripe. The court held that all signs in the Durham market constituted the appropriate unit for analysis of the impact of the amortization provision, not each individual affected sign. The court then examined the entire list of factors affecting the economic impact of the regulation set forth by the court of appeals in its earlier decision in this litigation. The court noted that the plaintiff had recovered nearly twice the fair-market value of its affected signs during the amortization period and was able to make a reasonable return on its remaining signs. The court concluded that the amortization requirement was not a taking.

Nello L. Teer Co. v. Orange County, 810 F. Supp. 679 (M.D.N.C. 1992), *aff'd in part, rev'd in part per curiam*, 993 F.2d 1538 (4th Cir. 1993)

Vested rights

The plaintiff challenged a county moratorium on permits for quarries and a subsequent zoning amendment that removed mining as a permitted use in the zoning district in which plaintiff's proposed rock quarry was located. The court held that since the quarry required a special use permit under the previous zoning and no such permit had been obtained, the plaintiff had no cognizable property right that could become vested. An owner has no property right to the continuation of a particular regulation. There can be no vested rights based on the expectation that a discretionary permit will issue in the future.

On appeal, the circuit court in an unpublished decision upheld this ruling and found that the state claims, which had been dismissed with prejudice by the district court as time-barred, raised different issues and should have been dismissed without prejudice.

Burch v. Federal Insurance Administration, 23 F.3d 849 (4th Cir. 1994)

Floodplain zoning and insurance

The plaintiff homeowners contacted the state coastal management program regarding relocation of their oceanfront home in Nags Head when the structure was forty feet from the vegetation line. The state determined that the structure was imminently endangered and thus eligible for relocation benefits under the Upton-Jones provision of the national flood-insurance program (42 U.S.C. § 4013(c)(1)). The state also determined that the site proposed for relocation of the cottage met the minimum oceanfront setbacks required under the Coastal Area Management Act. The Federal Emergency Management Agency paid for the cost of relocation but then cancelled future flood insurance. The minimum setback required for continuation of insurance was the same under the federal law (thirty times the annual erosion rate) as under state law, but the federal agency applied a rate of six feet per year at this site rather than the three feet per year used by the state. The court found that the federal agency could make the final determination of erosion rates for flood-insurance purposes and was not required to accept the state definition of these rates. The court held that there was adequate scientific evidence in the record to support the federal determination that the actual rate of erosion at this site was six feet per year.

United States v. City of Charlotte, 904 F. Supp. 482 (W.D.N.C. 1995)
Group homes

The federal government brought an action against the city for violation of the Fair Housing Act in conjunction with the city's denial of an application for construction of a group home for AIDS patients in a single-family zoning district. The applicant for the facility, Taylor Home, intervened and added equal-protection, Americans with Disabilities Act (ADA), and Rehabilitation Act claims. The city sought dismissal of Taylor's ADA and Rehabilitation Act claims. The court held that the zoning decision of the city did not constitute exclusion from a "service, program, or activity" of a municipality and thus was not subject to the ADA. The court further held that the protection of the Rehabilitation Act was not limited to persons with disabilities but that the statute's "any person aggrieved" term included persons providing services who were allegedly discriminated against based on the disabilities of those they serve. Accordingly, this claim was not to be dismissed.

Browning-Ferris Industries of South Atlantic, Inc. v. Wake County, 905 F. Supp. 312 (E.D.N.C. 1995)
Due process; Vested rights

The plaintiff company proposed to lease land in Morrisville near Lake Crabtree for a regional facility for its garbage trucks and containers. The town of Morrisville approved a site plan for the project and a building permit for the structures. The county approved a land-disturbing permit. The town of Cary approved a connection to its sewer system to receive effluent from the project site. At this point the county board of commissioners determined that the stormwater runoff from the project posed an unacceptable risk to Lake Crabtree. The commissioners urged the state to deny a water-quality permit for the project and notified Cary that the county did not approve allowing effluent from the project to use a county sewer interceptor to transport waste to the Cary treatment plant. The plaintiff terminated its contract with the landowner and challenged the county's action on due-process and equal-protection grounds.

The court held that the plaintiff had secured a vested property right in the project based on the building permit and substantial expenditures in good-faith reliance on the site-plan approval. The court held that the county's action was arbitrary and capricious in that the county had no authority to refuse effluent-transport approval on grounds unrelated to the effluent. The county had no authority to withhold this approval based on the proposed land use (as the land was within Morrisville, which was subject to town rather than county land use approval), water-quality impacts (which were within the purview of state agencies), or citizen objections. The court granted summary judgment for the plaintiff on the due-process claim. However, it granted summary judgment for the county on the equal-protection claim, noting that there was no showing that a similarly situated business was treated differently.

K. Hope, Inc. v. Onslow County, 911 F. Supp. 948 (E.D.N.C. 1995), *vacated*, 107 F.3d 866 (4th Cir. 1997)
Adult uses

The plaintiff owner of an adult use challenged an ordinance adopted by the defendant county under its general ordinance-making power that regulated the location of such businesses. The district court held that state law precluding more than one adult business in a single location preempted county regulation of minimum-separation requirements for adult uses. The court also held that since the ordinance regulated the location of these businesses, it was in effect a zoning ordinance rather than a general-police-power ordinance, but that the requisite procedures for zoning adoption had been met. The court then found that the ordinance met First Amendment protections. On appeal, the court of appeals held that the state law issues presented were difficult and unsettled and should be left to state courts. The court ruled that the district court should have abstained from deciding the state law issues. [Note: State law was subsequently amended to remove the possible state preemption.]

Mom N Pops, Inc. v. City of Charlotte, 979 F. Supp. 372 (W.D.N.C. 1997), *aff'd*, 162 F.3d 1155 (4th Cir. 1998)
Adult uses

The city issued a notice of zoning violation for operation of an adult bookstore and mini-motion-picture the-ater in a retail sales location that did not allow adult establishments. The determination that the establishment was an adult business and that it was in violation of zoning regulations was upheld by the board of adjustment and affirmed by the superior court, which issued an injunction prohibiting operation of an adult business at this location. The city then revoked the plaintiff's zoning use permit. The board of adjustment upheld this order. When subsequent investigation revealed that an adult business was still in operation, the city began assessing daily civil penalties and sought further injunctive relief. The superior court found the plaintiff in contempt and issued an order to cease operation. South Blvd. Video and News then ceased operation. Several months later, the plaintiff Mom N Pops was incorporated with the same principals and attorneys as South Blvd. Video and News; Mom N Pops subleased the South Blvd. premises and secured rights to the use of the name and goodwill of that business.

Mom N Pops then applied for a privilege license for a retail and video business at this site. The license application was referred to city zoning officials for a determination as to the type of business involved and ver-ification of zoning compliance. The zoning office requested documentation that the use would not be an adult business prior to issuing a zoning clearance or privilege license. The plaintiff did not submit the requested information and instituted this litigation.

The court held the privilege license to be a tax, not a regulatory scheme. The zoning administrator has no discretion as to the type of business allowed at a particular location. The court held that neither the tax nor the zoning-compliance review constituted a prior restraint on speech and that the restrictions on adult-business location included in the zoning ordinance were a reasonable time-place-and-manner restriction on speech and left reasonable alternative avenues for protected speech. The court found that the definition of an adult business as a use with "one of its principal business purposes" or "a substantial or significant portion of its stock or trade" being the sale or rental of adult materials was not impermissibly vague.

CMH Manufacturing, Inc. v. Catawba County, 994 F. Supp. 697 (W.D.N.C. 1998)
Manufactured housing

The plaintiff challenged the county zoning provisions establishing appearance standards for single-wide and double-wide manufactured housing. The ordinance required lap siding and a pitched roof with shingles. The court held that federal law preempted local construction and safety standards for manufactured housing but not local appearance or aesthetic standards. The court also held that the local regulations did not violate the Commerce Clause, Due Process Clause, or Equal Protection Clause.

Mermaids, Inc. v. Currituck County Board of Commissioners, 19 F. Supp. 2d 493 (E.D.N.C. 1998)
Adult uses

The plaintiff operated a bar in the Point Harbor area of Currituck County. The plaintiff began offering topless dancing at the bar without the requisite special use permit for adult entertainment. The ordinance limited adult uses to the "heavy manufacturing" zoning district and established a 1000-foot separation from various sensitive land uses and from residential zoning districts. The court upheld the county ordinance as a reason-able regulation aimed at preventing adverse secondary impacts.

AT&T Wireless PCS, Inc. v. Winston-Salem Zoning Board of Adjustment, 172 F.3d 307 (4th Cir. 1999)
Findings; Telecommunication towers

The plaintiff challenged the city's denial of a special use permit for a telecommunication tower proposed to be built on the property of the Southeastern Center for Contemporary Art. The site was located in a single-family residential neighborhood that included a structure on the National Register of Historic Places. The tower would be 500 feet from any other residences. The city's zoning board held a hearing on the permit application and received testimony both supporting and opposing it. The board voted to deny the permit on the grounds that the tower would not be in harmony with the area or consistent with the city's comprehensive plan. Immediately after the hearing, the board's secretary sent an official notice of the decision to the plaintiff, with the word "denied" written in the blank for case disposition. Three months later, the board adopted minutes for its hearing and a written decision that summarized the evidence and the board's reasons for its decision.

The plaintiff alleged that this procedure violated the requirement of the federal Telecommunications Act that denials be "in writing and supported by substantial evidence contained in a written record." 42 U.S.C. § 332(c)(7)(B)(iii). The district court agreed and ordered the permit issued. The Fourth Circuit reversed and upheld the city's decision. The court found that the prompt mailing of a letter with the word "denied" on the application met the requirement that the decision be in writing. The court further held that the subsequent transcription of the hearing, adoption of minutes, and adoption of written findings met the requirement of a written record to support the decision, as there was no requirement that the formal written decision be filed contemporaneously with the actual decision. Finally, the court ruled that while there was adequate evidence in the record to support the permit issuance, there was also competent, substantial evidence in the record to support denial, and thus the decision had to be affirmed.

Oxford House, Inc. v. City of Raleigh, No. 5:98-CV-113-BO(2), 1999 WL 1940013 (E.D.N.C. Jan. 26, 1999)
Group homes

Raleigh's zoning codes restricted homes in single-family zoning districts to no more than four unrelated persons but allowed "supportive housing units" with more than four unrelated persons with specified conditions (including battered individuals, abused children, pregnant teenagers, those recovering from drug or alcohol abuse, those with temporary or permanent mental, physical, or emotional disabilities, and those protected by the Americans with Disabilities Act); their family members; and support and supervisory personnel, provided they were 375 feet from another supportive-housing residence or any existing group or family-care home.

The plaintiffs, a group home and its residents, were cited for a violation of the separation requirement. The plaintiff contended that the 375-foot separation requirement violated the Fair Housing Act, the Americans with Disabilities Act, and the Fourteenth Amendment. The plaintiffs did not seek board of adjustment review of the citation. The city responded with a counterclaim seeking a declaration that the spacing requirement comported with federal law. The plaintiffs did not respond, and default judgment was entered for the city. The plaintiffs sought to vacate the default judgment, while the city sought a judgment on the pleadings.

The court upheld the entry of default judgment for the city, as the plaintiffs were unable to show a meritorious defense to the city's counterclaim. The court held that the city's regulations did not discriminate against these individuals but, rather, exempted them from the limit on numbers of residents, provided the separation requirement was observed. The court granted the city's motion for judgment on the pleadings.

Trinity Baptist Church, Inc. v. City of Asheville, 88 F. Supp. 2d 487 (W.D.N.C. 1999)
Abstention; Religious use; Standing

The plaintiff religious organization challenged the city's development regulation that excluded day-care and recreational and educational facilities incidental to a place of worship from its definition of a church. When the city issued a permit for completion of an auditorium and day care, a neighborhood association appealed the decision to the board of adjustment, which upheld the permit issuance. The plaintiff's suit raised a number of claims, including vested rights and violation of due process, equal protection, and freedom of religious expression. A state action raising many of the same issues was also pending.

The court dismissed the action on two grounds. First, since the city had permitted the plaintiff's proposed development, they had no injury and thus no standing for this suit. Second, given the availability of timely state-court review for resolution of these complex issues of state land use law, federal-court abstention was appropriate.

Frye v. City of Kannapolis, 109 F. Supp. 2d 436 (M.D.N.C. 1999)
Adult uses; Statutes of limitation

The plaintiff operated an adult newsstand in Kannapolis. Zoning regulations were adopted in 1994 to require a 2000-foot separation between individual adult businesses and between these businesses and sensitive land uses such as schools, parks, and churches. The plaintiff's store was nonconforming upon adoption of the regulations, and he was given sixty days to come into compliance. In 1999, the plaintiff brought a Section 1983 claim alleging a First Amendment violation on the grounds that the regulation totally excluded adult uses from the jurisdiction. The city moved to dismiss, contending that the claim was barred by the three-year statute of limitations of G.S. 1-52(5).

The court held that the plaintiff had made a facial challenge to the ordinance on First Amendment grounds, as an allegation that the ordinance left no site within the city as permissible for adult use would not provide the requisite reasonable alternative avenues for expression. The court then held that statutes of limitation do not bar facial challenges on First Amendment grounds, so the city's motion to dismiss could not be granted.

Steakhouse, Inc. v. City of Raleigh, 166 F.3d 634 (4th Cir. 1999), *cert. denied*, 534 U.S. 1113 (2002)
Adult uses

The plaintiff challenged Raleigh's denial of a special use permit for a proposed topless bar as an unlawful prior restraint under the First Amendment. The board of adjustment denied the permit on the grounds of insufficient parking and a failure to demonstrate that the use would not adversely affect public services or adjacent properties. Rather than seeking judicial review in superior court, the plaintiff filed this federal-court action. The district court refused to issue a preliminary injunction compelling issuance of the permit, and the Fourth Circuit affirmed.

The court held that the plaintiff had failed to show any irreparable harm without a preliminary injunction or that any harm it would suffer would outweigh the harm the city and neighbors would suffer if the injunction were to be issued. The court also held that the plaintiff was unlikely to succeed on the merits of the claim that Raleigh's regulations constituted an unlawful prior restraint. The court found that the standards for the permit decision sufficiently limited the board of adjustment's discretion to "concrete topics that generate palpable effects on the surrounding neighborhood" (including factors such as parking, traffic, police protection, noise, light, stormwater runoff, pedestrian circulation, and safety). The court held that the ordinance provided for a decision within a reasonably short time frame, as the ordinance mandated a final decision by the board within ninety days of receipt of a completed application. The court also ruled that the state statutory provisions for judicial review of special use permit denials provided the requisite prompt judicial review for First Amendment purposes. The court noted that permission to open a topless bar does not present particularly time-sensitive issues (as might be the case with a parade, demonstration, or exhibition of a film), that the petitioner must file for review within thirty days, and that the board's rules of procedure insured prompt submittal of its record and brief regarding such a petition.

Sandhills Ass'n of Realtors v. Village of Pinehurst, No. 1:98CV00303, 1999 WL 1129624 (M.D.N.C. Nov. 8, 1999)
Signs

Plaintiffs challenged sign regulations that limited the size of "For Sale" signs in residential zoning districts to a maximum of eight by ten inches with a height of no more than thirty inches, restricted colors to green and white, and specified that only the words "For Sale" or "For Rent" along with a contact name and telephone number could be displayed. These limitations were more restrictive than those for other types of "temporary signs" (including those for political signs; holiday decorations; and signs for fairs, church functions, construction sites, and yard sales).

The court invalidated the regulations as content-based regulations because they treated real-estate signs more harshly than other yard signs and specified the language that could be used for these signs. The court found that aesthetic interests, while important, were not a compelling enough governmental interest to support content-based regulation. The court also held that the restrictions were not reasonable time-place-and-manner restrictions, nor were they valid regulations of commercial speech under the *Central Hudson* tests. (See *Central Hudson Gas & Electric Corp. v. Public Service Commission*, 447 U.S. 557, 574 (1980).)

Carrico v. Village of Sugar Mountain, 114 F. Supp. 2d 422 (W.D.N.C. 2000)
Vested rights

The plaintiff had contracts to build condominiums in Sugar Mountain. After the defendant village revoked his permits, he initiated this litigation alleging violation of various constitutional and statutory rights. At discovery it was admitted that neither the plaintiff nor any of his corporations held the general contractors' licenses required for this construction, nor did they hold the real-estate licenses necessary to market them. The court found that since the plaintiff by law could not undertake this work, and as any contracts entered into by an unlicensed contractor are unenforceable, the plaintiff had no property rights to continue this business. The defendant was entirely within its rights in refusing to issue certificates of zoning compliance.

American Legion Post No. 7 v. City of Durham, 239 F.3d 601 (4th Cir. 2001)
Signs

The court upheld a Durham ordinance regulating the size of all flags (including the U.S. flag) as a reasonable time-place-and-manner restriction of speech that preserved adequate alternative avenues for expression and was supported by the city's substantial aesthetic interests. The regulation limited the height and number of flagpoles and the number and maximum size of all flags. In nonresidential districts, flagpoles were limited to a maximum height of 70 feet and flags were restricted to 216 square feet in size; in residential districts, the corresponding limits were 25 feet (flagpole height) and 40 square feet (flag size). There was also a limit of three flagpoles per property and two flags per flagpole and setback requirements.

Davis v. Town of Holly Springs, No. 5:00-CV-368-BR(3), 2001 WL 34013440 (E.D.N.C. Apr. 25, 2001), *aff'd*, 20 F. App'x 180 (4th Cir. 2001)
Immunity; Parties

The plaintiff sued the town and various specified town officials regarding the revocation and refusal to renew a special use permit. The court held that suits against individual defendants in their official capacities are equivalent to a suit against the town. Further, the complaint identified no acts by any of the individual plaintiffs. Therefore, all individual defendants were dismissed from the action. The court held that the town and its board of adjustment acting on a special use permit is performing a quasi-judicial function, so the board and its members are entitled to absolute immunity.

Tri-County Paving, Inc. v. Ashe County, 281 F.3d 430 (4th Cir. 2002)
Moratoria; Vested rights

The plaintiff unsuccessfully sought county approval to build an asphalt plant. The court upheld a one-year moratorium on such plants, and the county subsequently adopted a Polluting Industries Development Ordinance. Since the plaintiff had only applied for a permit and had not obtained a building permit or any other county approval prior to the adoption of the ordinance, the plaintiff had no vested right to construct the plant. The court held that the moratorium was rationally related to a legitimate public objective of protecting the health, safety, and well-being of county citizens.

Southern Blasting Services, Inc. v. Wilkes County, 288 F.3d 584 (4th Cir. 2002)

Due process; Preemption

The plaintiff challenged county ordinances regulating explosives operations and the storage and use of explosives. The court held that federal law on the manufacture, distribution, and storage of explosives did not preempt local regulation, noting an express congressional intent not to preempt the field (18 U.S.C. § 848) and pointing out that the county regulations were not in direct and positive conflict with federal provisions simply because they were more stringent in some respects. Since the county regulations addressed legitimate governmental interests and were rationally related to these objectives, they were found to meet substantive-due-process requirements. Since the plaintiff had not applied for a county permit, there was no standing to raise a procedural-due-process claim (and the court noted that, in any event, the standards and process to be followed by the county fire marshal met procedural-due-process requirements).

Giovani Carandola, Ltd. v. Bason, 303 F.3d 507 (4th Cir. 2002)

Adult uses

The plaintiff operated a bar that offered adult entertainment in Greensboro. The state Alcoholic Beverage Control (ABC) Commission cited the plaintiff for violation of state statutes prohibiting simulation of sexual intercourse or masturbation at facilities with ABC licenses. The court held that the state rules limiting the nature of erotic dancing were legitimate content-neutral rules designed to prevent adverse secondary impacts and were thus subject to intermediate rather than strict-scrutiny review. The court found that since the rules applied not only to bars and clubs but also to theaters offering ballet, plays, and other serious literary work for which no adverse secondary impact had or could be produced, they (and the state statutes) were impermissibly overly broad.

Sunkler v. Town of Nags Head, No. 2:01-CV-22-H(2), 2002 WL 32395571 (E.D.N.C. May 17, 2002), aff'd, 50 F. App'x 116 (4th Cir. 2002)

Inspections; Liability

The plaintiffs alleged that a building inspection pursuant to an administrative-inspection warrant constituted an unreasonable search and that the defendant town's building-code and zoning enforcement were negligent. The inspection was made to check for alleged unauthorized work to convert approved residential storage space to unapproved habitable space. The fact that the inspector had personal knowledge of the plaintiffs' plans to do this work and objective indicators of work underway in that portion of the building provided reasonable grounds for the warrant and search. Given the reasonableness of the search, the inspector has qualified immunity from personal damages while performing a discretionary act. The town likewise has immunity for a reasonable search. Without an appeal of the enforcement action to the board of adjustment, the plaintiff could not bring a claim of negligence against the town.

Eberhart v. Gettys, 215 F. Supp. 2d 666 (M.D.N.C. 2002)

Enforcement; Liability

The plaintiffs alleged that the defendants selectively enforced the Town of Spencer's ordinances regarding a nightclub, a boardinghouse, and rental properties because of the plaintiffs' race. The court refused to dismiss the claim, noting that there was a genuine issue of material fact as to whether the nightclub, which had been subject to repeated warnings and citations regarding excessive noise, was treated differently from similarly situated businesses. The court held that an allegation that the mayor made at least one racially biased statement, along with other circumstantial evidence of racial discrimination that was alleged, created a genuine issue of material fact on this allegation as well. The court held that the allegation of racial animus on the part of the mayor, if established, voided the qualified immunity he would have in his individual capacity; however, because no such personal animus was alleged regarding the defendant police officer and zoning-enforcement officer, those defendants retained immunity in their individual capacities. As a question of fact existed as to whether the alleged discrimination was pursuant to a municipal policy or by a final policy maker, summary judgment on town liability was not proper.

Hyatt v. Town of Lake Lure, 225 F. Supp. 2d 647 (W.D.N.C. 2002)
Liability; Statutes of limitation

The plaintiff sought and received permits to build a bulkhead and boathouse on Lake Lure. Town staff inspected the work during construction and raised no objections. After the construction, a neighbor complained that the bulkhead improperly extended onto his property. Upon investigation, the town concluded the plaintiff's construction violated the town's lake-structures regulation in several respects. The plaintiff appealed to the town council for permission for an after-the-fact approval to fill in a portion of the lake. The council denied this approval and ordered the plaintiff to bring the location of the bulkhead and boathouse into compliance with the rules. The town's order requiring such was appealed to the board of adjustment. Town staff provided written analysis of the matter to the board but did not provide copies to the plaintiff or a notice that the material had been provided to the board. Upon the board's upholding of the staff interpretation, this litigation was commenced. The plaintiff (1) alleged that the regulations should have been adopted following zoning procedures and that the town was estopped from enforcement since it made no objections during construction and (2) raised various constitutional claims.

The court dismissed some of the plaintiff's claims and allowed others to go forward. The court held that the town council's refusal to permit fill in the lake was quasi-judicial and that individual council members had absolute immunity from suit in their personal capacity on these decisions. However, the actions of the town manager and zoning administrator in sending letters to the board were ministerial and not immune from suit. The court found that the lake-structures regulations were adopted as development regulations, thus any facial challenge to the procedures used had to be brought within two months, which was not done here. Since the plaintiff alleged that the town acted with personal malice, her claims of selective enforcement and equal-protection violation were not dismissed. The court ruled that the town council's consideration of the plaintiff's appeals was quasi-judicial in nature. The court also held that an adequate allegation had been made that the town's definition of the shoreline of the lake was impermissibly vague.

Hyatt v. Town of Lake Lure, 314 F. Supp. 2d 562 (W.D.N.C. 2003), *aff'd*, 114 F. App'x 72 (4th Cir. 2004)
Vagueness

The court held that the definition of lake shoreline used (based on elevations and contours) was not impermissibly vague. The disagreement regarding shoreline location was not based on confusion in the definition but, rather, on the plaintiff's total disregard or lack of consideration of the definition. The court found that at each step of the enforcement proceedings, the plaintiff was given notice of the violation; she also had an opportunity to appear before the town council, was able to present an argument and evidence at the hearings, and had counsel present at all hearings. The court granted summary judgment to the town on these issues and dismissed the town's trespass claim (based on improper encroachment of the plaintiff's boathouse on the town-owned lake) without prejudice.

Fourth Quarter Properties IV, Inc. v. City of Concord, No. 1:02CV00908, 2004 WL 231303 (M.D.N.C. Jan. 22, 2004)
Jurisdiction; Takings

The plaintiff engaged in extended discussions with the city regarding a proposed shopping center to be developed adjacent to the Concord Regional Airport. The discussions were complicated by potential revisions to the defendant city's ordinances regarding restrictions on the height and location of buildings adjacent to the airport, potential runway-expansion proposals, utility-easement arrangements, and economic-incentive agreements. As a result, portions of the proposed development were not approved (even though objections were not raised during preliminary reviews), plans were required to be revised, and other approvals were delayed. The court held that a takings claim by the plaintiff was not ripe because its state inverse-condemnation claim was pending. The court granted the city's motion to stay the state claims, as those claims involved important matters of state zoning law more properly heard in state court, thus making federal abstention appropriate under *Burford v. Sun Oil Co.*, 319 U.S. 315 (1943).

Molamphy v. Town of Southern Pines, No. 1:02CV00720, 2004 WL 419789 (M.D.N.C. Mar. 8, 2004)
Adoption; Liability

The plaintiff approached the defendant town regarding a proposed convenience store and was advised to present an informal concept plan for staff review. After this information was submitted, the town council began consideration of a zoning-text amendment to remove convenience stores as a permitted use in the highway corridor overlay district, a designation that included the subject property. In subsequent meetings with the plaintiff, inconsistencies in his plan regarding the current ordinance were identified, but the proposed text amendment was not mentioned. The town subsequently held a hearing to effectuate this text amendment. The two published notices of the town-council hearing were published in the same week, rather than in separate weeks as required by state law. Also, the published notice simply noted a proposed amendment to a particular section of the ordinance, with no indication of the subject matter or content of the amendment. The plaintiff attended the hearing and objected to the proposed amendment.

The court held that the ordinance amendment was invalid due to the town's failure to strictly comply with both statutory and ordinance requirements for published notice (both on the basis that the notice was not timely and that it was so sparse as to fail to apprise persons of the nature and character of the action proposed). The fact that the plaintiff had actual notice of the hearing was legally irrelevant. The court noted that the violation of state statutory procedural requirements is not per se a constitutional violation. The facts that the plaintiff had actual notice of the hearing and that the plaintiff had no vested legal right to build a convenience store led to dismissal of federal due-process claims.

Giovani Carandola, Ltd. v. Fox, 470 F.3d 1074 (4th Cir. 2006)
Adult uses

In response to judicial invalidation of statutes limiting adult entertainment in facilities with Alcoholic Beverage Control licenses, the state amended its statutes and rules regarding sexual performances at these facilities. The relevant statute, G.S. 18B-1005.1, prohibited actual or simulated specified sex acts and the fondling of specified erogenous zones of the body. The statute excluded application to performances in theaters, concert halls, art centers, museums, or similar establishments devoted to the arts when presenting performances of serious literary, artistic, scientific, or political value. The court held that the prohibition of these specified acts was not impermissibly vague or facially overbroad.

Giovanni Carandola, Ltd. v. City of Greensboro, 258 F. App'x 512 (4th Cir. 2007), *aff'g* 457 F. Supp. 2d 615 (M.D.N.C. 2006) *and* No. 1: 05CV1166, 2007 WL 703333 (M.D.N.C. Mar. 1, 2007)
Adult uses; Attorney's fees; Mootness

When Greensboro amended its regulations on adult business in 2001 to increase minimum separations, several existing businesses became nonconforming and were required to close or relocate. After the U.S. district court held that the Greensboro ordinance did not prohibit the continuation of businesses already in existence, the city amended the ordinance to clearly prohibit continuation of nonconforming adult businesses.

The court held that the city's subsequent amendment of the ordinance made the question of interpretation of the ordinance as originally written moot. The court also held that the plaintiff adult-business owners were not entitled to attorney's fees here since they had prevailed on the question of statutory interpretation (for which attorney's fees are not available). Since the court did not reach their constitutional claims, the plaintiffs had not prevailed on a 42 U.S.C. § 1983 claim, and thus they could not be awarded attorney's fees.

Adams v. Village of Wesley Chapel, 259 F. App'x 545 (4th Cir. 2007)
Due process; Equal protection; Takings

The plaintiffs acquired land in Union County in 1964. In 1999, the mayor of the village discussed potential voluntary annexation with the plaintiffs and advised them that their zoning would not change if this happened. The plaintiffs then submitted an annexation petition to the village and were annexed in 1999. At that time, the village did not have a zoning ordinance, so the property remained subject to county zoning. A year later the village adopted its own zoning ordinance and, while leaving the plaintiffs' property in the same R-40 district as had been the case with the county, changed the density standard for the district in ways that resulted in thirty-five fewer potential residential lots on the property. The plaintiffs sold the land in 2004 for $3.7 million but alleged that the village zoning had reduced its value by $1.59 million.

The court held that the sale of the land had not mooted the plaintiffs' constitutional claims. However, the court then found for the village on all of those claims. The court applied a *Penn Central* balancing test to the takings claim (see *Penn Cent. Transp. Co. v. N.Y. City*, 438 U.S. 104 (1978)). The court noted that the plaintiffs could make a reasonable return on their investment, just not as much as they had hoped, and that the character of the governmental action here was "garden-variety zoning" intended to control growth, preserve a small-town atmosphere, and maintain a low tax rate, all legitimate governmental objectives. The plaintiffs' substantive-due-process claim failed, as the village regulations were reasonably related to the above-stated legitimate objectives. The plaintiffs were not misled by governmental misconduct, the court found, as even if the mayor's promise that the zoning would not change were to be accepted, the zoning did not change for a year and the village honored all vested rights that had been established under county zoning. There was no equal-protection violation in that the plaintiffs did not show different treatment from those who were similarly situated; those with vested rights to higher densities under the county ordinance were not similarly situated.

MLC Automotive, LLC v. Town of Southern Pines, No. 1:05CV1078, 2007 WL 128945 (M.D.N.C. Jan. 11, 2007)
Evidence; Public records

The plaintiff business challenged a rezoning that blocked its plans to use a site for multiple automobile-sales facilities. The plaintiff also contended that the defendant town intentionally delayed the permit-approval process in order to allow time for the rezoning. The town sought to compel discovery of email between the plaintiff's engineer (who was responsible for site evaluation and site design) and attorney in order to show that the delay was due to the plaintiff's own conduct. The plaintiff sought to depose town council members and discover communications between council members and the town attorney. This action dealt with those discovery issues.

The court held that most of the communications between the plaintiff's engineer and attorney were protected by the attorney-client privilege; these communications were made while the engineer was acting as an agent for the plaintiff to supply information for the attorney's use in the permit applications. The court also issued a protective order preventing deposition of the town council members, holding that legislative immunity bars inquiries regarding the members' motives or intentions regarding the rezoning and that the Architectural Compliance Permit here was sufficiently similar to a quasi-judicial determination (even though the town did not follow quasi-judicial procedures in deciding upon it) so that judicial immunity barred inquiries of the members about it. Finally, the court held that while the plaintiff could not discover communications from the town attorney to the town, communications from the town and its employees to the attorney were public records and were thus discoverable.

Y.K. Enterprises v. City of Greensboro, No. 1:07CV0289, 2007 WL 2781706 (M.D.N.C. Sept. 21, 2007)
Adult uses

A number of adult businesses sought to enjoin Greensboro's enforcement of an amortization provision requiring the relocation of nonconforming businesses. The court held that there were unresolved factual issues regarding the studies supporting the city's justification for the ordinance, the range of available alternative avenues for expression, and the rationale for differing amortization requirements for different types of adult businesses. Therefore, while the court did not issue a preliminary injunction, it did order an expedited consolidated hearing on that matter and the merits of the case. The court noted that the city had voluntarily delayed enforcement during the litigation and encouraged that to continue while this case remained pending.

Mickelsen v. Warren County, No. 5:06-CV-00360-F, 2007 WL 4245848 (E.D.N.C. Nov. 29, 2007)
Adoption; Notice; Plan consistency

The plaintiffs sought a rezoning from a residential to a neighborhood business zoning district. After a positive recommendation from the planning board and a duly advertised hearing, the county commissioners voted in favor of the rezoning. After the plaintiffs left the meeting but before the meeting adjourned, one of the commissioners who had supported the rezoning made a motion to reconsider the rezoning vote, which passed. Upon reconsideration, the rezoning motion failed. The court rejected a variety of challenges to the county's failure to rezone. First, the court held that the county's rules of procedure expressly provide for a motion to reconsider if made in the same meeting as the original vote and by a member of the prevailing side and that this is not inconsistent with state law. Second, the court found that additional notice, hearing, and planning-board referral were not required for the second vote because under the county ordinance, the property is not actually rezoned until the change is entered on the official zoning map, a step that had not been taken prior to the second vote. Third, the court held that there were policies in the county's comprehensive plan supporting either zoning of this property, so there was no plan inconsistency or arbitrary and capricious action by the board. Fourth, the court found that there could be no vested right to the briefly approved rezoning because it never took effect and there were no expenditures made in reliance on it between the first and second votes. Finally, the court concluded that there was no equal-protection violation because the plaintiffs had not established that they were treated differently from others who were similarly situated and, even if they had done this, there was no showing of purposeful discrimination.

MLC Automotive, LLC v. Town of Southern Pines, 532 F.3d 269 (4th Cir. 2008)
Abstention; Jurisdiction

The plaintiff corporation claimed a vested right to develop a site for multiple automobile-sales facilities and contended that a rezoning of the site by the defendant town from General Business to Office Services that blocked the project violated its substantive-due-process rights and constituted tortious interference with contract and prospective economic-advantage rights.

The district court held that the federal claim was inextricably woven with the state common law vested-right claim, which would be more appropriately heard in state court. The court thus abstained in deference to the state's domestic policy. Since the plaintiff sought damages as well as equitable relief, the court upheld a stay awaiting the state court decision on the case. The court later denied the town's motion to vacate the stay.

The circuit court affirmed, noting that the plaintiff's allegations and evidence, viewed in the light most favorable to it, were sufficient to withstand a motion for summary judgment. The court also held that the factual and legal issues on the vested-rights claim were not clearly and easily resolved under state law, and so abstention was not an abuse of discretion by the district court.

Independence News, Inc. v. City of Charlotte, 568 F.3d 148 (4th Cir. 2008), *cert. denied*, 558 U.S. 992 (2009)
Adult uses; Amortization; Variances

The city adopted an adult use regulation in 1994 that required minimum separations between adult uses and sensitive land uses and between each sort of use. The regulation had an eight-year amortization period. It also allowed a variance to the separation requirement upon a showing that manmade or natural features provided sufficient separation to prevent harmful secondary impacts. The plaintiff challenged the application of the amortization requirement, contending that evidence in the eight years since its adoption showed that the adult use at issue here had no adverse secondary impacts. The plaintiff also made a facial challenge to the variance standards, contending that they must provide an opportunity to show a lack of adverse secondary impacts in fact at a particular location.

The court held for the city on both challenges. The court found the ordinance to be a legitimate, content-neutral time-place-and-manner regulation. The city was required to consider adverse secondary impacts at the time of enactment, but it had no obligation to make a post-enactment study of actual impacts at particular locations. The city's consideration in enactment is properly focused on the overall problem to be addressed, not on its application to a particular case. As for documentation of adverse secondary impacts in a variance application, the rules are designed to prevent future adverse impacts before they occur, so consideration of actual past impacts in a particular location is not constitutionally required.

Covenant Media of North Carolina, LLC v. City of Monroe, 285 F. App'x 30 (4th Cir. 2008)
Signs; Standing

The defendant city denied the plaintiff's permit applications for billboards due to violations of the city's regulations restricting billboard size (250 square feet per side) and separation (1000 feet between billboards and 50 feet from buildings). The court held that the plaintiff had standing for an as-applied challenge to the size restriction, as all of its proposed signs were 672 square feet per side, well above the maximum size allowed. The court held that the size restriction was a permissible content-neutral regulation that furthered substantial city interests in traffic safety and aesthetics.

Templeton Properties, LP v. Town of Boone, No. 5:07CV62-V, 2008 WL 5839000 (W.D.N.C. Mar. 3, 2008)
Abstention

The plaintiff applied for a special use permit to locate a medical clinic in a residential zoning district. At the hearing on the permit, the mayor appeared and opined that commercial special uses should not be allowed in the district. The board of adjustment found the application incomplete and continued the hearing. The plaintiff then submitted a revised application. Prior to resumption of the hearing on the revised complete application, the town amended the ordinance to eliminate this special use in the district. The board of adjustment then denied the application. The plaintiff filed an action in state court contesting the denial, claiming that the town's action violated federal due-process and equal-protection rights, and seeking an order to issue the permit and award costs and fees. The town then removed the action to federal court, contending that there was original jurisdiction there for the federal constitutional claims.

The court held that resolution of the zoning claims depended on the construction of state land use law, noting a well-established line of abstention cases in the Fourth Circuit that the resolution of routine land use disputes properly rests with state courts. Therefore, the matter was remanded to state courts.

Griffin v. Town of Unionville, No. 3:05-CV-514-RJC, 2008 WL 697634 (W.D.N.C. Mar. 11, 2008)

Landfills; Vested rights

The plaintiffs operated a "Construction and Demolition" landfill beginning in 1992 as a permitted use under the county zoning ordinance. After the ordinance was amended to require a special use permit for these landfills, the plaintiff secured a special use permit in 1997 in conjunction with an expansion of the landfill. The permit limited the use to an inert-debris landfill and specified that any changes would require permit modification. In 1998, the county amended its definition of these landfills to include non-hazardous industrial wastes. In 1999, the plaintiff sought state permits for inclusion of industrial wastes in this landfill. The state advised the plaintiff that G.S. 130A-294(b1) required a local franchise as well as zoning approval. The plaintiff did not secure such a franchise, nor did it get an amended special use permit from the county. In 1998, the town became an incorporated municipality, and in 2003 the town adopted its own land use regulations, with the same provisions regarding landfills as were in the county ordinance. The town in 2003 issued the plaintiff a franchise for an inert debris landfill. In 2005, the plaintiff requested a town franchise for an industrial-debris landfill, which was not granted. In 2006, the town amended its land use ordinance to delete industrial waste from the range of uses that could be allowed within the special use permits within this zoning district.

The plaintiff brought this Section 1983 claim, contending that the town's actions violated substantive due process by depriving the plaintiff of vested rights in an industrial-waste landfill. The court held that the plaintiff's vested rights were limited to an inert-debris landfill and did not extend to include industrial wastes. The court noted that the plaintiff had never secured all required approvals for this use; the special use permit had not been amended to include industrial wastes. The zoning-text amendment authorized this, but that was not the same as securing a permit amendment. Further, the plaintiff did not secure a franchise for this aspect of the landfill, something clearly required by state law. The franchise is a personal right that is legally separate from, and addresses separate issues from, the special use permit. Also, investments made to secure state approval prior to securing all required local approvals is neither in reliance on a valid approval nor made in good faith.

Karagiannopoulous v. City of Lowell, No. 3:05-CV-00401-FDW, 2008 WL 2447362 (W.D.N.C. June 13, 2008), aff'd per curiam, 305 F. App'x 64 (4th Cir. 2008)

Discrimination; Estoppel

The plaintiff acquired a lot that had been used as a used-car sales lot from 1962 to 1990. The property was rezoned from residential to neighborhood commercial (C-2) in 1985 to accommodate the neighborhood business use (with the record not clearly indicating whether the prior car sales were deemed to be a lawful nonconformity). The site was later used successively as a laundry, a pottery shop, and a welding shop. The plaintiff acquired the lot in 2003. In 2004, she located a school on the site to provide computer and English-language-proficiency classes at no cost to students from low-income households. She acquired the appropriate licenses for the school. The plaintiff then proposed to resume selling used cars on site to raise funds to defray the costs of the school.

The city concluded that car sales were not a permitted use in the neighborhood business district but would be allowed in the more intensive C-3 district. The plaintiff petitioned for a zoning-text amendment to allow the use in a C-2 district, which was denied by the town. The plaintiff's husband then secured a privilege license for a used-car lot at another location and began to store cars on this property. The city cited the plaintiff for storing junk vehicles on the lot. When the plaintiff responded that the cars were inventory rather than junk, the city advised her that it would be a zoning violation to store used cars in a district where used-car sales are not allowed.

The plaintiff brought this action pro se, contending that the city discriminated against her in not allowing resumption of used-car sales because of her Hispanic heritage. The court noted that while the lot had been used in a manner inconsistent with its zoning from 1962 to 2004 (and had actually been operated more in keeping with activities in a C-3 zone), prior noncompliance did not rezone it from C-2 to C-3. Further, prior nonenforcement did not estop the town from present enforcement of a zoning violation. The plaintiff did not establish any intentional discrimination based on ethnicity nor show any stark pattern of discrimination against Hispanics. There was no evidence that previous nonenforcement had any racial or ethnic component. The city showed other denials to white applicants for approval to operate a used-car lot in a C-2 district, so there was no evidence of a failure to treat similarly situated applicants equally.

On appeal, the court of appeals held that the plaintiff had waived review of the summary-judgment order of the district court, that her motion for default judgment was entirely without merit, and that her claim of a conspiracy between the city and district court was delusional.

Quality Built Homes, Inc. v. Village of Pinehurst, No. 1:06CV1028, 2008 WL 3503149 (M.D.N.C. Aug. 11, 2008)

Aesthetics; Due process; Equal protection; Evidence

The plaintiffs challenged ordinance architectural-design and landscaping requirements adopted by the defendant village in 2006. The architectural-design standards required inclusion of three or four design elements for new construction in three of the village's seven residential zoning districts (those three districts were located near the downtown area and historic core of the village). The landscaping standards required a tree survey in most districts and required a certain number of plantings based on a point system. The standards were based on the recommendations of a broad citizen committee that had substantial citizen comment, as well as extensive staff analysis and an earlier comprehensive-plan update. The plaintiffs contended that the standards increased the costs of housing in the village and were unconstitutionally applied only in specified zoning districts.

The court first granted motions to strike several affidavits offered by the plaintiffs regarding the economic impacts of the regulations. In most instances, the affidavits were from persons identified but then not offered as expert witnesses or not identified as witnesses at all and thereby not available in the discovery process. The court noted that even if the evidence in the stricken affidavits were allowed, it would not change the outcome of the decision.

The court then held that the ordinance did not violate the substantive-due-process rights of the plaintiffs, as none of them had a protected property right since there is no constitutional right to build houses for a certain price or to earn a particular level of profit or wages, nor is there a right to build according to the regulations in effect at the time of property purchase. Also, the regulations were rationally related to the legitimate governmental objectives of protecting property values, promoting of tourism, and preserving community character. Aesthetic regulations legitimately preserve the special character, integrity, and ambiance of the village, found the court. The village clearly gave careful consideration to balancing the aims of the regulations with the economic burden they would impose.

The court dismissed the plaintiffs' exclusionary-zoning claim, noting that they likely did not have standing to raise it. The court held that the plaintiffs had not demonstrated the availability of affordable housing prior to the regulation nor shown that the village did not provide affordable-housing options within its jurisdiction. The court also dismissed the plaintiffs' equal-protection claim, noting that zoning regulations can be different in different zoning districts and that no suspect classifications were involved that would generate strict scrutiny.

The plaintiffs also alleged a violation of the state public-records law. The plaintiffs' employee appeared in the village offices the Friday before Christmas and requested certified copies of the amendments and council minutes. When they were not immediately produced, the employee refused to leave the premises and was eventually escorted out by village police. The records were made available the first working day after the Christmas holiday (the plaintiffs contended that they were not available until the day after the New Year's holiday). The court held that the plaintiffs' public-records claim was frivolous in that there was no legal right to immediate production and the records were clearly provided in a reasonable time period. The court thus awarded attorney's fees to the defendant for its defense of this claim.

United States v. Town of Garner, 720 F. Supp. 2d 721 (E.D.N.C. 2010)

Group homes; Ripeness

Oxford House opened a group home for eight occupants in a single-family residential zoning district in late 2003. After receiving a neighbor's complaint, the town issued a notice of violation in late 2004. Oxford House appealed, contending that the occupants were a "family" under the ordinance and alternatively requesting reasonable accommodation of their use. In response, the town amended its ordinance to create a new use for "handicapped and disabled homes" that allowed up to six persons with a disability to reside in a single-family home and to limit a "family" to no more than four unrelated individuals. In early 2006, the board of adjustment upheld the staff determination that the occupants of the facility did not meet the definition of a "family" under either the original or revised ordinance. The board also held that it had no authority to issue a use variance. Oxford House did not appeal but did submit a letter asking that it be allowed to retain eight residents and have relief from the minimum-separation requirements. The town responded that the market rental value of the house was substantially less than Oxford House claimed and requested studies to document Oxford House's claim that its therapeutic model required eight residents. After a year passed without response, the town notified Oxford House that they were in violation and sent a similar notice to the landlord. Oxford House again requested reasonable accommodation and submitted an expert report on its need for eight residents. The Department of Justice then advised the town of a complaint from Oxford House regarding a failure to make reasonable accommodation and subsequently brought this action alleging that the town's failure to establish a process by which requests for reasonable accommodation could be made violated the federal Fair Housing Act.

The court first held that the claim was ripe for judicial review once the town had considered and rejected a reasonable accommodation request. After three requests to the town, a plaintiff need not submit a particular text amendment or wait for a vote on such. An indeterminate delay by the town has the same effect as an outright denial. The court held that res judicata and collateral estoppel did not apply based on the board of adjustment's unappealed decision because the federal government was not a party to or participant in that action. Oxford House was, however, precluded from relitigating issues that were actually before the board and that were both critical and necessary for the board's decision (particularly, whether their use met the ordinance definition of a "family" or some other permitted use).

Dixon v. Town of Coats, No. 5:08-cv-489-BR, 2010 WL 2347506 (E.D.N.C. June 9, 2010)

Religious use; Standing

The plaintiff owned a small building in downtown Coats that had previously been used for various retail uses, a residence, and a church. The town rezoned the entire six-block downtown area to a "Mixed Use Village District." Churches were not a permitted use in the district. At the time of the rezoning, the plaintiff's structure had been vacant for several months. Some six months later, the plaintiff leased the building to a person who proposed using it for a church. The town informed the tenant that the use was not permitted and that prior church use did not have nonconforming status as that use had been discontinued for more than sixty days. Nonetheless, the town allowed the tenant to open a church on site but advised that this was a "one time" approval and if the church closed, another religious use would not be approved. The church operated briefly, closed, and the plaintiff then leased the property to another church. The town staff denied zoning approval and the denial was upheld by the board of adjustment.

The court first held that the plaintiff had standing to bring a claim under the Religious Land Use and Institutionalized Persons Act even though he had not made nor proposed to make any personal religious use of the site. The plaintiff's potential financial loss as a lessor prohibited from leasing to a religious user of his property was sufficient to establish standing. The court dismissed his "equal terms" claim, however, as the plaintiff was not a religious assembly or institution. The court held that the exclusion of places of worship from a relatively small area was not a "substantial burden" as it did not render religious exercise effectively impractical within the town as a whole.

FC Summers Walk, LLC v. Town of Davidson, No. 3:09-CV-266-GCM, 2010 WL 4366287 (W.D.N.C. Oct. 28, 2010)
Abstention; Adequate public facilities

The town adopted an adequate-public-facilities ordinance as part of its unified development ordinance. The regulation set requirements for the availability of law enforcement, fire protection, and parks to support proposed development. The ordinance required staff review of the timing of proposed developments, impacts on service availability, and recommendations for governing-board action. The plaintiff submitted four applications and received staff determinations on each that services were inadequate and that it could wait until services were available or pay its pro rata share of the costs to advance the deficient services. The first of these staff determinations was approved by the town board and not appealed by the plaintiff. The second and third determinations were appealed, but the fourth, which was labeled a "final determination," was not appealed. The plaintiff posted bonds to cover the costs identified in the second and third determinations and brought this action contending that the town's actions violated state and federal constitutional protections.

The court previously held that there was inadequate information in the record to support the town's motion to dismiss for failure to exhaust administrative remedies given the lack of clarity about appeals of the staff determination to the town board and that it was unclear if the two-month zoning statute of limitations was applicable to an as-applied challenge of the adequate-public-facilities ordinance. 2010 WL 323769 (W.D.N.C. Jan. 20, 2010). The court here concluded that while state law was relatively settled regarding school impact fees, state law on adequate-public-facility requirements for the public-safety and parks requirements at issue here were important and unsettled. The court therefore held that the *Burford* abstention was appropriate (see *Burford v. Sun Oil Co.*, 319 U.S. 315 (1943)). In order to avoid statute of limitations issues (as there was no parallel state case pending), the court did not dismiss the case but remanded it to state court for continuation.

Oxford House, Inc. v. City of Wilmington, No. 7:07-CV-61-F, 2010 WL 4484523 (E.D.N.C. Oct. 28, 2010)
Group homes

In 2002, the city formed a task force to study and update its zoning regulations for group homes and other care facilities for the disabled. Over the course of nine months, the city held eight public meetings on the topic and, in 2003, adopted regulations that set locational standards for small (six or fewer residents), medium (seven or eight residents), and large (nine to twelve residents) group homes. The rules also included a half-mile separation requirement for all group homes. The plaintiff had two group homes that did not meet the updated regulations as they had nine rather than the maximum eight residents allowed for those sites. These two homes were also within a half-mile of other existing group homes (where there were multiple group homes within the prescribed radius, the city held a random drawing to determine which homes would be permitted to remain as sited). The plaintiff brought this action contending that the city's subsequent enforcement action violated the Fair Housing Act, the Americans with Disabilities Act, and the Rehabilitation Act.

The court held that the plaintiff failed to meet its burden of establishing that its proposed accommodation was necessary or that the accommodation would be reasonable. The court found no evidence in the record that nine rather than eight residents was necessary (rather than simply preferred) and was less costly. The court held that there was no showing that the city's balancing the neighborhood concerns about traffic, parking, and law enforcement with the treatment needs of the residents was unreasonable.

Peterson v. City of Hickory, No. 5:07-CV-00074-RLV, 2010 WL 4791901 (W.D.N.C. Nov. 17, 2010)
Enforcement

The city issued a notice of violation regarding junk vehicles being stored on a property and tenants working there on a race car at night to the disturbance of neighbors. The notice gave the plaintiff four weeks to remedy the violation or face fines. At the end of the period, the site was inspected, and it was determined that the violation had been remedied. The court held that as no fines were imposed, there was no property deprivation to raise due-process concerns. Even if there had been fines, the graduated fines would not have been a substantial deprivation; the process provided was adequate (notice of violation, an opportunity to remedy, and appeal possibilities).

Marsh v. Black, No. 3:10cv547, 2011 WL 4747897 (W.D.N.C. Oct. 7, 2011)
Equal protection

Plaintiff obtained a special use permit from Union County to conduct rodeos on his 300-acre farm. The permit limited the plaintiff to conducting four rodeos in 2007. The county subsequently revoked the special use permit for conducting more than four rodeo events. The revocation was upheld by state courts. In this federal action, the plaintiff contended that the county's action was based on community opposition to his predominately Hispanic clientele for the rodeos, that failure to require other similar events to secure a special use permit violated equal protection, and that the county had hidden or destroyed a citizen petition opposing his rodeos that was circulated during the pendency of his permit application.

The court granted summary judgment to the county. The burden was on the plaintiff to submit admissible evidence that similarly situated persons were treated differently. In this instance, the allegations in the complaint were unsupported by affidavits, depositions, or any admissible evidence. Further, the alleged conduct by the county as a matter of law did not rise to the level of extreme and outrageous conduct necessary for a claim of intentional infliction of emotional distress. As for the petition, in addition to no admissible evidence of its existence and regardless of whether the alleged petition is a "public record," there is no legally cognizable claim for "concealment" or "destruction" of public records.

Griffin Farm & Landfill, Inc. v. Town of Unionville, No. 3:10-cv-250-RJC-DSC, 2012 WL 3257789 (W.D.N.C. Aug. 8, 2012)
Landfills; Vested rights

The plaintiffs claimed to have begun operation of a construction-and-demolition landfill pursuant to a county special use permit. The area was subsequently incorporated, and in 2004 the town issued the plaintiffs a five-year franchise (and a state five-year permit was also issued in 2004), but the town denied a permit to allow an industrial-solid-waste-landfill at the site. In 2008, the plaintiffs stopped accepting waste rather than complying with new state regulations. In 2009, the town denied a renewal of the franchise. The plaintiffs contested this denial, claiming a vested right to continued operation. The court held that no vested rights existed. At the time the franchise was denied, the plaintiffs had no valid state or local permits in hand. They had substantial notice that renewal of their franchise was not certain. They similarly had no statutory vested rights. The takings claim failed because they had no property right to a renewal authorization for the landfill and no reasonable investment-backed expectation of a franchise renewal.

Allison Outdoor Advertising, LP v. Town of Canton, 2012 WL 4061510 (W.D.N.C. Sept. 14, 2012)
First Amendment; Pleadings; Signs

The plaintiff applied for nine billboards, all of which were denied by the town because they were proposed to be located in a C-2 zoning district, and billboards were not allowed in that district. The plaintiff appealed to the board of adjustment, contending that the more recently adopted sign ordinance should be applied rather than the zoning restrictions. The board held that one billboard should be permitted, as it was actually in a different zoning district, and upheld denial of the remaining eight signs. The plaintiff also challenged the constitutionality of the sign and zoning ordinances.

The court held that the plaintiff had standing to challenge the constitutionality of only the provision of the zoning ordinance under which the denials were made, not all aspects of the two ordinances. The court dismissed the constitutional claims, noting they were conclusory allegations and thus improperly pled. Moreover, the allegation of a failure of the ordinance to enumerate a governmental interest to be advanced or societal purpose fails in that the zoning ordinance had a statement of purpose reflecting the state enabling law. An explicit declaration of a more specific purpose within the ordinance is not required.

Brown v. Town of Cary, 706 F.3d 294 (4th Cir. 2013)

First Amendment; Signs

The plaintiff and city engaged in an extended dispute after the city widened a street adjacent to his home. The plaintiff contended that the road project devalued his property and caused flooding problems. The city made a number of improvements to address drainage issues but refused the plaintiff's demand that his lot be purchased. In response, the plaintiff had "Screwed by the Town of Cary" painted in large letters across the front of his home. The city cited him for a violation of its sign ordinance, primarily on the grounds that the "sign" was approximately forty-eight square feet, well in excess of the maximum of five square feet allowed in this residential zoning district. The regulation exempted several types of signs from its coverage or this size limit. The exemptions included holiday decorations, public art, and temporary signs advertising town-recognized events. The district court held that this made the ordinance content-based rather than content-neutral, applied a strict-scrutiny review, and invalidated the regulation. The court of appeals reversed.

The court rejected an absolutist view of content neutrality, adopting instead a three-part test, finding that a regulation is not content-based if (1) it regulates the place some speech may take place; (2) it was not adopted in response to disagreement with the message; and (3) the government's interests are unrelated to the content of the affected speech. If the regulation is justified without reference to the content of the regulated speech, it is content neutral. Here, there is a reasonable fit between the legitimate interests in traffic safety and aesthetics and the exemption provided for public art and holiday decorations, given that these likely enhance rather than harm aesthetics and seasonal holiday displays have only a temporary traffic impact. There is not a requirement for an optimal fit, only a reasonable one. The ordinance was upheld as one that met substantial interests in aesthetics and traffic safety, was narrowly tailored to meet those interests, was a content-neutral reasonable time-place-and-manner restriction, and had sufficient definitions for exempted displays to avoid undue vagueness.

Sansotta v. Town of Nags Head, 724 F.3d 533 (4th Cir. 2013)

Beaches; Nuisances

The plaintiff's oceanfront beach cottage was one of six adjacent cottages severely damaged in a storm. The property involved had experienced serious erosion, averaging eight feet per year over the past several decades. As a result, the structures since 2001 had been located on the beach itself, with the vegetation line being landward of the cottages and with sandbags being placed around the structures. During the storm, the plaintiff hired contractors to bulldoze sand around the cottages in an effort to minimize damage. The road in front of the cottages was damaged in the storm, so the town barricaded the road as a safety hazard and required the contractors to stop their work. Several weeks after the storm, the town declared the structures a nuisance and ordered them demolished.

The court held that the town did not violate the procedural-due-process rights of the plaintiff. Assessing a fine, as distinct from collecting payment of it, is not a deprivation of property. Also, since an owner has no right to use property in a way that constitutes a nuisance, an action to abate a nuisance is a reasonable use of the police power, even if the nuisance action is later determined to have been mistaken and even if the cottages were rendered valueless. The court held that the town decision to declare some but not all cottages on the beach after the storm to be nuisances was not an equal-protection violation. Testimony established that the cottages cited were closer to the ocean than others and posed the most severe and continuous obstruction of the beach. This difference established a rational basis for the town's differential treatment. The court ruled that the plaintiff's takings claim should not have been dismissed on ripeness grounds (based on a failure to pursue a state compensation claim). The plaintiff did file in state court and made both a takings compensation claim and an inverse-condemnation compensation claim. The town's action to remove the case to federal court effectively waived the state-litigation requirement to seek compensation first in order to be ripe for federal litigation on the takings claim. The court remanded, noting that the district court could decide the claim on its merits, invoke abstention, or take some other approach. [Note: After remand, the plaintiff and town settled the matter, with the town making a payment to the plaintiff and acquiring title to the property.]

Town of Nags Head v. Toloczko, 728 F.3d 391 (4th Cir. 2013)
Abstention; Ripeness

The defendants owned an oceanfront beach cottage that was severely damaged in a storm. The storm left the structure on the beach with an exposed septic tank. Several weeks after the storm, the town declared the structure a nuisance and ordered it demolished. The town later cited the defendants for violation of an ordinance requiring permits prior to any development on the beach public-trust area. The case was removed to federal court by the plaintiffs. The defendants contended that the nuisance ordinance was invalid and alleged due-process, equal-protection, and takings violations. Given the unsettled, important policy issues raised relative to state law, as the court noted is often the case with complex land use law cases, the district court abstained and declined to exercise jurisdiction over the various claims and counterclaims.

The appeals court reversed and remanded. The court held that after the district court's decision, the North Carolina courts had conclusively determined that the town did not have jurisdiction to protect public-trust rights in the ocean-beach area. Because the town did not have jurisdiction, the unsettled state-law issues regarding the geographic reach of the public-trust doctrine were no longer applicable to this dispute. Therefore, because the grounds for a *Burford* abstention were no longer present (see *Burford v. Sun Oil Co.*, 319 U.S. 315 (1943)), the court remanded.

Fenner v. City of Durham, No. 1:10cv383, 2013 WL 704324 (M.D.N.C. Feb. 26, 2013), *adopted by* 2013 WL 1182240 (M.D.N.C. Mar. 21, 2013), *affirmed by* 535 F. App'x 314 (4th Cir. 2013)
Res judicata

The plaintiff contended that the city permitted an illegal nightclub to operate to the detriment of his property. As the same claim had previously been subject to state litigation, with a judgment on the merits for the city, this federal claim is barred by the doctrine of res judicata.

Hellbender, Inc. v. Town of Boone, No. 5:12CV45-RLV, 2013 WL 1349286 (W.D.N.C. Mar. 31, 2013)
First Amendment; Noise

The plaintiffs challenged a town ordinance that limited the level of sound generated by commercial establishments and live-music venues in specified zoning districts. The court held that the ordinance affected protected speech (music) in a traditional public forum (the zoning districts included the downtown area of the plaintiffs' businesses). The court held that limited exemptions for high-school, college, and nonrecurring community events were not based on an attempt to restrict the content of the speech, and the ordinance remained content neutral with these reasonable classifications. The ordinance advanced a legitimate governmental objective (protecting the character of the affected area and preventing undue intrusion into residential areas). It was narrowly tailored by limiting the level of noise (higher levels being allowed in daytime, in nonresidential areas, or on weekends). As the type and manner of entertainment that could be offered was unaffected, and only the level of sound generated was being regulated, adequate alternative avenues of expression were retained. Thus, the ordinance does not violate First Amendment protections.

Mt. Airy Business Center, Inc. v. City of Kannapolis, No. 10CV307, 2014 WL 229564 (M.D.N.C. Jan. 21, 2014), *order adopted*, 2014 WL 975516 (M.D.N.C. Mar. 12, 2014)
Federal jurisdiction

The plaintiff operated an Internet-sweepstakes business in the city beginning in 2008. The city in 2010 adopted zoning restrictions on these businesses that limited their location to certain districts and imposed separation and parking requirements, as well as operational restrictions. The city also adopted a privilege-license fee of $500 per terminal per year. The city cited the plaintiff for violation of the zoning provisions. The plaintiff challenged the city regulations and fees, alleging various federal constitutional and statutory claims, as well as a lack of state authority for the regulations. The city asked the court to abstain.

The court held that *Pullman* abstention was not applicable because the only unsettled issue of state law involved the criminal statutes regarding sweepstakes cafes, which are not at issue in this case. (See *Railroad Commission v. Pullman Co.*, 321 U.S. 496 (1941).) The court held that *Burford* abstention was also inapplicable. (See *Burford v. Sun Oil Co.*, 319 U.S. 315 (1943).) Zoning cases often present difficult questions of substantial public import where federal review would be disruptive of state efforts to establish a coherent policy, thus triggering *Burford* abstention. Here, however, there is no state review pending, and the plaintiff is challenging the regulatory scheme on constitutional and statutory grounds, so given the specific facts presented, abstention is not appropriate.

Town of Nags Head v. Toloczko, No. 2:11-CV-1-D, 2014 WL 4219516 (E.D.N.C. Aug. 18, 2014)
Beaches; Public-trust doctrine; Takings

The defendants owned an oceanfront cottage that was severely damaged in a storm. The town cited the defendants for violation of an ordinance requiring permits prior to any development on the beach public-trust area. The defendants contended that the nuisance ordinance was invalid and alleged due-process, equal-protection, and takings violations. The federal district court initially abstained, but state case law subsequently determined that the town did not have jurisdiction to protect public-trust rights in the ocean-beach area. On remand, the court concluded that the plaintiff's cottage was not located on the wet-sand beach; the town did not have a right to enforce the public-trust doctrine on the wet-sand beach pursuant to the state law; given the subsequent beach nourishment, the structure was not likely to cause personal injury; and the question of whether the public-trust area extended to the dry-sand beach was moot. As for the takings claims, the court held that the town's assertion that state law allowed public use of the dry-sand beach did not amount to a physical-invasion taking. The court noted that the town's good faith in use of its police power was irrelevant in a takings inquiry. It also noted that several of the *Penn Central* balancing factors weighed in favor of the plaintiffs, particularly that they had been allowed to repair the structure after past storm damage, they lost all rental income during the period of the dispute with the town, and removal of the structure would not provide them with a reciprocity of advantage. (See *Penn Central Transportation Co. v. City of New York*, 438 U.S. 104, 124 (1978).) Still, the town raised genuine issues of material fact on both the *Penn Central* factors and whether the town's actions were the proximate cause of the plaintiffs' losses. Thus, summary judgment was not appropriate.

CarSpa Automotive, LLC v. City of Raleigh, 57 F. Supp. 3d 505 (E.D.N.C. 2014)
Ripeness; Takings

Plaintiff contended that the city forced donation of a public-access right-of-way in order to get a building permit and that this was a takings, due-process, and equal-protection violation. The court held that the plaintiff's failure to apply for a variance meant no final administrative decision had been made, so the case was not ripe for judicial review. Further, as the plaintiff had not brought an inverse-condemnation claim in state court, failure to seek an available and adequate procedure for just compensation also rendered the takings claim unripe.

Sansotta v. Town of Nags Head, 97 F. Supp. 3d 713 (E.D.N.C. 2014)
Beaches; Nuisances; Public-trust doctrine; Takings

The plaintiff managed and was part owner of six oceanfront beach cottages that were severely damaged in a storm. Several weeks after the storm, the town declared the structures a nuisance and ordered them demolished. During the pendency of the litigation, the town completed a beach-nourishment project and eventually issued permits for repair of the cottages.

On remand, the court found that none of the damaged cottages were located on the wet-sand beach. The court also found that at the time of this action, under state law the state (rather than local government) had exclusive authority to enforce public-trust rights, so the town had no authority to declare a structure on the dry-sand beach to be a nuisance. As the town had no authority to protect public-trust rights on the dry-sand beach, the court held the plaintiff's claim that the dry-sand beach was not subject to public-trust rights to be moot. The court held that the public-duty doctrine precludes a claim of negligence against the town for its action preventing access to the structures during the storm.

The court addressed three regulatory-takings claims. First, the court held that blocking access to the property for repairs during the storm was not a taking because it was based on preventing grave threats to life and property. It held that the town's assertion of public-trust use rights in the dry-sand beach was not a physical-occupation taking. It found that there were genuine issues of material fact as to the *Penn Central* factors for a temporary regulatory taking and accordingly remanded for a jury trial on those issues. (See *Penn Central Transportation Co. v. City of New York*, 438 U.S. 104, 124 (1978).) [Note: The parties subsequently settled, with the town purchasing the property.]

Developers Surety & Indemnity Co. v. City of Durham, No. 1:11CV515, 2014 WL 4677181 (M.D.N.C. Sept. 18, 2014)
Performance guarantees

The plaintiff provided a surety bond for the completion of streets and stormwater-management facilities within a subdivision. When the developer defaulted, the city called the bond. The court held that the terms of the surety bond were controlling as to the scope of plaintiff's obligations. In this instance, the bond only required the completion of improvements already constructed, not the completion of those improvements not yet initiated.

Tommy Davis Construction, Inc. v. Cape Fear Public Utility Authority, 807 F.3d 62 (4th Cir. 2015)
Attorney's fees; Impact fees; Statutes of limitation

The plaintiff was required to pay water-and-sewer impact fees when it obtained building permits. However, the subdivision in question was not in an area for which the utility authority provided services, and a private company provided the water and sewer. As the public-utility authority had no plan for extension of service to this area, it discontinued requiring impact fees there, but refused to refund the fees previously paid. The court held that the defendant had no authority to impose a water-and-sewer impact fee for lots in a subdivision that was not served by public water and sewer and where there were no concrete plans to extend services to that area. While the federal claims under 42 U.S.C. § 1983 were barred by a three-year statute of limitations, the state-law claim was subject to a ten-year period. The court held that the trial court could, in its discretion, award attorney's fees for challenging the ultra vires action of collecting the fees as building permits were issued.

Combs v. Ashe County, No. 5:14-CV-136, 2016 WL 3625551 (W.D.N.C. July 6, 2016)
Appellate procedures; Junkyards

Ashe County cited the plaintiff for having a junkyard that violated the county's junkyard ordinance and constituted a public nuisance. The plaintiff failed to comply with an order to abate the nuisance, contending that this use of the property was "grandfathered." The county sought injunctive relief to order compliance and to have the nuisance abated. The district court found for the county, and when the plaintiff did not comply, the court authorized the county to remove the junk and to recover its costs. The county removed the junk, and the court subsequently entered a judgment lien of $22,907 for the costs of cleanup.

The plaintiff brought this federal action pro se, contending that removal of the junk (a camper, several vehicles, auto parts, and farm equipment) constituted trespass and violated various constitutional rights. The court dismissed the claim against the district judge based on judicial immunity. The court dismissed the claims against most of the individual county defendants because there was no plausible allegation as to their involvement in the alleged trespass and conversion of property. The court held that the request for dismissal of remaining claims based on collateral estoppel and the *Rooker-Feldman* rule (*Rooker v. Fidelity Trust Co.*, 263 U.S. 413 (1923); *D.C. Court of Appeals v. Feldman*, 460 U.S. 462 (1983)) against federal appeals of state-court rulings was not appropriate for a Rule 12(b)(6) motion to dismiss but would properly be addressed in a motion for summary judgment or a Rule 12(c) motion for judgment on the pleadings.

American Entertainers, LLC v. City of Rocky Mount, 888 F.3d 707 (4th Cir. 2018)

Adult uses; First Amendment

The plaintiff began operation of a club offering adult entertainment without a license from the city to operate a sexually oriented business. When the city threatened suit, the plaintiff sued the city, arguing that the city's adult-entertainment ordinance was unconstitutional. The city granted a temporary license to operate, pending resolution of the suit. The plaintiff then voluntarily dismissed the suit. Subsequently, city law enforcement investigated and determined that the club was operating without a permit, that it was violating the city adult-entertainment ordinance in several respects, and that criminal action would be taken if the club did not come into compliance. In response, the plaintiff brought this action contending that the ordinance was invalid.

The court held that the definitions of sexually oriented businesses and adult cabarets in the ordinance were not overly broad, that they were adopted to regulate deleterious secondary effects (particularly negative impacts on crime and property values), and that the licensing requirements furthered this substantial government interest. The court also held that the requirement for the applicant and business principals to be at least twenty-one years old did not violate the Equal Protection Clause or the First Amendment. However, the court held that a provision allowing the chief of police to deny a permit if the application would not comply with "all applicable laws" was an unconstitutional prior restraint. That provision was deemed to be too broad and left the officer with too much discretion as it was not limited to building codes, zoning, and health and safety regulations. The court remanded the case to determine if the offending provision was separable from the valid portions of the ordinance.

A Hand of Hope Pregnancy Resource Center v. City of Raleigh, 332 F. Supp. 3d 983 (E.D.N.C. 2018)

Religious use

The plaintiff proposed to locate a pregnancy-counseling center on a lot adjacent to an existing abortion clinic. In addition to counseling and prayer, the center proposed to offer pregnancy tests and, if positive, ultrasounds to view the fetus. The property was in a residential zoning district that allowed civic uses (which includes places of worship and educational facilities) but did not allow medical uses. The city advised the plaintiff that a rezoning would be required, but then provided a zoning certification that the use may be a permitted civic use if no medical services were provided. The adjacent abortion clinic appealed the determination to the board of adjustment. The board found that the use of ultrasound tests at the site, all performed by registered nurses as required by state law, constituted a medical service and was not allowed under the residential zoning. This suit was brought contending that the ordinance as applied violated the Religious Land Use and Institutionalized Persons Act and constitutional guarantees of free speech and equal protection.

The court held that summary judgment on the equal-terms claim under the act was inappropriate because there was a genuine issue of material fact as to whether the plaintiff had met its initial burden of showing that it fulfills the applicable zoning criteria in the same way as its identified comparable uses that provide only civic uses without medical uses on site. On the constitutional issues, assuming the provision of live ultrasound images to be protected speech, the court found no religious animus or basis for the regulation and thus no discrimination on the basis of content or viewpoint. As a content-neutral time-place-and-manner restriction, the limitation on medical uses in residential zoning districts was narrowly tailored and left adequate alternative avenues of expression available. The court found no Equal Protection claim because comparative uses offered by the plaintiff were not similarly situated. It was treated the same as other religious uses not offering medical services. The adjacent abortion clinic was zoned commercial by a prior owner who in fact used it for a commercial real-estate office, and this rezoning had been done under a different, prior ordinance.

Raynor v. Town of Chapel Hill, No. 1:18CV291, 2019 WL 503443 (M.D.N.C. Feb. 8, 2019)
Due process; Historic preservation

The plaintiffs applied for a certificate of appropriateness (COA) to construct a single-family home in a designated historic district. There was an existing 294-square-foot cottage on the site, and its future was the subject of considerable discussion. The plaintiffs originally proposed to move it to an adjacent lot, but they explored other options in light of concerns raised by the historic commission. As no mutually acceptable alternative was found, the plaintiffs proposed to demolish the cottage if no alternative was found to preserve or relocate it within 365 days. That request was eventually approved. However, the COA for the new residence was denied on the grounds that the structure was too large, there were inadequate setbacks, and the design was not consistent with neighborhood character.

Rather than appeal, the plaintiffs submitted a new application several months later. The historic commission refused to consider it on the grounds that it was not substantially different from the previously denied application. The board of adjustment overruled that decision and remanded the case for a decision on the merits. On remand, the historic commission denied the COA on the grounds that the relocation of the driveway and the visibility of the garage were incongruous with the district. The plaintiffs again appealed to the board of adjustment, and the board reversed the denial and remanded with instructions to issue the COA. On remand, the historic commission refused to issue the COA based on concerns that there were no findings on congruency by the board of adjustment. The town subsequently issued the COA administratively because the historic commission did not act on it within the statutorily mandated 180-day period for decision.

The plaintiffs contended that the sixteen-month period to reach a final decision violated federal substantive due process. The court rejected that contention, finding that (1) there was not a clear entitlement to a COA, as that decision involved considerable discretion by the historic commission, and (2) the protracted discussion and local appeals process was not arbitrary and irrational, nor did the process and rationales offered for decision shock the conscience of the court. The court likewise found no violation of procedural due process or equal protection. The remaining state-law claims were remanded to state court.

A Hand of Hope Pregnancy Resource Center v. City of Raleigh, 386 F. Supp. 3d 618 (E.D.N.C. 2019)
Religious use

Plaintiff sought to relocate its pregnancy resource center to a site adjacent to an abortion clinic. The site was in a residential zoning district with a special highway overlay district, which allowed places of religious assembly but not medical practices. So the plaintiff sought a rezoning to an office-mixed use zoning district. The planning commission found the rezoning consistent with the comprehensive plan and recommended approval, but the city council denied the rezoning. After this suit was commenced, the plaintiff sought an official interpretation as to whether its proposed use was consistent with the existing zoning. The zoning officials ruled the intended use was permissible within the existing district as a "civic use" provided it did not include any "medical uses." On appeal to the board of adjustment, the plaintiff contended that ultrasound tests performed to determine whether there is a viable pregnancy should be considered a means to communicate a religious message rather than a "medical use." The board ruled the use was not permitted in the residential district since ultrasound tests would be performed there.

The plaintiff contended the city's actions violated the Religious Land Use and Institutionalized Persons Act provisions by imposing a substantial burden on religious activities and failing to treat the use on equal terms with nonreligious assemblies. The court noted that the city allows religious exercise on the site, including prayer meetings, counseling, Bible studies, and the provision of educational materials. The prohibition of pregnancy testing and ultrasound imaging is not a substantial burden, since those services could be provided at the plaintiff's other appropriately zoned location and they would have constituted a small portion of the plaintiff's work at this site. The fact that the other location may be inconvenient or less preferred for the services does not constitute a substantial burden. The court did not decide the equal-terms challenge. As there were factual disputes related to the degree and scope of medical testing that would be conducted on site, the court ruled that summary judgment on the question of whether the testing constituted a principal or an accessory use was premature.

Cities4Life, Inc. v. City of Charlotte, No. 3:17-CV-670-KDB-DSC, 2019 WL 4127295 (W.D.N.C. July 26, 2019), *report and recommendation adopted*, 2019 WL 4121998 (W.D.N.C. Aug. 29, 2019)
Religious use

The plaintiffs, a group that gathers near a women's health clinic to express opposition to abortion, made numerous claims regarding enforcement of the city's zoning, picketing, and sign regulations. The court held that the city's preexisting ban on portable signs did not impose a substantial burden on the plaintiffs' religious exercise. The plaintiffs had no reasonable expectation that portable signs, which are banned throughout the city, would be allowed on a lot that they owned. They also failed to show how other permitted signs could not be used on their property. There was no individualized assessment involved as the portable-sign prohibition is universal and a decision that the plaintiffs were in violation was the application of that universal standard, not an "individualized determination" such as a special use permit or variance.

Mangum v. Town of Wrightsville Beach, No. 7:19-CV-29-FL, 2019 WL 6190648 (E.D.N.C. Nov. 20, 2019), *reconsideration denied*, 2020 WL 4938332 (E.D.N.C. Aug. 24, 2020), *appeal dismissed*, 2021 WL 672650 (4th Cir. Feb. 22, 2021)
Res judicata

The plaintiff was cited for zoning violations and assessed civil penalties relating to his operation of a jet-ski-rental business using an N.C. Wildlife Commission public-boating ramp and N.C. Department of Transportation bridge right-of-way. He and any successor to the business were enjoined from using that location for the business; eventually, the plaintiff was held in civil contempt by state courts for violation of a consent judgment. This federal action challenged the constitutional authority of the town to require a $500 fee to appeal zoning determinations, the authority of the town to regulate these areas, and the constitutionality of the zoning enforcement. The court dismissed the federal-law claims as barred by res judicata since there was a final judgment on these same issues with the same parties in the state-court-enforcement action. Having dismissed all federal claims, the court declined to exercise supplemental jurisdiction over the remaining state-law claims.

Currituck County v. LeTendre, No. 2-19-CV-27-BO, 2020 WL 707179 (E.D.N.C. Feb. 12, 2020)
Abstention

This case involved disputes over the construction of a 15,000-square-foot oceanfront structure in an area of the Currituck Outer Banks that is not accessible by public or paved roads. It was subject to several state court-of-appeals decisions prior to this litigation. This action for an injunction and order of abatement was initiated by the county in state court, but the plaintiff removed it to federal court on the basis of diversity jurisdiction and asserted takings, equal-protection, and vested-rights counterclaims against the county. When the state trial court issued enforcement injunctions and refused to stay them pending resolution of this federal case, the plaintiff sought an injunction to stay the state action and the county sought abstention by the federal court. The court exercised its discretion to decline to enjoin state enforcement action in the concurrent state case. As the court determined difficult or disputed questions of state law were not raised, it declined to abstain under *Burford v. Sun Oil Co.*, 319 U.S. 315 (1943). Also, because the county's motion to enforce the prior state ruling was filed after this case was removed to federal court, the court concluded abstention under *Younger v. Harris*, 401 U.S. 37 (1971), was not appropriate.

Ballantyne Village Parking, LLC v. City of Charlotte, 818 F. App'x 198, No. 19-1213, 2020 WL 3265007 (4th Cir. June 17, 2020)
Abstention; Ripeness

The plaintiff owner of a parking lot and parking deck contended that a building permit issued to an adjacent shopping center deprived it of various due-process rights. The adjacent shopping center had secured permission to use parking places in the plaintiff's deck to meet its minimum parking requirements under city zoning regulations. This dispute involved the use of additional parking in the plaintiff's deck for a planned expansion of office space at the adjacent shopping center. The court held that the matter was not ripe for judicial review. The court noted that two matters in addition to this federal litigation were still pending. First, the issue of whether the easement held by the adjacent shopping center allowed the additional parking was still in arbitration and that determination would be subject to judicial review in state courts. Second, the plaintiff had appealed the city's permit decision to the city's board of adjustment, which had stayed any action on the appeal upon filing of this federal litigation. This dispute—and the question of whether the plaintiff's constitutional due-process rights to participate in the city's permitting discussions were violated—is clearly related to the outcome of those two ongoing matters.

Currituck County v. LeTendre, No. 2-19-CV-27-BO, 2020 WL 6750429 (E.D.N.C. Nov. 17, 2020)
Interpretation

This case addressed ongoing disputes over the construction of a large oceanfront structure in the Currituck Outer Banks (the prior federal and state litigation is discussed above). The county originally permitted the structure as a single-family residence under the county unified development ordinance (UDO). The state court of appeals in 2016 held that the structure was three separate buildings connected by unconditioned walkways rather than a permissible single building. Although the State Building Code Council in 2015 had ruled that the structure was subject to the one- and two-family building code rather than the commercial building code, the state court of appeals in 2018 held that the Council's determination was applicable to the state building code but not to the county UDO. In 2019, the legislature amended state law to prohibit a local government from using any definition of a "building" that differs from the definitions in state statutes or in rules adopted by the Building Code Council. The court held that the 2019 legislation was intended "to clarify" rather than substantially alter the statute. For that reason, the 2019 legislation requires that the county's definition of a building or single-family dwelling in its UDO must be consistent with the Building Code Council's determination that the structure was in fact a single-family dwelling for local regulatory purposes.

Zito v. North Carolina Coastal Resources Commission, 8 F.4th 281 (4th Cir. 2021)
Immunity; Takings

The plaintiffs were denied a Coastal Area Management Act (CAMA) permit to replace a 1700-square-foot oceanfront beach cottage in South Nags Head that had been destroyed by a fire. At this site, the minimum CAMA setback for a structure of less than 5000 square feet was 180 feet from the first line of stable vegetation (thirty times the site's annual erosion rate of six feet). However, because the cottage was less than 2000 square feet and was built before 1979, it qualified for a relaxed setback minimum of sixty feet from the vegetation line. The plaintiffs had proposed to rebuild the cottage with a setback of only twelve feet. After the permit was denied by the Town of Nags Head, the Coastal Resources Commission denied the plaintiffs a setback variance upon finding a lack of requisite hardship.

The court dismissed the suit for lack of subject-matter jurisdiction under Rule 12(b)(1) as the Eleventh Amendment bars a Fifth Amendment claim against states in federal court where the state courts remain open to adjudicate such claims. Since the Coastal Resources Commission is an arm of the state, sovereign immunity applies to it and has not been waived. A state statute, G.S. 113A-123(b), and the Law of the Land Clause of the state constitution provide a state remedy for a regulatory taking. The court noted that the U.S. Supreme Court's ruling in *Knick v. Township of Scott*, 139 S. Ct. 2162 (2019), removed the state-litigation prerequisite for a federal court taking claim against a municipality, but that case did not affect the sovereign immunity of state governments.

Cities4Life, Inc. v. City of Charlotte, 52 F.4th 576 (4th Cir. 2022)
Attorney's fees

The plaintiffs, who regularly picketed an abortion clinic, challenged enforcement of the city's sign regulation, picketing regulation, and zoning regulations prohibiting portable signs. After dismissal of the zoning claim and resolution of the sign claim, the parties reached a settlement agreement regarding the picketing claim. The plaintiffs then sought attorney's fees and the city objected, contending the plaintiffs were not a "prevailing party" for attorney's fee purposes. The court held that even though the settlement did not condemn the city's pre-agreement picketing-enforcement actions, it did specify how the plaintiffs would be allowed to approach vehicles entering the clinic's parking area. This materially altered the legal relationship between the parties, so the plaintiffs were entitled to reasonable attorney's fees. The amount of the fee was reduced to exclude time devoted to unsuccessful portions of the plaintiffs' claims.

Nance v. City of Albemarle, 520 F. Supp. 3d 758 (M.D.N.C. 2021)
Due process; Equal protection

The plaintiffs proposed to convert an existing extended-stay motel to assisted low-income housing. The city, which had previously cited the motel for public nuisances related to illegal drug use, fights, and assaults at the site, denied approval for the renovations. The plaintiffs alleged numerous constitutional claims. The court dismissed all the federal claims and declined to exercise supplemental jurisdiction over the state claims. The court held that there was no factual support for a claim that the city had a custom or policy to unlawfully limit low-income housing. The equal-protection claim was dismissed as the plaintiffs presented no direct or indirect evidence that: (1) racial discrimination played any role in the city's permit denial; (2) there was a pattern of permit denial for affordable housing; (3) there was historical housing discrimination by the city; or (4) there were contemporaneous statements showing a reasonable inference of discrimination. Further, the permit denials were rationally related to abatement of the nuisance. The city's pursuit of a legitimate nuisance charge was not shown to be in retaliation for comments made by the plaintiffs at a public hearing. There was no showing that the process followed in denying the application violated due process, as the applicants were allowed multiple opportunities to meet with the planning director, to address the city council, and to submit multiple applications. As the plaintiffs did not show they had a property right to a nondiscretionary permit approval, there could be no substantive-due-process violation in the denial of city approval for their redevelopment plan for the motel.

Catherine H. Barber Memorial Shelter, Inc. v. Town of North Wilkesboro, 576 F. Supp. 3d 318 (W.D.N.C. Dec. 20, 2021)
Equal protection; Group homes; Special uses

The plaintiff in 1987 began operating out of a single-family home the only homeless shelter in Wilkes County. In 2018, the plaintiff began searching for a new location because the existing structure was not large enough to meet all of the shelter's needs. Prior to 2018, the town zoning ordinance did not regulate homeless shelters as a distinct use. In 2018, the ordinance was amended to define homeless shelters, limit their location to the highway-business district, set separation requirements from residences, parks, and schools, and require a special use permit. After temporary relocation to a church, the plaintiff in 2020 applied for a special use permit to relocate to a former dental office that had been donated to the shelter for its use. While the city found the application met all the objective standards of the zoning regulation, the special use permit was denied on three grounds: (1) that pedestrian traffic from the shelter would be close to the highway and pose a safety risk; (2) that neighboring property values would be harmed; and (3) that the use was not in harmony with the surrounding area.

The court held that the special use permit was improperly denied under state law. The applicant presented sufficient competent, material, and substantive evidence that all the permit standards were met. The board refused to allow the applicant to cross-examine the lay witnesses who presented testimony regarding problems at the shelter's prior location, evidence that was strongly disputed by the applicant. As failure to allow a party to cross-examine was a clear error of law, that evidence was incompetent and could not be considered to rebut the applicant's evidence of compliance. Also, while one of the opposing neighbors was a commercial-real-estate appraiser, he offered no analysis or data to support his opinion of a harm to property values.

The court further held that the special use permit requirement for homeless shelters violated the Equal Protection Clause as it treated similarly situated uses differently without a rational basis. The court found there were no factors relating to the intensity of the land use and the potential impact on surrounding properties that differentiated the shelter from other similar uses that were permitted in this zoning district without a special use permit (congregate-care facilities, emergency shelters, nursing homes, hospitals, lodges, and civic/fraternal/cultural/community facilities). While the court must show deference to legislative categorizations, it does not countenance intentional differential treatment of similarly situated land uses without a rational basis.

5-Star Athlete, Development, LLC v. City of Shelby, No. 1:21-CV-323-MR-WCM, 2022 WL 4287921 (W.D.N.C. May 26, 2022)
Discrimination

The plaintiff, a minority-owned company, applied for a rezoning to build eleven townhouses on property previously zoned commercial and single-family residential. The application was denied. The plaintiff alleged a violation of the state and federal fair-housing acts. The court granted a motion to dismiss, finding no allegation of disparate impact or disparate treatment based on racial or ethnic grounds. The plaintiff made no allegations about the demographics of the community or the race and color of those who would reside in the townhouses. Public opposition to the potential for low-income housing if the rezoning was approved, without any reference to race or color, does not constitute racial animus. The racial identity of the applicant, standing alone, does not in and of itself establish racial discrimination. There were no allegations about the racial identity of applicants whose rezonings were approved by the city during this time to support a claim of disparate treatment.

Fairway Outdoor Advertising, LLC v. City of High Point, No. 1:21-CV-00867, 2022 WL 17975990 (M.D.N.C. Dec. 28, 2022)
First Amendment; Signs

The city denied the plaintiff's applications for six new digital billboards and for the replacement of an existing vinyl billboard with a digital billboard. The city zoning ordinance allowed new billboards only in the heavy industrial zoning district; digital signs, however, were not allowed there, which effectively banned digital billboards citywide. The court held that the on-site/off-site distinction for signs was a content-neutral regulation. The court also held that traffic safety and aesthetics were significant governmental interests that were sufficient to justify the sign regulations. Adequate alternative avenues of expression remained given that nonconforming billboards were allowed to continue and new billboards, albeit not digital billboards, were permissible in the heavy industrial zoning district.

PEM Entities, LLC v. County of Franklin, 57 F.4th 178 (2023)
Standing; Vested rights

The plaintiff in 2012 acquired land that was within the area of a preliminary plat approved by the county in 2005. The preliminary plat showed fifteen "phases" for development and included a note stating that the area "will be served by Franklin County water and sewer to be installed by the developer." In 2019, the county adopted a water-and-sewer-allocation ordinance. The plaintiff contended they were not subject to this allocation ordinance because the 2005 preliminary plat had created a vested right to the service. Later in 2019, the plaintiff and other developers reached a settlement with the county providing that each developer could apply every year for service for up to fifty lots and that the county would review those applications in good faith without discriminating among the developers.

The court held that the plaintiff had standing to bring this action because its ability to obtain utility services on the terms it claims it was entitled to depend on the validity of its asserted vested rights. However, the court held that neither the 2005 preliminary plat nor the 2019 settlement agreement created a constitutionally protected property right. Under North Carolina law, a vested right requires substantial expenditures in good-faith reliance on a valid approval. No such valid approval exists in this case. Neither the required final-plan approval or building permits had been applied for or received. Preliminary approvals cannot be the basis of a vested right under state law. Without a valid property right at issue, the plaintiff's takings and due-process claims were properly dismissed. In addition, since the plaintiff did not show evidence of differential treatment compared to others who were similarly situated, the equal-protection claim was also properly dismissed.

Epcon Homestead, LLC v. Town of Chapel Hill, 62 F.4th 882 (4th Cir. 2023)
Statutes of limitation

The plaintiff's predecessors in interest secured a special use permit in 2014 for a planned development with sixty-three dwelling units. They opted to make an in-lieu payment of $803,250 rather than set aside 15 percent of the units for affordable housing. Payments were made as certificates of occupancy were issued, commencing in July 2017 and ending in March 2019. In October 2019, this suit was filed alleging violation of state law (lack of statutory authority to impose the fee) and claiming violation of substantive due process and an unconstitutional taking. The plaintiff sought a return of the full amount of the inclusionary-housing fees paid and attorney's fees.

The court held that the statute of limitations began to run when the plaintiff knew or had reason to know of the condition on the special use permit. This occurred when the plaintiff began to acquire the land that was already subject to the permit condition. The "continuing wrong" doctrine did not extend the time for beginning the case through the period of continuing payments because those fees were not separate and distinct fees but rather were partial payments toward a predetermined total. As under *Koontz* and *Knick*, the constitutionality of the condition became cognizable at the time of imposition (here, when the plaintiff became aware of it), which is when the statute of limitations began to run. Because the applicable three-year statute of limitations related to personal-injury actions had run, the case was properly dismissed.

Cases by Subject

This index organizes the case digests by their subject matter. The references to cases appear under subheadings, according to whether they were decided by the North Carolina Supreme Court (SC), the North Carolina Court of Appeals (CA), or federal courts (FC).

Amendments

SC: Markham (1963), Armstrong (1965), Sofran (1990), Wally (2012)

CA: Capps (1978), Johnson (1978), Lee (1980), Wenco Management (1981), Sherrill (1986), Brown (1994), Gossett (1996), Carter (1997), Gregory (1997), Devaney (2001), Massey (2001), Summers (2002), Ashby (2003), Keith (2006), Rakestraw (2008), Laurel Valley Watch (2008), Carroll (2008), Thrash (2009), Murdock (2009), Coucoulas/Knight Properties (2009), McMillan (2009), Sapp (2011), Atkinson (2014), Ring (2017), Walton North Carolina (2017)

Amortization

SC: Lawing (1913), Shannonhouse (1914), Joyner (1975), Capital Outdoor Advertising (1994), Naegele Outdoor Advertising v. City of Winston-Salem (1995)

CA: Eastern Federal (1980), Appalachian Poster Advertising (1981), R.O. Givens (1982), Goodman Toyota (1983), Summey Outdoor Advertising (1989), Maynor (1997), Whiteco Outdoor Advertising (1999), Bessemer City Express (2002)

FC: Major Media (1986), Naegele Outdoor Advertising (1988), Georgia Outdoor Advertising (1990), National Advertising (1991), Naegele Outdoor Advertising (1992), Independence News (2008)

Animals

CA: Maynard (2009)

Appeals

SC: Roberson (1929), White Oak Properties (1985), Empire Power (1994), North Buncombe Association of Concerned Citizens (1994), Martin Marietta Technologies (1998), Morningstar (2015)

CA: Smith (1970), Coleman (1971), Quadrant (1974), Greene (1976), Catawba Valley Machinery (1978), Pleasant (1982), Summerlin (1984), Goforth Properties (1984), Town & Country Civic Organization (1986), Ad/Mor (1988), Teen Challenge Training Center (1988), Cardwell (1989), North Buncombe Ass'n (1990), Allen (1990), Conservation Council of N.C. (1991), Pamlico Tar River Foundation (1991), Appalachian Outdoor Advertising (1991), Gaskill (1993), Grandfather Village (1993), Northwood Homeowners (1993), Hudson Belk (1994), Simpson (1994), Garrity (1994), Shell Island Homeowners (1999), Hemphill-Nolan (2002), Society for the Preservation of Historic Oakwood (2002), Bessemer City Express (2002), Fairway Outdoor Advertising (2013), Henderson (2016), Coates (2019), Appalachian Materials (2022)

Appellate Procedures

SC: W.P. Rose Builders' Supply (1931), Save Our Rivers (1995), Dobo (2003), Walsh (2007)

CA: Flynt (1970), Thurston (1974), Deffet Rentals (1975), Catawba Valley Machinery (1978), Jennewein (1980), LFM Enterprises (1980), Martin Marietta (1983), Mize (1986), Little (1986), Coastal Ready-Mix Concrete (1994), Moore (1997), Mercer (1998), Estates (1998), Water Tower Office Associates (1998), Darnell (1998), Piland (2000), Councill (2001), Hyatt (2008), MCC Outdoor (2012), MNC Holdings (2012), Royal Oak Concerned Citizens (2014), Hirschman (2016), Swan Beach Corolla (2017), Beroth Oil (2017), Weishaupt-Smith (2019)

FC: Combs (2016)

Applicants

SC: Lee (1946), MacPherson (1973), Humble (1974)

Application

CA: Wade (1997)

Attorney's Fees

CA: Walker (1996), Williams (2004), Table Rock Chapter of Trout Unlimited (2008), Izydore (2013), High Rock Lake Partners (2014), Batson (2022), Town of Midland (2022), TAC Stafford (2022)

FC: Giovanni Carandola (2007), Tommy Davis Construction (2015), Cities4Life (2022)

Beaches

CA: Fabrikant (2005), Koenig (2006), Fisher (2012), Town of Nags Head (2012), Riggings Homeowners (2013), Nies (2016), Hovey (2021)

FC: Sansotta (2013), Toloczko (2014), Sansotta (2014)

Bias
CA: *In re* Raleigh (1992), Rice Associates (1992), Vulcan Materials (1994), Cox (2003)

Board of Adjustment
SC: Harden (1926), Little (1928), Pine Hill Cemeteries (1941), Ornoff (1942), James (1948), Jarrell (1963), Brannock (1963), Craver (1966), Joyner (1966), Jamison (1967), Rea Construction (1968), Jackson (1969), Keiger (1971), Humble (1974), Town of Swansboro (1993)
CA: Long (1974), Washington Park Neighborhood Ass'n (1978), Burton (1980), Summerlin (1984), Brummer (1986), Tate (1986), Cardwell (1987), J.H. Carter Builder (1989), Garrity (1994), Willis (1998)

Bonds
CA: Smith (1970)

Buffer Zones
CA: P.A.W. (1989), Cary Creek (2010)

Building Permits and Inspection
SC: Lynn (1991)
CA: Law Building (1992), Sinning (1995), Simmons (1997), Coffey (2001), Eason (2003)

Cemeteries
SC: Ellison (1859)
CA: Stegall (1987), Northfield Development (2004)

Certificate of Compliance
SC: Lynn (1991)

Change in Use
SC: Mitchell (1950), Maddry & Co. (1985)

Civil Penalties
SC: Holly Ridge Associates (2007)

Coastal Area Management Act
SC: Adams (1978), Rhodes v. Gaskill (1989), Rhodes v. Simpson (1989), Cobey (1992)
CA: Pamlico Marine (1986), CAMA Minor Development Permit (1986), Weeks (1990), Conservation Council of N.C. (1991), Webb (1991), Pamlico Tar River Foundation (1991), Ballance (1992), Gaskill (1993), Flowers (1994), Leeuwenburg (1994), Coastal Ready-Mix Concrete (1994), Friends of Hatteras (1995), Rusher (1995), King (1997), Pine Knoll Associates (1997), Everhart & Associates (1997), Shell Island Homeowners (1999), Shell Island Homeowners (1999), Williams (2001), Williams (2004), Fabrikant (2005), Busik (2013), Long (2016), Batson (2022)

Commerce Clause
CA: Waste Industries USA (2012), PBK Holdings (2014)

Comprehensive Plan
SC: Shuford (1938), A-S-P Associates (1979)
CA: Piney Mountain Neighborhood Ass'n (1983), Willis (1985), Purser (1997), Everhart & Associates (1997), Schooldev (2022)

Condemnation
SC: Wayne (2015), Kirby (2016)
CA: Fisher (2012), Six at 109 (2014)

Conditional Zoning
CA: Massey (2001), Summers (2002), McMillan (2009), Sapp (2011)

Conditions
SC: Davidson County v. City of High Point (1987)
CA: Decker (1969), Kerik (2001), Mangum (2009), Northwest Property Group (2009)

Conflicts of Interest
SC: County of Lancaster (1993)
CA: JWL Investments (1999), Litvak (2006), Dellinger (2019)

Consistency with Enabling Statute
  SC: Eldridge (1939)
Contract Zoning
  SC: Allred (1971), Blades (1972), Chrismon (1988), Hall (1988)
  CA: Graham (1981), Godfrey (1983), Willis (1985), Nelson (1986), Alderman (1988), Dale (1991), Kerik (2001), Massey (2001), Childress (2007), Musi (2009), Morgan (2012)
Costs
  CA: Williams (2004), Schwarz Properties (2010)
Damages
  SC: Heath (1972)
  CA: Smith (1970), Baucom's Nursery (1988), Monroe (2003)
Delegation
  SC: Wilcher (1952), Adams (1978), Broad & Gales Creek (1980), Homebuilders Ass'n (1994), Appalachian Poster Advertising (1996), Town of Spruce Pine v. Avery County (1997), Smith Chapel Baptist (1999)
  CA: Peedin (1996)
Demolition
  SC: Horton (1970)
  CA: Wiggins (1985), Wiggins (1987), Newton (1989), Knotts (2001), Coffey (2001), Carolina Holdings (2002), Monroe (2003), Patterson (2012), Hillsboro Partners (2013), Six at 109 (2014), Askew (2022)
Determinations
  SC: Ashe County (2020)
Development Agreements
  CA: Bill Clark Homes (2021)
Discovery
  CA: Sapp (2011)
Discretion
  CA: Quadrant (1974)
Discrimination
  CA: Goforth Properties (1984)
  FC: McCauley (1989), Karagiannopoulous (2008), 5-Star Athlete (2022)
Downzoning
  SC: Helms (1961), Finch (1989)
  CA: Roberson's Beverages (1969), Wenco Management (1981)
Driveway Permits
  SC: High Rock Lake Partners (2012)
Due Process
  CA: Capital Outdoor (2003), Coventry Woods Neighborhood Ass'n (2010), Lipinski (2013), Patmore (2014), McDowell (2017)
  FC: Browning-Ferris Industries (1995), Southern Blasting Services (2002), Adams (2007), Quality Built Homes (2008), Raynor (2019), Nance (2021)
Easements
  SC: Concerned Citizens of Brunswick County (1991), Beechridge Development (1999)
  CA: Price (1989), Darbo (2005), Hovey (2021), Craig (2021)
Economic Development
  SC: Cheape (1987)

Enforcement
SC: Aydlett (1930), Aydlett (1930), Aydlett (1930), Mitchell (1950), Fisher (1950), Convent of Sisters of
St. Joseph (1956), Rhyne (1960), City of New Bern v. Walker (1961), Schloss (1962), Parrish (1967),
McBane (1969), Heath (1972), Ritter (1974), Woodhouse (1980), Tillett (1985), Grace Baptist (1987),
Civil Penalty (1989), Rhodes v. Gaskill (1989), Rhodes v. Simpson (1989), Lynn (1991), Evans (1991),
Cobey (1992)
CA: Upton (1973), York (1973), Price (1973), Auman (1975), Westbery (1977), Catawba Valley Machinery
(1978), Hoots Concrete (1980), National Advertising (1980), LFM Enterprises (1980), Pleasant (1982),
National Advertising (1983), Mize (1986), Sherrill (1986), Whiteco Metrocom (1987), Midgette (1989),
Vaughn (1989), North Topsail Water & Sewer (1989), Simmons (1991), Crowell Constructors (1992),
Abernathy (1993), Grandfather Village (1993), Cobey (1995), Midway Grading (1996), Moore (1999),
JWL Investments (1999), Brown (2000), McKillop (2000), Pisgah Oil (2000), Eller (2001), MMR
Holdings (2001), Woodell (2002), Moody (2002), Hewett (2002), Overton (2002), King (2003), Prewitt
(2003), Fantasy World (2004), Clark Stone (2004), McCormick (2004), Dejavue (2007), McDowell
(2007), Hill (2008), Graham (2008), Marts (2009), Moores (2009), Lawyer (2009), Patterson (2012),
Sanford (2012), Fairway Outdoor Advertising (2013), Hillsboro Partners (2013), Lipinski (2013), NCJS
(2017), LeTendre (2018), Nance (2019), Town of Midland (2022), Thompson (2022)
FC: Eberhart (2002), Peterson (2010)
Environmental-Impact Statements
CA: Marriott (2007)
Equal Protection
CA: Coucoulas/Knight Properties (2009), PBK Holdings (2014)
FC: South Shell Investment (1988), Adams (2007), Quality Built Homes (2008), Marsh (2011), Nance
(2021), Catherine Barber (2021)
Erosion
CA: Blackwell (1989)
Estoppel
SC: Fisher (1950), Quality Built Homes (2018)
CA: Hoots Concrete (1978), Hoots Concrete (1980), Goforth Properties (1984), Carolina Holdings (2002),
NCDENR (2002), Laurel Valley Watch (2008), Bailey & Associates (2010), Wake Forest Golf & Coun-
try Club (2011), Orange County v. Town of Hillsborough (2012), Hillsboro Partners (2013), MYC
Klepper/Brandon Knolls (2014)
FC: Karagiannopoulous (2008)
Evidence
SC: Jarrell (1963), Craver (1966), Joyner (1966), Parrish (1967), Northfield Development (2000), Mann
Media (2002), Guilford Financial Services (2003), Dobo (2003), PHG Asheville (2020)
CA: Carter (1972), Long (1974), Robinhood Trails Neighbors (1980), Burton (1980), National Advertis-
ing (1983), Jennewein (1983), Brummer (1986), Signorelli (1989), Petersilie (1989), Pamlico Tar River
Foundation (1991), Triple E Associates (1992), *In re* Raleigh (1992), Wolbarst (1994), Ballas (1996),
Baker (1997), Tate Terrace Realty Investors (1997), Whiteco Outdoor Advertising (1999), McKillop
(2000), Sun Suites Holdings (2000), Davis (2000), Howard (2002), Lamar Outdoor Advertising (2002),
Showcase Realty (2002), Humane Society (2003), MCC Outdoor (2005), Harding (2005), Elliott
(2005), Cumulus Broadcasting (2006), Stealth Properties (2007), Weaverville Partners (2008), Blue
Ridge (2008), Mangum (2009), Bailey & Associates (2010), Russell (2013), Blair Investments (2013),
Davidson County Broadcasting (2016), Dellinger (2016), Innovative 55 (2017), Ecoplexus (2017), Little
River (2017), Jubilee (2019), Violette (2022)
FC: MLC Automotive (2007), Quality Built Homes (2008)

Exactions
SC: Wilson Realty (1956), Batch (1990), River Birch Associates (1990)
CA: Sampson (1978), Emanuelson (1980), Messer (1982), Franklin Road Properties (1989), Price (1989), Dellinger (1994), Franklin-Sloan (1994), TAC Stafford (2022)

Exhaustion
SC: Roberson (1929)
CA: Wil-Hol (1984), Ward (2006), Laurel Valley Watch (2008), Meares (2008), Town of Kill Devil Hills (2009), Sanford (2012), Swan Beach Corolla (2014), Cheatham (2017), Askew (2022)

Extraterritorial Jurisdiction
SC: Rice (1912), Owen (1955), Morand (1957), State (2016), Town of Pinebluff (2020)
CA: Sellers (1977), Savage (1987), Raynor (1989), Odum (1989), Baggett (1999), Potter (2001), Town of Green Level v. Alamance County (2007), Macon County (2007)

Federal Jurisdiction
FC: Mt. Airy Business Center (2014)

Fees
SC: Homebuilders Ass'n (1994)
FC: South Shell Investment (1988)

Findings
SC: Capricorn Equity (1993)
CA: Dockside Discotheque (1994), Shoney's (1995), Ballas (1996), Crist (1998), Richardson (1999), Showcase Realty (2002), Robertson (2004), Childress (2007), Cary Creek (2010)
FC: AT&T Wireless (1999)

First Amendment
SC: Cheryl Humphrey (2021)
FC: Allison Outdoor Advertising (2012), Brown (2013), Hellbender (2013), American Entertainers (2018), Fairway Outdoor Advertising (2022)

Floodplain Zoning and Insurance
SC: Responsible Citizens (1983)
FC: Leland (1991), Burch (1994)

Government Uses
SC: McKinney (1953), Pharr (1960), Bryan (1963), Yancey (1966), Davidson County v. City of High Point (1987)
CA: Nash–Rocky Mount Board of Education (2005), McDonald (2008), Orange County v. Town of Hillsborough (2012)

Group Homes
CA: Mohr (1976), Taylor Home of Charlotte (1994), Parkwood Ass'n (1999), Dismas Charities (2022)
FC: U.S. v. City of Charlotte (1995), Oxford House (1999), U.S. v. Town of Garner (2010), Oxford House (2010), Catherine Barber (2021)

Hazardous Waste
CA: Seaboard Chemical (1994)

Hearings
SC: Freeland (1968), Cheryl Humphrey (2021)
CA: Washington Park Neighborhood Ass'n (1978), Burton (1980), Raynor (1989), Pisgah Oil (2000), Coffey (2001), Cook (2007), Patterson (2012)

Historic Preservation
SC: A-S-P Associates (1979)
CA: Jennewein (1983), Unruh (1990), Meares (2008), Meares (2008), Sanchez (2011), Cherry (2016)
FC: Raynor (2019)

Home Occupation
SC: Jamison (1967)

Judicial Review

SC: Harden (1926), Pine Hill Cemeteries (1941), Ornoff (1942), Jamison (1967), Coastal Ready-Mix Concrete (1980), Farr (1985)

CA: Long (1974), Rose (1982), Sherrill (1985), Weeks (1990), Capricorn Equity (1992), Gossett (1996), Willis (1998), Procter (1999), Village Creek Property Owners (1999), Nazziola (2001), Welter (2003), Northfield Development (2004), 321 News & Video (2005), Weaverville Partners (2008), McMillan (2009), Fort (2014), Henderson (2016), Thompson (2017), Appalachian Materials (2022)

Junkyards

SC: Brown (1959), Parrish (1967), Vestal (1972), Jones (1982)

CA: Byrd (1992)

FC: Combs (2016)

Jurisdiction

SC: Taylor (1968), Davidson County v. City of High Point (1987)

CA: Eastern Federal (1980), Tate (1986), Simmons (1991), Garrity (1994), Simmons (1994), Society for the Preservation of Historic Oakwood (2002), Slavin (2003), Meares (2008), Cary Creek (2010)

FC: Fourth Quarter Properties (2004), MLC Automotive (2008)

Jury Trial

SC: Rhodes v. Simpson (1989)

CA: Mize (1986)

Laches

SC: Taylor (1976)

CA: Stutts (1976), Capps (1978), Allen (1990), Abernathy (1993), MMR Holdings (2001), Woodell (2002), Capital Outdoor (2003), Point South Properties (2015)

Landfills

CA: Grassy Creek Neighborhood Alliance (2001), Greene Citizens for Responsible Growth (2001), NCDENR (2002), Waste Industries USA (2012), PBK Holdings (2014)

FC: Griffin (2008), Griffin Farm (2012)

Liability

SC: Clinard (1917), Cates (1997)

CA: Pigott (1981), Wiggins (1985), Wiggins (1987), EEE-ZZZ Lay Drain (1992), Robinette (1994), Leftwich (1999), Stephenson (2000), Block (2000), Tabor (2003), Kennedy (2003), Eason (2003), Russell (2013), Cline (2021)

FC: Sunkler (2002), Eberhart (2002), Hyatt (2002), Molamphy (2004)

Libel

CA: Martin-Marietta (1994)

Manufactured Housing

SC: Morand (1957), Weston (1965), Jolly (1970), Northwestern Financial Group (1991), Northfield Development (2000)

CA: Martin (1969), Strickland (1971), Upton (1973), Van Poole (1973), York (1973), Price (1973), Auman (1975), Stutts (1976), Willey (1980), Barber (1983), Duggins (1983), Alderman (1988), White (1989), Starr (1989), Hensley (1990), Forest Oaks Homeowners (1991), Angel (1993), Sutton (1993), Young (1996), Williams (1998), Koontz (1998), Andrews (1999), Clark (1999), Devaney (2001), Overton (2002), Jones (2004), Knight (2004), Five C's (2009), Schwarz Properties (2010)

FC: CMH Manufacturing (1998)

Marinas

CA: Walker (1993)

Mining

CA: Crowell Constructors (1992), Hewett (2002), Clark Stone (2004)

Minutes

CA: Washington Park Neighborhood Ass'n (1978), Burton (1980)

Nuisances

SC: Blount (1826), Hunter (1826), Mathews (1837), Bradsher (1844), Dargan (1848), Simpson (1851), Wilder (1856), Ellison (1859), Hyatt (1874), Hyatt (1875), Dorsey (1881), Black (1886), Hord (1898), Duffy (1902), Redd (1904), Hickory (1906), Cherry (1908), Barger (1909), Berger (1911), Berger (1912), Jones (1915), Wilkes (1915), Holton (1931), Everhardt (1932), King (1935), Aydlett (1939), Brown (1942), Ross (1946), Pake (1949), Barrier (1949), Wilcher (1952), Rhyne (1960), Pharr (1960), Parker (1999)

CA: Yates (1980), Mayes (1985), Mercer (1998), Neuse River Foundation (2002), Campbell (2005), Harris (2005), Elliott (2005), Broadbent (2006), Cherry (2012), Nance (2020)

FC: Sansotta (2013), Sansotta (2014)

Oaths

SC: Jarrell (1963), Craver (1966), Joyner (1966)

CA: Burton (1980)

Objectives

CA: Town of Green Level (2007)

Open Meetings

CA: Coulter (1990), Dockside Discotheque (1994)

Open Space

SC: River Birch Associates (1990)

CA: Harry v. Crescent Resources (1999), Wake Forest Golf & Country Club (2011)

Ownership

CA: Graham Court Associates (1981), Hill (2008)

Parking

SC: Chambers (1959), Grace Baptist (1987)

CA: Goforth Properties (1984), R.L. Coleman (1990), March (1997), Wooten (1997)

Parties

CA: Hudson Belk (1994), Piland (2000), Councill (2001), McDowell (2007), Macon County v. Town of Highlands (2007), Graham (2008), Hirschman (2016), Azar (2017), Weishaupt-Smith (2019)

FC: Davis (2001)

Performance Guarantees

CA: Lexon (2014), Brookline Residential (2017)

FC: Developers Surety (2014)

Permit Choice

CA: Ashe County (2022)

Permit Conditions

CA: Orange County v. Town of Hillsborough (2012)

Permit Extension

CA: Cambridge Southport (2012)

Permitted Uses

SC: Rea Construction (1968), Maddry & Co. (1985)

Phased Development

SC: Tadlock (1964)

CA: Pack (1988)

Plan Consistency

CA: Coucoulas/Knight Properties (2009), Sapp (2011), Morgan (2012), Atkinson (2014), McDowell (2017)

FC: Mickelsen (2007)

Planned-Unit Developments

SC: Woodhouse (1980)

CA: Roberts (1983)

Recusal
    CA: Sapp (2011)
Religious Use
    CA: Jirtle (2005)
    FC: Trinity Baptist (1999), Dixon (2010), Hand of Hope (2018), Hand of Hope (2019), Cities4Life (2019)
Remedies
    SC: Hickory (1906), Marriott Financial Services (1975)
    CA: Flowers (1994), Leeuwenburg (1994), Blue Ridge (2008)
Repairs
    SC: Groves (1952)
Repeal
    SC: Heath (1971)
Res Judicata
    FC: Fenner (2013), Mangum (2019)
Restrictive Covenants
    SC: Chapel Hill Title (2008), Belmont Ass'n (2022), C Investments (2022)
    CA: Strickland (1971), Van Poole (1973), Barber (1983), Midgette (1989), Westminster (1989), Starr (1989),
          Forest Oaks Homeowners (1991), Buie (1995), Young (1996), Parkwood Ass'n (1999), Sanford (2012),
          Russell (2012), Erthal (2012)
Rezoning
    CA: Martin-Marietta (1994), Brown (1994), Carter (1997), Gregory (1997), Devaney (2001), Massey (2001),
          Ashby (2003), Keith (2006), Murdock (2009), Ring (2017), Walton North Carolina (2017)
Riparian Access
    CA: Pine Knoll Associates (1997), Duke Energy (2021)
Ripeness
    FC: U.S. v. Town of Garner (2010), Toloczko (2013), CarSpa Automotive (2014), Ballantyne (2020)
Sales Contracts
    CA: Gardner Homes (1976), Lewis (1983), Litvak (2006)
Satellite Dishes
    CA: Sunderhaus (1989)
Schools
    CA: Fort (2012)
Scope of Authority
    SC: King (2014), Quality Built Homes (2016)
    CA: Meares (2008), Patmore (2014), Daedalus (2022)
Secondary Impacts
    SC: Broad & Gales Creek (1980)
Sedimentation
    SC: Civil Penalty (1989), Ocean Hill Joint Venture (1993), Holly Ridge Associates (2007), Hensley (2010),
          Applewood Properties (2013)
    CA: Cramer Mountain Country Club (1991), Ford (1992), Cobey (1995), Midway Grading (1996),
          Graham (2008)
Septic Tanks
    CA: Russell (2013)
Setbacks
    SC: Whitlock (1908), Appeal of Parker (1938)
Shooting Ranges
    SC: Byrd (2015), Hampton (2017), Jeffries (2018)

Short-Term Rentals
    CA: Schroeder (2022)

Signs
    SC: Whitlock (1908), Staples (1911), Schloss (1964), Naegele Outdoor Advertising (1994), Naegele Outdoor Advertising v. City of Winston-Salem (1995), Appalachian Poster Advertising (1996), Capital Outdoor (2002), Morris Communications (2002)
    CA: National Advertising (1980), Eastern Federal (1980), Appalachian Poster Advertising (1981), R.O. Givens (1982), National Advertising (1983), Dandy Signs (1983), Goodman Toyota (1983), Whiteco Metrocom (1987), Webb (1988), Raleigh Place Associates (1989), Summey Outdoor Advertising (1989), Appalachian Outdoor Advertising (1991), Stepp (1992), Abernathy (1993), Grandfather Village (1993), Whiteco Industries (1993), Adams Outdoor Advertising (1993), Naegele Outdoor Advertising v. Hunt (1995), Outdoor East (1996), Appalachian Outdoor Advertising (1997), Whiteco Outdoor Advertising (1999), PNE AOA Media (2001), Cain (2002), Eastern Outdoor (2002), Moody (2002), Capital Outdoor (2002), Lamar Outdoor Advertising (2002), Capital Outdoor (2003), Morris Communications (2003), MCC Outdoor (2005), MMR Holdings (2005), Lamar OCI (2007), Premier Plastic Surgery Center (2011), MCC Outdoor (2012), Fairway Outdoor Advertising (2013), MYC Klepper/Brandon Knolls (2014), Visible Properties (2022)
    FC: Major Media (1986), Georgia Outdoor Advertising (1987), Naegele Outdoor Advertising (1988), Georgia Outdoor Advertising (1990), National Advertising (1991), Naegele Outdoor Advertising (1992), Sandhills Ass'n of Realtors (1999), American Legion (2001), Covenant Media of N.C. (2008), Allison Outdoor Advertising (2012), Brown (2013), Fairway Outdoor (2022)

Special Uses
    SC: Convent of Sisters of St. Joseph (1956), Brannock (1963), Craver (1966), Jackson (1969), Ellis (1970), Keiger (1971), Humble (1974), Humble (1974), Woodhouse (1980), Coastal Ready-Mix Concrete (1980), Davidson County v. City of High Point (1987), County of Lancaster (1993), Mann Media (2002), PHG Asheville (2020)
    CA: Kenan (1972), Carter (1972), York (1973), Long (1974), Freewood Associates (1976), Washington Park Neighborhood Ass'n (1978), Robinhood Trails Neighbors (1980), Harts Book Stores (1981), Heery (1983), Jennewein (1983), Piney Mountain Neighborhood Ass'n (1983), Charlotte Yacht Club (1983), Goforth Properties (1985), Ghidorzi Construction (1986), Stegall (1987), Cardwell (1987), White (1989), Signorelli (1989), Raynor (1989), Petersilie (1989), Coulter (1990), Triple E Associates (1992), *In re* Raleigh (1992), Covington (1992), Rice Associates (1992), Franklin-Sloan (1994), Vulcan Materials (1994), Wolbarst (1994), Rauseo (1995), Ballas (1996), Wade (1997), Baker (1997), Tate Terrace Realty Investors (1997), C.C. & J. (1999), Village Creek Property Owners (1999), Clark (1999), Richardson (1999), Stephenson (2000), Sun Suites Holdings (2000), SBA (2000), Michael Weinman Associates (2001), Howard (2002), Hopkins (2002), Overton (2002), Hewett (2002), Sarda (2003), Butler (2003), Cox (2003), Humane Society (2003), Northfield Development (2004), Ward (2004), MCC Outdoor (2005), Harding (2005), Coleman (2005), Ward (2006), Cumulus Broadcasting (2006), Cook (2007), Davidson County Broadcasting (2007), Casper (2007), Habitat for Humanity (2007), Weaverville Partners (2008), McDonald (2008), Northwest Property Group (2009), Four Seasons Management Services (2010), McCrann (2011), American Towers (2012), Blair Investments (2013), Templeton Properties (2014), Davidson County Broadcasting (2016), Dellinger (2016), Hirschman (2016), Innovative 55 (2017), Ecoplexus (2017), Little River (2017), Dellinger (2019), Jubilee (2019), Dismas Charities (2022)
    FC: Catherine Barber (2021)

Spot Zoning
    SC: Walker v. Town of Elkin (1961), Zopfi (1968), Allred (1971), Heath (1971), Blades (1972), Allgood (1972), Chrismon (1988), Good Neighbors of South Davidson (2002)

CA: Stutts (1976), Lathan (1980), Graham (1981), Godfrey (1983), Nelson (1986), Alderman (1988), Mahaffey (1990), Dale (1991), Covington (1992), Budd (1994), Naegele Outdoor Advertising v. Hunt (1995), Purser (1997), McDowell (2007), Childress (2007), Friends of Mt. Vernon Springs (2008), Musi (2009), Etheridge (2014), Good Neighbors of Oregon Hill (2015), McDowell (2017)

Standing

SC: Lackey (1952), Lackey (1952), Fox (1956), Jackson (1969), Humble (1974), Taylor (1976), Save Our Rivers (1995), Northfield Development (2000), N.C. Forestry (2003), Holly Ridge Associates (2007), Walsh (2007), Mangum (2008), Applewood Properties (2013), Morningstar (2015), Willowmere Community Ass'n (2018), United Daughters of the Confederacy (2022)

CA: Coleman (1971), Duke Power (1974), Pigford (1980), Heery (1983), Piney Mountain Neighborhood Ass'n (1983), Wil-Hol (1984), Davis (1986), Concerned Citizens of Downtown Asheville (1989), Allen (1990), Kentallen (1993), Lloyd (1997), Darnell (1998), C.C. & J. (1999), Andrews (1999), Procter (1999), Village Creek Property Owners (1999), Northeast Concerned Citizens (2001), Councill (2001), Neuse River Foundation (2002), NCDENR (2002), Sarda (2003), Koenig (2006), Cook (2007), Casper (2007), Smith (2007), Marriott (2007), Habitat for Humanity (2007), Thrash (2009), North Iredell Neighbors (2009), Murdock (2009), McMillan (2009), Musi (2009), Templeton (2010), Sanchez (2011), Fort (2012), Morgan (2012), Cherry (2016), Ring (2017), Little River (2017), Cherry Community Organization (2018), Byron (2018), Sound Rivers (2020), Society for Historical Preservation (2022), Violette (2022)

FC: Trinity Baptist (1999), Covenant Media (2008), Dixon (2010), PEM Entities (2023)

Statements of Reasonableness

SC: Michael (1967), Wally (2012)

CA: Good Neighbors of Oregon Hill (2015)

Statutes of Limitation

SC: Ocean Hill Joint Venture (1993), Quality Built Homes (2018)

CA: Sherrill (1986), Baucom's Nursery (1988), Mahaffey (1990), Pinehurst Area Realty (1990), Thompson (1995), Reunion Land (1998), Piland (2000), Potter (2001), Meares (2008), Coventry Woods Neighborhood Ass'n (2010), Schwarz Properties (2010), Amward Homes (2010), Meier (2010), Templeton (2010), McCrann (2011), Patterson (2012), Lexon (2014), Point South Properties (2015), Bill Clark Homes (2021)

FC: Ocean Acres (1983), South Shell Investment (1988), National Advertising (1991), Frye (1999), Hyatt (2002), Tommy Davis Construction (2015), Epcon Homestead (2021)

Streets

CA: March (1997), Wooten (1997), Williamson (2001), Wright (2006), Ocean Hill Joint Venture (2006)

Structures

CA: Riggs (1991)

Subdivisions

SC: Wilson Realty (1956), McBane (1969), Marriott Financial Services (1975), Tillett (1985), Batch (1990), River Birch Associates (1990), Three Guys Real Estate (1997), Beechridge Development (1999), Guilford Financial Services (2003)

CA: Williamson (1974), Sampson (1978), Springdale Estates Ass'n (1980), Emanuelson (1980), Messer (1982), First American Federal Savings & Loan (1985), Lyerly (1986), Rice (1989), Shear (1992), Dellinger (1994), Derwort (1998), Harry v. Crescent Resources (1999), Buckland (2000), Nazziola (2001), Hemphill-Nolan (2002), William Brewster (2003), Jones (2004), Sanco (2004), Darbo (2005), Blue Ridge (2008), Tonter Investments (2009), Lexon (2014), Brookline Residential (2017), Hovey (2021), Craig (2021), TAC Stafford (2022)

Takings

SC: Privett (1875), Eno Cotton Mills (1906), Angelo (1927), Appeal of Parker (1938), McKinney (1954), Helms (1961), Long (1982), Responsible Citizens (1983), Finch (1989), Messer (1997), Kirby (2016), Anderson Creek Partners (2022)

Chronology of Amendments to North Carolina Development-Regulation-Enabling Statutes

Below is a chronology of amendments to the development-regulation-enabling statutes. The basic zoning statute for municipalities was enacted in 1923; the basic zoning statute for counties in 1959. Only the amendments with statewide applicability are included in the chronology. They are listed by biennial session of the General Assembly. The chapter numbers refer to the session laws for each biennium.

1905

Ch. 506—Municipal regulation of buildings authorized; fire districts required.

1919

Ch. 23—Municipal planning boards authorized.

1923

Ch. 25—Municipal-zoning-enabling act adopted.

1927

Ch. 90—Requirement added for two public notices for adoption or amendment of zoning ordinance.

1929

Ch. 94—Option of staggered terms for board of adjustment added.
Ch. 186—Municipal subdivision regulation authorized.

1931

Ch. 176—Provision added that when two corners of intersection are zoned one way, owners of other corners might obtain same zoning as of right ("four corners" statute); seven counties exempted.

1939

Ch. 287—Municipal housing codes authorized.

1945

Ch. 1040—County planning boards authorized; six counties exempted.

1947

Ch. 311—Option of appointing two alternate members of board of adjustment added.

1949

Ch. 979—Provision on alternate members of board of adjustment clarified to specify that no more than two might be appointed.

1951

Ch. 1203—Zoning made applicable to erection and construction of buildings by state and its political subdivisions.

1955

Ch. 489—Provision added setting planning-board membership at three to nine members.
Ch. 1252—Provision added authorizing planning boards to accept federal planning grants.
Ch. 1334—Subdivision-enabling statute adopted for municipalities; fifty-three counties exempted.

1957

Ch. 947—Expanded county planning boards authorized.

1959

Ch. 327—Provision added authorizing planning boards to accept state planning grants.

Ch. 434—Protest-petition provision amended to include sides of affected property as qualifying areas.

Ch. 1006—County-zoning-enabling authority enacted; thirty-one counties exempted.

Ch. 1007—County-enabling authority for subdivision ordinances enacted; twenty-six counties exempted.

Ch. 1204—Extraterritorial zoning of one mile authorized for cities with populations of 2500 or more; requirements for extraterritorial-jurisdiction membership on planning boards and boards of adjustment established; nineteen counties exempted.

1961

Ch. 548—Population requirement for extraterritorial jurisdiction reduced to 1250; municipalities authorized to appoint extraterritorial-jurisdiction members to boards if county failed to make appointments.

1963

Ch. 1058—Four-corners provision (see 1931, above) deleted; form and timing requirements for protest petition added; authority of chair of board of adjustment to administer oaths added.

Ch. 1129—Open-space protection authorized.

1965

Ch. 194—Technical amendments made to county-zoning-enabling statute, including authorization of compensation of members of board of adjustment.

Ch. 864—Provisions added making initial extraterritorial-jurisdiction zoning not subject to protest petitions; providing for compensation of members of municipal boards of adjustment; allowing interlocal agreements on extraterritorial-jurisdiction boundaries and exclusion of certain portions from zoning; allowing option of extraterritorial-jurisdiction members voting on inside matters; and allowing appointment of county members outside extraterritorial-jurisdiction area if necessary.

1967

Ch. 197—Limitation of not more than two alternate members of board of adjustment deleted.

Ch. 1208—Provision added allowing governing board or board of adjustment to issue special or conditional use permits; provision on planning-board preparation of initial zoning ordinance rewritten.

1969

Ch 1065—Local building inspection required.

1971

Ch. 698—Municipal law comprehensively revised, Chapter 160A created; zoning ordinance changed to include graduated extraterritorial-jurisdiction authority to three miles for larger cities.

Ch. 884—Historic preservation and landmark protection authorized.

Ch. 1058—Community appearance commissions authorized.

1973

Ch. 426—Technical corrections made to 1971 comprehensive revision.

Ch. 525—Extraterritorial statute amended to provide for vested rights when jurisdiction has shifted.

Ch. 669—Zoning ordinances enacted before 1972 validated.

Ch. 822—County law comprehensively revised, Chapter 153A created.

1977

Ch. 882—Provision added specifying use of most recent annual population estimate in setting maximum extraterritorial-jurisdiction boundary.

Ch. 912—Provision on planning-board approval of initial zoning rewritten; provisions added for county assumption of prior extraterritorial-jurisdiction area, for more than five members of board of adjustment, for planning-agency assumption of board-of-adjustment functions, and for thirty-day period for judicial appeals.

1979

Ch. 50—Provision added allowing board-of-adjustment decisions to be served in person or by registered or certified mail.

Ch. 611—Technical amendments made to county statutes.

Ch. 1247—Minor technical amendments made.

Ch. 413—Floodplain zoning authorized.

1981

Ch. 705—Nine-month statute of limitations for challenges to county zoning ordinances added.

Ch. 891—Provisions added regarding computation of date for notice of required hearing, nine-month statute of limitations for suits challenging city zoning ordinances, and simple-majority vote for special use permits issued by governing board.

1983

Ch. 441—Authority for counties to exercise zoning over estuarine and navigable waters added.

Ch. 584—Provision allowing separate extraterritorial advisory board deleted.

1985

Ch. 397—Provision regarding planning-board assumption of board of adjustment's duties clarified.

Ch. 442—Provision added establishing thirty-day statute of limitations for appeal of special use permits.

Ch. 540—Provision added creating vested right to zoning for current building permits.

Ch. 595—Provision added requiring mailed notice of rezoning proposals when tax maps are available.

Ch. 607—Explicit authority for overlay and special use districts added; provision for Council of State approval for state lands to be in overlay or special use district added.

Ch. 689—Technical amendment regarding oaths administered by chair of board of adjustment made.

1987

Ch. 747—Provision added regarding density credits; severable development rights established for right-of-way protection.

Ch. 805—Section added prohibiting total exclusion of manufactured homes from jurisdictions but allowing appearance and dimension criteria.

Ch. 807—Exemption added for mailed notice when total rezoning of jurisdiction was involved.

1989

Ch. 706—Historic-preservation provisions recodified.

Ch. 980—Provision added requiring mailed notice for total rezonings if downzoning was involved.

Ch. 996—Provisions added for vested rights upon approval of site-specific development plan or phased-development plan.

1991

Ch. 69—Provision added to county-zoning statute further defining "bona fide farm."

Ch. 512—Provisions added to municipal-zoning statute authorizing board of adjustment to subpoena witnesses, to provide that protest petitions do not apply to certain special or conditional use district amendments, and to clarify provision for appeal of stop-work orders to boards of adjustment.

1993

Ch. 469—Five exemptions to the mailed-notice requirements added.

Ch. 539—Failure to testify accurately defined as a misdemeanor.

1995

Ch. 261—Mailed-notice requirements completely rewritten, adding provisions regarding contents and timing of mailings and alternatives to mailing for large-scale zoning-map amendments.

1996

Ch. 746—Provisions added requiring mailed notice for amendment of extraterritorial-boundary ordinances, county hearings on appointment of extraterritorial members of planning boards and boards of adjustment, and proportional representation of extraterritorial members on city boards; statute of limitations for challenging legislative zoning decisions shortened from nine to two months.

1997

Ch. 458—Provision added allowing county zoning of large-scale swine farms.

2004

Ch. 75—Provision added requiring mailed notice of zoning changes to base commander for rezonings and text amendments affecting permitted uses within five miles of military bases.

2005

Ch. 418—Provisions added reducing publication of notice for large-scale rezonings; requiring posted notice for rezonings; revising protest-petition qualification, calculation, and voting; requiring planning-board review; prohibiting use variances; allowing unified-development ordinances; adding conflict-of-interest standards for quasi-judicial decisions; revising board-of-adjustment voting; allowing county board-of-adjustment subpoenas.

Ch. 426—Provisions added regarding development moratoria, planning-board voting on conditional use permits, conflict-of-interest standards for zoning amendments, allowing conditional zoning and specifying permissible conditions; requiring statements on reasonableness of all small-scale rezonings; requiring planning-board and governing-board statements on plan consistency for zoning amendments; allowing use of development and infrastructure agreements.

2006

Ch. 259—Provisions added clarifying mechanics for making a mandatory statement of planning consistency; provision added clarifying an agricultural exemption from county zoning.

2007

Ch. 147—Provision added regarding regulation of amateur radio antennae.
Ch. 279—Provision added regarding restriction regulation of solar collectors.
Ch. 526—Provision added regarding regulation of wireless telecommunications.

2009

Ch. 95—Authorization of density bonus for energy conservation.
Ch. 178—Provision added requiring actual notice to landowners for third-party rezoning proposals.
Ch. 406—Provision added mandating extension of all development approvals.
Ch. 421—Provisions added regarding judicial review of quasi-judicial decisions.
Ch. 533—Restrictions on discrimination based on affordable housing added.
Ch. 553—Restrictions on regulation of solar collectors extended to all residential uses.

2010

Ch. 177—Provision added further extending development approvals.

2011

Ch. 281—Reasonable-cause requirement added for inspection of residential properties.
Ch. 286—Limit imposed on use of residential moratoria for developing plans and ordinances.
Ch. 363—Definition of bona fide farms modified; bona fide farms made exempt from extraterritorial jurisdiction.
Ch. 367—Demolition-by-neglect provisions extended.
Ch. 384—Statute of limitations for challenges of legislative-zoning decisions extended; limit imposed on county restriction on residential use of parcels over ten acres.
Ch. 408—Campaign signs in state rights-of-way allowed.

2013

Ch. 59—Notice for proposed ordinance changes near military bases expanded.

Ch. 126—Provisions on quasi-judicial decisions and boards of adjustment rewritten.

Ch. 185—Provisions for cell-tower regulations modified.

Ch. 347—Grain drying added to county bona-fide-farm exemption.

Ch. 413—Regulation of fraternity and sorority houses clarified, development-agreement provisions for brownfield sites modified, and regulation of relocation or repair of billboards with N.C. Department of Transportation permits limited.

2014

Ch. 120—Permit-choice rule for pending applications adopted.

2015

Ch. 86—Limitations added to use of design standards for single-family residential structures.

Ch. 160—Protest-petition provisions repealed.

Ch. 187—Use of performance guarantees in subdivision regulation clarified.

Ch. 246—Zoning regulations added to permit-choice rule; limits for bee-hive regulation established; size and duration limits on development agreements removed.

2016

Ch. 90—Adoptions of official maps suspended.

Ch. 111—Statutory vested right for multiphase projects provided.

2017

Ch. 10—Requirements for plan-consistency statements modified; statute of limitations set on enforcement actions; estate-settlement exemption added to definition of subdivision; provision added for expedited plat reviews.

Ch. 40—Performance-guarantee rights for subdivisions clarified.

Ch. 108—Definition of bona fide farm modified; agritourism for county-zoning exemption defined.

Ch. 138—Process and standards created for water-and-sewer-system development fees.

Ch. 159—Regulatory programs allowed for small-cell wireless facilities specified.

2018

Ch. 5—Limitations provided for fees on schools for access and road improvements.

2019

Ch. 35—Official Map Act repealed.

Ch. 79—Performance-guarantee provisions modified.

Ch. 111—Development-regulation authority for cities and counties merged, reorganized, and modernized, Chapter 160D created; third-party downzoning prohibited; permit-choice and vested-rights provisions modified.

Ch. 174—Minimum house size prohibited.

2020

Ch. 3—Remote hearings allowed on quasi-judicial matters during state of emergency; period for development approvals extended.

Ch. 18—Bona-fide-farm exemption from zoning clarified.

Ch. 25—Chapter 160D effective date accelerated; 2019 legislation consolidated into Chapter 160D; clarifications made to Chapter 160D.

Ch. 61—Process for collection of water-and-sewer-system development fees modified and clarified.

2021

Ch. 117—Requirement of masonry curtain walls for manufactured housing prohibited.

Ch. 138—Violation of development regulations decriminalized.

Ch. 164—Redevelopment of property in water-supply watersheds allowed.

Ch. 168—Permit-choice rule clarified.

Ch. 180—Use of harmony standard for affordable housing prohibited.

2022

Ch. 11—Maximum space requirement for parking spaces limited; annual reporting requirement set for administrative fees.

Ch. 55—Commodity-storage facilities added to bona-fide-farm exemption from zoning.

Ch. 62—Appeals process regarding subdivision-plat decisions clarified.

Directory of North Carolina Statutes
on Topics Related to Land Use

Topic	Statute
ABC permits	18B-901
ABC permits in urban-renewal areas	18B-309
Adult establishments	14-202.10 to .12; 160D-902
Agriculture-nuisance limits	106-700, -701
Air quality	143-215.105 to .114C
Airport zoning	63-30 to -37.1
Annexation, Voluntary	160A-29 to -31.1
Annexation agreements	160A-58.21 to -58.28
Annexation of satellite areas	160A-58 to -58.8
Appointments, Cities	160A-60 to -62
Appointments, Counties	153A-25, -26
Balanced-growth policy	143-506.6 to .13
Billboard regulations	136-126 to -140.1; 160D-911
Brownfield redevelopment	130A-310.30 to .40
Building inspection	Ch. 160D, Art. 11
Capacity-use act	143-215.11 to .22B
Cemeteries	65-46 to -73
Closing streets, Cities	160A-299
Coastal-area management, beach access, coastal reserves	113A-100 to -134.3
Coastal wetlands	113-229, -230
Code-enforcement-official certification	143-151.8 to .21
Community appearance	Ch. 160D, Art. 13, Pt. 5
Community development	Ch. 160D, Art. 14, Pt. 2
Community Development Council	143B-437.1 to .3
Control of streets	160A-296
Controlled-access highways	136-89.48 to .56
Dams	143-215.23 to .43

Topic	Statute
Density transfers for rights-of-way	136-66.10 to .11
Development agreements	Ch. 160D, Art. 10
Directional signs	136-140.6 to .9
Disaster response and recovery	166A-1 to -16
Downtown development	160D-1315
Dual-office holding	128-1 to -2
Economic Development Board	143B-434.01
Economic-development commissions	158-8 to -15
Economic development, Counties	158-7.1, .2
Environmental Policy Act	113A-1 to -13
Erosion and sedimentation control	113A-50 to -66
Fair housing	41A
Family care homes	160D-906
Farmland preservation	106-735 to -744
Floodplain zoning	143-215.51 to .61
Graves, Unmarked-grave protection	70-26 to -40
Guns	14-409.40
Hearings, Cities	160A-81
Hearings, Counties	153A-52
Highway beautification	136-122 to -125
Historic preservation	Ch. 160D, Art. 9, Pt. 4
Historic-properties taxation	105-278
Historic-rehabilitation tax credit	105-129.35 to .37
Housing and disabled persons	168-9
Housing codes	Ch. 160D, Art. 12
Interbasin water transfers	Ch. 143, Art. 21, Pt. 2A
Interlocal coordination	160A-460 to -464
Junk-car controls, Cities	160A-303, -303.2
Junk-car controls, Counties	153A-132, -132.2
Junkyard controls	136-141 to -155
Jurisdiction	Ch. 160D, Art. 2
Manufactured-home definition	143-145(7)
Metropolitan-planning organizations	136-200 to -203
Mining	Ch. 74, Art. 7
Mountain-ridge protection	113A-205 to -214

Topic	Statute
Municipal boundary maps	160A-21, -22
Nature preserves	Ch. 143, Art. 25B
Newspaper definitions	1-597
Nonpoint source / agriculture cost share	106-850 to -852
Oaths	11-1 to -10
On-site waste disposal	130A-39, -333 to -343
Open meetings	143-318.9 to .18
Open-space protection	160D-1301 to -1307
Ordinance-making authority, Cities	160A-174 to -198
Ordinance-making authority, Counties	153A-121 to -142
Parking	160A-301
Parks and recreation	Ch. 160A, Art. 18; 153A-444
Pawnshops	66-385 to -399
Permit choice	143-755; 160D-108
Plats	47-30 to -32.2
Public-enterprise rates, Cities	160A-314
Public-enterprise rates, Counties	153A-277
Public records	132-1 to -10
Regional councils of government	160A-470 to -478
Regional-planning commissions	153A-391 to -398
Regional solid-waste authorities	153A-421 to -432
Register of historic places	121-4.1
Relocation assistance	Ch. 133, Art. 2
Rights of disabled persons	168-1
Road closing, Counties	153A-241
Road naming, Counties	153A-238, -239.1
Rural fire employment	160A-294
Rural-planning organizations	136-210 to -213
Sanitary-district powers	130A-55
Scenic rivers	143B-135.140 to .172
Shooting ranges	14-409.45 to .47
Solid waste	130A-309.01; 47-29.1
State Building Code	143-138
States of emergency	166A-19.20 to .31
State planning	143-341

Topic	Statute
State streets	160A-297
Stormwater	143-214.7
Streets in cities	136-66.1 to .7
Streets in subdivisions	136-102.6
Streets, traffic, and parking	160A, Art. 15; Ch. 153A, Art. 12
Subdivision regulation	Ch. 160D, Art. 8
Swine-farm siting	106-800 to -805
Tourist-oriented directional signs	136-140.15 to .19
Traffic control	160A-300
Trails	143B-135.70 to .118
Tree removal by DOT	136-18.6
Underground storage tanks	143-215.94A to .94Y
Urban redevelopment	160A-500 to -526
Use-value property taxes	105-277.2 to .7
Utility rates	162A-9
Water quality	143-211 to -215.9B
Water-and-sewer-system development fees	162A-200 to -215
Water-quality planning	143-215.8A
Water-supply planning	143-215.73A, -355
Watershed protection	143-214.5
Zoning	Ch. 160D, Art. 7

Charting Chapter 160D:
A Guide to North Carolina's New Land Use Laws

Chapter 160D of the North Carolina General Statutes was adopted in 2019 and became fully effective on July 1, 2021. The new legislation was the result of a painstaking, collaborative effort to completely reorganize and update the state's land use laws. The charts below, which show how the earlier planning and development regulations were consolidated in Chapter 160D, are intended to help citizens and local governments understand and navigate the changes.

Table D-1 shows where each section of Chapter 160D was located in the prior statutes, if there was a comparable preexisting statutory provision. Table D-2 shows the reverse, indicating where the principal prior statutes were relocated in Chapter 160D.

For a detailed comparison of the precise changes that were made in the statutory language when the prior statutes were integrated into Chapter 160D, see David W. Owens & Adam S. Lovelady, Chapter 160D: A New Land Use Law for North Carolina 97–255 (UNC School of Government, 2020).

Table D-1. Location of Chapter 160D Provisions in Prior Statutes

CHAPTER 160D	CHAPTER 153A	CHAPTER 160A
ARTICLE 1 *General Provisions*		
§ 160D-101. Application.	--	--
§ 160D-102. Definitions.	153A-344.1(b) 153A-349.2	160A-1(3) 160A-385(a)(2) 160A-385.1(b) 160A-393(a) 160A-400.9 160A-400.21 160A-442
§ 160D-103. Unified development ordinance.	153A-322(d)	160A-363(d)
§ 160D-104. Development approvals run with the land.	--	--
§ 160D-105. Maps.	--	--
§ 160D-106. Refund of illegal fees.	153A-324(b)	160A-363(e)
§ 160D-107. Moratoria.	153A-340(h)	160A-381(e)
§ 160D-108. Permit choice and vested rights.	153A-320.1 153A-344; 344.1	160A-360.1 160A-385; 385.1
§ 160D-108.1. Vested rights: Site specific vesting plans.	153A-344.1	160A-385.1
§ 160D-109. Conflicts of interest.	153A-340(g) 153A-355	160A-381(d) 160A-388(e) 160A-415

CHAPTER 160D	CHAPTER 153A	CHAPTER 160A
§ 160D-110. Chapter construction.	--	--
§ 160D-111. Effect on prior laws.	153A-2	160A-2 160A-5 160A-366

ARTICLE 2
Planning and Development Regulation Jurisdiction

§ 160D-201. Planning and development regulation jurisdiction.	153A-320	160A-360
§ 160D-202. Municipal extraterritorial jurisdiction.	--	160A-360
§ 160D-203. Split jurisdiction.	--	--
§ 160D-204. Pending jurisdiction.	--	--

ARTICLE 3
Boards and Organizational Arrangements

§ 160D-301. Planning boards.	153A-361	160A-321
§ 160D-302. Boards of adjustment.	--	160A-388
§ 160D-303. Historic preservation commission.	--	160A-400.7
§ 160D-304. Appearance commission.	--	160A-451
§ 160D-305. Housing appeals board.	--	160A-446
§ 160D-306. Other advisory boards.	--	--
§ 160D-307. Extraterritorial representation on boards.	--	160A-362
§ 160D-308. Rules of procedure.	---	--
§ 160D-309. Oath of office.	--	--
§ 160D-310. Appointments to boards.	--	--

ARTICLE 4
Administration, Enforcement, and Appeals

§ 160D-401. Application.	--	--
§ 160D-402. Administrative staff.	153A-351 153A-352 153A-353 153A-354	160A-411 160A-412 160A-413 160A-414
§ 160D-403. Administrative development approvals and determinations.	153A-357 153A-358 153A-359 153A-360 153A-362 153A-363	160A-388 160A-417 160A-418 160A-419 160A-420 160A-422 160A-423
§ 160D-404. Enforcement.	153A-324 153A-361	160A-365 160A-389 160A-400.11 160A-421
§ 160D-405. Appeals of administrative decisions.	--	160A-388
§ 160D-406. Quasi-judicial procedure.	--	160A-388

ARTICLE 5
Planning

§ 160D-501. Plans.	--	--
§ 160D-502. Grants, contracts, and technical assistance.	153A-322	160A-363
§ 160D-503. Coordination of planning.	--	--

CHAPTER 160D	CHAPTER 153A	CHAPTER 160A
ARTICLE 6 *Development Regulation*		
§ 160D-601. Procedure for adopting, amending, or repealing development regulations.	153A-323 153A-343	160A-364 160A-384
§ 160D-602. Notice of hearing on proposed zoning map amendments.	153A-343	160A-384
§ 160D-603. Citizen comments.	--	160A-385 160A-386
§ 160D-604. Planning board review and comments.	153A-341 153A-344	160A-383 160A-387
§ 160D-605. Governing board statement.	153A-341 153A-342	160A-382 160A-383
ARTICLE 7 *Zoning Regulation*		
§ 160D-701. Purposes.	153A-341	160A-383
§ 160D-702. Grant of power.	153A-340	160A-381
§ 160D-703. Zoning districts.	153A-342	160A-382
§ 160D-704. Incentives.	153A-340	160A-381 160A-383.4
§ 160D-705. Quasi-judicial zoning decisions.	153A-340	160A-381 160A-388
§ 160D-706. Zoning conflicts with other development standards.	153A-346	160A-390
ARTICLE 8 *Subdivision Regulation*		
§ 160D-801. Authority.	153A-330	160A-371
§ 160D-802. Applicability.	153A-335	160A-376
§ 160D-803. Review process, filing, and recording of subdivision plats.	153A-332	160A-373
§ 160D-804. Contents and requirements of regulation.	153A-331	160A-372
§ 160D-804.1. Performance guarantees.	153A-331	160A-372
§ 160D-805. Notice of new subdivision fees and fee increases; public comment period.	153A-102.1	160A-4.1
§ 160D-806. Effect of plat approval on dedications.	153A-333	160A-374
§ 160D-807. Penalties for transferring lots in unapproved subdivisions.	153A-334	160A-375
§ 160D-808. Appeals of decisions on subdivision plats.	153A-336	160A-377
ARTICLE 9 *Regulation of Particular Uses and Areas*		
Part 1. Particular Land Uses		
§ 160D-901. Regulation of particular uses and areas.		
§ 160D-902. Adult businesses.	--	160A-181.1
§ 160D-903. Agricultural uses.	153A-340	160A-360 160A-383.2
§ 160D-904. Airport zoning.	--	--
§ 160D-905. Amateur radio antennas.	153A-341.2	160A-383.3
§ 160D-906. Bee hives.	--	--

CHAPTER 160D	CHAPTER 153A	CHAPTER 160A
§ 160D-907. Family care homes.	--	168-20 168-21 168-22
§ 160D-908. Fence wraps.	153A-340	160A-381
§ 160D-909. Fraternities and sororities.	153A-340	160A-382
§ 160D-910. Manufactured homes.	153A-341.1	160A-383.1
§ 160D-911. Modular homes.	--	--
§ 160D-912. Outdoor advertising.	153A-143	160A-199
§ 160D-913. Public buildings.	153A-347	160A-392
§ 160D-914. Solar collectors.	153A-144	160A-201
§ 160D-915. Temporary health care structures.	153A-341.3	160A-383.5
§ 160D-916. Streets and transportation.	--	160A-458.4

Part 2. Environmental Regulation

CHAPTER 160D	CHAPTER 153A	CHAPTER 160A
§ 160D-920. Local environmental regulations.	--	--
§ 160D-921. Forestry activities.	153A-452	160A-458.5
§ 160D-922. Erosion and sedimentation control.	--	160A-458
§ 160D-923. Floodplain regulations.	--	160A-458.1
§ 160D-924. Mountain ridge protection.	153A-448	160A-458.2
§ 160D-925. Stormwater control.	153A-454	160A-459
§ 160D-926. Water supply watershed management.	--	--

Part 3. Wireless Telecommunication Facilities

CHAPTER 160D	CHAPTER 153A	CHAPTER 160A
§ 160D-930. Purpose and compliance with federal law.	153A-349.50	160A-400.50
§ 160D-931. Definitions.	153A-349.51	160A-400.51
§ 160D-932. Local authority.	153A-349.51A	160A-400.51A
§ 160D-933. Construction of new wireless support structures or substantial modifications of wireless support structures.	153A-349.52	160A-400.52
§ 160D-934. Collocation and eligible facilities requests of wireless support structures.	153A-349.53	160A-400.53
§ 160D-935. Collocation of small wireless facilities.	--	160A-400.54
§ 160D-936. Use of public right-of-way.	--	160A-400.55
§ 160D-937. Access to city utility poles to install small wireless facilities.	--	160A-400.56
§ 160D-938. Applicability.	--	160A-400.57

Part 4. Historic Preservation

CHAPTER 160D	CHAPTER 153A	CHAPTER 160A
§ 160D-940. Legislative findings.	--	160A-400.1
§ 160D-941. Historic preservation commission.	--	160A-400.7
§ 160D-942. Powers of the historic preservation commission.	--	160A-400.8
§ 160D-943. Appropriations.	--	160A-400.12
§ 160D-944. Designation of historic districts.	--	160A-400.3 160A-400.4
§ 160D-945. Designation of landmarks.	--	160A-400.5
§ 160D-946. Required landmark designation procedure.	--	160A-400.6
§ 160D-947. Certificate of appropriateness required.	--	160A-400.9
§ 160D-948. Certain changes not prohibited.	--	160A-400.13

CHAPTER 160D	CHAPTER 153A	CHAPTER 160A
§ 160D-949. Delay in demolition of landmarks and buildings within historic district.	--	160A-400.14
§ 160D-950. Demolition by neglect in contributing structures outside local historic districts.	--	160A-400.15
§ 160D-951. Conflict with other laws.	--	160A-400.10

Part 5. Community Appearance Commissions

CHAPTER 160D	CHAPTER 153A	CHAPTER 160A
§ 160D-960. Powers and duties of commission.	--	160A-452
§ 160D-961. Staff services; advisory council.	--	160A-453
§ 160D-962. Annual report.	--	160A-454
§ 160D-963. Receipt and expenditure of funds.	--	160A-455

ARTICLE 10
Development Agreements

CHAPTER 160D	CHAPTER 153A	CHAPTER 160A
§ 160D-1001. Authorization.	153A-349.1	160A-400.20
§ 160D-1002. Definitions.	153A-349.2	160A-400.21
§ 160D-1003. Approval of governing board required.	153A-349.3	160A-400.22
§ 160D-1004. Size and duration.	153A-349.4	160A-400.23
§ 160D-1005. Hearing.	153A-349.5	160A-400.24
§ 160D-1006. Content and modification.	153A-349.6	160A-400.25
§ 160D-1007. Vesting.	153A-349.7	160A-400.26
§ 160D-1008. Breach and cure.	153A-349.8	160A-400.27
§ 160D-1009. Amendment or termination.	153A-349.9	160A-400.28
§ 160D-1010. Change of jurisdiction.	153A-349.10	160A-400.29
§ 160D-1011. Recordation.	153A-349.11	160A-400.30
§ 160D-1012. Applicability of procedures to approve debt.	153A-349.12	160A-400.31

ARTICLE 11
Building Code Enforcement

CHAPTER 160D	CHAPTER 153A	CHAPTER 160A
§ 160D-1101. Definitions.	153A-350 153A-350.1	160A-442
§ 160D-1102. Building code administration.	153A-351	1160A-411
§ 160D-1103. Qualifications of inspectors.	153A-351.1	160A-411.1
§ 160D-1104. Duties and responsibilities.	153A-352	160A-412
§ 160D-1104.1. Remote inspection alternative.	--	--
§ 160D-1105. Other arrangements for inspections.	153A-353	160A-413
§ 160D-1106. Alternate inspection method for component or element.	--	160A-413.5
§ 160D-1107. Mutual aid contracts.	--	160A-413.6
§ 160D-1108. Conflicts of interest.	153A-355	160A-415
§ 160D-1109. Failure to perform duties.	153A-356	160A-416
§ 160D-1110. Building permits.	153A-357	160A-417
§ 160D-1111. Expiration of building permits.	153A-358	160A-418
§ 160D-1112. Changes in work.	153A-359	160A-419
§ 160D-1113. Inspections of work in progress.	153A-360	160A-420
§ 160D-1114. Appeals of stop orders.	153A-361	160A-421
§ 160D-1115. Revocation of building permits.	153A-362	160A-422

CHAPTER 160D	CHAPTER 153A	CHAPTER 160A
§ 160D-1116. Certificates of compliance; temporary certificates of occupancy.	153A-363	160A-423
§ 160D-1117. Periodic inspections.	153A-364	160A-424
§ 160D-1118. Defects in buildings to be corrected.	153A-365	160A-425
§ 160D-1119. Unsafe buildings condemned.	153A-366	160A-426
§ 160D-1120. Removing notice from condemned building.	153A-367	160A-427
§ 160D-1121. Action in event of failure to take corrective action.	153A-368	160A-428
§ 160D-1122. Order to take corrective action.	153A-369	160A-429
§ 160D-1123. Appeal; finality of order if not appealed.	153A-370	160A-430
§ 160D-1124. Failure to comply with order.	153A-371	160A-431
§ 160D-1125. Enforcement.	153A-372	160A-432
§ 160D-1126. Records and reports.	153A-373	160A-433
§ 160D-1127. Appeals.	153A-374	160A-434
§ 160D-1128. Fire limits.	153A-375	160A-435 160A-436 160A-437 160A-438
§ 160D-1129. Regulation authorized as to repair, closing, and demolition of nonresidential buildings or structures; order of public officer.	--	160A-439
§ 160D-1130. Vacant building receivership.	--	160A-439.1

ARTICLE 12
Minimum Housing Codes

§ 160D-1201. Authorization.	--	160A-441
§ 160D-1202. Definitions.	--	160A-442
§ 160D-1203. Ordinance authorized as to repair, closing, and demolition; order of public officer.	--	160A-443
§ 160D-1204. Heat source required.	--	160A-443.1
§ 160D-1205. Standards.	--	160A-444
§ 160D-1206. Service of complaints and orders.	--	160A-445
§ 160D-1207. Periodic inspections.	153A-364	160A-424
§ 160D-1208. Remedies.	--	160A-446
§ 160D-1209. Compensation to owners of condemned properties.	--	160A-447
§ 160D-1210. Additional powers of public officer.	--	160A-448
§ 160D-1211. Administration of ordinance.	--	160A-449
§ 160D-1212. Supplemental nature of Article.	--	160A-450

ARTICLE 13
Additional Authority

Part 1. Open Space Acquisition	--	
§ 160D-1301. Legislative intent.	--	160A-401
§ 160D-1302. Finding of necessity.	--	160A-402
§ 160D-1303. Local governments authorized to acquire and reconvey real property.	--	160A-403
§ 160D-1304. Joint action by governing bodies.	--	160A-404
§ 160D-1305. Powers of governing bodies.	--	160A-405

CHAPTER 160D	CHAPTER 153A	CHAPTER 160A
§ 160D-1306. Appropriations authorized.	--	160A-406
§ 160D-1307. Definitions.	--	160A-407

Part 2. Community Development and Redevelopment

CHAPTER 160D	CHAPTER 153A	CHAPTER 160A
§ 160D-1311. Community development programs and activities.	153A-376	160A-456
§ 160D-1312. Acquisition and disposition of property for redevelopment.	153A-377	160A-457
§ 160D-1313. Urban Development Action Grants.	--	160A-457.1
§ 160D-1314. Urban homesteading programs.	--	160A-457.2
§ 160D-1315. Downtown development projects.	--	160A-458.3
§ 160D-1316. Low- and moderate-income housing programs.	153A-378	--

Part 3. Miscellaneous

CHAPTER 160D	CHAPTER 153A	CHAPTER 160A
§ 160D-1320. Program to finance energy improvements.	153A-455	160A-459.1

ARTICLE 14
Judicial Review

CHAPTER 160D	CHAPTER 153A	CHAPTER 160A
§ 160D-1401. Declaratory judgments.	--	--
§ 160D-1402. Appeals in the nature of certiorari.	153A-349	160A-393
§ 160D-1403. Appeals of decisions on subdivision plats.	153A-336	160A-377
§ 160D-1403.1. Civil action for declaratory relief, injunctive relief, other remedies; joinder of complaint and petition for writ of certiorari in certain cases.	--	160A-393.1
§ 160D-1403.2. No estoppel effect when challenging development conditions.	--	160A-393.2
§ 160D-1404. Other civil actions.	--	--
§ 160D-1405. Statutes of limitation.	153A-348	160A-364.1

Table D-2. Location of Prior Statutes in Chapter 160D

CHAPTER 160A	CHAPTER 153A	CHAPTER 160D
ARTICLE 1 *Definitions and Statutory Construction* *(most also retained in 160A/153A)*	*ARTICLE 1*	
§ 160A-1. Application and meaning of terms.	153A-1	160D-102
§ 160A-2. Effect upon prior laws.	153A-2	160D-111
§ 160A-3. General laws supplementary to charters.	153A-3	160D-102; 111
§ 160A-4. Broad construction.	153A-4	160D-110
§ 160A-4.1. Notice of new fees and fee increases; public comment period.	--	160D-800
§ 160A-5. Statutory references deemed amended to conform to Chapter 160D.	153A-5	160D-111
ARTICLE 19 *Planning and Regulation of Development*	*ARTICLE 18*	
Part 1. General Provisions		
§ 160A-360. Territorial jurisdiction.	153A-320	160D-200; 202; 903
§ 160A-360.1. Permit choice.		160D-108(b)
§ 160A-361. Planning boards.	153A-321	160D-301
§ 160A-362. Extraterritorial representation.	--	160D-307
§ 160A-363. Supplemental powers.	153A-322	160D-102; 103; 106; 502
§ 160A-364. Procedure for adopting, amending, or repealing ordinances under Article.	153A-323	160D-601
§ 160A-364.1. Statute of limitations.	153A-348	160D-1405
§ 160A-365. Enforcement of ordinances.	153A-324	160D-106; 404(c)
§ 160A-366. Validation of ordinance.	--	160D-111
§§ 160A-367 through 160A-370. Reserved.	153A-327 to -329	--
Part 2. Subdivision Regulations		*ARTICLE 8*
§ 160A-371. Subdivision regulation.	153A-330	160D-801
§ 160A-372. Contents and requirements of ordinance.	153A-331	160D-804; 804.1
§ 160A-373. Ordinance to contain procedure for plat approval; approval prerequisite to plat recordation; statement by owner.	153A-332	160D-803
§ 160A-374. Effect of plat approval on dedications.	153A-333	160D-806
§ 160A-375. Penalties for transferring lots in unapproved subdivisions.	153A-334	160D-807
§ 160A-376. Definition.	153A-335	160D-802
§ 160A-377. Appeals of decisions on subdivision plats.	153A-336	160D-808; 1403
§§ 160A-378 through 160A-380. Reserved.	153A-337 to -339	--
Part 3. Zoning		*ARTICLE 7*
§ 160A-381. Grant of power.	153A-340	160D-107; 109; 406; 702; 704; 705; 903; 908
§ 160A-382. Districts.	153A-342	160D-502; 605(b); 703; 909
§ 160A-383. Purposes in view.	153A-341	160D-604(d); 605(a); 701
§ 160A-383.1. Zoning regulations for manufactured homes.	153A-341.1	160D-910

CHAPTER 160A	CHAPTER 153A	CHAPTER 160D
§ 160A-383.2. Voluntary agricultural districts.	--	160D-903
§ 160A-383.3. Reasonable accommodation of amateur radio antennas.	153A-341.2	160D-905
§ 160A-383.4. Local energy efficiency incentives.	--	160D-704
§ 160A-383.5. Temporary health care facilities.	153A-341.3	160D-915
§ 160A-384. Method of procedure.	153A-343	160D-601
§ 160A-385. Changes.	--	160D-102; 108(d); 603
§ 160A-385.1. Vested rights.	153A-344.1	160D-102; 108; 108.1
§ 160A-386. Protest petition; form; requirements; time for filing.	--	160D-603
§ 160A-387. Planning board; zoning plan; certification to city council.	153A-344	160D-604
§ 160A-388. Board of adjustment.	153A-345.1	160D-1-9(d); 302; 403(b); 405; 406; 702; 705; 1405
§ 160A-389. Remedies.	--	160D-404(c)
§ 160A-390. Conflict with other laws.	153A-346	160D-706
§ 160A-391. Other statutes not repealed.	--	--
§ 160A-392. Part applicable to buildings constructed by State and its subdivisions; exception.	153A-347	160D-913
§ 160A-393. Appeals in the nature of certiorari.	153A-349	160D-1-2; 1402
§ 160A-393.1. Civil action for declaratory relief, injunctive relief, other remedies; joinder of complaint and petition for writ of certiorari in certain cases.	--	160D-1403.1
§ 160A-393.2. No estoppel effect when challenging development conditions.		160D-1403.2
§ 160A-394. Reserved.	--	--
§§ 160A-395 through 160A-399. Repealed.	--	--
§§ 160A-399.1 through 160A-400. Repealed.	--	--
Part 3C. Historic Districts and Landmarks	--	*ARTICLE 9, PART 4*
§ 160A-400.1. Legislative findings.	--	160D-940
§ 160A-400.2. Exercise of powers by counties as well as cities.	--	--
§ 160A-400.3. Character of historic district defined.	--	160D-944
§ 160A-400.4. Designation of historic districts.	--	160D-944
§ 160A-400.5. Designation of landmarks; adoption of an ordinance; criteria for designation.	--	160D-945
§ 160A-400.6. Required landmark designation procedure.	--	160D-946
§ 160A-400.7. Historic Preservation Commission.	--	160D-303; 941
§ 160A-400.8. Powers of the Historic Preservation Commission.	--	160D-942
§ 160A-400.9. Certificate of appropriateness required.	--	160D-102; 947
§ 160A-400.10. Conflict with other laws.	--	160D-951
§ 160A-400.11. Remedies.	--	160D-404(c)
§ 160A-400.12. Appropriations.	--	160D-943
§ 160A-400.13. Certain changes not prohibited.	--	160D-948
§ 160A-400.14. Delay in demolition of landmarks and buildings within historic district.	--	160D-949
§ 160A-400.15. Demolition by neglect to contributing structures outside local historic districts.	--	160D-950
§§ 160A-400.16 through 160A-400.19. Reserved.	--	--

CHAPTER 160A	CHAPTER 153A	CHAPTER 160D
Part 3D. Development Agreements		***ARTICLE 10***
§ 160A-400.20. Authorization for development agreements.	153A-349.1	160D-101
§ 160A-400.21. Definitions.	153A-349.2	160D-102; 102
§ 160A-400.22. Local governments authorized to enter into development agreements; approval of governing board required.	153A-349.3	160D-1-2; 103
§ 160A-400.23. Developed property must contain certain number of acres; permissible durations of agreements.	153A-349.4	160D-104
§ 160A-400.24. Public hearing.	153A-349.5	160D-105; 106
§ 160A-400.25. What development agreement must provide; what it may provide; major modification requires public notice and hearing.	153A-349.6	160D-106
§ 160A-400.26. Law in effect at time of agreement governs development; exceptions.	153A-349.7	160D-107
§ 160A-400.27. Periodic review to assess compliance with agreement; material breach by developer; notice of breach; cure of breach or modification or termination of agreement.	153A-349.8	160D-108
§ 160A-400.28. Amendment or cancellation of development agreement by mutual consent of parties or successors in interest.	153A-349.9	160D-109
§ 160A-400.29. Validity and duration of agreement entered into prior to change of jurisdiction; subsequent modification or suspension.	153A-349.10	160D-1010
§ 160A-400.30. Developer to record agreement within 14 days; burdens and benefits inure to successors in interest.	153A-349.11	160D-1011
§ 160A-400.31. Applicability to local government of constitutional and statutory procedures for approval of debt.	153A-349.12	160D-1012
§ 160A-400.32. Relationship of agreement to building or housing code.	153A-349.13	160D-101(c)
Part 3E. Wireless Telecommunication Facilities		***ARTICLE 9, PART 3***
§ 160A-400.50. Purpose and compliance with federal law.	153A-349.50	160D-930
§ 160A-400.51. Definitions.	153A-349.51	160D-931
§ 160A-400.51A. Local authority.	153A-349.52	160D-932
§ 160A-400.52. Construction of new wireless support structures or substantial modifications of wireless support structures.	153A-349.53	160D-933
§ 160A-400.53. Collocation and eligible facilities requests of wireless support structures.	153A-349.54	160D-934
§§ 160A-400.54 through 160A-400.58. Reserved.		
Part 4. Acquisition of Open Space		***ARTICLE 13, PART 1***
§ 160A-401. Legislative intent.	--	160D-1301
§ 160A-402. Finding of necessity.	--	160D-1302
§ 160A-403. Counties or cities authorized to acquire and reconvey real property.	--	160D-1303
§ 160A-404. Joint action by governing bodies.	--	160D-1304
§ 160A-405. Powers of governing bodies.	--	160D-1305
§ 160A-406. Appropriations authorized.	--	160D-1306
§ 160A-407. Definitions.	--	160D-1307
§§ 160A-408 through 160A-410. Reserved.	--	--

CHAPTER 160A	CHAPTER 153A	CHAPTER 160D
Part 5. Building Inspection		*ARTICLE 11*
"Building" defined.	153A-350	160D-1101
Tribal lands.	153A-350.1	160D-1101
§ 160A-411. Inspection department.	153A-351	160D-402(b); 404(c); 1102
§ 160A-411.1. Qualifications of inspectors.	153A-351.1	160D-1103
§ 160A-412. Duties and responsibilities.	153A-352	160D-402(b); 1104
§ 160A-413. Joint inspection department; other arrangements.	153A-353	160D-402(c); 1105
§ 160A-413.5. Alternate inspection method for component or element.	--	160D-1106
§ 160A-413.6. Mutual aid contracts.	153A-353.1	160D-1107
§ 160A-414. Financial support; fee collection, accounting, and use limitation.	153A-354	160D-402(d)
§ 160A-415. Conflicts of interest.	153A-355	160D-109(c); 1108
§ 160A-416. Failure to perform duties.	153A-356	160D-1109
§ 160A-417. Permits.	153A-357	160D-403; 1110
§ 160A-418. Time limitations on validity of permits.	153A-358	160D-403(c); 1111
§ 160A-419. Changes in work.	153A-359	160D-403(d); 1112
§ 160A-420. Inspections of work in progress.	153A-360	160D-403(e); 1113
§ 160A-421. Stop orders.	153A-361	160D-404(b); 1114
§ 160A-422. Revocation of permits.	153A-362	160D-403(f); 1115
§ 160A-423. Certificates of compliance.	153A-363	160D-403(g); 1116
§ 160A-424. Periodic inspections.	153A-364	160D-1117; 1207
§ 160A-425. Defects in buildings to be corrected.	153A-365	160D-1118
§ 160A-425.1. Repealed.	--	--
§ 160A-426. Unsafe buildings condemned in localities.	153A-366	160D-1119
§ 160A-427. Removing notice from condemned building.	153A-367	160D-1120
§ 160A-428. Action in event of failure to take corrective action.	153A-368	160D-1121
§ 160A-429. Order to take corrective action.	153A-369	160D-1122
§ 160A-430. Appeal; finality of order if not appealed.	153A-370	160D-1123
§ 160A-431. Failure to comply with order.	153A-371	160D-1124
§ 160A-432. Enforcement.	153A-372	160D-1125
§ 160A-433. Records and reports.	153A-373	160D-1126
§ 160A-434. Appeals in general.	153A-374	160D-1127
§ 160A-435. Establishment of fire limits.	153A-375	160D-1128
§ 160A-436. Restrictions within primary fire limits.	--	160D-1128
§ 160A-437. Restriction within secondary fire limits.	--	160D-1128
§ 160A-438. Failure to establish primary fire limits.	--	160D-1128
§ 160A-439. Ordinance authorized as to repair, closing, and demolition of nonresidential buildings or structures; order of public officer.	153A-372.1	160D-1129
§ 160A-439.1. Vacant building receivership.		160D-1130
§ 160A-440. Reserved.	--	--

CHAPTER 160A	CHAPTER 153A	CHAPTER 160D
Part 6. Minimum Housing Standards		**ARTICLE 12**
§ 160A-441. Exercise of police power authorized.	--	160D-1201
§ 160A-442. Definitions.	--	160D-102; 1101; 1202
§ 160A-443. Ordinance authorized as to repair, closing, and demolition; order of public officer.	--	160D-1203
§ 160A-443.1. Heat source required.	--	160D-1204
§ 160A-444. Standards.	--	160D-1205
§ 160A-445. Service of complaints and orders.	--	160D-1206
§ 160A-446. Remedies.	--	160D-305; 1208
§ 160A-447. Compensation to owners of condemned property.	--	160D-1209
§ 160A-448. Additional powers of public officer.	--	160D-1210
§ 160A-449. Administration of ordinance.	--	160D-1211
§ 160A-450. Supplemental nature of Part.	--	160D-1212
Part 7. Community Appearance Commissions		**ARTICLE 9, PART 5**
§ 160A-451. Membership and appointment of commission; joint commission.	--	160D-304
§ 160A-452. Powers and duties of commission.	--	160D-960
§ 160A-453. Staff services; advisory council.	--	160D-961
§ 160A-454. Annual report.	--	160D-962
§ 160A-455. Receipt and expenditure of funds.	--	160D-963
Part 8. Miscellaneous Powers		
§ 160A-456. Community development programs and activities.	153A-376	160D-1311
§ 160A-457. Acquisition and disposition of property for redevelopment.	153A-377	160D-1312
§ 160A-457.1. Urban Development Action Grants.	--	160D-1313
§ 160A-457.2. Urban homesteading programs.	--	160D-1314
§ 160A-458. Erosion and sedimentation control.	--	160D-922
§ 160A-458.1. Floodway regulations.	--	160D-923
§ 160A-458.2. Mountain ridge protection.	153A-448	160D-924
§ 160A-458.3. Downtown development projects.	--	160D-1315
§ 160A-458.4. Designation of transportation corridor official maps.	--	160D-916
§ 160A-458.5. Restriction of certain forestry activities prohibited.	153A-452	160D-921
§ 160A-459. Stormwater control.	153A-454	160D-925
§ 160A-459.1. Program to finance energy improvements.	153A-455	160D-1320
Low- and moderate-income housing programs	153A-378	160D-1316
Others		
§ 160A-181.1. Adult businesses.	--	160D-902
§ 160A-199. Outdoor advertising.	153A-143	160D-912
§ 160A-201. Solar collectors.	153A-143	160D-914
§§ 168-20 to -22. Family care homes.	--	160D-907

Case Index

Andrus v. Sierra Club, 442 U.S. 347 (1979) *144*

Andy's Restaurant & Lounge, Inc. v. City of Gary, 466 F.3d 550 (7th Cir. 2006) *548*

Angelo v. City of Winston-Salem, 193 N.C. 207, 136 S.E. 489 (1927) *366, 507*

Angel v. Truitt, 108 N.C. App. 679, 424 S.E.2d 660 (1993) *455*

Anheuser-Busch, Inc. v. Schmoke, 63 F.3d 1305 (4th Cir. 1995) *611*

Anheuser-Busch, Inc. v. Schmoke, 101 F.3d 325 (4th Cir. 1996) *611, 614*

Animas Valley Sand & Gravel, Inc. v. Board of Commissioners, 38 P.3d 59 (Colo. 2001) *509*

Annex Books, Inc. v. City of Indianapolis, 581 F.3d 460 (7th Cir. 2009) *552*

Anselmo v. County of San Diego, 873 F. Supp. 2d 1247 (E.D. Cal. 2012) *580*

Anundson v. City of Chicago, 44 Ill. 2d 491, 256 N.E.2d 1 (1970) *630*

APAC-Atlantic, Inc. v. City of Salisbury, 210 N.C. App. 668, 709 S.E.2d 390 (2011) *373, 656*

Apartment Ass'n of South Central Wisconsin v. City of Madison, 2006 WI App 192, 296 Wis. 2d 173, 722 N.W.2d 614 *118*

Appalachian Materials, LLC v. Watauga County, 262 N.C. App. 156, 822 S.E.2d 57 (2018) *320*

Appalachian Materials, LLC v. Watauga County, 283 N.C. App. 117, 872 S.E.2d 591 (2022) *660*

Appalachian Outdoor Advertising Co. v. Town of Boone, 103 N.C. App. 504, 406 S.E.2d 297 (1991) *402, 622, 644*

Appalachian Poster Advertising Co. v. Zoning Board of Adjustment, 52 N.C. App. 266, 278 S.E.2d 321 (1981) *365, 370, 376*

Appeal of CAMA Permit No. 82-0010 v. Town of Bath, 82 N.C. App. 32, 345 S.E.2d 699 (1986) *133, 175, 329, 638*

Appeal of Parker, 214 N.C. 51, 197 S.E. 706 (1938) *193, 507, 520, 650*

Appeal of Realen Valley Forge Greenes Associates, 576 Pa. 115, 838 A.2d 718 (2003) *518*

Apple Group, Ltd. v. Granger Township Board of Zoning Appeals, 41 N.E.3d 1185 (Ohio 2015) *438*

Applewood Properties, LLC v. New South Properties, LLC, 366 N.C. 518, 742 S.E.2d 776 (2013) *632*

APT Pittsburgh Ltd. Partnership v. Penn Township, 196 F.3d 469 (3d Cir. 1999) *491, 492*

Arcara v. Cloud Books, Inc., 478 U.S. 697 (1986) *559, 567*

ARC of New Jersey, Inc. v. New Jersey, 950 F. Supp. 637 (D.N.J. 1996) *482*

Arkansas Game & Fish Commission v. United States, 133 S. Ct. 511 (2012) *501*

Arkell v. Middle Cottonwood Board of Zoning Adjustment, 2007 MT 160, 338 Mont. 77, 162 P.3d 856 *298*

Arlington County Republican Committee v. Arlington County, 983 F.2d 587 (4th Cir. 1993) *613*

Armstrong v. Manzo, 380 U.S. 545 (1965) *232*

Armstrong v. McInnis, 264 N.C. 616, 142 S.E.2d 670 (1965) *215*

Arnel Development Co. v. City of Costa Mesa, 28 Cal. 3d 511, 169 Cal. Rptr. 904, 620 P.2d 565 (1980) *195*

Arnold Bernhard & Co. v. Planning & Zoning Commission, 194 Conn. 152, 479 A.2d 801 (1984) *102*

Artistic Entertainment, Inc. v. City of Warner Robins, 331 F.3d 1196 (11th Cir. 2003) *559, 566*

ASF, Inc. v. City of Seattle, 408 F. Supp. 2d 1102 (W.D. Wash. 2005) *540*

Ashby v. Town of Cary, 161 N.C. App. 499, 588 S.E.2d 572 (2003) *184, 217, 219, 232, 517, 518, 650*

Ashe County v. Ashe County Planning Board, 284 N.C. App. 563, 876 S.E.2d 687 (2022) *106, 329*

Ashe County v. Ashe County Planning Board, 376 N.C. 1, 852 S.E.2d 69 (2020) *306*

Ashton v. Kentucky, 384 U.S. 195 (1966) *543*

Asian Americans for Equality v. Koch, 72 N.Y.2d 121, 531 N.Y.S.2d 782, 527 N.E.2d 265 (1988) *195*

Askew v. City of Kinston, ___ N.C. App. ___, 883 S.E.2d 85 (2022) *645*

A-S-P Associates v. City of Raleigh, 298 N.C. 207, 258 S.E.2d 444 (1979) *120, 383, 438, 439, 520, 521, 524, 525, 528*

Asselin v. Town of Conway, 137 N.H. 368, 628 A.2d 247 (1993) *525, 600*

Associated Home Builders v. City of Walnut Creek, 4 Cal. 3d 633, 94 Cal. Rptr. 630, 484 P.2d 606 (1971) *511*

Associated Home Builders v. Livermore, 18 Cal. 3d 582, 135 Cal. Rptr. 41, 557 P.2d 473 (1976) *115*

Associated Mechanical Contractors, Inc. v. Payne, 342 N.C. 825, 467 S.E.2d 398 (1996) *653*

Association for the Advancement of the Mentally Handicapped v. City of Elizabeth, 876 F. Supp. 614 (D.N.J. 1994) *484*

Athens Cellular, Inc. v. Oconee County, 886 F.3d 1094 (11th Cir. 2018) *488*

Atkinson v. City of Charlotte, 235 N.C. App. 1, 760 S.E.2d 395 (2014) *188*

Atkins v. Zoning Board of Adjustment, 53 N.C. App. 723, 281 S.E.2d 756 (1981) *319, 370, 374*

Atlantic Construction Co. v. City of Raleigh, 230 N.C. 365, 53 S.E.2d 165 (1949) *91*

Atlas Roofing Co. v. Occupational Safety & Health Review Commission, 430 U.S. 442 (1977) *231*

ATL Corp. v. City of Seattle, 758 F. Supp. 2d 1147 (W.D. Wash. 2011) *557, 568*

ATM Express, Inc. v. City of Montgomery, 376 F. Supp. 2d 1310 (M.D. Ala. 2005) *567*

I

N

War Eagle, Inc. v. Belair, 204 N.C. App. 548, 694 S.E.2d 497 (2010) *399*

Warner v. W & O, Inc., 263 N.C. 37, 138 S.E.2d 782 (1964) *344, 346, 350, 355*

Warren County v. North Carolina, 528 F. Supp. 276 (E.D.N.C. 1981) *144*

Warth v. Seldin, 422 U.S. 490 (1975) *479, 634*

Washington *ex rel.* Seattle Title Trust Co. v. Roberge, 278 U.S. 116 (1928) *184*

Washington Park Neighborhood Ass'n v. Winston-Salem Board of Adjustment, 35 N.C. App. 449, 241 S.E.2d 872 (1978) *254, 262*

Waste Industries USA, Inc. v. State, 220 N.C. App. 163, 725 S.E.2d 875 (2012) *148, 344, 352, 357*

Water Tower Office Associates v. Town of Cary Board of Adjustment, 131 N.C. App. 696, 507 S.E.2d 589 (1998) *237, 253*

Ways v. City of Lincoln, 331 F.3d 596 (8th Cir. 2003) *551, 560*

Wayte v. United States, 470 U.S. 598 (1985) *411*

Weaverville Partners, LLC v. Town of Weaverville Zoning Board of Adjustment, 188 N.C. App. 55, 654 S.E.2d 784 (2008) *279, 285, 287*

Webb v. Department of Environment, Health, & Natural Resources, 102 N.C. App. 767, 404 S.E.2d 29 (1991) *133*

Weeks v. North Carolina Department of Natural Resources & Community Development, 97 N.C. App. 215, 388 S.E.2d 288 (1990) *135, 139, 509*

Weinberger v. Hynson, Westcott & Dunning, Inc., 412 U.S. 609 (1973) *231*

Weinberg v. Whatcom County, 241 F.3d 746 (9th Cir. 2001) *233*

Weishaupt-Smith v. Town of Banner Elk, 264 N.C. App. 618, 826 S.E.2d 734 (2019) *633*

Welch v. Swasey, 214 U.S. 91 (1909) *20, 76*

Welter v. Rowan County Board of Commissioners, 160 N.C. App. 358, 585 S.E.2d 472 (2003) *261, 653*

Welton v. Hamilton, 344 Ill. 82, 176 N.E. 333 (Ill. 1931) *293*

Wenco Management Co. v. Town of Carrboro, 53 N.C. App. 480, 281 S.E.2d 74 (1981) *526*

Wensmann Realty, Inc. v. City of Eagan, 734 N.W.2d 623 (Minn. 2007) *501*

Wesleyan Methodist Church of Canisteo v. Village of Canisteo, 792 F. Supp. 2d 667 (W.D.N.Y. 2011) *580*

Westchester Day School v. Village of Mamaroneck, 386 F.3d 183 (2d Cir. 2004) *585*

Westchester Day School v. Village of Mamaroneck, 504 F.3d 338 (2d Cir. 2007) *585, 586*

Westgate Tabernacle, Inc. v. Palm Beach County, 14 So. 3d 1027 (Fla. Dist. Ct. App. 2009) *584*

Westminster Homes, Inc. v. Town of Cary Zoning Board of Adjustment, 354 N.C. 298, 554 S.E.2d 634 (2001) *309, 317, 318*

West Virginia Ass'n of Club Owners and Fraternal Services, Inc. v. Musgrave, 553 F.3d 292 (4th Cir. 2009) *610*

West v. Slick, 313 N.C. 33, 326 S.E.2d 601 (1985) *139*

Wheeler v. Commissioner of Highways, 822 F.2d 586 (6th Cir. 1987) *604*

Whichard v. Oliver, 56 N.C. App. 219, 387 S.E.2d 461 (1982) *82*

White Coat Waste Project v. Greater Richmond Transit Co., 35 F.4th 179 (4th Cir. 2022) *597*

Whiteco Industries, Inc. v. Harrington, 111 N.C. App. 839, 434 S.E.2d 234 (1993) *401*

Whiteco Outdoor Advertising v. Johnston County Board of Adjustment, 132 N.C. App. 465, 513 S.E.2d 70 (1999) *249, 376, 656*

Whitehead Oil Co. v. City of Lincoln, 245 Neb. 660, 515 N.W.2d 390 (1994) *360*

White Oak Properties, Inc. v. Town of Carrboro, 313 N.C. 306, 327 S.E.2d 882 (1985) *236, 642*

White River Amusement Pub, Inc. v. Town of Hartford, 481 F.3d 163 (2d Cir. 2007) *553*

Whiteside Estates v. Highlands Cove, 146 N.C. App. 449, 553 S.E.2d 431 (2001) *151*

White v. Pate, 308 N.C. 759, 304 S.E.2d 199 (1983) *536*

White v. Union County, 93 N.C. App. 148, 377 S.E.2d 93 (1989) *452, 621, 639*

Whitfield v. Longest, 28 N.C. (6 Ired.) 268 (1846) *36*

Whitton v. City of Gladstone, 54 F.3d 1400 (8th Cir. 1995) *613*

Wiener v. United States, 357 U.S. 349 (1958) *16*

Wiggins v. City of Monroe, 73 N.C. App. 44, 326 S.E.2d 39 (1985) *408, 419*

Wiggins v. City of Monroe, 85 N.C. App. 237, 354 S.E.2d 365 (1987) *419*

Wilcher v. Sharpe, 236 N.C. 308, 72 S.E.2d 662 (1952) *184*

Wild River Estates, Inc. v. City of Fargo, 2005 ND 193, 705 N.W.2d 850 *107, 505*

Wil-Hol Corp. v. Marshall, 71 N.C. App. 611, 322 S.E.2d 655 (1984) *238, 402, 630, 644*

William Brewster Co. v. Town of Huntersville, 161 N.C. App. 132, 588 S.E.2d 16 (2003) *228, 276*

Williamson County Regional Planning Commission v. Hamilton Bank of Johnson City, 473 U.S. 172 (1985) *506*

Williamson v. Avant, 21 N.C. App. 211, 203 S.E.2d 634 (1974) *84*

Williamson v. Town of Surf City, 143 N.C. App. 539, 545 S.E.2d 798 (2001) *140*

Williams v. Blue Cross Blue Shield of North Carolina, 357 N.C. 170, 581 S.E.2d 415 (2003) *643*

Table of Statutes

Subject Index

Page numbers with an appended italic *f*, *i*, or *t* indicate the presence of a figure, illustration, or table.

Printed in the USA
CPSIA information can be obtained
at www.ICGtesting.com
LVHW011738091123
763522LV00013B/561